AUTHORS AND THEIR WORKS

WITH DATES

BEING THE APPENDICES TO

"*THE READER'S HANDBOOK*"

BY THE REV.

E. COBHAM BREWER, LL.D.

TRINITY HALL, CAMBRIDGE

AUTHOR OF "GUIDE TO SCIENCE" (THREE HUNDRED AND EIGHTIETH THOUSAND)
"HISTORY OF FRANCE" (TENTH EDITION) ; "HISTORY OF GERMANY"
"THEOLOGY IN SCIENCE" (EIGHTH EDITION); "READER'S HANDBOOK" (FOURTH EDITION)
"DICTIONARY OF PHRASE AND FABLE" (SIXTEENTH EDITION)
"A DICTIONARY OF MIRACLES;" "RULES FOR ENGLISH SPELLING;" ETC., ETC.

DETROIT
Gale Research Company • Book Tower
1970

This is a facsimile edition of the revised
appendices to *The Reader's Handbook*
published in 1898 by Chatto & Windus,
London.

Library of Congress Catalog Card Number 71-134907

NEW PREFACE

This supplement to the ever popular reference work *The Reader's Handbook* was first published as a separate volume London, 1884, but in later revised editions of the British printing was included at the end of the single volume format of the main work.

The final revised edition of *The Reader's Handbook* was published after the author's death London, 1898; Philadelphia 1899. By that time the original three appendices had been reduced to two; the facts in the short Appendix II of "Dates of Foreign Poems and Novels" had been incorporated into the text of the main work. All the information in the remaining two appendices had been thoroughly checked and revised by librarians.

Although the final 1898 British edition of *The Reader's Handbook* included these two appendices with the main work in one rather unwieldy volume, the American edition of 1899 omitted them. These appendices were therefore not included in the Gale Research Co. reprint of 1966 (published in two volumes for more convenient handling).

However, as these appendices give useful bibliographical information relevant to the basic work, they are now reissued as a supplementary volume. The page numbering continues from the last page of the second volume of the Gale reprint. This reissue will have special interest for all owners of the Gale reprint of *The Reader's Handbook*.

1970   LESLIE SHEPARD

APPENDIX I.

ENGLISH AUTHORS AND THEIR WORKS, WITH DATES.

(Appendix II. contains the titles of Dramas, with names of authors and dates.)

A personal comment, rarely exceeding a word or two, has, in a few instances, been added to books which I have been struck with.

ABBOTT, D.D. (*Edwin Abbott*), London, 1838–
. Anglican Career of Cardinal Newman, 1892; Bacon and Essex, 1877; Bacon (*Francis*), 1885; Bacon's Essays, 1876; Bible Lessons, 1872; Cambridge Sermons, 1875; Common Tradition of the Synoptic Gospels, 1884 (with W. G. Rushbrooke); English Lessons, 1871 (with Prof. J. R. Seely); Flatland, 1884; Hints on Home Teaching, 1883; How to write clearly, 1872; How to tell Parts of Speech, 1875; Kernel and the Husk (*The*), 1886; Latin Gate (*The*), 1889; Latin Prose, 1873; Newman, 1892; Onesimus, 1882, a religious romance; Oxford Sermons, 1879; Parables for Children, 1875; Philochristus, 1878, a religious romance; Philomythus, 1891; Shakesperian Grammar (*A*), 1870; Spirit on the Waters, 1897; Through Nature to Christ, 1877; Via Latina, 1880.

N.B.—The "Concordance to Pope," 1875, was by Edwin Abbott (1803–1882). It has an *Introduction* by Edwin Abbott Abbott, D.D.

ABBOTT (*Jacob*), Hallowel, in Maine, U.S., 1803–1879. Corner Stone (*The*), 1826; Way to do Good (*The*), 1836; Young Christian (*The*), 1825.

∴ These books were enormously popular at the time.

ABBOTT, D.D. (*John S. C.*), brother of the preceding, 1806–1877. Mother at Home (*The*), 1845.

A'BECKETT (*Arthur William*), Hammersmith, 1844– . About Town, 1873, a three-act comedy; Comic Guide to the Royal Academy, 1863–64; Doom of St. Quirec (*The*), 1875 (with Burnand); Faded Flowers, 1874, a play; Fallen among Thieves, 1869, a novel; Ghost of Grimstone Grange (*The*), and the Mystery of Mostyn Manor, 1877–78; Green-Room Recollections, 1896; L. S. D., 1872, a three-act comedy; Member for Wrottenborough (*The*), 1895; Modern Arabian Nights (*The*), 1885; On

Strike, 1873, a play; Our Holiday in the Highlands, 1874; Papers from Pump-handle Court, 1884; Shadow Witness (*The*), 1876 (with Burnand); Tracked Out, Hard Luck, Stone Broke, 1879–81.

A'BECKETT (*Gilbert Abbot*), father of the above, humourist, etc., 1811–1856. Comic Blackstone (*The*), 1846; Comic History of England (*The*), 1847–48; Comic History of Rome, 1851–52; Quizziology, etc., 1846. And above thirty dramatic pieces.

ABERCROMBIE, M.D. (*John*), Aberdeen, 1781–1844. Inquiry concerning the Intellectual Powers, 1830–32; Philosophy of the Moral Feelings (*The*), 1833; Researches on the Diseases of the Brain, etc., 1828.

ABERCROMBIE (*John*), near Edinburgh, 1726–1806. Every man his own gardener, 1767.

ABERCROMBY, M.D. (*David*), Scotland, 1620–1695. Academia Scientiarium, 1687; Discourse on Wit (*A*), 1685.

ABERNETHY (*John*), 1763–1831. Surgical and Physiological Essays, 1793–97. His Life, by Macilwain, 1853.

ADAM (*Alexander*), near Forres, in Scotland, 1741–1805. Dictionary of Classical Biography (*A*), 1800; Latin Dictionary (*A*), 1809; Principles of Latin and English Grammar, 1772; Roman Antiquities, 1791.

ADAMS, D.D. (*William*), Colchester, in Connecticut, U.S., 1807–1880. Conversations of Christ with Representative Men, 1868; In the World, 1866; Thanksgiving, 1867; The Three Gardens (Eden, Gethsemane, Paradise), 1867.

ADAMS (Rev. *William*), sacred allegorist, died 1848. Distant Hills (*The*), 1844; King's Messenger (*The*), 1846; Old Man's Home (*The*), 1847; Shadow of the Cross (*The*), 1842.

ADAMS (*William Davenport*), born 1851. Anthologies: Comic Poets, 1875; English Epigrams, 1878; Latter-Day Lyrics, 1878; Lyrics of Love, 1873; Songs of Society,

1879 ; Songs from the Novelists, 1885 ; Quids and Quiddities, 1881. Book of Burlesque (*A*), 1891; By-ways in Bookland, 1888 ; Dictionary of English Literature, 1877; Dictionary of the Drama, 1897 ; Famous Books, 1875; Modern Anecdotes, 1886 ; Rambles in Bookland, 1889 ; Sunshine and Shadow, 1888; Witty and Humorous Side of the English Poets (*The*), 1880 ; With Poet and Player, 1891.

ADAMS (*Estelle Davenport*), wife of above. Flower and Leaf, 1884 ; Poet's Praise of Poets (*The*), 1894 ; Rose Leaves, 1883 ; Sea Song and River Rhyme, 1889.

ADDERLEY (*James Granville*), born July 1, 1861. Fight for the Drama at Oxford, 1885 ; God's Fast, 1896 ; Looking Upwards, 1896 ; Social Prayers, 1896; Stephen Remarx, 1893, a religious novelette ; New Floreat, a Letter to an Eton Boy (*The*), 1895.

ADDISON (*Joseph*), Milston, in Wiltshire, 1672–1719.
   Prose Works: Dissertation on [the Chief] Roman Poets, 1718 ; Evidences of the Christian Religion, 1730 ; Freeholder (*The*), 1715–16 ; Guardian (*Contributions to the*), 1713 ; Letter to Lord Halifax, 1703; Notes on Paradise Lost, 1719; Spectator (*The*),1711–12, 1714 (his sketches of sir Roger de Coverley, sir Andrew Freeport, and William Honeycomb, in these papers, are admirable); Tatler (*Contributions to the*), 1709–11.
   Poetical Works: Campaign (*The*), *i.e.* The Victory of Blenheim (10-syl. rhyme), 1704 ; Cato, 1713, a tragedy (the best drama in the language, containing the French unities); Divine Poems, 1728 ; Ode to Dr. Thos. Burnet, 1727 ; Poems, 1712, 1719 ; Poems to the Princess of Wales, etc., 1716. Life by Richard Steele, 1724; Tickell, 1765 ; Sprengel, 1810 ; Lucy Aikin, 1843 ; Macaulay, 1843 ; Elwin, 1857.

ADOLPHUS (*John*), London, 1764–1845. History of England, 1802 (from the Accession of George III. to the Peace of 1783) ; History of France, 1803 (from 1790 to the Peace of 1802).

AIDÉ (*Hamilton*), Paris, novelist and poet, 1830– . Carr of Carlyon, 1862 ; Cliff Mystery (*The*), 1888 ; Confidences, 1859; Eleanore and other Poems, 1856 ; Elizabeth's Pretenders, 1895 ; In that State of Life, 1871 ; Introduced to Society, 1884 ; Marstons (*The*), 1868 ; Morals and Mysteries, 1872 ; Mr. and Mrs. Faulconbridge, 1864 ; Nine Days' Wonder (*A*), (played by the Kendalls and John Hare ,1874); Passages in the Life of a Lady, 1887 ; Penruddocke, 1873 ; Philip, a drama (played by sir H. Irving, 1872) ; Poet and Peer, 1880 ; Rita, 1864; Romance of the Scarlet Leaf, and other Poems, 1865 ; Songs without Music, 1882 ; Voyage of Discovery (*A*), 1892. And the words of several songs.

AIKIN, M.D. (*John*), Kibworth-Harcourt, in Lincolnshire, 1747–1822. Annals of the Reign of George III., 1822 (between 1813 and 1820) ; Calendar of Nature, 1784 ; England Delineated, 1788 ; Evenings at Home, 1795 (with his daughter, Mrs. Barbauld) ; General Biography, 1799–1815 ; Lives of John Selden and Archbishop Usher, 1773. His Life, by Lucy Aikin, 1823.

AIKIN (*Lucy*), Warrington, in Lancashire, daughter of the preceding, 1781–1864. Life of Addison, 1845 ; Memoir of Dr. John Aikin (her father), 1823 ; Memoirs of the Court of Queen Elizabeth, 1818. Her Life, by Le Breton.

AINGER (Rev. *Alfred*), London, 1837– . Charles Lamb, 1882.

AINSWORTH (*Henry*), Hebraist, died 1622. Annotations on the Five Books of Moses, 1627.

AINSWORTH (*Robert*), Eccles, in Lancashire, 1660–1743. Latin Dictionary, 1714–36.

AINSWORTH (*William Francis*), Exeter, 1807– . Researches in Assyria, etc., 1838 ; Researches in Asia Minor, etc., 1842 ; Travels in the Track of the " Ten Thousand Greeks," 1844.

AINSWORTH (*William Harrison*), Manchester, novelist, 1805–1882.
   Novels: Auriol and other Tales, 1880 ; Beatrice Tyldesley, 1878 ; Beau Nash, 1880 ; Boscobel, or the Royal Oak, 1872 ; Cardinal Pole, 1863 ; Chetwynd Calverley, 1876 ; Constable de Bourbon, 1866 ; Constable of the Tower, 1861 ; Crichton, 1837 ; Fall of Somerset, 1877 ; Flitch of Bacon (*The*), 1854 ; Goldsmith's Wife (*The*), 1875 ; Good Old Times (*The*), 1873 ; Guy Fawkes, 1841 ; Hilary St. Ives, 1870 ; Jack Sheppard, 1839 ; John Law, the Projector, 1864 ; Lancashire Witches, 1848 ; Leaguer of Lathom (*The*), 1876 ; Lord Mayor of London (*The*), 1862 ; Manchester Rebels (*The*), 1873 ; Merry England, 1874 ; Mervyn Clitheroe, 1857 ; Miser's Daughter (*The*), 1842 ; Myddleton Pomfret, 1868 ; Old Court (*The*), 1867 ; Old St. Paul's, 1841–43 ; Ovingdean Grange, 1860 ; Preston Fight (*The*), 1875 ; Rookwood, 1834 ; St. James's, or Court of Queen Anne, 1844 ; Sir John Chiverton, 1826 (? J. P. Aston) ; South Sea Bubble, 1868 ; Spanish Match (*The*), 1867 ; Spendthrift (*The*), 1856 ; Stanley Brereton, 1881 (his last); Star Chamber (*The*), 1854 ; Talbot Harland, 1870; Tale of the Plague, 1841 ; Tower Hill 1871 ; Tower of London, 1840 (his best) ; Windsor Castle, 1843 (good).
   Poetry: Ballads, 1855 ; Combat of the Thirty (*The*), 1860.

AIRD (*Thomas*), Bowden, Roxburghshire, poet, 1802–1876. Captives of Fez, and other Poems, 1857, 1878 ; Devil's Dream (*The*), 1856, a weird poem ; Poetical Works, 1842, 1856, 1878 ; Religious Characteristics, 1827 ; Summer's Day (*The*), 1842, a poem full of word-painting ; The Old Bachelor, 1848, tales and sketches.

AIRY, LL.D. (Sir *George Biddell*), Alnwick, Northumberland, astronomer, 1801–1892. Astronomical Observations, 1829–38 ; Errors of Observation, 1861 ; Figure of the Earth (*The*) (for the *Metropolitana*) ; Gravitation, 1834 (for the *Penny Cyclopædia*) ; Invasion of Britain by J. Cæsar, 1865 ; Ipswich Lectures on Astronomy, 1849 ; Magnetism, 1870 ; Sound, 1869 ; Trigonometry, 1855 (for the *Encyclopædia Metropolitana*).

AITON (*William*), near Hamilton, in Lanark-shire, Scotland, botanist, 1731–1793. Hortus Kewensis, 1789.

AKENSIDE (*Mark*), Newcastle-on-Tyne, poet, 1721–1770. British Philippic (blank verse), 1738 ; Epistle to Curio (10-syl. rhyme), 1744, altered to Ode to Curio, in Spenserian stanzas, 1744 ; Naiades (*Hymn to the*), 1746 ; Odes, 1740, 1744, 1747, 1749, 1750, 1751, 1754, 1757, 1763 ; Pleasures of the Imagination (three books, in blank verse), 1744 (his chief poem), recast in 1757, but the first cast is by far the best. His Life, by Bucke, 1832 ; by Dyce. (See also Dr. Johnson, *Lives of the Poets.*) Satirically sketched by Smollett, in *Peregrine Pickle*, as a pe-dant who gives a classical entertainment.

ALABASTER (*William*), Hadleigh, in Suffolk, 1567–1640. Lexicon Pentaglotton, 1637 ; Roxana, 1632, a tragedy acted at Cam-bridge.

ALAN, abbot of Tewkesbury, (?) 1141–1201. Life of Thomas à Becket, about 1190.

ALAN OF LYNN, (?) 1350–1420 ; Moralia Bi-bliorum, about 1400.

ALCOCK, LL.D. (*John*), bishop of Ely, born at Beverley, Yorkshire, 1435–1500, founder of Jesus College, Cambridge, 1496. Mons Perfectionis, 1497 ; Spousage of a Virgin to Christ, 1486.

ALCUIN (*Flaccus Albinus*), York, 735–804. Charlemagne invited him to his court, 793. The best of his numerous works are his *Dia-logue on Rhetoric* and his *Book on the Seven Arts.* His works were compiled by André Duchesne, 1617, in folio ; by the abbot Frobenius, 1777 ; and by the abbot Migne, in his *Patrologie*, 1851. His Life was written both by Duchesne and by Fro-benius ; by professor Lorenz in 1829, trans-lated by Jane Mary Slee, 1837. (See also Morley's *English Writers*, vol. ii.)

ALDRICH, D.D. (*Henry*), Westminster, 1647–1710. Artis Logicæ Rudimenta, 1692 ; Ele-ments of Civil Architecture, 1789 ; Pleasant Musical Companion (*The*), 1726. (Dr. Aldrich composed the round, *Hark! the bonny Christ-church bells.*)

ALEXANDER (*Mrs.*), real name *Mrs. A. Hector*, Dublin, novelist, 1825– . Ad-miral's Ward (*The*), 1882 ; At Bay, 1885 ; Beaton's Bargain, 1886 ; Blind Fate, 1890 ; For his Sake, 1891 ; Freres (*The*), 1882 ; Her Dearest Foe, 1875 ; Heritage of Langdale (*The*), 1876 ; Look before you Leap, 1864 ; Maid, Wife, or Widow, 1879 ; Mammon, 1893 ; Mrs. Creighton's Creditor, 1897 ; Ralph Wilton's Weird, 1874 ; Second Life (*A*), 1884 ; Snare of the Fowler (*The*), 1892 ; Which shall it be? 1865 ; Woman's Heart, 1891 ; Wooing o't (*The*), 1873.

ALEXANDER (*William*), first earl of Stirling, poet, 1580–1640. Aurora, 1604 ; Mon-archicke Tragedies (Crœsus, Darius, the Alexandræans, and Julius Cæsar), 1607 ; Recreations with the Muses, 1637.

ALEXANDER OF HALES, called "The Irre-fragable Doctor," died 1215. Commentaries, printed 1490 ; Summa Universa Theologia, written at the command of pope Innocent IV. (the two best editions are that of

1575 and that published at Cologne in 1622).

ALEYN (*Charles*), poet, died about 1640. Battle of Crecy and Poictiers, 1632 ; His-tory of Euriolus and Lucretius, 1639 ; His-tory of Henry VII., 1638.

ALFORD, D.D. (*Henry*), London, 1810–1871. Chapters on the Poets of Greece, 1841 ; Greek Testament, edited 1841–52 (his chief work); New Testament for English Readers, 1863–69 ; Queen's English (*The*), 1864.

Poetry : Abbot of Muchelnage, and other Poems, 1841 ; Poems and Poetical Frag-ments, 1831 ; School of the Heart, and other Poems, 1835.

ALFRED THE GREAT, king of England, born at Wantage, in Berkshire, 849, 871–901.

Translations : Bede's *Ecclesiastical His-tory ;* The Bible, about 870 ; Boëthius, *On the Consolation of Philosophy ;* Orosius, *Universal History ;* The Pastoral of Gregory I., *On the Care of the Soul ;* Selections from St. Augustine.

Original Works : Chronicles ; Institutes ; Laws of the West Saxons ; Meditations, etc. His Life, by Asser, 1574 ; Robert Powell, 1634 ; Spelman, 1678 ; A. Bicknell, 1777 ; Stolberg, 1815 ; Dr. Pauli. (See also Morley, vol. ii.)

ALISON (*Alexander*), 1812– . Church and the World Reconciled (*The*), 1864 ; Im-provement of Society (*The*), 1862 ; New Reformation in Europe and America, 1861 ; Philosophy and History of Civilization (*The*), 1860.

ALISON (Rev. *Archibald*), Edinburgh, 1757–1839. Essay on Taste, 1790 ; Memoirs of Lord Woodhouse Lee, 1818 ; Sermons, 1814, 1815.

ALISON (Sir *Archibald*), son of the preceding, Kenley, in Shropshire, 1792–1867. Criminal Law of Scotland (*The*), 1833 ; England in 1815, published 1845 ; Essays, 1850 ; Free Trade and Fettered Currency, 1847 ; His-tory of Europe during the French Revolu-tion (10 vols.), 1839–1842 ; History of Europe from the Fall of Napoleon (9 vols.), 1853–59 ; Life of Marlborough, 1848 ; Lives of Lord Castlereagh and Sir C. Stewart, 1861 ; Practice of the Criminal Law, 1834 ; Prin-ciples of the Criminal Law of Scotland, 1832 ; Principles of Population, 1840.

ALLEIN (*Richard*), 1611–1681. Companion for Prayer (*A*), 1680 ; Godly Fear, 1674 ; Heaven Opened, 1665 ; Vindiciæ Pietatis, 1665 ; World Conquered (*The*), 1668.

ALLEINE (*Joseph*), Devizes, in Wiltshire, minister, 1633–1668. Alarm to the Uncon-verted, 1672 ; Assembly's Shorter Cate-chism (*Explanation of the*), 1656 ; Call to Archippus (*A*), 1664. Life, by R. Baxter, 1672 ; Geo. Newton, 1673.

ALLEINE (*William*), son of Richard Alleine, 1623–1677. Millennium (*The*).

ALLEN (*Charles Grant*) (his early pseudonym was Cecil Power), Kingston, in Canada, 1848– . Anglo-Saxon Britain, 1881 ; At Market Value, 1894 ; Babylon, 1887 ; Beck-oning Hand (*The*), 1887 ; Blood Royal, 1893 ; British Barbarians, 1895 ; Charles

Darwin, 1885; Colin Clout's Calendar, 1882; Colour Sense (*The*), 1879; Colour of Flowers (*The*), 1882; Devil's Die (*The*), 1888; Dr. Palliser's Patient, 1889; Duchess of Powysland, 1892; Dumaresq's Daughter, 1891; Evolutionist at Large (*The*), 1881; Falling in Love, with other essays, 1889; Flowers and their Pedigrees, 1883; For Maimie's Sake, 1886; Force and Energy, 1888; Great Taboo (*The*), 1890; In All Shades, 1886; Ivan Greet's Masterpiece, 1893; Jaws of Death (*The*), '1896; Lower Slopes (*The*), 1894, poems; Michael Crag, 1893; Moorland Idylls, 1892-96; Mortal Coil (*This*), 1888; New Novel (*A*), 1896; Philistia, 1885; Physiological Æsthetics, 1877; Post-prandial Philosophy, 1894; Recalled to Life, 1891; Scallywag (*The*), 1893; Science in Arcady, 1892; Splendid Sin (*A*), 1896; Story of the Plants, 1895; Strange Stories, 1884; Tents of Shem (*The*), 1889; This Mortal Coil, 1889; Under Sealed Orders, 1896; Vignettes from Nature, 1881; What's Bred in the Bone, 1891; White Man's Foot, 1888; Woman who did (*The*), 1895.

ALLEN, M.D. (*John*), Redford, near Edinburgh, miscellaneous writer, 1770–1843. Illustrations of Hume's Essay on Liberty and Necessity, 1795; Inquiry into the Rise and Growth of the Royal Prerogative in England, 1830; Vindication of the Independence of Scotland, 1833; *Translated* Cuvier's *Animal Economy*, 1801.

ALLEN (Rev. *John*), 1771–1839. Modern Judaism, 1816 (the best book extant on the subject).

ALLEN (*Richard*), died 1717. Biographia Ecclesiastica, 1671; Vindiciæ Pietatis, 1664–66.

ALLEN (*Thomas*), 1608–1673. Chain of Scripture Chronology, 1659; Practice of a Holy Life.

ALLEN (*Thomas*), 1803–1833. Antiquities of London, 1824–27; History of Lincolnshire, 1832; History of London, 1829; History of Yorkshire, 1830.

ALLEN (*William*), cardinal of England, born at Rossall, Sutherland, 1532–1594 (called *Alanus*). Admonition to the Nobles and People of England and Ireland, 1588; Apologie for the Institution of Two Colleges, Rome and Rheims, 1581; Authoritie of the Priesthood to remitte Sinnes, 1567; Defense of the Bull excommunicating Queen Elizabeth, 1586; Defense of the Doctrine touching Purgatory, etc., 1565; True, Sincere, and Moderate Defense of Christian Catholics, 1563.

ALLIBONE, LL.D. (*Samuel Austin*), Philadelphia, U.S., 1816–1888. A Critical Dictionary of English Literature, and British and American Authors, 1854–71, also a Supplement, in 2 vols., edited by John Foster Kirk, 1891.

ALLIES (*Thomas William*), Bristol, 1813– . Church of England cleared from the Charge of Schism, 1846; Dr. Pusey and the Ancient Church, 1866; Formation of Christendom (in three parts), 1865–75; Royal Supremacy, etc., 1850; St. Peter, his Name and Office, etc., 1852; See of St. Peter (*The*), 1850.

ALLINGHAM (*William*) (pseudonym Patricius Walker), Ballyshannon, in Donegal, Ireland, 1823–1889. Ashby Manor, 1882; Blackberries, 1884; Choice Lyrics, 1891; Choicest British Ballads, 1864; Day and Night Songs, 1854; Evil May Day, 1882; Fairies (*The*), 1883; Fifty Modern Poems, 1865; Flower Pieces, 1888; In Fairy-land, 1870; Irish Songs and Poems, 1887; Laurence Bloomfield in Ireland, 1864, a poem in twelve chapters; Life and Phantasy, 1889; Music-Master (*The*), and other Poems, 1855; Nightingale Valley, 1854; Peace and War, 1854; Poems, 1850; Rambles, 1873; Rhymes for the Young, 1887; Songs, Ballads, and Stories, 1877.

ALLIX, D.D. (*Pierre*), a refugee in England at the revocation of the Edict of Nantes, 1641–1714. Diatriba de Anno et Mense Natali Jesu Christi, 1710; Dissertation on the Rise of the Trisagium or Doxology, 1674; Reflexions on the Books of the Holy Scripture, 1688; Remarks on the History of the Albigenses, 1692; Remarks on the History of the Churches of Piedmont, 1690.

A.L.O.E. (see TUCKER, *Miss*), 1821–1893.

ALSTON, M.D. (*Charles*), Eddlewood, 1683–1760. Tirocinium Botanicum Edinburgense, 1753.

AMES (*Joseph*), Great Yarmouth, 1689–1759. Catalogue of [2000] English Heads, 1748; Parentalia, 1750; Typographical Antiquities, 1749 (this is an account of printing in England, etc.).

AMES, D.D. (*William*), Norfolk, 1576–1633. De Conscientiæ et ejus Jure, 1630; Fresh Suit against Roman Ceremonies, etc., 1633; Medulla Theologiæ, 1623; Puritanismus Anglicanus, 1610.

AMHURST (*Nicholas*), Marden, in Kent, 1706–1742. Craftsman (*The*), 1729–30; Terræ Filius, 1721.

ANDERDON (Rev. *William Henry*), London, 1816–1889. Afternoons with the Saints, 1863; Bonneval, a Story of the Fronde, 1857; Christian Æsop (*The*), 1871; In the Snow, 1866; Tales of Mount St. Bernard; Is Ritualism Honest? 1877; Owen Evans, the Catholic Crusoe, 1862; Seven Ages of Clarewell (*The*), 1867.

ANDERSON (*Adam*), 1692–1765. Historical and Chronological Deduction of Trade and Commerce, 1762.

ANDERSON (*Alexander*), Aberdeen, 1582–1619. Exercitationum Mathematicarum Decas Prima, 1619; Supplementum Apollonii redivivi, 1612.

ANDERSON (Sir *Edmund*), Broughton, 1540–1605. Reports, 1664, posthumous.

ANDERSON (Rev. *James*), Edinburgh, *-1595. Ane Godly Treatis calit the First and Second Cumming of Christ, with the Tone of the Wintersnycht, 1595.

ANDERSON (*James*), Edinburgh, 1662–1728. Collections relating to the History of Mary, Queen of Scotland, 1724–28; Genealogical History of the House of Yvery, posthumous 1742; Selectus Diplomatum et Numismatum Scotiæ Thesaurus, 1739, posthumous.

ANDERSON, LL.D. (*James*), Hermiston, Edinburgh, 1739-1808. Account of the Hebrides, etc., 1785; The Bee, 1790-94, a periodical; Encouragement of the National Fisheries, 1784; Essays of Agricola, 1777; Recreations in Agriculture, Natural History, Arts, and General Literature, 1799-1802.

ANDERSON (*Robert*), Carnwath, in Scotland, 1750-1830. British Poets (edited), 1790-1807; Life of Tobias Smollett, M.D., 1803.

ANDERSON (*Robert*), Carlisle, poet, 1770-1833. Ballads in the Cumberland Dialect, 1805; Betty Brown, 1801; Lucy Gray, 1794; Essay on the Character and Manners of the Peasantry of Cumberland (in prose), 1820.

ANDERSON, D.D. (*Walter*), 1720-1800. History of France, during the Reigns of Francis I. and Charles IX., 1769; History of France, from Henri III. to the Peace of Munster, 1775-82; Philosophy of Ancient Greece investigated, 1791

ANDERSON (*William*), Kilsyth, in Stirlingshire, 1800-1833. Mass, Penance, Regeneration, etc. (*The*).

ANDERTON (*James*), polemical writer, flourished 1600. Explanation of the Liturgy of the Mass, 1620; Protestant's Apology for the Roman Catholic Church (*A*), 1609; Religion of St. Augustine, 1620.

ANDREWE (*Laurence*), 16th century. The Wonderful Shape and Nature of Man, Beastes, Serpents, Fowles, Fishes, and Monsters, 1610.

ANDREWES (*George*), *-*. Dictionary of Slang and Cant (no date).

ANDREWES (*Launcelot*), bishop of Winchester, born in London, 1555-1626. Manual of Devotion, or Præces Privatæ, posthumous 1674; Manual for the Sick, posthumous 1629; Orphan Lectures, posthumous 1657 (his most popular work); Sermons, 1631; Selected Sermons, 1868; Tortura Torti (a Defence of Royalty, in answer to Bellarmine's treatise against James I., published under the pseudonym of Matthew Tortus), 1609; Works, 1589-1610. His Life, by Henry Isaacson, his amanuensis, 1628; by A. T. Russell.

ANDREWS (*James Pettit*), Newbury, Berkshire, 1737-1797. History of Great Britain, 1794.

ANGUS, D.D. (*Joseph*), Bolam, in Northumberland, 1816- . Christian Churches, 1862; Handbook of English Literature, 1865; Handbook of the English Tongue, 1861.

ANSON (*George*, lord), Shackborough, Warwickshire, 1697-1762. Voyage round the World, 1740 (written by B. Robins from Anson's notes, and supervised by Anson). His Life, by sir J. Barrow, 1838.

ANSTED (*David Thomas*), London, 1814-1880. Ancient World (*The*), 1847; Application of Geology to the Arts and Manufactures, 1865; Channel Islands (*The*), 1862; Correlation of the Natural History Sciences, 1863; Earth's History (*The*), 1869; Elementary Course of Geology, Mineralogy, and Physical Geography, 1850; Geological Gossip, 1860; Geological Science, 1855; Geologist's Text-book (*The*), 1845; Geology, In-

troductory, Descriptive, and Practical, 1844; Gold-seekers' Manual (*The*), 1849; Great Stone-book of Nature (*The*), 1863; Ionian Islands (*The*), 1863; Physical Geography, 1867; Physiography, 1877; Scenery, Science, and Art, 1854; Short Trip to Hungary and Transylvania, 1862; Water, 1878; World we live in (*The*), 1869 (the most popular of all his works).

ANSTEY (*Christopher*), poet, 1724-1805. Election Ball (*The*), 1776; New Bath Guide, 1766; Priest Dissected (*The*), 1774, a poem suppressed. (N.B.—This Anstey is buried in Westminster Abbey! where Byron is not recognized.)

ANSTEY (*F.*), real name *Thomas Anstey Guthrie*, Kensington, 1856- . Black Poodle, etc. (*The*), 1884; Burglar Bill, etc., 1888; Fallen Idol (*A*), 1886; Giant's Robe (*The*), 1884; Lyre and Lancet, 1895; Man from Blankley's (*The*), etc., 1893; Mr. Punch's Model Music-hall Songs and Dramas, 1892; Mr. Punch's Pocket Ibsen, 1895; Pariah (*The*), 1889; Talking Horse (*The*), etc., 1892; Tinted Venus (*The*), 1885; Tourmalin's Time Cheques, 1891; Travelling Companions, 1892; Under the Rose, 1894; Vice Versâ, 1882; Voces Populi, 1895.

APPERLEY (*Charles James*), pseudonym "Nimrod," 1777-1845. Chase (*The*), the Turf, and the Road, 1835; Horse (*The*) and the Hound, 1842; etc., etc.

ARBUTHNOT, M.D. (*John*). Arbuthnot, near Montrose, 1675-1735. Examination of Dr. Woodward's Account of the Deluge, etc., 1697; History of John Bull, 1713; Tables of Ancient Coins, Weights, and Measures, 1705-1708; etc., etc.

ARCHER (*William*), Perth, 1856- . About the Theatre, 1886; English Dramatists of To-day, 1882; Irving (*Henry*), 1883; Macready, 1896; Masks or Faces, 1888. *Translations*: Ibsen's Prose Dramas, 5 vols.; Peer Gynt (with his brother).

ARGYLL (*George John Douglas Campbell*, duke of), 1823- . Administration of Lord Dalhousie, 1855; Afghan Question (*The*), 1879; Burdens of Belief, and other Poems, 1864; Eastern Question (*The*), 1879; Geology of the Deluge, 1885; Highland Nurse (*The*), 1889; History and Antiquity of Iona, 1871; Irish Nationalism, 1893; Landlord and Tenant, 1877; Letter to the Peers, etc., 1842; New British Constitution (*The*), 1887; Philosophy of Belief, 1896; Plantagenet Act (*The*), 1874; Poems, 1894; Presbytery Examined (*The*), 1848; Primeval Man, 1869; Progress of the Highlands, 1886; Prophet of San Francisco (*The*), 1884; Reign of Law (*The*), 1866; Scotland as it was and as it is, 1887; Unity of Nature (*The*), 1884; Unseen Foundations of Society (*The*), 1893; What is Truth? 1889.

ARMSTRONG (*Archibald*, or *Archee*), jester, died 1672. Archee's Banquet of Jests, 1639. His Life, by Cecil; Dr. Doran, *Court Fools*.

ARMSTRONG (*George Francis Savage*), Dublin, poet, 1845- . Garland from Greece (*A*), 1882; King David, 1874; King Saul, 1872; King Solomon, 1876, a dramatic trilogy; Mephistopheles in Broadcloth, 1888, a

4 L

satire; One in the Infinite, poem; Poems, Lyrical and Dramatic, 1869; Stories of Wicklow, 1886, poems; Ugonê, 1870, a tragedy; Victoria Regina, 1887.

ARMSTRONG, M.D. (*John*), Castleton, in Roxburghshire, poet, 1709-1779. Art of Preserving Health (*The*), a didactic poem in four books, blank verse, 1744 (his best poem); Benevolence, 1751; Day, 1761, a poem; Economy of Love (*The*), 1737 (his first poem, suppressed as obscene); Essays, 1758, in prose; Short Ramble through Parts of France and Italy, by Lancelot Temple, Esq., 1771; Taste, 1753, a poetical epistle.

ARMSTRONG, M.D. (*John*), Ayres Quay, Bishop Wearmouth, in Durham, 1784-1829. Lectures, 1834; Puerperal Fever, 1813; Typhus, 1816. His Life, by Boott, 1832.

ARMYN (*Robert*), died 1611. Nest of Ninnies (*A*), 1608, a comedy.

ARNALD (*Richard*), 1696-1756. Commentary on the Apocrypha, 1744.

ARNE, Mus.D. (*Thomas Augustine*), London, 1710-1778. Artaxerxes, 1762, an opera, paraphrased from Metastasio; Comus, 1738, a masque; Eliza, an opera; Guardian Outwitted (*The*), 1759; words by Massinger, altered by Garrick; Rosamond, 1733, an opera; libretto by Addison; Rose (*The*), comic opera, adapted from the French; Rule, Britannia, 1740, a national song, words by Thomson; Tom Thumb, or the Opera of Operas, 1735, a burletta, words by Fielding, altered 1778 by O'Hara.

ARNOLD (Sir *Arthur*), Whartons, Framfield, Sussex, 1833-   . Cotton Famine (*The History of the*), 1864; Free Land, 1880; From the Levant, 1868; Hever Court, 1867, a novel; Letters from the Levant, 1868; Ralph, 1863, a novel; Social Politics, 1878; Through Persia by Caravan, 1877.

ARNOLD (Sir *Edwin*), brother of the above, poet, 1832-   . Adzuma, 1893; Book of Good Counsels, 1861; East and West, 1896; Education in India, 1860; Feast of Belshazzar, 1852, a Newdegate prize; Griselda, 1856, a drama; Hero and Leander, 1873, a translation; Hitopadesa, 1861, a translation; In my Lady's Praise, 1889; India Revisited, 1886; India under Lord Dalhousie, 1862-64; Indian Idylls, 1883; Indian Poetry, 1881; Indian Song of Songs, 1875; Japonica, 1871; Light of Asia (*The*), 1879; Light of the World (*The*), 1891; Lotus and Jewel, 1887; Pearls of Faith, 1882; Poems (Narrative and Lyrical), 1853; Poems (National and Non-Oriental), 1888; Poetical Works, complete edition in 8 vols., 1888; Poets of Greece, 1869; Potiphar's Wife, and other Poems, 1892; Seas and Lands, 1891; Secret of Death (*The*), 1885; Song Celestial (*The*), 1885; Tenth Muse (*The*), 1895; Wandering Words, 1894; With Sadi in a Garden, 1888; Wreck of the *Northern Belle*, 1857.

ARNOLD, D.C.L. (*Matthew*), Laleham, Middlesex, 1822-1888.
   Poetry: Balder (his best); Cromwell, 1843, Newdegate prize; Empedocles on Etna, and other Poems, 1853; England and the Italian Question, 1859; Merope, 1857, a tragedy; New Poems, 1867; Poems, 1853-57;

Sohrab and Rustum; Strayed Reveller (*The*), and other Poems, 1849.
   Prose: Bible Readings for Schools, 1872; Culture and Anarchy, 1869; Discourses in America, 1885; Essays in Criticism, 1865; French Eton (*A*), 1864; Friendship's Garland, 1871, conversations; God and the Bible, 1875; Higher Schools of Germany, 1874; Irish Essays, 1882; Isaiah, 1875; Last Essays on Church and State, 1877; Last Words on Translating Homer, 1803; Literature and Dogma, 1873; Mixed Essays, 1879; Popular Education of France, 1861; Schools and Universities on the Continent, 1868; St. Paul and Protestantism, 1870; Study of Celtic Literature, 1867; Three Lectures on Translating Homer, 1861-62.

ARNOLD (*Samuel*), London, 1740-1802. Prodigal Son (*The*), 1770, an opera.

ARNOLD, D.D. (*Thomas*), West Cowes, Isle of Wight, 1795-1842. History of Rome, 1838-42; Lectures on Modern History, 1842; Roman Commonwealth, 1845; Sermons, 1845. His Life, by A. P. Stanley, 1844.

ARNOLDE (*Richard*), 1450-1521. Customes of London, 1502.

ARNOTT, M.D. (*Neil*), Arbroath, in Scotland, 1788-1873. Elements of Physics, or Natural Philosophy, General and Medical, 1827-1864; On the Smokeless Fire-place, Chimney-valves, etc., 1855; Survey of Human Progress, 1861; Warming and Ventilating, 1838.

ARTEMUS WARD. See BROWNE (*C. F.*).

ARTHINGTON (*Henry*), poet, died 1610. Principall Points of Holy Profession: (1) The Creation, (2) The Subversion, and (3) The Restoration of Man, 1607 (a few months before the birth of Milton).

ASCHAM (*Roger*), Kirby-Wiske, Yorkshire, 1515-1568. Apologia pro Cœna Dominica, etc., posthumous 1577; Epistolarum Libri Tres, 1578; Letters and Poems, posthumous 1570; Scholemaster (*The*), 1570 (his chief work); Toxophilus, and the Schole of Schootinge, 1544. His Life, by James Bennet, 1761; Dr. Johnson, 1767; Grant, etc.

ASGILL (*John*), 1650-1738. Argument respecting Eternal Life, 1698; De Jure Divino, 1710.

ASH, LL.D. (*John*), 1724-1779. Dictionary of the English Language, 1775; Introduction to Lowth's English Grammar, 1766.

ASHBURNHAM (*John*), 1604-1671. Narrative of Attendance on Charles I., posthumous 1830.

ASHMOLE (*Elias*), Lichfield, Staffordshire, 1617-1692. Antiquities of Berkshire, posthumous 1719; History and Antiquities of Berkshire, posthumous 1736; History of the Order of the Garter, 1672; Theatrum Chemicum Britannicum, 1652; Way to Blisse (*The*), *i.e.* The Philosopher's Stone, 1658. Life, by himself, and edited 1717 by Charles Burman.

ASHTON (*John*), *-*. Adventures of John Smith, 1884; Century of Ballads (*A*), 1887-88; Eighteenth-Century Waifs, 1887; English Caricature and Satire of the Seventeenth Century, 1884; History of the Chap-books of the Eighteenth Century, 1882; Humour, Wit, and Satire of the Seventeenth Century,

1883; Men, Maidens, and Manners a Hundred Years Ago, 1888; Modern Street-Ballads, 1888; Old Times, 1885; Romances of Chivalry, 1886; Social Life in the Reign of Queen Anne, 1882.

ASSER (*John*), surnamed "Menevensis," a monk of Menevia (St. David's), died 910. Annales Rerum Gestarum Ælfredi Magni (posthumous), first published 1574, best edition 1722.

ASTELL (*Mary*), Newcastle-on-Tyne, 1668–1731. Christian Religion (*The*), 1705; Defence of the Female Sex, 1696; Fair Way with Dissenters (*A*), 1704; Moderation truly stated, 1704; Vindication of the Royal Martyr, 1704.

ASTLE (*Thomas*), Needwood Forest, Staffordshire, 1735–1803. Origin and Progress of Writing, 1784 (the best work on the subject in any language); Seals of the Kings, etc., of Scotland, 1792.

ATHERSTONE (*Edwin*), poet, 1788–1872. Fall of Nineveh (*The*), 1828; Handwriting on the Wall (*The*), 1858; Israel in Egypt, 1861; Last Days of Herculaneum (*The*), 1821; Midsummer Day's Dream, 1822; Sea Kings of England (*The*), 1830.

ATKINSON, F.C.S. (*Thomas William*), Yorkshire, 1799–1861. Oriental and Western Siberia, 1858; Travels on the Amoor, 1860.

ATKYNS (Sir *Robert*), 1621–1710. Ancient and Present State of Gloucestershire, 1712, posthumous; Power, etc., of Parliament, 1689.

ATTERBURY, D.D. (*Francis*), bishop of Rochester, born at Milton-Keynes, Buckinghamshire, 1662–1732. *Absalom and Achitophel* of Dryden, Latinized, 1682; Considerations on the Spirit of Martin Luther, 1687; Posthumous Sermons, 1740; Works, 1789.

(N.B.—"The Examination of Dr. Bentley's Dissertation on the Epistles of Phalaris," by the Hon. Charles Boyle, was mainly the work of Dr. Atterbury. His Life, by Stackhouse, 1727.)

ATTWOOD (*George*), 1746–1807. Construction and Properties of Arches, 1801; Ordinances of Assize, 1801; Review of Statutes and Ordinances of Assize, 1801; Supplement of "Construction, etc., of Arches," 1804; Treatise on Rectilinear and Rotatory Motion, 1784 (a valuable work).

ATTWOOD (*Thomas*), 1765–1838. Coronation Anthem, "The king shall rejoice," 1820 (for the coronation of George IV.); Coronation Anthem, "O Lord, grant the king a long life," 1830 (for the coronation of William IV.).

AUBERTIN (*John James*), 1818– . Fight with Distances (*A*), 1888; Flight to Mexico (*A*), 1882; Lusiads (*The*) of Camoëns in English Verse, 1884; Seventy Sonnets of Camoëns, with Original Poems, 1881; Six Months in Cape Colony, 1886.

AUBREY(*John*), Easton-Piers, Wiltshire, 1626–1697. Letters and Lives of Eminent Men, 1813; History of Wiltshire, 1821; Miscellanies (on ghosts, dreams, omens, etc.), 1696; Natural History and Antiquities of Surrey, 1719. His Life, by J. Walker, 1813; John Britton, 1845.

AUDUBON (*John James*), Louisiana, U.S., 1780–1851. American Ornithological Biography, 1831–39; Birds of America, 1828–39–44; Quadrupeds of America (with Dr. Buchanan), 1853.

AUSTEN (*Jane*), Steventon, Hampshire, novelist, 1775–1817. Emma, 1816; Lady Jane, 1872, posthumous; Mansfield Park, 1814; Northanger Abbey, 1818, posthumous; Persuasion, 1818, posthumous; Pride and Prejudice, 1812; Sense and Sensibility, 1811. Memoir, by Austen Leigh, 1870; and by Goldwin Smith, 1890.

AUSTIN (*Alfred*), poet-laureate. Headingley, near Leeds, 1835– . Artist's Proof (*An*), 1864, a novel; At the Gate of the Convent, 1885; Conversion of Winckelmann, and other Poems, 1897; Days of the Year, 1887; England's Darling, 1896; England's Destiny, 1896, in verse; England's Policy and Peril, 1877, political; Five Years of it, 1858, a novel; Fortunatus the Pessimist, 1892; Garden that I love (*The*), 1894; Golden Age (*The*), 1871, a satire; Human Tragedy (*The*), in four cantos, 1862; Hibernian Horrors, 1880; Interludes, 1872; In Veronica's Garden, 1895; Jameson's Ride, 1896, a poem; Leszko the Bastard, 1877, a tale in verse of Polish grief; Love's Widowhood, and other Poems, between the years 1881–90; Madonna's Child, 1873; Millais (*Sir John Everett*), an Ode on his death, 1896; My Satire and its Censors, 1861, in verse; Note of Admiration (*A*), etc., 1861, prose; Poems (*Lyrical*), 1891; Poems (*Narrative*), 1891; Poetry of the Period (*The*), 1870; Prince Lucifer, 1887; Randolph, 1854, in verse; Rome or Death, 1873, in verse; Russia before Europe, 1876, political; Savonarola, 1881, a tragedy; Season (*The*), 1861, a satire; Soliloquies in Song, 1882; Tory Horrors, 1876, political; Tower of Babel (*The*), 1874, a drama; Vindication of Lord Byron, 1869, in answer to Mrs. Beecher Stowe's attack; Won by a Head, 1865, a novel.

AUSTIN (*Samuel*), poet, 1646–1664. Naps upon Parnassus, 1658; Urania, 1629, a poem.

AUSTIN (*Mrs.*), maiden name *Sarah Taylor*, of Norwich, miscellaneous writer, 1793–1867. Carové's "Story without an End" (translated), 1844; Falk's "Characteristics of Goethe" (translated), 1833; Fragments from German Prose-writers (translated), 1841; Guizot's "Causes of the Success of the English Revolution" (translated), 1850; Letters on Girls' Schools, and on the Training of Working Women, 1857; National Education, 1839; Ranke's "History of Germany during the Reformation" (translated), 1845; Ranke's "Popes of Rome" (translated), 1866; Sketches of Germany, 1854.

AYLETT, LL.D. (*Robert*), poet, 1584– . Divine and Moral Speculations, 1654; Humble Man's Prayer (*The*), 1655; Peace with her Four Garders, 1622; Wife not Ready-made, but Bespoken (*A*), 1653.

AYLIFFE, LL.D. (*John*), 1684–1750. Ancient and Present State of the University of Oxford, 1714; Pandect of Roman Civil Law, 1734; Parergon Juris Canonici Anglicani,

1726; State of the University of Oxford, 1714.

AYLMER (*John*), bishop of London, born at Aylmer Hall, Norfolk, 1521-1594. Harborowe for Faithfull and Trewe Subiects against the Late Blowne Blaste, etc., 1559.

AYLOFFE (Sir *Joseph*), 1708-1781. Calendars of the Ancient Charters, etc., 1772; Sepulchral Monuments, 1781 (completed by Gough).

AYRE (*John*), 1801-1869. Treasury of Bible Knowledge, 1866. Edited bishop Jewel's Works, 1845; and Horne's "Introduction to the Criticism of the Old Testament," 1860.

AYSCOUGH (Rev. *Samuel*), 1745-1805. Catalogue of MSS. in the British Museum, hitherto undescribed, 1782; Catalogue of Books in the British Museum, 1788; Index to Shakespeare, 1790 (*superseded by Mrs. Cowden Clarke's Concordance to Shakespeare*).

AYTON (Sir *Robert*), poet, 1570-1638. Buried in Westminster Abbey. Several of his songs and lyrics were published in the collections called *Deliciæ Poetarum Scotorum*, and Watson's *Collections of Scottish Poems*.

AYTON (*William*), 1731-1793. Hortus Kewensis, 1789.

AYTOUN (*William Edmonstoune*), Edinburgh, 1813-1865.

Poetry: Ballads of Scotland (edited), 1858; Bothwell, 1856, a narrative poem in the style of sir Walter Scott; Firmilian, 1854, a spasmodic tragedy; Lays of the Scottish Cavaliers and other Poems, 1849 (his chief poetical work: "The Execution of Montrose" and "The Burial-March of Dundee," especially good); Nuptial Ode on the Marriage of the Prince of Wales, 1863; Poland, and other Poems.

Prose: Glenmutchkin Railway, a tale; How I became a Yeoman (his best tale); Life and Times of Richard I., 1840; Norman Sinclair, 1861. His Life, by Martin, 1867.

BABBAGE (*Charles*), Teignmouth, Devonshire, 1792-1871; noted for his calculating-machine. Comparative View of . . . Assurances of Life, 1826; Decline of Science, 1830; Differential and Integral Calculus, 1816; Economy of Manufactures, 1832; Exhibition (*The Great*), 1851; Letters to Sir H. Davy, 1822; Ninth Bridgewater Treatise (*The*), 1837; On the Economy of Manufactures and Machinery, 1832; Passages from the Life of a Philosopher, 1864; Table of Logarithms, 1826, from 1 to 180,000; Turning and Planing Tools, 1846.

BABINGTON, M.D. (*Benjamin Guy*), 1794-1866. Adventures of the Gooroo Paramatan, 1822, a tale in the Tamil language.

BABINGTON (*Charles Cardale*), Ludlow, Shropshire, 1808-1895. Ancient Cambridge-shire, 1851; British Rubi (*The*), 1869; Flora Bathoniensis, 1836; Flora in Cambridge-shire, 1860; Flora of the Channel Islands, 1839; History of St. John's College, Cambridge, 1874; Manual of English Botany, 1843.

BABINGTON (Rev. *Churchill*), 1821-1888.

Edited from MS. recently discovered, "The Oration of Hyperides against Demosthenes." Edited from papyrus in the British Museum, "The Funeral Oration of Hyperides;" Hulsean Prize Essay, 1846.

BABINGTON, M.D. (*William*), Portglenone, in Ireland, 1756-1833. New System of Mineralogy, 1799; Systematic Arrangement of Minerals, 1795.

BACK (Sir *George*), Stockport, Cheshire, 1796-1878. Narrative of the Arctic Land Expedition to the Mouth of the Great Fish (*or* Back) River, and along the Shores of the Arctic Ocean, in 1833-35.

BACON (*Francis*, baron Verulam and viscount St. Albans), London, 1561-1626, "Father of Experimental Philosophy." Advancement of Learning, 1605; Apologie, 1604; Apophthegms, 1625; Charge touching Duels, 1614; De Augmentis Scientiarum, 1623 ("Advancement of Learning," in Latin, and enlarged); De Sapientia Veterum, 1609; Discourse on the Happy Union of England and Scotland, 1603; Elements of the Laws of England, 1636, posthumous; Essays (fifty-eight), 1597, 1612, 1624; Felicities of Queen Elizabeth, 1650, posthumous; Historia Naturalis et Experimentalis, etc., 1622; Historia Ventorum, 1638, posthumous in English, 1653; Historia Vitæ et Mortis, etc., 1623; History of Henry VII., 1623; Instauratio Magna, 1620; NewAtlantis (*The*), 1635, posthumous (unfinished); Novum Organum, 1620 (his great work, edited, with Introduction and Notes, by J. S. Brewer, 1856); Of the State of Europe, 1580; Opera (very scarce), 1623; Psalmes in Verse, 1625; Reading on the Statute of Uses, 1643, posthumous; Relation of the Poysoning of Sir Thomas Overbury, 1651, posthumous; Sermones Fideles, 1638, posthumous; Sylva Sylvarum (in ten centuries), 1627, posthumous; Wisdom of the Ancients (in Latin), 1609. His Life, by viscount of St. Albans, 1626; Rawley, 1657; Robert Stephens, 1736; David Mallet, 1740; Birch, 1763; P. L. Courtier, 1803; Basil Montagu, 1825; J. Sortain; Macaulay, 1843; lord Campbell, 1846-47; Macvey Napier, 1857; Ellis, 1858; W. Hepworth Dixon, 1862; Spedding, 1870.

BACON (*John*), Southwark, Surrey, sculptor, 1740-1799. Monument to Lord Chatham in Westminster Abbey, 1778-83.

BACON (*Roger*), Ichester, in Somersetshire; generally called "Friar Bacon," "Doctor Mirabilis," 1214-1292. Compendium Philosophiæ, 1271; Compendium Studii Theologiæ, 1292; De Nullitate Magiæ, posthumous, edited by J. S. Brewer, 1859; De Potestate Artes et Naturæ, 1542, posthumous; Libellus de Retardantis Senectutis, etc., 1590, posthumous; Means of Avoiding the Infirmities of Old Age (in Latin), 1289, first published 1590, translated by Browne, 1683; Miracles of Art, Nature, and Magick, 1659, posthumous; Mirror of Alchimy, 1597, posthumous; Opus Majus, 1267 (his great work), edited by Jebb, 1733; Opus Minus, posthumous, edited by J. S. Brewer, 1859; Opus Tertium posthumous, edited by J. S.

Brewer, 1859; Speculum Alchemiæ, 1541, posthumous. Works, edited by J. S. Brewer, 1859.

BAGE (*Robert*), Darley, near Derby, novelist, 1728-1801. Barham Downs, 1784; Fair Syrian (*The*), 1787; Hermstrong, or Man as He is not, 1796; James Wallace, 1788; Man as He is, 1792; Mount Heneth, 1781. His Life, by sir Walter Scott, 1836.

BAGEHOT (*Walter*), 1826-1877. Economic Studies, 1880, posthumous. English Constitution (*The*), 1867; Essays on Silver, 1877; Literary Studies, 1878, posthumous; Lombard Street, 1873; Physics and Politics, 1870.

BAILEY (*Nathaniel*), died 1742. Universal Etymological English Dictionary, 1726, very scarce (the best edition is in folio by Joseph Nicol Scott, M.D., 1755, very scarce).

BAILEY (*Peter*), Nantwich, Cheshire, died 1823. Idwal, a poem connected with the conquest of Wales; Queen's Appeal (*A*), in the Spenserian stanza; Sketches from St. George's-in-the-Fields.

BAILEY (*Philip James*), poet, Nottingham, 1816- . Age (*The*), 1858, a colloquial satire in verse; Angel World (*The*), 1850, in verse; Festus, 1839 (his chief work), a dramatic poem; Mystic (*The*), 1855, in verse; Universal Hymn, 1867.

BAILEY (*Samuel*), Sheffield, 1791-1870. Berkeley's Theory of Vision (*Review of*), 1842; Berkeley's Letter to a Philosopher in Reply . . . 1843; Discourses of Various Subjects, Literary and Philosophical, 1852; Formation and Publication of Opinion (*Essays on the*), 1829, a sequel to the "Pursuit of Truth;" Joint Stock Banks and Country Issues (*A Defence of*), 1840; Money and its Vicissitudes in Value, 1837; Parliamentary Reform (*A Discussion of*), 1831; Philosophy of the Human Mind (*Letters on the*), 1st series 1855, 2nd series 1858, 3rd series 1868; Political Representation (*Rationale of*), 1835; Pursuit of Truth, etc. (*Essays on the*), 1821; Questions for Discussion on Politics, etc., 1823; Right of Primogeniture Examined, 1837; Shakespeare's Dramatic Writings (*On the Received Text of*), 1862, 1868; Theory of Reasoning (*The*), 1851; Value (*Critical Discussion on the Nature, etc., of*), 1825; Value (*Letters to a Political Economist on*), 1826.

BAILLIE (*Joanna*), Bothwell, in Lanark, Scotland, dramatist, 1762-1851. Dramas, 1836, sequel to the "Plays of the Passions;" Family Legend (*The*), 1810; Fugitive Verses, 1823; Metrical Legends, 1821; Miscellaneous Plays, 1804; Plays of the Passions, 1st series 1798, 2nd series 1802, 3rd series 1812, 4th series 1836. (The best of her plays is "De Montfort," a tragedy.) Works, with a Life, 1858.

BAILLIE, M.D. (*Matthew*), Shotts, in Scotland, 1761-1823 (brother of Joanna, the poet). The Morbid Anatomy of some of the most Important Parts of the Human Body, 1795.

BAILY, D.C.L. (*Francis*), Newbury, Berkshire, 1774-1844. Life of Flamsteed, 1835.

BAIN, LL.D. (*Alexander*), Aberdeen, 1818- . Emotions and the Will, 1859 (one of his chief works); Higher English Grammar, 1872, and its Companion, 1874; Logic, Deductive and Inductive, 1870; Manual of English Composition, 1866; Mental and Moral Sciences, 1868; Mill (*John Stuart*), 1882; Mind and Body, 1873; Moral Philosophy, 1852; On Teaching English, 1887; Practical Essays, 1884; Senses and the Intellect (*The*), 1855 (one of his chief works); Science of Education (*The*), 1879; Study of Character (*The*), 1861.

BAINES (*Edward*), Walton-le-Dale, in Lancashire, 1774-1848. History, etc., of the County of York, 1822-23; History, etc., of the County Palatine and Duchy of Lancaster, 1824-25; History of the Reign of George III., 1814; History of the Wars of the French Revolution (*A*), 1818; His Life, by his son Edward, 1849.

BAIRD (*Robert*), Fayette, in Pennsylvania, U.S., 1798-1863. Christian Retrospect and Register (*The*), 1851; History of Temperance Societies, 1836; View of Religion in America (*A*), 1842.

BAKER (*David Erskine*), eldest son of Henry Baker, 1723-1770. A Companion to the Playhouse, 1764 (enlarged into the *Biographia Dramatica*).

BAKER (*George*), Northamptonshire, 1780-1851. History and Antiquities of the county of Northampton, 1822-38 (an excellent work).

BAKER (*Henry*), London, naturalist and poet, founder of the Bakerian Oration, 1698-1774. Attempt towards a Natural History of the Polype, 1743; Employment for the Microscope, 1753; Microscope made easy, (*The*), 1743; Microscopical Observations, 1768.
  Poetry: Invocation to Health, 1722; Medulla Poetarum Romanorum, 1737; Original Poems, 1725-26; Universe (*The*), 1740, a philosophical poem.

BAKER (*James*), Hampshire, 1847- . By the Western Sea, 1889, a novel; Days Afoot and European Sketches, 1881; Forgotten Great Englishman (*A*), *i.e.* Peter Payne, 1894; Gleaming Dawn (*The*), 1896; John Westacott, 1886, a novel; Mark Tillotson, 1892, a novel; Our Foreign Competitors, 1892; Pictures from Bohemia, 1894.

BAKER, F.L.S. (*John Gilbert*), Guisborough, in Yorkshire, 1834- . An Attempt to classify the Plants of Britain Geologically, 1855; Elementary Lessons in Botanical Geography, 1875; Flora of the Mauritius, etc., 1877; Flora of Northumberland and Durham, 1868 (with Dr. G. R. Tate); Monograph of British Mints, 1865; Monograph of British Ferns, 1869; Monograph of British Roses, 1869; Monograph of the Ferns of Brazil, 1870; Monographs of the Papilionaceæ of Tropical Africa, 1868-71; Monographs of the Papilionaceæ of India, 1876; North Yorkshire: its Botany, Geology, etc., 1863; On the Geographical Distribution of Ferns, 1868; Popular Monograph of the Narcissus, Crocus, Lily, Iris, and Agave, 1870-77; Revision of the Order Liliaceæ (in seven parts), 1870-80; Synopsis

Filicum (commenced by sir W. Hooker), 1868, completed 1872; Systema Iridacearum, 1877.

BAKER (Sir *Richard*), Sittinghurst, Kent, 1568-1644. Chronicle of the Kings of England (*A*), 1641; Theatrum Redivivum, 1661.

BAKER, K.B. (Sir *Samuel White*), 1821-1893. Albert N'yanza (*The*), Great Basin of the Nile, and Exploration of the Nile Sources (2 vols.), 1866; Cast up by the Sea, 1869, a story from the French; Egyptian Question (*The*), 1884; Eight Years' Wanderings in Ceylon, 1855; Ismaïlia, 1874 (on the suppression of the slave-trade ; so called because the expedition was arranged by Ismaïl, khedive of Egypt); Nile Tributaries of Abyssinia (*The*), 1871; Rifle and Hound of Ceylon (*The*), 1853; True Tales for my Grandson, 1883; Wild Beasts and their Ways, 1890.

BAKER (Rev. *Thomas*), Crook, in Durham, 1656-1740. Reflections on Learning, 1710, to show the necessity of a revelation. His Life, by Dr. Zachary Grey, 1784.

BAKEWELL (*Robert*), 1768-1843. Introduction to Geology, 1813; Introduction to Mineralogy and Crystallography, 1819.

BALCANQUAL (*Walter*), Scotch divine, died 1645. Declaration of King Charles I. concerning the late Tumults in Scotland, 1630.

BALDWIN (*William*), poet, 1510?-1564. Cantacles or Balades of Solomon, in Metre, 1549; Funerailes of Edward VI., 1560; Mirrours for Magistraytes (*One of the Authors and Editors of*), 1559 (this valuable work occupies the annals of English poetry from Surrey to Spenser). *Prose:* Moral Philosophy, 1547.

BALE (*John*), bishop of Ossory, in Ireland, born at Cove, in Suffolk, 1495-1563. Summary of the Illustrious Writers of Great Britain (Latin), 1549.

BALES (*Peter*), penman, 1547-1610. The Writing-Master (in three parts), 1590. (He wrote out the entire Bible in shorthand, so small that it could be enclosed in an ordinary walnut-shell.)

BALFE (*Michael William*), Dublin, 1808-1870. *Operas :* Armourer of Nantes, 1863; Bianca, 1859; Bohemian Girl, 1843; Bondman, 1846; Catherine Grey, 1837; Dame Voilée (*La*), 1838; Daughter of St. Mark, 1844; Elfrida, 1856; Enchantress (*The*), 1849; Enrico IV., 1834; Falstaff, 1838; Four Sons of Aymon (*The*), 1843; Joan of Arc (*Jean d'Arc*), 1839; Kiolanthe, 1840; L'Etoile de Seville, 1842; Maid of Artois (*Manon Lescaut*), 1836; Maid of Honour, 1847; Puritan's Daughter (*The*), 1861; Rivals (*The*), (*I Rivali*), 1830; Rose of Castile (*The*), 1857; Satanella, 1858; Siege of Rochelle (*Assedio di la-Rochelle*), 1835.

BALFOUR (*Arthur James*), 1848- . Defence of Philosophic Doubt (*A*), 1879; Essays and Addresses, 1893; Foundations of Belief (introductory to the "Study of Theology"), 1895; Pleasures of Reading (*The*), 1887; Religion of Humanity (*The*), 1888.

BALFOUR, M.D. (*John Hutton*), 1808-1888.

Botany in the *Encyclopædia Britannica*; First Book of Botany, 1872; Introduction to Palæontological Botany, 1873; Manual of Botany (*The*), 1849; Phylo-Theology, 1851; Plants of Scripture (*The*), 1858.

BALL (*John*), puritan divine, 1585-1640. Short Treatise containing all the Principal Grounds of the Christian Religion (printed sixteen times before 1618); Treatise on Faith, 1632.

BALL (Sir *Robert*), Dublin, 1840- . Astronomy, 1877; Atlas of Astronomy, 1892; Experimental Mechanics, 1871; Great Astronomers, 1895; In Starry Realms; In the High Heavens, 1889; Mechanics, 1879; Starland, 1889; Story of the Heavens (*The*), 1886; Story of the Sun (*The*), 1893; Theory of Screws (*The*), 1876.

BALLANTINE (*James*), 1808-1877. Gaberlunzie Wallet (*The*), 1843; Life of David Roberts (*The*), 1866; Lilias Lee, 1872; Miller of Deanhaugh (*The*), 1844; Ornamental Art, 1847; Poems, 1856; Songs, 1865; Stained Glass, 1845; Whistle Binkie, 1878, posthumous.

BALLANTYNE (*James Robert*), Kelso, in Roxburgh, died 1864. Christianity contrasted with Hindoo Philosophy, 1859; First Lessons in Sanscrit Grammar, 1862; Synopsis of Science, in Sanscrit and English, 1856; Translation of the *Sahitya Darpana*, 1848.

BANCROFT, M.D. (*Edward*), died 1821. Essay on the Natural History of Guiana, in South America, 1769; Experimental Researches concerning the Philosophy of Permanent Colours, etc., 1813 (a valuable work).

BANCROFT (*George*), Worcester, in Massachusetts, U.S., 1800-1891. History of the Revolution in North America, 1852; History of the Colonization of the United States of North America, vol. i. 1834, iii. 1840, vii. 1858, viii. 1860 (a great work); Poems, 1823.

BANCROFT (*Richard*), archbishop of Canterbury, born at Farnworth, Lancashire, 1544-1610. Daungerous Proceedings under Pretence of Reformation, 1593; Survay of the Pretended Holy Discipline, 1593. Life, Hook's "Lives of the Archbishops."

BANCROFT (*Thomas*), epigrammatist, seventeenth century. Epigrams and Epitaphs, 1639; Glutton's Feaver, 1633; Heroical Lover, 1658; Two Bookes of Epigrammes and Epitaphs, 1639.

BANIM (*John*), near Kilkenny, novelist, 1800-1842. Tales of the O'Hara Family, 1825.

BANKS (*Mrs. George Linnæus*), Oldham Street, Manchester, 1821-1897. Bond Slaves, 1893; Bridge of Beauty, 1894; Caleb Booth's Clerk, 1878; Daisies in the Grass, 1865, poems; Forbidden to Marry, 1883, a novel; From the same Nest, 1891; Geoffrey Ollivant's Folly, 1886; Glory, 1877, a novel; God's Providence House, 1865, a novel; In his own Hand, 1885, a novel; Ivy Leaves, 1844 (her first poems); Manchester Man (*The*), 1876, a novel; More than Coronets, 1881; Poems, 1884; Ripples and Breakers, 1878; Slowly-grinding Mills (*The*), 1893; Stung to the Quick, 1867, a novel; Sybilla, 1884; Through the Night,

1882 ; Watchmaker's Daughter (*The*), 1883 ; Wooers and Winners, 1880, a novel.

BANKS (*John*), dramatist (seventeenth century). Cyrus the Great, 1696 ; Destruction of Troy, 1679 ; Innocent Usurper (*The*), 1694 ; Island Queens (*The*), 1684 ; Rival Kings (*The*), 1677 ; Unhappy Favourite (*The*), *i.e.* the Earl of Essex, 1632 ; Virtue Betrayed, 1682.

BANKS (Sir *Joseph*), London, 1743–1820. Catalogus Bibliothecæ Historico-Naturalis, 1798 (most comprehensive extant); Causes of Blight, Mildew, and Rust in Corn, 1803 ; Circumstances relative to Merino Sheep, 1809.

BANKS (*Thomas Christopher*), 1764–1854. Dormant and Extinct Baronage since the Conquest, 1807 ; History of the . . . Family of Marmyun, 1817 ; History of the Families of the Ancient Peerage, 1826 ; Stemmata Anglicana, 1825.

BANNATYNE (*George*), 1545–1606. Ancient Scottish Poems, published posthumously from his MS., 1770. (The Bannatyne Club, so called from George Bannatyne, 1823–1859.)

BARBAULD (*Mrs.*), maiden name *Anna Letitia Aikin*, born at Kibworth-Harcourt, in Leicestershire, 1743–1825; Devotional Pieces, 1775 ; Early Lessons for Children, 1774 ; Eighteen Hundred and Eleven, 1812 ; Evenings at Home, 1792-95 (with Dr. Aikin); Female Spectator (*The*), 1811 ; Hymns in Prose, 1774 ; Life of Samuel Richardson, 1805 ; Miscellaneous Poems, 1773 ; Miscellaneous Pieces in Prose, 1773 (with Dr. Aikin) ; Poetical Epistle to Mr. Wilberforce, 1790 ; Remarks on Gilbert Wakefield's "Inquiry," 1792. Memoir, by Lucy Aikin, 1827.

BARBOUR (*John*), 1316–1395. The Bruce, 1375, a metrical chronicle (it embraces the period between 1306-1329), first published from MS. in 1489.

BARCLAY (*Alexander*), 1476-1552. Castle of Labour (*The*), 1506 ; Egloges (50 in number), 1548 ; Mirror of Good Manners (*The*), posthumous ; Shyp of Folys of the Worlde (*The*), 1509.

N.B.—The *Narenschiff*, by Sebastian Brandt, was published 1494.

BARCLAY (*John*), a Scotchman born in France, 1582-1621. Argenis, 1621, a political allegory (Cowper says, "It is the most amusing ever written ;" Disraeli (lord Beaconsfield) much admired it also); Conspiratio Anglicana, 1605 ; De Potestate Papæ, 1611 ; Euphormio, 1603-29, a satire in Latin ; Icon Animarum, 1614, a capital book ; Phœniro (*The*), translated by Clara Reeve in 1771.

(*A Scot by blood, and French by birth, this man At Rome speaks Latin as no Roman can. Grotius.*)

His Life, by sir D. Dalrymple, 1786.

BARCLAY (*Robert*), Gordonstown, in Scotland, 1648-1690. Apology for the True Christian Divinity, 1678 ; Catechism and Confession of Faith, 1675 ; Treatise on Universal Love (*A*), 1677 ; Truth cleared of Calumnies, 1670 ; Universal Love, etc., 1677.

BARCLAY (*William*), Aberdeen, 1541-1605. De Regno et Regali Potestate, 1600.

BARHAM (*Richard Harris*), Canterbury, 1788–1845. Ingoldsby Legends, 1837, in verse and prose ; My Cousin Nicholas, a novel. Life, by his son.

BARING-GOULD (Rev. *Sabine*), Exeter, 1834-. Arminell, 1889 ; Birth of Jesus (*The*), 1885 ; Bladys of the Stewponey, 1897 ; Book of Fairy Tales ; Book of Nursery Songs and Rhymes (edited by B. Gould) ; Book of Were-Wolves (*The*), 1865 ; Broom Squire (*The*), 1896 ; Cheap Jack Zita, 1893 ; Church in Germany (*The*), 1891 ; Church Songs, 1884 ; Conscience and Sin, 1890 ; Court Royal (*The*), 1886 ; Curiosities of the Olden Time, 1869 ; Curious Myths of the Middle Ages, 1866-68 ; Curious Survival, 1892 ; Dartmoor Idylls ; Death and Resurrection of Jesus (*The*), 1888 ; Deserts of Southern France, 1894 ; Difficulties of the Faith (*The*), 1874 ; Eve, 1888 ; Freaks of Fanaticism ; Garland of Country Song (*A*), 1894 ; Gaverocks (*The*), 1887 ; Germany, Past and Present, 1879-83 ; Golden Gate (*The*), 1870 ; Gretter the Outlaw, 1889 ; Guavas the Tinner, 1897 ; Historic Oddities, 1889-91 ; Iceland, its Scenes and Sagas, 1862 ; Icelander's Sword (*The*), 1893 ; In Exitu Israel, 1870, a novel ; In the Roar of the Sea, 1892 ; In Troubadour Land, 1890 ; John Herring, 1883 ; Kitty Alone, 1894 ; Legendary Lives of Old Testament Characters, 1871 ; Life of Napoleon Bonaparte, 1896 ; Life of the Rev. J. S. Hawker, 1876 ; Lives of the Saints, 1872-77 ; Lost and Hostile Gospels (*The*), 1874 ; Margery of Quether, 1891 ; Mehalah, 1880 ; Mrs. Curgenven of Curgenven, 1893 ; My Prague Pig, 1890 ; Mystery of Suffering (*The*), 1877 ; Nazareth and Capernaum, 1886 ; Noemi, 1895 ; Old Country Life, 1889 ; Old English Fairy Tales (collected by B. Gould), 1894 ; Origin and Development of Religious Belief, 1869-70 ; Our Inheritance, 1888 ; Our Parish Church, 1886 ; Passion of Christ (*The*), 1885-86-87 ; Path of the Just (*The*), 1854 ; Pennycomequicks (*The*), 1889 ; Postmediæval Preachers, 1865 ; Preacher's Pocket (*The*), 1880 ; Queen of Love (*The*), 1894 ; Red Spider, 1887 ; Richard Cable, 1888 ; Saint Paul, 1897 ; Silver Store (*The*), 1870 ; Some Modern Difficulties, 1875 ; Strange Survivals, 1892 ; Through all the Changing Scenes of Life, 1892 ; Tragedy of the Cæsars (*The*), 1892 ; Urith, 1890 ; Village Pulpit (*The*), 1881-87 ; Village Sermons for a Year, 1875 ; Yorkshire Oddities, 1874 ; Way of Sorrows (*The*), 1887.

BARKER (*Edmund Henry*), Hollym, in Yorkshire, 1788-1839. Aristarchus Anti-Blomfieldianus, 1818 (in reply to Blomfield, who attacked his *Thesaurus* in the *Quarterly Review*) ; Classical Recreations, 1812 ; Parriana, 1828-29. (His *magnum opus*, however, is his edition of Stephen's "Thesaurus Linguæ Græcæ," which contains 11,752 double-columned closely printed pages, 1816-28.)

BARKER (Lady), maiden name *Mary Ann Stewart*, Jamaica ; afterwards married sir F. N. Broome. Christmas Cake in Four

Quarters (A), 1871; First Principles of Cooking, 1874; Ribbon Stories, 1872; Spring Comedies, 1872, a novelette; Station Life in New Zealand, 1869; Stories About, 1870; Travelling About, 1871; Year's Housekeeping in South Africa (A), 1877.

BARKSTED (William), 1577-1620. Hirem, or the Faire Greek, 1611, a poem (referred to by Shakespeare, 2 Henry IV. act ii.); Myrrha, the Mother of Adonis, 1607, a poem.

BARLOW (Jane), Clontarf, County Dublin, 1860-   . Battle of the Frogs and Mice (The), 1894; Bogland Studies, 1892; End of Elfintown (The), 1894; Irish Idylls, 1892; Kerrigan's Quality, 1893; Maureen's Fairing, 1895; Mockers of the Shallow Waters, 1893; Mrs. Martin's Company, 1897; Strangers at Lisconnel, 1895.

BARLOW (Joel), Reading, in Connecticut, U.S., 1755-1812. Conspiracy of Kings (The), 1792, a poem; Vision of Columbus (The), 1787, a poem (afterwards enlarged into The Columbiad, 1805).

BARLOW (Peter), Norwich, 1776-1862. Elementary Investigation of the Theory of Numbers, 1811; Essay on Magnetic Attractions, etc., 1822; Essay on the Strength and Stress of Timbers, 1817; New Mathematical and Philosophical Dictionary, 1813; New Mathematical Tables, 1814.

BARNES (Albert), New York State, 1798-1870. Notes on the New Testament, 1832-48; Notes on the Old Testament, 1851.

BARNES (Barnaby), 1569-1607. Devil's Charter (The), 1607, a tragedy on pope Alexander VI.; Divine Centurie of Spiritual Sonnets, 1595; Four Books of Offices, 1606; Parthenophil and Parthenophe: Sonnets, Madrigals, and Odes, 1593; Praise of Musike, 1587.

BARNES (Rev. William), Rushhay, in Dorsetshire, 1810-1886. An Anglo-Saxon Delectus (called S. Geflysta), 1849; Arithmetical and Commercial Dictionary (An), 1840; Early England, 1869; Elements of Linear Perspective, 1842; Grammar and Glossary of the Dorset Dialect, 1864; Hwomely Rhymes, etc., 1859; Notes on Ancient Britain, 1858; Philological Grammar, 1854; Poems of Rural Life (in Dorset dialect), 1844; Rural Poems (in common English), 1862; Song of Solomon (in the Dorset dialect), 1859; Tiw, or a View of the Roots and Stems of English, 1862; Views of Labour and Gold, 1859.

BARNETT (John), near Bedford, 1802-1889. Fair Rosamond, 1836, an historic opera; Farinelli 1839, an opera; Mountain Sylph (The), 1834 (his best opera). (And many hundred ballads, vaudevilles, canzonets, etc., as " Strike the Light Guitar," " Not a Drum was heard . . ." " Rise, Gentle Moon," etc.)

BARNFIELD (Richard), born 1574. Affectionate Shepherd, 1524, a vol. of poems; Cynthia, 1595, a poem, with sonnets; Lady Pecunia, 1598, in praise of money; Legend of Cassandra (The), 1595; Poems (reprinted by James Boswell, 1816).

BARNFIELD (Richard), poet, born 1574. Affectionate Shepherd (The), 1594 (very rare); Cynthia, with Sonnets, and the Legend of Cassandra, 1595; Encomion of

Lady Pecunia (The), 1598, on the praise of money. (Barnfield wrote the beautiful ode, "As it fell upon a Day," generally ascribed to Shakespeare.)

BARNHAM (Lady Anne), 1750-1825. Auld Robin Gray, 1771, a ballad.

BARR (Mrs.), maiden name Amelia Edith Huddleson, Ulverston, Lancashire, novelist, 1831-   . Beads of Tasmer, 1893; Between Two Loves, 1886; Border Shepherdess (A), 1887; Bow of Orange Ribbons (The), 1886; Cluny Macpherson, 1884; Daughter of Fife (A), 1886; Feet of Clay, 1889; Friend Olivia, 1890; Hallam Succession (The), 1885; Household of MacNeil (The), 1888; In Spite of himself, 1888; Jan Vedder's Wife, 1885; Last of the MacAllisters (The), 1886; Lone House (The), 1894; Lost Silver of Briffault (The), 1886; Love for an Hour is Love for Ever, 1892; Paul and Christina, 1887; Preacher's Daughter (The), 1892; Remember the Alamo, 1888; Scottish Sketches, 1890; She loved a Sailor, 1892; Singer from the Sea (A), 1893; Sister of Esau (A), 1892; Squire of Sandal-side (The), 1887; Women of Love and Glory, 1890.

BARR (Robert), novelist, 1850-   . Face and the Mask, 1894; From whose Bourne, etc., 1893; In a Steamer Chair, etc., 1892; In the Midst of Alarms, 1897; Luke Sharp, 1891; Mutable Many (The); Revenge, 1896; Woman Intervenes (A), 1896.

BARRETT, D.D. (John), died 1821. Inquiry into the Origin of the Constellations of the Zodiac. (It is said that Dr. Barrett, professor of Oriental languages in Trinity College, Dublin, was unable to tell a sheep from an ox.)

BARRI (Girald de). (See GIRALDUS CAMBRENSIS.)

BARRIE (James Matthew), Kerriemuir, 1860-   . Auld Licht Idylls, 1888; Better Dead, 1887; Edinburgh Eleven (An), 1889; Little Minister (The), 1891; Margaret Ogilvy, 1896; My Lady Nicotine, 1890; Sentimental Tommy, 1896; When a Man's Single, 1888; Window in Thrums (A), 1889 (Kerriemuir is the Thrums of the story).

Plays: Jane Annie, 1893; Little Minister (The), 1897 (adapted from the novel); Professor's Love Story (The), 1894; Walker, London, 1892.

BARRINGTON (The Hon. Daines), 1727-1800. Miscellanies, 1781; Observations on the Statutes, 1765 (a valuable work).

BARRINGTON (John Shute, lord viscount), Theobalds, Hertfordshire, 1678-1734. Essay on the Several Dispensations of God to Mankind; Miscellanea Sacra, 1725 (a valuable work).

BARRINGTON (Sir Jonah), 1767-1834. Historic Anecdotes, etc., relative to the . . . Union . . . [of] Ireland, 1809-1835; Personal Sketches of his own Time, 1830.

BARROW, D.D. (Isaac), London, 1630-1677. Archimedis Opera, 1675; Euclidis Data, 1675; Euclidis Elementa, 1655; Lectio de Sphæra et Cylindro, 1678, posthumous; Lectio Geometricæ, 1670; Lectiones Mathematicæ, 1734, posthumous; Lectiones Opticæ, 1669; Opuscula (containing Latin sermons, speeches, poems, etc.), 1687, posthumous ; Selected Writings, 1866, posthumous ; Theological Works, 1675, 1683, posthumous ; Life, by Hill.

BARROW (Sir *John*), Ulverstone, in Lancashire, 1764–1848. Autobiographical Memoir (*An*), 1847 ; Chronological History of Arctic Voyages, 1818 ; Life of Lord Macartney, 1807 ; Memoirs of Naval Worthies of Queen Elizabeth's Reign, 1845 ; Mutiny of the *Bounty*, 1831 ; Sketches of the Royal Society, 1848 ; Travels in China, 1804 ; Travels in Southern Africa, 1799 (valuable) ; Voyage to Cochin-China, 1806 (admirable).

BARRY, D.C.L. (Rev. *Alfred*), 1826-   . Bampton Lectures, 1892 ; Boyle Lectures (*The*) for 1876-77-78 ; England's Mission to India, 1894 ; First Words in Australia, 1884 ; Hulsean Lectures, 1895 ; Introduction to the Old Testament, 1850 ; Lectures on Christianity and Socialism, 1891 ; Life of Sir Charles Barry, R.A., 1867 ; Notes on the Catechism, 1867 ; Parables of the Old Testament, 1889 ; Religion for Every Day, 1873 ; Sermons, 1884 ; Sermons for Boys, 1868 ; Some Lights of Science on the Faith, 1892 ; What is Natural Theology ? 1876, Boyle Lecture.

BARRY, R.A. (Sir *Charles*), Westminster, 1795–1860. Built the Palace of Westminster, 1840–59. His Life, by Dr. Alfred Barry, 1867.

BARRY, D.D. (*George*), 1747–1805. History of the Orkney Islands, 1805 (an excellent work).

BARRY (*James*), Dublin, 1598–1673. The Case of Tenures upon the Commission of Defective Titles, 1637.

BARRY, R.A. (*James*), Cork, 1741–1806. An Inquiry into the Real and Imaginary Obstructions to the Acquisition of the Arts in England, 1775 ; Progress of Civilization, 1777–84. (As an artist his fame rests on his *Victors of Olympia*.) His Life, by Dr. Fryer, 1809.

BARRY (*Lodowick*), *-*. Ram Alley, or Merry Tricks, 1611, a comedy.

BARRY, M.D. (*Martin*), Hampshire, 1802–1855. Researches in Embryology, etc. (published in the *Philosophical Transactions*), 1838–43.

BARTON, M.D. (*Benjamin Smith*), Lancaster, U.S., 1766–1816. Elements of Botany, 1804 ; Fragments of the Natural History of Pennsylvania, 1799.

BARTON (*Bernard*), London, poet, 1784–1849. Household Verses, 1845 ; Metrical Effusions, 1812 ; Napoleon, and other Poems, 1822 ; Poems by an Amateur, 1818 ; Poems, 1820, 1849, 1853 ; Reliquary (*The*), 1836 ; Widow's Tale (*The*), 1827.

BARTRAM (*William*), Kingsessing, in Pennsylvania, U.S., 1739–1823. Travels through North and South Carolina, Georgia, etc., 1791 (the botany of this book is excellent).

BASSE (*William*), poet, seventeenth century. Great Brittaines Sunnes set . . . 1613, poem on the death of prince Henry ; Pastorals (prepared for publication, 1653) ; Sword and Buckler (*The*), 1602.

BASTIAN, M.D. (*Henry Charlton*), Truro, in Cornwall, 1837-   . Beginnings of Life (*The*), 1872 ; Brain as an Organ of Mind

(*The*), 1880 ; Clinical Lectures on Paralysis from Brain Disease, 1875 ; Evolution and the Origin of Life, 1874 ; Modes of Origin of Lowest Organisms, 1871 ; Paralysis, . . . 1886-93.

BASTWICK, M.D. (*John*), Writtle, in Essex, 1593-1648. Apologeticus ad Præsules Anglicanos, 1636 ; New Discovery of the Prelates' Tyranny, 1641 ; Elenchus Religionis Papisticæ, 1624 ; Flagellum Pontificis, 1635 ; New Letany, 1637 (once very famous).

BATEMAN, M.D. (*Thomas*), Whitby, in Yorkshire, 1778–1821. Delineations of Cutaneous Diseases, 1817 ; Synopsis of Cutaneous Diseases, 1813.

BATES, D.D. (*William*), 1625-1699. Vitæ Selectorum aliquot Virorum, 1681 (thirty-two lives : valuable).

BATESON (*Thomas*), seventeenth century. English Madrigals, 1604-18.

BATMAN (*Stephen*), poet, etc., 1537-1587. Doome (*The*), 1581 ; Golden Booke of the Leaden Goddess (*The*), 1577 ; Travayled Pilgrim (*The*), 1569.

BAXTER (*Andrew*), Aberdeen, 1686-1750. Inquiry into the Nature of the Human Soul, 1728 (an appendix was added in 1750); Matho, 1745.

BAXTER (*Richard*), Rowton, in Shropshire, 1615-1691. Aphorisms of Justification, 1649 ; Biographies, 1696, posthumous ; Call to the Unconverted, 1657 ; Catholic Theology, 1675 ; Certainty of the World of Spirits, 1691 ; Christian Directory, 1675 ; Church History of the Government of Bishops, 1680 ; Confessions of Faith, 1655 ; Dying Thoughts, 1688 ; Episcopacy, 1681 ; Gildas Silvianus, the Reformed Pastor, 1656 ; Life of Faith, 1670 ; Life of Mrs. Baxter, 1681 ; Methodus Theologiæ Christianæ, 1681 ; Now or Never, 1663 ; Paraphrase of the New Testament, 1685 ; Poetical Fragments, 1681 ; Poor Man's Family Book (*A*), 1674 ; Reasons for the Christian Religion, 1667 ; Reformed Liturgy (*The*), 1661 ; Reformed Pastor, 1656 ; Reliquiæ Baxterianæ, 1696, posthumous ; Saint's Everlasting Rest (*The*), 1649 ; Treatise on Episcopacy, 1681 ; Universal Concord, 1658 ; Universal Redemption, 1694. Life, by himself and Sylvester, 1696 ; Dr. E. Calamy, 1713 ; Orme, 1830.

BAXTER (*Robert Dudley*), 1827-   . National Income, 1868 ; Railway Extension and its Results, 1866 ; Taxation of the United Kingdom, 1869.

BAXTER (*William*), Llangollen, in Wales, 1650-1723. Glossarium Antiquitatum Britannicarum, 1719.

BAXTER (*William Edward*), Dundee, 1825-1889. America and the Americans, 1855 ; Free Italy, 1860 ; Hints to Thinkers, 1860 ; Impressions of Central and Southern Europe, 1850 ; Tagus and the Tiber, 1850-51 ; Winter in India, 1882.

BAYLE (*Pierre*), 1647-1706. Historical and Critical Dictionary, 1715 (originally in French, 1695-96 : useful).

BAYLY (*Lewis*), bishop of Bangor, born at Carmarthen, in Wales, 1565-1632. Practice of Piety (*The*), about 1600, the 11th edition was in 1619.

BAYLY (*Miss*). (See LYALL, EDNA.)
BAYLY (*Thomas Haynes*), 1797-1839. Thirty-six Dramatic Pieces; Weeds of Kitchery, 1837. (His poetical works were collected and published, with a memoir, in 1844.)
BAYNE (*Alexander*), 1690-1737. Institutions of Criminal Law of Scotland, 1730; Notes, 1731. (Also an edition of *Hope's Minor Practicks*, 1726.)
BAYNE (*Peter*), Fodderty, in Scotland, 1830-
. Chief Actors in the Puritan Revolution, 1878; Christian Life (*The*), 1855; Church's Curse and Nation's Claim (*The*), 1868; Days of Jezebel, 1872, an historical drama; Essays in Biographical Criticism, 1857-58; Free Church of Scotland (*The*), 1894; Lessons from my Master, 1872; Life of Hugh Miller, 1870; Martin Luther, 1887; Six Christian Biographies, 1887; Testimony of Christ to Christianity, 1862; Two Great English-women (*The*), 1880.
BAYNES, LL.D. (*Thomas Spencer*), Wellington, in Somersetshire, 1823-1886. New Analytic of Logical Forms, 1852; Port Royal Logic, 1851.
BEACONSFIELD. (See DISRAELI.)
BEALE, M.D. (*Lionel Smith*), London, 1828-
. Anatomy of the Liver, 1874; How to work the Microscope, 1871; Lectures, 1889; Life Theories, 1871; Microscope in its Application to Practical Medicine (*The*), 1868; Mystery of Life (*The*), 1871; Our Morality, etc., 1887; Protoplasm; or Life, Matter, and Mind, 1870.
BEATTIE (*James*), Laurencekirk, in Scotland, poet, etc., 1735-1803. Judgment of Paris, 1765; Minstrel (*The*), in two parts, Spenserian metre, part i. 1771, part ii. 1774 (incomplete : Merivale added a third part); Poems and Translations, 1760.
    Prose : Dissertations, 1783; Elements of Moral Sciences (*The*), 1790-93; Essay on Poetry and Music, 1778; Essay on Truth, 1770; Essays, 1776; Evidences of Christianity, 1786. Life, by sir William Forbes, 1806; Mudford, 1809; Dyce, 1831.
BEATTIE, M.D. (*William*), poet, etc., 1793-1875. Courts of Germany (*The*), 1827; Heliotrope (*The*), 1838; John Huss, 1829, in verse; Life of Campbell, 1847.
BEAUMONT (*Francis*), Gracedieu, in Leicestershire, dramatist and poet, 1586-1616. Bloody Brother (*The*), a tragedy published in 1639; Knight of the Burning Pestle (*The*), 1611, a comedy; Letter to Ben Jonson (*A*), published in 1640; Masque (*The*), 1613; Ovid's "Salāmis and Hermophrodītus," translated, 1602; Poems, 1640, 1653, posthumous.
    N.B.—Some sixty plays have been published under the names of Beaumont and Fletcher, either separately or in conjunction; of these, twenty-four bear the date of 1647, and seven others were published between the death of both dramatists and the year 1647.

BEAUMONT AND FLETCHER IN CONJUNCTION.

    (1) *Before the death of Beaumont in* 1616; Captain (*The*), 1613; Coxcomb (*The*), 1612; Cupid's Revenge, 1615; Honest Man's Fortune (*The*), 1613; Mad World, 1608;

Right Woman (*The*), 1615; Wit at Several Weapons, 1614; Woman-Hater (*The*), 1607.
    (2) *Between the death of both dramatists and* 1647: Coronation (*The*), 1640; Merchant of Bruges (*The*), 1630; Night-Walkers, 1633; Rollo, 1639; Two Noble Kinsmen, 1634 (excellent : ? B.and F.); Wit without Money, 1639.
    (3) *Plays published in* 1647, *and ascribed to Beaumont and Fletcher* (C. stands for comedy, T. *for tragedy*) : Bonduca, a tragedy; Custom of the Country (*The*), T.; Fair Maid of the Inn (*The*), C.; Faithful Friend (*The*); Four Plays in One, C.; Humorous Lieutenant (*The*), C. (? B. and F.); Island Princess (*The*); Jeweller of Amsterdam (*The*); Knight of Malta (*The*); Laws of Candy (*The*); Little French Lawyer (*The*), C.; Love's Cure, C. (? B. and F.); Love's Pilgrimage, C. (? B. and F.); Maid in the Mill, C. (? B. and F.); Nice Valour, C.; Noble Gentleman (*The*) (? B. and F.); Prophetess (*The*); Queen of Corinth (*The*) (? B. and F.); Sea Voyage (*The*), C. (? B. and F.); Woman's Place, C.; Woman's Prize, C.; Women Pleased, C. (? B. and F.). (For a list of the sixty plays, see FLETCHER, *John*.)
BEAUMONT (Sir *John*), poet, 1582-1628. Bos-worth Field, and other Poems, 1629.
BEAUMONT, D.D.(*Joseph*), 1615-1699. Poems, 1749, posthumous; Psyche (2 *syl.*), or Love's Mystery, 1647-48, posthumous.
BEAVAN (Rev. *James*), 1800-1871. An Account of the Life and Writings of St. Irenæus, 1841.
BECHE (Sir *Henry Thomas de la*), London, 1796-1855. Classification of European Rocks, 1828; Discovery of a New Fossil Animal, 1823; Geological Manual, 1831; Geological Observer, 1851; Geology of Cornwall, etc., 1839; Geology of Jamaica, 1826; How to observe in Geology, 1835 (a masterly work); Researches in Theoretical Geology, 1834.
BECKFORD (*William*), 1760-1844. Biographical Memoirs of Extraordinary Painters, 1870, a satire; Dreams, Incidents, etc., 1783; Italy, with Sketches of Spain and Portugal, 1780, published 1834; Memoirs of Extraordinary Painters, 1780; Recollections of an Excursion, 1835; Vathek, 1786, an Eastern tale. Life, by Cyrus Redding, 1858.
BECON (*Thomas*), 1511-1570. Actes of Christ and of Antichrist (*The*), 1577; Boke of Matrimony (*The*), 1542; Christmas Banket (*The*), 1542; David's Harpe, 1542; Fortres of the Faithfull, 1560; Gouvernaunce of Vertue (*The*), 1550; Inuctiue against Swearyng, 1543; Newes out of Heauen, 1541; Newyeare's Gift (*The*), 1543; Pathwaye unto Prayer, 1542; Physicke of the Soule, 1549; Policie of Warre (*The*), 1543; Pomaunder of Prayer (*The*), 1582; Popish Masse displayed, 1559; Potation for Lent, 1542; Reliques of Rome (*The*), 1553; Sicke Man's Salue, 1561; Solace of the Soul, 1548; Worckes (in folio), 1563-64.
BEDDOES (*Thomas Lovell*), Clifton, 1803-1849, son of Dr. Thomas Beddoes. Bride's Tragedy (*The*), 1822, a drama; Death's Jest Book, or

the Fool's Tragedy, 1850, a play; Improvisatore (*The*), 1821; Poems (with memoir), 1851, posthumous.

BEDDOES, M.D. (*Thomas*), Shifnall, in Shropshire, 1760–1808. Advice to Husbandmen in Harvest, 1808; Alexander's Expedition to the Indian Ocean, 1792; Chemical Experiments, 1790; Cure for Calculus, etc., 1792; Defence of Bill of Rights against Gagging Bills, 1796; History of Isaac Jenkins, 1793 (rules for sobriety for working men); Hygeia, 1801–2 (a very judicious treatise); On the Nature of Demonstrative Evidence, etc., 1792; On Consumption, 1799; On Fever, 1807; Public Merits of Mr. Pitt, 1796; Several Translations. Life, by Dr. Stock, 1811.

BEDE (" The Venerable"), Jarrow, in Durham, 672–735. A book on Metrical Art; another on Orthography; Lives of the Abbots of Wearmouth; Commentaries on most of the books of the Bible, including the Apocrypha; De Sex Ætatibus Mundi (all in Latin). Historia Ecclesiastica Gentis Anglorum (in five books), 734 (his best work); Homilies, Hymns, Epigrams, etc.; Martyrology. Life, by J. Stevens, 1723; Gehle, 1838; Wright, *Biographia Britannica Literaria*, 1843.

BEDE (*Cuthbert*). (See BRADLEY, Rev. *Edward*.)

BEE (*John*), *i.e.* John Badcock. Slang Dictionary (*A*), 1823.

BEECHER-STOWE (*Mrs.*), maiden name *Harriet Elizabeth Beecher*, born at Lichfield, Connecticut, U.S., 1812–1896. Agnes of Sorrento, 1862; Betty's Bright idea, and other Tales, 1875; Chimney Corner (*The*), 1868; Christian Slave (*The*), 1855, a drama, based on "Uncle Tom's Cabin;" Daisy's First Visit, and other Stories, 1867; Dog's Mission (*A*), 1881; Dred, a Tale of the Great Dismal Swamp, 1856; Footsteps of the Master, 1876; House and Home Papers, 1864; Key to "Uncle Tom's Cabin," 1853; Lady Byron's Vindication, 1870; Little Foxes, 1865; Little Pussy Willows, 1870; May Flower (*The*), 1849 (her first), a series of tales; Men of our Times, 1868; Minister's Wooing (*The*), 1859, a tale of the 18th century; My Wife and I, 1872; Old Town Folks, 1869; Our Charley, and what to do with him, 1859; Palmetto Leaves, 1873; Pearl of Orr's Island (*The*), 1862, a New England tale; Peep into Uncle Tom's Cabin, 1853; Pink and White Tyranny, 1871; Poems, 1865; Poganuc People, their Loves and Lives, 1878; Queer Little People, 1867; Ravages of a Carpet (*The*), 1864; Religious Rhymes, 1865; Sam Lawson's Fireside Stories, 1871; Stories about our Dogs, 1865; Sunny Memories of Foreign Lands, 1854; True Story of Lady Byron, 1869 (caused great indignation in England); Uncle Tom's Cabin, 1852 (her chief production); We and our Neighbours, 1875.

BEESLEY (*Edward Spencer*), Fakenham, in Worcestershire, 1831– . Catiline, Clodius, and Tiberius, 1878; Queen Elizabeth, 1892; Social Dynamics, or the General Theory of Human Progress, 1876 (this is vol. iii. of Comte's " System of Positivism ").

BEHN (*Mrs. Aphra*), Canterbury, 1642–1689.

Seventeen Dramatic Pieces: Adelazar, or the Moor's Revenge, 1677; Amorous Prince (*The*), 1671; City Heiress (*The*), 1682; Debauchee (*The*), 1677; Dutch Lover (*The*), 1673; Emperor of the Moon, 1687; False Count (*The*), 1682; Feigned Courtesans, 1679; Forced Marriage (*The*), a tragedy, 1671; Lucky Chance (*The*), 1687; Roundheads (*The*), 1682; Rover, part i. 1677, part ii. 1681; Sir Patient Fancy, 1678; Town Fop (*The*), 1677; Widow Ranter (*The*), 1690; Young King (*The*), 1683; Younger Brother (*The*), 1696.

Histories and Novels, 1698, posthumous: Lover's Watch, 1686; Lycidus, or the Lover in Fashion, 1688; Miscellany, 1685; Oroonoko, 1668, a novel; Poems, 1684. Her Life, by Gildon, 1735.

BEKE (*Charles Tilstone*), London, 1800–1874. Abyssinia, a Statement of Facts, etc., 1845; British Captives in Abyssinia, 1867; Essay on the Nile and its Tributaries (*An*), 1847; History of Nilotic Discovery, 1860; Nile and its Tributaries (*The*), 1847; On the Geographical Distribution of Languages in Abyssinia, 1849; Origines Biblicæ, 1834; Sources of the Nile, 1848, 1849.

BELL (Sir *Charles*), Edinburgh, 1774–1842. Anatomy of the Brain, 1802; Anatomy and Physiology of the Human Body, 1816; Course of the Nerves Explained, 1804; Essays on the Anatomy of the Human Face in Painting, 1806; Exposition of the Natural System of the Nerves in the Human Body (*An*), 1824; Institutes of Surgery, 1838; Letters, 1870, posthumous; Natural System of the Nerves in the Human Body, 1834; Nervous System of the Human Body (*The*), 1830; On Gunshot Wounds, 1814; Operative Surgery, 1807; System of Dissection, 1799–1801; System of Operative Surgery, 1807; Treatise on the Hand, 1833, a Bridgewater treatise. His Life, by Pichot, 1860.

BELL (*George Joseph*), Edinburgh, 1770–1843. Commentaries on the Cessio Bonorum, etc., 1840; Commentaries on the Laws of Scotland, 1810; Principles of the Laws of Scotland, 1829.

BELL (*Henry Thomas Mackenzie*), Liverpool, 1856– . Forgotten Genius (*A*), 1884; Keeping the Vow, and other Verses, 1879; Old Year's Leaves, 1883; Spring's Immortality, and other Poems, 1893; Verses of Varied Life, 1882.

BELL (*Mrs. Hugh*), Christian name *Florence*, Paris, *. Chamber Comedies, 1890; Nursery Comedies, 1892; Story of Ursus (*The*), 1895; Will o' the Wisp, 1890.

BELL, M.D. (*John*), Auchtermony, in Scotland, 1691–1780. Travels from St. Petersburg to Various Parts of Asia, 1763.

BELL, F.R.C.S. (*John*), Edinburgh, 1763–1820. Anatomy of the Human Body, 1793–1802; Discourses on the Nature and Cure of Wounds, 1793–95; Present State of Military Surgery, 1805; Principles of Surgery, 1801.

BELL (*Robert*), Cork, in Ireland, novelist, etc., 1800–1867. Hearts and Altars, 1852, a collection of tales; History of Russia (for Lardner's series); Ladder of Gold, 1850, a novel; Life of Canning, 1846; Lives of the

English Poets ; Memorials of the Civil War ; Outlines of China ; Wayside Pictures through France, etc. An edition of the British poets commenced 1854.

BELL (*Thomas*), Poole, in Dorsetshire, 1792–1880. History of British Quadrupeds, 1836 ; History of British Reptiles, 1829 ; History of British Stalk-eyed Crustacea, 1853 ; Monograph of the Testudinata, 1833.

BELLENDEN (Sir *John*), 1490–1560. Proheme of the Cosmographie ; Topography of Scotland, 1577. He also translated Boethius's " History of Scotland," 1536.

BELLENDEN (*William*), Scotch author, 1573–1635. Caroli Primi et Henriettæ Mariæ . . . Epithalamium, 1625 ; Ciceronis Consul, etc., 1612 ; Ciceronis Princeps, etc., 1608 ; De Statu Prisci Orbis, 1618 ; De Tribus Luminibus Romanorum (Cicero, Seneca, and Pliny), 1634.

BELOE (Rev. *William*), Norwich, 1756–1817. Anecdotes of Scarce Books, etc., 1812 ; "Attic Nights" of Aulus Gellius (translated), 1795 ; History of Herodotus, 1799 ; Miscellanies, 1795 ; Poems and Translations, 1788 ; Sexagenarian (*The*), *i.e.* himself, 1817.

BELSHAM (Rev. *Thomas*), Bedford, 1750–1829. Evidences of Christianity, 1800 ; Improved Version of the New Testament, 1808 ; Inquiry into the Scripture Doctrine of the Person of Christ, 1811. Life, by the Rev. J. Williams, 1836.

BELSHAM (*William*), 1753–1827. History of Great Britain, 1805.

BENEDICT (Sir *Julius*), Stuttgart, in Würtemberg, 1804–1885. Bride of Song (*The*), 1864, an operetta ; Gipsy's Warning (*The*), 1838, an opera ; Lily of Killarney (*The*), 1862, an opera ; Richard Cœur de Lion, 1863, a cantata ; St. Cecilia, 1866, a cantata ; St. Peter, 1866, an oratorio ; Undine, 1860, a cantata.

BENNETT, LL.D. (*William Cox*), Greenwich, 1820–1895. Baby May, etc., 1861 ; Ballad History of England, 1880 ; Our Glory Roll, 1866 ; Poems, 1850, 1862 ; Queen Eleanor's Vengeance, and other Poems, 1857 ; Sea Songs, 1878 ; Songs by a Song-writer, 1859 ; Songs for Sailors, 1873 ; Songs of a Song-writer, 1876 ; Verdicts, 1852 ; War Songs, 1855 ; Worn Wedding Ring (*The*), 1861.

BENSON (E. F.), 1867–   . Babe, B.A. (*The*), 1897 ; Dodo, a Detail of the Day, 1893 ; Judgment Book (*The*), 1895 ; Limitations, 1896 ; Rubicon (*The*), 1894 ; Six Common Things, 1894.

BENT (*James Theodore*), Yorkshire, 1852–   . Cyclades, or Life amongst the Insular Greeks (*The*), 1885 ; Ruined Cities of Mashonaland (*The*), 1892 ; Sacred City of the Ethiopians (*The*), 1893.

BENTHAM (*James*), 1708-1794. History and Antiquities of the Conventual and Cathedral Church of Ely, 1771.

BENTHAM (*Jeremy*), London, 1748-1832. Art of Packing Special Juries (*The*), 1821 ; Book of Fallacies, 1824 ; Chrestomathia, 1816-17 ; Church of Englandism, 1818 ; Codification of Public Instruction, 1817 ; Constitutional Code, 1830 ; Defence of Usury, 1787 ; Draft of a Code for Judicial

Establishment in France, 1791 ; Emancipate your Colonies, 1793 ; Fragment on Government, 1776 ; Hard Labour Bill (*The*), 1778 ; Introduction to the Principles of Morals and Legislation, 1780 ; Liberty of the Press, 1821 ; Mother Church relieved by Bleeding, 1825 ; Not Paul, but Jesus, 1823 ; On the Law of Evidence, 1813 ; Panopticon, 1791 ; Pauper Management, 1797 ; Plea for the Constitution, 1803 ; Political Tactics, 1791 ; Principles of Morals and Legislation, 1780 ; Rationale of Judicial Evidence, 1827 ; Restrictive and Prohibitory Commercial System, 1821 ; Scotch Reform, 1808 ; Springs of Action, 1817 ; Supply without Burden, 1796 ; Swear not at all, 1817 ; Table of the Springs of Action, 1817 ; Truth *v.* Atheism, 1823 ; Usefulness of Chemistry, 1783. Life, by Bowring, 1838.

BENTLEY, D.D. (*Richard*), Oulton, Yorkshire, 1662–1742. Boyle Lecture, 1724 ; Discursus on Latin Metres, 1726 ; Dissertation on the Epistles of Phalaris, 1690 ; Remarks on a Late Discourse on Freethinking, 1743 ; Sermons, 1809. He also edited Milton, and some classics, as Horace and Terence. Life, by bishop Monk, 1823.

BERDOE (*Edward*), L.R.C.P., M.R.C.S., London, 1836–   . Adventures in Search of a Religion, 1873 ; Bibliographical and Historical Notes to Browning's Complete Works, 1894 ; Browning and the Christian Faith, 1896 ; Browning Cyclopædia (*The*), 1891 ; Browning's Message to his Time, 1890 ; History of Medicine in all Ages and Countries (*A*), 1893 ; St. Bernard's, the Romance of a Medical Student ; Dying Scientifically, 1883.

BERINGTON (Rev. *Joseph*), Shropshire, 1743–1827. Faith of Catholics proved from Scripture, 1812 ; Gregory Panzani, 1793 ; History of Abelard and Heloïse, 1787 ; History of the Reign of Henry II., 1790 ; Immaterialism Delineated, 1779 ; Literary History of the Middle Ages, 1814 ; Memoirs of Gregorio Panzani, 1793 ; Reflections, 1787.

BERKELEY (*George*), bishop of Cloyne, born at Kilerin, in Kilkenny, metaphysician, 1684–1753. Alciphron (in seven dialogues), 1732 ; Analyst, 1734 ; Arithmetic [independent of] Algebra and Geometry, 1707 ; Defence of Freethinking in Mathematics, 1739 ; (3) Dialogues between Hylas and Philonous (to prove that material objects have no existence except in the human brain), 1713 ; Letters, posthumous, 1771 ; Minute Philosopher (*The*), 1732, against infidelity ; New Theory of Vision (*A*), 1709 ; On the Virtues of Tar-Water, 1744, 1752 ; Principles of Human Knowledge, 1710 (same object as the " Dialogues") ; Principles of Motion, 1721 ; Proposal for converting the Savage Americans to Christianity, 1725 ; Querist, 1736 ; Siris, 1744 (the title of the book about tar-water) ; Three Dialogues, 1713. Life, by George Berkeley, 1776 ; Prior, 1784 ; Wright, 1843 ; Fraser, 1871.

BERKELEY (Rev. *Miles Joseph*), Biggin, in Northamptonshire, 1803–   . Antarctic and New Zealand Flora, 1860 ; English Flora, 1836.

BERNARD (*Edward*), near Towcester, in

Northamptonshire, 1638-1697. Catalogus Manuscriptorum Angliæ et Hiberniæ, 1697.

BERNARD (*Richard*), 1566-1641. Bible Battels, 1629; Isle of Man, 1627, a religious allegory; Key to . . . the Revelation [of St. John], 1617; Look beyond Luther, 1623; Thesaurus Biblicus, 1639.

BERNERS (Dame *Juliana*), prioress of Sopewell Nunnery, in St. Albans, died 1490. Bokys of Haukynge, Huntynge, and Fysshynge, 1486; Book of St. Albans (*The*), 1486.

BERRY (*Mary* and *Agnes*, sisters), Yorkshire, 1763-1852, 1764-1852. Comparative View of Social Life in England and France, 1828-31; Journal and Correspondence, 1865.

BESANT (*Annie, née* Wood), 1847- . Autobiography, 1893; Building of the Kosmos, 1894; Death and After, 1893; In the Outer Court, 1895; Karma, 1895; Man and his Bodies, 1896; Path of Discipleship, 1896; Seven Principles of Man, 1892; Self and its Sheaths (*The*), 1895.

BESANT (Sir *Walter*), Portsmouth, novelist, 1838- . All in a Garden Fair, 1883; All Sorts and Conditions of Men, 1882; Armorel of Lyonese, 1890; Art of Fiction (*The*), 1884; Bell of St. Paul's (*The*), 1889; Beyond the Dreams of Avarice, 1893; Captain Cook, 1889, a biography; Captains' Room (*The*), 1883, a novel; Children of Gibeon, 1886; City of Refuge (*The*), 1896; Coligny, 1879, a biography; Dorothy Forster, 1884; Fifty Years Ago, 1888; For Faith and Freedom, 1889; Fountain Sealed (*A*), 1897; Herr Paulus, 1888; History of Jerusalem (with professor Palmer), 1871; History of London, 1893; Holy Rose (*The*), 1890; In Deacon's Orders; Ivory Gate (*The*), 1892; Life of E. H. Palmer, 1883; London, 1892; Rabelais, 1877, a biography; Readings in Rabelais, 1883; Rebel Queen (*The*), 1893; Revolt of Man (*The*), 1882; Richard Jefferies, 1888; St. Katherine's by the Tower, 1891; Studies in Early French Poetry, 1866; To Call her Mine, 1889; Uncle Jack, 1885; Whittington, 1881, a biography; World Went very well then (*The*), 1887.

Novels and plays written in conjunction with James Rice: By Celia's Arbour, 1878; Case of Mr. Lucraft, 1876; Chaplain of the Fleet (*The*), 1880-1; French Humourists (*The*), 1873; Golden Butterfly (*The*), 1876; Monks of Thelema (*The*), 1878; My Little Girl, 1873; Ready-Money Mortiboy, 1872; Seamy Side (*The*), 1880; Studies in Early French Poetry, 1868; Such a Good Man, 1874, a comedy; Ten-Years' Tenant (*The*), and other Stories, 1881; This Son of Vulcan, 1877, a novel; 'Twas in Trafalgar's Bay, and other Stories, 1879; With Harp and Crown, 1877, a novel.

BETHAM (Sir *William*), Stradbroke, in Suffolk, antiquary, 1779-1853. Etruria Celtica, 1842; Gael and Cimbri (*The*), 1842; Irish Antiquarian Researches, 1826-27; Origin and History of the Constitution of England, 1834.

BETHAM-EDWARDS (*Matilda Barbara*), Westerfield, Suffolk, novelist, etc., 1836- . Bridget, 1877; Brother Gabriel, 1895; Disarmed, 1883; Dr. Jacob, 1864; France of

To-day, 1892; John and I, 1862; Kitty, 1869; Love and Marriage, 1884; Parting of the Ways (*The*), 1888; Pearla, 1883; Roof of France (*The*), 1889; Sylvestres (*The*), 1871; Year in Western France (*A*), 1876.

BETHUNE (*Alexander*), 1804-1841. Scottish Peasant's Fireside, 1843; Tales and Sketches of the Scottish Peasantry, 1838.

BETTERTON (*Thomas*), dramatist. Amourous Widow (*The*), or The Wanton Wife, 1700; Bondman (*The*), or Love and Liberty, 1719; Henry IV., with the humours of sir John Falstaff, 1700, Sequel 1719; Prophetess (*The*), or The History of Dioclesian, 1790; Revenge (*The*), or A Match at Newgate, 1688; Roman Virgin (*The*), or The Unjust Judge, 1679; Woman made Justice (*The*), 1720.

BEVER, LL.D. (*Thomas*), Mortimer, in Cheshire, 1758-1791. History of the Legal Polity of the Roman State, 1781.

BEVERIDGE (*William*), bishop of St. Asaph, born at Barrow, in Leicestershire, 1638-1708. Codex Canonum Ecclesiæ Primitivæ vindicatus, 1678; Exposition of the Thirty-nine Articles, posthumous 1721; Institutiones Chronologicæ, 1669; Private Thoughts upon Religion, posthumous 1709; Synodicon, 1672; Syriac Grammar, 1658; Thesaurus Theologicus, 1710-11. His Life, by J. Kimber, 1729; T. H. Horne, 1824.

BEWICK (*Thomas*), Cherry-Burn, in Northumberland, wood-engraver, 1753-1828. Figures of British Land Birds, 1800; Figures of Land and Water Birds, 1817; Illustrations to *Gay's Fables*, 1779; History of British Birds, 1797-1804 (tail-pieces noted); History of Quadrupeds, 1790 (tail-pieces noted); Select Fables, 1784. (He drew the diagrams for Hutton's *Mensuration*, 1770.)

BICKERSTAFF (*Isaac*), Ireland, 1735-1800. Absent Man (*The*), 1768, a comedy; Captive (*The*), 1769; Daphne and Amintor, 1765; Dr. Last in his Chariot, 1769, a farce (with Foote); Ephesian Matron (*The*), 1769; He Would if he Could, 1771, a comedy; Hypocrite (*The*), 1768, a comedy; Judith, 1764, an oratorio; Leucothe, 1750, a comedy; Lionel and Clarissa, 1760, an opera; Love in a Village, 1762, an operatic farce; Love in the City, 1767, a comedy; Maid of the Mill (*The*), 1765, an operatic farce; Padlock (*The*), 1768, an operatic farce; Plain Dealer (*The*), 1766, a comedy; Recruiting Sergeant (*The*), 1770, a musical entertainment; Royal Garland (*The*), 1768; School for Fathers (*The*), 1770, a comedy; Sultan (*The*), 1775, a farce; Thomas and Sally, 1760, a comic opera; 'Tis Well 'tis no Worse, 1770, a comedy.

N.B.—Sir Richard Steele assumed the name of Isaac Bickerstaff, but had no hand in the plays mentioned above.

BICKERSTETH, D.D. (*Edward*), Acton, in Suffolk, 1814-1892. Sermons, such as the "Anthem of Creation;" "Enoch," 1869; "The Victor on his Throne," 1867; etc.

BICKERSTETH, D.D. (*Edward Henry*), bishop of Exeter, 1825- . Commentary on the New Testament, 1864; Hymnal Companion (*The*), 1870; Poems, 1848; Reef (*The*), and other Parables, 1873; Rock of Ages, or Scripture Testimony to the Trinity, 1858; Shadowed Home (*The*), and the Light Beyond, 1874; Two Brothers (*The*), and other Poems, 1871; Water from the Wellspring, 1853; What is revealed of the Blessed Dead, 1863; What is revealed of the Risen Saints, 1863; Yesterday, To-day, and For Ever (a poem in 12 books), 1866.

BICKERSTETH, D.D. (*Robert*), bishop of Ripon, born at Acton, in Suffolk, 1816-1884. Bible Landmarks, 1850; Lent Lectures, 1861; Sermons, 1866.

BIGSBY, LL.D. (*Robert*), Nottingham, 1806-1873. Memoir of the Order of St. John of Jerusalem, 1869; Omba, 1853, a dramatic romance; Poems and Essays, 1842; Triumph of Drake, 1839, a poem; Visions of the Time of Old, or The Antiquarian Enthusiast, 1848.

BINGLEY (Rev. *William*), 1779-1823. Animal Biography, 1803 (very amusing); Biographical Dictionary of Musical Composers of the Last Three Centuries, 1813; Memoirs of British Quadrupeds, 1809; Tour round North Wales, 1800 (excellent).

BINNEY, D.D. (*Thomas*), Newcastle-upon-Tyne, 1799-1874. Closet and the Church (*The*); Dissent not Schism; Is it possible to make the Best of Both Worlds? (his most popular work).

BIRCH, LL.D. (*Samuel*), London, 1813- . Analecta Simensia (short stories from the Chinese), 1841; Catalogue of Greek and Etruscan Vases in the British Museum (assisted by Mr. Newton), 1851; Description of the Papyrus of Nas-khem, 1863; Elfin Foxes (*The*), 1863, a romance from the Chinese; Friends till Death, 1845, a tale from the Chinese; Gallery of Antiquities, etc., 1842; History of Ancient Pottery, 1857; Introduction to the Study of Hieroglyphs, 1857; Rhind Papyri (*The*), 1866; Views on the Nile, etc., 1843.

BIRCH, D.D. (*Thomas*), London, 1705-1766. Biographical Sketches, 1743-1752; Courts and Times of James I. and Charles I., posthumous 1848; General Dictionary, Historical and Critical, 1734-1741; Historical View of the Negotiations between the Courts of England, France, and Belgium (from 1592 to 1617), 1749; History of the Royal Society, 1756-57; Inquiry into the Part which Charles I. took in the Glamorgan Transaction, 1747; Life of Henry, Prince of Wales, 1760; Life of the Hon. Robert Boyle, 1744; Life of Tillotson, 1752; Lives of Illustrious Persons in Great Britain, 1743-1752; Memoirs of the Reign of Elizabeth, 1754.

BIRKENHEAD (Sir *John*), Northwich, Cheshire, 1615-1679. Assembly Man (*The*), 1662-63; Mercurius Aulicus, 1642-45.

BIRRELL (*Augustine*), Wavertree, 1850- . Lectures on the Duties and Liabilities of Trustees, 1896; Life of Charlotte Brontë, 1887; Men, Women, and Books, 1894; Obiter Dicta, 1884, 1887; Res Judicata, 1892.

BISHOP (Sir *Henry Rowley*), London, musical composer, 1780-1855. He composed about seventy operas, ballads, glees, and musical entertainments. His best known operas are:

Barber of Seville (*The*); Guy Mannering, 1816; Marriage of Figaro (*The*); Miller and his Men (*The*), 1813; Maid Marian (*The*), 1822; Native Land, 1823; Slave (*The*), 1816; Virgin of the Sun (*The*), 1812.

BISHOP (*Samuel*), London, 1731-1795. Poetical Works, posthumous, 1796. His Life, by T. Clare, 1796.

BISSETT, LL.D. (*Robert*), 1759-1805. Douglas, 1800; History of the Reign of George III., 1803; Life of Edmund Burke, 1800.

BLACK, M.D. (*Joseph*), Bordeaux, in France, 1728-1799. Experiments upon Magnesia Alba, etc., 1756. Black evolved the theory of "latent heat:" his lectures were published in 1803.

BLACK (*William*), Glasgow, novelist, 1841- . Adventures in Thule; Autobiography, 1877; Briseis, 1896; Daughter of Heth (*A*), 1871; Green Pastures and Piccadilly, 1877; Handsome Humes (*The*), 1893; Highland Cousins, 1894; In Far Lochaber; In Silk Attire, 1869; Judith Shakespeare, 1884; Kilmeny, 1870; Lady Silverdale's Sweetheart, 1876; Love or Marriage, 1867; Macleod of Dare, 1878; Madcap Violet, 1876; Magic Ink, and other Tales, 1892; Maid of Killeena (*The*), and other Stories, 1874; Monarch of Mincing Lane (*The*), 1871; Nanciebel, 1889; New Prince Fortunatus (*The*), 1890; Penance of John Logan (*The*), 1889; Princess of Thule (*A*), 1873; Sabina Zembra, 1887; Shandon Bells, 1883; Stand Fast Craig-Royston, 1891; Strange Adventures of a House-Boat, 1888; Strange Adventures of a Phaeton, 1872; Sunrise, 1881; That Beautiful Wretch, 1881; Three Feathers, 1875 (scene laid in Cornwall); White Heather, 1885; White Wings, 1880; Wise Women of Inverness (*The*), 1885; Wolfenberg, 1892; Yolande, 1883. Life of Oliver Goldsmith, 1878.

BLACKBURN (*Henry*), 1830-1897. Academy Notes, 1875-96; Art in the Mountains, 1870; Art of Illustration, 1894; Artistic Travels in Normandy, etc., 1892; Artists and Arabs, 1868; Breton Folk, 1880; Harz Mountains, 1873; Normandy Picturesque, 1869; Pyrenees (*The*), 1867; Randolph Caldecott, 1886; Travelling in Spain, 1866.

BLACKBURNE (*Francis*), Richmond, in Yorkshire, 1705-1787. Confessional (*The*), 1766; Intermediate State (*The*), 1772.

BLACKIE (*John Stuart*), Glasgow, 1809-1895. Altavona, 1882; Christianity and the Ideal of Humanity in Old Times and Now, 1893; Democracy, 1867; (3) Discourses on Beauty, 1858; Essays (moral and social), 1890; Four Phases of Morals, 1871; Homer and the Iliad, 1866; Horæ Hellenicæ, 1874; Lay Sermons, 1881; Lays and Legends of Ancient Greece, 1857; Lays of the Highlands and Islands, 1872; Life of Burns, 1887; Lyrical Poems in English and Latin, 1860; Musa Burschicosa, 1869; Natural History of Atheism, 1877; Poems, chiefly Mythological, 1857, 1860; Pronunciation of Greek, 1852; Scottish Songs, 1889; Self-culture, 1877; Song of Heroes (*A*), 1890; War-Songs of Germany, 1870; Wisdom of Goethe (*The*), 1883; Wise Men of Greece

(*The*), 1877. He translated Goethe's *Faust*, 1834; and *Æschylus*, 1850.

BLACKLOCK, D.D. (*Thomas*), Annan, in Scotland, poet, 1721–1791. Grahame (*The*), 1774; Panegyric on Great Britain (*A*), 1773; Paracelsis, 1767; Poems, 1745, 1754. Collected poems and Life, by H. Mackenzie, 1793.

BLACKMORE, M.D. (Sir *Richard*), Corsham, in Wiltshire, 1650–1729. Creation (*The*), in seven books, 10 syl. rhymes, 1712 (his best. Addison calls it "one of the most noble productions in our English verse;" and Dr. Johnson says it shows him to be "among the first favourites of the English Muse"); Eliza, 1700; "Job" (paraphrased), 1700; King Alfred (in 12 books), 1718; King Arthur (in 12 books), 1697; Lay Monk (*The*), 1713; Prince Arthur (in 10 books), 1696; Eliza, *i.e.* Queen Elizabeth (in 10 books), 1703; Redemption (in 6 books), 1715; Satire upon Wit (*A*), 1700; The Nature of Man (in 3 books), 1720. And a host of miscellaneous treatises, written in 1700.

All hail him victor in both gifts of song,
Who sings so loudly and who sings so long.
The Dunciad.

BLACKMORE (*Richard Doddridge*), Longworth, in Berkshire, novelist, 1825– . Alice Lorraine, 1875, a tale of the South Downs; Christowell, 1882, a Dartmoor tale; Clara Vaughan, 1864; Cradock Nowell, 1866, a tale of the New Forest; Cripps the Carrier, 1876, a woodland tale; Eréma, or my Father's Sin, 1877; Fate of Franklin (*The*), 1860, a poem; Fringilla, 1895; Georgics (*The*) translated, 1871; Kit and Kitty, 1889; Lorna Doone, 1869, a romance of Exmoor; Maid of Sker, 1872; Mary Anerley, 1890; Perlycross, 1894; Springhaven, 1887; Tales from the Telling House, 1896; Tommy Upmore, 1882.

BLACKSTONE (*John*), died 1753. Fasciculus Plantarum, 1737; Plantæ rariores Angliæ, 1737; Specimen Botanicum, 1746.

BLACKSTONE, LL.D. (Sir *William*), London, 1723–1780. Commentaries on the Laws of England (4 vols.), 1765–69 (his great work); Considerations on Copyholders, 1758; Essay on Collateral Consanguinity, 1750; Great Charter and Charter of the Forest (*The*), 1759; Reports of Cases, 1781, posthumous; Tracts, 1771; Lawyer's Farewell to his Muse (*The*), 1740, poetry. Life, by James Clitherow, 1780.

BLACKWALL (*Anthony*), 1674–1730. Introduction to the Classics, 1740 (a valuable book); Sacred Classics (*The*), 1727–31.

BLACKWELL (*Elizabeth*), about 1703–1797. Herbal (*The*), 1737–39 (once much esteemed).

BLACKWELL, M.D. (*Elizabeth*), Bristol, 1821. The first woman who obtained a medical diploma (1849). She practises in New York, U.S. Her sister Emily took her diploma in 1854. Laws of life considered with reference to the Physical Education of Girls, 1852.

BLACKWELL (*Thomas*), Aberdeen, 1701–1757. Inquiry into the Life and Writings of Homer,

1735; Letters on Mythology, 1748; Memoirs of the Court of Augustus, 1753.

BLADES (*William*), 1824– . Life of Caxton, 1863 (valuable).

BLAGRAVE (*John*), Reading, in Berkshire, mathematician, 1550–1611. Art of Dialling, 1609; Astrolabium Uranicum Generale, 1596; Mathematical Jewel (*The*), 1585.

BLAIR, D.D. (*Hugh*), Edinburgh, 1718–1799. Lectures on Rhetoric, 1783; Ossian (in defence of the poems so called), 1763; Sermons, 1777 (once very popular). His Life, by Dr. T. Hill, 1807.

BLAIR (*John*), died 1782. Chronological Tables, 1756.

BLAIR (*Patrick*), Dundee, 1680–1728. Botanical Essays (in two parts), 1720; Pharmaco-Botanology, 1723–28.

BLAIR (Rev. *Robert*), Edinburgh, 1699–1747. Grave (*The*), 1743, in blank verse. (In this occurs the celebrated line, "Like angels' visits, short and far between.")

BLAKE (*William*), London, 1757–1827. Book of Ahania, 1795; Book of Thel, 1790; The Gates of Paradise, 1793, a book of symbolic designs; Ghost of Abel (*The*), 1822; Marriage of Heaven and Hell, 1791; Milton, 1804; Poetical Sketches, 1783; Songs of Experience (with etchings on copper by himself), 1794; Songs of Innocence (with etchings on copper by himself), 1787; Song of Los (America, Europe, Africa, and Asia, prophecies), 1793–95; Urizen, 1794; Visions of the Daughters of Albion, 1793. He illustrated on copper Blair's *Grave*, 1805; Chaucer's *Canterbury Pilgrims*; *The Book of Job*, 1826; Milton, 1804; Dante's *Inferno*, 1827; Young's *Night Thoughts*, 1797; his own Poems, etc. His Life, by Gilchrist, 1863; A Critical Essay, Swinburne, 1868. All Blake's poems now issued in one volume, edited by W. M. Rossetti, 1885.

BLAKEY, Ph. D. (*Robert*), Morpeth, in Northumberland, 1795–1878. Essay on Logic, 1834; Freedom of the Divine and Human Wills, 1829; History of Moral Science, 1833; History of the Philosophy of Mind, 1848; History of Political Literature, 1855; Lives of the Primitive Fathers of the Church, 1834.

BLANCHARD (*Laman*), Yarmouth, 1803–1845. Essays and Sketches, 1849; Lyric Offering (*The*), 1828.

BLAND (Rev. *Robert*), London, 1779–1825; Edwy and Elgiva, about 1810, poems; Four Slaves of Cytherea (*The*), about 1803.

BLAND (*William*), 1788–1872. Experimental Essays on the Principles of Construction in Arches, Piers, and Buttresses, 1862.

BLANE, M.D. (Sir *Gilbert*), Blanefield, in Ayrshire, 1749–1834. Elements of Medical Logic, 1819; Lectures on Muscular Motion, 1790; Observations on the Diseases of Seamen, 1783; Select Dissertations, 1822.

BLAYNEY, D.D. (*Benjamin*), died 1801. Dissertation on Daniel's "Weeks," 1775; Jeremiah (translated from the original), 1784.

BLESSINGTON (*Marguerite*, countess of), near Clonmel, in Ireland, 1789–1849. Conversations with Lord Byron, 1832 (her best work);

Desultory Thoughts, 1838; Idler in France, 1841; Idler in Italy, 1839.
Novels and Tales: Belle of the Season (*The*), 1840; Confessions of an Elderly Gentleman, 1835; Confessions of an Elderly Lady, 1836; Country Quarters, 1850; Governess (*The*), 1841; Repealers (*The*), 1833; Two Friends (*The*), 1834; Victims of Society, 1837. Her Life, by Madden, 1855.

BLIGH (*William*), Farningham, in Kent, 1753–1817. Narrative of the Mutiny on board H.M.S. *Bounty*, 1790 (Lord Byron's *Island* is based on this narrative); Voyage to the South Sea, 1792.

BLIND (*Mathilde*), 1847–1896. Ascent of Man (*The*), 1889; Birds of Passage, 1895; Dramas in Miniature, 1891; George Eliot, 1888; Heather on Fire (*The*), 1886; Madame Roland, 1886; Songs and Sonnets, 1893; Tarantella, 1884.

BLOMEFIELD (*Francis*), Fersfield, in Norfolk, 1705–1752. Collectanea Cantabrigiensia, 1750; History of Thetford [in Norfolk], 1739; Topographical History of Norfolk (continued by Parkin), 1739–75.

BLOMFIELD (*Charles James*), bishop of London, Bury St. Edmunds, Suffolk, 1786–1857. Lectures on the Gospel of St. John, 1823. His Life, by A. Blomfield, 1863.

BLOOMFIELD (*Robert*), Honington, in Suffolk, 1766–1823. Ballads and other Pieces, 1800–1806; Banks of the Wye, 1822; Fakenham Ghost (*The*), 1814; Farmer's Boy (in 4 parts, 10 syl. rhymes), 1800; Good Tidings, 1804; May-day with the Muses, 1822; Poems (miscellaneous), 1806; Rural Tales, 1802; Wild Flowers, 1806.

BLORE (*Thomas*), Stamford, 1753–1814. History and Antiquities of Rutland, 1811 (of great merit); History of the Manor of South Winfield, in Derbyshire, 1793.

BLOUNT (*Charles*), Upper Holloway, deist, 1654–1693. Anima Mundi, 1679; Great is Diana of the Ephesians, 1680; Oracles of Reason, 1693; Two First Books of Philostratus concerning the Life of Apollonius of Tyana, 1680.

BLOUNT (Sir *Henry*), Tittenhanger Park, Surrey, 1602–1682. Journey to Jerusalem, 1669; Voyage into the Levant (*A*), 1636.

BLOUNT (*Thomas*), Bardsley, Lancashire, 1618–1679. Boscobel (a history of the escape of Charles II.), 1660; Fragmenta Antiquitatis, 1679; Glossographia, or Dictionary of Hard Words, 1656; Law Dictionary and Glossary (*A*), 1670.

BLOUNT (Sir *Thomas Pope*), Upper Holloway, 1649–1697. Censura celebrium Authorum, 1690 (a learned treatise); De re Poetica, 1694; Essays, 1687 (Chalmers says they are equal to Montaigne's); Natural History, 1693.

BLUNDELL (Mrs. *Francis*), Dublin. Among the Untrodden Ways, 1896; Daughter of the Soil (*A*), 1895; Frieze and Fustian, 1896; In a North Country Village, 1893; Story for Children (*A*), 1894; Story of Dan (*The*), 1894; Town Mice in the Country, 1894; Whither? 1892.

BLUNT (*Wilfred Scawen*), 1840–   . Esther, 1892; Future of Islam, 1882; Griselda, 1893; Ideas about India, 1885; In Vinculis, 1889;

Love Sonnets of Proteus, 1880; New Pilgrimage (*A*), 1889; Stealing of the Mare, 1892; Wing and the Whirlwind (*The*), 1883.

BOETHIUS, or BOECE, D.D. (*Hector*), Dundee, 1470–1550. Scotorum Historiæ, etc., 1520; Vitæ Episcoporum Murthlacensium et Aberdonensium, 1522.

BOGAN (*Zachary*), Devonshire, 1625–1659. Additions to Rous's *Attic Archæology*, 1685; Homeri comparatio cum Scriptoribus Sacris, 1658.

BOLDREWOOD, ROLF (*Thomas Alexander Browne*), London, novelist, 1826–   . Colonial Reformer (*A*), 1890; Miner's Right (*The*), 1890; Modern Buccaneer (*A*), 1894; Robbery under Arms, 1888; Squatter's Dream (*The*); Crooked Stick (*The*), 1895; Sydney-side Saxon (*A*), 1891; and other stories.

BOLINGBROKE (*Henry St. John*, viscount), Battersea, 1678–1751. Dissertation on Parties, 1735; Idea of a Patriot King, 1743; Letter on the Spirit of Patriotism, 1749; Letter to Sir William Wyndham, 1753; Letters on the Study and Use of History, 1752; Remarks on the History of England, 1743; Letters and Correspondence, 1798, posthumous. His Life, by Mallet, 1754; St. Lambert, 1796; G. H. Cooke, 1835; Thomas Macknight, 1863.

BONER (*Charles*), died 1870. C. B.'s Book, 1848; Chamois Hunting in Bavaria, 1853; Forest Creatures, 1861; Transylvania, 1865.

BONNYCASTLE (*John*), died 1821. General History of Mathematics, 1803; Introduction to Algebra, 1782; Scholar's Guide to Arithmetic, 1780.

BOOLE (*George*), Lincoln, 1815–1864. Calculus of Finite Differences, 1860; Differential Equations, 1859; Investigation of the Laws of Thought, 1854; Mathematical Analysis of Logic, 1847.

BOOTHBY (*Guy Newell*), Adelaide, South Australia, 1867–   . Beautiful White Devil, 1896; Bid for Fortune (*A*), 1895; Dr. Nikola, 1896; Fascination of the King, 1897; In Strange Company, 1894; In the Wallaby, 1894; Lost Endeavour (*A*), 1895; Marriage of Esther (*The*), 1895; Sheila McLeod, 1897.

BORDE, M.D. (*Andrew*), Pevensey, in Sussex, 1500–1549. Breviarie of Health, 1547; Compendyous Regimente, or Dietary of Helthe, 1562; Boke of the Introduction of Knowledge, 1542; Merye Tales of the Madmen of Gotham, 1565.

BORROW (*George*), East Dereham, in Norfolk 1803–1881. (Knew 27 languages.) Bible in Spain (*The*), 1843; Lavengro, the Scholar, Gipsy, and Priest, 1851; Romano Lavo Lil, 1874; Romany Rye (*The*), a sequel to Lavengro, 1857; Wild Wales, 1862; Zincali (*The*), or an Account of the Gipsies in Spain, 1841.

BOSTON (*Thomas*), Dunse, in Berwick, 1676–1732. Crook in the Lot (*The*), 1805, posthumous (it is in this excellent little treatise that he warns the profligate from expecting "to leap from Delilah's lap into Abraham's bosom"); Human Nature in its Fourfold State, 1720 (well-known, especially in Scotland); Memoirs, by himself, 1776, posthumous.

BOSWELL (Sir *Alexander*), son of James Boswell, 1775-1822. Edinburgh, or the Ancient Royalty, 1810; Sir Allan, 1811; Songs (chiefly in the Scottish dialect), 1803; Spirit of Tintoc, or Jonnie Bell and the Kelpie, 1808. (His brother James, 1779-1822, wrote a "Life of Malone.")

BOSWELL (*James*), father of the preceding brothers, Auchinleck, in Scotland, 1740-1795. Account of Corsica (*An*), 1768; Essays in favour of the Corsicans, 1769; Journal of a Tour to the Hebrides with Dr. Johnson, 1785; Letters to the Rev. W. T. Temple, 1856, posthumous; Life of Dr. Samuel Johnson, 1791 (a model of biography). Boswelliana, 1874.

BOSWORTH, D.D. (*Joseph*), Derbyshire, 1788-1876. Anglo-Saxon Dictionary, 1838; Compendious Anglo-Saxon and English Dictionary, 1868; Elements of Anglo-Saxon Grammar, 1825.

BOUCHER (Rev. *Jonathan*), Cumberland, 1737-1804. Causes and Consequences of the American Revolution, 1797; Supplement to Johnson's *Dictionary*, 1807, posthumous (valuable).

BOUCICAULT (*Dion*), Dublin, 1820-1890. Wrote above 50 dramatic pieces. After Dark, 1868; Arrah-na-Pogue; Colleen Bawn, 1860, a comedy; Corsican Brothers (*The*), 1848; Daddy O'Dowd, 1859; Dark Night's Work (*A*), 1870; Dead Secret (*The*), 1878; Don Cæsar de Bogan; Dot; Faust and Marguérite, 1877; Flying Scud (*The*), 1866; Formosa; Foul Play (with Charles Reade); Girl's Romance (*A*), 1879; How she Loves Him, 1867, a comedy; Janet Pride, a sensational drama; Jilt (*The*), 1885; Led Astray, 1873, a comedy; London Assurance, 1841 (his first comedy); Long Strike (*The*); Lost at Sea; Louis XI., 1846, an historic drama; Love in a Maze, 1844; Man of Honour (*The*), a comedy; Octoroon (*The*), 1861; O'Dowd (*The*), 1880; Old Heads and Young Hearts, 1843; Paul Lafarge, 1870; Rapparee (*The*), or Treaty of Limerick, 1870; Shaughraun, 1873; Streets of London (*The*), 1862; Used up, 1846; Willow Copse (*The*).

BOURNE (*Vincent*), Latin poet, 1700-1747. Poemata, 1734, 1750 (the best Latin poems by any foreigner). His Life, by J. Mitford, 1846.

BOWDICH (*Thomas Edward*), Bristol, 1790-1824. Excursions to Madeira, 1825; Mission to Ashantee, 1819.

BOWDLER (*Thomas*), Ashley, near Bath, 1754-1825. The Family (or expurgated) Shakespeare, 1818 (this work has given to us the word "bowdlerise,"—to mutilate an author).

BOWER (*Archibald*), born at Dundee, 1686-1766. History of the Popes, 1748-66.

BOWLES, D.D. (*William Lisle*), King's Sutton, in Northamptonshire, 1762-1850. Battle of the Nile (*The*), 1799; Elegiac Verses, 1796; Hope, 1796; Life of Thomas Ken, 1830-31; Missionary of the Andes, 1815, in blank verse; Paulus Parochialis, 1826, in prose; Poems, 1798-1809; St. Michael's Mount, 1798; Scenes and Shadows, etc.; (14) Sonnets, 1789 (his best production); Sorrows of Switzerland (*The*), 1801; Spirit of Discovery, 1805, in blank verse; Village Verse Book, 1837. (Noted for the "Pope and Bowles Controversy," which arose from his "Essay on Pope," 1819-28.)

BOWRING (Sir *John*), Exeter, poet, linguist, etc., 1792-1872. Decimal System, 1853; Kingdom and People of Siam (*The*), 1857; Visit to the Philippine Islands, 1858-59. Some excellent translations from the Batavian *anthology*, the Danish, German, Magyar, Polish, Portuguese, and Russian poets. An edition, in 11 vols., of Jeremy Bentham, 1838-39.)

BOYCE, Mus.D. (*William*), London, 1710-1779. Collection of Church Music, 1760; Serenata of "Solomon," 1743.

BOYD, D.D. (*Andrew Kennedy Hutchinson*), Auchinleck, in Scotland, 1825-   . Autumn Holidays of a Country Parson; Best Last (*The*), 1888; Common-place Philosopher; East Coast Days and Memories, 1887; Graver Thoughts of a Country Parson (*The*); Landscapes, Churches, and Moralities, 1874; Leisure Hours in Town, etc.; Memorials of St. Andrew's Sundays, 1870; Recreations of a Country Parson, 1859 (originally in *Fraser's Magazine*); St. Andrew's and Elsewhere, 1894; Twenty-five Years of St. Andrew's, 1892.

BOYD (*Henry*), Ireland, 1750-1832. Dante's *Divine Comedy*, 1785-1802, translated into English verse.

BOYD (*Zachary*), 1589-1653. Crosses, Comforts, and Counsels, 1643; Garden of Zion (*The*), 1644; Last Battell of the Soule in Death, 1629; Psalmes of David in Meeter (3rd edit.), 1646; Two Oriental Pearls, Grace and Glory, 1718; Zion's Flowers (usually called "Zachary Boyd's Bible," in rhyme), never published.

BOYLE (*Charles*, earl of Orrery), Chelsea, 1676-1731. Edited the *Epistles of Philaris*, 1695.

BOYLE (Hon. *Robert*), Lismore, in Ireland, 1626-1691. Considerations touching the Usefulness of Experimental Natural Philosophy, 1663; Discourse of Things above Reason, 1682; Experiments and Considerations upon Colours, 1663; Experiments and Observations upon Cold, 1665; Free Inquiry into the vulgarly received Notion of Nature, 1679; General History of the Air, 1692; Medicina Hydrostatica, 1690; Memoirs for the Natural History of Human Blood, 1684; New Experiments, Physico-mechanical, touching the Spring of the Air, 1660; Physiological Essays, etc., 1661; Sceptical Chemist, 1662. Life, by Thomas Birch, 1744.

BRABOURNE (Lord *Edward Knatchbull-Hugessen*), Mersham Hatch, Kent, 1829-1893. Crackers for Christmas, 1870; Ferdinand's Adventures, 1883; Friends and Foes from Fairyland, 1885; Higgledy Piggledy, 1875; Moonshine, 1871; Queer Folk, 1873; River Legends, 1874; Stories for my Children, 1869; Tales at Tea-time, 1872; Uncle Joe's Stories, 1878; Whispers from Fairyland, 1874.

BRACKENBURY (*Charles Booth*), Bayswater, 1831– . European Armaments, 1867; Winter Campaign of Prince Frederick Charles in 1870–71.

BRACKENBURY (Colonel *Henry*), Bolingbroke, in Lincolnshire, 1837– . Fanti and Ashanti, 1873.

BRACTON (*Henry de*), 1185–1267. De Legibus et Consuetudinibus Angliæ, 1569, posthumous ("best of judicial classics").

BRADDON (*Mary Elizabeth*), "Mrs. Maxwell," London, novelist, 1837– . All along the River, 1893; Asphodel, 1881; Aurora Floyd, 1863; Barbara, etc., 1880; Birds of Prey, 1870; Captain of the Vulture (*The*), 1870, a tale; Charlotte's Inheritance, 1871; Christmas Hirelings (*The*), 1894; Cloven Foot (*The*), 1878; Cut by the County, 1887; Day will Come (*The*), 1889; Dead Men's Shoes, 1876; Dead Sea Fruit, 1872; Doctor's Wife (*The*), 1867; Eleanor's Victory, 1865; Fatal Three (*The*), 1888; Fenton's Quest (contributed to *Belgravia*); Gerard, 1891; Golden Calf (*The*), 1883; Henry Dunbar, 1865; Hostages of Fortune, 1875; Ishmael, 1884; John Marchmont's Legacy, 1866; Joshua Haggard's Daughter, 1876; Just as I am, 1880; Lady Audley's Secret, 1862; Lady Lisle (contributed to *Temple Bar*), 1869; Lady's Mile (*The*), 1869; Like and Unlike, 1887; London Pride, 1896; Lost for Love, 1874; Lovells of Arden, 1871; Lucius Davoren, 1873; Milly Darrell, 1872; Mohawks, 1886; Mount Royal, 1882; One Thing Needful, 1886; Only a Clod, 1868; Open Verdict (*An*), 1878; Phantom Fortune, 1883; Ralph the Bailiff (a tale in *St. James's Magazine*); Robert Ainsleigh, 1871; Run to Earth, 1872; Rupert Godwin, 1871; Sir Jasper's Tenant, 1868; Sons of Fire, 1896; Story of Barbara, 1880; Strange World (*A*), 1875; Strangers and Pilgrims, 1873; Taken at the Flood, 1874; Thou art the Man, 1894; To the Bitter End, 1872; Trail of the Serpent (*The*), 1868; Under Love's Rule, 1897; Venetians (*The*), 1894; Weavers and Weft, 1877; Wyllard's Weird, 1885; Vixen, 1879. Garibaldi, and other Poems, 1861; Griselda, 1873, a drama; Loves of Arcadia, 1860, a comedietta. She has written other novels.

BRADFORD (*William*), Austerfield, in Lancashire, 1588–1657. History of Plymouth Colony, 1856.

BRADLEY (Rev. *Edward*), pseudonym "Cuthbert Bede," Kidderminster, in Worcestershire, 1827–1889. Adventures of Verdant Green, 1853, a tale; Curate of Cranston, etc., 1862; Fotheringay and Mary Queen of Scots, 1886; Glencreggan, 1861, a descriptive work; Mattins and Muttons, 1866, a novel; Rook's Garden (*The*), 1865; Tour in Tartan Land (*A*), 1863; White Wife (*The*), 1864, legends and tales; Wild Cantire, 1864.

BRADLEY, D.D. (*James*), Sherborne, astronomer, 1692–1762. Astronomical Observations, 1798, 1805, posthumous. He discovered the *Aberration of Light*, 1727; and *Nutation*, 1747.

BRADLEY (*Richard*), 1700–1732. Dictionarum Botanicum, 1728; New Improvement of Planting, etc., 1717; Plantæ Succulentæ,

1716–27; Survey of Ancient Husbandry and Gardening, 1725.

BRADSHAW (*George*), Manchester, died 1853. Bradshaw's Continental Railway Guide, 1847; Railway Companion, 1839; developed into the Railway Guide, 1841.

BRADSHAW (*Henry*), Chester, 1450–1513. Lyfe of St. Radegunde (no date); Lyfe of St. Werburgh, 1495.

BRADWARDINE (*Thomas*), archbishop of Canterbury, born at Chichester, 1290–1349. De Arithmetica Speculativa, 1495; De Causa Dei contra Pelagium, 1618; De Geometria Speculativa, 1495; De Proportionibus Velocitatum, 1505 (all posthumous). His Life, by Dr. Hook, in his *Lives of the Archbishops of Canterbury*, 1861–75.

BRADY (*Nicholas*), Bandon, in Ireland, 1659–1726. Translations of Psalms, 1696 (with Tate).

BRADY, M.D. (*Robert*), died 1700. Complete History of England, 1685; Introduction to Old English History, 1684.

BRAMAH (*Joseph*), Stanborough, in Devonshire, 1749–1825. Dissertation on the Construction of Locks, 1787. (Took out his patent for *locks*, 1784; for his *hydraulic press*, 1796.)

BRAND (*John*), Newcastle-on-Tyne, in Northumberland, 1741–1806. History and Antiquities of Newcastle, 1789; Popular Antiquities, 1776.

BRANDE (*William Thomas*), 1786-1866. Dictionary of Materia Medica, 1839; Dictionary of Science, Literature, and Art, 1842 (recast by W. T. Brande and Rev. G. W. Cox, 1865–67); Manual of Chemistry, 1819.

BRANDON (*Robert*), 1810– . Analysis of Gothic Architecture; Open Timber Roofs of the Middle Ages (*The*), 1842; Parish Churches, 1854.

BRATHWAYTE (*Richard*), near Appleby, 1588–1673. Ar't Asleep, Husband? a Boulster Lecture, 1640; Astræa's Tears, 1641, an elegy; Barnabees Journal, 1648–50; Bessie Bell, 1648, in Latin and English verse; Drunken Barnabees Journal . . . (in Latin and English verse), 1716, posthumous; Lives of the Roman Emperors from Julius Cæsar to Ferdinand II., 1636; Mercurius Britannicus, 1641, a tragi-comedy; Muster Roll of the Evill Angels embatteld against S. Michael, 1655; Penitent Pilgrim (*The*), 1641; Philocles and Doroclea, two Lancashire Lovers, 1640; Psalmes of David paraphras'd, 1638; Spiritual Spicerie, 1638. His Life, by J. Haslewood, 1820.

BRAY (Mrs.), maiden name *Anna Eliza Kempe*, Surrey, novelist, 1799–1883. Borders of the Tamar and the Tavy (*The*), 1836, a descriptive work; Courtenay of Walreddon 1844, a romance; De Foix, 1826, a romance; Fitz of Fitzford, 1830, a legend of Devon; Good St. Louis and his Times, 1870; Handel, his Life, etc., 1857; Hartland Forest, 1871, a legend; Henry de Pomeroy, 1842, a legend; Joan of Arc, 1873, historical; Life of Thomas Stothard, R.A., 1851; Memoirs of Charles Alfred Stothard (her first husband), 1823; Mountains and Lakes of Switzerland, 1841; Peep at the Pixies, 1854, a

Christmas tale; Protestant (*The*), 1828, a novel; Revolt of the Protestants of the Cevennes, 1870; Roseteague, 1874; Talba (*The*), or Moor of Portugal, 1830; Trelawny of Trelawne, 1837, a legend of Cornwall; Trials of Domestic Life, 1848; Trials of the Heart, 1839; Warleigh, or the Fatal Oak, 1834, a legend of Devon; White Hoods (*The*), 1828, a novel.

BRAY (Sir *Reginald*), died 1503. Henry VII.'s Chapel, Westminster Abbey (begun), 1502; St. George's Chapel, Windsor (begun), 1476;

BRAY, F.S.A. (*William*), Shere, in Surrey, 1736–1832. History of the County of Surrey, 1804–14.

BRAYBROOKE (*Richard Cornwallis Neville*, lord), 1820–1861. Antiqua Explorata, 1847; Sepulchra Exposita, 1848; Saxon Obsequies, 1852.

BREEN (*Henry Hegart*), Kerry, Ireland, 1805– . Diamond Rock (*The*), and other Poems, 1849; Modern English Literature, 1857; St. Lucia, Historical, Statistical, and Descriptive, 1844; Warrawarra, the Carib Chief, 1776, a tale.

BRENTON (*Edward Pelham*), 1774–1839. Naval History of Great Britain from 1783 to 1822 (in 5 vols.), 1823.

BREREWOOD (*Edward*), Chester, 1565–1613. De Ponderibus et Pretiis Veterum Nummorum, 1614; Inquiries touching the Diversity of Languages and Religions, etc., 1614.

BRETON (*Nicholas*), poet, 1558–1624. Arbor of Amorous Devices, 1597; Barley Break (*The*), or Warning for Wantons, 1607; Britton's Bowre of. Delights, 1591, epitaphs, sonnets, pastorals, etc.; Cornv-copiæ; Pasquil's Nightcap, an Antidot for the Headache, 1612; Crossing of Proverbs (*The*), 1616; Dialogue between Antonio, Meandro, and Dinarco, 1603; Divine Poem (*A*), part i. The Ravisht Soule, part ii. The Blest Weeper, 1601; Floorish upon Fancie (*A*), 1577; Good and Badde (*The*), 1606, in prose; Honest Counsaile, 1605, in verse; I Would and Would Not, 1614, in verse; Mad World, my Masters (*A*), 1603, a dialogue between Taker and Mistaker; Marie Magdalene's Love (The Soul's Love), 1595; Melancholike Humours, 1600, in verse; Mother's Blessing (*The*), 1602, in verse; Old Madcappe's New Gallymaufry, 1602; Old Man's Lesson and a Young Man's Love (*An*), 1605, an interlude; Pasquil's Madcappe and Madcappe's Message, 1600, a satire in verse; Pilgrimage to Paradise, 1592; Pleasant Quippes for Upstart Gentlewomen, 1595; Post with a Packet of Mad Letters (*A*), 1603; Small Handful of Fragrant Flowers gathered from the Sacred Scriptures, 1575; Solemn Passion of the Sowles Love, 1623, in verse; Soules Immortal Crowne (*The*), twined of Virtue, Wisdome, Love, Constancie, Patience, Humilitie, and Infiniteness, 1605, in verse; Will of Wit (*The*), 1597, in prose and verse; Wit's Private Wealth, 1603; Wits Trenchmore, 1597; Wonders worth the hearing, 1602; Works of a Young Wyt (descriptive of the manners of the time), 1577.

BREWER (*Antony*), in the time of Charles I.

and Cromwell. Wrote six dramas, one called *The Five Senses*, about 1620.

BREWER, LL.D. (Rev. *E. Cobham*), 1810–1897. Dictionary of Miracles, 1884; Dictionary of Phrase and Fable, 1868 (greatly enlarged 1895); Guide to Science, 1850; Historic Note-book, 1891; History of France, 1863; History of Germany, 1881; History of Greece, 1859; History of Rome, 1858; La Clef de la Science, in French, 1854 (based on the *Guide to Science*, but quite a new work); Reader's Handbook (*The*), 1880 (enlarged 1898); Theology in Science, 1859.

BREWER (Rev. *John Sherren*), elder brother of the preceding, 1809–1879. Athanasian Creed vindicated, 1871; Athanasian Origin of the Athanasian Creed, 1872; Elementary Atlas of History and Geography: revised editions, 1865, 1871; Endowments and Establishment of the Church of England, 1873; English Studies, 1881, posthumous; Prefaces 'to Henry VIII., vol. i. 122 pp., vol. ii. 279 pp., vol. iii. 435 pp., vol. iv. 666 pp.; Report to the Master of the Rolls on the Carte and Carew Papers, 1867; What is Establishment, etc.? 1868.

Edited: Aristotle's *Ethics*, with English Notes, 1836; Bacon's *Novum Organum*, with Introduction and Notes, 1856; *Court of King James I.*, by C. Goodman, now first published, 1839; Fuller's *Church History*, 1845; *History of Popish Transubstantiation*, by J. Cosin, with Memoir, 1850; Student's *Hume* (new edition), 1880.

Record Office Publications: Calendar of the Carew MSS., 1874 (with Bullen); Carte and Carew Papers relating to Ireland, 1867; Fr. Rogeri Baconi opera quædam hactenus inedita, 1859; Giraldi Cambrensis Opera; Letters and Papers of the Reign of Henry VIII., with prefaces, vol. i. 1861, vol. ii. 1864, and six more "part-volumes" (his great work); Monumenta Franciscana, 1858; Registrum Malmburiense, 1881 (with C. T. Martin).

BREWER (*Thomas*), poet, 17th century. Knot of Fooles (*A*), 1624; Weeping Lady (*The*), or London like Ninivie in Sackcloth, 1625.

BREWSTER, LL.D. (Sir *David*), Jedburgh, in Scotland, 1781–1868. Depolarisation of Light, 1813; Elliptical Polarisation, 1830; Kaleidoscope (invented), 1819; Laws of Polarisation (*The*), 1818; Letters on Natural Magic, 1831; Life and Letters of Euler, 1813; Life of Sir Isaac Newton, 1828 (republished and enlarged in 1855); Martyrs of Science, 1841; Memoirs of Life, Writings, and Discoveries of Sir I. Newton, 1855; More Worlds than One, 1854; New System of Illumination for Lighthouses, 1827; On the Production of Polarising Structure by Pressure, 1816; Optics, 1831; Polarisation of Light by Reflection, 1815; Treatise on Burning Instruments, 1812; Treatise on Optics, 1831. Life, by his daughter, 1869.

BRIDGES (*John*), Binfield, in Berkshire, 1666–1724. History and Antiquities of Northamptonshire, 1762–91.

BRIDGES (*Noah*), about 1610–1670. Art of Short and Secret Writing, 1659; Lux

Mercatoria, Arithmetik Natural and Decimal, 1661.

BRIDGES (*Robert Seymour*), 1844- . Achilles in Scyros, 1892; Christian Captives (*The*); Eden, 1891; Eros and Psyche; Feast of Bacchus, 1889; Growth of Love (*The*), 1876; Humours of the Court, 1893; "Keats," 1895, a critical essay; Milton's Prosody, 1893; Nero, part i.; Nero, part ii.; Overheard in Arcady, 1894; Palicio Plays, 1885; Shorter Poems, 1890, 1893-4; Prometheus the Firegiver, 1884; Return of Ulysses.

BRISCOE (*John Potter*), Leverbridge, in Lancashire, 1848- . Biographical Sketch of R. Millhouse, 1881; Book of Nottinghamshire, 1878, anecdotes; Literature of Tim Bobbin, 1872, a bibliography; Midland Notes, four series, 1879-82; Nottinghamshire Facts and Fictions (folklore, etc.), 1st series 1876, 2nd series 1877.

BRITTON (*John*), near Chippenham, in Wiltshire, 1771-1857. Architectural Antiquities of Great Britain, 1805-26; Architectural Illustrations of the Public Buildings of London, 1828; Autobiography, 1849-50; Beauties of Wiltshire, 1801-25; Cathedral Antiquities of England, 1814-35; Dictionary of the Architecture and Archæology of the Middle Ages, 1830-38.

BRODIE (Sir *Benjamin Collins*), Winterlow, in Wiltshire, 1783-1862. Experiments and Observations on the Influence of the Nerves of the Eighth Pair on the Secretions of the Stomach, 1814; Lectures on Diseases of the Urinary Organs, 1833; Lectures on Local Nervous Affections, 1837; Lectures on Pathology and Surgery, 1840; Pathological and Surgical Observations on Diseases of the Joints, 1813; Physiological Researches, 1851; Psychological Inquiries, 1854. Autobiography.

BROME (*Alexander*), dramatist, etc., son of the succeeding, called "The English Anacreon," 1620-1666. Covent Garden Drollery, 1672; Cunning Lovers (*The*), 1654; Fancy's Festivals, 1657; Poems and Songs, 1660; Translation of Horace (*A*), 1666.

BROME (*Richard*), died 1652. (*Ten of his comedies were published by the preceding in 1653.*) Antipodes (*The*), 1653, a comedy; City Wit (*The*), 1653, a comedy; Covent Garden Weeded, 1653, a comedy; Damoiselle (*The*), 1653, a comedy; English Moor (*The*), 1653, a comedy; Jovial Crew (*The*), or The Merry Beggars, 1652, a comedy; Lacrymæ Musarum, 1650, elegies; Lovesick Court (*The*), 1653, a comedy; New Academy (*The*), 1653, a comedy; Northern Lass (*The*), 1632, a comedy; Novella, 1653, a comedy; Queene and the Concubine (*The*), 1653; Queene's Exchange (*The*); Royal Exchange (*The*), 1653, a comedy; Sparagus Garden (*The*), 1640.

BRONTË (*Anne*), sister of Charlotte (see below), novelist, 1820-1849. Agnes Grey, 1847; Tenant of Wildfell Hall (*The*), 1845.

BRONTË (*Charlotte*), pseudonym "Currer Bell," novelist, Thornton, in Yorkshire, 1816-1855. Jane Eyre, 1847 (her best); Poems, 1856; Professor (*The*), 1856; Shirley, 1849; Villette, 1852. Life, by Mrs. Gaskell, 1857.

BRONTË (*Emily*), sister of the preceding, 1818-1848. Wuthering Heights, 1847.

BROOKE (*Frances*), novelist and dramatist, 1745-1789. Excursion (*The*), 1777; History of Charles Mandeville, 1790; History of Emily Montague, 1769; History of Lady Julia Mandeville, 1763; Marian, 1788, a tragedy; Memoirs of the Marquis of St. Forbaix, 1770; Old Maid (*The*), 1755; Rosina, 1782, a play; Siege of Sinope, 1781, a tragedy.

BROOKE (*Fulke Greville*, lord). See GREVILLE.

BROOKE (*Henry*), Ireland, 1706-1783. Constantia, or the Man of Law's Tale, 1741; Earl of Essex (*The*), 1760, a tragedy; Earl of Westmoreland (*The*), 1748, a tragedy; Fairy Tales, 1750; Farmer's Letters, 1745; Fool of Quality (*The*) 1766, a novel; Gustavus Vasa, 1739, a tragedy; Juliet Grenville, 1774, a novel; Redemption, 1772, a poem; Translations of Tasso, 1737; Trial of the Roman Catholicks, 1762; Universal Beauty, 1735, in verse.

BROOKE (*Ralphe*), 1552-1625. Catalogue of the Kings, Princes, Dukes, etc., of England, 1619 (a valuable work); Discoverie of Certain Errors in the much commended *Britannia* [by Camden], 1594; A Second Discovery of Errors, 1724.

BROOKE (Rev. *Stopford Augustus*), Dublin, 1832- . Christ in Modern Life, 1881; Development of Theology, 1893; Dove Cottage, 1890; History of Early English Literature, 1892; Irish Literature, 1893; Life of Frederick W. Robertson, 1865; Milton, 1879; Old Testament and Modern Life, 1896; Poems, 1888; Primer of English Literature, 1878; Sermons, 1868-77; Studies of Old Testament Heroes, 1880 (in *Good Words*); Tennyson (his art and relation to modern life), 1894; Theology in the English Poets, 1874.

BROOKS (*Charles Shirley*), Brill, in Oxfordshire, wrote novels, plays, etc., 1815-1874. Aspen Court, 1855, a novel; Creole (*The*), a comedy; Daughter of the Sun (*The*), a comedy; Gordian Knot (*The*), 1858, a novel; Honours and Tricks, a comedy; Naggletons (*The*), (written for *Punch*); Our New Governess, a comedy; Poems of Wit and Humour, 1875, posthumous; Silver Cord (*The*), 1841, a novel; Sooner or Later, 1868, a novel.

BROOME (*Mary Ann*, lady), novelist. About over New and Old Ground, 1870; Bedroom and Boudoir, 1878; Christmas Cake in Four Quarters (*A*), 1871; Stories About, 1870; Year in South Africa (*A*), 1877. And many others.

BROOME, LL.D. (*William*), 1689-1745. Poems on Several Occasions, 1727.

BROTHERS (*Richard*), 1760-1824. A Revealed Knowledge of the Prophecies and Times, etc., 1794.

BROUGHAM and VAUX (*Henry*, lord), Edinburgh, 1778-1868. Albert Lunel, 1844, a novel; Analytical View of Newton's *Principia*, 1855; Dialogues on Instinct, 1849; Discourses of Natural Theology, 1835; Dissertations on Subjects of Science, 1839; Experiments and Observations on the Properties of Light, 1850; Historic Sketches of Statesmen, 1839-43; Lives of Men of Arts and

Science, 1845; Paley's *Natural Theology* (edited), 1842; Political Philosophy, 1840–44; Revolution in France (*The*), 1849; Speeches, 1838; Statesmen of the Time of George III., 1839–43; Voltaire and Rousseau, 1845; Works, collected by himself, 1855–57. Autobiography, 1871, posthumous.

BROUGHTON (Rev. *Hugh*), 1549–1612. Comment upon Coheleth or Ecclesiastes, 1605; Consent of Scripture, 1596, defended, 1609; Daniel his Chaldie Visions, 1596; Daniel his Weekes, 1589; Exposition of the Common Prayer, 1603; Lamentation of Jeremiah, from the Original Hebrew, 1608; Melchisedek proved to be Sem, 1591; Mordochai his Age, 1590; Our Lorde died at the time foretold to Daniel, 1592; Our Lordes Famile, 1608; Seder Olam, 1594.

BROUGHTON (*John Cam Hobhouse*, lord), Redland, near Bristol, in Gloucestershire, 1786–1869. Journey through Albania, etc., 1820; Last Reign of Napoleon (*The*), 1876; Letters of an Englishman, 1816; Poems, 1809.

BROUGHTON (*Richard*), 1569–1634. Ecclesiastical History of Great Britain, 1633; Monastichon Britannicum, 1655, posthumous.

BROUGHTON (*Rhoda*), North Wales, novelist, 1840– . Alas! 1890; Beginner (*A*), 1894; Belinda, 1883; Cometh up like a Flower, 1867; Dear Faustina, 1897; Dr. Cupid, 1886; Good-bye, Sweetheart, Good-bye, 1872; Joan, 1876; Mrs. Bligh, 1892; Nancy, 1873; Not Wisely, but too Well, 1867; Red as a Rose is She, 1870; Scylla or Charybdis, 1896; Second Thoughts, 1880; Widower Indeed! (*A*), 1891.

BROUGHTON (*Thomas*), London, 1704–1774. Defence of the commonly received Doctrines of the Human Soul, 1766; Historical Dictionary of All Religions, 1756.

BROUGHTON (*William Robert*), Gloucestershire, 1763–1822. Voyage of Discovery to the North Pacific Ocean, 1804.

BROWN, M.D. (*John*), Rothbury, in Northumberland, 1715–1766. Barbarossa, 1755; Essays on the Characteristics of the Earl of Shaftesbury, 1751; Estimate of the Manners and Principles of the Times, 1757–58 (seven editions in one year).

BROWN (*John*), Carpow, in Perthshire, 1722–1787. Christian Journal, 1765; Dictionary of the Holy Bible, 1769; General History of the Church, 1771; Help for the Ignorant (*A*), 1758; History of the Church from the Birth of the Saviour, 1771; Self-Interpreting Bible (*The*), 1778 (his *magnum opus*).

BROWN (*John*), Buncle, in Scotland, 1736–1788. Elementa Medicinæ, 1779; Observations on the Old System of Physic, 1804, posthumous. Memoir, by Dr. W. C. Brown, 1804.

BROWN, D.D. (*John*), Bolton-le-Moors, Lancashire, 1830– . Bunyan's Home, 1890; God's Book for Man's Life, 1881; Historic Episcopate (*The*), 1891; John Bunyan, 1885.

BROWN, M.D. (*John*), Biggar, in Scotland, 1810–1882. Horæ Subsecivæ, 1858, a volume of essays.

BROWN (Rev. *Robert*), founder of the " Brownists," Northampton, 1549–1630. Life and Manners of True Christians (*The*), to which

is prefixed A Treatise of Reformation, 1582.

BROWN (*Robert*), Montrose, in Scotland, 1773–1858. General Remarks, Geographical and Systematical, on the Botany of Terra Australis, 1814; Prodromus Floræ Novæ Hollandiæ, 1810; Supplement, 1830 (works of great merit).

BROWN, M.D. (*Thomas*), Kirkmabreck, in Scotland, 1778–1820. Inquiry into Cause and Effect, 1804; Lectures on Philosophy, 1820; Observations on the Zoönomia of Dr. Darwin, 1798; Philosophy of the Human Mind, 1822; Poetical Works, 1803. His Life, by Welsh, 1825.

BROWN, D.D. (*William Lawrence*), Utrecht, in the Netherlands, 1755–1833. Comparative View of Christianity and of other Forms of Religion, 1826; Essay on the Existence of a Supreme Creator, 1816 (a prize of £1200 adjudged to it).

BROWNE (*Charles Farrer*), pseudonym "Artěmus Ward," Maine, U.S., 1834–1867. Artemus Ward among the Fenians, 1866; Artemus Ward among the Mormons, 1864; Artemus Ward his Book, 1862; Artemus Ward in London, 1868, posthumous; Artemus Ward's Complete Works, 1870; Artemus Ward's Lecture (at the Egyptian Hall), 1869.

BROWNE (*Charles Thomas*), Wellington, in Somersetshire, 1825– . Astrello, or the Prophet's Vision, 1850; Irene, 1848; Life of Southey, 1854; Tower of London (*The*), 1844; United States, its Constitution and Powers (*The*), 1856.

BROWNE (*Edward Granville*), born at Uley, Orientalist, 1862– . Catalogue of Persian MSS. in Cambridge University Library, 1896; New History of Mírzá Ali Muhammad the Báb (*The*), translated from the Persian, 1893; Traveller's Narrative (*A*), written to illustrate the Episode of the Báb, Persian text and English translation with notes, 1891; Year amongst the Persians (*A*), 1893.

BROWNE (*Frances*), Stranorlar, in Ireland (blind from infancy), 1816– . Ericksons (*The*), 1849; Hidden Sin (*The*), 1865, a novel; Legends of Ulster, 1848; My Share of the World, 1861; Songs of our Land, 1840.

BROWNE (*Hablot Knight*), pseudonym "Phiz," 1815–1882. Illustrated most of the novels of Charles Dickens, Charles Lever, W. H. Ainsworth, and Mayhew; also the Abbotsford edition of Scott's Works, etc.

BROWNE (*Isaac Hawkins*), Burton-upon-Trent, 1706–1760. De Animi Immortalite, 1754.

BROWNE (Rev. *Moses*), 1703–1787. Piscatory Eclogues, 1729; Poems on Various Subjects, 1739.

BROWNE, M.D. (*Patrick*), Crossboyne, in Ireland, 1720–1790. Civil and Natural History of Jamaica, 1756 (a valuable work).

BROWNE (Sir *Thomas*), London, 1605–1682. Discourse on Sepulchral Urns (*A*), 1648; Garden of Cyrus (*The*), or the Quincunxiai Lozenge, 1658; Hydriotaphia, or Urn-burial, 1658; Pseudoxia Epidemica (Vulgar Errors), 1646; Religio Medici, 1642 (his chief work).

Treatise on Christian Morals, 1756, posthumous. His Life, by Dr. Johnson, 1756.

BROWNE (*William*), Tavistock, in Devonshire, 1590–1645. Britannia's Pastorals (two books, each five songs), 1613, 1616 ; Inner Temple Masque (*The*), 1620 ; Shepherd's Pipe (*The*), seven eclogues, 1614.

BROWNING (Mrs.), maiden name *Elizabeth Barrett*, London, poetess, 1809–1861 ; generally called Mrs. Barrett Browning, wife of Robert Browning. Aurora Leigh, 1856 (her longest production) ; Battle of Marathon, 1822 ; Casa Guidi Windows, 1851, a poem on the Tuscans' struggle for freedom ; Curse for a Nation (*A*), 1861 ; Dead Pan, 1844 ; Drama of Exile, 1840 ; Essay on Mind, and other Poems, 1826 ; Greek Christian Poets, 1863 ; Lady Geraldine's Courtship, 1850, poem ; Last Poems, 1862 ; Poems, 1844 ; Poems before Congress, 1860 (1862, posthumous) ; Prometheus Bound (translated), 1833 ; Romaunt of the Page (*The*), 1839 ; Seraphim, and other Poems (*The*), 1838 ; Sonnets from the Portuguese, 1850. Memoirs, by Stedman.

BROWNING (*Oscar*), 1837–   . Age of the Condottieri (*The*), 1895 ; Aspects of Education, 1888 ; Cornelius Nepos, 1868 ; Dante : Life and Works, 1891 ; Earl Gower's Despatches, 1885 ; Goethe : Life and Work, 1891 ; Guelphs and Ghibellines, 1894 ; History of England (in 4 vols.), 1890 ; Life of George Eliot, 1890 ; Milton's Tractate on Education, 1883 ; Modern England, 1879 ; Modern France, 1880 ; and other works.

BROWNING (*Robert*), poet, 1812–1889. Agamemnon of Æschylus (transcripts from the Greek), 1877 ; Alkestis of Euripedes (transcript from the Greek), 1871 ; Aristophanes' Apology, being the last adventure of Balaustion, 1875 ; Asolando, 1889 (his last work, published December 12th, 1889, the day of his death) ; Balaustion's Adventure, 1871 ; Blot on the 'Scutcheon, 1843, a tragedy (performed at Drury Lane, 1843, at Sadler's Wells, 1848) ; Christmas Eve and Easter Day, 1850 ; Colombe's Birthday, 1844 (performed at the Haymarket, 1853 ; also at Boston in 1853 or 1854 : Miss Helen Faucit was Colombe) ; Dramatic Idyls (1st series), 1879 ; Dramatic Idyls (2nd series), 1880 ; Dramatic Lyrics, 1842 ; Dramatic Romances and Lyrics, 1845 ; Dramatis Personæ, 1864 ; Ferishtah's Fancies, 1884 ; Fifine at the Fair, 1872 ; In a Balcony, 1853, a dramatic fragment ; Inn Album (*The*), 1875, a tragedy ; "Jocoseria," 1883 ; King Victor and King Charles, 1842 ; "La Saisiaz" (Savoyard for "the sun"), 1878 ; Luria, 1846, a poetic drama ; Men and Women, 1855 ; Pacchiarotto, 1876 ; Paracelsus, 1835 ; Parleyings with certain People, 1887 ; Pauline, 1833 ; Pippa Passes, 1841 ; Prince Hohenstiel Schwangau, 1871 ; Red Cotton Night-Cap Country, 1873 ; Return of the Druses, 1843, a tragedy ; Ring and the Book, 1868–69 (poem founded on an Italian *cause célèbre*) ; Sordello, 1840 ; Soul's Tragedy (*A*), 1846 ; Strafford, 1837, a tragedy ; Two Poets of Croisic (*The*), 1878. Handbook to his works, by Mrs. Sutherland Orr ; Browning Cyclopædia, by Dr. E, Berdoe. All the poems in "Bells and

Pomegranates," 1841–46, are to be found in the volumes enumerated above.

BROWNRIGG, M.D. (*William*), Cumberland, 1711–1800. De Praxi Medica Ineunda, 1737 ; Treatise on the Art of making Salt, 1748 (a masterly treatise).

BRUCE (*James*), Kinnaird, in Scotland, 1730–1794. Travels to discover the Sources of the Nile, 1790. His Life, by Salt, 1805 ; A. Murray, 1808.

BRUCE (*John*), Nuthill, in Scotland, 1744–1826. Annals of the East India Company, 1810 ; Ethics, 1786 ; First Principles of Philosophy, 1780 ; Report on the Internal Defence of England, 1798 ; Review of the Events and Treaties which established the Balance of Power in Europe, 1796.

BRUCE (*John*), London, 1802–1869. Restoration of Edward IV. (*The*), 1838 ; Verney's Notes on the Long Parliament, 1844.

BRUCE, LL.D. (Rev. *John Collingwood*), Newcastle-upon-Tyne, 1805–   . Bayeux Tapestry elucidated (*The*), 1856 ; Handbook of English History (*A*) ; Handbook of Newcastle(*A*) ; Roman Wall (*The*), 1851.

BRUCE (*Michael*), Kinnesswood, in Scotland, 1746–1767. Poems, 1770, posthumous. Memoir by Grosart, 1865.

BRUNTON (*Mary*), in Burra, Orcades, novelist, 1778–1818. Discipline, 1814 ; Self-Control, 1810.

BRYANT (*Jacob*), Plymouth, 1715–1804. Analysis of Ancient Mythology, 1774–76 ; Authenticity of the Scriptures, 1792 ; Dissertation concerning the War of Troy, etc., 1796 ; Observations and Inquiries relating to Various Parts of Ancient History, 1767 ; Plagues of Egypt, 1794 ; Sentiments of Philo-Judæus concerning the Logos, 1797 ; Treatise on the Authenticity of the Scriptures, etc., 1792 ; Trojan War (*On the*), 1796 ; Vindiciæ Flavianæ, 1780 (to prove Josephus's testimony to Christ).

BRYANT (*William Cullen*), Cummington, U.S., 1794–1878. Ages (*The*), 1828 (his longest and best poem) ; Among the Trees, 1874 ; Battle-field ; Embargo (*The*), 1807, a satire ; Fountain (*The*), and other Poems, 1842 ; History of the United States, 1877 ; Hymn of the City ; Indian at the Burying-place of his Fathers ; Letters from the East, 1869 ; Little People of the Snow, 1872 ; Poems collected, 1832 ; Spanish Revolution (*The*), and other Poems, 1848 ; Thanatopsis, 1812 ; White-footed Deer (*The*), and other Poems, 1844. Also a translation of Homer's *Iliad* and *Odyssey*, 1870–1.

BRYCE (The Right Hon. *James*), Belfast, 1838–   . American Commonwealth (*The*), 1888 ; Holy Roman Empire (*The*), 1864 ; Transcaucasia and Ararat, 1877.

BUCHAN, M.D. (*William*), Ancram, in Scotland, 1729–1805. Domestic Medicine, 1769 (once enormously popular).

BUCHANAN (*George*), Killearn, Stirlingshire, 1506–1582. Baptistes (tragædia), 1578 ; De jure Regni apud Scotos, 1579 ; Detectio Mariæ Reginæ, 1572 ; Franciscanus, 1564, a satire, by order of king James V. ; Jephthes tragædia, 1554 ; Latin Version of the Psalms, 1550 ; Rerum Scoticarum Historia, 1582 (his principal work) ; Rudimenta Grammaticæ, 1550 ; Somnium, 1536, a satire. His Life, by Dr. David Irving, 1807.

BUCHANAN (*Robert Williams*), Caverswall, in Staffordshire, 1841-   .   Annan Water, 1883, a novel ; Balder the Beautiful, 1877 ; Ballad Stories of the Affections, 1866 ; Ballads of Love, Life, and Humour, 1882 ; Book of Orm, 1868 ; Charlatan (a novel in conjunction with H. Murray) ; Child of Nature, 1870, a novel (printed in 1881) ; City of Dream (*The*), 1888 ; Come, Live with me and be my Love, 1891 ; Coming Terror (*The*), 1891 ; David Gray, and other Essays, 1868 ; Drama of Kings (*The*), 1871 ; Fleshly School of Poetry (*The*), 1871 ; Foxglove Manor, 1884 ; God and the Man, 1881, a novel ; Heir of Linne (*The*), 1888, a novel ; Idyls and Legends of Inverburn, 1865 ; Lady Kilpatrick, 1892 ; Land of Lorne (*The*), 1871 ; London Poems, 1866 ; Poems, 1860 ; Look round Literature (*A*), 1887 ; Love me for Ever, 1883, a novel ; Martyrdom of Madeline, 1882, a novel ; Master of the Mine (*The*), 1885, a novel ; Master Spirits, 1873 ; Matt, 1835, a story of a caravan ; Moment After (*The*), 1890 ; Napoleon Fallen, 1871, a lyrical drama ; New Abelard (*The*), 1884, a novel ; North Coast, and other Poems, 1867 ; Outcast (*The*), 1891 ; Poems for the People, 1892 ; Poetical Works, 1874 ; Rachel Dene, 1894, a novel ; Red and White Heather, 1894, a novel ; St. Abe and his Seven Wives, 1872 ; Shadow of the Sword (*The*), 1875, a romance ; Stormy Waters, 1885 ; Undertones, 1860 ; Wandering Jew (*The*), 1893, a novel ; White Rose and Red, 1873, a love story ; Woman and the Man, 1893, a novel. With C. Gibbon : Storm-Beaten, and the following plays : Madcap Prince (*The*), 1874 ; Piper of Hamelin (*The*) ; Sophia ; and Witchfinders (*The*), a tragedy.

BUCKINGHAM (*George Villiers*, duke of), Wallingford, 1627-1688. Rehearsal (*The*), 1671, a satirical drama ; Works, 1704, posthumous.

BUCKINGHAM (*James Silk*), Cornwall, 1786-1855. Travels in Arabia, 1825 ; Travels in Assyria, Persia, etc., 1828 ; Travels in Mesopotamia, 1827 ; Travels in Palestine, 1822.

BUCKLAND (*Francis Trevelyan*), Oxford, son of the geologist, 1826-1880. Curiosities of Natural History, 1857 ; Familiar History of British Fishes, 1873 ; Fish-hatching, 1863 ; Logbook of a Fisherman and Zoologist, 1876.

BUCKLAND, D.D. (*William*), Axminster, in Devonshire, 1784-1856. Annals of Philosophy ; Geology and Mineralogy considered with reference to Natural Theology, 1836 (a Bridgewater Treatise) ; Reliquiæ Diluvianæ, or Observations on Organic Remains, attesting the Action of a Universal Deluge, 1823 ; Vindiciæ Geologicæ, 1820.

BUCKLE (*Henry Thomas*), 1822-1862. History of Civilization in Europe, 1857-61.

BUCKMAN (*James*), Cheltenham, 1816-   .   Flora of the Cotteswolds (*The*), 1844 ; Geology of the Cotteswolds (*The*), 1845 ; History of British Grasses, 1858 ; Letters on the Geology, Botany, and Archæology of the Neighbourhood of Cheltenham, 1842 ; Re-

mains of Roman Art (*The*), 1850 ; Science and Practice in Farm Cultivation, 1863.

BUCKSTONE (*John Baldwin*), suburbs of London, 1802-1879. He wrote about 150 pieces for the stage. Dream at Sea (*The*), 1837, a melodrama ; Flowers of the Forest, 1847, a romantic drama ; Green Bushes, 1845 (his best) ; Irish Lion (*The*) ; Leap Year, 1850 ; Luke the Labourer, 1828, a melodrama ; Married Life, 1834, a comedy ; Popping the Question, a comedy ; Rural Felicity, 1834 ; Wreck Ashore (*The*), 1830, a melodrama. (Others given in APPENDIX II.)

BULL, D.D. (*George*), bishop of St. David's, born at Wells, in Gloucestershire, 1634-1710. Apologia pro *Harmonia*, 1673 ; Defensio Fidei Nicenæ, 1685-88 ; Examen "Censuræ" (*i.e.* of his *Harmonia*), 1671 ; Judicium Ecclesiæ Catholicæ, 1694 ; Harmonia Apostolica, 1669 ; Primitive and Apostolic Tradition, 1709. His Life, by R. Nelson, 1713.

BULWER (*John*), seventeenth century. Anthropometamorphosis, 1653 ; Chirologia, or the Naturall Language of the Hand, 1644 ; Chironomia, 1644 ; Pathomyotomia, or a Dissection of the Muscles of the Mind, 1649 ; Philocophus, or the Deafe and Dumbe Man's Friend, 1643.

BUNNEY (*Edmund*), 1540-1617. Admonition out of the Prophet Joel, 1588 ; Corner Stone (*The*), 1611 ; Coronation of David, 1588 ; Divorce for Adulterie, 1610 ; Summe of the Christian Religion (*The*), 1576.

BUNNEY (Right Rev. *Francis*), 1543-1617. Comparison between the Auncient Fayth and the Romish, 1595 ; Exposition of Romans iii. 28, 1616 ; Guide to Godlinesse, 1617 ; Survey of the Pope's Supremacie, 1595.

BUNYAN (*John*), Elstow, in Bedfordshire, 1628-1688. Barren Figtree (*The*), 1683 ; Defence of Justification, 1672 ; Grace Abounding, 1666 ; Gospel Truths opened, 1656 ; Holy City (*The*), 1665 ; Holy War, 1684, an allegory ; Jerusalem Sinner saved (*The*), 1688 ; Justification by Christ, 1671 ; Life and Death of Mr. Badman, 1680, an allegory ; Pharisee and Publican (*The*), 1685 ; Pilgrim's Progress part i. 1678, part ii. 1684, an allegory (his great work) ; Sighs from Hell, 1650 ; Water Baptism, 1673. Posthumous Works, 1691. His Life, by Ivimey, 1809 ; Southey, 1830 ; Philip, 1839 ; George Offor, 1853 ; Froude, 1880.

BURCKHARDT (*John Lewis*), a Swiss by birth, 1784-1817. Arabic Proverbs, 1830 ; Travels in Arabia, 1829 ; Travels in Nubia, 1819 ; Travels in Syria and the Holy Land, 1822. His Life, prefixed to *Travels in Nubia*.

BURGESS, C.I.E., LL.D. F.R.S.E. (*James*), born at Kirkmahoe, Aug., 1832. Antiquities of Dabhoi for the Gaikwar of Baroda, 1888 ; Archæological Survey of Western India, 1874-83 ; Buddhist Stupas of Amaravati, 1887 ; Epigraphia Indica, 1889-94 ; Rock Temples of Elephanta (*The*), 1871 ; Temples of Shatrunjaya (*The*), 1869 ; Temples of Somanath, Junagadh, and Girnar, 1872 ; and other books on India.

BURGESS (Rev. *Richard*), 1796-1881. Greece, and the Levant, 1835 ; Ludi Circenses, 1827 ;

Topography and Antiquities of Rome (*The*), 1831.

BURGH (*James*), Perthshire, 1714-1775. Britain's Remembrancer, 1745 ; Crito, etc., 1766-67 ; Political Disquisitions, 1774-75.

BURGIN (*George Brown*), novelist, 1856– . Dance at the Four Corners (*The*), 1894 ; Gascoigne's Ghost, 1896 ; His Lordship and Others, 1894 ; Judge of the Four Corners (*The*), 1896 ; Old Man's Marriage, 1897 ; Tomalyn's Quest, 1896 ; Tuxter's Little Maid, 1895.

BURGON, D.D. (*John William*), dean of Chichester, 1819-1888. Athanasian Creed to be retained (*The*), 1872 ; Century of Verses on Dr. Routh (*A*), 1856 ; Disestablishment the Rejection of God, 1868 ; Divergent Ritual, 1881 ; England and Rome, 1869 ; Historical Notices of the Colleges of Oxford, 1857 ; Inspiration and Interpretation, 1861 ; Life and Times of Sir Thomas Gresham, 1839 ; Memoir of the Panathenaic Vases, 1833 ; Oxford Reformers, 1854 ; Petra, 1846 ; Portrait of a Christian Gentleman (*i.e.* P. F. Tytler), 1861 ; Protest against Dr. Temple's Consecration, 1870 ; Prayer-book (*The*), 1876 ; Revised Version, (*The*), 1883 ; Treatise on the Pastoral Office, 1864.

BURGOYNE (*John*), died 1792. Heiress (*The*), 1786, a comedy ; Lord of the Manor (*The*), 1783, a comedy ; Maid of the Oaks (*The*), 1780, a dramatic entertainment. Memoirs, prefixed to his *Dramatic and Poetic Works*, 1808.

BURKE (*Edmund*), Dublin, statesman, 1729-1797. Appeal from the New to the Old Whigs, 1791 ; Letter to a Noble Lord, 1795 ; Present State of the Nation (*The*), 1769 ; Reflections on the French Revolution, 1790 ; Speeches, 1801, posthumous ; Sublime and Beautiful (*The*), 1757 (excellent) ; Thoughts on French Affairs, 1791 (the "Thoughts" on the queen of France are admirable) ; Thoughts on a Regicide's Peace, 1796 ; Thoughts on the Cause of the Present Discontents, 1770 ; Vindication of Natural Society, 1756. His Life, by MacCormick, 1797 ; Bisset, 1798 ; James Prior, 1824 ; George Croly, 1840 ; Thomas Macknight, 1858-60 ; Joseph Napier, 1862 ; Morley, 1867 ; etc.

BURLEY (*Gauthier*), called "Doctor Planus," Oxford, 1275-1357. De Vita ac Moribus Philosophorum, 1467, posthumous.

BURN, LL.D. (*Richard*), Winton, in Westmoreland, 1720-1785. Ecclesiastical Law, 1760-65 ; Justice of the Peace, 1755.

BURNABY (*Frederick G.*), Bedford, 1842-1885. On Horseback through Asia Minor, 1877 ; Ride to Khiva, 1873.

BURNAND (*Francis Cowley*), editor of *Punch*. Written about a hundred plays, amongst them "The Colonel," which was a big success ; wrote "Happy Thoughts," which first appeared in *Punch*, June 23, 1866 ; "Happy Thought Series"—many burlesques on popular novels, etc.

BURNES (Sir *Alexander*), Montrose, Scotland, 1805-1842. Cabool, 1842 ; Travels in Bokhara, 1834.

BURNET (*Gilbert*), bishop of Salisbury, born in Edinburgh, 1643-1715. Exposition of the Thirty-nine Articles, 1699 ; History of his own Time, 1723-34, posthumous ; History of the Reformation, vol. i. 1679, vol. ii. 1681, vol. iii. 1715 ; Letters (on the corruptions of Popery), 1686 (the best work on the subject extant) ; Life of Dr. Bedell, 1692 ; Life of Sir Matthew Hale, 1682 ; Memoirs of the Dukes of Hamilton, 1676 ; Rome's Glory (Miracles of the Saints), 1673 ; Some Passages in the Life and Death of the Earl of Rochester, 1680. His Life, by Le Clerc, 1715 ; by his son Thomas, 1724-34.

BURNET (*John*), Fisherrow, in Scotland, 1784-1868. Education of the Eye, 1837 ; Landscape Painting in Oil Colours, 1849 ; Life of J. M. W. Turner, 1852 (with P. Cunningham) ; Practical Treatise on Painting, 1827 ; Rembrandt and his Works, 1849 ; Turner and his Works, 1852. Of his paintings, "Greenwich Pensioners receiving the news of the Battle of Trafalgar" is the best known.

BURNET, M.D. (*Thomas*), 1638-1715. Hippocrates Contractus, etc., 1685 ; Thesaurus Medicinæ Practicæ, 1673.

BURNET, D.D. (*Thomas*), of Yorkshire, 1678-1750. Archæologiæ Philosophicæ, etc., 1692 (in which he treats the Mosaic account of "The Fall" as an allegory) ; De Fide et Officiis Christianorum, 1722 ; De Statu Mortuorum, 1720 ; Telluris Theoria Sacra, part i. 1680, part ii. 1689 (the second edition was in English). His Life, by Ralph Heathcoat, 1759.

BURNETT (*James*). See MONBODDO.

BURNETT (Mrs.), maiden name *Frances Hodgson*, Manchester, novelist, 1849– . Children I have known, 1891 ; Dolly, 1893 ; Fair Barbarian (*A*), 1881 ; Fortunes of Philippa Fairfax, 1888 ; Haworth's, 1879 ; Kathleen, 1878 ; Lady of Quality (*A*), 1896, a novel ; Lass o' Lowrie (*The*), 1877 ; Little Lord Fauntleroy, 1886 (a very pretty tale) ; Little St. Elizabeth, 1890 ; Louisiana, 1880 ; Pretty Sister of Jose (*The*), 1889 ; Sara Crewe, 1888 ; Surly Tim, 1878 ; The One I knew best of all, 1893 ; Two Little Pilgrims' Progress, 1895.

BURNEY, Mus. D. (*Charles*), Shrewsbury, 1726-1814. General History of Music, 1776-89 ; Life of Metastasio, 1796 ; Present State of Music in France and Italy, 1771. His Life was written by his daughter, Mme. D'Arblay.

BURNEY (*Francisca*), afterwards *Mme. D'Arblay*, novelist, 1752-1840. Diary and Letters, 1841-46, posthumous ; Dramas for Private Representation, 1818 ; Edwin and Elgitha, 1795 ; Evelina, or a Young Lady's Entrance into Society, 1778 ; Camilla, or a Picture of Youth, 1796 ; Cecilia, or Memoirs of an Heiress, 1782 ; Georgina, 1788 ; Memoirs of her father, Dr. Charles Burney, 1832 ; Wanderer (*The*), or Female Difficulties, 1814.

BURNEY (*James*), 1749-1821. History of Discoveries in the South Sea, 1803 (a masterly work) ; History of North-Eastern Voyages of Discovery, 1819.

BURNS (*Robert*), Ayr, Scotland, 1759-1796. Auld Lang Syne, 1793 (not original) ; Cotter's

Saturday Night (*The*) (Spenserian metre), 1787; Death and Dr. Hornbook (6-line stanza), 1787; Duncan Gray, 1792; For a' that an' a' that, 1796; Green grow the Rashes O, 1787; Hallowe'en (8-line stanza), 1787; Highland Mary (8-line stanza), 1792; Mary Morison (8-line stanza), 1793; Poems, 1780; Scots wha hae (Sapphic), 1793; Tam O'Shanter, 1791; To Mary in Heaven, 1788; To a Mountain Daisy, 1786; To a Mouse, 1785; Twa Dogs (Cæsar and Luath), 1787, a dialogue. His Life, by Heron (*i.e.* John Pinkerton), 1797; James Currie, 1800; Hamilton Paul, 1819; J. G. Lockhart, 1828; Allan Cunningham, 1834; sir H. Nicolas, 1839; J. Wilson, 1841; R. Chambers, 1851–52; Mackie, 1875.

BURRITT (*Elihu*), of Connecticut, master of 50 languages, 1811–1879. Chips from Many Blocks, 1878; Olive Leaves, 1853; Sparks from the Anvil, 1848; Thoughts on Things . . . 1854; Voice from the Forge (*A*); Walk from John o' Groat's to Land's End, 1865.

BURROUGHS (*John*), writer, born Roxbury, New York, 1837. Birds and Poets, 1877; Fresh Fields, 1884; Indian Studies, 1889; Locusts and Wild Honey, 1879; Peperston, 1881; Riverley, 1894; Signs and Seasons, 1886; Wake-Robin, 1871; Whitman, 1896; Winter Sunshine, 1875.

BURTON (Rev. *Edward*), Shrewsbury, 1794–1836. Attempt to ascertain the Chronology of the Acts of the Apostles, etc., 1830; Description of the Antiquities of Rome, 1821; Greek Testament, with Notes, 1830, Inquiry into the Heresies of the Apostolic Age, 1829; Lectures on Ecclesiastical History, 1833.

BURTON, LL.D. (*John Hill*), Aberdeen, 1809–1881. Benthamiana, 1838; Book-hunter (*The*), 1862; Cairngorm Mountain (*The*), 1864; History of Queen Anne; History of Scotland from Agricola's Invasion to the Revolution, 1867–70; History of Scotland from the Revolution to Extinction of the Last Jacobite Insurrection, 1853; Life and Correspondence of David Hume, 1846; Lives of Lovat and Forbes, 1847; Political and Social Economy, 1849; Reign of Queen Anne, 1880; Scot Abroad (*The*), 1864.

BURTON (Sir *Richard Francis*), Norfolk, master of 29 languages, 1821–1890. Abeokuta, or the Cameroon Mountains, 1863; Book of the Sword (*The*), 1884; Camoëns, his Life, and his *Lusiads*, 1881; Canoeing . . . from Sahara to the Sea, 1868; City of the Saints (*The*), 1861; Etruscan Bologna, 1876, a study; Explorations of the Highlands of Brazil, 1869; Falconry in the Valley of the Indus, 1852; First Footsteps in East Africa, 1856; Goa and the Blue Mountains, 1851; Lake Regions of Central Africa, 1860; Mission to Gelile, King of Dahomey, 1864; Nile Basin (*The*), 1864; Personal Narrative of a Pilgrim to . . . Mecca, 1855; Pilgrimage to El Medina and Mecca, 1856; Sindh, 1851, Revisited, 1877; Trips to Gorilla Land, 1875; Ultima Thule, 1875; Vikram and the Vampire, 1869, Hindu tales; Wit and Wisdom from West Africa, 1865; Zanzibar, 1872. Life, by Lady Burton, his widow.

BURTON (*Robert*), pseudonym "Democritus,

Junior," Lindley, Leicestershire, 1576–1639. Anatomy of Melancholy, 1621 (a wonderful mass of quotations, chiefly Latin); Philosophaster, with poems, 1862, posthumous.

BUTLER (Rev. *Alban*), of Northampton, 1710–1773. Lives of the Saints, 1745. His Life, by sir T. Matthews, 1795; Charles Butler, 1838.

BUTLER (*Arthur John*), Putney, 1844– . Companion to Dante (*A*), 1893; Dante (translated): "Hell," 1891, "Paradise," 1885, "Purgatory," 1880; Dante (his time and work), 1895; Letters of Count Cavour, 1894.

BUTLER (*Charles*), Wycombe, in Buckinghamshire, 1560–1647. Feminine Monarchie, a Treatise on Bees, 1609.

BUTLER (*Charles*), London, 1750–1832. Life of Erasmus, 1825; Life of Fénelon, 1810; Life of Grotius, 1826; Horæ Biblicæ, 1797–1807; Horæ Juridicæ Subsecivæ, 1807.

BUTLER, D.D. (*Joseph*), bishop of Durham, born at Wantage, in Berkshire, 1692–1752. Analogy of Religion, 1736; Sermons, 1726 (three of them are *On Human Nature*).

BUTLER (*Samuel*), Strensham, in Worcestershire, 1612–1680. Elephant in the Moon (satire, in verse, on the Royal Society), 1654; Hudibras (satire, in verse, on the Puritans), part i. 1663, part ii. 1664, part iii. 1678.

BUTLER (*William Archer*), Annerville, in Ireland, 1814–1848. Lectures on the History of Ancient Philosophy (his principal work), 1856, posthumous; Letters on the Development of Christian Doctrine, 1850, posthumous; Letters on Romanism, 1854, posthumous; Sermons, 1849, posthumous.

BUTLER (Major-general sir *William Francis*), Tipperary, 1838– . Akinfoo, 1874; Campaign of the Cataracts, 1887; Far out, 1881; Gordon (*C. G.*), 1889; Great Lone Land (*The*), 1872; Napier (*Sir Charles*), 1890; Red Cloud, the Solitary Sioux, 1882; Sixty-ninth Regiment (*Memorabilia of the*), 1870; Wild North Land (*The*), 1873.

BUXTON (Sir *Thomas Fowell*), Castle Hedingham, in Essex, 1786–1845. African Slave Trade (*The*), 1839. His Life, by C. Buxton.

BYRD, or BIRDE (*William*), 1537–1623. Gradualia, ac Cantiones Sacræ (3, 4, and 5 voices), 1610 (admirable compositions); Liber Primus and Secundus Sacrarum Cantionum (6 voices), 1589; Musica Transalpina (madrigals), 1588, 1597; Psalms, Sonnets, and Songs (5 parts), 1588; Songs (for 3, 4, 5, and 6 voices), 1589. (Prince of vocal part-music.)

BYROM (*John*), pseudonym "John Shadow," near Manchester, 1691–1763. Poems, 1773, posthumous; Universal English Shorthand (*The*), 1749. He wrote the beautiful pastoral "To Phœbe" in the *Spectator*, 1747; and the famous lines about Handel and Bononcini ending—

> *Strange all this difference should be*
> *'Twixt Tweedledum and Tweedledee.*

BYRON (*Gordon George Noel*, lord), London, 1788–1824. Age of Bronze, 1823, Napoleon's fall; Beppo, 1818, a Venetian story; Bride of Abydos (*The*), 1813; Cain, 1821, a dramatic poem ; Childe Harold, canto i. 1809, ii. 1810, iii. 1816, iv. 1818 (Spenserian metre); Corsair (*The*), 1814 (see *Lara*); Curse of Minerva (*The*), 1812 ; Deformed Transformed (*The*), 1824, a drama ; Don Juan, cantos i. and ii. 1819, iii.-v. 1821, vi.-viii. 1823, ix.- xi. 1823, xii.-xiv. 1823, xv. and xvi. 1824 (incomplete) ; English Bards and Scotch Reviewers,1809 ; Giaour(*The*), 1813 ; Heaven and Earth, a Mystery, 1822, dramatic ; Hebrew Melodies, 1815 ; Hints from Horace, 1811 ; Hours of Idleness, 1807 (edit. of 1806 suppressed); Island (*The*), 1823 (mutiny of the *Bounty*); Lament of Tasso, 1817 ; Lara (sequel to *The Corsair*), 1814 ; Manfred, 1817, a tragedy ; Marino Faliero, 1821, a tragedy ; Mazeppa, 1819 ; Memoirs of my own Life, 1825, posthumous ; Monody on Sheridan, 1817 ; Morgante Maggiore, etc., 1823 ; Ode to Napoleon Buonaparte, 1814 ; Parisina, 1816 ; Parliamentary Speeches, 1824; Poems, 1808 ; Prisoner of Chillon, 1816 ; Prophecy of Dante (three cantos), 1821; Sardanapālus, 1821, a tragedy; Siege of Corinth, 1816 ; Two Foscari (*The*), 1821, a drama ; Vision of Judgment (skit on Southey's deification of George III.), 1822 ; Waltz (*The*), 1813 ; Werner, 1822, a tragedy. Letters and Journal, 1831, posthumous. His Life, anon., 1816 ; by A. R. C. Dallas, 1824; J. Galt, 1825 ; Noel Byron, 1825; J. W. Lake, 1826 ; L. Hunt, 1828 ; sir H. Bulwer, 1826 ; Brydges, 1828 ; Clinton, 1828 ; Armstrong, 1846 ; John Galt, 1830–37 ; T. Moore, 1830 ; Karl Elze, 1871.

BYRON (*Henry James*), Manchester, 1835–1883. (*Since* 1858 *he produced a host of dramatic pieces.*) Aladdin, 1859 ; American Lady (*An*), 1874, a comedy ; Babes in the Wood ; Bad Debt (*A*), a novel ; Cyril's Success ; Der Frieschutz, a travestie ; Dundreary Married and Done for, 1859 ; Esmeralda, 1860 ; Fra Diavolo, 1858 (his first play); Grin Bushes, a parody ; Hundred Thousand Pounds (*A*), a comedy ; Ill-treated Il Trovatore, 1865 ; Jack the Giant-killer, a pantomime ; La Sonnambula, a travestie ; Lady of Lyons, 1861, a parody ; Little Don Giovanni ; Lucia di Lammermoor ; Maid and Magpie (*The*); Married in Haste ; Mazeppa, a travestie ; Miss Eily O'Connor ; Not such a Fool as I Look, 1869 ; Old Sailors, 1874, a comedy ; Old Story, a comedy ; Our Boys, 1873, a comedy (it ran 1150 nights) ; Paid in Full, a novel ; War to the Knife, 1865, a comedy. (*Others will be found in* APPENDIX II.)

CABLE (*George Washington*), author, born New Orleans, 1844. Bonaventure, 1887 ; Creoles of Louisiana (*The*), 1883 ; Dr. Sevier, 1884 ; Grandissimes (*The*), 1879 ; John March, 1894 ; Madame Delphine, 1881 ; Old Creole Days, 1873 ; Silent South (*The*), 1884 ; Strange True Stories of Louisiana, 1888.

CÆDMON, first of our English poets ; he wrote in Latin ; died at Whitby, 630. Paraphrasis Poetica Geneseos, printed 1655.

CAFFYN (*Kathleen Mannington*). Children

of Circumstances, 1894 ; Comedy in Spasms (*A*), 1895 ; Quaker Grandmother (*A*), 1896 ; Yellow Aster (*A*), 1894.

CAINE (*Thomas Henry Hall*), Runcorn, in Cheshire, novelist, dramatist, 1853– . Bondman (*The*), 1890; Captain Davy's Honeymoon, 1892 ; Christian (*The*), 1897 ; Cobwebs of Criticism, 1883 ; Coleridge (*Life of*), 1887 ; Deemster (*The*), 1887, a novel ; Good Prophet (*The*), 1892 ; Little Manx Nation (*The*), 1891 ; Manxman (*The*), 1893 ; Richard III. and Macbeth, 1877 ; Rossetti (D. G.)" (*Recollections of*), 1882 ; Scapegoat (*The*), 1891 ; Shadow of a Crime (*The*), 1885, a novel ; Son of Hagar (*A*), 1886, a novel ; Sonnets of Three Centuries, 1882.

CAIRD (*Edward*), Greenock, in Scotland, 1835– . Comte (his social philosophy, etc.), 1885 ; Essays on Literature, etc., 1892 ; Evolution of Religion, 1893 ; Hegel, 1883 ; Kant (his critical philosophy, etc.), 1877.

CAIRD, D.D. (*John*), Greenock, in Scotland, 1820– . Introduction to the Philosophy of Religion, 1880 ; Religion of Common Life, 1856 ; Religions of India (*The*), 1881 ; Spinoza, 1888 ; Universal Religion, (*The*), 1874.

CAIRNS, D.D. (*John*), Ayton, in Berwickshire, 1818–1892 (pupil and successor of Charles Simeon). Christ the Morning Star, 1892 ; Life of Dr. John Brown, 1860 ; Unbelief in the Eighteenth Century, 1881. His Life, by Dr. Alexander McEwen, 1895.

CAIUS (Latin form of *Key* or *Kaye*), M.D., (*John*), Norwich, 1510–1573. De Antiquitate Cantabrigiensis Academiæ, 1568 ; De Canibus Britannicis et Raris Animalibus, 1570; De Ephemera Britannica, 1556.

CALAMY, D.D. (*Edmund*), London, 1671–1732. Account of Ministers, etc., ejected in 1662, printed 1727; Defence of Moderate Non-conformity, 1703. His Life, by himself, edited by J. T. Rutt, 1829.

CALLCOTT, Mus.D. (*John Wall*), Kensington, 1766–1821. Musical Grammar, 1805 (much esteemed).

CALLCOTT (Lady), maiden name *Maria Graham*, wife of sir A. W. Callcott, 1788–1843. Essay towards the History of Painting, 1836 ; Little Arthur's History of England, 1836 ; Memoirs of Poussin, 1820.

CALVERLEY (*Charles Stuart*), poet, etc., 1831–1884. Fly-leaves, etc., 1871 ; Literary Remains, 1885 ; Theocritus (translated into English verse), 1869 ; Verses and Translations, 1862 ; Works (uniform edition), 1888.

CALVERT (Rev.*William*), 1819– . Pneuma, or the Wandering Soul, 1856 ; Wife's Manual (*The*), 1854.

CAMBRIDGE (*Richard Owen*), London, 1717–1802. Scribleriad (*The*), 1742–51, a mock-heroic poem in six books ; War (1750–60) in India, 1761 ; Works, 1803, posthumous. His Life, by G. O. Cambridge, his son, 1803.

CAMDEN (*William*), London, 1551–1623. Account of the Monuments, etc., of Westminster Abbey (Latin), 1606 ; Anglica, Normanica, Hibernica, Cambrica, 1602 ; Annales Rerum Anglicarum, etc., regnante

Elizabetha, 1615; Britanniæ Descriptio, 1586–1607 (his great work); Description of Scotland, 1695; Remains concerning Britain, 1605. His Life, by Thomas Smith, 1691; Gough, 1551.

CAMOËNS' *Lusiad*, in ten books, translated by sir R. Fanshawe, 1655; Mickle, 1775; sir T. Mitchell, 1854; Aubertin, 1878; and by R. F. Burton, 1880. One of the four epic poems of the world.

CAMPBELL (*George*), Argyllshire, 1696–1757. Defence of the Christian Religion, 1736.

CAMPBELL, D.D. (*George*), Aberdeen, 1719–1796. Dissertation on Miracles, 1763; Lectures on Ecclesiastical History, 1800, posthumous (an excellent work); Philosophy of Rhetoric, 1776.

CAMPBELL, LL.D. (*John*), Edinburgh, 1708–1775. Biographia Britannica, begun 1745; Hermippus Redivivus, 1743; Political Survey of Britain, 1774.

CAMPBELL (*John*, lord), near Cupar, in Scotland, 1781–1861. Lives of the Chief Justices, 1849–57; Lives of the Lord Chancellors, 1845–48; Shakespeare's Legal Acquirements, 1860.

CAMPBELL, D.D. (*John M'Leod*), 1801–1872. Christ the Bread of Life, 1851; Nature of the Atonement, 1856; Thoughts on Revelation, 1862.

CAMPBELL (*Thomas*), Glasgow, 1777–1844. Battle of the Baltic (*The*), 1801 (an admirable song); Exile of Erin (*The*), 1801; Gertrude of Wyoming (three parts), 1809 (Spenserian metre); Hohenlinden, 1801 (the best English Sapphic); Pilgrim of Glencoe (*The*), and other Poems, 1842; Pleasures of Hope (two parts), 1799 (his chief poem); Poems, 1803; Reullura, the Beautiful Star, 1817; Theodoric, and other Poems, 1824; Ye Mariners of England, 1801 (a capital song). *Prose:* Annals of Great Britain, from George II. to the Peace of Amiens (3 vols.), 1807; Frederic the Great, 1843; History of our own Times, 1843–45; Letters from the South, 1837; Life of Petrarch, 1841; Life of Mrs. Siddons, 1834. His Life, by Dr. Beattie, 1849; C. Redding, 1859.

CANDLISH, D.D. (*Robert Smith*), 1806–1873. Atonement (*The*), 1860; Fatherhood of God (*The*), 1865; Gospel of Forgiveness (*The*), 1873; Life in a Risen Saviour, 1858; Reason and Revelation, 1859; Scripture Characters, 1850. His Life, by J. L. Watson.

CANNING (*George*), London, 1770–1827. Friend of Humanity (*The*), or the Needy Knife-grinder, 1798, comic verse; Rovers (*The*), 1820, a satirical tragedy.

CANTON (*William*), poet and prose writer. Lost Epic (*A*), and other Poems, 1887; Shining Waif (*The*), 1879; W. V., her Book; Invisible Playmate (*The*).

CAPEL (*Edward*), Troston, Suffolk, 1713–1781. Notes and Various Readings of Shakespeare, etc., 1775; Prolusions, 1760.

CARDWELL (Rev. Dr. *Edward*), Blackburn, in Scotland, 1787–1861. Coinage of the Greeks and Romans, 1832; Documentary Annals of the Reformed Church of England, 1839; History of Conferences, etc., connected with the Book of Common Prayer,

1558–1690, 1840 (his chief work; Reformatio Legum Ecclesiasticarum, 1850; Synodalia, 1848.

CAREW (*George*), 1557–1629. Pacata Hibernia, 1633 (a history of the wars in Ireland).

CAREY (*George Savile*), son of Henry Carey the poet, song-writer, 1740–1807. Balnea, 1799; Eighteen-hundred, 1800; Poetical Efforts, 1787. Also a large number of songs.

CAREY, Mus.D. (*Henry*), father of the preceding, 1663–1743. Amelia and Teraminta, 1732, a drama; Cantatas, etc., 1724; Chrononhotonthologos, 1734, a mock tragedy; Contrivances (*The*), 1715, a broad farce; Dragon of Wantley (*The*), 1737, a burlesque opera; God save the King, published in 1742 (Chappell says that Dr. Carey wrote both the words and music of " God save the King " for a birthday of George II. ; Dr. Finck is of the same conviction); Hanging and Marriage, 1722, a farce; Honest Yorkshireman (*The*), 1736, a farce; Margery, or the Dragoness, 1738, a farce; Musical Century (*The*), or a Hundred Ballads, 1734–40; Nancy, or the Parting Lover, 1739, an interlude; Poems, 1713, 1720, 1729; Sally in our Alley (his best ballad); Thomas and Sally, a musical entertainment; Verses on *Gulliver's Travels*, 1727.

CAREY (*Rosa Nouchette*), novelist. Writes books for girls, amongst others: Barbara Heathcote's Trial, 1871; Basil Lyndhurst, 1889; For Lilias, 1885; Heriot's Choice, 1879; Lover or Friend, 1890; Mary St. John, 1882; Men must Work, 1892; Mistress of Brae Farm (*The*), 1896; Mrs. Romney, 1894; Nellie's Memories, 1868; Not like other Girls, 1884; Old Old Story (*The*), 1894; Only the Governess, 1888; Queenie's Whim, 1881; Robert Ord's Atonement, 1873; Sir Godfrey's Granddaughters, 1892; Uncle Max, 1887; Wee Wifie, 1869; Wooed and Married, 1875.

CAREY, D.D. (*William*), Orientalist, etc., born at Paulers-Pury, in Northamptonshire, 1762–1834. Grammars and Dictionaries of several Indian languages, 1801–17.

CARLETON (*William*), Prillish, in Tyrone, Ireland, novelist, 1794–1869. Art Maguire, 1847; Blank Prophet (*The*), 1847; Clarionet (*The*), 1850; Double Prophecy (*The*), 1862; Emigrants (*The*), 1847; Evil Eye (*The*), 1860; Fair of Emyvale (*The*), 1870; Fardorougha, the Miser, 1839; Fawn of Springvale (*The*), 1841; Jane Sinclair, 1852; Parry Sastha, 1845; Red Hall (*The*), 1852; Redmond Count O'Hanlon, 1862; Rody the Rover, 1845; Silver Acre (*The*), 1862; Squanders of Castle Squanders (*The*), 1852; Tales of Ireland, 1834; Tithe Proctor (*The*), 1849; Traits and Stories of the Irish Peasantry, 1830–32; Valentine M'Clutchy, the Irish Agent, 1845; Willy Reilly, 1855.

CARLISLE, F.R.S. (Sir *Anthony*), Stillington, in Durham, 1768–1840. Alleged Discovery of the Use of the Spleen, etc., 1829; Essay on the Disorders of Old Age, 1817.

CARLISLE (*Frederick Howard*, earl of), 1748–1826. Father's Revenge (*The*), 1783, a tragedy; Poems, 1773; Present Condition of the Stage (*The*), 1808; Stepmother (*The*), 1800, a tragedy. (See Byron's *English Bards*, etc., and *Childe Harold*, canto iii.)

CARLISLE (*Nicholas*), 1771–1847. Endowed Grammar Schools, 1818; Foreign Orders of Knighthood conferred on British Subjects, 1839; Topographical Dictionary: England 1808, Ireland 1810, Scotland 1813.

CARLYLE (*Thomas*), Dumfriesshire, in Scotland, 1795–1881 (the most German of all our authors). Chartism, 1839; French Revolution (*The*), 1837; Friedrich II., the Great, vols. i., ii. 1858, iii., iv. 1862; Heroes and Hero-worship, 1840; Life of Schiller, 1823–24, recast 1825; Life of John Sterling, 1851 (a model of biography); Oliver Cromwell's Letters and Speeches, 1845 (a master work); Past and Present, 1843; Reminiscences, 1881, posthumous; Sartor Resartus, or the Autobiography of Herr Teufelsdröckh of Weissnichtwo (*i.e.* Mr. Shoddy of Nowhere), 1833–34. Several translations, as Goethe's *Wilhelm Meister*, 1824; Legendre's *Geometry*, 1824, etc.; and numerous articles for *Reviews*, *Magazines*, *Encyclopædias*, etc. His Life, by M. D. Conway, 1881; W. H. Wylie, 1881; Shepherd, 1881.

CARNARVON (*Henry Howard Molyneux Herbert*, earl of), London, 1831–1889. Druses of Mount Lebanon (*The*), 1860.

CARPENTER (*Edward*). Chants of Labour, a Song-book of the People, 1888; Civilization, its Cause and Cure—Essays: England's Ideal, 1887; From Adam's Peak to Elephanta, 1892; Modern Science, 1885.

CARPENTER, LL.D. (*Lant*), Kidderminster, in Worcestershire, 1780–1840. Harmony of the Gospels, 1835; Introduction to the Geography of the New Testament, 1805; Principles of Education, etc., 1820.

CARPENTER (Miss *Mary*), 1820–1877. Reformatory Schools for Children, 1851; Reformatory Schools and their Present Position, 1855.

CARPENTER, M.D. (*William Benjamin*), Bristol, 1813–1885. Alcoholic Liquors (a prize essay), 1848; Animal Physiology, 1847; Microscope (*The*), etc., 1856; Physiology of Temperature, 1853; Popular Cyclopædia of Science, 1843; Principles of General and Comparative Physiology, 1854; Principles of Human Physiology, 1846 (his best work); Principles of Mechanical Physiology, 1847; Principles of Mental Physiology, 1874; Zoölogy, 1848.

CARPENTER, D.D. (*William Boyd*), bishop of Ripon, 1841– . After-Hints for those recently Confirmed, 1875; District Visitor's Companion (*The*), 1881; Footprints of the Saviour, 1872; Heart and Healing, 1885; My Bible, 1884; Narcissus, 1879; Prophets of Christendom (*The*), 1876; Revelation of St. John the Divine (*The*), 1883; Thoughts on Prayer, 1872; Truth in Tale, 1885; Victor Crowned (*The*), 1870; Witness of the Heart to Christ (*The*), 1880.

CARPENTER (*William Hookham*), London, 1792–1866. Pictorial Notices of Vandyke and Rubens, 1844.

CARR (Sir *John*), 1772–1832. Caledonian Sketches, 1809; Descriptive Travels, 1811;

Poems, 1803, 1809; Rove through Holland (*A*), 1807; Stranger in France (*The*), 1803; Stranger in Ireland (*The*), 1806.

CARROLL (*Lewis*), the assumed name of the *Rev. C. L. Dodgson*, 1833– . Alice's Adventures in Wonderland, 1865; Alice's Adventures Underground, 1886; Curiosa Mathematica, 1885; Doublets, 1879; Elementary Treatise on Determinants, 1867; Euclid and his Modern Rivals, 1879; Euclid, Book V., 1874; Facts, Figures, and Fancies, 1871; Formulæ of Plane Trigonometry, 1861; Game of Logic (*The*), 1887; Guide to the Mathematical Student, 1864; Hunting of the Snark (*The*), 1876; Phantasmagoria, 1869; Songs from Alice in Wonderland, 1870; Syllabus of Plane Algebraical Geometry (*A*), 1860; Sylvie and Bruno; Rhyme? and Reason? 1883; Symbolic Logic, 1896; Tangled Tale (*A*), 1885; Through the Looking-glass, and what Alice found there, 1871.

CARTE (*Thomas*), Clifton, in Warwickshire, 1686–1754. Catalogue of Gascon, Norman, and French Rolls, preserved in the Archives of the Tower, 1743; Collection of Letters and Memoirs concerning the Affairs of England, from 1641 to 1660, published 1730; History of England, 1747–55; Life of James, Duke of Ormond, 1735–36 (contains the best account of the Irish rebellion).

CARTWRIGHT (*George*), Marnham, in Nottinghamshire, 1739–1819. Journal of Facts and Events during a Stay of Sixteen Years on the Coast of Labrador, 1792.

CARTWRIGHT (*John*), Marnham, in Nottinghamshire, 1740–1824. Independence of America considered as supremely useful, etc., to Great Britain, 1774.

CARTWRIGHT (*William*), Gloucestershire, 1611–1643. Comedies and Poems, 1651, posthumous; Lady Errant (*The*), 1651, posthumous, a comedy; Offspring of Mercy (*An*), 1652; Ordinary (*The*), 1651, posthumous; Royal Slave (*The*), 1639, a tragi-comedy; Siege (*The*), 1651, posthumous, a comedy; Signal Days of November, 1641, posthumous, a poem.

CARWITHEN (*John Bayly Somers*), Devonshire, ecclesiastical historian, 1781–1832. History of the Church of England, 1829–33; Views of the Brahminical Religion, 1810.

CARY (Rev. *Henry Francis*), Birmingham, 1772–1844. Dante (translated into blank verse), 1813 (excellent); Early French Poets (*The*), 1847, posthumous; Lives of the English Poets from Jonson to Kirk White, 1846, posthumous; Sonnets and Odes, 1788. He also translated The Odes of Pindar, and The Birds of Aristophanês.

CARYL (*Joseph*), London, 1602–1673. Commentary on Job, 1648–66 (a learned and judicious work).

CASE, M.D. (*John*), 1529–1599. Apologia Musices, 1588; Speculum Moralium Quæstionum, 1585; Sphæra Civitatis, 1588; Summa Veterum Interpretum in Universam Dialecticam Aristotelis, 1592 (his chief work).

CASTELL, D.D. (*Edmund*), Cambridgeshire, 1606–1685. Lexicon Heptaglotton, 1669 (a lexicon to Walton's *Polyglot*, highly commended by Dr. A. Clarke).

CASTLE-EGERTON (*Lewis Anthony*), 1858– . Bibliotheca Dimicatoria, 1891 ; Consequences, 1891, a novel ; English Book Plates, 1892 ; Jerningham Letters (*The*), 1896 ; la Bella, and Others, 1892 ; Light of Scarthey (*The*), 1895, a romance ; Schools and Masters of Fence, 1884.

CASWELL (*Henry*), Hampshire, 1810–1871. America and the American Church, 1839 ; City of the Mormons, 1842–43 ; Scotland and the Scottish Church, 1853 ; Western World revisited (*The*), 1854.

CATHCART (General sir *George*), London, 1784–1854. Commentaries on the War in Russia and Germany, 1850 (a valuable work).

CATULLUS, the Latin poet, has been translated into English verse by Dunlop and Lander ; by Cranston, by Martin, by Robins Ellis in 1871, etc.

CAVE (*Edward*), 1691–1754. Started the *Gentleman's Magazine* in 1731.

CAVE, D.D. (*William*), Pickwell, in Leicestershire, 1637–1713. Ecclesiastici (Lives of the Fathers of the fourth century), 1683 ; Lives of the Apostles and Apostolic Fathers of the first three centuries, 1677 (these two were once standard works) ; Primitive Christianity, 1672 ; Scriptorum Ecclesiasticorum Historia Literaria a Christo usque ad Sæculum XIV., 1688–98 ; Tabulæ Ecclesiasticæ, 1674.

CAVENDISH (*George*), real name Rev. *J. Hunter*, published in 1814 a pamphlet entitled, *Who wrote Cavendish's Life of Wolsey ?* Life of Cardinal Wolsey, 1825 (an excellent biography).

CAVENDISH (Sir *William*), gentleman usher to cardinal Wolsey, 1505–1557. Life and Death of Cardinal Wolsey, 1607, posthumous.

CENTLIVRE (*Susanna*), 1680–1723. (*Wrote 19 comedies, the three best are marked *.*) Artifice, 1721, a comedy ; Basset Table (*The*), 1706, a comedy ; * Bold Stroke for a Wife (*A*), 1817, a comedy ; * Busybody (*The*), 1708, a comedy ; Cruel Girl (*The*), 1707, a comedy ; Don Felix (see "Wonder"), a comedy ; Gotham Election, 1715, a comedy ; Love at a Venture, 1706, a comedy ; Love's Contrivances, 1705, a comedy ; Man Bewitched, 1716, a comedy ; Platonic Lave, 1707, a comedy ; Wife well Managed (*A*), 1715, a comedy ; * Wonder (*The*), a Woman keeps a Secret, 1714, a comedy.

CHALLIS (Rev. *James*), 1803–1882. Creation in Plan and Progress, 1861.

CHALMERS (*Alexander*), Aberdeen, 1759–1834. British Essayist, 1803 ; English Poets, 1810 ; General Biographical Dictionary, 1812 –17 (his chief work) ; History of the Colleges, etc., of Oxford, 1810.

CHALMERS (*David*), Ross-shire, in Scotland, 1530–1592. Discours de la Légitimée Succession des Femmes, etc., 1573 ; Histoire Abrégée de tous les Roys de Francæ, d'Angleterre, et d'Ecosse, 1572 ; La Recherche des Singularites, etc., 1579.

CHALMERS (*George*), Fochabers, in Scotland, 1742–1825. Allan Ramsay, 1800 ; Caledonia (historical and topographical), 1807–24 (his great work) ; Chronological Account of the Commerce and Coinage of Great Britain, 1810 ; Collection of Treaties between Great Britain and other Powers, 1790 (a good work) ; Estimate of the Comparative Strength of Great Britain during the Present and the Four Preceding Reigns, 1782 ; Life of Daniel Defoe, 1785 ; Life of Mary Queen of Scots, 1818 ; Life of Thomas Ruddiman, 1794 ; Political Annals of the United Colonies, 1780 ; Use and Abuse of Endowments, 1827. (He had no appreciation of the internal evidence of style, seeing he pronounced Ireland's *Vortigern and Rowena* to be decidedly Shakespeare's composition, whereas it is no more like Shakespeare than Klopstock is like Milton.)

CHALMERS, D.D. (*Thomas*), Anstruther, in Scotland, 1780–1847. Adaptation of Nature to the Constitution of Man, 1833 (a Bridgewater Treatise) ; Astronomical Discourses, 1817 (best known of all his works) ; Christian and Civic Economy of Large Towns, 1819, 1823, 1826 ; Ecclesiastical and Literary Endowments, 1827 ; Inquiry into the Extent and Stability of the National Resources, 1808 ; Lectures in Defence of Church Establishments, 1838 ; Political Economy, 1831. His Life, by Dr. W. Hanna, 1851.

CHALMERS (*William*), Aberdeen, 1600–1678. Ecclesiastical History of Scotland, 1643 ; Selectæ Disputationes Philosophicæ, 1630.

CHAMBERS (*Ephraim*), Kendal, in Westmoreland, 1680–1740. Cyclopædia, 1728.

CHAMBERS (*Robert*), Peebles, in Scotland, 1802 –1871. Biographical Dictionary of Eminent Scotchmen, 1832–35 ; Book of Days (*The*), 1863–64 (his best work) Essays, 1847 ; Exploration (a sequel to *Vestiges*), 1845 ; Histories of Scottish Rebellion, 1826 ; History of Scotland, 1849 ; History of the English Language and Literature, 1837 ; Life of James I., 1827 ; Picture of Scotland, 1827 ; Popular Rhymes of Scotland, 1826 ; Scottish Ballads and Songs, 1829 ; Scottish Jests and Anecdotes, 1856 ; Traditions of Edinburgh, 1823–30 ; Vestiges of the Natural History of Creation, 1844 ; Walks in Edinburgh, 1825. His Memoirs, by W. Chambers, 1871.

CHAMBERS, LL.D. (*William*), brother of the preceding, 1800–1883. Ailie Gilroy, 1872, a novel ; Book of Scotland, 1830 ; History of Peeblesshire, 1864 ; History of the Gipsies, 1822 ; Memoir of Robert Chambers, 1872 ; Sketches, 1866 ; Stories of Old Families, 1878 ; Story of a Long and Busy Life, 1882. The Two Brothers : Ancient Sea Margins, 1848 ; Cyclopædia of English Literature, 1843–44 ; Domestic Annals of Scotland, 1858 ; Essays, 1866 ; *Edinburgh Journal*, started 1832 ; Information for the People, commenced 1834 ; Gazetteer of Scotland, 1829–30.

CHAMIER (Captain *Frederick*), London, writer of sea-stories, etc., 1796–1870. Arethusa (*The*), 1836 ; Ben Brace, 1835 ; Jack Adams, 1838 ; Life of a Sailor (*The*), 1834 ; Passion and Principle, 1843 ; Saucy Arethusa, 1836 ; Tom Bowline, 1839 (a capital sea-song) ; Trevor Hastings, 1841. He also published, in 1849, a review of the French Revolution of 1848.

CHANDLER (*Edward*), bishop of Durham, born in Dublin, 1670–1750. Defence of Christianity, 1725 ; Vindication of the *De-fence*, 1728 (a masterly work).

CHANDLER, D.D. (*Richard*), Hampshire, 1738-1810. History of Ilium, 1802 ; Inscriptiones Antiquæ, etc., 1774 (a standard work); Ionian Antiquities, 1769 (with Revett and Pars) ; Life of William Waynflete, 1811 ; Marmora Oxoniensia, 1763 ; Travels in Asia Minor, 1775 (valuable especially to antiquaries) ; Travels in Greece, 1776.

CHANDLER, D.D. (*Samuel*), Hungerford, in Berkshire, 1693-1766. Critical History of the Life of David, 1766 (his best work, and very excellent) ; History of Persecution, 1736 ; Reflections on the Conduct of Modern Deists, 1727 ; Vindication of the Christian Religion, 1725 ; Witnesses of the Resurrection, etc., 1744. His Life, by Thomas Amory.

CHANNING, D.D. (*William Ellery*), Newport, U.S., 1780-1842. Character and Writings of Fénélon, 1829 ; Character and Writings of Milton, 1826 ; Essay on National Literature, 1823 ; Essay on Self-culture, 1638. His Life, by W. H. Channing, 1848.

CHAPMAN (Dr. *George*), Hitching Hill, in Hertfordshire, 1557-1634.

Dramas : All Fooles, 1605, a comedy; Andromeda Liberata, 1614 ; Ball (*The*), 1632 (with Shirley) ; Blinde Beggar of Alexandria, 1598, a comedy ; Bussy d'Ambois, 1607, a tragedy ; Cæsar and Pompey, 1621, a tragedy ; Conspiracie of Charles, Duke of Byron, 1608, a tragedy ; Eastward Hoe, 1605, a comedy ; Gentleman Usher (*The*), 1606 ; Humerous Dayes Myrth (*An*), 1599 ; May Day, a Wittie Comedie, 1611 ; Memorable Maske of the Two Honourable Inns of Court, 1614 ; Monsieur d'Olive, 1606, a comedy ; Revenge for Honour, 1654, posthumous, a tragedy ; Revenge of Bussy d'Ambois, 1613, a tragedy ; Second Maiden's Tragedy, 1655, posthumous (composed before 1620) ; Tragedie of Chabot, Admirall of France, 1639, posthumous ; Tragedie of Alphonsus, Emperor of Germany, 1654, posthumous ; Two Wise Men and all the Rest Fooles, 1619 ; Widowes Teares (*The*), 1612, a comedy.

Translations : Hesiod, 1612 ; Homer's *Iliad*, 1603 ; Homer's *Odyssey*, 1614 ; Juvenal, *Satire* v. (Nero justified), 1629 ; Musæus, 1616.

Miscellaneous : Epicede (*An*), or Funerall Song on Henry Prince of Wales, 1612 ; Eugenia, or True Nobilities Trance, 1614 ; Euthymiæ Raptus, or the Tears of Peace, 1609 ; Ovid's *Banquet of Sense*, 1595 ; Pro Vere Autumni Lachrymæ, 1622 ; Shield of Achilles (*The*), 1596 ; Skianuktos, or Shadow of Night, 1595.

CHAPMAN (*Matthew James*), poet, 1786-1865. Barbadoes, and other Poems, 1833 ; Hebrew Idylls and Dramas, 1866 ; Translations of Bion, Moschus, and Theocritus.

CHAPONE (Mrs. *Hester*), 1727-1801. Letters on the Improvement of the Mind, 1773 ; Miscellanies, in Prose and Verse, 1775.

CHAPPELL (*William*), 1809-1887. Collection of National English Airs, 1838-40 (to refute the notion that the English are not a musical people); History of Music, 1874 ; Popular

Music of Olden Time, 1855-59 ; Roxburghe Ballads (*The*), 1869.

CHARKE (Mrs.), maiden name *Charlotte Cibber*, youngest daughter of Colley Cibber, *-1760. Art of Management (a satire on Fleetwood), 1735, a dramatic piece ; History of Henry Dumont and Charlotte Evelyn (no date). Narrative of [her own] Life, 1755.

CHARLES (Mrs. *Elizabeth*), 1828-1897. Against the Stream, 1873 ; Bertram Family (*The*), 1876 ; Chronicles of the Schönberg-Cotta Family, 1863 ; Diary of Mrs. Kitty Trevylyan, 1864 ; Draytons and Davenants (*The*), 1841 ; Joan the Maid, 1879 ; Lapsed, but not Lost, 1881 ; Martyrs of Spain (*The*), 1870 ; Winifred Bertram, 1866. And many religious works.

CHARLESWORTH (*Maria Louisa*), 1819-1880. Ministering Children, 1854, a Sequel, 1867 ; Ministry of Life (*The*), 1858 ; Sabbath Given (*The*), 1854 ; Sabbath Lost (*The*), 1856 ; Sailor's Choice (*The*), 1863. And many other similar works.

CHARLETON, M.D. (*Walter*), Shepton Mallet, in Somersetshire, 1619-1707. Chorea Gigantum (an account of Stonehenge), 1663 ; Enquiries into Human Nature, 1680; Natural History of Nutrition, etc., 1658 ; Onomasticon Zoicon, etc., 1668-71 ; Physiologia Epicuro-gassendo-charletoniana, 1654.

CHATTERTON (*Thomas*), Bristol, 1752-1770. Rowley Correspondence begins 1768.

Posthumous : Godwin, 1771, a tragedy ; Miscellanies (in prose and verse), 1778, supplement 1784 ; Poems, 1771 (the lament in *Ælla* is unsurpassed in tenderness) ; Rowley Pieces in a Collective Form, 1777. His Life, by Dr. Gregory, 1789 ; Davis, 1809 ; John Dix, 1837 ; Martin, 1865 ; Dr. D. Wilson, 1869 ; Masson, 1875 ; Bell, 1875.

N.B.—Chatterton professed that his poems were written by Thomas Rowley, in the fifteenth century.

CHAUCER (*Geoffrey*), called "The Father of English Poetry," London, 1328-1400. Analida and Arcite, about 1387 (excellent) ; Boke of Cupid, or the Cuckow and the Nightingale, 1364, first printed 1532 ; Boke of Fame (*The*), printed by Caxton, no date, by Pynson, 1526 ; Boke of the Duchesse (*The*), 1371, printed 1532 ; Canterbury Tales (*The*), 1383, printed by Caxton, 1475 (his best work); Chaucer's A B C ; Chaucer's Prophecy ; Compleynte of a Loveres Lyfe (*The*), 1362 ; Compleynte of Chaucer to his Purse (*The*), 1377, first printed 1532 ; Compleynte of Mars and Venus (*The*), 1364 ; Flower and the Leaf (*The*), first printed 1598; House of Fame (*The*), 1373, first printed 1532; Jacke Upland, first printed 1602 ; Legende of Goode Women (*The*) ; Parlement of Briddes, or Assembly of Fowles (*The*), 1358, or Scipio's Dream, printed by Wynkyn de Worde, 1530 ; Ploughman's Tale (*The*), first printed 1542 ; Praise of Women (*A*), 1366, first printed 1532 ; Prosperity ; Quene Anelyda and the False Arcite ; Romaunt of the Rose (*The*), 1360, printed 1532 ; Treatise on the Astrolabie, 1391-92 ; Troylus and Creseyde, 1369, printed by Caxton, no date, by Wynkyn de Worde, 1517. His Life, by **J.**

Urry, 1721 ; Godwin, 1804 ; Todd, 1810 ; Singer, 1822 ; Schmitz, 1841 ; sir H. Nicholas, 1843 ; R. Bell, 1855 ; Skeat, 1878.
N.B.—*Mrs. Haweis published a "Chaucer for Children" and a "Chaucer for Schools."*

CHAUNCY (Sir *Henry*), 1632-1719. Historical Antiquities of Hertfordshire (*The*), 1700 (an excellent county history).

CHAVASSE (*Pye H.*), nineteenth century. Advice to a Mother on the Management of her Children, 1839 ; Advice to a Wife on the Management of her Own Health, 1843 ; Aphorisms on Mental Culture and Training of a Child, 1872 ; Counsel to a Mother on the Care and Rearing of her Children, 1869 ; Young Wife's Book (*The*), 1842.

CHERRY (*Andrew*), Irish dramatist, 1762-1812. All for Fame, 1805, a comedy ; Soldier's Daughter (*The*), 1804, a comedy ; Travellers (*The*), 1806, a comedy ; Village (*The*), 1805, a comedy.

CHESELDEN (*William*), Barrow-on-the-Hill, in Leicestershire, 1688-1752. Anatomy of the Human Body, 1713, a text-book ; Osteology, or Anatomy of the Bones, 1733 ; Treatise on the Operation for the Stone, 1723.

CHESNEY (*Francis Rawdon*), Ballyrea, in Ireland, 1787-1872. Narrative of the Euphrates Expedition, 1868 ; On Fire-arms, 1852 ; Russo-Turkish Campaigns of 1828-29, published 1854 ; Survey of the Euphrates and Tigris, 1850.

CHESTERFIELD (*Philip Dormer Stanhope*, earl of), London, 1694-1773. Letters to his Son, 1774, posthumous, supplement, 1777 (best known by this work) ; Miscellanies, 1777, posthumous. His Life, by Dr. Maty, 1777-78.

CHETTLE (*Henry*), about 1535-1610. Doleful Ditty of the Lord Darby, 1567 ; Hoffman, 1631, a tragedy ; Kindeheart's Dreame, 1593, a comedy ; Piers Plainnes Seauen Yeres Prentiship, 1595 ; Popes Pittifull Lamentation (*The*), 1603. He wrote, or assisted in writing, some 200 plays.

CHEVALLIER (Rev. *Temple*), 1794 – 1873. Translations of the Epistles of Clement of Rome, Ignatius, Polycarp, etc.

CHEYNE, M.D. (*George*), Scotland, 1671-1742. Account of himself and his Cures, 1743, posthumous ; English Malady (*The*), 1733 ; Essay on Health and Long Life, 1725 ; Observations on Gout, 1722 ; On Fluxions, 1703 ; Philosophical Principles of Natural Religion, 1715 ; Theory of Fevers, 1702.

CHEYNE, D.D. (*T. Kelly*), London, 1841– . Aids to the Devout Study of Criticism, 1892 ; Book of Psalms, 1884-88 ; Founders of the Old Testament Criticism, 1894 ; Hallowing of Criticism (*The*), 1885 ; Introduction to the Book of Isaiah, 1895 ; Isaiah Chronologically Arranged, 1870 ; Isaiah, 1897 ; Job and Solomon, 1887 ; Notes and Criticisms to Isaiah, 1868 ; Origin of the Psalter, 1891 ; Prophecies of Isaiah, 1880-81.

CHEYNELL (*Francis*), Oxford, 1608-1665. Chillingworthi Novissima, 1644 ; Rise, Growth, and Danger of Socinianism, 1643.

CHILD (Sir *Josiah*), 1630-1699. Brief Observa-

tions concerning Trade and the Interest of Money, 1668 (his chief work) ; New Discourse of Trade, 1690 ; Treatise proving that the Abatement of Interest on Money is the Effect and not the Cause of the Riches of a Nation, 1751.

CHILLINGWORTH (*William*), Oxford, 1602-1644. Religion of Protestants a Way to Salvation, 1638 ; Unlawfulness of resisting the Lawful Prince, 1642. His Life, by F. Cheynell, 1644 (a vile calumny) ; Dr. Birch, 1742.

CHITTY (*Joseph*), 1776-1841. Reports, 1820-23 (highly valued by lawyers). He also wrote practical treatises on criminal law, the laws of commerce, medical jurisprudence, pleading, etc.

CHORLEY (*Henry Fothergill*), Lancashire, 1808-1872. Authors of England, 1838 ; Modern German Music, 1854 ; Memorials of Mrs. Hemans, 1836 ; Music and Manners in France and Germany, 1841 ; Thirty Years of Musical Recollections, 1862.

CHRISTIE (*James*), 1773-1831. Disquisition on Etruscan Vases, 1806 ; Disquisition on Painted Greek Vases, 1825 ; Essay on the Earliest Species of Idolatry, 1814 ; Inquiry into the Game of Palamedes, 1801 ; Inquiry into Greek Sculpture, 1832.

CHRISTISON, M.D. (*Robert*), Scotland, 1797-1882. Biography of Edward Turner, M.D., 1837 ; Dispensatory (*The*), 1842 ; On Granular Degeneration of the Kidneys, 1839 ; Treatise on Poisons, 1829.

CHUBB (*Thomas*), East Harnham, in Wiltshire, 1679-1746. Doctrine of Vicarious Suffering refuted ; On Future Judgment and Eterna Punishment, 1748, posthumous ; Supremacy of God the Father vindicated, 1715 ; Tracts, 1727, 1730 ; True Gospel of Jesus asserted (*The*), 1738 ; Posthumous Works, 1748.

CHURCH (Rev. *Alfred John*), London, 1829– . Account of Pliny, 1871 ; Carthage, 1886 ; Chantry Priest of Barnet, 1884 ; Early Britain, 1889 ; Fall of Athens (*The*), 1894 ; Heroes and Things, 1883 ; Horæ Tennysonianæ, 1870 ; Milton's *Samson Agonistes*, 1872 ; Roman Life in the Days of Cierco, 1883 ; Sea of Galilee (*The*), 1884 ; Stories from the Early Comedians, 1892 ; Stories of the Last Days of Jerusalem, 1880 ; Stories of the Magicians, 1886 ; Stories from Homer, Virgil, Greek Tragedians, Livy, etc., 1877-82 ; Stories of the East, 1880 ; Story of the Persian War, 1881 ; Three Greek Children, 1888 ; Two Thousand Years Ago, 1885 ; With the King at Oxford, 1885.

CHURCH (The Very Rev. *Richard William*), 1815-1890. Bacon, 1878 ; Beginning of the Middle Ages, 1877 ; Civilization before and after Christianity, 1872 ; Dante and other Essays, 1888 ; Human Life and its Conditions, 1876-78 ; Influences of Christianity upon National Character, 1873 ; Life of St. Anslem, 1871 ; Oxford Movement (*The*), 1891 ; Sacred Poety of Early Religions, 1874 ; Spenser, 1878. And other similar works. His Life, by his daughter.

CHURCHILL (Rev. *Charles*), Westminster, 1731-1764.
Satires in Verse: Apology to Critical

Reviewers, 1761; Author (*The*), 1764 (his best satire); Conference (*The*), 1763; Candidate (*The*), 1764; Duellist (*The*), 1763; Epistle to Hogarth, 1763; Farewell (*The*), 1764; Ghost (*The*), 1762 (against Dr. Johnson); Gotham (three books), 1764; Independence, 1764; Night, an Epistle to Lloyd, 1761; Prophecy of Famine, 1762, a political squib; Rosciad (*The*), on actors and managers, 1761; Scot's Pastoral (*A*); Times (*The*), 1764. His Life, by W. Tooke, 1804.

CHURCHYARD (*Thomas*), Shrewsbury, 1520-1604. Challenge (*The*), 1593; Chippes (contayning 12 labours), 1565; Davie Dicar's Dream, 1562-63, in verse; Description of the Wofull Warres in Flaunders, 1578; Discourse of Rebellion, 1570; Miserie of Flaunders, etc., 1579; Pleasaunte Laborinth (*A*), 1580; Warning to the Wise, 1580; Worthines of Wales, 1587. And scores of others. His Life, by G. Chalmers, 1817.

CHURTON (Ven. *Edward*), 1800-1874. Early English Church (*The*), 1840; Vindiciæ Ignatii, 1852.

CIBBER (*Colley*), London, 1671-1757. Apology for his own Life, 1740 (most amusing); Careless Husband (*The*), 1704, a comedy; Love's Last Shift, 1695, a comedy; Nonjuror (*The*), 1717, a comedy; Woman's Wit, 1697, a comedy; Works, 1721; Xerxes, 1699, an historic drama.

CIBBER (*Theophilus*), son of the preceding, 1703-1758. Apology for the Life of Mr. T. C. [Theophilus Cibber], comedian, 1740; Auction (*The*), 1757, a farce; Civil Wars of Henry VI. (*The*), 1724, a tragedy; Harlot's Progress (*The*), 1733, an extravaganza; Lives of Eminent Actors and Actresses (*The*), 1753; Lives of British and Irish Poets from the Time of Swift, 1753; Lover (*The*), 1730, a comedy; Mock Officer (*The*), 1733, a comedy; Patie and Peggie (see APPENDIX II.), 1730.

CLAPPERTON (*Hugh*), Annan, in Scotland, 1788-1827. Travels and Discoveries in Northern and Central Africa, 1826; a Second Expedition, 1829; a Final Expedition, 1830.

CLARE (*John*), Peterborough, 1793-1864. Moments of Forgetfulness, 1824, in verse; Poems descriptive of Rural Life, 1820; Shepherd's Calendar, and other Poems, 1827; Rural Muse (*The*), 1835; Village Minstrel (*The*), and other Poems, 1821. His Life, by Martin, 1865; by Cherry, 1873.

CLARENDON (*Edward Hyde*, earl of), Dinton, in Wiltshire, 1608-1674. Brief View of the Dangerous Errors in Hobbes's *Leviathan*, 1676; History of the Grand Rebellion, 1702-4, continuation 1759, posthumous. His own Life, 1759, posthumous.

CLARENDON (*Henry Hyde*, second earl of), Dinton, in Wiltshire, 1638-1709. History of the Rebellion and Civil War in England, 1702-4, posthumous (a standard work); Letters on the Affairs of the Times, 1763, posthumous. His Life, by T. H. Lister, 1838.

CLARICARDE (Marquis of), London, 1604-1659. Memoirs concerning the Affairs in Ireland from 1640 to 1653, 1722, posthumous.

CLARIDGE (*John*), called "The Shepherd of Banbury," seventeenth century. Shepherd's

Legacy (*The*), or Weather Rules, 1670 (showing how to forecast the weather by observing the moon, the stars, the mist, the rainbow, the clouds, and the winds; how to keep sheep sound, and how to cure the rot).

CLARK, F.R.S. (Sir *James*), Banffshire, Scotland, 1788-1870. Pulmonary Consumption, 1835; Sanative Influence of Climate, 1829.

CLARKE, LL.D. (*Adam*), Ireland, 1762-1832. Bibliographical Dictionary, 1802, supplement, 1806; Commentary on the Holy Scriptures, 1810-26. He edited and enlarged the *Fœdera*, but not with good judgment. His Life, by J. B. B. Clarke, 1833; Dr. Etheridge, 1858; S. Dunn, 1863.

CLARKE (*Charles Cowden*), Enfield, in Middlesex, 1787-1877. Molière Characters, 1865; Shakespeare Characters (chiefly subordinate), 1863; Tales from Chaucer, 1833.

CLARKE (Mrs. *Cowden*), maiden name *Mary Novello*, wife of the preceding, 1809- . Adventures of Kit Bam, Mariner, 1848; Complete Concordance to the Works of Shakespeare (*A*), 1845 (a great work, well done); Girlhood of Shakespeare's Heroines (*The*), 1850; Iron Cousin (*The*), 1854, a novel; Many Happy Returns of the Day, 1860 (a birthday book); Rambling Story (*A*), 1874; Song of a Drop o' Wather, etc., 1856; Trust and Remittance, 1873, love-stories in poetic prose; World-noted Women, 1857.

CLARKE, LL.D. (*Edward Daniel*), Willington, in Sussex, 1769-1822. Tomb of Alexander (*The*), 1805; Travels, 1810-23 (excellent); Travels through Denmark, Sweden, Norway, England, etc., 1819-24, posthumous. His Life, by bishop Otter, 1824.

CLARKE, D.D. (*James Stanier*), died 1834. Life of James II., from Memoirs written by himself, 1816; Life of Lord Nelson, from his Lordship's MSS., 1809; Naufragia, or Historical Memoirs of Shipwrecks, 1805; Progress of Maritime Discoveries, 1803.

CLARKE (Rev. *Samuel*), 1599-1689. General Martyrologie, 1677; Lives of Sundry Eminent Persons, part i. divines, part ii. nobility and gentry, 1683; Looking-glass for Saints, 1671; Marrow of Ecclesiastical History (*The*), part i. Christ and the Fathers, part ii. Christian monarchs, 1650.

CLARKE, D.D. (*Samuel*), Norwich, 1675-1729. Being and Attributes of God (*The*), 1704 (his best work); Evidences of Natural and Revealed Religion, 1703; Scripture Doctrine of the Trinity, 1712.

Literal Translations: Cæsar's *Commentaries*, 1712; Homer's *Iliad*, 1729-32; Works Collected, 1738.

His Life, by bishop Hoadly, 1738; W. Whiston, 1748.

CLARKE (*William*), Shropshire, 1696-1771. Connexion of the Roman, Saxon, and English Coins, 1767.

CLARKSON (*Thomas*), Wisbeach, in Cambridgeshire, 1760-1846. History of the Abolition of the Slave Trade, 1808; Memoirs of William Penn, 1813; Portraiture of Quakerism, 1806. His Life, by Thomas Taylor.

CLAYDEN (*Peter William*), Wallingford, in Berkshire, 1827- . Early Life of Samuel

Rogers, 1887; England under Lord Beaconsfield, 1880; England under the Coalition, 1892; Religious Value of the Doctrine of Continuity, 1866; Rogers and his Contemporaries, 1889; Samuel Sharpe, 1883; Scientific Men, 1874.

CLAYTON (*Ellen Creathorne*), Dublin, *–* Celebrated Women, 1860; Cruel Fortune, 1865, a novel; Crying for Vengeance. 1877, a novel; Female Artists, 1876; Female Warriors, 1879; Miss Milly Moss, 1862, a tale; Notable Women, 1860; Playing for Love, 1876, a novel; Queens of Song, 1863; Women of the Reformation, 1861.

CLAYTON (*Robert*), bishop of Clogher, 1695-1758. Chronology of the Hebrew Bible vindicated, 1747 (a work of great merit); Essay on Spirit, 1751; Introduction to the History of the Jews, 1746.

CLEMENS (*Samuel Langhorne*), pseudonym "Mark Twain," Florida, U.S., 1835– . Adventures of Huckleberry Finn, 1884; Adventures of Tom Sawyer (*The*), 1876; American Claimant (*The*), 1892; Gilded Age (*The*), 1873; Idle Excursion (*An*), 1878; Joan of Arc, 1896; Innocents Abroad (*The*), 1869; Jumping Frog (*The*), 1867; Life on the Mississippi, 1883; Mark Twain's Choice Works, 1897; Mark Twain's Library of Humour, 1888; £1,000,000 Bank Note, 1893; Prince and Pauper, 1881; Pudd'nhead Wilson, 1894; Roughing it, and the Innocents at Home, 1872; Stolen White Elephant (*The*), 1882; Tom Sawyer Abroad, 1884; Tom Sawyer, Detective, 1896; Tramp Abroad (*A*), 1880; More Tramps Abroad, 1897; Yankee at the Court of King Arthur, 1889.

CLEVELAND (*John*), at Loughborough, in Leicestershire, 1613-1658. Poems, 1651, 1654, 1657; Works, 1687, posthumous. (Once more esteemed than Milton.)

CLIFFORD (*Arthur*), 1788-1830. Cliffordia Collectanea, 1817; Historical and Topographical Description of the Parish of Tixall, etc., 1817; State Papers, etc., of Sir Ralph Sadler, 1809.

CLIFFORD, D.D. (*John*), Sawley, near Derby, 1836– . Christian Certainties, 1893; Dawn of Manhood (*The*), 1886; Familiar Talks with the Young, 1872; George Mostyn, 1874; Inspiration and Authority of the Bible (*The*), 1892; Is Life worth Living? 1880. And other similar works.

CLIFFORD (*William Kingdon*), 1845-1879. Classification of Loci, 1879; Common Sense of the Exact Sciences (*The*), 1885; Elements of Dynamics (*The*), 1878, 1887; Seeing and Thinking, 1879.

CLIFFORD (Mrs. *William Kingdon*), maiden name *Lucy Lane*, Liverpool. Anyhow Stories, 1882; Aunt Anne, 1893; Dingy House at Kensington (*The*), 1881; Flash of Summer (*A*), 1895; Last Touches (*The*), 1893; Love-Letters of a Worldly Woman, 1891; Mere Stories, 1896; Mrs. Keith's Crime, 1885; Very Short Stories, 1886; Wild Proxy (*A*), 1894.

CLINTON (*Henry Fynes*), Gamston, in Nottinghamshire, 1781-1852. Epitome of Rome and Constantinople, 1853; Fasti Hellenici, 1824-34 (a standard work); Fasti Romani,

1845-50 (a standard work). His Life, by himself, edited by C. J. F. Clinton, 1854.

CLIVE (Mrs. *Archer*), 1801-1873. John Greswold, 1864; Morlas (*The*), 1853; Paul Ferroll, 1855; Poems, 1840; Queen's Ball (*The*), 1847; Why Paul Ferroll killed his Wife, 1860; Year after Year, 1858.

CLODD (*Edward*), 1840– . Jesus of Nazareth, 1880; Myths and Dreams, 1885; Pioneers of Evolution, 1897; Primer of Evolution, 1895; Story of Primitive Man, 1895; Story of Creation, 1888. And other works.

CLOUGH (*Arthur Hugh*), Liverpool, 1819-1861. Ambarvalia, 1840 (a volume of poems of great merit); Amours de Voyage, 1840 (in English hexameters); Bothie of Tober-na-Vuolich, 1848; Dipsychus, 1840 (a dialogue in verse between Dipsychus and a spirit); Mari Magno, 1840, three stories in verse; Poems and Essays, 1871, posthumous. His Life, by F. T. Palgrave, 1863; A. Symonds, 1871.

CLUTTERBUCK (*Robert*), Hertfordshire, 1772-1831. History and Antiquities of Hertfordshire, 1815-27.

COBBE (*Frances Power*), Dublin, 1828– . Alone to the Alone, 1871; Broken Lights, 1864; Cities of the Past, 1864; Confessions of a Lost Dog, 1867; Criminals, Idiots, Women, and Minors, 1869; Darwinism in Morals, 1872; Dawning Lights, 1868; Doomed to be Saved, 1874; Duties of Women, 1880; Essays on the Pursuits of Women, 1863; False Beasts and True, 1875; Female Education, 1862; Friend of Man, etc., 1889; Friendless Girls and how to Help them, 1861; Hopes of the Human Race, 1874; Hours of Work and Play, 1867; Modern Rack (*The*), 1889; Moral Aspects of Vivisection, 1875; Peak in Darien (*The*), 1882; Red Flag in John Bull's Eye (*The*), 1863; Re-echoes, 1876; Religious Duty, 1864; Scientific Spirit of the Age, 1888; Studies of Ethical and Social Subjects, 1865; Thanksgiving, 1863; Why Women desire the Franchise, 1877; Workhouse as an Hospital (*The*), 1861.

COBBETT (*William*), Farnham, in Surrey, 1762-1835. Advice to Young Men, 1831; Cottage Economy, 1822; English Grammar, 1819; French Grammar, 1824; History of the Protestant Reformation in England, etc., 1810; Legacy to Labourers, 1834; Legacy to Parsons, 1835; Paper against Gold, 1817; Parliamentary History of England, 1803; Political Registers, 1802-13; Poor Man's Friend (*The*), 1826; Rural Rides, 1830; Weekly Register, 1802-35; Works of Peter Porcupine, 1801; Year's Residence in the United States, 1818-19. His Life, by Huish, 1835; by his son, 1837; by Smith, 1878.

COBBOLD (Rev. *Richard*), 1797-1877. Margaret Catchpole, 1845, an historical novel; Freston Tower, 1850; John H. Steggall, 1850; Mary Ann Wellington, 1846; Young Man's Home (*The*), 1849; Zenon the Martyr, 1847.

COCHRANE (*Alexander Dundas Ross Wishart Baillie*), 1814– . Ernest Vane, 1849; Exeter Hall, 1841; Florence the Beautiful, 1854; Francis I., and other Historic Studies, 1870; Historic Studies, 1870; Morea (*The*), a poem (2nd edition), 1841; Young Italy, 1865.

COCHRANE (*John Dundas*), 1780-1825. Narrative of a Pedestrian Journey through Russia and Siberian Tartary, 1824.

COCKBURN (Mrs. *Catherine*), 1679-1749. Agnes de Castro, a play; Fatal Friendship, a tragedy; Gustavus Erikson, King of Sweden, an historic drama; Love at a Loss, a comedy.

COCKBURN (*Henry Thomas*, lord), Edinburgh, 1779-1854. Life of Lord Jeffrey, 1852; Memorials of his Time, 1856, posthumous.

COCKER (*Edward*), London, 1631-1677. Arithmetick, 1654; Penna Volans, 1660; Pen's Triumph, 1657.

COCKTON (*Henry*), humorous novelist. Sylvester Sound the Somnambulist, 1844; Valentine Vox the Ventriloquist, 1840.

COKAINE (Sir *Aston*), 1608-1684. Chaine of Golden Poems (*A*), 1658; Choice Poems, 1669; Obstinate Lady (*The*), 1657, a comedy; Ovid, 1669, a tragedy; Plays, 1669; Small Poems, 1658; Trapolin, a supposed Prince, 1658, a play.

COKE (Sir *Edward*), chief justice of England, born at Mileham, in Norfolk, 1551-1633. Book of Entries, 1614; Complete Copyholder, 1640, posthumous; Institutes, part i. (Coke upon Littleton) 1628, part ii. (Magna Charta) 1642, posthumous, part iii. (High Treason) 1644, posthumous, part iv. (Jurisdiction of Courts) 1644, posthumous; Reading on Fines, 1662, posthumous; Reports, 1600-16.

COKE (Hon. *Henry John*), 1827- . Ride over the Rocky Mountains, etc., 1852; Vienna in 1848; Will and a Way (*A*), 1858.

COLDEN (*Cadwallader*), Dunse, in Scotland, 1688-1776. History of the Five Indian Nations, 1747; Plantæ Novæboracenses, 1743-44.

COLE (*William*), herbalist, 1626-1662. Adam in Eden, or a History of Plants, Herbs, and Flowers, 1657; Art of Simpling (*The*), *i.e.* where to gather plants, 1656.

COLEBROOKE (*Henry Thomas*), London, 1765-1837. Amera Cosha, etc., 1808; Digest of Hindu Law on Contracts and Successions, 1797; Essays, 1837; Grammar of the Sanscrit Language, 1805; Remarks on the Agriculture and Commerce of Bengal, 1806.

COLENSO, D.D. (*John William*), bishop of Natal, 1814-1883. Criticism on *The Speaker's Commentary*, 1871; *Epistle to the Romans* (*The*), 1861; Lectures on the Pentateuch, 1873; Natal Sermons, 1866; Pentateuch and Book of Joshua critically examined (*The*), 1662-72; Ten Weeks in Natal, 1855; Village Sermons, 1853. His Life, by Rev. sir G. W. Fox, 1888.

COLERIDGE (Rev. *Derwent*), son of S. T. Coleridge the poet, Keswick, in Cumberland, 1800-1883. Biographical Sketch of his brother Hartley, 1850; Life of Praed, 1864; Scriptural Character of the English Church, 1839.

COLERIDGE (*Hartley*), son of S. T. Coleridge the poet, Clevedon, near Bristol, 1796-1849. Biographia Borealis, 1833, prose; Life of Andrew Marvell, 1835; Life of Massinger;

Marginalia, 1851, posthumous; Poems, 1833; Worthies of Yorkshire and Lancashire, 1836 (his best prose work). His Life, by his brother, Derwent Coleridge, 1851.

COLERIDGE (*Henry Nelson*), nephew of the poet, 1800-1843. Introduction to the Study of the Greek Classic Poets, 1830; Six Months in the West Indies, 1825; Specimens of the Table Talk of S. T. Coleridge, 1835.

COLERIDGE (*Samuel Taylor*), Ottery St. Mary, in Devonshire, 1772-1834.

Poetry and Fiction: Ancient Mariner (in seven parts), 1798 (his best poem); Christabel, part i. 1797, part ii. 1800, published 1816; Fall of Robespierre, 1794, a play; Kubla Khan, 1816 (said to have been dreamt); France, 1798, an ode; Ode to the Departed Year, 1796; Poems, 1794; Raven, 1848, posthumous, a Christmas tale; Religious Musings, 1796; Remorse, 1813, a tragedy; Sibylline Leaves, 1817; Translation of Wallenstein, 1800; Zapolya, 1818, a Christmas tale in two parts.

Prose: Aids to Reflection, 1825; Biographia Literaria, 1817 (his chief prose work); Confessions of an Inquiring Spirit, 1840, posthumous; Constitution of Church and State, 1830; Essays on his own Times, 1850, posthumous; Friend (*The*), 27 numbers, 1812; Lay Sermons, 1816-17; Notes and Lectures on Shakespeare, etc., 1849, posthumous; Remains, 1836; Table Talk, 1835, posthumous; Theory of Life, 1849, posthumous; Treatise on Method, 1848, posthumous; Watchman (*The*), a weekly miscellany (10 parts), 1796.

His Life, by J. Gilman, 1838; Cottle, 1847.

COLERIDGE (*Sara*), Keswick, in Cumberland, daughter of the poet, and wife of her cousin, Henry Nelson Coleridge, 1803-1852. Account of the Abipones, etc. (translation), 1822; Phantasmion, 1837, a fairy tale. Her Memoir, by her daughter, 1873.

COLES (*Elisha*), 1640-1716. Dictionary (*A*), English-Latin and Latin-English, 1677; English Dictionary (*An*), 1706; Nomenclatura Trilinguis, or an Anglo-Latino-Græca, 1707; Shorthand, 1674.

COLET, D.D. (*John*), dean of St. Paul's, London, 1466-1519. Construction of the Eight Parts of Speech, etc., 1530, posthumous; Rudimenta Grammatices, 1510. His Life, by T. Fuller, 1693; Dr. Samuel Knight, 1726; Erasmus in *Phœnix*, vol. ii.

COLGAN (*John*), an Irish mendicant, 1590-1658. Acta Sanctorum . . . Scotiæ seu Hiberniæ, 1645; Tractatus de Joannis Scoti . . . Vita, 1655 (very rare); Triadis Thaumaturgæ . . . Acta, 1647 (containing the Lives of St. Patrick, St. Colomb, and St. Brigid).

COLLIER (*Jeremy*), Stow Quy, in Cambridgeshire, 1650-1726. Desertion discussed (*The*), 1688; Ecclesiastical History of Great Britain, 1708-14 (his chief work); Essays on Moral Subjects, 1697, 1705, 1709; Great Historical, Geographical, and Genealogical Dictionary (*The*), 1701, supplement, 1721; Short View of the Immorality, etc., of the English Stage, 1698; Translation of Moreri's *Historical Dictionary*, 1701-21. His Life, by P. Lathbury, 1852.

COLLIER (*John Payne*), London, philologist, 1789-1883. Bibliographical Account of Rare Books, 1865; History of English Dramatic Poetry, 1831; Memoirs of Actors in the Plays of Shakespeare, 1846; New Facts regarding Shakespeare, 1835, 1836, 1839; Notes and Emendations to the Text of Shakespeare's Plays, 1852; Poetical Decameron, 1820; Poet's Pilgrimage (*The*), an allegorical poem, in four cantos, 1822; Sculptor (*The*), 1878.
    Editor of Shakespeare's Works, 1842, 1853; Spenser, 1862.

COLLINGWOOD (*Cuthbert*), Greenwich, in Kent, 1826– . Rambles of a Naturalist on the Shores of the China Sea, 1868; Travelling Birds (*The*), 1872; Vision of Creation (*A*), 1872, a poem.

COLLINS (*Anthony*), Middlesex, a freethinker, 1676-1729. Discourse on Freethinking, 1713 (his chief work); Essay concerning the Use of Human Reason, 1707; Grounds and Reasons of the Christian Religion, 1724; Philosophical Inquiry concerning Liberty and Necessity, 1715; Priestcraft in Perfection, 1709; Reply to Dr. Rogers, 1727; Scheme of Literal Prophecy, 1726; Vindication of the Divine Attributes, 1710.

COLLINS (*Arthur*), 1682-1760. Baronetage, 1720; History of the Peerage of England, 1709.

COLLINS, F.R.S. (*John*), Wood Eaton, Oxfordshire, 1624-1683. Commercium Epistolicum, etc., de Analysi Promota, 1712.

COLLINS (*Mortimer*), Plymouth, in Hampshire, 1827-1876. Blacksmith and Scholar, 1875, a novel; British Birds (a vision from Aristophanes), 1872; Fight with Fortune (*A*), 1876, a novel; Frances, 1874, a novel; From Midnight to Midnight, 1875; Idyls and Rhymes, 1855; Inn of Strange Meetings (*The*), and other Poems, 1871; Ivory Gate (*The*), 1869, a novel; Letter to Disraeli, in Verse, 1869; Marquis and Merchant, 1871, a novel; Miranda, 1873, a novel; Mr. Carington, 1873, a novel; Princess Clarice, 1872, a novel; Secret of Long Life (*The*), 1871; Squire Silchester's Whim, 1873, a novel; Summer Songs, 1860; Sweet and Twenty, 1879, a novel; Sweet Anne Page, 1868, a novel; Transmigration, 1873, a novel; Two Plunges for a Pearl, 1872, a novel; Village Comedy (*A*), 1874, a novel (with Frances Collins); Vivian Romance (*The*), 1870, a novel; Who is the Heir? 1865, a novel; You play me False, 1878, a novel (with his wife, Frances).

COLLINS (*William*), Chichester, 1720-1756. Odes, 1745, 1746, 1747; Ode to Evening, 1746 (the best Alcaic in the language); Oriental Eclogues, 1742; Passions (Ode on the), 1746; Persian Eclogues and Odes, 1742; Poems, 1765, posthumous. His Life, by Dr. Johnson, 1798; Dyce, 1827; sir Harris Nicolas, 1830; Moy Thomas, 1858.

COLLINS (*William Wilkie*), London, novelist, 1824-1889. After Dark, and other Stories, 1856; Alicia Warlock, 1875; Antonina, or the Fall of Rome (fifth century), 1850; Armadale, 1866; Basil (a story of modern life), 1852; Black Robe (*The*), 1881; Blind Love, 1890, posthumous; Dead Secret (*The*), 1857; Evil Genius, 1886; Fallen Leaves (*The*), 1879; Frozen Deep (*The*), 1874; Guilty River (*The*), 1886; Haunted Hotel (*The*), 1878; Heart and Science, 1883; Hide and Seek, 1854; I say No, 1884; Jezebel's Daughter, 1880; Law and the Lady (*The*), 1875; Legacy of Cain (*The*), 1888; Little Novels, 1887; Man and Wife, 1870; Memoirs of his Father, 1848; Miss or Mrs.? and other Stories, 1873; Mr. Wray's Cashbox, 1852, a Christmas tale; Moonstone (*The*), 1868; My Miscellanies, 1862; New Magdalen (*The*), 1873; No Name, 1862; Poor Miss Finch, 1871; Queen of Hearts (*The*), 1859; Rambles beyond Railways, 1851; Rogue's Life (*A*), 1879; Two Destinies, 1876; Woman in White (*The*), 1860 (his best).
    Plays: Black and White; Frozen Deep (*The*), dramatized, 1857; Lighthouse (*The*), 1855; Moonstone (*The*), dramatized, 1877; No Name, dramatized.

COLLINSON (Rev. *John*), died 1793. History and Antiquities of the County of Somerset, 1791.

COLMAN (*George*), born at Florence, 1733-1794. Clandestine Marriage, 1766, a comedy (with Garrick); Jealous Wife (*The*), 1761, a comedy; Pieces in Prose and Verse, 1787; Polly Honeycombe, 1760, a dramatic novel; Translation of Horace's De Arte Poetica, 1873; of Terence, 1765 (praised by Dr. Adam Clarke). His Life, by himself, 1795, posthumous.

COLMAN (*George*), "the Younger," son of the preceding, born in Florence, 1762-1836.
    Plays: Africans (*The*), 1808; Battle of Hexham (*The*), 1789, an historic play; Blue Beard, 1798, a musical spectacle; Broad Grins (same as "My Nightgown and Slippers," with additions), 1802; Eccentricities for Edinburgh, 1820; Female Dramatists (*The*), a musical farce; Gay Deceivers, 1804, a farce; Heir-at-Law (*The*), 1797, a comedy; Inkle and Yarico, 1787, a musical drama; Iron Chest (*The*), 1796, a musical drama; John Bull, 1805, a comedy; Law of Java (*The*), 1822, a musical drama; Love Laughs at Locksmiths, 1803, a farce; Man of the People (*The*); Mountaineers (*The*), 1793, a comedy; My Nightgown and Slippers, 1797, a comedy; Poetical Vagaries, 1812; Poor Gentleman (*The*), 1802, a comedy; Random Records, 1830; Review (*The*), or the Wags of Windsor, 1798, a farce; Surrender of Calais (*The*), 1791, a comedy; Turk and No Turk, 1785, a musical comedy; Vagaries Vindicated (a poem to Reviewers), 1814; Ways and Means, 1788, a comedy; We Fly by Night, 1806, a farce; Who wants a Guinea? 1805, a farce; X Y Z, 1810. Memoirs of the Colman family, by R. B. Peeke, 1842.

COLQUHOUN(*Archibald Ross*), 1848- . Across Chrysê, 1883; Amongst the Shans, 1885; Burmah and the Burmans, 1885; English Policy in the Far East, 1885; Key of the Pacific (*The*), 1895; Matabeleland, 1893; Opening of China (*The*), 1884; Report on the Railway Connection of Burmah and

China, 1888; Truth about Tonquin (*The*), 1884.

COLQUHOUN, LL.D. (*Patrick*), Dumbarton, in Scotland, 1745-1820. Treatise on the Functions, etc., of a Constable, 1803; Treatise on the Police of the Metropolis, 1796 (a valuable work); Treatise on the Police, etc., of the River Thames, 1800; Treatise on the Wealth, Power, and Resources of the British Empire, 1814.

COLQUHOUN (Sir *Patrick MacChombaich*), 1815-1890. A Summary of the Roman Civil Law, 1849-60.

COLQUHOUN (Rev. *William Gifford*), Brasted, in Kent, 1802-1880. Account of the Ancient City of Rome, 1850; Account of the Map of Athens, 1851.

COLTON (Rev. *Caleb C.*), died 1832. Lacon, or Many Things in Few Words, 1822.

COLVIL (*S.*), *-*. Grand Impostor discovered (*The*), 1673.

COLVIL (*Samuel*). Whiggs' Supplication (*The*), or the Scotch Hudibras, a satirical poem on the Scotch Covenanters, 1710.

COLVILE (Sir *Henry Edward*), 1852- . Accursed Land (*The*), 1884; History of the Sudan Campaign, 1887; Ride in Petticoats and Slippers (*A*), 1880.

COLVIN (*Sidney*), Norwich, 1845- . Children in Italian and English Design, 1872; Keats, 1887; Edited Letters of Keats, 1887, and Edinburgh Edition of R. L. Stevenson's Works; Landor, 1881.

COMBE, M.D. (*Andrew*), Edinburgh, 1797-1847. Management of Infancy, 1840 (edited afterwards by sir James Clark, who appended a sketch of the character, etc., of the writer); On Mental Derangement, 1831; Physiology of Digestion, etc., 1836; Principles of Physiology applied to Health (*The*), 1834. His Life, by George Combe, 1850.

COMBE, M.D. (*Charles*), 1743-1817. Nummorum Veterum Populorum, etc., qui in Musæo Gulielmi Hunter asservantur, Descriptio, etc., 1780 (much esteemed).

COMBE (*George*), Edinburgh, 1788-1858. Constitution of Man (*The*), 1828 (his best work); Edinburgh Phrenological Journal, 1823; Elements of Phrenology, 1824; Essays on Phrenology, etc., 1819; Life, etc., of Dr. Andrew Combe, 1850; Moral Philosophy, 1840; Notes on the United States, 1841; Phrenology applied to Painting and Sculpture, 1843, 1855; Principles of . . . Prison Discipline, 1854; Relation between Science and Religion, 1857; System of Phrenology (*A*), 1835. His Life, by C. Gibbon, 1878.

COMBER, D.D. (*Thomas*), 1644-1699. Companion to the Altar, 1658; Companion to the Temple (in three parts), 1672, 1674, 1675; On the Roman Forgeries in Councils (in four parts), 1689. His Life, by Thomas Comber, 1799.

COMBER (*Thomas*), died 1778. History of the Parisian Massacre of St. Bartholomew, 1810, posthumous; Vindication of the Revolution in England, 1758.

COMERFORD (*T.*), *-*. History of Ireland (for 3000 years), to the Invasion by Henry II., 1754.

COMYNS (Sir *John*), lord chief baron of the

Exchequer, 1667-1740. Digest of the Laws of England, 1762-67, posthumous (a sixth volume was added in 1776) Reports, 1744, posthumous.

CONDER, LL.D., M.R.A.S. (*Claude Regnier*), 1848- . Altaic Hieroglyphs, 1887; Bible and the East, 1896; Heth and Moab, 1883; Judas Maccabæus, 1879; Latin Kingdom of Jerusalem, 1897; Memoirs of Eastern Palestine, 1890; Memoirs of Western Palestine, 1883; Palestine, 1891; Tel Amarna Tablets, 1893; Tent Work in Palestine, 1878.

CONDER (*James*), *-*. Coins, Tokens, and Medalets, issued by Great Britain, Ireland, and the Colonies, etc., 1799.

CONDER (*Josiah*), London, 1789-1855. Modern Traveller (*The*), 1824; Protestant Nonconformity, 1818. His Life, by E. R. Conder, 1857.

CONE, COWNE, or CONEI (*George*), died 1640. Vita Mariæ Stuartæ, etc., 1624.

CONGLETON (*Henry Brooke Parnell*, lord), 1776-1842. Financial Reform, 1830; History of Penal Laws against Irish Catholics, 1808; Principles of Currency and Exchange, 1805.

CONGREVE (*William*), Stafford, 1670-1729. Double Dealer (*The*), 1694, a comedy; Love for Love, 1695 (his best comedy); Mourning Bride (*The*), 1697, a tragedy; Old Bachelor (*The*), 1693, a comedy; Poems, 1710; Way of the World (*The*), 1700, a comedy. His Life, by Charles Wilson, 1730.

CONGREVE (Sir *William*), of Middlesex, 1772-1828. Elementary Treatise on the Mounting of Naval Ordnance, 1812.

CONINGTON (*John*), Boston, in Lincolnshire, 1825-1869. Translations into English verse of the Æneid of Virgil, 1866; of the Agamemnon of Æschylus, 1848; of the Odes of Horace, 1863 (all excellent). His Miscellanies and a Memoir, 1872.

CONOLLY, M.D. (*John*), Lincolnshire, 1794-1866. Construction and Government of Lunatic Asylums, 1847; Inquiry concerning the Indications of Insanity, 1830; Study of Hamlet, 1863; Treatment of the Insane, 1856.

CONSTABLE (*Archibald*), Scotland, 1776-1827. Miscellany, 1826.

C[ONSTABLE] (*Henry*), 1560-1612. Diana, 1584, sonnettes; Spiritual Sonnettes in Honour of God and Hys Sayntes, 1590.

CONSTABLE (*John*), Epigrammata, 1520 (printed by Pynson).

CONWAY (*Henry Seymour*), 1720-1795. False Appearances; Poems.

CONWAY (*Hugh*), the assumed name of F. Fargus, 1847-1885. At What Cost, 1885; Bound Together, 1884; Called Back, 1883; Cardinal Sin (*A*), 1886; Carriston's Gift, 1886; Dark Days, 1884; Family Affair (*A*), 1885; Lays and Lyrics, 1887; Life Idylls (*A*), 1879; Living or Dead? 1886; Slings and Arrows, 1885.

CONWAY (*Moncure Daniel*), Virginia, born 1832. Barons of the Potomac, 1892; Demonology and Devil Lore, 1879; Emerson at Home and Abroad, 1882; Earthward Pilgrimage (*The*), 1872; Idols and Ideals, 1874; Life of Edmund Randolph, 1887; Life of Thomas Paine, 1892; Nathaniel Hawthorne, 1890; Pine and Palm, 1887;

Rejected Stone (*The*), 1861–62; Sacred Anthology, 1872; Thomas Carlyle, 1886; Travels in South Kensington, 1875; Wandering Jew (*The*), 1880; Works of Thos. Paine, 1893–96.

CONWAY (Sir *William Martin*), Rochester, 1856– . Albert Dürer (*Literary Remains of*),1889; Alps from End to End (*The*), 1895; Climber's Guide (*The*), 1890, 1891; Dawn of Art in the Ancient World, 1891; Early Flemish Artists, 1886; Gallery of Art (Liverpool), 1884; Reynolds and Gainsborough (*Artistic Development of*), 1885; Woodcutters of the Netherlands in Fifteenth Century, 1884; Zermatt Pocket-book, 1881.

CONYBEARE (*John*), bishop of Bristol, born at Exeter, 1692–1755. Defence of Revealed Religion, etc., 1732.

COOK (*Dutton*), London, 1832–1883. Art in England, 1869; Banns of Marriage (*The*), 1875; Book of the Play, 1876; Dr. Muspratt's Patients, 1868; Doubleday's Children, 1877; Hobson's Choice, 1866; Hours with the Players, 1881; Leo, 1864; Over Head and Ears, 1868; Paul Foster's Daughter, 1861; Prodigal Son (*The*), 1862; Sir Felix Foy, Bart., 1865; Studies, etc., of Historic Story, Life, and Character, 1876; Trials of the Tredgolds (*The*), 1864; Young Mr. Nightingale, 1874.

COOK (*Eliza*), 1818–1888. Journal, 1849–54; New Echoes, and other Poems, 1864; Poems, 1840.

COOK, D. D. (*George*), Scotland, 1795–1845. History of the Church of Scotland, etc., 1815; History of the Reformation in Scotland, 1811 (a valuable work).

COOK (Captain *James*), Marton, in Yorkshire, 1728–1779. Three Voyages round the World, first published in 1773; second in 1777; third in 1784. His Life, by D. Samwell, 1786; Dr. A. Kippis, 1788.

COOKE (Captain *Edward*), *-*. Voyage round the World (*A*), 1712.

COOKE, D.D. (*George*), 1773–1845. Historical Review of Christianity (*An*), 1822; History of the Church of Scotland (*A*), 1815; History of the Reformation (*A*), 1811.

COOKE (*George Wingrove*), 1813–1865. China and Lower Bengal, 1858; Conquest and Colonization of North Africa, 1860; History of Party, 1836; Inside Sebastopol, 1856; Memoirs of Lord Bolingbroke, 1835.

COOKE (*John*), *-*. Preacher's Assistant (*The*), 1783 (a list of texts of sermons by Churchmen and Dissenters since the Reformation).

COOKE (*John Esten*), Winchester, in Virginia, U.S., novelist, 1830– . Dr. Van Dyke, 1872; Hammer and Rapier, 1870; Henry St. John, Gentleman, 1858; Her Majesty the Queen, 1873; Hilt to Hilt, 1869; Last of the Foresters (*The*), 1856; Leather Stockings and Silk, 1854; Life of Robert E. Lee 1871, biography; Life of Stonewall Jackson 1866, biography; Mohun, or the Last Days of Lee and his Paladins, 1868; Out of the Foam, 1871; Virginia Comedians (*The*), 1855; Wearing of the Grey, 1867; Youth of Jefferson (*The*), 1855.

COOKE (*Robert*), died 1614. Censura quorundam Scriptorum, quæ sub Nomine Sanctorum, etc., [a] Pontificiis Citari Solent, 1614 (an excellent work, pointing out the forgeries of quotations and counterfeit authorities).

COOKE (*William*), died 1814. Enquiry on Patriarchal and Druidical Religion, Temples, etc., 1755; Medallic History of Imperial Rome, etc., 1781.

COOKE (*William*), *-*. Picture of the Isle of Wight, etc., 1808.

COOKESLEY (Rev. *William Gifford*), Brasted in Kent, 1802–1880. Account of the Ancient City of Rome, 1850; Account and Map of Athens,1851.

COOKSEY (*Richard*), *-*. Life and Character of John Lord Somers, Baron of Evesham, 1791 (an esteemed work).

COOLEY (*Arnold James*), *-*. Cyclopædia of Practical Receipts, 1851; Pharmaceutical Latin Grammar, 1845.

COOMBE (*William*), Bristol, 1741–1823. Devil upon Two Sticks in England, 1790; Diabolad (*The*), a satire; English Dance of Death; Three Tours of Dr. Syntax, (1) In Search of the Picturesque, 1812, (2) In Search of Consolation, 1820, (3) In Search of a Wife, 1821. N.B.—The Tour of Dr. Syntax through London, 1810, Dr. Syntax in Paris, 1820, and Dr. Syntax's Life of Napoleon, 1823, were not by Coombe. Plates and Illustrations by Rowlandson.

COOPER, LL.D. (Sir *Astley Paston*), Brooke, in Norfolk, 1768–1841. Anatomy and Diseases of the Breast, 1829–40; Anatomy of the Thymus Gland, 1832; Medical Records and Researches, 1798; Principles and Practice of Surgery, 1824; Treatise on Dislocations and Fractures, 1822; Treatise on Hernia, 1804–7; Treatment of Hernia, 1827, His Life, by B. B. Cooper, 1843.

COOPER (*Basil Henry*), Maidenhead, in Berkshire, 1819– . Chronology of the Bible, 1874; Cleopatra's Needle, 1878; Free Church of Ancient Christianity, 1852; Hieroglyphical Date of the Exodus in the Annals of Thothmes the Great, 1861; Life of Count Cavour, 1860.

COOPER (*Bransby Blake*), Great Yarmouth, 1792–1853. Lectures on Anatomy, 1829; Lectures on the Principles and Practice of Surgery, 1851; Life of Sir A. Cooper, 1843.

COOPER (*Charles Henry*), Great Marlow, in Buckinghamshire, 1808–1866. Annals of Cambridge, 1842–52; Athenæ Cantabrigienses, 1858–61; Memorials of Cambridge, 1858.

COOPER (*James Fenimore*), Burlington, U.S., novelist, 1789–1851. Afloat and Ashore, 1844; Borderers, or the Heathcotes, 1850; Bravo (*The*), 1831; Chainbearer (*The*), 1845; Crater (*The*), or Vulcan's Peak, 1847; Deerslayer (*The*), 1841; Eve Effingham, 1849; Headsman of Berne, 1833; Heidenmauer, 1832; History of a Pocket-handkerchief, 1843; Home as Found, 1838; Homeward Bound, 1838; Jack Tier (*The Red Rover* recast), 1848; Last of the Mohicans (*The*), 1826; Lionel Lincoln, 1825; Mercedes of Castile, 1840; Miles Wallingford, 1844; Monikins (*The*), 1835; Ned Myers, 1843; Notions of a Travelling Brother, 1828; Oak Openings,

1848; Outward Bound, 1836; Pathfinder, 1840; Pilot (*The*), 1823; Pioneers (*The*), 1823; Prairie (*The*), 1827; Precaution, 1821; Red Rover (*The*), 1827; Red Skins (*The*), 1846; Satanstoe, 1845; Sea Lions, 1849; Spy (*The*) (the War of Independence), 1821; Two Admirals (*The*), 1842; Water Witch (*The*), 1830; Ways of the Hour, 1850; Wept of Wishton-Wish (*The*), 1829; Wing and Wing, 1842; Wyandotte, 1843.

American Democrat (*The*), 1835; History of the Navy of the United States, 1839; Lives of American Naval Officers, 1845; Travelling Bachelor (*The*), 1828.

COOPER (*Thomas*), Leicester, 1805-1891. Alderman Ralph, 1853, a novel; Autobiography, 1872; Baron's Yule Feast (*The*), 1846, a poem; Bridge of History over the Gulf of Time (*The*), 1871; Condition of the People (*The*), 1846; Family Feud (*The*), 1854, a novel; Poetical Works, 1878; Purgatory of Suicides (*The*), 1845, an epic poem; Triumphs of Enterprise (*The*), 1847; Triumphs of Perseverance (*The*), 1847; Verity of Christ's Resurrection (*The*), 1875; Wise Saws and Modern Instances, 1844 (a series of stories).

COOTE, LL.D. (*Charles*), London, 1759-1835. History of Ancient Europe, 1815; History of England, 1791-1803; History of Europe from the Peace of Amiens, 1802; History of the Union, etc., 1802. Translated Mosheim's *Ecclesiastical History*, 1811.

COPLAND, M.D. (*James*), Deerness, in the Orkneys, 1792-1870. Dictionary of Practical Medicine, 1830-58 (his chief work); Elements of Physiology, 1824; Outlines of Pathology and Practical Medicine, 1822; Pestilential Cholera, 1832.

COPLESTON, D.D. (*Edward*), bishop of Llandaff, born in Devonshire, 1776-1849. Enquiry into the Doctrines of Necessity and Predestination, etc., 1821 (a valuable work); Prælectiones Academicæ, 1813. His Life, by W. J. Copleston, 1851.

COPPING (*Edward*), London, 1828- . Alfieri and Goldoni, their Lives and Adventures, 1826; Aspects of Paris, 1858; Home at Rosefield (*The*), 1861.

CORBET (*Richard*), bishop of Norwich, poet, born at Ewell, in Surrey, 1582-1635. Distracted Puritan (*The*), about 1610, a mad song; Poetica Stromata, 1648, posthumous.

CORELLI (*Marie*), 1864- . Ardath, 1889; Barabbas, 1893; Cameos, 1896; Jane, 1897; Mighty Atom (*The*), 1896; Murder of Delicia, 1896; Romance of Two Worlds (*A*), 1886 (her first book); Sorrows of Satan (*The*), 1895; Soul of Lilith (*The*), 1892; Thelma, 1887; Vendetta, 1886; Wormwood, 1890; Ziska, 1897.

CORNWALL (*Barry*), the pseudonym of Bryan Waller Procter, Wiltshire, 1787-1874. Dramatic Scenes, 1819; Effigies Poeticæ, 1824; English Songs, 1831; Essays and Tales in Prose, 1851; Flood of Thessaly (*The*), 1823; Kean and Lamb, 1860; Marcian Colonna, 1820; Mirandola, 1821, a play; Poetical Works, 1822; Sicilian Story (*A*), 1820.

CORNWALLIS (*Caroline Frances*), Kent, 1786-1858. Letters and Remains, 1864, post-

humous; Pericles, a Tale of Athens, 1847; Philosophical Theories and . . . Experience, by a Pariah, 1842; State of Man after the Coming of Christ (*The*); State of Man before the Coming of Christ (*The*).

CORNWALLIS (Sir *William*), 1530-1618. Discourse upon Seneca, 1601; Essays, 1568; Miraculous and Happie Union of England and Scotland, 1604; Praise of King Richard III.!! 1617.

CORYAT (*Thomas*), Odcombe, in Somersetshire, 1577-1617. Coryat's Crudities, 1611, a Supplement, or "Second Course," 1611 (very rare); Odcombian Banquet (*The*), 1611; Traveller for the English Wits, 1616.

COSIN, D.D. (*John*), bishop of Durham, born at Norwich, 1594-1672. Collection of Private Devotion, 1627; History of the Canon of Holy Scripture, 1657.

COSIN (*Richard*), dean of the Arches, 1517-1597. Apologie for Sundrie Proceedings by Jurisdiction Ecclesiasticall, 1593 (a very learned work); Conspiracy for Pretended Reformation, 1591 (that is, in Presbyterian discipline).

COSTA (Sir *Michael*), born in Naples, but settled in England, 1810-1884. Don Carlos, 1844 (his best opera); Eli, 1855, an oratorio (his best production); Naaman, 1864, an oratorio.

COSTELLO (*Louisa Stuart*), 1815-1870. Anne of Brittany, 1855, a memoir; Clara Fane, 1848; Lay of the Stork (*The*), 1856, a poem; Lives of Eminent Englishmen, 1844; Mary Duchess of Burgundy, 1853, a memoir; Pilgrimage to Auvergne, 1842; Queen's Prisoner (*The*), 1841; Rose Garden of Persia (*The*), 1841; Specimens of the Early Poetry of France, 1835.

COTES (*Roger*), Burbage, in Leicestershire, 1682-1716. Harmonia Mensurarum, etc., 1722 (much esteemed).

COTTLE (*Amos Simon*), died 1800 (immortalized by lord Byron). Edda of Shemend (*The*), 1797, in English verse.

Oh, Amos Cottle! Phœbus, what a name
To fill the speaking trump of future fame!
Oh, Amos Cottle, for a moment think
What meagre profits spread from pen and ink
    English Bards and Scotch Reviewers.

COTTLE (*Joseph*), Bristol, in Somersetshire, 1774-1853. Alfred, 1801, an epic; Fall of Cambria (*The*), 1809, a poem; John the Baptist, 1801, a poem; Malvern Hills (*The*), 1798, a poem; Poems, 1795; Recollections of Coleridge, 1837.

Bœotian Cottle, rich Bristowa's boast,
Imports old stories from the Cambrian coast,
And sends his goods to market—all alive,—
Lines forty thousand, cantos twenty-five.
    English Bards and Scotch Reviewers.

COTTON (*Charles*), Beresford Hall, in Staffordshire, burlesque poet, 1630-1687. Burlesque upon Burlesque, 1675; Compleat Gamester (*The*), 1674; Compleat Angler, 1676, in prose; Paneygyrick to the King's . . . Majesty, 1675; Poems on Several Occasions, 1680; Scarronides, or Virgil, book i., 1678, a travestie; Valiant Knight (*The*), a legend of Sir Peregrine, 1663; Voyage to Ireland in burlesque, 1673; Wonders of the Peake (*The*), 1681.

COTTON (Very Rev. *Henry*), 1790–1879. Fasti Ecclesiæ Hibernicæ, 1845-62 ; List of Editions of the Bible, 1821; Rheims and Douay, 1855; Typographical Gazetteer, 1831.

COTTON, M.D. (*Nathaniel*), 1707–1788. Eight Visions in Verse, 1751.

COTTON (Sir *Robert Bruce*), Denton, in Huntingdonshire, 1570–1631. His library was transferred to the British Museum. Cottoni Posthuma, 1679; Defence of the Oath of Allegiance, 1641, posthumous; Henry III., or a Short View of a Long Life, 1627; No Post from Heaven, nor yet from Hell, 1643, posthumous; Rolls of Parliament in the Tower, 1657, posthumous.

COTTON (*Roger*), 1548–1618. Armour of Proofe from the Tower of David to fight against the Spannyardes and other Enimies of the Trueth, 1596, in verse ; Spirituall Song (*A*), a History of the World from Creation, 1596.

COUCH (*Arthur Thomas Quiller*), signs himself "Q.," Bodmin, in Cornwall, 1863– . Adventures in Criticism, 1896; Astonishing History of Troy Town (*The*), 1888; Blue Pavilions, 1891; Dead Man's Rock, 1887, melodramatic ; Delectable Duchy (*The*), 1893 ; Golden Pomp (*The*), 1895 ; Green Bays, 1893; Ia, 1896 ; I saw Three Ships, 1892 ; Noughts and Crosses, 1891 (good) ; Poems, 1896; Splendid Spur (*The*), 1889 ; Wandering Heath, 1895 ; Warwickshire Avon (*The*), 1892.

COURTHOPE (*William*), Somerset herald, 1808-1866. Memoir of Daniel Chamier, 1852 ; Sir Harris Nicholas's Synopsis, 1857 ; Spanish Maid (*A*), 1897. Revised and edited Debrett's *Peerage*, 1834-36 ; ditto Debrett's *Baronetage*, 1857.

COURTHOPE (*William John*), Malling, in Sussex, 1842– . Addison, 1882 ; Genius of Spenser (*The*), 1868 ; History of English Poetry, vol. i. 1895; Liberal Movement in English Literature, 1885 ; Ludibra Lunæ, 1869 ; Paradise of Birds (*The*), 1870; Tercentenary of Corydon, 1864.

COURTNEY, M.A., LL.D. (*William Leonard*), Poona, 1850– . Constructive Ethics, 1886; Kit Marlowe (produced at St. James's), 1893 ; Life of John Stuart Mill, 1889 ; Metaphysics of John Stuart Mill, 1879; Studies at Leisure, 1892; Studies New and Old, 1818 ; Studies on Philosophy, 1882.

COVERDALE (*Miles*), bishop of Exeter, born at Coverham, in Yorkshire, 1485–1565. Cranmer's (or the Great) Bible, 1539 ; Latin-English Testament, 1538; Olde Fayth (*The*), 1541; Translation of the Bible, 1535.

COVERTE (*Robert*), 1582–1635. True and almost Incredible Narrative, etc., 1612.

COWELL, LL.D. (*John*), Devonshire, 1534–1611. Institutiones Juris Anglicani, etc., 1605; Interpreter (*The*), 1607 ; Law Dictionary, 1607.

COWLEY (*Abraham*), London, poet, 1618-1667. Books of Plants, 1662–78 ; Carmina, 1662 ; Cutter of Coleman Street, 1663, a comedy ; Davideis (in four books), 1635 (incomplete) ; Four Ages of England, 1648 ;

Guardian (*The*), 1650, a comedy ; History of Plants (a poem in six books), 1705, posthumous ; Love's Riddle, 1638, a pastoral comedy ; Mistresse (*The*), 1647, a collection of love verses; Naufragium Joculare, 1638, a comedy ; Ode on the Restoration of Charles II., 1660; Pindaric Odes, 1663 ; Plantarum Libridus, 1662 ; Poem on the Civil War, 1662 ; Poemata Latina, 1668 ; Poetical Blossoms, 1633 ; Satyr (*A*), The Puritan and Papist, 1643; Satyr against Separativity (*A*), 1642 ; Tragical History of Pyramus and Thisbe, 1628 ; Verses upon Several Occasions, 1663 ; Vision concerning the late Pretended H. Cromwell the Wicked, 1661. His Life, by Sprat, 1680 ; Dr. Johnson, 1779.

COWPER (*William*), Great Berkhampstead, in Hertford, poet, 1731–1800. Anti-Thelyphthora, 1781 (his first publication) ; Boadicea, 1790 ; Castaway (*The*), 1799 ; Charity, 1782 ; Conversation, 1782 ; Expostulation, 1781, published 1782 ; *Homer* translated into blank verse, 1784–91 ; Hope, 1782 ; John Gilpin, 1782, a humorous ballad ; Miscellaneous Poems, 1793 ; Olney Hymns, 1779 ; On the Receipt of my Mother's Picture, 1798 ; Progress of Error, 1781, published 1782 ; Retirement, 1782 ; Table Talk, 1781, published 1782 ; Task (*The*), in six books, 1783–85 ; Tirocinium, 1784 ; Truth, 1781, published 1782. His Life, by J. Corry, 1803; W. Hayley, 1803; by himself, 1816, posthumous ; T. Taylor, 1835 ; Grimshawe, 1836; Southey, 1838 ; H. F. Cary, 1839 ; sir H. Nicolas, 1843 ; T. Wright, 1892.

COX (Rev. sir *George William*), 1827– . British Rule in India, 1881 ; Concise History of England (*A*), 1887; Crusades (*The*), 1874 ; History of Greece (*A*), 1874 ; Great Persian War (*The*), 1861; Introduction to the Science of Comparative Mythology and Folke Lore, 1881; Life of Colenso, 1888 ; Life of St. Boniface, 1853; Mythology of the Aryan Nations (*The*), 1870 ; Poems, Legendary and Historical, 1850 ; Tales of Ancient Greece, 1868, 1877 ; Tales of Thebes and Argos, 1863 ; Tales of the Gods and Heroes, 1862.

COX, D.D. (*Samuel*), London, 1826–1893. Balaam, 1884 ; Biblical Expositions, 1874 ; Book of Ruth (*The*), 1876 ; Expositions, 1885, 1888 ; Expositor's Note-book (*An*), 1872 ; Expository Essays, 1877 ; Genesis of Evil (*The*), 1880; House and its Builder (*The*), 1888 ; Inductive Theology, 1874 ; Job (*Commentary on the Book of*), 1880 ; Latter Hope (*The*), 1883 ; Miracles, 1884 ; Pilgrim Psalms (*The*), 1874; Quest of the Chief Good, 1868 ; Resurrection (*The*), 1869; Salvator Mundi, 1877 ; Secret of Life (*The*), 1866.

COXE (*William*), London, 1747–1828. Anecdotes of Handel, 1799 ; Historical Tour in Monmouthshire, 1801 ; History of the House of Austria, 1807 (his chief work) ; Memoirs of Sir Robert Walpole 1798, of Lord Walpole 1804, of the Bourbon Kings of Spain 1813, of the Duke of Marlborough, 1817–19, of the Pelham Administration, 1829 ; Travels in Switzerland, 1778–1801 ; in Poland, Russia, and Denmark, 1778–84.

COYNE (*Joseph Stirling*), Birc, in Ireland, 1805–1868. Bad Lovers (*The*), 1836, a comedy; Black Sheep, a comedy; Honest Cheats (*The*), 1836, a comedy; Hope of the Family (*The*), a comedy; How to Settle Accounts with your Landlord, 1847; Little Rebel (*The*), a comedy; My Wife's Daughter, a comedy; Phrenologist (*The*), 1835, a comedy; Presented at Court, 1848, a comedy; Queer Subject (*A*), 1837, a comedy; Tipperary Legacy (*The*), 1847, a comedy; Urgent Private Affairs, a comedy; Water Witches (*The*), 1843; English Hermit's Spade at the . . . Root of Idolatry (*The*), 1849, a comedy.

CRAB (*Roger*), called "The English Hermit," in the time of Cromwell: he lived on three farthings a week, *–1680. Dagon's Downfall; English Hermite (*The*), 1655; English Hermit's Spade at the . . . Root of Idolatry (*The*).

CRABBE, LL.D. (*George*), Aldborough, in Suffolk, poet, 1754–1832. Borough (*The*), 24 Letters in Verse, 1810 (his chief work); Candidate (*The*), 1779; Hall of Justice (*The*), in dialogue, 1807; Inebriety, 1775 (his first publication); Library (*The*), 1781; Natural Theology, 1840, posthumous; Newspaper (*The*), 1785; Parish Register (*The*), in three parts, 1807; Religion, 1817; Sir Eustace Gray (The Madhouse), in dialogue, 1807; Tales in Verse (21 tales based on facts), 1812; Tales of the Hall (22 tales based on facts), 1819; Village (*The*), 1783. His Life, by his son, 1838.

CRADOCK (*Samuel*), 1620–1706. Apostolica History (*The*), 1672; Harmony of the Four Evangelists, 1668; Knowledge and Practice, 1702.

CRAIG (*Isa*), Edinburgh, poetess, 1831– . Duchess Agnes, and other Poems, 1865; Ode (first prize at the Burns centennial), 1859; Poems by Isa, 1857, 1865.

CRAIG (Sir *Thomas*), Scotland, 1538–1608. Right of Succession to the Throne of England, 1602; Treatise on the Feudal Law, 1655 (a standard work); Treatise on Homage, 1695, posthumous (to prove that Scotland never owed homage to England). His Life, by P. F. Tytler, 1823.

CRAIK (*George Lillie*), Fifeshire, Scotland, 1799–1866. Bacon, his Writings and Philosophy, 1846–47; English of Shakespeare (*The*), 1857; History of British Commerce, 1844; Pursuit of Knowledge under Difficulties, 1831; Romance of the Peerage, 1848–50; Outlines of the History of the English Language, 1855; Sketches of the History of Literature and Learning in England, 1844–45; Spenser and his Poetry, 1845.

CRAIK (Mrs. *George Lillie*), better known as Miss *Dinah Maria Mulock*, Stoke-upon-Trent, in Staffordshire, novelist, 1826–1887. About Money, and Other Things, 1886; Adventures of a Brownie (*The*), 1872; Agatha's Husband, 1852; Brave Lady (*A*), 1870; Children's Poetry, 1881; Christian's Mistake, 1866; Concerning Man, and Other Things, 1888; Domestic Stories, 1860; Fair France, 1871; Fairy Book, 1863 (the best popular fairy stories); Fifty Golden Years,

1887; French Country Family (*A*), 1867 (trans.); Hannah, 1871; Head of the Family (*The*), 1851; His Little Mother, 1881; Is it True? 1872; John Halifax, Gentleman, 1857; King Arthur, 1886; Laurel Bush (*The*), 1877; Legacy (*A*), 1878; Life for a Life (*A*), 1859; Little Lame Prince and his Travelling Cloak, 1875; Little Sunshine's Holiday, 1871; Miss Tommy, 1884; Mistress and Maid, 1862; My Mother and I, 1874; New Year's Gift to Sick Children, 1865; Noble Life (*A*), 1866; Nothing New; Ogilvies (*The*), 1849; Olive, 1850; Only Sister (*An*), 1873 (trans.); Our Year, A Child's Book in Prose and Verse, 1860; Plain Speaking, 1882; Poems, 1859; Romantic Tales, 1859; Sermons out of Church, 1875; Songs of our Youth, 1874; Studies from Life, 1861; Thirty Years' Poems, 1880; Twenty Years Ago, 1871; Two Marriages, 1867; Unkind Word (*The*), 1869; Unknown Country (*An*), 1887; Unsentimental Journey through Cornwall (*An*), 1884; Will Denbigh, 1877; Woman's Kingdom (*The*), 1868; Woman's Thoughts about Women; Young Mrs. Jardine, 1879.

CRAKANTHORPE (*Richard*), Westmoreland, 1567–1624. Defensio Ecclesiæ Anglicanæ contra M. Anton, etc., injurias, 1625 (much esteemed).

CRANE (*Lucy*), 1842–1882. Grimm's Fairy Tales, 1882; Lectures on Art and the Formation of Taste, 1882. She wrote some of the original verses and rhymed versions of well-known nursery legends for her brother's (Walter Crane) coloured toy-books.

CRANE, A.R.W.S. (*Walter*), painter, decorator, designer, book-illustrator, writer, and socialist, 1845– . Baby's Banquet, 1879; Baby's Opera, 1877; Baby's Own Æsop, 1886; Claims of Decorative Art, 1892; Decorative Illustration of books (*The*), 1896; First of May, 1883; Flora's Feast, 1889; Grimm's Household Stories, 1882; Legends for Lionel, 1887; Mrs. Mundi, 1875; Old Garden (*The*), 1893; Pan-Piper, 1882; Picture Books, 1865–76; Queen Summer, 1891; Renascence : a Book of Verse, 1891; Shepheard's Calendar, 1897; Sirens Three, 1886, a poem; Slate and Pencilvania, 1885; Wonder Book (*A*), 1892.

CRANMER (*Thomas*), archbishop of Canterbury, born at Aslacton, in Nottinghamshire, 1489–1556. Answer [to] Stephen Gardner . . . agaynst the Trewe and Godly Doctrine of the Moste Holy Sacrament, 1551; Catechisms (for children, etc.), 1548; Confutation of Unwritten Verities, etc., 1558, posthumous; Defence of the Trewe and Catholicke Doctrine of the Sacrament, etc., 1550; Works, compiled and edited by Jenkyns, 1834. His Life, by Strype, 1694; Gilpin, 1784; H. J. Todd, 1831; Cox, 1844; dean Hook, in his *Lives of the Archbishops*, 1861, etc. ; J. N. Norton, 1863.

CRASHAW (*Richard*), London, 1616–1650. Carmen Deo Nostro . . . 1652; Delights of the Muses, 1648; Epigrammata Sacra, 1634; Sacred Poems, 1652; Steps to the Temple, etc., 1646.

•.• Crashaw is the author of that celebrated

line relating to the water turned to wine in the marriage banquet of Cana of Galilee—

Lympha pudica Deum vidit et erubuit.
(*The modest water saw its God, and blushed.*)

CRAWFORD (*Adair*), chemist, 1749–1795. Experiments and Observations on Animal Heat, 1779.

CRAWFORD and BALCARRES (*Alexander William*, lord Lindsay, earl of), 1812–1880. Argo, 1876 ; Case of Gorham *v.* the Bishop of Exeter (*The*), 1850 (made a great sensation) ; Etruscan Inscriptions, 1872 ; Evidence and Theory of Christianity, 1841 ; Letters on Egypt, Edom, etc., 1838 ; Lives of the Lindsays (*The*), 1849 ; Œcumenicity, 1870 ; Progression by Antagonism, 1846 ; Scepticism and the Church of England, 1861 ; Sketches of the History of Christian Art, 1847.

CRAWFORD (*David*), Scotland, 1665–1726. Memoirs of Scotland under the Reign of Mary, 1706 ; Peerage of Scotland, 1716.

CRAWFORD (*F. Marion*), an American novelist, 1845–   . Adam Johnstone's Son, 1895 ; American Politician, 1884 ; Casa Braccio, 1895 ; Children of the King (*The*), 1892 ; Cigarette-maker's Romance (*A*), 1890 ; Constantinople, 1895 ; Corleone, 1897 ; Don Orsino, 1892 ; Dr. Claudius (a true tale), 1883 (excellent) ; Greifenstein, 1889 (a German student's tale) ; Katherine Lauderdale, 1894 ; Khaled, 1891, an Arabian tale ; Love in Idleness, 1894 ; Marion Darche, 1893 ; Marzio's Crucifix, 1887 ; Mr. Isaacs, 1882, a tale of modern India ; Novel (*The*), what it is, 1893 ; Paul Patoff, 1887 ; Pietro Ghisleri, 1893 ; Ralstons (*The*), 1894 ; Roman Singer (*A*), 1894 ; Rose of Yesterday (*A*), 1897 ; Sant Ilario, 1889 ; Saracinesca (the author's favourite work), 1887 ; Tale of a Lonely Parish (*A*), 1886, an English tale ; Taquisara, 1896 ; Three Fates (*The*), 1892 ; To Leeward, 1883 ; Witch of Prague (*The*), 1891 (good) ; With the Immortals, 1888 ; Zoroaster (in the time of Daniel and Darius), 1885, (excellent).

CRAWFORD (Mrs.). See "Kathleen Mavourneen."

CRAWFURD (*John*), Edinburgh, 1783–1868. Descriptive Dictionary of the Indian Islands, etc., 1856 ; History of the Indian Archipelago, 1820 ; Malay Grammar and Dictionary, 1852.

CRAUFURD (*Quintin*), Ayrshire, in Scotland, 1743–1819. Essais Historiques sur le Docteur Swift, 1808 ; Researches concerning the Laws, etc., of Ancient and Modern India, 1817 ; Sketches . . . relating to the . . . Hindoos, 1792.

CREASY (Sir *Edward Shepherd*), Bexley, in Kent, 1812–1878. Fifteen Decisive Battles of the World (*The*), 1851 ; History of England, 1869–70 ; History of the Ottoman Turks, 1854–56 ; Imperial and Colonial Institutions of the Britannic Empire, 1872 ; Rise and Progress of the British Constitution, 1853.

CREECH (Rev. *Thomas*), Blandford, in Dorsetshire, 1659–1701. Poetical Translations of

Horace, 1684 ; of *Lucretius*, 1682 ; of *Theocritus*, 1690.

CREIGHTON, D.D. (*Mandell*), Carlisle, 1843–   . Age of Elizabeth (*The*), 1876 ; Carlisle, 1889 ; History of the Papacy (Reformation period), 1882–86 ; Life of Simon de Montford, 1876 ; Life of Thomas Wolsey, 1888 ; Persecution and Tolerance, 1895 ; Tudors and the Reformation (*The*), 1876.

CROCKETT (*S. R.*), Duchrae, New Galloway, 1860–   . Bog, Myrtle, and Peat, 1895 ; Cleg Kelly, 1896 ; Dulce Cor, 1886 ; Grey Man (*The*), 1896 ; Lad's Love, 1897 ; Lilac Sun-bonnet (*The*), 1894 ; Lochinvar, 1897 ; Mad Sir Ochtred, 1894 ; Men of the Moss Hags (*The*), 1895 ; Play Actress (*The*), 1894 ; Raiders (*The*), 1894 ; Surprising Adventures of Sir Toady Lion, 1897 ; Stickit Minister (*The*), 1893 ; Sweetheart Travellers, 1896.

CROFT, Mus.D. (*William*), of Warwickshire, 1677–1727. Musica Sacra, 1724.

CROKER (Mrs. *B. M.*), novelist. Beyond the Pale, 1897 ; Bird of Passage (*A*), 1886 ; Diana Barrington, 1888 ; Family Likeness (*A*), 1892 ; Interference, 1891 ; In the Kingdom of Kerry, 1896 ; Married or Single ? 1895 ; Miss Balmaine's Past, 1898 ; Mr. Jervis, 1894 ; Pretty Miss Neville, 1883 ; Proper Pride, 1884 ; Real Lady Hilda (*The*), 1895 ; Some one Else, 1885 ; Third Person (*A*), 1893 ; "To Let," 1893 ; Two Masters, 1890 ; Village Tales and Jungle Tragedies, 1895.

CROKER (*John Wilson*), Galway, in Ireland, 1780–1857. Battle of Albuera, 1811 ; Battle of Talavera, 1809 ; Familiar Epistles on the Irish Stage, 1803 ; Intercepted Letter from Canton (*An*), 1805 ; Sketch of Ireland (past and present), 1807 ; Songs of Trafalgar, 1806 ; State of Ireland (*The*), 1807. Edited Boswell's *Life of Dr. Johnson*, 1831.

CROKER (*Thomas Crofton*), Cork, in Ireland, 1798–1854. Barney Mahoney, 1832 (one of his best) ; Daniel O'Rourke (an Irish Munchausen), 1828 ; Fairy Legends, etc., of the South of Ireland, 1825 ; Legends of the Lakes, 1828 ; Memoirs of Joseph Holt, General of the Irish Rebels, 1833 ; My Village, 1832 (one of his best) ; Popular Songs of Ireland, 1839 ; Researches in South Ireland, 1824 ; Tour of M. Boullaye le Gour in Ireland, 1844.

CROLY, LL.D. (Rev. *George*), Dublin, 1780–1860. Angel of the World (*The*), 1820 ; Catiline, 1822, a tragedy ; Historical Sketches, etc., 1842 ; Life of Burke, 1840 ; Marston, or the Soldier and Statesman, 1846, a novel ; Modern Orlando (*The*), 1846 ; Paris (a poem), 1815 (his first work) ; Personal History of George IV., 1830 ; Pride shall have a Fall, 1825, a comedy ; Salathiel, 1827, a prose romance (his best-known work) ; Tales of the Great St. Bernard, 1813. He also edited Jeremy Taylor's Works, 1838.

CROOKES (*William*), London, 1832–   . Aniline and its Derivatives, 1876 ; Chemical Technology, 1877 ; Handbook of Dyeing and Calico Printing, 1879 ; Repulsion resulting from Radiation, 1872; Select Methods of Chemical Analysis, 1877.

CROSBY, D.D. (*Howard*), New York, U.S., 1826-1891. Lands of the Moslem, 1850; Life of Christ, 1871; Notes on the New Testament, 1861.

CROSLAND (*Mrs.*), maiden name *Camilla Toulmin*, London, 1812-1895. Diamond Wedding (*The*), and other Poems, 1871; Hubert Freeth's Prosperity, 1873, a novel; Island of the Rainbow (*The*), 1865, a fairy tale; Light in the Valley, 1853; Memorable Women, 1850; Mrs. Blake, 1862, a novel; My Experiences of Spiritualism, 1857; Stories of London, 1881.

CROSSE (*Andrew*), Somersetshire, 1784-1855. Spontaneous Production of *Acari*, 1837 (this caused a storm of indignation, quite contemptible). His Life, by his widow, 1857.

CROTCH, Mus.D. (*William*), Norwich, 1775-1847. Elements of Musical Composition, etc., 1812.

CROUCH (the musical composer), 1808-1896. See " Kathleen Mavourneen."

CROWE (Mrs.), maiden name *Catherine Stevens*, Borough Green, in Kent, novelist, 1800-1876. Adventures of a Beauty, 1852; Aristodemus, 1838; Last Portrait (*The*), 1871; Light in Darkness, 1850; Lilly Dawson, 1847; Linny Lockwood, 1850; Night Side of Nature, 1848, ghost stories; Pippie's Warning, 1848; Susan Hopley, 1844.

CROWE (*Eyre Evans*), 1799-1868. History of France, 1858-68; Lives of Eminent Foreign Statesmen, 1830; Reigns of Louis XVIII. and Charles X., 1854; Greek and the Turk (*The*), 1853.

CROWE (*Joseph Archer*), London, 1825- . Early Flemish Painters, 1857, 1872; History of Painting in Italy, 1864; History of Painting in North Italy, 1871; Life of Titian, 1877.

CRUDEN (*Alexander*), Aberdeen, 1700-1770. Concordance of the Holy Scriptures, 1737; Scripture Dictionary, 1770.

CRUIKSHANK (*George*), London, 1792-1878. *Didactic Designs:* The Bottle (in eight pictures); The Ginshop : Sunday in London; The Upas Tree; The Worship of Bacchus, 1863.

Comic Illustrations: Box; Comic Almanac (12 years); Grimm's Goblins; The Man in the Moon; My Sketch-book; Oliver Twist; Peter Schlemihl; Points of Humour; *Punch* and *Judy*; Tom Thumb.

Oil Paintings: Disturbing the Congregation; Dressing for the Day; A Runaway Knock; Tam O'Shanter; Titania and Bottom the Weaver.

CRUIKSHANK (*William*), Edinburgh, 1746-1800. Anatomy of the Absorbing Vessels of the Human Body, 1786; Experiments on the Insensible Perspiration, etc., 1795; Memoirs on the Yellow Fever, etc., 1799.

CRUTTWELL (Rev. *Clement*), 1743-1808. Concordance of Parallels, 1790; Tour through Great Britain, 1801; Universal Gazetteer, 1808.

CUDWORTH, D.D. (*Ralph*), Aller, in Somersetshire, 1617-1688. Treatise on Eternal and Immutable Morality, 1731, posthumous;

True Intellectual System of the Universe, 1678 (his best work); True Nature of the Lord's Supper, 1642; Union of Christ and the Church shadowed, 1642. His Life, by Birch, 1743-52.

CULLEN, M.D. (*William*), Hamilton, in Scotland, 1710-1790. First Lines of the Practice of Physic, 1775; Institutions of Medicine, 1777; Synopsis Nosologiæ Methodicæ, 1780; Treatise of the Materia Medica, 1789.

CULPEPPER (*Nicholas*), 1616-1654. English Physician or Herbal, 1652.

CUMBERLAND, D.D. (*Richard*), bishop of Peterborough, born in London, 1632-1718. De Legibus Naturæ Disquisitio, 1672 (against Hobbes' philosophy); Essay on Jewish Weights and Measures, 1686; Fragment of Sanchoniathon on *Phœnician History*, 1720; Origines Gentium, 1724.

CUMBERLAND (*Richard*), Cambridge, 1732-1811. Amelia, 1768, an after-piece; Anecdotes of Spanish Painters, 1782, in prose; Arab (*The*), 1783, a tragedy; Armourer (*The*), 1793, a comic opera; Arundel, 1789, a novel; Banishment of Cicero (*The*), 1761, a dramatic poem; Battle of Hastings (*The*), 1778, a tragedy; Bondman (*The*), 1780, a play; Box Lobby Challenge (*The*), 1794, a comedy; Brothers (*The*), 1769, a comedy; Calvary, or the Death of Christ, a poem in eight books, 1792; Calypso, 1779, a play; Carmelite (*The*), 1785, a tragedy; Choleric Man (*The*), 1775, a comedy; Country Attorney (*The*), 1793, a comedy; Days of Yore, 1796, a comedy; Defendant (*The*), 1798, a comedy; Eccentric Love, 1799, a comedy; Exodiad (*The*), a poem in two parts, 1807-8; False Impressions, 1796, a comedy; Fashionable Lover (*The*), 1772, a comedy; First Love, 1795, a comedy; Henry, 1795, a novel; Hints for Husbands, 1806, a comedy; Impostor (*The*), 1789, a comedy; Jew (*The*), 1795, a comedy; Joanna Montfaucon, 1808, a dramatic romance; John de Lancaster, 1800, a novel; Last of the Family (*The*), 1795, a comedy; Memoirs (of himself), 1806; Mysterious Husband (*The*), 1782, a comedy; Natural Son (*The*), 1780, a comedy; Observer (*The*), in prose, 1785; Retrospection, 1811, a poem; Sailor's Daughter (*The*), 1800, a comedy; Summer's Tale (*A*), 1760, a comic opera; Timon of Athens (altered), 1778, a tragedy; Walloons (*The*), 1771, a comedy; West Indian (*The*), 1771, a comedy; Wheel of Fortune (*The*), 1779, a comedy; Word of Nature (*The*), 1797, a comedy. His Memoirs, written by himself, 1800; his Life, by W. Mudford, 1812.

CUMMING (*Roualeyn George Gordon*), Scotland, the African lion-hunter, 1820-1866. Hunter's Life in South Africa (*A*), 1850.

CUNNINGHAM (*Alexander*), Ettrick, in Scotland, 1654-1737. History of Great Britain, etc., 1787; posthumous. His Life, by W. Thomson, 1787.

CUNNINGHAM (*Allan*), Blackwood, in Scotland, 1785-1842. Biographical and Critical History of Literature, etc., 1833; Life and Works of Burns, 1834; Life of Sir David Wilkie, 1843; Lives of British Painters,

Sculptors, and Architects, 1829-33 (his chief prose work); Lord Roldan, 1822, a romance; Maid of Elwar (*The*), 1825, a romance; Memoirs of Mark Macrabin, 1820; Otterburn, a novel; Paul Jones, 1822, a romance; Poems and Songs, 1847, posthumous; Sir Marmaduke Maxwell, 1822, a drama; Sir Michael Scott, 1822, a romance; Songs of Scotland, etc., 1826; Traditionary Tales of the Peasantry, 1822. His Life, by David Hogg, 1875.

CUNNINGHAM (*Peter*), London, 1816-1869. Handbook to London, 1849; Handbook to Westminster Abbey, 1842; Life of Drummond of Hawthornden, 1833; Life of Inigo Jones, 1848; Memoir of J. M. W. Turner, 1852; Modern London, 1851; Songs of England and Scotland, 1835; Story of Nell Gwynn, 1852.

CURETON (*William*), Westbury, in Shropshire, 1808-1864. Catalogue of Arabic MSS. in the British Museum, 1846; Spicilegium Syriacum, 1855; Vindiciæ Ignatianæ, 1846.

CURRIE, M.D. (*James*), Dumfriesshire, 1756-1805. Medical Reports on the Effects of Water, Cold and Warm, in Febrile Diseases, 1794-1804. He edited Burns, adding notes and a memoir, for the benefit of Burns's widow.

CURRIE (Lady *Mary Montgomerie*), pseudonym "Violet Fane." Autumn Songs, 1889; Collected Verses, 1880; Denzil Place, 1875; Edwin and Angelina Papers (*The*), 1878; From Dawn to Noon, 1872; Memoirs of Marguerite de Valois, Queen of Navarre, 1892; Sophy, or the Adventures of a Savage, 1881; Queen of the Fairies (*The*), 1877; Thro' Love and War, 1886; Under Cross and Crescent, 1896; etc.

CURTIS (*William*), Alton, in Hampshire, 1746-1799. Botanical Magazine, 1787-98, continued by sir W. J. Hooker to 1859; Companion to the *Botanical Magazine*, 1788; Flora Londinensis, etc., 1777.

DAHLGREN (*John A.*), admiral in the United States, 1798-1870. Shells and Shell-guns, 1856; System of Boat Armament, 1852. Inventor of the Dahlgren gun.

DALE, D.D. (*Robert William*), London, 1829-1895. Atonement (*The*), 1874; Christ and the Controversies of Christendom, 1869; Christian Doctrines, 1894; Epistle to the Ephesians (*The*), 1882; Evangelical Revival (*The*), 1880; Fellowship of Christ (*The*), 1891; Holy Spirit (*The*), 1869; Impressions of Australia, 1889; Impressions of America, 1878; Jewish Temple and the Christian Church (*The*), 1863; Laws of Christ for Common Life, 1884; Life of John Angell James, 1861; Living Christ (*The*), and the Four Gospels, 1890; Manual of Congregationalism, 1884; Protestantism, 1874; Sermons on the Ten Commandments, 1871; Week-day Sermons, 1867.

DALE, M.D. (*Samuel*), Braintree, in Essex, 1659-1739. Pharmacologia, 1693.

DALE (*Thomas*), dean of Rochester, born at Pentonville, London, 1797-1870. Golden Psalm (*The*), 1846; Poetical Works, 1836;

Sermons preached in Great St. Mary's, Cambridge, 1832-36; Translation of *Sophocles*, 1824; Widow of Nain, 1818.

DALGARNO (*George*), Aberdeen, 1627-1687. Ars Signorum, Vulgo Character Universalis, et Lingua Philosophica, 1661; Didascolocophus, or the Deaf and Dumb Man's Tutor, 1680.

DALLAS (*Charles Robert*), Jamaica, 1754-1824. History of the Maroons, 1803-4; Recollections of the Life of Lord Byron, 1824.

DALLAWAY (Rev. *James*), Bristol, 1763-1834. Constantinople, etc., 1797; Enquiries into the Origin and Progress of Heraldry in England, 1793; History of Western Sussex, 1815-32.

DALLING AND BULWER (*Lord*), 1801-1872. Autumn in Greece (*The*), 1826; Crimean Questions (*The*), 1863; Historical Characters, 1867; Life of Lord Byron, 1835; Life of Lord Palmerston, 1870; Monarchy of the Middle Classes (*The*), 1834; Ode on the Death of Napoleon, 1822; Poems, 1822; Sir Robert Peel, 1874.

DALRYMPLE (Sir *David*), generally called "lord HAILES," Edinburgh, 1726-1792. Annals of Scotland, from the Accession of Robert I. (the Bruce) to the House of Stuart, 1776-79 (his chief work); Discourse on the Gowrie Conspiracy, 1757; Memorials and Letters relating to the History of Britain in the Reign of James I., 1762; Memorials and Letters relating to the History of Britain in the Reign of Charles I., 1766; Works of the Ever-memorable John Hailes of Eton, 1765.

DALRYMPLE (*John*), Norwich, 1804-1852. Anatomy of the Human Eye, 1834.

DALTON, LL.D. (*John*), near Cockermouth, in Cumberland, 1766-1844. Meteorological Observations, etc., 1793; New System of Chemical Philosophy, 1808, 1810, 1827. His Life, by Dr. H. Lansdale, 1874.

DAMPIER (*William*), Somersetshire, 1652-1712. Treatise on Winds and Tides; Vindication of the South Sea Voyage, etc, 1707; Voyage round the World, 1697; Voyages to Campeachy Bay, 1709.

DANIEL (*Samuel*), Taunton, in Somersetshire, poet-laureate, 1562-1619. Civile Wares betwene the Two Roses (a poem in eight books), i.-iv. 1595, v. 1599, vi. 1602, vii., viii. 1609 (his chief work); Cleopatra, 1594, a tragedy; Complaint of Rosamond, 1594; Delia (57 sonnets), 1592; Epistles, 1601, in verse; Hymen's Triumph, 1615; Musophilus and Philocosmus, 1599, a poetic dialogue in praise of learning; Philotas, 1597, a tragedy; Queenes Arcadia (*The*), 1606, a pastoral tragi-comedy; Tethys' Festival, 1610; Vision of the Twelve Goddesses, 1604.
Prose: A History of England, from the Conquest to Edward III., 1613.

DANIELL, D.C.L. (*John Frederick*), London, 1790-1845. Essay on Artificial Climates, 1824; Introduction to Chemical Philosophy, 1839; Meteorological Essays, 1823.

DANIELL (*Thomas* and *William*), 1749-1840, 1769-1837. Antiquities of India, 1799; Oriental Scenery, or Views in Hindûstan (four series), 1795-1808 (the finest work on

India ever published). The plates in Wood's *Zoography* are by William Daniell.

DANIELL (Rev. *William Barker*), died 1833. Rural Sports, 1801-2 (highly esteemed); Supplement, 1813.

DANVERS (*John*), seventeenth century. The Royal Oake, 1660 (the flight of Charles II.).

D'ARBLAY (*Madame*). See BURNEY (*Francisca*).

DARLEY (*George*), 1800-1846. Errors of Extasie, 1822; Ethelstan; Sylvia, or the May Queen, 1827; Thomas à Becket.

DARMESTETER (*Madame*). See ROBINSON (*Agnes*).

DARRELL (*John*), seventeenth century. Narration of the Possession, Dispossession, and Repossession of William Sommers, 1598; Narration of the Vexation by the Devill [of eight persons], 1600.

DART (*John*), eighteenth century. Westmonasterium (History and Antiquities of Westminster Abbey), 1723.

DARWIN (*Charles Robert*), Shrewsbury, 1809-1882. Cross and Self Fertilization, etc., 1876; Descent of Man, and Selection in Relation to Sex (*The*), 1871; Different Forms of Flowers in Plants of the same Species, 1877; Domesticated Animals and Cultivated Plants, etc., 1867; Effects of Cross-fertilization in Plants, 1876; Expression of Emotion in Man and Animals (*The*), 1872; Fertilization of Orchids, 1862; Formation of Vegetable Mould through the Action of Worms, 1881; Fossil Lepodidæ of Great Britain (*The*), 1855; Geological Observations on South America, 1846; Geological Observations on Volcanic Islands, 1844; Habits of Climbing Plants, 1875; Insectivorous Plants, 1875; Journal of Researches in Various Countries visited by H.M.S. *Beagle* in 1831-36; Monograph of the Family Cirripedia, 1851; Movements and Habits of Climbing Plants, 1875; Nutation of Plants, 1880; Origin of Species by Means of Natural Selection (*The*), 1859 (his great work); Structure and Distribution of Coral Reefs (*The*), 1842; Voyage of a Naturalist, 1845; Zoology of the Voyage of H.M.S. *Beagle*, 1840-43. His Life, by J. G. Romanes, 1882; Grant Allen, 1885; Francis Darwin, 1887; T. G. Bettany, 1887.

DARWIN, M.D. (*Erasmus*), Elton, in Nottinghamshire, poet, 1731-1802. Botanic Garden (*The*), part i. The Economy of Vegetation, 1781, part ii. The Loves of the Plants, 1791, in verse (his chief work); Phylologia, or Philosophy of Gardening, 1799; Plan for the Conduct of Female Education in Boarding Schools (*A*), 1797; Shrine of Nature (*The*), 1803, posthumous; Temple of Nature (*The*), 1803, posthumous; Zoönomia, or the Laws of Organic Life, 1794-96; Works collected, 1809. His Memoir, by Anna Seward, 1804.

DASENT (Sir *George Webbe*), St. Vincent, 1820-   . Annals of an Eventful Life, 1870, a novel; Half a Life, 1874; Jest and Earnest, 1873; Norseman in Iceland (*The*), 1855; Popular Tales from the Norse, etc., 1859; Prose of the Younger Edda (*The*), 1842; Saga of Burnt Nial (*The*), 1861; Story

of Gisli from the Icelandic (*The*), 1866; Tales from the Fjeld, 1874; Theophilus Eutychianus, etc., 1845; Three to One, 1872; Vikings of the Baltic (*The*), 1875.

DAUBENY, M.D. (*Charles Giles Bridle*), Gloucestershire, 1795-1867. Christianity and Rationalism, 1867; Climate, 1863; Description of Volcanoes, 1826 (much esteemed); Final Causes of the Sexuality of Plants, 1860; Introduction to the Atomic Theory, 1831; Lectures on Agriculture, 1841; Supplement to the Atomic Theory, 1840.

DAVENANT, LL.D. (*Charles*), 1656-1714. Circe, 1677, a tragedy; Discourse upon Grants and Resumptions (*A*), 1700; Discourses on the Public Revenues and Trade of England, 1698; Essay upon the Balance of Power (*An*), 1701; Essay upon Ways and Means of Supplying the War (*An*), 1695; Essays upon Peace at Home and War Abroad, 1704; Right of making War, Peace, and Alliances (*The*), 1701.

DAVENANT (Sir *William*), Oxford, 1605-1668. Albovine, 1629, a tragedy; Britannia Triumphans, 1637, a masque; Cruel Brother (*The*), 1630, a tragedy; Cruelty of the Spaniards in Peru, 1658; Gondibert, 1651, an heroic poem, unfinished; History of Sir Francis Drake, 1659; Just Italian (*The*), 1630; London, King Charles his Augusta, 1648; Love and Honour, 1649; Madagascar, and other Poems, 1638; Man's a Master (*The*), 1668, a comedy; Panegyric to . . . Generall Monck, 1659; Platonick Lovers, 1636, a tragi-comedy; Poem on the Restoration, 1660; Salmacida Spolia, 1639, a masque; Siege of Rhodes, 1663; Rivals (*The*), 1668, a comedy; Temple of Love (*The*), 1634, a masque; Triumphs of Prince d'Amour, 1635, a masque; Unfortunate Lovers (*The*), 1643, a tragedy; Voyage to the other World, 1668; Witts (*The*), 1636, a comedy; Works collected, 1672-73.

DAVENPORT (Rev. *Francis*), chaplain to queen Henrietta, 1610-1672. Manuale Missionarium Regularium . . . S. Francisci, 1658 (a most interesting account of the English Franciscans).

DAVENPORT (*Robert*), 1612-1671. Bloodie Banquet (*The*), 1639, a tragedy; City Nightcap (*The*), 1661, a tragi-comedy; Crowne for a Conqueror, 1639; King John and Matilda, 1655, a tragedy; New Tricke to Cheat the Divell, 1639, a comedy Too late to call back Yesterday, 1639.

DAVIDS, LL.D. (*Thomas William Rhys*), Colchester, 1843-   . Ancient Coins and Measures of Ceylon, 1877; American Lectures, 1896; Buddhism, 1878; Buddhist Birth Stories, 1880; Buddhist Suttas from the Pali, 1881; Hibbert Lectures, 1881; Jātaka (tales of the anterior births of Gotama Buddha), 1877; Origin and Growth of Religion, as illustrated by Buddhism, 1881; Questions of King Milinda, 1890-94.

DAVIDSON (*John*), Barrhead, in Scotland, poet, 1857-   . Ballads and Songs, 1894; Baptist Lake, 1894; Bruce, 1886; Fleet Street Eclogues, 1893, second series, 1896; Great Men (*The*), and a Practical Novelist, 1891;

In a Music-Hall, 1891 ; Miss Armstrong's and other Circumstances, 1896, essays ; New Ballads, 1896 ; Perfervid, 1891 ; Plays, 1894; Random Itinerary (*A*), 1893 ; Sentences and Paragraphs, 1893; Smith, 1888, a tragedy ; Wonderful Mission of Earl Lavender (*The*), 1894.

DAVIDSON, D.D. (*Samuel*), Ballymena, in Ireland, 1807– . Canon of the Bible (*The*), 1877 ; Doctrine of Last Things (*The*), 1882 ; Ecclesiastical Polity of the New Testament (*The*), 1848, 1858 ; English Old Testament (*Revision of the*), 1873 ; Interpretation of the Bible (*The*), 1856 ; Introduction to the New Testament (*An*), 1848 ; Sacred Hermeneutics, 1843 ; Tischendorf's New Testament (translated), 1875.

DAVIDSON (*Thomas*), Aberdeen, in Scotland, 1623-1679. Cantus, or songs in 3, 4, and 5 parts, 1666 (contains the first known collection of Scotch songs).

DAVIDSON, F.R.S. (*Thomas*), Edinburgh, 1817-1885. British Fossil Brachiopoda (5 huge vols., a magnificent work, with 230 plates), 1850-70.

DAVIDSON (*William Leslie*), Meikle Wartle, 1848– . English Words Explained, 1886 ; Logic of Definition (*The*), 1885 ; Theism as Grounded in Human Nature, 1893.

DAVIES (Mrs. C. M.), died 1863. Life and Times of P. Quintus Ondaatje, 1871 ; History of Holland, 1841-44.

DAVIES, D.D. (*John*), 1594-1644. Antiquæ Linguæ Britannicæ Rudimenta, etc., 1621 ; Dictionarium Latino-Britannicum, 1632.

DAVIES (Sir *John*), Westbury, in Wiltshire, 1570-1626. Book of Epigrams (*A*), 1596 ; Discovery of the Cause why Ireland has never been subdued until this Reign, 1612 (earl Chatham calls it "a masterly work") ; Hymns of Astrea, 1599 ; Nosce Teipsum, 1599, a poem on the immortality of the soul (his chief work) ; Orchestra, or Poem on Dancing, 1596 ; Original Nature and Immortality of the Soul, 1697, a poem ; Poems, 1622; Reports of Cases in the King's Courts of Ireland, 1615. His Life, by G. Chalmers, 1786.

DAVIES (Rev. *John Llewelyn*), Chichester, 1826– . Christian Calling (*The*), 1875 ; Gospel and Modern Life (*The*), 1869 ; Manifestation of the Son of God (*The*), 1864 ; Morality according to the Sacrament of the Lord's Supper, 1865; Order and Growth, 1891; Theology and Morality, 1873 ; Warnings against Superstition, 1874.

DAVIS (*John*), Sandridge, in Hertfordshire, 1540-1605. Seaman's Secrets, wherein is taught the Three Kinds of Sailing, etc. (*The*), 1595 ; World's Hydrographical Description, etc. (*The*), 1595.

DAVIS (Sir *John Francis*), London, 1795-1889. China, a General Description of that Empire, 1857 ; China, during the War and since the Peace, 1852.

DAVIS, M.D. (*Joseph Barnard*), York, 1801-1881. Crania Britannica, 1865 ; Thesaurus Craniorum, 1867.

DAVIS (*Nathan*), 1812-1882. Carthage and her Remains, 1861; Israel's True Emancipation, 1852 ; Tunis, 1841 ; Voice from North Africa, 1844.

DAVY (Sir *Humphrey*), Penzance, in Cornwall, 1778-1829. Consolations in Travel, 1830, posthumous ; Elements of Agricultural Chemistry, 1813 ; Elements of Chemical Philosophy, 1812 ; On the Safety Lamp, 1818 ; On Some Chemical Agencies of Electricity, 1806 (a valuable work); Researches, Chemical and Philosophical, 1800 (his chief work) ; Salmonia, or Days of Fly-fishing, 1828 ; Six Discourses before the Royal Society, 1827. His Memoirs, by Ayton, 1830 ; Dr. Paris, 1831 ; Dr. John Davy, 1836.

DAWE, R.A. (*George*), London, 1781-1829. Life of George Morland, 1807.

DAWES (*Richard*), Market-Bosworth, in Leicestershire, 1708-1766. Miscellanea Critica, 1745 (a valuable work).

DAWKINS, M.A., F.R.S. (*William Boyd*), 1838. British Pleistocene Mammalia, 1866-87; Cave-hunting, 1874 ; Early Man in Britain, 1880.

DAWSON (Sir *J. William*), Pictou, Nova Scotia, 1820. Acadian Geology, 1855; Agriculture for Schools, 1864 ; Archaia, 1857; Chain of Life in Geological Time (*The*), 1881 ; Fossil Men and their American Analogues, 1880; Geological History of Plants (*The*), 1888 ; Handbook of Canadian Geology, 1889 ; Handbook of Canadian Zoology, 1871 ; Ice Age in Canada (*The*), 1894 ; Life's Dawn on Earth, 1875 ; Meeting-place of Geology and History (*The*), 1891 ; Modern Ideas of Evolution, 1890 ; Modern Science in Bible Lands, 1888 ; Origin of the World (*The*), 1878 ; Salient Points in the Science of the Earth, 1893-94 ; Story of Earth and Man, 1872.

DAY, M.D. (*George Edward*), 1815-1872. Physiology and Medicine, 1860 ; Practical Treatise on the Diseases of Advanced Life (*A*), 1849.

DAY (*John*), about 1584-1661. Blind Beggar of Bednal-Green, 1659, a comedy ; Humour out of Breath, 1608, a comedy ; Ile of Guls, 1606, a comedy ; Law Trickes, or Who would have thought it? 1603, a comedy ; Parliament of Bees (*The*), being 12 satirical colloquies in rhyme, 1641 ; Travailes of Three English Brothers, 1607, a tragicomedy.

DAY (*Thomas*), London, 1748-1789. Desolation of America (*The*), 1777 ; Devoted Legions (*The*), 1776 ; Dying Negro (*The*), 1773; History of Little Jack, 1780 ; History of Sandford and Merton, 1783-89 (a tale which stands its ground still). His Life, by James Keir, 1791.

DEE, D.C.L. (*John*), London, 1527-1608. Apologie sent to the Archbishop of Canterbury, 1594-95 ; Brevis quædam Epistola, etc., 1556 ; Diary (published in 1842 by the Camden Society); General and Rare Memorials pertaining to the Art of Navigation, 1577; Monas Hieroglyphica, 1564 ; Parallaticæ Commentationis Praxeosque Nuclius quidam, 1573 ; Propaidetmata Aphoristika (120 aphorisms), 1558 ; Relation of what passed between Dr. John Dee and some Spirits, etc., 1514 ; Triple Almanacke (*A*), 1591.

DEERING, M.D. (*Charles*), 1690-1759. Catalogue of Plants growing about Nottingham, 1738; Nottinghamia Vetus et Nova, 1751.

DEFOE (*Daniel*), London, 1661-1731. Adventures of Roxana, 1724; Appeal to Honour and Justice, 1715; Captain Carleton (*Life of*), 1728, a biographical romance; Captain Singleton, 1720, a biographical romance; Colonel Jack, 1721, a biographical romance; Duncan Campbell, 1720, a biographical romance; Essays on Projects, 1697; Jonathan Wild (*An Account of*), 1725, a biographical romance; John Sheppard (*History of*), 1724, a biographical romance; Journal of the Plague Year, 1722, an excellent romance; Jure Divino, 1706; History of Apparitions, 1727; History of the Union, 1709; Hymn to the Pillory (*A*), 1703 (written in jail); Memoirs of a Cavalier, 1724, a novel (Chatham calls it "the best account of the Civil War extant"); Moll Flanders (*Fortunes of*), 1721, a biographical romance; New Voyage round the World (*A*), 1725; Political History of the Devil (*The*), 1726, a serious memoir; Presbytery Rough Drawn, 1683; Reasons against the Hanoverian Succession, 1713; Religious Courtship, 1722; Review (*The*), 1704-13; Robinson Crusoe (*Adventures of*), 1719 (his best work: refused, like Carlyle's *Sartor Resartus*, by nearly all the trade!); Roxana, 1724; Shortest Way with Dissenters (*The*), 1702 (he was pilloried for this satire); Speculum Crape-gownorum, 1682; Tour through Great Britain, 1724-27; Tracts, 1687, 1689; Treatise against the Turks, 1683; True-born Englishman (*The*), 1701, a satirical poem in defence of William III. (a great hit) His Life, by George Chalmers, 1790; Walter Wilson, 1830; J. Ballantyne, 1840; J. Foster, 1855; W. Chadwick, 1859; Lee, 1869.

DEKKER (*Thomas*), 1570-1637. Bachelor's Banquet (*The*), 1603; Belman of London (*The*), 1608, continuation 1609; English Villanies, 1632, 1637, 1638, 1648; Foure Birds—the Dove, the Eagle, the .Pelican, and the Phœnix, 1609; Gul's Hornbook, 1609, not a play (it contains many details of the manners of the times); History of Sir Thomas Wyat, 1607; Honest Whore (*The*), 1604, a comedy; If it is not Good the Divel is in it, 1612, a comedy; Jests to make you Merrie, 1607 (with Wilkins); Knights conjuring, done in Earnest, discovered in Jest, 1607, a comedy; Match mee in London, 1631, a tragi-comedy; Newes from Hell, 1606; Northward Hoe! 1607, a comedy; O per se O, 1612; Old Fortunatus, 1600, a comedy; Owles Almanacke (*The*), 1618; Patient Grissell, 1603, a comedy (with Haughton); Phaeton, 1597; Raven's Almanacke (*The*), 1609; Roaring Girl (*The*), 1611, a comedy (with Middleton); Satiromastix, 1602, a satirical comedy; Seven Deadly Sins of London (*The*), 1606; Shoemaker's Holiday, 1600, a comedy; Troia Nova Triumphans, 1612; Westward Hoe! 1607, a comedy (with Webster); Whore of Babylon (*The*), 1603, a comedy; Wonderful Yeare (*The*), . . . London lying Sicke of the Plague, 1603.

DE LA BECHE, F.R.S. (Sir *Henry Thomas*), near London, 1796-1855. Geological Manual, 1831; Geological Observer, 1851; On the New Fossil Animal, a Link between the Ichthyosaurus and the Crocodile, 1823; On the Temperature and Depth of the Lake of Geneva, 1820; Researches in Theoretical Geology, 1834.

DE LA RAMÉ (*Louise*), better known as "Ouida," Bury St. Edmunds, 1840- . Altruist (*The*), 1897; Ariadne, 1877, the story of a dream; Bimbi, 1882; Cecil Castlemaine's Gage, 1867; Chandos, 1866; Dog of Flanders (*A*), 1872 (a pretty tale); Folle Farine, 1871; Frescoes, 1883; Friendship, 1878; Guilderoy, 1889; Held in Bondage, 1863; House Party (*A*), 1886; Idalia, 1867; In a Winter City, 1876; In Maremma, 1882; Leaf in a Storm (*A*), 1873; Lemon Tree (*The*), 1894; Massarenes (*The*), 1897; Moths, 1880; New Priesthood (*The*), 1893; Othmar, 1887; Pascarel, 1873; Pipistrello, and other Stories, 1880; Princess Napraxine, 1884; Puck, his Vicissitudes and Adventures, 1869; Ruffino, 1890; Santa Barbara, 1891; Signa, 1875, a story; Silver Christ (*The*), 1894; Strathmore, 1865, a romance; Syrlin, 1890; Tower of Taddeo, 1890; Tricotrin, a Story of a Waif and Stray, 1860; Two Little Wooden Shoes, 1874; Two Offenders, 1894; Under Two Flags, 1868 (her best novel); Views and Opinions, 1895; Village Commune (*A*), 1881; Wanda, 1883. The Wisdom, Wit, and Pathos of Ouida, by F. Sydney Morris, 1883.

DELAND (*Margaret*), American authoress, 1857- . Florida Days, 1889; John Ward, Preacher, 1888; Mr. Tommy Dove, 1893; Old Garden (*The*), 1886; Philip and his Wife, 1894; Sidney, 1890; Story of a Child (*The*), 1892; Wisdom of Fools (*The*), 1897.

DELANY (*Mary*), Wiltshire, 1700-1788. Autobiography and Correspondence, 1861-62; Flora (*The*), 1774-88.

DELANY, D.D. (*Patrick*), Ireland, 1686-1768. History of the Life and Reign of David, 1741-42 (not equal to Dr. Chandler's); Revelation examined with Candour, 1732-36.

DELOLME (*Jean Louis*), Geneva, 1740-1806. Constitution de l'Angleterre, 1771 (Delolme was not an Englishman, but his book was once a standard work, and is still held in good estimation).

DELONEY (*Thomas*), about 1582-1660, called by Kempe "the great ballade-maker" (*Nine Days' Wonder*). Garland of Delight; Garland of Good Will (*A*), historical ballads, published by the Percy Society, 1851; Jack of Newbury, 1633, a ballad; Strange Histories, or Songs of Kings and Princes, Lords and Ladyes, 1612; Shoemaker's Holiday (*The*), 1618, a ballad; Thomas of Reading, or the Six Worthy Yeomen of the West, 1632.

DE MORGAN (*Augustus*), East Indies, 1806-1871. Arithmetical Books, 1847, Book of Almanacs, 1851; Connection of Number and Magnitude, 1836; Differential and Integral Calculus, 1842; Elements of Algebra, 1835; Elements of Arithmetic,

1830; Elements of Trigonometry, 1837; Essay on Probabilities, 1838 ; Formal Logic, 1847; Trigonometry and Double Algebra, 1849.

DEMPSTER (*Thomas*), Muiresk, in Scotland, 1579-1625. De Etruria Regali, 1723-24; Historia Ecclesiastica Gentis Scotorum, 1627; Nomenclatura Scriptorum Scotorum, 1619.

DENHAM (*Dixon*), London, 1786-1828. Narrative of Travels and Discoveries in Northern and Central Africa, 1826.

DENHAM (Sir *John*), Dublin, 1615-1668. Cooper's Hill, 1642 (his best production); Poems, 1642, collected 1709, 1719 ; Sophy (*The*), 1642, a tragedy.

DENNIS (*John*), London, 1657-1734. Battle of Ramillia, 1706, a poem in five books ; Blenheim, 1705, a poem ; Britannia Triumphans, 1704 ; Court of Death (*The*), 1695 ; Essay on Taste, 1702 ; Monument (*The*), 1702, a poem ; Pindaric Ode on William III., 1692.

Dramas: Appius and Virginia, 1705, a tragedy ; Comical Gallant (*The*), or the Amours of Sir John Falstaff, 1702 (Shakespeare's *Merry Wives of Windsor* altered); Gibraltar, 1704, a play ; Iphigenia, 1704, a tragedy ; Invader of his Country (*The*), 1705 (Shakespeare's *Coriolanus* altered) ; Liberty Asserted, 1704, a tragedy ; Orpheus and Eurydice, 1704, a tragedy ; Plot (*A*), and no Plot, 1697, a comedy ; Rinaldo and Armida, 1699. (The best abused man in English literature, being lampooned by Swift, gibbeted in Pope's *Essay on Criticism*, and enrolled in the *Dunciad*.)

DENTON (*Daniel*), 1630-1682. Description of New York, with the Customs of the Indians, 1670.

DENTON (Rev. *William*), Newport, in the Isle of Wight, 1815- . Christians of Turkey (*The*), 1863; Commentaries, 1860-63, 1864; Montenegro, its People, etc., 1877 ; Servia and the Servians, 1862.

DE QUINCEY (*Thomas*), Manchester, 1786-1859. Confessions of an Opium-Eater, 1821 ; Logic of Political Economy, 1844. He wrote many essays and articles, which have been collected into 16 vols., 1862-74, Edinburgh Edition. Also his collected writings by David Masson, 1889.

DERBY (*Edward Geoffrey Smith Stanley*, earl of), Knowsley, in Lancashire, 1799-1869. Translation of Homer's *Iliad*, 1864.

DERHAM, D.D. (*William*), Stowton, in Worcestershire, 1657-1735. Artificial Clockmaker (*The*), 1696 ; Astro-theology, 1714; Christo-theology, 1730 ; Miscellania Curiosa, 1705-7 (remarkable natural phenomena); Physico-theology, 1713.

DE TABLEY (*John Byrne Leicester*, lord), 1835-1894. Guide to the Study of Bookplates, 1880; Philoctetes, 1866 ; Poems, (dramatic and lyrical), 1890, 1895 ; Rehearsals, 1870; Searching the Net, 1873; Soldier of Fortune (*The*), 1876.

DE VERE (*Aubrey Thomas*), Curragh Chase, in Limerick, 1814- .
Poetry : Alexander the Great, 1874, a dramatic poem ; Foray of Queen Meave,

and other Irish Legends, 1882 ; Household Poetry Book, 1893 ; Infant Bridal (*The*), and other Poems, 1864; Irish Odes, and other Poems, 1869; Legends of St. Patrick, 1872 ; Legends of Saxon Saints, 1879 ; May Carols, 1857, 1881 ; Mediæval Records and Sonnets, 1893 ; Poems (miscellaneous and sacred), 1853 ; Proteus and Amadeus, 1879 ; Religious Poems of the Nineteenth Century, 1893 ; St. Peter's Chains, 1888 ; St. Thomas of Canterbury, 1876, a dramatic poem ; Search after Proserpine (*The*), and other Poems, 1843 ; Sisters (*The*), and other Poems, 1861 ; Waldenses (*The*), 1842, a lyrical tale.

Prose : Church Establishment in Ireland (*The*), 1867 ; Church Settlement of Ireland, 1868; Constitutional and Unconstitutional Political Action, 1881; English Misrule and Irish Misdeeds, 1843 ; Essays, 1887 ; Essays, 1889 ; Ireland's Church Property, 1867 ; Legends and Records of the Church and Empire, 1887 ; Picturesque Sketches of Greece and Turkey, 1850; Pleas for Secularization, 1867; Religious Problems of the Nineteenth Century, 1893.

D'EWES (Sir *Symonds*), Coxden, in Dorsetshire, 1602-1650. Autobiography and Correspondence, 1845 ; Journals of all the Parliaments in the Reign of Queen Elizabeth, 1682.

DIBDIN (*Charles*), Southampton, 1745-1814, famous for his sea-songs. Complete History of the English Stage (*A*), 1795 ; Musical Tour, 1788 ; Observations on a Tour through England, 1801 ; Sea-songs, 1790 ("Poor Tom Bowling" is his best song); Shepherd's Artifice (*The*), 1761, an opera ; Whim of the Moment (*The*), containing " Poor Jack," 1789. His Life, by T. Dibdin, 1850.

DIBDIN, D.D. (*Thomas Frognall*), Calcutta, 1776-1847. Ædes Althorpianæ, 1822 ; Bibliographical, Antiquarian, and Picturesque Tour in France and Germany, 1821 ; Bibliographical, Antiquarian, and Picturesque Tour in the Northern Counties of England and Scotland, 1838 ; Bibliographical Decameron (*The*), 1817 ; Bibliomania, 1811 (written in dialogue, the speakers being well-known book-collectors) ; Bibliotheca Spenseriana, 1814-15 ; Introduction to the Knowledge of Rare and Valuable Editions of the Greek and Latin Classics, 1802 ; La Belle Marianne, 1824, a tale of woe ; Library Companion (*The*), 1824 ; Poems, 1797 ; Reminiscences of a Literary Life, 1836; Sermons, 1820-25 ; Sunday Library (*The*), 1831 ; Typographical Antiquities of Great Britain, 1810-19.

DICEY (*Edward*), Claybrook Hall, in Leicestershire, 1832- . Battle-fields of 1866 (*The*), 1866 ; Bulgaria, 1895 ; England and Egypt, 1884 ; Memoir of Cavour, 1859 ; Month in Russia (*A*), 1867 ; Morning Land (*The*), 1870; Rome in 1860; Schleswig-Holstein War (*The*), 1864 ; Six Months in the Federal States, 1863 ; Victor Emmanuel, 1882.

DICEY (*Thomas*), Guernsey, 1711-1767. Historical Account of Guernsey, etc., 1751 (held in good esteem).

DICK, LL.D. (*Thomas*), Dundee, in Scotland, called "The Christian Philosopher," 1772–1857. Celestial Scenery, 1838; Christian Philosopher (*The*), 1823; Philosophy of Religion (*The*), 1825; Philosophy of a Future State (*The*), 1828; Practical Astronomer (*The*), 1845; Sidereal Heavens (*The*), 1840; Solar System (*The*), 1846.

DICKENS (*Charles*), Landport, Portsmouth, in Hampshire, 1812–1870. Barnaby Rudge, 1840; Battle of Life, 1846; Bleak House, 1853; Chimes (*The*), 1844; Cricket on the Hearth (*The*), 1846; Christmas Carol (*A*), 1843; David Copperfield, 1850; Dr. Marigold's Prescription, 1865 (C. N.); Dombey and Son, 1848; Going into Society, 1858 (C. N.); Great Expectations, 1861; Hard Times, 1854; Haunted House (*The*), 1859 (C. N,); Haunted Man (*The*), 1848; Holiday Romance (*The*), 1868; Holly-tree Inn (*The*), 1858 (C. N.); Hunted Down, 1871; Little Dorrit, 1857; Martin Chuzzlewit, 1843; Master Humphrey's Clock, 1840–41; Memoirs of Grimaldi, 1838; Message from the Sea (*A*), 1860 (C.N.); Mr. and Mrs. Gamp, 1858 (C. N.); Mrs. Lirriper's Lodgings, 1863–64 (C. N.); Mudfog Papers, 1880; Mugby Junction, 1866 (C. N.); Mystery of Edwin Drood, 1870 (unfinished); Nicholas Nickleby, 1839; No Thoroughfare, 1867 (C. N.); Old Curiosity Shop (*The*), 1840; Oliver Twist, 1838; Our Mutual Friend, 1865; Perils of Certain English Prisoners, 1857; Pickwick Papers (*The*), 1837; Poor Traveller (*The*), 1858 (C. N.); Round of Stories (*A*), 1852 (C.N.); Seven Poor Travellers, 1854; Sketches by Boz, 1836; Sketches of Young Couples, 1840; Sketches of Young Gentlemen, 1838; Somebody's Luggage, 1862 (C. N.); St. George and the Dragon, 1866 (C. N.); Stories from Household Words, 1859; Strange Gentleman (*The*), 1836 (C. N.); Tale of Two Cities (*A*), 1859; Tenants at Will, 1864 (C. N.); Tom Tiddler's Ground, 1861 (C. N.); Two Ghost Stories, 1865–66 (C. N.); Uncommercial Traveller (*The*), 1860; Village Coquettes (*The*), 1836; Wreck of the Golden Mary, 1856. N.B.—C. N. (Christmas Number) only in part by Dickens.

Not Works of Fiction: American Notes, 1842; Child's History of England (*The*), 1853–54; Letters, 1879, posthumous; Pictures from Italy, 1846; Plays and Poems, 1882; Speeches, 1871, posthumous; Sunday under Three Heads, 1836. His Life, by Theodore Taylor, 1870; R. S. Mackenzie, 1870; John Forster, 1873; Shepherd, 1881; Mary Dickens, 1885; T. Marzial, 1887.

DICKENS (*Mary Angela*), novelist (eldest daughter of Charles Dickens), 1838– . Cross Currents, 1891; Mere Cypher (*A*), 1893; Prisoners of Silence, 1895; Valiant Ignorance, 1894.

DICKSON (*Adam*), died 1776. Treatise on Agriculture, 1762; Treatise on the Husbandry of the Ancients, 1788, posthumous.

DICKSON (*James*), died 1822. Collection de Plants Diverses, 1789–99; Fasiculi Quatuor Plantarum Cryptogamicarum Britanniæ, 1783–1801.

DIGBY (Sir *Kenelm*), Buckinghamshire, 1603–1665. Broad Stone of Honour (*The*), 1826–27; Conference with a Lady about the Choice of a Religion, 1638; Discourse on Vegetation, 1661; Five Books of Peripatetic Institutions, 1651; Mores Catholici, or Ages of Faith, 1844–47; Observations on Religio Medici, 1643; Private Memoirs, 1827, posthumous; Treatise on the Soul (*A*), 1645.

DIGGES (Sir *Dudley*), 1583–1639. Compleat Ambassador, 1655; Defence of Commerce, 1615.

DILKE (Sir *Charles Wentworth*), London, 1843– . British Army (*The*), 1888; Eastern Question (*The*), 1878 ; European Politics, 1887; Fall of Prince Florestan, 1874; a satire; Greater Britain, 1868; Imperial Defence, 1892; Papers of a Critic (*i.e.* his grandfather), 1875; Parliamentary Reform, 1879; Problems of Greater Britain, 1890; Two Recess Speeches, 1876.

DILKE (Lady *Emilia Frances*), formerly Mrs. *Mark Pattison, née Strong*. Art in the Modern State, 1880; Biography of Lord Leighton, 1881; Claude Lorraine, 1884 (in French); Renaissance of Art in France, 1879; Shrine of Death (*The*), 1886; Shrine of Love (*The*), 1891.

DIRCKS, LL.D. (*Henry*), Liverpool, 1806–1873. Electro-Metallurgy, 1863; Inventors and Inventions, 1867; Joseph Anstey, 1863, a novel; Jordantype, 1852; Life, Times, etc., of Edward Somerset. 1865; Memoir of S. Hartlib (Milton's friend), 1865; Naturalistic Poetry, etc., 1872; Nature Study, 1869; Optical Illusions, 1863; Worcesteriana, 1866.

DISRAELI (*Benjamin*), earl of Beaconsfield), London, novelist, etc., 1804–1881. Alarcos, 1839, a tragedy; Alroy (*The Wondrous Tale of*), 1833; Coningsby, or the New Generation, 1844; Contarini Fleming, 1833; Endymion, 1880; Henrietta Temple, 1836; Ixion in Heaven, 1847; Lothair, 1870; Revolutionary Epic (*The*), 1834, a poem; Rise of Iskander (*The*), 1833; Sybil, or the Two Nations,1845; Tancred, or the New Crusade, 1847; Venetia, 1837; Vivian Grey, 1826–27; Voyage of Captain Popanilla (*The*), 1828; Young Duke (*The*), 1831.

Not works of Fiction: Address at Glasgow University, 1873; Crisis Examined (*The*), 1834; Letters of Runnymede, 1836; Lord George Bentinck, 1851.

Speeches: Church and Queen, 1860–65; Conservative Policy, 1870; Constitutional Reform, 1859–65; Parliamentary Reform, 1867; Vindication of the English Constitution (*A*), 1835; Wit and Wisdom, 1881. His Life, by Hitchman, 1876, 1881; O'Connor, 1879; Brandes, 1880; Clarigny, 1880; Foggo, 1881; Froude, 1890.

DISRAELI, D.C.L. (*Isaac*), Enfield, Middlesex, literary virtuoso, 1766–1848. Amenities of Literature, 1841; Calamities of Authors, 1812; Crisis Examined (*The*), 1834; Curiosities of Literature, 1791, 1793, 1823 (his best-known work); Defence of Poetry (*A*), 1790; Despotism, or the Fall of the Jesuits, 1811; Dissertation on Anecdotes, 1793; Eliot, Hampden, and Pym, 1832; Flim-

Flams, 1805 ; Genius of Judaism (*The*), 1833 ; History of Cupid and Psyche (*The*), 1813 ; Illustrations of the Literary Character, 1828 ; Life and Reign of Charles I., 1828–31 ; Literary Character (*The*), 1795 ; Literary and Political Character of James I. (*The*), 1816 ; Miscellanies of Literature, 1812–22 ; Narrative Poems, 1803 ; Poetical Epistle on the Abuse of Satire (*A*), 1789 ; Quarrels of Authors (*The*), 1814 ; Romances, 1799 ; Vaurien, 1797, a novel. His Life, by his son, Benjamin Disraeli, earl of Beaconsfield.

DITTON (*Humphrey*), Salisbury, 1675-1715. Discourse on the Resurrection of Jesus Christ, 1712 (a book of good repute) ; General Laws of Nature and Motion, 1705 ; Institution of Fluxions, etc., 1706 ; New Law of Fluids (*The*), 1714 ; Treatise on Perspective (*A*), 1712.

DIXON (*William Hepworth*), Newton Heath, in Yorkshire, 1821-1879. British Cyprus, 1879 ; Diana, Lady Lyle, 1877, a novel ; Free Russia, 1870 ; Her Majesty's Tower, 1869-71 ; Holy Land (*The*), 1865 ; John Howard (*Memoir of*), 1849 ; Lady Morgan's Memoirs, 1862 ; Life of Lord Bacon, 1860 ; Life of Admiral Blake, 1852 ; Life of William Penn (*A*), 1851 ; New America, 1867 ; Personal History of Lord Bacon (*The*), 1860 ; Proof-Private : Lord Bacon's Confession, 1861 ; Robert Blake, Admiral, etc., 1852 ; Royal Windsor, 1878-80 ; Ruby Grey, 1878, a novel ; Spiritual Wives, 1868 ; Story of the Life of Bacon, 1862 ; Switzers (*The*), 1872 ; Two Queens, 1873-74 ; White Conquest, 1875.

DOBELL (*Sydney*), London, 1824-1874. Balder, 1854 ; England in Time of War, 1856 (his best) ; England's Day, 1871 ; Parliamentary Reform, 1865 ; Poetical Works, 1875, posthumous ; Roman (*The*), 1850 ; Sonnets on the War, 1853 (with A. Smith) ; Thoughts on Art, Philosophy, and Religion, 1876, posthumous.

DOBSON (*Henry Austin*), Plymouth, in Hampshire, poet, 1840- . At the Sign of the Lyre, 1885 ; Civil Service Handbook of English Literature, 1874 ; Eighteenth Century Vignettes (3 series), 1892, 1894, 1896 ; Eighteenth Century Essays, 1882 ; Fables of John Gay, 1882 ; Fielding, 1883 ; Four Frenchwomen, 1890 ; Horace Walpole, 1890 ; Life of Goldsmith, 1886 ; Life of Hogarth, 1879 ; Life of Steele, 1886 ; Old World Idylls, 1883 ; Poems, 1889 ; Poems on Several Occasions, 1895 ; Proverbs in Porcelain, 1877 ; Thomas Bewick and his pupils, 1884 ; Vers de Société, 1873 ; Vignettes in Rhyme, 1873. His collected poems were published in 1897.

DODD (*Charles*), Worcestershire, died 1745. Church History of England, 1737-42 ; List of the Writers (Protestant and Catholic) since the Reformation, 1724.

DODD, D.D. (*William*), Bourne, in Lincolnshire, 1729-1777. Beauties of *Shakespeare*, 1752 ; Commentary on the Old and New Testaments, 1765 ; Comfort for the Afflicted, 1764 ; Poems, 1767 ; Practical Discourses on Miracles, etc., 1757 ; Reflection on Death, 1763 ; Sermons to Young Men, 1771 ; Sisters

(*The*), 1754 ; Thoughts in Prison (in five parts, blank verse), 1777 ; Visitor (*The*), 1764. His Life, by Reed, 1777.

DODDRIDGE, D.D. (*Philip*), London, 1702-1751. Colonel Gardiner, 1747 ; Course of Lectures, etc., 1763 ; Family Expositor (*The*), 1739-56 ; Passages in the Life of Colonel Gardiner, 1747 ; Rise and Progress of Religion in the Soul, 1750 (his chief work). Also some excellent poems. His Life, by Job Orton, 1766.

DODDRIDGE (Sir *John*), Barnstaple, 1555-1628. Compleat Parson (*The*), 1602 ; English Lawyer (*The*), 1631 ; Law of Nobility and Peerage (*The*), 1642.

DODS, D.D. (*Marcus*), Belford, in Northumberland, 1834- . Epistles to the Seven Churches (*The*), 1865 ; Erasmus, and other Essays, 1891 ; Handbook on Haggai, Zechariah, and Malachi, 1879 ; Introduction to the New Testament (*An*), 1888 ; Isaac, Jacob, and Joseph, 1880 ; Israel's Iron Age, 1874 ; Mohammed, Buddha, and Christ, 1877 ; Parables of our Lord (*The*), 1886 ; Prayer that teaches to pray (*The*), 1863. And other works.

DODSLEY (*Robert*), Mansfield, in Nottinghamshire, 1703-1764. Annual Register, begun 1758 ; Blind Beggar of Bethnal Green, 1745, a comedy ; Cleone, 1740, a tragedy ; Economy of Human Life, 1751 ; King and the Miller of Mansfield (*The*), 1737, a farce ; Muse in Livery (*The*), 1732, a comedy ; Preceptor (*The*), 1748 ; Public Register (*The*), 1741-42 ; Rex et Pontifex, 1745 ; Select Collection of Old Plays (12 vols.), 1780 ; Sir John Cockle at Court, 1737, a farce, the second part of *The King and the Miller of Mansfield ;* Toy-shop (*The*), 1735, a drama ; Trifles, 1748 ; World (*The*), 1754-57.

DODSON (*James*), died 1757. Antilogarithmic Canon (*The*), 1742 ; Calculator (*The*), 1747 ; Mathematical Repository, 1748-55.

DODSWORTH (*Roger*), St. Oswald, in Yorkshire, 1585-1654. Collections for a History of Yorkshire, in MS. (in the Bodleian Library).

DODWELL (*Henry*), Dublin, 1641-1711. Annales Thucydidei et Xenophontei, 1696 ; Chronologia Græco-Romana pro hypothesibus ; De Veteribus Græcorum Romanorumque Cyclis, etc., 1701 ; Dionis Halicarnassei, 1692 ; Prælectiones, etc., 1692. His Life, by F. Brokesby, 1715.

DONALDSON, LL.D. (*James*), Aberdeen, 1831- . Ante-Nicene Christian Library (*The*) (24 vols.), completed 1872 ; Apostolic Fathers (*The*), 1874 ; Critical History of Christian Literature (up to the Nicene Council), 1864 ; 66 ; Lyra Græca (specimens of the Greek lyric poets), 1884 ; Sacrifices of the Greeks, etc., 1875. And other works.

DONALDSON, D.D. (*John William*), London, 1811-1861. Comparative Grammar of the Hebrew Language, 1853 ; Greek Grammar, 1848 ; Jashar (*The Book of*), 1854 ; Latin Grammar, 1852 ; New Cratylus, 1839 ; Theatre of the Greeks, 1837 ; Varronianus, 1844.

DONALDSON, Ph.D. (*Thomas Leverton*), London, 1795-1885. Architectural Maxims and Theories, 1847; Architectura Numismatica, 1859; Examples of Doorways, 1833; Pompeii Illustrated, 1837; Practical Guide to Architects, 1860; Temple of Apollo at Bassa, 1838.

DONNE, D.D. (*John*), London, poet, 1573–1631. Anatomy of the World (*An*), 1625; Biathanatos, 1644, posthumous; Death's Duel, 1632, posthumous; Devotions upon Emergent Occasions, etc., 1624; Elegy on . . . Prince Henry, 1613; Ignatius his Conclave, 1611; Juvenilia, 1633, posthumous; Letters, 1651, posthumous; Poems, 1593; Polydoron, 1631; Pseudo-Martyr (*The*), 1610; Satyr, 1662, posthumous; Sermons, 1640, posthumous; Sheaf of . . . Epigrams, 1632. His Life, by I. Walton, 1640; H. Alford, 1839.

DONOVAN (*Dick*), pseudonym of *J. E. Muddock*. Caught at Last, 1889; Dark Deeds, 1892; Detective's Triumphs (*A*), 1891; From Information received, 1893; In the Grip of the Law, 1894; Link by Link, 1893; Man from Manchester (*The*), 1890; Man-hunter (*The*), 1888; Michael Danevitch, 1897; Mystery of Jamaica Terrace (*The*), 1896; Riddles Read, 1896; Suspicion Aroused, 1893; Tracked and Taken, 1890; Tracked to Doom, 1891; Wanted, 1892; Who poisoned Hetty Duncan? 1890.

DONOVAN (*Edward*),—died 1837. Insects of Asia (*The*), commenced 1798; Natural History of British Birds, 1794–1797; Natural History of British Insects, 1792–1816.

DORAN, LL.D. (*John*), 1807–1878. Bentley Ballads (*The*), 1861; Filia Dolorosa, etc., 1852 (with Mrs. Romer); Habits and Men, 1855; History and Antiquities of . . . Reading, 1835; History of Court Fools, 1858; Knights and their Days, 1856; Lady of the Last Century (*A*), *i.e.* Mrs. Montague, 1873; Last Journals of Horace Walpole, 1859; Life of Dr. Young, 1854; Lives of the Princes of Wales, 1860; Lives of the Queens of the House of Hanover, 1855; London in Jacobite Times, 1878; Mann' and Manners at the Court of Florence in 1740–86, 1875; Memoir of Queen Adelaide (*A*), 1861; Memories of our Great Towns, 1876; Monarchs retired from Business, 1857 (this and his "Court Fools" are his best-known books); New Pictures and Old Panels, 1859; Saints and Sinners, etc., 1868; Table Traits, etc., 1854; Their Majesties' Servants, 1863; Wandering Jew (*The*), 1822, a melodrama.

DORSET (*Thomas Sackville*, earl of), Sussex, 1536–1608. Induction (to the *Mirrour of Magistraytes*), 1557; poetry; Gorboduc, 1561, a tragedy.

DOUCE (*Francis*), 1762–1834. Dance of Death, 1833; Illustrations of Shakespeare, etc., 1807.

DOUDNEY (*Sarah*), novelist, 1842– . Principally stories for girls.

DOUGLAS (*Gawin*), bishop of Dunkeld, in Scotland, 1474–1522. Æneis of Virgil, translated 1512–13, published 1553; King Hart, a Poem on Human Life, 1519; Palis of Honoure, 1553 (strikingly like *Pilgrim's Progress*). His Memoirs, by Scott, 1787.

DOUGLAS (Sir *Howard*), Gosport, in Hampshire, 1776–1861. Essay on Military Bridges, 1817 (a valuable manual); Naval Evolutions, 1832; Treatise on Naval Gunnery, 1819.

DOUGLAS, M.D. (*James*), Scotland, 1677–1742. Arbor Yemensis, 1727; Bibliographiæ Anatomicæ Specimen, 1715; History of the Lateral Operation, 1726; Myographiæ Comparatæ Specimen, 1707.

DOUGLAS (Sir *Robert*), eighteenth century. Baronetage of Scotland (*The*), 1798; Peerage of Scotland (*The*), 1764.

DOVER (*George James Welbore Agar Ellis*, lord), 1797–1833. Ellis Correspondence, 1829; Historical Inquiries respecting the Character of Clarendon, 1828; Life of Frederick the Great, 1832.

DOWDEN, LL.D. (*Edward*), Cork, in Ireland, 1843– . Introduction to Shakespeare, 1893; New Studies in Literature, 1895; Percy Bysshe Shelley, 1886; Poems, 1876; Shakespeare (his Mind and Art), 1875; Shakespeare's Sonnets, with Notes, 1881; Shakespeare's Primer, 1877; Southey, 1880; Studies in Literature, 1878; Transcripts of Studies, 1888.

DOWNMAN (Rev. *Hugh*), Exeter or its vicinity, poet, 1740–1809. Infancy, 1771; Land of the Muses (*The*), 1768.

DOYLE (*Arthur Conan*), Edinburgh, novelist, etc., 1859– . Adventures of Sherlock Holmes (*The*), 1891; Captain of the Polestar (*The*), 1888; Doings of Ruffles Haw, 1892; Exploits of Brigadier Gerard (*The*), 1896; Great Shadow (*The*), 1892; Jane Annie, 1893; Firm of Girdlestone (*The*), 1896; Memoirs of Sherlock Holmes, 1893; Micah Clarke, 1889; Mystery of Cloomber (*The*), 1888; Parasite (*The*), 1894; Refugees (*The*), 1891; Rodney Stone, 1896; Round the Red Lamp, 1894; Sign of Four (*The*), 1889; Stark-Munro Letters (*The*), 1895; Study in Scarlet (*A*), 1888; Tragedy of the Korosco (*The*), 1897; Uncle Bernac, 1897; White Company (*The*), 1890.

DOYLE (Sir *Francis Hastings*), Nunappleton, in Yorkshire, verse-writer, etc., 1810–1888. Lectures on Poetry, 1868–69; Return of the Guards, and other Poems, 1866; Verses, 1834.

DOYLE (*Richard*), London, 1824–1883. Continental Tour of Messrs. Brown, Jones, and Robinson, 1854; In Fairyland, 1869 (a Christmas book); Sketches of Modern Society, 1861.

D'OYLY (*George*), 1778–1846. Life of William Sancroft, 1821 (much esteemed); Notes . . . on the Bible, 1845 (with Mant).

DRAKE (Sir *Francis*), Devonshire, on the banks of the Tavy, 1545–1595. Voyage round the Globe, 1577; Voyage to America, 1586.

DRAKE, F.R.S. (*Francis*), died 1770. Eboracum, or History and Antiquities of York, 1736.

DRAKE, M.D. (*Nathan*), York, 1766–1836. Essays, etc., 1805, 1808–9; Evenings in Autumn, 1822; Gleaner (*The*), 1811; Literary Hours, 1798; Memorials of Shakespeare, 1828; Mornings in Spring, 1828;

Shakespeare and his Times, 1817; Winter Nights, 1820.

DRAYTON (*Michael*), Hartshill, in Warwickshire, poet-laureate, 1563-1631. Barons' Wars (*The*) (in 8-line stanzas), 1596; Bataile of Agincourt (in 8-line stanzas), 1627; Endimion and Phœbe, 1596; England's Heroical Epistles, 1598, poetry; Idea, 1594; Man in the Moone (*The*), 1605; Matilda, Daughter of Lord Robert Fitzwalter, 1594, a legend; Mortimeriados, 1605; Moses' Birth and Miracles, 1593, poetry; Muses Elizium (*The*), 1630, poetry; Nymphidia, or the Court of Fairy (in 8-line stanzas), 1627; Owle (*The*), 1604; Piers Gaveston, 1596, a legend; Robert, Duke of Normandy, 1596, a legend; Polyolbion, songs, i.-ix. 1612, xi.-xviii. 1613, xix.-xxx. 1622 (his great work); Shepherd's Garland, 1593 (his first work).

DREW (*Samuel*), St. Austell, in Cornwall, 1765-1833. Essay on Immateriality and Immortality of the Soul, 1802; Essay on the Identity and the General Resurrection of the Human Body, 1809; History of Cornwall, 1820-24. His Life, by his son, J. H. Drew, 1834.

DRIVER, D.D. (*S. Rolles*), 1846– . Commentary on Deuteronomy (*A*), 1895; Introduction to the Literature of the Old Testament (*An*), 1894; Isaiah, 1893; Treatise on the Use of the Tenses in Hebrew (*A*), 1892. And other valuable theological books.

DRUMMOND (*Henry*), Stirling, in Scotland, 1852-1897. Ascent of Man (*The*), 1894; Baxter's Second Innings; Changed Life (*The*); Greatest Thing in the World (*The*), 1893; Natural Law in the Spiritual World, 1883 (excellent); Pax Vobiscum; Programme of Christianity; Tropical Africa, 1888.

DRUMMOND, LL.D. (*James*), Dublin, 1835– . Communion, 1884; Introduction to the Study of Theology, 1884; Jewish Messiah (*The*), 1877; Philo-Judæus, 1885; Philo and the Principles of the Jewish-Alexandrian Philosophy, 1879; Religion and Liberty, 1882; Spiritual Religion, 1870; Via, Veritas, Vita, 1894. And other works.

DRUMMOND (*William*), Hawthornden, in Scotland, poet, 1586-1649. Cypress Grove (*The*), 1613; Flowers of Sion, 1623; Forth Feasting (a panegyric on the king), 1617; Poems, Sonnets, Songs, etc., 1616; Polemo-Middinia, Carmen Macaronicum, 1684, posthumous; Tears on the Death of Meliades, 1613.

Prose: Conversations with Ben Jonson, 1619; History of Scotland, from 1423 to 1542, 1655, posthumous; Notes of Ben Jonson's Conversations, etc., 1619. His Life, by P. Cunningham, 1823; David Laing, 1842; W. B. Turnbull, 1857; Masson, 1873.

DRUMMOND (Sir *William*), died 1828. Academical Questions, 1805; Herculanensia, 1810 (with Walpole); Œdipus Judaicus, 1811; Œdipus Romanus (to prove that the 12 Cæsars are the 12 signs of the Zodiac), 1819; Origines (or the origin of certain

empires), 1828; Review of the Governments of Sparta and Athens, 1794.

DRURY (*Dru*), London, 1725-1804. Illustrations of Exotic Entomology, 1773-82 (of high repute); Illustrations of Natural History, 1770-73.

DRYDEN (*John*), born at Aldwinkle, in Northamptonshire, poet-laureate, 1631-1701.

Poetry not dramatic: Absalom and Achitophel, part i. 1681, part ii. 1682 (on Monmouth's rebellion; a political satire in verse); Alexander's Feast, 1697, a Pindaric ode; Annus Mirabilis (A.D. 1666), 1667, in verse; Astræa Redux (on the Restoration), 1660, in verse; Britannia Rediviva, 1689; Coronation of Charles II. (*On the*), 1661; Cromwell (*Death of*), 1658, an elegy; Eleonora, a Panegyric on the Late Countess of Abingdon, 1695; Fables, 1698-1700; Hind and the Panther (*The*), 1687, in defence of the Church of Rome, an allegory in verse (the "Hind" is the Church of Rome, and the "Panther" the Church of England); Lord Hastings (*An Elegy on*); MacFlecknoe, 1682, a satire on Shadwell, in verse; Medal (*The*), 1681, a satire against sedition; Ovid's *Epistles* translated, 1679; Religio Laici, 1682, a poem against deists and dissenters; Song of St. Cecilia, 1687, a choral ode; Tales from Chaucer, 1700; Threnonia Augustalis, a Funeral Pindarick on Charles II., 1685; Virgil translated, 1694-97.

Dramatic poetry (28 plays): Albian and Albanus, 1684; All for Love, or the World Well Lost, 1668, a tragedy; Amboyna, 1673; Amphitrion, 1690, a comedy; Arthur (*King*), 1691, an opera; Assignation (*The*), 1672, a comedy; Aurungzeba, or the Great Mogul, 1695; Cleomènes (4 *syl.*), 1692; Cymon and Iphigenia; Don Sebastian, 1690, a tragedy; Duke of Guise (*The*), 1682, a tragedy; Evening's Love (*An*), 1668; Indian Emperor (*The*), 1668, an heroic play; Indian Queen (*The*), 1664, an heroic play; Limhorham, 1679; Love Triumphant, 1694, a comedy; Marriage à-la-Mode, 1672, a comedy; Œdipus, 1679, a tragedy; Rival Ladies, 1663, a comedy; Royal Martyr (*The*), 1669, a tragedy; Secret Love, 1667, a comedy; Siege of Grenada (*The*), 1671, historic play; Sir Martin Marrall, 1667, a comedy; Spanish Fryar (*The*), 1680, a comedy; Tempest (*The*), 1668, a comedy; Troilus and Cressida, 1679, a tragedy; Tyrannic Love, 1669, a tragedy; Wild Gallant (*The*), 1663, a comedy.

Prose: Essay on Dramatic Poets (*An*), 1667; Essay on Heroic Plays (*An*), 1672; Letter to the Duke of Ormond, 1699. His Life, by S. Derrick, 1760; Malone, 1800; sir Walter Scott, 1808; Bell; R. Hooper Mitford, 1832; G. Saintsbury, 1881.

DUDLEY (Sir *Henry Bate*), 1743-1824. Flitch of Bacon, 1779, a musical farce; Rival Candidates, 1775, a musical interlude.

DUFF, D.D. (*Alexander*), Pitlochry, in Scotland, 1808-1878. India and Indian Missions, 1839; Indian Rebellion, its Causes and Results (*The*), 1858; Jesuits, their Origin, etc. (*The*), 1842; Missions the Chief End of the Christian Church, 1839; Missionary

Addresses, 1850; New Era of the English Language and Literature, 1837.

DUFF (*Mountstuart Elphinstone Grant*), 1829–   . East India Financial Statement, 1869; Elgin Speeches, 1871; Ernest Renan, 1893; Expedit Laboremus, 1872; Glance over Europe (*A*), 1867; Miscellanies, etc., 1879; Notes of an Indian Journey, 1870; Political Survey (*A*), 1868; Studies in European Politics, 1866.

DUFFERIN (*Frederick Temple Blackwood*, earl of), born in Florence, 1826–   . Honourable Impulsia Gushington (*The*), a satire on high life; Irish Emigration, 1867; Letters from High Latitudes, 1856; Narrative of a Journey from Oxford to Skibbereen, 1848; Speeches, 1882; Various Pamphlets on the Irish Land Question, 1870–78.

DUFFERIN (Marchioness of). ʊ My Canadian Journal, 1891; Our Vice-regal Life in India, 1889.

DUFFY (Sir *Charles Gavan*), Monaghan, Ireland, 1816–   . Ballad Poetry of Ireland, 1845 (ran through forty editions in ten years).

DUGDALE (Sir *William*), Shustoke, in Warwickshire, 1605-1686. Antient Usage in bearing . . . Arms, etc., 1682; Antiquities of Warwickshire, 1656 (Gough says, "It stands at the head of our county histories"); Baronage of England (*The*), 1675–76; History of imbanking and drayning divers Fenns, etc., 1662 (very scarce); History of St. Paul's Cathedral, 1658; Monasticon Anglicanum, 1655-73 (his great work); Origines Juridiciales, etc., 1666; Short View of the Late Troubles in England, 1681. His Life, by Hamper, 1827.

DU MAURIER (*George Louis Palmella Busson*), educated in Paris, but a British subject, 1834-1896. English Society, 1897; Martian (*The*), 1896–97, a novel; Peter Ibbetson, 1891; Trilby, 1894, a novel (extremely popular; dramatized). ("In Bohemia with Du Maurier," by Felix Moscheles, 1896.)

DUNBAR (*William*), Scotland, 1465-1529. Dance of the Seven Deadly Sins, 1505; Fliars of Berwick (*The*), 1512, a comic story; Golden Targe (*The*), 1508 (good); Justes between the Tailyour and Souter, Flyting (*The*), 1509; Manner of the Crying of ane Play, 1520; Thrissil and the Rose (*The*), (in 7-line stanzas), 1503 (James IV. was the *thistle*, and his bride Margaret the *rose*).

DUNCAN (*William*), Aberdeen, 1671-1770. Elements of Logic, 1748; Translation of *æsar*, 1752; Translation of Cicero's *Orations*, 1771.

DUNLOP (*John*), about 1778-1842. History of Fiction, 1814 ("an able and interesting work"); History of Roman Literature, 1823 –28; Memoirs of Spain during the Reigns of Philip IV. and Charles II., 1834.

DUNS SCOTUS, called "The Subtile Doctor," famous for his defence of the "immaculate conception," 1265-1308. Commentary on Aristotle; Commentary on the Bible; Contemplations of Divine Love, printed 1662; Opus Oxoniense; Works, in 12 vols., printed 1639. His Life, by John Colgan, 1655 (rare and valuable).

DUNSTER (Rev. *Charles*), died 1816. Considerations on Milton's Early Reading, and the Prima Stamina of his *Paradise Lost*, 1800.

DUNTON (*John*), Graffham, in Huntingdonshire, 1659-1733. Athenian Mercury, 1691– 97; Athenian Sport (2000 paradoxes), 1707; Bull Baiting, 1702 (the "bull" is Sacheverell); Cat may look on a Queen (*A*), 1701, a satire; Death-bed Charity, 1728; Life and Errors of John Dunton, 1705; Mordecai's Memorial, 1716; Neck or Nothing, 1713; Whipping Post, 1706, a satire upon everybody. His Life, by J. Nichols, 1818.

DUPPA (*Richard*), 1755-1831. Life, etc., of Michael Angelo, 1806; Life, etc., of Raffaelo, 1816.

D'URFEY (*Thomas*), Exeter, in Devonshire, 1630-1723. Archerie revived, 1676, an heroic poem; Ballads, 1716; Butler's Ghost, 1682 (forming a fourth part to *Hudibras*); Collection of New Ballads (*A*), 1715; Collin's Walk through London, etc., 1690, a burlesque poem; Dido and Æneas, 1727, a dramatic entertainment; Merry Musician (*The*), 1716; New Operas, 1721; Pills to purge Melancholy (sonnets), 1719–20 (his best-known work); Progress of Honesty, 1681, a Pindaric ode; Satires, Elegies, and Odes, 1690; Songs, 1687.

Dramatic works (he wrote 26 plays): Ariadne (4 *syl.*), 1721, a comedy; Banditti (*The*), or Lady in Distress, 1686; Bussy d'Ambois, 1691, a tragedy; Campaigners (*The*), 1698, a comedy; Commonwealth of Women (*The*), 1686, a tragi-comedy; Cynthia and Endymion, 1697, a dramatic opera; Dido and Ænēas, 1727, a dramatic entertainment, posthumous; Fond Husband (*The*), 1676, a comedy; Fool turned Critic (*The*), 1678, a comedy; Fool's Preferment (*The*), 1688, a comedy; Grecian Heroine (*The*), 1721, a comedy; Injured Princess (*The*), 1682, a tragi-comedy; Intrigues of Versailles (*The*), 1697, a farce; Massaniello, 1699, a tragedy; Modern Prophets, 1709, a comedy; Old Mode (*The*) and the New, 1709, a comedy; Plotting Sisters (*The*), 1676, a comedy; Richmond Heiress (*The*), 1693, a comedy; Royalist (*The*), 1682, a comedy; Siege of Memphis, 1876, a tragedy; Sir Barnaby Whigg, 1681, a comedy; Sq ire Oldsapp, 1679, a comedy; Trick for Trick, 1678, a comedy; Two Queens of Brentford, 1721, a comedy; Wonders in the Sun, 1706, a comic opera.

Prose works: Stories (moral and comical), 1691; Tales (tragical and comical), 1704.

DWIGHT, D.D. (*Timothy*), Massachusetts, U.S., 1752-1817. Conquest of Canaan, 1785, an epic poem; Sermons, 1828, posthumous; Theology explained and defended (173 sermons), 1819 (his principal work); Travels in New England and New York, 1821, posthumous (a valuable work).

DYCE (Rev. *Alexander*), 1798-1869. Recollections of . . . Samuel Rogers, 1858; Secret Translations of Quintus Smyrnæus, 1821; Specimen of the English Poetesses, 1823.

DYER (*George*), London, 1755-1841. History of the University and Colleges of Cambridge, 1814 ; Privileges of the University, 1824. He was joint editor of Valpy's *Classics*.

DYER (Rev. *John*), poet, 1700-1758. Fleece (*The*), (in four books), 1758 ; Grongar Hill, 1727 (his best) ; Ruins of Rome (*The*), 1740.

DYER, D.C.L. (*Thomas Henry*), London, historian, 1804—　Ancient Athens, 1873 ; History of Modern Europe, 1861 ; History of the City of Rome, 1865 ; History of the Kings of Rome, 1868 ; Life of Calvin, 1850 ; Pompeii, 1867.

DYER (*W. T.| Thiselton*), 1843-　. Joint author of *Flora of Middlesex*, 1869 ; edited English Edition of Sach's *Text-Book of Botany*, 1875 ; editor of *Flora Capensis*, vol. vi., 1896.

DYKES, D.D. (*James Oswald*), Port Glasgow, 1835-　. Beatitudes of the Kingdom, 1872 ; Gospel according to St. Paul (*The*), 1888 ; Law of the Ten Words (*The*), 1884 ; Laws of the Kingdom, 1873 ; Plain Words on Great Themes, 1892 ; Problems of Faith, 1875 ; Relations of the Kingdom, 1874 ; Sermons, 1882 ; Written Word (*The*), 1868.

DYMOND (*Jonathan*), Exeter, 1796-1838. Essay on the Principles of Morality, 1829.

EADIE, LL.D. (*John*), Alloa, in Clackmannan, Scotland, 1810-1876. Classified Bible (*The*), 1861 ; Commentary of the Greek Text of Philippians 1859, Galatians 1869, Thessalonians 1877 ; History of the English Bible, 1876 ; Paul the Preacher, 1859.

EADMER OF CANTERBURY, a Benedictine monk, twelfth century. Historia Novorum (History of his own Times), printed 1623 ; Vita Anselmi, printed 1551.
　·.· His Lives of SS. Bregwyn, Dunstan, Odo, Oswald, and Wilfrid, are in the *Anglia Sacra* of Wharton, 1691.

EARLE, D.D. (*John*), York, 1601-1665. Microcosmography, 1628. He translated the *Ikon Basilikè* into Latin, 1649.

EARLE, M.A., LL.D. (Rev. *John*), 1824-　. Anglo-Saxon Literature, 1884 ; Bath, Ancient and Modern, 1864 ; Book for the Beginner in Anglo-Saxon (*A*), 1877 ; Deeds of Beowulf (*The*), 1892 ; English Plant-Names from the Tenth to the Fifteenth Century, 1880 ; English Prose, 1890 ; Philology of the English Tongue (*The*), 1871 ; Psalter of 1539 (*The*), 1894. And other works.

EASTLAKE, R.A. (Sir *Charles Lock*), Plymouth, 1793-1865. Materials for a History of Oil Painting, 1847. He also translated Goethe's *Farbenlehre*, or Theory of Colours, 1847 ; and Kugler's *Handbook of Painting*, 1843.

EASTLAKE (*Charles Locke*). Hints on Household Taste, 1868 ; History of the Gothic Revival in England, 1871 ; Pictures at the National Gallery, 1896 ; Square and Circle, 1895.

EASTLAKE (Lady *Elizabeth*), 1816-1892. Five Great Painters, 1883 ; Life of John Gibson, 1870 ; Mrs. Grote, 1880 ; Music, and the Art of Dress, 1852. Lady Eastlake completed Mrs. Jamieson's *History of Our Lord in Works of Art*, 1863.

ECHARD, F.S.A. (*Lawrence*), Suffolk, 1671-1730. General Ecclesiastical History, 1702 (Prideaux says, " It is the best of its kind ") ; History of England, 1707-18 ; Roman History, 1713.

EDEN (Hon. *Emily*), 1795-1869. People and Princes of India, 1844 ; Semi-detached House (*The*), 1859 ; Up the Country, 1866.

EDEN (Sir *Frederick Morton*), 1766-1809. State of the Poor (a History of the Labouring Classes from 1066 to the present time), 1797 (a storehouse of useful information).

EDGEWORTH (*Maria*), Hare-hatch, in Berkshire, 1767-1849. Belinda, 1803, a novel ; Castle Rackrent, 1801 (her first novel) ; Comic Drama, 1815 ; Dun (*The*), 1808 ; Early Lessons, 1810 ; Essays on Practical Education, 1798 (her first work) ; Eunice (3 *syl.*) ; Harrington and Ormond, 1817, a novel ; Harry and Lucy, 1823 ; Helen, 1834 (her best novel) ; Irish Bulls (*An Essay on*), 1802 (in conjunction with her father) ; Leonora, 1806, a novel ; Memoir of her Father, 1820 ; Moral Tales, 1856, posthumous ; Ormond, 1817 ; Parents' Assistant (*The*), 1823 ; Patronage, 1814 ; Popular Tales, 1804 ; Practical Education, 1798 (with her father) ; Rosamond, 1823 ; Self-justification, 1807 ; Tales and Novels, 1812 ; Tales of Fashionable Life, 1809, 1812 (the best are *Ennui* and *The Absentee*) ; Thoughts on Bores. Her Memoirs, by Mrs. Edgeworth, 1867. Coll. edition of her novels and tales published in 18 vols., 1832.

EDWARDES (Sir *Herbert*), of Shropshire, 1809-1868. Year on the Punjaub Frontier (*A*), 1850. His Memoirs, by Lady Edwardes, 1888.

EDWARDES (Mrs. *Annie*), novelist,*-*. Adventuress (*The*) ; Archie Lovell, 1866 ; Ball-Room Repentance (*A*), 1882 ; Blue Stocking (*The*), 1877 ; Creeds, 1859 ; Girton Girl (*A*), 1885 ; Jet, 1878 ; Leah, 1875 ; May Fair, 1858 ; Miss Forrester, 1865 ; Ordeal for Wives, 1864 ; Ought we to visit her? 1871 ; Playwright's Daughter (*The*), 1886 ; Point of Honour (*A*), 1863 ; Steven Laurence, 1868 ; Susan Fielding, 1869 ; Vagabond *Heroine* (*A*), 1873 ; Vivian the Beauty, 1879 ; World's Verdict (*The*), 1861.

EDWARDS (*Amelia Blandford*), novelist, 1831-1892. Ballads, 1865 ; Barbara's History 1864 ; Debenham's Vow, 1870 ; Half a Million of Money, 1865 ; Hand and Glove, 1859 In the Days of my Youth, 1872 ; Ladder of Life (*The*), 1856 ; Lord Brackenbury, 1880 ; Miss Carew, 1865 (short tales) ; Mons. Maurice, 1873 ; My Brother's Wife, 1855 ; Young Marquis (*The*), 1857.
　Not works of Fiction : History of France, 1858 ; Pharaohs, Fellahs, and Explorers, 1891 ; Story of Cervantes, 1862 ; Summary of English History (*A*), 1856 ; Thousand Miles up the Nile (*A*), 1877 ; Untrodden Peaks, etc., 1873.

EDWARDS (*Bryan*), Wiltshire, 1743-1800. Historical Survey of St. Domingo, 1797 ; History of the British Colonies in the West Indies, 1793 (in good repute).

EDWARDS (*Edward*), London, 1812- .
Economy of the Fine Arts in England, 1840 ;
Life of Sir Walter Raleigh, 1868.
EDWARDS (*Eliezer*). Words, Facts, and
Phrases, 1882.
EDWARDS, F.R.S. (*George*), Essex, 1693-1773.
Gleanings of Natural History, 1758-64 ; His-
tory of Uncommon Birds, 1743-51. His
Memoirs, by J. S. Miller, 1776.
EDWARDS (*Henry Sutherland*), 1828- .
Germans in France (*The*), 1874 ; Life of
Bossini, 1869 ; Lyrical Drama, 1881 ; Mal-
vina, 1871, a novel ; Russians at Home (*The*),
1861.
EDWARDS, D.D. (*Jonathan*), Windsor, in Con-
necticut, U.S.,1703-1758. Doctrine of Original
Sin, 1758 ; Inquiry into the Freedom of the
Will, 1754 (his best-known work) ; Redemp-
tion, 1788 ; Treatise concerning Religious
Affections, 1740 ; Works, including Sermons
and Life (in 10 vols.), 1830.
EDWARDS (*Matilda Barbara Betham*), Wes-
terfield, in Suffolk, 1836- . Dr. Jacob,
1864, a novel ; Kitty, 1869, a novel ; White
House by the Sea (*The*), 1857 ; Winter with
the Swallows (*A*), 1866 ; Year in Western
France (*A*), 1877.
EDWARDS, or EDWARDES (*Richard*), Somer-
setshire, 1523-1566. Damon and Pythias,
1566, a comedy ; Palamon and Arcite, 1560,
a comedy in two parts ; Paradise of Daintie
Devices (which Shakespeare quotes from),
1563.
EDWARDS (*Sydenham*), about 1770-1850.
Botanical Register, 1815-47 (continued by Dr.
Lindley) ; Cynographia Britannica (*i.e.* Bri-
tish Dogs), 1800 ; Rare Plants, 1809.
EDWARDS (*Thomas*), 1591-1647 (Milton calls
him "Shallow Edwards "). Gangræna (*i.e.*
Church Heresies), 1646.
EGAN (*Pierce*), Ireland, 1772-1849. Anecdotes
of the Turf, etc., 1827 ; Book of Sports and
Mirror of Life, 1832 ; Life in London (Tom and
Jerry), about 1824, a continuation, called
"Tom, Jerry, and Logic," appeared subse-
quently) ; Life of an Actor, 1825 ; Panorama
of the Sporting World, 1827 ; Pilgrims of the
Rhine, 1828 ; Pilgrims of the Thames, 1838 ;
Rambles through London, 1821-22 ; Show
Folks (*The*), 1831 ; Trial of J. Thurtell, etc.,
1824 ; Walks in Bath, 1834.
EGAN (*Pierce*), London, novelist, son of the
above, 1814-1880. Adam Bell, 1842 ; Black
Prince (*The*) ; Clifton Grey ; Flower of the
Flock (*The*), 1865 ; My Lady Maude, 1881 ;
Paul Jones, 1842 ; Poor Girl (*The*), 1880 ;
Quintin Matsys, 1839 ; Robin Hood and
Little John, 1840 ; Wat Tyler, 1841 ; Waits,
1883.
EGERTON (*George*), Mrs. *Egerton Clairmonte*.
Discords, 1894 ; Key-notes, 1893 ; Young
Ofeg's Ditties, 1895 ; Symphonies, 1897.
ELIOT (*George*), a name assumed by *Marian
Evans*, subsequently Mrs. *J. W. Cross*,
novelist, 1819-1880. Adam Bede, 1859 (her
best novel) ; Agatha, 1869, a poem (in the
Atlantic Monthly) ; Daniel Deronda, 1876 ;
Essays and Leaves from a note-Book,
1884 ; Felix Holt, the Radical, 1866 ; Impres-
sions of Theophrastus Such, 1879 ; Legend
of Jubal, and other Poems, 1874 ; Lifted Veil

(*The*), and Brother Jacob, 1860 (in *Blackwood's Magazine*) ; Middlemarch, 1871-72 ;
Mill on the Floss (*The*), 1860 ; Romola,
1863 (originally published in *Cornhill*, July,
1862, to August, 1863) ; Scenes of Clerical
Life, 1856, 1857 ; Silas Marner, the Weaver
of Raveloe, 1861 ; Spanish Gypsy (*The*),
1868, a poem.
Translations : Essence of Christianity, by
Feuerbach, 1854 ; *Life of Jesus*, by Strauss,
1846. Her Life, by J.W. Cross. Wise, Witty,
and Tender Sayings of G. Eliot, 1874.
ELLESMERE (*Francis Leveson Gower*, earl of),
London, 1800-1857. Life and Character of
the Duke of Wellington, 1852 ; Mediterranean Sketches, 1843 ; History of Liberty,
1849-53.
ELLICOTT, D.D. (*Charles John*), bishop of
Gloucester and Bristol, born at Whitwell,
near Stamford, 1819- . Being of God
(*The*), 1880 ; Comfort of the Scripture, 1862 ;
Commentaries on the Pauline Epistles, 1854,
1855, 1856, 1858 ; Destiny of the Creature,
1862 ; Fundamental Doctrine, 1885 ; History
and Obligation of the Sabbath, 1844 a prize
essay ; Life of our Lord Jesus Christ, 1860,
a Hulsean lecture ; Modern Vorbeliet, 1877 ;
New Testament Commentary, edited 1877-79;
Old Testament Commentary (*An*), edited
1882-84 ; Present Dangers of the Church,
1878 ; Sermons preached at St. Mary's,
Cambridge, 1858 ; Spiritual Needs, 1888 ;
Treatise on Analytical Statics, 1851 ; What
is the Real Distinction between England and
Rome ? 1876.
ELLIOT (*George*), born 1784. Life of the Duke
of Wellington, 1815.
ELLIOTSON, M.D. (*John*), London, 1788-1868.
Human Physiology, 1835-40 ; Lumleyan
Lectures, 1830 ; Zoist, 1843-54.
    ∴ Translated Blumenbach's *Physiology*,
1817.
ELLIOTT (Rev. *Charles*), Donegal, Ireland,
1792-1869. History of the Great Secession
from the Methodist Episcopal Church, 1855 ;
Treatise on Baptism, 1834.
ELLIOTT (*Ebenezer*), Masborough, in York-
shire, the "corn-law rhymer," 1781-1849.
Corn-Law Rhymes, 1831-46 ; Love, 1823 ;
More Prose and Verse, 1850, posthumous ;
Ranter (*The*), 1828 ; Vernal Walk (*The*),
1798 (his first poem) ; Village Patriarch (*The*),
1829 ; Works compiled, 1876. His Life, by
Searle, 1852.
ELLIOTT (Rev. *Edward Bishop*), 1795-
Warburtonian Lectures (*The*), 1849-52.
ELLIS, F.R.S. (*Alexander John*), born *Sharpe*,
at Hoxton, in Middlesex, 1814-1890. Alpha-
bet of Nature, 1845 ; Basis of Music, 1877 ;
Early Pronunciation, 1869, 1871, 1875, etc. ;
Essentials of Phonetics, 1848 ; History of
Musical Pitch, 1880 ; Logic for Children,
1882 ; On the Musical Pitch, 1877 ; On the
Pronunciation of Greek, 1877 ; Original
Nursery Rhymes, 1864 ; Practical Hints on
the Quantitative Pronunciation of Latin,
1875 ; Pronunciation for Singers, 1877 ; Re-
port on Dialect Work, 1885-87 ; Speech in
Song, 1878 ; Universal Writing and Printing,
1856.
ELLIS (*George*), 1745-1815. Poetical Tales and

Trifles, by sir Gregory Gander, 1778 ; Specimens of Early English Poetry, 1790; Specimens of Ancient English Romances, 1805.

ELLIS (*George James Welbore Agar*), lord Dover, 1797–1833. See DOVER.

ELLIS (*Henry*), Arctic voyager, 1721–1806. Voyage to Hudson's Bay, etc. (*A*), 1748 (a valuable work).

ELLIS, F.S.A. (Sir *Henry*), London, 1777–1869. Introduction to Domesday Book, 1816 ; Letters Illustrative of English History, 1824, 1827, 1846.
  ∴ An edition of Brand's *Popular Antiquities*, 1813 ; and of Dugdale's *Monasticon*, 1817–30.

ELLIS (*John*), London, 1710–1776. Description of the Mangostan and Bread Fruit, 1775 ; Essay towards a Natural History of Corallines, 1755 ; Historical Account of Coffee, 1774 ; Natural History of Uncommon Zoophytes, 1786, posthumous.

ELLIS (Rev. *William*), London, 1789–1872. History of Madagascar (*A*), 1839 ; Madagascar revisited, etc., 1867 ; Martyr Church of Madagascar (*The*), 1870 ; Narrative of a Tour through Owhyhee, 1826 ; Polynesian Researches, 1829 ; Three Visits to Madagascar, 1853–56 ; Vindication of the South Sea Missions, 1831.

ELLIS (Mrs. *William*), maiden name *Sarah Stickney*, wife of the Rev. William Ellis, 1812–1872. Brewer's Family (*The*), 1863 ; Daughters of England, 1842 ; Education of Character, 1856 ; Hearts and Homes, 1848–49 ; Hints on Formation of Character, 1848 ; Janet, 1862 ; Mothers of Great Men (*The*), 1859 ; Mother's Mistake, 1856 ; Pictures of Private Life, 1845 ; Prevention Better than Cure, 1847 ; Social Distinction, 1854 ; Summer and Winter in the Pyrenees (*A*), 1841 ; Value of Health, 1854 ; Widow Green, 1859 ; Wives of England, 1843 ; Women of England, 1838.

ELLISTON (*Robert William*), London, 1774–1831. Venetian Outlaw (*The*), 1805.

ELLWOOD (*Thomas*), Crowell, in Oxfordshire, 1639–1713. Autobiography, 1714, posthumous ; Davideis, or Life of David, 1712, a poem (Cowley wrote a poem so called); Foundation of Tithes shaken (*The*), 1682 ; Sacred History, 1705–9.
  ∴ He suggested to Milton the subject of *Paradise Regained*, in 1665.

ELPHINSTONE (Hon. *Mountstuart*), 1778–1859. Account of the Kingdom of Cabul (*An*), 1815 ; History of India, 1841.

ELPHINSTONE (*William*), bishop of Aberdeen, 1430–1514. Breviarium Aberdonense, printed 1509–10.

ELYOT (Sir *Thomas*), 1495–1546. Bantrette of Sapience (*The*), 1542 ; Boke named "The Governor" (*The*), 1531 ; Castell of Helthe (*The*), 1533 ; Defence of Good Women, 1545 ; Dictionarium, 1538 ; Pasquil the Playne, 1533 ; Preservation agaynste Deth, 1545.

EMERSON, LL.D. (*Ralph Waldo*), the "Sage of Concord," Boston, U.S., 1803–1882. Conduct of Life (*The*), 1860 ; Emancipation of the Negroes (*The*), 1844 ; English Traits, 1856 ; Essays, 1844, 1847, 1871 ; Fortune of the Republic, 1878 ; Lectures on the Times,

1841 ; Letters and Social Aims, 1876 ; Literary Ethics, 1838 ; Man the Reformer, 1844 ; Margaret Fuller, 1852 ; May-day, and other Pieces, 1867 ; Method of Nature (*The*), 1841 ; Miscellanies, 1849 ; Nature, 1844 ; Nature and Man thinking, 1844 ; Orations, Lectures, etc., 1844–66; Parnassus, 1875 ; Poems, 1847–81 ; Poetry and Criticism, 1874 ; Representative Men, 1850 ; Society and Solitude, 1870 ; Young American (*The*), 1844.

ENFIELD, LL.D. (*William*), Suffolk, 1741–1797. History of Philosophy, 1791 ; Sermons, 1768–70, 1777, 1798 ; Speaker (*The*), 1775, a selection of pieces for school recitations, etc. (once largely used in schools).

ENT (Sir *George*), 1604–1689. On the Circulation of the Blood (in Latin), 1641. Harvey wrote his treatise in 1628.

ERSKINE (*John*), 1695–1765. Institute of the Law of Scotland, 1773, posthumous ; Principles of the Law of Scotland, 1754.

ERSKINE, D.D. (*John*), Scotland, 1721–1803. Sketches, etc., of Church History and Theological Controversy, 1790–97. His Life, by sir H. M. Wellwood, 1818.

ESPY (*James P.*), Western Pennsylvania, U.S., 1786–1860 ; Philosophy of Storms, 1841.

ETHEREGE (Sir *George*), Oxfordshire, wit and dramatist, 1636–1694. Comical Revenge (*The*), or Love in a Tub, 1664, a comedy ; Man of Mode (*The*), or Sir Fopling Flutter, 1676, a comedy ; She would if she could, 1668, a comedy ; Trial of the Poets for the Bays (*The*).

EVANS (*David Morier*), 1819–1874. City Men and City Manners, 1853 ; Commercial Crisis, 1847–48 ; Facts, Failures, and Frauds, 1859.

EVANS, D.C.L. (*John*), 1823– . Ancient British Coins, 1864 ; Ancient Bronze Implements, 1881 ; Implements of the Drift, 1868.

EVANS (*Marian*), Mrs. *J. W. Cross*. See under GEORGE ELIOT, 1820–1880.

EVANSON (Rev. *Edward*), Warrington, in Lancashire, 1731–1805. Dissonance of the Four Evangelists, etc., 1792.

EVELYN (*John*), Wotton, in Surrey, 1620–1706. Acetaria, a Discourse of Sallets, 1699 ; Diary and Correspondence, 1818 and 1857, posthumous (highly appreciated) ; French Gardener (*The*), 1658 ; Fumifugium, 1661 ; Gardener's Almanac (*The*), 1664 ; Kalendarium Hortense, 1664 ; Memoirs, 1818, posthumous (sir W. Scott says he "never saw so rich a mine"); Mundus Muliebris, 1690 ; Navigation and Commerce, 1674 ; Numismata, 1697 ; Parallel of Ancient and Modern Architecture, 1669 ; Sculptura (or engraving on copper), 1662 ; Sylva (Forest Trees), 1664 (his chief work) ; Terra, 1675 ; Tyrannus, or the Mode, 1662. His Memoir, by W. Bray, 1818.

EWBANK (*Thomas*), Barnard Castle, in Durham, 1792–1870. Life in Brazil, 1858 ; World a Workshop (*The*), 1855.

EWING (*Juliana Horatia Orr*), 1841–1885. (Most of her stories appeared in *Aunt Judy*.) Baby Puppy, 1885 ; Bluebells on the Lea (*The*), 1884 ; Brothers of Pity, 1882 ; Brownies (*The*), and other Tales, 1870 ; Convalescence, 1885 ; Daddy Darwin's Dovecot, 1884 ; Dandelion Clocks, 1887 ; Doll's

Housekeeping, 1884; Flat-Iron for a Farthing (*A*), 1872; Grandmother's Spring, 1885; Great Emergency (*A*), and other Tales, 1877; Jackanapes, 1883 (34,000 copies sold in one year); Jan of the Windmill, 1876; Little Boys and Wooden Horses, 1884; Lob-lie-by-the-fire, 1873; Mary's Meadow, 1856; Melchior's Dream, 1862; Mill Stream (*The*), 1885; Mother's Birthday Review, 1885; Mrs. Overtheway's Remembrances, 1868; Old-fashioned Fairytales, 1882; Papa Poodle, 1884; Peace Egg, 1887; Poems of Child Life and Country Life, 1885; Poet and Brook, 1885; Red and Blue, 1883; Six to Sixteen, 1875; Story of a Short Life (*The*), 1885; Sweet Little Dear (*A*), 1883; Tongues in Trees, 1884; Touch him if you dare, 1884; We and the World, 1873; Week spent in a Glass Pond by the Great Water-Beetle (*A*), 1882.

EXELL (Rev. *J. S.*). Editor of Pulpit Commentary, 50 vols., 1880–97 (a masterly work); Biblical Illustrator, 1890–   .

EYRE (*Vincent*), 1810–1881. Metallic Boats and Floating Waggons, etc., 1856; Military Operations in Cabul, 1843; Observations on American Life-preserving Cars, 1856.

FABER (Rev. Dr. *Frederick William*), Durham, poet, 1814–1863. All for Jesus, 1855; Cherwell Water-lily, etc., 1840; Essay on Beatification, 1848; Ethel's Book, 1858; Fathers of the Oratory, 1849; Foot of the Cross (*The*), 1858; Jesus and Mary, 1848; Oratory of St. Philip Vere, 1850; Rosary, 1845; Sir Lancelot, 1844; Styrian Lake, 1842; Thoughts on Great Mysteries, 1883.

FABER (Rev. *George Stanley*), 1773–1854. Cabiri (*The*), or Gods of Phenicia, 1803; Difficulties of Infidelity (*The*), 1824; Eight Dissertations upon the Prophetic Promises of a Mighty Deliverer, 1845; Genius and Object of the Patriarchal, Levitical, and Christian Dispensations, 1823; Horæ Mosaicæ, published in a complete form in 1818 (his chief work); Origin of Pagan Idolatry, 1816; Primitive Doctrine of Election (*The*), 1836; Primitive Doctrine of Justification, 1837; Primitive Doctrine of Regeneration, 1840; Sacred Calendar of Prophecy, 1828.

FABYAN (*Robert*), historian, 1450–1512. Chronicle, printed by R. Pynson, 1516; Concordance of Historyes (*The*), printed 1533.

FAIRBAIRN, D.D (*Andrew Martin*), Edinburgh, 1838–   . Christ in the Centuries, 1893; City of God (*The*), 1883; New Sacerdotalism (*The*), 1886; Place of Christ in Modern Theology, 1893; Religion in History and in the Life of To-day, 1884, revised 1893; Studies in the Life of Christ, 1880; Studies in the Philosophy of Religion and History, 1876.

FAIRFAX (*Edward*), Yorkshire, died 1632. Demonology (in which he was a firm believer); Eclogues; Tasso's *Jerusalem Delivered* translated into English verse, 1600.

FAIRHOLT (*Frederick William*), London, 1814–1866. Antiquities of Richborough,

1850; Dictionary of Terms of Art, 1854; England under the House of Hanover, 1848; History of Costume in England, 1846; Home of Shakespeare (*The*), 1847; Up the Nile, 1861.

FAITHORNE (*William*), London, 1616–1691. Art of Graving and Etching, etc., 1662.

FALCONER, F.R.S. (*Hugh*), Forres, in Scotland, 1808–1865. Fauna Antiqua Sivalensis, 1846; Palæontological Memoirs, 1868.

FALCONER (*William*), Edinburgh, poet, 1732–1769. Demagogue (*The*), 1765; Marine Dictionary (*The*), 1769; Shipwreck (*The*), (in three cantos), 1762. His Life, by Rev. J. S. Clarke, 1804; Rev. J. Mitford, 1836.

FALCONER, M.D. (*William*), Chester, 1741–1824. Dissertation on the Influence of the Passions on the Disorders of the Body, 1788; Remarks on the Influence of Climate, etc., 1781.

FALKLAND (*Henry Cary*). Marriage Night (*The*), 1664, a tragedy.

FANSHAW (Sir *Richard*), Ware, in Hertfordshire, 1608–1666. Translated the *Lusiad* of Camoëns, 1655; the *Pastor Fido* of Guarini; the Fourth Book of the *Æneid;* the *Odes* of Horace; etc.

FARADAY, D.C.L. (*Michael*), born at Stoke Newington, 1791–1867. Chemical History of a Candle, 1861; Chemical Manipulation, 1827; Experimental Researches in Electricity, 1839, 1844, 1855 (his chief work); Experimental Researches in Chemistry and Physics, 1859; Also Lectures on "Nonmetallic Elements," 1858, and on "Physical Forces, and their Relations to each other." His Life, by Tyndall, 1870.

FAREY (*John*), London, 1791–1851. Treatise on the Steam Engine, 1827; View of the Agriculture and Minerals of Derbyshire, 1811.

FARJEON (*Benjamin Leopold*), London, novelist, 1833–   Aaron the Jew, 1894; At the Sign of the Silver Flagon, 1876; Basil and Annette, 1890; Blood-white Rose (*The*), 1889; Christmas Angel, 1885; Christmas Stories (Blade o' Grass, Golden Grain, Bread and Cheese and Kisses), 1874; Devlin the Barber, 1888; Dr. Glennie's Daughter, 1889; Duchess of Rosemary Lane (*The*), 1876; For the Defence, 1891; Golden Land, 1886; Great Porter Square, 1884; Grif, 1870; House of White Shadows, 1884; In a Silver Sea, 1886; Jessie Trim, 1874; Joshua Marvel, 1871; Last Tenant, (*The*), 1893; London's Heart, 1873; Love's Victory, 1875; March of Fate (*The*), 1892; Miser Fairbrother, 1888; Molka Christmas Angels, 1886; Mystery of M. Felix, 1890; Nine of Hearts (*The*), 1886; Peril of Richard Pardon (*The*), 1890; Sacred Nugget (*The*), 1885; Secret Inheritance (*The*), 1887; Self-doomed, 1885; Solomon Isaacs, 1877; Something occurred, 1893; Strange Enchantment (*A*), 1889; Three Times tried, 1886; Toilers of Babylon (*The*), 1888; Tragedy of Featherstone, 1886; Young Girl's Life (*A*), 1889.

FARMER (Rev. *Hugh*), near Shrewsbury, 1714–1787. Dissertation on Miracles, 1771; Essay on the Demoniacs of the New Testament, 1774; Inquiry into the Nature and

Origin of our Lord's Temptation, etc., 1761; Prevalence of the Worship of Human Spirits in Ancient Heathen Nations, 1783. His Life, by Michael Dodson, 1805.

FARMER, D.D. (*Richard*), Leicester, 1735-1797. Essay on the Learning of Shakespeare, 1766.

FARNABY (*Thomas*), London, philologist, 1575-1647. Florilegium Epigrammatum Græcorum, etc., 1629; Index Rhetoricus Scholis Accommodatus, 1625; Systema Grammaticum, 1641.

FARNELL (*Lewis Richard*). Cults of the Greek States, 1896.

FARQUHAR (*George*), London, 1678-1707. Beaux's Stratagem (*The*), 1707 (his best comedy); Constant Couple (*The*), 1700, a comedy; Inconstant (*The*), 1703, a comedy; Love and a Bottle, 1698, a comedy; Recruiting Officer (*The*), 1706, a comedy; Sir Harry Wilder, 1701, a comedy; Stage Coach (*The*), 1704, a comedy.

FARRAR, D.D. (*Frederic William*), Bombay, 1831- . Between the Living and the Dead, 1878; Chapters on Language, 1865; Darkness and Dawn, 1891; Defects in Public School Education, 1867; Early Days of Christianity, 1882; Ephphatha, 1880; Eric, or Little by Little, 1858, a tale of Roslyn School; Eternal Hope, 1878; Every-Day Christian Life, 1887; Fall of Man (*The*), and other Sermons, 1868; Families of Speech, 1869; Gathering Clouds (the new edition), 1896, a tale of the days of St. Chrysostom; Individual Responsibility, 1885; In the Days of thy Youth, 1876; Julian Home, 1859; Language and Languages, 1878; Lecture on Public School Education (*A*), 1867; Life of Christ (*The*), 1874 (his chief work); Life and Work of St. Paul (*The*), 1879; Lives of the Fathers (*The*), 1889; Lyrics of Life, 1859; Mercy and Judgment, 1881; Message of the Books (*The*), 1884; Minor Prophets (*The*), 1890; Music in Religion and in Life, 1882; My Object in Life, 1883; Origin of Language (*The*), 1860; Passion-Play of Ober-Ammergau (*The*), 1890; People of England (*The*), 1857; St. Winifred's, or the World of School, 1865; Saintly Workers, 1876; Seekers after God, 1868; Silence and Voices of God (*The*), 1873; Social and Present-day Questions, 1891; Truths to Live by, 1890; Voices from Sinai (*The*), 1892; Wider Hope (*The*), 1890; Witness of History (*The*), 1870; With the Poets 1883.

FAULKNER (*Thomas*), 1776-1855. Historica and Topographical Description of Brentford, Ealing, and Chiswick, 1845; Chelsea and its Environs, 1810; Fulham, 1813; Hammersmith, 1839; Kensington, 1820.

FAWCETT (*Henry*), Salisbury, 1833-1884. Economic Position of the British Labourer (*The*), 1865; Free Trade and Protection, 1878; Manual of Political Economy (*A*), 1863 (his chief work); Mr. Hare's Reform explained, 1860; Pauperism, its Causes and Remedies, 1871.

FAWCETT (Mrs.), wife of the above, maiden name *Millicent Garrett*, 1847- . Essays, 1872; Janet Doncaster, 1875; Life of Queen

Victoria, 1894; Political Economy for Beginners, 1870; Some Eminent Women of our Time, 1889; Tales in Political Economy, 1874.

FAWKES (*Francis*), Yorkshire, poet, 1721-1777; Bramham Park, a Poem, 1758; Poems, 1761; Poetic Calendar, 1763; Translations of Anacreon, Bion, Moschus, and Sappho, 1760; Translation of Theocritus, 1767.

FAY (*Theodore Sedgwick*), New York, U.S., novelist, 1807- . Countess Ida (*The*), 1840; Dreams, etc., of a Quiet Man, 1832; Great Outlines of Geography, 1867; History of Switzerland, 1860; Hoboken, 1843, a romance of New York; Minute Book (*The*), 1835; Norman Leslie, 1835; Robert Rueful, 1844; Sidney Clifton, 1839; Ulrick, or the Voices, 1815, a tale.

FELLOWES, LL.D. (*Robert*), 1770-1847. Anti-Calvinist (*The*), 1800; Body of Theology (*A*), 1807; Christian Philosophy, 1798; Guide to Immortality (*A*), 1804; Manual of Piety (*A*), 1807; Picture of Christian Philosophy (*A*), 1798; Poems, 1806; Religion of the Universe (*The*), 1836; Religion without Cant, 1801.

FELLOWS (Sir *Charles*), Nottingham, 1799-1860. Account of the Ionic Trophy Monument, 1848; Coins of Ancient Lycia, etc., 1855; Journal during an Excursion in Asia Minor, 1839; Journal of a Second Excursion, 1841; Xanthian Marbles (*The*), etc., 1843.

FENN (*George Manville*), Pimlico, novelist, 1831- . Black Bar (*The*), 1893; Bent, not Broken, 1866; Book of Fair Women (*A*), 1873; By Birth a Lady, 1871; Cabby, 1864; Commodore Junk, 1888; Dick o' the Fens, 1887; Double Cunning, 1886; Featherland, 1865; Fire Island, 1894; Hollowdell Grange, 1866; Lady Maud's Mania, 1890; Lass that loved a Sailor (*The*), 1889; Little World (*A*), 1877; Mad, 1868; Midnight Webs, 1872; New Mistress (*The*), 1893; Off to the Wilds, 1881; Ocean Waif, 1874; Parson o' Dumford, 1879; Poverty Corner, 1882; Pretty Polly, 1878; Queen's Scarlet (*The*), 1895; Sapphire Cross (*The*), 1871; Story of Antony Grace (*The*), 1887; Sweet Mace, 1885; Thereby hangs a Tale, 1876; White Virgin (*The*), 1895; Witness to the Deed, 1893; Woman worth Winning (*A*), 1898. He wrote a great many more novels, and boys' stories.

FENN (Sir *John*), Norwich, 1739-1794. Three Chronological Tables, 1784. He edited the *Paston Letters*, 1787.

FENTON (*Elijah*), 1683-1730. Life of Milton, 1727; Mariamne, 1723, a tragedy; Poems, 1707-1717. He also contributed books i., iv., xix., xx., to Pope's *Odyssey*.

FENTON (Sir *Geoffrey*), died 1608. History of the Wars of Italy, by Guicciardini, 1570; Monophylo (a philosophical treatise about love), 1572.

FERGUSON, LL.D. (*Adam*), Logierait, in Scotland, 1724-1816. Essay on the History of Civil Society, 1767; History of the Progress and End of the Roman Republic, 1783 (his chief work); Institutes of Moral Philosophy, 1770; Principles of Moral and Political Science, 1792.

FERGUSON (*James*), Keith, in Scotland, 1710–1776. Art of Drawing in Perspective, etc., 1775; Astronomy explained, etc., 1756; Astronomical Tables, 1763; Introduction to Astronomy, 1769; Introduction to Electricity, 1770; Lectures on . . . Mechanics, Hydrostatics, etc., 1760.

FERGUSON (*James*), Ayr, Scotland, 1808–1885. Handbook of Architecture, 1855; History of Ancient and Modern Architecture (*A*), 1865; Illustrations of the Rock-cut Temples of India, 1845; Palaces of Nineveh and Persepolis restored, 1851; Rude Stone Monuments, 1872.

FERGUSON (*Robert*), Edinburgh, 1750–1774. Poems, 1774, posthumous; Scripture Metaphors, 1675. His Life, by D. Irving, 1799; A. Peterkin, 1807–9.

FERGUSON (Sir *Samuel*), Belfast, 1810–1886. Congal (a poem in five books), 1872; Cromlech in Howth (*The*), 1864; Father Tom and the Pope, 1868; Forging of the Anchor (*The*), 1883; Hibernian Nights, 1887, a series of tales; Lays of the Western Gael, 1864; Leabhar Breac, 1876; Ogham's Inscriptions in Ireland, Wales, and Scotland, 1887; Poems, 1880; Shakesperian Breviates, 1882; Widow's Cloak (*The*), 1884.

FERNE (*Henry*), bishop of Chester, born at York, 1602–1662. Episcopacy and Presbytery, 1647; Resolving of Conscience, 1642.

FERRIER, LL.D. (*James Frederick*), Edinburgh, 1808–1864. Institutes of Metaphysics, 1854; Lectures on Greek Philosophy, 1866; Theory of Knowing and Being (*The*), 1854.

FERRIER (*Susan Edmonston*), Edinburgh, novelist, 1782–1854. Destiny, or the Chief's Daughter, 1831; Inheritance (*The*), 1824; Marriage, 1818; Works, 1841.

FIELD (Rev. *John*), Wallingford, in Berkshire, 1813–1884. Convict Discipline, 1855; Correspondence of John Howard, 1856; Life of John Howard, 1850; Prison Discipline, 1848; Remarks on the Lord's Prayer, 1857; University and other Sermons, 1853.

FIELD (*Michael*), the name assumed by Miss *Bradley* and Miss *Cooper*. Brutus Ultor, 1886; Callirrhoë, 1884; Canute the Great, 1887; Father's Tragedy (*The*), 1885; Long Ago, 1889; Question of Memory (*A*), 1893; Sight and Song, 1892; Stephania, 1892; Tragic Mary (*The*), 1890; Underneath the Bough, 1893.

FIELD (*Nathaniel*), dramatist, died 1641 (lived in the time of James I. and Charles I.). Amends for Ladies, 1639, a comedy; Fatal Dowry (*A*), 1632, a tragedy (in combination with Massinger); Woman's a Weathercock, 1612, a comedy.

FIELD, D.D. (*Richard*), Herefordshire, 1561–1616. Of the Church, 1606–10. His Life, by his son, 1617.

FIELDING (*Henry*), near Glastonbury, in Somersetshire, 1707–1754. Amelia, 1751, a novel; Covent Garden Journal, 1751–52; Jacobite Journal (*The*), 1748; Jonathan Wild (*The History of*), 1754; Joseph Andrews (*The Adventures of*), 1742; Journal of his Voyage to Lisbon, 1755; Journey from this World to the Next, 1743;

Tom Jones (*The History of*), 1749 (the best novel in the language); True Patriot (*The*), 1745.

Dramas: Author's Farce (*The*), 1731, a farce; Coffee-house Politician (*The*), 1730, a comedy; Covent Garden Tragedy (*The*), 1732; Debauchees (*The*), 1733; Don Quixote in England, 1733, a comedy; Eurydice, 1735; Eurydice hissed, 1737; Fathers (*The*), 1778; Grub Street Opera (*The*), 1731; Historical Register (*The*), 1736, a comedy; Intriguing Chambermaid (*The*), 1734, a farce; Letterwriters (*The*), 1731; Lottery (*The*), 1731; Love in Several Masques, 1728, a comedy; Miser (*The*), 1733, a comedy; Mock Doctor (*The*), 1733, a farce; Modern Husband (*The*), 1732, a comedy; Old Man taught Wisdom (*An*), 1734; Pasquin, 1736, a comedy; Temple Beau (*The*), 1730, a comedy; Tom Thumb, 1733, a comic opera; Tragedy of Tragedies (*The*), 1731; Tumble-Down Dick, 1737; Universal Gallant (*The*), 1735; Wedding-day (*The*), 1743, a comedy. His Life, by Murphy, 1802; sir W. Scott, 1821; Lawrence, 1855.

FILMER (Sir *Robert*), died 1647. Anarchy of a Limited and Mixed Monarchy, 1646; Freeholder's Grand Inquest (*The*), 1679; Original of Government, 1652; Patriarcha, or the Natural Power of the Kings of England, 1680 (this book called forth Locke's famous treatise on Government); Political Discourses, 1680.

FINDLAY, D.D. (*Robert*), 1721–1814. Divine Inspiration of the Jewish Scriptures, 1804 (a reply to Dr. Geddes); Vindication of the Sacred Books and of Josephus, 1770 (in refutation of Voltaire).

FINLAY, LL.D. (*George*), Scotland, 1799–1875. Greece under the Romans, 1843; History of the Byzantine Empire, 1852; History of the Byzantine and Greek Empires, 1853–54; History of Greece, from its Conquest by the Crusaders to its Conquest by the Turks, 1851; History of Greece under Othoman, etc., 1854; History of the Greek Revolution, 1861.

FINLAYSON (*George*), 1790–1823. Mission to Siam and Hué, 1825, posthumous. His Memoirs, by T. S. Raffles, 1825.

FISHER (Rev. *James*), *-*. Martha Hatfield, the Wise Virgin, 1653.

FISHER (*Payne*), poet-laureate to Cromwell, pseudonym "Paganus Piscator," 1616–1693. Marston-moore, 1650; Oratio Anniversaria, 1854; Piscatoris Poemata, 1656; Threnodia Gratulatoria, 1652.

FITZGERALD (*Edward*), 1809–1883. Agamemnon (*The*), 1876; Euphranor, 1851, a dialogue on Youth; Letters and Literary Remains; Omar Khayyám, and Salaman, and Absal, 1878; Polonius, a collection of Wise Saws, etc., 1852; Six Dramas of Calderon (translated), 1853.

FITZGERALD (*Percy Hetherington*), Fane Valley, in Louth, Ireland, novelist, etc., 1834– . (*A large number of his stories, etc., appeared in "All the Year Round," and in "Once a Week," some of which have been published separately*.) Autobiography of a Small Boy (*The*), 1869; Beauty Talbot,

1870; Bella Donna, 1864; Book of Theatrical Anecdotes, 1873; Boswell and Croker's Boswell, 1886; Bridge of Sighs; Charles Lamb, his Friends, his Haunts, and his Books, 1865; Chronicles of Bow Street Police Office, 1888; Day's Tour (*A*), through France and Belgium, 1887; Dear Girl (*The*), 1868; Diana Gay, 1868; Doctor's Mixture (*The*); Fairy Alice, 1865; Famous Forgery (*A*), 1865 (this is a life of Dr. Dodd); Great Canal of Suez (*The*), 1876; Jenny Bell, 1866; Jewels of the Mass, 1887; Kembles (*The*), 1871; Kings and Queens ot an Hour (Records of Love, Romance, Oddity and Adventure), 1883; Lady of Brantome (*The*), 1884; Le Sport at Baden, 1864; Life and Adventures of Alexandre Dumas, 1872; Life of Charles Lamb, 1865; Life of Charles Townshend, 1866; Life of Garrick, 1868; Life of George IV., 1881; Life of Samuel Johnson, 1874; Life of Sterne, 1864; Life of William IV., 1884; Life, Letters, and Writings of Charles Lamb, 1875-76; Middleaged Lover (*The*), 1873; Mildrington the Barrister; Never Forgotten, 1865; New History of the English Stage (*A*), 1882; Night Mail (*The*), 1862; Parvenu Family (*The*), 1876; Pictures of School Life and Boyhood, 1873; Polly, 1867; Principles of Comedy, 1870; Proverbs and Comedettas, 1869; Puppets, 1884; Recreations of a Literary Man, 1882; Rev. Alfred Hoblush, 1869; Romance of Book Collecting (*The*), 1886; Romance of the English Stage (*The*), 1874; Royal Dukes and Princesses of George III., 1882; Savoy Opera (*The*); School Days at Saxonhurst, 1868; Second Mrs. Tillotson (*The*), 1866; Seventy-five, Brooke Street, 1867; Sheridans (*The Lives of the*), 1887; Sir Henry Irving; Story of my Uncle Toby (*Bayard Series*), 1871; Sword of Damocles (*The*); Two Fair Daughters, 1870; Travels of Young Cœlebs; Woman with the Yellow Hair (*The*), (for *Household Words*); World behind the Scenes (*The*), 1881.

FITZHERBERT (Sir *Anthony*), died 1538. Book of Husbandry, 1523; Grand Abridgment of the Law (*A*), 1516; New *Natura Brevium*, 1534; Office and Authority of Justices of Peace, 1538.

FITZROY (*Robert*), meteorologist, 1805-1865. Barometer Manual, 1861; Narrative of the Surveying Voyages of H.M.S. *Adventurer* and *Beagle*, 1824-33; Weather Book (*The*), 1863.

FLAMMARION (*Camille*), a French astronomer, 1842– . Popular Astronomy (translated by J. Ellard Gore), (in 1880 the French Academy awarded the Montyon prize for this work); Urania, a romance.

FLAMSTEED (*John*), Denby, near Derby, 1646-1719. Atlas Cœlestis, 1729; Historia Cœlestis Britannica, 1675-1720.

FLAVEL (Rev. *John*), 1627-1691. Divine Conduct, 1678; Husbandry spiritualized, 1669; Saint Indeed (*A*), 1673.

FLAXMAN, R.A. (*John*), York, sculptor, 1755-1826. Mercury and Pandora, 1805; Monument to Lord Mansfield in Westminster Abbey, 1795; Monument to Sir W. Jones,

Oxford, 1797; Shield of Achilles, 1818 (very famous).
Illustrations: Æschylus, 1795; Dante, 1793-94; Hesiod, *Works and Days*, 1817; Homer, 1793-95 (his most celebrated work).

FLECKNOE (*Richard*), died 1678 (immortalized by Dryden). Affections of a Pious Soule unto . . . Christ, 1640; Damoiselles à la Mode (*The*), 1667, a comedy; Diarium (*The*), in 12 Jornadas, 1656, in burlesque rhyme; Enigmaticall Characters . . . from Life, 1658; Epigrams, 1665, 1672, etc.; Erminia, 1665, a tragi-comedy; Euterpe Revised, 1675; Heroic Portraits, 1660; Hierothalamium (Nuptials of Christ and the Soul), 1626; Love's Dominion, 1654, a dramatic piece; Love's Kingdom, 1664, a pastoral tragi-comedy; Marriage of Oceanus and Britannia (*The*), 1659; Miscellania, or Poems of All Sorts, 1653; Relation of Ten Years' Travells, etc. (*A*), 1654; Sir William Davenant's Voyage to the other World, 1668, a poetical fiction; Treatise on the Sports of Wit (*A*), 1675.

FLEETWOOD, D.D. (*John*), *-*. Christian Dictionary, 1773; Life of Christ, Lives of John the Baptist, and of the Virgin Mary, all about 1770, but often reprinted.

FLEETWOOD (*William*), bishop of Ely, surnamed "Silver-tongued," London, 1656-1723. Chronicon Pretiosum, 1707; Inscriptionum Antiquarum Sylloge, etc., 1691.

FLETCHER (*Andrew*), Saltoun, in Scotland, 1653-1716. Political Works, 1737, posthumous. His Life, by D. S. Erskine, 1792.

FLETCHER (Rev. *Giles*), 1588-1623. Christ's Victory and Triumph (in four poems), 1610; Licia (excellent).

FLETCHER (*John*), Rye, in Sussex, 1576-1625.
N.B.—Between 1616 (when Beaumont died) and 1621, he wrote 11 plays. (*C.*=comedy; *T.*=tragedy.) Beggar's Bush (*The*), 1622, C.; Boadicea, 1611, T.; Chances (*The*), 1620, C.; Faithful Shepherdess (*The*), 1610, a beautiful pastoral; False One (*The*), 1619, T.; King and No King, 1619, T.; Loyal Subject (*The*), 1616; Mons. Thomas, 1619, C.; Philaster, or Love Lies a-bleeding, 1620 (excellent); Pilgrims (*The*), 1621; Rule a Wife and Have a Wife, 1624, C.; Spanish Curate (*The*), 1622, C.; Valentinium, 1617, T.; Wife for a Month (*A*), 1624; Wild Goose Chase (*The*), 1619. His Life, by the Rev. A. Dyce, 1843.

FLETCHER, BEAUMONT, and the two in conjunction. (61 *dramas*. *B.*=*Beaumont*, *F.*=*Fletcher*, ?=*doubtful*, *C.*=comedy, *T*=*tragedy*.) N.B.—Between 1616 the date of Beaumont's death, and 1625 when Fletcher died, presumably all the dated plays were by Fletcher, and generally those previous to 1616 were by the two coadjutors. Beggar's Bush (*The*), 1622, C. by F.; Bloody Brother, published 1639, T. by B.; Boadicea, 1611, T. by F.; Bonduca, published 1647, T. by B. and F.; Captain (*The*), 1613 (? B. and F.); Chances (*The*), 1620, by F.; Coronation (*The*), published 1640, by B. and F.; Coxcomb (*The*), 1612, C. by B. and F.; Cupid's Revenge, 1615, C. by B. and F.; Custom of the Country, published 1647, T. by B. and

F. ; Double Marriage, published 1647, C. by F. ; Elder Brother (*The*), published 1637, C. by F. ; Fair Maid of the Inn (*The*), published 1647, C. (? B. and F.); Faithful Friend (*The*), published 1647, by B. and F. ; Faithful Shepherdess (*The*), 1610, an exquisite pastoral by F. ; False One (*The*), 1619, T. by F. ; Four Plays in One, published 1647, C. by B. and F. ; History of Madoc, published 1647, by B. and F. ; Honest Man's Fortune (*The*), 1613, C. by B. and F. ; Humorous Lieutenant (*The*), published 1647, C. (? B. and F.); Island Princess (*The*), published 1647, by B. and F. ; Jeweller of Amsterdam (*The*), published 1647, by B. and F. ; King and No King, 1619, T. by F. ; Knight of Malta, published 1647, by B. and F. ; Knight of the Burning Pestle (*The*), 1611, C. by B. ; Laws of Candy, published 1647, by B. and F. ; Little French Lawyer (*The*), published 1647, C. by B. and F. ; Love's Cure, published 1647, C. (? B. and F.); Love's Pilgrimage, published 1647, C. (? B. and F.); Lovers' Progress, published 1647, C. (? B. and F.); Loyal Subject, 1618, by F. ; Mad Lover, 1617, by F. ; Mad World, 1608, C. by B. and F. ; Maid in the Mill, published 1647, C. (? B. and F.); Maid's Tragedy, 1610, T. by B. and F. ; Masque (*The*), 1612, C. by B. ; Merchant of Bruges (*The*), published 1630, by B. and F. ; Mons. Thomas, 1619, C. by F. ; Nice Valour, published 1647, C. by B. and F. ; Night Walkers, published 1633, C. (? B. and F.); Noble Gentleman (*The*), published 1647 (? B. and F.) ; ? Noble Valour, (? B. and F.); Philaster, or Love Lies a-Bleeding, 1620, T. by F. (excellent) ; Pilgrim (*The*), 1621, by F. ; Prophetess (*The*), published 1647 (? B. and F.); Queen of Corinth (*The*), published 1647 (? B. and F.); Right Woman (*A*), 1615, by B. and F. ; Rollo, published 1639, by B. and F. ; Rule a Wife and Have a Wife, 1624, C. by F. ; Sea Voyage (*The*), published 1647, C. (? B. and F.); Spanish Curate (*The*), 1622, C. by F. ; Thiery and Theodoret, 1621, T. by F. ; Two Noble Kinsmen, published 1634 (? B. and F.), (one of the three best) ; Valentinian, 1617, T. by F. ; Wife for a Month, 1624, C. by F. ; Wild Goose Chase, 1619, C. by F. ; Wit at Several Weapons, 1614, C. by B. and F. ; Wit without Money, published 1639, C. by B. and F. ; Woman-Hater (*The*), 1607, C. by B. and F ; Woman's Place, published 1647, C. by B. and F. ; Woman's Prize, published 1647, C. by B. and F. ; Women Pleased, published 1647, C. (? B. and F.). N.B.—The three best are *Philaster*, *The Two Noble Kinsmen*, and *The Faithful Shepherdess*.

FLETCHER (*Phineas*), poet, brother of Giles Fletcher, the poet, 1584–1650. Locustes, 1627, a satire ; Piscatorie Eclogs, 1633 ; Purple Island (*The*), an allegorical poem in twelve cantos, 1633 (the "Purple Island' is the human body; his chief work); Sicelides, 1631, a piscatory. His Life, by W. Jaques, 1816.

FLINDERS (*Matthew*), Lincolnshire, 1760–1814. Voyage to Terra Australis, etc., 1814.

FLORIO (*John*), London, 1550–1625. Ridiculed by Shakespeare in *Love's Labour's Lost*, as "Holofernes.") Florio his First Frutes, yielding Familiar Speech, Merrie Proverbes, Wittie Sentences, and Golden Sayings, 1575 ; Florio his Second Frutes, being 6000 Italian Proverbes, 1591 ; New World of Words : an Italian-English Dictionarie, 1595.

FLOWER, LL.D. (*William Henry*), Stratford-on-Avon, in Warwickshire, 1831–   . Diagrams of the Nerves of the Human Body, 1871 ; Introduction to the Osteology of the Mammalia (*An*), 1870.

FLUDD, M.D. (*Robert*), surnamed "The Searcher," Kent, 1574–1637. Clavis Philosophiæ et Alchimiæ, 1617 ; De Supernaturalis, Naturalis, Præternaturalis, et Contranaturalis Microcosmi Historia, 1619 ; Mosaicall Philosophy, 1659, posthumous ; Summum Bonum, etc., 1629 ; Utriusque Cosmi Metaphysica, Physica, atque Technica Historia, 1617.

FOLKES, LL.D. (*Martin*), Westminster, 1690–1754. Table of English Silver Coin, etc. (*A*), 1745 ; Tables des Monnaies d'or d'Angleterre, 1743.

FOOTE (*Samuel*), "The English Aristophanes," Truro, in Cornwall, 1719–1777. Prelude on opening the Theatre, 1767. (*His twenty-five dramatic works all farces. The two best are marked with a* *.) Auction of Pictures (*The*), 1748, a farce * ; Author (*The*), 1757, a farce * ; Bankrupt (*The*), 1776, a farce * ; Capuchin (*The*), 1776 ; Commissary (*The*), 1765, a farce ; Cozeners (*The*), 1774, a farce ; Devil upon Two Sticks (*The*), 1768, a farce ; Diversions of the Morning, 1747, a farce ; Dr. Last in his Chariot, 1769 (in connection with Bickerstaff), a farce ; Englishman in Paris (*The*), 1753, a farce ; Englishman returned from Paris, 1756, a farce * ; Knights (*The*), 1754, a farce ; Lame Lover (*The*), 1770, a farce (after he broke his leg) ; Lindamira, 1805, posthumous ; Lyar (*The*), 1762, a farce * ; Maid of Bath (*The*), 1771, a farce ; Mayor of Garratt (*The*), 1764, a farce * ; Minor (*The*), 1760, a farce * ; Nabob (*The*), 1772, a farce ; Orators (*The*), 1762, a farce ; Patron (*The*), 1764, a farce ; Piety in Pattens, 1773, a farce ; Slanderer (*The*), 1778, posthumous ; Taste, 1752, a farce ; Trip to Calais (*A*), 1778, a farce ; Tryal of Samuel Foote (*The*), 1763, a farce ; Young Hypocrite (*The*), 1778, posthumous. His Life, by Cooke, 1806.

FORBES (*Archibald*), 1838–   . Chinese Gordon, 1884 ; Glimpses through the Cannon Smoke, 1880 ; History of the War between Russia and Turkey, 1878 ; Life of Napoleon III., 1898 ; Soldiering and Scribbling, 1872 ; Souvenirs of Some Continents, 1885 ; War Correspondence of the *Daily News* (*The*), 1877–88 ; William I. of Germany, 1888.

FORBES (*Duncan*), Culloden, in Scotland, 1685–1747. Reflections on the Sources of Incredulity in . . . Religion, 1750, posthumous ("a little jewel"); Thoughts on Religion, 1735. His Life, by Bannatyne, 1816 ; J. H. Burton, 1847.

FORBES (*Edward*), Isle of Man, 1815–1854. History of British Star-fish, 1841 ; History of British Mollusca, 1853 (with S. Hanley);

On the Distribution of the Pulmonifera Mollusca of the Ægean, 1843 ; Travels in Lycia, 1848 (with lieutenant Spratt). His Life, by G. Wilson and A. Geikie, 1861.

FORBES (*James*), London, 1749–1819. Letters from France, 1806 ; Memoir of Eliza Dalton, 1813 ; Oriental Memoirs, etc., 1813.

FORBES, D.C.L. (*James David*), Edinburgh, 1809–1868. Norway and its Glaciers, 1853 ; Theory of Glaciers (*The*), 1859 ; Tour of Mont Blanc, 1855 ; Travels through the Alps of Savoy, 1843. His Life, by Shairp, 1873.

FORBES (Rev. *John*), Aberdeen, 1593–1648. Institutiones Historico-Theologicæ, 1646.

FORBES, M.D. (Sir *John*), Scotland, 1778–1861. Cyclopædia of Practical Medicine, 1833–35 ; Homœopathy, Allopathy, and Physic, 1846 ; Manual of Medical Bibliography, 1836 ; Nature and Art in the Cure of Diseases, 1857 ; Physician's Holiday (*The*), 1849.

FORBES (*William*), bishop of Edinburgh, born at Aberdeen, 1585–1634. Considerationes Modestæ Controversiarum, de Justificatione, Purgatorio, Invocatione Sanctorum, etc., 1658.

FORBES-ROBERTSON (*John*), Aberdeen, 1822– . Great Painters of Christendom (*The*), 1877.

FORD (*John*), Ilsington, in Devonshire, 1586–1640. Fame's Memorial (In Memoriam of Ben Jonson), 1606.

His dramas: Beauty in a Trance, 1653, a comedy ; Bristowe Merchant (*The*) (with Dekker) ; Broken Heart (*The*), 1635 (his best) ; Fairy Knight (*The*) (with Dekker) ; Fancies Chaste and Noble, 1638, a tragi-comedy ; Ill Beginning has a Good Ending (*An*), 1613, a comedy ; Lady's Trial (*The*), 1638, printed 1639 ; Late Murther of the Sonne upon the Mother (with Webster) ; Love's Sacrifice, 1633, a tragedy ; Perkin Warbeck, 1634, an historic play ; Sun's Darling (*The*), 1657, posthumous, a melodrama ; 'Tis Pity she's a Whore, 1633 (an excellent tragedy spoilt by its title).

FORD (*Richard*), London, 1796–1858. Gatherings in Spain, 1848 ; Handbook of Spain, 1845.

FORDUN (*John de*), Fordun, in Scotland, 1303–1386. Scotichronicon, part i. printed 1703, part ii. printed 1722, with supplement 1759 (this book is the authority for all the early history of Scotland).

FORDYCE (*David*), Scotland, 1711–1751. Dialogues concerning Education, 1745–48 ; Elements of Moral Philosophy, 1743 ; Temple of Virtue (a dream), 1750 ; Theodorus, or Dialogue concerning the Art of Preaching, 1746 (his chief work).

FORDYCE, D.D. (*James*), Aberdeen, 1720–1796. Addresses to the Deity, 1785 ; Addresses to Young Men, 1777 ; Poems, 1787 ; Sermons to Young Women, 1766.

FORDYCE (*George*), Aberdeen, 1750–1802. Elements of the Practice of Physick, 1768–70 ; Four Dissertations on Simple Fever, 1794 ; Treatise on the Digestion of Food, 1791.

FORMAN (*Henry Buxton*), London, 1842– . Letters of Keats to Fanny Brawne, 1878 ;

Our Living Poets, 1871 ; Poetical Works of Keats, 1883 ; Shelley Library (*The*), 1886.

FORSTER (*George*), 1754–1792. Journey from Bengal to England, etc., 1790 ; Voyage round the World, 1777.

FORSTER (*John*), Newcastle, 1812–1876. Arrest of the Five Members by Charles I., 1860 (a valuable work) ; Biographical and Historical Essays, 1859 ; Debates on the Grand Remonstrance, 1860 ; Life of Charles Dickens, 1872–74 ; Life of Sir John Eliot, 1864 ; Life of Oliver Goldsmith, 1848 (very good) ; Life of Walter Savage Landor, 1868 ; Life of Jonathan Swift, 1876 (unfinished) ; Statesmen of the Commonwealth of England, 1831–34 (a valuable work).

FORSTER, D.D. (*Nathaniel*), Devonshire, 1717–1757. Arts and Sciences of Egypt, 1743 ; Dissertation upon the Account . . . of Christ by Josephus, 1749 ; Platonis Dialogi Quinque, 1745.

FORSTER (*Thomas Ignatius Maria*), London, 1789–1850. Anecdotes about Dogs, 1828 ; Observations on the Influence of Comets, 1836 ; Observations on the Influence of Particular States of the Atmosphere on Human Health, 1817 ; Observations on the Natural History of the Swallow, and its Brumal Retreat, 1817 ; Perennial Calendar (*The*), 1824 ; Pocket Encyclopædia of Natural Phenomena, 1827 ; Researches about Atmospheric Phenomena, 1823 (an esteemed work) ; Synoptical Catalogue of British Birds, 1817.

FORSYTH (*William*), Aberdeen, 1737–1804. Treatise on the Culture of Fruit Trees, 1802 (a standard work).

FORSYTH (*William*), botanist, *–*. Botanical Nomenclator, 1794 (an esteemed work).

FORSYTH, LL.D. (*William*), Greenock, in Scotland, 1812– . Cases in Constitutional Law, 1869 ; Essays (Critical and Historical), 1874 ; Hannibal in Italy, 1872, a drama ; History of Trial by Jury, 1852 ; Hortensius, or the Duty, etc., of an Advocate, 1849 ; Letters from Lord Brougham to William Forsyth, 1872 ; Life of Cicero, 1864 ; Napoleon at St. Helena and Sir Hudson Lowe, 1853 ; Novels, etc., of the XVIII. Century in Illustration of the Manners and Morals of the Time, 1871 ; On the Custody of Infants, 1850 ; On the Law of Composition with Creditors, 1841 ; Rome and its Ruins, 1865 ; Slavonic Provinces . . . (*The*), 1876.

FOSBROOKE (Rev. *Thomas Dudley*), London, antiquary, 1770–1842. British Monachism, etc., 1802 ; Encyclopædia of Antiquities, 1823–25 ; Foreign Topography, 1828 ; History of Gloucestershire, 1807 ; Manners and Customs of the Monks and Nuns of England, 1810 ; Monastic Life, 1795, a poem.

FOSS (*Edward*), London, 1787–1870. Biographia Juridica, 1870 ; Judges of England, 1848–64 ; Tabulæ Curiales, 1865.

FOSTER, D.D. (*James*), Exeter, 1697–1753. Essay on Fundamentals, etc., 1720 ; Natural Religion, 1749–52 ; Usefulness, Truth, and Excellency of the Christian Revelation, 1731.

FOSTER (*John*), Halifax, in Yorkshire, 1770–1843. Essay on the Evils of Popular

Ignorance, 1819; Essays (in a series of letters), 1805; Introduction to Doddridge's *Rise and Progress of Religion*, 1825. His Life, by Dr. Ryland, 1846; J. Shepherd, 1846.

FOSTER (Sir *Michael*), Marlborough, in Wiltshire, 1689-1763. Examination of the Scheme of Church Power laid down in the *Codex Juris Ecclesiastici Anglicani*, 1735; Reports of Crown Cases, 1763. His Life, by Michael Dodson, 1811.

FOSTER (*Samuel*), 1598-1652. Art of Dialling, 1638; Four Treatises of Dialling, 1654; Lucubrationes Mathematicæ, 1659; Posthuma Fosteri, 1652; Sector altered (*The*), 1661.

FOTHERGILL, M.D. (*John*), Yorkshire, 1712-1780. Works, 1871, posthumous. His Life, by Gilbert Thompson, 1782; Lettsom, 1783.

FOUNTAINE (Sir *Andrew*), 1726-1755. Numismata Anglo-Saxonica, etc., 1704.

FOWLER, M.D. (*Thomas*), York, 1736-1801. Medical Reports on Acute and Chronic Rheumatism, 1795; Medical Reports on the Effects of Arsenic, 1786; Medical Reports on the Effects of Tobacco, 1785.

Fox (*Charles James*), 1749-1806. History of the Reign of James II., 1808, posthumous; Speeches, 1815, posthumous. His Life, by R. Fell, 1808; J. B. Trotter, 1811; J. Allen, 1820; lord John Russell, 1859.

Fox (*George*), Drayton, in Leicestershire, 1624-1691. Great Mystery of the Great Whole unfolded (*The*), 1659; Works, 1694-1706, posthumous. His Life, by J. S. Watson; Josiah Marsh, 1848; Janney, 1853.

Fox (*Luke*), 1585-1635. North-West Fox (*The*), 1635.

FOXE (*John*), Boston, in Lincolnshire, the martyrologist, 1517-1587. Acts and Monuments (the Book of Martyrs), part i. 1554, complete edition 1563 (his great work, immensely popular at one time); De Censura seu Excommunicatione Ecclesiastica, 1551; De Christo Crucifixio, etc., 1571; De Christo Triumphante, 1551, a Latin drama; De Non Plectendis morte Adulteris Consultatio, 1548; Ecclesiastical History, 1570. His Life, by S. R. Catley, 1843.

FRANCILLON (*Robert Edward*), Gloucester, novelist, 1841- . Dog and his Shadow (*A*), 1876; Earl's Dene, 1870; Esther's Glove, 1882; Grace Owen's Engagement, 1868 (his first novel); In the Dark, 1877; Jack Doyle's Daughter, 1895; King or Knave, 1888; Olympia, 1874; One by One, 1883; Pearl and Emerald, 1872; Queen Cophetua, 1880; Rare and Good Luck, 1876; Real Queen (*A*), 1884; Romance of the Law, 1889; Ropes of Sand, 1893; Strange Waters, 1878; Under Slieve-Ban, 1881; Zelda's Fortune, 1873.

FRANCIS, D.D. (*Philip*), Dublin, died 1773. Translated the *Orations* of Demosthenês, etc., 1757; translated *Horace* into poetry, 1747.

FRANCKLIN, D.D. (*Thomas*), London, 1720-1784. Dissertation on Ancient Tragedy (*A*), 1760; translated *Lucian* 1780, *Sophoclês* 1759.

FRANKLIN, LL.D. (*Benjamin*), Boston, U.S., 1706-1790. Poor Richard's Almanac, 1732-57; Way to Wealth (*The*), 1795; Works,

1836-40, posthumous. His Life, by Brissot, 1793; W. T. Franklin, 1818; Walker, 1819; J. Sparks, 1844.

FRANKLIN (*Eleanor Ann*), first wife of sir John Franklin, the Arctic voyager, 1795-1825. Cœur de Lion, 1822; Triumphs of Constancy, 1815.

FRANKLIN (Sir *John*), Spilsby, in Lincolnshire, 1786-1847. Narrative of a Journey to the Shores of the Polar Sea, 1823; Narrative of a Second Expedition to the Polar Sea, 1828.

FRASER (*Alexander*), **-**. A Key to the Prophecies of the Old and New Testaments, not yet accomplished, 1795.

FRASER, D.D. (*Alexander Campbell*), 1819- . Annotated Selections from Berkeley, 1881; Collected Works of Bishop Berkeley annotated with Dissertations and Life (4 vols.), 1871; Locke, a Monograph, 1890; Philosophy of Theism, 1896; etc.

FRASER (*James Baillie*), Scotland, 1783-1856. Highland Smugglers (*The*), a novel; Journal of a Tour through the Snowy Range of the Himalaya Mountains to the Sources of the Jumna and Ganges, 1820; Kuzzilbach, a novel; Narrative of a Journey into Khorassan, 1825; Travels and Adventures on the Shore of the Caspian Sea, 1826; Winter's Journey from Constantinople to Tehran (*A*), 1838.

FRAUNCE (*Abraham*), noted for his English hexameters, 1565-1630. Countesse of Pembroke's Yuychurch (three parts, in English hexameters), 1591; Death of Phillis and Amyntas (a "funeral," in English hexameters), 1585; Lament of Amintas for the Death of Phillis (in English hexameters), 1592; Lawiers' Logike, 1588; Nativity, Passion, Burial, and Resurrection of Christ (in English hexameters), 1591.

FRAZER, LL.B., C.E. (*R. W.*), 1854- . British India (*Story of Nations Series*), 1897; Silent Gods and Sun-steeped Lands, 1896.

FREEMAN, D.C.L. (*Edward Augustus*), Harborne, in Staffordshire, 1823-1892. Ancient Greece and Mediæval Italy, 1858; Architecture of Llandaff Cathedral, 1851; Cathedral Church of Wells (*The*), 1870; Chief Periods of European History, 1886; Church Restoration, 1846; Comparative Politics, 1873; Disestablishment and Disendowment, 1874; English People in its Home (*The*), 1884; Essay of Window Tracery, 1850; Exeter, 1887; General Sketch of European History 1872; Growth of the English Constitution, 1872; Historical and Architectural Studies, 1876; Historical Essays, 1872-73; Historical Geography of Europe, 1881; History and Antiquities of St. David, 1860 (with Dr. B. Jones); History and Conquests of the Saracens, 1856; History of Architecture, 1849; History of Federal Government, 1863, in Greece and Italy, 1893, posthumous; History of Sicily, 1891, vol. v. 1895, posthumous; History of the Norman Conquest, 1867-76; Methods of Historical Study, 1886; Old English History for Children, 1869; Ottoman Power in Europe (*The*), 1877; Practical Bearing of . . . European History, 1884; Sicily, etc., 1892; Studies of Travel, 1893, posthumous; Unity of History (*The*), 1872; William Rufus, 1881;

William the Conqueror, 1888. His Life, by
W. R. W. Stephens, 1895.
FREMANTLE (Hon. and Very Rev. *William
Henry*), Swanbourne, in Buckinghamshire,
1831- . Gospel of the Secular Life (*The*),
1882; World (*The*), as the Subject of Re-
demption, 1885.
FRERE (Rev. *John Alexander*), 1814- .
Inspiration of Scripture (*The*), 1850; Testi-
mony of the Spirit to the Incarnation, 1853.
FRISWELL (*James Hain*), Newport, 1827-
1878. About in the World, 1864; Better
Self (*The*), 1875; Daughter of Eve (*A*),
1863; Francis Spira, and other Poems, 1865;
Gentle Life (*The*), 1864; Houses with the
Fronts off, 1854; Life Portraits of Shake-
speare, 1864; Man's Thoughts (*A*), 1872;
One of Two, 1871; Other People's Windows,
1868; Out and About, 1860; Varia, 1866.
FROBISHER (Sir *Martin*), 1536-1594. Three
Voyages for the Discovery of the North-
West Passage, 1578.
FROST (*Thomas*), Croydon, 1821- . Alice
Leighton, 1857; Circus Life and Circus
Celebrities, 1875; Emma Mayfield, 1857;
Forty Years' Recollections, 1880; Half-hours
with Early Explorers, 1873; In Kent with
Charles Dickens, 1880; Life of Thomas,
Lord Lyttelton, 1876; Lives of Conjurors,
1875; Modern Explorers, 1882; Obi, 1851;
Old Showmen (*The*), and Old London Fairs,
1874; Reminiscences of a Country Journalist,
1886; Secret Societies of the European
Revolution, 1876.
FROUDE, LL.D. (*James Anthony*), Dartington,
in Devonshire, 1818-1894. Beaconsfield
(*Lord*), 1890; Bunyan, 1880; Cæsar, 1879;
Calvinism, 1871; Carlisle (*Jane Welsh*),
1884; Carlisle (*Thomas*), 1882, his Remini-
scences 1884; Cæt's Pilgrimage (*The*), 1870;
Divorce of Catherine of Aragon, 1891;
English in Ireland in the XVIII. Century
(*The*), 1872-74; English in the West Indies
(*The*), 1888; English Seamen in the XVIII.
Century, 1895, posthumous; Erasmus (his
Life and Letters), 1891; History of England
from the Fall of Wolsey to the Death of
Queen Elizabeth, 1856-70; Life of Bunyan,
1880; Life of Julius Cæsar, 1879; Lives of
the English Saints, 1844; Luther, 1883;
Nemesis of Faith (*The*), 1848; Oceana, 1886;
Pilgrim (*The*), 1861; Shadows of the Clouds,
1847, stories; Short Studies on Great Subjects, 1867, 1872, 1877, 1882; Spanish Story
of the Armada (*The*), 1892; Two Chiefs of
Dunboy (*The*), 1889.
FRY (*Edmund*), type-founder, died 1835. Pan-
tographia, 1799 (it contains copies of all the
known alphabets in the whole world, and
is highly interesting).
FRY (Sir *Edward*), Bristol, in Gloucestershire,
1827- . Adaptation of Christianity to
the Nature of Man, 1857; Darwinism and
Theology, 1872; Doctrine of Election (*The*),
1864.
FRY (*John*), a Socinian, 1599-1660. Clergy
in their Colours (*The*), 1650 (burnt by the
sheriffs of London); Pair of Bellows to blow
off the Dust cast on John Fry, M.P., 1648;
Theiss, with a Cordial to heal the Corasives
which John Fry hath engendered, 1651.

FULKE, D.D. (*William*), London, 1550-1589.
Antiprognosticon contra . . . Astrologorum
Prædictiones, 1560; Astrologus Luctus, 1571;
Comment on the Rhemish Testament, 1580
(his best-known work); Confutation of a
Libelle, etc., 1571; Confutation of William
Allen, 1585; De Successione Ecclesiastica,
etc., 1584; Goodly Gallery (*A*), 1563 (on
meteors); Metromachia, 1597 (a geometrical
game); Ouranomachia, 1573 (a game resem-
bling chess); Philosopher's Game (*The*), 1563
(on chess); Prelections upon Revelation,
1573; Responsio ad Thomæ Stapletoni
Calumnias, 1579; Retentive to stay Good
Christians in the True Faith, 1580 (against
the motives of Richard Bristow); Scripture
Translation into the English Tong Defended
(*Our*), 1583; Sermons at Alphages, 1577;
Sermons at Hampton Court, 1571; Text of
the New Testament . . . translated out of
. . . Latin by the Papists of the Traitorous
Seminarie at Rhemes, 1580.
FULLER (*Andrew*), called "The Franklin of
Theology," Wicken, in Cambridgeshire, 1754-
1815. Backslider (*The*), 1801; Calvinistic and
Socinian Systems examined, 1794; Expository Discourse . . . of Genesis, 1806; Discourses on the Book of Genesis, 1806; Gospel
its own Witness (*The*), 1799-1800. His Life,
by Dr. Ryland, 1824.
FULLER, D.D. (*Thomas*), Aldwinkle, in
Northamptonshire, 1608-1661. Abel Redivivus, or the Dead yet Speaking, 1651;
Andronicus, or the Unfortunate Politician,
1646; Appeal of Injured Innocence (*The*),
1659; Christ's Temptation, 1652; Church
History of Britain, etc., to 1648, 1648-55
(his great work), (edited by J. S. Brewer,
1845); David's Sin, Repentance, and Punishment, 1631, a poem (his first publication);
Ephemeris Parliamentaria, 1654; Good
Thoughts in Bad Times, 1645; Good
Thoughts in Worse Times, 1646; Historie
of the Holy Warre (*The*), 1639, 1640, 1642,
1647, 1651; History of the University of
Cambridge, 1655; History of the Worthies
of England (*The*), 1662 (a valuable and
interesting work); Holy and Profane States
(*The*), 1642, 1648, 1652, 1658; Joseph's Party-
coloured Coat, 1640; Life of Dean Colet,
1635; Mixt Contemplations in Better Times,
1660; Ornithologie, or the Speech of Birds,
1663; Pisgah-sight of Palestine (*A*), 1650;
Triania, 1654. His Life, by A. T. Russell,
1844; H. Rogers, 1856; J. E. Bailey, 1874.
FULLERTON (Lady *Georgina*), maiden name
Lady *Georgina Granville*, novelist, 1812-
1885. Constance Sherwood, 1865, an autobiography; Dramas from the Lives of
the Saints, 1872; Ellen Middleton, 1844, a
domestic story (her first work); Gold-digger
(*The*), and other Verses, 1872; Grantley
Manor, 1847; Lady-bird, 1852; La Comtesse
de Bonneval, 1857; Laurentia, 1861, a tale
of Japan; Life of Father Henry Young,
1874; Life of Louisa de Carvajal, 1873,
Life of St. Frances of Rome, 1857; Mrs.
Gerald's Niece, 1869; Rose Leblanc, 1861;
Stormy Life (*A*), 1867; Too Strange not to
be True, 1864, a novel; Will and a Way (*A*),
1881, a novel. Her Life, by A. Craven.

FUNK and WAGNALL, New York, U.S. Chief editor, J. K. Funk, D.D.: Analytical Concordance to the Bible, by Dr. Young, 1895 (admirable); Preachers' Commentary on the Old Testament, by various contributors, 1890, New Testament 1896; Standard Dictionary of the English Language, 1893 (most excellent).

FUSELI, R.A. (*Henry*), born in Switzerland, but lived in England, 1741-1825. Three Lectures on Painting, 1801 (much esteemed). His Life, by J. Knowles, 1831.

GAINSFORD (*Thomas*), 1588-1629. Glory of England (*The*), 1619; Historie of Trebizonde (in four books), 1616, tales; Secretaries Studie, 1616; True and Wonderfull Historie of Perkin Warbeck, 1618; Vision of Henry VII., 1610, a poem.

GAIRDNER (*James*), Edinburgh, 1828- Early Chroniclers of Europe, 1879; Henry VII. (*History of*), 1858, 1889; Henry VIII., continuation of Brewer's *Letters and Papers of Henry VIII.* (*q.v.*); Historical Collection of a London Citizen, 1876; Houses of York and Lancaster (*The*), 1874; Richard III. (*Life and Reign of*), 1878; Richard III. and Henry VII. (*Letters and Papers illustrative of the Reigns of*), 1861-63; Studies in English History, 1881; Three XV. Century Chronicles, 1880.

GAISFORD, D.D. (*Thomas*), dean of Christ Church, born in Wiltshire, critic, 1779-1855. Ethnologicon Magnum, 1848; Hephæstionis Enchiridion, 1810; Herodotus, 1824; Homeri *Ilias* 1821, *Odyssea* 1827; Poetæ Græci Minores (edited, with critical notes), 1814-20; Suidæ Lexicon, 1834.

GALE (*Norman Rowland*), Kew, in Surrey, 1862- . Country Muse (*A*), 1892, 1895; Cricket Songs, 1894; June Romance (*A*), 1894; Orchard Songs, 1893; Songs for Little People, 1896.

GALE (*Roger*), London, 1672-1744. Knowledge of Medals, 1697; Registrum Honoris de Richmond, 1722.

GALE (*Samuel*), London, 1682-1754. History of Winchester Cathedral, 1715.

GALE (Rev. *Theophilus*), Devonshire, 1628-1678. Court of the Gentiles (*The*), 1669-78 (still in good repute).

GALE (*Thomas*), Yorkshire, 1636-1702. Historiæ Anglicanæ Scriptores Quinque, 1687; Historiæ Britannicæ Saxonicæ, Anglo-Danicæ Scriptores, xv., 1691; Jamblichus, 1678; Opuscula Mythologica, etc., 1671; Rerum Anglicarum Scriptores Veteres, 1684.

GALFRID. See GEOFFREY OF MONMOUTH.

GALL (*Richard*), Scotland, 1776-1801. Farewell to Ayrshire (a poem falsely ascribed to Burns); My only Jo and Dearie O, about 1787, a poem.

GALT (*John*), Irvine, in Scotland, 1779-1839. Autobiography, 1833; Life of Benjamin West, 1816; Life of Cardinal Wolsey, 1812; Life of Lord Byron, 1830; Literary Life and Miscellanies, 1834; Lives of the Players, 1831; Ouranoulogos, 1833; Voyages and Travels, 1812; Wandering Jew (*The*), no date.

Novels: Annals of the Parish, 1821 (his best novel); Ayrshire Legatees, 1821; Boyle Corbet, or the Emigrant, 1831; Eben Erskine, or the Traveller, 1813; Entail (*The*), 1823; Forester (*The*), 1825; Gathering of the West, 1823; Last of the Lairds (*The*), 1826; Lawrie Todd, or the Wood Settlers, 1830; Majolo, 1820; Member (*The*), 1832, an autobiography; Omen (*The*), 1824, an historical romance; Provost (*The*), 1822 (very good); Ringan Gilhaize (a tale of the Covenanters), 1823; Sir Andrew Wylie of that Ilk, 1822; Southennan, 1830 (Queen Mary's time); Steamboat (*The*), 1822; Stolen Child (*The*), 1833; Stories of the Study, 1833; Trials of Margaret Lyndsay, 1823. And several others in *The Novelist's Library, The Romancist*, etc.

GALTHER (*Philip*), *-*. Gestorum Alexandri Magni Libri Decem, printed by Pynson (it contains the proverb, *Incidis in Scyllam cupiens vitare Charybdis*).

GALTON (*Francis*), 1822- Art of Campaigning, 1855; Art of Travel (*The*), 1855; Englishmen of Science, their Nature and Nurture, 1874; Experiences on Prehension, 1887; Finger Prints, 1892; Hereditary Genius, 1869; Inquiries into Human Faculties, 1883; Life History Album, 1883; Meteorographica, 1863; Natural Inheritance, 1889; Record of Family Faculties, 1883; Teletype (*The*), 1850; Vacation Tourist, 1861-64.

GARDINER, LL.D. (*Samuel Rawson*), Ropley, in Hampshire, 1829- . Charles I. (*The Fall of the Monarchy of*), 1879-80; Charles I. (*The Personal Government of*), 1877; Debates in the House of Commons in 1625, 1873; England under the Duke of Buckingham and Charles I., 1875; First Two Stuarts (*The*), and the Puritan Revolution, 1875; Fortescue Papers (*The*), 1871; History of England from the Accession of James I. to the Disgrace of Chief Justice Coke, 1863; History of the Commonwealth and Protectorate, 1894; History of the Great Civil War, 1886-91; Prince Charles and the Spanish Marriage, 1869; Thirty Years' War (*The*), 1874.

GARDINER, D.D. (*Stephen*), bishop of Winchester, born at Bury St. Edmunds, 1483-1555. De Vera Obedientia, 1534; Detection of the Devil's Sophistrie, 1546; Necessary Doctrine of a Christian Man (*A*), 1543; Rescvynge of the Romishe Foxe, 1543.

GARDNER, M.D. (*John*), Coggeshall, in Essex, 1804- . Great Physician (*The*), 1843; Household Medicine, 1863; Treatise on Consumption, 1854.

GARDNER (*Percy*), 1846- . New Chapters in Greek History, 1892; Numismatic Commentary on Pausanias, 1887. And various books on Greek coins.

GARNETT, LL.D. (*Richard*), Lichfield, in Hampshire, 1835- . Biographies of Carlyle 1887, Emerson 1888, Milton, etc.; Idylls and Epigrams, 1869; Io in Egypt, and other Poems, 1859; Iphigenia in Delphi, 1890; Poems, 1893; Poems from the German, 1862; Primula, a Book of Lyrics, 1858; Relics of Shelley, 1862; Twilight of the Gods, 1888

GARRICK (*David*), Hereford, 1716–1779. Clandestine Marriage, 1796, a comedy (with Colman); Guardian (*The*), 1759 (altered from Massinger's comedy); Irish Widow (*The*), 1757, a farce; Lethe, 1743; Lying Valet, 1740, a farce; Miss in the Teens, 1747, a farce. With about thirty other dramatic pieces, most of them adaptations. His works were compiled and published 1785–98. His Life, by Tom Davies, 1780; A. Murphy, 1801; Percy Fitzgerald, 1872.

GARTH, M.D. (Sir *Samuel*), Cambridge, 1657–1719. Claremont, 1715, a poem; Dispensary (*The*), in six cantos, 8-syl. rhymes, 1699, a poetical satire (his chief work).

GASCOIGNE (*George*), poet, 1530–1577. Complaynt of Philomene (*The*), 1576; Flowres, Hearbes, and Weedes, 1566; Fruits of War, 1587; Glasse of Government (*The*), 1575, a play; Grief of Joy (*The*), 1576; Hermit's Tale at Woodstock (*The*), 1575; Hundreth Sundrie Flowres in One Small Posie (*A*), 1572; Iocasta, 1587, posthumous, a tragedy; Pleasures at Kenilworth Castle (*The*), 1575; Steele Glas (*The*), 1576, a satyre; Storie of Ferdinando Jeronimi (*The*), 1587, posthumous; Supposes, 1560, a comedy from Ariosto; Wyll of the Deuyll, 1825, posthumous. His "Remembravnce," by G. Whetstone, 1577.

GASCOIGNE (Mrs.), maiden name *Caroline Leigh Smith*, Dale Park, 1813– . Aunt Prue's Railway Journey, 1865, a novel; Belgravia, 1851, a poem; Crystal Palace (*The*), 1852, a poem; Dr. Harold, 1865, a novel; Evelyn Harcourt, 1842, a novel; Next-door Neighbours (*The*), 1855, a novel; School for Wives (*The*), 1839; Spencer's Cross Manor-House, 1852, a tale for children; Temptation, or a Wife's Perils, 1839 (her first production).

GASKELL (Mrs.), maiden name *Elizabeth Cleghorn Stevenson*, Chelsea, novelist, 1811–1865. Cousin Phyllis, 1865; Cranford, 1853; Dark Night's Work (*A*), 1863; Gray Woman (*The*), 1865; Lizzie Leigh, 1854; Lois the Witch, 1861; Mary Barton, 1848; Memoir of Charlotte Brontë, 1857; Moorland Cottage, 1850; My Lady Ludlow, 1859–61; North and South, 1855; Novels and Tales, 1872–73; Right at Last, 1860; Round the Sofa, 1859; Ruth, 1853; Sylvia's Lovers, 1863; Wives and Daughters, 1866 (unfinished).

GASTRELL (*Francis*), bishop of Chester, 1662–1725. Christian Institutes, 1707, a concordance of parallel texts.

GATAKER (Rev. *Thomas*), London, 1574–1654 De Nomine Tetragrammate, etc., 1645; De Novi Testamenti Puritate, 1648; Dialogue on the Unlawfullness of Playing at Cards, etc., 1593; Opera Critica, 1697–98, posthumous.

GATTY, D.D. (*Alfred*), London, 1813– . Baptism Misunderstood, 1849; Bell (*The*), its Origin, History, and Uses, 1847; Key to Tennyson (*A*), 1881; Life at One Living (*A*), 1885; Literature and the Literary Character, 1858; Poems, 1833; Poetical Character (*The*), 1860; Sermons, 1846, 1854, 1858; Sheffield, Past and Present, 1873; St.

Wandville's Abbey, 1887; Testimony of David (*The*), 1870; Vicar and his Duties (*The*), 1853.

With Mrs. Gatty: Book of Sun-dials, 1863 (her last work); Life of Dr. Scott (his wife's father), 1842.

GATTY (Mrs.), pseudonym "Aunt Judy," wife of the preceding, maiden name *Margaret Smith*, Essex, 1809–1873 (a great invalid for the last ten years of her life). Aunt Judy's Letters, 1862; Aunt Judy's Tales, 1858; Aunt Sally's Life, 1865; Book of Emblems, 1872; British Seaweeds, 1863; Children's Mission Army (*The*), 1869; Domestic Pictures and Tales, 1865; Fairy Godmothers (*The*), and other Tales, 1851 (her first book); History of a Bit of Bread (from the French of Jean Macé), 1864; Human Face Divine (*The*), 1859; Hundredth Birthday (*The*), and other tales, 1862; Legendary Tales, 1857; Mission Shillings, 1869; Mother's Book of Poetry (*The*), 1871; Old Folks from Home (*The*), 1861; Parables from Nature, 1851–71; Poor Incumbent (*The*), 1858; Proverbs Illustrated, 1857; Waifs and Strays of Natural History, 1870; Worlds not Realized, 1856. (In conjunction with her husband, see above.)

GAUDEN, D.D. (*John*), bishop of Worcester, born at Mayfield, in Essex, 1605–1662. Eikon Basilikê, 1649 (he claimed the authorship of this book).

GAY (*John*), Barnstaple, in Devonshire, 1688–1732. Ballads (*Eleven*), 1725; Beggar's Opera (*The*), 1727, an opera; Black-eyed Susan, 1725, a song; Captives (*The*), 1724, a play; Dione (a pastoral tragedy); Epistles (*Fourteen*), 1709–22; Fables (50 in part i., 16 in part ii.), 1727–38; Fan (*The*), (in three books), 1713; Polly, a Sequel to the "Beggar's Opera," 1729; Rural Sports (in two cantos), 1711; Shepherd's Week (in six pastorals), 1714; Three Hours after Marriage, 1715, a farce; Trivia (in three books), 1712; What d'ye call it? 1715, a poem on the Royal family; Wife of Bath (*The*), 1713, a comedy. His Life, by Coxe, 1796; Owen, 1804.

GEDDES, LL.D. (Rev. *Alexander*), Arradowl, in Scotland, 1737–1807. Apology for the Roman Catholics of Great Britain, 1801; Bardomachia, or Battle of the Bards, 1803, posthumous; Battle of Bangor, or the Church's Triumph (a comic-heroic poem in nine cantos); Confessional (*The*), a poem; Critical Remarks on the Hebrew Scriptures, 1800; Holy Bible . . . translated, etc., 1792–1807; Idea of a New Version of the Holy Bible for the Use of the English Catholics, 1780. Select *Satires of Horace*, translated, 1778. His Life, by Dr. Mason Good, 1803.

GEDDES (*James*), Scotland, 1710–1749. Essay on the Composition and Manner of Writing of the Ancients . . . 1748.

GEDDES, LL.D. (Rev. *Michael*), Edinburgh, 1671–1714. Church History of Æthiopia, 1696; Church History of Malabar, 1694; Tracts on Divers Subjects, 1714.

GEE, D.D. (*Edward*), 1636–1698. Steps of Ascension to God, or a Ladder to Heaven, 1677 (printed about 30 times).

GEE (*John*), 1582–1648. Foot out of the

4 P

Snare (*The*), 1624 (an *exposé* of the imposi-
tions of English priests).

GEE (*Joshua*), 1726-1788. Trade and Commerce of Great Britain (*The*), 1767 (in good
esteem).

GEIKIE, LL.D. (*Archibald*), Edinburgh, 1835-
. Life of Sir Roderick I. Murchison,
1874; Life of Edward Forbes, 1861 (with Dr.
G. Wilson); Phenomena of the Glacial Drift
of Scotland, 1863; Scenery of Scotland, viewed
in Connection with its Physical Geography,
1865; Story of a Boulder (*The*), 1858;
Student's Manual of Geology, 1871 (with
J. B. Jukes).

GEIKIE, D.D. (*John Cunningham*), Edinburgh, 1824- . Bible by Modern Light
(*The*), 1894; English Reformation (*The*),
1879; George Stanley, 1864; Holy-land and
the Bible, 1887; Hours with the Bible,
1880-84; Landmarks of Old Testament
History, 1894; Life, 1868; Life and Works
of Christ, 1877; Light from Beyond, 1872;
Old Testament Characters, 1884; Science of
Common Life (*The*), 1879; Short Life of
Christ (*A*), 1888.

GELL (Sir *William*), Hopton, in Derbyshire,
1777-1836. Attica, 1817; Geography and
Antiquities of Ithaca, 1807; Itinerary of
Greece, 1810; Itinerary of the Morea, 1817;
Pompeiiana, 1817-19 (with J. P. Gandy);
Topography of Rome and its Vicinity, 1834;
Topography of Troy, 1804.

GENT (*Thomas*), Yorkshire, 1691-1778. An-
nales Regioduni Hullini (*i.e.* Kingston-upon-
Hull), 1735; Customs and Orders of the
Lord Mayor, etc., of York, 1730; Divine
Entertainments, 1724; History of the Eastern
Window of York Cathedral, 1762; History of
England and Rome (*A*), 1741; Miscellanea
Curiosa, 1734; Rippon (*Ancient and Modern
History of*), 1713; York (*Ancient and Modern
History of*), 1730; Yorkshire Militia (*History
of the*), 1760.
Poetry: Divine Mercy and Justice Dis-
played in the Life and Death of Judas Is-
cariot, 1772; Life and Death of Job, 1784;
Life and Death of St. Robert the Hermit (no
date); Life and Death of St. Winefred,
1743; Life and Miracles of Jesus Christ (no
date). His Life, by himself; edited by J.
Hunter, 1832.

GEOFFREY OF MONMOUTH, bishop of St.
Asaph, chronicler, 1082-1154. Chronicon,
sive Historia Britonum, 1128, first printed
1508 (historically worthless); Vita et Vati-
cinia Merlini (in hexameter verse), printed
1830.

GERARD (*Emily*), Mme. de Laszowska, novelist, 1849- . Wrote various stories in collaboration with her sister, Dorothea Gerard.

GIBBON (*Charles*), about 1847-1889. Amoret,
1886; Beyond Compare, 1888; Blood Money,
1896; Braes of Yarrow (*The*), 1881; By
Mead and Stream, 1885; Clare of Clares-
mede, 1886; Dangerous Connections, 1864;
Dead Heart (*The*), a Tale of the Bastile,
1865; Fancy Free, 1884; Flower of the
Forest (*The*), 1882; For Honour's Sake,
1876; For Lack of Gold, 1871; For the
King, 1872; Garvock, 1885; Golden Shaft

(*The*), 1882; Hard Knot (*A*), 1885; Heart's
Delight, 1885; Heart's Problem (*A*), 1881;
In Honour Bound, 1874; In Love and War,
1877; In Pastures Green, 1880; Life of
George Combe, 1878; Loving a Dream,
1884; Of High Degree, 1883; Queen of the
Meadow, 1880; Robin Gray, 1869; What
will the World say? 1875.

GIBBON (*Edward*), Putney in Surrey, 1737-
1794. Antiquities of the House of Bruns-
wick, 1799, posthumous; Autobiography,
1799, posthumous; Decline and Fall of the
Roman Empire, 1776-88 (his great work);
Essais sur l'Etude de la Littérature, 1761.
His Life, by lord Sheffield, 1799; H. H.
Milman, 1839; W. Youngman, 1844; J. C.
Morison, 1879.

GIBBONS, Mus.D. (*Orlando*), Cambridge,
1583-1625. Anthems (these are masterpieces,
especially "Almighty and Everlasting God,"
"Hosannah to the Son of David," and "O
clap your Hands"); Madrigals and Mottets
for five voices, 1612 ("Dainty Sweet Bird,"
and "The Silver Swan," are gems of rare
value).

GIBSON (*Edmund*), bishop of London, born in
Westmoreland, 1669-1748. Chronicon Sax-
onicum, 1692; Codex Juris Ecclesiastici
Anglicani, 1713. Also translated Camden's
Britannia, 1695.

GIBSON (Rev. *John Monro*), 1838- . Ages
before Moses, 1879; Christianity according
to Christ, 1888; Rock *versus* Sand, 1883.
And many other works on divinity.

GIFFORD (*John*), real name *John Richard
Green*, 1758-1818. Address to the People of
England, 1792; Anti-Jacobin Review, 1798;
History of France, 1791-93; Political Life of
W. Pitt, 1809; Reign of Louis XVI., and
History of the Revolution, 1801.

GIFFORD (*William*), Ashburton, in Devonshire, 1756-1826. Baviad (*The*), 1794, a satire
in verse; Mæviad (*The*), 1795, a satire in
verse. Also an Autobiography prefixed to his
translation of *Juvenal*, 1802.

GILBART (*James William*), London, 1794-
1863. History and Principles of Banking,
1834; Logic of Banking, 1859; Logic for the
Million, 1851; Practical Treatise on Banking, 1827.

GILBERT (Sir *Humphrey*), Devonshire, 1539-
1583. Possibility of a North-West Passage,
1576.

GILBERT (Sir *Jeffrey*), Goudhurst, in Kent,
1674-1726. Historical View of the Court of
Exchequer, 1738; History and Practice of
the Court of Chancery, 1758; Law of Devises,
1730; Law of Evidence, 1760; Law of Uses
and Trusts, 1734; Reports in Equity, 1734;
Treatise of Tenures, 1738.

GILBERT (*William Schwenck*), London, 1836-
. Ages Ago, 1869, a play; Bab Ballads
(*The*), 1868 (contributed to *Fun*, but published
separately); Broken Hearts, 1875, an original
fairy play; Charity, 1874, a play, in four acts;
Comedy and Charity, 1884; Creatures of Impulse, 1869, a play; Dan'l Druce, 1876, a
drama, in three acts; Dulcamara, 1866 (his
first dramatic piece); Engaged, 1877, a farcical
comedy, in three acts; Foggerty's Fairy,
1877, a play; Gondoliers (*The*), 1889;

Gretchen, 1879 (based on the legend of *Faust*) ; Happy Arcadia, 1869, a play ; H.M.S. *Pinafore*, 1878, a nautical comic opera ; Iolanthe ; Mikado (*The*), 1885 ; More Bab Ballads, 1872 ; Mountebanks (*The*), 1892 ; Ne'er-do-Weel, 1878, a comedy ; Old Score (*An*), 1867, a play ; On Bail (from the French), 1877, a comedy ; Palace of Truth (*The*), 1870, a fairy comedy, in three acts ; Patience, Bunthorne's Bride, 1881, an æsthetic opera; Pirates of Penzance (*The*), 1880, a comic opera ; Princess (*The*), 1868 (based on Tennyson's poem) ; Princess Ida, 1884, a play ; Pygmalion and Galatea, 1871, a mythological comedy ; Randall's Thumb, 1879, a play ; Rosencrantz and Guildenstern, a play ; Ruddigore, 1887, a play ; Sensation Novel (*A*), 1869 ; Sorcerer (*The*), 1877, a comic opera, in two acts ; Sweethearts, 1874, a dramatic contrast, in two acts ; Tom Cobb, 1875, a farce, in three acts ; Trial by Jury, 1876, an operetta ; Utopia, Limited, 1893 ; Wedding March (*The*), 1873 ; Wicked World (*The*), 1873, a farcical comedy, in three acts ; Yeomen of the Guard (*The*), 1884.

GILCHRIST, LL.D. (*John Borthwick*), Edinburgh, 1759-1841. Anglo-Hindostanee Dictionary, 1786-90 ; British Indian Monitor, 1806-8 ; Hindee Story-teller (*The*), 1802-3 ; Hindostanee Grammar, 1796.

GILDAS, "The Wise," chronicler, 516-570. De Excidio Britanniæ, 560, printed in 1525.

GILES, D.C.L. (Rev. *John Allen*), 1802- . History of the Ancient Britons ; Life and Letters of Thomas Becket ; Life of Alfred the Great. His works extend to 160 volumes.

GILFILLAN (Rev. *George*), born at Comrie, in Perthshire, 1813-1878. Alpha and Omega, 1860 ; Bards of the Bible, 1850 ; Book of British Poesy, 1851 ; Christianity and our Era, 1857 ; Comrie and its Neighbourhood, 1872 ; Gallery of Literary Portraits, 1845 ; Second Gallery of Literary Portraits, 1849 ; Third Gallery of Literary Portraits, 1849, 1854, 1855 ; Grand Discovery (*The*), 1854 ; History of a Man, 1856 ; Life of W. Scott, 1870 ; Life of Rev. W. Anderson, 1873 ; Martyrs, Heroes, and Bards of the Scottish Covenant, 1852 ; Modern Christian Heroes, 1869 ; Night, 1867 ; Remoter Stars in the Church Sky, 1867 ; Sketches (literary and theological), 1881, posthumous.

GILL, D.D. (*John*), Kettering, in Northamptonshire, 1697-1771. Body of Doctrinal Divinity, 1769-70 ; Cause of God and Truth, 1735-38 ; Exposition of the Bible, 1746-66 ; Exposition of Solomon's Song, 1728 ; Prophecies . . . relating to Christ, 1728.

GILLIES, LL.D. (*John*), Scotland, 1747-1836. History of Ancient Greece, 1786-1810 ; History of the World from Alexander to Augustus, 1807-10 ; View of the Reign of Frederick II. of Prussia, 1789.

GILLRAY (*James*), London, 1750-1815. Caricatures, 1779, 1810.

GILLY, D.D. (*William Stephen*), 1789-1855. Excursion to the Mountains of Piedmont, 1825 ; Memoir of Felix Neff, etc., 1832 ; Our Protestant Forefathers, 1835 ; Vigilantius

and his Times, 1844 ; Waldensian Researches, 1831.

GILPIN (Rev. *William*), Carlisle, 1724-1804. Exposition of the New Testament, 1790 ; Forest Scenery, 1791 ; Life of Lord Cobham, 1764 ; Life of Cranmer, 1784 ; Life of Bernard Gilpin, 1751 ; Life of Latimer, 1755 ; Lives of Wicliff, Huss, etc., 1764 ; Observations relative to Picturesque Beauty, 1787.

GINSBURG, LL.D. (*Christian*), born at Warsaw, 1830- . Essenes (*The*), 1864 ; Kabbalah (*The*), 1865 ; Karaites (*The*), their history and literature, 1864.

GIRALDUS CAMBRENSIS, or Sylvester Gerald de Barri, Pembrokeshire, 1147-1220. De Principis Instructione, 1216 ; Descriptio Walliæ, Symbolum Electorum, Speculum Duorum, De Rebus a se Gestis, 1200-1 ; Expugnatio Hiberniæ, 1187 ; Gemma Ecclesiastica, 1197 ; Itinerarium Cambriæ, 1189, printed 1585 ; Topographia Hiberniæ, 1187 ; Vita Galfridi, 1193.

GIRDLESTONE (Rev. *Charles*), 1797-1881. Family Commentary on the Bible, 1832-1842 ; Number, a link between Divine and Human Intelligence, 1875.

GISBORNE (Rev. *Thomas*), Derby, 1758-1846. Duties of Women, 1797 ; Familiar Survey of the Christian Religion, 1797 ; Inquiry into the Duties of Men in the Higher and Middle Classes, 1794 ; Poems, Sacred and Moral, 1799 ; Principles of Moral Philosophy, 1789 ; Testimony of Natural Theology to Christianity, 1818 ; Walks in a Forest, 1796.

GISSING (*George*), 1857. Demos, 1886 ; Isabel Clarendon, 1884 ; Life's Morning (*A*), 1888 ; Nether World (*The*), 1889 ; New Grub Street, 1891 ; Thyrza, 1887 ; Unclassed (*The*), 1884 ; Whirlpool (*The*), 1897.

GLADSTONE (*William Ewart*), Liverpool, 1809-1898. Academic Sketch (*An*), 1892 ; Ancient Greece, 1865, an address ; Butler's Works (arranged), 1896 ; Chapter of Autobiography (*A*), 1868 ; Church considered in Relation with the State, 1840 ; Church Principles, etc., 1841 ; Eastern Crisis (*The*), 1897 ; Ecce Homo (*On*), 1868 ; Gleanings of Past Years, 1879, 1897 ; Homeric Synchronisms, 1876 ; Horace, Odes, etc., translated, 1895 ; Impregnable Rock of . . . Scripture (*The*), 1890-92 ; Irish Question (*The*), 1886 ; Juventus Mundi, 1869 ; Landmarks of Homeric Study, 1890 ; Letters to the Earl of Aberdeen, 1850-51 ; Psalter (*The*), 1895 ; Remarks on Recent Commercial Legislation, 1845 ; Rome and the Latest Fashions in Religion, 1875 ; State considered in its Relation to the Church (*The*), 1838 ; Studies on Homer and the Homeric Age, 1858 ; Studies Subsidiary to the Work of Bishop Butler, 1896-7 ; Turk in Europe (*The*), 1876 ; Vatican Decrees (*The*), 1874 ; Vaticanism, 1875 ; Wedgwood, 1863, an address. His Life, by Barnett Smith, 1879 ; G. W. E. Russell ; G. R. Emerson, 1881 ; Justin M'Carthy, 1898.

GLAISHER (*James*), Scotland, *- . Travels in the Air, etc., 1870.

GLANVIL (Rev. *Joseph*), Plymouth, philosopher, 1636-1680. Considerations touching Witches, 1666 ; Lux Orientalis, 1662 ; Plus

Ultra, 1668 (the advancement of knowledge since the time of Aristotle); Sadducismus Triumphatus, 1681; Scepsis Scientifica, 1665; Vanity of Dogmatizing.

GLANVIL (*Ranulph de*), "Father of English Jurisprudence," died 1190. Tractatus de Legibus et Consuetudinibus Angliæ, 1181 (the first of the kind ever written), printed in 1780.

GLAPTHORNE (*Henry*), 1602–1653. Albertus Wallenstein, 1630, a tragedy; Argalus and Parthenia, 1639, a play; Hollander (*The*), 1640, a comedy; Ladies' Privilege (*The*), 1640, a comedy; Poems, 1639; Whitehall, 1643, a poem; Wit in a Constable, 1640, a comedy.

GLEICHEN (*Albert Edward Wilfrid*, count), 1863– . Armies of Europe (translated), 1890; With the Camel Corps, 1888.

GLEIG (Rev. *George Robert*), Stirling, in Scotland, 1796–1887. Campaigns of Washington and New Orleans, 1821; Life of the Duke of Wellington, 1859 (his chief work); Story of the Battle of Waterloo (*The*); Subaltern (*The*), 1825, a novel.

GLIDDON (*George Robins*), Egypt, 1807–1857. Ancient Egypt, her Monuments, Hieroglyphics, History, etc., 1840 (his first work, and held in high estimation); Indigenous Races of the Earth, 1857; Types of Mankind . . . based on the Ancient Monuments, Paintings, Sculptures, etc.

GLOVER (*Richard*), London, 1712–1785. Admiral Hosier's Ghost, 1739 (this was a very parallel case to that of sir Richard Glenville, the subject of Tennyson's ballad); Boadicea, 1753, a tragedy; Athenaïd (*The*), a continuation of "Leonidas" (in blank verse), 1787; Jason, 1799, a tragedy (suppressed); Leonidas (an epic in 12 books, in blank verse), 1737–38; London, 1739; Medea, 1761, a tragedy.

GLOVER (*Thomas*), Somerset herald, 1530–1588. Catalogue of Honour, 1610; De Nobilitate Politica vel Civili, 1608.

GODWIN (Rev. *Benjamin*), Bath, in Somersetshire, 1785–1871. Examination of Dr. Pusey's Sermon on the Eucharist, 1843; Lectures on Colonial Slavery, 1830; Lectures on the Atheistic Controversy, 1834.

GODWIN, D.D. (*Francis*), bishop of Hereford, born in Northamptonshire, 1561–1633. Catalogue of the Bishops of England, 1601; De Præsulibus Angliæ Commentarius, 1616 (an excellent and useful book); Man in the Moon (*The*), 1638, a philosophical romance (his best-known work); Nuncius Inanimatus in Utopia, 1629; Rerum Anglicarum . . . Annales, 1616.

GODWIN (*George*), Brompton, in Middlesex, 1815– . Churches of London, 1838; Essay on Concrete (*An*), 1835; History in Ruins, 1853; London Shows, 1854.

GODWIN (*Mary*). See WOLSTONECRAFT.

GODWIN, D.D. (*Thomas*), 1587–1643. Moses and Aaron, or the Civil and Ecclesiastical Rites of the Hebrews, 1610 (for many years a text-book); Romanæ Historiæ Anthologia, 1613.

GODWIN (*William*), Wisbech, in Cambridgeshire, 1756–1836. Antonio, 1800, a tragedy; Caleb Williams, 1794 (his best novel, drama-

tized by Coleman as "The Iron Chest"); Cloudesley, 1830, a novel; Damon and Delia, 1831; Deloraine, 1833, a novel; Enquirer (*The*), 1834; Essay on Sepulchres, 1809; Faulkner, 1808, a tragedy; Fleetwood, 1805, a novel (a "man of feeling"); Genius of Christianity Unveiled, 1819; Herald of Literature (*The*), 1821; History of the Commonwealth of England, 1824–28; Imogen, 1830, a novel; Inquirer (*The*), 1797, essays; Life of Chatham, 1810; Life of Chaucer, 1803; Lives of Edward and John Philips, 1815; Lives of the Necromancers, 1834; Mandeville, 1817, a tale of the 17th century; On Population, 1820; Political Justice, 1793; St. Godwin, 1800, a tale of the 17th and 18th centuries; St. Leon, 1799, a tale of the 16th century; Sketches of History, 1784 (his first work); Thoughts on Man, 1831; Treatise on Population, 1820. His Life, by Kegan Paul, 1876.

GOFFE (Rev. *Thomas*), 1592–1627. Careless Shepherdess (*The*), 1656, a tragi-comedy; Couragious Turke (*The*), 1632, a tragedy (Amurath I.); Orestes, 1663, a tragedy; Raging Turke (*The*), 1631, a tragedy (Bajazet II.).

GOLDING (*Arthur*), died 1590. Discourse upon the Earthquake, 1580; Translation of Ovid's *Metamorphoses*, 1565–67.

GOLDSMITH (*Oliver*), Pallas, in Ireland, 1728–1774. Bee (*The*), 1759–60; Captivity (*The*), 1774, an oratorio; Citizen of the World (*The*), 123 letters, 1759–62; Deserted Village (*The*), 1770, his best poem; Double Transformation (*The*), 1765, a tale in verse; Edwin and Angelina, 1765, a ballad; Elegy on a Mad Dog, 1765; Essays (*Twenty-four*), 1758–65; Good-natured Man (*The*), 1768, a comedy; Haunch of Venison (*The*), 1765, a poetic epistle; Hermit (*The*), 1765, a ballad; History of the Earth and Animated Nature, 1774; Life of Bolingbroke, 1770; Life of Richard Nash (*i.e.* Beau Nash), 1762; Life of Thomas Parnell, 1768; Life of Voltaire, 1759; Present State of Literature in Europe, 1759; Retaliation, 1774, a poem; She Stoops to Conquer, 1773, a comedy; Traveller (*The*), 1764, a poem; Vicar of Wakefield (*The*), 1766, a novel. His Life, by bishop Percy, 1774; sir James Prior, 1837; John Forster, 1848; Washington Irving, 1849; Dr. Kalisch, 1860; W. Black, 1879; H. Austin Dobson, 1888.

GOOD, M.D. (*John Mason*), Epping, in Essex, 1764–1827. Book of Job (translated metrically), 1812; Book of Nature, 1826 (his chief work); Proverbs and Psalms (from the Hebrew), 1826; Short History of Medicine, 1795; Song of Songs (*The*), from the Hebrew, 1803; Study of Medicine, 1822 (his best medical work); Translation of *Lucretius* into verse, 1805. His Life, by Dr. Olinthus Gregory, 1828.

GOODCOLE (Rev. *Henry*), 1579–1637. Account of Francis Robinson hanged and quartered for stealing the Great Seale of England, 1618; Elizabeth Sawyer, the Witch of Edmont . . . with the Devil's Access to her, and their Conference, 1621.

GOODWIN (*Charles Wycliffe*), King's Lynn,

in Norfolk, 1817–1878. Essays and Reviews, 1860; Hieratic Papyri, 1858; Mosaic Cosmogony (*The*), 1860.

GOODWIN, D.D. (*Harvey*), bishop of Carlisle, born at King's Lynn, 1818–1891. Christ in the Wilderness, 1855; Commentary on St. Mark, 1860; Commentary on St. John 1865; Creation, 1886; Essays on the Pentateuch, 1867; Foundations of the Creed (*The*), 1889; Gradual Development of Revelation, 1871; Hulsean Lectures, 1855–56; Memoirs of Bishop Mackenzie, 1864; Walks in the Regions of Science and Faith, 1883.

GOODWIN (Rev. *John*), 1593–1665. Imputatio Fidei, 1640; Obstructors of Justice, 1649 (in defence of the decapitation of Charles I. : this book was burnt by the common hangman); Redemption Redeemed, 1651; Right and Might Well Met, 1648 (in favour of lord Fairfax).

GORDON (Lady *Duff*), maiden name *Lucy Austen*, died 1869. Letters from Egypt, 1863–65; Last Letters from Egypt, 1875; Letters from the Cape, 1864.

GORDON, D.D. (*James*), Scotland, 1543–1620. Controversiarum Fidei Christianæ Epitome, 1612–20.

GORDON (*James Lesmore*), Aberdeen, 1560–1641. Biblia Sacra, 1636; Opus Chronologicum, 1617.

GORDON (*Robert*), Straloch, in Scotland, 1580–1661. History of Scots Affairs, 1637–41; Origo et Progressus Familiæ . . . Gordoniorum (still in MS.); Theatrum Scotiæ, 1648.

GORDON (Sir *Robert*), 1791–1847. Genealogical History of the Earldom of Sutherland, etc., 1813 (a valuable publication for details bearing on the early history of Scotland).

GORDON (*Thomas*), Ireland, 1684–1750. Independent Whig (*The*), 1728; Pillars of Priestcraft . . . shaken, 1768, posthumous. *Translations :* Cato's *Letters*, 1737; *Sallust*, 1744; *Tacitus*, 1728–31.

GORDON (*William*), Old Aberdeen, in Scotland, *–*. History of the . . . Family of Gordon, 1726–1727 (very rare).

GORDON, D.D. (*William*), Hitchin, in Hertfordshire, 1729–1807. History of the Rise . . . and Independence of the United States of America, 1788.

GORDON-CUMMING (*Constance Frederica*), Altyre, in Scotland, 1837– . At Home in Fiji, 1881; Fire Fountains, 1882; From the Hebrides to the Himalayas, 1876; Granite Crags, 1883; In the Hebrides, 1883; In the Himalayas, 1884; Lady's Cruise in a French Man-of-War (*A*), 1882; Two Happy Years in Ceylon, 1891; *Viâ* Cornwall to Egypt, 1885; Wanderings in China, 1885; Work for the Blind in China, 1888.

GORE (Rev. *Charles*), 1853– . Bampton Lectures, 1891; Church and the Ministry, 1893; Creed of the Christian (*The*), 1895; Dissertations, 1895; Hints for the Study of Theology, 1888; Incarnation of the Son of God (*The*), 1891; Leo the Great, 1880; Mission of the Church, 1891; Roman Catholic Claims, 1888; Sermon on the Mount (*The*), 1896.

GORE (Mrs.), maiden name *Catherine Grace Frances Moody*, East Retford, in Nottinghamshire, novelist, 1799–1861. Ambassador's Wife (*The*), 1842; Banker's Wife (*The*), or Court and City, 1843; Book of Roses (*The*), 1838, a rose manual; Cabinet Minister (*The*), 1839 (R. B. Sheridan); Cecil, or the Adventures of a Coxcomb, 1841; Cecil, a Peer; Courtier of the Days of Charles II., and other Tales, 1839; Dacre of the South, 1841, a drama; Diary of a Désennuyée, 1838; Dowager (*The*), or the New School for Scandal, 1840; Fair of May-Fair (*The*), 1832; Fascination, 1842; Greville, or a Season in Paris, 1841; Heir of Selwood (*The*), 1838; Hungarian Tales, 1829; Lettre de Cachet (*The*), 1827; Lover and her Husband (*The*), 1841; Mary Raymond, 1837; Mothers and Daughters, 1831; Mrs. Armytage, 1836; Preferment, or My Uncle the Earl, 1839; Reign of Terror (*The*), 1827; Theresa Marchmont, or the Maid of Honour, 1823; Woman of the World (*The*), 1838; Women as they are, 1830.

Her *dramatic works :* The Bond, a dramatic poem; Lord Dacre of the South, a tragedy; School for Coquettes, a prize comedy.

GORTON (*John*), *–*. Biographical Dictionary (*A*), 1828 (of considerable merit); Topographical Dictionary of Great Britain and Ireland, 1833.

GOSSE (*Edmund William*), London, poet, etc., 1849– . Browning (*Robert*), 1890; Critical Essay on George Tinworth, 1883; Critical Kit-Kats, 1895; Discourses of Sir Joshua Reynolds, 1884; English Odes, 1881; Firdawsi in Exile, 1885; From Shakespeare to Pope, 1885; Gossip in a Library, 1891; Gray (*Thomas*), 1882 (his works, 1884); History of XVIII. Century Literature, 1889; In Russet and Silver, 1894, poems; Jacobean Poets (*The*), 1894; King Erik, 1876; Life of Congreve, 1888; Life of P. H. Gosse (his father), 1890; Life of Gray, 1882; Life of Sir W. Raleigh, 1886; Madrigals; Memoir of Thomas Locke, 1882; Memoir of Cecil Lawson (*A*), 1883; New Poems, 1879; On Viol and Flute, 1873; Questions at Issue, 1893; Raleigh, 1806; Secret of Narcisse (*The*), 1892; Selections of English Odes (*A*), 1881; Seventeenth Century Studies, 1883; Student in the Literature of Northern Europe, 1879; Unknown Lover (*The*), 1878; Works of L. T. Beddoes (*The*), 1894.

GOSSE (*Philip Henry*), Worcester, 1810–1887. Actinologia Britannica (Sea Anemones and Corals), 1860; Aquarium (*The*), 1854; Canadian Naturalist (*The*), 1840; Naturalist's Rambles on the Devonshire Coast (*A*); Naturalist's Sojourn in Jamaica; Omphalos, 1857; Year at the Shore (*A*), 1865.

GOSSON (Rev. *Stephen*), Kent, 1554–1623. Captain Mario, 1577, a comedy; Cataline's Conspiracies, an historic drama; Speculum Humanum, 1581, a poem.

Against Dramatic Entertainments : Ephemerides of Phialo (*The*), in three books, 1586; Plays Confuted in Five Actions, 1580; Schoole of Abuse, 1579 (an attack on the stage).

GOUGH (*Richard*), London, 1735–1777. Ancient

Monuments of India, 1785, posthumous ; Anecdotes of British Topography, 1768 ; Coins of Canute, 1777 ; Coins of the Seleucidæ, Kings of Syria, 1804, posthumous ; History of Crowland Abbey, 1816, posthumous ; History of the Society of Antiquaries of London, 1770 ; On the Round Towers of Scotland and Ireland, 1779, posthumous ; Sepulchral Monuments of Great Britain, 1786–1799 (this valuable work was almost entirely destroyed by fire).

GOULBURN, D.D. (*Edward Meyrick*), 1818–1889. Athanasian Creed (*The*), 1872 ; Book of Rugby School (*The*), 1856 ; Doctrine of the Resurrection of the Body (eight sermons), 1851 ; Functions of our Cathedrals (*The*), 1869 ; Holy Catholic Church (*The*), 1873 ; Home and Foreign Missions, 1872 ; Idle World (*The*), 1855 ; Inspiration of the Scriptures, 1857 ; Introduction to the Devotional Study of the Scriptures, 1854 ; Manual of Confirmation (*The*), 1855 ; Office of the Holy Communion (*The*), 1863 ; Pursuit of Holiness (*The*), 1869 ; See and Cathedral of Norwich (*The*), 1872 ; Thoughts on Personal Religion, 1862.

GOULD (*John*), Lyme, in Dorsetshire, 1804–1881. Birds of Asia (*The*), 1850–60 ; Birds of Australia (*The*) (in seven folio volumes), 1837–48 ; Birds of Europe (*The*) (in five folio volumes), 1832–37 ; Birds of Great Britain ; Century of Birds from the Himalayan Mountains, 1832 ; Handbook of the Birds of Australia, 1865; Humming Birds, 1852 ; Icones Avium, etc., 1837–38 ; Introduction to the Birds of Australia, 1848 ; Macropodidæ or Kangaroo Family (*The*), 1841–42 ; Mammals of Australia (*The*), 1845 ; Odontophorinæ or Partridges of America (*The*), 1844–50 ; Ramphastidæ or Toucans (*The*), 1833–35, Supplement 1855 ; Synopsis of the Birds of Australia, 1837–38 ; Trochilidæ or Humming Birds (*The*), 1850 ; Trogonidæ (*The*), 1835–38.

GOULD (*Robert*), 1645–1708. Lydus Scacchiæ (a satyre), with other Poems, 1675 ; Poems, chiefly Satyres, 1689.

GOWER, M.D. (*Foote*), 1730–1792. Materials of a History of Cheshire, 1771.

GOWER (*John*), 1327–1402. (Chaucer calls him "The Moral Gower.") (50) Balades (in French), 1350, printed 1813 ; Confessio Amantis (a poetical dialogue in English), 1393, printed by Caxton 1483 (? 1493) ; Pyrgomachia, printed 1675 ; Speculum Meditantis (in French), 1370 ; Vox Clamantis (in Latin), 1381 (never printed). His Life, by Dr. R. Pauli, 1857.

GRACE (*William Gilbert*), surgeon, 1848– . Cricket, 1891.

GRADY (*Thomas*), *–*. Nosegay (*The*), 1815 (the most violent invective in the language ; it is dedicated to T. Moore, the poet).

GRAEME (*John*), Scotland, 1748–1772. Poems, 1773.

GRAFTON (*Richard*), chronicler, died 1573. Abridgment of the Chronicles of England, 1562 ; Chronicles at Large, 1568–69 ; Hall's Chronicle, 1548 ; Manuell of the Chronicles of England, 1565.

GRAHAM (*Maria*), afterwards Mrs. *Calcott*,

1788–1842. Journal of a Residence in Chili, 1824 ; Journal of a Residence in India, 1812 ; Journal of a Voyage to Brazil, etc., 1824 ; Journal of a Voyage to the Sandwich Islands, 1827 ; Letters on India, 1815 ; Memoirs of Nicholas Poussin, 1820 ; Three Months on the Mountains East of Rome, 1819.

GRAHAM, D.C.L. (*Thomas*), Glasgow, 1805–1869. Elements of Chemistry, 1842 ; Liquid Diffusion applied to Analysis, 1861 ; On the Diffusion of Liquids, 1850–51 ; On the Formation of Alcoates . . . and Alcohol, 1831 ; On the Law of the Diffusion of Gases, 1834 ; On the Motion of Gases, 1846, 1849 ; On Osmotic Force, 1854 ; Researches on the Arseniates, Phosphates, etc., 1833.

GRAHAME (Rev. *James*), Glasgow, 1765–1811. Biblical Pictures, 1805, in verse; Birds of Scotland (*The*), 1806 ; British Georgics, 1809 ; Mary Stewart, 1801, a dramatic poem ; Poems, 1807, 1810 ; Sabbath (*The*), 1804 (his chief poem) ; Wallace, 1799, a tragedy.

GRAINGER, M.D. (*James*), Dunse, in Berwick, 1723–1767. Sugar Cane (*The*), 1764. He translated into English verse the *Elegies* of Tibullus, 1758.

GRAND (*Sarah*), real name Mrs. *Frances E. MacFail*, *– . Beth Book (*The*), 1897 ; Domestic Experiment (*A*), 1891 ; Heavenly Twins (*The*), 1893 ; Ideala, 1888 ; Our Manifold Nature, 1894 ; Singularly Deluded, 1893.

GRANGER (Rev. *James*), Berkshire, 1716–1776. Biographical History of England (*A*), 1769–74, supplement 1774, continuation to the reign of George I. 1806 (with the Rev. Mark Noble), further continuation to the close of George III.'s reign by W. Miller, 1820 ; Letters, etc., 1805, posthumous.

GRANT (Mrs.), afterwards Mrs. *Murray*, Aberlour, in Scotland, 1745–1814. Roy's Wife of Aldivalloch, a song.

GRANT (Mrs.), of Laggan, maiden name *Anne McVicar*, Glasgow, 1755–1838. Eighteen Hundred and Thirteen, 1814, a poem ; Essays on the Superstitions of the Highlanders of Scotland, 1811 ; Highlanders (*The*), and other Poems, 1803 ; Letters from the Mountains, 1806 ; Memoirs of an American Lady, 1808 ; Poems, 1803. Her Life, by herself, finished by her son, 1844.

GRANT (*James*), Elgin, Scotland, 1802–1879. Bench and the Bar (*The*), 1837 ; British Senate (*The*), 1838 ; Brother born for Adversity (*The*), 1856 ; Comforter (*The*), 1859 ; Divinity of Christ, 1868 ; Dying Command of Christ (*The*), 1863 ; End of All Things, etc., 1866 ; Foes of our Faith, etc., 1862 ; Glorious Gospel of Christ (*The*), 1861 ; God is Love, 1858 ; God's Unspeakable Gift, 1861 ; Grace and Glory, 1863 ; Great Metropolis (*The*), 1836 ; Hymns of Heaven, 1867 ; Impressions of Ireland, 1844 ; Joseph Jenkins, 1843 ; Lights and Shadows of London Life, 1842 ; Memoirs of Sir George Sinclair, 1870 ; Metropolitan Pulpit (*The*), 1839 ; Newspaper Press (*The*), 1871–72 ; Our Heavenly Home, 1859 ; Paris and its People, 1844 ; Personal Visits to the Scenes of Irish Revivals, 1859 ; Pictures of Popular People, 1842 ; Plymouth Brethren, 1875 ;

Portraits of Public Characters, 1841; Random Recollections of the House of Commons, 1835; Random Recollections of the House of Lords, 1836; Records of a Run through Continental Countries, 1853; Religious Tendencies of the Times, 1869; Sketches in London, 1838; Sources of Joy in Seasons of Sorrow, 1811; Steps and Stages on the High-road to Glory, 1865; Travels in Town, 1839; Truths for the Day of Life, 1864.

GRANT (*James*), novelist, Edinburgh, 1822–1887. Adventures of an Aide-de-Camp, 1848; Adventures of Rob Roy, 1864; Arthur Blane, or the Hundred Cuirassiers, 1858; Bothwell, or the Days of Mary Queen of Scots, 1851; British Battles on Land and Sea, 1873–75; British Heroes in Foreign Wars, 1873; Captain of the Guard (*The*), 1862; Cassell's Old and New Edinburgh, 1880–83; Cavaliers of Fortune (*The*), 1859; Constable of France (*The*), 1866; Derval Hampton, 1881; Dick Rodney, or the Adventures of an Eton Boy, 1862; Did She Love Him? 1876; Edinburgh Castle, 1850; Fairer than a Fairy, 1874; First Love and Last Love, 1868; Frank Hilton, or the Queen's Own, 1857; Girl he Married (*The*), 1869; Harry Ogilvie, or the Black Dragoon, 1856; Highlanders of Belgium (*The*), 1847; History of India, 1880–81; Hollywood Hall, 1859; Jack Challoner, 1883; Jack Manly, his Adventures, 1861; IJane Seton, or the King's Advocate, 1853; King's Own Borderers (*The*), 1865; Lady Gwendonwyn (a romance of war), 1881 (The Cameronians); Lady Wedderburn's Wish, 1870, a tale of the Crimean War; Laura Everingham, 1857; Legends of the Black Watch, 1859; Letty Hyde's Lovers, 1863; Lucy Arden, 1859, a tale of 1715; Mary of Loraine, 1860; Master of Aberfeldie, 1884; Memoirs of Kirkcaldy of Grange, 1849; Memoirs of Morley Ashton, 1876; Memoirs of Sir John Hepburn, etc., 1851; Memoirs of the Marquis of Montrose, 1858; Memorials of Edinburgh Castle, 1850; Miss Cheyn of Essilmont, 1883; Morley Ashton, 1876; Old and New Edinburgh, 1882; Oliver Ellis, or the Fusiliers, 1861; One of the Six Hundred, 1875; Only an Ensign, 1871; Phantom Regiment (*The*), 1856; Philip Rollo, or the Scottish Musketeers, 1854; Playing with Fire, 1887; Queen's Cadet (*The*), 1874; Romance of War (*The*), or Highlanders in Spain, 1846 (his first production); Royal Regiment (*The*), 1879; Royal Highlanders, 1885; Second to None, 1864; Secret Despatch (*The*), 1869; Shall I win her? 1874; Six Years ago, 1877; Under the Red Dragon, 1872; Vere of Ours, 1878; Violet Jermyn, 1882; Yellow Frigate (*The*), 1855; Walter Fenton, or the Scotch Cavalier, 1850; White Cockade, or Faith and Fortitude, 1867.

GRANT (Rev. *Johnson*), about 1780–1840. Josuah, 1837, a poem, in 13 books (never published); Summary of the History of the English Church, etc., 1811–26 (held in good repute).

GRANT ALLEN. See ALLEN (*Charles Grant*).

GRANTHAM (Rev. *Thomas*), 1600–1672. Wife and no Wife (*A*), or Leah instead of Rachel, 1641, a sermon (ordered to be burnt by the common hangman).

GRANVILLE (*George*), viscount Lansdowne, 1667–1735. British Enchanters (*The*), 1701, a dramatic poem; Gallants (*The*), 1696, a comedy; Heroic Love, 1698, a tragedy.

GRATTAN (*Henry*), Dublin, 1746–1820. Speeches, 1822, posthumous. His Life and Times, by his son, 1839–46; D. O. Madden, 1847.

GRATTAN (*Thomas Colley*), 1796–1864. Agnes of Mansfeldt; Ben Nazir, 1827, a tragedy; Heiress of Bruges; Highways and Byeways, 1827; History of the Netherlands, 1840; Jacqueline of Holland; Legends of the Rhine, 1837; Philibert, 1819, a poetical romance; Traits of Travels.

GRAUNT (*John*), London, 1620–1674. Bills of Mortality, 1661.

GRAVES (*George*), naturalist, *-*. British Ornithology, 1821; Monograph of the British Grasses, 1822; Naturalist's Pocket-book (*The*), 1818; Ovarium Britannicum, 1816.

GRAVES (Rev. *John*), 1729–1809. History of Cleveland, in the North Riding of Yorkshire, 1808.

GRAVES (Rev. *Richard*), Gloucestershire, 1705–1804. Euphrosyne, or Amusements on the Road of Life, 1776; Spiritual Quixote (*The*), a satire on illiterate preachers, 1772 (his best work).

GRAY (*Maxwell*) (*M. G. Tuttiett*), novelist. Costly Freak (*A*), 1893; In the Heart of the Storm, 1891; Innocent Impostor (*An*), 1892; Last Sentence (*The*), 1893; Days of the Dragon Slayer, 1894; Reproach of Annesley, 1889; Silence of Dean Maitland (*The*), 1886; Westminster Chimes and other poems, 1889; etc.

GRAY, M.D. (*Asa*), Paris, in New York, U.S., 1810–1887. Botany of the United States, 1840; Elements of Botany, 1836; Flora of North America, begun 1838 (with Dr. Torrey); Manual of Botany for the Northern States, 1848; Pacific Exploring Expedition under Captain Wilkes, 1854.

GRAY (*David*), Glasgow, 1838–1861. Luggie (*The*), and other Poems, 1862.

GRAY (*John Edward*), 1800–1875. Bibliography of Zoölogy and Geology, 1852; Gleanings from the Menagerie and Aviary of Knowsley Hall, 1846–50; Spicelegia Zoölogica, 1828–30; Synopsis of the Contents of the British Museum, 1840; Zoölogical Miscellany, 1835–45. His brother, George Robert (1808–1872), was also a distinguished naturalist, and author of *The Genera of British Birds*, etc.

GRAY, D.D. (*Robert*), bishop of Bristol, 1762–1834. Connexion between the Sacred Writings and the Literature of [secular] Authors, 1819 (an admirable work); Key to the Old Testament and Apocrypha, 1790; Sermons and Discourses, 1793, 1796; Theory of Dreams, 1808.

GRAY (*Thomas*), London, 1716–1771. Bard (*The*), 1757, a Pindaric ode; Elegy in a Country Churchyard, 1749 (the best elegy in the language); Eton College, 1742, an ode; Hymn to Adversity, 1750; Installation of the Duke of Grafton (*The*), 1769; Ode to Vicissitude, 1756; Progress of Poesy, 1757, a Pindaric ode; Spring, 1751, an ode. His Life, by W. Mason, 1775; J. Mitford, 1814.

GREAVES (*John*), Alresford, in Hampshire, 1602–1652. Astronomicæ quædam, ex Traditione Shah Cholgii Persæ . . . 1652; Bina Tabulæ Geographicæ, 1652; Chorasmiæ et Mawarnalnabræ . . . Descriptio, 1650; Discourse on the Roman Foot and Denarius, 1647; Elementa Linguæ Persicæ, 1648; Epochæ Celebriores ex Traditione Ulug-Beigi, 1650; Origine and Antiquity of our English Weights and Measures, etc., 1706, posthumous; Pyramidographia, 1646. His Memoirs, by Dr. Birch, 1737.

GREEN (*John Richard*), 1837–1883. Conquest of England (*The*), 1884; History of the English People, 1877–80; Making of England (*The*), 1882; Stray Studies from England and Italy, 1876.

GREEN (*Joseph Henry*), 1791–1863. Spiritual Philosophy, 1865; Vital Dynamics.

GREEN (*Matthew*), 1696–1737. Spleen (*The*), and other Poems, 1737.

GREEN (Mrs.), maiden name *Mary Ann Everett Wood*, Sheffield, 1818–1895. Diary of John Rous (*The*), 1856; Letters of Queen Henrietta Maria, 1857; Letters of Royal and Illustrious Ladies, 1846; Lives of the Princesses of England, 1849–55. N.B.— Mrs. Green has calendered several State Papers under the direction of the Master of the Rolls; she calendered the papers of James I., 1857–59; of Charles II., 1860–68; The Interregnums, 1875–83, etc.

GREEN (*Thomas Hill*), 1836–1882. Lectures on the Principles of Political Obligations, 1895; Liberal Legislation and Freedom of Contract, 1881; Prolegomĕna to Ethics, edited by A. C. Bradley, 1883; Witness of God and Faith (*The*), with Introductory notice by Arnold Toynbee, 1883. Works, edited by R. L. Nettleship, 1885–88.

GREEN (*Valentine*), Warwickshire, 1739–1813. History and Antiquities of Worcester, 1796, supplement, containing an account of the discovery of the body of king John in Worcester Cathedral, 1797. He also engraved West's *Stoning of St. Stephen*, 1776.

GREENE (*Robert*), Norwich, 1560–1592. Alcida, 1588, a play; Alfonsus, King of Arragon, 1594, posthumous, a comedy; Arbasto, King of Denmark, 1617, a romance; Blacke Bookes Messenger (*The*), 1592; Ciceronis Amor, 1589; Euphues his Censure to Philautus, 1587; Farewell to Folly, 1591; Frier Bacon and Frier Bongay, 1594, a comedy; Groat'sworth of Wit . . . 1592, a romance; Gwydonius, 1584; History of Dorastus and Faunia, 1588; James IV. of Scotland, 1598, posthumous, an historical play; Looking-glass for London, etc., 1594, posthumous, a comedy; Mamillia, or the Triumph of Pallas (in two parts), 1593, a play; Menaphon, 1587, a romance; Morando, the Tritameron of Love, 1584; Myrrour of Modestie (Susanna and the Elders), 1584; Never too Late (a lament of the follies and faults of his youth), 1590; News both from Heaven and Hell,

1593, posthumous; Notable Discovery of Coosnage, 1591; Orlando Furioso, 1594, posthumous, a play; Orpharion, 1599, posthumous; Pair of Turtledoves (Bellora and Fidelio), 1606, posthumous, a romance; Pandosto, the Triumph of Time, 1588, a romance (same as "Doraustus and Faunia"); Perimedes the Blacksmith, 1588, a collection of stories and poems; Philomela, the Lady Fitzwalter's Nightingale, 1592; Planetomachia, 1585; Quip for an Upstart Courtier (*A*), 1592; Repentance of Robert Greene, 1592 (his most valuable prose work); Spanish Masquerado (*The*), 1589; Vision (*Greene's*), 1592, a lament for the folly of his pen. His Life, by Dyce, 1831.

GREENFIELD (*William*), 1800–1831. Polymierian Lexicon to the Greek Testament, 1829.

GREENWELL (*Dora*), poetess, etc., 1821–1882. Camera Obscura, 1876; Carmina Crucis, 1869; Christina, 1860; Colloquia Crucis, 1871 (sequel to "The Two Friends"); Covenant of Life and Peace, 1867; Essays, 1866; John Woolman, 1871; Patience of Hope, 1867; Poems, 1848, 1867; Stories that might be True, 1851; Two Friends (*The*), 1866.

GREENWOOD (*James*), *-*. Adventures of Reuben Davidger (*The*); Curiosities of Savage Life; Dining with Duke Humphrey, 1884; Gaol Birds at Large, 1882; History of a Little Ragamuffin (*The*); Humphrey Dyot, 1867; Legends of Savage Life, 1866; Little Ragamuffins (*The*), 1884; Low Life Depths, 1875; On Tramps, 1877; Seven Curses of London (*The*), 1869; Silas the Conjurer, 1866; Tag, Rag, and Co., 1883; Unsentimental Journeys, 1867; Wild Man at Home (*The*), 1879; Wilds of London (*The*), 1874.

GREG (*William Rathbone*), Manchester, 1809–1881. Creed of Christendom, 1851; Enigmas of Life, 1872; Essays, 1870, 1880–82; Great Duel (*The*), 1853; Literary and Social Judgments, 1877; Mistaken Aims . . . of the Artisan Class, 1876; Rocks Ahead, or Warnings of Cassandra, 1874; Truth *versus* Edification, 1873; Why are Women redundant? 1869.

GREGORY (Dr. *David*), Aberdeen, 1661–1708. Astronomiæ Physicæ et Geometriæ Elementa, 1702 (his great work); Catoptricæ et Dioptricæ Sphæricæ Elementa, 1695; Exercitatio Geometrica de Dimensione Figurarum, 1684. He left a MS. on the Catenary.

GREGORY, D.D. (*George*), Ireland, 1754–1808. Dictionary of Sciences and Arts, 1806; Economy of Nature, 1796; History of the Christian Church (*A*), 1795; Life of Thomas Chatterton, 1789.

GREGORY (*James*), Aberdeenshire, 1636–1675. Exercitationes Geometricæ, 1668; Geometriæ pars Universalis, 1668; Great and New Art of weighing Vanity, etc. (*The*), 1672; Optica Promota, 1663; Vera Circuli et Hyperbolæ Quadratura, 1667.

GREGORY, M.D. (*James*), Aberdeen, 1753–1821. Conspectus Medicinæ Theoreticæ, 1776–82; Essays, 1792.

GREGORY, M.D. (*John George*), Aberdeen, in Scotland, 1724–1773. Comparative View of the State and Faculties of Man, etc., 1765; Elements of the Practice of Physic, 1772; Father's Legacy to his Daughters (A), 1793, posthumous. His Life, by Mr. Tytler (lord Woodhouselee), 1788 ; W. Smellie, 1800.

GREGORY, LL.D. (Olinthus Gilbert), Huntingdonshire, 1774–1841. Elements of Trigonometry, 1816 ; Evidence, Doctrine, and Duties of the Christian Religion, 1810 ; Life of Robert Hall, 1833 ; Treatise on Astronomy, 1802 ; Treatise on Mechanics, 1806. His Life, by Hall, 1849.

GREGSON (Matthew), about 1776-1837. History and Antiquities of . . . Lancaster, 1817.

GRENVILLE (Robert Kaye), Scotland, *-*. Algæ Britannicæ, 1830 ; Flora Edinensis, 1824 ; Scottish Cryptogamic Flora (The), 1822 (a good supplement to Sowerby's English Botany).

GRESWELL (Edward), Denton, in Lancashire, 1797–1869. Fasti Temporis Catholici, 1852; Origines Kalendariæ Hellenicæ, 1862 ; Origines Kalendariæ Italicæ, 1854 ; Prolegomena ad Harmoniam Evangelicam, 1840.

GREVILLE (Fulke, lord Brooke), Alcaster, in Warwickshire, 1554–1628. Alaham Mustapha, 1609, a tragedy ; Cælica (109 songs), 1633, posthumous ; Inquisition upon Fame and Honour (68 stanzas), 1663, posthumous ; Life of Sir Philip Sidney, 1652, posthumous; Treatise on Human Learning (15 stanzas), 1633, posthumous ; Treatise on Wars (68 stanzas), 1633, posthumous.

GREVILLE (Robert Kaye), Durham, 1794–1866. Algæ Britannicæ, 1830 ; Flora Edinensis, 1824 ; Scottish Cryptogamic Flora, 1823–28.

GREW (Nehemiah), Coventry, 1628 – 1711. Anatomy of Plants, 1682 ; Cosmologia Sacra, 1701; Idea of a Philosophical History of Plants, 1673 ; Musæum Regalis, Societatis, 1681.

GREY (Sir George), 1812–1882. Journals of Discovery in Australia, 1841 ; Polynesian Mythology . . . of New Zealand, 1855 ; Proverbial Sayings of . . . New Zealand, 1858.

GREY, D.D. (Richard), Newcastle, 1694-1731. Memoria Technica, 1730.

GREY (William), about 1609–1660. Chronographia, or a Survey of Newcastle-upon-Tine, 1649.

GREY, LL.D. (Rev. Zachary), Yorkshire, 1687-1766. Attempt towards the Character of Charles I., 1738; Church of England vindicated, 1740 ; Critical, Historical, and Explanatory Notes on Shakespeare, 1754 ; Examination of Neal's History of the Puritans, 1736–39 ; History of the Donatists, 1741; Ministry of Dissenters Null and Void, 1725 ; Popery in its Proper Colours, 1750.

GRIFFIN (Gerald), novelist, etc., 1803–1840. Collegians (The), 1828 ; Gisipus, 1842, a tragedy ; Hollandtide, 1827 ; Rivals (The), 1830 ; Tales of the Five Senses, 1832 ; Tales of the Munster Festivals, 1827 ; Tracy's Ambition, 1830. His Memoirs, by Dr. D. Griffin, 1857.

GRIFFIN (Sir Lepel Henry), 1840- . Famous Monuments of Central India, 1888 ; Great

Republic (The), 1884 ; Law of Inheritance to Chiefships, 1869 ; Punjab Chiefs (The), 1865 ; Rajahs of the Punjab (The), 1870 ; Ranjit Singh, 1894.

GRIMOALD (Nicholas), 1519-1562 ; the second writer of blank verse in the English language, lord Surrey being the first. Archiropheta, 1548, a tragedy ; John the Baptist, 1548, a tragedy.[1]

GRIMSHAWE (Rev. Thomas Shuttleworth), 1777–1850. Life of Cowper, 1835; Life of Legh Richmond, 1828.

GRISWOLD, D.D. (Rufus Wilmot), New York, U.S., 1815–1857. Curiosities of American Literature, 1851 ; Female Poets of America, 1849 ; Poets and Poetry of America, 1842 ; Prose Writers of America (The), 1847.

GROSE (Francis), Middlesex, 1731–1791. Antiquities of England and Wales, 1773-87 ; Antiquities of Scotland, 1789–91 ; Antiquities of Ireland, 1791-95, posthumous ; Classical Dictionary of the Vulgar Tongue, 1785 ; Humourous Advertisements (to attain beauty, health, honour, and riches), 1785 ; Local Proverbs and Popular Superstitions, 1787 ; Military Antiquities, 1786-88 ; Olio (The), 1792, posthumous ; Rules for drawing Caricatures, 1788 ; Treatise on Ancient Armour and Weapons, 1786, supplement, 1789 ; Views of the Antiquities in England and Wales, 1773-76 ; Views of the Antiquities in Ireland, 1794, posthumous ; Views of the Antiquities in Scotland, 1785.

GROSSETESTE (Robert), bishop of Lincoln, 1175-1253. Castle of Love, first printed 1849 ; De Cessatione, Legalium, printed 1652 ; Treatyse of Husbandry, printed by Wynkyn de Worde. His Life, by Bardney ; Pegge, 1761.

GROTE (George), Clayhill, in Kent, 1794-1871. Aristotle, 1872, posthumous ; Essentials of Parliamentary Reform, 1831 ; History of Greece, 1846–56 (his chief work); Plato and the other Companions of Sokratês, 1865. His Life, by his widow, 1873.

GROTE (John), Beckenham, in Kent, 1813-1866. Examination of the Utilitarian Philosophy, 1870 ; Exploratio Philosophica, 1865.

GROVE (Sir George), Clapham, 1820- . Dictionary of Music and Musicians, 1879-89 (editor ; but the lives of Beethoven, Mendelssohn, and Schubert are original).

GROVE (Henry), 1683-1738. Sermons and Tracts, 1741-42, posthumous ; System of Moral Philosophy, 1749-50, posthumous; Works, 1740, posthumous. His Life, by T. Amory.

GROVE (Joseph), died 1764. History of the Life and Times of Cardinal Wolsey, 1742-44 (his chief work); Lives of all the Earls and Dukes of Devonshire, 1764 ; Two Dialogues in the Elysian Fields, etc., 1761.

GROVE (Matthew), about 1559-1635. Historie of Pelops and Hippodamia, 1587, a poem ; Witty Proverbs, Pithy Sentences, and Wise Similes, 1638.

GROVE (Hon. sir William Robert), Swansea, in Wales, 1811- . Address to the British Association, 1867 ; On the Correlation of Physical Forces, 1846 (a standard work); Progress of Physical Science, etc., 1842 ;

Voltaic Ignition, and the Decomposition of Water, etc., 1847, a Bakerian lecture.

GRUNDY (*Sydney*), dramatic author, 1848– . Arabian Nights, 1887; Bells of Haslemere, 1887; Bunch of Violets, 1894; Clito, 1886; Dean's Daughter, 1888; Esther Sandraz, 1889; Fool's Paradise (*A*), 1889; Glass of Fashion, 1883; Greatest of These, 1895; Haddon Hall, 1892; Late Mr. Castello (*The*), 1895; Little Change (*A*), 1872; Mamma, 1888; Marriage of Convenience (*A*), 1897; New Woman (*The*), 1894; Pair of Spectacles (*A*), 1890; Pompadour (*The*), 1888; Queen's Favourite (*The*), 1883; Silver Key (*The*), 1897; Silver Shield (*The*), 1885; Slaves of the Ring, 1894; Sowing the Wind, 1893; Union Jack (*The*), 1888; Vicar of Bray (*The*), 1882; Village Priest (*A*), 1890.

GUILD (Rev. *William*), Scotland, 1586–1657. Antidote against Popery, 1639; Harmonie of all the Prophets, 1619; Ignis Fatuus, or the Elfe-fire of Purgatorie, 1625; Issachar's Asse braying under a Double Burden, 1622; Limbo's Battery, 1630; Moses unveiled, 1620; New Sacrifice of Christian Incense (*The*), 1608; Novelty of Popery proved out of themselves, 1656; Only Way of Salvation (*The*), 1608; Popish Glorying in Antiquitie turned to their Shame, 1626; Sealed Book opened (*The*), 1656; Throne of David (*The*), 1659. His Life, by Dr. Shirreffs.

GUILFORD (*Francis North*), 1637–1685. Philosophical Essay on Music, 1677.

GUILLIM (*John*), Herefordshire, 1565–1621. Display of Heraldry, 1610 (still a standard work).

GUNTER, C.E. (*Archibald Clavering*), Liverpool, 1847– . Baron Montey of Panama, 1893; First of the English, 1895; Mr. Barnes of New York, 1887; Mr. Potter of Texas, 1888; Miss Nobody of Nowhere, 1890. And other novels.

GUNTER (Rev. *Edmund*), Hertfordshire, 1581–1626. Canon Triangulorum, 1620; Description and Use of H.M. Dials, 1624; Of the Sector, Cross-staff, etc., 1624. (Inventor of Gunter's chain in surveying, 1624.)

GUNTON (*Symon*), Peterborough, in Northamptonshire, 1642–1710. History of the Church of Peterborough, 1686.

GURNELL (*William*), Lavenham, in Suffolk, 1617–1679. Christian in Complete Armour (*The*), 1656–58.

GURNEY (*Hudson*), 1774–1864. Cupid and Psyche; Observations on the Bayeux Tapestry, 1817.

GURNEY (*Joseph*). The original author of "Brachygraphy, or an Easy and Compendious System of Shorthand;" but the system was considerably improved in 1753 by Thomas Gurney, to whom it is generally ascribed. Thomas Gurney lived 1705-1770.

GURNEY (*Joseph John*), Earlham, near Norwich, 1788-1847. Essays on the Evidences . . . of Christianity, 1827; Notes on Prison Discipline, 1819; Observations on the Religious Peculiarities of the Society of Friends, 1824; Winter in the West Indies, 1840. His Life, by Braithwaite, 1851.

GUTHRIE (*James Cargill*), Airniefoul Farm, in Scotland, 1814– . First False Step (*The*), 1854; My Lost Love, etc., 1865; Rowena, 1871, a semi-dramatic poem in blank verse; Summer Flowers, 1867; Vale of Stathmore, 1875, in prose; Village Scenes, 1852, a descriptive poem (his first production); Wedded Love, 1859; Woodland Echoes, 1882, poems and songs.

∴ Several Scotch songs of great merit.

GUTHRIE, D.D. (*Thomas*), Brechin, in Scotland, 1803-1873. Angel's Song (*The*), 1865; Christ and the Inheritance of Saints, 1858; City (*The*), its Sins and Sorrows, 1857; Gospel in Ezekiel (*The*) 1855; Out of Harness, 1867; Parables (*The*), 1866; Plea for Drunkards, etc., 1856; Plea for Ragged Schools, 1847; Seed-time and Harvest of Ragged Schools, 1860; Speaking to the Heart, 1862; Studies of Character from the Old Testament, 1868-70; Sundays Abroad, 1871; Way of Life (*The*), 1862. Autobiography, with Memoir by his sons, 1874-75.

GUTHRIE (*Thomas Anstey*). See ANSTEY.

GUTHRIE (*William*), Brechin, in Scotland, 1708-1770. Geographical Grammar, 1770; History of England, 1744-50; History of Scotland, 1767; History of the World, 1764-67 (with John Gray).

GWILLIM (Sir *Henry*), *-*. Collection of Acts and Records, 1801 (much esteemed).

GWILT (*Joseph*), London, architect, 1784-1833. Encyclopædia of Architecture, 1842; Notitia Architectonica Italiana, 1818; Rudiments of Architecture, 1837; Rudiments of Grammar of the Anglo-Saxon Tongue, 1829; Sciography, or Rules for the Projection of Shadows, 1822; Treatise on . . . Arches, 1811. He also translated *Vitruvius*, 1826.

HABBERTON (*John*), Brooklyn, U.S., novelist, 1842– . Barton Experiment (*The*), 1876; Brueton's Bayou, 1886; Canoeing in Kanuckia, 1878 (with C. L. Norton); Country Luck, 1887; Crew of Sam Weller (*The*), 1878; Grown - up Babies, 1877; Helen's Babes, 1876 (his best; the sale very large indeed); Jericho Road (*The*), 1876; Just One Day, 1879; Little Guzzy, 1878; My Mother-in-Law, 1877; Other People, 1878; Other People's Children, 1877; Scripture Club of Valley Rest, 1877; Some Folks, 1877; Who was Paul Grayson? 1881; Worst Boy in the Town (*The*), 1880.

HACKET, D.D. (*John*), bishop of Lichfield, etc., London, 1592-1670. Century of Sermons, 1675; Christian Consolations, 1671; Comædia Loila, 1669; Life of Archbishop Williams, 1692 (said to be "the worst-written book in the language"). His Life, by T. Plume, D.D., 1675.

HADDON, LL.D. (*Walter*), Buckinghamshire, 1516-1572. Cantabrigienses, sive Exhortatio ad Literas,*1552; Lucubrationes, 1567 (with sir John Cheke); Reformatio Legum Ecclesiasticorum, 1567.

HAGGARD, LL.D. (*John*), *-*. Reports in the High Court of Admiralty, 1822-38; in the Consistory Court, 1822; in the Ecclesiastical Courts, 1827-32; in the Prerogative Court of Canterbury, 1826 (very valuable).

HAGGARD (*H. Rider*), novelist, 1856– . Allan Quatermain, 1887; Allan's Wife, and other Tales, 1889; Beatrice, 1890; Cetewayo and his White Neighbours, 1882; Cleopatra, 1889; Colonel Quaritch, V.C., 1888; Dawn, 1884; Eric Brighteyes, 1891; Heart of the World, 1896; Jess, 1887; Joan Haste, 1895; King Solomon's Mines, 1885; Maiwa's Revenge, 1888; Mr. Meeson's Will, 1888; Montezuma's Daughter, 1894; Nada the Lily, 1892; People of the Mist (*The*), 1894; She, 1887; Witch's Head (*The*), 1884; Wizard (*The*), 1896; World's Desire (*The*), 1891 (with A. Lang).

HAILES (Sir *David Dalrymple*, lord), Edinburgh, antiquary, 1726–1792. Annals of Scotland, 1776–79 (his chief work); Canons of the Church of Scotland, etc., 1769; Davidis Humei . . . vita, 1787; Historical Memoirs concerning the Provincial Councils of the Church of Scotland, 1769; Lives of John Barclay, Mark Alexander Boyd, George Leslie, John Hamilton, James Ramsay, and (in MS.) of Montrose; Remains of Christian Antiquity, 1776-80.

HAKE (*A. Egmont*), son of Dr. Thomas Hake (see below). Coming Individualism (*The*), 1895; Events of the Taeping Rebellion, 1891; Flattering Tales, 1882; General Gordon's Journals from Khartoum; Irish Finance, an Un-royal Commission and a Lady, 1897; New Dance of Death, 1884 (with J. G. Lefebre); Paris Originals, 1878; Story of Chinese Gordon (*The*), 1883; Suffering London, 1892 (our voluntary hospitals), 1892; Unemployed Problem solved (*The*), 1888.

HAKE (*Edward*), poet, about 1552–1612. Touchstone of Wittes (*The*), 1588.

HAKE, M.D. (*Thomas Gordon*), poet, 1809–1895. Legends of the Morrow, 1878; Madeline, etc., 1871; Maiden Ecstasy, 1880; Memoirs of Eighty Years, 1892; New Day (*The*), 1890; New Symbols, 1875; On Vital Force, 1867; Parables and Tales, 1873; Piromides (*The*), 1839; Poetic Lucubrations, 1828; Selected Poems, 1894 (edited by Mrs. Meynell); Serpent Play (*The*), 1883; Vates, 1840; World's Epitaph (*The*), 1866.

HAKE (*Thos. St. Edmund*), son of the poet, brother of Egmont Hake, novelist. In Letters of Gold, 1886; Within Sound of the Weir, 1891; Ye Historical Sketch of ye Olde London Streete, 1885. And various magazine articles.

HAKEWELL (Rev. *George*), 1579–1649. Power and Providence of God in the Government of the World, 1627; Scutum Regum, 1612.

HAKLUYT (Rev. *Richard*), Herefordshire, 1553–1616. Divers Voyages touching the Discoverie of America . . . 1582; Four Voyages to Florida, 1587; Historie of the West Indies (in Latin), translated by Saunders, 1818; Principal Navigations and Discoveries of the English Nation, 1589, supplement compiled from his MSS. 1812 (very valuable).

HALDANE (*Robert*), Austrey, Worcestershire, 1764–1842. Evidences and Authority of

Divine Revelation, 1816; Exposition of the Epistle to the Romans, 1835. His Life, by Alexander Haldane, the enlarged edition, 1852.

HALE (Sir *Matthew*), Alderley, in Gloucestershire, 1609–1678. Analysis of the Law, 1739; Contemplations, 1676; Historia Placitorum Coronæ, 1739; History of the Common Law, 1713; Nature of Religion (*The*), 1684; Pleas of the Crown, 1678. His Life, by bishop Burnet, 1682; Roscoe, 1830; Dr. Williams, 1835.

HALE (Mrs.), maiden name *Sarah Josepha Buell*, Newport, in New Hampshire, U.S., poetess and novelist, 1795–1879. Alice Ray, 1837-46, a romance in rhyme; Bible Reading Book (*The*), 1854; Flora's Interpreter, 1830; Genius of Oblivion (*The*), and other Poems, 1823 (her first work); Grosvenor, 1838, a tragedy; Harry Guy, the Widow's Son, 1848; Judge (*The*), a Drama of American Life, 1846; Letters of Mme. de Sevigny to her Daughter, 1856; Letters of Lady Mary Wortley Montague, 1856; Northwood, a Tale of New England, 1827; Sketches of American Character, 1830; Three Hours, or the Vigil of Love, and other Poems, 1848; Traits of American Life, 1835; Way to Live Well, and to be Well (*The*), 1833; Woman's Record, 1856, sketches of distinguished women from the beginning to 1850–51.

HALES (*John*), called "The Ever-Memorable," Bath, in Somersetshire, 1584-1656. Golden Remains, 1659. His Life, by Des Maizeaux, 1719.

HALES, D.D. (*Stephen*), Bookesbourn, in Kent, natural philosopher, 1677–1761. Hæmastatics, 1733; Statickal Essays, 1733; Vegetable Staticks, 1727 (his best-known work).

HALES (Dr. *William*), chronologist and mathematician, died 1831. Analysis Æquationum, 1784; Analysis Fluxionum, 1800; New Analysis of Chronology, 1809-14 (his best-known work); Sonorum Doctrina Rationalis et Experimentalis, 1778.

HALIBURTON, D.C.L. (*Thomas Chandler*), popularly known as "Sam Slick," Windsor, in Nova Scotia, 1796–1865. Americans at Home (*The*), 1854; Attaché (*The*), or Sam Slick in England, 1843-44; Bubbles of Canada, 1839; English in America (*The*), 1851; Historical and Statistical Account of Nova Scotia, 1829; Letter-bag of the Great Western, 1839; Nature and Human Nature, 1855; Old Judge (*The*), 1839; Rule and Misrule of the English in America, 1851; Sam Slick, the Clockmaker, 1837, 1838, 1840; Sam Slick's Wise Saws and Modern Instances, 1853; Traits of American Humour, 1852; Yankee Stories, 1852.

HALIFAX (*Samuel*), bishop of St. Asaph, 1733–1790. Analysis of the Roman Civil Law, 1774 (a text-book at the Cambridge University); Sermons on the Prophecies, 1776.

HALL (Captain *Basil*), Edinburgh, 1788–1844. Extracts of a Journal written on the Coasts of Chili, Peru, and Mexico, 1823 (excellent); Fragments of Voyages and Travels (three series), 1831-33; Patchwork, or Travels in Stories, 1841; Travels in North America,

1829; Voyage of Discovery to the Western Coast of Corea, etc., 1817.

HALL (Rev. *Christopher Newman*), Maidstone, in Kent, 1816– . Divine Socialism, 1851; From Liverpool to St. Louis, 1870; Hints on Preaching, 1858; Homeward Bound, and other Sermons, 1869; Land of the Forum and the Vatican, 1854; Now! 1858; Pilgrim Songs in Cloud and Sunshine, 1870; Prayer: its Reasonableness and Efficacy, 1875.
∵ Some of his tracts, as "The Sinner's Friend," "Come to Jesus," and its sequel, "Follow Jesus," have an unprecedented circulation.

HALL (*Edward*), Shropshire, 1499–1547. Union of the . . . Families of Lancaster and Yorke, 1542 (valuable).

HALL, D.D. (*Joseph*), bishop of Norwich, called "The Christian Seneca," Ashby-de-la-Zouch, in Leicestershire, 1574–1656. Apologie of the Church of England, etc., 1610; Balm of Gilead (*The*), 1660, posthumous; Characters of Vertues and Vices, 1608; Contemplations, 1612–15 (Dr. Doddridge calls it "incomparable for language, criticism, and devotion'); Devout Soul (*The*), 1644; Episcopacy by Divine Right, 1640; Epistles (in six decades), 1608–11; Henochismus, 1762; King's Prophecie (*The*), or Weeping Joy, 1603, a poem; Mundus Alter et Idem, 1643; Paraphrases of Hard Texts, 1633; Peace of Rome (*The*), 1609; Quo Vadis? 1617 (in ridicule of foreign travels); Satires (in three books), poetical (Pope says they are "the best in the language"); Solomon's Divine Arts, 1609; Virgidemiarum, Byting Satyres, 1599. His Life, by Pratt, 1808; Jones; Morris, 1846.

HALL, M.D. (*Marshall*), Basford, in Nottinghamshire, 1790–1857. Essay on the Circulation of the Blood, 1831; Lectures on the Nervous System, 1836; Medical Essays, 1824; Memoirs on the Nervous System, 1837; New Memoir on the Nervous System, 1843; Reflex Function of the Medulla Oblongata and Medulla Spinalis, 1833 (his great discovery); Synopsis of the Diastaltic Nervous System, 1850; Theory and Practice of Medicine, 1837; Theory of Convulsive Diseases, 1847; Treatise on Diagnosis, 1817. His Life, by his widow, 1858.

HALL (Rev. *Peter*), *–*. Ductor Vindogladiensis, 1830 (a guide to Wimborne Minster); Fragmenta Liturgica, 1848; Picturesque Memorials of Salisbury, 1834; Picturesque Memorials of Winchester, 1829; Reliquiæ Liturgicæ Anglicanæ, 1847; Tekmeria Metrica, 1824.

HALL (Rev. *Robert*), Arnsby, in Leicestershire, 1764–1831. Apology for the Freedom of the Press, 1793; Modern Infidelity considered, 1795; Sermons, 1831–33, posthumous. His Life, by sir J. Mackintosh, 1832; J. W. Morris, 1846.

HALL (*Samuel Carter*), Topsham, in Devonshire, 1801–1889. Book of Memories of Great Men and Women of the Age (*A*), 1870; Book of South Wales, 1861 (with Mrs. Hall); Book of the Thames, 1859; Ireland, 1841–43; Memory of T. Moore (*A*), 1879;

Poems, 1850; Retrospect of a Long Life (*A*), 1883. He wrote or edited 340 vols.

HALL (Mrs. *S. C.*), maiden name *Anna Maria Fielding*, Dublin, 1804–1881. Alice Stanley, 1868; Buccaneers (*The*), 1832 (her first novel); Can Wrong be Right? 1862; Chronicles of a Schoolroom, 1830; Daddy Dacre's School, 1859; Digging a Grave with a Wine-glass, 1871; Fight of Faith (*The*), 1869, a story of Ireland; French Refugee (*The*), 1836, a play; Groves of Blarney, 1838, a tale; Ireland, its Scenery, etc., 1840 (with her husband); Lights and Shadows of Irish Character, 1838; Lucky Penny (*The*), 1857; Marian, or a Young Maid's Fortunes, 1840 (her best novel); Merchant's Daughter (*The*), 1874; Midsummer Eve, 1847, a fairy tale; Outlaw (*The*), 1835 (a novel, time James II.); Pilgrimages to English Shrines; Playfellow (*The*), 1868; Prince of the Fair Family, 1866, a fairy tale; Ronald's Reason, or the Little Cripple, 1865; Sketches of Irish Character, 1828 (his first production); Stories of the Irish Peasantry, 1840; Tales of Woman's Trials, 1834; Uncle Horace, 1835, a novel; Uncle Sam's Money-box (for the young); Union Jack, 1863; Village Garland (*The*), 1863; White Boy (*The*), 1845, a novel; Woman's Story (*A*), 1857.

HALL, D.D. (*Thomas*), 1610–1665. Loathsomeness of Long Hair, with an Appendix against Painting, Spots, Naked Backs, and Exposed Bosoms, 1656; Funebria Floræ, 1660; Vindiciæ Literarum, 1655.

HALLAM (*Arthur Henry*), London, 1811–1833. Remains in Verse and Prose, 1862, posthumous (this is the "A. H. H." of Tennyson's *In Memoriam*).

HALLAM, D.C.L. (*Henry*), Windsor, 1777–1859. Constitutional History of England, 1827; Introduction to the Literature of Europe in the Fifteenth, Sixteenth, and Seventeenth Centuries, 1837–39; View of the State of Europe during the Middle Ages, 1818 (his chief work).

HALLE (*Edwarde*), contemporary with Henry VIII. Chronicle from Henry IV. to Henry VIII., 1548.

HALLECK (*Fitz-Green*), Guildford, U.S., 1795–1867. Fanny, 1849, a satire in the metre of Don Juan (his longest poem); Poems, 1827, 1835; Twilight, 1818 (his first poem). His Life, by F. S. Cozzens, 1868.

HALLEY, LL.D. (*Edmund*), Haggerston, near London, 1656–1742. Catalogus Stellarum Australium, 1679; Circulation of the Vapours of the Sea, 1691; General Chart showing the Variation of the Compass, etc., 1692; Tabulæ Astronomicæ, 1749, posthumous.

HALLIDAY (*Andrew*), 1830–1877. Adventures of Mr. Wilderspin, 1860; Everyday Papers, 1864; Great City (*The*), 1867; Savage Club Papers (*The*), 1867–68; Sunnyside Papers, 1866; Town and Country, 1866.
Plays (chiefly based on the novels of Scott or Dickens): Amy Robsart; Checkmate; For Love or Money, a comedy; Fortunes of Nigel (dramatized); Great City (*The*), a comedy; Heart's Delight, a comedy; King o' Scots, a comedy; Lady of the Lake (*The*), dramatized; Little Em'ly (Dickens's

tale dramatized); Nell, a comedy; Nicholas Nickleby (dramatized); Notre Dame (dramatized); Rebecca, a comedy; Richard Cœur de Lion, an historic play.

HALLIDAY, M.D. (Sir *Andrew*), Dumfries, in Scotland, died 1840. Annals of the House of Brunswick, 1820; Annals of the House of Hanover, 1826; Memoir of the Campaign of 1815, published 1816; Observations on Emphysema, 1807.

HALLIWELL (*James Orchard*), Chelsea, 1820-1888. Dictionary of Archaic and Provincial Words, 1847 (a standard work); Life and Works of Shakespeare, 1851-61; Popular Rhymes and Nursery Tales, 1849.

HALYBURTON (Rev. *Thomas*), called "The Holy Halyburton," Scotland, 1674-1712. Great Concern of Salvation (*The*), 1821, posthumous; Natural Religion Insufficient, etc., 1714, posthumous; Sermons (*Ten*) on the Lord's Supper, 1722, posthumous. His Memoirs, by himself, 1715; by D. Young, 1824.

HAMERTON (*Philip Gilbert*), Laneside, in Lancashire, 1834-1894. Chapters on Animals, 1873; Contemporary French Painters, 1867; Drawing and Engraving, 1892; Etcher's Handbook (*The*), 1871; Etching and Etchers, 1868; French and English, 1889; Graphic Arts (*The*), 1882; Harry Blount, 1875, a story for boys; Human Intercourse, 1884; Imagination in Landscape Painting, 1886; Intellectual Life (*The*), 1873; Isles of Loch Awe, and other Poems, 1855; Landscape, 1885; Life of Turner (the artist), 1879; Man in Art, 1892; Marmorne, 1878; Modern Frenchmen, 1878; Painter's Camp in the Highlands (*A*), 1862; Paris in Old and Present Times, 1884; Portfolio Papers, 1889; Present State of the Fine Arts, 1892; Rome in 1849 (a series of articles), 1849-50; Round my House, 1875; Saône (*The*), a Summer Voyage, 1887; Sylvan Year (*The*), 1876; Unknown River (*The*), 1870; Wenderholme, 1869, a story of Lancashire, etc.

HAMILTON (*Alexander*), Island of Nevis, one of the Lesser Antilles, 1757-1804. Federalist (*The*), begun 1787. Works (in seven vols.), edited by his son, 1851.

HAMILTON (*Anthony*, Count de), Ireland, 1646-1720. Contes de Féerie, 1805, posthumous (charming tales); Mémoires du Comte de Grammont (a faithful delineation of the court of Charles II.).

HAMILTON (*Elizabeth*), Belfast, in Ireland, 1758-1816. Agrippina, 1803; Cottagers of Glenburnie, 1808; Elementary Principles of the Human Mind, 1809; Letters of a Hindoo Rajah, 1796 (a covert satire on English manners and customs); Letters on the Elementary Principles of Education, 1801-2; Memoirs of the Life of Agrippina, 1811; Memoirs of Modern Philosophers, 1800; Modern Philosopher (*The*), 1800. Her Life, by Miss Benger, 1818.

HAMILTON (Lady), maiden name *Emma Harte*, the favourite of lord Nelson, 1761-1815. Attitudes after the Antique, 1807; Memoirs, with Illustrative Anecdotes of . . . Contemporaries, 1815.

HAMILTON (*George Baillie*), 1798-1850). Codex

Criticus of the Hebrew Bible, 1821; Introduction to the Study of the Hebrew Scriptures, 1814 (a very learned work); Observations on the . . . Roman Catholic English Bible, 1826.

HAMILTON, D.D. (*Hugh*), bishop of Ossory, 1729-1805. De Sectionibus Conicis Tractatus Geometricus, 1758 (a valuable work); Existence and Attributes of the Supreme Being, 1792. Works, with Life, 1809.

HAMILTON, D.D. (*John*), about 1540-1610. Ane Catholik and Facile Traictise drauin out of the Halie Scriptures . . . on the Real and Corporall Presence of Crystis Pretious Bodie and Blude in the Sacrament of the Alter, 1581. His Life, by lord Hailes, 1784.

HAMILTON (Captain *Thomas*), 1789-1842. Annals of the Peninsular Campaign, 1849; Cyril Thornton, 1827, a novel; Men and Manners in America, 1833.

HAMILTON, K.B. (Sir *William*), Scotland, 1730-1803. Antiquités Etrusques, Grecques, et Romaines, 1766 (a splendid work), a sequel, 1791-95; Campi Phlegræi, 1776-77, supplement, 1779; Observations on Mount Vesuvius, 1772.

HAMILTON (Sir *William*), Glasgow, in Scotland, 1788-1856. Discussions on Philosophy and Literature, 1852; Lectures on Metaphysics, 1859-61, posthumous.

HAMILTON (*William Gerard*), better known as "Single-speech Hamilton," 1729-1796. Parliamentary Logick, 1808 (his famous speech is appended).

∴ Some have fathered *Junius's Letters* on William Gerard Hamilton.

HAMILTON, LL.D. (Sir *William Rowan*), Dublin, 1805-1865. Elements of Quaternions, 1866; General Method in Dynamics (*A*), 1834; Lectures on Quaternions, 1853; Theory of Systems of Rays, 1828.

HAMLEY (Lieutenant-general sir *Edward Bruce*), Bodmin, in Cornwall, 1824-1892. Chapter on Outposts (*A*), 1875; Last French Hero (*The*), 1879; Life of Alexander Innes Shand, 1895; National Defence, 1889; Operations of War (*The*), 1866; Our Poor Relations, 1872; Shakespeare's Funeral, 1889; Staff College Exercises, 1874; Story of the Campaign of Sebastopol (*The*), 1855; Thomas Carlyle, 1881; Voltaire, 1877; War in the Crimea (*The*), 1890; Wellington's Career, 1860.

HAMMOND, D.D. (*Henry*), Chertsey, in Middlesex, 1605-1660. Paranæsis, printed separate from his Works, 1841; Paraphrase and Annotations on the New Testament, 1653 (a celebrated work); ditto on the Psalms. His Life, by bishop Fell, 1661; R. Fulman, 1684.

HAMMOND (*James*), poet, 1710-1742 (son of Anthony Hammond, also a poet, called the "Silver-tongued"). Love Elegies (once very popular, written between 1731 and his death, but first published by lord Chesterfield in 1743; they are contained in vol. 49 of Johnson's *British Poets*).

HAMPDEN, D.D. (*Renn Dickson*), bishop of Hereford, born in Barbadoes, 1793-1868. Fathers of Greek Philosophy, 1862; Lectures Introductory to the Study of Moral Philosophy, 1835 ; Philosophical Evidence of Christianity, 1827 ; Scholastic Philosophy . . . in its Relation to Christian Theology, 1833.

HANNA, LL.D. (Rev. *William*), 1808–1882. Close of the Ministry (*The*), 1869 ; Earlier Years of our Lord's Life on Earth, 1864 ; Essays by Ministers of the Free Church of Scotland, 1858 ; Forty Days after our Lord's Resurrection (*The*), 1863 ; Last Days of our Lord's Passion, 1862 ; Ministry of Galilee (*The*), 1868 ; Notes on a Visit to Hayti, 1836 ; On Religion, 1857 ; Our Lord's Life on Earth, 1869 ; Passion Week (*The*), 1866 ; Wars of the Huguenots, 1871 ; Wycliffe and the Huguenots, 1860.

HANNAFORD (*Samuel*), 1828–   . Catalogue of the Flowering Plants and Ferns in the Neighbourhood of Totnes, in Devonshire, 1851 ; Flora Tottonensis, 1852 ; Jottings in Australasia, or Notes on the Flora and Fauna of Victoria, 1856 ; Wild Flowers of Tasmania, 1866.

HANNAY (*James*), Dumfries, 1827–1873. Biscuits and Grog, 1848 ; Blackwood and Carlyle, 1850 ; Brief Memoir of Mr. Thackeray, 1864 ; Characters and Criticisms, 1865 ; Charles Dickens, 1870 ; Claret Cup (*A*), 1848 ; Course of English Literature, 1866 ; Eustace Conyers, 1855 ; Hearts are Trumps, 1849 ; King Dobbs, 1848 ; Satire and Satirists, 1854 ; Singleton Fontenoy, 1850 ; Sketches in Ultramarine, 1853 ; Studies on Thackeray, 1869 ; Three Hundred Years of a Norman House, 1866.

HANWAY (*Jonas*), Portsmouth, 1712–1786. Farmer Trueman ; Journal, 1756–57 ; Historical Account of British Trade over the Caspian Sea, etc., 1753 ; Virtue in Humble Life, 1774. His Life, by Pugh, 1787.

HARDIMAN (*J.*), *–*. History of the Town and County of Galway, 1820 (a valuable work). He also published two volumes of "Irish Minstrelsy").

HARDING (*James Duffield*), Deptford, in Kent, 1798–1863. Lessons on Art, 1849 ; Lessons on Trees, 1850 ; Park and Forest, 1841 ; Principles and Practice of Art, 1845.

HARDING (*John*), 1378–1468. Chronicle in Metre fro the Begynnyng of Englād vnto ye Reigne of Edwarde IV., 1543.

HARDY (*Iza Duffus*), daughter of sir Thomas Duffus and lady Hardy (*q.v.*), born at Enfield, in Middlesex, about 1855–   . Between Two Fires, 1873 ; Between Two Oceans, 1884 ; Broken Faith (*A*), 1878 ; Buried Sin (*A*), 1893 ; For the Old Love's Sake, 1877 ; Friend and Lover, 1880 ; Girl he did not Marry (*The*), 1887 ; Glencairn, 1877 ; Hearts or Diamonds, 1885 ; Love, Honour, and Obey, 1881 ; Love in Idleness, 1887 ; Love that he passed by (*The*), 1884 ; New Othello, 1890 ; Not easily Jealous, 1872 ; Only a Love-story, 1877 ; Oranges and Alligators, 1886 ; Westhorpe Mystery (*The*), 1886 ; Woman's Loyalty, 1893.

HARDY (Lady *Mary*), mother of Iza Hardy, . Artist Family (*The*), 1855 ; Beryl Fortescue, 1881 ; Casual Acquaintance (*A*), 1866 ; Daisy Nichol, 1870 ; Dangerous Experiment (*A*), 1888 ; Down South, 1883 ;

Hero's Work (*A*), 1867 ; Paul Wynter's Sacrifice, 1869 ; Through Cities and Prairie Lands, 1881.

HARDY (*Thomas*), Dorsetshire, novelist, 1840– . Desperate Remedies, 1871 ; Dorsetshire Labourer (*The*), 1893 ; Far from the Madding Crowd, 1874 (first appeared in *Cornhill*, vols. xxix.–xxx., January to December, 1874) ; Group of Noble Dames (*A*), 1891 ; Hand of Ethelberta (*The*), 1876 (first appeared in *Cornhill*, vols. xxxii.–xxxiii., July, 1875, to May, 1876) ; Jude the Obscure, 1895 ; Laodicean (*The*), 1881 (*Harper*, December, 1880–81) ; Life's Little Ironies, 1894 ; Mayor of Casterbridge, 1886 (the *Graphic*, January 2 to May 15, 1886) ; Pair of Blue Eyes (*A*), 1873 (first appeared in *Tinsley's*, vols. xi.–xii., September, 1872, to July, 1873) ; Return of the Native (*The*), 1878 (first appeared in *Belgravia*, vols. xxxiv.–xxxvii., January to December, 1878) ; Spectre of the Real (with Hon. Henniker), 1896 ; Tess of the d'Urbervilles, 1892 (the *Graphic*, July 4 to December 26, 1891) ; Trumpet-Major (*The*), 1880 (*Good Words*, January to December, 1880) ; Two on a Tower, 1882 (*Atlantic Monthly*, vols. xlix.–l., January to December, 1882) ; Under the Greenwood Tree, 1872) ; Well-beloved (*The*), 1897 ; Wessex Tales, 1888 ; Woodlanders (*The*), 1887 (*Macmillan*, May, 1886, to April, 1887). "The Art of Thomas Hardy," by Lionel Johnson, including a Bibliography by John Lane (admirable essays on Thomas Hardy's work, the best book possible for students).

HARDY (Sir *Thomas Duffus*), Port Royal, in Jamaica, 1804–1878. Catalogue of the Lord Chancellors, etc., 1843 ; Description of the Close Rolls in the Tower of London, 1833 ; Life of Lord Langdale, Master of the Rolls.

    ·.· He edited several of the MS. Records under the Master of the Rolls ; the Introduction to the *Monumenta Historica Britannica*, 1848 ; and the *Willelmi Malmesburiensis Gesta*, 1840, for the "English Historical Society." He also edited *Modus Tenendi Parliamentum*, 1840 ; *Rotuli Literarum Clausarum*, 1833–34, etc.

HARDY (*William John*), record searcher and translator, 1857–   . Book Plates, 1893 ; Documents illustrative of English Church History, 1896 (with Rev. H. Gee) ; Lighthouses, 1895 ; Handwritings of the Kings and Queens of England, 1893.

HARE (*Augustus John Cuthbert*), the Villa Strozzi, in Rome, 1834–   . Biographical Sketches, 1895 ; Cities of Central and Northern Italy, 1884 ; Cities of Northern and Central Italy, 1876 ; Cities of Southern Italy and Sicily, 1883 ; Days near Rome, 1875 ; Days near Paris, 1887 ; Epitaphs from Country Churchyards, 1856 ; Florence, 1884 ; Gurneys of Earlham (*The*), 1895 ; Life and Letters of Frances, Baroness Bunsen, 1878 ; Life and Letters of Maria Edgeworth, 1894 ; Memorials of a Quiet Life, 1872 (supplementary vol. 1876). North-Eastern France, 1890 ; North-Western France, 1895 ; Paris, 1887 ; Rivieras (*The*), 1896 ; Sketches in Holland, etc., 1885 ; South-Eastern France,

1890; South-Western France, 1890; Story of my Life, 1896; Studies in Russia, 1885; Sussex, 1894; Two Noble Lives, 1893; Venice, 1884; Walks in London, 1878; Walks in Rome, 1871; Wanderings in Spain, 1873; Winter in Mentone (*A*), 1861.

∴ Also Murray's Handbooks of Berkshire, 1860; Bucks, 1860; Durham, 1863; Northumberland, 1863; and Oxford, 1860.

HARE, D.D. (*Francis*), bishop of Chichester, 1665-1740. He is known as the opponent of Hoadly, bishop of Bangor, in the famous Bangorian controversy, "My Kingdom is not of this World," 1717. Hoadly maintained that Christ never delegated His authority to any man, and that "apostolic succession" is not scriptural. The controversy is more distinguished for "shuffling" and ill temper than anything else.

HARE (Ven. *Julius Charles*), Hurstmonceux, in Sussex, 1795-1855. Guesses at Truth, 1847 (with A. W. Hare); Memoir of John Sterling, 1848; Mission of the Comforter, 1846; Victory of Faith, 1847 (his chief work); Vindication of Luther, 1855.

HARGRAVES (*Edmund Hammond*), Gosport, in Hampshire, 1815-1890. Australia and its Gold-fields, 1855.

HARINGTON (Sir *John*), Kelston, near Bath, in Somersetshire, poet, 1561-1612. Apologie (*An*), 1596; Epigrams (in four books), 1615, posthumous; History of Polindor and Flostella, with other Poems, 1651, posthumous; Metamorphosis of Ajax, 1596; Nugæ Antiquæ (in prose and verse), 1769, posthumous; Schoole of Salerne (*The*), (in 10-line stanzas), 1609; State of the Church of England, 1608 (an attack on the bishops); Translation into English verse of *Orlando Furioso*, 1591; Ulysses upon Ajax, 1596.

HARIOT or HARRIOTT (*Thomas*), Oxford, 1560-1621. Artis Analyticæ Praxis, 1631; Report of the New-found Land of Virginia, 1588.

HARMER (Rev. *Thomas*), Norwich, 1715-1788. Observations on Various Passages of Scripture, 1764 (useful). His Memoir, by Dr. A. Clarke, 1816.

HARNESS (Rev. *William*), Hampshire, 1790-1869. Boyle Lecture, 1822; Memoir of Mary R. Mitford, 1870; Welcome and Farewell, 1837, a tragedy.

HARPSFELD, LL.D. (*Nicholas*), died 1583. Dialogi Sex contra Summi Pontificatus, 1566; Historia Anglicana Ecclesiastica, 1622, posthumous.

HARRADEN (*Beatrice*), 1864- . Fairy Folk, 1897; Hilda Strafford, 1897; In Varying Moods, 1894; Ships that pass in the Night, 1893.

HARRIES, M.D. (*Walter*), Gloucester, 1647-1709. De Morbis Acutis Infantium, 1694; Pharmacologia Anti-Empirica, 1683.

HARRINGTON, M.D. (*Henry*), 1729-1816. Nugæ Antiquæ, 1769.

HARRINGTON (*James*), Upton, in Northamptonshire, 1611-1677. Oceana (an ideal republic), 1556 (Dugald Stewart calls it "one of the boasts of English literature"); Political Discourses, 1660. His Life, by Toland, 1771.

HARRIS (*Benjamin*), eighteenth century. Ghost of Moll King, or a Night at Derry's, 1785; List of Covent-Garden Ladies, or the New Atlantis (an annual), commenced in 1760, suppressed in 1793.

HARRIS, LL.D. (*George*), 1809-1889. Life of Lord Chancellor Hardwicke, 1847; Philosophical Treatise on the Nature and Constitution of Man, 1870 (highly esteemed).

HARRIS (*James*), Salisbury, 1709-1780. Hermes, 1751 (a learned work on language and grammar); Philological Inquiries, 1781, posthumous; Philosophical Arrangements, 1775; Treatises on (1) Art, (2) Music, Poetry, and Painting, (3) Happiness, 1744. His Life, by his son, the earl of Malmesbury, 1801.

HARRIS (*Joel Chandler*), American, 1848. Free Joe, 1887; Mingo, 1884; Nights with Uncle Remus, 1883; Uncle Remus, 1880.

HARRIS, D.D. (*John*), 1667-1719. History of Kent, 1719; Lexicon Technicum, 1704-10 (his chief work); Navigantium atque Itinerantium Bibliotheca, 1705.

HARRIS, D.D. (*John*), Devonshire, 1802-1856. Great Teacher (*The*), 1835; Mammon, 1836; Pre-Adamite Earth (*The*), 1847.

HARRIS (*Moses*), 1735-1806. Aurelian (*The*), 1766; English Lepidoptera, 1775; Exposition of English Insects, 1776.

HARRIS, D.D. (*Thaddeus Mason*), Boston, U.S., 1768-1842. Natural History of the Bible, 1820 (a valuable work).

HARRIS (*Walter*), eighteenth century. Hibernica, 1770 (interesting and valuable); History and Antiquities of Dublin, 1766; History of William, Prince of Nassau and Orange (William III.), 1749; Histriographarum Aliorumque Scriptores Hiberniæ Commentarium (Irish authors), 1736.

N.B.—His father, Walter Harris, M.D., lived 1647-1725, and wrote several medical works.

HARRIS (*Thomas Lake*), 1823 (established the Brotherhood of the New Life in Duchess County, N.Y.). Arcana of Christianity, 1858-68; Breath of God, 1867; Great Republic (*The*), 1867; Holy City (*The*), 1880; Hymns, 1848; Luminous Life (*The*), 1882; Modern Spiritualism, 1860; Regina, 1860; Song of Satan, 1858; Star Flowers, 1886; Wisdom of the Adepts (*The*), 1884.

HARRIS, D.D. (*William*), 1720-1770. Life and Writings of Charles I., 1758; Life of Charles II., 1765; Life of Oliver Cromwell, 1761; Life and Writings of James I. of Great Britain, 1753; Life of Hugh Peters, 1751.

HARRIS (*William*), 1765-1829. Catalogue of the Library of the Royal Institution of Great Britain, 1809 (a most useful work).

HARRISON (*Frederic*), London, 1831- . Annals of an Old Manor House, 1893; Choice of Books (*The*), 1886; Comte's Social Statics translated, 1875; Crisis in Egypt (*The*), 1882; England and France, 1866; Lectures on Education, 1883; Martial Law in Cabul (*The*), 1880; Meaning of History (*The*), 1862; Oliver Cromwell, 1888; On the Choice of Books, 1886; Order and Progress, 1875; Present (*The*) and the

Future, 1880; Questions for a Reformed Parliament, 1867.

HARRISON (*Mary St. Leger*), pseudonym "Lucas Malet," daughter of Charles Kingsley, 1852–   . Carissima (*The*), 1896; Colonel Enderby's Wife, 1885; Counsel of Perfection (*A*), 1888; Little Peter, 1887; Modern Grotesque (*A*), 1896; Mrs. Lorimer, 1882; Wages of Sin (*The*), 1891.

HARRY, called "The Blind Harry," about 1440–1499. Life of Wallace (an historical rhyming epic, in 11 books), 1483.

HARTE (*Francis Bret*), Albany, U.S., 1839–   . Argonauts of North Liberty (*The*), 1888; Barker's Luck, 1896; Bell-ringer of of Angel's (*A*), 1894; By Shore and Sedge, 1885; Californian Stories, 1884; Clarence, 1895; Colonel Starbottle's Client, 1892; Condensed Novels, 1867; Cressy, and the Heritage of Dedlow Marsh, 1889; Crusade of the "Excelsior" (*The*), 1887; Devil's Ford, 1887; Drift from Redwood Camp, 1888; Drift from Two Shores, 1887; East and West Poems, 1871; Echoes of the Foot Hills, 1874; Episode of Fiddletown (*An*), 1873; Flip, 1882; Found at Blazing Star, 1882; Gabriel Conroy, 1876; Heiress of Red Dog (*An*), 1879; Hoodlum Band (*The*), 1878; In the Carquinez Woods, 1883; Jeff Briggs's Love Story, 1880; Luck of Roaring Camp, and other Sketches (*The*), 1870; Maruja, 1885; Millionaire of Rough and Ready (*A*), 1887; Mrs. Skaggs's Husbands, 1872; On the Frontier, 1884; Phyllis of the Sierras (*A*), 1888; Poems, 1871; Protégé (*A*) of Jack Hamlin's, 1894; Queen of the Pirate Isle, 1886; Sally Dows, 1893; Sappho of Green Springs (*A*), 1891; Snow-bound at Eagle's, 1886; Stories of the Sierras, 1872; Story of a Mine, 1878; Susy, 1893; Tales of the Argonauts, 1875; Tales of Trail and Town, 1898; Thankful Blossom, 1877; Three Partners, 1897; Twins of Table Mountain (*The*), 1879; Two Men of Sandy Bar, 1876; Waif of the Plains (*A*), 1890; Ward of the Golden Gate (*A*), 1890.

HARTE (Rev. *Walter*), 1700–1774. Essay on Satire, 1730; History of Gustavus Adolphus, 1759 (the best military biography in the language); Poems on Several Occasions, 1727.

HARTLEY, M.D. (*David*), Armley, in Yorkshire, 1705–1757. Observations on Man, 1749 (in high esteem). His Life, by his son, 1791.

HARTLIB (*Samuel*), a naturalized Englishman, 1606–1670. Compleat Husbandman (*The*), 1659; Considerations concerning England's Reformation, 1647; Discourse of Husbandry used in Brabant and Flanders, 1651.

HARTSHORNE (Rev. *Charles Henry*), Broseley, in Shropshire, 1802–1865. Ancient Metrical Tales, 1829; Book of Rarities in the University of Cambridge, 1829; Feudal and Military Antiquities of Northumberland, etc., 1858; Historical Memorials of Northampton, 1848; Home of the Working-Man, 1856; Salopia Antiqua, 1841; Sepulchral Remains in Northamptonshire.

HARVEY, M.D. (*Gideon*), Surrey, 1625–1700. Ars Curandi Morbos Expectatione, 1689;

De Vanitatibus, Dolis, et Mendaciis Medicorum, 1683.

HARVEY (*Richard*), about 1540–1610. Astrological Discourse on the Conjunction of Saturn and Jupiter, 1582 (this tract threw the whole kingdom into a panic; all looked with consternation for the fatal Sunday, April 28, 1583); Philadelphus, or a Defence of Brute, etc., 1593.

HARVEY, M.D. (*William*), Folkestone, in Kent, 1578–1657. Exercitatio Anatomica de Motu Cordis et Sanguinis in Animalibus, 1628 (an immortal treatise on the "circulation of the blood"); Exercitationes de Generatione Animalium, 1651; Exercitationes duæ Anatomicæ de Circulatione Sanguinis, etc., 1649. His Life, by Dr. Lawrence, 1766; Dr. Willis, 1847.

HARWOOD, D.D. (*Edward*), Lancashire, 1729–1794. Biographica Classica, 1778; Introduction to the Study of the New Testament, 1767–71; New Translation of the New Testament, 1768; View of Various Editions of the Greek and Roman Classics, 1775.

HARVINGTON (Sir *John*). See HARINGTON.

HASTED (*Edward*), Hawley, in Kent, 1732–1812. History of Canterbury, 1801; History of Kent, 1778–99.

HASTINGS (*Warren*), governor-general of India, Daylesford, in Worcestershire, 1732–1818. Narrative of the Insurrection in the Zemendary of Benares, 1782. His Life, by G. R. Gleig, 1841; Macaulay wrote an essay on him.

HATCH, D.D. (*Edwin*), Derby, 1835–1889. Growth of Church Institutions, 1887; Organization of Early Christian Churches, 1881; Progress in Theology, 1885; Student's Handbook to the University and Colleges of Oxford, 1873; Studies in Biblical Greek, 1889; Study of Ecclesiastical History, 1885.

HATTON (Sir *Christopher*), Holdenby, Peterborough, 1540–1591. Treatise concerning Statutes, etc., 1677. His Life, by sir N. H. Nicholas.

HATTON (*Joseph*), Andover, in Hampshire, novelist, etc., 1839–   . Abbey Murder (*The*), 1888; Against the Stream, 1866; Banishment of Jessop Blythe (*The*), 1895; Behind a Mask, 1885; Bitter Sweets, 1865, a love-story; By Order of the Czar, 1890; Captured by Cannibals, 1888; Christopher Henrick, 1869; Cigarette Papers, 1892; Clytis, 1874, a novel dramatized; Cruel London, 1878; Gay World (*The*), 1887; Henry Irving's Impressions on America, 1884; In Jest and Earnest, 1893; In the Lap of Fortune, 1873; John Needham's Double, 1885; Journalistic London, 1882; Kites and Pigeons, 1872; Lyceum Faust (*The*), 1886; Memorial Window (*The*), 1870; Modern Ulysses (*A*), 1883; New Ceylon (*The*), 1882; Not in Society, 1877; Old House at Sandwich (*The*), 1886; Pit and Pitmen, 1864; Princess Mazaroff (*The*), 1891; Provincial Papers, 1861; Queen of Bohemia (*The*), 1877; Reminiscences of J. L. Toole 1888; Tallants of Barton (*The*), 1867; Three Recruits, 1880; To-day in America, 1881; Under the Great Seal, 1893; Valley of Poppies (*The*), 1871.

HATTON (*Joseph L.*), Liverpool, 1815–
Pascal Bruno, 1844, an opera; Rose, or
Love's Ransom, 1864, an opera; Queen of
the Thames (*The*), 1844, an operetta.
∵ About 200 songs, part-songs, glees, etc.
HAUGHTON (*William*), about 1558–1610.
Englishmen for my Money, 1596, a comedy;
Pleasant Comedie of Patient Grissill, 1603. (It
seems that the former of these two comedies
was by Thomas Haughton. There are
three editions of it in the British Museum.
Whether Thomas and William are the same
person, or brothers, is uncertain. The latter
seems to have been the joint work of Haughton, Dekker, and Chettle.)
HAUSTED (*P.*), seventeenth century. Ad
Populum, 1644, a poem; Rival Friends
(*The*), 1632, a comedy; Senile Odium, 1633,
a Latin comedy.
HAVELOCK (Sir *Henry*), Bishop Wearmouth,
in Durham, 1795–1857. History of the Ava
Campaigns, 1827. His Life, by J. T. Headley,
1859; Dr. W. Brock; J. C. Marsham, 1860.
HAVERGAL (*Frances Ridley*), Astley, in Worcestershire, 1836–1879. Devotional Poems
in 3 vols., 1881, posthumous.
HAVERS, M.D. (*Clopton*), 17th century (he
discovered the "Haversian canals" in bone).
Osteulogia Nova, 1691 (long a standard work).
HAWEIS (Rev. *Hugh Reginald*), Egham, in
Surrey, 1838–   . American Humourists,
1883; Amy Arnold, 1863; Arrows in the
Air, 1878; Ashes to Ashes, 1874; Christ and
Christianity, 1886–87; Current Coin (essays
on current topics), 1876; Key of Doctrine
and of Practice, 1884; Life of Queen Victoria,
1887; Music and Morals, 1871 (brought him
into notice); My Musical Life, 1884; Old
Ballads, 1886; Pet (for children), 1874;
Poets in the Pulpit, 1880; Select Poems,
1886; Shakespeare and the Stage, 1878; Sir
Morell Mackenzie, 1893; Speech in Season,
1875; Thoughts for the Times, 1872; Travel
and Talk, 1885, 1893, 1895; War, 1878, a
sermon; Winged Words, 1885; Worship and
Praise, 1872, a sermon; Unsectarian Family
Prayers, 1874.
HAWEIS (Mrs.), maiden name *Mary Eliza
Joy*, wife of the above, *-*. Art of Beauty,
1877; Art of Decoration, 1881; Art of Dress,
1879; Beautiful Houses, 1882; Chaucer for
Children, 1876; Chaucer for Schools, 1880;
Chaucer's Beads, 1884; Rus in Urbe, 1886;
Tales from Chaucer, 1887.
HAWES (*Stephen*), 1483–1512. Comfort of
Lovers (printed by Wynkyn de Worde); Con-
version of Seweres, 1509, a poem in octave
stanzas; Example of Vertu, printed 1530,
a poem; Joyfull Medytacyon, etc. (printed
by Wynkyn de Worde); Passe-Tyme of
Plesure (*The*), printed 1517, an allegorical
poem; Temple of Glasse (*The*), a poem,
also attributed to John Lydgate.
HAWKER, D.D. (*Robert*), 1753–1827. Com-
mentary on the Bible, 1808; Poor Man's
Commentary, 1822; Poor Man's Commentary
on the Psalms, 1846; Portion (*Morning and
Evening*), 1845 (his best-known work);
Reeds shaken with the Wind, 1843–44;
Record of the Western Shore, 1836; Rural
Synods, 1844; Tendrils, 1821.

HAWKER (*Robert Stephen*), 1803–1875. Aishah
Shoechinab, 1860; Cornish Ballads, 1869;
Ecclesia, 1841; Echoes from Old Cornwall,
1846; Footprints of Former Men in Cornwall,
1870; Quest of the Sangrail (*The*), 1864.
His Life, by F. G. Lee.
HAWKESWORTH, LL.D. (*John*), London,
1715–1773. Adventurer (*The*), 1752–54;
Voyages of Byron, Wallis, Carteret, and
Cook, 1773 (he received £6000 for the copy-
right of this book).
HAWKINS (*Benjamin Waterhouse*), London,
1807–1889. Artistic Anatomy of the Horse,
Cattle, and Sheep, 1865; Atlas of Elemen-
tary Anatomy, 1865 (with Huxley); Com-
parative View of the Human and Animal
Frame, 1860; Elements of Form, 1842;
Popular Comparative Anatomy, 1840.
HAWKINS (Sir *John*), London, 1719–1789.
General History of Music, 1776 (much
esteemed); Life of Dr. Johnson, 1787.
HAWKS, D.D. (*Francis Lister*), Newbern,
U.S., 1798–1866. Auricular Confession in
the Protestant Church, 1850; Commodore
Perry's Expedition to the China Sea and
Japan, 1852–54; Contributions to the Eccle-
siastical History of the United States, 1836–
40; Egypt and its Monuments, 1849;
History of North Carolina (unfinished at his
death); Reports of the Supreme Court of
North Carolina, 1823–28.
HAWORTH (*Adrian Hardy*), Chelsea, died
1833. Genus Mesembryanthemum, 1794;
Lepidoptera Britannica, 1803–28 (excellent);
Saxifragearum Enumeratio, 1821; Synopsis
Plantarum Succulentarum 1812, supplement
1819.
HAWTHORNE (*Julian*), son of Nathaniel
Hawthorne, 1846–   . Archibald Mal-
maison, 1879; Beatrix Randolph, 1883;
Bressant, 1873, a novel; David Pointdexter's
Disappearance, 1888; Dust, 1883; Ellice
Quentin, 1880; Fortune's Fool, 1883; Garth,
1877, a novel; Idolatry, 1874, a novel;
Laughing Mill (*The*), 1879; Love—or a
Name, 1885; Miss Cadogna, 1885; Mrs.
Gainsborough's Diamonds, 1878; Nathaniel
Hawthorne and his Wife, 1884; Noble
Blood, 1885; Prince Saroni's Wife, 1882;
Saxon Studies, 1876; Sebastian Strome,
1879; Septimus, 1871, a novel; Spectre of
the Camera (*The*); Yellow Cap, 1880.
HAWTHORNE (*Nathaniel*), Salem, in Massa-
chusetts, U.S., 1804–1864. American Note-
Books, 1868; Blithedale Romance (*The*),
1852; Dr. Grimshawe's Secret, 1883; House
of the Seven Gables (*The*), 1851, a novel;
Life of President Pierce, 1852; Mosses from
an Old Manse, 1846; Our Old Home, 1863,
a novel; Pansie, 1864; Passages from the
American Note-Books of N. Hawthorne,
1870; Passages from the Italian and French
Note-Books, 1871; Scarlet Letter (*The*), 1850
(an excellent romance); Septimus Felton,
1872; Sketches and Studies, 1883; Tales of
the White Hills, 1877; Transformation, 1860
(his best work); Twice-told Tales, 1837 (so
called because they had been published first
in periodicals); Virtuoso's Collection (*A*),
1877. His Life, by H. James, junr.
HAY (*William*), 1695–1755. Essay on De-

formity, 1794, posthumous; Religio Philosophi, 1753.

HAYDON (*Benjamin Robert*), artist, Plymouth, 1786–1846. Autobiography. Life, by Tom Taylor, 1853.

HAYES (*Charles*), 1678–1760. Chronographiæ Asiaticæ et Ægyptiacæ Specimen, 1759; Treatise on Fluxions, 1704; Vindication of the History of the Septuagint, 1736.

HAYES (*William*), eighteenth century. Natural History of British Birds, with their Portraits, 1775; Portraits of Rare and Curious Birds, 1794.

HAYLEY (*William*), Chichester, 1745–1820. Afflicted Brother (*The*), 1800; Ballads on Animals, 1805; Essays in Verse, on Epic Poetry 1782, History 1780, Painting 1778, Sculpture 1800; Odes, Elegies, and Plays, 1785; Plays of Three Acts, 1784; Plays with a Preface, 1811; Triumphs of Music, 1804; Triumphs of Temper (six cantos), 1781.
Prose: Essay on Old Maids, 1785; Life of Cowper, 1803; Life of Milton, 1796; Life of G. Romney, 1809. His Life, by himself, was published 1823.

HAYMAN, D.D. (*Henry*), Devonshire, 1823– A Fragment of the Jason Legend, 1874; Homer's *Odyssey*, completed 1881; Latin and Greek Translations, 1865; On the Indwelling of the Holy Spirit, 1875; Rugby Sermons, 1875.

HAYMAN (*Robert*), 17th century. Quodlibets lately come from New Britaniola, 1628.

HAYWARD (*Abraham*), Wishford, in Wiltshire, 1803–1884. Art of Dining, 1852; Autobiography, etc., of Mrs. Piozzi, 1861; Biographical and Critical Essays, first series 1858, second 1873, third 1874; Diaries of a Lady of Quality, 1864; Goethe, 1877; Goethe's *Faust* (a prose translation), 1883; Juridical Tracts, 1856; Letters and Remains of Mrs. Piozzi, 1861; Sketches of Eminent Statesmen and Writers, 1880; Whist and Whist-players, 1878.

HAYWARD (Sir *John*), died 1627. Certain Yeeres of Queen Elizabeth's Reign, 1640; History of Edward IV., 1630; Life of Henry IV., 1599; Lives of the Norman Kings of England, 1613; Of Supremacie in Matters of Religion, 1624.

HAYWARD (*William Stephens*), novelist,*– . Barbara Home, 1880; Black Angel (*The*), 1871; Caroline, 1875; Cloud King (*The*), 1865; Demons of the Sea, 1866; Diamond Cross (*The*), 1868; Ethel Gray, 1875; Eulalie, or the Red and White Rose, 1869; Fiery Cross (*The*), 1866, a tale of the great American War; High-road to Ruin (*The*), 1876; Hunted to Death, 1862; John Hazel's Vengeance, 1880; Lord Scatterbrain, or the Rough Diamond, 1869; Lost Lucy, 1881; Love against the World, 1875; Love's Treason, 1874; Maud Luton, 1875; Mutiny of the *Thunderer*, 1878; Perils of a Pretty Girl, 1875; Ran away from Home, 1875; Rebel Privateer (*The*), 1874; Rodney Ray, 1874; Star of the South, 1871 (sequel to "The Black Angel"); Tales of the Wild and Wonderful, 1870; Three Red Men, 1876; Tom Holt's Log, 1868, a sea tale.

HAYWOOD (Mrs. *Eliza*), 1693–1756. Court

of Caramania (*The*), 1722 (this and "The New Utopia" gave her a place in the *Dunciad*); Female Spectator (*The*), 1744–46; History of Jenny and Jessamy; New Utopia (*The*), 1723; History of Miss Betsy Thoughtless, 1751; Spy on the Conjuror (*A*), 1725, a collection of stories. Said to be the most voluminous female writer this kingdom ever produced; about her only (?) merit. She is introduced in the *Dunciad*, and her name is inscribed on the rail of the stairs in Hogarth's *Rake's Progress*.

HAZLITT (*William*), Maidstone, 1778–1830. Characteristics, 1823; Characters of Shakespeare's Plays, 1817; Conversations of James Northcote, 1830; Dramatic Scorpion (*The*), 1818, a satire; Eloquence of the British Senate (*The*), 1807; Essay on the Principles of Human Action, 1805; Free Thoughts on Public Affairs, 1806; Lectures on the Dramatic Literature of the Age of Elizabeth, 1821; Lectures on the English Comic Writers, 1819; Lectures on the English Poets, 1818; Liber Amoris, or the New Pygmalion, 1823; Life of Napoleon, 1828; Life of Titian, 1830; Memoirs of Holcroft, 1816; Notes of a Journey through France and Italy, 1825; Plain Speaker (*The*), etc., 1826; Political Essays, with Sketches of Public Characters, 1819; Reply to Maltush, 1807; Round Table (*The*), 1817, essays on men and manners; Sketches of the Principal Picture Galleries of England, 1824; Spirit of the Age, 1825; Table Talk, 1821–22; View of the English Stage (*A*), 1818. His Life, by his son, 1836; grandson, 1867.

HAZLITT (*William Carew*), grandson of the above, 1834– . Bibliography of Old English Literature, 1867; English Proverbs and Provincial Phrases, 1869; Handbook of Early English Literature, 1868; History of the Venetian Republic, 1860; Memoirs of W. Hazlitt (his grandfather), 1867; Popular Antiquities of Great Britain, 1870; Sophie Laurie, 1865, a novel.

HEAD (Sir *Edmund Walker*), born near Maidstone, in Kent, 1805–1868. Ballads, and other Poems, 1868; Chapters on Shall and Will, 1856; Handbook of Spanish Painting, 1848.

HEAD (Sir *Francis Bond*), Hermitage, near Rochester, in Northumberland, 1793–1875. Bubbles from the Brunnen, etc., 1833 (his best-known work); Defenceless State of Britain (*The*), 1850; Descriptive Essays, 1857; Emigrant (*The*), 1846; Fagot of French Sticks (*A*), 1851; Fortnight in Ireland (*A*), 1852; Life of Bruce the Traveller, 1830; Horse and his Rider (*The*), 1860; Rough Notes on the Pampas, 1826; Royal Engineer (*The*), 1860; Stokers and Pokers, 1856.

HEAD (Sir *George*), Rochester, 1782–1855. Forest Scenes and Incidents in the Wilds of North America, 1829; Home Tour through the Manufacturing Districts, 1836–37; Rome, 1849. He also translated the *Metamorphoses* of Apuleius, 1851.

HEAD (*Richard*), pseudonym "Meriton Latroon," etc., died 1678. Almansir, or the Rhodomontadoes of Sir Frederick Fightall, 1672; Canting Academy (*The*), 1674; English Rogue (*The*), a Witty Extravagant,

1671; Floating Island (*The*), 1673; Jackson's Recantation, 1674; Hic et Ubique, 1663, a comedy; Madam Wheedle, 1678; News from the Stars, 1673; Nugæ Venales, 1686 (jests, bulls, and witticisms); Porteus Redivivus, or the Art of Wheedling, 1667; Venus's Cabinet unlocked, 1674.

HEARNE (*Thomas*), White Waltham, in Berkshire, 1678-1715. Camden's *Annals*, 1717; De Rebus Britannicis Collectanea, 1715; Ductor Historicus, 1704; Fordun's *Scotichronicon*, 1722; Leland's *Itinerary*, 1710-12; Life of Alfred the Great, 1709; Reliquiæ Bodleianæ, 1703; Reliquiæ Hearnianæ, 1857.
∵ He edited a host of ancient authors, so that his complete works occupy 100 volumes.
His Life, by Huddesford, 1772; Henry Headley, 1780; Kett, 1810.

HEATH, D.C.L. (*Benjamin*), Exeter, died 1766. Notæ . . . ad Æschyli, Sophoclis, et Euripidis . . . Dramata, 1762 (a work of great merit); Proof of the Divine Existence and Unity, 1740.

HEATH (*Charles*), London, 1784-1848. Book of Beauty, 1833-49; Descriptive Account of Petersfield and Chepstow, etc.; Excursion down the Wye, etc., 1808; Historical and Descriptive Account of Monmouth, 1804, Ragland Castle 1801, Tintern Abbey 1805; Shakespeare Gallery (*The*), 1836.

HEATH (Rev. *Dunbar Isidore*), 1816- . Defence of my Professional Character, 1862; Exodus Papyri (*The*), 1855; Future Kingdom of Christ (*The*), 1852-53; Proverbs of Aphobis (*The*), 1858 (these were supposed to exist B.C. 1900); Sermons on Important Subjects, 1859 (condemned as unorthodox).

HEATH (*Francis George*), Totnes, in Devonshire, 1843- . Autumn Leaves, 1881; Burnham Beeches, 1879; English Peasantry (*The*), 1874; Fern Paradise (*The*), 1878; Fern World (*The*), 1877; My Garden Wild, and what I grew there, 1881; Our Woodland Trees, 1878; Peasant Life in the West of England, 1880; Romance of Peasant Life (*The*), 1873; Sylvan Spring, 1880; Where to find Ferns, 1881.

HEATH (*James*), London, 1629-1664. Chronicle of the Late War in the Three Kingdoms (in four parts), 1661-63; Elegy on Dr. Thomas Fuller 1661, on Dr. Sanderson 1662; Flagellum, 1663 (Oliver Cromwell, "The Usurper"); Glorious . . . Restitution of . . . His Sacred Majesty Charles II., 1662; History of Loyal English Martyrs, 1663.

HEATHCOTE, D.D. (*Ralph*), Leicestershire, 1721-1795. Historia Astronomiæ, 1746·Irenarch, 1771, a manual for justices of the peace; Sylva, 1786, a collection of anecdotes. His autobiography, 1771.

HEBER (*Reginald*), bishop of Calcutta, born at Malpas, in Cheshire, 1783-1826. Hymns, 1812; Hymns written and adapted to the Weekly Church Service of the Year, 1827; Life of Jeremy Taylor, D.D., 1824; Narrative of a Journey through the Upper Provinces of India, from Calcutta to Bombay, 1828 (very interesting and valuable); Omnipotence of God (*The*), 1825; Palestine, 1803 (Newdigate prize poem); Personality and Office of the Christian Comforter, 1815;

Poems and Translations, 1812; Sermons, 1829, 1837. His Life, by his widow, 1830; Potter; Taylor.

HEBERDEN, M.D. (*William*), London, 1710-1801. Commentarii de Morborum Historia et Curatione, 1802 (a valuable work); Essay on Methridatium Theriaca (*An*), 1745.

HEDLEY (*John Edward*), bishop of Cæsaropolis, born at Morpeth, in Northumberland, 1837- . Light of the Holy Spirit in the World, 1873; Spirit of Faith (*The*), 1875; Who is Jesus Christ? 1874.

HELPS (Sir *Arthur*), 1817-1875. Brevia, or Short Essays and Aphorisms, 1870; Casimir Maremma, 1870; Catherine Douglas, 1843, a tragedy; Claims of Labour, 1845, an essay; Companions of my Solitude, 1851 (a sequel to "Friends in Council"); Conquerors of the New World, 1848; Conversations on War, etc., 1871; Essays, etc., 1841 (his first production); Friends in Council 1847, 1859, second series 1859; History of the Spanish Conquests of America, 1855-61; Ivan de Biron, 1874; King Henry II., 1843, an historic play; Life of Cortez, 1871; Life of Pizarro, 1869; On Organization, 1860, an essay; Oulita the Serf, 1858, a play; Realmah, 1869; Social Pressure, 1874; Spanish Conquest in America (*The*), 1855-57; Thoughts in the Cloister and the Crowd, 1835; Thoughts upon Government, 1871.

HEMANS (*Mrs.*), maiden name *Felicia Dorothea Browne*, Liverpool, poetess, 1794-1835. Dartmoor, 1821; Domestic Affections, and other Poems, 1812; Early Blossoms, 1808; England and Spain, 1808; Forest Sanctuary (*The*), 1826; Hymns of Childhood, 1834; Last Constantine (*The*), and other Poems, 1827; Lays of Leisure Hours, 1829; Meeting of Wallace and Bruce (*The*), 1819; Modern Greece, 1817; National Lyrics, 1834; Poetical Remains, 1836, posthumous; Records of Women, 1828; Restoration of Works of Art in Italy, 1817; Scenes and Hymns of Life, 1834; Sceptic (*The*), 1820; Siege of Valencia, and other Poems, 1823; Songs of the Affections, 1830; Vespers of Palermo, 1823, a tragedy; Welsh Melodies, 1822. Her Life, by H. F. Chorley, 1837; Mrs. Hughes, 1839.

HEMINGFORD (*Walter de*), Gisborough, in Yorkshire, chronicler, died 1347. Historia de Rebus Gestis Edwardi I., II., et III., printed by Bale 1548, reprinted 1731.

HENDERSON (Rev. Dr. *Ebenezer*), 1784-1858. Biblical Researches and Travels in Russia, 1826 (useful); Book of Isaiah translated from the Hebrew, 1840, Jeremiah 1851, the Twelve Minor Prophets 1845; Iceland, or the Journal of a Resident, 1818; Vaudois (*The*), 1845. His Life, by J. S. Henderson, 1859.

HENLEY (Rev. *John*), called "Orator Henley," Melton Mowbray, Leicestershire, 1692-1756. Compleat Linguist (*The*), a grammar of all known languages, 1719-21; Primitive Liturgy for the Use of Oratory, 1726.

HENLEY, LL.D. (*W. E.*), Gloucester, 1849-Book of Verses, 1888; London Volunteers, etc., 1893; Song of the Sword (*The*), 1892; Three Plays, 1892 (with Stevenson); Views and Reviews, 1890.

HENRY VIII., king of England, born at Greenwich, 1491–1547. On the Seven Sacraments, 1521 (against Luther); for this book the pope called him "The Defender of the Faith."

HENRY OF HUNTINGDON, chronicler, died 1160. Historia Anglorum, 1135.

HENRY (*David*), Aberdeen, 1710–1792. Complete English Farmer, 1772; Historical Account of Voyages round the World, 1774.

HENRY (*Matthew*), Broadoak Farmhouse, in Wales, 1662–1714. Communicant's Companion (*The*), 1704; Direction for Daily Communion, 1712; Discourse against Vice and Immorality, 1705; Discourse concerning Meekness, 1698; Exposition of the Old and New Testaments, 1704–10 (his great work); Life of the Rev. Philip Henry, 1696; Method of Prayer (*A*), 1710; Pleasantness of a Religious Life, 1714. His Life, by W. Tong, 1716; Burder and Hughes, 1811; J. B. Williams, 1830.

HENRY, D.D. (*Robert*), St. Ninians, in Scotland, 1718–1790. History of Great Britain, 1771–95.

HENRY, M.D. (*William*), Manchester, 1775–1836. Elements of Experimental Chemistry, 1799.

HENRYSON (*Robert*), Scotland, died 1508. Bludy Serf (*The*) (printed in the *Select Remains of the Ancient Popular Poetry of Scotland*); Fabils, printed 1621; Orpheus Kyng, and how he zeid to Hewyn and Hel to seek his Quene, printed 1508; Robin and Makyne, printed in 1824 by the Bannatyne Club; Taile of the Uplandis Mous and the Burges Mous, printed 1815; Testament of Faire Creseide, printed 1593.

HENSLOW (*John Stevens*), Rochester, in Northumberland, 1796–1861. Dictionary of Botanical Terms, 1849; Principles of Botany, 1836. His Life, by Jenyns, 1862.

HENTY (*George Alfred*), Trumpington, in Cambridgeshire, 1832–   . All but Lost, 1869, a tale; Colonel Thorndyke's Secret, 1898; Condemned as a Nihilist, 1892, a tale; Dorothy's Double, a novel; In the Heart of the Rockies, 1894, a tale; March to Coomassie (*The*), 1874, a tale; March to Magdala (*The*), 1868, a tale; Out on the Pampas, 1870, a tale; Rujub the Juggler, a novel; Search for a Secret (*A*), 1868, a tale; Young Colonist (*The*), 1884, a tale; Young French-Tireurs (*The*), 1871, a tale. And many other boys' books.

HEPBURN (*James Buonaventura*), Scotland, 1573–1620. Dictionarium Hebraicum et Chaldaicum, 1591.

HERAUD (*John Abraham*), poet, London, 1799–1886. Agnola Diora; Descent into Hell (*The*), 1830, a poem; Ingathering, 1870, a war epic; Judgment of the Flood (*The*), 1834, a poem; Legend of St. Loy, 1821; Macée de Lésdepart, 1878, an historical romance; Roman Brother (*The*), a tragedy; Salvator, or the Poor Man of Naples, a tragedy; Shakspere, his Inner Life, etc., 1865; Tottenham, 1820, a poem; Uxmal, 1877, an antique love-story; Videna, 1854, a tragedy; War of Ideas (*The*), 1871, a war epic; Wife or No Wife, a comedy; Wreck of the London (*The*), 1870.

HERBERT (Hon. *Auberon*). Windfall and Waterdrift, 1896.

HERBERT (Lord *Edward*), Montgomery Castle, Cherbury, 1581–1648. De Causis Errorum, 1645; De Religione Gentilium, 1663, posthumous; De Religione Laica, 1645; De Veritate, 1624; De Vita Humana, 1647; Expeditio Buckinghami Ducis in Ream Insulam, 1630; Life and Reign of King Henry VIII., 1649, posthumous; Memoirs, 1764, posthumous; Own Life, written by himself, 1764, posthumous.

HERBERT (Rev. *George*), called "The Holy Herbert," Montgomery Castle, Wales, 1593–1633 Priest to the Temple, or the Country Parson, 1652, prose; Temple (*The*), or the Church, 1631, poetry. His Life, by Izaak Walton, 1670; Gilfillan, 1853; W. Jerdan, 1853; Duyckinck, 1858. Edition of his *Works*, with a Memoir, by A. B. Grosart, 1875.

HERBERT (Sir *Thomas*), York, 1610–1682. Charles I. (Memoirs of the last two years), 1663; Travels in Africa and Asia, etc., 1634; Threnodia Carolina, 1678, published 1702 (the last days of Charles I.).

HERON (*Robert*), New Galloway, in Scotland, 1764–1807. General History of Scotland, 1794–99.

HERRICK (Rev. *Robert*), London, 1591–1674. Hesperides, 1647–48, a poem; Noble Numbers, or Pious Pieces, 1647. His *Complete Poems*, edited by A. B. Grosart, 1877.

HERSCHEL (Sir *John Frederick William*), Slough, near Windsor, astronomer, 1792–1871. Application of the Calculus of Finite Differences, 1820 (his first work); Essays, 1857; Familiar Letters on Scientific Subjects, 1866; Manual of Scientific Enquiry, 1849; Outlines of Astronomy, 1850; Physical Geography, 1861; Preliminary Discourse on the Study of Natural Philosophy, 1830; Results of Astronomical Observation at the Cape of Good Hope, 1847; Treatise on Astronomy 1833, on Sound 1830, on the Theory of Light 1831.

∴ His sister, Caroline Lucretia, was also an astronomer, 1750–1848.

HERVEY (Mrs.), maiden name *Eleonora Louisa Montague*, Liverpool, 1811–   . Double Claim (*The*), 1842, a tale; Feasts of Camelot (*The*), 1863; Landgrave (*The*), 1839, a dramatic poem; Margaret Russell, 1840.

HERVEY (Rev. *James*), Northamptonshire, 1714–1758. Contemplations, 1747; Meditations among the Tombs, 1746–47; Reflections in a Flower Garden, 1750; Theron and Aspasia, 1755. His Life, by John Brown, 1822; John Cole, 1822–26.

HERVEY (Lord *John*), 1696–1743. (He was attacked as "Sporus" in Pope's *Epistle to Dr. Arbuthnot*, and as "Lord Fanny" in Pope's *Imitation of the First Book of Horace*, and in Byron's *English Bards and Scotch Reviewers*.) Memoirs of the Reign of George II., published in 1848.

HEWITSON (*William*), Newcastle-upon-Tyne, 1806–1878. British Oology, 1831; Exotic Butterflies, 1852; Illustrations of Diurnal Lepidoptera.

HEWSON (*William*), Hexham, in Northumberland, 1739–1774. Experimental Inquiries

into the Properties of the Blood, 1771;
Lymphatic System (*The*), 1774.
HEYDON (Sir *Christopher*), astrologer, about
1568-1653. Defence of Judicial Astrology
(*A*), 1603 (a learned book); Validity of
Astrology justified, 1650.
HEYDON (*John*), about 1616-1668. Elhava-
reuna and Psonthonphancia, 1665; Eugenius
Theodidactus, 1655, in verse; Harmony of
the World (*The*), 1662; Holy Guide (*The*),
leading the Way to the Wonders of the
World, 1662; Idea of the Law charactered,
etc. (*The*), 1660; New Method of Rosie-
crucian Physick, 1658; Ocia Imperialia,
1663; Quintuple Rosie-crucian Scourge, etc.,
1665; Rosie-crucian Axiomata, 1660; Rosie-
cross Uncovered, 1662; Theomagia (in three
parts), 1669; Wise Man's Crown (*The*), or
the Glory of the Rosie-cross, 1664.
HEVLIN, D.D. (*Peter*), Burford, in Oxfordshire, 1600-1662. Ærius Redivivus, 1636-47;
Certamen Epistolare, 1659; Cosmographie
(in four books), 1622 (first called "Microcosmus"); Cyprianus Anglicus (that is, a Life
of W. Laud), 1644; Ecclesia Restaurata,
1661; Ecclesia Vindicata, 1657 (anti-
Puritan); Examen Historicum, 1659 (an
attack on Fuller's *Church History*); Help to
English History, 1641; Historia Quinquarti-
cularis, 1660 (a defence of Arianism); Historie of Episcopie, 1642; Historie of St.
George of Cappadocia, 1631; Historie of the
Reformation of the Church of England, 1661;
Life, etc., of Charles II., 1658; Parable of
the Tares (in ten sermons), 1659; Theologia
Veterum, 1673, posthumous. His Life, by
G. Veron, 1681; Dr. J. Barnard, 1682.
HEYWOOD (*John*), North Mimms, in Herts,
1506-1565. Breefe Balet (*A*), 1557; Dialogue
of Wit and Folly, 1546; Dialogue on Marriage, containing all the Proverbs in the
Language, 1547; Four P's (*The*), *i.e.*
Palmer, Pardoner, Poticarry, Pedlar, 1530,
an interlude; Mery Play between Johan
... Tyb ... and the Prester, 1533, a
comedy; Mery Play between the Pardoner
and the Frere, 1533, a comedy; Of Gen-
tylnes and Nobylyte, 1535, a dialogue; Play
of Love (*The*), 1533, an interlude; Spider
and the Flie, 1556, a parable.
HEYWOOD (*Thomas*), 1576-1645, wrote partly
or entirely 220 plays, 28 of which are extant.
Dramas : Brazen Age (*The*), 1603; Challenge for Beautie, 1606, a tragi-comedy;
Edward IV. (in two parts), 1600; English
Traveller (*The*), 1633, a tragi-comedy; Fair
Maid of the Exchange (*The*), 1607, a
comedy; Fair Maid of the West (*The*), 1611,
a comedy; Fortune by Land and Sea, 1655,
a tragi-comedy; Four Prentises of London,
1615, an historic play; Golden Age (*The*),
1611, a comedy; Iron Age (*The*), (in two
parts), 1632, a comedy; Lancashire Witches,
1634, a comedy; Life and Death of Hector,
1614, an historic play; Love's Maistresse,
1636, a masque; Maydenhead Well Lost
(*A*), 1634, a comedy; Queen Elizabeth's
Troubles (in two parts), 1606, 1609, an historic play; Rape of Lucrece (*The*), 1608, a
tragedy; Royall King and Loyall Subject
(*A*), 1637, a tragi-comedy; Silver Age

(*The*), 1613, a comedy; Wise Woman of
Hogsdon, 1638, a comedy; Woman kilde
by Kindnesse (*A*), before 1603, third edition
1617, a tragedy.
Not Dramas : Apology for Actors (three
treatises), 1612; Description of H.M.S. *The
Great Harry*, 1637; England's Elizabeth,
from her Cradle to her Crown, 1631; Epithalamium on the Marriage of Princess Elizabeth, 1613; Funeral Elegie of Henry Prince
of Wales, 1613; Funeral Elegie on James I.,
1625; Gunaikeion (in nine books, inscribed
with the names of the nine Muses), 1624;
Hierarchie of the Blessed Angels (a poem in
nine books), 1635; Life of Merlin, etc.,
1641; Life of the Duchess of Suffolk, 1631;
Lives of the Nine Most Worthy Women of
the World, 1640; Lives of the Most Famous
and Infamous Women of all Ages, 1657,
posthumous; Londini Artium, etc., 1632,
a pageant; Londini Speculum, 1637, a
pageant; Londini Status Pacatus, 1639, a
pageant; London's Harbour of Health and
Happiness, 1635, a pageant; London's Jus
Honorarium, 1631, a pageant; Porta
Pietatis, 1638, a pageant; Priest (*A*), a
Judge, and a Patentee (*i.e.* Laud, lord
Finch, and alderman Abel), 1641; Troia
Britannica (a poem in 17 cantos), 1609.
His Life, by J. P. Collier, 1856.
HIBBERD (*Shirley*), nineteenth century.
Epitome of the Russian War, 1857; Fresh-
water Aquaria, 1856; Garden Favourites,
1858.
HIBBERT, M.D. (*Samuel*), nineteenth century.
Description of the Shetland Islands, 1822
(a valuable work); History of the College
and Collegiate Church of Manchester, 1828;
History of Extinct Volcanoes, etc., 1832;
Sketches of the Philosophy of Apparitions,
1824.
HICKES, D.D. (*George*), Newsham, in York-
shire, 1642-1715. Devotions, 1712 (a stock
book); Institutiones Grammaticæ Anglo-
Saxonicæ, 1689; Thesaurus Linguarum
Veterum Septentrionalium, 1703-5 (his great
work).
HIGDEN (*Ralph*), Chester, chronicler, died
1367. Polychronycon, 1357 (printed by
Caxton 1482, and by Wynkyn de Worde
1495).
HIGGINS (*Godfrey*), 1771-1833. Anacalypsis,
1836; Celtic Druids, 1827; Horæ Sabbaticæ,
1826; Mohammed, 1829.
HIGGINS (Rev. *John*), 1544-1605. Mirror
for Magistrates, 1574 (sixteen legends).
HIGGONS (*Bevil*), 1670-1735. Generous Con-
queror (*The*), 1702; Historical and Critical
Remarks on Burnet's *Own Times*, 1725;
Short View of the English History, 1723.
HIGHMORE (*Anthony*), London, 1758-1829.
History of the Artillery Company of London,
1804; Pietas Londinensis, 1810; Review of
the History of Mortmain, 1787; Treatise on
Idiocy and Lunacy, 1807.
HIGHMORE (*Joseph*), London, 1692-1780.
Practice of Perspective, 1763.
HILL (*Aaron*), London, 1684-1749. Camillus,
1716; Elfrid, or the Fair Inconstant, 1710, a
tragedy; History of the Ottoman Empire,
1709; Northern Star (*The*), 1718, a poem in

praise of Peter the Great; Rinaldo, 1711, an opera.

HILL, D.D. (*George*), Scotland, 1748-1820. Lectures on Divinity, 1821, posthumous (much esteemed); Lectures to illustrate Jewish History, 1812; Theological Institutes (in three parts), 1803; View of the Constitution of the Church of Scotland, 1817.

HILL, M.D. (Sir *John*), Spalding, in Lincolnshire, 1716-1775. British Herbal (*The*), 1756; Construction of Timber (*The*), (in five books), 1770; Eden, or a Compleat Body of Gardening, 1773; Exotic Botany, 1752; Flora Britannica, 1760; General Natural History (*A*), 1748; Herbarum Britannicum, 1770; History of the Materia Medica, 1751; Hortus Kewensis, 1768; Mrs. Glasse's Cookery, 1749; Review of the Works of the Royal Society, 1751; Sleep of Plants (*The*), 1752; Vegetable System (*The*), 1756-76.
∴ He also wrote some farces, which called forth from Garrick the following couplet :—

For physic and farces his equal there scarce is; His farces are physic, his physic a farce is.

HILL (Rev. *Rowland*), Hawkestone, near Shrewsbury, 1744-1833. Village Dialogues, published in 1801. His Life, by W. Jones, 1842; E. Sidney, 1844.

HILL (Rev. *Thomas*), about 1530-1602. Art of Physiognomy, 1571; Contemplation of Mysteries (no date); Interpretation of Dreams, 1563; Proffitable Arte of Gardening, 1568; Proffitable Instruction for the Ordering of Bees, 1574; Schoole of Skil (*The*), (in two books), 1599.

HILTON (*John*), died 1655. Ayres and Falas (for three voices), 1627; Catch that catch can (a collection of catches, etc.), 1652 (in this collection "Non Nobis, Domine," first appeared: a great favourite with the royal family).

HILTON (*Walter*), monk of Sheen, contemporary with Henry VI. Ladder of Perfection (*The*), the "Scala Perfectionis" (printed by Wynkyn de Worde), translated 1494; Walter Hilton's *Devoute Boke*, 1506 (printed by R. Pynson).

HILTON, R.A. (*William*), Lincoln, 1786-1839. Christ crowned with Thorns, 1825; Edith and the Monks searching for the Body of Harold, 1834; Infant Warrior (*The*), 1836; Sir Calepine rescuing Serena, 1831; Una entering the Cave of Corceca, 1832.

HINCKS (*Edward*), Cork, 1792-1866. Assyrio-Babylonian Measures of Time, 1865; Catalogue of Egyptian MSS. in Trinity College, Dublin, 1843; On Egyptian Steel, 1842.

HIND (*John Russell*), Nottingham, 1823– . Astronomical Vocabulary, 1852; Comets (*The*), 1852; Descriptive Treatise on Comets, 1857; Elements of Algebra, 1855; Illustrated London Astronomy, 1853; Recent Comets and . . . their Orbits, 1845; Replies to Questions on the Comet of 1566..1852; Solar System (*The*), 1846; Unexpected Return of the Great Comet, 1848.

HINDS, D.D. (*Samuel*), bishop of Norwich, born in Barbadoes, 1793-1872. Nature and Extent·of Inspiration, 1831; Poems, 1834; Rise and Early Progress of Christianity, 1828.

HINKSON (Mrs.), maiden name *Katherine Tynan*, Dublin, 1861– . Ballads and Lyrics, 1891; Cluster of Nuts (*A*), 1894; Cuckoo Songs, 1894; Isle in the Water (*An*), 1895; Land of Mist and Mountains (*The*), 1895; Louise de la Vallière, 1885; Lover's Breast Knot (*A*), 1896; Miracle Plays, 1896; Nun (*A*), etc., 1892; Oh what a Plague is Love! 1896; Shamrocks, 1887; Way of a Maid (*The*), 1895.

HINTON (*James*), Reading, 1822-1875. Chapters on the Art of Thinking, 1879, posthumous; Life in Nature, 1862; Man and his Dwelling-place, 1859; Mystery of Pain (*The*), 1866; Selections from MSS., 1870-74. His Life, by Jane Ellice Hopkins, 1878.

HINTON (Rev. *J. Howard*), 1791-1873. Acquaintance with God, 1856; God's Government of Man, 1856; History and Topography of the United States, 1832; Man's Responsibility, 1842; Moderate Calvinism Reexamined, 1861; Redemption, 1859; Test of Experience (*The*), 1851; Theological Works, 1864; Tour in Holland, etc., 1851; Voluntary Principle in the United States (*The*), 1851.

HITCHCOCK, D.D. (*Edward*), Deerfield, in Massachusetts, U.S., 1793-1864. Elementary Geology, 1840; Fossil Footmarks in the United States, 1848; Geology of the Connecticut Valley, 1824; Ichnology of New England, 1858; Outlines of Geology, 1853; Religion of Geology, 1851; Religious Truth illustrated from Science, 1857; Report on the Geology of Massachusetts, 1833-41.

HOADLY, D.D. (*Benjamin*), bishop of Winchester, born at Westerham, in Kent, 1676-1761. "My Kingdom is not of this World," 1717 (a sermon which originated the famous "Bangorian controversy;" Hoadly maintained that Christ did *not* delegate His authority to any human being, and therefore denied the dogma of "apostolic succession." His chief opponent was W. Law. The *odium theologicum* is the most striking feature of this battle of books); Plain Account of the Nature and End of the Lord's Supper, 1735; Reasonableness of Conformity to the Church of England, 1703; Sermons, 1754-55. His Life, by his son.

HOADLY, M.D. (*Benjamin*), London, son of the above, 1705-1757. Suspicious Husband (*The*), 1747, a comedy; Tatlers (*The*), 1797, posthumous, a comedy; Three Letters on the Organs of Respiration, 1737.

HOARE (Sir *Richard Colt*), Stourhead, in Worcestershire, 1758-1838. Ancient History of Wiltshire, 1810-19; British Antiquities in Dorsetshire (no date); Chronicon Vilodunense, 1830; Classical Tour through Italy and Sicily, 1818; History of Modern Wiltshire, 1822-32; Hungerfordiana, 1823; *Itinerarium Cambriæ*, by Giraldus Cambrensis, 1806; Recollections of a Classical Tour, 1818; Registrum Wiltunense, Saxonicum et Latinum, 1827; Tour through the Isle of Elba, 1814; Tumuli Wiltunenses, 1820 (Stonehenge).

HOBBES (*Thomas*), Malmesbury, in Wiltshire, one of the five great philosophers of Great Britain, 1588-1679. Behemoth (*The*), 1679

(History of the Civil Wars); Decameron Physiologicum, 1678; De Cive (2 *syl.*), 1646; De Corpore Politico, 1650; Ecclesiastical History from Moses to Luther, 1688, posthumous; Elementa Philosophica de Cive, 1642; *Homer* translated into English Verse, 1675; Human Nature, 1650; Leviathan, 1651 (on forms of government; his great work); Liberty and Necessity, 1654; Life of himself, in Latin Verse, 1672; Wonders of the Peak, 1636, a poem. His Life, by R. Blackburne, 1681.

HOBBES (*John Oliver*), real name Mrs. *Pearl Mary Craigie*, 1867–   Bundle of Life (*A*), 1894; Gods (*The*), some Mortals and Lord Twickenham, 1895; Herb-Moon (*The*), 1896 (*Herb-moon*, a long courtship, which is bitter in comparison to *Honey-moon*; it is her own expression); Journeys end in Lover's Meeting (one act written for Ellen Terry), 1894; Sinner's Comedy (*The*), 1892; Some Emotions and a Moral, 1891; Study in Temptations (*A*), 1893.

HOCKING (*Silas*), Kitto, 1850–   . Alec Green, 1878; Caleb Carthew, 1884; Cricket, 1885; Crookleigh, 1888; Dick's Fairies, 1883; For such is Life, 1896; Her Benny, 1879. And other stories.

HODDER (*Edwin*), Staines, Middlesex, 1838–   Cities of the World, 1881–84; George FitzAngus, 1891; Heroes of Britain, 1878–80; History of South Australia, 1893; John MacGregor (Rob Roy), 1894; Junior Clerk (*The*), 1862; Life of the Seventh Earl of Shaftesbury, 1886; Life of Samuel Morley, 1887; Lost in Paris, 1868; Reconciled, 1869; Sir George Burns, 1890; Tossed on the Waves, 1864.

HODGES (*J. Sydney Willes*), 1829–   . Among the Gibjigs, 1881, a child's romance; Among the Woblins, 1882; Geoffrey's Wife, 1874, a novel; New Godiva (*A*), 1876, a novel; Poems, 1854; When Leaves were Green, 1896.

HODGES, M.D. (*Nathaniel*), 1630–1684. Loimologia, 1672 (the Plague of London).

HODGETTS (*Edward Arthur Brayley*), 1859–   . Death-Trap in the House (*The*), 1889; In the Track of the Russian Famine, 1892; Life of Robert Greene; Personal Reminiscences of General Skobeleff (translated from the Russian); Round about Armenia, 1896; Russian Wild Flower (*A*), 1897; Swiss Family Robinson (*The*), 1897.

HODY, D.D. (*Humphrey*), Odcombe, in Somersetshire, 1659–1706. Case of Sees vacant by Uncanonical Deprivation, 1693; De Bibliorum Textibus Originalibus, 1705 (in high estimation); De Græcis Illustribus Linguæ Græcæ . . . Instauratoribus, 1742; History of English Councils, etc., 1701.

HOEY (Mrs. *Cashel*), maiden name *Frances Sarah Bolton*, Bushy Park, Dublin, novelist, 1830–   . All or Nothing, 1879; Blossoming of an Aloe (*The*), 1874; Buried in the Deep, 1873; Falsely True, 1870; Griffith's Double, 1876; Golden Sorrow, 1872; House of Cards (*A*), 1868; Lover's Creed (*The*), 1884; Nazareth, 1873; No Sign, 1876; Out of Court, 1874; Question of Cain (*The*), 1882; Stern Chase (*A*), 1886. She has translated many books.

HOFLAND (Mrs.), Sheffield, 1770–1844. Decision, 1824; Poems, 1805; Son of a Genius, 1822.

HOGG (*James*), "The Ettrick Shepherd," born at Ettrick, in Scotland, 1772–1835. Forest Minstrel (*The*), 1810; Mador of the Moor, 1816, in Spenserian stanzas; Mistakes of a Night (*The*), 1794; Mountain Bard (*The*), 1807 (the "Skylark" is beyond all praise); Pilgrims of the Sun (*The*), 1815, a poem; Poetic Mirror (*The*), 1814; Queen Hynde (a poem in six books), 1825; Queen's Wake (*The*), 1813 (his best; the Story of Kilmeny is admirable); Scottish Pastorals, Poems, and Songs, 1801.

Prose: Altrive Tales (*The*), 1832; Brownie of Bodsbeck (*The*), 1818, a tale of the Covenanters; Lay Sermons, 1834; Life of Sir Walter Scott; Montrose Tales, 1835; Shepherd's Guide (*The*), 1807; Three Perils of Man (*The*), 1822; Three Perils of Woman (*The*), Love, Teasing, and Jealousy, 1823; Winter Evening Tales, 1820. His Life, in Wilson's Edition, 1838.

HOGG, LL.D. (*Robert*), Dunse, in Scotland, 1818–   . British Pomology, 1851; Dahlia (*The*), 1852; Fruit Manual (*The*), 1860; Gardener's Year-book (an annual); Handbook of Hardy Annuals (*A*), 1837; Manual of Fruits, 1848; Vegetable Kingdom and its Products (*The*), 1858; Wild Flowers of Great Britain (*The*), 1865.

HOLCROFT (*Thomas*), London, 1745–1809. Alwyn, or the Great Comedian, 1780, a novel (his first literary work); Anna St. Ives, 1790, a novel in seven vols.; Brian Perdue, a novel; Gaffer Gray, a capital song in "Hugh Trevor;" Hugh Trevor, 1794–97, a novel; Marriage of Figaro (his best novel); Tour in Germany and France; Travels through Westphalia, etc., 1804.

Plays (*above* 30 *between* 1778 *and* 1805): Deaf and Dumb, 1785, an historic play; Deserted Daughter (*The*), 1785, a comedy; Duplicity, 1781, a comedy; Follies of a Day (*The*), a comedy; He's Much to Blame, 1790, a comedy; Joseph made known to his Brethren, 1789 (see APPENDIX II.); Road to Ruin (*The*), 1792 (his best play, and a very good one); School for Arrogance, a comedy; Tale of Mystery, a melodrama. His Life, by Self and Hazlitt, 1816.

HOLDEN (Rev. *Henry*), Lancashire, 1596–1662. Discourse concerning Time, 1694; Divinæ Fidei Analysis, 1652; Marginal Notes on the New Testament, 1660.

HOLDER, D.D. (*William*), Nottinghamshire, 1614–1697. Elements of Speech, 1669; Treatise on the Principles of Harmony, 1694.

HOLDSWORTH (*Edward*), North Stoneham, in Hampshire, 1688–1746. Muscipula, or the Mouse-trap, 1709, a poem in Latin (translated by Lewis in 1728); Remarks, etc., on Virgil, 1768.

HOLE (Rev. *Richard*), Exeter, 1750–1803. Arthur, 1789, a poetical romance in seven books (praised by Dr. Drake); Remarks on Sinbad's Voyages, 1797 (good).

HOLE, D.D. (*Samuel Reynolds*), 1819–   Book about the Garden, etc., 1892; Book about Roses, 1869; Hints to Preachers, 1880;

Little Tour in Ireland (*A*), 1859; Memories of Dean Hole (*The*), 1892; More Memories, 1894; Nice and her Neighbours, 1881; Six of Spades, 1872.

HOLINSHED (*Raphael*), chronicler, born of a Cheshire family, died 1580. Chronicles of Englande, Scotlande, and Irelande, 1577–87.

HOLLAND, M.D. (Sir *Henry*), Knutsford, in Cheshire, 1788–1873. Chapters on Mental Physiology, 1852; Essay on Scientific Subjects, 1862; Medical Notes and Reflections, 1840; Medical Science and Philosophy, 1840; Travels in Albania, etc., 1815.

HOLLAND (*Henry Richard Vassall Fox*, lord), Wiltshire, 1773–1840. Foreign Reminiscences, 1850, posthumous; History of the Whig Party; Life and Writings of Lope Felix de Vega Carpio, 1806; Memoirs of the Whig Party, 1852, posthumous; Three Comedies from the Spanish, 1807.

HOLLINGSHEAD (*John*), London, 1827– . Footlights (*The*), 1883; Grasshopper (*The*), 1877 (an adaptation of *La Cigale*); Miscellanies, 1874; Niagara Spray; Odd Journeys, 1860; Plain English, 1880; Ragged London, 1861; Rough Diamonds, 1861; Rubbing the Gilt off, 1860; Stories and Essays, 1874; To-day, 1864; Under Bow Bells, 1859 (from *Household Words*); Underground London, 1861; Ways of Life, 1861.

HOLMAN (Lieutenant *James*), "The Blind Traveller," 1787–1857. Journey in France, 1824; Narrative of a Journey in 1819, 1820, 1821, published 1822; Travels through Russia, Siberia, etc., 1825; Voyage round the World, 1840.

HOLMAN (*Joseph George*), 1764–1817. Abroad and At-Home, a comic opera; Red-Cross Knight (*The*), 1794, a play; Votary of Wealth (*The*), 1792, a comedy; What a Blunder! a comedy.

HOLME (*Randle*), about 1629–1692. Academy of Armory, etc., 1688.

HOLMES, D.D. (*Abiel*), Cambridge, U.S., 1763–1830. American Annals . . . from its First Discovery, 1805 (a very valuable work).

HOLMES, D.D. (*Nathaniel*), 1610–1678. Resurrection Revealed (*The*), 1653 (a very learned work).

HOLMES, M.D. (*Oliver Wendell*), Cambridge, Massachusetts, U.S., 1809–1894. Autocrat of the Breakfast Table, 1857, prose; Before the Curfew, 1888; Currents and Counter-Currents, 1861; Elsie Venner, 1861, a romance of destiny; Guardian Angel (*The*), 1867; Humourous Poems, 1865; Iron Gate (*The*), 1880; John Lothrop Motley, 1878; Mechanism in Thought and Morals, 1870; Our Hundred Days in Europe, 1887; Pages from an Old Volume of Life, 1857–81; Poet at the Breakfast Table (*The*), 1872; Professor at the Breakfast Table (*The*), 1860; Ralph Waldo Emerson, 1885; Report on Medical Literature, 1848; Songs in Many Keys, 1861; Songs of Many Seasons, 1874; Soundings from the Atlantic, 1863. His Life and Letters, by his nephew, Mr. Moss, 1896.

HOLT (*Emily Sarah*), afterwards Mrs. *John Avery*, novelist, born 1840– . Ashcliffe Hall, 1870; Clare Avery, 1876; For the Master's Sake, 1877; Imogen, 1876;

Isoult Barry, 1871; Lady Sybil's Chain, 1879; Lettice, Eden, 1877; Maiden's Lodge (*The*), 1880; Margery's Son, 1878; Memoirs of Royal Ladies, 1861; Mistress Margery, 1868; Robin Tremayne, 1872; Sister Rose, 1870; Verena, 1873; Well in the Desert (*The*), 1872; White Rose of Langley (*The*), 1878.

HOLWELL, M.D. (*John Zephaniah*), Dublin, 1711–1798. Dissertations on the Origin, Nature, and Pursuits of Intelligent Beings, 1788; Historical Events relating to Bengal, etc., 1765–71; Narrative of the . . . Deaths . . . of those suffocated in the Black Hole of Calcutta, 1758; India Tracts, 1774.

HOLYDAY, D.D. (*Barten*), 1593–1661. Shoemaker's Holiday (*The*), 1660, a comedy; Survey of the World (in 10 books), 1661; Technogamia, or the Marriage of the Arts, 1630, a comedy.

HOLYOAKE (*Francis*), Warwickshire, 1567–1653. Etymological Dictionary of Latin Words, 1606. (Thomas Holyoake published a Latin Dictionary, 1677.)

HOME (*Daniel Douglas*), 1833–1889. Incidents of my Life, 1863.

HOME (Sir *Everard*), Edinburgh, 1756–1832. Lectures on Comparative Anatomy, 1814–23.

HOME (*Henry*, lord Kames), born at Kames, in Scotland, 1696–1782. Decisions of the Court of Session, 1741–80; Elements of Criticism, 1762 (his chief work); Essays on . . . Natural Religion, 1751 (celebrated); Essays upon Several Subjects concerning British Antiquities, 1747; Gentleman Farmer (*The*), 1777; Historical Law Tracts, 1758; Introduction to the Art of Thinking, 1761; Loose Thoughts on Education, 1781; Principles of Equity, 1760; Principles of the Law of Scotland, 1754; Remarkable Decisions of the Court of Sessions, 1716–28; Sketches of the History of Man, 1773. His Life, by lord Woodhouselee, 1807.

HOME (*James*), eighteenth century. Scripture History of the Jews, etc., 1737 (recommended by bishop Tomline).

HOME (Rev. *John*), Leith, in Scotland, 1724–1808. Alfred, 1778, an historic play; Alonzo, 1773, a tragedy; Douglas, 1756, a tragedy (still well known); Fatal Discovery (*The*), 1769, a tragedy; History of the Rebellion . . . 1802. His Life, by Mackenzie, 1822.

HONE (*William*), Bath, in Somersetshire, 1779–1842. Ancient Mysteries, 1823; Apocryphal New Testament, 1820; Bullet Te Deum (*The*), 1817; Everyday Book, 1825–27; Facetiæ and Miscellanies, 1827; Memoirs of Sheridan, 1817; Political House that Jack built, 1816; Table-book, 1827–28; Year-book, 1832.

HOOD (Rev. *Edwin Paxton*), Westminster, 1820–1885. Age and its Architects (*The*); Binney (*Life of the Rev. Thomas*); Blind Amos; Bye-path Meadow; Carlyle (*Thomas*); Christmas Evans, the Preacher of Wild Wales, 1881; Cromwell and his Contemporaries, 1882; Dark Days of Queen May (*The*); Dark Sayings on a Harp; Day (*The*), the Book, and the Teacher, 1880; Dream-land and Ghost-land; Earnest Minister (*The*); Genius and Industry; Golden Times of

Queen Bess ; Lamps, Pictures, and Trumpets; Literature of Labour ; Mental and Moral Philosophy of Laughter ; Maid of Nuremburg (*The*), in verse; Old England ; Oliver Cromwell, etc., 1882 ; Peerage of Poverty (*The*); Romance of Biography (*The*); Scottish Characteristics, 1883 ; Self-Education ; Self-Formation ; Swedenborg (*Life of*) ; Uses of Biography (*The*) ; Vignettes of the Great Revival of the Eighteenth Century, 1881 ; Villages of the Bible (*The*); World of Anecdote (*The*) ; World of Religious Anecdote (*The*) ; Wordsworth (*Biography of*), 1856.

HOOD (*Thomas*), London, 1799-1845. Comic Annual, 1829-39 (called "Hood's Own"); Dream of Eugene Aram, 1845 ; Epping Hunt, 1829 ; Hood's Own, 1838-39 ; National Tales, 1827 ; Odes and Addresses to Great People, 1825 (with J. H. Reynolds); Tylney Hall, 1834, a novel ; Up the Rhine, 1840; Whims and Oddities, 1826-27 ; Whimsicalities, 1843-44.
  Poems: Bridge of Sighs ; Eugene Aram's Dream ; Plea for the Midsummer Fairies, and other Poems, 1827 ; Poems of Wit and Humour, 1847 ; Song of the Shirt, 1843 ; etc. His Life, by his son and daughter, 1860.

HOOD (*Tom*), son of the preceding, 1835-1874. Captain Masters' Children, a novel ; Disputed Inheritance (*The*), a novel ; From Nowhere to the North Pole ; Golden Heart, a novel ; Lost Link (*The*), a novel ; Love and Valour, a novel ; Money's Worth, a novel ; Poems collected and reprinted, 1877.

HOOK, D.D. (*James*), dean of Worcester, 1763-1828. Anguis in Herba, 1802.

HOOK (*Theodore Edward*), London, 1788-1841. Adventures of an Actor, 1842 ; All in the Wrong, 1839, a novel; Births, Deaths, and Marriages, 1839 ; Cousin Geoffrey, the Old Bachelor, 1840 ; Fathers and Sons, 1841 ; Gilbert Gurney, 1835 (an autobiography worked into a novel) ; Gurney Married, 1837, a novel ; Jack Brag, 1837, a novel ; Killing no Murder, 1811, a drama ; Life of Sir David Baird, 1832 ; Love and Pride, 1833, a novel ; Man of Sorrow (*The*), 1809 (his first novel) ; Maxwell, 1830, a novel ; Parson's Daughter (*The*), 1835 ; Pascal Bruno, 1837, a Sicilian story ; Pen Owen, 1855 ; Percy Mallory, 1824 ; Perigrine Bunce, or Settled at Last, 1842 ; Peter and Paul, 1815, a drama ; Precept and Practice, 1840 ; Reminiscences of Michael Kelly, 1826 ; Sayings and Doings, 1824, 1825, 1828 ; Soldier's Return (*The*), 1805, an operatic farce.

HOOK, D.D. (*Walter Farquhar*), dean of Chichester, born at Worcester, 1798-1875. Church and its Ordinance (*The*), 1876 ; Church Dictionary, 1842 ; Ecclesiastical Biography, 1845-52 ; Hear the Church, 1838 ; Last Days of our Lord's Ministry (*The*), 1832 ; Lives of the Archbishops of Canterbury, 1875 (his chief work) ; Sermons suggested by the Miracles of Christ, 1847 ; Three Reformations (*The*), 1847. His Life, by the Rev. W. R. W. Stephens, his son-in-law, 1881.

HOOKE, D.D. (*Luke Joseph*), Dublin, 1716-1796. Religionis Naturalis Revelatæ et Catholicæ Principia, 1754.

HOOKE (*Nathaniel*), 1690-1763. Roman History, 1733-71.

HOOKER (*John*), Exeter, 1524-1601. Catalogue of the Bishops of Exeter, 1584 ; Order and Usage of Keeping the Parliaments in England, 1572.

HOOKER, M.D.(*Joseph Dalton*), Glasgow,1816- Botany of Sir James Ross's Antarctic Voyage (in three parts): i. The Flora of New Zealand, of Tasmania, of Lord Auckland's Islands ; ii. Illustrations of Sikkim-Himalayan Plants ; iii. The Rhododendrons of Sikkim-Himalaya) ; Flora of British India (*The*), 1874 ; Himalayan Journals, 1852 ; Student's Flora of the British Islands (*The*), 1870.

HOOKER (*Richard*), Heavytree, near Exeter, 1553-1600. Laws of Ecclesiastical Polity, first four books 1594, fifth book 1597, last two 1604, posthumous (a standard work). His Life, by Walton, 1665.

HOOKER, F.R.S. (Sir *William Jackson*), Norwich, 1785-1865. Botanical Miscellany, 1830-33 ; Botany of Captain Beechy's Voyages to the Pacific, 1831-41 (with Dr. W. Arnott) ; British Ferns, 1862 ; British Flora (*The*), 1830 ; Century of Ferns, 1854 ; Century of Orchidaceous Plants (*A*), 1848 ; Exotic Flora, 1823-27 ; Flora Boreali-Americana, 1829-40 ; Flora Scotica, 1821 ; Garden Ferns, 1862 ; Icones Filicum, 1829-31 (with Dr. Greville) ; Icones Plantarum, 1837-60) ; Illustrations of the Genera of Ferns, 1838-42 ; Journal of Botany, 1834-42, 1842-51, 1849-55 ; Journal of a Tour in Iceland, 1811 (his first) ; Monograph of the British Jungermanniæ, 1812-16 ; Musci Exotici, 1818-20 ; Muscologia Britannica, 1818 (with Taylor) ; Species Filicum, 1846-51 ; Victoria Regia (*The*), 1851.

HOOLE (*John*), Tenterden, in Kent, 1727-1803. Cleonice, 1775, a tragedy ; Cyrus, 1768, a tragedy ; Tymanthes, 1770, a tragedy. Translations in English verse of Ariosto's *Orlando Furioso*, 1773-83 ; Tasso's *Jerusalem Delivered*, 1762 ; Tasso's *Rinaldo*.

HOOPER (*John*), bishop of Gloucester, born in Somersetshire, 1493-1555 (this is the Hooper who was burnt alive). Answer unto my Lord of Wynchester's Booke, *The Deuyls Sophistrie*, 1547 ; Declaricion of Christe and of his Offyce (*A*), 1547 ; Exposition of Psalms, 1562, 1580 ; Funerall Oratyon (*A*), 1549 ; Godley Annotations on "Romaynes Chapyter XIII.," 1551 ; Godley . . . Protestacion of the Christian Fayth, 1550 ; Homelye in Tyme of Pestylence, 1553 ; Lesson of the Incarnation (*A*), 1549 ; Prophete Jonas (*The*), in seven sermons, 1550.

HOOPER, M.D. (*William*), *-*. Medical Dictionary, 1825; Morbid Anatomy of the Human Brain, 1826 ; Morbid Anatomy of the Human Uterus, 1832.

HOPE, LL.D. (*Alexander James Beresford Beresford*), generally called "Beresford Hope," 1820-1886. Brandreths (*The*), 1882, a novel ; Strictly Tied up, 1880, a novel ; Worship in the Church of England, 1874.

HOPE (*Anthony*), full name *Anthony Hope Hawkins*, London, 1863-   Change of

Air (*A*), 1893; Chronicles of Count Anthonio, 1895; Comedies of Courtship, 1896; Dolly Dialogues (*The*), 1894; Father Stafford, 1891; God in the Car (*The*), 1894; Half a Hero, 1893; Heart of Princess Osra, 1896; Man of Mark (*A*), 1890; Mr. Witt's Widow, 1892; Phroso, 1897, a romance; Prisoner of Zenda (*The*), 1894; Sport Royal, 1893.

HOPE (*Thomas*), 1774-1831. Anastasius, 1819 (his master-work); Costume of the Ancients, 1809 (much esteemed); Designs of Modern Costumes, 1812; Essay on Architecture (*An*), 1835, posthumous; Household Furniture, 1805; Origin and Prospects of Man, 1821.

HOPKINS (*Matthew*), "The Witch-finder," about 1610-1660. Discovery of Witches (*The*), 1647.

HOPTON (*Arthur*), "The Miracle of his Age," 1589-1614. Baculum Geodeticum, 1610; Concordancy of Yeares (*A*), 1615; Speculum Topographicum, 1611.

HORNE, D.D. (*George*), bishop of Norwich, born at Otham, in Kent, 1730-1792. Commentary on the Psalms, 1776; Letters on Infidelity, 1784. His Life, by Jones of Nayland, 1795.

HORNE (*Richard Hengist*), London, 1803-1884. Ballads and Romances, 1846; Cosmo de' Medici, 1837, a drama; Death Fetch (*The*), 1839; Death of Marlowe, 1838, a drama; Dreamer and Worker (*The*), 1851; Exposition of the . . . Barriers to Men of Genius, etc., 1838; Gregory VII., 1840, a tragedy; Judas Iscariot, 1848, a miracle play; Laura Dibalzo, 1880; Life of Napoleon, 1841; New Spirit of the Age, 1844; Orion, 1843, an epic poem (price one farthing); Undeveloped Characters of Shakespeare, 1880.

HORNE, D.D. (*Thomas Hartwell*), London, generally called "Hartwell Horne," 1780-1862. Bibliographical Notes on the "Book of Jasher," 1833; Deism refuted, 1826; Introduction to a Critical Study of the Holy Scriptures, 1818 (unrivalled); Life of Bishop Beveridge, 1824; Mahomedan Empire in Spain (*The*), 1816; Manual of Biblical Bibliography, 1839; Mariolatry, 1841; Necessity and Truth of the Christian Revelation, 1800; Protestant Memorial (*A*), 1850; Romanism Contradictory to Scripture, 1827; Scripture Doctrine of the Trinity, 1820. His Life, by Cheyne.

HORNER (*Leonard*), Edinburgh, 1785-1864. Memoirs and Correspondence of Francis Horner, 1843; Translation of Villari's *Life of Savonarola*, 1862.

HORNUNG (*Ernest William*), Middlesbrough, in Northumberland, novelist, 1860– . Bride from the Bush (*A*), 1890; Boss of Taroomba (*The*), 1894; Ting Luttrell, 1893; Unbidden Guest (*The*), 1894; Under Two Skies, 1892.

HORSLEY (Rev. *John*), Scotland, 1685-1731. Britannia Romana, 1732 (admirable).

HORSLEY, D.D. (*Samuel*), bishop of St. Asaph, born in London, 1733-1806. Biblical Criticism, 1820, posthumous; Power of God deduced from the Solar System, 1767; Theo-

logical Works, 1829, posthumous; Tracts in Controversy with Dr. Priestley, 1783, 1784, 1786 (*The Quarterly Review* calls them "models of clear and powerful reasoning;" many consider them rude, unmannerly, and unseemly).

HORTON, D.D. (*Robert Forman*), London, 1855– . Apostles' Creed (*The*), 1895; Book of Proverbs (*The*), 1888; Cartoons of St. Mark (*The*), 1894; History of the Romans, 1884; Inspiration of the Bible, 1888; Revelation and the Bible, 1892; Verbum Dei, 1893.

HOUGHTON (*Richard Monckton Milnes*, baron), Great Houghton, in Yorkshire, 1809-1885. Boswelliana, 1855; Events of 1848 (especially in relation to Great Britain), 1849; Good Night and Good Morning, 1859; Life, etc., of Keats, 1848; Memorials of a Residence on the Continent, 1838; Memorials of a Tour in Parts of Greece, 1833; Memorials of Many Scenes, 1844; Monographs, Personal and Social, 1873; Palm Leaves, 1844; Poems, Legendary and Historical, 1844; Poems of Many Years, 1838; Poetry for the People, 1840. His Life, by Wemyss Reid, 1890.

HOUGHTON (*Thomas*), 1630-1715. Ancient Laws, Customs, and Orders of the Miners in Mendipp Forest, 1687; Compleat Miner (*The*), 1688; Laws and Customs of the Miners in the Forest of Dean, 1687.

HOVEDEN (*Roger de*), Howden, Yorkshire, twelfth century. Annals, printed 1595, in a compilation called *Rerum Anglicarum Scriptores post Bedam.*

HOWARD (*John*), Hackney, near London, 1726-1790. Account of the Lazarettos in Europe, 1789; State of the Prisons in Great Britain, etc., 1777. His Life, by John Aikin, 1792; J. B. Brown, 1818; Thomas Taylor, 1836; W. H. Dixon, 1848; J. Field, 1850.

HOWARD (*Henry*), earl of Surrey, 1518-1547. Poems, 1557, posthumous. His Life, by Nott, 1815.

HOWARD (Sir *Robert*), 1626-1698. Committee (*The*), 1670, a comedy; Historical Observations upon the Reigns of Edward I., II., III., and Richard II., their Favourites and Counsellors, 1689; History of Religion, 1694; Poems, 1660. (He wrote ten plays, as *The Duke of Lerma*, 1665, but they are all without merit, except *The Committee.*)

HOWE (Rev. *John*), "The Platonic Puritan," chaplain to Cromwell, Loughborough, in Leicestershire, 1630-1706. Blessedness of the Righteous, 1700; Calm . . . Inquiry concerning the . . . Trinity, 1695; Carnality of Religious Contention, 1693; Delighting in God, 1700; Living Temple of God (*The*), 1676-1702 (his great work); Patience in Expectation, etc., 1705; Reconcilableness of God's Prescience of Sin with His Wisdom, etc., 1677; Redeemer's Dominion, etc. (*The*), 1699; Redeemer's Tears (*The*), 1688; Self-dedication, 1682; Thoughtfulness for the Morrow, 1681; Union among Protestants, 1683. His Life, by Calamy, 1708; Hunt, 1823; Rogers, 1836.

HOWEL (Rev. *Lawrence*), 1660-1720. Compleat History of the Bible, 1729, posthumous;

Synopsis Canonum, etc., 1710–15; View of the Pontificate, etc., 1712.

HOWELL (*James*), Wales, 1594–1660. Ah! Ha! Tumulus Thalamus, 1653, two poems; Bella Scoto-Anglica, 1648; Dendrologia, or the Vocal Forest, 1640; Discourses between Patricius and Peregrine, 1643; Dodona's Grove, 1640; England's Teares for the Present Wars, 1644; Epistolæ Ho-Elianæ, 1645–55; Instructions for Forreine Travell, 1642; Lexicon Tetraglotton (English, French, Italian, and Spanish), 1660; Londinopolis, 1657; Lustra Ludovici (Life of Louis XIII.), 1646; Nuptials of Peleus and Thetis, 1654, a masque and comedy; Parley of Beasts, or Morphandra, Queen of the Enchanted Island, 1660; People of Scotland (*The*), 1649 (scurrilous); Poems on Divers Occasions, 1664; Precedency of Kings, 1664; Preheminence and Pedigree of Parliament (*The*), 1644; Vision (*The*), a Dialogue between Soule and Bodie, 1651.

HOWELL (*Lawrence*). See HOWELL.

HOWELL (*Thomas*), sixteenth century. Arbor of Amitie, 1568, poems and posies; Delightful Discourses, etc., 1580; Devises for [my] own Exercise, and Friends' Pleasure, 1581; Fable of Narcissus (in English metre), 1560.

HOWELL, LL.D. (*William*), 1630–1683. History from the Beginning of the World to the Conquest, 1662–80 (praised by Gibbon); Medulla Historiæ Anglicanæ, continued after his death, 1712 (an excellent epitome).

HOWELLS (*William Dean*), Martin's Priory, Ohio, U.S., 1837-   . He has written about 70 books. Chance Acquaintance (*A*), 1874; Counterfeit Presentment, 1877, a comedy; Day's Pleasure (*A*), 1876; Foregone Conclusions, 1875; Italian Journeys, 1867; Lady of the Aroostook, 1879; Life of Lincoln, 1860; Life of R. B. Hayes, 1877; Modern Instance (*A*), 1882; No Love Lost, 1868; Parlor Car (*The*), 1876; Poems, 1860, 1875; Suburban Sketches, 1871; Their Wedding Journey, 1871; Undiscovered Country (*The*), 1880; Venetian Life, 1866.

HOWES (Rev. *Thomas*), called "The Learned" by Dr. Parr, Norwich, eighteenth century. Critical Observations on Books, Ancient and Modern, 1776.

HOWIE (*John*), Scotland, about 1730–1790. Biographia Scoticana, 1781.

HOWITT (Mrs.), Uttoxeter, in Staffordshire, maiden name *Mary Botham*, wife of William Howitt, 1800–1888. Ballads and other Poems, 1847; Birds and Flowers, 1870; Cost of Caergwyn (*The*), 1864, a work of fiction; Deal of Love (*The*), 1839, a tale; Father and Daughter, 1895; Heir of West Wayland (*The*), 1837, a tale; Improvisatore (*The*), 1857 (Andersen's novel); Libieslea, 1860; Little Arthur's Letters, 1861; Marian's Pilgrimage, 1859; Poet's Children (*The*), 1863; Seven Temptations (*The*), 1830, a series of dramatic sketches; Sketches of Natural History, in verse; Stories of Stapleford, 1863; Wood Leighton, 1835, a novel. And several books for children.

With William Howitt, her husband: Desolation of Eyam, 1827; Forest Minstrel (*The*), 1823; History of Scandinavian Litera-

ture, 1852; Literature and Romance of Northern Europe.

HOWITT (*Samuel*), *-*. British Sportsman (*The*), 1812; Field Sports, 1807; Foreign Field Sports, 1814; New Work of Animals for *Æsop, Gay*, and *Phædrus*, 1811.

HOWITT (*William*), Heanon, in Derbyshire, 1795–1879. Aristocracy of England (*The*), 1846; Book of the Season, 1831; Boy's Adventures in the Wilds of Australia, 1853; Boy's Country Book (*The*), 1839; Colonization and Christianity, 1837; Hall and Hamlet (*The*), 1847; Haunts and Homes of British Poets (*The*), 1847; History of Priestcraft (*The*), 1833; History of the Supernatural (*The*), 1863; Illustrated History of England, 1854–61 (called "Cassell's History of England"); Land, Labour, and Gold, 1855; Mad War Planet (*The*), and other Poems, 1871; Madame Dorrington of the Dene, 1851, a novel; Man of the People (*The*), 1860; Ruined Castles and Abbeys of England (*The*), 1861; Rural and Domestic Life of Germany (*The*), 1842; Rural Life of England (*The*), 1837; Student's Life in Germany, 1841; Talangetta, 1857; Tales of the Pantika, 1836; Visits to Remarkable Houses, 1846; Year-book of the Country, 1849.

HUBERT (Sir *Francis*), seventeenth century. Egypt's Favourite, 1631, a poem; History of Edward II., etc., 1629, an epic poem (not without merit both in plan and execution).

HUDDESFORD (Rev. *George*), about 1760–1810. Bubble and Squeak, 1801, in burlesque verse; Champignons du Diable (*La*), 1800, mock heroic; Salmagundi, 1793, an olio of original poetry; Topsy-turvy, with Anecdotes, 1790; Wiccamical Chaplet (*The*), 1804, poetry.

HUDSON, D.D. (*John*), Cumberland, 1662–1719. Introductio ad Chronographiam, 1691.

HUDSON (*William*), Westmoreland, 1730–1793. Flora Anglica, 1762.

HUGHES (*John*), 1677–1720. Court of Neptune (*The*), 1699; Ode on the Peace of Ryswick (*An*), 1697; Peace of Ryswick (*The*), 1697; Siege of Damascus (*The*), 1720, a tragedy.

HUGHES (*Thomas*), well known also as "Tom Brown," Uffington, in Berkshire, 1823–1896. Alfred the Great, 1869; Gone to Texas, 1884; Manliness of Christ (*The*), 1879; Memoir of a Brother, 1873; Memoir of Daniel Macmillan, 1882; Memoir of Bishop Fraser, 1887; Memoir of David Livingstone, 1889; Our Old Church, 1878; Scouring of the White Horse, 1859; Tom Brown's Schooldays, 1857 (his best production); Tom Brown at Oxford, 1861.

HUISH (*Robert*), *-*. Life of George III.; Memoirs of Charlotte Augusta, Princess of Wales, 1818; Memoir of Queen Charlotte; Memoir of George IV., 1830; Mysteries of Fermoy Castle, 1809; Peruvians (*The*), 1813, a poem; Solomon, 1809, a sacred drama (from Klopstock); Sorcerer (*The*), 1811, a romance.

HULL (*Edward*), Antrim, in Ireland, 1820-   Building and Ornamental Stones, 1872; Coal-fields of Great Britain (*The*), about 1879; Geological Survey of the United

Kingdom, 1860–62; History, Structure, and Resources of the Coal-fields of Great Britain, 1870; On the Geology of the Leicestershire Coal-field 1860, Country round Cheltenham 1857, Country round Oldham and Manchester 1863; On the Triassic and Permian Rocks of the Midland Counties of England, 1869; Physical Geology and Geography of Ireland, 1878.

HUME, LL.D. (Rev. *Abraham*), Scotland, 1815–1884. Geographical Terms as an Addition to the Language, 1859; Learned Societies and Printing Clubs of the United Kingdom, 1847; Philosophy of Geographical Names, 1851; Sir Hugh of Lincoln, 1849 (the tradition investigated).

HUME (*Alexander*), Edinburgh, 1560–1609. Flyting betwixt Montgomery and Polwart, 1629, posthumous; Hymnes, 1599; Triumphs of Love, Chastitie, and Death, 1644, posthumous.

Prose: Catholick Meaning of the Words, "This is my Body," 1602; Elementa Grammatica, 1612; Rejoynder to Dr. A. Hill concerning the Descence into Hell, 1593; Treatise of Conscience, quhairin Divers Secreats are discouered, 1594; Triumph of the Lord (*The*), the defeat of the Armada, a poem.

HUME (*David*), Edinburgh, 1711–1776. Dialogues concerning Natural Religion, 1779; Essays, 1741–42 (his essay *On Miracles* is the most noted); History of England, 1754–61; History of the Stuarts, 1754, 1756, 1759, 1761; Inquiry concerning Human Understanding, 1748; Inquiry into the Principles of Morals, 1751; Natural History of Religion, 1755; Political Discourses, 1751; Treatise of Human Nature, 1738. His Life, by himself, 1777; Pratt, 1777; David Dalrymple, 1787; Adam Smith, 1789; T. E. Ritchie, 1807; J. H. Burton, 1846.

HUME (*David*), Scotland, 1756–1838. Commentaries on the Law of Scotland Relative to the . . . Punishment of Crimes, 1797.

HUMPHREY, D.D. (*Lawrence*), Newport Pagnell, in Buckinghamshire, 1527–1590. Jesuitism (in two parts, Latin), 1852–54; Life of Bishop Jewell (Joannis Juelli . . . Vita), 1573; Nobles (*The*), in three books, 1563; Oratio ad Reginam Elizabetham, 1575; Seven Sermons against Treason, 1588.

HUMPHREYS (*Henry Noel*), Birmingham, 1810–1878. Ancient Coins and Medals, 1850; Art of Illumination (*The*), 1849; British Butterflies and their Transformations, 1840; British Moths and their Transformations, 1844; Butterfly Vivarium (*The*), 1858; Coinage of the British Empire (*The*), 1854; Collector's Manual (*The*), 1853; Goethe in Strasburg, 1860, a dramatic novelette; History of the Art of Printing, 1867; Holbein and his "Dance of Death," 1868; Masterpieces of the Early Painters and Engravers, 1870; Ocean Gardens, 1857; Rembrandt and his Etchings, 1871; Stories by an Archæologist and his Friends, 1856.

HUMPHRY (Rev. *William Gilson*), 1815– . Doctrine of a Future State (*The*), 1849, a Hulsean lecture; Early Progress of the Gospel (*The*), 1850, a Hulsean lecture;

Historical . . . Treatise of the Book of Common Prayer, 1853; Miracles (*The*), 1857, a Boyle lecture.

HUNGERFORD (Mrs.), *-1897.

Novels: Airy Fairy Lilian, 1879; Anxious Moment (*An*), 1896; April's Lady, 1891; Beauty's Daughters, 1880; Doris, 1884; Duchess (*The*), 1887; Faith and Unfaith, 1881; Green Pastures and Grey Grief, 1886; Herbert's Amusement, 1886; Hon. Mrs. Vereker, 1888; In Durance Vile, 1885; Lady Branksmere, 1886; Lady Patty, 1892; Lady Valworth's Diamonds, 1886; Lady Verner's Flight, 1892; Lovice, 1897; Loys, etc., 1883; Maiden all Forlorn (*A*), 1885; Marvel, 1888; Mental Struggle (*A*), 1886; Modern Circe (*A*), 1887; Molly Bawn, 1878; Mrs. Geoffrey, 1881; Nora Creina, 1892; "O Tender Dolores," 1885; Peter's Wife, 1894; Phyllis, 1877; Point of Conscience (*A*), 1895; Portia, 1882; Professor's Experiment (*The*), 1895; Red-House Mystery (*The*), 1893; Rossmoyne, 1883; Three Graces (*The*), 1895; Under-currents, 1888; Unsatisfactory Lover (*An*), 1894.

HUNT, Ph.D. (*James*), Swanage, in Dorsetshire, 1833–1869. Philosophy of Voice and Speech, 1859; Stammering and Stuttering, 1861.

HUNT (*James Henry Leigh*), Southgate, Middlesex, 1784–1859 (imprisoned two years for calling George IV. a "fat Adonis of fifty"). Autobiography and Reminiscences, 1850; Amyntas, 1820 (a tale of the woods); Bacchus in Tuscany, 1816; Book for a Corner (*A*), 1849; Captain Sword and Captain Pen, 1835, a poem; Christianism, 1846; Companion (*The*), a sequel to the Indicator, 1828; Day by the Fire, 1852; Descent of Liberty, 1815, a masque; Feast of the Poets, and other Pieces in Verse, 1814; Foliage, 1818, poems; Francesca and Rimini, 1816; Hero and Leander, 1816; Imagination and Fancy, 1844; Indicator (*The*), 1819–21, a periodical; Jar of Honey from Mount Hybla (*A*), 1848; Legend of Florence (*A*), 1840, a play; Liberal (*The*), 1822, verse and prose; Men, Women, and Books, 1847; Old Court Suburbs (*The*), i.e. Kensington, topographical, etc., 1855; One Hundred Romances of Real Life, 1843; Palfrey (*The*), 1842 (a love-story of olden times, in verse, well told); Reading for Railways, 1850; Recollections of Lord Byron and his Contemporaries, 1828; Religion of the Heart (*The*), 1853; Seer (*The*), 1840–41; Sir Ralph Esher, 1832, a novel in the time of Charles II.; Stories in Verse, 1855; Stories from the Italian Poets, 1846; Story of Rimini, 1846, in poetry (an excellent narrative, composed in prison); Table Talk, 1851; Tale for a Chimney Corner (*A*), 1848; Town (*The*), a description of London, with its noted characters, 1848 (his best book); Ultra-Crepidarius, 1819, a satire on W. Gifford; Wishing Cap Papers, 1850; Wit and Humour, 1846. His Life and Letters, by his son; by Cosmo Monkhouse.

HUNT (*Margaret*), pseudonym "Averil Beaumont" (she married Alfred Hunt the artist), born 1831. Barrington's Fate, 1883; Basildon,

1879 ; Hazard of the Die (*The*), 1878 ; Leaden Casket (*The*), 1880 ; Magdalen Waynward, 1871 ; Mrs. Juliet ; Self Condemned, 1883 ; That Other Person, 1886 ; This Indenture witnesseth, 1875 ; Thornicroft's Model, 1873 ; Under Seal of Confession, 1874.

HUNT (*Violet*), daughter of the preceding. Hard Woman (*The*), 1895 ; Maiden's Progress (*The*), 1894 ; Unkist, Unkind ! 1897 ; Way of Marriage (*The*), 1896.

HUNT (*Robert*), Devonport, 1807-1886. Elementary Physics, 1851 ; Manual of Photography, 1842 ; Panthea, or the Spirit of Nature, 1849 ; Poetry of Science, 1845 ; Popular Romances of the West of England, 1881 ; Researches on Light, 1844 ; Treatise on Physics. In 1860 a testimonial of the value of 500 guineas was presented to him for his "Mineral Statistics."

HUNT, D.D. (*Thomas*), 1696-1774. De Antiquitate, Elegantia, et Utilitate Linguæ Arabicæ, 1739 ; De Usu Dialectorum Orientalium, 1748 ; On the Book of Proverbs, 1775, posthumous.

HUNTER, D.D. (*Henry*), Perthshire, in Scotland, 1741-1802. History of London and its Environs (in parts), part i. 1776 ; Sacred Biography, 1783-94 (much esteemed).

HUNTER (*John*), Long Calderwood, near Glasgow, 1728-1793. Natural History of the Human Teeth, part i. 1771, part ii. 1778 ; Observations on Certain Parts of Animal Economy, 1786 ; Treatise on the Blood, Inflammation, and Gunshot Wounds, 1794, posthumous ; Treatise on the Venereal Disease, 1786. (Mrs. John Hunter, 1742-1821, wrote the popular song, "My Mother bids me bind my Hair.") His Life, by Everard Home, 1794 ; Jesse Foot, 1794 ; Joseph Adams, 1816 ; Drewry Otley, 1835.

HUNTER (Rev. *Joseph*), 1783-1861. Agincourt, 1850 ; Connection of Bath with Literature, etc., 1827 ; Gens Sylvestrina, 1846 ; Golden Sentences, 1826 ; Hallamshire, 1816 (a first-class antiquarian history) ; Hallamshire Glossary, 1829 ; History and Topography of Doncaster, 1828, of Sheffield, 1819 ; Life of Oliver Heywood, 1842 ; Robin Hood, his Period and Character, 1852 ; South Yorkshire, 1828-31.

HUNTER, M.D. (*William*), Long Calderwood, near Glasgow, 1718-1783. Anatomia Uteri Humani Gravidi, 1774 (a superb work) ; Medical Commentaries, with Supplement, 1762-64. His Life, by Simmons, 1783.

HUNTER, M.D. (*William*), Montrose, in Scotland, 1760-1815. Concise Account of Pegu, 1784 ; Hindostanee-English Dictionary, 1868.

HUNTINGFORD (*George Isaac*), bishop of Hereford, 1748-1832. (24) Discourses, 1795-97 ; Introduction to the Writing of Greek, 1782 (incomparable) ; Metrica quædam Monostrophica, 1781, Apology for the Monostrophics, 1784 ; Thoughts on the Trinity (enlarged), 1832.

HUNTINGTON (Rev. *William*), "S.S.," born near Cranbrook, in Dorsetshire, 1744-1813. Bank of Faith (*The*).
N.B.—"S.S." means a "Sinner Saved."

HUNTON (Rev. *Philip*), died 1682. Treatise on Monarchy, 1643-44 (the best ever written).

HURD, D.D. (*Richard*), bishop of Worcester, born at Congreve, in Staffordshire, 1720-1808. Commentary on the *Ars Poetica* of Horace, 1749 ; Dialogues, 1759 ; Introduction to the Study of the Prophecies, 1772 ; Letters on Chivalry and Romance, 1762 ; Life of Warburton, 1795. His Life, by himself ; by Kilvert.

HURDIS, D.D. (*James*), Bishopstone, in Sussex, 1763-1801. Adriana, 1791 ; Favourite Village (*The*), 1800, a poem ; Sir Thomas More, 1792, a tragedy ; Village Curate (*The*), 1788, a poem.

HUTCHESON, LL.D. (*Francis*), "Father of the Scotch School of Metaphysicians," Ireland, 1694-1747. Inquiry into the Original of our Ideas of Beauty and Virtue, 1720 ; Nature and Conduct of the Passions, etc., 1728 ; Philosophiæ Moralis Institutio, 1742 ; Reflections on Laughter, 1750, posthumous ; System of Moral Philosophy, 1755, posthumous, (his largest and chief work). His Life, by Leechman, 1755.

HUTCHINS (Rev. *John*), Bradford Peverel, 1698-1773. History and Antiquities of the County of Dorset, 1774.

HUTCHINSON (*Benjamin*), 1729-1810. Biographica Medica, 1799.

HUTCHINSON (*Francis*), bishop of Down and Connor, 1670-1729. Historical Essay on Witchcraft, 1718 (contains table of the persons burnt for "witchcraft,") ; Life of Archbishop Tillotson, 1718.

HUTCHINSON (Rev. *John*), Spennithorne, in Yorkshire, 1674-1737. Confusion of Tongues, 1731 ; Moses's Principia, 1724-27 (in defence of Gen. i., and an attack on Newton's *Theory of Gravitation*) ; Moses sine Principio, 1729 ; Works, including *Hutchinsoniasm*, 1748, posthumous.

HUTCHINSON (Mrs.), maiden name *Lucy Apsley*, born in the Tower, 1620-1664. Life of Colonel Hutchinson, 1806, posthumous (interesting). Her Life, by herself, 1806.

HUTCHINSON (*Thomas*), Boston, U.S., 1711-1780. Collection of Original Papers relative to the History of the Colony of Massachusetts, 1769 ; History of the Colony of Massachusetts, 1760-67.

HUTCHINSON, M.D. (*Thomas Joseph*), Stonyford, in Ireland, 1820- . Buenos Ayres and Argentine Gleanings, 1865 ; Impressions of Western Africa, 1858 ; Narrative of Niger Tshadda Binue Exploration, 1855 ; Parana and South America Recollections, 1868 ; Ten Years' Wanderings among the Ethiopians, 1861 ; Two Years in Peru, 1874.

HUTCHINSON (*William*), 1732-1814. History and Antiquities of . . . Durham, 1785-1794 ; History of Cumberland, 1794-98 ; View of Northumberland, 1778-80.

HUTTON, LL.D. (*Charles*), Newcastle-upon-Tyne, 1737-1823. Abridgment of the Philosophical Transactions, 1809 ; Course of Mathematics, 1798-1801 (with Pearson and Shaw) ; Mathematical and Philosophical Dictionary, 1795 ; Mathematical Recreations (4 vols.), 1803 (his most popular production) ; Mathematical Tables, 1785 ; Principles of Bridges . . . and the Laws of Arches, 1772 ; Tables of Products and the Powers of Numbers, 1781; Tracts, Mathematical and Philosophical, 1786, 1812; Treatise on Arithmetic and Book-keeping, 1764; Treatise on Mensuration, 1771. His Life, by Dr. Olinthus Gregory, 1824.

HUTTON, M.D. (*James*), Edinburgh, 1726–1797. Dissertation on Natural Philosophy, 1792; Investigation of the Principles of Knowledge, 1794; Theory of the Earth, 1796, advocating the *Plutonian System*, or central heat, opposed by Werner, who advocated the *Neptunian System*, or aqueous agency.

HUTTON (*William*), Derby, 1723–1815. Autobiography, 1816; Court of Requests, 1784; History of Birmingham, 1781; History of Derby, 1790; Roman Wall (*The*), 1861.

HUXHAM, M.D. (*John*), Halberton, in Devonshire, 1694–1768. Antimony, 1756; Essay on Feyers, 1739; Observationes de Aëre et Morbis Epidemicis, 1739–71; Ulcerous Sore Throat, 1750.

HUXLEY, LL.D. (*Thomas Henry*), Ealing, in Middlesex, 1825–1895. American Addresses, with a Lecture on Biology, 1877; Classification of Animals (*The*), 1869; Cray-fish (*The*), 1880; Critiques and Addresses, 1873; Elementary Atlas of Osteology, 1864; Elementary Biology, 1875; Elementary Physiology, 1866; Essays, 1892; Evolution and Ethics, 1893; Hume, 1879; Introduction to the Classification of Animals, 1869; Lay Sermons, etc., 1870; Lectures on Comparative Anatomy, 1864; Lessons in Elementary Physiology, 1866; Man's Place in Nature, 1863; Manual of the Anatomy of Vertebrated Animals, 1871; Observations on the Glaciers, 1857 (with Dr. Tyndall); Oceanic Hydrozoa, 1859 (his great work); On the Educational Value of the Natural History Sciences, 1854; On the Theory of the Vertebrate Skull, 1858, a Croonian lecture; Physiography, 1877; Physiology, etc., 1877; Science and Culture, 1881; Science Primers, 1880; Social Diseases and Worse Remedies, 1891; Tape and Cystic Worms, 1857.

HYDE, D.D. (*Thomas*), Billingsley, in Yorkshire, 1636–1703. De Ludis Orientalibus, 1694; Tabulæ Stellarum Fixarum, etc., 1665; Veterum Persarum et Magorum Religionis Historia, 1700 (his chief work).

HYDE. See CLARENDON.

INCHBALD (Mrs.), maiden name *Elizabeth Simpson*, Standyfield, in Suffolk, 1753–1821. Nature and Art, 1796, a novel; Simple Story, 1791, a novel (her best work).
    Of her 19 *plays the best known are:* Case of Conscience (*The*); Child of Nature (*The*); Everyone has her Fault, 1794 (one of her best comedies); Lovers' Vows, 1798; Married Man (*The*), 1789, a comedy; Midnight Hour (*The*), 1793, a petit comedy; Mogul Tale (*The*), 1784, a farce (her first production); Such things are, 1787 (her best comedy); To Marry, or Not to Marry, a comedy; Wedding Day (*The*), 1790; Wives as they were, and Maids as they are, 1797, a comedy. Her Life, by J. Boaden, 1832.

INGELOW (*Jean*), Boston, 1830–1897. Allerton

and Dreux, 1851, a novel; Deborah's Book, etc., 1867; Don John, 1881, a tale; Fated to be Free, 1875; Golden Opportunity (*The*), 1867; Grandmother's Shoe (*The*), 1867; High Tide on the Coast of Lincolnshire (*The*), 1883; Home Thoughts, 1865; John Jerome, 1886; Life of John Smith, 1867; Little Rie and the Rosebuds, 1867; Little Wonder-box (*The*), 1887; Little Wonder-horn (*The*), 1872; Minnows with Silver Tails, 1868; Moorish Gold, and the One-eyed Servant, 1867; Mopsa the Fairy, 1869; Off the Skelligs, 1872, a novel; Poems, 1863, 1876, 1879, 1885; Rhyming Chronicle of Incidents and Feelings, 1850; Round of Days (*The*), 1861; Sarah de Berenger, 1879, a novel; Sister's Bye-hours (*A*), 1868; Stories told to a Child, 1865; Story of Doom, and other Poems, 1867; Studies for Stories, 1864; Suspicious Jackdaw (*The*), 1867; Tales of Orris, 1860; Two Ways of telling a Story, 1867; Very Young, etc., 1890; Wild Duck Shooter (*The*), etc., 1868.

INGERSOLL (*Charles Jared*), Philadelphia, U.S., 1782–1862. Chismara, 1800; Julian, 1831; Historical Sketch of the Second War between the United States and Great Britain, 1845; History of the Territorial Acquisitions of the United States, 1852.

INGLEBY, LL.D. (*Clement Mansfield*), Edgbaston, in Warwickshire, 1823–1886. Introduction to Metaphysics, 1869; Outlines of Theoretical Logic, 1856; Revival of Philosophy at Cambridge, 1870; Shakspere Controversy (*The*), 1861; Shakspere Fabrications (*The*), 1859; Shakspere Hermeneutics, 1875; Shakspere, the Man and the Book, 1877; Still Lion (*The*), 1867, 1874; Theoretical Logic, 1856; Was T. Lodge an Actor? 1867.

INGOLDSBY (*Thomas*). See BARHAM (*R. H.*).

INGRAM (*John H.*), London, 1849– . Annotated Edition of Lockhart's *Life of Burns*, 1890; Biographical Essay, 1884; Bird of Truth (translated from the Spanish of Fernan Caballero), 1881; Claimants to Royalty, 1882; Darley's *May Queen*, 1892; E. B. Browning's Poetical Works, with Memoir, 1888; Eminent Women Series, edit. 1883; Flora Symbolica, 1868; Haunted Homes, 1883, 2nd series 1884; Life of E. A. Poe, 1880; Life of E. B. Browning, 1888; Oliver Madox Brown, 1884; Poe's Tales and Poems, 1884; Poe's Works, with Memoir, 1874.

INGRAM (*John Kells*), 1823– . History of Political Economy (*A*), 1888; History of Slavery and Serfdom (*A*), in *Encyclopædia Britannica* (separately, 1895); Political Economy; Work and the Workman, 1892. Edited first English translation of *De Imitatione Christi*, 1892.

INGULPHUS, abbot of Croyland, 1030–1109. Ingulphi Croylandensis Historia, edited by Gale and Fell, 1684.

INNES (*Alexander Taylor*), 1833– . Church and State, 1890; John Knox, in Famous Scots Series, 1896; Law of Creeds in Scotland (*The*), 1867; Studies in Scottish History, 1892.

INNES (*Thomas*), Drumgask, in Scotland, 1662–1744. Civil and Ecclesiastical History

of Scotland (incomplete), published 1853; Critical Essay on the Ancient Inhabitants of Scotland, 1729 (a work of great merit).
IRELAND (*John*), 1720-1808. Graphic Illustrations of Hogarth, 1794-99; Life and Letters of John Henderson, 1786.
IRELAND, D.D. (*John*), dean of Westminster, born at Ashburton, 1761-1842. Nuptiæ Sacræ, 1821; Paganism and Christianity compared, 1809; Vindicia Regiæ, 1797.
IRELAND (*Samuel*), London, 1750-1800. Graphic Illustrations of Hogarth, 1794; Picturesque Tour through Holland, 1790; Picturesque Views of the Medway, 1793; Picturesque Views of the River Thames, 1792; Picturesque Views of the River Wye, 1797; Picturesque Views on the Upper Avon, 1795.
IRELAND (*William Henry*), son of the preceding, 1777-1835. Authentic Account of the Shakesperian MSS., 1796; Catholic (*The*), 1807, a romance; Chalcographimania, 1814, a satirical poem; Confessions relative to the Shakespeare Papers, 1805; Gandez, the Monk, 1804, a romance; Henry II., 1799, an historical drama; Miscellaneous Papers under the Hand and Seal of W. Shakespeare, including the Tragedy of King Lear, etc., 1796; Modern *Ship of Fools* (*The*), 1807, a poem; Mutius Scævola, 1801, an historic drama; Vortigern, 1796, an historic play . . . attributed to him to Shakespeare; printed 1832; Woman of Feeling (*The*), 1803, a novel.
IRONS, D.D. (*William Josiah*), 1812-1883. Athanasius contra Mundum, 1872; Apostolical Succession, 1837; Ecclesiastical Jurisdiction (*On*), 1847; Holy Catholic Church (*The*), 1838; Indifference (*On*), 1871.
IRVING, LL.D. (*David*), about: 1770-1820. Elements of English Composition, 1801; Lives of Scottish Authors, 1801; Lives of the Scottish Poets, 1810; Memoirs of George Buchanan, 1807; Memorial of Anne Margaret Anderson, 1815.
IRVING (Rev. *Edward*), Annan, in Scotland, 1792-1834. Babylon and Infidelity foredoomed of God, 1826; Church and State, 1829; Exposition of the Book of Revelation, 1831; Homilies on the Sacraments, 1828; Judgments to Come, 1823; Last Days (*The*), 1828; Lectures on Baptism, 1828; Missionary Sermon, 1824; Orations for the Oracles of God, 1838; Sermons on the Trinity, 1828. His Life, by W. Wilks, 1854; by Mrs. Oliphant, 1862.
IRVING (Sir *Henry Brodribb*), Keinton, in Somersetshire, 1838- . (A Record of over twenty years at the Lyceum; he removed thither in 1871.) The Drama, 1893.
IRVING, LL.D. (*Washington*), (nom de plume "Jonathan Old Style"), New York, U.S., 1783-1859. Abbotsford and Newstead Abbey, 1835; Adventures of Captain Bonneville, 1837; Astoria, 1836; Bracebridge Hall, 1822; Chronicles of Wolfert's Roost, 1855; Companions of Columbus (*The*), 1831; Conquest of Florida, 1838; Conquest of Granada, 1829; Crayon Miscellany, 1835; History of New York, by Diedrich Knickerbocker, 1809 (a burlesque chronicle); Legends of the Con-

quest of Spain, 1835; Life and Voyages of Columbus, 1828; Life of Margaret Davidson, 1841; Life of Oliver Goldsmith, 1849; Life of Washington, 1855-59 (his great work, in 15 vols.); Mahomet and his Successors, 1849-50; Salmagundi, 1807-8; Sketch-book (*The*), 1820 (this was refused by Murray and Constable); Tales of the Alhambra, 1832; Tales of a Traveller, 1824; Tour on the Prairies, 1835; Voyages of the Companions of Columbus, 1831; Wolfert's Roost (stories contributed to the *Knickerbocker Magazine*), 1839-40.
IVIMY (*Joseph*), *-*. History of the English Baptists, 1811-23 (much esteemed); Life of John Bunyan, 1809; Life of Milton, 1833.

JACK (*Richard*), 1706-1760. Existence of God Geometrically Demonstrated, 1747 (a curious and excellent treatise).
JACKSON (*Arthur*), 1593-1666. Annotations upon the Historical Part of the Old Testament, 1643-46 (excellent); Annotations upon Isaiah, 1682, posthumous; Annotations on Job, the Psalms, etc., 1658, posthumous.
JACKSON (*James Grey*), about 1761-1830. Account of the Empire of Marocco, etc., 1809 (valuable and interesting); Account of Timbuctoo and Housa, 1820.
JACKSON (Rev. *John*), Yorkshire, 1686-1763. Chronological Antiquities, 1752 (highly recommended by bishop Watson); Scripture Doctrine of the Trinity, 1714. His Life, by Dr. Sutton, 1764.
JACKSON, D.D. (*Thomas*), Durham, 1579-1640. Works, 1673, posthumous. (His great work is "On the Creed.") His Life, by E. Vaughan, 1673; J. H. Todd, 1838.
JACOB (*Giles*), 1686-1744. Lives, etc., of the English Dramatic Poets, 1719-23.
∴ His *Law Dictionary* was greatly enlarged and improved by J. E. Tomlins, 1820. Giles Jacob figures in the *Dunciad* as "the scourge of grammar."
JACOB (Rev. *Henry*), 1561-1626. Institution of Christ's . . . Visible Church, 1610; Reasons . . . for reforming our Churches of England, 1604; Sufferings and Victories of Christ, 1598; Survey of Christ's Sufferings, etc., 1604.
JAMES I., Scotland, 1394-1437. Christis Kirk of the Grene (a poem of 23 stanzas), printed 1783; King's Quhair (*The*), (a poem in six cantos, in which he celebrates his lady-love, lady Jane Beaufort), printed in 1783; Peebles at the Play (a humorous poem on the festival called "Bettane Day," held at Peebles), printed 1783. His Life, by Wilson and Chalmers, 1830.
JAMES I., king of England, born in Edinburgh Castle, 1566-1625. (Called by Sully "the wisest fool in Christendom.") Anagrammata, 1613; Apothegmes, or Table Talk, 1643, posthumous; Basilikon Doron (in three books), 1599; Counterblaste to Tobacco, 1616; Dæmonologie (in three books), 1597; Discourse of the Gowrie Conspiracie, 1600; Essayes of a Prentise in the Divine Art of Poesie, 1584; Lepanto, or Heroicall Song, 1603; His Majesty's Poetical Exercises, 1591;

Facill and Plaine Expositioun of Chap. xx. Revelatioun, 1589; Poetical Exercises, 1591; Premonition to all Most Mighty Monarchies, 1608; Prince's Looking-glass (*A*), 1603; Prose Works, 1616; Remonstrance for the Right of Kings, 1615; Triplici Nodo Triplex Cuneus, 1605; True Law of Free Monarchies (*The*), 1598. His Life, by Arthur Wilson, 1653; W. Sanderson, 1656; William Harris, 1753; Laing, 1804; Thomas Thomson, 1823.

JAMES (*George Payne Rainsford*), novelist and biographist, London, 1801–1860. (*He wrote about* 180 *novels. From his initials he was sometimes nicknamed* "*G*[*eorge*] *P*[*rince*] *R*[*egent*] *James*.") Agincourt, 1844, an historical romance; Agnes Sorrel, 1853, a novel; Arabella Stuart, 1844, a romance; Arrah Neil, or Times of Old, 1845; Attila, 1837, an historical romance; Beauchamp, or the Error, 1848, a novel; Blanche of Navarre, 1839, a play; Brigand (*The*), 1841, a romance; Cameralzaman, 1848, a fairy drama; Castelneau, 1841, a tale; Castle of Ehrenstein (*The*), 1847, a novel; Charles Tyrel, 1839, a novel; Convict (*The*), 1847, a tale; Darnley, 1830, a novel; Delaware, or Thirty Years Since, 1848; De L'Orme, 1830, a novel; De Lunatico Inquirendo, 1842; Desultory Man (*The*), 1836; Eva St. Clare, and other Tales, 1843; False Heir (*The*), 1843, a novel; Fate, 1851, a novel; Fight of the Fiddlers (*The*), 1848; Forest Days, 1843; Forgery, or Best Intentions, 1848; Gentleman of the Old School (*The*), 1838; Gowrie, or the King's Plot, 1847; Heidelberg, 1846, a romance; Henry Masterton, 1832, a novel; Henry of Guise, 1839, a novel; Henry Smeaton, 1850; Huguenot (*The*), 1839, a novel; Jacquerie (*The*), 1841, an historical romance; John Jones's Tales from English History, 1849; John Marston Hall, 1834; King's Highway (*The*), 1840; Lady Montagu's Page, 1858 (his last novel); Last of the Fairies (*The*), 1847, a tale; Man at Arms (*The*), 1840, a romance; Margaret Graham, 1847; Mary of Burgundy, 1833, an historical novel; Morley Ernstein, 1842, a novel; Old Dominion, or the Southampton Massacre, 1856; One in a Thousand (Henri IV.), 1835; Pequinillo, 1852; Philip Augustus, 1831, an historical novel; Prince Life, 1855; Revenge, 1851; Richelieu, 1828, an historical novel (his first); Robber (*The*), 1838, a tale; Rose d'Albret, 1840, a romance; Russell, 1847, a tale (time, Charles II.); Sir Theodore Broughton, 1847; Smuggler (*The*), 1845, a novel; Stepmother (*The*), 1846, a novel; Story without a Name (*A*), 1852; String of Pearls (seven Eastern tales), 1849; Ticonderaga, or the Black Eagle, 1854; Whim (*The*), and its Consequences, 1847; Woodman (*The*), 1849, a novel.

Poems, Biographies, etc.: Adra, or the Peruvians, a poem; Book of the Passions (*The*), 1839; City of the Silent (*The*), a poem; History of Charlemagne, 1832; History of Chivalry, 1849; Life and Times of Louis XIV., 1838; Life of the Black Prince, 1822; Life of Richard Cœur de Lion, 1841–42; Lives of Eminent Foreign States-

men, 1832-38; Memoirs of Celebrated Women, 1837; Memoirs of Great Commanders, 1832.

JAMES (*Henry*), American author, 1843– . Americans (*The*), 1877; Aspern Papers (*The*), 1888; Beltraffio, 1885; Bostonians (*The*), 1886; Bundle of Letters (*A*), 1879; Confidence, 1880; Daisy Miller, 1878; Diary of a Man of Fifty, 1880; Embarrassments, 1896; Essays in London; Europeans (*The*), 1878; French Poets and Novelists, 1878; International Episode (*An*), 1879; Life of Hawthorne, 1879; Little Tour in France (*A*), 1884; London Life (*A*), 1889; Madonna of the Future (*The*), 1879; Other House (*The*), 1896; Partial Portraits, 1888; Passionate Pilgrim (*A*), 1875; Portraits of Places, 1884; Portrait of a Lady (*The*), 1881; Princess Casamassima, 1886; Reverberator (*The*), 1888; Roderick Hudson, 1875; Siege of London, 1883; Tales of Three Cities, 1884; Terminations, 1896; Tragic Muse (*The*), 1890; Transatlantic Sketches, 1875; Washington Square, 1880; Watch and Ward, 1878; What Maisie knew, 1897.

JAMES (Rev. *John Angell*), Blandford, in Dorsetshire, 1785–1859. Anxious Inquirer, 1834 (enormous sale). His Life, by R. W. Dale, 1862.

JAMES, M.D. (*Robert*), Staffordshire, 1703–1776. (Inventor of "James's Powders.") Dissertation upon Fevers, 1751; Medicinal Dictionary, 1743-45; Vindication of the Fever Powders, 1778.

JAMES, D.D. (*Thomas*), Newport, in the Isle of Wight, 1571-1629. Apology for J. Wicliffe (*An*), 1608; Catalogus Librorum Bibliothecæ Publicæ, etc., 1605; Catalogus Librorum in Bibliotheca Bodleianæ, 1605; Corruption of the Scripture, Councils, and Fathers, 1611 (his best work); Ecloga Oxonio-Cantabrigiensis, 1600; Index Librorum Prohibitorum Pontificus in usum Bibliothecæ Bodleianæ Designus, etc., 1627.

JAMES (*William*), died 1827. Naval History of Great Britain, 1862.

JAMESON (Mrs.), maiden name *Anna Murphy*, Dublin, 1797-1860. Beauties of the Court of Charles II., 1833; Celebrated Female Sovereigns, 1831; Characteristics of Shakespeare's Women, 1832; Commonplace Book, etc., 1854; Diary of an Ennuyée, 1826; Early Italian Painters (*The*), 1845; Handbook of the Public Galleries of Art in and near London, 1842; History of our Lord, etc., as represented in Art, 1860; Legends of the Madonna, 1852; Legends of the Monastic Orders, 1850; Lives of the Early Italian Poets, 1845; Lives of . . . Female Sovereigns, 1831; Loves of the Poets, 1829; Memoirs and Essays, 1846; Pictures of Social Life in Germany, etc., 1840; Poetry of Sacred and Legendary Art, 1848; Rubens, his Life and Genius, 1840; Sacred and Legendary Art, 1848; Scriptural and Legendary History of our Lord, as represented in Christian Art, 1860; Sketches of Germany, 1837; Visits and Sketches, etc., 1834; Winter Studies and Summer Rambles in Canada, 1838. Her Life, 1878.

JAMESON, D.D. (*John*), Glasgow, Scotland,

1759–1838. Etymological Dictionary of the Scottish Language, 1808–9, Supplement 1825 (his chief work); Hermes Scythicus, etc., 1814; Historical Account of the Ancient Culdees of Iona, 1811; Historical Account of the Royal Palaces of Scotland, 1818.

JAMESONE (*Robert*), Leith, in Scotland, 1774–1854. Characters of Minerals, 1805; Elements of Geognosy, 1809; Elements of Mineralogy, 1837; Geology of the Arran and Shetland Isles, 1800; Manual of Minerals and Mountain Rocks, etc., 1821; Mineralogical Description of the County of Dumbarton, 1805; Mineralogy of the Scottish Isles, 1800; Outline of the Mineralogy of the Shetland Islands, 1798; System of Mineralogy, 1820 (excellent).

JAMIESON, D.D. (*John*), Glasgow, 1759–1838. Etymological Dictionary of the Scottish Language, 1808 (a standard work), Supplements 1825; Hermes Scythicus, 1814 (excellent); History of the Culdees of Iona, 1811; Use of Sacred History . . . [to] Revelation, 1802 (of great merit); Vindication of the . . . Deity of Christ, 1794.

JARDINE (*George*), of Glasgow, 1743–1827. Outlines of Philosophical Education, 1818 (valuable).

JARDINE (Sir *William*), Scotland, 1800–1874. British Salmonidæ, 1839–41; Contributions to Ornithology, 1848–52; Ichnology of Annandale, etc., 1851; Naturalist's Library (40 vols.), 1844–55.

JARROLD, M.D. (*Thomas*), *-*. Anthropologia (on the form and colour of man), *-*. Dissertations on Man, etc., 1806 (much praised by the *Quarterly Review*).

JAY (*Harriett*), 1857– . Dark Colleen, 1876; Madge Dunraven, 1878; Priest's Blessing, 1881; Queen of Connaught, 1875 (her first, dramatized in 1870); Two Men and a Maid, 1881.

JAY, D.D. (*William*), generally called the Rev. William Jay of Bath, Tisbury, in Wiltshire, 1769–1853. Autobiography, 1854, posthumous; Essay on Marriage, 1845; Lectures on Female Scripture Characters, 1847; Life of John Jay, 1832; Morning and Evening Exercises, 1829–32; Prayers for the Use of Families, 1821; Sermons, 1802; Works (in 12 vols.), 1841–47. His Life, by C. Winter, 1808; Redford and James, 1854.

JEAFFRESON (*John Cordy*), Framlingham, in Suffolk, 1831– . Crew Rise, 1854 (his first novel); Isabel, the Young Wife, etc., 1856; Live it Down, 1863; Lottie Darling, 1873; Miriam Copley, 1859; Noble Woman (*A*), 1868; Not Dead Yet, 1864; Olive Blake's Good Work, 1862; Sir Everard's Daughter, 1863; Woman in Spite of Herself (*A*), 1872.

Not Novels : Annals of Oxford, 1871; Book about the Clergy (*A*), 1870; Book about Doctors (*A*), 1860; Book about Lawyers (*A*), 1866; Book about the Table (*A*), 1874; Book of Recollections (*A*), 1893; Brides and Bridals, 1872; Lady Hamilton and Lord Nelson, 1887; Life of Robert Stephenson, 1864; Novels and Novelists from Elizabeth to Victoria, 1858; Queen of Naples and Lord Nelson, 1889; Real Lord

Byron (*The*), 1883; Real Shelley (*The*), 1885; Victoria, Queen and Empress, 1893; Young Squire of the Seventeenth Century (*A*), 1877.

JEBB, M.D. (*John*), London, 1736–1786. Works, Theological, Medical, Political, etc., 1878, posthumous. His Memoirs, by Dr. J. Disney, 1787.

JEBB, D.D. (*John*), bishop of Limerick, born at Drogheda, in Ireland, 1775–1833. Essay on Sacred Literature (*An*), 1820 (one of the best in the language); Practical Theology, 1830; Sermons . . . chiefly Practical, 1816. His Life, etc., by C. Foster, 1836.

JEBB, M.D. (*Samuel*), died 1772. Bibliotheca Literaria from 1722; Life of Mary Queen of Scots, 1725.

JEFFERIES (*Richard*), Wiltshire, essayist and novelist, 1848–1887. After London, 1885; Amaryllis at the Fair, 1887; Amateur Poacher (*The*), 1879; Bevis, 1882; Dew of Morn (*The*), 1884; Field and Hedgerow, 1889, posthumous; Gamekeeper at Home (*The*), 1878; Green Ferne Farm, 1880; Hodge and his Masters, 1880; Life of the Fields (*The*), 1884; Nature near London, 1883; Open Air (*The*), 1885; Red Deer, 1884; Restless Human Hearts, 1875; Round about a Great Estate, 1880; Scarlet Shawl (*The*), 1874; Story of my Heart (*The*), 1883; Toilers of the Field (*The*), 1892, posthumous; Wild Life in a Southern County, 1879; Wood Magic, 1881; World's End, 1877. His Life, by H. S. Salt, 1894; and the Eulogy by sir Walter Besant, 1888.

JEFFERYS (*Thomas*), 1720–1780. Dresses of Different Nations, Ancient and Modern, 1757–72; Probability of a North-West Passage, 1768.

JEFFREY OF MONMOUTH. See GEOFFREY.

JEFFREY (*Francis*, lord), Edinburgh, 1773–1850. Editor of the *Edinburgh Review*, 1803–50. Essays, 1843. His Life, by lord Cockburn, 1852.

JELF, D.D. (*Richard William*), 1798–1871. Evidence of Unsoundness, in *Essays and Reviews*, 1861; Means of Grace, 1844, a Bampton lecture; Sermons, 1835.

JENKIN, D.D. (*Robert*), 1656–1727. Reasonableness of the Christian Religion (*The*), 1721 (a learned work).

JENKINS (*David*), Wales, 1586–1667. Eight Centuries of Reports, 1777 (a standard work).

JENKINS (*Edward*), Bangalore, in India, 1838– . Captain's Cabin (*The*), 1872; Contemporary Manners, 1882; Coolie, his Rights and Wrongs (*The*), 1864; Devil's Chain (*The*), 1868; Fatal Days, 1874; Ginx's Baby, 1860 (his best); Glances at Inner England; Haverholme, 1863; Jobson's Enemies, 1880–81; Lisa Lena, 1880; Little Hodge, 1866; Lord Bantam, 1862; Lutchmee and Dilloo, 1870; Paladin of Romance (*A*), 1876.

JENNER, M.D. (*Edward*), Berkeley, in Gloucestershire, 1749–1823. Inquiry into the Causes and Effects of the Variolæ Vaccinæ, 1798; Natural History of the Cuckoo, 1788 (good); New Observations on the Variolæ Vaccinæ, 1799. His Life, by Dr. J. Baron, 1827; J. C. Lettsom.

4 R

JENYNS (*Soame*), London, 1704-1787. Art of Dancing (*The*), 1761, a poem ; Free Inquiry into the Nature and Origin of Evil, 1756 ; Internal Evidences of the Christian Religion, 1786. His Life, by C. N. Cole, 1790.

JEPHSON (*Robert*), 1736-1803. Braganza, 1775, a tragedy ; Conspiracy (*The*), 1796, a tragedy ;। Court of Narbonne (*The*), 1781, a drama ; Hotel (*The*), 1783, a drama ; Julia, 1787, a tragedy ; Law of Lombardy (*The*), 1779, a tragedy ; Roman Portraits, 1794, a poem in heroic verse ; Two Strings to your Bow, 1791, a farce.

JEROME (*Jerome Klapka*), Walsall, Stratford, 1859- . Barbara, 1856 ; Diary of a Pilgrimage, 1891 ; Idle Thoughts of an Idle Fellow, 1886 (subsequently he introduced a periodical called *The Idler*) ; John Ingerfield, 1894 ; New Lamps for Old, 1890 ; Novel Notes, 1893 ; On the Stage and Off, 1885 ; Prude's Progress (*The*), 1895, a comedy ; Rise of Dick Halward, 1896 ; Ruth, 1890 ; Sketches in Lavender, Blue, and Green, 1897 ; Stageland, 1889 ; Sunset, 1888 ; Three Men in a Boat, 1889 (good) ; Told after Supper, 1891 ; Wood Barrow Farm, 1891.

JERROLD (*Douglas William*), London, 1803-1857. Barber's Chair (*The*) ; Black-eyed Susan, 1829, a nautical play ; Bubbles of the Day, 1842, a comedy ; Cakes and Ale, 1841 ; Catspaw (*The*), 1850 ; Caudle Lectures (contributed to *Punch*), 1845 ; Chronicles of Clovernook, 1846 (his best novel) ; Heart of Gold (in three acts), 1854 ; Hedgehog Letters (*The*) ; Housekeeper (*The*), 1835, a two-act play ; Man made of Money (*A*), 1849, a novel ; Men of Character, 1838 ; Nell Gwynne, 1832, a two-act comedy ; Prisoner of War (*The*), 1837, a three-act comedy ; Punch's Letters to his Son (contributed to *Punch*), 1846 ; Rent-day (*The*), 1832, a play in two acts ; Retired from Business, 1851, a three-act comedy ; St. Giles and St. James, 1851 (his most elaborate novel) ; Story of a Feather, 1843, a novel ; Time works Wonders, 1845, a comedy. His Life, by W. B. Jerrold, 1858.

His grandson published, in *Notes and Queries* (February 13, 1897), a list of 68 dramatic pieces by Douglas Jerrold.

JERROLD (*William Blanchard*), son of the preceding, London, 1826-1883. At Home in Paris, 1864, 1870 ; Beau Brummel, 1858, a comedy ; Chatterbox (*The*), 1857, a comedy ; Children of Lutetia, 1863 ; Christian Vagabond (*The*), 1871 ; Chronicles of a Crutch, 1860 ; Cockaignes (*The*), 1871 ; Cool as a Cucumber, 1851, a farce ; Cupboard Papers (*The*), in *All the Year Round*, 1873, as a vol. 1881 ; Cupid in Waiting, 1871, a comedy ; Disgrace to the Family (*The*), 1847, a novel ; Epicure's Year-book, by Fin-Bec, 1867-68 ; French under Arms (*The*), 1860 ; Imperial Paris, 1855 ; Life of George Cruikshank, 1882 ; Life of Douglas Jerrold (his father), 1858 ; Life of Napoleon III., 1874-82 ; London a Pilgrimage, 1872 ; Old Woman who lived in a Shoe (*An*), a series of papers on emigration ; On the Boulevards (*Sketches*), 1853-66 ; Passing the Time, 1865 ; Progress

of a Bill, 1848, a tale ; Story of Madge and the Fairy Content, 1871 ; Swedish Sketches, 1852 ; Trip through the Vineyards of Spain, 1864 ; Trips to Normandy, etc., 1867 ; Two Lives, 1865, a novel ; Up and Down in the World, 1866, a novel.

JESSE (*Edward*), Halifax, 1780-1868. Anecdotes of Dogs, 1846 ; Angler's Rambles (*An*), 1836 ; Favourite Haunts and Rural Studies, 1847 ; Gleanings in Natural History, 1832-35 ; Handbook to Hampton Court, 1841 ; Scenes, etc., of Country Life, 1844 ; Summer's Day at Hampton Court (*A*), 1839 ; Summer's Day at Windsor (*A*), and a Visit to Eton, 1841 ; Windsor Castle and its Environs, 1848.

JESSE (*John Heneage*), historian, 1815-1874. London and its Celebrities, 1847-50 ; Memoirs of the Court of England (Stuarts), 1839 ; Memoirs of King Richard III. ; Memoirs of the Pretender, etc., 1845.

JESSOPP, D.D. (*Augustus*), Cheshunt, Herts, 1824- . Arcady for Better for Worse, 1887 ; Autobiography of Roger North, 1887 ; Coming of the Friars, etc. (*The*), 1888 ; History of the Diocese of Norwich, 1884 ; Norwich School Sermons, 1864 ; One Generation of a Norfolk House, 1878 ; Random Roaming, etc., 1894 ; Studies by a Recluse, 1892 ; Trials of a Country Parson, 1896. Editor of Essays in Divinity by John Doune, D.D., with Life, 1855.

JEWELL, D.D. (*John*), bishop of Salisbury, born in Devonshire, 1522-1571. Apology for the Church of England, in Latin, 1562, translated in 1864 ; Defence of the "Apology," 1567-69. His Life, by Dr. Humfrey, 1573 ; Featley, 1645 ; E. Bohun, 1685 ; G. W. Le Bas ; Isaacson, 1823.

JEWSBURY (*Geraldine Endsor*), Measham, in Warwickshire, novelist, 1820-1880. Constance Herbert, 1855 ; Half-Sisters (*The*), 1848 ; Marian Withers, 1851 ; Right and Wrong, 1859 ; Zoe, or the History of Two Lives, 1845.

JEWSBURY (*Maria Jane*), subsequently Mrs. Fletcher,ʼ 1800-1833. Essays of Leisure Hours ; Life and Literature, 1825.

JODRELL, D.C.L. (*Richard Paul*), 1745-1831. Illustrations of Euripidês, 1781-90 ; Knight and Friars (*The*), 1785 ; Seeing is Believing, 1786.

JOHN OF OXNEAD, chronicler, in the reign of Edward I. Chronicle from 449 to 1292 (this is the Chronicle of Wendover supplemented).

JOHN OF SALISBURY (*Joannes Sarisberiensis*), bishop of Chartres, 1110-1182. Opera Omnia, first compiled and sent to press by J. A. Giles, 1848 ; Polycraticus de Nugis Curialium, etc., 1156.

JOHNSON (*Charles*), 1679-1748. (*He wrote* 19 *plays.*) Gentleman Cully (*The*), 1702, a play ; History of the Most Famous Highwaymen and Murderers . . . 1734 ; History of the Most Notorious Pyrates, 1724 ; Life and Intrigues of Elizabeth Mann, 1724.

JOHNSON (*Cuthbert William*), 1799-1879. On the Uses of Salt for Agricultural Purposes, 1820.

JOHNSON (*George William*), Bromley, in Kent, 1802- . British Ferns ; Cottage

Gardener's Dictionary, 1860; Dictionary of Modern Gardening, 1846; History of Gardening, 1865; Science and Practice of Gardening, 1862.

JOHNSON (*James*),*-*. Scot's Musical Museum (*The*), 1787-1803 (a very valuable work).

JOHNSON (*Richard*), 1570-1630. Anglorum Lacrimæ, 1603; Crowne Garland of Golden Roses . . . 1612; Dainty Conceits, 1630; Golden Garland of Princely Pleasures, etc., 1620; Life of Robert Cecill, 1612; Nine Worthies of London (*The*), 1592; Pleasant Walks of Muorfields (*The*), 1607; Seven Champions of Christendom (*The*), 1595; Tom-à-Lincoln (*History of*), 1599.

JOHNSON (Rev. *Samuel*), 1649-1703. Julian the Apostate, 1682 (this book was burnt by the common hangman, 1684).

JOHNSON (*Samuel*), 1705-1773. All Alive and Merry, 1737; Cheshire Comics, 1730; Hurlo-thrumbo, 1729, an extravaganza; Mad Lover (*The*), 1732; Playing Comet (*The*); Poet made Wise (*A*); Sir John Falstaff in Masquerade, 1741.

JOHNSON, LL.D. (*Samuel*), Lichfield, Stafford, 1709-1784. Dictionary of the English Language, 1755; Idler (*The*), 1758-60, a periodical; Irene, 1749, a tragedy; Journey to the West Islands of Scotland, 1775; Life of Dr. Isaac Watts, 1785, posthumous; Life of Richard Savage, 1744 (interesting); Lives of the Poets, 1779-81; London, 1738, a satire in verse; Miscellaneous Observations on Hamlet, 1745; Rambler (*The*), 1750-52, a periodical; Rasselas, 1759, a tale (written in a week); Taxation no Tyranny, 1775; Vanity of Human Wishes, 1749, a satire in verse (his best poetical work); Visit to the Hebrides, 1773; Voyage to Abyssinia, 1735. His Life, by T. Trotter, 1785; J. Walker, 1785; Tyers, 1786; sir J. H. Hawkins, 1787; Boswell, 1791 (admirable); Dr. Robert Anderson, 1795; J. F. Russell, 1847; J. T. Hewlett, 1851; Thomas Carlyle, 1853.

JOHNSON, M.D. (*Thomas*), botanist, 1561-1644. Descriptio Plantarum in Agram Cantianum, 1632; Iter Cantianum et Ericetum Hamstedianum, 1629; Mercurius Botanicus, etc., 1634. Edited Gerard's *Herbal*, 1633.

JOHNSTON (*Alexander Keith*), Kirkhill, near Edinburgh, 1804-1871. Astronomy, 1855; Chart of the Distribution of Health and Disease, 1852; Classical Geography, 1853; Dictionary of Geography, 1850; General Geography, 1852; National Atlas, 1843; Physical Atlas of Natural Phenomena, 1848 (a splendid work); Royal Atlas, 1861 (his greatest work); School Atlases of Physical Geography.

JOHNSTON, M.D. (*Arthur*), Aberdeenshire, 1587-1641. Delitiæ Poetarum Scotorum . . . 1637; Elegiæ, 1628; Epigrammata, 1632; Musæ Aulicæ, 1635; Musæ Querulæ . . . 1633; Paraphrasis Poetica Psalmorum Davidis, 1637; Parerga, 1632; Poetarum Scoticorum Deliciæ, 1637.

JOHNSTON (*Charles*), died 1800. Chrysal, or Adventures of a Guinea, 1760-61 (this tale was suggested by *The Adventures of a Halfpenny*, 1753); History of Arsaces, 1774;

History of John Juniper, Esq., 1781; Pilgrim (*The*), 1775; Reverie (*The*), 1762.

JOHNSTON, M.D. (*George*), 1798-1855. History of British Sponges and Lithophytes, 1842; History of British Zoophytes, 1838; Introduction to Conchology, 1850.

JOHNSTON (*James F. Weir*), Paisley, in Scotland, 1796-1855. Catechism of Agricultural Chemistry and Geology, 1844; Chemistry of Common Life, 1853-55; Elements of Agricultural Chemistry and Geology, 1842; Lectures on Agricultural Chemistry and Geology, 1844; Notes on America, 1851.

JOHNSTON, LL.D. (*Robert*), 1612-1680. Historia Rerum Britannicarum, 1655 (a work of great merit); Historie of Scotland during the Minority of King James, 1644.

JOHNSTON (*William*), Downpatrick, in Ireland, 1829- . Freshfield, 1870, a novel; Nightshade, 1857, a novel; Under which King? 1872, a novel.

JOHNSTONE, D.D. (*Bryce*), Annan, in Scotland, 1747-1805. Commentary on Revelation, 1794 (good); Influence of Religion on Civil Society, 1801.

JOHNSTONE (*Chevalier de*), Edinburgh, 1720-1795. Memoirs of the Rebellion of 1745-46, 1820, posthumous.

JOHNSTONE (*James*), Scotland, about 1730-1795. Anecdotes of Olave the Black, King of Man, 1780; Antiquitates Celto-Normannicæ, 1786; Antiquitates Celto-Scandicæ, etc., 1786 (interesting); Lodbrokar-Quida, or the Death-Song of Lodbroc, 1782; Norwegian Account of Haco's Expedition against Scotland, 1782.

JOHNSTONE, M.D. (*John*), 1768-1836. Life and Works of Parr, 1828; Medical Jurisprudence, 1800.

JONES (*Ernest Charles*), 1814-1869. Battleday, 1855; Songs of Democracy, 1856-57; Wood-Spirit (*The*), 1841.

JONES, R.A. (*George*), 1786-1869. Life of Chantrey, 1849.

JONES (*Henry*), pseudonym "Cavendish," London, 1831- . Game of Drôle, 1869; Improved Table Croquet, 1866; Laws of Ecarté, 1878; Laws of Piquet, 1873; Pocket Laws of Whist, 1864; Principles of Whist, 1862; and many books on games. .·. Also edited Bennett's *Billiards*, 1873.

JONES (*Henry Arthur*), Grandborough, in Bucks, dramatic author, 1851- . Bauble Shop (*The*), 1893; Case of Rebellious Susan (*The*), 1894; Clerical Error (*A*), 1879; Crusaders (*The*), 1891; Dancing Girl (*The*), 1891; Judah, 1890; Masqueraders (*The*), 1894; Michael and his Lost Angel, 1896; Middleman (*The*), 1889; Renascence of the English Drama, 1895; Rogue's Comedy (*The*), 1896; Saints and Sinners, 1894; Silver King, 1882; Tempter (*The*), 1893; Triumph of the Philistines (*The*), 1895.

JONES (*Inigo*), London, 1572-1652. He built the Banqueting House, Whitehall, 1619-22; the Piazza and Church, Covent Garden, 1631-38, etc. Journal and Sketch-book, 1611; Stonehenge restored, 1655, posthumous. His Life, by Peter Cunningham, 1848.

JONES (*Jeremiah*), 1693-1724. Gospel of St. Matthew (*The*), 1719; Method of settling the Canonical Authority of the New Testament, 1726-27 (esteemed).

JONES, LL.D. (Rev. *John*), 1765-1827. Ecclesiastical Researches, 1812; Greek and English Lexicon, 1823.

JONES (*Owen*), 1740-1814. Myvyrian Archæology of Wales, 1801-7.

JONES (*Theophilus*), *-*. History of Brecknockshire, 1805-9 (a work of great merit).

JONES (*Thomas Rymer*), 1809-1880. General Outline of the Animal Kingdom, 1838.

JONES (*Thomas Wharton*), St. Andrews, in Scotland, 1808-   . Essay on Inflammation, 1850 (sir Astley Cooper's prize); Failure of Sight from Spinal Disturbance, 1869; Physiology, etc., of Body, Sense, and Mind, 1869; Wisdom and Beneficence of [God, shewn] in the Sense of Vision, 1851 (Actonian prize).

∴ He pooh-poohs Dr. Darwin's doctrine of Evolution as "wholly unsupported by sound science." See MIVART.

JONES (Rev. *William*), generally called "Jones of Nayland," Northamptonshire, 1726-1800. Art of Music, 1784; Catholic Doctrine of the Trinity, 1756; Figurative Language of Scripture, 1790; Letter from Thomas Bull to his Brother John, 1792; Life of Bishop Horne, 1795; Passages of Scripture not Commonly Understood; Physiological Disquisitions, 1781; Scholar Armed, etc. (*The*), 1792. His Life, by W. Steevens, 1810.

JONES (Sir *William*), London, 1746-1794. Commentaries on Asiatic Poetry, 1774; Enchanted Fruit, or the Hindû Wite, a story in verse; Hitopadesa (translated); Institutes of Hindû Law, 1794; Laws of Manu, 1794; Life of Nadir Shah, 1770; Moallákat (seven Arabic poems), 1782; Persian Grammar, 1771; Poeseos Asiaticæ Commentariorum, libri vi. 1774; Principles of Government (*The*), 1797, posthumous; Sacontala, or the Fatal Ring (an Indian drama translated). His Life, by lord Teignmouth, 1799.

JONES, D.D. (*William Basil Tickell*), bishop of St. David's, born in Wales, 1822-   . History and Antiquities of St. David's, 1856 (with Dr. Freeman); New Testament . . . with Commentary, 1864; Peace of God (*The*), 1869, sermons; Vestiges of Gael in Gwynedd, 1851.

JONSON (*Ben*), Westminster, poet laureate, 1574-1637. "Drink to me only with thine Eyes" (to Celia): this very beautiful song is in *The Forest*, 1616; Execration against Vulcan, with Divers Epigrams, 1640, posthumous; Jests, or the Wit's Pocket Companion, 1731; Last Legacy to the Sons of Mirth, etc., 1756, posthumous.

Dramas: Alchemist (*The*), 1610, a comedy; Bartholomew Fair, 1614, a comedy; Catiline, 1611, a tragedy; Cynthea's Revels, 1600, a satirical comedy; Devil's an Ass (*The*), 1616, a comedy; Eastward Hoe! 1605 (with Chapman and Marston), a satirical comedy; Epicene, or The Silent Woman, 1609, a comedy; Every Man in his Humour, 1596 (his best), a comedy; Every Man out of his Humour, 1599, a comedy; Forest (*The*), 1616 (this contains the song "Drink to me only . . ."); Magnetic Lady (*The*), 1632, a comedy; New Inn (*The*), 1630, a comedy; Poetaster (*The*), 1601, a satiric comedy; Sad Shepherd (*The*), 1637, a pastoral unfinished; Sejanus, 1603, a tragedy; Staple of News (*The*), 1625, a comedy; Tale of a Tub (*A*), 1633 (his last comedy); Volpone, 1605, a comedy. His Life, by Chetwood, 1756; Gifford, 1816; Barry Cornwall, *i.e.* B. W. Procter, 1838; Cunningham and Bell, 1870; and J. A. Symonds, 1887.

JORDAN (*Thomas*), London, poet laureate for the city, 1611-1688. Box of Spikenard newly broken, etc., 1661-62; Cabinet of Mirth (*The*), in two parts, 1674; Divine Raptures, 1646; Divinity and Morality in Robes of Poetry, 1651; Fancy's Festival, 1657, a masque; Goldsmith's Jubilee (*The*), 1674; Jewels of Ingenuity in a Coronet of Poetry (no date); London in Lustre (November 9), 1679; London in Splendour, 1673; London Triumphant, 1672; London's Glory, 1680; London's Joy, 1681; London's Joyful Gratulation, etc., 1642; London's Resurrection to Joy, 1671; London's Triumphs, 1653, 1675, 1676, 1677, 1678, 1684; Lord Mayor's Show, etc. (*The*), November 9, 1682; Money is an Asse, 1668, a comedy; Muses' Melody (*The*), (no date); New Droll (*A*), 1660; Pictures of Passions, etc. (no date); Poetical Varieties, 1637; Rosary of Rarities (*A*), 1659; Royal Arbor of Loyall Poesie, 1663; Rules to know a Royall King, etc., 1642; Tricks of Youth, etc., 1657; Wit in a Wilderness, 1660-67, promiscuous pieces of poetry.

JORDEN, M.D. (*Edward*), 1569-1632. Discourse of Natural Bathes and Mineral Waters, 1631 (a learned treatise); Suffocation of the Matrix . . . (on possession of evil spirits), 1603 (very scarce indeed).

JORTIN, D.D. (*John*), London, 1698-1770. Life of Erasmus, 1758-60; Lusus Poetici, 1748; Observations on Authors, Ancient and Modern, 1731-32; On the Truth of the Christian Religion, 1748; Remarks on Ecclesiastical History, 1751-54; Remarks on Spenser and Milton, 1734; Truth of the Christian Religion (*The*), 1732. His Life, by Dr. J. Disney, 1792.

JOWETT, LL.D. (Rev. *Benjamin*), Camberwell, 1817-1893. Aristotle translated, 1885; Dialogues of Plato, 1871; Epistles to Romans, Galatians, etc., 1855; Plato translated, 1892; Politics of Aristotle, 1885; Thucydidês translated, 1881.

JOYCE (*Jeremiah*), 1764-1816. Arithmetic, 1808; Dialogues on Chemistry, 1807; Scientific Dialogues, 1807.

JUDSON, D.D. (*Adoniram*), Massachusetts, U.S., 1788-1850. Burmese and English Dictionary, 1852; Burmese Bible (*i.e.* the Bible in Burmese), 1835. His Life, by Wayland, 1853; Mrs. H. C. Conant, 1856; Clements; Gillette.

JUKES (*Joseph Beete*), near Birmingham, 1811-1869. Excursions in Newfoundland,

1842 ; Physical Structure of Australia, 1850 ; Student's Manual of Geology, 1858.

JUNIUS, Letters of, 1769–72 ; compiled 1783, 1796, 1800, etc. ; Woodfall's edition, 1812. N.B.—The original " Junius " ceased in the spring of 1772. *The Author of these Letters*: Barré, Col. *Isaac* (" Authorship of the *Letters of Junius*, by John Britton "), 1848. Boyd, *Hugh* (" Author of *Junius* ascertained by George Chalmers "), 1817. Burke, *Edmund* (" Inquiry into the Author of *Junius*, by John Roche "), 1813 ; (" Junius proved to be Burke," no name), 1826 ; Prior, in his *Life of Burke*, takes the same view, 1839. Burke, *William* (" The Author of *Junius*, by J. C. Symons "), 1859. Chatham, *William Pitt*, lord (" Another Guess at Junius," by (?) Fitzgerald), 1809 ; Earl Chatham " proved to be Junius," by John Swinden, 1833 ; by W. Dowe, U.S., 1857 ; (" Who was Junius?" no name), 1837 ; also an essay to prove this, by Dr. B. Waterhouse, of Boston, U.S., 1831. Chesterfield, Earl of (" Author of *Junius* discovered," by W. Cramp), 1821, 1851. De Lolme, *John Lewis* (" Arguments and Facts demonstrating " this, by Dr. Thomas Busby), 1816. Francis (Dr.) and his son sir Philip (" Discovery of the Author of *Junius*, by John Taylor "), 1813. Francis, Sir *Philip* (" Identity of *Junius* . . . established by John Taylor "), 1816 ; sir F. Dwarris, 1850, and lord Campbell, in his *Lives of the Chancellors*, take the same view (" Handwriting of Junius professionally investigated, by Charles Chabot "), 1871 ; Macaulay espoused this "identity." Glover, *Richard* (" An Inquiry into the Author of the *Letters of Junius*," no name), 1814. Gibbon (" Junius unmasked," no name), 1819. Lee, Major-general *Charles* (proved " from facts" to be Junius by Dr. T. Girdlestone), 1813. M'Lean, *Laughlin* (said to be Junius in Galt's *Life of West*, pp. 57–69) ; sir David Brewster takes the same view. Portland, Duke of (" Letters to a Nobleman proving " this, by A. G. Johnston), 1816. Pownall, Governor (" Junius discovered," by F. Griffin, Boston, U.S."), 1854. Rich, Sir R. (" The Ghost of Junius, by F. Ayerst "), 1853. Sackville, Viscount (" The Real Author of the *Letters of Junius*, by George Coventry "), 1825 ; (" Junius unmasked," no name), 1770 ; the same proved by John Jaques, 1843. Suett, the comedian (" Junius with his Visor up," a skit, no name), 1819. Temple, *R. Grenville*, earl (" Letters on Junius showing " this, by Isaac Newhall, Boston, U.S.), 1831. Tooke, *John Horne* (" Junius discovered, by P[hilip] T[hicknesse] "), 1789 ; the same " proved " by J. B. Blakeway, 1813 ; and Dr. A. Graham, 1828. Wray, *Daniel* (" The Secret revealed, by James Falconar "), 1830. Wilmot, *James*, D.D., proved to be "Junius" by O. W. Serres, 1813. N.B.—To these add Mr. Sergeant Adair ; Gerard Hamilton, called " Single-Speech ; " lord Lyttelton ; and John Wilks. Other pamphlets or books have been published to disprove all these "proofs." Byron says—

> *I've an hypothesis . . .*
> *'Tis that what Junius we are wont to call*
> *Was really, truly, nobody at all.*
> *The Vision of Judgment.*

KAMES (Lord *Henry Home*), Kames, in Berwickshire, 1696–1782. Decisions of the Court of Sessions, 1741, 1766, 1780 (a very valuable work) ; Elements of Criticism, 1762 (his best-known work) ; Gentleman Farmer (*The*), 1777 ; Hints on Education, 1781 ; Historical Law Tracts, 1758 ; Introduction to the Art of Thinking, 1761 ; Principles of Equity, 1760 ; Principles of the Law of Scotland, 1754 ; Principles of Morality and Natural Religion (*The*), 1751 ; Sketches of the History of Man, 1774. His Life, by W. Smellie, 1800 ; lord Woodhouselee, 1807.

KANE (*Elisha Kent*), Philadelphia, U.S., 1820–1857. Second Grimmell Expedition in Search of Sir John Franklin, 1856. His Life, by Dr. W. Elder, 1857.

KANE (Sir *Robert*), Dublin, 1810–1889. Elements of Chemistry, 1841–42 ; Industrial Resources of Ireland, 1884.

KAVANAGH (*Julia*), Thurles, in Ireland, novelist, etc., 1824–1877. Adèle, 1858 ; Beatrice, 1865 ; Bessie, 1872 ; Daisy Burns, 1853 ; Dora, 1868 ; English Women of Letters, 1862 ; Forget-me-nots, 1878 ; French Women of Letters, 1861 ; Grace Lee, 1855 ; John Dorrien, 1875 ; Madeleine, 1848 ; Nathalie, 1851 ; Pearl Fountain (*The*), 1855 ; Queen Mab, 1863 ; Rachel Gray, 1856 ; Seven Years, 1860 ; Summer and Winter in the Two Sicilies (*A*), 1858 ; Sybil's Second Love, 1867 ; Sylvia, 1870 ; Three Paths (*The*), 1847 ; Two Lilies, 1877 ; Women in France during the Eighteenth Century, 1850 ; Women of Christianity, 1852.

KAYE, D.D. (*John*), bishop of Lincoln, born at Hammersmith, 1783–1853. Council of Nicæa in Connection with Athanasius, 1853 ; Ecclesiastical History of the Second and Third Centuries, 1826 ; External Government, etc., of the Church in the First Three Centuries, 1855 ; Writings and Opinions of Clement of Alexandria, 1835.

KAYE (Sir *John William*), London, 1814–1876. Administration of the East India Company (*The*), 1853 ; Biographies of Sir John Malcolm 1856, Lord Metcalfe 1854, Sir George Tucker 1854 ; Christianity in India, 1859 ; Essays of the Optimist, 1870 ; History of the Sepoy War (1857-58), 1864–76 ; History of the War in Afghanistan, 1851 ; Lives of Indian Officers, 1867.

KEACH (Rev. *Benjamin*), 1640–1704. Banqueting House (*The*), 1692 ; Breach repaired (*The*), 1661 (by singing) ; Grand Impostor discovered (*The*), 1675, a poem (against the Quaker sect) ; Parables explained, 1701 (much esteemed) ; Scripture Metaphors opened, 1681 (his chief work) ; Spiritual Songs, 1700 ; Trumpet blown in Zion, 1694.

KEARY (*Anna Maria*), 1825–1879, Castle Daly, 1875 ; Clemency Franklyn, 1866 ; Doubting Heart (*A*), 1878 ; Janet's Home,

1863; Mia and Charlie, 1856; Nations Around, 1870; Oldbury, 1869.
With her sister : Heroes of Asgard (*The*), 1857; Wanderlin, 1864.

KEATS (*John*), London, 1796–1821 Endymion, 1818, a poetic romance ; Eve of St. Agnes, 1820, Spenserian stanza; Hyperion, 1820, blank verse ; Isabella, 1820 ; Lamia, and other poems, 1820 ; Ode to the Nightingale, 1820; Poems, 1817. His Life, by M. Milnes, 1845 ; lord Houghton, 1848.

KEBLE (Rev. *John*), born at Fairford, in Gloucestershire, 1792–1866. Christian Year (*The*), 1827 (his chief work) ; De Poeticæ Vi Medica, 1844; Letters of Spiritual Guidance, 1870, posthumous ; Life of Bishop Wilson, 1863 ; Lyra Innocentium, 1846 ; Sermons, 1848. His Life, by sir J. T. Coleridge ; and by Walter Lock.

KEELING (*Elsa d'Esterre*). Appassionata ; Bib and Tucker, 1884 ; How the First Queen of England was Wooed and Won, 1884 ; In Thoughtland and in Dreamland ; Music of the Poets, 1897 ; Old Maids and Young; Orchards Croft ; Professor's Wooing (*A*), 1886; Three Sisters, 1884 ; True Story of Catherine Parr (*The*), 1884.

KEIGHTLEY (*Thomas*), Dublin, 1789–1872. Crusaders (*The*), 1833 ; Fairy Mythology, 1828, enlarged 1850 ; History of England, 1837 ; History of Greece, 1836; History of India, 1847 ; History of Rome, 1835 ; Life of Milton, 1855 ; Mythology of Greece and Italy, 1831; Tales and Popular Fictions, 1834.

KEILL, M.D. (*John*), Edinburgh, 1671–1721. Examination of Dr. Burnet's Theory of the Earth, 1698 ; Introductio ad Veram Astronomiam, 1718; Introductio ad Veram Physicam, 1702.

KEITH, D.D. (*Alexander*), Keithall, in Scotland, 1791–1880. Demonstration of the Truth of the Christian Religion, 1838 ; Evidences of Religion from the Fulfilment of Prophecy, 1823 (a text-book) ; Harmony of Prophecy (*The*), 1851 ; History and Destiny of the World and of the Church, according to Scripture, part i., 1861 ; Land of Israel (*The*), 1843 ; Narrative of the Mission to the Jews ; Signs of the Times, 1832.

KEITH (*Thomas*), Yorkshire, 1759–1824. Practical Arithmetician (*The*), 1789 ; Romance of an Hour (*The*), 1771 ; Use of the Globes, 1804.

KELLY (*Hugh*), 1739–1777. Clementina, 1774 ; False Delicacy, 1763, a comedy ; Man of Reason (*The*), 1776 ; School for Wives (*The*), 1774, a comedy ; Thespis, 1762, a drama ; Word to the Wise (*A*), 1765, a comedy. Works, with Life, 1778.

KELLY, LL.D. (Rev. *John*), Douglas, in the Isle of Man, 1750–1809. Gaelic Grammar, 1803 ; Manx Translation of the Bible, 1772.

KELLY (*Michael*), Ireland, 1762–1826. Reminiscences, etc., 1820 (the best addition to our theatrical literature since Cibber's *Apology*).

KELLY, LL.D. (*Patrick*), Ireland, *-*. Universal Cambist (*The*), 1811 (excellent).

KELTON (*Arthur*), chronicler in the reign of Edward VI. Cronycle . . . declaryng that

Britons and Welshmen are lineally descended from Brute (in verse), printed 1547.

KEMBLE (*Frances Anne*), afterwards Mrs. *Pierce Butler*, London, 1809–1893. Francis I., 1880, an historical play ; Journal of a Residence. in America, 1835 ; Poems, 1842 ; Record of a Girlhood, 1878 ; Records of Later Life, 1882 ; Residence in a Georgian Plantation, 1863 ; Star of Seville (*The*), 1837, a drama ; Year of Consolation (*A*), 1847.

KEMBLE (*John Mitchell*), London, 1807–1857. Anglo-Saxon Poems of Beowulf, 1833 ; Codex Diplomaticus Ævi Saxonici, 1839–40 ; History of the English Language (first period), 1834 ; Saxons in England, 1849 (his chief work).

KEMP, Mus.Doc. (*Joseph*), Exeter, in Devonshire, 1778–1824. System of Musical Education, 1819.

KEN, D.D. (*Thomas*), bishop of Bath and Wells, born at Berkhampstead, in Hertfordshire, 1637–1711. Edmund, an epic poem ; Morning, Evening, and Midnight Hymns, 1674 (by which he is best known) ; Works collected and published, 1721. His Life, by W. Hawkins, 1713 ; canon W. L. Bowles, 1830 ; a Layman, *i.e.* J. L. Anderdon, 1853.

KENEALY (*Arabella*), 1864– . Dr. Janet, 1893 ; Hon. Mrs Spoor (*The*), 1895 ; Molly and her Man-of-War, 1894 ; Some Men are such Gentlemen, 1894.

KENNAN (*George*), 1845– . Siberia and the Exile System ; Tent-Life in Siberia, 1870.

KENNEDY (*John*), Bradley, in Derbyshire, 1700–1770. Scripture Chronology, 1752.

KENNEDY (*John Pendleton*), Baltimore, U.S., novelist, 1795–1870. Annam of Quodlibet, 1840 ; Horse-shoe Robinson, 1835 ; Life of William Wirt, 1849 ; Red Book (*The*), 1817–19.

KENNET, D.D. (*White*), bishop of Peterborough, born at Dover, 1660–1728. Complete History of England, 1706, composed by different authors, the third vol. by himself ; Family of Cavendish (*The*), 1707 ; Parochial Antiquities of Ambrosden, Burcester, etc., 1695 (a valuable work) ; Register and Chronicle, Ecclesiastical and Civil, 1728. His Life, by Newton, 1730.

KENNEY (*James*), Ireland, 1780–1849. Ella Rosenberg, 1807, a comedy ; False Alarms, 1807, an operetta; Illustrious Stranger (*The*), 1827, a comedy ; Love, Law, and Physic, a comedy ; Masaniello, 1829 ; Matrimony, 1804, a comedy ; Raising the Wind, 1803, a farce (his first and best) ; Sicilian Vespers (*The*), 1840 ; Spring and Autumn, 1827, a comedy ; World (*The*), 1808, a comedy.

KENNICOTT, D.D. (*Benjamin*), Totnes, in Devonshire, 1718–1783. Dissertation on the "Tree of Life," the Creation, and Fall, 1747 ; Hebrew Bible, 1776–80 ; On the State of the Printed Hebrew Text of the Old Testament, 1753–59 (valuable) ; Variæ Lectiones Veteris Testamenti, 1784–88.

KENRICK, LL.D. (*William*), Watford, in Hertfordshire, 1720–1779. English Dictionary, 1773; Epistles, 1759, in verse ; Falstaff's Wedding, 1766, a comedy ; Immortality of the Soul (*The*), 1751 ; Pasquinade (*The*), 1753.

KENT (*James*), Winchester, 1700-1771. Twelve Anthems, 1773, posthumous.

KENT (*James*), Fredericksburg, New York, U.S., 1763-1847. Commentaries on American Law, 1826-30.

KENT (*William Charles Mark*), generally called " Charles Kent," London, 1823–   . Aletheia, and other Poems, 1850 ; Assumptione Epigramma Carolo Kent, 1880 ; Cameldriver's Turban (*The*), 1842 ; Catholicity in the Dark Ages, 1864 ; Charles Dickens as a Reader, 1872 ; Dreamland, and other Poems, 1862 ; Footprints on the Road, 1864, in prose ; Napoleon's Slippers, 1842 ; Poems (collected, etc.), 1870 ; Seagulls of Iona (a tale of the escape of the Young Pretender), 1842 ; Shakespeare's Frolic on the Thames, 1842 ; Wit and Wisdom of . . . Lord Lytton, 1883.

KER (*David*), writer of tales for boys. Afloat in a Volcano, 1893 ; Amid Siberian Forests, 1894 ; Captives of the Ocean ; Champion of the Kremlin (*The*), 1891, a Russian tale ; Death Spring (*The*), 1893 ; Eagle's Rock (*The*), 1895, a story of the Polar Seas ; Tale of the Russian Conquest of Asia, 1894 ; Through the Darkness, the Portuguese Conquest of Angola (his best) ; Tiger Chief of Burmah (*The*), 1893 ; Unseen Depths.

KER (*John Bellenden*), *-*. Archaiology of our Popular Phrases and Nursery Rhymes, 1834 (to prove they are perversions of Dutch words, mainly anti-monkish).

KERNAHAN (*Coulson*), Ilfracombe, in Devonshire, 1858–   . Book of Strange Sins (*A*), 1893 ; Captain Shannon, 1897 ; Child (*The*), the Wise Man and the Devil, 1896 ; Dead Man's Diary (*A*), 1890 ; God and the Ant, 1895 ; Literary Gent (*A*), 1897 ; Sorrow and Song, 1894.

KERR (*Robert*), Scotland, 1755-1814. Collection of Voyages and Travels, 1811-17 (a valuable work) ; History of Scotland (Robert the Bruce), 1811 (a good epitome) ; Life of William Smellie, 1811.

KETT (Rev. *Henry*), 1761-1825. Elements of General Knowledge, . . . with Lists of the most Approved Authors, 1812 ; Emily, 1809, a moral tale ; History the Interpreter of Prophecy, 1799 (an excellent work) ; Juvenile Poems, 1793.

KIDD (*Benjamin*), 1858–   . Social Evolution, 1894.

KIDD, M.D. (*John*), 1775-1851. Adaptation of External Nature to the Physical Condition of Man, 1833 (a Bridgewater treatise) ; Outlines of Mineralogy, 1809 (good).

KIDD (*William*), Hammersmith, 1803-1867. British Song-birds, 1856.

KIDDER, D.D. (*Richard*), bishop of Bath and Wells, born in Sussex, 1635-1703. (He and his wife were killed in bed during the storm of November 26.) Commentary on the Pentateuch, 1694 ; Demonstration of the Messias, 1694-1700.

KILLIGREW (*Thomas*), " King Charles's Jester," Middlesex, 1611-1682. Parson's Wedding (*The*), 1663, a comedy ; several other plays printed in 1664.

KILLIGREW (Sir *William*), vice-chamberlain to queen Henrietta, poet, brother of the preceding, 1605-1693. Artless Midnight

Thoughts of a Gentleman at Court, 1684 ; Imperial Tragedy (*The*), 1669, a tragedy ; Love and Friendship, 1666, a play ; Midnight and Daily Thoughts, 1694 ; Ormasdes, 1665, a play ; Pandora, 1664, a play ; Selindra, 1665, a play ; Siege of Urbin, 1666, a play.

KING, F.R.S. (*Edward*), Norfolk, 1735-1807. Essay on the English Government, 1767 ; Morsels of Criticism, 1788 ; Munimenta Antiqua, 1799-1805.

KING (*Gregory*), Lichfield, in Hampshire, 1648-1712. Observations on the State of England, 1710.

KING (*Henry*), bishop of Chichester, etc., 1591-1669. Deep Groan fetched at the Funeral of . . . Charles I. (*A*), 1649 ; Poems, Elegies, and Paradoxes, 1657 ; Psalms (*The*), in metre, 1657.

KING (*Peter*, lord), Exeter, 1669-1734. History of the Apostles' Creed, 1702 ; Inquiry into the Constitution, etc., of the Primitive Church, 1691.

KING, D.D. (*William*), archbishop of Dublin, born at Antrim, in Ireland, 1650-1729. State of the Protestants in Ireland, 1691 ; De Origine Mali, 1702.

KING, LL.D. (*William*), London, 1663-1712. Animadversions on the Pretended Account of Ireland, 1694 ; Art of Cookery (in imitation of Horace), 1703, a poem ; Art of Love (in imitation of Ovid), no date ; Dialogues of the Dead, 1699 ; Joan of Hedington, 1712, a tragi-comedy ; Journey to London (*A*), 1698 (excellent piece of irony); Transactioner (*The*), two satires on the Royal Society, 1700 ; Vindication of Dr. Sacheverell, 1710. His Memoir, by Nichols, 1776.

KINGLAKE (*Alexander William*), near Taunton, in Somersetshire, 1811-1891. Eothen, 1844 (a model book of travels) ; History of the Crimean War, 1863-68-75-80-87.

KINGSLEY (Rev. *Charles*), Holne Vicarage, in Devonshire, 1819-1875. Ancien Régime (*The*), 1867 ; Andromeda and other Poems, 1858 ; Alexandra and her Schools, 1854 ; Alton Locke, Tailor and Poet, a novel on the social anarchy of the day, 1849 ; At Last, 1871 ; Cheap Clothes and Nasty, 1850 (by Parson Lot) ; Glaucus, or the Wonders of the Shore, 1855 ; Health and Education, 1874 ; Hereward the Wake, 1866, a novel ; Hermits (*The*), 1869 ; Heroes (*The*), 1856, Greek fairy tales ; Hypatia, 1853, a novel (to show the struggle of Christianity with paganism and Greek philosophy of the fifth century) ; Lectures delivered in America, 1875 ; Limits of Exact Science as applied to History (*The*), 1860 ; Madam How and Lady Why, 1869 ; Miscellanies, 1859 ; Phaeton, 1852, a dialogue against the Emersonian school ; Plays and Puritans, 1873 ; Prose Idylls, 1873 ; Roman (*The*) and the Teuton, 1864, lectures ; Saints' Tragedy (*The*), 1848, a dramatic poem (Elizabeth of Hungary) ; Sermons, 1859 ; Sermons, 1872 ; Sermons for the Times, 1855 ; Sermons on National Subjects, 1852-54 ; Sermons on the Pentateuch, 1863 ; Town Geology, 1872 ; Town and Country Sermons, 1861 ; Two Years Ago, 1857, a novel ; Village Sermons, 1849 ; Water Babies (*The*), 1863 ; Water of Life, 1867 ; Westminster

Sermons, 1874; Westward Ho! (voyages and adventure of sir Amyas Leigh in the reign of queen Elizabeth), 1855 (this and "Alton Locke" are his two best); What then does Dr. Newman mean? 1864; Yeast, 1849, a philosophical novel. His Life, by his widow, 1876.

KINGSLEY (*Henry*), Holne Vicarage, in Devonshire, brother of the above, novelist, 1830–1876. Austin Elliot, 1863; Boy in Grey (*The*), 1870; Fireside Studies, 1876; Geoffry Hamlyn (*Recollections of*), 1859; Grange Garden, 1876; Harveys (*The*), 1872; Hetty, and other Stories, 1871; Hillyars and the Burtons (*The*), 1865; Hornby Mills, and other Stories, 1872; Leighton Court, 1866; Lost Child (*The*), 1871; Mademoiselle Mathilde, 1868; Mystery of the Island, 1877; Number Seventeen, 1875; Oakshott Castle, 1873; Old Margaret, 1871; Ravenshoe, 1861 (his best novel); Reginald Hetheredge, 1874; Silcote of Silcotes, 1867; Stretton, 1869; Tales of Old Travel, 1869; Valentin, 1872, a story of Sedan.

KIPLING (*Rudyard*), Bromley, 1865– . Barrack-room Ballads, etc., 1892; Black and White, 1888, reissued 1897; Captains Courageous, 1897; City of Dreadful Night (*The*), and other Places, 1891 (this book and "Letters of Marque," being published without the author's sanction, were withdrawn from circulation); Departmental Ditties, 1888; Jungle Book (*The*), 1894; Letters of Marque, 1891; Life's Handicap, 1891; Light that Failed (*The*), 1890 (published originally in *Lippincott's Magazine*, afterwards revised and altered); Many Inventions, 1893; Naulahka, 1892 (with C. Walcott Balestier); Phantom Rickshaw (*The*), 1888; Plain Tales from the Hills, 1888; Second Jungle Book, 1895; Seven Seas (*The*), 1896, poems; Soldiers Three, Story of the Gadsbys (*The*), Under the Desdars, Wee Willie Winkle (these four were written in 1888).

KNIGHT (*William Angus*), 1836– . Aspects of Theism, 1894; Christian Ethic (*The*), 1894; Colloquia Peripatetica, 1870; English Lake District, as interpreted in the Poems of Wordsworth, 1878; Essays in Philosophy, 1890; Memoir of John Nichol, 1895; Memorials of Coleorton, 1887; Philosophical Classics for English Readers (edited), 1886; Philosophy of the Beautiful, its History, 1891; Poems from the Dawn of English Literature to the Year 1699, 1863; Principal Shairp, 1888; Rectorial Addresses, 1894; Selections from Wordsworth, 1889; Stories and Rhymes of Golf, 1893; Studies in Philosophy, 1879; Theory, 1893; Through the Wordsworth Country, 1892; Transactions of the Wordsworth Society, 1880–86; White Doe of Rylstone (edited), 1891; Wordsworthiana, 1889; Wordsworth's Prose, 1893; Works of Wordsworth, etc. (in preparation).

KNOLLIS (Sir *Francis*), statesman, born at Grays, in Oxfordshire, 1530–1596. Treatise against the Usurpation of Papal Bishops, 1608, posthumous.

KNOTT (*Edward*), his pseudonym was "Matthias Wilson," Northumberland, 1580–1656.

Charity mistaken, 1630; Infidelity unmasked, 1652.

KNOWLES (*James Sheridan*), Cork, in Ireland, 1784–1862. Idol demolished by its own Priest (*The*), a reply to cardinal Wiseman on *transubstantiation*, 1851; Rock of Rome (*The*), or the Arch-Heresy, 1849.

Plays: Alfred the Great, 1831, historical play; Beggar's Daughter of Bethnal Green, 1898, a comedy; Brian Boroihme, 1814; Caius Gracchus, 1815, an historical play; Hunchback (*The*), 1832, a comedy; John of Procida, 1840, a tragedy; Leo, or the Gipsy, 1813, a comedy; Love, 1840, a comedy; Love Chase (*The*), 1837, a comedy; Love's Disguises, 1838, a comedy; Maid of Mariendorpt (*The*), 1838; Old Maids, 1841, a comedy; Rose of Aragon (*The*), 1842; Secretary (*The*), 1843; Virginius, 1828, a tragedy; Wife (*The*), 1833; William Tell, 1825, a tragedy; Woman's Wit, 1838, a comedy.

KNOX (*John*), Gifford Gate, in Scotland, 1505–1572. Admonition (*An*), 1554; Faithfull Admonition, 1554; First Blast of the Trumpet against the Monstrous Regiment of Women, 1558; Fort for the Afflicted, etc., 1556; History of the Reformation . . . in Scotland, 1584, posthumous; What True Praier is, 1534. His Life, by Smeaton, 1579; McCrie, 1812; Niemeyer, 1824; Laing, 1847; T. Brandes, 1863.

KNOX (*Robert*), born 1641– . Historical Relation of the Island of Ceylon, 1681 (a standard work).

KNOX, M.D. (*Robert*), Edinburgh, 1791–1862. Manual of Artistic Anatomy, 1852; Manual of Human Anatomy, 1853; Races of Men, 1850.

KNOX, D.D. (*Vicesimus*), London, 1752–1821. Christian Philosophy, 1795; Family Lectures, 1791; Liberal Education, etc., 1781; Moral and Literary Essays, 1778–79; Winter Evenings, 1788.

KYNASTON (Sir *Francis*), Shropshire, 1587–1642. Corona Minervæ, 1635, a masque; Leoline and Sydanis, 1642, a poetical romance; Muses' Complaint (*The*), 1633, in Latin.

LAING (*Alexander*), Brechin, in Scotland, 1787–1857. Called "The Brechin Poet." Archie Allan, 1827; Thistle of Scotland (*The*), 1823, ancient ballads; Wayside Flowers, 1846.

LAING (*Alexander Gordon*), Edinburgh, 1794–1826. Travels, 1826, posthumous.

LAING (*David*), 1792–1878. Early Metrical Tales, 1826; Fugitive Scottish Poetry (17th century), 1823–25, 1853; Select Remains of the Ancient Popular Poetry of Scotland, 1822.

LAING (*Malcolm*), Orkney, 1762–1818. History of Scotland, with Critical Dissertation on . . . Ossian, 1800; On the Gowrie Conspiracy; On the Participation of Mary (Queen of Scots) in the Darnley Murder (appended to the second edition of his "History").

LAING (*Samuel*), Edinburgh, 1810–1897. Human Origins, 1892; India and China, 1863; Modern Science and Modern Thought, 1885; Modern Zoroastrian (*A*), 1887; Prehistoric Remains of Caithness, 1865; Problems of the Future, 1889; Sporting Quixote (*A*), 1886.

LAMB (Lady *Caroline*), maiden name *Caroline Ponsonby*, 1785–1828.   Ada Reis, 1823; Glenarvon, 1816, a new canto 1819; Graham Hamilton, 1822, a novel.

LAMB (*Charles*), London, 1775–1834.   Adventures of Ulysses, 1808; Blank Verse by Charles Lloyd and Charles Lamb, 1798; Essay on the Genius of Hogarth (his best work); Essays of Elia (a volume of essays under the pseudonym of "Elia"), 1st series 1820–22, 2nd series 1823–25, last 1833 (his most popular production); John Woodvil, 1801, a tragedy; Last Essays, and Popular Fallacies, 1833; Mrs. Lacester's School, 1805 (with his sister Mary); Old Blind Margaret, 1798, a tale; Poems, 1797 (with Coleridge); Poems, 1836, posthumous; Poetry for Children, 1809; Rosamond Gray, 1798, a tale; Specimens of English Dramatic Poets, 1808; Tales from Shakespeare (*i.e.* the tales of Shakespeare's chief dramas, not historic), 1806.   His Life, by Talfourd, 1836; by Procter, 1866; and Percy Fitzgerald, 1895.

LAMBARD or LAMBORDE (*William*), London, 1536–1601.   Archaionomia (ancient laws, books, and customs of the English), 1568; College of the Poor (*i.e.* Greenwich), 1576; Dictionarium Angliæ Topographicum et Historicum, 1730, posthumous; Duties of Constables, etc., 1582; Eirenarcha, in two books (office of J.P.), 1581; Pandecta Rotulorum, 1601; Perambulation of Kent, 1570, 1576 (the first county history, and still a model of the class).   His Life, added to the edition of his works, Chatham, 1826.

LAMBERT (*Aylmer Bourke*), 1761–1842.   Description of the Genus Pinus, 1803–37; Illustration of the Genus Cinchona, 1797.

LANDEN (*John*), Peakirk, near Peterborough, 1719–1790.   Mathematical Lucubrations, 1755; Mathematical Memoirs, 1780, 1790; Residual Analysis, 1758, 1764.

LANDER (*Richard*), Truro, in Cornwall, 1804–1834.   Journal of an Expedition to explore . . . the Niger, 1832; Records of Captain Clapperton's Last Expedition in Africa, 1830.

LANDON (*Letitia Elizabeth*), Mrs. *Maclean*, wrote under the initials "L. E. L.," London, 1802–1838.   Duty and Inclination, 1838; Ethel Churchill, 1837, a novel; Fate of Adelaide (*The*), 1821, a Swiss tale in verse (her first work); Francisca Carrara, 1834, a romance; Golden Violet (*The*), and other Poems, 1827; Improvisatrice (*The*), and other Poems, 1824; Lady Anne Granard, 1841, a novel, posthumous; Lost Pleiad (*The*), 1829; Romance and Reality, 1832, a novel; Traits and Trials of Early Life 1836, tales; Troubadour (*The*), and other Poems, 1825; Venetian Bracelet (*The*), and other Poems, 1829; Vow of the Peacock (*The*), 1835; Zenana (*The*), and minor Poems, 1839, posthumous.   Her Life, by Miss Roberts, 1839; L. Blanchard, 1841.

LANDOR (*Walter Savage*), Ipsley Court, in Warwickshire, 1775–1864.   Admonition to Detractors, 1837; Andrea of Hungary, 1839, a drama; Anthony and Octavius, 1856; Count Julian, 1812; Dry Sticks

faggoted, 1857; Examination of William Shakespeare (*The*), 1834; Fra Ruperto, 1841; Gebir, 1798, a poem, translated into Latin 1813; Giovanni of Naples, 1839, a drama; Hebrew Lyrics, 1859; Hellenics (*The*), 1847; Heroic Idylls, with Additional Poems, 1863; Idyllia Heroica (in Latin), 1820; Imaginary Conversations of Greeks and Romans, 1853; Imaginary Conversations of Literary Men, 1824–28, second series 1829; Imaginary Conversations . . . on Italian Affairs, 1848; Last Fruit off an Old Tree, 1853; Latin Poems, 1824; Letters of an American (under the pseudonym of "Pottinger"), 1854; Letters of a Conservative, 1836; Pentameron and Pentalogia (*The*), 1837; Pericles and Aspasia, 1836; Poems, 1795; Poems from the Arabic, etc., 1800; Popery, British and Foreign, 1851; Simoniaca, 1806, a poem; Satire on Satirists, 1836.   His Life, by Foster, 1876; Sidney Colvin, 1881.)

LANE (*Edward William*), 1801–1870.   Arabian Nights (translated), 1841 (last edited 1853); Arabian Society in the Middle Ages, 1883; Arabian Tales, 1845; Arabic Lexicon, parts i.–vii., 1867 (the first fasciculus of part viii. was published in 1887); Manners and Customs of the Modern Egyptians, 1836; Selections from the Kur-ân, 1843.

LANE (Sir *Richard*), died 1650.   Reports in the Court of Exchequer in the Reign of King James, 1657, posthumous.

LANE-POOLE (*Stanley*), London, 1854–   .   Additions to the Oriental Coins, 1890; Arabian Society in the Middle Ages, 1883; Art of the Saracens in Egypt, 1886; Aurangzib, 1893; Barbary Corsairs (*The*), 1890; Cairo, 1892; Catalogue of Arabic Glass Weights, 1891; Catalogue of Indian Coins, 1884–92; Catalogue of Oriental Coins, 1875–83 (for British Museum); Catalogue of the Mohammedan Coins in the Bodleian, 1888; Coins and Medals, 1885; Coins of the Urtuki Turkomans, 1874; Essays in Oriental Numismatics, 1872–77; Life of E. W. Lane, 1877; Life of Stratford Canning, 1888; Life of Sir Henry Parkes, 1894 (with F. V. Dickens); Mogul Emperors (*The*), 1892; Mohammedan Dynasties, 1893; Moors in Spain (*The*), 1886 (with A. Gilman); Picturesque Egypt, 1883; Prose Writings of Jonathan Swift, 1884; Social Life in Egypt, 1884; Speeches of Mohammed, 1882; Studies in a Mosque, 1883; Turkey, 1888.

LANFRANC, archbishop of Canterbury, born at Pavia, in Italy, 1005–1089.   De Corpore et Sanguine Domini Nostri, 1080; Opera Omnia, ex editione L. Dacherii, 1648.

LANG (*Andrew*), Selkirk, in Scotland, pseudonym "Hugo Longway," 1844–   .   Angling Sketches, 1891; Animal Story Book (*The*), 1896; Aucassin and Nicolète (trans.), 1887; Ballades (xxii.) in Blue China, 1880; Ballades (xxxii.) in Blue China, 1881; Ballads and Lyrics of Old France, 1872; Ballads and Verses Vain, 1884; Ballads of Books, 1888; Ban et Arrière Ban, 1894; Blue Poetry Book (*The*), 1891 (edited by A. Lang); Books and Bookmen, 1886; Book of Dreams and Ghosts, 1897; Cock-Lane and Common Sense, 1894; Collection of Ballads, 1897 (edited by A. Lang, first of a series to be known as "The Diamond Library"); Custom and Myth, 1884; Days of Jeanne D'Arc, 1896, a romance; Essays in Little, 1891; Gold of Fairnilee, 1888; Grass of Parnassus, 1888; He, 1887 (with W. Pollock); Helen of Troy, 1882; Homer and the Epic, 1893; How to fail in Literature, 1890; In the Wrong Paradise, 1886; Johnny Nut and the Golden Goose (trans.), 1887; Letters on Literature, 1889; Letters to Dead Authors, 1886; Library (The), 1881; Life of John Gibson Lockhart, 1896; Life, etc., of Sir Stafford Northcote, 1890; Lost Leaders, 1889; Mark of Cain, 1886; Modern Mythology, 1897; Monk of Fife (A), 1896 (3rd edition); Much Darker Days, 1884; Myth, Ritual, and Religion, 1887; Old Friends, 1890; Oxford, 1880; Pickle the Spy, 1897; Politics of Aristotle, 1886; Prince Prigio, 1889; Prince Ricardo, etc., 1893; Princess Nobody, 1884; Red True Story Book, 1895 (edited by Andrew Lang); Rhymes à-la-Mode, 1884; St. Andrews, 1893; True Story Book (The), 1893; World's Desire (The), 1890 (with Rider Haggard). He translated Bion, Theocritus, etc., 1880. He edited Blue Fairy Book (The), 1890; Green Fairy Book (The), 1892; My Own Fairy Book, 1895; Pink Fairy Book (The), 1897; Red Fairy Book (The), 1890; Yellow Fairy Book (The), 1894.

LANGBAINE (Gerard), Oxford, 1656-1692. Account of the English Dramatick Poets, 1691; Lives, etc., of the English Dramatick Poets, 1699; Momus Triumphans, or the Plagiaries of the English Stage exposed, 1688; New Catalogue of English Plays, 1688 (the only catalogue to be relied on).

LANGFORD, LL.D. (John Alfred), Birmingham, in Warwickshire, 1823-   . Century of Birmingham Life (A), 1868; Drama of Life (A), 1852; English Democracy, 1855; Lamp of Life (The), 1856, a poem; Modern Birmingham, 1874-77; Pleasant Spots, etc., 1862; Poems of the Fields, etc., 1860; Prison Books and their Authors, 1861; Religion and Education, 1852; Staffordshire and Warwickshire, 1874.

LANGHORNE, D.D. (John), Westmoreland, 1735-1779. Country Justice (The), 1774-75, in three parts (verse); Death of Adonis (The), in verse; Enlargement of the Mind (The); Genius and Valour, 1765, a pastoral poem (for which the Scotch conferred on him the degree of D.D.); Solyman and Alcmēna, 1762, a tale in verse; Tables of Flora (translated into verse); Tears of the Muses (The); Visions of Fancy. Prose: Letters of Theodosius and Constantia, 1763; Plutarch's Lives (translated), 1771. His Life, by his son, 1802; by Anderson.

LANGLAND (William), Cleobury Mortimer, in Cheshire, 1332-1400. Vision of Piers Plowman, 1362, a satirical poem in alliterative verse.

LANKESTER (Edwin Ray), London, 1847-   . Advancement of Science, 1889; Comparative Longevity, 1870; Degeneration, 1880; Developmental History of the Mollusca,

1875; Limulus, an Arachnid, 1881; Monograph of the Cephalaspidian Fishes, 1870; Spolia Maris, 1889; Zoological Articles, 1891.

LANOE (Falconer), pseudonym of Mary Elizabeth Hawker. Cecilia de Noel, 1891; Mlle. Ixe, 1890; Hotel d' Angleterre, 1891.

LARDNER, LL.D. (Dionysius), Dublin, 1793-1859. Cabinet Cyclopædia (62 treatises by different authors), 1829-46; Cabinet Library (The), 1830-32; Discourse on the Advantages of Natural Philosophy, 1828; Handbook of Natural Philosophy and Astronomy, 1851-53; Lectures on the Steam Engine, 1828; Museum of Science and Art, 1853-56; Treatise on Algebraic Geometry, 1825; Treatise on Differential and Integral Calculus, 1825.

LARDNER, D.D. (Nathaniel), Hawkhurst, in Kent, 1684-1768. Counsels of Prudence, 1735; Credibility of the Gospel History, 1727-57; Supplement, 1756-57,(invaluable); Demoniacs of the New Testament (The), 1758; Jewish and Heathen Testimonies, 1764-67; Histories of the Apostles and Evangelists, 1760; Vindication of Three of our . . . [Lord's] Miracles, 1729. Paley's Evidences are borrowed wholesale from these books. His Life, by Kippis, 1788.

LARWOOD (Jacob) (pseudonym of S. R. Sadler). Book of Clerical Anecdote, 1871; Forensic Anecdotes, 1882; History of Sign Boards, 1867 (with J. C. Hotten); Story of the London Parks (The), 1872; Theatrical Anecdotes, 1882.

LATHAM, M.D. (John), Eltham, in Kent, 1740-1837. General History of Birds, 1821-24; General Synopsis of Birds, 1781-87 (good); Index Ornithologicus, 1791.

LATHAM, M.D. (Robert Gordon), Billingborough, in Lincolnshire, 1812-   . Descriptive Ethnology, 1859; English Grammar, 1843; English Language (The), 1855; Ethnology of Europe, 1852; Ethnology of the British Colonies, 1851; Frithiof's Saga and Axell, 1840 (trans. from the Swedish); History and Etymology of the English Language; Johnson's Dictionary (a new edition), 1870; Man and his Migrations, 1851; Nationalities of Europe, 1863; Natural History of the Varieties of Man, 1850; Norway and the Norwegians, 1840 (his first work); Outlines of General Philology, 1878; Russian and Turk (The), 1878; Varieties of Man, 1851.

LATIMER (Hugh), bishop of Worcester, born at Thurcaston, in Leicestershire, 1490-1555. Seven Sermons before Edward VI., 1562, posthumous; Seven Sermons preached in Lincolnshire, 1571, posthumous; Seven Sermons on the Lord's Prayer, 1562, posthumous; Sermons on the Ploughers, 1549. His Life, by Gilpin, 1780; Watkins, 1824; and Demaus, 1869.

LAUD, D.D. (William), archbishop of Canterbury, born at Reading, in Berkshire, 1573-1645. Autobiography, 1839, posthumous; Diary, 1694, posthumous; History of his Troubles and Trials, 1695-1700, posthumous. His Life, by Prynne, 1644; Heylyn, 1668; C. W. Lebas; J. Parker, 1829; Lawson, 1829; Baines, 1855. (See LAUD, p. 594.)

LAUDER (*George*), called "the Scottish Souldier," seventeenth century. Aretophel, 1634, an elegy on Walter, earl of Buccleugh ; Breda Exultans, 1667, a poem on the Peace ; Caledonia's Covenant, 1641 ; Souldier's Wish (*The*), 1628 ; Sunt Artibus Arma Decori, 1629 ; Tears on the Death of Evander, 1630; Tweed's Tears of Joy to King Charles, 1639.

LAUDER (Sir *Thomas'Dick*), near Edinburgh, 1784-1848. Great Floods in Moray, 1829 ; Highland Rambles, 1837 ; Legendary Tales of the Highlands, 1841 ; Lochander, 1825, a romance ; Tour round the Coast of Scotland, 1842 ; Wolf of Badenoch (*The*), 1827.

LAUDER (*William*), Scotland, 1710-1771. Essay on Milton's Use and Imitation of the Moderns, 1750 (this essay contains false quotations from Masenius, Taubmann, and Staphorstius, with intent of proving Milton to have been a plagiarist) ; Grand Impostor detected (*The*), 1754 (the confession of his imposition).

LAURENCE (*Richard*), archbishop of Cashel, 1761-1838. Dissertation on the "Logos" of St. John, 1808 ; Doctrine of Baptismal Regeneration (*The*), 1815 ; Efficacy of Baptism, 1816 ; Tracts, Theological and Critical, 1819 (admirable).

LAVINGTON (*George*), bishop of Exeter, 1683-1762. Enthusiasm of Methodists and Papists compared (in three parts), 1749-51 (much esteemed).

LAW, D.D. (*Edmund*), bishop of Carlisle, born at Cartmel, in Lancashire, 1703-1787. Considerations on the Theory of Religion, 1745 (a very valuable work); Enquiry into the Ideas of Space and Time, 1735 ; Translation of King's Essay on the *Origin of Evil*, 1731. His Life, by Dr. Paley, 1820.

LAW (Rev. *William*), Kingscliffe, in Northamptonshire, 1686-1761. Remarks on the Fable of the Bees, 1724 (one of the best essays in the language) ; Serious Call, 1729 (his chief work) ; Unlawfulness of Stage Entertainments (*The*), 1726 ; Ways to Divine Knowledge, 1752. His Life, by R. Tighe, 1813.

LAWES (*Henry*), 1600-1662. Ayres and Dialogues, 1653, 1655, 1698 ; Choice Psalmes put into Musick for Three Voices, 1648 ; Music to Milton's *Comus*, 1634.

LAWLESS (Hon. *Emily*), 1845- . Grania, 1892 ; Hurrish, 1886 ; Maelcho, 1894 ; Major Lawrence, F.L.S., 1887 ; Millionaire's Cousin (*A*), 1885 ; Plain Frances Mowbray, 1889 ; Story of Ireland, 1887 ; With Essex in Ireland, 1890.

LAWRENCE (*Frederick*), Bisham, in Berkshire, 1821-1867. Life of Fielding, 1855.

LAWRENCE (Sir *William*), Cirencester, in Gloucestershire, surgeon, 1783-1867. Comparative Anatomy, etc., 1819 ; Lectures on the Physiology, Zoology, and Natural History of Man, 1819 (this book was suppressed, and is scarce) ; Treatise on Hernia, 1807 ; Treatise on Venereal Diseases of the Eye, 1830 (very valuable).

LAYAMON, priest of Ernely, in Worcestershire, thirteenth century. Brut d'Angleterre (*The*), a translation of Wace's *Brut* in French.

∵ Sir Frederick Madden edited the entire

chronicle for the Society of Antiquaries, 1847. It is probably the oldest specimen of native verse extant. The lines are in six or seven syllables; sometimes the yrhyme, but generally the metre is alliterative only ; thus—

> *He gef seolver, he gef gold,*
> *He gef hors, he gef lond,*
> *Castles and cluthes eke.*

LAYARD (Sir *Austin Henry*), born in Paris of English parents, 1817- . Monuments of Nineveh, 1849-53; Nineveh and its Remains, 1848-49 (a standard work).

LEACH (*Thomas*), *-*. Cases of Crown-Law determined by the Twelve Judges in the Court of King's Bench, 1730-55, 1815 (highly esteemed).

LEACH, M.D. (*William Elford*), Plymouth, 1790-1836. History of the British Crustacea, 1815; Malacostraca Podophthalma Britanniæ, 1817-21; Mollusca of Great Britain arranged (*The*), 1852; Systematic Catalogue of the Mammalia and Birds . . . in the British Museum, 1816; Zoological Miscellany (*The*), 1814-17.

LEADE (*Jane*), mystic, 1623-1704. Fountain of Gardens, etc. (*The*), 1678-86; Heavenly Cloud now breaking (*The*), 1681 ; Revelation of God and His Glory, 1665 ; Revelation of Revelations, 1683; Tree of Faith (*The*), 1696 ; Wars of King David, etc., 1680 ; Wonders of God's Creation manifested, 1695.

LEAKE (*Stephen Martin*), 1702-1774. Life of Sir John Leake (admiral), 1750 ; Nummi Britannici Historia, 1726; Statutes of the . . . Order of the Garter, 1766 ; Statutes of the . . . Order of St. George, 1766.

LEAKE, LL.D. (*William Martin*), 1777-1860. Historical Outline of the Greek Revolution, 1826 ; Journal of a Tour in Asia Minor, etc., 1824 ; Numismata Hellenica, 1854 (valuable) ; Peloponnesiaca, 1824 (supplement to "Travels in the Morea"); Researches in Greece, etc., 1814 ; Topography of Athens (*The*), 1821 ; Travels in Northern Greece, 1835, 1841; Travels in the Morea, 1830.

LEATHES, D.D. (*Stanley*), Ellesborough, in Buckinghamshire, 1830- . Characteristics of Christianity, 1884 ; Christ and the Bible, 1885 ; Christian Creed (*The*), its Theory and Practice, 1878 ; Foundations of Morality (*The*), 1882; Gospel its own Witness (*The*), 1874 (a Hulsean lecture) ; Law in the Prophets (*The*), 1891 ; Old Testament Prophecy, 1880 ; Religion of Christ (*The*), 1874 (a Bampton lecture) ; Structure of the Old Testament (*The*), 1873 ; Truth and Life, 1872 ; Witness of St. John to Christ, 1870 ; Witness of the Old Testament to Christ, 1868 (a Boyle lecture).

LECKY (*William Edward Hartpole*), Dublin, 1838- . Democracy and Liberty, 1896 ; Empire (*The*), its Value and its Growth, 1893 ; History of England in the eighteenth century, 1878-1890 ; History of European Morals, 1869 ; History of Rationalism, 1865; History of the Rise and Influence of Rationalism, etc., 1865; Leaders of Public Opinion in Ireland, 1861 ; Poems, 1891; Political Value of History, 1892.

LEDWICH (*Edward*), Ireland, 1739-1823. Antiquities of Ireland, 1793 (valuable).

LEE, D.C.L. (Rev. *Frederick George*), Stantonbury, in Buckinghamshire, 1832– . Beauty of Holiness (*The*), 1860; Bells of Botteville Tower, and other Poems, 1871; Book of the Epistles, 1867; Book of the Gospels, 1867; Christian Doctrine of Prayer for the Departed, 1872; Church under Queen Elizabeth (*The*), 1880; Communion of the Church of Scotland, 1869; Death, Judgment, Hell, and Heaven (in four sermons), 1858; Dictionary of Liturgical and Ecclesiastical Terms, 1871; Directorium Anglicanum, 1865; Glimpses of the Supernatural, 1874, 1878; Glossary of Liturgical and Ecclesiastical Terms, 1876; Historical Sketch of the Reformation, 1879; Gospel Message (*The*), 1860; King's Highway (*The*), and other Poems, 1866; Lyrics of Life and Light, 1874; Manual of Devotion for the Blessed Sacrament, 1866; Manuale Clericorum, 1874; Martyrs of Vienne and Lyons (*The*), 1861; Memorials of R. S. Hawker, 1876; Message of Reconciliation, 1859; Paraphrastica Expositis Articulorum Confessionis Anglicane, 1865; Petronilla, and other Poems, 1858; Poems, 1854; Rest in Death, 1872; Truth as it is in Jesus, 1868; Validity of the Holy Orders of the Church of England, 1869; Words from the Cross, 1856.

LEE (*Harriet*), the younger of two sisters, London (published two novels and three dramas), 1756-1851. Canterbury Tales, 1797-1805 (with her sister Sophia); Clara Lennox, 1797, a novel; Errors of Innocence, 1786, a novel; Mysterious Marriage (*The*), 1795, a drama; New Peerage (*The*), 1787, a drama; Three Strangers (*The*), 1835, a drama. See LEE (*Sophia*).

LEE (*Henry*), Virginia, U.S., 1756-1816. Memoirs of the War in the Southern . . . States, 1809 (an excellent work).

LEE (*James*), Hammersmith, 1730-1795. Introduction to the Linnæan System of Botany, 1760 (much esteemed).

LEE (*John Edward*), Newland, near Hull, 1808– . Isca Silurum, 1862; Roman Imperial Photographs, 1874; and 160 Profiles, 1874; Translations of Dr. Keller's *Lake Dwellings*, 1866; and C. Merk's *Excavations at the Kesslerloch*, 1876.

LEE (*Nathaniel*), Hatfield, in Hertfordshire, 1657-1691. *Wrote 11 tragedies:* Alexander the Great, or the Rival Queens, 1671 (his best); Lucius Junius Brutus, 1679; Massacre of Paris (*The*), 1690; Mithridātes (4 *syl.*), 1674; Nero, Emperor of Rome, 1675; Œdipus, 1679 (with Dryden); Princess of Cleves (*The*), 1689; Rival Queens; see above, "Alexander," etc.; Theodosius, 1680. ∴ Helped Dryden in *The Duke of Guise*, 1682.

LEE, D.D. (*Samuel*), Longnor, in Shropshire, 1783-1852. Book of Job, 1837; Events and Times of the Visions of Daniel, etc., 1851 (well esteemed); Hebrew, Chaldaic, and English Lexicon, 1844; Hebrew Grammar, 1827; Sermons on the Study of the Holy Scriptures, 1830; Travels of Ibn Batuta, 1833; Visions of Daniel, 1851.

LEE (*Sophia*), elder sister of Harriet Lee, London (she published three dramas and two tales), 1750-1824. Almeyda, Queen of Grenáda, 1796, a tragedy; Assignation (*The*), 1807, a comedy; Chapter of Accidents, 1780, a comedy; Life of a Lover (*The*), 1804, a comedy; Recess (*The*), 1784, a comedy. The two sisters published *The Canterbury Tales*. These are original stories quite independent of Chaucer's tales. See LEE (*Harriet*).

LEE (*Vernon*), pseudonym of *Violet Paget*, 1857– . Althea, 1893; Baldwin, 1886; Belcaro, 1882; Countess of Albany, 1884; Euphorion, 1884; Hauntings, 1890; Juvenilia, 1887; Miss Brown, 1884; Ottilie, 1883; Phantom Lover, 1886; Prince of the Hundred Soups, 1882; Renaissance Fancies and Studies, 1895; Story of a Puppet Show, 1889; Studies of the 18th Century in Italy, 1880; Vanitas, 1892.

LEE, D.D. (*William*), Ireland, 1815-1883. Inspiration of Holy Scripture, 1852 (Donnelan lectures); Introductory Lectures on Ecclesiastical History, 1858.

LEECH (*John*), London, 1817-1864 (known by his contributions to *Punch*). Pictures of Life and Character, 1854; Rising Generation, (*The*), 1848.

LEES (*Edwin*), Worcester, 1800– . Affinities of Plants and Animals; Botany of Worcestershire, 1868; Forest and Chase of Malvern, etc., 1877; Scenery and Thought in Poetical Pictures, etc., 1880.

LEES, Phil. Doc. (*Frederic Richard*), Meanwood Hall, near Leeds, 1815– . Argument for the Suppression of the Liquor Traffic, 1856 (100-guinea prize); Metaphysics of Owenism dissected (*The*), 1837; Science of Symbolism, etc., 1845; Temperance Bible Commentary (*The*), 1866 (with D. Burns); Text-book of Temperance (*The*), 1863; Truth-seeker in Literature, etc. (*The*), 1845-50.

LE GALLIENNE (*Richard*), Liverpool, 1866– . Book-Bills of Narcissus, 1891; English Poems, 1892; George Meredith, 1890; If I were God, 1897; My Ladies' Sonnets, etc., 1887; Prose Fancies, etc., 1894-96; Quest of the Golden Girl, 1896; Religion of a Literary Man, 1893; Retrospective Reviews, 1896; Robert Louis Stevenson, 1895, an elegy; Student (*The*) and the Body-Snatcher, 1890 (with R. K. Leathes); Volumes in Folio, 1888.

LEIGH (*Charles*), Lancashire, 1650-1710. Natural History of Lancashire, Cheshire, and the Peak in Derbyshire, 1700; Phthisiologia Lancastriensis, 1694.

LEIGH (Sir *Edward*), Leicestershire, 1602-1671. Annotations on the Poetical Books of the Old Testament, 1657; Critica Sacra, 1639 (an excellent work); Observations Concerning the Twelve Cæsars, 1635; Observations on all the Kings of England, 1662; Treatise of Religion and Learning, 1656.

LEIGHTON (*Robert*), archbishop of Glasgow, 1613-1684. Commentary of the First Epistle of St. Peter, 1693, posthumous; Posthumous Tracts, 1708; Prælectiones Theologicæ, 1693, posthumous; Rules for a Holy Life, 1708, posthumous; Sermons, 1692, posthumous. His Life, by W. Wilson, D.D., 1746; West, 1871; G. Jerment, 1808; Pearson, 1825; Burnet.

LELAND (*Charles Godfrey*), pseudonym "Hans Breitman," of Philadelphia, U.S., 1824– . Egyptian Sketch-book (*The*), 1873; English Gipsies and their Language (*The*), 1873; English Gipsy Songs, 1875; Fu-Sang, or the Discovery of America by Buddhist Priests, 1875; Gipsy Sorcery and Fortune-telling, 1896; Hans Breitmann's Ballads, 1867, 1870; Legends of Birds, 1863; Manual of Mending and Repairing, 1896; Meister Karl's Sketch-book, 1855; Music Lessons of Confucius (*The*), and other Poems, 1870; Poetry and Mystery of Dreams (*The*), 1855; Sunshine in Thought, 1862.

LELAND (*John*), 1506-1552. Assertio Inclytissimi Arturi Regis Britanniæ, 1554, posthumous; Commentarii de Scriptoribus Britannicis, 1709, posthumous; De Rebus Britannicis Collectanea, 1715, posthumous; Genethliacon Illustrissimi Eduardi Principis Cambriæ, 1543; Itinerary of England, 1710–12, posthumous; Laudatio Pacis, 1546; Næniæ in Mortem Henrici Duddolegi Equitatis, 1544; Thomæ Viati Equitatis, 1542; Principum ac Illustrium Aliquot . . . in Anglia Virorum Encomia, 1589, posthumous; Serche for Englandes Antiquitees, 1549. His Life, by Huddesford, 1772.

LELAND, D.D. (*John*), Wigan, in Lancashire, 1691-1766. Advantage and Necessity of the Christian Religion (*The*), 1764; Chief Deistical Workers of the XVII. and XVIII. Centuries, 1754; Christianity as Old as Creation, 1733; Defence of Christianity, 1740; Divine Authority of the [Bible], 1739–1740; View of the Principal Deistical Writers, 1754.

LELAND, D.D. (*Thomas*), Dublin, 1722-1785. History of Ireland, 1773 (much praised); History of Philip of Macedon, 1758.

LEMON (*Mark*), London, 1809-1870. Christmas Hamper (*A*), 1859, a novel; Enchanted Doll (*The*), 1849, a novel; Falkner Lyle, 1866, a novel; Jest-Book, 1864, a compilation of anecdotes; Loved at Last, 1864, a novel; Wait for the End, 1863, a novel. And 60 dramatic pieces.

LEMPRIÈRE, D.D. (*John*), Jersey, a Channel Isle, 1765-1824. Classical Dictionary, 1788 (once a standard work); Universal Biography, 1808.

LE NEWE (*John*), London, 1679-1741. Fasti Ecclesiæ Anglicanæ, 1716; Lives, etc., of the Protestant Bishops of the Church of England, 1720; Monumenta Anglicana, 1717-19.

LENNOX (*Charlotte*), New York, U.S., 1720-1804. Female Quixote (*The*), 1752; Novels and Histories on which the Plays of Shakespeare are founded, 1753-54; Poems, 1747.

LENNOX (Lord *William Pitt*), 1799-1881. Adventures of a Man of Family, 1864; Celebrities I have Known, 1867; Compton Audley, 1841; Drafts on my Memory, 1865;

Fifty Years' Biographical Reminiscences, 1863; Merrie England, its Sports and Pastimes, 1857, 1863; Percy Hamilton, 1852; Philip Courtenay, 1857; Pictures of Sporting Life and Character, 1859; Recreations of a Sportsman, 1862; Story of my Life (*The*), 1857 : Tuft Hunters, 1843.

LESLEY (*John*), bishop of Ross, born in Scotland, 1527-1596. Defence of Marie Quene of Scotland, 1569; De Origine Moribus et Rebus Gestis Scotorum, 1578 (his chief work); De Titulo et Jure Mariæ Scotorum Reginæ, 1580.

LESLIE (Rev. *Charles*), Ireland, 1650-1722. Short and Easy Method with Deists, 1694.

LESLIE, R.A. (*Charles Robert*), London, 1794–1859. Autobiographical Recollections, 1866 (edited by Tom Taylor); Handbook for Young Painters, 1845; Life of Constable, 1845 (a first-class biography).

LESLIE (Sir *John*), Largo, in Fifeshire, Scotland, natural philosopher, 1766-1832. Elements of Geometry, 1809; Inquiry into the Nature and Propagation of Heat, 1804 (valuable); Philosophy of Arithmetic, 1817. His Life, by Macvey Napier, 1834.

LESTRANGE (Sir *Roger*), Norfolk, 1616-1704. Brief History of the Times (*A*), 1687; Memento, 1662; Translation of Æsop's Fables, 1692, of Josephus, 1702, Colloquies of Erasmus, etc.

LETTSOM, M.D. (*John Coakley*), West Indies, 1744-1815. Life of Fothergill, 1783; Natural History of the Tea Tree, 1772; Naturalist's and Traveller's Companion, 1772. His Life, by T. J. Pettigrew, 1817. His epigram contains a pun on his name—

When people's ill they comes to I;
I physics, bleeds, and sweats 'em.
Sometimes they live, sometimes they die;
What's that to I?—I let's 'em (Lettsom).

LETTSOM (*William Nanson*), 1796-1865. Translated into English verse the Nibelungenlied (called the "German *Iliad*"), 1850.

LEVER (*Charles James*), Dublin, novelist, 1809-1872. Barrington, 1863; Bramleighs of Bishop's Folly (*The*), 1858; Charles O'Malley, 1841; Con Cregan, or the Irish Gil Blas, 1850; Daltons (*The*), 1852; Davenport Dunn, 1859; Day's Ride (*A*), 1863; Diary of Horace Templeton, 1861; Dodd Family Abroad (*The*), 1854; Fortunes of Glencore (*The*), 1857; Harry Lorrequer (*Adventures of*), 1839; Jack Hinton, 1842; Knight of Gwynne (*The*), 1847; Lord Kilgobbin, 1872; Luttrel of Arran, 1865; Martins of Cro' Martin (*The*), 1856; O'Donoghue (*The*), 1845; Paul Gosslett's Confession, 1871; Roland Cashel, 1849; Sir Brooke Fosbrooke, 1866; That Boy of Norcott's, 1869; Tom Burke of Ours, 1844; Tony Butler, 1865. His Life, 1879.

LEVI (*David*), London, 1740-1799. Defence of the Old Testament, 1797; Dissertation on the Prophecies of the Old Testament, 1793; Lingua Sacra, 1785-89 (valuable); Pentateuch in Hebrew and English, 1789; Rites and Ceremonies of the Jews, 1783.

LEWES (*George Henry*), London, 1817-1878. Aristotle, 1861; Biographical History of

Philosophy, 1847; Comte's Philosophy of the Sciences, 1859; History of Philosophy (from Thales to Comte), 1867 ; Life of Goethe, 1859 (the best "Life") ; Life of Robespierre, 1850l; Noble Heart (*The*), 1850, a tragedy; Physical Basis of Mind, 1877; Physiology of Common Life, 1860; Problems of Life and Mind, 1873-76; Ranthorpe, 1847, a tale; Rose, Blanche, and Violet, 1848; Seaside Studies, 1859; Spanish Drama (*The*), 1848 (Lope de Vega and Calderon); Studies in Animal Life, 1861.

N.B.—For "Mrs. George Henry Lewes," see ELIOT (*George*).

LEWIN (*Thomas*), 1805-1877. Cæsar's Invasion of Britain, 1862; Jerusalem, a Sketch of the City and Temple, 1861; Life and Epistles of St. Paul, 1851.

LEWIS (Sir *George Cornewall*), Radnorshire, 1806-1863. Astronomy of the Ancients, 1861 ; Dialogue on the Best Form of Government, 1863; Glossary of Herefordshire Provincial Words, 1839; Influence of Authority in Matters of Opinion, 1849; Inquiry into the Credibility of the Early Roman History, 1855; On Local Disturbances in Ireland, etc., 1836; On the Government of Dependencies, 1841; Origin and Formation of the Romance Languages, 1835; Remarks on the Use and Abuse of Political Terms, 1832; Treatise on the Method of Observation, etc., in Politics, 1852.

LEWIS (Rev. *John*), "of Margate," born at Bristol, antiquary, 1675-1746. Antiquity and Use of Seals in England, 1736; Apology for the Church of England, 1714 ; Complete History of the Several Translations of the Bible into English, 1739; History and Antiquities of Faversham Church, Kent, 1727 ; History and Antiquities of the Isle of Tenet, in Kent, 1723; History of Anabaptism, 1738; Life and Sufferings of Wickliffe, 1720 ; Life of Bishop Pecocke, 1744 ; Life of Mayster Wyllyam Caxton, 1737; Wickliffe's Translation of the New Testament, 1731.

LEWIS (*Matthew Gregory*), called "Monk Lewis," London, 1775-1818. Alonzo the Brave and the Fair Imogene, a ballad ; Bravo of Venice (*The*), 1804, a novel; Feudal Tyrants, in verse ; Jamaica Journal (excellent); Journal of a West India Proprietor, 1834 ; Monk (*The*), 1795, a romance (which gave him the sobriquet of "Monk Lewis"); Romantic Tales, 1808 ; Tales of Terror, 1799 ; Tales of Wonder, 1801 (called by Byron "Tales of Plunder").

Plays : Adelgitha, 1806 ; Adelmorn, or the Outlaw, 1801; Alonzo, King of Castile, 1801, an historic play ; Captive (*The*), 1839, posthumous, a melodrama ; Castle Spectre (*The*), 1797, a dramatic romance ; East Indian (*The*), 1800, a comedy ; Minister (*The*), 1797, a tragedy ; One O'clock, or the Wood Demon, 1811, an operatic romance ; Rich and Poor, 1812, a comic opera ; Rolla, 1799, a tragedy ; Runantio, 1806 ; Timour the Tartar, 1812, a melodrama ; Veroni, 1809.

LEWIS (*Samuel*), topographer, 1799-1854. Topographical Dictionary of England, 1831-33 ; Topographical Dictionary of Ireland, 1837 ;

Topographical Dictionary of Scotland, 1846 ; Topographical Dictionary of Wales, 1833.

LEWIS (*Taylor*), Northumberland, in the state of New York, U.S., 1802-1877. Science and the Bible, 1856 ; Six Days of Creation, etc. (*The*), 1855.

LEWIS (Lady *Theresa*), 1803-1865. Clarendon and his Contemporaries, 1852; Journals and Correspondence of Miss Berry, 1865.

LEWIS (*Thomas*), 1684-1730. History of the Parthian Empire, 1728; Origines Hebrææ, 1724-25; Scourge (*The*), 1717, 1720.

LEYDEN, M.D. (*John*), 1775-1811. Discoveries and Travels in Africa, 1799 (a valuable work); Poems and Ballads, 1858. posthumous ; Poetical Remains, 1819, posthumous ; Scottish Descriptive Poems, 1803. His Life, by Rev. J. Morton, 1819 ; sir Walter Scott, 1858.

LIDDEL, M.D. (*Duncan*), Aberdeen, 1561-1613. Artis Conservandi Sanitatem, 1651, posthumous. His Life, by J. Stuart, 1790.

LIDDELL, D.D. (*Henry George*), 1811- . Greek Lexicon, 1843 (with Scott); History of Rome, 1855.

LIDDON, D.D. (*Henry Parry*), Stoneham, in Hampshire, 1829-1890. Clerical Life and Work, 1894 ; Divinity of . . . Jesus Christ (*The*), 1867, a Bampton lecture ; Divine Indwelling (*The*), 1868 ; Easter in St. Paul's, 1887 ; Essays and Addresses, 1892 ; Lenten Sermons, 1858 ; Life of E. B. Pusey, 1893 ; Magnificat (*The*), 1889 ; Our Founder's Vow, 1865 ; Passion-tide Sermons, 1891 ; Phœbe in London, 1877 ; Purchas Judgment (*The*), 1871 ; Sermons on Old Testament Subjects, 1891 ; Some Elements of Religion, 1870 ; Some Words for God, 1865 ; Some Words of Christ, 1892 ; There is a Holy Ghost, 1867 ; Thoughts on Present Troubles, 1882; Walter Ken Hamilton, 1869 ; Whole Counsel of God (*The*), 1864. And many other sermons.

LIGHTFOOT, D.D. (*John*), Stoke, in Staffordshire, 1602-1675. Battell with a Wasp's Nest, 1649 ; Description of the Temple Service in the Dayes of Christ, 1650 ; Eurubhim, 1629 ; Harmony of the Gospels, 1644-50 ; Horæ Hebraicæ et Talmudicæ, 1648 (his chief work, but all his works are admirable).

LIGHTFOOT (*John*), Gloucestershire, 1735-1788. Floræ Scoticæ, 1775 (valuable).

LIGHTFOOT, D.D. (*Joseph Barber*), bishop of Durham, born at Liverpool, 1828 – 1890. Apostolic Fathers (*The*), 1869-85, appendix, Clement of Rome, 1877 ; Essays on Supernatural Religion, 1889 ; Leaders in the Northern Church, 1890, posthumous ; Many Members and One Body, 1883, a sermon ; Notes on the "Epistle to the Colossians" 1875, the "Corinthians" 1869, the "Galatians" 1865, the "Philippians" 1868 ; Ordination Addresses, 1890 ; Primary Charge to the Clergy, 1884.

LILBURNE (*John*), Durham, 1618-1657. England's New Chains discovered, 1649 ; Truth's Victory over Tyrants, 1649.

LILLO (*George*), London, 1693-1739. Arden of Feversham, 1762, a tragedy; Elmerick, 1739 (his last tragedy); Fatal Curiosity, 1736, a tragedy (by far his best) ; George Barnwell,

1730, a tragedy (once a stock piece for Boxing-night); Silvia or Sylvia, 1731 (her first play). His Life, by T. Davies, 1770.

LILLY or LYLYE (*John*), called "The Euphuist," Kent, dramatist, 1553-1601. Alexander and Campaspe, 1584, a play; Anatomy of Wit (Euphues), 1579; (Six) Court Comedies, 1632; Endymion, the Man in the Moone, 1591, a play; Euphues, 1581, a description of character; Euphues and his England, 1580; Euphues' Shadow, 1592 (ascribed to T. Lodge, *q.v.*); Euphues and Lucilla, published 1716; Gallathea, 1593, a play; Love's Metamorphoses, 1601, a pastoral; Maydes Metamorphosis (*The*), 1600; Midas, 1592, a play; Mother Bombie, 1594, a play; Pap with a Hatchet, 1589; Sapho and Phao, 1591, a play; Woman in the Moone (*The*), 1597, a mythological drama.

LILLY (*William*), Leicestershire, 1602-1681. Christian Astrology (in three books), 1659; Collection of the Prophecies which concern these Times, 1645; Compleat Book of Fortune (*The*), 1728, posthumous; Merlinus Anglicus, Junior, 1644; Monarchy and no Monarchy in England, 1651; Starry Messenger (*The*), 1645; World's Catastrophe (*The*), 1647. His Life, by himself, published 1715.

LILLY (*William Samuel*), Fifehead, in Dorsetshire, 1840- . Ancient Religion and Modern Thought, 1884; Century of Revolution (*A*), 1889; Chapters in European History, 1886; Claims of Christianity (*The*), 1894; Four English Humourists of the Nineteenth Century, 1895; Great Enigma (*The*), 1892; On Right and Wrong, 1890; On Shibboleths, 1892.

LILY (*William*), Hampshire, 1466-1523. Antibossicon, 1521; Brevissima Institutio (Lily's Grammar), 1513; Fairest Fairing (*The*), 1776, posthumous.

LINACRE, M.D. (*Thomas*), Canterbury, 1460-1524. De Emendata Structura Latini Sermonis (six books), 1524; De Temperamentis, 1521; Methodus Medendi, 1519. Translation of Galen's *De Sanitate*, 1517. His Life, by J. N. Johnson, 1854.

LINDLEY, Ph.D. (*John*), Catton, near Norwich, 1799-1865. Collectanea Botanica, 1821; Descriptive Botany, 1858; Digitalium Monographia, 1821; First Principles of Botany, 1836; First Principles of Horticulture, 1832; Flora Medica, 1838; Folia Orchidacea, 1852-55; Fossil Flora of Great Britain, 1831-37 (with Hutton); Genera and Species of Orchidaceous Plants, 1837-38; Icones Plantarum Sponte China Nascentium, 1821; Introduction to Botany, 1835; Introduction to the Natural System of Botany, 1830; Introduction to the Structure and Physiology of Plants, 1832; Ladies' Botany, 1848; Medical Botany, 1849; Pomologia Britannica, 1841; Rosarum Monographia, 1820; School Botany, 1849; Synopsis of British Flora, 1829; Theory, etc., of Horticulture, 1840; Vegetable Kingdom (*The*), 1846 (a standard work).

LINDSAY (*Alexander William Crawford*, lord), 1812-1877. Edom and the Holy Land, 1838; Lives of the Lindsays, 1849; Sketches of the History of Christian Art, 1847.

LINDSAY (Sir *David*), called "Lindsay of the Mount," born at Garmylton, in East Lothian, Scotland, 1490-1555. Booke . . . of Armes, 1542; Complaynt of the King's Papyngo, 1530; Deploration of Queen Magdalene, 1536; Dialog betuix Experience and ane Courteour, 1554; Dreme (*The*), 1528; Historie of Squyer William Meldrum, 1550; Monarchie (*The*), 1553; Plesant Satyre of the Three Estaitis (*Ane*), 1602, posthumous; Testament of the Papyngo (*The*), 1530; Tragedie of Fader David [Beatoun], 1558.

LINDSAY (Lady *R. T.*). Flower Seller (*The*), 1896; King's Last Vigil, 1894; Lyrics, 1890; Philosopher's Window (*The*), 1892; String of Beads (*A*), 1892; Tangled Web (*A*), 1892.

LINDSEY (Rev. *Theophilus*), Cheshire, 1723-1808. Apology for resigning the Cure of Catterick, 1773, the Sequel, 1776; Historical View of the State of the Unitarian Doctrine and Worship, 1783; Vindiciæ Priestleianæ, 1788. His Life, by T. Belsham, 1812.

LINGARD, D.D. (*John*), Winchester, 1771-1851. Antiquities of the Saxon Church, 1806; History of England (from Cæsar to William and Mary), 1819-30. His Memoirs, by canon Tierney, 1855.

LINTON (Mrs.), maiden name *Eliza Lynn*, wife of the late W. J. Linton, novelist, generally called "Mrs. Lynn Linton," Keswick, in Cumberland, 1822- . About Ireland, 1890; About Ulster, 1892; Amymone, 1848, a romance (time, Pericles); Atonement of Leam Dundas (*The*), 1876; Autobiography of Christopher Kirkland (*The*), 1885; Azeth, the Egyptian, 1846 (her first novel); Dulcie Everton, 1876; Girl of the Period (*The*), 1883; Grasp your Nettle, 1865; In Haste and at Leisure, 1895; Ione, 1883; Lake Country (*The*), 1864; Lizzie Lorton of Greyrigg, 1866; Mad Willoughbys (*The*), 1875; "My Love!" 1881; Octave of Friends (*An*), 1891; One too Many (*The*), 1894; Ourselves, 1884; Paston Carew, 1886; Patricia Kemball, 1875; Realities, 1851, a story of modern times; Rebel of the Family, 1880; Rift in the Lute, 1885; Sowing the Wind, 1867; Stabbed in the Dark, 1885; Through the Long Night, 1888; True History of Joshua Davidson (*The*), 1872; 'Twixt Cup and Lip, 1896; Under which Lord? 1879; Witch Stories, 1861; With a Silken Thread, 1880; World Well Lost (*The*), 1877.

LINTON (*William James*), husband of the preceding, London, 1812-1898. American Odyssey (*The*), 1876; Claribel, and other Poems, 1865; European Republicans, 1893; Ferns, 1856; Flower of the Star (*The*), 1869; Golden Apples of Hesperus, 1882; History of Wood Engraving in America (*A*), 1882; Ireland for the Irish, 1867; James Watson, 1880; Life of Paine, 1866; Life of J. G. Whittier, 1893; Love-lore, 1887; Masters of Wood Engraving (*The*), 1889; Memories, 1895; Poems, etc., 1889; Poetry of America (*The*), 1878; Pot Pourri, 1875; Practical Hints on Wood Engraving, 1879; Voices of the Dead, 1879; Works of Deceased British Artists, 1860; Wood Engraving, 1884.

LIPPINCOTT (Mrs.), maiden name *Sara Jane Clarke*, pseudonym "Grace Greenwood," born at Pompey, New York, U.S., 1823- . Forest Tragedy (*A*), and other Tales, 1856 ; Greenwood Leaves, 1850-52 ; Haps and Mishaps, etc., 1855 ; History of my Pets, 1850 ; Merrie England, 1855 ; New Life in New Lands, 1873 ; Poems, 1851 ; Recollections of my Childhood, 1851 ; Records of Five Years, 1867 ; Stories and Legends of Travel, 1858 ; Stories and Sights in France, etc., 1867 ; Stories from Famous Ballads, 1860 ; Stories of Many Lands, 1867.

LIPSCOMB, M.D. (*George*), *-*. History and Antiquities of the County of Buckingham, 1831-43 ; Journey into Cornwall (*A*), 1799 ; Journey into South Wales (*A*), 1799.

LISTER, M.D. (*Martin*), Buckinghamshire, 1638-1712. De Cochleis, etc., 1685 ; De Fontibus Medicatis, 1682 ; Historia sive Synopsis Conchyliorum, 1685-93 (a standard work) ; Historiæ Animalium Angliæ Tres Tractatus, 1678.

LISTON (*Robert*), Ecclesmachan, in Scotland, 1794-1848. Elements of Surgery, 1831 ; Practical Surgery, 1837.

LISTON (*Thomas Henry*), novelist and dramatist, 1801-1842. Arlington, 1832 ; Epicharis, 1829 ; Granby, 1826, a novel ; Herbert Lacy, 1827 ; Life of Clarendon, 1838.

LITHGOW (*William*), Lanarkshire, Scotland, foot traveller, 1583-1640. Adventures of XIX. Yeares Travayles, 1614, 1623, 1632, 1640 ; Gushing Teares, etc., 1640 ; Last Siege of Breda, 1637 ; Pilgrimes Farewell to . . . Scotland, 1618, a poem ; Scotland's Teares (for James I.), 1625 ; Scotland's Welcome to King Charles, 1633 ; Siege of Newcastle (*The*), 1645 ; Tracts on London, 1643.

LITTLE (*William*), called "William of Newbury," chronicler, 1128-1198. History of England from the Conquest to his own Times (one of the best of the chronicles ; he rejects the fable of Brutus and the Trojan descent of our race).

LITTLE (*William John Knox*), 1839- . Broken Vow, 1887 ; Child of Stafferton, 1888 ; Christian House, 1891 ; Light of Hope, 1888 ; Meditations, 1880 ; Mystery of the Passion, 1881 ; Witness of the Passion, 1886.

LITTLETON, D.D. (*Adam*), Shropshire, 1627-1694. Latin and English Dictionary, 1678 (noted for the blunder "concurro, to condog," a pun between -*cur* and -*dog*).

LITTLETON (Sir *Thomas*). See LYTTELTON.

LIVINGSTONE (Dr. *David*), Blantyre, in Scotland, 1817-1873. Expedition to the Zambesi, 1865 ; Last Journal, 1874, posthumous ; Missionary Travels and Researches in South Africa, 1857. His Life, by W. G. Blaikie, 1881.

LLEWELLYN, M.D. (*Martin*), 1616-1680. Elegy on the Death of Henry, Duke of Gloucester, 1660 ; Marrow of the Muses (*The*), 1661 ; Men, Miracles, and other Poems, 1656 ; Wickham Wakened, 1672.

LLOYD (Rev. *David*), Wales, 1625-1691. Countess of Bridgewater's Ghost (*The*), 1663 (he was imprisoned for this) ; History of Plots and Conspiracies, 1664 ; Legend of Captain Jones, 1636 (a capital burlesque) ;

Life of General Monk, 1660 ; Memoires of those who Suffered for the Protestant Faith, 1637-66 ; Statesmen and Favourites of England, 1665 ; Wonders no Miracles, 1666.

LLOYD (*Henry Humphrey Evans*), Wales, 1729-1783. Introduction to the History of the War in Germany, 1781 (the war referred to is that of 1756) ; Memoir on the Invasion and Defence of Great Britain, 1798.

LLOYD, D.D. (*Humphrey*), Dublin, 1800-1881. Magnetical and Meteorological Observations, 1865-69 ; Magnetical Observatory of Dublin, 1842 ; Miscellaneous Papers on Physical Science, 1877 ; Power of the Keys (*The*), 1873 ; Treatise on Light and Vision, 1831 ; Treatise on Magnetism, 1874 ; Treatise on the Wave Theory of Light, 1870.

LLOYD (Rev. *Nicholas*), Flintshire, North Wales, 1634-1680. Dictionarum Historicum, etc., 1670.

LLWYD (*Edward*), Wales, 1660-1709. Archæologia Britannica, 1707 ; Lithophylacii Britannici Iconographia, 1699.

LLWYD (*Humphrey*), Wales, died 1570. Commentarioli Britannicæ Descriptionis Fragmentum, 1572.

LOCK (*Matthew*), Exeter, 1635-1677. Music in *Macbeth*, 1672.

LOCKE (*John*), Wrington, in Somersetshire, one of our five philosophers, 1632-1704. Adversariorum Methodus, 1686 ; Essay on the Human Understanding (to prove there are no innate ideas), 1670-87, printed 1690 (a book of profound thought) ; Inspiration of the Holy Scriptures (*The*), 1699 ; (Three) Letters on Toleration, 1667, 1689, 1692 ; Method of a Commonplace Book, 1685 ; Of the Conduct of the Understanding, 1706 ; On Education, 1693 ; On the Reasonableness of Christianity, 1695 ; Thoughts on Education, 1693 ; Treatise on Civil Government, 1690. His Life, by Le Clerc, 1713 ; lord King, 1829 ; Fox Bourne, 1876 ; T. Fowler, 1881.

LOCKER (*Arthur*), Greenwich Hospital, 1828- . On a Coral Reef, 1869 ; Sir Godwin's Folly, 1864 ; Stephen Scudamore, 1868 ; Sweet Seventeen, 1866 ; Village Surgeon (*The*), 1874.

LOCKER (*Frederick*), 1821-1895. London Lyrics, 1857 ; Patchwork, 1879.

LOCKHART (*John Gibson*), Cambusnethan, in Scotland, 1794-1854. Adam Blair, 1832, a story of Scottish life ; Essays on Cervantes, 1822 ; Life of Burns, 1828 ; Life of Napoleon, 1830 ; Life of Scott, 1837-39 ; Matthew Wald, 1824, a novel ; Peter's Letters to his Kinsfolk, 1819 (with Wilson) ; Reginald Dalton, 1823, a tale of University life ; Spanish Ballads, 1821 (very popular) ; Valerius, 1821, a Roman story. His Memoirs, by Dr. R. S. Mackenzie, 1855.

LOCKYER (*Joseph Norman*), Rugby, in Warwickshire, 1836- . Chemistry of the Sun, 1887 ; Contributions to Solar Physics, 1873 ; Dawn of Astronomy (*The*), 1894 ; Elementary Astronomy, 1871 ; Movements of the Earth, 1887 ; Primer of Astronomy, 1874 ; Researches in Spectrum Analysis, 1882 ; Solar Physics, 1873 ; Spectroscope and its Applications (*The*), 1873 ; Studies in

Spectrum Analysis, 1878 ; Star-gazing, Past and Present, 1878.

LODGE (*Edmund*), London, 1756-1839. Illustrations of British History 1798 ; Life of Sir Julius Cæsar, 1810 ; Portraits of Illustrious Personages in Great Britain, 1821-34 (his chief work).

LODGE (*Thomas*), poet, 1555-1625. Alarum against Usurers (*An*), 1584 ; Catharos, 1591 ; Defence of Stage Plays (in reply to Gosson's *School of Abuse*), 1579 ; Divel conjured (*The*), 1596 ; Euphues' Shadow, 1592 (see G. LILLY) ; Fig for Momus (*A*), 1595, satires, eclogues, etc.; Glaucus and Scylla, 1589 ; Life of W. Longbeard, 1593 ; Lookingglasse for London, etc., 1594, a comedy (with Greene) ; Margarite of America (*A*), 1596 ; Paradoxes . . . for Young Wittes, 1602 ; Phillis, 1593, sonnets, elegies, etc. ; Rosalynde, or Euphues' Golden Legacie, 1590, a novel (to which Shakespeare owes his *As You Like It*) ; Scille's Metamorphosis, 1589 ; Seneca's Works, translated, 1614 ; Spider's Webbe (*A*), no date ; Treatise on the Plague (*A*), 1603 ; Wit's Miserie, and the World's Madness, 1596 ; Works of Josephus, translated, 1602 ; Wounds of Civill War (two tragedies, 1, Marcus, 2, Sylla), 1594 (probably with Greene).

LOGAN (Rev. *John*), Scotland, 1748-1788. Charges against Warren Hastings, 1784 ; Government of Asia (*The*), 1782 ; Lectures on the Philosophy of History, 1781 ; Poems, 1781 ; Runnimede, 1783, a tragedy ; Sermons, 1790-91 ; View of Ancient History, 1788.

LONG (*George*), Poulton, in Lancashire, 1800-1879. Decline of the Roman Republic, 1864-74 ; History of France and its Revolutions, 1849.

LONGFELLOW (*Henry Wadsworth*), Portland, in Maine, U.S., poet, 1807-1882. Aftermath, 1873 ; Ballads, etc., and other Poems, 1842 ; Belfry of Bruges, and other Poems, 1842 ; *Dante*, translated, 1867-70 ; Divine Tragedy (*The*), 1871 ; Evangeline (in two parts), 1848, English hexameters ; Flower de Luce, 1866 ; Golden Legend (*The*), 1851, a dramatic poem (based on the German story of *Poor Henry*) ; Hanging of the Crane (*The*), 1874 ; Hiawatha (in 22 staves), 1855 (the most original poem of the century) ; Hyperion, 1839, a romance ; Kavanagh, 1849, a poetico-philosophical tale ; Keramos, 1878 ; Masque of Pandora (*The*), 1875 ; Miles Standish, 1858, in English hexameters ; New England Tragedies, 1869 ; Outre-mer, 1835 (his first work in prose) ; Poems on Places, 1877 ; Poems on Slavery, 1843 ; Poets and Poetry of Europe (*The*), 1847 ; Seaside (*The*), and the Fireside, 1851 ; Spanish Student (*The*), 1845, a dramatic poem in three acts ; Tales of a Wayside Inn, 1863, in verse ; Three Books of Song, 1872 ; To a Child, 1848 ; Voices of the Night, 1841.

LORNE (Sir *John George Edward Henry Campbell*, called complimentarily the marquis of), born at Stafford House, London (he married the princess Louise), 1845- . Guido and Lita, 1875, a tale in verse ; Psalms (*The*) Versified, 1877.

LOSSING, LL.D. (*Benson*), Beekman, in New York, U.S., 1819- . Brief Memoirs of Eminent Americans, 1854 ; Illustrated History of the United States, 1854-56 ; Life, etc., of P. Schuyler, 1860 ; Life of Washington, 1860 ; Lives of the Signees of the Declaration of Independence, 1848 ; Mount Vernon and its Associations, 1859 ; Outline History of the Fine Arts (*An*), 1841 ; Pictorial Field-Book of the Revolution, 1848-52 ; Pictorial History of the Civil War, 1866-69 ; Seventeen Hundred and Seventy-Six, 1847.

LOUDON (*John Claudius*), Cambuslang, in Scotland, landscape gardener, etc., 1783-1843. Arboretum. etc., Britannicum, 1838 ; *Architectural Magazine*, 1839 ; Cultivation of the Pine Apple, 1823 ; Derby Arboretum (*The*), 1841 ; Designs for . . . Farms and Farm Buildings, 1812 ; Encyclopædia of Agriculture 1825, of Cottage, Farm, and Villa Architecture 1812, of Gardening 1822, of Plants 1829 (Supplement, 1838), of Trees and Shrubs 1842 ; Formation and Management of Country Residences 1806, of Plantations 1804 ; *Gardener's Magazine*, 1826-34, new series, 1835-43 ; Greenhouse Companion (*The*), 1824 ; Horticulturist (*The*), 1849 ; Hortus Britannicus, 1830 ; Hortus Lignosus Londinensis, 1838 ; Illustrations of Landscape Gardening, etc., 1830-33 ; *Magazine of Natural History*, 1829-36 ; On laying out Cemeteries, 1843 ; Paper Roofs used at Tew Lodge, 1811 ; Self-instruction to Young Gardeners, 1845 ; Suburban Gardener (*The*), 1836-38 ; Suburban Horticulture, 1842. His Life, by his wife, 1845.

LOUDON (Mrs.), wife of the preceding, maiden name *Jane Webb*, born near Birmingham, in Warwickshire, 1800-1858. *Amateur Gardener's Monthly Calendar* (*The*), 1847 ; Botany for Ladies, 1849 ; British Wild Flowers, 1844-46 ; Entertaining Naturalist (*The*), 1850 ; Flower Garden of . . . Annuals 1840, of Bulbous Plants 1841, of Perennials 1843 ; Gardening for Ladies, 1840 ; Ladies' Companion to the Flower Garden, 1841 ; Ladies' Country Companion, 1845 ; Ladies' Flower Garden, 1843 ; Mummy (*The*), 1827, a tale of the xxii. century.

LOVELACE (*Richard*), Kent, 1618-1658. Lucasta, 1649, odes, songs, sonnets, etc. ; Scholar (*The*), 1649, a comedy ; Soldier (*The*), 1649, a tragedy.

LOVER (*Samuel*), Dublin, 1797-1868. Angels' Whispers, a song ; Four-leaved Shamrock (*The*), 1839, a song ; Handy Andy, 1842, an Irish tale (it first appeared in *Bentley's Miscellany*, 1838) ; Happy Man (*The*), an opera ; Irish Sketches, 1837 ; Legends and Stories of Ireland, 1832-34 ; Low-backed Car (*The*), 1838 ; Lyrics of Ireland, 1858, a compilation ; May Dew (*The*), 1839, a song ; Metrical Tales, and other Poems, 1860 ; Molly Bawn, 1839, a song ; Molly Carew, 1838, a song ; Rory O'More (a romance 1837, a song 1838, and an opera) ; Songs and Ballads, 1839 ; Treasure Trove, 1844, a novel about Irish heirs (first published as "L.S.D.") ; True Love can ne'er Forget, a song; White Horse of the Peppers (*The*), an opera. His Life, by B. Bernard, 1874.

LOWE (*Edward Joseph*),Highfield, in Nottingham, 1825-   . Atmospheric Phenomena, 1847; Beautiful Leaved Plants, 1861 (with Howard); British Grasses, 1858; Chronology of the Seasons (*The*); Climate of Nottinghamshire (*The*), 1853 (valuable); Conchology of Nottinghamshire (*The*), 1853 (valuable); Ferns, British and Exotic, 1867 (a standard work); Natural History of British and Exotic Ferns, 1856-62; New and Rare Ferns, 1862; Prognostications of the Weather, 1840.

LOWE (Rev. *Richard Thomas*); 1801-   . Fishes of Madeira, 1843; Manual of the Flora of Madeira.

LOWELL (*James Russell*), born at Boston, U.S., 1819-1891. Among my Books, 1870; Biglow Papers (*The*). 1848, political poems, second series, 1862; Cathedral (*The*), 1869; Conversations on Some of the Old Poets, 1845; Fable for Critics (*A*), 1848, in verse; Fireside Travels, 1864; Legend of Brittany, 1844; My Study Windows, 1871l; Poems, 1844, 1848; Prometheus, 1844; Under the Willows, 1869; Vision of Sir Launfal (*The*), 1848; Year's Life (*A*), 1841, poems.

LOWER (*Mark Antony*), Chiddingley, in Sussex, 1813-1870. Curiosities of Heraldry, 1845; English Surnames, etc., 1842; History of Sussex, 1876; Patronymica Britannica, 1860; Worthies of Sussex (*The*), 1865.

LOWER (Sir *William*), seventeenth century. Amorous Fantasms, 1660, a tragi-comedy; Enchanted Lovers (*The*), 1663, a pastoral; Noble Ingratitude (*The*), 1659, a pastoral tragedy; Phœnix in the Flames (*The*), 1639, a tragedy.

LOWMAN (Rev. *Moses*), Clapham, 1680-1752. Argument from Prophecy that Jesus is the Messiah, 1733; Dissertation on the Civil Government of the Hebrews, 1740; Isaiah retranslated; Three Tracts (1, Were the "appearances" mentioned in the Bible really God? 2, the Schechinah; 3, the Logos), 1756, posthumous. His Life, by P. Hall, 1834.

LOWNDES (*William Thomas*), died 1843. Bibliographer's Manual (*The*), 1834, 1858 (a standard work).

LOWTH, D.D. (*Robert*), bishop of London, born at Winchester, son of Dr. William Lowth, 1710-1787. De Sacra Poesi Hebræorum, 1753; Introduction to English Grammar, 1762; Life of William of Wykeham, 1758 ("a model biography," *Quarterly Review*); Translation of Isaiah, with Prolegomena, 1778 (his chief work). (See BLAYNEY.) His Life, by P. Hall, 1834.

LOWTH, D.D. (*William*), London, 1661-1732. Commentaries on the Prophets, 1714-23; Vindication of the Divine Authority of the [Bible], 1692. His Life, by his son Robert.

LUARD, D.D. (*Henry Richard*), 1825-1890. Life of Porson, 1857. Edited *Annales Monastici*, 1864-69; *Mathew Paris*, 1872-82, etc.

LUBBOCK (Sir *John*), London, 1834-   . Ants, Bees, and Wasps, 1882; Beauties of Nature (*The*), 1892; Contribution to our Knowledge of Seedlings, 1892; Fifty Years of Science, 1882; Monograph on the Thysanura, etc., 1873; On the Origin and Metamorphosis of Insects, 1873; Origin of Civilization . . . 1870; Our British Wild Flowers considered in their Relation to Insects, 1873; Pleasures of Life (*The*), 1887; Prehistoric Times illustrated, etc., 1865; Use of Life (*The*), 1894; Volume of Scientific Lectures (*A*), 1879.

LUBBOCK (Sir *John William*), London, 1803-1865. Classification of Different Branches of Human Knowledge, 1838; Researches on Physical Astronomy, 1830; Theory of the Moon and Perturbations of the Planets, 1833; Treatise on the Tides, 1831-37.

LUCAS (*Samuel*), Bristol, 1818-1865. Biography and Criticism, 1860; Causes and Consequences of National Revolutions, 1840; Eminent Men and Popular Books, 1859; History and Condition of Social Progress, 1853; Mornings of the Recess, 1804.

LUCY (*Henry W.*), Crosby, near Liverpool, 1847-   . Diary of the Salisbury Parliament, 1892; Diary of Two Parliaments (*A*), 1885-86; East by West, 1885; Faces and Places, 1892; Gideon Fleyce, 1882, a novel; Gladstone, 1893; Men and Manners in Parliament, 1881; Popular Handbook of Parliamentary Procedure, 1880.

LUKIS (Rev. *William Collings*), 1817-   . Church Bells and Bell Founders, 1847; Danish Cromlechs, etc., compared with those of Great Britain, etc., 1861; Guide for Archiologists, 1875; History of the Salisbury Bellfoundry, 1858; Rude Stone Monuments, and Errors concerning them, 1875; Specimens of Ancient Church Plate, 1847.

LUPTON (*Donald*), about 1590-1660. Description of Flanders, 1658; Emblems of Rarities, 1636; England's Command of the Seas, 1653; Jesuit turned Quaker (*The*), 1655; Historie of Moderne Protestant Divines, 1637; Lives of the Primitive Fathers, 1640; London and the Country carbonadoed, 1632; Objectorum Reductio, 1634.

LUPTON (*Thomas*), sixteenth century. All for Money, 1578, a tragi-comedy; Christian (*The*) *v.* the Jesuit, 1582; Dream of the Devill, etc., 1589; Thousand Notable Things (*A*), 1586; Too Good to be True, 1581.

LYALL (*Edna*), real name *Ada Ellen Bayly*, Brighton, novelist, about 1858-   . Autobiography of a Slander, 1887; Autobiography of a Truth (*The*), 1896; Donovan, 1882; Doreen, 1894; Derrick Vaughan, Novelist, 1889; Hardy Norseman (*A*), 1889; Hope the Hermit, 1898; How the Children raised the Wind, 1895; In the Golden Days, 1885; Knight Errant, 1887; Their Happiest Christmas, 1886; To Right the Wrong, 1892; Wayfaring Men, 1897; We Two, 1884; Won by Waiting, 1879.

LYDGATE (*John*), monk of Bury, in Suffolk, poet, about 1370-1460. Chorle and the Bryde (*The*), printed by Wynkyn de Worde; Cronycle of the Kynges Names, printed 1500, by Wynkyn de Worde; Daunce of Machabre (*The*), printed 1554; Falls of Prynces (*The*), printed 1494; Life and

Death of Hector, printed 1614 ; Lytell Treatis of the Horse, Shepe, and Goos (*A*), printed by Wynkyn de Worde ; Lyf of our Ladye (*The*), printed by Caxton ; Lyf of St. Edmund ; Maidens Crosse Rewe (*The*); P[ro]verbes of Lydgate, printed by Wynkyn de Worde, no date ; Sege and Destruccyon of Troye, printed 1513, by Pynson ; Serpent of Division (*The*), printed 1590; Story of Thebes (*The*), published 1561 ; Temple of Glass (*The*), printed by Wynkyn de Worde ; Testament of John Lydgate, whiche he made hymselfe by his Lyfe-Days, printed by Richard Pynson; Worke of Sapience, printed by Caxton.

LYDYAT (*Thomas*), Oxfordshire, 1572-1646. Canones Chronologici, 1675, posthumous ; Tractatus de Variis Annorum Formis, 1605.

LYE (*Edward*), Totnes, in Devonshire, 1704-1767. Anglo-Saxon and Gothic Dictionary, 1772, posthumous (a valued work).

LYELL (Sir *Charles*), Kinnordy, Scotland, 1797-1875. Antiquity of Man (*The*), etc., 1863; Atheisms of Geology, 1857 ; Elements of Geology, 1838 ; Manual of Elementary Geology, 1863 ; Principles of Geology, 1830-33 (his great work) ; Travels in North America, 1845, 1849. His Life, by Mrs. Lyell, his sister-in-law, 1881.

LYLY (*John*), the euphuist. See LILLY.

LYNCH (Rev. *Thomas Toke*), Dunmow, in Essex, 1818-1871. Lectures on Some Forms of Literature, 1853 ; Lectures to Young Men, 1853 ; Memorials of Theophilus Trinal, 1850 ; Mornington Lectures, 1870 ; Sermons for my Curates, 1871.

LYNDSAY. See LINDSAY.

LYNN (*William Thynne*), Chelsea, 1835-Celestial Motions, 1884 ; Remarkable Comets, 1893 ; Remarkable Eclipses, 1896.

LYONS (*Israel*), Cambridge, 1739-1775. Fasciculus Plantarum circa Cantabrigiam Nascentium, 1763 ; Treatise on Fluxions, 1758.

LYONS (Rev. *Daniel*), Rodmarton, in Gloucestershire, 1760-1834. Environs of London, 1792-96, Supplements, 1800, 1811 ; Magna Britannia, 1806-22 (with S. Lysons).

LYSONS (*Samuel*), Rodmarton, in Gloucestershire, 1763-1819. Britannia Depicta, 1806 ; Collection of Gloucester Antiquities, 1804 ; Magna Britannica, 1806-22 (with D. Lysons); Mosaic Pavements, 1801, 1808 ; Roman Remains discovered 1797, 1813-17 (splendid works).

LYTTELTON (*George*, lord), Hagley, in Worcestershire, 1709-1773. Blenheim, a poem ; Conversion of St. Paul (*The*), 1747 ; Dialogues of the Dead, 1760, 1765 ; History of Henry II., 1764-67 ; Letters from a Persian in England to his Friend in Ispahan, 1735 ; Miscellaneous Works, 1774, posthumous ; Monody (*A*), 1747, a Pindaric ode ; Observations on the Conversion, etc., of St. Paul, 1747 ; Poetical Works, 1787 ; Progress of Love (four eclogues), 1732. His Life, by R. Phillimore, 1845.

LYTTELTON (Sir *Thomas*), Frankley, in Cheshire, 1421-1481. Treatise on Tenures, 1841 (invaluable).

∵ This is the Lyttelton so well known in his connection with the ghost story.

LYTTON (*Edward George Earle Lytton, Bulwer-Lytton*, lord), born at Woodalling, in Norfolk, poet and novelist, 1805-1873. He published first under the name of Lytton Bulwer. Alice, or the Mysteries, 1838 ; Arthur (*King*), 1848, an epic in six-line stanzas ; Athens, its Rise and Fall, 1836 ; Caxtoniania, 1863, a novel ; Caxtons (*The*), 1849, a domestic novel ; Coming Race (*The*), 1871 ; Confessions of a Water Patient, 1845 ; Devereux, 1829, a novel ; Disowned (*The*), 1828, a novel ; England and the English, 1833 ; Ernest Maltravers, 1837, a novel ; Eugene Aram, 1831, a novel ; Eva, 1842, a poem ; Falkland, 1827 (his first novel); Godolphin, 1833, a novel ; Harold, 1850, an historic novel ; Ill-omened Marriage (*The*), 1842 ; Ismael, 1820, an Oriental tale, with other poems ; Kenelm Chillingly, 1873, a novel ; Last Days of Pompeii, 1834, an historic novel ; Last of the Barons (*The*), 1843, an historic novel ; Leila and Calderon, 1838 ; Lost Tales of Miletus (*The*), 1866 ; Lucretia, 1847, a novel ; My Novel, 1853, a novel ; New Timon (*The*), 1846 ; Night and Morning, 1841, a novel ; O'Neill, or the Rebel, 1827, a tale in verse ; Parisians (*The*), 1873, a novel ; Paul Clifford, 1830, a novel ; Pausanias, the Spartan, 1876 ; Pelham, 1827 (his second novel); Pilgrims of the Rhine, 1834, a novel ; Poems, etc., of Schiller, translated, 1844 ; Rienzi, 1835, an historic novel ; St. Stephen's, 1861, a poem ; Sculpture, 1825, a prose poem ; Strange Story (*A*), 1862, a novel ; Walpole, 1869 ; Weeds and Wild Flowers, 1826, in verse (his first production) ; What will he do with it ? 1858, a novel ; Zanoni, 1842, a novel.

Plays : Duchess de la Vallière (*La*), 1836, a tragedy ; Lady of Lyons (*The*), 1838, a comedy ; Money, 1840, a comedy ; Not so Bad as we seem, 1851, a comedy ; Richelieu, 1839, an historic play ; Rightful Heir (*The*), 1868, a tragedy; Sea Captain (*The*), 1839, a tragedy. His Memoirs, by his son, Edward Robert Bulwer Lytton, 1874.

LYTTON (*Edward Robert Bulwer Lytton*, lord), pseudonym "Owen Meredith," poet, 1831-1891. After Paradise, 1887 ; Clytemnestra, and other Poems, 1855 ; Chronicles and Characters, 1868 ; Fables in Song, 1874 ; Glenaveril, or the Metamorphoses, 1885 ; Julian Fane, 1871, a memoir ; King Poppy, 1892, posthumous ; Life of Lord Lytton (his father), 1874 ; Lucile, 1860, a novel in verse ; Orval, or the Fool of Time, 1869, a dramatic poem ; Poetical Works of Owen Meredith, 1867 ; Ring of Amasis (*The*), 1863, a romance ; Serbski Pesme, 1861, national Servian songs ; Tannhaüser, or the Battle of the Bards, 1861 (with Julian Fane); Wanderer (*The*), 1859, a collection of poems.

MAARTENS (*Maarten*), born in Holland. God's Fool, 1892 ; Greater Glory (*The*), 1894 ; My Lady Nobody, 1895 ; Old Maid's Love (*An*), 1891 ; Question of Time (*A*), 1891 ; Sin of Joost Avelingh, 1890.

MACADAM (*John London*), Scotland, 1756-

1836. Practical Essay on the . . . Repair, etc., of Public Roads, 1819; Remarks on the Present State of Road-making, 1820.

MACARTNEY (*George Macartney*, earl of), near Belfast, in Ireland, 1737-1806. Journal of the Embassy to the Emperor of China in 1792-94, 1807, posthumous.

MACAULAY (Mrs.), maiden name *Catherine Sawbridge*, Olantigh, in Kent, 1733-1791. History of England from James I. to the House of Hanover, 1763-83; Immutability of Moral Truth (*The*), 1783; Letters on Education, 1790.

MACAULAY (*Thomas Babington*, lord), Rothley Temple, Leicestershire, 1800-1859. Armada (*The*), 1832, a fragment in Alexandrine verse; Essay on Milton, 1825 (*Edinburgh Review*); Essays (in three vols.), 1843; Evening, 1820 (Chancellor's medal); History of England from James II., 1849-61; Ivry, 1824, a song of the Huguenots, in Alexandrine verse; (Four) Lays of Ancient Rome, 1842; Pompeii, 1819 (Chancellor's medal); Speeches, 1854. His Life, by dean Milman, 1862; Rev. F. Arnold, 1862; G. O. Trevelyan, 1876.

MACBRIDE, M.D. (*David*), Antrim, Ireland, 1726-1778. Experimental Essays, 1764; Introduction to the Theory and Practice of Medicine, 1772.

MACCABE (*William Bernard*), Dublin, 1801-1885. Agnes Arnold, 1860, a novel; Bertha, 1851, a romance of the Dark Ages; Catholic History of England (*A*), 1848-54; True History of the Hungarian Revolution (*A*), 1851.

MACCARTHY (*Denis Florence*), Ireland, 1820-1882. Ballads, Poems, and Lyrics, 1850; Bell-founder (*The*), and other Poems, 1857; Poets and Dramatists of Ireland; Shelley's Early Life, 1872; Under-glimpses, and other Poems, 1857.

MACCARTHY (*Justin*), Cork, Ireland, 1830-. Camiola, 1885; Charing Cross to St. Paul's, 1892; Comet of the Season (*The*), 1881; Con Amore, 1868, critical essays; Dear Lady Disdain, 1875; Dictator (*The*), 1893; Donna Quixote, 1879; Epoch of Reform (*The*), 1882; Fair Saxon (*A*), 1873; Grey River (*The*), 1889; History of our own Times, 1878-80; History of the Four Georges, 1884; Ireland's Cause, etc., 1888; Ladies' Gallery, 1888 (with Mrs. C. Praed); Lady Judith, 1871; Life of Mr. Gladstone, 1898; Life of Sir Robert Peel, 1891; Linley Rochford, 1874; Maid of Athens, 1883; Miss Misanthrope, 1877; My Enemy's Daughter, 1869; Paul Massie, 1866; Prohibitory Legislation in the United States, 1872; Rebel Rose (*The*), 1888 (with Mrs. C. Praed); Red Diamonds, 1893; Riddle Ring (*The*), 1896; Right Honourable (*The*), 1886 (with Mrs. C. Praed); Rival Princesses, 1891 (with Mrs. C. Praed); Roland Oliver, 1889; Short History of our own Time (*A*), 1883; Three Disgraces (*The*), 1897; Waterdale Neighbours (*The*), 1867.

MACCARTHY (*Justin Huntly*), son of the above, 1860-. Case for Home Rule (*The*), 1887; Dolly, 1889; Doomed, 1886; England under Gladstone, 1884; French

Revolution (*The*), 1890, 1897; Hafiz in London, 1886; Harlequinade, 1889; Ireland since the Union, 1887; Lily Lass, 1889; London Legend (*A*), 1895; Our Sensation Novel, 1886; Outlines of Irish History, 1883; Persian Tales, 1893; Royal Christopher (*The*), 1896; Serapion, and other Poems, 1883; Thousand and One Days (*The*), 1892. Also a translation of *Omar Khayyam*, 1889.

MACCAUL (Rev. *Joseph Benjamin*), Warsaw, 1827-. Dark Sayings of Old, 1873; Last Plague of Egypt (*The*), and other Poems, 1880; Paraphrastic Commentary on the Epistle to the Hebrews, 1871; Sunday Reflections, 1872.

MACCOSH, D.D. (*James*), Ayrshire, Scotland, 1811-. Christianity and Positivism, 1871; Intuitions of the Mind, 1860; Method of Divine Government, etc., 1850; Scottish Philosophy (*The*), 1874; Supernatural in Relation to the Natural (*The*), 1862; Typical Forms, etc., in Creation, 1856.

MACCRIE, D.D. (*Thomas*), Dunse, in Berwick, 1772-1835. History of the Progress and Suppression of the Reformation in Italy, 1829; History of the Progress and Suppression of the Reformation in Spain, 1827; Life of Andrew Melville, 1819; Li~e of John Knox, 1811. His Life, by Thomas MacCrie, 1840.

MACCULLOCH, M.D. (*John*), Guernsey, 1773-1835. Description of the Western Isles of Scotland, 1819 (his chief work); Essay on the Remittent and Intermittent Diseases, 1828; Geological Classification of Rocks, etc., 1821; Highlands, etc., of Scotland (*The*), 1824; Malaria (on the propagation thereof), 1827; Proofs and Illustrations of the Attributes of God, 1837; Remarks on the Art of Making Wine, 1817; System of Geology (*A*), etc., 1831.

MACCULLOCH (*John Ramsay*), Whithorn, in Scotland, 1789-1864. Dictionary of Commerce, 1832; Geographical Dictionary, 1842; Literature of Political Economy, 1845; Principles of Political Economy, 1825; Rise and Progress of Political Economy, 1824; Statistical Account of the British Empire, 1837.

MACCURTIN (*Hugh*), eighteenth century. Anglo-Irish Dictionary, 1732; Elements of the Irish Language, 1728.

MACDIARMID (*John*), born in Perthshire, Scotland, 1779-1808. Inquiry into the System of National Defence, 1805; Lives of British Statesmen, 1807 (in esteem).

MACDONALD, D.D. (*George*), Huntly, in Scotland, 1824-. Adela Cathcart, 1864, a novel; Alec Forbes of Howglen, 1865, a novel; Annals of a Quiet Neighbourhood, 1866; At the Back of the North Wind, 1870; Book of Strife (*A*), 1885; Castle Warlock, 1882; Cross Purposes and the Shadows, 1890; David Elginbrod, 1862, a novel; Dealings with the Fairies, 1867; Disciple (*The*), and other Poems, 1868; Donald Grant, 1883; Elect Lady (*The*), 1888; England's Antiphon, 1868; Exotics (*i.e.* translations), 1876; Flight of the Shadow (*The*), 1891; Gifts of the Child Christ (*The*), 1882; Guild Court, 1867;

Gutta Percha Willie, 1873 ; Heather and Snow, 1893 ; Hidden Life, and other Poems, 1864 ; Home Again, 1887 ; Hope of the Gospel (*The*), 1892 ; Imagination (*The*), etc., 1883 ; Light Princess (*The*), 1890 ; Lilith, 1894, a romance ; Malcolm, 1874, a novel ; Marquis of Lossie (*The*), 1877 ; Mary Marston, 1881 (his best novel); Miracles of our Lord (*The*), 1870 ; Orts, 1882 ; Paul Faber, Surgeon, 1878 ; Phantastes, 1858, a fairy romance ; Poems and Essays, 1851 ; Poetical Works, 1893 ; Portent (*The*), 1864, a story of second sight ; Princess (*The*) and the Curdie, 1882 ; Princess (*The*) and the Goblin, 1871 ; Ranald Bannerman's Boyhood, 1870 ; Robert Falconer, 1868 (his second-best novel) ; Rough Shanking (*A*), 1890 ; St. George and St. Michael, 1875 ; Salted with Fire, 1897 ; Seaboard Parish (*The*), 1868 ; Sir Gibbie, 1879, a novel ; Stephen Archer, 1883 ; There and Back, 1891 ; Thomas Wingfold, Curate, 1876 ; Three-fold Cord (*A*) ; Unspoken Sermons, 1866 ; Vicar's Daughter (*The*), 1872 ; Weighed and Wanting, 1882 ; What's Mine's Mine, 1886 ; Wilfred Combermede, 1871, a novel ; Wise Woman (*The*), 1875 ; Within and Without, 1855, a dramatic poem (his first publication) ; Wow O' Rivven, or the Idiot's Home, 1868.

MACDONALD (*John*), Kingsborough, 1759–1831. Telegraphic Dictionary, 1816 ; Treatise on Telegraphic Communication, etc., 1808.

MACE (Rev. *Thomas*), 1613–1709. Musicks Monument, 1676 ("a most delectable book," *Burney*).

MACEWIN (*William*), 1734–1762. Grace and Truth, 1763 (highly esteemed).

MACFARREN, Mus.D. (*George Alexander*), London, 1813–1880. Christmas, 1859, a cantata ; Devil's Opera (*The*), 1838, an opera ; Don Quixote, 1846, an opera ; Emblematical Tribute, 1841 ; Freya's Gift, 1863 ; Helvellyn, 1864, an opera ; Jessy Lee, 1863, an opera di camera ; King Charles II., 1849, an opera ; (Six) Lectures on Harmony, 1867 ; Lenore, 1851, a cantata ; May-day, 1856, a cantata ; Robin Hood, 1860, an opera (his best) ; Rudiments of Harmony, 1860 (in repute) ; St. John the Baptist, 1866, an oratorio ; She Stoops to Conquer, 1864, an opera ; Sleeper awakened (*The*), 1850, a cantata ; Soldier's Legacy (*The*), 1864 ; Songs in a Cornfield, 1869.

∴ With hundreds of smaller pieces.

MACGILLIVRAY, LL.D. (*William*), died 1852. History of British Birds, 1848 ; History of the Molluscous Animals of Aberdeen, etc., 1843 ; Lives of Zoölogists, 1834.

MACGREGOR (*John*), of Scotland, 1797–1857. British America, 1832 ; Commercial Statistics, 1842 ; History of the British Empire from James I., 1852 ; Maritime Colonies of British America (*The*), 1828 ; My Notebook, 1835 ; Progress of America, 1847.

MACKAY (*Andrew*), died 1809. Complete Navigator (*The*), 1804 ; Mathematical Tables, 1804.

MACKAY, LL.D. (*Charles*), Perth, in Scotland, 1814–1889. Cavalier Songs, 1863 ;

Egeria, 1850 ; Forty Years' Recollections, 1878 ; Gideon Brown, 1877 ; Gouty Philosopher (*The*), 1862 ; Home Affections, 1857 ; Hope of the World (*The*), and other Poems, 1837 ; Interludes and Undertones, 1883 ; Legendary and Romantic Ballads of Scotland, 1861 ; Legends of the Isles, and other Poems, 1845 ; Liberal Party (*The*), 1880 ; Life and Liberty in America, 1859 ; Lost Beauties of the English Language, 1874 ; Luck, 1881 ; Lump of Gold (*The*), 1856 ; Man's Heart (*A*), 1860 ; Medora Leigh, 1869 ; Memoirs of Popular Delusions, 1841, prose ; Poems, 1834 ; Poetical Works, 1857 ; Poetry and Humour of the Scottish Language, 1882 ; Salamandrine (*The*), 1842 ; Scottish Songs, 1857 ; Songs collected, 1858 ; Studies from the Antique, 1864 ; Through the Long Day, 1887 ; Town Lyrics, 1847 ; Twin Soul (*The*), 1888 ; Under Green Leaves, 1857 ; Under the Blue Sky, 1871 ; Voices from the Crowd, 1844 ; Voices from the Mountains, 1846.

MACKAY (*George Eric*), pseudonym "George Eric Lancaster," poet, 1851– . Ad Reginam, 1881 ; Arrows of Song ; Gladys the Singer, 1887 ; Love-letters of a Violinist, 1886 ; Lover's Litanies (*A*), 1888 ; Lover's Missal (*The*), 1897 ; Marriage Ode, 1893 ; My Lady of Dreams ; Nero and Actia, 1891 ; Pygmalion in Cyprus, 1880 ; Song of the Sea (*A*), 1895 ; Songs of Love and Death, 1865 ; Song of the Flag, 1893 ; White Rose of the Crown, 1894.

MACKELLER (*Thomas*), New York, 1812– . American Printer (*The*), 1866 ; Rhymes atween Times, 1873. (The author of "Let me kiss him for his Mother," once a most popular song.)

MACKENZIE (Sir *Alexander*), 1760–1820. Journeys from Montreal . . . to the Frozen and Pacific Oceans, 1801.

MACKENZIE, M.D. (*George*), Scotland, died 1726. Lives and Characters of the Most Eminent Writers of the Scots Nation, 1708–22.

MACKENZIE (Sir *George*), Dundee, in Scotland, 1636–1691. Antiquity of the Royal Line of Scotland, 1685 ; Aretina, 1661, a serious romance ; Coelia's Counting-House and Closet, 1664, a poem ; Discourse on the Laws and Customs of Scotland in Matters Criminal, 1678 ; Essays in Praise of Solitude, 1665 ; Institutions of the Laws of Scotland, 1684 ; Jus Regium, 1684 ; Moral Gallantry, 1667 ; Moral History of Frugality, 1691 ; Moral Paradox (*A*), 1667 ; Reason, 1690, an essay ; Religio Stoici, 1663 ; Science of Heraulдry, 1680.

MACKENZIE, M.D. (*Henry*), Edinburgh, 1745–1831. Julia de Roubigné, 1777 ; *Edits* the Lounger, 1785–87, a periodical ; Life of Blacklock, 1793 ; Life of John Home, 1812 ; Man of Feeling (*The*), 1771 (his best novel) ; Man of the World (*The*), 1773.

MACKINTOSH (Sir *James*), Aldourie, in Inverness, Scotland, 1765–1832. Dissertation on Ethical Philosophy, 1830 ; History of England, 1830–32, 1838 ; History of the Reformation (in 1688) in England, 1834, posthumous ; Life of Sir Thomas More, 1844, posthumous; On the Study of the Laws of Nature and Nations, 1799; Regency Question (*The*), 1788; Trial of John Peltier, 1803 (very eloquent); View of the Reign of James II., 1835; Vindiciæ Gallicæ, 1791 (in reply to Burke). His Memoirs, by his son, Robert Mackenzie, 1835.

MACKLIN (*Charles*), Ireland, real name *Maclaughlin*, 1690-1797. Love à-la-Mode, 1759, a farce; Man of the World, 1781, a comedy; Married Libertine (*The*), 1761. His Life, by J. T. Kirkman, 1799.

MACKNIGHT, D.D. (*James*), Scotland, 1721-1800. Harmony of the Four Gospels, 1756 (a standard work, based on Osiander); New Translation of the Apostolic Epistles (*A*), 1795; Truth of the Gospel History, 1763.

MACLAINE, D.D. (*Archibald*), Ireland, 1722-1804. Discourses, 1799 (in high estimation); Letters to Soame Jenyns, 1777; Translation of Mosheim's *Ecclesiastical History*, 1765.

MACLAREN, D.D. (*Alexander*), Glasgow, 1826- . Christ in the Heart, 1886; Conquering Christ (*The*), 1891; Counsels for the Study and the Life, 1864; Epistles to the Colossians and Philemon, 1887; God of the Amen (*The*), 1891; Holy of Holies (*The*), 1890; Life of David as reflected in his Psalms, 1880; Modern Miracles, 1888; Paul's Prayers, 1893; Pictures and Emblems, 1885; Secret of Power (*The*), 1882; Spring Holiday in Italy (*A*), 1865; Unchanging Christ (*The*), 1890; Wearied Christ (*The*), 1893; Year's Ministry (*A*), 1884.

MACLAREN (*Charles*), 1782-1866. Dissertation on the Topography of Troy, 1822; Geology of Fife, 1839.

MACLAREN (*Ian*), pseudonym of Rev. *John Watson*, 1850- . Beside the Bonnie Brier Bush, 1894; Cure of Souls (*The*), 1896; Days of Auld Lang Syne, 1895; Kate Carnegie, 1896; Mind of the Master, 1896; Upper Room (*The*), 1895.

MACLEOD, D.D. (*Norman*), Campbelltown, Argyleshire, 1812-1872. Across the River, 1864; Character-Sketches, 1872; Daily Meditations, 1861; Deborah, 1857; Earnest Student (*The*), 1854; Eastward, 1866; Gold Thread, 1861; How can we best relieve our Deserving Poor? 1867; Job Jacobs, 1862; Life and Travels of St. Paul, 1861; Old Lieutenant (*The*) and his Son, 1862; Parish Papers, 1862; Peeps at the Far East, 1871; Prevailing Prayer, 1859; Reminiscences of a Highland Parish, 1867; Simple Truths spoken to Worknig People, 1866; Starling (*The*), 1867; Temptation of our Lord (*The*), 1872; War and Judgment, 1876, a sermon; Wee Davie, 1865. His Life, by his brother, 1876.

MACLURE (*William*), U.S., 1763-1840. Geology of the United States of America, 1817 (very valuable).

MACMILLAN, LL.D. (Rev. *Hugh*), Aberfeldy, Perthshire, 1833- . Bible Teachings in Nature, 1866; Daisies of Nazareth (*The*), 1894; First Forms of Vegetation (*The*), 1861; Garden (*The*), and the City, 1872; Gate Beautiful (*The*), 1891; Holidays on High Lands, 1869; Marriage of Cana in Galilee (*The*), 1892; Ministry of Nature (*The*), 1871;

My Comfort in Sorrow, 1891; Mystery of Grace (*The*), 1893; Olive Leaf (*The*), 1886; Our Lord's Three Raisings from the Dead, 1876; Sabbath of the Fields (*The*), 1876; Sun-glints in the Wilderness, 1872; Riviera (*The*), 1885; Roman Mosaics, 1888; True Vine, (*The*), 1871; Worlds are Ours (*The*), 1880.

MACNICOL (Rev. Dr. *Donald*), 1735-1802. Remarks on Dr. Johnson's Journey to the Hebrides, 1779 (highly esteemed).

MACNISH, M.D. (*Robert*), called the "Modern Pythagorean," Glasgow, 1802-1837. Anatomy of Drunkenness, 1827; Book of Aphorisms, 1833; Tales, Essays, and Sketches, 1839, posthumous; Philosophy of Sleep, 1830 (his chief work).

MACPHERSON (*James*), Ruthven, in Scotland, 1738-1796. Fingal (in six books), 1762; Fragments of Ancient Poetry collected in the Highlands of Scotland, 1760; Highlander (*The*), 1758, a poem; History of Great Britain from the Restoration, 1776; *Iliad* of Homer (*The*), 1775, a prose translation; Introduction to the History of Great Britain and Ireland, 1771; Original Papers containing the History of Great Britain (1688-1714), with Extracts from the Autobiography of James II., 1775; Poems of Ossian, 1762-63, in poetic prose; Temora (in eight books), 1763.

MACQUOID (Mrs.), 1824- . About Yorkshire, 1883; Appledore Farm, 1894; At an Old Chateau, 1891; At the Peacock, 1887; At the Red Glove, 1885; Bad Beginning (*A*), 1862; Berkshire Lady (*The*), 1879; Berries, 1893; Beside the River, 1881; By the Sea, 1865; Charlotte Burney, 1867; Cosette, 1890; Diane, 1875; Doris Barugh, 1877; Drifting Apart, 1891; Elizabeth Morley, 1889; Evil Eye (*The*), and other Stories, 1875; Faithful Lover (*A*), 1882; Forgotten by the World, 1869; Haunted Fountain (*The*), 1890; Her Sailor Lover, 1883; His Last Card, 1895; In the Ardennes, 1881; In the Sweet Spring Time, 1880; In the Volcanic Eifel, 1896 (with Gilbert S. Macquoid); Joel Wentworth, 1886; Little Fifine, 1881; Little Vagabond (*A*), 1886; Lost Rose, and other Stories, 1876; Louisa, 1885; Maisie Derrick, 1892; Mère Suzanne, 1886; Miriam's Marriage, 1872; Miss Eyon, 1892; My Story, 1874; Patty, 1871; Pepin, 1889; Pictures across the Channel, 1892; Pictures and Legends from Normandy and Brittany, 1878; Player's Progress (*A*) (forthcoming); Prince's Whim (*The*), 1891; Puff, 1888; Roger Ferron, 1889; Rookstone, 1871; Sir James Appleby, 1886; Strange Company (*A*), 1885; Through Brittany, 1877; Through Normandy, 1874; Too Soon, 1873; Under the Snow, 1884; Wild as a Hawk, 1868.

MADAN, D.D. (*Martin*), 1726-1790. Thelyphthora, 1781 (to prove that polygamy was a Mosaic law).

MADDEN (Sir *Frederick*), 1801-1873. Wrote numerous historical, literary, and genealogical works. Edited *Historia Anglorum* of Matthew Paris, 1866-69; Layamon's *Brut*, 1847; and other metrical romances; the Wycliffite version of the Bible; etc. Translated and abridged Silvestre's *Universal Palæography*.

MADDEN, M.D.(*Richard Robert*),Dublin,1798-1873. Connection of Ireland with the Crown of England, 1845; Egypt and Mahommed Ali, 1841; History of Irish Periodical Literature, 1867; History of the Penal Laws against Roman Catholics, 1847; Infirmities of Genius (*The*), 1833; Island of Cuba, its Resources, etc., 1849; Life of Savonarola, 1854; Lives and Times of the United Irishmen, 1842, 1843, 1846 (his chief work); Memoirs of the Countess of Blessington, 1855; Mussulman(*The*),1830; Phantasmata, 1857; Poems on Cuban Slavery, 1840; Poems on Sacred Subjects, 1838; Shrines and Sepulchres of the Old and New Worlds, 1851; Travels in the West Indies, 1838, 1840; Travels in Turkey and Egypt, 1829; Turkish Empire in Relation to Christianity, etc., 1860.

MADDOX (*Isaac*), bishop of Worcester, born in London, 1697-1759. Vindication of the Church of England, 1733.

MADOX (*Thomas*), died 1730. Baronia Anglica, 1736, posthumous; Firma Burgi, 1726; Formulare Anglicanum, 1702; History and Antiquities of the Exchequer, etc., 1711.

MAGEE, D.D. (*William*), archbishop of Dublin, 1765-1831. Scriptural Doctrines of the Atonement, etc., 1801 (in high estimation). His Memoir, by Dr. Kenney, 1842.

MAGEE, D.D. (*William Connor*), bishop of Peterborough, born at Cork, in Ireland, 1821-1891. Sermons, the most important being "Christ the Light of All Scripture," 1860; "The Gospel of the Age," 1860; "The Church's Fear and the Church's Hope," 1864; "The Christian Theory of the Origin of the Christian Life," 1868; "The Breaking Net," 1868; "The Defence, etc., of the Faith;" etc.

MAGUIRE (*John Francis*), 1815-1872. Father Mathew, 1863; Rome and its Rulers, 1857.

MAGUIRE (Rev. *Robert*), Dublin, 1826-1888. Lectures on the *Pilgrim's Progress*, 1859; Miracles of Christ (*The*), 1863; Mottoes for the Million, 1866; Perversion and Conversion, 1854; St. Peter non-Roman, 1871; Self, its Dangers and Duties, 1862; Seven Churches of Asia (*The*), 1857; Things Present and Things to Come, 1860.

MAHAFFY, D.D. (*John Pentland*), Chapponaire, in Switzerland, 1839- . Art of Conversation, 1889; Decay of Modern Preaching, 1882; Empire of the Ptolemies, 1896; Greek Antiquities, 1876; Greek Education, 1879; Greek Life and Thought, 1888; Greek Pictures, 1890; Greek Social Life from Homer to Menander, 1874; Greek World under Roman Sway (*The*), 1890; History of Classical Greek Literature, 1880; Kant's Philosophy for English Readers, 1871; Primitive Civilization, 1868 (12 lectures); Problem of Greek History, 1892; Prolegomena to Ancient History, 1871; Rambles and Studies in Greece, 1876; Report on the First Grammar Schools, 1881; Sketch of the Life of Descartes, 1883-86; Story of Alexander's Empire (*The*), 1887.

MAHONY (*Francis*), better known as "Father Prout," 1809-1866. Facts and Figures from Italy, 1847; Reliques of Father Prout, 1836.

MAINE (Sir *Henry James Sumner*),Caversham Grove, Oxfordshire, 1822-1888. Ancient Law . . ., 1861; Dissertation on Early Law Customs, 1883; Early History of Institutions, 1875; Effect of Observation on India . . ., 1875; International Law, 1888; Popular Government, 1885; Roman Law and Legal Education, 1856; Village Communities . . ., 1871, six lectures.

MAITLAND, D.D. (*Samuel Roffey*), London, 1792-1866. Attempt to elucidate the Prophecies concerning Antichrist (*An*), 1830; Chatterton, 1857, an essay; Dark Ages (*The*), 1844; Eruvin, 1850; Essays on . . . the Reformation in England, 1849; Facts, etc., [about] the Albigenses and Waldenses, 1832.

MAITLAND (*William*), Brechin, in Scotland, 1693-1757. History and Antiquities of Scotland, 1757; History of Edinburgh, 1753; History of London, 1739.

MAJOR, D.D. (*John*), Scotland, 1470-1550. De Historia Gentis Scotorum, 1521.

MAJOR (*Richard Henry*), London, 1818-1890. Life of Prince Henry the Navigator, 1868.

MALAN (Rev. *Solomon Cæsar*), 1812- . Catalogue of the Eggs of British Birds (*A*), 1848; Coast of Tyre and Sidon (*The*), 1857; Exposition of the Apostles' Creed, 1847; On Ritualism, 1867; Philosophy of Truth, 1865; Three Months in the Holy Land, 1843; Threefold San-toze-king (*The*), 1856; Who is God in China, etc.? 1855. ∴ Numerous translations.

MALCOLM (*James Peller*), 1760-1815. Anecdotes of the Manners and Customs of London, 1808, 1811; Excursions into the Counties of Kent, etc., 1807; Lives of Topographers and Antiquaries, 1815; Londinum Redivivum, 1803-7; Miscellaneous Anecdotes of the Manners, etc., of Europe, 1811.

MALCOLM (Sir *John*), Westerkirk, Scotland, 1769-1833. History of Persia, 1815 (highly valued); Life of Lord Clive, 1836; Memoir of Central India, 1823 (esteemed); Political History of India, 1826 (esteemed); Sketch of the Sikhs, 1812. His Life, by J. W. Kaye, 1856.

MALET (*Lucas*), true name Mrs. *Mary St. Leger Harrison*, maiden name *Kingsley*, novelist, etc., 1852- . Carissima (*The*), 1896; Colonel Enderby's Wife, 1885; Counsel of Perfection (*A*), 1888; Little Peter, 1887; Mrs. Lorimer, 1882; Wages of Sin (*The*), 1891.

MALLET (*David*), Perthshire, Scotland, 1700-1765. Amyntor and Theodora, 1747, a tale in blank verse; Edwin and Emma, 1760, a ballad; Elvira, 1763; Excursion (*The*), 1728, a descriptive poem in blank verse (Wordsworth has a poem called *The Excursion*, also in blank verse); Eurydice, 1731; Life of Lord Bacon, 1740; Mustapha, 1739; Truth in Rhyme, 1761; Verbal Criticism, 1733, a satire in verse; William and Margaret, 1727, a ballad.

MALLOCK (*William Hurrell*), Devonshire, 1849- . Art of Life (*The*), 1895; Atheism and the Value of Life, 1884; Every Man his own Poet, 1872; Heart of Life (*The*), 1895;

Human Document (*A*), 1892; In an Enchanted Island, 1889; Is Life worth Living? 1879; Labour and the Popular Welfare, 1893; Landlords and the National Income, 1884; Lucretius, 1878; New Paul and Virginia (*The*), 1878; New Republic (*The*), 1877; Old Order changes (*The*), 1886; Poems, 1880; Property and Progress, 1884; Romance of the Nineteenth Century (*A*), 1881; Social Equality, 1882; Studies of Contemporary Superstitions, 1895; Verses, 1893.

MALMESBURY (*William of*), Somersetshire, chronicler, 1095-1143. De Antiquitate Glastoniensis Ecclesiæ (Gale's edition, 1691); De Gestis Regum Anglorum (in five books), 1127, continued in the "Historiæ Novellæ" (in three books), 1142, translated 1815; De Gestis Pontificum Anglorum (in four books), 1124; Life of Aldhelm, 1126 (Gale's edition, 1691); Life of Wulstan (Wharton's edition, 1691).

MALONE (*Edmond*), Dublin, 1741-1812. Life of W. Wyndham, 1810; Memoir of Sir Joshua Reynolds, 1797; Rise and Progress of the English Stage, 1800. Edits *Shakespeare*, with numerous notes, 1790-1821. His Life, by sir J. Prior, 1860.

MALORY (Sir *Thomas*), 1430-*. Morte d'Arthur (History of Prince Arthur), in three parts, 1465-70, printed by Caxton 1485.

MALTBY, D.D. (*Edward*), bishop of Durham, 1770-1859. Greek Gradus, 1830; Illustrations of the Truth of the Christian Religion, 1802 (recommended by bishop Tomline).

MALTHUS (Rev. *Thomas Robert*), near Dorking, in Surrey, 1766-1834. Crisis (*The*), 1792 (not published); Definitions in Political Economy, 1827; Essay on the Principle of Population, 1798, 1803 (his best-known work); Inquiry into the Nature, etc., of Rent, 1815; Measure of Value, etc. (*The*), 1823; Principles of Political Economy, 1820. His Life, by bishop Otter, 1836.

MALTON (*Thomas*), 1750-1804. Treatise on Perspective, 1776-83.

MANBY (Captain *George William*), Hilgay, in Suffolk, 1765-1854. Essay on the Preservation of Shipwrecked Persons, etc., 1812; Practical Observations on the Preservation of Mariners from Stranded Vessels, etc., 1827.

MANDEVILLE, M.D. (*Bernard de*), 1670-1733 (he must have been born before 1670, or else he would be only 15 years old when he made his *Oratio de Medicina*). Esop dressed, 1704, in familiar verse; Fable of the Bees, 1708 (a philosophical poem of some 400 lines, to which, in 1714, were added prose notes,—the object is to show the *benefits* of vices, such as gin-drinking, etc.; in 1729 a second part, in six dialogues, was added); Free Thoughts on Religion, etc., 1720; Grumbling Hive (*The*), 1714; Oratio de Medicina, 1685; Planter's Charity (*The*), 1704, a poem; Typhon in Verse, 1704; Virgin Unmasked, 1709; World Unmasked (*The*), 1736.

MANDEVILLE (Sir *John de*), St. Albans, in Hertfordshire, 1300-1372. Voyaige and Travaile, 1356 (a book of marvels connected

with Jerusalem, the East Indies, and Islands of the Indian Ocean).

MANLEY (*Mary de la Rivière*), Guernsey, a Channel island, 1672-1724. Adventures of Rivella, 1710; Bath Intrigues, a novel; Court Intrigues, 1711; Lost Lover (*The*), a comedy; Lucius, 1717, a tragedy; Memoirs of Europe towards the Close of the Eighteenth Century; New Atalantis, 1709 (love-scandals of distinguished contemporaries); Power of Love (*The*), 1720, in seven novels; Royal Mistress (*The*), 1696, a tragedy; Secret Memoirs, etc., of Several Persons of Quality, 1736, a satire (for which the publisher was arrested). Her Memoirs, 1717.

MANNERS (Lord *John James Robert*), Belvoir Castle, in Leicestershire, 1818- . (One of the "Young Englanders.") England's Trust, and other Poems, 1841 (in which occurs the couplet—

Let wealth and commerce, laws and learn-
ing die,
But leave us still our old nobility);

English Ballads, and other Poems, 1850; Importance of Literature to Men of Business, 1852; Notes of an Irish Tour, 1839; Plea for National Holy-days, 1843.

MANNING (*Anne*), novelist, 1807- . Belforest, 1864, a tale of English life; Cherry and Violet, 1853; Chronicles of Merrie England, 1854; Claude, the Colporteur, 1857; Duchess of Trajetto (*The*); Good Old Times, 1856; Household of Sir Thomas More, 1851; Mary Powell, 1850; Masque at Ludlow, and other Romanesques, 1866; Miss Biddy Frobisher, 1866; Noble Purpose nobly won (*A*); Passages in the Life of a Fair Gospeller, 1866; Poplar House Academy, 1859; Royal Mischief; Salt-Water Story (*A*), 1866; Tasso and Leonora.

MANNING (*Charlotte*), died 1871. Ancient and Mediæval India, 1856.

MANNING, D.D. (*Henry Edward*), Totteridge, in Hertfordshire, 1808-1892. Blessed Sacrament, etc. (*The*), 1864; Cæsarism and Ultramontanism, 1874; Catholic Church and Modern Society, 1880; Crown in Council (*The*), first letter 1864, second letter 1864; Dæmon of Socrates (*The*), 1872; Devotional Readings, 1868; England and Christendom, 1867; Eternal Priesthood (*The*), 1883; Fourfold Sovereignty of God (*The*), 1871; Four Great Evils of the Day (*The*), 1871; Grounds of Faith (*The*), 1853; Holy Baptism, 1843; Internal Mission of the Holy Ghost, 1875; Ireland, 1868; Last Glories of the Holy See greater than the First, 1861; Miscellanies, 1877-88; National Education, 1889; Œcumenical Council (*The*), and Infallibility of the Roman Pontiff, 1869; Oxford University Sermons, 1845; Petri Privilegium, 1871; Present Crisis of the Holy See tested by Prophecy, 1861; Religio Viatoris, 1887; Reunion of Christendom (*The*), 1866; Rome and the Revolution, 1867, a sermon; Rule of Faith (*The*), 1838; Sermons on Ecclesiastical Subjects, 1863; Sin and its Consequences, 1876; Temporal Mission of the Holy Ghost, 1865; Temporal Power of the Pope (*The*), 1866; Temporal Sovereignty of the Popes

(*The*), 1860; Thoughts for those that Mourn, 1850; True Story of the Vatican Council (*The*), 1877; Unity of the Church (*The*), 1845; Vatican Council (*The*), 1870; Vatican Decrees (*The*), 1875; Working of the Holy Spirit, 1864. His Life, by A. W. Hutton, 1892.

MANNING (Rev. *Owen*), Northamptonshire, 1721–1801. History and Antiquities of Surrey, 1804.

MANSEL, D.D. (*Henry Longueville*), dean of St. Paul's, born at Cosgrove, in Northamptonshire, 1820–1871. Demons of the Winds, and other Poems, 1838; Lectures on History, 1861–62; Limits of Religious Thought, 1858, a Bampton lecture; Metaphysics . . . 1860; Philosophy of Kant, 1856; Philosophy of the Conditioned, 1866 (with Veitch); Prolegomena Logica, 1851; Witness of the Church . . . 1864.

MANT, D.D. (*Richard*), bishop of Dromore, born at Southampton, in Hampshire, 1776–1848. Bampton Lectures, 1812; Bible, with Notes and Commentaries, 1817 (with D'Oyly); Biographical Notices of the Apostles, etc., 1828; Book of Psalms (*The*), 1824; British Months, 1835; Christian Sabbath (*The*), 1830; Gospel Miracles, 1832; History of the Church of Ireland, 1839–41; Life of Christ, 1840; Metrical Version of the Psalms, 1824; Poems, 1806–7; Simpliciad (*The*), 1809. His Life, by Berens, 1849.

MANTELL, LL.D. (*Gideon Algernon*), Lewes, in Sussex, 1790–1852. Atlas of Fossil Remains, 1850; Fossils of the South Downs, 1822; Fossils of the Tilgate Forest, 1836; Geological Excursions in the Isle of Wight, etc., 1847; Geology of Sussex (*The*), 1827; Geology of the South Coast of England (*The*), 1833; Illustrations of the Geology of Sussex, 1822; Medals of Creation, 1844; Petrifactions and their Teachings, 1851; Thoughts on Animalcules, 1846; Thoughts on a Pebble, 1840, 1849; Wonders of Geology (*The*), 1838 (his most popular work).

MANTON, D.D. (*Thomas*), 1620–1677. Exposition of the Epistle of St. James 1653, of the Epistle of St. Jude 1658, of the Lord's Prayer 1684, posthumous, of Psalm cxix. 1681. His Life, by Harris, 1725.

MAPES (*Walter*), archdeacon of Oxford, 1143–1210 (author of the famous drinking-song, "Meum est propositum in tabernâ mori"). De Nugis Curialium, printed 1850, satires and songs. (There was a *De Nugis Curialium* by John of Salisbury, 1156, printed 1475.)
∴ Mapes wrote in French (then the vernacular tongue) the *Mort Artus, Lancelot of the Lake*, and the *Quest of the St. Graal*.

MAPOTHER, M.D. (*Edward Dillon*), Fairview, in Ireland, 1835– . Lectures on Public Health, 1869; Manual of Physiology, 1871.

MARBECK (*John*), died 1585. Booke of Common Praier with Notes, 1550; Booke of Notes and Common-Places, 1581; Concordance of the Bible, 1500 (the first ever compiled in English); Dialog betweene Youth and Olde Age, 1584; Historie of King David in Meetre, 1579; Lives of the Saincts, etc., 1574; Ripping up of the Pope's Fardel, 1581.

MARCET (Mrs.), 1769–1858. Conversations on

Chemistry, 1819; Natural Philosophy, 1819; Political Economy, 1816; Vegetable Physiology, 1821.

MARGOLIOUTH, LL.D. (Rev. *Moses*), 1820–1881. Abyssinia; its Past, Present, and Future, 1866; Anglo-Hebrews (*The*), their Wrongs, etc., 1856; Apostolic Triple Benediction (*An*), 1853; England's "Crown of Rejoicing," 1853; Essay on the Poetry of the Pentateuch, 1871; Exposition of Isaiah, 1846; Gospel (*The*), and its Mission, 1860; Haidad (*The*), 1864; History of the Jews of Great Britain, 1851; Israel's Ordinance examined, 1844; Jews of Great Britain (*The*), 1846; Lord's Prayer no Adaptation, etc. (*The*), 1876; Oracles of God (*The*), 1870; Pilgrimage to the Land of my Fathers, 1850; Principles of Modern Judaism, 1843; Quarrel of God's Covenant (*The*), 1857; Sacred Minstrelsy, 1853; Sermons, 1851, 1861, 1874; Spirit of Prophecy (*The*), 1864; True Light (*The*), 1862; Vestiges of Historic Anglo-Hebrews, 1869.

MARINER (*William*), *–*. Account of the Natives of the Tonga Islands, 1818 (excellent).

MARKHAM (*Clement Robert*), born at Stillingfleet, in Yorkshire, 1830– . Cuzco and Lima, 1856; Franklin's Footsteps, 1852; History of the Abyssinian Expedition, 1869; History of Persia, 1873; Life of Lord Fairfax, 1870; Memoir of the Countess of Chinchon, 1875; Ollanta, a Quichua drama, 1871; Quichua Grammar and Dictionary, 1863; Spanish Irrigation, 1867; Threshold of the Unknown Region (*The*), 1874; Travels in Peru and India, 1856.

MARKHAM (*Gervase*), 1570–1655. Art of Archerie, 1634; Cavelarie, or the English Horseman, 1607; Cheap and Good Husbandry, 1614; Countrey Contentment, 1611; Countrey Farmer (*The*), 1616; Cure for Diseases in Horses, 1610; Discourse of Horsemanship, 1593; Dumbe Knight (*The*), 1608, a comedy (also attributed to Machin); English Arcadia (*The*), 1607, 1613; English Housewife, 1615; English Husbandman, 1613–14; Farewell to Husbandry, 1620; Gentleman's Academy (*The*), 1595; Herod Antipater, 1622, a tragedy; Honour in Perfection, 1604; How to chuse, etc., Horses, 1596; How to train Horses, 1605; Pleasures of Princes (fishing and cock-fighting), 1615; Poem of Poems (*The*), 1596, eight eclogues; Sir Richard Grinvile, 1595, a tragedy; Souldier's Accidence (*The*) 1625, Grammar 1639, Exercise 1643; Teares of the Beloved, 1600 (the lament of John on the death of Christ); Vox Militis (in two parts), 1625; Way to get Wealth (*The*), 1625 (by farming); Young Sportsman's Instructor (*The*), no date.

MARLOWE (*Christopher*), Canterbury, 1565–1593. (*He wrote nine tragedies*.) Dido, 1594, a tragedy (with Nash); Edward II., 1594, historic tragedy; Faustus (*Dr.*), 1604, a tragedy; Hero and Leander, 1598, a tragedy; Jew of Malta (*The*), 1586, printed 1633, a tragedy; Lucan, book i., translated, printed 1600; Lust's Dominion, 1593, a tragedy; Massacre of Paris (*The*), 1590, a tragedy;

Ovid's *Elegies*, translated, 1596; Tamburlaine the Great, parts i., ii., 1590, tragedies. His Life, by Cunningham; Dyce, 1850.

MARMION (*Shackerley*), 1602–1639. Antiquary (*The*), 1633, printed 1641, a comedy; Cupid and Psyche, 1637, an epic poem; Fine Companion (*A*), 1633, a play; Holland's Leaguer, 1632, a comedy (excellent).

MARRIOTT (*Wharton Booth*), 1823–1871. Vestiarium Christianum, 1867.

MARRYAT (Captain *Frederick*), London, naval novelist, 1792–1848. Children of the New Forest (*The*), 1847; Code of Signals for . . . the Merchant Service, 1837; Diary in America (*A*), two series, 1839; Frank Mildmay, or the Naval Officer, 1829; Jacob Faithful, 1834; Japhet in Search of a Father, 1836; Joseph Rushbrook, 1841; King's Own (*The*), 1830; Little Savage (*The*), 1847; Masterman Ready, 1841 (his best); Mission (*The*), or Scenes in Africa, 1845; Mr. Midshipman Easy, 1836; Monsieur Violet, 1842; Newton Forster, 1832; Olla Podrida, 1840; Pacha of Many Tales (*The*), 1835; Percival Keene, 1842; Peter Simple, 1834; Phantom Ship (*The*), 1839; Pirate and the Three Cutters (*The*), 1836; Poor Jack, 1840; Privateer's Man (*The*), 1844; Settlers in Canada (*The*), 1843; Snarley-Yow, or the Dog-Fiend, 1837; Valerie, 1849, an autobiography. His Life, by his daughter Florence, 1872.

MARRYAT (*Florence*), subsequently Mrs. Francis Lean (her first husband was Ross Church), daughter of the preceding, Brighton, novelist, 1837– . Beautiful Soul (*The*), 1896; Blindfold, 1890; Broken Blossom (*A*), 1879; Confessions of Gerald Estcourt, 1867; Crown of Shame (*The*), 1888; Daughter of the Tropics (*A*), 1887; Driven to Bay, 1887; Facing the Foot-lights, 1883; Fair-haired Alda, 1880; Fighting the Air, 1875; For Ever and Ever, 1866; Gentleman and Courtier, 1888; Girls of Feversham, 1869; Gup, 1868, sketches of Anglo-Indian life; Hampstead Mystery (*The*), 1893; Harvest of Wild Oats (*A*), 1877; Heart of Jane Warner, 1885; Heir Presumptive (*The*), 1885; Her Father's Name, 1876; Her Lord and Master, 1871; Her Own; Her Word against a Lie, 1878; Hidden Chains, 1876; How like a Woman! 1892; How she Loved him, 1882; Life and Letters of Captain Marryat, 1872; Little Stephen, 1878; Little Stepson (*A*), 1888; Love's Conflict, 1865; Mad Dumaresq, 1875; Master Passion (*The*), 1886; Miss Harrington's Husband, 1891; Moment of Madness (*A*), 1883; Mount Eden, 1889; My Own Child, 1876; My Sister, the Actress, 1881; Nelly Brooke, 1868; No Intentions, 1874; No Valentines, 1873; Nobler Sex (*The*), 1892; On Circumstantial Evidence, 1889; Open, Sesame, 1875; Parson Jones, 1893; Peeress and Player, 1883; Petronel, 1870; Phyllida, 1882; Prey of the Gods (*The*), 1871; Root of All Evil (*The*), 1879; Scarlet Sin, 1890; Spiders of Society, 1886; Spirit-World (*The*), 1894; Sybil's Friend, etc., 1873; There is no Death, 1891; Tom Tiddler's Ground, 1886; Too Good for him, 1865; Verdique, 1868; Veronique, 1869, a romance;

With Cupid's Eyes, 1880; Woman against Woman, 1865; World against a Lie, 1878; Written in Fire, 1878. And other novels.

MARSDEN, D.C.L. (*William*), Dublin, 1754–1836. Catalogue of Dictionaries, etc., 1796; Essays, 1832; Grammar and Dictionary of the Malayan Language, 1812; History of Sumatra, 1782 (a model work); Memoirs of a Malayan Family, 1830; Numismata Orientalia, 1823–25; Travels of Marco Polo, 1817. His Memoir, by himself, printed by his widow, 1838.

MARSH, LL.D. (*George Perkins*), born at Woodstock, U.S., 1801–1882. Camel (*The*), his Habits and Uses, 1856; Grammar of the Icelandic Language, 1838; Lectures on the English Language, 1861; Origin and History of the English Language, 1862 (now called "The Earth as modified by Human Action," 1874).

MARSH, D.D. (*Herbert*), bishop of Peterborough, born in London, 1758–1839. Authenticity, etc., of the New Testament, 1840, posthumous; Authenticity of the Pentateuch, 1792; Course of Lectures on Divinity, 1809–23 (most valuable); Dissertation on the First Three Gospels, 1801; History of the Politics of Great Britain and France, 1800; History of the Translations of the Holy Scriptures, 1812; Horæ Pelasgicæ, 1815; National Religion, 1811; Politics of Great Britain and France, posthumous; Translation of Michaelis's *Introduction to the New Testament*, 1792–1801.

MARSH (*John B.*), Chester, 1835– . Dick Whittington, 1874; For Liberty's Sake, 1873; Robin Hood, 1865; Sayings from Shakespeare, 1863; Story of Harecourt (*The*), 1871; Venice and the Venetians, 1873; Wise Sayings of the Great and Good, 1864.

MARSH, D.D. (*Narcissus*), archbishop of Armagh, born in Wiltshire, 1638–1713. Introductory Essay to the Doctrine of Sounds, 1683; Manuductio ad Logicam, 1678.

MARSH-CALDWELL (*Anne*), novelist, 1796–1874. Evelyn Marston, 1853; Norman's Bridge, 1847; Rose of Ashurst (*The*), 1855; Time, the Avenger, 1849; Triumphs of Time (*The*), 1836; Two Old Men's Tales, 1834.

MARSHALL (*Alfred*), 1842– . Economics of Industry, 1879; Elements of Industry, 1892; Principles of Economics, 1890.

MARSHALL (*Frances*), pseudonym "Alan St. Aubyn." Author of many novels.

MARSHALL (*Francis Albert*), London, 1840– . Biorn, 1873, a romantic drama; Brighton, 1874, a comedy; Corrupt Practices, 1870, a play in two acts; False Shame, 1872, a comedy (his best); Family Honours, 1878; Gold, 1874, a comic opera, in two acts; Mad as a Hatter, 1863, a farce; Saratoga, 1874, a comedy; Study of Hamlet (*A*), 1875; Q.E.D., 1871, a comedietta.

MARSHALL (*John*), biographer, born in Virginia, U.S., 1755–1835. Life of Washington, 1804–7; Royal Naval Biography (12 vols.), 1823–35.

MARSHALL, D.D. (*Thomas*), Leicestershire, 1621–1685. Observationes in Evangeliorum Versiones, 1665.

MARSHALL (*William Humphrey*), 1745–1818. Landed Property of England (*The*), 1804; Management of Landed Estates (*The*), 1806; Minutes of Agriculture, 1778; Observations on Agriculture and the Weather, 1779; Planting and Ornamental Gardening, 1785; Rural Economy of Norfolk, 1787; Gloucestershire, etc., 1789; the Midland Counties, 1790; the Southern Counties, 1798; the West of England, 1796; Yorkshire, 1788.

MARSHAM (Sir *John*), London, 1602–1685. Canon Chronicus Ægyptiacus, Ebraicus, Græcus, 1672 (a learned work).

MARSHES (*A Son of the*), pseudonym of *Jean A. Owen* (Mrs. *Owen Visger*), 1841– . After Shipwreck, 1882; Our Honolulu Boys, 1877. And numerous books published under the signature of "A Son of the Marshes."

MARSHMAN, D.D. (*Joshua*), Westbury Leigh, in Wiltshire, 1767–1837. Bengalee and English Dictionary, 1825; Clavis Sinica, 1814 (an excellent work); Dissertation on the Characters and Sounds of the Chinese Language, 1800; Sanskrit Grammar, 1815; Works of Confucius, with a Translation, 1811.

MARSTON (*John*), 1575–1633. Antonio and Mellida, 1602, a tragedy; Antonio's Revenge, 1602, a tragedy; Dutch Courtezan, 1605, a comedy; Eastward Hoe, 1605 (with Chapman, etc.); Insatiate Countess (*The*), 1613, a tragedy; Malcontent (*The*), 1604, a tragi-comedy; Metamorphosis of Pigmalion's Image, 1598, a satire; Parasitaster, or the Fawn, 1606, a comedy; Scourge of Villanie (*The*), 1598, three books of satires; What you Will, 1607, a comedy; Wonder of Women (*The*), 1606 (Sophonisba), a tragedy. His Life, by Halliwell, 1856.

MARSTON, LL.D. (*John Westland*), generally called "Westland Marston," Boston, in Lincolnshire, 1820–1890. Ann Blake, 1852, a play; Death-ride at Balaclava, 1855; Dramatic and Poetic Works, 1876; Family Credit, and other Tales, 1861; Favourite of Fortune (*The*), 1866, a comedy; Gerald, and other Poems, 1842; Heart and the World (*The*), 1847, a play; Hero of Romance (*A*), 1867 (from the French); Lady in her Own Right (*A*), 1860, a novel; Life for Life, 1868, a play; Life's Ransom (*A*), 1853; Our Recent Actors, 1888; Patrician's Daughter (*The*), 1841, a tragedy (his best work); Strathmore, 1849, a tragedy.

MARSTON (*Philip Bourke*), son of the preceding, 1850–1887. All in All, 1874, poems and sonnets; For a Song's Sake, and other Stories, 1887; Garden Secrets, 1887; Song-tide, and other Poems, 1871; Wind-voices, 1884. (He was the subject of Mrs. Craik's Poem, *Philip my King*.)

MARTIN (*John*), painter, born near Hexham, in Northumberland, 1789–1854. His autobiography, 1854.

MARTIN (*Robert Montgomery*), Tyrone, in Ireland, 1803–1870. British Colonial Library (*The*), 1843; China, Political, Commercial, and Social, 1847; History of the British Colonies, 1834–38; History, Antiquities, etc., of Eastern India, 1833.

MARTIN (Sir *Theodore*), Edinburgh, 1816– . Bon Gaultier Ballads, 1854 (with Aytoun); Correggio, 1854, a play (from the German); Essays on the Drama; King René's Daughter, translated, 1850; Life of Aytoun, 1867; Life of Lord Lyndhurst, 1883; Life of the Prince Consort (five vols.), 1874–79 (his chief work); Madonna Pia, 1855; Memoir of W. E. Aytoun, 1867; Odes of Horace, 1860; Poems, 1863; Princess Alice (*The*), 1885; Shakespeare or Bacon? 1888; Vita Nuova of Dante (*The*), 1862. He contributed articles to *Fraser's Magazine*, and tales under the signature of "Bon Gaultier." With Aytoun, several translations from Catullus, Horace, Goethe, Schiller, Heine, Uhland, etc.

MARTIN (*Violet B.*), Ross, co. Galway (writes in collaboration with *Edith Œnone Somerville*). Beggars on Horseback, 1895; In the Vine Country, 1893; Irish Cousin (*An*), 1889; Naboth's Vineyard, 1891; Real Charlotte (*The*), 1894; Silver Fox (*The*), 1897; Through Connemara in a Governess's Cart, 1893.

MARTINEAU (*Harriet*), Norwich, 1802–1876. Autobiography, 1877, posthumous; Billow and the Rock (*The*), 1846; Biographical Sketches, 1872; British Rule in India, 1857; Christmas Day, 1824, a tale (its sequel is called "The Friend"); Complete Guide to the Lakes, 1854; Comte's *Philosophie Positive*, condensed, 1853; Corporate, Traditional, and Natural Rights, 1857; Crofton Boys (*The*), 1840; Deerbrook, 1839; Devotional Exercises . . . for the Young, 1823; Eastern Life, etc., 1847; Endowed Schools in Ireland, 1859; England and her Soldiers, 1859; Factory Controversy (*The*), 1855; Feats of the Fiord, 1840; Forest and Game Law Tales, 1845; Friend (*The*), 1825; Health, Husbandry, and Handicraft, 1861; History of England during the Thirty Years' Peace, 1816–46, 1849–50, introduction 1851 (her chief work); History of the American Compromise, 1856; Hour and the Man (*The*), 1840; Household Education, 1854; Illustrations of Political Economy, 1833, a series of tales; Illustrations of Taxation, 1834, a series of tales; Laws of Man's Nature, etc., 1851 (with Atkinson); Letter on Mesmerism, 1845; Life in the Sick-Room, 1843; Local Dues on Shipping, 1857; Poor Laws and Paupers, 1834, a series of tales; Principle and Practice, 1826; (Three) Prize Essays, 1830; Retrospect of Western Travel, 1838; Rioters (*The*), 1826; Society in America, 1837; Traditions of Palestine, 1830; Turn-out (*The*), 1827. Her Life, by Fenwick Miller.

MARTINEAU, D.D. (*James*), born at Norwich, 1805– . Endeavours after the Christian Life, 1843–47; Essays, 1869, 1879, 1890–91; Home Prayers, 1891; Hours of Thought, 1876-80; Hymns, 1840, 1874; Ideal Substitutes for God, 1878; Miscellanies, 1852; Rationale of Religious Inquiry, 1837; Religion and Modern Materialism, 1874; Seat of Authority in Religion, 1890; Studies of Christianity, 1858; Study of Religion, 1887; Study of Spinoza 1882; Types of Ethical Theory, 1885.

MARTYN, F.R.S. (*John*), London, 1699–1768. Edited Virgil's *Bucolics*, 1749 ; *Georgics*, 1741 (with botanical notes and plates).

MARTYN (*Thomas*), Chelsea, 1735–1825. Aranei, 1793 ; English Entomologist, 1792 ; Flora Rustica, 1792–94 ; Universal Conchologist, 1784.

MARVELL (*Andrew*), Kingston-upon-Hull, in Yorkshire, 1620–1678. Account of the Growth of Popery, etc., 1678, posthumous ; Flagellum Parliamentarium, 1661 ; Miscellaneous Poems, 1681, posthumous ; Mr. Smirke, 1674, prose ; Rehearsal transposed (*The*), 1672, prose ; Seasonable Argument (*A*), 1681, posthumous (a sarcastic notice of some 200 members of the first parliament of Charles II.). His Life, by Cooke, 1772 ; Thompson, 1776.

MASKELL (*William*), Bath, in Somersetshire, 1814– . Ancient and Mediæval Ivories, 1872 ; Ancient Liturgy of the Church of England, 1844 ; History of the "Martin Marprelate" Controversy, 1845 ; Monumenta Ritualia Ecclesiæ Anglicanæ, 1846–47 ; Odds and Ends, 1872.

MASKELYNE, D.D. (*Nevil*), London, 1732–1811. Astronomical Observations, 1776 ; British Mariner's Guide (*The*), 1763 ; Catalogue of the Stars, 1790 ; Nautical Almanac, 1767–1811 ; Tables for computing the . . . Places of the Fixt Stars, 1774.

MASON (Rev. *John*), called "Mason of Stratford ;" with the exception of George Wither, the earliest writer of English hymns : Dr. Watts has borrowed largely from him. Angel's Oath (*The*), "Time is no longer," 1694, a prophecy ; Midnight Cry (*The*), 1694, the parable of the Ten Virgins ; Songs of Praise, 1683.

MASON (Rev. *John*), called "Mason of Dorking," Dunmow, in Essex, 1706–1763. Christian Morals, 1761 ; Lord's-Day Evening Entertainment (*The*), 1751 ; Self-Knowledge, 1745 (excellent).

MASON (Rev. *William*), Hull, Yorkshire, 1725–1797. Caractacus, 1759, a dramatic poem ; Elfrida, 1753, a dramatic poem ; English Garden (*The*), 1772–82, a poem in four books, blank verse ; Fall of Tyranny (*The*), 1756 ; Heroic Epistle (*An*), 1773 ; Isis, 1748, a poetical attack on Oxford ; Life of Gray (the poet), 1775 ; Melancholy, 1756 ; Memory, 1756 ; Odes on Independence, 1756 ; Religio Clerici, 1810, a poem in two parts.

MASON (*William Monck*), Dublin, about 1780–1830. History and Antiquities of the Cathedral of St. Patrick, near Dublin, 1820.

MASSEY (*Gerald*), Tring, in Hertfordshire, 1828– . Ballad of Babe Christabel, and other Poems, 1855 ; Craigcrook Castle, and other Poems, 1856 ; Havelock's March, and other Poems, 1861 ; My Lyrical Life, 1889 ; Poems and Chansons, 1846 (his first work) ; Shakespeare's Sonnets and his Private Friends, 1866 ; Tale of Eternity (*A*), and other Poems, 1869 ; Voices of Freedom and Lyrics of Love, 1849.

MASSIE (Rev. *James William*), 1799–1869. America, 1864 ; Continental India, 1840 ;

Evangelical Alliance, 1847 ; Revivals in Ireland, 1859–60.

MASSINGER (*Philip*), Salisbury, 1584–1640. Alexius, or the Chaste Lover, 1639, a comedy ; Antonio and Vallia, 1660, posthumous ; Bashful Lover (*The*), 1636, printed 1655, a comedy ; Believe as You Like, 1653, posthumous, a comedy ; Bondman (*The*), 1624, a tragedy (with Field) ; City Madam (*The*), 1659, posthumous, a comedy ; Duke of Milan (*The*), 1623 ; Emperor of the East (*The*), 1632 ; Fair Anchoress (*The*), 1640, a comedy ; Fast and Welcome, 1660, posthumous, a comedy ; Fatal Dowry (*The*), 1632, a tragedy (with Field) ; Great Duke of Florence (*The*), 1636, a comedy ; Guardian (*The*), 1637, published 1655, a comedy ; Honour of Women (*The*) ; Judge (*The*) ; King and the Subject (*The*) ; Maid of Honour (*The*), 1632, a tragi-comedy ; Minerva's Sacrifice, 1653, posthumous ; New Way to pay Old Debts (*The*), 1625, printed 1633, a comedy ; Noble Choice (*The*), 1653 ; Old Law (*The*), 1599, printed 1656, a comedy ; Orator (*The*) ; Parliament of Love (*The*), 1625, a comedy ; Philenzo and Hippolyta, 1653, posthumous ; Picture (*The*), 1630, a tragi-comedy ; Renegade (*The*), 1624, printed 1630, a tragi-comedy ; Roman Actor (*The*), 1629 ; Spanish Viceroy (*The*), 1653, posthumous ; Tragedy of Cleander (*The*) ; Tyrant (*The*), 1660, posthumous ; Unfortunate Piety ; Unnatural Combat (*The*), 1639, a tragedy ; Very Woman (*A*), 1655, a tragi-comedy ; Virgin Martyr (*The*), 1622, a tragedy (with Dekker) ; Wandering Lover (*The*), 1653, a tragi-comedy. His Life, by T. Davies, 1789 ; H. Coleridge, 1859.

MASSON (*David*), Aberdeen, 1822– . British Novelists, etc., 1859 ; Carlyle, 1885 ; Critical Sketch . . . of British Prose Fiction, 1859 ; De Quincey, 1878 ; Drummond of Hawthornden, 1873 ; Edinburgh Sketches, etc., 1892 ; Essays, Biographical and Critical, etc., 1856 ; Goldsmith, 1879 ; Life of John Milton, 1858–79 ; Recent British Philosopher, 1865 ; Three Devils (*The*), Luther's, Milton's, and Goethe's, 1874 ; Wordsworth, Shelley, Keats, etc., 1874.

MATHER, D.D. (*Cotton*), Boston, U.S., 1663–1728. Christian Philosopher (*The*) ; Curiosa Americana, 1712 ; Ecclesiastical History of New England ; Magnalia Christi Americana, 1702 ; Memorable Providences relating to Witchcraft, 1685 (an investigation into the famous "Salem Witchcraft") ; Wonders of the Invisible World, 1692 (trials of witches). His Life, by his son Samuel, who also wrote the life of Dr. Nathaniel Mather, under the title of "Early Piety Exemplified," 1689.

MATHER, D.D. (*Increase*), Dorchester, Massachusetts, U.S., 1639–1723. Remarkable Providences, 1684. And above 90 other works.

MATHESON, D.D. (*George*), Glasgow, 1842– . Aids to the Study of German Theology, 1874 ; Can the Old Faith live with the New ? 1885 ; Confucianism, 1882 ; Distinctive Messages of the Old Religions, 1892 ; Growth of the Spirit of Christianity, 1877–78 ; Landmarks of New Testament Morality, 1888; Moments on the Mount, 1884; My Aspirations, 1883; Natural Elements of Revealed Theology, 1881; Pessimist; Psalmist (*The*) and the Scientist, 1887; Religion of China, 1881; Sacred Songs, 1890; Searchings in the Silence, 1894; Spiritual Development of St. Paul, 1890; Voices of the Spirit, 1888.

MATHIAS (*Thomas James*), 1757–1835. Odes, 1798; Political Dramatist, 1795; Pursuits of Literature, 1794–95 (his chief work); Works of Thomas Gray, 1814.

MATTHEW OF PARIS, or MATTHEW PARIS, monk of St. Albans, thirteenth century. Historia Major, 1067–1273 (this history up to 1235 is ascribed to Roger of Wendover, and only the supplement (1235–12) is attributed to Matthew Paris. See MATTHEW OF WESTMINSTER); Lives of the Kings of Mercia and Abbots of St. Albans.

MATTHEW OF WESTMINSTER, chronicler, fourteenth century. Flores Historiarum (this is for the most part drawn from the *Flowers of History* by Roger of Wendover, but the reigns of John, Henry III., and Edward I. are original: it brings the history to 1307), first printed in 1567. See MATTHEW OF PARIS.

MATURIN (Rev. *Robert Charles*), Dublin, 1782–1824. Albigenses (*The*), 1814; Bertram, 1816, a tragedy; Controversial Sermons, 1824; Fatal Revenge, 1807, a tragedy; Manuel, 1817, a tragedy; Melmoth the Wanderer, 1820, a novel; Women, or "Pour et Contre," 1818, a novel.

MATY, M.D. (*Matthew*), born in Holland, but settled in England, 1718–1776. Journal Britannique, 1750–47; Memoirs of Richard Mead, D.D., 1755.

MAUNDER (*Samuel*), Islington, 1790–1849. Biographical Treasury, 1838; Treasury of Knowledge, 1830; Treasury of Literature and Science, 1840; Treasury of Natural History, 1848.

MAUNDRELL (Rev. *Henry*), 1650–1710. Journey from Aleppo to Jerusalem, 1697.

MAURICE (Rev. *John Frederick Denison*), 1805–1872. Bible and Science (*The*), 1863; Christian Ethics, 1867; Commandments (*The*), 1866; Conflict of Good and Evil (*The*), 1865; Conscience (*The*), 1868; Doctrine of Sacrifice (*The*), 1854; Eustace Conyers, 1831, a novel; Friendship of Books (*The*), 1873; History of Moral and Physical Philosophy, 1853–62; Kingdom of Christ, 1842; Kingdom of Heaven, 1864; Lectures on Ecclesiastical History, 1854; On the Lord's Prayer, 1848; Patriarchs and Law-givers of the Old Testament, 1855; Prophets and Kings of the Old Testament, 1853; Religions of the World, 1847; Social Morality, 1869; Theological Essays, 1854; Word "Eternal" (*The*), and the Punishment of the Wicked, 1853. His Life, by his son, 1884.

MAURICE (Rev. *Thomas*), Hertford, 1755–1824. History of Hindostan, 1795–98. Indian Antiquities, 1793–1800 (highly commended by bishop Tomline); Memoirs, 1819–22; Modern History of Hindostan, 1802–10; Poems, Sermons, etc.; Richmond Hill, 1807,

a poem; Westminster Abbey, and other Poems, 1784.

MAURIER (*George Louis Palmella Busson du*), born in Paris, March 6, 1834, son of a Frenchman of old family, died 1896. Introduced by Mr. Edward Lawson to Mark Lemon, and engaged on the staff of *Punch*; succeeded John Leech. Late in life he wrote Peter Ibbetson, 1891, a dream-story; Trilby, 1894 (which had an enormous success, and was dramatized); then The Martians, 1897, posthumous.

MAURY (*Matthew*), Spottsylvania County, U.S., 1806–1873. Physical Geography of the Sea, 1854.

MAVOR, LL.D. (Rev. *William*), of Aberdeenshire, Scotland, 1758–1837. British Tourist (*The*), 1807; Spelling-Book (*The*) (had an almost unprecedented sale); Universal History (in 25 vols), 1802–13; Voyages, Travels, etc. (in 25 vols.), 1796–1802.

MAWE (*John*), 1764–1829. Familiar Lessons on Mineralogy and Geology, 1799; Linnæan System of Conchology (*The*), 1823; Mineralogy of Derbyshire, 1802; Shell Collector's Pilot, 1825; Travels in Brazil, 1812 (his chief work); Treatise on Diamonds and Precious Stones, 1813.

MAX MÜLLER (*Friedrich*), Dessau, in Germany, a naturalized Englishman, member of both our universities, and elected in 1896 on the Privy Council; the greatest Sanskrit scholar that ever lived in Europe, 1823– . Anthropological Religion, 1892; Biographical Essays, 1883; Biography of Words, 1888; Chips from a German Workshop, 1868–70; Coincidences, 1896 (to show how Buddhism has overlaid Christianity in the Roman Catholic Church—read before the Royal Society of Literature); Comparative Mythology, 1858; Contributions to the Science of Mythology, 1897; History of Sanskrit Literature, 1859; Meghaduta, 1847, an Indian elegy (from the Sanskrit); Natural Religion, 1889; On Missions, 1873; On the Stratification of Languages, 1870, a Rede lecture; Origin and Growth of Religion, as illustrated by the Religions of India, 1878; Philosophy of Mythology, 1873, an essay; Physical Religion, 1891; Prātisâkhya (*The*), an ancient work on Sanskrit Grammar and Pronunciation, 1857; Proposals for a Uniform Missionary Alphabet, 1854; Rig-Veda (six vols.), 1840–74 (the four Vedas are very ancient Sanskrit works, on which the Indian religion is based; the oldest is the Rig-Veda, said to be divinely inspired; each is divided into two parts, one of which consists of hymns; "Rig" means *praise* or thanksgiving, and "Veda" means knowledge or *belief;* the "hymns" of the Rig-Veda were published by Max Müller in 1857; the Rig-Veda is the oldest book in existence); Sanskrit Grammar for Beginners (*A*), 1870 (second edition); Science of Language (*The*), 1861–64, 1891; Science of Thought (*The*), 1887; Survey of Languages (*A*), 1855; Theosophy, 1893; Upanishada (*The*), 1879 (the word means "the identity of Brahman and the soul," and the object of these books is to enforce faith in one Supreme

Spirit, the Creator of all things, in whom and by whom they subsist); Vagrakkhediks (*The*), 1881 (from a Japanese Buddhist MS.); Vedânta Philosophy, 1894. All these Vedic books should be deeply studied by theological students.

MAXWELL (*James*), seventeenth century. Carolana, 1614, a poem; Golden Legend (*The*), 1611 (Abraham, Isaac, and Jacob, with their wives); Notable Prophecies, 1615; Prince Henry, and other Poems, 1612; Queen Elizabeth's Looking-glass, 1612.

MAXWELL, LL.D. (*James Clerk*), Edinburgh, 1831–1879. Electrical Researches of . . . Cavendish (*The*), 1879; Faraday's Lines of Force; Kinetic Theory of Gases (*The*); Matter and Motion, 1876; Stability of the Motion of Saturn's Rings, 1859; Telephone (*The*), 1878 (the Rede lecture); Theory of Heat, 1871; Treatise on Electricity and Magnetism, 1873. His Life, by Campbell and W. Garnett, 1882.

MAXWELL (*William Hamilton*), 1795–1850. Stories of Waterloo, 1829

MAXWELL (Sir *William Stirling*), Kinmure, in Scotland, 1818–1878. Annals of the Artists of Spain, 1848; Cloister Life of Charles V. (*The*), 1852; Soliman the Magnificent, 1877; Songs of the Holy Land, 1847; Velasquez, 1855.

MAY (*Phil*), 1864– . On the staff of *Punch*. Parson and the Saintes (*The*), 1891; Phil May's Annual, from 1892; Phil May's Sketch-Book, 1896.

MAY (*Thomas*), Mayfield, in Sussex, 1594–1650. Antigone, 1631, a classical play; Breviary of the History of the Parliament of England, 1650; Cleopatra, 1639, a tragedy; Heir (*The*), 1622, a play; History of the Parliament of England, etc., 1643–47 (praised by bishop Warburton); Julia Agrippina, Empresse of Rome, 1639, an historical play; Life of the Satirical Puppy called Nim, 1657; Old Couple (*The*), 1658, a comedy; Reigne of King Henry II., 1633, an historic poem, in seven books; Supplementum Lucani, 1640; Victorious Reigne of King Edward III., 1635, an historic poem, in seven books. ∴ Translation of Lucan's *Pharsalia*, Virgil's *Georgics*, etc.

MAY (Sir *Thomas Erskine*), 1815–1886. Constitutional History of England since the Accession of George III., 1861–63, 1871; Democracy in Europe, 1877, a history; Treatise on the Law, etc., of Parliament, 1844.

MAYER (*Brantz*), Baltimore, U.S., 1809– . Mexico as it was, and as it is, 1844; Mexico, Aztec, Spanish, and Republican, 1851.

MAYHEW (*Henry*), Westminster, 1812–1876. Great World of London (*The*), 1856; Greatest Plague of Life; London Characters, etc.; London Labour and London Poor, 1851 (his best-known work); Magic of Kindness (*The*); Mormons, or Latter-day Saints (*The*), 1852; Peasant-boy Philosopher (*The*); Rhine (*The*) and its Scenery, 1856–58; Tricks of Trade (*The*); Wandering Minstrel (*The*), 1841, a farce (with Beckett); Whom to Marry, and how to get Married; Wonders of Science (*The*), 1855.

MAYNE, D.D. (*Jasper*), Devonshire, 1604–1672. Amorous Warre, 1648, a tragi-comedy to satirize the Puritans; Citye Match (*The*), 1639, a comedy.

MAYNE (*John*), 1759–1836. Hallowe'en, 1780; Logan Braes, 1781, a ballad (from this Burns borrowed); Siller Gun (*The*), first in 12 stanzas 1777, afterwards expanded into four cantos, 1808.

MAYO (*Herbert*), died 1852. Letters on the Truths contained in Popular Superstitions, 1849; Outlines of Human Physiology, 1827; Philosophy of Living, 1837.

MAYO, M.D. (*Thomas*), London, 1790–1871. Elements of the Pathology of the Mind, 1838; Outlines of Medical Proof revised, 1850.

MEAD, M.D. (*Richard*), near London, 1675–1754. Dissertation on the Scurvy, 1749; Mechanical Account of Poisons, 1702; Medica Sacra, 1748; Moneta et Præcepta Medica, 1751. His Life, by Matthew Maty, 1755.

MEDE (Rev. *Joseph*), Essex, 1586–1638. Clavis Apocalypta, 1627.

MEDWIN (Captain *Thomas*), nineteenth century. Angler in Wales (*The*), 1834; Conversations of Lord Byron, 1824; Lady Singleton, 1842, a novel; Shelley Papers (*The*), 1833.

MELMOTH (*William*), called "Melmoth of Lincoln's Inn," 1666–1743. Importance of a Religious Life, 1711. His Life, by his son William, 1796.

MELMOTH (*William*), called "Melmoth of Bath," son of the preceding, 1710–1799. Letters (at one time immensely admired), called "Fitzosborne's Letters," 1742; Life of William Melmoth, K.C., 1796. Translation of Pliny's *Letters*, 1746; parts of *Cicero*, 1753, 1773, 1777 (considered models of translation).

MELVILLE (*Andrew*), Scotland, 1545–1622. Gathelus, sive de Origine Gentis Scotorum, 1602 Melvini Musæ, etc., 1620; Satyra Menippæa, 1619 (supposed to be by Scioppius, and not Melville); Stephaniskion, 1590. His Life, by MacCrie, 1819.

MELVILLE (*George John Whyte*), novelist, 1821–1878. Black, but Comely, 1879, posthumous; Bones and I, 1868; Brookes of Bridlemere (*The*), 1864; Cerise, 1865; Contraband, 1870; Digby Grand, 1853; General Bounce, 1854; Gladiators (*The*), 1863 (his best novel); Good for Nothing, 1861; Holmby House, 1860; Interpreter (*The*), 1858; Kate Coventry, 1856; Katerfelto, 1875; M. or N., 1869; Market Harborough, 1861; Poems; Queen's Maries (*The*), 1864; Rosine, 1876; Roy's Wife, 1878; Sarchedon, 1871; Satanella, 1872; Sister Louise, 1875; Tilbury Nogo, 1861; True Cross (*The*), 1873; Uncle John, 1874; White Rose (*The*), 1868.

MELVILLE (*Herman*), novelist, New York, U.S., 1819– . Battle Pieces, 1866; Confidence Man (*The*), 1857; Israel Potter, 1855; Mardi, 1848, a philosophical romance; Moby Dick, or the White Whale, 1851; Omoo, or Adventures in the South Seas, 1847; Piazza Tales (*The*), 1856; Pierre, or the

Ambiguities, 1852 ; Redburn, 1849 ; Refugee (*The*), 1865 ; Typee, 1846 (his first literary work); White Jacket, or the World in a Man-of-war, 1850.

MELVILLE (Sir *James*), 1535–1617. Memoirs, first printed 1683 (it is an account of the most remarkable affairs of state not mentioned by other historians).

MENDHAM (*Joseph*), nineteenth century. Account of the "Indexes," 1826 ; Clavis Apostolica, 1821 ; Index Librorum Prohibitorum, by Gregory XVI. 1835, by Sextus V. 1835 ; Life of Pius V., 1832 ; Memoirs of the Council of Trent, 1834 ; Venal Indulgences, 1839.

MENNIS, or MENNES (Sir *John*), 1591–1671. Musarum Deliciæ, 1656 (here may be found the famous lines, imitated in *Hudibras*—

He that fights and runs away
May live to fight another day ;
But he that is in battle slain
Can never rise to fight again).

MERCER (Lieutenant-colonel *William*), poet, seventeenth century. Angliæ Speculum (part i. a long poem, part ii. short poems), 1646 ; Edinburgh Vertues, and other Poems, 1632 ; Elegy on the Earl of Essex, 1646 ; Moderate Cavalier (*The*), 1675, in verse ; News from Parnassus, 1682 ; Welcome to the Lord-Lieutenant of Ireland, 1669.

MEREDITH (Mrs. *C.*), maiden name *Louisa Twamley*, Birmingham, 1812– . Autumn Tour on the Wye, 1838 ; Loved and Lost, 1860, in verse ; Notes and Sketches of New South Wales, 1843 ; Our Wild Flowers described, 1839 ; Over the Straits, 1856 ; Poems, 1832 ; Some of my Bush Friends, 1859.

MEREDITH (*George*), novelist and poet, Hampshire, 1828– . Adventures of Harry Richmond (*The*), 1871 (this appeared originally in *Cornhill*, September, 1870, to November, 1871) ; Amazing Marriage (*The*), 1895 ; Ballads and Poems of Tragic Life, 1887 ; Beauchamp's Career, 1876 (originally in the *Fortnightly Review*, August, 1874, to December, 1875) ; Diana of the Crossways, 1885 (enlarged from the *Fortnightly Review*, June to December, 1884) ; Egoist (*The*), 1879 (a masterpiece) ; Emilia in England, 1864 (reprinted in the coll. edit. of 1887–9 under the title "Sandra Belloni") ; Essay on Comedy (*An*), 1897 ; Evan Harrington, 1861 ; Farina, 1857, a legend of Cologne (reprinted with "The Shaving of Shagpat" in the coll. edit. of 1887–9) ; Jump-to-Glory Jane (a poem in the *Universal Review*, October, 1889, since reprinted, and illustrated by Laurence Housman) ; Lord Ormont and his Aminta, 1895 ; Mary Bertrand, 1862 ; Modern Love, and Poems of the English Roadside, with Poems and Ballads, 1862 ; One of our Conquerors, 1891 ; Ordeal of Richard Feveril (*The*), 1859 ; Poems and Lyrics of the Joy of Earth, 1883 ; Reading of Earth (*A*), 1888 ; Rhoda Fleming, 1865 ; Shaving of Shagpat (*The*), 1856 ; Tale of Chloe (*The*), House on the Beach (*The*), Case of General Ople (*The*) and Lady Camper, 1895 ; Tragic Comedians (*The*), 1880 (origin-

ally in the *Fortnightly Review*, October, 1880, to February, 1881) ; Vittoria, 1867 (the references to "the Chief" in this work are to Mazzini). (A new edition of George Meredith's works is being (1898) issued under his supervision.)

MEREDITH (*Owen*). See LYTTON.

MERES (*Francis*), 1569–1646. God's Arithmeticke, 1597 ; Granada's Devotion, 1598 ; Palladis Tamia, 1598 ; Sinner's Guide (*The*), 1596 ; Wit's Commonwealth, 1597.

MERIVALE, D.D. (*Charles*), son of John H., 1808–1893. Boyle Lectures, 1875 ; General History of Rome, 1875 ; History of the Romans under the Empire, 1850–62.
∴ He also translated Homer's *Iliad* 1869.

MERIVALE (*Herman*), brother of Charles, 1805–1874. Lectures on the Colonies and Colonization, 1841.

MERIVALE (*Herman Charles*), play-writer, 1839– . All for Her, 1874 ; Binko's Blues, 1884 ; Cynic (*The*), 1882 ; Faucit of Balliol, a story in two parts, 1882 ; Fédore (from Sardou), 1883 ; Florien, 1884 ; Forget-me-not, 1879 ; Our Joan, 1885 ; White Pilgrim, and other Poems (*The*), 1883.

MERIVALE (*John Herman*), Exeter, 1779–1844. Beatie's *Minstrel* continued, 1836 ; Orlando in Roncesvalles (a poem in five cantos), 1814 ; Poems, Original and Translated, 1836–44.

MERRICK (Rev. *James*), Reading, in Berkshire, 1720–1769. Messiah (*The*), 1734, a divine comedy ; Metrical Version of the Psalms, 1765 ; Poems on Sacred Subjects, 1763.

MERRIMAN (*Henry Seton*), *nom de plume* of *Hugh S. Scott*. Flotsam, 1896 ; From One Generation to Another, 1892 ; Grey Lady (*The*), 1895 ; In Kedar's Tents, 1897 ; Money-Spinner (*The*), 1896 (Merriman and S. G. Tallentyre) ; Phantom Futures, 1889 ; Prisoners and Captives, 1891 ; Slave of the Lamp (*The*), 1892 ; Sowers (*The*), 1896 ; Suspense, 1890 ; With Edged Tools, 1894.

METCALFE (Rev. *Frederick*), 1817– . History of German Literature, 1858.

METEYARD (*Eliza*), pseudonym "Silverpen," 1801–1879. Ancient London, 1861 ; Doctor's Little Daughter (*The*), 1850 ; Dr. Oliver's Maid, 1857 ; Group of Englishmen (*A*), 1871 ; Hallowed Spots of London (*The*), 1861 ; Industrial and Household Tales, 1872 ; Josiah Wedgwood, 1865–66 ; Juvenile Depravity, 1849, a prize essay ; Lady Herbert's Gentlewoman, 1862 ; Lilian's Golden Hours, 1856 ; Little Museum-keepers (*The*), 1863 ; Maidstone's Housekeeper, 1860 ; Struggles for Fame, 1845 (his first work).

MEYNELL (*Mrs.*), maiden name *Alice Thompson*. Children (*The*), 1896 ; Colour of Life (*The*), 1896 ; Poems, 1892, republished with some changes and additions from "Preludes," a volume of poems written in early girlhood ; Rhythm of Life, 1893.

MEYRICK (Sir *Samuel Rush*), London, 1783–1848. Antiquities of Cardigan, 1810 ; Critical Inquiry into Ancient Armour, 1824 (sir W. Scott calls it "an incomparable armory") ; Costume of the Original Inhabitants of the

British Islands, 1815 ; Illustrations of Ancient Arms, etc., 1830.

MIALL (*Edward*), Portsmouth, 1806–1881. Bases of Belief (*The*), 1853 ; British Churches [and] the British People, 1849 ; Editor off the Line (*An*), 1865 ; Ethics of Nonconformity, 1848 ; Politics of Christianity (*The*), 1863 ; Title-deeds of the Church of England, 1861 ; Views of the Voluntary Principle, 1845 ; Voluntary Principle (*The*), 1845.
∴ He started the *Nonconformist*, 1841.

MICKLE (*William Julius*), Scotland, 1734–1789. Almada Hill, 1781 ; Concubine (*The*), 1767 ; Eskdale Braes, 1788 ; Lusiad (*The*), translated, 1775 ; Mary Queen of Scots, 1770 ; Pollio, 1765 ; Prophecy of Queen Emma (*The*), 1782 ; Providence, 1762 ; Translates into English verse Camoën's *Lusiad*, 1775 ; Voltaire in the Shades, 1770. His Life, by J. Sim, 1806.

MIDDLETON, D.D. (*Conyers*), Richmond, in Yorkshire, 1683–1750. Dissertation on the Origin of Printing in England, 1735 ; Free Inquiry into the Miraculous Powers . . . of the Christian Church, 1749 ; Letter from Rome, 1729 ; Letters of Cicero to Brutus, and *vice versâ*, 1743 ; Life of M. Tullius Cicero, 1741 (esteemed) ; Method for the Management of a Library, 1729.

MIDDLETON (*Thomas*), 1570–1627. Account of Sir Robert Sherley, 1609 ; *Wisdom of Solomon* paraphrased, 1597.
Dramas: Anything for a Quiet Life, 1662, a comedy, posthumous ; Blurt Master Constable, 1602, a comedy ; Changeling (*The*), printed 1653, a tragedy ; Chaste Mayd in Cheapside (*The*), 1620, a comedy ; Civitatis Amor ; Courtly Masque (*A*), 1620, a masque ; Fair Quarrel, 1617, a comedy (with Rowley) ; Familie of Love (*The*), 1608, a comedy ; Four Fine Gallants, 1607, a comedy ; Game of Chesse (*The*), 1624 ; Mad World, my Masters (*A*), 1608, a comedy ; Masque of Honour (*The*), 1619, a masque ; Mayor of Quinborough (*The*), printed 1657 ; Michaelmas Term, 1607 ; More Dissemblers besides Women, printed 1657, a comedy ; No Wit, no Help like a Woman's, printed 1657, a comedy (with Greene) ; Old Law (*The*), printed 1657, a comedy ; Patient Grissel, 1607, a comedy ; Phœnix (*The*), 1607 ; Spanish Gipsie (*The*), printed 1653, a comedy (with Rowley) ; Sun in Aries (*The*), 1621, a comedy ; Trick to Catch the Old One (*A*), 1608, a comedy ; Widow (*The*), 1628, printed 1653, a comedy ; Witch (*The*), 1604, printed 1778, a tragi-comedy ; Women beware of Women, printed 1657, a comedy.
∴ Also numerous "Solemnities" for Lord Mayors' Days, *e.g.* : The Triumphs of Health and Prosperity, 1626 ; The Triumphs of Love and Antiquity, 1617 ; The Triumphs of Honour and Industry, 1617 ; The Triumphs of Honour and Virtue, 1622 ; The Triumphs of Integrity, 1623 ; The Triumphs of Love and Antiquity, 1619 ; The Triumphs of Truth ; and many more. His Life, by Dyce, 1840.

MIDDLETON, D.D. (*Thomas Fanshawe*), bishop of Calcutta, born in Derbyshire, 1769–1822. Greek Article (*The*), 1808

(profound). His Life, by Bonney, 1824 ; C. W. Lebas, 1831.

MILEY (Rev. *John*), Ireland, 1805– . History of the Papal States, from their Origin to the Present Day, 1850 ; Rome under Paganism and the Popes, 1832–34.

MILL (*James*), Northwater-Bridge, in Montrose, Scotland, 1773–1836. Analysis of the Phenomena of the Human Mind, 1829 ; Elements of Political Economy, 1821–22 ; Essay on the Impolicy of Exporting Grain, 1804 ; History of British India, 1817–18 (his chief work) ; Principles of Toleration (*The*), 1837. His Biography, by Bain, 1882.

MILL, D.D. (*John*), Shap, in Westmoreland, 1643–1707. Novum Testamentum Græcum, cum Lectionibus Variantibus, 1707.

MILL (*John Stuart*), London, 1806–1873. Address to the Students of St. Andrew's, 1867 ; Auguste Comte and " Positivism," 1865; Autobiography, 1873, posthumous ; Dissertations and Discussions, 1859–67 ; England and Ireland, 1868 ; Essay on Liberty, 1858 ; Essays on . . . Political Economy, 1844 ; Examination of Sir W. Hamilton's Philosophy, 1865 ; Irish Land Question (*The*), 1870 ; Liberty, 1859, an essay of 16 pages, which has found an immense sale (the subject is, the right of liberty of thought and speech, as well as of conscience, pursuit, and combination) ; Logic ; Nature, and other Essays, 1874 ; Principles of Political Economy, 1848 (his chief work) ; Representative Government, 1861 ; Subjection of Women (*The*), 1869, an essay (admirable) ; System of Logic, 1843 ; Thoughts on Parliamentary Reform, 1859 ; Utilitarianism, 1862, an essay.

MILLAR (*John*), Shotts, Scotland, 1735–1801. Origin and Distinction of Ranks in Society, 1771 ; View of the English Government, 1787–90. His Life, by Craig, 1806.

MILLER, Mus.D. (*Edward*), Doncaster, in Yorkshire, 1731–1807. History of Doncaster, 1791 ; Institutes of Music, 1771 ; Selection of Psalms, 1774 ; Thorough Bass and Composition, 1787.

MILLER (Mrs. *Florence Fenwick*). Atlas of Anatomy, 1879 ; House of Life (*The*), 1878 ; In Ladies' Company, 1892 ; Life of Harriet Martineau, 1884 ; Physiology for Schools, 1880 ; Readings in Social Economy, 1883 ; Simple Lessons for Home Use, 1877.

MILLER (*Hugh*), Cromarty, in Scotland, 1802–1856. Cruise of the *Betsy*, 1858, posthumous ; Edinburgh and its Neighbourhood, posthumous ; First Impressions of England, etc., 1847 ; Footprints of the Creator, 1850 ; Headship of Christ (*The*), posthumous ; My Schools and Schoolmasters, 1854 ; Old Red Sandstone (*The*), 1841 ; Poems, 1829 ; Scenes and Legends in the North of Scotland, 1834 ; Sketch-book of Popular Geology, posthumous ; Tales and Sketches, posthumous ; Testimony of the Rocks, 1857, posthumous. His Life, by Peter Bayne, 1870.

MILLER (*Joaquin*), real name *Cincinnatus Hiner Miller*, Indiana, U.S., poet, 1841– . Baroness of New York (*The*), 1877 ; Chicago, 1876 ; Danites (*The*), 1877 ; Destruction of Gotham, 1886 ; First Fam'lies of the Sierras, 1875, a tale ; Goldseekers of the Sierras, 1884 ; Life among the Madocs, 1873 ; Memorie and Rime, 1884 ; One Fair Woman (*The*), 1876, a novel ; Pacific Poems, 1864 ; Poetical Works, 1882 ; Shadows of Shasta, 1881 ; Ship in the Desert (*The*), 1875, a poem ; Songs of Far-away Lands, 1878 ; Songs of Italy, 1878 ; Songs of the Mexican Seas, 1887 ; Songs of the Sierras, 1871 ; Songs of the Sunlands, 1873 ; Unwritten History, 1873.

MILLER (*John*), botanist, eighteenth century. Sexual System of . . . Plants, 1777 (praised by Linnæus).

MILLER (*Philip*), Scotland, 1691–1771. Catalogue of Trees, Shrubs, etc., near London, 1730 ; Catalogus Plantarum . . . quæ in . . . Chelseiano Aluntur, 1730 ; Gardener's Dictionary, 1731 (his chief work).

MILLER (*Thomas*), the " Basket-maker," Gainsborough, in Lincolnshire, 1807–1874. Beauties of Country Life, 1839 ; Boy's Own Country Book, 1867 ; Boy's Own Library, 1856 ; Brampton among the Roses, 1863 ; British Wolf-hunters, 1859 ; Common Wayside Flowers, 1841 ; Country Year-book (*The*), 1847 ; Day in the Woods (*A*), 1836 (his first prose work) ; Dorothy Dovedale's Trials, 1864 ; English Country Life, 1858 ; Fair Rosamond, 1839 ; Fortune and Fortitude, 1848 ; Fred and the Gorillas, 1869 ; Fred Holdersworth, etc., 1852 ; Gaboon (*The*), 1868 ; Geoffrey Malvern, 1847 ; Gideon Giles, the Roper, 1841 ; Goody Plats and her Two Cats, 1864 ; History of the Anglo-Saxons, 1856 ; Jack-of-all-Trades, 1867 ; Lady Jane Grey, 1840 ; Langley on the Sea, 1858 ; Life and Adventures of a Dog, 1856 ; Lights and Shadows of London Life ; Little Blue-hood, 1863 ; My Father's Garden, 1866 ; No-man's Land, 1863 ; Old Fountain (*The*), in verse ; Old Park Road, 1876 ; Original Poems for my Children, 1850 ; Our Old Town, 1857 ; Pictorial Sketch-book of London (*The*), 1852 ; Poacher (*The*), and other Tales, 1858 ; Poems, 1856 ; Poetical Language of Flowers, 1847 ; Royston Gower, 1838 ; Rural Sketches, 1839 ; Sketches of English Country Life ; Song of the Sea-Nymphs, 1857 (his first volume of poetry) ; Songs for British Riflemen, 1860 ; Songs of the Season, 1865 ; Sports and Pastimes of Merry England, 1856 ; Spring, Summer, Autumn, and Winter, 1847 ; Tales of Old England, 1849.

MILLER (*William Allen*), Ipswich, 1817–1870. Elements of Chemistry, 1855–57.

MILLES, D.D. (*Jeremiah*), antiquary, 1713–1784. Rowley's Poems, 1782.

MILLES (*Thomas*), antiquary, seventeenth century. Catalogue of Honor, 1610 (a judicious work) ; Nobilitas Politica vel Civilis, 1608 ; History of the Holy War (the first crusade), 1604 ; Mysterie of Iniquitie, 1615.

MILLINGEN (*James*), London, 1774–1845. Ancient Coins of Greek Cities and Kings, 1821 ; Ancient Unedited Monuments of Grecian Art, 1822–26 ; Considerations sur la Numismatique de l'Ancienne Italie, 1841 ; Medallic History of Napoleon [I.], 1819 ; Peintures Antiques Inédites de Vases Grecs,

1813–17 ; Recueil de quelques Médailles Grecques Inédites, 1812.
∵ All the works of this author are admirable.

MILLS (*Charles*), Greenwich, 1788–1825. History of Chivalry, 1825 ; History of the Crusades, 1818 (his chief work) ; History of Mohammedanism, 1817 ; Travels of Theodore Ducas, 1822.

MILMAN, D.D. (*Henry Hart*), dean of St. Paul's, London, 1791–1868. Alexander Tumulum Achillis Invisens, 1813 ; Anne Boleyn, 1826, a dramatic poem ; Apollo Belvidere, 1812, Newdegate prize poem ; Bampton Lectures, 1827 ; Belshazzar, 1822, a classical drama ; Character and Conduct of the Apostles . . . as Evidence of Christianity, 1828 ; Comparative View of Sculpture and Painting, 1816, a prize essay ; Fall of Jerusalem, 1820, a dramatic poem ; Fazio, 1815, a tragedy ; History of Christianity, 1840 ; History of Latin Christianity, 1854–55 (his master-work, and a first-class history) ; History of the Jews, 1829–30 ; Life of E. Gibbon, 1839 ; Life of Horace, 1849 ; Martyr of Antioch, 1822, a dramatic poem ; Nala and Damayanti, 1834, from the Sanskrit ; Office of the Christian Teacher (*The*), 1826 ; Poems, 1826 ; Samor, 1818, an heroic poem ; Translations from the Sanskrit, 1834.

MILNE (Rev. *Colin*), Aberdeen, 1744–1815. Botanical Dictionary, 1770 (with A. Gordon) ; Indigenous Botany, 1793 ; Institutes of Botany, 1770–72.

MILNE (*Joshua*), 1773–1851. Treatise on Annuities, 1815.

MILNER, D.D. (*John*), London, 1752–1826. Ecclesiastical Architecture of England, 1811 ; End of Religious Controversy, 1818 ; History and Antiquities of Winchester, 1798.

MILNER (Rev. *Joseph*), ecclesiastical historian, near Leeds, 1744–1797. History of the Church of Christ, 1794–1812 (from a Calvinistic standpoint). His Life, by his brother, Dr. Isaac Milner, 1799.

MILTON (*John*), London, 1608–1674. One of the five epic poets : Homer, Virgil, Dante, Camoëns, being the other four.

Poetry: Arcades, 1633, an entertainment in rhyming verse ; Comus, 1634, a masque, published 1637 ; Death of an Infant (*On the*), 1626 ; Hymn on the Nativity, 1629 ; L'Allegro (trochaic, 7 feet, rhymes), 1637 ; Lycidas, 1637, a monody ; May Morning, 1630, a song ; Morning of Christ's Nativity, 1629 ; Paradise Lost (an epic in 12 books), 1667 ; Paradise Regained (an epic in four books), 1671 ; Penseroso (*Il*), (trochaic, 7 feet, rhymes), 1637 ; Psalms, 1648, 1653 ; Samson Agonistes, 1671, a sacred drama ; Sonnet on Reaching the Age of Twenty-three Years, 1631 ; University Carrier (*The*), 1631, two poems on Hobson ; Vacation Exercise, 1628.

Prose: Areopagitica, 1644 (his best prose work) ; Christian Doctrine, 1823, posthumous ; Colasterion, 1645 ; Considerations . . . for removing Hirelings from the Church, 1659 ; Defence of the Civil Powes in Ecclesiastical Causes, 1659 ; Defensio Populi Anglicani, 1650–51 (burnt by the public hangman) ; Doctrine, etc., of Divorce,

4 T

1644 ; Eikonoklastes, 1649 (burnt by the public hangman) ; History of Britain, 1670 ; Judgment of Bucer touching Divorce, 1644 ; Latin Letters, 1674 ; Observations on the Articles of Peace, 1649 ; On Shakespeare, 1630 ; Prelatical Episcopacy, 1641 ; Pro Populo Anglicano Defensio, 1651, 1654 ; Reasons of Church Government . . . against Prelacy, 1641-42 ; Reformation in England (*The*), 1641 ; Tenure of Kings, etc. (*The*), 1648-49 ; Tetrachordon, 1645. His Life, by Philips, 1694 ; Toland, 1699 ; J. Richardson, 1734 ; Rev. F. Peck, 1740 ; Newton, 1749 ; Birch, 1753 ; Dr. Johnson, 1779 ; W. Hayley, 1794 ; Mosneron, 1803 ; Mortimer, 1805 ; Dr. C. Symmons, 1806 ; H. T. Todd, 1809 ; Byerley, 1822 ; Ivimey, 1833 ; Brydges, 1835 ; Stebbing, 1840 ; Montgomery, 1843 ; Hunter, 1850 ; Edmonds, 1851 ; Hood, 1851 ; J. Mitford, 1853 ; Cleveland, 1855 ; Keightley, 1855 ; Masson, 1858 ; J. W. Morris, 1862.

N.B.—Concordance to Milton: by Prendergast, 1857-59 ; by Cleveland, 1867 ; by Dr. John Bradshaw, 1895.

MINTO (*William*), Auchintoul, in Aberdeenshire, 1845-1893. Characteristics of English Poets, 1874 ; Crack of Doom (*The*), 1886 ; Defoe, 1879 ; English Prose Literature, 1872 ; Literature of the Georgian Era, 1894 ; Logic, etc., 1893 ; Mediation of Ralph Hardelot, 1888 ; Was she Good or Bad? 1889.

MITCHELL (*John*), Stirlingshire, Scotland, 1785-1859. Biographies of Eminent Soldiers, 1865 ; Fall of Napoleon, 1845 ; Life of Wallenstein, 1837 ; Thoughts on Tactics, 1838.

MITCHELL (*Joseph*), 1684-1738. Fatal Extravagance, 1721, a tragedy ; Highland Fair (*The*), 1729, a ballad opera ; Poems, 1729 ; Three Poetical Epistles, etc., 1731.

MITCHELL (*Thomas*), London, 1783-1845. Translated into English verse *Aristophanes* (five plays), 1820-22, 1834-38.

MITCHELL (Sir *Thomas Livingstone*), Stirlingshire, Scotland, 1792-1855. Journal of an Expedition into the Interior of Tropical Australia, 1848 ; Origin, etc., of the Boomerang . . . 1853 ; Outlines of Military Surveying, 1827 ; Three Expeditions into the Interior of Eastern Australia, 1838.

MITFORD (*Bertram*), novelist, . Curse of Clement Waynflete ; Expiation of Wynne Palliser ; Gun-runner (*The*), 1893 ; King's Assegai (*The*), 1894 ; Luck of Gerard Ridgeley (*The*), 1893 ; Renshaw Fanning's Quest, 1894 ; Sign of the Spider (*The*) ; Through the Zulu Country, 1883 ; 'Tween Snow and Fire ; Veldt Official (*The*) ; Weird of Deadly Hollow ; White Shield (*The*).

MITFORD (Rev. *John*), 1782-1859. Agnes, the Indian Captive, 1811, a poem ; Christina, Maid of the South Seas, 1811 ; Correspondence of Walpole and Mason, 1851 ; Life of Gray, 1814 ; Memoirs of Butler, Dryden, Milton, Spenser, etc., 1830 ; Narrative Poems on the Female Character in Different Relations of Life, 1812 ; Poems, 1810, 1858.

MITFORD (*Mary Russell*), Alresford, in Hampshire, 1786-1855. American Stories for the Young, 1832 ; Atherton, and other Tales,

1854 ; Belford Regis, 1835, sketches of a country town ; Charles I., 1832, an historical play ; Christine, 1811, a novel ; Country Stories, 1837 ; Dramatic Works, 1854 ; Foscari, 1826, an historical play ; Julian, 1823, a tragedy ; Letters, etc., 1870, posthumous ; Lights and Shadows of American Life, 1832 ; Our Village, 1824-32 (her best work) ; Poems on the Female Character, 1812 ; Recollections of a Literary Life, 1851 ; Rienzi, 1828, an historical play ; Watlington Hill, 1812, a poem.

MITFORD (*William*), London, 1744-1827. History and Doctrine of Christianity, 1823 ; History of Greece, 1784-1818 (his chief work); Inquiry into the Principles of Harmony in Languages, etc., 1774 ; Mechanism of Verse, Ancient and Modern, 1774 ; On the Military Force . . . of the Kingdom, 1774. His Life, by lord Redesdale, 1829.

MIVART (*St. George*), London, 1827- . Birds, the Elements of Ornithology, 1892 ; Cat (*The*), 1881 ; Contemporary Evolution, 1876 ; Dogs, Jackals, and Wolves, 1890 ; Essays and Criticisms, 1892 ; Genesis of Species (*The*), 1871 (opposed to Darwin: see JONES *T. W.*); Introduction to the Elements of Science, 1893 ; Lessons in Elementary Anatomy, 1872 ; Lessons in Nature, 1876 (showing the gulf between man and other animals) ; Man and Apes, 1873 ; Nature and Thought, 1883 ; On Truth, 1889, a systematic inquiry ; Origin of Human Reason, 1889 ; Philosophical Catechism, 1884 ; Types of Animal Life, 1893.

MOBERLY, D.C.L. (*George*), bishop of Salisbury, born in St. Petersburg, 1803-1885. Administration of the Holy Spirit in the Body of Christ, 1868 (a Bampton lecture); Admission of Dissenters into the University, 1834 ; Great Forty Days (*The*), 1846 ; Introduction to Logic (*An*), 1838 ; Law of the Love of God, 1854 ; Memoir of Bishop Ken (*A*), 1840 ; Sayings of the Great Forty Days, 1844 (between the Resurrection and Ascension) ; Sermons, 1838, 1844, 1848, 1860, 1869.

MOFFAT, D.D. (*Robert*), Inverkeithing, in Scotland, 1795-1883. Farewell Services, 1843 ; Life's Labour in South Africa, 1871 ; Missionary Labours in South Africa, 1842 ; Missionary (*The*), and other Stories, 1871 ; Translation of the New Testament and the Psalms into the Bechuana Language.

MOGRIDGE (*George*), pseudonyms "Peter Parley" and "Old Humphrey," United States, 1787-1854. Amos Armfield, etc., 1845 ; Articles of War, 1863 ; Aunt Mary's Tales, 1867 ; Aunt Rose and her Nieces, 1852 ; Calls of Usefulness, 1846 ; Corner Houses, 1868 ; Elsie Lee, 1868 ; Ephraim Holding's Sunday School, 1864 ; Family Walkingsticks, 1864 ; Footprints of Popery, or Places where Martyrs have suffered, 1843 ; Frank's Victory, 1868 ; Help for Every Hour, 1846 ; Jenny's Waterproof, 1874 ; Learning to act, 1846 ; Learning to converse, 1854 ; Learning to think, 1844 ; Little Messengers, 1868 ; Little Year-book (*The*), 1867 ; Loiterings among the Lakes, etc., 1849 ; Luke and Little Lewis, 1852 ; Memoirs of Old Humphrey, 1855 ; Milly and her Two Friends,

1868 ; Nevers (*The*), 1867 ; Old Anthony's Hints to Young People, 1844 ; Peter and Patty, 1852 ; Peter Parley's Tales, 1828 ; Play-hours, 1843 ; Points and Pickings of Information about China, 1844 ; Rural Pickings, 1846 ; Sketches from my Note-book, 1866 ; Sunny Season of Boyhood, 1859 ; Susie's Mistakes, 1868 ; Things that have Wings, 1857 ; Wanderings in the Isle of Wight, 1846 ; Who is my Neighbour ? 1868 ; Willie Maitland, 1867.

MOIR (*David Macbeth*), pseudonym "Delta," Musselburgh, Scotland, 1798 1851. Autobiography of Mansie Waugh, 1828 ; Bombardment of Algiers, and other Poems, 1818 ; Domestic Verses, 1843 ; Legends of Geneviève, and other Tales, 1824 ; Outlines of the Ancient History of Medicine, 1831 ; Sketches of the Poetical Literature of the Past Half-century, 1851. His Life, by Thomas Aird, 1852.

MOLESWORTH (*Guilford Lindsay*), Millbrook, in Hampshire, 1828– . Conversion of Wood by Machinery, 1858 (obtained the "Watt" medal) ; Pocket-book of Engineering Formulæ (a standard work).

MOLESWORTH (*Mary Louisa*), 1839– . Hathercourt Rectory, 1878 ; Leona, 1892 ; Marrying and Giving in Marriage, 1867 ; My New Home, 1894 ; Next-door House (*The*), 1893 ; Neighbours, 1889 ; Studies and Stories, 1893. And many other publications.

MOLESWORTH (*Robert*, viscount), Dublin, 1656-1725. Account of Denmark, 1694 (an elegant work).

MOLESWORTH (Rev. *William Nassau*), Millbrook, in Hampshire, 1816– . England and France, 1860, a prize essay ; History of England from William IV., 1871-1873 ; History of the Reform Bill, 1864 ; New System of Moral Philosophy (*A*), 1867, a prize essay ; Religious Importance of Secular Instruction, 1857.

MOLYNEUX (*William*), Dublin, 1656-1698. Dioptrica Nova, 1692 ; Sciothericum Telescopicum, 1686.

MONBODDO (*James Burnet*, lord), Monboddo, in Kincardineshire, 1714-1799. Ancient Metaphysics, 1779 ; Origin and Progress of Language, 1773-92.

MONCRIEFF (*W. Thomas*), died 1857. (His real name was *W. Thomas;* he assumed that of Moncrieff when he began to write for the stage.) Giovanni in London, 1829, an operatic extravaganza (the amatory poems of Thomas Shuffleton, Esq., are attributed to him).

MONIER-WILLIAMS (Sir *Monier*), Bombay, 1819– . Brahmanism and Hinduism, 1877 ; Buddhism, 1889 ; Indian Epic Poetry, 1863 ; Indian Wisdom, 1877 ; Modern India and the Indians, 1878 ; Religious Thought and Life in India, 1887 ; Sakuntala, 1887, a translation.

MONKHOUSE (*William Cosmo*), 1840– . Christ upon the Hill (*The*), 1895 ; Corn and Poppies, 1890 ; Dream of Idleness (*A*), 1865, poems ; Earlier English Water-Colour Painters, 1890 ; In the National Gallery, 1895 ; Italian Pre-Raphaelites, 1887 ; Leigh Hunt, 1893 ; Masterpieces of English Art,

1868 ; Question of Honour (*A*), 1868 ; Turner, 1879 ; Works of John Henry Foley, 1875.

MONRO, M.D. (*Alexander*), London, 1697-1767. Essay on Comparative Anatomy, 1744 ; Inoculation for the Small-Pox, 1765 ; Observations, Anatomical and Physiological, 1758 ; Osteology, 1726. His Life, by his son Alexander [*secundus*], 1781.

MONRO, M.D. (*Alexander*), *secundus*, son of the preceding, Edinburgh, 1733-1817. De Venis Lymphaticis Valvulosis, 1757 ; Description of the *Bursæ Mucosæ* of the Human Body, 1788 ; Structure and Functions of the Nervous System, 1783 ; Structure and Physiology of Fishes, 1785 ; System of Anatomy and Physiology, 1795 ; Treatises on the Brain, Eye, and Ear, 1797.

MONRO (*Alexander*), *tertius*, son of the preceding, Edinburgh, 1773-1859. Elements of the Anatomy of the Human Body, 1825 ; Morbid Anatomy of the Gullet, Stomach, etc., 1811 ; Observations on Crural Hernia, 1803 ; Outlines of the Anatomy of the Human Body, 1813.

MONTAGU (*Basil*), London, 1770-1851. Digest of Bankrupt Laws, 1805 ; Essays, etc., 1837 ; Life of Lord Bacon, 1834 ; Thoughts on Laughter, 1830.

MONTAGU (*Edward Wortley*), Yorkshire, 1713-1776. Memorial, 1752 ; Rise and Fall of the Ancient Republics, 1759.

MONTAGU (Lady *Mary Wortley*), maiden name *Mary Pierrepoint* (daughter of the duke of Kingston), born at Thoresby, in Nottinghamshire, 1690-1762. Letters, first printed in 1763 ; Poetical Works, printed 1768 ; Town Eclogues, 1716. Her Life, by Dallaway, 1863 ; by lord Wharncliffe, 1836 ; by Moy Thomas, 1861.

MONTAGU (Lord *Robert*), 1825– . Mirror in America, 1861 ; Naval Architecture, etc., 1852 ; Some Popular Errors, 1871.

MONTAGUE (Mrs. *Elizabeth*), York, 1720-1800. Dialogues of the Dead ; Essay on Shakespeare, 1769.

MONTAGUE (*George*), Devonshire, 1747-1815. Ornithological Dictionary, 1802 (esteemed) ; Testacea.Britannica, 1813, Supplement 1823.

MONTAIGU, D.D. (*Richard de*), bishop of Norwich, born in Buckinghamshire, 1578-1641. Apparatus ad Origines Ecclesiasticas, 1635 ; Origines Ecclesiasticæ, 1636-40.

MONTGOMERIE (*Alexander*), Hazelhead Castle, in Ayrshire, poet, 1540-1607. Cherrie and the Slae (*The*), 1597 ; Flyting betwixt Montgomerie and Polwart (*The*), printed in 1629, a poem (" Flyting " means a contention between two poets : Virgil's *Eclogue* iii. is a " Flyting ") ; Mindes Melody (*The*), 1605. His Life, by David Irving, LL.D., 1821.

MONTGOMERY (*Florence*), novelist, 1847– . Blue Veil (*The*), 1883 ; Children with the India Rubber Ball, 1872 ; Fisher Daughter (*The*), 1888 ; Herbert Manners, 1880 ; Misunderstood, 1869 ; My Walk with God, 1883 ; Peggy, and other Tales, 1868 ; Seaforth, 1878 ; Thrown Together, 1872 ; Thwarted, 1873 ; Transformed, 1886 ; Very Simple Story (*A*), 1867 ; Wild Mike and his Victim, 1875.

MONTGOMERY (*James*), Irvine, in Ayrshire, 1774–1854. Christian Poet (*The*), 1825; Christian Psalmist (*The*), 1852; Climbing Boy's Soliloquy (*The*), 1824; Greenland (in five cantos), 1819; Hymns, 1853; Lectures on Poetry, etc., 1833; Miscellaneous Poems, 1803–20; Ocean (*The*), 1805; Pelican Island (*The*), 1827, a dramatic poem; Poet's Portfolio (*A*), 1835; Prison Amusements, 1795–96 (he was imprisoned for publishing, in a periodical called the *Iris*, an article upon the demolition of the Bastille); Songs of Zion, 1822; Thoughts on Wheels, 1817; Wanderer of Switzerland (*The*), in six parts, 1806; West Indies (*The*), in four parts, 1810 (a poem on the abolition of the slave-trade : the verses on "Home," at the beginning of part iii., are by far his best); World before the Flood (*The*), in 10 cantos, 1813. His Life, by Holland and Everitt, 1856; King, 1858; Ellis, 1864.

MONTGOMERY (Rev. *Robert*), Bath, in Somersetshire, 1807–1855. Christ our All in All, 1845; Christian Life (*The*), 1848; Church of the Invisible (*The*), 1851; Death, 1828; God and Man, 1850; Gospel in Advance of the Age (*The*), 1844; Great Salvation (*The*), 1846; Ideal of the Christian Church, 1845; Luther, 1842, a poem; Messiah (*The*), 1832, a poem; Omnipresence of the Deity (*The*), 1828, a poem; Oxford, 1831, a poem; Religion and Poetry, 1847; Sacred Gift (*The*), 1842; Sacred Meditations, 1847; Sanctuary (*The*), 1855; Satan, 1800, a poem (whence the author was nicknamed "Satan Montgomery"); Scarborough, 1846, a poetic glance; Vision of Heaven, 1828; Vision of Hell, 1828; Woman, the Angel of Life, 1833, a poem; World of Spirits (*The*), 1847.

MOORE (*Edward*), Abingdon, in Berkshire, 1712–1757. Fables for the Female Sex, 1744; Gamester (*The*), 1753, a tragedy; Gil Blas, 1750, a comedy; Trial of Selim, the Persian, 1748, an ironical poem in defence of lord Lyttleton.

MOORE (*Frank Frankfort*), Limerick, Ireland, novelist, 1855–   . Coral and Cocoanut, 1870; Daireen, 1879; Dr. Koomassi of Ashantee, 1896; Fate of the *Black Swan* (*The*), 1885; Fireflies and Mosquitoes, 1888; From the Bush to the Breakers, 1893; Gray Eye or So (*A*), 1893; Great Orion (*The*), 1886; Highways and High Seas, 1888; Ice Prison (*The*), 1891; I forbid the Banns, 1893; Impudent Comedians (*The*), 1896; In our Hours of Ease, 1896; Jessamy Bride (*The*), 1897 (an excellent story); Journalist's Notebook (*A*), 1894; Mate of the *Jessica*, 1879; Mutiny on the *Albatross*, 1884; One Fair Daughter, 1894; Phillis of Philistia, 1895; Sailing and Sealing, 1892; Sale of a Soul (*The*), 1895; Silver Sickle, 1890; Secret of the Court (*The*), 1895; Slaver of Zanzibar, 1889; Sojourners Together, 1872; They call it Love, 1895; Told by the Sea, 1877; Tre, Pol, and Pen, 1887; Two Clippers (*The*), 1894; Two in the Bush, 1895; Under Hatches, 1888; Where the Rail runs, 1876; Will's Voyages, 1886.

Plays : Broken Fetters, 1881; Forgotten,

1889; Kitty Clive, 1895; March Hare (*A*), 1877; Mayflower (*The*), 1892; Moth and Flame, 1878; Oliver Goldsmith, 1892; Queen's Room (*The*), 1891.

MOORE (*George*), *–   . Celibates, 1895; Confessions of a Young Man, 1888; Drama in Muslin (*A*), 1886; Esther Waters, 1894; Flowers of Passion, 1877; Impressions and Opinions, 1891; Literature at Nurse, 1885; Mere Accident (*A*), 1887; Miss Fletcher, 1889; Modern Lover (*A*), 1883; Modern Painting, 1893; Mummer's Wife (*A*), 1884; Parnell and his Island, 1887; Pagan Poems, 1881; Spring Days, 1888; Strike at Arling. ford (*The*), 1893, a play; Vain Fortune, 1891.

MOORE, M.D. (*John*), 1730–1802. Edward, 1796, a novel ("Views of Human Nature . . . England"); Journal during a Residence in France, 1793–94; Medical Sketches, 1786; Mordaunt, 1799, a novel ("Views of Human Nature . . . France"); Mooriana, 1803; View of the Causes, etc., of the French Revolution, 1795; View of Society and Manners in France, Switzerland, and Germany, 1779; View of Society and Manners in Italy, 1781; Zeluco, 1789, a novel ("Views of Human Nature . . . Italy"). His Life, by Robert Anderson, 1820.

MOORE (*Thomas*), Dublin, 1779–1852. Alciphron, 1839; *Anacreon* translated into English verse, 1800 (whence he was called "Anacreon Moore"); Ballads and Songs, from 1806; Epicurean (*The*), 1827, a poetical prose romance; (Six) Fables for the Holy Alliance, 1820; Fudge Family in Paris (*The*), 1818, twelve letters, in verse; History of Ireland, 1827; Intercepted Letters (see "Twopenny Post-bag"); Intolerance, 1808; Irish Melodies, in nine numbers, 1807–34; Lalla Rookh, 1817, an Oriental poetical romance, in four tales; Life of Lord Byron, 1830; Life of Lord Edward Fitzgerald, 1831; Life of Sheridan, 1825; Loves of the Angels, 1823, in three stories, poetry; Memoirs of Captain Rock, 1824; M.P., or the Blue Stocking, 1811; National Airs, 1815, in three numbers; Ode to Nothing, 1800; Odes, etc., 1806; Odes upon Cash, Corn, and Catholics, 1828; Rhymes on the Road, 1820, in eight extracts; Sacred Songs, 1816, in two numbers; Sceptic (*The*), 1809; Tom Crib's Memorial to Congress, 1819, in five numbers; Tom Little's Poems, 1801, chiefly amatory (the pseudonym of Tom Moore); Torch of Liberty (*The*), 1814; Travels of an Irish Gentleman in Search of a Religion, 1827; Twopenny Post-bag, 1811, eight intercepted letters, in verse (one of his best); World of Westminster (*The*), 1816. His Life, by R. H. Montgomery, 1850; earl Russell, 1855.

MOORE (*Thomas*), Stoke-next-Guildford, in Surrey, 1806–1886. Cultivation of the Cucumber and Melon, 1844; Elements of Botany, 1865; Ferns and the Allied Plants, 1856; Ferns of Great Britain and Ireland, 1856; Field Botanist's Companion, 1862; Handbook of British Ferns (*The*), 1848; Index Filicum, 1857; Nature-printed Ferns, 1859–60; Orchidaceous Plants, 1857.

MOORHOUSE, D.D. (*James*), bishop of Manchester, born at Sheffield, in Yorkshire, 1826– . Expectation of Christ (*The*), 1879 ; Genuineness of the Gospels, 1885 ; Jacob, 1870, three sermons ; Nature and Revelation, 1861, four sermons ; Our Lord . . . the subject of "Growth in Wisdom," 1866, a Hulsean lecture.

MORANT (*Philip*), Jersey, a Channel Island, 1700–1770. History and Antiquities of Colchester, 1748 ; History of Essex, 1760–68.

MORE (*Hannah*), Stapleton, in Gloucestershire, 1745–1833. Bas Bleu, 1786, a satire, in verse, against the Blue-Stocking Club ; Bible Rhymes, 1821 ; Bleeding Rock (*The*), 1778, a poem ; Christian Morals, 1813 ; Cœlebs in Search of a Wife, 1809, a novel ; Essay on . . . St. Paul, 1815 ; Essays for Young Ladies, 1789 ; Estimate of the Religion of the Fashionable World, 1790 ; Fatal Falsehood, 1779, a tragedy ; Florio, 1786, a satire, in verse, on the "exquisites" of the day ; Inflexible Captive (*The*), 1774, a tragedy ; Modern System of Female Education, 1799 ; Moral Sketches, etc., 1819 ; Percy, 1777, a tragedy ; Poems on the Slave Trade, 1789 ; Practical Piety, 1811 ; Regulus, 1774, a tragedy ; Sacred Dramas, 1782 ; Search after Happiness, 1773, a pastoral drama ; Sensibility, 1782, a poem ; Shepherd of Salisbury Plain, 1800 ; Sir Eldred of the Bower, 1776, a poem ; Stories for the Middle Ranks, 1818 ; Tales for the Common People, 1818 ; Thoughts on the Manners of the Great, 1788 ; Village Politics, 1793. Her Life, by Shaw, 1802 ; W. Roberts, 1834 ; Rev. H. Thompson, 1838 ; Smith, 1844 ; A. Roberts, 1859.

MORE, D.D. (*Henry*), Grantham, 1614–1687. Conjectura Cabalistica, 1662 ; Divine Dialogues, 1743, posthumous ; Enchiridion Ethicum, 1668 ; Enchiridion Metaphysicum, 1671 ; Opera Philosophica, 1662, 1679 ; Philosophical Poems, 1647 ; Psychodia, 1642, a Platonic song of the soul ; Theological Works, 1708, posthumous. His Life, by R. Ward, 1710.

MORE (Sir *Thomas*), London, 1480–1535. Apologye, 1533 ; Confutacyon of Tyndale's Answere, 1532–33 ; Debellacyon of Salem and Bizance, 1533 ; Dyaloge of Comfort against Tribulacyon, 1553, posthumous ; Dyaloge . . . touching the Pestilent Sect of Luther . . . 1529 ; Historie of . . . Edward V. and his Brother . . . 1557, posthumous ; Letters [against] John Fryth, 1533–34 ; Sergeant and the Frere, 1514 ; Supplycacyon of Soulys against [that] of Beggars (no date) ; Utopia, 1516, translated into English, 1551. His Life, by F. de Herrara, 1617 ; C. More, 1626 ; J. Hoddesdon, 1652 ; Stapleton, 1689 ; W. Roper, 1716 ; F. Warner, 1758 ; Cayley, 1808 ; Dr. T. F. Dibden, 1808 ; T. More, 1828 ; Emily Taylor, 1834 ; W. Rastall ; sir James Mackintosh, 1844 ; Campbell, 1848 ; T. E. Bridget, 1891.

MORELL, D.D. (*Thomas*), Eton, in Buckinghamshire, 1703–1784. Thesaurus Græcæ Poeseos, 1762 (excellent).

MORES (*Edward Rowe*), 1730–1778. English Typographical Founders and Founderies, 1778 (valuable) ; Nomina et Insignia Gentilitia Nobilium, 1749.

MORGAN (*Augustus de*). See DE MORGAN.

MORGAN (*Lady*), maiden name *Sydney Owenson*, Dublin, 1783–1859. Absenteeism, 1825 ; Book of the Boudoir, 1829 ; Book without a Name (*The*), 1841 (with sir T. C. Morgan, her husband) ; Dramatic Scenes from Real Life, 1833 ; Florence Macarthy, 1818, an Irish tale ; France, 1817, 1830 (on its social state) (the period of the first was 1816, of the second 1829–30) ; Italy, 1821 ; Lay of an Irish Harp, 1807 ; Life and Times of Salvator Rosa, 1824 ; Luxima the Prophetess, 1859 ; Missionary (*The*), 1811 ; Novice of St. Dominick (*The*), 1806 ; O'Brians (*The*) and the O'Flahertys, 1827 (her best work) ; O'Donnell, 1814, a national tale ; Passages from my Autobiography, 1859 ; Patriotic Sketches of Ireland, 1807 ; Poems, 1797 ; Princess (*The*), 1835 ; St. Clair, or the Heiress of Desmond, 1810 ; Wild Irish Girl (*The*), 1801, a novel ; Woman and her Master, 1840 ; Women, or Ida of Athens, 1809. Her Memoirs, by J. Fitzpatrick, 1860.

MORGAN (*Sylvanus*), died 1693. Armilogia sive Ars Chromocritica, 1666 ; Horologiographia Optica, 1652 ; Sphere of Gentry (in four books), 1661 ; Treatise of Honor, 1642.

MORGAN (Dr. *Thomas*), died 1741. Moral Philosopher (*The*), 1738, a dialogue between a Deist and a Jew against revelation.

MORGAN, M.D. (Sir Thomas Charles), 1783–1843. Sketches of the Philosophy of Life, 1818 ; Sketches of the Philosophy of Morals, 1822.

MORGANN (*Maurice*), *-*. On the Dramatic Character of Falstaff, 1777 (Dr. Symmons says it is "the most honourable monument reared to the genius of Shakespeare ").

MORIER (*James*), 1780–1849. Abel Allnutt, 1837, a novel ; Adventures of Hajji Baba, 1824, a novel ; Ayesha, the Maid of Kars, 1834, a tale ; Banished (*The*), 1839, a Swabian tale ; Hajji Baba in England, 1828 ; Hajji Baba of Ispahan (*The Adventures of*), 1824, a Persian romance ; Journey through Persia, etc., 1812, 1818 ; Martin Toutrond (a Frenchman in London), 1849 ; Mirza (*The*), 1841 ; Zohrab, the Hostage, 1832, an historical novel.

MORISON (*James Cotter*), London, 1831–1888. Gibbon, 1878 ; Irish Grievances, 1868 ; Life and Times of St. Bernard, 1863 ; Macaulay, 1882 ; Madame de Maintenon, 1885 ; Service of Man (*The*), 1887.

MORISON, M.D. (*Robert*), Aberdeen, 1620–1683. Plantarum Historia Universalis Oxoniensis, 1680 (a valuable work) ; Plantarum Umbelliferarum Distributio Nova, 1672.

MORLAND (Sir *Samuel*), near Reading, in Berkshire, 1625–1695. Description and Use of Two Arithmetical Machines, 1673 ; Description of the Tuba Stentorophonica, 1671 ; History of the . . . Churches in the Valleys of Piedmont, 1658 (a religious butchery). His Life, by J. O. Halliwell, 1838.

MORLEY (*Henry*), London, 1822–1894. Defence of Ignorance (*A*), 1851 ; English Literature (*A First Sketch of*), 1873 ; English Writers before Chaucer, 1864, from Chaucer to Dunbar, 1867, and 1887–95 ; Fairy Tales,

1859, 1860, 1881; How to make Home Un-healthy, 1850; Journal of a London Play-goer, 1866; Life of Clement Marot, 1870; Life of Cornelius Agrippa, 1856; Life of Jerome Cardan, 1854; Life of Palissy the Potter, 1852; Memoirs of Bartholomew Fair, 1858; Shorter English Poems, 1876; Sketches of Longer Works, in English Verse and Prose, 1881; Sketches of Russian Life, 1866; Sunrise in Italy, and other Poems, 1848; Tables of English Literature, 1870. Memoir, by F. Martin, *Contemporary Biography.* This is the Morley who published *Cassell's English Literature* and *National Library.*

MORLEY (The Right Hon. *John*), Blackburn, in Lancashire, 1838-   . Aphorisms, 1887; Burke (English Men of Letters), 1879; Critical Miscellanies, 1871, 1877; Diderot and the Encyclopædists, 1878; Edmund Burke, 1867; Emerson, 1884; Life of Cobden, 1881; On Compromise, 1874; On the Study of Literature, 1887; Rousseau, 1873; Sketch, 1879; Struggle for National Education (*The*), 1873; Studies in Literature, 1891; Voltaire, 1871; Walpole, 1888.

MORLEY (*Thomas*), musical composer, 1550-1604. Book of Ballets to Five Voices, 1595; Canzonets for Three Voices, 1598; Madri-galles for Four Voices, 1594; Plaine and Easie Introduction to Practical Musicke, 1597; Triumphe of Oriana, 1601, an opera.

MORRIS (Rev. *Francis Orpen*), Yorkshire, 1810-1892. All the Articles of the Darwin Faith, 1877; Anecdotes of Natural History, 1859; Bible Natural History (*A*), 1852; Book of Natural History (*A*), 1852; Difficul-ties of Darwinism, 1870; Dogs and their Doings, 1871; Essay on the Eternal Dura-tion of the Earth (*An*); History of British Birds (in six vols.), 1851-57; Natural His-tory of British Butterflies, 1853; Natural History of British Moths, 1859-71; Natural History of the Nests and Eggs of British Birds, 1853; Records of Animal Sagacity, 1861.

MORRIS (*George P.*), born at Philadelphia, U.S., poet, 1802-1864. Complete Poetical Works, 1858; Maid of Saxony (*The*), 1842; "Wood-man, spare that Tree," 1853, a song. His Life, by his son, 1896.

MORRIS (Sir *Lewis*), Carmarthen, in Wales, poet, 1833-   . Epic of Hades (*The*), 1876-77; Gwen, 1879, a drama in monologue, in six acts; Gycia, 1886; Idylls and Lyrics, 1896; Love and Sleep, 1893; Odatis, 1892; Ode of Life (*The*), 1880; Songs of Britain, 1887; Songs of Two Worlds, 1871, and after; Songs Unsung, 1883; Songs without Notes, 1894; Vision of Saints (*A*), 1890.

MORRIS (*William*), Walthamstow, in Essex, poet, etc., 1834-1896. Chants for Socialists, 1885; Decorative Arts (*The*), 1878; De-fence of Guenevere, 1858, a poem; Dream of John Ball (*A*), 1888, in prose; Earthly Paradise (*The*), 1868-70, a poem in four parts (so called because the 24 tales are told in verse by travellers in search of the Earthly Paradise); Glittering Plain (*The*), 1892; Gothic Architecture, 1893; Hopes and Fears for Art, 1878-81, lectures; House of the Wolfings (*The*), 1888, a romance in prose and verse; Life and Death of Jason, 1867, a narra-

tive poem; Love is Enough, 1872; News from Nowhere, 1892, in prose; Poems by the Way, 1891; Roots of Mountains (*The*), 1890, a romance in prose and verse; Signs of Change, 1888, seven lectures; Sir Galahad, 1858; Socialism, its Growth and Outcome, 1893 (with E. B. Bax); Story of Grettir the Strong, 1869; Story of Sigurd . . . and Fall of the Nibelungs, 1876; Sundering Flood (*The*), 1898 (posthumous); Three Northern Love Stories, 1875; Under an Elm Tree, 1891; Well at the World's End (*The*), 1896; Wood beyond the World (*The*), 1894.
∴ Translations from the Icelandic, 1869-75; Virgil's *Æneid*, 1875; Homer's *Odyssey*, 1887. (He wrote various socialist tracts.)

MORRISON (*Arthur*), 1863-   . Adventures of Martin Hewitt, 1896; Child of the Jago, 1896; Chronicles of Martin Hewitt, 1895; Martin Hewitt, 1894; Tales of Mean Streets, 1894.

MORRISON, D.D. (*Robert*), Morpeth, in North-umberland, 1782-1834. Chinese Dictionary, 1822; Chinese Grammar, 1815; Chinese Mis-cellany, 1825; Chinese Translation of the Bible, 1810-18; Horæ Sinicæ, 1812. His Life, by his widow, 1839.

MORTON (*Ann*, countess of), seventeenth century. Devotions, 1665, 14th edition 1689 (from this book Horace Walpole quotes the words, "Lord, wilt Thou hunt after a flea?").

MORTON (*James Maddison*), 1811-1891. Box and Cox, a farce; Give a Dog a Bad Name, a comedy; Phenomenon in a Smock Frock (*A*), a farce. And many others: see APPENDIX II.

MORTON, M.D.(*Samuel George*), Philadelphia, U.S., 1799-1851. Crania Americana, 1839; Crania Egyptiaca, 1844 (his great work); Illustrated System of Human Anatomy, 1849. His Memoir, prefixed to Nott and Gliddon's *Types of Mankind*, 1854.

MORTON (*Thomas*), Durham, 1764-1834. (*The best of his plays are marked with a* *.) Cure for the Heart-ache,* 1811, a comedy; Invincibles (*The*), 1820, a comedy; Roland for an Oliver (*A*), 1819, a comedy; School for Grown Children, 1826, a comedy; School for Grown Gentlemen, 1827, a comedy; School of Reform (*The*),* 1817, a comedy; Secrets worth Knowing, 1798, a comedy; Speed the Plough,* 1798, a comedy; Town and Country, 1807 (for this comedy he re-ceived £1000); Way to Get Married (*The*),* 1796, a comedy; Zorinski, 1809.

MORYSON (*Fynes*), Lincolnshire, 1566-1614. History of Ireland, 1735; Itinerary of Travels through Germany, etc., 1617 (much es-teemed).

MOSELEY (*Henry*), 1802-1872. Lectures on Astronomy, 1836; Mechanical Principles of Engineering and Architecture, 1842.

MOSER (*Joseph*), about 1760-1810. Adventures of Timothy Twig, Esq., 1784, in poetical epistles; Tales and Romances of Ancient and Modern Times, 1800; Turkish Tales, 1794.

MOSS (*Thomas*), Trentham, in Staffordshire, 1740-1808. Imperfections of Human Enjoy-ments, 1783; Poems, 1769 (containing *The Beggar's Petition*, "Pity the Sorrows of a Poor Old Man"); Vanity of Human Wishes, 1783, in blank verse.

MOTHERWELL (*William*), Glasgow, 1797-1835. Harp of Renfrewshire, 1819; Minstrelsy, Ancient and Modern, 1827; Poems, Narrative and Lyrical, 1832; Poets of Renfrewshire (*The*), 1819. His Life, by Dr. J. M'Conechy, 1849.

MOTLEY, LL.D. (*John Lothrop*), Dorchester, U.S., 1814-1877. Life and Death of John Barneveldt, 1874; History of the Rise of the Dutch Republic, 1856 (his best work); History of the United Netherlands, etc., 1860-65; Merry Mount, 1849, a romance; Morton's Hope, 1839, a novel. His Life, by Holmes, 1878.

MOTTEUX (*Peter Antony*), a Frenchman by birth, 1660-1718. Translated *Don Quixote*, 1719; and *Pantagruel*, by Rabelais.

MOTTLEY (*John*), 1692-1750. Catherine, Empress of Russia, 1744; Peter I., Emperor of Russia, 1739.

MOULE (*Thomas*), 1784-1851. Antiquities of Westminster Abbey; Bibliotheca Heraldica Magnæ Britanniæ, 1822 (accurate and valuable); Heraldry of Fish, 1842; Roman Villas of the Augustan Age, 1833; Topographical Description of England, 1837.

MOULTON (Mrs. *Ellen Louise*), maiden name *Chandler*. (Mrs. Moulton was the literary executor of Philip Bourke Marston; she has edited and prefaced a collected edition of his poems.) Bedtime Stories, 1873; Firelight Stories, 1883; Juno Clifford, 1855; More Bedtime Stories, 1874; My Third Book, 1859; New Bedtime Stories, 1880; Ourselves . . . 1887; Poems, 1877; Random Rambles, 1881; Some Women's Hearts, 1874; Swallow-flights, 1878, poems.

MOULTRIE (Rev. *John*), 1804-1874. Altars, Hearths, and Graves, 1853; Dream of Life (*The*), 1843; Lays of the English Church; My Brother's Grave, and other Poems, 1837. Memoirs, by prebendary Coleridge, 1876.

MOZLEY, D.D. (*James Bowling*), Lincolnshire, 1813-1878. Baptismal Controversy (*The*), 1862; Doctrine of Baptismal Regeneration (*The*), 1856; Essays, 1878; On Miracles, 1865 (a standard book); Predestination, 1855; Review of the Baptismal Question, 1862; Sermons, 1876; Subscription to the Articles, 1863; Treatise on the Augustinian Doctrine of Predestination, 1855.

MOZLEY (Rev. *Thomas*), Gainsborough, in Lincolnshire, 1806-1893. Creed (*The*), 1893; Letters from Rome, 1891; Reminiscences of the Oxford Movement, 1882; Reminiscences of Towns, Villages, and Schools, 1885; Son (*The*), 1891; Word (*The*), 1889.

MUDDOCK (*E. J.*), writer of tales, under the pseudonym of "Dick Donovan," 1843- . As the Shadows Fall, 1876; Alps and How to See them (*The*), 1883; Bastile the Jester; Dead Man's Secret (*The*), 1880; Doll, 1880; From the Bosom of the Deep, 1886; Maid Marian and Robin Hood; Shadow Hunter (*The*), 1887; Snowdrop, 1887; Stories Weird and Wonderful; Stormlight, 1888; Wingless Angel (*The*), 1875.

MUDIE (*Robert*), Forfarshire, Scotland, 1777-1842. Air (*The*), 1835; Autumn, 1837; British Birds, 1835 (his best publication); Channel Islands, 1840; China and its Re-sources, 1840; Domesticated Animals, 1839; Earth (*The*), 1837; First Lessons in Natural Philosophy, 1832; First Lessons in Zoölogy, 1831; Gleanings from Nature, 1838; Guide to the Observations of Nature, 1832; Heavens (*The*), 1835; History of Hampshire, 1840; Isle of Wight, 1840; Lessons in Astronomy, 1841; Man as a Moral and Accountable Being, 1840; Man in his Intellectual Faculties, 1839; Man in his Physical Structure, 1838; Man in his Relations to Society, 1840; Mental Philosophy, 1838; Sea (*The*), 1835; Spring, 1837; Summer, 1837; Winter, 1837; World described (*The*), 1840.

·.· These are called Mudie's books, but they were written by divers persons under his direction.

MUIR, D.C.L. (*John*), Glasgow, Scotland, 1810-1882. Comparison of the Vedic with Later Representations of the Indian Deities, 1863; Contributions . . . to the Cosmogony, Mythology, etc., in the Vedic Age, 1870; Mythical, etc., Accounts of Caste, 1866; Origin of the People of India, 1858; Trans-Himalayan Origin of the Hindus, 1860; Vedas (*The*) . . . 1861.

MÜLLER (*Frederick Max*). See MAX MÜLLER.

MULOCH (*Dinah Maria*). See CRAIK (Mrs.).

MULREADY, R.A. (*William*), Ennis, in Ireland, 1786-1863.

·.· He devised a very "shoppy" government envelope, which happily was soon abandoned, 1840.

MUNDAY (*Anthony*), poet, etc., 1554-1633. Archaioplutos, or the Riches of Elder Ages, 1592; Banquet of Daintie Conceits (*A*), 1588; Breefe Chronicle . . . from Creation to this Instant, 1611; Breefe Discourse of the Taking [of] Edmond Campion and other Papists, 1581; Defence of Contraries (*A*), 1593; Downfall of Robert, Earl of Huntington, 1601 (Robin Hood); English Romayne Life (*The*), 1582; Falsehood in Friendship, 1605; Fountaine of Fame, etc. (*The*), 1580; Godly Exercise . . . 1586; Life of Sir John Oldcastle, 1600; Masque of the League, etc. (*The*), 1593; Mirrour of Mutabilitie (*The*), 1579; Paine of Pleasure (*The*), 1580; Strangest Adventure that ever happened (*The*), 1601; Union's Vizard, or Wolves in Lambskins, 1605; Watchword to Englande (*A*), 1584.

Inauguration of Lord Mayors: Chrysanaleia, or the Golden Fishing, 1616 (the Lord Mayor was of the Fishmongers' Company); Chryso-thriambos, or the Triumph of Golde, 1611 (the Lord Mayor was of the Goldsmiths' Company); Metropolis Coronata, 1615; Triumphs of Old Drapery, 1614 (the Lord Mayor was of the Drapers' Company); Triumphs of Reunited Britannia, 1605 (James I. dined with the Lord Mayor).

MUNFORD (Rev. *George*), Great Yarmouth, 1795-1871. Analysis of the Doomsday-book of the County of Norfolk, 1858; List of Flowering Plants found growing in West Norfolk, 1841; Local Names of Norfolk (their derivations), 1870.

MURCHISON (Sir *Roderick Impey*), Ross-shire, Scotland, 1792-1871. Geological Atlas of Europe, 1856; Geology of Cheltenham, 1834;

Geology of Russia and the Ural Mountains, 1845; Geology of Scotland, 1860; Siluria, 1854; Silurian System (*The*), 1839; Tertiary Deposits of Lower Styria, etc., 1830.

MURE (*William*), historian, 1799–1860. Calendar of the Egyptian Zodiac, 1832; Critical History of the Language and Literature of Ancient Greece, 1850–57; Journal of a Tour in Greece, 1838; On the Chronology of the Egyptian Dynasties, 1829.

MURFREE (*Mary Noailles*), pen-name "Charles Egbert Craddock," 1850– . Despot of Broomsedge Cove, 1888; Down the Ravine, 1885; His Vanished Star, 1894; In the Clouds, 1887; In the Stranger-People's Country, 1891; In the Tennessee Mountains, 1884; Juggler (*The*), 1897; Mystery of Witch-face Mountain (*The*), 1895; Phantoms of the Footbridge (*The*), 1895; Prophet of the Great Smoky Mountains (*The*), 1885; Story of Keedon Bluffs (*The*), 1887; Where the Battle was Fought, 1884.

MURPHY (*Arthur*), Ireland, 1727–1805. All in the Wrong, printed 1761, a comedy; Citizen (*The*), printed 1761, a comedy; Essay on Dr. Johnson, 1786; Grecian Daughter (*The*), 1712, a tragedy; Life of Fielding, 1802; Life of Garrick, 1801; Life of Miss Ann Elliot, 1769; Orphan of China (*The*), printed 1761, a tragedy (his first play); Three Weeks after Marriage, 1776, a farce; Upholsterer (*The*), 1758; Way to Keep him (*The*), 1760, a comedy. His Life, by Jesse Foote, 1811.

MURPHY (*James Cavanan*), 1760–1816. Arabian Antiquities of Spain, 1813–15 (a splendid work); General View of the State of Portugal, 1798; History of the Mahometan Empire in Spain, 1816; Travels in Portugal, 1795; Views, etc., of the Church of Batalha, in Portugal, 1795.

MURPHY (*Robert*), Ireland, 1806–1843. Treatise on the Theory of Algebraical Equations, 1839.

MURRAY, D.D. (*Alexander*), Scotland, 1775–1813. History of the European Languages, 1823.

MURRAY (Sir *Charles Augustus*), 1806– . Hasoan, or the Child of the Pyramids, 1857; Prairie Bird (*The*), 1844, an Indian story; Travels in North America, 1854.

MURRAY (*David Christie*), West Bromwich, Staffordshire, 1847– . Aunt Rachel, 1866; Bishops' Bible (*The*), 1890; Bit of Human Nature (*A*), 1885; Bob Martin's Little Girl, 1892; By the Gate of the Sea, 1883; Capful o' Nails (*A*), 1896; Coals of Fire, 1882; Collection of Short Stories (*A*), 1881; Contemporaries in Fiction (*My*), 1897; Cynic Fortune, 1886; Dangerous Catspaw (*A*), 1889; First Person Singular, 1886 (good); He fell among Thieves, 1891; Hearts, 1883; In Direct Peril, 1894; Investigations of John Pym (*The*), 1895; John Vale's Guardian, 1890; Joseph's Coat, 1881; Life's Atonement (*A*), 1880; Little World (*This*), 1897; Making of a Novelist (*The*), 1893; Martyred Fool (*The*), 1895; Model Father (*A*), 1883; Mount Despair, 1895; Novelist's Note-book (*A*), 1887; Old Blazer's Hero, 1887; One Traveller Re-

turns, 1887 (with H. Herman); Only a Shadow, 1891; Paul Jones's Alias, 1890; Queen's Scarf, 1887; Race for Millions (*A*), 1898; Rainbow Gold, 1885; Rising Star (*A*), 1894; Schwartz, 1889; Tales in Prose and Verse, 1898; Time's Revenges, 1893; Traveller returns (*One*), 1887; Val Strange, 1882; Wasted Crime (*A*), 1893; Way of the World (*The*), 1884; Weaker Vessel (*The*), 1888; Wild Dorrie, 1889.

MURRAY (*Hugh*), North Berwick, in Scotland, 1779–1846. Character of Nations (*The*), 1808; Discoveries and Travels in Africa, 1818; British America, 1848; North America, 1829; Asia, 1820; the Polar Seas; Encyclopædia of Geography, 1834 (his chief work); History of British India, 1822; History of the United States of America, 1844.

MURRAY (Rev. *James*), died 1782. Advice to Bishops, with a Discourse on Ridicule, 1774; Essay on Redemption, 1768; History of the Churches of England and Scotland, 1771; History of the American War; History of Religion, 1764; Lectures on the Lives of the Patriarchs, 1777; Sermons on the Revelation, 1778; Sermons to Asses, 1768, 1773; Sermons to Doctors of Divinity (part ii. of "Sermons to Asses"), 1775; Sermons to Ministers of State, 1781; Travels of the Imagination, 1773.

MURRAY (*Lindley*), Pennsylvania, U.S., 1745–1826. English Grammar, 1795 (once in general use); English Exercises, etc., 1797; Power of Religion on the Mind, 1787. His Life, by himself and Elizabeth Frank, 1826.

MURRAY (Rev. *Nicholas*), pseudonym "Kirwan," Ireland, 1802–1861. Decline of Popery and its Cause, 1850; Letters to the Catholic Archbishop of New York, 1847; Men and Things in Europe, 1853; Parish Pencillings, 1854; Romanism at Home, 1852.

MUSGRAVE (Rev. *George*), London, 1798– . Hebrew Psalter in Blank Verse (*The*), 1833; Nooks and Corners of Old France, 1867; Parson, Pen, and Pencil (*The*), 1847; Pilgrimage into Dauphiné, 1857; Ramble in Brittany (*A*), 1870; Rambles in Normandy, 1855; Ten Days in a French Parsonage, 1864; Translation into blank verse of Homer's *Odyssey*, 1869.

MYERS (*Ernest James*), Keswick, poet, 1844– . Defence of Rome, and other Poems, 1880; Judgment of Prometheus, 1886; Lord Althorp, 1890; Poems, 1877; Puritans (*The*), 1869; Selected Prose Writings of Milton, 1884.

∴ He translated Pindar, 1874.

MYERS (*Frederic W. H.*), Keswick, brother of the preceding, 1843– . Essays (Classical), 1883; Essays (Modern), 1883; Phantoms of the Living, 1886; Poems, 1870; Renewal of Youth, 1882; Saint Paul, 1867; Science and a Future Life, 1886; Wordsworth, 1880.

NABBES (*Thomas*), 1600–1643. Bride (*The*), 1640, a comedy; Covent Garden, 1638, a comedy; Entertainment on the Prince's Birthday, 1639; Hannibal and Scipio, 1637, a tragedy; Microcosmus, 1637, a masque; Spring's Glorie (*The*), 1638, a masque;

Tottenham Court, 1638, a comedy; Unfortunate Mother (*The*), 1640, a tragedy.

NADEN (*Constance C. W.*), Edgbaston, in Warwickshire, 1858-1891. Songs and Sonnets of Spring-time, 1881.

NALSON, LL.D. (Rev. *John*), 1638-1686. Common Interest of King and People, 1678; Countermine, 1677; Foxes and Firebrands, 1682; Impartial Collection of Great Affairs of State, 1682-83; Journal of the High Court of Justice, 1684; Translation of Maimbourg's *History of the Crusade*, 1685.

NANSEN (*Fridtjof*), 1861 - . Across Greenland; Esquimaux Life; Farthest North, 1897.

NAPIER (*John*), lord of Merchiston, Merchiston, in Scotland, 1560-1617. Mirifici Logarithmorum Canonis Constructio, 1619, posthumous; Mirifici Logarithmorum Canonis Descriptio, 1614; Plaine Discovery of the Revelation of St. John, 1593; Rabdologiæ, seu Numerationis per Virgulas, 1617 (called "Napier's Bones"). His Life, by the earl of Buchan, 1778; Mark Napier, 1834.

NAPIER (*Mark*), 1798- . Life and Times of Montrose, 1840; Memoirs of the Marquis of Montrose, 1856; Memoirs of Napier of Merchiston, 1834; Memorials of Graham of Claverhouse, 1859; Memorials of Montrose, etc., 1848-50; Montrose and the Covenanters, 1838.

NAPIER (Sir *William Francis Patrick*), Castletown, in Ireland, 1785-1860. Conquest of Scinde, 1845; History of General Sir C. Napier's Administration of Scinde, 1851; History of the Peninsular War, 1828-40.

NARES, D.D. (*Edward*), 1762-1841. Elements of General History, 1822; Evidences of Christianity, 1813; Heraldic Anomalies, 1824; Memoirs . . . of William Cecil, Lord Burghley, 1828-31; Plurality of Worlds [put to the Scripture test]; Remarks on the Version of the New Testament edited by the Unitarians, 1810, 1814; Thinks I to Myself, 1811, a novel (his best-known work).

NARES, Mus.D. (*James*), Stanwell, in Middlesex, 1715-1783. Anthems, 1778, 1788.

NARES (Rev. *Robert*), York, 1753-1829. Elements of Orthoëpy, 1784; Glossary of Words and Phrases in the Time of Elizabeth, 1822 (excellent); View of Prophecy relating to the Christian Church, 1787.

NARY (*Cornelius*), Kildare, Ireland, 1660-1738. New History of the World (*A*), 1720; New Testament newly translated from the Original Greek (*The*), 1718.

NASH (*Joseph*), artist, 1812-1878. Architecture in the Middle Ages, 1838; Mansions of England in the Olden Time, 1839, 1849.

NASH (*Thomas*), Lowestoft, Suffolk, 1564-1601. Almond for a Parrot (*An*), 1590, a satire on the Puritans; Anatomie of Absurditie, 1589; Apologie of Pierce Penilesse, 1592, a pamphlet on his own poverty; Christ's Teares over Jerusalem, 1593; Countercuffe to Martin Junior (*A*), 1593, a satire on the Puritans; Dido, 1594, a tragedy (with Marlowe); Have with you to Saffron Waldron, 1596, a pamphlet in ridicule of Dr.

Gabriel Harvey; Isle of Dogs (*The*), 1597, a satirical play; Martin's Months Minde, no date, about 1589, a satire on the Puritans; Nashes Lenten Stuffe, 1599; Pappe with a Hatchet, 1589, a satire on the Puritans; Pasquil's Apologie, 1590; Pierce Penilesse his Supplication to the Divell, 1592, a pamphlet on his own poverty; Plaine Percevall the Peace-maker of England, no date, about 1589; Returne of the Knight-of-the-Poste from Hell with the Divell's Answere, 1606; Return of the Renowned Cavaliero Pasquill of England, 1589; Strange Newes, etc., 1592, a pamphlet in ridicule of Dr. Gabriel Harvey; Summer's Last Will and Testament, 1600, a comedy; Terrors of the Night, 1594 (apparitions); Tom Nash, his Ghost, no date; Unfortunate Traveller (*The*), 1594 (with J. Wilton); Wonderful . . . Astrological Prognostication, 1591. His Life, by J. Collier, 1842.

NASH, D.D. (*Treadway Russel*), 1726-1811. Collections for a History of Worcestershire, 1781-99.

NAUNTON (Sir *Robert*), Suffolk, 1563-1635. Fragmenta Regalia, 1641; enlarged by J. Caulfield, and called "The Court of Queen Elizabeth," 1814. His Memoirs, by J. Caulfield, 1814.

NEAL (Rev. *Daniel*), London, 1678-1743. History of New England, 1720; History of the Puritans, 1732-38.

NEAL (*John*), nicknamed "Jehu O'Cataract," Portland, in Maine, U.S., 1793-1876. Downeasters, 1831; Errata, 1823, a novel; Keep Cool, a novel, 1817; Logan, 1823, a novel; One Word More, 1854; Otho, 1819, a tragedy; Poems, 1818; Rachel Dyer, 1828; Randolph, 1823, a novel; Ruth Eider, 1833; Seventy-six, 1822; True Womanhood, 1859, a novel.

NEALE, D.D. (*John Mason*), London, 1818-1866. Agnes de Tracy, 1843; Commentary on the Psalms, 1860; Essays on Liturgiology and Church History, 1863; History of Pews, 1841; History of the Eastern Church, 1850-51; Hymns of the Eastern Church, 1862; Hymns, 1865; Rhythm of Bernard of Morlaix, 1859; Seatonian Poems, 1864; Triumphs of the Cross, 1845-46.

NEATE (*Charles*), Adstock, in Buckinghamshire, 1807-1879. Lectures on the Currency, 1859; Three Lectures on Taxation, 1861.

NEEDELL (Mrs. *John Hodder*). Julian Karslake's Secret, 1881; Lucia, Hugh and Another, 1884; Noel Chetwynd's Fall, 1888; Passing the Love of Women, 1892; Stephen Ellicott's Daughter, 1891; Story of Philip Methuen, 1886; Unequally Yoked, 1892.

NEEDHAM (*John Turberville*), London, 1713-1781. New Microscopical Discoveries, 1745; On Microscopical and Generation of Organized Bodies, 1769.

NEEDHAM (*Marchamont*), Burford, in Oxfordshire, 1620-1678. Digitus Dei, 1649; Mercurius Britannicus, 1643, a journal; Mercurius Politicus, 1649-60, a journal; Mercurius Pragmaticus (The Levellers levelled), 1647, a journal.

NELSON (*Robert*), 1656-1715. Festivals and Fasts of the Church of England, 1704 (the sale almost unparalleled); Great Duty of frequenting the Christian Sacrifice (*The*), 1714; Life of Bishop Bull, 1714; Practice of True Devotion, 1708; Whole Duty of a Christian (*The*), 1727. His Life, by Secretan, 1716.

NESBIT (*Edith*), afterwards Mrs. *Hubert Bland*, Kensington, 1858– . Grim Tales, 1893; In Homespun, 1896; Lays and Legends, 1886, 1892; Leaves of Life, 1888; Marden Mystery (*The*), 1896; Pomander of Verse (*A*), 1895; Something Wrong, 1893; Songs of Two Seasons, 1890.

NETTLETON, M.D. (*Thomas*), 1683–1742. Treatise on Virtue and Happiness, 1751.

NEUBRIGENSIS (*Gulielmus*). See below.

NEWBURGH (*William* of), chronicler, 1136–1208. Historia, sive Chronica Rerum Anglicarum (from 1066 to 1197), printed 1567.

NEWCASTLE (*Margaret Lucas Cavendish*, duchess of), born in Essex, 1624–1673. Country Captain (*The*), a comedy; Grounds of Natural Philosophy, 1668; Humourous Lovers (*The*), 1671, a comedy; Nature's Picture drawn by Fancie's Pencil, 1656; Life of William, Duke of Newcastle, 1667; Orations of Divers Sorts, 1662; Philosophical Fancies, 1653; Philosophical Letters, 1664; Philosophical Opinions, etc., 1655; Plays, 1662–68; Poems and Fancies, 1653; Sociable Letters, 1664; Triumphant Widow (*The*), 1677; Variety (*The*), 1649, a comedy; World's Olio (*The*), 1655. Her Life, by herself; published by sir Egerton Brydges, 1814.

NEWCASTLE (*William Cavendish*, duke of), husband of the preceding, 1592–1676. General System of Horsemanship, 1743, posthumous; La Methode . . . Nouvelle de Dresser les Chevaux, 1657, in English 1667; New Method . . . to dress Horses, 1667 (not identical with the above).

NEWCOMB, LL.D. (*Simon*), Wallace, in Nova Scotia, 1835– . A B C of Finance (*The*), 1877; Investigation of the Solar Parallax, 1867; On the Action of the Planets on the Moon, 1871; On the Secular Variations of the Asteroids, 1860; Our Financial Policy during the Southern Rebellion, 1865; Popular Astronomy, 1878; Tables of the Planet Neptune, 1865; Tables of the Planet Uranus, 1873.

NEWCOMB (Rev. *Thomas*), 1675–1766. Last Judgment, 1723; Library (*The*), 1718; Odes and Epigrams, 1743; Poems, Odes, Epistles, etc., 1756.

NEWCOMBE, D.D. (*William*), archbishop of Armagh, born in Bedfordshire, 1729–1800. Attempt towards revising the Translation of the Greek Scriptures, 1880; Chief Difficulties in the Gospel History relating to our Lord's Resurrection, 1791; Duration of our Lord's Ministry, 1780; Harmony of the Gospels, 1778 (good); Historical View of English Biblical Translations, 1792; New Version of Ezekiel, 1788; New Version of the Twelve Minor Prophets, 1785; Our Lord's Conduct as a Divine Instructor, 1782.

NEWMAN (*Edward*), 1801–1876. History of British Ferns; Letters on the Natural History of Godalming, 1849; List of British Ornithology; Natural History of British Butterflies.

NEWMAN (*Francis William*), brother of John Henry, London, 1805– . Catholic Union, 1854; Christian Commonwealth (*A*), 1883; Christianity in its Cradle, 1884; Church of the Future (*A*), 1854; Contrasts of Ancient and Modern History, 1847; Crimes of the House of Hapsburg, 1853; Early History of Cardinal Newman (*The*), 1891; Essays towards a Church of the Future, 1854; History of the Hebrew Monarchy, 1847; Introduction to Roman History, 1852; Kabail Vocabulary, 1888; Lectures on Ancient and Modern History, 1851; Lectures on Logic, 1838; Lectures on Political Economy, 1851; Libyan Vocabulary (*A*), 1882; Life after Death, 1887; National Debt (*The*), 1849; Passages from My Own Creed, 1850; Phases of Faith, etc., 1850 (his best-known work); Radical Reforms, etc., 1848; Rebilius, or Robinson Crusoe in Latin, 1884; Regal Rome, 1852; Reminiscences of Two Exiles and Two Wars, 1888; Soul (*The*), her Sorrows and Aspirations, 1849; State Church not defensible (*A*), 1846; Theism, or Didactic Religious Utterances, 1858.

NEWMAN, D.D. (*John Henry*), generally called "Cardinal Newman," brother of the preceding, London, 1801–1890. Apologia pro Vita Sua, 1864; Arians of the Fourth Century, 1838; Callista, 1856, a third-century sketch; Church of the Fathers, 1842; Development of Christian Doctrine, 1846 (his chief work); Dream of Gerontius (*The*), 1865; Essay on Assent, 1870; Essays, 1871; Grammar of Assent (*The*), 1870; Historical Sketches, 1872; Kingsley and Newman, 1864 (correspondence); Lectures on Justification, 1838; Lectures on Romanism, etc., 1837; Lectures on University Subjects, 1859; Letter to Dr. Pusey, 1866; Life of Apollonius Tyanæus, 1824; Lives of the English Saints, 1844; Loss and Gain, 1848, the story of a convert; Maxims of the Kingdom of Heaven, 1867; Miracles of the Middle Ages (*The*), 1843; Office and Work of Universities (*The*), 1854–56; Pincerna . . . 1880; Poems, 1868; Prophetical Office of the Church, etc., 1837; Sermons, 1838–44, 1844, 1857–68; Theory of Religious Belief (*The*), 1844; Tracts for the Times (No. 90), 1840; Turks (*The*), and Christianity, 1854; Via Media, 1877. His Life, by H. J. Jennings, 1881.

NEWMARCH (*William*), Yorkshire, 1820–1882. Loans raised (1793–1807) by Mr. Pitt, etc., 1855; New Supplies of Gold, 1853.

NEWTON (Sir *Isaac*), one of the five English Philosophers, etc., Woolsthorpe, Lincolnshire, 1642–1727. Analysis per Quantitatum Series, 1711; Arithmetica Universalis, 1707; Chronology of Ancient Kingdoms, 1728, posthumous; De Mundi Systemate, 1728, posthumous; Letters on Disputed Texts, 1754, posthumous; Letters to Bentley, 1693; Method of Fluxions, etc., 1669 (published 1711, 1736); Optical Lectures, 1728, posthumous; Opticks, 1704; Observations on Daniel and the Apocalypse, 1733, posthumous; Principia Philosophiæ Naturalis Mathematica, 1684, published 1687–1726 (his great work, best edition, 1871); Quadrature of Curves, 1700. His Life, by

Fontenelle, 1728; Frisi, 1778; Biot, 1822; De Morgan, 1833; Dr. Whewell, 1836; sir David Brewster, 1853, 1855; Conduitt.

NEWTON, D.D. (*John*), London, 1725–1807. Cardiphonia, or Utterance of the Heart, 1781; Messiah (*The*), in 50 sermons, 1786; Narrative of his own Life, 1764; Olney Hymns, 1779 (with Cowper); Omicron's Letters, 1762; Review of Ecclesiastical History, 1770.

NEWTON, D.D. (*Thomas*), bishop of Bristol, born at Lockfield, in Hampshire, 1704–1782. Dissertation on the Prophecies, 1758–58.
∴ He edited the *Paradise Lost*, with notes, concordance, and life of Milton, 1749 (excellent); *Paradise Regained*, 1752.

NICCOLS (*Richard*), poet, 1584– . Beggar's Ape (*The*), no date; Cuckow (*The*), 1607; England's Eliza, 1610; Furies (*The*), 1614; London's Artillerie, 1616; Monodia, 1615; Sir Thomas Overberrie's Vision, 1616; Three Sisters' Tears (*The*), 1613; Twynnes Tragedye (*The*), 1611; Virtue's Encomium, 1614.

NICHOL, LL.D. (*John*), Montrose, in Scotland, 1833–1894. American Literature, 1882; Byron, 1880; Death of Themistoclês, and other Poems, 1881; Francis Bacon, his Life and Philosophy, 1888–89; Fragments of Criticism, 1860; Hannibal, 1872, a dramatic poem; Leaves, 1854; Robert Burns, 1882; Tables of Ancient History, 1876; Tables of English Literature, 1876–88; Thomas Carlyle, 1892.

NICHOL, LL.D. (*John Pringle*), Montrose, in Scotland, 1804–1859. Architecture of the Heavens, 1838; Cyclopædia of Physical Sciences, 1857; Planet Neptune (*The*), 1848; Planetary System (*The*), 1851; Stellar Universe (*The*), 1848.

NICHOLLS, M.D. (*Frank*), London, 1699–1778. De Anima Medica, 1748; De Motu Cordis et Sanguinis, 1772.

NICHOLLS (Sir *George*), Cornwall, 1786–1851. History of the English Poor Law (*The*), 1855; Irish Poor Law (*The*), 1856; Scotch Poor Law (*The*), 1856.

NICHOLLS, D.D. (*William*), Donnington, in Buckinghamshire, 1664–1712. Commentary on the Book of Common Prayer, 1710; Conference with a Theist, 1723; Defence of the Church of England (first published in Latin).

NICHOLS (*James*), died 1861. Calvinism and Arminianism compared, 1824 (much praised by the *Quarterly Review*).

NICHOLS (*John*), Islington, 1745–1826. Anecdotes of Bowyer, etc., 1782 (his chief work); Bibliotheca Topographica Britannica, 1780–90 (with Gough); Biographical Anecdotes of Hogarth, 1781 (continued by his son, see below); History and Antiquities of Hinckley, in Leicestershire, 1813; History and Antiquities of Leicestershire, 1795–1815; Illustrations of the Literary History of the Eighteenth Century, 1795–1811 (continued by his son, see below, to 1858); Illustrations of the Manners and Expenses of Ancient Times in England, 1797; Literary Anecdotes of the Eighteenth Century, 1812–15; Memoirs of Mr. Bowyer, 1778; Origin of Printing, 1774 (with Bowyer); Progresses

and Processions of Queen Elizabeth, 1788–1807; Progress and Processions of James I., 1828, posthumous. Memoir, by Alexander Chalmers, 1826.

NICHOLS (*John Bowyer*), son of the preceding, London, 1779–1863. Anecdotes of Hogarth, 1833; Collectanea Topographica, etc., 1834–43; Fonthill and its Abbey, 1836; Illustrations of the Literary History of the Eighteenth Century, continued and completed, 1848–58 (see above); London Pageants, 1831.

NICHOLSON, M.D. (*Henry Alleyne*), Penrith, in Cumberland, 1844– . Fossil Corals of the State of Ohio, 1875; Geology of Cumberland and Westmoreland, 1866; Monograph of the British Graptolitidæ, 1872; Palæontology of Ontario, 1874–75. Many other similar works.

NICHOLSON I (*William*), London, 1753–1815. Dictionary of Chemistry, 1795.

NICOLAS (Sir *Nicholas Harris*), Cornwall, 1799–1848. Alphabetical Lists of the Knights, 1725; Catalogue of Heralds' Visitations, 1823; Chronology of History, 1835 (a standard work); Despatches and Letters of Nelson, 1844–46; History of the Battle of Agincourt, 1827; History of the British Navy, 1847 (left unfinished); History of the Orders of Knighthood in the British Empire, 1841–42; History of Rugby, 1827; Life of William Davison, 1823; Life and Times of Sir Christopher Hatton, 1847; Lives of Izaac Walton and Charles Cotton, 1837; Memoirs of Augustus Vincent, 1827; Notitia Historica, 1824; Roll of Arms, etc., 1828–29; Siege of Carlaverock (*The*), 1828; Statutes of the Order of the Thistle, and Catalogue of the Knights, 1828; Synopsis of the Peerage of England, 1825; Testamenta Vetusta, 1826.

NICOLSON (*William*), archbishop of Cashel, born in Cumberland, 1655–1727. English Historical Library, 1696–99; Irish Historical Library, 1724; Leges Marchiarum, or Border Laws, 1705; Scottish Historical Library, 1702.

NIGHTINGALE (*Florence*), Florence, 1820– . Hints on Hospitals, 1859; Life or Death in India, 1874; Notes on Lying-in Institutions, 1871; Notes on Nursing, 1860; On the Sanitary State of the Army in India, 1863.

NISBET (*Alexander*), 1672–1725. Additional Figures and Marks of Cadency, 1702; Ancient and Modern Use of Armories, 1718; System of Heraldry (*A*), 1722–42 (valuable).

NIXON (*Anthony*), about 1566–1622. Blacke Year (*The*), 1606; Cheshire Prophecy (*The*), 1719, posthumous; Christian Navy (*The*), . . . the Course to sayle to the Haven of Happiness, 1602; Dignitie of Man (*The*), 1612; Eliza's Memoriall, 1603; Ground . . . of the Wars of Swetheland, 1609; London's Dove (*i.e.* Robert Dove), 1612; Oxford's Triumph, 1605 (visit of the queen and prince); Scourge of Corruption, or a Crafty Knave needs no Broker, 1615; Strange Foot-post (*A*), 1613.

NOBLE (Rev. *Mark*), biographer, died 1827. Genealogical History of the Royal Families of Europe, 1781; Historical Genealogy of the House of Stuart, 1795; History of the College of Arms, 1804; Lives of English Regicides, 1798; Memoirs of the House of Cromwell, 1784; Memoirs of the Medici, 1797.

NOBLE (Rev. *Samuel*), London, 1779-1853. Appeal in Behalf of Certain Doctrines of the New Church, 1826; Plenary Inspiration of the Scriptures, 1824.

NOEL (Hon. and Rev. *Baptist Wriothesley*), 1799-1873. Essay on the External Act of Baptism, 1850; Essay of the Union of Church and State, 1848; Protestant Thoughts in Rhyme.

NOEL (Hon. *Roden Berkeley Wriothesley*), poet, 1834-1896. Beatrice, 1869; Behind the Veil, 1863; Essays on Poetry, 1886; Home of Ravensburg (*The*), 1877; Little Child's Monument (*A*), 1881; Livingstone in Africa, 1874; Modern Faust (*A*), 1888; My Sea, 1896; Philosophy of Immortality (*A*), 1882; Red Flag (*The*), 1872.

NOLAN (Captain *Lewis Edward*), 1817-1854. Organization, Drill, etc., of Cavalry Corps, 1853.

NORDEN (*John*), Wiltshire, 1548-1625. Antithesis, or Contrarietie between the Wicked and Godly, set forth in a Pair of Gloves fit for Every Man to wear, 1590; England, or a Guide for Travellers, 1625; Eye to Heaven and Earth (*An*), 1619; Labyrinth of Man's Life (*The*), 1614, a poem; Loadstone to a Spiritual Life, 1614; Mirror for the Multitude (*A*), 1586; Mirror of Honour (*The*), 1597; Pathway to Patience, 1626; Pensive Man's Practise (*A*), 1585; Pensive Soules Delight (*A*), 1615; Poor Man's Rest, 1620; Progress of Pietie,1596; Reforming Glass(*A*), 1596; Sinful Man's Solace, 1592; Speculum Britanniæ, 1593-1620; Surveyor's Dialogue, 1607; Vicissitudo Rerum, 1600, a poem.

NORMAN (*Henry*), Leicester, 1858 – . Account of the Havard Greek Play (*An*); Near East (*The*), 1897; People and Politics of the Far East, 1895; Preservation of Niagara Falls (*The*), 1882; Real Japan (*The*), 1892.

NORMAN (*Menie Muriel*), wife of the above, 1867– . Gallia, 1895; Girl in the Karpathians, 1891.

NORMANBY (*Constantine Henry Phipps*, marquis of), 1797-1863. Congress (*The*) and the Cabinet, 1859; Louise de Bourbon, 1861; Matilda, 1825, a novel; Year of Revolution (*A*), 1857; Yes or No, 1818, a novel.

NORRIS (Rev. *John*), the "English Plato," born in Wiltshire, 1657-1711. Discourse concerning the Immortality of the Soul, 1708; Discourses on the Beatitudes, 1690; Idea of Happiness (*The*), 1688; Picture of Love unveiled, 1682; Reason and Faith, 1697; Reason and Religion, 1689; Reflections on the Conduct of Human Life, 1690; Theory and Regulation of Love, 1688; Theory of an Ideal World, 1691-1701 (his chief work).

NORRIS (*W. E.*), novelist, 1847– . Adrian Vidal, 1885; Bachelor's Blunder (*A*), 1886; Baffled Conspirators (*The*), 1890; Billy Bellew, 1895; Chris, 1888; Clarissa Furiosa, 1897; Dancer in Yellow (*A*), 1896; Deplorable Affair (*A*), 1893; Fight for the Crown (*The*), 1898; Heaps of Money, 1877; Hearts; His Grace, 1892; Jack's Father,

etc., 1891; Major and Minor, 1887; Man of his Word (*A*), 1885; Marcia, 1890; Matrimony, 1881; Matthew Austin, 1894; Misadventure, 1890; Miss Shafto, 1889; Miss Wentworth's Idea, 1891; Mlle. de Mersac, 1880; Mr. Chain's Sons, 1891; Mrs. Fenton, 1889; My Friend Jim, 1886; No New Thing, 1883; Rogue (*The*), 1888; Saint Ann's, 1894; Style in Fiction, 1894; Thirlby Hall, 1884; Victim of Good Luck (*A*), 1894.

NORTH (Sir *Dudley*), 1641-1691. Discourses on Trade, 1691 (commended by MacCulloch). His Life, by Roger North, 1740-42.

NORTH (*Roger*), biographer, 1650-1733. Discourse on the Study of the Laws, 1824, posthumous; Examen, 1740, a defence of Charles II.; Fish and Fishponds, 1713; Lives of the Norths, 1742-44; Memoirs of Musick, 1846, posthumous.

NORTH (Sir *Thomas*), 1535-1579. Translated Doni's *Moral Philosophy*, 1570; Guevara's *Dial of Princes*, 1557; Plutarch's *Lives*, 1578 (his best-known work).

NORTHCOTE, R.A. (*James*), Plymouth, 1746-1831. Life of Titian, 1820 (with Hazlitt); Memoirs of Sir Joshua Reynolds, 1813-15; One Hundred Fables,1828,second series 1828.

NORTON (Rev. *Andrews*), Hingham, U.S., 1786-1853. Genuineness of the Gospels, 1837, 1844, 1855; On the Latest Forms of Infidelity, 1839; Reasons for not believing the Doctrine of the Trinity, 1833; Tracts concerning Christianity, 1852.

NORTON (Hon. Mrs.), maiden name *Caroline Elizabeth Sarah Sheridan*, 1808-1877. Aunt Carry's Ballads for Children, 1847; Child of the Islands (*The*), 1845, a poem; Coquette (*The*), and other Stories, 1834; Dandies' Rout (*The*), 1829, a satire; Dream (*The*), and other Poems, 1840; English Laws for Women, 1854; Lady of La Garaye, 1862, in verse; Lost and Saved, 1863, a novel; Martyr (*The*), 1849, a tragedy; Old Sir Douglas, 1867 (one of her best); Residence in Sierra Leone, 1849; Rose of Jericho (*The*), 1870; Sorrows of Rosalie, 1829 (her first work); Stuart of Dunleath, 1851, a novel; Tales and Sketches, in Prose and Verse, 1850 (same as "The Coquette"); Undying One (*The*), 1831 (her best poem); Wife (*The*), and Woman's Reward, 1835.

NORTON (*Thomas*), called "Archicarnifex," Sharpenhoe, Bedfordshire, 1532 – 1584. Epistle to the Queen's Poor Deceived Subjects of the North Country; Ferrex and Porrex (the first three acts), 1561 (the first English tragedy); Twenty-seven of the *Psalms of David*, in Sternhold and Hopkins' version, 1549; Warning against the Dangerous Practices of Papists.

NORWOOD (*Richard*), about 1590-1645. Seaman's Practice (*The*), 1637; Trigonometry, 1631.

NOTT, M.D. (*John*), Worcester, 1751-1826. Poems, 1780; Translations from *Hafiz*, 1787, and *Petrarch*, 1777, 1808.

NOWELL, D.D. (*Alexander*), 1507-1602. Catechism(the third),1577; Catechismus Parvus, 1574, an English version 1587; Christianæ Pietatis Prima Institutio,1570,an English version 1571. His Life, by R. Churton, 1809.

Noy (*William*), Cornwall, 1577–1634. Compleat Lawyer (*The*), 1651, posthumous; Grounds and Maximes of the Lawes of England, 1641 ; Reports, 1656 ; Rights of the Crown, 1715. His Life, by sir John Doddridge, 1821.

Nugent (*George Grenville*, lord), Buckingham Castle, 1788–1850. Essay on Duelling, 1807 ; Lands, Classical and Sacred, 1845 ; Legends of the Library at Lilies, 1832 ; Memorials of Hampden, 1831 ; Oxford and Locke, 1829 ; Portugal, 1812, a poem.

Nugent (*Robert Craggs*, earl), Ireland, 1709–1788. Faith, 1774, a poem ; Ode to Mankind, 1741 ; Odes and Epistles, 1739.

Nugent, LL.D. (*Thomas*), died 1772. Dictionnaire Portatif des Langues Française et Anglaise, 1774, posthumous ; History of Vandalia, 1766 ; Principles of Political Law, 1756, posthumous (this is a translation of Burlamaqui's work).

Oakeley (Rev. *Frederick*), Shrewsbury, 1802–1880. Catholic Worship, 1872 ; Church of the Bible (*The*), 1857 ; Historical Notes on the Tractarian Movement, 1833–45 ; Lyra Liturgica, 1867 ; Practical Sermons, 1848 ; Priest on the Mission (*The*), 1871 ; Sacrifice of the Mass (*The*), 1848 ; Voice of Creation (*The*), 1875 ; Whitehall Sermons, 1839 ; Youthful Martyrs of Rome, 1856 (adaptation of Wiseman's *Fabiola*).

O'Brien (*Henry*), Ireland, nineteenth century. Round Towers of Ireland (*The*), 1834 (prize essay).

O'Brien (*William*), 1852–   . Irish Ideas, 1893 ; When we were Boys, 1890 (written in prison).

Occam (*William of*), called "Doctor Singularis et Invincibilis," born in Surrey, 1270–1347. Centilcquium Theologicum, printed 1494 ; Compendium Errorum Johannis Popæ XXII., printed 1496 ; De Sacramento Altaris, printed 1514 ; Dialogorum Libri Septem adversus Hæreticos, etc., printed 1476 ; Disputatio inter Clericum et Militem, printed 1475 ; Expositio Aurea, etc., printed 1496 ; Opus Nonaginta Dierum . . . contra Johannem XXII., printed 1481 ; Questiones et Decisiones, in quatuor libros, etc., printed 1495 ; Quodlibeta Septem, printed 1487 ; Scriptum in Primum Librum Sentenciarum, etc., printed 1483 ; Summa Totius Logicæ, printed 1498 ; Tractatus Logicæ, etc., printed 1488.
∴ He was the best logical writer of the Middle Ages.

Ockley (*Simon*), Exeter, 1678–1720. History of the Present Jews, 1707 ; History of the Saracens, 1708–18 ; Introductio ad Linguas Orientales, 1706 ; South-West Barbary, 1713.

O'Connor, M.D. (*Bernard*), Kerry, Ireland, 1666–1698. Evangelium Medici, 1697 ; Letters on Poland, 1698.

O'Connor (*Thomas Power*), Athlone, Ireland, 1848–   . Benjamin Disraeli, 1876 ; Charles Stewart Parnell, 1891 ; Gladstone's House of Commons, 1885 ; Lord Beaconsfield, 1879 ; Napoleon, 1896 ; Parnell Movement (*The*), 1886 ; Sketches in the

House, 1893 ; Some Old Love Stories, 1895.

O'Conor (*Charles*), Belanagare, Ireland, eighteenth century. Dissertation on the History of Ireland, 1766 (valuable). His Life, by Dr. Charles O'Conor, 1796 (rare).

O'Conor, D.D. (*Charles*), 1760–1828. Bibliotheca MS. Stowensis, 1818–19 ; Columbanus ad Hibernos, 1810–16 ; Memoirs of Charles O'Conor, Esq., 1796 ; Rerum Hibernicarum Scriptores, 1814–26.

Odell (*Thomas*), seventeenth century. Brief . . . Treatise called "The Christian's Fatherland," 1635. (N.B.—This probably is the first instance of the word "Fatherland " in the language.)

O'Donovan, LL.D. (*John*), Kilkenny, in Ireland, 1809–1861. Annals of the Four Masters (translated), 1848–51 ; Irish Grammar, 1845 ; Topographical Poems of O'Dubhagain and O'Hindbrin (translated, 1862).

O'Driscol (*John*), Ireland, *-*. History of Ireland, 1827 (excellent) ; Moral, Political, and Religious Views of Ireland, 1823 (highly praised).

Offor (*George*), 1787–1864. Tyndale's New Testament, 1836.

O'Flaherty (*Roderic*), seventeenth century. Ogygia, sive Rerum Hibernicarum Chronologia, 1685 (a vast fund of information).

O'Flanagan (*James Roderick*), Fermoy barracks, Cork, 1814–   . Bar-Life of O'Connell, 1866 ; Bryan O'Ryan, 1866, a sporting novel ; Historical Guide . . . to Blackwater, in Munster, 1844 ; History of Dundalk, 1861 (with D'Alton) ; Impressions at Home and Abroad, 1857 ; Irish Rivers, 1845–52 ; Lives of the Lord Chancellors of Ireland, 1870 (his chief work).

Ogden, D.D. (*Samuel*), 1716–1778. Sermons, with an Account of the Author's Life, 1780, posthumous. (Gilbert Wakefield says of Ogden, "Like Cicero, he lacks nothing to complete his meaning ; like Demosthenes, he can suffer no deduction." Dr. Johnson says that Ogden "fought infidels with their own weapons.")

Ogilby (*John*), Edinburgh, 1600–1676. Africa, 1670 ; America, 1671 ; Asia, 1673 ; Atlas Chinensis, 1671–73 ; Atlas Japanensis, 1670 ; Britannia, 1675 ; Book of Roads, 1649 ; Relation of His Majestie's [coronation] Entertainment, 1662 (Charles II.). Translated Virgil's *Æneid*, 1649 ; Æsop's *Fables*, 1651 ; Homer's *Iliad*, 1660 ; *Odyssey*, 1665.
∴ He was satirized by Pope in *The Dunciad*, and by Dryden in *MacFlecknoe*.

Ogilvie (Rev. *Charles Almore*), 1793–1873. Divine Glory manifested in the Conduct and Discourses of our Lord, 1836, Bampton lectures.

Ogilvie (Sir *George*), *-*. True Account of the Preservation of the Regalia of Scotland from falling into the Hands of the English Usurpers, 1701.

Ogilvie, D.D. (*John*), 1733–1814. Britannia (an epic in 20 books), 1801 ; Inquiry into the Causes of the Infidelity . . . of the Times, 1783 ; Observations on . . . Composition, 1774 ; Poems, 1769 ; Rona, 1777, a poem in seven books; Sermons, 1767; Theology of Plato (*The*), 1793.

OGILVIE, LL.D. (*John*), Banffshire, Scotland, 1797–1867. Comprehensive English Dictionary, 1863; Imperial Dictionary, 1850, supplement 1856; Student's English Dictionary, 1865.

O'HARA (*Kane*), Ireland, dramatist, 1722–1782. April Day, 1766; Golden Pippin (*The*), 1765; Midas, 1764, a burletta (his best); Tom Thumb, 1766; Two Misers (*The*), 1767.

O'KEEFFE (*John*), Dublin, 1747–1833. (*Wrote about 50 plays.*) Agreeable Surprise (*The*), 1798, a comedy (his best, it contains the excellent character of Lingo); Fontainebleau, 1798, a comedy; Highland Reel (*The*), 1798; Love in a Camp, 1798, a comedy; Modern Antiques, 1798, a comedy; Poems, 1824, a legacy to his daughter; Poor Soldier (*The*), 1798, an opera; Recollections of the Life of John O'Keeffe, 1826, an autobiography; Sprigs of Laurel (*The*), 1798; Tony Lumpkin, 1778, a musical farce; Wild Oats, 1798, a comedy. N.B.—Of course these plays were not produced on the stage all in one year, but were printed and published in 1798.

OLDHAM (*John*), 1653–1684. Satires, Odes, Poems, etc., 1770, posthumous. His Memoir, by E. Thompson, 1770.

OLDMIXON (*John*), 1673–1742. Amores Britannica, 1703 (in imitation of Ovid's *Epistles*); Amyntas, 1698, a pastoral; Anacreontic Poems, 1696; British Empire in America, 1708; Clarendon and Whitlock, compared, 1727; Court Tales, or the Amours of the Present Nobility, 1717; Critical History of England, 1726; Governor of Cyprus (*The*), 1713, a play; Grove (*The*), or Lover's Paradise, 1700, a play; History of England, 1730–39; Memoirs of Ireland, 1716; Memoirs of North Britain, 1715; Memoirs of the Press, 1742; Poems and Translations, 1714.

∴ Pope says—

In naked majesty
Oldmixon stands.
Dunciad, ii. 283.

OLDYS (*William*), bibliographer, etc., 1696–1761. British Librarian, 1737 (unpublished books); Catalogus Bibliothecæ Harleianæ, 1743; Harleian Miscellany, 1753; Life of Sir Walter Raleigh, 1735.

O'LEARY (Rev. *Arthur*), generally called "Father O'Leary," Cork, 1729–1802. Loyalty asserted, 1777; Plea for Liberty of Conscience, 1780. His Life, by T. R. England, 1822.

OLIPHANT (*Laurence*), 1829–1888. Altiora Peto, 1883; Episodes in the Life of an Adventurer, 1887; Fashionable Philosophy, 1887; Haifa, 1887; Incidents of Travel, 1865; Journey to Katmandhu (*A*), 1850; Land of Gilead (*The*), 1880; Land of Khemi, 1882; Masollam, 1866; Minnesota and the Far West, 1855; Narrative of the Earl of Elgin's Mission to China and Japan, etc., 1860; Patriots and Filibusters, 1860; Piccadilly, 1870; Russian Shores of the Black Sea (*The*), 1853; Scientific Religion, 1888; Sympneumata, 1885; Tender Recollections

of Irene MacGillicuddy, 1878; Traits and Travesties, 1882; Trans-Caucassian Campaign under Omer Pasha, 1856; Universal Suffrage, 1860. His Memoirs, by Mrs. Margaret Oliphant, 1891.

OLIPHANT (*Thomas Lawrence Kington*), Henleaze, near Bristol, 1831–1888. Jacobite Lairds of Gask, 1870; Life of the Duc de Luynes, etc., 1875;; Life of the Emperor Frederick II., 1862; New English, 1886; Old and Modern English, 1870; Sources of Standard English, 1873.

OLIPHANT (Mrs.), maiden name *Margaret Wilson*, Liverpool, novelist and biographer, 1828–1897. Adam Græme of Mossgray, 1852, a novel; Agnes, 1866, a novel; Agnes Hopetoun's Schools, etc., 1859; At the Gates, 1872, a novel; Beleaguered City (*A*), 1880; Brownlows (*The*), 1868, a novel; Caleb Field, 1851; Carita, 1877, a novel; Cervantes, 1880; Child's History of Scotland (*A*), 1896; Chronicles of Carlingford (*The*), 1863 (see "Salem Chapel," etc.); Country Gentleman and his Family (*A*), 1886; Cousin Mary, 1888, a novel; Cuckoo in the Nest (*The*), 1892, a novel; Curate in Charge (*The*), 1876, a novel; Dante, 1877; Diana Trelawny, 1892, a novel; Dress, 1878; Duke's Daughter (*The*), 1890, a novel; Effie Ogilvie, 1886; For Love and Life, 1874, a novel; Francis of Assisi, 1871; Greatest Heiress in England (*The*), 1879; Harry Jocelyn, 1881; Harry Muir, 1853, a novel; Heart and Cross, 1863; Heir Presumptive (*The*), and the Heir Apparent, 1892, a novel; Hester, 1883, a novel; He that will not when he may, 1880, a novel; Historical Sketches in the Reign of Queen Anne, 1894; Historical Sketches in the Reign of George II., 1869; History of the Monks of the West, 1867–79 (translated); House divided against itself (*A*), 1886; House in Bloomsbury (*A*), 1894; House on the Moor, 1860; Innocent, 1873, a tale of modern life; In Trust, 1882, a novel; It was a Lover and his Lass, 1883, a novel; Janet, 1891, a novel; Jeanne d'Arc, her Life and Death, 1896; Jerusalem, 1891; John, 1870, a love-story; Joyce, 1888, a novel; Katie Stewart, 1856, a novel; Kirstein, 1890, a novel; Ladies Lindores (*The*), 1883, a novel; Lady Car, 1889, a novel; Lady William, 1894, a novel; Laird of Worlow, 1858; Land of Darkness (*The*), 1888; Last of the Mortimers (*The*), 1861; Lilliesleaf, 1855, a novel; Literary History of England (*A*), 1882; Little Pilgrim in the Unseen (*A*), 1882; Lucy Crofton, 1859; Madam, 1885, a novel; Madonna Mary, 1866; Magdalen Hepburn, 1854, a novel; Makers of Florence (*The*), 1874, viz. Dante, Giotto, and Savonarola; Makers of Modern Rome (*The*), 1895; Makers of Venice (*The*), 1887; Marriage of Elinor (*The*), 1892, a novel; May, 1873, a novel; Memoir of John Tulloch, 1888; Memoir of Laurence Oliphant and of Alice Oliphant, 1892; Memoir of Montalembert, 1872; Memoir of Thomas Chalmers, 1893; Memoirs of Edward Irving, 1862; Merkland, 1851, a novel; Minister's Wife (*The*), 1869, a novel; Miss Marjoribanks (one of the "Chronicles of Carlingford"), 1866; Mrs. Arthur, 1877, a novel; Mrs. Margaret Maitland of Sunnyside, 1849 (her first work); Mystery of Mrs. Blencarrow, 1890, a novel; Neighbours on the Green, 1889, a novel; Old Mr. Tredgold, 1896, a novel; Oliver's Bride, 1886; Ombra, 1872, a novel; Passages in the Life of "Mrs. Margaret Maitland" (*q.v.*), 1849; Perpetual Curate (*The*), (one of the "Chronicles of Carlingford"), 1864; Phœbe Junior (the last "Chronicle of Carlingford"), 1876; Poor Gentleman (*A*), 1889, a novel; Primrose Path (*The*), 1878, a novel; Prodigals and their Inheritance (*The*), 1894; Quiet Heart (*The*), 1856, a novel; Railway Man and his Children (*The*), 1891; Rector (*The*), (one of the "Chronicles of Carlngford"), 1863; Rose in June (*A*), 1874, a novel; Royal Edinburgh, 1891; Salem Chapel (the first "Chronicle of Carlingford"), 1863; Second Son (*The*), 1888, a novel; Sheridan, 1883; Sir Robert's Fortune, 1895; Sir Tom, 1884, a novel; Son of his Father (*The*), 1887, a novel; Son of the Soil (*A*), 1866, a novel; Sons and Daughters, 1890; Sorceress (*The*), 1893, a novel; Squire Arden, 1871, a novel; Three Brothers, 1870, a novel; Three Gifts (*The*),1857; Two Stories of the Seen and the Unseen, 1884; Valentine and his Brothers, 1875, a novel; Whiteladies, 1876; Within the Precincts, 1879, a novel; Wizard's Son (*The*), 1884, a novel; Young Musgrave, 1877, a novel; Zaidee, 1856, a novel.

OLIVER, D.D. (*George*), Paplewick, in Nottinghamshire, 1781-1861. Account of Corpus Pageants, Miracle Plays, etc., at Sleaford, with Traditions of Lincoln Heath, 1838; Antiquities of Freemasonry, 1823; Apology for Freemasons, 1846; Booke of the Lodge, or [Masonic] Manual, 1849; Collections . . . illustrating the Biography of . . . the Members of the Society of Jesus, 1838; Collections . . . illustrating the Catholic Religion in Cornwall, etc., 1857; Dictionary of Symbolical Masonry, 1853; Ecclesiastical Antiquities of Devon, 1844; Existing Remains of the Ancient Britons, 1847; Golden Remains of Early Masonic Writers, 1847-50 (edited); Historic Account of the Ancient Britons, 1847; Historic Account of the Church of Wolverhampton, 1836; Historic Account of the Religious Houses in [Lincolnshire], 1846; Historical Collections relating to the Monasteries of Devon, 1820; Historical Landmarks . . . of Freemasonry, 1844-46; History and Antiquities of Beverley, in Yorkshire, 1829; History of Exeter, 1821; History of Freemasonry, 1841; History of St. James's Church, Grimsby, 1825; History of Witham [Masonic] Lodge, 1840; Illustrations of Masonry, 1829 (Preston's book continued); Institutes of Masonic Jurisprudence, 1840; Jacob's Ladder, 1845; Lives of the Bishops and History of Exeter Cathedral, 1861; [Masonic] Schism (*The*), 1847; Mirror for the Johannite Masons (*A*), 1848; Monasticon Diœcesis Exoniensis, 1847, supplement 1854; Origin of the "Royal Arch Degree" [in Masonry], 1847; Revelations of a Square [in Masonry], 1855; Signs and Symbols of Freemasonry, 1826-29; Star in the East

(*The*), 1825 (Freemasonry); Symbol of Glory (*The*), or the End and Object of Freemasonry, 1850; Theocratic Philosophy of Freemasonry, 1825; Visit to Exeter (*A*), 1841.

OLIVER, LL.D. (*Peter*), about 1780-1825. Scripture Lexicon of above Four Thousand Proper Names, 1810 (a useful work).

O'NEIL, A.R.A. (*Henry*), historical and genre painter, 1817– . Age of Stucco (*The*), (a satire in three cantos), 1871; Modern Art in England and France, 1869.

OPIE, R.A. (*John*), called "The Cornish Wonder," born at St. Agnes, in Cornwall, 1761-1807. Lectures on Painting, 1809, posthumous; Life of Reynolds, in Pilkington's *Dictionary of Painters*. His Life, by his widow, 1809.

OPIE (Mrs.), maiden name *Amelia Alderson*, Norwich, 1769-1853. Adeline Mowbray, 1804, a novel; Dangers of Coquetry (*The*), 1800; Detraction Displayed, 1828; Elegy (*An*), 1802; Father and Daughter, 1810, a novel; Illustrations of Lying in All its Branches, 1827; Lays for the Dead, 1833; Madeline, 1822; Mother and Son, 1800; New Tales, 1818; Poems, 1802-8; Simple Tales, 1806; Tales of the Heart, 1811; Tales of Real Life, 1813; Temper, or Domestic Scenes, 1812; Valentine Eve, 1812; Warrior's Return (*The*), and other Poems, 1809. Her Life, by Lucy Brightwell, 1854.

ORFORD (*Horace Walpole*, fourth earl of), London, 1717-1797. Ædes Walpolianæ, etc., 1752; Anecdotes of English Painters, 1761-71; Castle of Otranto, 1764, a tale; Catalogue of English Authors (royal and noble), 1758 (his chief work); Catalogue of English Engravers, 1763; Catalogue of the Pictures of the Duke of Devonshire, 1760; Correspondence, 1820, 1831, 1837, posthumous; Description of Strawberry Hill, 1772; Essay on Modern Gardening, 1785; Fugitive Pieces in Prose and Verse, 1758; Hasty Productions, 1791; Hieroglyphic Tales, 1785; Historic Doubts about Richard III., 1768; Journal of the Reign of George III., 1859, posthumous; Letter [about] Chatterton, 1779; Memoirs of the Last Ten Years, 1751-60; Memoirs of the Reign of George II., 1822, posthumous; Memoirs of the Reign of George III., 1844, posthumous; Miscellaneous Antiquities, 1772; Mysterious Mother (*The*), 1768; Reminiscences, 1818, posthumous. His Life, by Coxe, 1798; Macaulay, 1843; E. Warburton, 1851.

ORME (*Robert*), Hindûstan, 1728-1801. Historical Fragments on the Mogul Empire, etc., 1782; History of the Military Transactions of the British in Hindûstan, 1763-78 (excellent).

ORME (*William*), 1787-1830. Bibliotheca Biblica, 1824; Memoirs of William Kiffin, 1823; Memoirs of John Owen, D.D., 1820; Memoirs of John Urquhart, 1827.

ORMEROD, D.C.L. (*George*), 1789-1873. Arderne of Cheshire and the Ardens of Warwickshire, 1843; British and Roman Remains Illustrative of Antonine's *Iter*. xiv., 1852; History of Chester, 1819 (much esteemed); Line of Earthquakes called Offa's

Dyke, 1859 ; Miscellanea Palantina, 1851 ; Parentalia, 1851 ; Stanley Legend (*The*), 1839 ; Strigulensia, 1841.

ORRERY (*Charles Boyle*, earl of). See BOYLE.

ORRERY (*Roger Boyle*, earl of), 1621–1679. Art of War (*The*), 1677 ; English Adventures, etc., 1676 ; Parthenissa, 1677, a romance ; Poems on the Church Festivals, 1681. His Life, by T. Morrice, 1742.

ORTON (Rev. *Job*), Shrewsbury, 1717–1783. Exposition of the Old Testament, 1788–91, posthumous ; Life of Dr Doddridge, 1766.

OSBORN (*Sherard*), 1820–1875. Career (*The*), Last Voyage, and Fate of Sir John Franklin, 1860; Cruise in Japanese Waters (*A*); Past and Future of British Relations in China, 1860.

O'SHAUGHNESSY (*Arthur William Edgar*), London, 1846–1881. Epic of Women (*The*), 1870 ; Lays of France, 1871 (free translations); Music and Moonlight, 1874 ; Songs of a Worker, 1881 ; Thoughts in Marble, 1881 ; Toyland, 1875 (with Eleanor O'Shaughnessy) ; Translations from the French (see "Lays of France "), 1881.

OSSIAN, Celtic warrior-poet, said to have lived in the third century.

Poems published by James Macpherson consist of two epics, viz. "Fingal" and "Temora," and several smaller prose-poems, 1760–63.

N.B.—Dr. Blair, lord Kames, Gray (the poet), and sir John Sinclair maintained that Macpherson's poems were genuine.

Dr. Johnson, David Hume, Laing, and Pinkerton maintained they were more or less fabrications of Macpherson.

No man can wish a higher honour than to be the author of such a series of poems, so wholly original, and so full of poetic inventions, beautiful similes, happy turns of thought, and poetic gems. No doubt the style is too abrupt, probably much of the scenery is purely imaginary ; but there never was but one Ossian.

O'SULLIVAN (*Vincent*), poet. Book of Bargains (*A*), 1896; House of Sin, 1897; Poems, 1895.

OTTLEY (*William Young*), 1771–1836. Inquiry into the Origin and Early History of engraving on Copper and Wood, 1816 ; Italian School of Design, 1808–23 ; Notices of Engravers and their Works, 1831 ; Scarce and Curious Prints, etc., 1826.

OTWAY (*Thomas*), Trotten, in Sussex, 1651–1685. Alcibiades, 1675, a tragedy ; Caius Marius, 1680, a tragedy ; Don Carlos, 1676, a tragedy ; Friendship in Fashion, 1683, a comedy ; Orphan (*The*), 1680, a tragedy ; Soldier's Fortune (*The*), 1681, a comedy ; Titus and Berenice (4 *syl.*), 1672 ; Venice Preserved, 1682, a tragedy ; Windsor (in verse), 1686, posthumous. His Life, by Thomas Thornton, 1813.

∴ His fame rests on "The Orphan " and "Venice Preserved."

OUGHTRED (Rev. *William*), called "The Prince of Mathematicians," Eton, in Buckinghamshire, 1573–1660. Arithmeticæ in Numero et Speciebus Institutio, etc., 1631 ; Clavis Mathematica, 1631 (his chief work) ; Description and Use of the Double Horizontal Dyall, etc., 1633 ; Geometrical Dialling, 1647; Opuscula Mathematica, 1676, posthumous ; Treatise on Trigonometry, 1657.

OUIDA. See DE LA RAMÉ.

OVERBURY (Sir *Thomas*), Compton Scorfen, in Warwickshire, 1581–1613. Characters, 1614 (witty and vigorous) ; Crumms fallen from King James's Table, 1715, posthumous (his table-talk) ; Downfall of Ambition, etc., 1615 ; Observations on the State of the Seventeen Provinces, 1626 ; Remedy of Love (*The*), 1620, posthumous ; Wife (*The*), 1614, a didactic poem.

OWEN, D.D. (*Henry*), in Monmouthshire, 1716–1795. Brief Account of the Septuagint, 1787 (excellent) ; Collatio Codicis Cottoniani Geneseos, 1778 ; Critica Sacra, 1774-75 ; Critical Disquisitions, 1784 ; Inquiry into the Present State of the Septuagint, 1769 (much esteemed) ; Intent and Propriety of the Scripture Miracles, 1773 ; Modes of Quotation by the Evangelists vindicated, 1789 ; Observations on the Four Gospels, 1764 ; Sermons, 1797.

OWEN, D.D. (*John*), Stadham, in Oxfordshire, 1616–1683. Christologia, 1679 ; Communion with God, 1657 ; Discourse concerning the Holy Spirit, 1674 ; Display of Arminianism, 1642 ; Exposition of the *Epistle to the Hebrews*, 1668 (his chief work) ; Exposition of *Psalm* cxiii., 1668 ; On Justification, 1677 ; On the . . . Study of Theology, 1661 ; Salus Electorum, Sanguis Jesu, 1679 ; Theologoumena, 1661 ; Treatise on Original Sin ; Truth and Innocence vindicated, 1669 ; Vindiciæ Evangelicæ (against the Unitarian doctrine), 1655. His Life, by Dr. Owen, 1720 ; W. Orme, 1826.

OWEN, M.D. (Sir *Richard*), called "The Newton of Natural History," Lancaster, 1804–1892. Affinities of Thylacoleo, 1884 ; Archetype and Homologies of the Vertebrate Skeleton, 1848 ; Catalogue of Recent Osteology, 1854 ; Crocodilia and Ophidia of the London Clay, 1859 ; Experimental Physiology, 1882 ; Fossil Mammals of Australia, 1877 ; Fossil Reptiles, 1884 ; Fossil Reptilia of South Africa, 1876 ; History of British Fossil Mammals and Birds, 1846; History of British Fossil Reptiles, 1849–51 ; Lectures on Comparative Anatomy, 1843 ; Lectures on the Invertebrate Animals, 1843 ; Lectures on the Vertebrate Animals, 1846; Life of R. S. Owen, 1894 ; Memoir on the Gigantic Extinct Sloth, 1842 ; Memoir on the Pearly Nautilus, 1832 ; Odontography, 1840-45 (his great work) ; On the Anatomy of Vertebrates, 1866-68 ; On the Aye-aye, 1863 ; On the Dodo, 1866 ; On the Extinct Wingless Birds of New Zealand, 1878 ; On the Gorilla, 1865 ; On the Megatherium, 1861 ; On the Nature of Limbs, 1849 ; On the Structure of the Brain, 1837 ; Ova of the Echidna Hystrix, 1881 ; Palæonotology, 1860 ; Parthenogenesis, 1849 ; Principles of Comparative Osteology, 1855 ; Remains of the Gigantic Land Lizard from Australia, 1881-82.

OWEN (*Robert*), Newton, in Montgomeryshire, 1771–1858. Book of the New Moral World, 1836 ; New Moral World, 1839 ; New View of Society (*A*), 1816. His Life, by Sargant.

OWEN (*Robert Dale*), New Lanark, in Scotland, 1800-1877. Authenticity of the Bible, 1832; Beyond the Breakers, 1870; Debatable Land (*The*), 1871; Footfalls on the Boundary of Another World, 1860; Moral Physiology, 1831; Personality of God, 1832; System of Education at New Lanark, 1824; Threading my Way, 1874, an autobiography; Wrong of Slavery (*The*), 1864.

OWEN (*William*), Wales, eighteenth century. Cambrian Biography, 1803; Dictionary of the Welch Language, 1793 (it contains 100,000 words).

OXLEE (Rev. *John*), 1779-1854. Confutation of Diabolarchy; Futility of any Attempt to convert the Jews, 1842; Mysterious Stranger (*The*), 1859, posthumous; Presumption of Gentiles in requiring Jews to forsake the Law of Moses (*The*), 1845-47.

PACE (Rev. *Richard*), 1482-1532. Conclusiones de Veniis Potificum, etc., 1518; De Fructu qui ex Doctrina Percipitur, 1517; De Utilitate Studiorum, 1518.

PAGET (Rev. *Francis Edward*), 1806- . Luke Sharp, 1845, a tale of modern education; St. Antholin's, 1842; Warden of Berkenholt (*The*), 1843.

PAIN (*Barry Eric Odell*). Graeme and Cyril, 1893; In a Canadian Canoe, etc., 1891; Kindness of the Celestial, etc., 1894; Playthings and Parodies, 1892; Stories and Interludes, 1892.

PAINE (*Thomas*), Thetford, in Norfolk, 1737-1809. Age of Reason, 1792-95, 1896 (his chief work); Agrarian Justice, 1797; American Crisis (*The*), 1776-85; Common Sense, 1776; Crisis (*The*), 1776-80; Dissertation on the First Principles of Government, 1795; Political and Moral Maxims, 1792; Prospects on the Rubicon, 1787; Public Good, 1780; Rights of Man (*The*), 1791-92. His Life, by George Chalmers (Francis Rydys), 1791; Oldys, 1791; W. Cobbett, 1796; James Cheetham, 1809; Rickman, 1814; R. Carlile, 1819; Sherwan, 1819; Harford, 1820; Vale, 1853.
∴ Few men have had so many biographers.

PAINTER (*William*), sixteenth century. Palace of Pleasure, 1566-67 (a collection of tales from Boccaccio, Biondello, etc.; Shakespeare derived from it several of his plots).

PALEY (*Frederick Apthorp*), grandson of the succeeding, Easingwold, in Yorkshire, 1816-1888. Ecclesiologists' Guide to the Churches near Cambridge (*The*), 1844; Gospel of St. John, 1887; Greek Wit, 1880-81; Homeri, etc., 1878; Manual of Gothic Architecture, 1846; Manual of Gothic Mouldings, 1847; Notes on Twenty Churches round Peterborough, 1860; Religious Tests, etc., 1871; Remarks on Peterborough Cathedral, 1854; Short Treatise on Greek Particles, 1881; Thœtetus of Plato (translated), 1875; Truth about Homer, 1887.

PALEY D.D. (*William*), Peterborough, in Northamptonshire, 1743-1805. Evidences of Christianity, 1794 (borrowed largely from Lardner and bishop Douglas, his chief work); Horæ Paulinæ, 1790 (his most original work); Moral and Political Philosophy, 1785; Natural Theology, 1802 (borrowed largely from the *Religious Philosopher*, by Nieuwentyt); Sermons, 1808, posthumous. His Life, by G. W. Meadley, 1809; Paley.

PALGRAVE (Sir *Francis*), London, 1788-1861; his name before he married was *Cohen*. Antient Kalendars and Inventories of His Majesty's Exchequer, 1836; Documents, etc., Illustrative of the History of Scotland, 1837; History of Normandy and of England, 1851-57 (his chief work); History of the Anglo-Saxons, 1831; Merchant and Friar, 1837 (Marco Polo and Friar Bacon); Parliamentary Writs, etc., 1827-34 (valuable); Rise and Progress of the English Commonwealth (Anglo-Saxon period), 1832; Rotuli Curiæ Regis, 1835; Truths and Fictions of the Middle Ages, 1837.

PALGRAVE, LL.D. (*Francis Turner*), London, 1824-1897. Amenophis, and other Poems, 1892; Chrysomela, 1877; Essays on Art, 1866; Five Days' Entertainments at Wentworth Grange, 1868; Golden Treasury of English Songs, etc., 1861; Golden Treasury of Sacred Song, 1889; Hymns, 1867; Idylls and Songs, 1854; Life of Jesus Christ illustrated from the Italian Painters, etc., 1885; Life of Sir Walter Scott, 1867; Lyrical Garlands, 1874; Lyrical Poems, 1871, 1875; Lyrical Poems of Tennyson, 1885; Songs and Sonnets of Shakespeare, 1879; Visions of England (*The*), 1881, poems.

PALGRAVE (Sir *Reginald Francis Douce*), London, 1829- . Chairman's Handbook (*The*), 1877; House of Commons (*The*), 1869; Law and Practice of Parliament (edited), 1893; Oliver Cromwell, 1890.

PALGRAVE (*William Gifford*), Westminster, 1826-1888. Dutch Guiana, 1076; Hermann Agha, 1872, a novel; Narrative of a Year's Journey through Arabia, 1862-63.

PALMER (Rev. *Charles Ferrers*), known as "Father Raymond," Tamworth, in Staffordshire, 1819- . Dominican Tertiary's Guide, 1868; History of Tamworth, 1845; History of the Baronial Family of Marmion, 1875; History of the Collegiate Church of Tamworth, 1871; Life of Beato Angelico da Fiesole, 1865; Life of Philip Thomas Howard, 1867.

PALMER (*Edward Henry*), Cambridge, 1846-1882. Arabic Grammar (*An*), 1874; Desert of the Exodus (*The*), 1871; Haroun Alraschid, 1880; History of Jerusalem, 1871; History of the Jewish Nation, 1874; Korân (*The*), 1880; Niger (*The*), or South Country of Scripture, 1871; Oriental Mysticism, 1867; Outlines of Scripture Geography, 1874; Persian-English and English-Persian Dictionary, 1875; Poems of Beha-ed-din Zoheir, 1876-77; Song of the Reed (*The*), 1876. He translated the Qur'ân, 1880 (Sacred Books of the East), and wrote many Arabic and Persian grammars, dictionaries, etc. His Life, by sir Walter Besant.

PALMER (Rev. *William*), 1803-1879. Compendious Ecclesiastical History (*A*), 1841; Episcopacy, 1840; Origines Liturgicæ, etc.,

1832; Treatise of the Church of Christ, 1838.

PALSGRAVE (*John*), 1480–1554. Lesclarecissement de la Langue Françoyse, 1530 (first attempt to reduce French to rules).

PARIS (*Matthew*). See MATTHEW OF PARIS.

PARK (*Mungo*), Selkirk, in Scotland, 1771–1805. Travels (in 1795–97) in the Interior of Africa, 1799. His Life, by Rennell, 1815.

PARK (*Thomas*), 1759–1834. Memoirs of W. Stevens, 1814 ; Nugæ Antiquæ, 1803 ; Nugæ Modernæ, 1818, prose and verse; Poems, 1797 ; Sonnets, and other Poems, 1797.

PARKER (*Gilbert*), Canada, 1862– . Adventuress of the North (*An*), 1895 ; Lover's Diary (*A*), 1894 ; Mrs. Falchion, 1893 ; No Defence, 1889 ; Pierre and his People, 1892 ; Round the Compass in Australia, 1892 ; Seats of the Mighty (*The*), 1896 ; Translation of a Savage (*The*), 1894 ; Trespasser (*The*), 1893 ; Trial of the Sword (*The*), 1894 ; Vendetta (*The*), 1889 ; When Valmond came to Pontiac, 1895.

PARKER (*John Henry*), 1806– . Archæology of Rome, 1874 ; Domestic Architecture of the Middle Ages, 1853–59 ; Glossary of Architecture, 1836 ; Introduction to the Study of Gothic Architecture, 1849.

PARKER, D.D. (*Joseph*), Hexham, Northumberland, 1830– . Adam, Noah, and Abraham, 1880 ; Ad Clerum, 1870 ; Apostolic Life (*The*), 1882–84 ; Church Questions, 1862 ; City Temple Sermons, 1869–70–71 ; Detached Links, 1873 ; Ecce Deus, 1868 ; Every Morning, etc., 1888 ; Henry Ward Becher, 1887 ; Homiletic Analysis of the New Testament, 1863 ; Inner Life of Christ (*The*), 1881 ; Might have Been, 1896 ; None Like it, 1893 ; Paraclete (*The*), 1874 ; People's Bible, 1885–88 ; People's Family Prayer-book, 1889 ; Priesthood of Christ (*The*), 1880 ; Pulpit Notes, 1873 ; Some One, 1895 ; Springdale Abbey, 1868 ; Tyne Childe, 1883, autobiography ; Weaver Stephen, 1885 ; Well Begun, 1893.

PARKER (*Martin*), about 1605–1645. Harry White, his Humour, 1633 ; Legend of Sir Leonard Lackwit, 1635 ; Poet's Blind Man's Bough (*The*), 1641 ; Rape of the Nightingale, 1632, in verse ; Robin Conscience, his Progresse thorow Court, City, and Countrey, 1635, in verse.

PARKER, D.D. (*Matthew*), archbishop of Canterbury, born at Norwich, 1504–1575. De Antiquitate Britannicæ Ecclesiæ, 1572 ; Life off the Seventy Archbishopp off Canterbury, etc., 1574. His Life, by Strype, 1711 ; Dr. Hook, in the *Lives of the Archbishops of Canterbury*, 1861–74.

PARKER (*Samuel*), bishop of Oxford, born at Northampton, 1640–1688. De Rebus sui Temporis, 1726, posthumous (his chief work); Ecclesiastical Polity, 1669 ; Reasons for Abrogating the Test, 1688 ; Tentamina Physico-Theologica, 1665.

PARKER (Rev. *Theodore*), born at Lexington, U.S., 1810–1860. Discourse of Matters pertaining to Religion, 1842 ; Sermons, 1852–53 ; Speeches, 1855. His Life, by Weiss, 1863 ; Reville, 1865.

PARKES (*Bessie Rayner*), afterwards Mrs.

Belloc, *-*. Ballads and Songs, 1863 ; Cat Aspasia (*The*), 1860 ; Gabriel, 1856 ; La Belle France, 1868 ; Peoples of the World (*The*), 1870 ; Poems, 1855.

PARKES (*Joseph*), 1796–1865. History of the Court of Chancery, 1828 (commended by lord Brougham).

PARKES (*Samuel*), 1759–1825. Chemical Catechism, 1800 ; Chemical Essays (Arts and Manufactures), 1823.

PARKES (*William*), seventeenth century. Curtaine-drawer of the World (*The*), showing how Vice in a Riche Embroidered Gowne of Velvet rides Ahorsebacke, and Vertue in Thrid-bare Cloake goes Afoote, 1612.

PARKHURST (*John*), Catesby, in Northamptonshire, 1728–1797. Divinity and Pre-existence of . . . Christ Demonstrated, 1787 ; Greek and English Lexicon to the New Testament, 1769 ; Hebrew and English Lexicon, 1762.

PARKINSON (*Anthony*), 1668–1728. Collectanea Anglo-Minoritica (*i.e.* the Grey Friars), 1726 (well digested) ; Legend of the Foundation of St. Begas Abbey, 1826.

PARKINSON (*James*), *-*. Introduction to the Study of Fossils, 1823 ; Organic Remains of a Former World, 1804.

PARKINSON (*John*), London, 1567–1641. Paradisi in Sole, Paradisus Terrestris, 1629 ; Theatrum Botannicum, 1640 (a work of merit).

PARKINSON (*Joseph Charles*), London, 1833– . Government Examinations, 1860 ; Shakespeare a Freemason ; Under Government, 1859, a guide to the Civil Service.

PARKINSON, D.D. (*Richard*), Lancashire, 1798–1858. Old Church Clock (*The*), 1844 ; Poems, 1845.

PARKINSON (*Thomas*), Kirkham, in Lancashire, 1745–1830. System of Mechanics and Hydrostatics, 1789.

PARNELL, D.D. (*Thomas*), Dublin, 1679–1717. Battle of the Frogs and Mice (in three books, mock-heroic), 1700 ; Fairy Tale (*A*), Edwin and Sir Topaz (in the ancient English style), 1798 ; Hermit (*The*), 1710, a story, in verse, from the Talmud ; Life of Zoilus, published 1770 ; Night-piece on Death (Goldsmith preferred this poem to Gray's *Elegy*) ; Poems, 1721, posthumous. His Life, by Goldsmith, 1770.

PARR (*Louisa*). Adam and Eve, 1880 ; Can this be Love? 1893 ; Dorothy Fox, 1870 ; Dumps, 1891 ; Gosau Smithy (*The*), 1875 ; How it all happened, 1871 ; Prescotts (*The*), 1874 ; Loyalty George, 1888 ; Robin, 1882 ; Squire (*The*), 1892.

PARR, LL.D. (Rev. *Samuel*), Harrow-on-the-Hill, in Middlesex, 1747–1825. Aphorisms, etc., 1826, posthumous ; Bibliotheca Parriana, 1827, posthumous ; Characters of Charles James Fox, 1809 ; Letter from Irenopolis, etc., 1792 ; Prefatio ad Bellendenum de Statu Prisci Orbis, 1788. His Life, by William Field, 1828 ; John Johnstone, M.D., 1828.

PARROT (*Henry*), about 1578–1633. Cures for the Itch (epigrams, epitaphs, etc.; (160) Epigrams, 1608 ; Laquei Ridiculosi, or Springes for Woodcocks (in two books), 1613 ; Mastive (*The*), or the Young Welpe of the Old Dogge, 1613, epigrams and satires ; More the Merrier (*The*), 1608, epigrams ; Mous-Trap (*The*), 1608, epigrams.

PARRY, Mus.Doc. (*Charles Hubert Hastings*), Bournemouth, 1848-   . Art of Music (*The*), 1893 ; History and Development of . . . European Music, 1877 ; Studies of Great Composers, 1886.

PARRY (Sir *William Edward*), Bath, in Somersetshire, arctic voyager, 1790-1855. Journal of a Voyage for the Discovery of a North-west Passage, 1821 ; Journal of a Second Voyage 1824, of a Third, 1826 ; Narrative of an Attempt to reach the North Pole, 1827. His Life, by E. Parry, D.D., 1857.

PARSONS, M.D. (*James*), Barnstaple, in Devonshire, antiquary, 1705-1770. Remains of Japhet, 1767 (European languages).

PARSONS (*Robert*), Somersetshire, 1546-1610. Christian Directory, 1583-91 ; Christian Exercise (*The Book of*), 1584 ; Conference about the Next Succession to the Crowne of England, 1594 (showing it to be the Spanish Infanta, and not James Stuart) ; Decachordon of Ten Quodlibical Questions, 1600 ; De Persecutione Anglicana Libellus, 1582 ; Liturgy of the Mass (*The*), 1620 ; Memorial of the Reformation, 1596 ; Responsio ad Elizabethæ . . . Edictum, 1592 (showing that the pope can dethrone monarchs) ; Three Conversions of Ingland (*The*), 1603-4 ; Why Catholiques refuse to goe to Church, 1580. His Life, by Thomas James, 1612.

PASLEY (General sir *Charles William*), military engineer, 1781-1844. Course of Elementary Fortification, 1822 ; Military Policy and Institutions of the British Empire, 1808 ; Natural Water Cements of England (*The*), 1830 ; Rules for conducting . . . a Siege, 1843 ; Universal Telegraphs for Day and Night Signals, 1823.

PATER (*Walter H.*), 1839-1894. Appreciations, 1889 ; Gaston de Latour, 1888, an unfinished romance (appeared in *Macmillan's*) ; Greek Studies, 1895 ; Imaginary Portraits, 1887, 1894 ; Marius the Epicurean, 1885 ; Miscellaneous Studies, 1895 ; Plato and Platonism, 1893 ; Renaissance (*The*), 1873 (enlarged edition, 1888) ; Studies in the History of the Renaissance, 1873. He wrote articles in the *Fortnightly Review*, *Contemporary Review*, *Macmillan's Magazine*, *New Review*, *Harper's*, *Nineteenth Century*.

PATERSON (Lieut.-colonel *Daniel*), eighteenth century. British Itinerary, 1785 ; Roads of England and Wales, etc., 1771 ; Topographical Description of the Island of Grenada, 1780.

PATMORE (*Coventry Kearsay Dighton*), Woodford, in Essex, 1823-1896. Amelia, 1878 ; Angel in the House (*The*), in four parts, 1855 (part i. the Betrothal, 1854 ; part ii. the Espousal, 1856 ; part iii. Faithful for Ever, 1860 ; part iv. the Victories of Love, 1862) ; Florilegium Amantis, 1879 (edited by Richard Garnett) ; Garland of Poems for Children (*A*), 1862 ; Memoir of Barry Cornwall, 1878 ; Poems, 1844, 1886 ; Principle in Art, 1889 ;

Religio Poetæ, 1893 ; Rod (*The*), the Root, and the Flower, 1895 ; Tamerton Church Tower, and other Poems, 1878 ; Unknown Eros (*The*), 1877.

PATRICK (*St.*), primate of Ireland, 372-493. S. Patricio . . . adscripta Opuscula, printed 1656 (Confessions, Letter to Corotil, etc.). His Life, by B. B., 1625 ; Juan Perez de Montalvan, 1627 ; Probus ; Jocelin, translated into English by E. L. Swift, 1809 ; J. H. Todd, 1863.

PATRICK (*Symon*), bishop of Chichester, then of Ely, 1626-1704. Aqua Genitalis, 1659 (on baptism) ; Commentary upon the Old and New Testament, 1809 (with Lowth, Arnald, and Whitby) ; Divine Arithmetic (Psalm xc. 12), 1659 ; Friendly Debate between a Conformist and a Nonconformist, 1669 ; Glorious Epiphany (*The*), 1678 ; Heart's Ease (*The*), 1671 ; Jewish Hypocrisy, 1660 ; Life of Dr. Walter Raleigh, 1679 ; Mensis Mystica (the " Lord's Table "), 1660 ; Parable of the Pilgrim, 1665 ; Paraphrase of Ecclesiastes and Canticles 1729, Job 1679, Proverbs 1683, Psalms 1680 ; Pillars and Ground of Truth (*The*), 1687 ; Search the Scriptures, 1685 ; Treatise on Repentance and Fasting, 1686 ; Virgin Mary misrepresented by the Roman Catholics, 1688 ; Witnesses of Christianity, 1675-77. His Life, by himself, 1839.

PATTERSON (*Robert*), 1802-1872. First Steps to Zoology, 1849 ; Introduction to Zoology, 1846-48 ; Natural History as a Branch of Education, 1847 ; On the Insects mentioned by Shakespeare, 1842.

PATTERSON (*Robert Hogarth*), Edinburgh, 1821-   . Economy of Capital (*The*), 1864 ; Essays in History and Art, 1861 ; New Revolution (*The*), 1860 (Napoleon III.) ; Science of Finance (*The*), 1867 ; State (*The*), the Poor, and the Country, 1870.

PATTISON (Rev. *Mark*), Hornby, in Yorkshire, 1813-1884. Isaac Casaubon, 1875 ; Milton, 1879 ; Suggestions on Academical Organization, 1868 ; Tendencies of Religious Thought in England, 1860. Memoirs, by his widow (who married sir Charles Dilke), 1838.

PAULDING (*James Kirke*), humourist, Pleasant Valley, U.S., 1779-1860. Book of St. Nicholas (*The*), 1830 ; Diverting History of John Bull and Brother Jonathan (*The*), 1816 ; Dutchman's Fireside (*The*), 1831, a novel ; John Bull in America, 1824, a satire in prose ; Konigsmarke, 1825, a novel ; Lay of the Scottish Fiddle, 1813, a parody ; Letters from the South by a Northerner, 1817 ; Life of Washington, 1835 ; Merry Tales of the Three Wise Men of Gotham, 1826 ; New Pilgrim's Progress (*The*), 1828 ; Old Continental (*The*), 1846, a novel ; Puritan (*The*) and her Daughter, 1849 ; Salmagundi, 1819, a new series ; Sketch of Old England by a New Englander (*A*), 1822 ; Slavery in the United States, 1836 ; Tales of a Good Woman, 1829 ; United States (*The*) and England, 1814 ; Westward Ho ! 1832, a novel. His Life, by his son, 1867.

PAYN (*James*), Rodney Lodge, Cheltenham,

1830-1898. Another's Burden, 1897; At Her Mercy, 1874; Bateman Household (*The*), 1860; Bentinck's Tutor, 1868; Best of Husbands, 1874; Blondel Parva, 1868; Burnt Million (*The*), 1890; By Proxy, 1878; Canon's Ward (*The*), 1884; Carlyon's Year, 1868; Cecil's Tryst, 1872; Clyffards of Clyffe, 1866; Confidential Agent (*A*), 1880; County Family (*A*), 1869; Disappearance of George Driffell, 1896; Eavesdropper, 1888; English Lakes, 1859; Fallen Fortunes, 1876; For Cash Only, 1882; Foster Brothers, 1859; Found Dead, 1869; From Exile, 1881; Furness Abbey, 1858; Gleams of Memory, 1894; Glow-worm Tales, 1887; Grape from a Thorn, 1881; Gwendoline's Harvest, 1870; Halves, 1876; Heir of the Ages, 1885; High Spirits, 1879; Holiday Tasks, 1887; In Market Overt, 1895; In Peril and Privation, 1885; Kit, 1883; Lakes in Sunshine, 1867, 1870; Leaves from Lakeland, 1858; Less Black than we're painted, 1878; Lights and Shadows of London Life, 1867; Like Father, like Son, 1871; Lost Sir Massingberd, 1864; Luck of the Darrells, 1885; Marine Residence (*A*), 1879; Married beneath him, 1865; Maxims, 1869; Meliboeus in London, 1862; Mirk Abbey, 1866; Modern Dick Whittington, 1892; Murphy's Master, 1873; Mystery of Mirbridge (*The*), 1888; Notes from the "News," 1890; Not Wooed, but Won, 1871; People, Places, and Things, 1865; Perfect Treasure, 1869; Poems, 1853; Prince of the Blood, 1888; Richard Arbour (The Family Scapegrace), 1861; Some Literary Recollections, 1884; Some Private Views, 1882; Stories and Sketches, 1857; Stories from Boccaccio, 1852; Stumble (*A*) on the Threshold, 1892; Sunny Stories, 1891; Talk of the Town (*The*), 1885; Thicker than Water, 1883; Trying Patient (*A*), 1893; Two Hundred Pounds Reward, 1879; Under One Roof, 1879; Walter's Word, 1875; What he Cost her, 1877; Woman's Vengeance (*A*), 1872; Word (*The*) and the Will, 1890.

PAYNE (*John*), London, 1842- . Book of the Thousand-and-One Nights (translated), 1882-84; Francis Villon, 1881, a biography; Intaglios, 1871, sonnets; Lautrec, 1878, a poem; Life and Death, 1872; Masque of Shadows (*The*), and other Poems, 1870; New Poems, 1880; Songs, 1872.

PAYNE-SMITH, D.D. (*Robert*), Gloucestershire, dean of Canterbury, 1818-1895. Daniel, 1886; Genesis, 1885; Prophecy as a Preparation for Christ, 1869; Thesaurus Syriacus, etc., 1868-85. Also Commentaries.

PEACHAM (*Henry*), London, 1576-1650. April Shower (*An*), for Richard Sacvile, earle of Dorset, 1624; Art of Living in London, 1642; Commons Complaint (*The*), 1611; Compleat Gentleman (*The*), 1622; Dialogue between the Crosse in Cheap and Charing Crosse, 1641; Duty of Subjects (*The*), 1639; Epigrams and Satyrs, 1600; Gentleman's Exercise (*The*),1634; Graphice, etc., 1606; History of the Five Wise Philosophers, 1672; Merry Discourse between Meum and Tuum, 1639; Minerva Britanna, 1612; Paradox in Praise of a Dunce, 1642; Period of Mourning (for

prince Henry), in six visions, 1613; Prince Henry revived, 1615, a poem; Thalia's Banquet, 1620; Truth of our Times revealed (*The*), 1638; Valley of Varietie (*The*), 1638; Worth of a Penny (*The*), 1664.

PEACOCK (*Edward*), Hemsworth, Lincolnshire, 1831- . Glossary of Words used in the Wapentakes of Manley and Corringham, in Lincolnshire, 1877; John Markenfield, 1874; Mabel Horn, 1872; Ralf Skislaugh, 1870.

PEACOCK, D.D. (*George*), *-1858. Algebra (arithmetical and symbolical), 1842-45; Trigonometry, 1839.

PEACOCK (*Thomas Love*), Weymouth, in Dorsetshire, 1785-1866. Ælia Lælia, 1862; Crotchet Castle, 1831, a novel; Genius of the Thames (*The*), a poem, part i. 1810, part ii. 1812; Gryll Grange, 1861, a novel; Gl'Ingannati, 1862, a comedy; Headlong Hall, 1816, a novel; London, 1856; Maid Marian, 1822, a novel; Melincourt, 1817, a novel; Misfortunes of Elphin (*The*), 1829, a novel; Nightmare Abbey, 1818, a novel; Palmyra (a poem in 25 stanzas), 1806; Phila, 1817; Philosophy of Melancholy, 1812, a poem; Rhododaphnê, or the Thessalian Spell, 1818, a poem. His Life, by Edith Nicolls, his granddaughter, 1875.

PEARCE (*Zachary*), bishop of Rochester, born in London, 1690-1774. Commentary on the Four Evangelists, etc., 1777. His Life, by Derby, with additions by Dr. Johnson, 1777.

PEARSE (Rev. *Mark Guy*), Cranborne, in Dorsetshire, 1842- . Christianity of Jesus Christ (*The*), 1888; Cornish Stories, 1883; Daniel Quorm and his Religious Notions, 1875-79; Elijah, the Man of God, 1891; Good Will, 1877; Gospel for the Day (*The*), 1893; Homely Talks, 1880; Jesus Christ and the People, 1891; John Tregenoweth, 1873; Mister Horn and his Friends, 1872; Moses, 1894; Naaman the Syrian, 1893; Old Miller and his Mill (*The*), 1881; Praise, 1887; Sermons for Children, 1875; Short Stories, 1877; Short Talks for the Times, 1889; Simon Jasper, 1882; Some Aspects of a Blessed Life, 1885; Thoughts on Holiness, 1883.

PEARSON (*Charles Henry*), Islington, 1830-1894. Early and Middle Ages of England, 1866; English History in the Fourteenth Century, 1876; Historical Maps of England, etc., 1869; History of England during the Early and Middle Ages, 1867; National Life and Character, 1893.

PEARSON, D.D. (*Edward*), 1760-1811. Twelve Lectures on . . . the Prophecies relating to the Christian Church, 1811. His Memoir, by T. Green, 1819.

PEARSON, D.D. (*John*), bishop of Chester, born at Snoring, in Norfolk, 1612-1686. Annales Cyprianici, 1682; Annales Paulini, 1685; Exposition of the Creed, 1659 (a standard work); Golden Remains of . . . John Hales of Eton, 1659; Opera Posthuma Chronologica, was published in 1688; Vindiciæ Epistolarum S. Ignatii, 1672 (to prove its genuineness). *Posthumous:* Orationes, Conciones, Determinationes Theologicæ,etc., 1688. His Memoirs, by E. Churton, 1842.

PECK (Rev. *Francis*), Stamford, in Lincolnshire, 1692-1743. Academia Tertia Anglicana, 1727; Antiquarian Annals of Stamford, 1727; Catalogue of all the Discourses for and against Popery in the Reign of James II., 1735; Desiderata Curiosa, 1732-35; Memoirs of Cromwell 1740, of Milton 1740; Monasticon Anglicanum, still in the British Museum in MS. His Life, by Evans.

PECKHAM (*John*), archbishop of Canterbury, born in Sussex, 1240-1292. De Summa Trinitate et Fide Catholica, 1510, posthumous; Perspectiva Communis, 1504, posthumous.

PECOCK (*Reginald*), bishop of Chichester, 1390-1460. Donet, 1440, a dialogue on the chief truths of Christianity; Repressor of Overmuch Blaming of the Clergy (*The*), 1449. His Life, by Lewis; by James Gardner, in Nos. 6 and 7 of the *Fortnightly Review;* and by Morley, vol. ii. part i. *English Writers.*

PEELE (*George*), dramatist, 1546-1597. Absalom, printed 1599, a tragedy; Arraignment of Paris, 1584, a masque; Battle of Alcazor (*The*), 1594, a tragedy; Chronicle of Edward I., 1593, an historic play; Descensus Astraeae, 1591; Device of the Pageant, October 29, 1585; Eclogue Gratulatorie (*An*), 1589; Farewell (*A*), 1589; Historie of Two Valiant Knights, 1599, posthumous, a tragedy; Honour of the Garter (*The*), 1593, a poem; Hunting of Cupid (*The*), 1591, a pastoral; King Edward I. (see above " Chronicle "); Love of King David for Fair Bethsabe, 1599, posthumous, a sacred drama; Merrie Conceited Jests, 1627, posthumous (a lampoon on himself); Old Wives' Tale (*The*), 1595, a legendary story in prose and verse; Polyhymnia, 1590, a .poem; Turkish Mahomet and Hyren the Faire Greek, 1584, a comedy. His Life, by Dyce, 1828.

PEGGE, LL.D. (*Samuel*), Chesterfield, in Derbyshire, 1704-1796. Annales Eliæ de Trickingham, etc., 1789; Anonymiana, 1809; Coins fabricated by . . . the Archbishops of Canterbury, 1772; Coins of Cunobelin, 1766; Croyland Boundary Stone, 1776; Dissertation on . . . Anglo-Saxon Remains of Coins, 1756; History of Beauchief Abbey, Derbyshire, 1801; History of Bolsover and Peak Castles, 1795; History of Eccleshall Castle, Staffordshire, 1784; Life of Robert Grosseteste, 1793; Memoirs of Roger de Weseham, 1761. His Life, by his son Samuel.

PEGGE (*Samuel*), son of Dr. S. Pegge, 1731-1800. Anecdotes of the English Language, 1813; Curialia, 1782; Curialia Miscellanea, 1818; Supplement to Grose's *Glossary*, 1814.

PEMBERTON, M.D. (*Henry*), London, 1694-1771. View of Sir Isaac Newton's Philosophy, 1728. (He assisted Newton in preparing the new edition of *Principia*.)

PEMBERTON (*Max*), Birmingham, 1863- . Christine of the Hills, 1897; Diary of a Scoundrel (*The*), 1891; Gentleman's Gentleman (*A*), 1896; Impregnable City (*The*), 1895; Iron Pirate (*The*), 1893; Jewel Mysteries I have known, 1894; Little Huguenot (*The*), 1895; Puritan's Wife (*A*), 1896; Sea Wolves (*The*), 1894. Editor of *Chums*, 1892-93; Editor of *Cassell's Magazine*, 1896.

PEMBROKE (Countess of), maiden name *Mary Herbert Sidney*, sister of sir Philip Sidney, 1556-1621. Antony, a tragedy; Discourse of Life and Death; Elegy on Sir Philip Sidney; Pastoral Dialogue in Praise of Astræa.
N.B.—To this lady Sidney's *Arcadia* is dedicated, and on this lady the famous epitaph was written by W. Browne, 1645—

Sidney's sister, Pembroke's mother,—
Death, ere thou hast killed another,
Fair, and good, and learned as she,
Time shall throw his dart at thee.
(Often ascribed to *Ben Jonson*.)

PENGELLY (*William*), Cornwall, 1812-1894. Lignite Formation of Bovey Tracey, in Devonshire, 1863. His Memoirs, edited by his daughter, Hester Pengelly, 1897.

PENN (*Granville*), 1761-1844. Bioscope on the Dial of Life, 1814; Christian Survey of the Periods of the World, etc., 1812; Comparative Estimate of the Mineral and Mosaical Geologies, 1822 (to show their agreement); Ezekiel's "Gogue," 1814; Isaiah, 1799; Memoirs of Admiral Sir William Penn, 1833. And many other works.

PENN (*William*), London, founder of " Pennsylvania," 1644-1718. Account of the People called Quakers, 1694; Account of the Provinces of Pennsylvania, 1681; Account of his Travels, 1677; Christian (*The*) a Quaker, and the Quaker a Christian, 1674; Journal; Libels no Proofs, 1674, a broadside; Light shining out of Darkness, 1699; Naked Truth needs no Shift, 1674, a broadside; No Cross, no Crown, 1669. His Life, by Marsillac, 1791; T. Clarkson, 1813; W. H. Dixon, 1855; S. Janney, U.S.

PENNANT, LL.D. (*Thomas*), Downing, in Wales, 1726-1798. Account of London, 1790; Arctic Zoology, 1784-87; British Zoology, 1766; Genera of Birds, 1773; History of the Parishes of Whiteford and Holywell, 1796; History of Quadrupeds, 1781(the "Synopsis" enlarged); Indian Zoology, 1769; Journey from Chester to London 1782, London to Dover, etc., 1801; Journey to Snowdon, 1778-81; Literary Life, 1793 (his autobiography); Of the Patagonians, 1788; Some Account of London, 1790; Synopsis of Quadrupeds, 1771; Tour from Downing to Alston Moor 1801, from Alston Moor to Harrowgate, etc., 1804; Tour in Scotland, 1771; Tours in Scotland, 1776; Tours in Wales, 1773.

PENNELL (*Henry Cholmondely*), 1837- . Angler-Naturalist (*The*), 1864; Book of the Pike (*The*), 1866; Crescent (*The*), 1866, poetry; Fishing Gossip, 1868; Fly Fishing, 1875-76; From Grave to Gay, 1884-85; Modern Babylon, 1873, poetry; Modern Practical Angler, 1873; Muses of Mayfair, 1874, poetry; Pegasus Resaddled, 1877; Puck on Pegasus, 1861, poetry.

PENNICUICK, M.D. (*Alexander*), Scotland, 1652-1722. Blue Blanket (*The*), 1722, a tract; Blythe Muses' Banquet (*The*), 1734, poems; Caledonia Triumphans, 1699, a poem; Poems, 1762; Streams from Helicon, 1720, poems.

PEPYS (*Samuel*), Brampton, in Huntingdon-

shire, 1632-1703. Diary, in shorthand, de-
ciphered by the Rev. John Smith, and
published 1825; Memoirs of the Royal
Navy, 1690. His Life, by Smith, 1840;
H. B. Wheatley, 1881.

PERCIVAL, M.D. (*James Gates*), Connecticut,
U.S., 1795-1856. Clio, 1822-27, prose and
verse; Poems, 1820; Report on the Geology
of Connecticut, 1842; Zamor, 1815. His
Life, by Ward, 1859.

PERCIVAL, M.D. (*Thomas*), Warrington, in
Lancashire, 1740-1804. Essays, Medical
and Experimental, 1767-78; Medical Ethics,
1803 (his best work).

PERCIVALL (*William*), *-*. Anatomy of the
Horse, 1836; Hippopathology, 1834; Lectures on Horses, their Form and Action,
1859; Lectures on the Veterinary Art,
1823-26.

PERCY, M.D. (*John*), Nottingham, 1817- .
Metallurgy, or the Art of Extracting Metals
from their Ores, 1861; Metallurgy of Gold,
Silver, and Lead, 1869; Metallurgy of Lead,
Desilverisation, and Cupellation, 1871.

PERCY, D.D. (*Thomas*), bishop of Dromore,
born at Bridgnorth, in Shropshire, 1728-1811.
Essay on the Origin of the English Stage,
1793; Five Pieces of Runic Poetry, 1763;
Hermit of Warkworth, 1771; Key to the
New Testament, 1779; Mallet's *Northern
Antiquities* (translated), 1770; Reliques of
Ancient English Poetry, 1765 (his chief
work); Songs of Solomon, 1764.

PERCY ANECDOTES, compiled by Thomas
Byerley, of Mount Benger, in Scotland,
under the pseudonyms of "Sholto" and
"Reuben Percy," brothers of the Benedictine Monastery, Mount Benger, 1820-23;
the sale was enormous. History of London,
1824.

PETTIGREW (*Thomas Joseph*), London, 1791-
1865. Bibliotheca Sussexiana, 1827-39
(admirable); Chronicles of the Tombs,
1847; History of Egyptian Mummies, 1834;
Medical Portrait Gallery, 1840; Memoirs of
Dr. Lettsom, 1817; Memoirs of Lord Nelson, 1849; Superstitions connected with
Medicine and Surgery, 1844.

PETTY (Sir *William*), Romsey, in Hampshire,
political economist, 1623-1687. Colloquium
Davidis cum Anima sua, 1679; Hiberniæ
Delineatio, etc., 1685; Political Anatomy of
Ireland, 1691; Political Arithmetic, 1682-90
(his chief work); Political Survey of Ireland,
1719, posthumous; Treatise on Taxes and
Contributions, 1662.

PETYT (*William*), 1636-1707. Ancient Right
of the Commons of England, 1680; Jus
Parliamentarium, 1739; Miscellanea Parliamentaria, 1681.

PHELPS-WARD (*Elizabeth Stuart*), Massachu-
setts, 1844- . Austin Phelps, 1891; Be-
yond the Gates, 1883; Chapters from a
Life, 1896; Come Forth, 1890 (with H. D.
Ward); Doctor Zay, 1882; Donal Marcy,
1893; Fourteen to One, 1891; Friends, 1881;
Gates Ajar (*The*), 1869; Gates Between
(*The*), 1887; Hedged in, 1870; Jack the
Fisherman, 1887; Madonna of the Tubs
(*The*), 1887; Master of the Magicians (*The*),
1890 (with Ward); My Cousin and I, 1879;

Poetic Studies, 1875; Sealed Orders, 1879;
Silent Partner (*The*), 1870; Story of Avis
(*The*), 1877; Struggle for Immortality, 1889;
Trotty Book (*The*), 1870; Trotty's Wedding
Tour, 1873.

PHILIPS (*Ambrose*), the Whig poet, nicknamed
"Nambypamby" Phillips, born in Leices-
tershire, 1671-1749. (See PHILIPS, *John*.)
Briton (*The*), 1722, a tragedy; Distressed
Mother (*The*), 1712, a tragedy; Humphrey,
Duke of Gloucester, 1722, a tragedy; Life of
John Williams, Archbishop of York, 1700;
Pastorals (six in number), 1708 (called by
Tickell "the finest in the language"); Per-
sian Tales, 1709; Poems, 1748; Poetical
Letter from Copenhagen (*A*), 1709. His
Life, by Dr. Johnson.

PHILIPS (*Francis Charles*), novelist, 1849- .
As in a Looking-glass, 1885; Constance,
1893; Dean and his Daughter (*The*), 1887;
Devil in Nun's Veiling (*A*), 1895; Doctor in
Difficulties (*A*), 1894; Extenuating Circum-
stances, 1891; French Marriage (*A*), 1890;
Jack and Three Jills, 1886; Little Mrs.
Murray, 1888; Luckiest of Three (*The*),
1896; Lucky Young Woman (*A*), 1886;
Madame Valérie, 1892; Mrs. Bouverie,
1894; One Never Knows, 1893; Question of
Taste (*A*), 1895; Social Vicissitudes, 1886;
Strange Adventures of Lucy Smith, 1887;
Undeserving Woman (*An*), 1896; Worst
Woman in London (*The*), 1895; Young Mr.
Ainslie's Courtship, 1889.

PHILIPS (*John*), the Tory poet, Oxfordshire,
1676-1708. (See PHILIPS, *Ambrose*.) Blenheim, 1705; Cyder (in two books), 1708;
Splendid Shilling (*The*), 1703, a parody on
the style of Milton. His Life, by Sewell,
1709.

PHILLIMORE (*John George*), 1809-1865. History of England during the Reign of George
III., 1863; History of the Law of Evidence,
1850; Introduction to the Study of the
Roman Law, 1848; Principles and Maxims
of Jurisprudence, 1856.

PHILLIPS (*Charles*), 1789-1859. Consolations
of Erin (*The*), 1818; Emerald Isle (*The*),
1812; Garland for the Grave of Sheridan,
1816; Historical Character of Napoleon,
1817; Lament of the Emerald Isle (*The*),
1812, a poem; Loves of Celestine and St.
Aubert (*The*), 1811, a romance; Recollections of Curran, etc., 1818.

PHILLIPS (*Edward*), 1630-1680. Coronation
Ode, 1685 (James II.); Enchiridion, 1684;
Life of Milton, 1694; Mysteries of Love
and Eloquence (*The*), 1658; New World of
Words (*A*), 1720; Speculum Linguæ
Latinæ, 1684; Theatrum Poetarum, 1675.
His Life, by W. Godwin, 1815.

PHILLIPS (*John*), 1800-1874. Geology (in the
Cabinet Cyclopædia), 1837; Geological Map
of the British Isles; Illustrations of the Geology of Yorkshire; Map of the Strata of
England and Wales; Rivers, Mountains,
and Sea-coast of Yorkshire, 1855; Three
Years' Observations on Rain.

PHILLIPS (Sir *Richard*), pseudonyms "James
Adair," "Rev. S. Barrow," "Rev. D. Blair,"
"Rev. C. C. Clarke," "Rev. J. Goldsmith,"
"M. Pelham," etc. It is scandalous for a

publisher to palm off his books under such false names, expressly intended to deceive the public, and to trade on the reputation of another's name. It also does irreparable harm to the young learner, as all false teaching must do. 1768–1840. Million of Facts, 1832 (worthless); Morning's Walk from London to Kew (*A*), 1817; Practices of Anonymous Critics (*The*), 1806; Proximate Causes of Material Phenomena, 1821, 1824. (*Why and Because*, and *First Catechism*, as Rev. David Blair; *Readings in Science*, as Rev. C. C. Clarke; editions of *Goldsmith's Historia*, as Rev. J. Goldsmith; etc.)

PHILLIPS, LL.D. (*Samuel*), 1815–1854. Caleb Stukely, 1843, a novel; Eminent Men and Popular Books, 1852–54; We are all Low People here (in *Blackwood's Magazine*).

PHILLIPS, R.A. (*Thomas*), Dudley, in Worcestershire, 1770–1845. Lectures on Painting, its History and Principles, 1833.

PHILLIPS (*William*), London, 1773–1828. Elementary Introduction to the Knowledge of Mineralogy, 1816 (excellent); Outline of the Geology of England and Wales, 1818.

PHILPOTTS (*Eden*), novelist, Mount Aboo, India, 1862– . Deal with the Devil (*A*), 1895; Down Dartmoor Way, 1895; End of a Life (*The*), 1890; Folly and Fresh Air, 1892 (charming essays); Lying Prophets, 1896; My Laughing Philosopher, 1896; Sugar-Cane Land (*In*), 1893; Some Every-day Folks, 1894; Tiger's Cut (*A*), 1892.

PHILPOTTS, D.D. (*Henry*), bishop of Exeter, born at Bridgewater, 1778–1869. Letter to the Archbishop of Canterbury on the Gorham Case, 1850; Letters to Mr. Canning on the Roman Catholic Claims, 1827; Letters to Charles Butler, 1825–26.

PICKEN (*Andrew*), Paisley, in Scotland, novelist, 1788–1833. Black Watch (*The*), 1833; Club Book (*The*), 1831; Domine's Legacy (*The*), 1830; Sectarian (*The*), 1829; Tales and Sketches of West Scotland, 1828; Tractarian (*The*), 1829; Traditionary Stories of Old Families, 1833; Travels and Researches of Eminent English Missionaries, 1830; Waltham, 1832.

PICKEN (*Andrew Belfrage*), Scotland, 1802–1849. Bedouins (*The*), and other Poems, 1828; Lights and Shadows of a Sailor's Life; Plague Ship (*The*), and other Tales.

PINDAR (*Peter*). See WOLCOT.

PINERO (*Arthur Wing*), London, 1855– . Hobby Horse (*The*), 1886; Lords and Commons, 1883; Low Water, 1884; Magistrate (*The*), 1885; Money Spinner (*The*), 1880; Notorious Mrs. Ebbsmith (*The*), produced at Garrick, 1893; Plays, 1891; Profligate (*The*), 1889; Rocket, 1883; Second Mrs. Tanqueray (*The*), produced 1893; Sweet Lavender, 1888; £200 a Year, 1877.

PINKERTON (*John*), Edinburgh, 1758–1826. Ancient Scottish Poems, 1786 (valuable); Antiquities of Western Scotland, 1793; Dissertation on . . . the Scythians and Goths, 1787; Essay on Medals, 1782; Enquiry into the History of Scotland before Malcolm III., 1789; General Collection of Voyages and Travels, 1808–14; History of Scotland

(House of Stuart), 1797; Iconographia Scotica, 1795–97; Letters on Literature, 1785; Medallic History of England, 1790; Modern Geography, 1802–7; Ode to Craigmillar Castle, 1776; Petralogy, 1811, a treatise on rocks; Rimes, 1782; Scottish Gallery, 1799; Scottish Poems, 1792; Scottish Tragic Ballads, 1781; Select Scottish Ballads, 1783; Vitæ Antiquæ Sanctorum, etc., 1789; Walpoliana, 1799.

PIOZZI (*Mrs.*), maiden name *Hester Lynch Salusbury* (her first husband was Mr. Thrale), born at Bodvel, in Wales, 1739–1821. Anecdotes of Dr. Johnson, 1786; British Synonymy, 1794; Letters to and from Dr. Johnson, 1788; Observations, etc., on a Journey through France, Italy, and Germany, 1789; Retrospection . . . of the Most Striking Events, Characters, etc., of the Last Eighteen Hundred Years, etc., 1801. Her Autobiography, published by Hayward, 1861. In 1833 E. Mangan published his *Piozziana*.

PITMAN (*Isaac*), Trowbridge, Wiltshire, 1813–1897. Phonography, or Writing of Sound, 1840; Stenographic Sound-hand, 1837.

PITT (*Christopher*), Blandford, in Dorsetshire, 1699–1748. Poems, 1727; Translations into verse of Vida's *Art of Poetry* 1725, and Virgil's *Æneid* 1740. (Dr. Johnson says, "Pitt's *Æneid* pleases the critics, but Dryden's the people; Pitt's is quoted, but Dryden's read." Dryden's name has made his *Virgil* pass muster; with an inferior name it could not have survived.)

PLANCHÉ (*James Robinson*), London, 1796–1880. (*He wrote about 200 plays. See below.*) Ash-next-Sandwich, 1864; Conqueror and his Companions (*The*), 1874; Continental Gleanings, 1836; Costumes for Shakespeare's *King John*, 1823–25; Costumes for Shakespeare's *Richard III.*, 1830; Cyclopædia of Costume, 1876–79; Danube (*The*), from Ulm to Vienna, 1836 (the same as Descent of the Danube, 1828); History of British Costume, 1834, 1847; Introduction to Heraldry, 1866; King Nutcracker, 1853, a fairy tale; Lays and Legends of the Rhine, 1826–27 (music by Bishop); Maid Marian, 1822, an opera (music by Bishop); Oberon, 1826, the libretto (music by Weber); Popular Fairy Tales, 1857; Pursuivant at Arms, etc., 1851; Recollections and Reflections, 1872, an autobiography; Regal Records (coronation of queens), 1838; Songs and Poems (from 1819 to 1879), 1880; Souvenir of the Bal Costumé, 1842; William with the Ring, 1872.

Plays: the subjoined are well known: Amoroso, King of Little Britain, produced 1818, a burlesque (his first); Babil and Bijou, 1872; Brigand (*The*), 1829 (this play contains the song of "Gentle Zitella"); Charles XII., 1828, an historic drama; Court Beauties (*The*), 1835, a comedy; Daughter to Marry (*A*), 1828, a comedy; Fair One with the Golden Locks (*The*), 1843; Fortunate Isles (*The*), 1840; Fortunio, 1842; Golden Branch (*The*), 1847; Golden Fleece (*The*), 1843; Green-eyed Monster (*The*), 1823; Invisible Prince (*The*), 1846; King Charming, 1850;

King Christmas, 1871; Loan of a Lover (*The*), 1833; Love and Fortune, 1859, a comedy; Maid Marian, 1822, the libretto (music by Bishop); My Lord and my Lady, 1861; Norma, the libretto; Oberon, 1826, the libretto (music by Weber); Olympic Revels, 1831; Red Mask (*The*), 1834; Rencontre (*The*), 1827; Riquet, 1836; Sleeping Beauty (*The*), 1848; Success, 1825, a farce; Theseus and Ariadne, 1848; Vampire (*The*), 1820; Yellow Dwarf (*The*), 1854.

PLAYFAIR (*John*), Bervie, Scotland, 1748–1819. Elements of Geometry, 1794; Illustrations of the Huttonian Theory of the Earth, 1802; Outlines of Natural Philosophy, 1812–16. His Memoirs, by F. Jeffrey and J. G. Playfair, 1822.

PLAYFAIR, LL.D. (*Lyon*), Meerut, in Bengal, 1819–   . Food of Man in Relation to Useful Work, 1865; Primary and Technical Education, 1870.

PLAYFAIR (*William*), 1759–1823. British Family Antiquary, 1809–11; Commercial and Political Atlas, 1786; History of Jacobinism, 1795; Inquiry into the Decline and Fall of Nations, 1790.

PLOT, LL.D. (*Robert*), Kent, 1641–1696. Natural History of Oxfordshire, 1677 (good); Natural History of Staffordshire, 1686.

PLOWDEN (*Edmund*), Shropshire, 1517–1584. Reports, 1571 (much esteemed).

PLOWMAN (*Pierce*), before 1350. Praier and Complaynte of the Ploweman unto Christe, about 1300; Visio Willi de Petro Plouhman (a religious allegorical satire generally attributed to Robert Langland, and supposed to have been written in the first quarter of the 14th century), printed by R. Cowley, 1550. The Appendix to the *Vision* is called "Pierce Ploughman's Crede," and was published by R. Wolfe, 1553.

PLUKENET (*Leonard*), 1642–1710. Almagestum Botanicum, 1696; Phytographia, 1691–96.

PLUMPTRE, D.D.(*Edward Hayes*), 1821–1891. Bible Educator (*The*), edited 1873; Biblical Studies, 1870; Book of Proverbs, 1864; Byways of Scripture, 1869; Calling of a Medical Student (*The*), 1849; Calmness in Times of Trouble, 1868; Christ and Christendom, 1867, a Boyle lecture; Confession and Absolution, 1874; Dangers Past and Present, 1861; Dante, 1886; Decalogue, etc. (*The*), 1866; Delays and Difficulties in the Churches' Work, 1872; Education of the Clergy, 1862; Epistle of St. James (*The*), 1876; Epistles of St. Peter and of St. Jude, 1876; Epistles to the Seven Churches, 1877; Gospels (*The First Three*), 1878; Infidelity refuted, 1876; Lazarus, and other Poems, 1864; Life of Thomas Ken, 1888; Master and Scholar, with other Poems, 1865; Mission of the Comforter, 1871; Movement of Religious Thought, 1879; Our Life in Heaven, 1856; Perversions to Rome, 1877; Respice, Aspice, Prospice, etc., 1876; Sermons at King's College, 1859; "Spirits in Prison," 1871; St. Paul in Asia Minor, etc., 1877; Study of Theology, etc., 1853; Theology and Life, 1866, sermons; Things Old and New, 1844; Tragedies of Æschylus (translated), 1870, of Sophocles

1866; Twilight Hours, 1868; Victory of Faith,1874; Who is Sufficient? 1878. ∴ He translated Sophocles in 1866, and Æschylus in 1870.

POCOCKE, D.D. (*Edward*), Oxford, 1604–1691. Commentary on Micah, etc., 1677; Porta Mosis, 1655; Specimen Historiæ Arabum, 1650; Translation of Abul-Pharajius into Latin, 1663; Translation of Grotius's *De Veritate Religionis Christianæ* into Arabic, 1660. His Life, by Leonard Twells, 1740.

POCOCKE, LL.D. (*Richard*), bishop of Meath, traveller in the East, born at Southampton, in Hampshire, 1704–1765. Observations on Egypt, 1743; Observations on Palestine, etc., 1745.

POE (*Edgar Allen*), Baltimore, U.S., 1811–1849. Al Aaraff, and Minor Poems, 1829; Annabel Lee, a ballad; Bells (*The*), 1831, a poetical word-painting; Conchologist's First Book (*The*), 1840; Eureka, 1848, a prose poem on the cosmogony; Mystery of Marie Roget (*The*), a tale; Narrative of Arthur Gordon Pym, 1838; Poems, 1831; Raven (*The*), and other Poems, 1831; Tales, 1845; Tales of the Grotesque, etc., 1840; Tamerlane, and some Minor Poems, 1827; Two Volumes of Tales, 1850, posthumous. His Life, by Hannay, 1863; Dr. Griswold, 1864; Ingram, 1874–75.

POLE (*Reginald*), cardinal - archbishop of Canterbury, born at Stourton Castle, in Staffordshire,1500–1558. De Concilio Liber, 1562, posthumous; Pro Ecclesiasticæ Unitatis Defensione, libri iv., 1536 (called by Wythers "seditious and blasphemous;" it certainly gave great alarm to the king [Henry VIII.], and Pole promised not to publish it); Reformatio Angliæ, 1556. His Life, "ex officina Guerrei fratrum," 1563; another, "London, J. Adamson," 1690.

POLLOCK (Sir *Frederick*), 1845–   . Introduction to the History of . . . Politics, 1890; Essays in Jurisprudence, etc., 1882; History of English Law before the Time of Edward I., 1895; Land Laws (*The*), 1883; Leading Cases done into English, 1876; Law of Torts (*The*), 1887; Oxford Lectures, etc., 1890; Principles of Contract at Law, 1875; Spinoza (his life and philosophy), 1880.

POLLOCK (*Walter Herries*), 1850–   . Amateur Theatricals, 1880; Charm (*The*), and other Drawing-room Plays, 1896 (with sir Walter Besant); Lectures on French Poets, 1879; Paradox of Acting (*The*), 1883; Picture's Secret (*The*), 1883; Songs and Rhymes, 1882; Verses of Two Tongues, 1884 (with lady Pollock).

POLLOK (*Robert*), Scotland, 1799–1827. Course of Time (*The*) (an epic poem in blank verse, in 10 books), 1827 (twenty-first edition, 1857). His Life, by his brother, 1843; Hannay, 1863; J. H. Ingram, with Works, 1874–75.

POLWHELE (Rev. *Richard*), Cornwall, 1760–1838. Cornish-English Vocabulary of Local Names, 1836; History of Cornwall, 1803; History of Devonshire, 1793–1806; Poems, 1794, 1796, 1806, 1810; Traditions and Recollections, 1826.

POMFRET (Rev. *John*), Luton, in Bedford-shire, 1667-1703. Choice (*The*), 1699, **a** didactic poem ; Dies Novissima, 1704, post-humous ; Poems, 1699 ; Reason, 1700. Life, by Dr. Johnson, who says, "No poem has been more read than Pomfret's *Choice*."

POND (*John*), astronomer royal, 1767-1836. Astronomical Observations from 1811 to 1835 (continued by G. B. Airy); Catalogue of the Stars, 1833.

PONT (Rev. *Robert*), Scotland, 1525-1606. Against Sacrilege, 1599 ; De Sabbaticorum Annorum Periodis Chronologica a Mundi Exordio Digestio, 1619 ; De Unione Britanniæ, etc., 1604 ; On the Right Reckoning of the Ages of the World, 1619 (he says the year 1600 is A.M. 5548).

POOLE (Rev. *George Ayliffe*), 1809- . History of Ecclesiastical Architecture in England, 1848 ; History of England from a Churchman's Point of View, 1845.

POOLE (*John*), humourist, etc., 1786-1872. Christmas Festivities, 1845 ; Comic Miscellany, 1845 ; Comic Sketch-book, 1835 ; Hamlet travestied, 1811 ; Little Pedlington, etc., 1839, a satire on humbug and all shams ; Oddities of London Life, 1838 ; Patrician and Parvenu (*The*), 1835, a comedy ; Paul Pry, 1825, a comedy ; Phineas Quiddy, **or** Sheer Industry, 1842.

POOLE (*Matthew*), York, 1624-1679. Annotations on Scripture, 1685 ; Synopsis Criticorum Biblicorum, 1669-76 (150 Biblical critics ; his chief work).

POPE (*Alexander*), London, 1688-1744. Bathos, or the Art of Sinking, 1727 ; Correspondence, 1735-36 ; Dunciad (in four parts), 1726, published 1728, part iv. 1742-43 ; Elegy on an Unfortunate Lady, 1717 ; Eloisa to Abelard, 1717 ; Epilogue to the Satires, 1738 ; Epistle on Taste, 1731 ; Epistle to Arbuthnot, 1735 ; Essay on Criticism (in verse), 1711 (excellent) ; Essay on Man (in four poetical epistles), 1732-34 (excellent) ; Grub Street Journal (*The*), 1730-37 ; Imitations of Horace, 1733, 1734, 1737 ; *Iliad* translated into English verse, bks. i.-iv. 1715, completed 1719, begun 1713 ; Messiah (*The*), 1712, a sacred eclogue ; Miscellaneous Poems, 1709 ; Moral Essays (in five poetical epistles), 1731-35 ; New Dunciad (*The*), 1742-43 (forming part iv. of *The Dunciad*) ; Ode for St. Cecilia's Day, 1713 ; *Odyssey* translated into English verse, 1725, begun 1721 ; Pastorals (four in number), 1709 ; Prologue to Addison's *Cato*, 1713 ; Rape of the Lock (in five cantos), 1711, 1714 (excellent) ; Satires, 1734 ; Temple of Fame, 1712 ; Treatise on the Bathos, 1727 ; Three Hours after Marriage, 1717 ; Windsor Forest, 1704, 1713. His Life, by W. Ayre, 1745 ; Owen Ruffhead, 1767 ; Bowles, 1807 ; Roscoe, 1824 ; R. Carruthers ; Mark Pattison, 1869 ; Ward, 1869 ; W. Elwin, 1872 ; C. Clarke, 1873 ; Rossetti, 1873.

·.· His *Iliad* and *Odyssey* are not Homer's epics, but Pope's parodies. The same may be said of Dryden's *Æneid*.

N.B.—Dr. Edwin Abbot published, in 1875, a *Concordance* to Pope.

N.B.—No man, except Shakespeare, has furnished so many quotable lines and phrases. His verbiage is unsurpassed, and yet he had no ear for music.

POPHAM, D.D. (*Edward*), about 1740-1812. Extracts from the Pentateuch compared with Passages from Greek and Latin Authors, 1802 ; Illustrium Virorum Elogia, 1778.

PORDAGE (*Samuel*), contemporary with Dryden. Azaria and Hushai, a counter-satire to Dryden's *Absalom and Achitophel*; Eliana, a romance ; Herod and Mariamne, 1673, a tragedy ; Mundorum and Explicatio, 1661, a sacred poem ; Poems, 1660 ; Siege of Babylon (*The*), 1678, a tragedy.

PORSON (*Richard*), East Ruston, Norfolk, Greek critic, 1759-1808. Adversaria, 1812, posthumous ; *Hecuba* edited, 1797 ; Letters to Archdeacon Travis, 1790 ; *Medea* edited, 1801 ; *Orestes* edited, 1798 ; *Phænissæ* edited, 1799 ; Photii Græcum Lexicon, 1822, posthumous ; Tracts, etc., 1815, posthumous. His Life, by Rev. S. Weston, 1808 ; Rev. J. S. Watson, 1861.

·.· Best known by his editions of four plays of Euripidês: *Hecuba*, 1797 ; *Orestes*, 1798 ; *Phænissæ*, 1799 ; and *Medea*, 1801.

PORTER (*Anna Maria*), Durham, 1781-1832. Artless Tales, 1793 ; Ballads, and other Poems, 1811 ; Barony, 1830, a romance ; Don Sebastian, 1809 ; Fast of St. Magdalen (*The*), 1818 ; Honor O'Hara, 1826, a novel ; Hungarian Brothers (*The*), 1685 (her chief work); Knight of St. John (*The*), 1821 ; Lakes of Killarney (*The*), 1804 ; Octavia, 1798, a novel ; Recluse of Norway (*The*), 1814 ; Roche Blanche, 1822 ; Sailor's Friendship (*A*), and a Soldier's Love, 1805 ; Tales round a Winter Hearth, 1826 (with her sister Jane) ; Village of Mariendorpt (*The*), 1821 ; Wash Colville, 1819.

PORTER (*Jane*), Durham, sister of the preceding, 1776-1850. Coming Out, 1828, a novel ; Duke Christian of Luneberg, 1824 ; Field of the Forty Footsteps, 1828 (interesting) ; Pastor's Fireside (*The*), 1815, a novel ; Scottish Chiefs (*The*), 1810, a romance (the favourite book of George IV.); Sir Edward Seaward's Narrative, 1831 ; Tales round a Winter Hearth, 1826 (with her younger sister Anna Maria) ; Thaddeus of Warsaw, 1803, a romance.

PORTER (Sir *Robert Ker*), Durham, brother of the two preceding novelists, an historical artist, 1775-1842. Napoleon's Campaign in Russia, 1813 ; Travels in Georgia, Persia, etc., 1821-22.

PORTEUS, D.D. (*Beilby*), bishop of London, born at York, 1731-1808. Death, 1759, a poem ; Evidences for the Truth of Revelation, 1800 ; Lectures on St. Matthew, 1802 ; Life of Archbishop Secker, 1797 ; Sermons, 1783-94 ; Temporal Benefits of Christianity, 1806 ; Works, 1811, posthumous. His Life, by a layman of Merton College, 1810 ; R. Hodgson, D.D., 1811.

POTE (*Joseph*), Eton, in Buckinghamshire, 1709-1787. History and Antiquities of Windsor Castle, 1749-62.

POTTER (*Humphrey Tristram*), eighteenth century. Cant and Flash Dictionary, 1795.

POTTER, D.D. (*John*), archbishop of Canterbury, born at Wakefield, in Yorkshire, 1674-1747. Antiquities of Greece, 1691-99 (a standard work); Archæologia Græca, 1697-98; Discourse on Church Government, 1707; Theological Works, 1753, posthumous. His Life, by Anderson; Dunbar; dean Hook, in the *Archbishops of Canterbury*, 1861-75.

POTTER (Rev. *Robert*), 1721-1804. Translated into English verse *Æschylus*, 1777; *Euripidês*, 1781-82; *Sophoclês*, 1788.

POTTS (*Thomas*), about 1575-1630. Discovery of Witches in Lancashire, 1613 (containing the trial of nineteen "witches").

POVEY (*Charles*), about 1660-1750. Torments after Death, 1740; Virgin in Eden (*The*), 1741; Visions of Sir Heister Ryley (no date).

POWELL (Rev. *Baden*), Stamford Hill, near London, 1796-1860. Christianity without Judaism, 1857; Connection of Natural and Divine Truth, 1838; Experimental and Mathematical Optics, 1833; History of Natural Philosophy, 1842; Order of Nature and Claims of Revelation, 1858; Progress of Physical and Mathematical Sciences, 1834; Revelation and Science, 1833; Study and Evidences of Christianity, 1860; Tradition Unveiled, 1839; Unity of Worlds and of Nature, 1855; View of the Undulatory Theory of Light, 1841.

POWELL (*Gabriel*), Wales, 1575-1611. De Antichristo et ejus Ecclesia, libri ii., 1605; Unlawfulness of Toleration.

POWELL (*Robert*), about 1590-1650. Parallell between Alfred and Charles I., 1634.

POWELL (*Thomas*), Wales, about 1573-1645. Arte of Thriving, 1635-36; Love's Leprosie, 1598; Passionate Poet (*The*), 1601; Tom of all Trades, 1631; Welch Bayte to spare Provender, 1603; Wheresoever you see Mee Trust unto Yourselfe, 1623 (against lending and borrowing).

POWNALL (*Thomas*), Lincoln, 1722-1805. Administration of the British Colonies, 1765; Antiquarian Romance (*An*), 1795; Antiquities of the "Provincia Romana" of Gaul, 1788; Currents of the Atlantic (*The*), 1787; Study of Antiquities (*The*), 1782.

POYNET (*John*), bishop of Winchester, 1514-1556. Defence for the Marriage of Priests, 1549; Politik Power, 1556; Right Use of the Lordes Supper, 1550.

PRAED (Mrs. *Campbell*), maiden name *Rosa Caroline Prior*, Queensland, Australia, novelist, 1852- . Affinities, 1885; Ariane, 1888; Australian Heroine (*An*), 1880; Australian Life, 1885; Bond of Wedlock (*The*), 1887; Brother of the Shadow (*The*), 1885; Christina Chard, 1894; December Roses, 1893; Head Station (*The*), 1885; Longleat of Kooralbyn, 1887; Miss Jawbsen's Chance, 1887; Moloch, 1883; Mrs. Tregaskiss, 1896; Nadine, 1882; Nulma, 1897; Outlaw and Law-maker, 1893; Policy and Passion, 1881; Romance of a Chalet, 1891; Romance of a Station (*The*), 1889; Soul of Countess Adrian, 1891; Zero, 1884. See McCARTHY, *Justin*.

PRAED (*Winthrop Mackworth*), London, 1802-1839. Poems, 1864, posthumous. His Life, by D. Coleridge, 1864.

PRATT (The Ven. *John Henry*), 1809-1871. Scripture and Science not at Variance, 1856; Treatise on Attractions, etc., 1860.

PRATT (*Samuel Jackson*); he assumed the name of "Courtney Melmoth;" St. Ives, in Cornwall, 1749-1814. Apology for David Hume, 1777; Cabinet of Poetry, 1808; Emma Corbett, 1776, a novel; Fair Circassian, a tragedy; Family Secrets, 1797, a novel; Gleanings in England, 1796; Gleanings through Wales, Holland, etc., 1795; Landscapes in Verse; Liberal Opinions, 1775, a novel; Pupils of Pleasure, 1779, a novel; Sympathy, a poem; Tears of Genius, 1774, a poem on Goldsmith.
∴ He translated Goethe's *Sorrows of Werther*, 1813.

PRESCOTT (*William Hickling*), Salem, U.S., 1796-1859. Biographical and Critical Essays, 1843; History of Ferdinand and Isabella, 1837; History of Philip II., King of Spain, 1855-59; History of the Conquest of Mexico, 1843; History of the Conquest of Peru, 1847. His Life, by Ticknor, 1863.

PRESTON (*Thomas*), 1537-1598. Lamentable Tragedy of King Cambisês (*The*), 1569.
For I must speak in passion, and I will do it in Cambyses' vein.
    Shakespeare : 1 *Henry V.* act ii. sc. 4.

PRESTWICH (*Joseph*), Clapham, near London, 1812-1896 Conditions under which the Drift Deposits . . . were accumulated, 1865; Geological Conditions affecting the Construction of a Tunnel between England and France, 1874; Occurrence of Flint Implements, etc., 1865; Past and Future of Geology (*The*), 1875.

PRICE, D.D. (*Richard*), Llangeinor, Glamorganshire, Wales, 1723-1791. American Revolution (*The*), 1784; Civil Liberty, 1776 (60,000 copies sold in a few months); Four Dissertations on Prayer, etc., 1766; Free Discussion on Materialism, 1778; Meeting after Death, etc., 1767; Miraculous Evidences of Christianity, 1776; Northampton Mortality Tables; Principal Questions, etc., in Morals, 1758; Treatise on Reversionary Payments, 1769. His Life, by W. Morgan, 1815.

PRICE (Rev. *Thomas*), Builth, in Wales, 1787-1848. Hanes Cymru, 1836-42; Literary Remains, 1854-55, posthumous. His Life, by Jane Williams, 1854.

PRICE (Sir *Uvedale*), Foxley, in Herefordshire, 1747-1829. Essay on the Modern Pronunciation of Greek and Latin, 1827; Essay on the Picturesque, 1794.

PRICE (*William*), 1780-1830. English Embassy to Persia, 1825; Grammar of Hindûstani, 1828; Grammar of Hindûstani, Persian, and Arabic, 1823.

PRICHARD, M.D. (*James Cowles*), Ross, in Herefordshire, 1785-1848. Analysis of Egyptian Mythology, 1819; Diseases of the Nervous System, 1822; Eastern Origin of the Celtic Nations, 1831; History of the Epidemic Fevers of 1817-1819 which prevailed in Bristol, 1820 ; Natural History of Man, 1843 ; On Different Forms of Insanity, etc., 1842 ; Researches into the Physical History of Mankind, 1813, 1849 (his best and first work) ; Treatise on Insanity, 1834 ; Treatise on the Diseases of the Nervous System, 1822.

PRICKET (*Robert*), about 1570–1650. Honor's Fame in Triumph Riding, 1604, in verse ; Newes from the King's Bath, 1645, in verse ; Souldier's Resolution (*A*), 1603, in prose ; Souldier's Wish unto . . . King James, 1603, in verse ; Time's Anatomie, 1606, in verse.

PRIDEAUX, D.D. (*Humphrey*), dean of Norwich, Padstow, in Cornwall, 1648–1724. Connection of the History of the Old and New Testament, 1715–18 (his chief work) ; Directions to Churchwardens, 1707 ; Ecclesiastical Tracts, 1716 ; Life of Mahomet, 1607 ; Marmora Oxoniensia et Arundellianis, 1676 ; Origin and Right of Tithes, 1710 ; Validity of Orders in the Church of England (*The*). His Life, 1748.

PRIESTLEV, LL.D. (*Joseph*), Fieldhead, near Leeds, in Yorkshire, 1733–1802. Answer to Paine's *Age of Reason*, 1795 ; Autobiography, 1795 ; Chart of Biography, 1765 ; Comparison of the Institutes of Moses and those of other Ancient Nations, 1799 ; Correspondence, 1818, posthumous ; Discourses of the Evidences of Revealed Religion, 1794 ; Disquisition on Matter and Spirit, 1777 ; Doctrine of Philosophical Necessity (affirmative), 1777 ; Doctrines of Heathen Philosphers compared with those of Revelation, 1804 ; Examination of Reid, Beattie, etc., 1774 ; Experiments, etc., on Air, 1774–79 (his great work) ; General History of the Christian Church, 1790–1803 ; Harmony of the Evangelists, 1777 ; History of the Corruptions of Christianity, 1782 ; History of the Early Opinions concerning Christ, 1786 ; History and Present State of Electric Science, 1767 ; History of the Present State of Vision, Light, and Colour, 1772 ; Institutes of Natural and Revealed Religion, 1772 ; Lectures on History, etc., 1788 ; Lectures on Oratory and Criticism, 1777 ; Lectures on the Theory of Language, etc., 1762 ; Letters to a Philosophical Unbeliever, 1780–87 ; Notes on all the Books of Scripture, 1803 ; Rudiments of English Grammar, 1769 ; Scripture Doctrine of Remission, 1761 ; Theological Repository, 1769–88 ; Theory of Language, etc., 1762. His Life, by J. Corry, 1805 ; by self and his son, 1806–7 ; by J. T. Rutt, 1823.

PRIME (Rev. *John*), contemporary with queen Elizabeth. Exposition of the Epistle to the Galathians, 1587 ; Nature and Grace, 1583 ; Queen Elizabeth and King Solomon compared, 1585 ; Sacraments of Baptism and the Supper (*The*), 1582.

PRINCE (*John*), Axminster, Devonshire, 1643–1723. Worthies of Devonshire, 1701.

PRINGLE, M.D. (Sir *John*), Scotland, 1707–1782. Diseases of the Army, 1752 ; Six Discourses, 1783 (much admired). His Life, by Andrew Kippis, D.D., 1783.

PRINGLE (*Thomas*), Teviotdale, Scotland,

1789–1834. African Sketches, 1834, in verse (good) ; Ephemerides, 1828, in verse ; Narrative of a Residence in South Africa, 1835. Scenes of Teviotdale, 1816, in verse. His Life, by L. Ritchie, 1839.

PRIOR (Sir *James*), 1790–1869. Life of Edmund Burke, 1824 ; Life of Oliver Goldsmith, 1837.

PRIOR (*Matthew*), Wimborne, in Dorsetshire, 1664–1721. Alma (in three cantos), 1717 ; Carmen Seculare, 1700 ; City and Country Mouse, 1687 (in ridicule of Dryden's *Hind and Panther*) ; Solomon (in three books), 1718. His Life, by Dr. Johnson ; J. Mitford, 1835 ; Geo. Gilfillan, 1857.

PRITCHARD (*Andrew*), *-- . History of Infusoria, Living and Fossil, 1841 ; List of Patents and Inventions, 1844 ; Micrographia, 1837 ; Microscopic Illustrations, 1840 ; Natural History of Animalcules, 1834 ; Notes on Natural History, 1844.

PROCTER (*Adelaide Anne*), London, daughter of Bryan Waller Procter, 1825–1864. Chaplet of Verse, 1862 ; Legends and Lyrics, 1858, 1861. Memoir, by C. Dickens, 1866.

PROCTER (*Bryan Waller*), pseudonym " Barry Cornwall," London, 1788–1874. Autobiography, 1877, posthumous ; Biography of Kean, 1835 ; Biography of Lamb, 1836 ; Dramatic Scenes, 1819 ; Effigies Poeticæ, 1832 ; English Songs, 1832 ; Essays and Tales, 1851, in prose ; Flood of Thessaly (*The*), 1822 ; Marcian Colonna, 1820 ; Mirandola, 1821, a play ; Sicilian Story (*A*), 1820. His Memoirs, by Miss Martineau, 1872.

PROCTOR (*Richard Anthony*), Chelsea, 1837–1888. Borderland of Science, 1873 ; Chance and Luck, 1887 ; Cyclonic Curves . . . the Motions of the Planets, etc., 1878 ; Easy Lessons in Differential Calculus, 1887 ; Easy Star Lessons, 1881 ; Elementary Astronomy, 1871 ; Essays on Astronomy, 1872 ; Expanse of Heaven (*The*), 1873 ; Familiar Science Studies, 1882 ; Flowers of the Sky, 1879 ; First Steps in Geometry, 1887 ; Gnomonic Star-Atlas, 1866 ; Great Pyramid (*The*), 1882 ; Half-hours with the Stars, 1869 ; Half-hours with the Telescope, 1868 ; Hand-book of the Stars (*The*), 1866 ; Home Whist, 1885 ; How to Play Whist, 1885 ; Light Science, etc., 1871, 1883 ; Moon (*The*), 1873–88 ; Mysteries of Time and Space, 1883 ; Myths and Marvels of Astronomy, 1877 ; Orbs around us (*The*), 1872 ; Other Suns than Ours, 1887 ; Other Worlds than Ours, 1870 ; Our Place among Infinities, 1875 ; Pleasant Ways in Science, 1878 ; Poetry of Astronomy (*The*), 1880 ; Rough Ways made Smooth, 1879 ; Saturn and his System, 1865 ; Seasons Pictured (*The*), 1885 ; Science By-ways, 1875 ; Star Atlas, 1870 ; Star Primer, 1886 ; Stars and the Earth (*The*), 1880 ; Stars in their Seasons (*The*), 1883 ; Strength, 1889 ; Strength and Happiness, 1885 ; Sun (*The*), 1871 ; Sun-views of the Earth, 1867 ; Transits of Venus, 1874 ; Treatise on the Cycloid, etc., 1878 ; Universe of Stars (*The*), 1874 ; Universe of Suns (*The*), 1884 ; Use and

Abuse of Food, 1879; Wages and Wants of Science-Workers, 1876; Watched by the Dead, 1888.

PROUT, M.D. (*William*), 1786–1850. Chemistry and Meteorology, 1834, a Bridgewater treatise; On the Nature and Treatment of Stomach and Renal Diseases, 1840.

PRYME (*George*), 1781–1868. Autobiographic Recollections, 1870, posthumous; Introductory Lecture, etc., to . . . Political Economy, 1823.

PRYNNE (*William*), Swainswick, in Somersetshire, 1600–1669. Antipathie of the English Lordly Prelacie to Regall Monarchy and Civill Unity, 1641; God's Judgments on Sabbath-Breakers, 1636; History of Archbishop Laud, 1644; Histrio-mastix, or Scourge for Stage-Players, 1633 (for which he was sentenced to imprisonment for life); Lame Giles, etc., 1630; Lives of John, Henry III., and Edward I. (third vol. of Prynne's "Records"); Newes from Ipswich, 1637 (against the bishops, for which he was pilloried, and lost both his ears); Pleasant Purge for a Roman Catholic, 1642; Pride's Purge, 1648; Records of the Tower, etc., 1666–68 (by far his most valuable production).

PUGHE (Dr. *William Owen*), Wales, 1759–1835. Cambrian Register, 1796–1818; Myvyrian Archæology of Wales, 1801–7; Translation of *Paradise Lost* into Welsh, 1819.

PUGIN (*Augustus Northmore Welby*), London, 1811–1852. Ancient Timber Houses, 1836; Architectural Illustrations of the Public Buildings of London, 1827; Chancel Screens and Rood Lofts, 1848; Contrasts (between Mediæval and Present Buildings), 1841; Designs for Floriated Ornaments, 1849; Examples of Gothic Architecture, 1831–38; Glossary of Ecclesiastical Ornaments, 1844; Gold and Silver Ornament and Costume, 1846; Gothic Furniture (15th century), 1836; Gothic Ornaments . . . from Ancient Buildings, 1831; Iron and Brass Work Designs, 1836; Ornamental Timber Gables (16th century), 1831; Paris and its Environs (200 views), 1829–31; Present State of Ecclesiastical Architecture, 1842; Specimens of Gothic Architecture, 1821–23; Specimens of the Architectural Antiquities of Normandy, 1828; True Principles of Pointed or Christian Architecture, 1843.

PULTENEY, M.D. (*Richard*), Loughborough, in Leicestershire, 1730–1801. General View of the Writings of Linnæus, 1782; Historical and Biographical Sketches of the Progress of Botany in England, 1790. His Life, by Maton.

PULTOCK or PALTOCK (*Robert*), about 1720–1765. Life and Adventures of Peter Wilkins, 1750, a romance.

PUNCH, the comic weekly paper that doth "cleanse the foul body of the infected world," was started 1841.

PURCELL (*Henry*), Westminster, 1658–1695. Collection of Ayres, 1697, posthumous; Dido and Æneas, 1680, a cantata; Ode for St. Cecilia's Day, 1683; Orpheus Britannicus,

1697, posthumous; (12) Sonatas, 1683; Te Deum and Jubilate, 1697.

PURCHAS (Rev. *Samuel*), Thaxted, Essex, 1577–1628. Haklytus Posthumus, or Purchas his Pilgrimmes, 1625–26, a history of the world; King's Tower, etc., of London (*The*), 1623; Microcosmus, or the Historie of Man, 1619; Purchas his Pilgrimage, etc., 1613 (this is an account of all the religions of the world since the creation).

PUSEY, D.D. (*Edward Bouverie*), 1800–1882. Advice on hearing Confession, 1878; Church of England a Portion of Christ's One Holy Catholic Church (*The*), 1865; Church's Seasons, 1883; Coloniarum apud Græcos atque Romanos inter se Comparatio, 1824; Daniel the Prophet, 1864; Doctrine of the Real Presence vindicated (*The*), 1855; Everlasting Punishment, 1880; History of the Councils of the Church, 1857; Holy Eucharist (*The*), 1843 (for this sermon he was suspended for three years); Minor Prophets (*The*), 1862, complete work issued 1876; Private Prayers, 1883; Real Presence, etc., 1855; Remarks on Cathedral Institutions, 1845; Royal Supremacy, etc., 1850; Sermons (Parochial), 1880; Sermons (University), 1859, 1872; Tracts for the Times (Nos. 18, 66, 67, 69), 1835; Unscience, not Science, adverse to Faith, 1878. His Life, by Liddon, 1893.

PUTTENHAM (*George*), sixteenth century. Arte of English Poesie, 1589; Partheniades, 1579. Memoir, by Hazlewood, 1811.

PYCROFT (Rev. *James*), 1813–1894. Agony Point, 1861 (warning against living at "Agony Point" from debt or other difficulties); Collegian's Guide, 1845; Dragon's Teeth, 1863 (sown by bad education); Elkerton Rectory, 1860, a tale; Greek Grammar Practice, 1844; Latin Grammar Practice, 1844; Recollections of College Life, 1845; Remarks on School Education, 1842; Student's Guide to University Honours, 1842; Twenty Years in the Church, 1859, a tale; Ways and Works of Men of Letters, 1860.

PYE, LL.D. (*Henry James*), London, poet laureate, 1745–1813. Alfred (an epic poem in six books), 1801; Commentary illustrating the *Poetics* of Aristotle, 1792; Comments, etc., on Shakespeare, 1807; Progress of Refinement, 1783; Shooting, 1784.

PYNE (*William Henry*), pseudonym "Ephraim Hardcastle," London, 1770–1843. History of Royal Residences, 1819; Microcosm, 1803–6; Wine and Walnuts, 1823.

QUARLES (*Francis*), Romford, Essex, 1592–1644. Alphabet of Elegies (*The*), 1625 (on Dr. Aylmer); Argalus and Parthenia, 1621, a pastoral romance in three books; Barnabas and Boanerges, 1646; Divine Fancies, 1632; Divine Poems, 1630; Emblems, etc., 1635 (his best-known work); Enchiridion of Meditations, 1652, posthumous; Feast for Wormes, 1620, a history of Jonah; Hadassa, 1621, a history of queen Esther; Hieroglyphikes of the Life of Man, etc., 1638; History of Argalus and Parthenia, 1621; History of Samson, 1631; Job Militant, 1624;

Loyal Convert (*The*), 1644, posthumous; Pentalogia, or Quintessence of Meditation, 1620; Shepherd's Oracles (*The*), 1644; Sion's Elegies (the *Lamentations* of Jeremie the prophet), 1624; Sion's Sonnets (Solomon's *Song*), 1625; Virgin Widow, 1649, posthumous, a comedy. His Life, by R. A. Willmott, 1835.

QUARLES (*John*), son of the preceding, 1624–1665. Argalus and Parthenia continued, 1659 (see above); Banishment of Tarquin, 1655, sequel to "The Rape of Lucrece;" Divine Meditations, 1655; Fons Lachrymarum, 1648 (Jeremiah paraphrased; see above, "Sion's Elegies"); Poems, 1648; Regale Lectum Miseriæ, 1648; Triumphant Chastity, 1684 (Joseph).

QUARTERLY REVIEW (*The*), Tory in politics, started 1809.

QUILLER-COUCH (*Arthur Thomas*). See COUCH (*Arthur Thomas Quiller*).

QUILTER, M.A. (*Harry*), 1851– . Anonymous Book of Poems (*An*); Art and Life; Art of Europe (*The*); Life of Giotto, 1881; Preferences in Art, Life, and Literature; Sententiæ Artis, 1886.

QUINCEY (*Thomas de*), Manchester, 1785–1859. Autobiographic Sketches, 1853; Confessions of an English Opium-Eater, 1821, 1822 (his best-known work); Logic of Political Economy, 1844; Works (in 20 volumes), 1856–60. His Life, by Dr. R. S. Mackenzie, U.S., 1855; Miss Martineau, 1872; Page, 1877.

QUINCY, M.D. (*John*), London, died 1723. Lexicon Physiomedicum, 1719; Pharmacopæia, 1733, posthumous.

QUINCY (*Josiah*), Boston, U.S., 1772–1864. History of the Boston Athenæum, 1851; History of Harvard University, 1840; Life of John Quincy Adams, 1858; Municipal History of Boston, 1852.

RADCLIFFE (Mrs.), maiden name *Anne Ward*, London, 1764–1823. Castles of Athlin and Dunbayne, 1789; Gaston de Blondeville, 1826; Italian (*The*), 1797, a romance (copyright £800); Journey through Holland, 1795; Mysteries of Udolpho (*The*), 1794 (her best novel, copyright £500); Poems, 1834; Romance of the Forest (*The*), 1791 (I prefer this to the "Udolpho"); Sicilian Romance (*The*), 1790; St. Alban's Abbey, 1826.

RAFFLES (Sir *Thomas Stamford*), Jamaica, 1781–1826. History of Java, 1817 (excellent).

RAGG (Rev. *Thomas*), Nottingham, 1808– . Creation's Testimony to its Author, 1855; Deity (*The*), 1834, a poem, in which the "Incarnation" forms a part; Heber, and other Poems, 1840; Incarnation (*The*), and other Poems, 1833; Lays from the Prophets, 1841; Lyrics from the Pentateuch, 1837; Man's Dreams and God's Realities, 1858; Martyr of Verulam (*The*), and other Poems, 1835; Scenes and Sketches, 1847.

RALEIGH (Sir *Walter*), Hayes, Devonshire, 1552–1618 (he himself spelt his name Ralegh). Discovery of . . . Guiana, 1596;

History of the World, 1611; Poems, 1813, posthumous. His Life, by Whitehead; Oldys, 1738; Birch, in *Biographical Sketches*, 1748–52; Cayley, 1805; Mrs. A. T. Thomson, 1830; P. F. Tytler, 1833; C. Whitehead, 1854; Macvey Napier, 1857; St. John, 1868; Edwards, 1870.

RALSTON (*William Ralston*), 1829–1888. Early History of Russia (*The*), 1874; Kriloff and his Fables, 1869; Nest of Gentlemen (*A*), 1869; Russian Folk Tales, 1873; Songs Illustrative of Slavonic Mythology, etc., 1872.

RAMSAY (*Allan*), Leadhills, Lanarkshire, in Scotland, 1686–1758. Evergreen (*The*), 1724, a collection of songs; (30) Fables, 1730; Fables and Tales, 1722; Fair Assembly, 1723; Gentle Shepherd, 1725 (the best pastoral in either the Scotch or English language); Health, 1724, a poem; Monk and the Miller's Wife (*The*), 1723; Poems, 1721, 1728, 1731; Scots Proverbs, 1736; Tartana, or the Plaid, 1721; Tea-Table Miscellany, 1724, 1725, 1727, 1740, a collection of songs. His Life, by G. Chalmers, 1800.

RAMSAY, LL.D. (*Andrew Crombie*), 1814– . Geology of Arran, 1858; Geology of North Wales, 1858; Old Glaciers of North Wales and Switzerland, 1860; Physical Geology, etc., of Great Britain, 1878.

RAMSAY (*Andrew Michael*), called "Le Chevalier Ramsay," Ayr, Scotland, 1686–1743. Essai de Politique, 1719; Histoire de la Vie de Fénelon, 1723; Histoire de la Vie de Turenne, 1735; Voyages de Cyrus, 1727.

RAMSAY, M.D. (*David*), Pennsylvania, U.S., 1749–1815. History of the American Revolution, 1790; History of the Revolution of South Carolina, 1785; History of the United States, 1817; Universal History Americanized, 1819.

RAMSAY, LL.D. (Very Rev. *Edward Bannerman*), Aberdeen, in Scotland, 1793–1872. Reminiscences of Scottish Life and Character, 1857. Memoir, by C. Rogers, 1873; Cosmo Innes, 1874.

RAMSAY (*William*), 1806–1865. Manual of Latin Prosody, 1859; Manual of Roman Antiquities, 1848.

RANDOLPH (Rev. *Thomas*), Newnham, in Northamptonshire, 1605–1635. Amyntas, or the Impossible Dowry, 1638, posthumous, a pastoral; Aristippus, or the Jovial Philosopher, 1630, a comedy; Cornelianum Dolium, 1638, posthumous; Hey for Honesty, 1638, posthumous, a comedy; Jealous Lovers, 1629, a comedy; Muses' Looking-glass (*The*), 1638, posthumous, a comedy; Poems, 1638, posthumous.

RANKINE (*William John Macquorn*), 1802–1872. Civil Engineering, 1862.

RASTALL (*John*), died 1536. Boke of Purgatorye, 1530; Existens of God (*The*), 1530; Pastyme of the People, 1529.

RAVENSCROFT (*Thomas*), 1592–1640. Brief Discourse, 1614, part-songs; Deuteromelia, 1609; Melismata, 1611; Musical Phansies, 1611, twenty-three part-songs; Whole Book of Psalms, 1621.

RAWLINS (*Thomas*), dramatist, 1610–1670. .

Calanthe, 1648, a volume of poems ; Rebellion (*The*), 1640, a tragedy ; Tom Essence, or the Moorish Wife, 1677, a comedy ; Tunbridge Wells, 1678, a comedy.

RAWLINSON (Rev. *George*), Chadlington, in Oxfordshire, brother of sir Henry, 1815– . Biblical Topography, 1887 ; Christianity and Heathenism contrasted, 1861 ; Egypt and Babylon, 1885 ; Five Great Monarchies of the Ancient World (*The*), 1862, 1864 ; Historic Evidences of the Truth of Christian Records, 1860, a Bampton lecture ; History of Ancient Egypt, 1881 ; History of Herodotus, 1858–60 ; History of Phœnicia, 1893 ; History, etc., of the Sassanian Empire, 1876 ; Isaac and Jacob, 1890 ; Kings of Israel and Judah (*The*), 1889 ; Manual of Ancient History (*A*), 1869 ; Moses (his life and times), 1887 ; New Version of Herodotus, 1858–62 ; Parthia, 1886 ; Religions of the Ancient World, 1882 ; Seventh Great Oriental Monarchy (*The*), 1876 ; Sixth Great Oriental Monarchy (*The*), 1873.

RAWLINSON (Sir *Henry Creswicke*), Chadlington, in Oxfordshire, the great Assyrian antiquary, 1810–1895. Cuneiform Inscriptions of Babylon and Assyria, 1850 (his great book) ; Cuneiform Inscriptions of Western Asia, 1861–70 ; England and Russia in the East, 1874 ; Inscription of Tiglath-Pileser (*The*), 1857 ; Notes on the Early History of Babylonia, 1854 ; Outline of the History of Assyria, 1852 (a standard work) ; Persian Cuneiform Inscription at Behistan, 1846.

∵ All these books are invaluable.

RAWLINSON, LL.D. (*Richard*), 1700–1755. Chief Historians of all Nations, and their Works, 1728–30 ; English Topographer (*The*), 1720 ; History and Antiquities of Hereford, 1747.

RAY (Rev. *John*), Black Notley, in Essex, 1628–1705. Catalogus Plantarum Angliæ, 1670 ; Catalogus Plantarum circa Cantabrigiam Nascentium 1660, Supplements 1663, 1685 ; Collection of English Words not generally used, 1674 ; Collection of Proverbs, 1672 (now his best-known work) ; Historia Piscium, 1686 ; Historia Plantarum, 1686–1704 ; Methodus Plantarum Nova, 1682 ; Observations in a Journey . . ., 1673 ; Ornithologia, 1676 (this was from Willoughby's MS.) ; Physico-Theological Discourses on Chaos, the Deluge, and the Dissolution of the World, 1693 ; Synopsis Methodica Animalium, 1693 ; Synopsis Methodica Stirpium Britannicarum, 1690 ; Wisdom . . . manifested in Creation (*The*), 1691. His Life, by W. Derham, 1760.

RAYLEIGH (Lord *John Willian Strutt*), 1852– . Theory of Sound, 1877–78.

∵ He edited Clerk Maxwell's *Heat*, 1891–94.

REACH (*Angus Bethune*), 1821–1856. Claret and Olives, etc., 1852 ; Clement Lorimer, 1848, a novel ; Comic Bradshaw (*The*) ; Leonard Lindsay, 1850, a novel ; Natural History of Bores, 1854.

READE, D.C.L. (*Charles*), 1814–1884. Autobiography of a Thief, 1858 ; Bible Characters, 1888 ; Christie Johnstone, 1853 ; Cloister and the Hearth (*The*), 1861 (a portion of this story was originally published in *Once a Week*, under the title of "A Good Fight ") ; Course of True Love never did run Smooth (*The*), 1857 ; Double Marriage (*The*), (originally entitled " White Lies "), 1857 ; Drink, 1879, a melodrama ; Eighth Commandment (*The*), 1860 ; Foul Play, 1868 (with Boucicault) ; Gold, 1850, a drama ; Good Stories of Man and other Animals, 1884 ; Griffith Gaunt, 1867 ; Hard Cash, 1863 ; Jilt (*The*), and other Stories, 1884 ; King's Rival (*The*), 1854, a drama ; Love and Money, 1883, a drama ; Love me Little, Love me Long, 1859 ; Masks and Faces, 1854, a play (with Tom Taylor) ; Never Too Late to Mend, 1856 ; Peg Woffington, 1852 ; Perilous Secret (*A*), 1884 ; Put Yourself in his Place, 1870 ; Readiana, 1884 ; Scuttled Ship (*The*), 1877, a drama ; Simpleton (*A*), 1873 ; Singleheart and Doubleface, 1884 ; Terrible Temptation (*A*), 1871 ; Two Loves and a Life, 1854, a drama ; Wandering Heir (*The*), 1875 ; Woman-hater (*A*), 1877. His Life, by C. L. and Compton Reade, 1887. Selections from his Works, by Mrs. Alex. Ireland, 1891.

READE (*John Edmund*), Broadwell, in Gloucestershire, 1806–1870. Broken Heart (*The*), and other Poems, 1825 ; Cain, the Wanderer, 1830 ; Catiline, 1839 ; Deluge (*The*), 1839 ; Italy, 1838 ; Laureate Wreath (*The*), 1863 ; Life's Episode, 1843 ; Man in Paradise, 1856 ; Memnon, 1844 ; Poetical Works, 1851–58 ; Record of the Pyramids (*A*), 1842 ; Revelations of Life, 1849 ; Revolt of the Angels (*The*), 1830 ; Sacred Poems, 1843 ; Vision of the Ancient Kings (*The*), 1841.

RECORDE, M.D. (*Robert*), Tenby, Wales, 1500–1558. Castle of Knowledge (spherical trigonometry), 1551 ; Grounde of Artes (arithmetic, etc.), 1549 ; Pathway to Knowledge (geometry), 1551 ; Urinal of Physicke, 1548, in dialogue ; Whetstone of Witte, 1557, a treatise on algebra. (He invented the symbol =, meaning "equal to.")

REDDING (*Cyrus*), Penrhyn, Wales, 1785–1870. Gabrielle, 1829, a Swiss tale ; History of Shipwrecks, etc., 1833 ; Keeping up Appearances, 1860, a novel ; Modern Wines, 1833 ; Mount Edgecumbe, 1812, a poem ; Remarkable Misers ; Retirement, and other Poems, 1810 ; Velasco, or Memoirs of a Page, 1846 ; Wife and not a Wife (*A*) ; Yesterday and To-day.

∵ And thirty other books, with scores of pamphlets, etc.

REDGRAVE, R.A. (*Richard*), Pimlico, near London, 1804–1888. A Century of Painters, 1864 (from Hogarth to the international gathering, with his brother S. Redgrave).

REED, D.D. (*Andrew*), London, 1787–1862. No Fiction, 1819, a religious novel. His Life, by A. and C. Reed, 1863.

REED (*Isaac*), London, 1742–1807. Biographia Dramatica, 1782 ; Repository, 1777–83.

REES, D.D. (*Abraham*), Wales, 1743–1825. Cyclopædia (in 85 quarto parts), 1803–19. This was a continuation and extension of the Cyclopædia of Ephraim Chambers.

REEVE (*Clara*), Ipswich, 1738–1803. Memoirs of Sir Roger de Clarendon; Old English Baron, 1777, a Gothic tale (by which she is best known); Phœnix (*The*), 1772 (a translation of the *Argenis*, a romance in Latin by Barclay); Poems, 1769; Progress of Romance, 1785, in dialogue.

REEVE (*Lovell Augustus*), naturalist, 1808–1869. Conchologia Iconica, 1843, *et seq.*; Initiamenta Conchologica, 1846–60.

REEVES (Mrs. *Henry*), maiden name *Helen Buckingham Mathers*, Crewkerne, in Somersetshire, novelist, 1852– . As he Comes up the Stair, 1878; Blind Justice, 1889; Cherry Ripe, 1877; Comin' through the Rye, 1875; Eyre's Acquittal, 1884; Fashion of this World (*The*), 1886; Found out, 1885; Jock of Hazelgreen, 1884; Land of the Leal (*The*), 1878; Man of To-day (*A*), 1894; Murder or Manslaughter? 1885; My Jo, John, 1891; My Lady Green-sleeves, 1879; Mystery of No. 13, 1891; Sam's Sweetheart, 1883; Story of a Sin (*The*), 1881; Study of a Woman (*A*), 1893; Token of the Silver Lily (*The*), 1876; T'other Dear Charmer, 1892; What the Glass told, 1893.

REEVES (*John*), 1752–1829. History of English Law, 1783–84 (valuable); History of the Law of Shipping and Navigation, 1792; Proposal for a "Bible Society" on a New Plan, 1805.

REID (*Mayne*), Ulster, Ireland, 1818–1883. Afloat in the Forest, 1866; Boy Hunters (*The*), 1852; Bruin, or the Grand Bear Hunt, 1860; Bush Boys (*The*), 1855; Castaways (*The*), 1870; Child Wife (*The*), 1868; Cliff Climbers (*The*), 1864; Croquet, 1863; Death Shot (*The*), 1873; Desert Home, or the Family Robinson, 1851; Fatal Cord (*The*), 1870, a tale; Finger of Fate (*The*), 1872; Flag of Distress (*The*), 1876; Forest Exiles (*The*), 1854; Giraffe Hunters (*The*), 1867; Guerilla Chief (*The*), 1867; Gwen Wynn, 1877, a romance; Headless Horseman (*The*), 1865; Hunter's Feast (*The*), 1860, a novel; Maroon (*The*), 1862, a novel; Mountain Marriage (*The*), 1876; Ocean Waifs, 1864; Oceola, 1859, a novel; Plant Hunters (*The*), 1857; Quadroon (*The*), 1856, a novel; Quadrupeds: what they are, and where found, 1867; Ran Away to Sea, 1861; Rifle-Rangers (*The*), 1849 (his first); Scalp Hunters (*The*), 1850; Tiger Hunters (*The*), 1860; War Trail (*The*), 1858; White Chief (*The*), 1855; White Gauntlet, 1864, a romance; White Squaw (*The*), 1870; Wild Huntress (*The*), 1861; Wood Rangers (*The*), 1860, a novel; Yellow Chief (*The*), 1870; Young Voyageurs (*The*), 1853; Young Yägers (*The*), 1856.

REID, D.D. (*Thomas*), Strachan, in Scotland, 1710–1796. Active Powers of the Human Mind (*The*), 1788; Essay on Quantity, 1745; Intellectual Powers of Man (*The*), 1785; Inquiry into the Human Mind, etc., 1764; Logics of Aristotle, etc., 1773. His Life, by Dugald Stewart, 1802; sir William Hamilton, 1846.

REID (Sir *Thomas Wemyss*), Newcastle-on-Tyne, in Northumberland, 1842– . Cabinet Portraits, 1872; Charlotte Bronté, 1877. Gabrielle Stuart, 1883; Gladys Fane,

1883; Land of the Bey (*The*), 1882; Life of W. E. Forster, 1888; Life of R. Monckton Milnes (lord Houghton), 1890; Mauleverer's Millions, 1885; Memoir of John Deakin Heaton, M.D., 1883; Politicians of To-day, 1879.

REID (Sir *William*), Scotland, 1791–1858. Law of Storms, 1838 (his chief work); Progress of the Development of the Law of Storms, 1849.

RENNEL (*James*), near Chudleigh, in Devonshire, 1742–1830. Atlas of Bengal, 1781; Chart of the Bank and Currents of Cape Agulhas, 1768; Comparative Geography of Western Asia, 1831, posthumous; Geographical System of Herodotus, etc., 1800 (of unrivalled merit); Illustrations, chiefly Geographical, of the Expedition of Cyrus, and the Retreat, 1816; Investigation of the Currents of the Atlantic Ocean, etc., 1832, posthumous; Map of Hindustan, 1788 (excellent); Memoir of the Geography of Africa, 1792; Topography of the Plain of Troy (*The*), 1814.

REPTON (*Humphrey*), Bury St. Edmunds, 1752–1818. Fragments on the Theory . . . of Landscape Gardening, 1816; Sketches and Hints on Landscape Gardening, 1795; Theory and Practice of Landscape Gardening, 1803.

REYNOLDS (*Frederick*), 1765–1841. Blind Beggar (*The*), a comedy; Delinquent (*The*), a comedy; Dramatist (*The*), 1789, a comedy (his best, containing the character of "Vapid," the author); Eloisa, 1786, a comedy; Folly as it Flies, a comedy; Fortune's Fool, a comedy; How to grow Rich, a comedy; Laugh when you can, a comedy; Life, a comedy; Management, a comedy; Notoriety, a comedy; Rage, a comedy; Speculation, a comedy; Werther, 1786, a comedy; Will (*The*) a comedy. His Life, by himself, 1826.

REYNOLDS (Rev. *James*), 1803– . History of Jerusalem, 1837 (from the Arabic); Kitab-i-Yamini, 1859 (from the Persian).

REYNOLDS (Sir *Joshua*), Plympton, near Plymouth, Devonshire, artist, 1723–1792. Discourses on Painting, 1771 (15 in number); Literary Works published in 1797; Notes on a Tour through Holland and Flanders, 1781. His Life, by Malone, 1794; Northcote, 1813; Farrington, 1819; Cunningham, 1854; Cotton, 1856; C. R. Leslie, edited by Tom Taylor, 1863.

RHYMER. "Thomas the Rhymer," the earliest poet of Scotland (his son calls him "Thomas Rymour de Ercildon"), real name *Thomas Learmouth*, Tweeddale, Scotland, about 1240–1298. Prophecies of the Rhymer, first published 1603; Sir Tristrem, edited by sir W. Scott, 1804.

RHYMER, "The Corn-Law Rhymer," Ebenezer Elliott, 1781–1849. Corn-Law Rhymes, 1846.

RICARDO (*David*), London, 1772–1823. High Price of Bullion a Proof of the Depreciation of Bank Notes, 1809; On Protection to Agriculture, 1822; On the Influence of a Low Price of Corn, etc., 1815; Plan for . . . a National Bank, 1824; Principles of Political Economy, etc., 1817; Proposals for an

Economical and Secure Currency, 1816. His Life, by MacCulloch, 1846.

RICARDO (*Joseph Lewis*), 1812–1862. Anatomy of Navigation Laws, 1857.

RICH (*Barnaby*), about 1540–1622. Adventures of Brusanus, Prince of Hungary, 1592; Adventures of Simonides, 1581, 1584; Allarme to England, 1578; Conference between Tady MacMarcall and Patricke Plaine, 1602; Dialogue between Mercury and an English Souldier, 1574; Excellencie of Good Women, 1613; Farewell to the Militarie Profession, 1606; Faultes and Nothing Else but Faultes, 1606, 1609; Fruites of Long Experience, 1604; Ingins, etc., to catch Opinion, 1613; Irish Hubbub (*The*), 1619; Looking Glasse for Ireland, 1599; My Ladies Looking Glasse, 1616; Pathway to Militarie Practise, 1587; Short Survey of Ireland, 1609; World never Honest till Now (*The*), 1614.

RICH (*Claudius James*), born in France, 1787–1821. Memoir on the Ruins of Babylon, 1811, 1818; Narrative of a Residence in Kurdistan, 1839, posthumous.

RICHARD DE BURY, bishop of Durham, 1281–1345. Philobiblon, 1345, first printed 1473. His Life, by E. Foss, in *The Judges of England*, 1848–64.

RICHARD OF CIRENCESTER, born at Cirencester, in Gloucestershire, one of the six old chroniclers, 1325?–1402. De Situ Britanniæ, 1355, first printed 1757; Historia ab Hengista ad Annum 1348; Liber de Officiis Ecclesiasticis; Tractatus super Symbolum Majus et Minus; Public Record Series, 1863, 1869. His Life, by Hatchard.

RICHARD OF DEVIZES, Wiltshire, twelfth century. Chronicle, translated and edited by Dr. Giles, 1841.

RICHARDS (*Alfred Bate*), poet, 1820–1875. Crœsus, King of Lydia, 1845, a tragedy; Cromwell, 1847, a drama; Death of the Magdalen, and other Poems, 1847; Dream of the Soul (*The*), and other Poems, 1848; Medea, 1869, a poem; Minstrelsy of War (*The*), and other Poems, 1854; Religio Animæ, and other Poems, 1866; So Very Human, 1871, a novel; Vandyck, 1850, a play.

RICHARDS (*Nathaniel*), about 1595–1660. Celestial Publican (*The*), 1620, a poem; Messalina, 1640, a tragedy; Poems, Sacred and Satyrical, 1641.

RICHARDSON, M.D. (Sir *Benjamin Ward*), Somerby, in Lincolnshire, 1828–   . Hygeia, 1876; Ministry of Health (*A*), 1879; Son of a Star (*The*), 1888; Thomas Sopwith, 1891.

RICHARDSON (*Charles*), 1775–1865. Dictionary of the English Language, 1835–37, Supplement 1855; Illustrations of English Philology, 1815; Study of Languages (*The*), 1854.

RICHARDSON, M.D. (Sir *John*), Dumfries, in Scotland, arctic explorer, 1787–1865. Arctic Searching Expedition, 1851; Fauna Boreali-Americana, 1829–37; Polar Regions, 1861; Zoology, 1839, 1844–47.

RICHARDSON (*Jonathan*), London, 1665–1745. Essay on the Art of Criticism as it relates to Painting, 1719; Theory of Painting, 1773.

RICHARDSON (*Joseph*), dramatist, 1758–1803.

One of the writers of *The Rolliad*, a series of political satires, started in 1784. It received its name from colonel (lord) Rolle, who was the subject of an early criticism in its pages; Fugitive (*The*), a comedy.

RICHARDSON (*Samuel*), Derbyshire, 1689–1761. Clarissa Harlowe, 1748, a novel (his masterpiece); Correspondence, 1804, posthumous; Pamela, 1740, a novel; Sir Charles Grandison, 1753, a novel. His Life, by Mrs. Barbauld, 1805; Rev. E. Mangin, 1811.

RICHARDSON (*William*), 1743–1814. Anecdotes of the Russian Empire, 1784; Essays on Shakespeare, 1783, 1789, 1797; Indiana (*The*), 1812; Maid of Locklin, 1801, a lyrical drama; Poems, 1781 (chiefly rural).

RICHMOND (Rev. *Legh*), Liverpool, 1772–1827. Annals of the Poor, 1814 (his best-known work, containing the world-famous memoir, "The Dairyman's Daughter"); Fathers of the English Church, 1807–11. His Life, by T. S. Grimshaw, 1829.

RICKMAN (*Thomas*), Maidenhead, in Berkshire, 1776–1841. Attempt to discriminate the Styles of Architecture in England, from the Conquest to the Reformation, 1817.

RIDDELL (*Henry Scott*), Scotland, 1798–1870. Christian Politician (*The*), 1844; Poems and Miscellaneous Pieces, 1847; Songs of the Ark, 1831.

RIDDELL (Mrs. *J. H.*), maiden name *Charlotte Elisa Lowson Cowan*, early pseudonym "F. G. Trafford," Carrickfergus, in Antrim, Ireland, novelist, 1837–   . Above Suspicion, 1875; Alaric Spenceley, 1881, a high-ideal novel; Austin Friars, 1870; Banshee's Warning (*The*), 1894; Berna Boyle, 1884; City and Suburbs, 1861; Daisies and Buttercups, 1882; Dearly Bought; Did he deserve it? 1897; Disappearance of Mr. Jeremiah Redworth, 1879; Earl's Promise (*The*), 1873; Fairy Water, 1878; Far above Rubies, 1867; George Geith, 1864; Head of the Firm (*The*), 1892; Her Mother's Darling, 1877; Home, Sweet Home, 1873; Idle Tales, 1888; Joy after Sorrow, 1873; Life's Assize (*A*), 1870; Mad Tour (*A*), 1891; Maxwell Drewitt, 1865; Miss Gascoigne, 1887; Mitre Court, 1885; Moor and the Fens (*The*), 1858; Mortomley's Estate, 1874; My First Love, 1876; Mystery in the Palace Garden (*The*), 1880; Nun's Curse (*The*), 1887; Phemie Keller, 1866; Prince of Wales' Garden Party (*The*), and other Stories, 1882; Princess Sunshine, 1889; Race for Wealth (*The*), 1866; Rich Husband (*The*), 1866; Ruling Passion (*The*), 1876; Rusty Sword (*The*), 1893; Senior Partner (*The*), 1881; Silent Tragedy (*A*), 1893; Struggle for Fame, 1884; Susan Drummond, 1884; Too much Alone, 1860; Uninhabited House (*The*), 1883; Weird Stories, 1882; World in the Church (*The*), 1862.

RIDDLE (Rev. *Joseph Esmond*), 1804–1859. Ecclesiastical Chronology, 1840; Latin-English Dictionary, 1849; Luther and his Times, 1827; Manual of Christian Antiquities, 1839; Manual of Scripture History, 1857; Natural History of Infidelity and Superstition, 1852.

RIDLEY (Rev. *Gloucester*), 1702–1774. Life

of Bishop Ridley (the progress of the Reformation), 1763; On the Use of the Syriac Version of the New Testament, 1761; Psyche (a poem in Dodsley's *Collection*).

RIDLEY (*James*), pseudonym "Sir C. Morell," son of the preceding, 1722-1777. Tales of the Genii, 1765.

RIDLEY, D.D. (*Nicholas*), bishop of London, 1500-1555. De Cœna Dominica Assertio, 1555; Way to Peace (*The*), 1688; Works, 1841, published for the Parker Society. His Life, by Gloucester Ridley, 1763.

RIDPATH (Rev. *George*), Stitchell, in Scotland, 1663-1717. Border History of England and Scotland (*The*), 1776, posthumous.

RIGG, D.D. (*James Harrison*), Newcastle-on-Tyne, in Northumberland, 1821- . Character, Life, and Works of Dr. Pusey, 1883; Comparative View of the Church Organizations, 1887; Discourses, etc., on the Leading Truths of Religion . . ., 1880; Living Wesley (*The*), 1875; Modern Anglican Theology, 1857; National Education, 1873; Principles of Wesleyan Methodism, 1850; Relations of J. Wesley . . . to the Church of England, 1868.

RIPLEY (*George*), 1425?-1490. Compounde of Alchemie (in eight-syllable verse), 1471 (a metrical description of the way to make *aurum potabile*).

RISHANGER (*William de*), a monk of St. Albans, about 1235-1320. De Bellis Leues et Eusham, about 1265 (fought 1264); Gesta Edwardi I., about 1310; Opus Chronicorum, about 1270 (the barons' wars of 1265, printed by the Camden Society, 1840).

RITA, true name Mrs. *Eliza M. J. von Booth*, Scotland, novelist. *- After long Grief and Pain, 1883; Brought Together, 1892; Corinna, 1888; Countess Daphne, 1885; Countess Pharamond, 1893; Dame Durden, 1883; Darby and Joan, 1886; Ending of my Day (*The*), 1895; Faustine, 1886; Fragoletta, 1881; Gender in Satin (*A*), 1895; Gretchen, 1887; Kitty the Rag, 1896; Lady Nancye, 1887; Laird o' Cockpen (*The*), 1891; Like Dian's Kiss, 1886; Man in Possession (*The*), 1893; Miss Kate, 1889; My Lady Coquette, 1881; My Lord Concert, 1884; Peg the Rake, 1895; Sheba, 1889; Sinless Secret (*The*), 1881; Two Bad Blue Eyes, 1884; Vignette Stories, 1896; Vivienne, 1877.

RITCHIE (*Leitch*), Greenock, novelist, 1801-1865. Game of Life (*The*), 1851; Headpieces and Tailpieces, 1828; London Night Entertainments; Magician (*The*), 1853; Romance 'of History: Ireland 1837-38, France 1831; Schinderhannes, the Rhine Robber, 1848; Tales and Confessions, 1856; Wearyfoot Common, 1855; Windsor Castle, 1840; Winter Evenings, 1858.

RITSON (*Joseph*), Stockton-on-Tees, in Durham, 1752-1803. Ancient Popular Poetry, 1791; Ancient Songs (from Henry III. to the Revolution), 1790; Annals of Caledonia, 1828, posthumous; Bibliographia Poetica, 1802; Caledonian Muse (*The*), 1821, posthumous; English Anthology, 1793-94; English Songs, 1783; Fairy Tales, 1831, posthumous; Gammer Gurton's Garland,

1810, posthumous; Life of King Arthur, 1825, posthumous; Memoirs of the Celts and Gauls, 1827, posthumous; Minot's Poems, 1795; Northern Garlands, 1810, posthumous; Observations on Warton's . . . English Poetry, 1782; Robin Hood Poems, 1795 (best known by); Scottish Songs, 1794. His Life, by Haslewood, 1824; sir Harris Nicholas, 1833.

ROBERTS, R.A. (*David*), Edinburgh, 1796-1864. Sketches of the Holy Land (in four vols.), 1842-48 (a splendid work).

ROBERTS (*Morley*), 1857- . Adventure of the Broad Arrow, 1897; Adventures of a Ship's Doctor, 1895; Degradation of Geoffrey Alwell, 1895; Earth Mother (*The*), 1896; Great Jester (*The*), 1896. And other similar works.

ROBERTSON (*Frederick William*), London, 1816-1853. Analysis of Tennyson's *In Memoriam*, 1862; Expository Lectures on the Epistle to the Corinthians, 1859; Lectures, etc., on Literary and Social Subjects 1858; Notes of Genesis, 1877. His Life, by Stopford Brooke, 1865.

ROBERTSON (*James Burton*), 1800-1877. Edmund Burke, his Life, Times, etc., 1868; Lectures, 1854, 1868; Prophet Enoch (*The*), 1860, an epic poem in blank verse.

ROBERTSON (Rev. *James Craigie*), Aberdeen, Scotland, 1813-1882. Biography of Thomas Becket, 1859; Growth of the Papacy (*The*), 1876; History of the Christian Church (in eight vols. 1873-75, in four vols. 1853-73); How shall we conform to the Liturgy? 1843; Sketches of Church History, 1855, 1878.

ROBERTSON (*Joseph*), Aberdeen, 1810-1866. Circumnavigation of the Globe, 1836; Concilia Scotiæ, 1866; Deliciæ Literariæ, 1840; Guide to the City of Aberdeen, 1839; Statuta Ecclesiæ Scotianæ, 1864.

ROBERTSON (*Thomas William*), 1829-1871. (*Author of a great number of plays.*) Caste, 1867, a comedy; David Garrick, 1864, a comedy; Dreams, a comedy; Home, a comedy; M.P., 1870, a comedy; Ours, 1866, a comedy (which met with enormous success); School, 1869, a comedy; Society, 1865, a comedy.

ROBERTSON, D.D. (*William*), Bothwick, in Scotland, 1721-1793. History of America, 1777, 1788; History of Charles V., 1769 (his best work); History of Scotland, 1759, 1787; Of the Knowledge of India before the Discovery of . . . the Cape of Good Hope, 1791. His Life, by Dugald Stewart, 1801; Gleig, 1828.

ROBERTSON (*William*), born 1686. Gates to the Holy Tongue, 1653; Index Alphabeticus Hebraico-Biblicus, 1683; Thesaurus Linguæ Sanctæ, 1680.

ROBERTSON (*William*), Fordyce, in Scotland, 1740-1803. History of Greece, 1768; Index of Charters, 1798; Proceedings Relative to the Peerage of Scotland, 1794.

ROBINS (*Benjamin*), Bath, Somersetshire, 1707-1751. Anson's Voyage round the World, 1740-44; New Principles of Gunnery, 1742. His Life, by Dr. Wilson.

ROBINSON (*A. Mary F.*), afterwards Mme. *Darmesteter*, Leamington, in Warwickshire, 1857– . Arden, 1883; Crowned Hippolytus, 1881; Emily Brontë, 1883; End of the Middle Ages (The), 1888; Handful of Honeysuckles, 1878; Italian Garden (An), 1886; Margaret of Angoulême, 1889; New Arcadia, and other Poems, 1884; Retrospect, and other Poems, 1893; Songs, Ballads, etc., 1888.

ROBINSON (Clement), sixteenth century. Handfull of Pleasant Delights, 1854 (Shakespeare often quotes from these songs).

ROBINSON, D.D. (Edward), Southington, U.S., 1794–1863. Biblical Researches in Palestine, 1841; Greek and English Lexicon of the New Testament, 1836; Harmony of the Four Gospels, 1846; Holy Land (The), 1851; Physical Geography of Palestine, 1865.

ROBINSON (F. W.), Spitalfields, London, novelist, 1830– . Anne Judge, Spinster, 1867; As Long as she Lives, 1876; Beyond the Church, 1866; Bridge of Glass (A), 1879; Carrie's Confessions, 1865; Christie's Faith, 1867; Church and Chapel, 1863; Courting of Mary Smith (The), 1886; Coward Conscience, 1879; Dark Street, 1887; Fair Maid (A), 1886; Fate of Sister Jessica (The), 1893; Female Life in Prison, 1863; For her Sake, 1869; Hands of Justice (The), 1883; Her Face was her Fortune, 1873; Her Love and his Life, 1891; In Bad Hands, 1887; Jane Cameron, 1863; Keeper of the Keys (The), 1896; Lazarus in London, 1885; Little Kate Kirby, 1873; Man she Cared for (The), 1884; Mattie, 1864; Mrs. Stewart's Intentions, 1864; No Church, 1862; No Man's Friend, 1867; Owen, 1870; Poor Humanity, 1868; Poor Zeph, 1880; Prison Characters, 1866; Second Cousin Sarah, 1874; Stern Necessity, 1870; True to Herself, 1870; Very Strange Family (A), 1896; Woman's Ransom (A), 1863; Women are Strange, etc., 1883; Wrong that was Done (The), 1892; Youngest Miss Green (The), 1888.

ROBINSON (Henry Crabb), Bury St. Edmunds, Suffolk, 1775–1867. Diary and Correspondence, 1869, posthumous.

ROBINSON (Rev. Robert), Swaffham, in Norfolk, 1735–1790. Arcana, 1774; Ecclesiastical Researches, 1792; History and Mystery of Good Friday, 1777; History of Baptism, 1790; On Nonconformity, 1778; Plea for the Divinity of Christ, 1776; Sermons, 1786. His Life, by George Dyer, 1796.

ROBINSON (Rev. Thomas), 1749–1813. Christian System unfolded, 1805; Prophecies relating to the Messiah, 1812; Scripture Characters, 1796. His Life, by the Rev. E. T. Vaughan, 1815.

ROBINSON (Rev. Thomas), 1790–1873. Last Days of Bishop Heber, 1827; Twin Fallacies of Rome (The), 1851.

ROBISON, LL.D. (John), Boghall, in Scotland, 1739–1805. System of Mechanical Philosophy, 1804 (much esteemed).

ROBY (John), Rochdale, in Lancashire, 1793–1850. Seven Weeks in Belgium, 1838; Sir Bartram (in six cantos), 1815; Traditions of Lancashire, 1829–31. His Life, by his widow, 1854.

ROCHESTER (John Wilmot, earl of), Ditchley in Oxfordshire, 1647–1680. "My Dear Mistress has a Heart," 1668; Poems, 1680; Upon Nothing, 1671; Valentinian, 1685, posthumous, a tragedy. His Life, by bishop Burnet, 1680.

ROCK (Rev. Daniel), Liverpool, 1799–1871. Church of Our Fathers, 1849–53; Hierurgia, 1848; Textile Fabrics, 1870.

ROEBUCK (John Arthur), Madras, 1803–1879. History of the Whig Party from 1830 to the Reform Bill, 1852; Plan for the Government of our Colonies, 1849.

ROGER OF HOVEDEN, or Howden, in Yorkshire, 1129–1202. Bede's Ecclesiastical History continued.

ROGER OF WENDOVER, prior of Belvoir, in Leicestershire, chronicler, born 1237. Flores Historiarum, 1236 (a history of the world from the Creation to 1235).

ROGERS (Henry), 1814–1877. Eclipse of Faith (The), 1882 (his chief work); Essays, 1850, 1868, 1874; Life of Thomas Fuller, 1856; Reason and Faith, 1866; Superhuman Origin of the Bible, 1874; Theological Controversies of the Time, 1874.

ROGERS (Henry Darwin), Philadelphia, U.S., 1809–1866. Geological Survey of Pennsylvania, 1858.

ROGERS, D.D. (John), Oxfordshire, 1679–1729. Necessity of a Divine Revelation, 1727; Visible and Invisible Church of Christ, 1719.

ROGERS (Samuel), Newington Green, near London, 1763–1855. Columbus (in 12 cantos), 1812; Epistle to a Friend, 1798; Human Life, 1819; Italy (in two parts), 1822 (part i. contains 22 subjects, part ii. 24 subjects); Jacqueline, 1814, a tale; Ode to Superstition, and other Poems, 1786; Pleasures of Memory (in two parts), 1792 (his chief poem); Recollections 1859, posthumous (his autobiography); Table Talk, 1856, 1859, posthumous. His Autobiography, called "Recollections," with Memoir, 1856, edited by W. Sharpe in 1859.

ROGET, M.D. (Peter Mark), London, 1779–1869. Animal and Vegetable Physiology, 1834; Physiology and Phrenology, 1838; Thesaurus of English Words and Phrases, 1852 (a useful book).

ROMAINE (Rev. William), Hartlepool, Durham, 1714–1795. Discourses (12) upon the Law and the Gospel, 1760; Essay on Psalmody, 1775; Life of Faith (The), 1763; Scripture Doctrine of the Lord's Supper, 1765; Sermons (12) upon Solomon's Song, 1759; Triumph of Faith (The), 1795; Walk of Faith (The), 1771. His Life, by the Rev. W. B. Cadogan, 1796.

ROMANES, LL.D. (George John), 1848–1894. Animal Intelligence, 1882; Candid Examination of Theism, 1878; Charles Darwin, 1882; Christian Prayer and General Laws, 1874; Darwin and After Darwin, 1892; Examination of Weismannism, 1893; Jellyfish, 1885; Locomotor System of Medusæ, 1878–80; Mental Evolution, 1878; Mental Evolution in Animals, 1883; Mental Evolution in Man, 1888; Mind, Motion, and Monism, 1895, posthumous; Scientific

Evidences of Organic Evolution, 1882; Starfish (*The*), Jellyfish, and Sea-urchins, 1885; Thoughts on Religion, 1895, posthumous.

ROSCOE (*Henry*), 1800-1836. Law of Evidence in Criminal Cases, 1836; Life of William Roscoe (his father), 1833; Lives of British Lawyers, 1830.

ROSCOE, LL.D. (*Henry Enfield*), London, 1833- . Elementary Chemistry; Lectures on Spectrum Analysis, 1869; Treatise on Chemistry, 1877.

ROSCOE (*Thomas*), Liverpool, 1791-1871. German Novelist, 1826; Italian Novelist, 1825; Life and Writings of Cervantes, 1839; Life of William the Conqueror, 1848; Memoirs of Scipio de Ricca, 1829; Memoirs of Silvio Pellico, 1833 (from the Italian); Spanish Novelist, 1826; Tourist in Italy, 1831-33; Tourist in Spain, etc., 1838; Translation of *Memoirs of Benvenuto Cellini* 1823, Lanzi's *History of Painting* 1828, Sismondi's *Literature* 1823.

ROSCOE (*William*), Liverpool, 1753-1831. Life and Pontificate of Leo X., 1805; Life of Lorenzo de' Medici, 1796 (admirable); On the Origin and Vicissitudes of Literature, 1817. His Life, by his son Henry, 1833.

ROSCOE (*William Caldwell*), Liverpool, 1823-1859. Impressions of America, 1868; Match in the Dark (*A*), 1878; Poems and Essays, 1860, posthumous.

ROSE (*George*), pseudonym "Arthur Sketchley," Brechin, in Scotland, 1817-1882. Mrs. Brown, a series of humorous sketches (once very popular); Observations on the Historical Work of Charles James Fox, 1809.

ROSE (*William*), Scotland, 1762-1790. Last Day of Love (*The*), and other Poems, 1834. N.B.—His "Praise of the Highland Mary" is a masterpiece of pastoral poetry.

ROSE (*William Stewart*), 1775 1843. Crusade of St. Louis, and other Poems, 1810; Naval History of the late War, 1802.
∵ He translated the *Amadis de Gaul*, 1803; and into English verse the *Orlando Innamorato* in 1823; and the *Orlando Furioso* in 1831.

ROSEBERY (*Archibald Philip Primrose*, earl of), London, 1847- . Pitt, 1891.

ROSS (*Alexander*), 1590-1654. Arcana Microcosmi, 1652; Centurie of Divine Meditations (*A*), 1646; History of the World (*The*), 1652; Medicus Medicatus, 1645; Mel Heliconium, 1642; Mystagogus Poeticus, 1647; Rerum Judaicarum Memorabilium, libri iii. 1617-19, libri iv. 1632; Three Decads of Divine Meditations, 1630; View of all Religions (*A*), 1653; Virgilius Evangelizans, 1634.
∵ This is the Ross to whom S. Butler refers in *Hudibras*—

There was an ancient sage philosopher
That had read [all] Alexander Ross over.

ROSS (*Alexander*), Aberdeenshire, Scotland, 1699-1784. Helenore, 1768, a pastoral tale (the first publication, aged 70). His Life, by the Rev. Alexander Thomson, 1812.

ROSS, M.D. (*Alexander Milton*), Belleville,

in Canada, 1832- . Architecture of Birds' Nests, 1875; Birds of Canada (*The*), 1872; Butterflies and Moths of Canada (*The*), 1873; Elephas Americanus, etc., 1875; Flora of Canada (*The*), 1874; Food of Canadian Birds (*The*), 1875; Forest Trees of Canada (*The*), 1874; Mammals and Fish of Canada (*The*), 1878; Migration of Canadian Birds, 1875.

ROSS (Sir *James Clark*), London, 1800-1862. Voyage of Discovery (1839-43) in the Southern Seas, 1847.

ROSS (Sir *John*), Balsarroch, in Scotland, 1777-1856. Narrative of a Second Voyage in Search of a Northern Passage, 1835; Residence in Arctic Regions, etc., 1829-31; Voyage of Discovery . . . for the . . . Exploring of Baffin's Bay, 1819.

ROSS (Rev. *John Lockhart*), 1810- . Druidical Temples at Avebury, 1859; Lectures on the History of Moses, 1837.

ROSS-CHURCH. See MARRYAT (*Florence*).

ROSSCOMMON (The earl of), 1663-1684. Essay on Translated Verse, 1684.
∵ He translated *Horace* into English verse, 1683.

ROSSETTI (*Christina Georgina*), pseudonym "Ellen Alleyn," London, 1830-1894. Annus Domini, a prayer for every day in the year, 1874; Called to be Saints, 1881; Commonplace, and other Short Stories, 1870; Face of the Deep (*The*), 1892; Goblin Market, and other Poems, 1862; Letter and Spirit, 1883; Pageant (*A*), and other Poems, 1881; Poems 1875, collected 1875; Prince's Progress (*The*), and other Poems, 1866; Seek and Find, 1879; Short Studies of the "Benedicite," 1879; Singsong, 1872, a nursery rhyme-book; Speaking Likenesses, 1874; Time Flies, 1885; Verses, 1847 (her first volume privately printed).

ROSSETTI (*Dante Gabriel*), London, 1828-1882. Ballads and Sonnets, 1881; Collected Works, 1886; Dante and his Circle, 1874; Early Italian Poets (*The*), 1861; Life of William Blake, 1863; Poems, 1870. His contributions in The Germ, 1850, were:— Pt. i., Songs of One Household and Hand and Soul; pt. ii., The Blessed Damozel; pt. iii., The Carillon, Sea Limits (called here From the Cliffs), Noon; pt. iv., Pax Vobis and six sonnets. His Biography, by W. Sharp, 1882; J. Knight, 1887; also by his brother.

ROSSETTI (*Maria Francesca*), London, 1827-1876. Letters to my Bible Class, 1872; Shadow of Dante (*A*), 1871.

ROSSETTI (*William Michael*), London, 1829- . Criticisms on Swinburne, 1866; Dante's *Hell* translated into English, 1865; Dante Gabriel Rossetti, 1889; Fine Arts, 1867; Life of Keats, 1887; Lives of Famous Poets, 1878; Memoir of Dante G. Rossetti, 1895; Mrs. Holmes Grey, 1869, blank verse. He edited the works of many English poets; amongst others: Blake, 1874; Campbell, 1872; Chaucer's *Troylus and Cryseyde* compared with Boccaccio's *Filostrato*, 1873-83; Coleridge, 1871; Dante and Christina Rossetti, 1886-1896; Shakespeare, 1880; Shelley, 1870.

ROUTH, D.D. (*Martin Joseph*), South Elmham, in Suffolk, 1755-1854. Reliquiæ Sacræ, 1814-15 (valuable); Scriptorum Ecclesiasticorum Opuscula, 1832.

ROWBOTHAM (*John Frederick*), 1852- . Death of Roland, 1887; History of Music, 1885-87; History of Rossal School, 1894; Human Epic (*The*), 1890; Private Life of Great Composers, 1892; Troubadours (*The*), and the Courts of Love, 1895.

ROWE (*Nicholas*), Little Bradford, in Derbyshire, poet laureate, 1673-1718, buried in Westminster Abbey. Ambitious Stepmother (*The*), 1698 (his first tragedy); Biter (*The*), 1705, a comedy; Fair Penitent (*The*), 1703, a tragedy (it contains the character of the "Gay Lothario"); Jane Shore, 1713, a tragedy (his best); Lady Jane Grey, 1715, a tragedy; Royal Convert (*The*), 1708, a tragedy; Tamerlane, 1702, a tragedy; Ulysses, 1706, a mythological drama.
∴ He translated Lucan's *Pharsalia* into English verse, and edited Shakespeare.

ROWE (Mrs. *Thomas*), maiden name *Elizabeth Singer*, pseudonym "Philomela," born at Ilchester, in Somersetshire, 1674-1737. Devout Exercises of the Heart, 1737; Friendship in Death (in 20 letters), 1721; History of Joseph (*The*), 1736, a poem; Letters, Moral, etc., 1729-33.

ROWLANDS (*Henry*), Wales, died 1722. Mona Antiqua Restaurata, 1723 (excellent).

ROWLANDS (*Samuel*), 1570-1625. Crew of Kind London Gossips, 1663, posthumous; Betrayal of Christ, and other Poems, 1598; Democritus, or Dr. Merryman his Medicine, 1607; Diogenes his Lanthorne, 1607; Goode Newes and Bad Newes, 1622; Haile Fellow, Well Met, 1612; Heaven's Glory, Earth's Vanitie, Hell's Horror, 1628; History of Guy, Earle of Warwicke, 1607; Humor's Looking-glasse, 1608, satires and stories in verse; Knave of Clubbs, 1609; Knave of Harts, 1612; Letting Humors Blood in the Head-vayne, 1600; Looke to it, for I'le Stabbe ye, 1604, a poem; Martin Mark-all, Beadle of Bridewell, 1610; Melancholie Knight (*The*), 1615; More Knaves yet, 1612; Night Raven (*The*), 1618; 'Tis Merrie when Gossips mete, 1602.

ROWLEY (*William*), time James I. All Lost by Lust, 1633, a tragedy; Birth of Merlin (*The*), 1662, a comedy; Booke of the 400 Loves (*The*), a comedy; Fair Quarrel (*A*), 1617 (with Middleton); Fool without Book (*The*), a comedy; Knave in Print (*A*), a comedy; Match at Midnight (*A*), 1633, a comedy; New Wonder (*A*), a Woman never Vext, 1632, a comedy; None-such (*The*), a comedy; Parliament of Love (*The*), 1625, a comedy (with Massinger); Search for Money, 1609, a pamphlet; Shoemaker a Gentleman (*A*), 1638, a comedy; Travailes of Three English Brothers, 1607, a tragi-comedy (with J. Day); Witch of Edmonton, a tragi-comedy (the joint work of Rowley, Dekker, and Ford).

ROXBURGH, M.D. (*William*), Ayrshire, Scotland, 1759-1815. Coromandel Plants, 1795-98; Flora Indica, 1820-24; Hortus Bengalensis, 1814.

ROY (*William*), of Scotland, 1726-1790.

Military Antiquities of the Romans in North Britain, 1793.

RUDDIMAN (*Thomas*), Scotland, 1674-1757. Grammaticæ Latinæ Institutiones, 1725-31; Rudiments of the Latin Tongue, 1714. His Life, by G. Chalmers, 1794.

RUDING (Rev. *Rogers*), Leicester, 1751-1820. Annals of the Coinage of Great Britain, etc., 1817.

RUSHWORTH (*John*), Northumberland, 1607-1690. Historical Collections of Private Passages of State (1659), 1701, posthumous.

RUSKIN, LL.D. (*John*), London, 1819- . Aratra Pentilici, 1870 (on sculpture); Ariadne Florentina, 1872; Arrows of the Chase, 1840-80; Art of England (*The*), 1883; Bibliotheca Pastorum, 1876-77; Cambridge School of Art (*The*), 1858; Catalogue of the Turner Sketches in the National Gallery, 1857; Cœli Enarrant, 1884; Crown of Wild Olives (*The*), 1866; Decoration and Manufacture, 1859; Deucalion, 1875-78; Dilecta, 1887; Eagle's Nest (*The*), 1872; Elements of English Prosody, 1880; Elements of Perspective, 1859; Elements of Sculpture (*The*), 1872; Ethics of the Dust, 1863; Fiction Fair and Foul, 1880; Fors Clavigera, 1871-84, index 1887; Frondes Agrestes, 1875; Giotto and his Works, 1855; Harbours of England, 1856; Hortus Inclusus, 1887; Instructions in Elementary Drawing, 1872; King of the Golden River, 1851 (a capital fairy tale); Laws of Fésole, 1877-79; Lectures on Architecture and Painting, 1854; Lectures on Art, 1870, in England 1883; Lectures on the Political Economy of Art, 1857; Letter to Young Girls, 1876; Lord's Prayer (*The*), 1880; Love's Meinie, 1873; Michael Angelo and Tintoret, 1870-71; Modern Painters, 1843-46, 1860; Mornings in Florence, 1875-77; Munera Pulveris, 1872; Nature of Gothic Architecture (*The*), 1854; Nature of St. George's Guild, 1882; Notes on Millais, 1886; Notes on Samuel Prout and William Hunt, 1880; Notes on the Academy, 1853-60-75; Notes on the Construction of Sheepfolds, 1851; Notes on Turner, 1878; On the Nature of Gothic Architecture, 1854; On the Old Road, 1834-85; Opening of the Crystal Palace (*The*), 1854; Our Fathers have told us, 1881; Oxford Museum (*The*), by Henry W. Ackland and John Ruskin, 1859; Pleasures of England (*The*), 1884; Poems, 1850; Poetry of Architecture (*The*), 1892; Political Economy of Art (*The*), 1857; Prætorita, 1887-88; Pre-Raphaelism, 1850; Proserpina, 1875-79; Queen of the Air, etc., 1869; St. Mark's Rest, 1877-79; Salsette and Elephanta, 1839, a poem; Sepulchral Monuments of Italy, 1872; Sesame and Lilies, 1865; Seven Lamps of Architecture (*The*), 1849; Sir Herbert Edwardes, 1885; Stones of Venice, 1851-53; Storm-Cloud of the Nineteenth Century, 1884; Study of Architecture in Schools, 1865; Time and Tide, etc., 1867; Two Paths, 1854; Unity of Art (*The*), 1859; Unto this Last, 1862; Val d'Arno, 1873; Verona and other Lectures, 1894. His Biography, by Shepherd, 1878; Collingwood, 1893.

RUSSELL, M.D. (*Alexander*), born 1768.

Natural History of Aleppo, 1754 (excellent).

RUSSELL (Rev. *John Fuller*), 1816–1883. Judgment of the Church on the Sufficiency of Holy Scripture, 1838 ; Life of Dr. Johnson, 1847.

RUSSELL (*John*, earl), pseudonym "Joseph Skillet, a gentleman who has left his lodgings," London, 1792–1878. Affairs of Europe since the Peace of Utrecht, 1824–25 ; Causes of the French Revolution, 1832 ; Correspondence of C. J. Fox ; Correspondence of John, Fourth Duke of Bedford ; Don Carlos, 1822, a tragedy ; Essay on . . . the English Government (*An*), 1823 ; Essays and Sketches by Joseph Skillet, 1820 ; Establishment of the Turks in Europe, 1828 ; Foreign Policy of England, etc., 1871 ; History of the British Constitution, 1821 ; Letters for the Post, not the Press, 1820 ; Letters on the State of Ireland, 1868 ; Life of Lady Rachel Russell, 1820 ; Life of Lord William Russell, 1819 ; Life, Diary, and Letters of Thomas Moore, 1852–56 ; Life and Times of Charles James Fox, 1859 ; Memoirs of the Affairs of Europe, 1824–29 ; Nun of Arrouca (*The*), 1822, a tale ; Rise and Progress of Christianity in the West, 1873.

RUSSELL (Lady *Rachel*), daughter of Thomas Wriothesley, earl of Southampton, 1636–1723. Letters to her Husband and Others, 1718. Her Life, by lord J. Russell, 1820.

RUSSELL, D.C.L. (*Michael*), bishop of Glasgow, etc., born in Edinburgh, 1781–1848. Connection of Sacred and Profane History, 1827–37 ; History of the Church of Scotland, 1834.

RUSSELL, M.D. (*Patrick*), Scotland, 1726–1805. Notice on the Serpents of India, 1796 ; Treatise on the Plague, 1791.

RUSSELL (*Thomas*), Beaminster, in Dorsetshire, 1762–1788. Sonnets and Poems, 1789, posthumous.
∴ His sonnet on *Philoctetes* is celebrated.

RUSSELL, LL.D. (*William*), Scotland, 1746–1794. History of America, 1779 ; History of Ancient Europe, 1793 ; History of Modern Europe, 1779–84. His Life, by Irvine, 1801.

RUSSELL (Sir *William Howard*), Lilyvale, in Dublin, Ireland, 1821– . Adventures of Dr. Brady, 1868, a novel ; Canada, its Defences, Condition, etc., 1865 ; Crimea (*The*), 1854–55 ; Diary in the East, 1869 ; Diary in the Last Great War, 1873 ; Diary in India, 1860 ; Diary, North and South, 1863 ; Great War with Russia (*The*), 1895 ; Hesperothen, 1882 ; Letters from the Crimea, 1855–56 ; Prince of Wales's Tour in India, 1877 ; Rifle and Volunteer Clubs, 1859 ; Visit to Chili (*A*), 1890.

RUTHERFORD (Rev. *Samuel*), Scotland, 1600–1661. Covenant of Life opened (*The*), 1655 ; Christ, dying and drawing Sinners to Himself, 1647 ; Disputatio Scholastica de . . . Providentia, 1650 ; Divine Right of Church Government, 1646 ; Due Rights of Presbyteries, 1644 ; Exercitationes Apologeticæ, 1636 ; Free Disputation against Pretended Liberty of Conscience, 1649 ; Lex Rex, 1644 (burnt by the Committee of Estates);

Survey of the Spiritual Antichrist (*A*), 1648 ; Tryall and Triumph of Faith (*The*), 1645. His Life, by Murray, 1828 ; Thomson, 1836

RUTHERFORTH, D.D. (*Thomas*), Cambridgeshire, 1712–1771. Institutes of Natural Law, 1754–56 ; System of Natural Philosophy, 1748.

RYLE (Bishop *John Charles*),near Macclesfield, in Cheshire, 1816– . Bible Inspiration, 1877 ; Bishops and Clergy of Other Days, 1869 ; Christian Leaders of [Last Century], 1868 ; Coming Events and Present Duties, 1869 ; Expository Thoughts on the Gospels, 1856-59 ; Facts and Men, 1882 ; Plain Speaking, 1860 ; Practical Religion, 1878 ; Spiritual Songs, 1861. And many other theological works.

RYMER (*Thomas*), Northallerton, in York, 1638–1713. Antiquity, Power, and Decay of Parliament, 1684 ; Edgar, or the English Monarch, 1677, an historic play ; Fœdera, etc., 1703, continued by Robert Sanderson 1717–35, enlarged by Dr. Adam Clarke (invaluable) ; Short View of Tragedy in the Last Age, 1693 ; Tragedies of the Last Age considered (*The*), 1678.

SACKVILLE (*Thomas*), earl of Dorset, etc., Buckhurst, in Sussex, 1527–1608. Gorboduc (the last two acts), 1562, a tragedy (the first three acts by Norton, 1561) ; Induction to the *Mirrour for Magistraytes* (in seven-line stanzas), 1557 (excellent).

SADLER (*Michael Thomas*), Snelstone, in Derbyshire, 1780–1835. Ireland, its Evils and their Remedies, 1828 ; Law of Population, 1830.

ST. AUBYN (*Alan*). See MARSHALL (*F.*).

ST. JOHN (*Henry*). See BOLINGBROKE.

ST. JOHN (*James Augustus*), Carmarthenshire, Wales, 1801–1875. Anatomy of Society (*The*), 1831 ; Education of the People (*The*), 1858 ; Egypt and Mehemet Ali, 1834 ; Egypt and Nubia, 1844 ; Hellenes (*The*), 1842 ; History, Manners, etc., of the Hindoos, 1832 ; History of the Four Conquests of England, 1862 (Romans, Saxons, Danes, and Normans) ; History of the Manners and Customs of Ancient Greece, 1842 ; Isis, an Egyptian Pilgrimage, 1852 ; Journal of a Residence in Normandy, 1831 ; Life of Louis Napoleon, 1857 ; Life of Sir Walter Raleigh, 1868 ; Lives of Celebrated Travellers, 1831 ; Margaret Ravenscroft, or Second Love, 1835 ; Nemesis of Power (*The*), 1854 ; Oriental Album (*The*), 1851 ; Philosophy at the Foot of the Cross, 1854 ; Ring (*The*) and the Veil, 1856 ; Sir Cosmo Digby, 1843 ; Tales of the Ramadhan, 1835 ; There and Back Again in Search of Beauty, 1853 ; Views in Borneo, 1847 ; Weighed in the Balance, 1864, a novel.

SAINTSBURY (*George Edward Bateman*), Southampton, Hampshire, 1845– . Corneille's Horace, 1882 ; Corrected Impressions, 1895 ; Dryden, 1881 ; Earl of Derby (*The*), 1892 ; Essays in English Literature, 1890, French Lyrics 1883 ; Essays on French Novelists, 1891, miscellaneous 1891 ; Flourishing of a Romance, 1897 ; History of Elizabethan Literature, 1887 ; Manchester, 1887 ;

Marlborough, 1885; Miscellaneous Essays, 1892; Nineteenth Century Literature, 1896; Primer of French Literature, 1880; Scenes of Travel by Théophile Gautier, 1886; Short History of French Literature, 1882; Specimens of English Prose Style, 1885; Specimens of French Literature from Villon to Hugo, 1883.

SALA (*George Augustus Henry*), London, 1828–1895. Accepted Addresses, 1862; After Breakfast, etc., 1864; America in the Midst of War, 1864; America Revisited, 1882; Baddington Peerage, 1860; Bow Bells Annual, 1887 (Right Round the World); Breakfast in Bed, 1863; Captain Dangerous, a tale; Charles Dickens, 1870; Dead Men tell no Tales, 1884; Down among the Dutchmen; Dumb Poor Porter (*The*), 1862; Dutch Pictures, 1861; Echoes of the Year, 1883; From Waterloo to the Peninsula, 1866; Gaslight and Daylight, 1872; Hogarth (in the *Cornhill Magazine*); How I tamed Mrs. Cruiser, 1858; Journey due North (*A*), 1859 (notes of residence in Russia); Journey due South, 1885; Life and Adventures, 1895; Living London, 1883; London up to Date, 1894; Looking at Life, 1860; Make your Game, 1860; Notes, etc., of the Paris Exhibition, 1868; Papers, Humorous and Pathetic, 1872; Paris herself Again, 1879; Quite Alone, 1864, a story; Residence in Russia, 1859; Right Round the World, 1887; Rome and Venice, 1869; Seven Sons of Mammon; Ship-chandler (*The*), and other Tales, 1862; Story of the Comte de Chambord, 1873; Strange Adventures of Captain Dangerous, 1886; Things I have Seen and People I have Known, 1894; Trip to Barbary, etc., 1865; Twice round the Clock, 1859; Two Kings and a Kaiser, 1875; Two Prima Donnas, and other Stories, 1862; Under the Sun, and other Essays, 1872; Wat Tyler, 1869, a burlesque; Yankee Drolleries, 1866–70.

SALE (*George*), 1680–1736. Translation of the *Korân*, 1734 (with notes).

SALESBURY (*William*), sixteenth century. Baterie of the Pope's Botereulx (High Altar), 1550; Englyshe and Welshe Dictionarie, 1547; Introduction, teaching how to pronounce the Letters in the Brytishe Tongue, 1550.

"SALESBURY MISSAL." (or Missale ad Usum Ecclesiæ Sarisburiensis), printed by R. Pynson, 1500 (scarce).

SALMON (*Nathaniel*), died 1742. Antiquities of Essex, 1740; Antiquities of Surrey, 1736; History of Hertfordshire, 1728; Lives of the Bishops since the Restoration, 1733; New Survey of England, 1731; State Trials, 1735; Survey of the Roman Stations in Britain, 1726; Survey of the Roman Antiquities in the Midland Counties of England, 1726.

SALMON (*Thomas*), died 1710. Essay on the Advancement of Music, 1672; Proposal to perform Music in Mathematical Proportions, 1689.

SALMON (*Thomas*), Bedfordshire, *-1743. Families of the Present English Nobility, 1751; Families of the Present Irish Nobility, 1759; Families of the Present Scottish Nobility, 1759; Geographical Grammar (*A*), 1749 (once very popular); Historical Collection relating to Britain, 1706; History of all Nations from the First Governments erected after the Flood, 1751; Marriage, with its Rites among the Ancient Greeks, Romans, Saxons, etc., 1724; Modern History, 1739; Noblemen who have died for their Princes, 1725; Original of the Order of the Garter, 1704; Present State of all Nations, 1725; Review of the History of England, 1722–24; State Trials since the Reign of Richard II., 1738; Universal Traveller, 1754.

SALMON (*William*), 1640–1715. Botanologia, 1710, a herbal; Horæ Mathematicæ seu Uraniæ, 1679; Palladio Londinensis, 1743; posthumous; Polygraphice, etc., 1675; Sephorum, or the Druggist's Shop opened, 1693.

SALT (*Henry*), Lichfield, 1785–1827. Correspondence, 1854, posthumous; Egypta, 1824, a poem; Voyage to Abyssinia, 1814. His Life, by J. G. Halls, 1834.

SALTMARSH (Rev. *John*), 1590–1647. Dawning of Light, 1644; Free Grace, 1645; Holy Discoveries and Flames, 1640; Poemata Sacra, 1636; Smoke in the Temple, 1646; Wonderfull Predictions declared . . . to Sir Thomas Fairfax, 1648.

SANCROFT, D.D. (*William*), archbishop of Canterbury, born at Fressingfield, in Suffolk, 1616–1693. Fur Prædestinatus, 1651 (a dialogue between a thief condemned to the gallows, and a Calvinistic preacher); Modern Policies, 1652. His Life, in dean Hook's *Lives of the Archbishops*.

SANDAY, D.D. (*William*), Holme Pierrepont, in Nottinghamshire, 1843– . Appendices ad Novum Testamentum Stephanicum, 1889; Fourth Gospel (*The*), 1872; Gospels in the Second Century (*The*), 1876; Inspiration, 1893; Oracles of God (*The*), 1891; Two Present-day Questions, 1892.

SANDERS, D.D. (*Nicholas*), Charlewood, in Surrey, 1527–1581. De Origine ac Progressu Schismatis Anglicani, libri iii. 1585; De Visibili Monarchia Ecclesiæ, 1571; Images of Saints Lawful, etc., 1567; Rocke of the Church (*The*), 1567; Supper of our Lord set foorth in Six Bookes, 1565; Treatise of Usurie, 1568.

SANDERSON, D.D. (*Robert*), bishop of Lincoln, born at Rotherham, in Yorkshire, 1587–1663. De Juramenti Obligatione, 1647; Episcopacy . . . not Prejudicial to Regal Power, 1661; Logicæ Artis Compendium, 1615; Nine Cases of Conscience resolved, 1678, posthumous; Physicæ Scientiæ Compendium, 1671, posthumous. His Life, by Walton, 1678.

SANDERSON (*Robert*), Durham, 1660–1741. Continuation of Rymer's *Fœdera*, 1717–35; Life of Henry V.; Sandys (*Sir Edwin*), 1561–1629; Europæ Speculum, 1605.

SANDFORD (*Francis*), 1630–1693. Genealogical History of the Monarchs of England, 1707 (a useful work); Genealogical History of the Kings of Portugal, etc., 1662; History of the Coronation of James II. and his Queen, 1687; Order and Ceremonies used at the Interment of George Monk, Duke of Albermarle, 1670.

SANDFORD (*James*), 1525–1590. Amorous Tales and Sentences of the Greeke Sages, 1567 ; Hours of Recreation, or Afterdinners, 1576, tales, bon-mots, etc. ; Mirror of Madness, 1567.

SANDYS (*George*), York, 1577–1644. Christ's Passion, 1640 (this is the *Christus Patiens* of Grotius) ; Ovid's *Metamorphoses* Englished, 1632 ; Paraphrase on the Psalms of David, 1636 ; Paraphrase on Solomon's Song, 1642 ; Relation of a Journey, etc., 1615 (a description of the Turkish empire, of Egypt, the Holy Land, etc.).

SANDYS (*William*), 1794–1863. Christmas Carols, Ancient and Modern, with the Airs, 1833 ; Christmastide, its History, Festivities, and Carols, 1852 ; Specimens of Macaronic Poetry, 1831.

SAVAGE (*Richard*), London, 1698–1743. Bastard (*The*), 1728 (a poem on himself, in which he holds his mother up to ridicule) ; Love in a Veil, 1718 ; Wanderer (*The*), in five cantos, 1729. His Life, by Dr. Johnson, 1744.

SAVILE (Sir *Henry*), near Halifax, in Yorkshire, 1549–1622. Lectures on Euclid (book i.), 1621 ; Rerum Anglicarum Scriptores post Bedam, 1596.

SAWYER (*William*), 1828–1882. Legend of Phillis, 1872 ; Ten Miles from Town, 1867 ; Thought and Reverie, 1849 ; Year of Song (*A*), 1872.

SAXON CHRONICLE (Annales Rerum in Anglia gestarum a Christo nato ad Annum 1154). It is inserted in the *Monumenta Historica Britannica*.

SAYCE, D.D. (*Archibald Henry*), Shire-hampton, near Bristol, prof. of Assyriology, Oxford University, since 1891, born 1846. Ancient Empires of the East (*The*), 1884 ; Assyria, its Princes, Priests, and People, 1885 ; Assyrian Grammar, 1872 ; Babylonian Literature, 1877 ; Egypt of the Hebrews, 1895 ; Fresh Light from the Monuments, 1883 ; Hibbert Lectures, 1887 ; Higher Criticism, 1894 ; Higher Criticism (*The*), and Verdict of the Monuments, 1893 ; Hittites (*The*), 1888 ; Inscriptions of the Mal-Amir, 1885 ; Monuments of the Hittites, 1881 ; Patriarchal Palestine, 1895 ; Principles of Comparative Philology, 1874 ; Races of the Old Testament (*The*), 1891 ; Religion of the Ancient Babylonians, 1887 ; Social Life among the Assyrians and Babylonians, 1893 ; Transl. in Records of the Past, 1874–77.

SAYERS, M.D. (*Frank*), 1763–1817. Disquisitions, Metaphysical and Literary, 1793 ; Dramatic Sketches of Ancient Northern Mythology, 1790 ; Miscellanies, 1805 ; Nugæ Poeticæ, 1803. His Life, by W. Taylor, of Norwich, 1823.

SCHOOLCRAFT (*Henry Rowe*), New York State, U.S., 1793–1864. Algic Researches, 1839 ; Ethnological Researches respecting the Red Man of America, 1845 ; Historical and Statistical Information respecting the Indian Tribes of the United States, 1851–60 ; Indian Tribes (*The*), their History, Condition, and Prospects, 1851–57 ; Narrative of an Expedition to Haska Lake, the Source of the Mississippi, 1834 ; Notes on the Iroquois,

1848 ; Travels in the . . . Mississippi Valley, 1825 ; View of the Lead Mines of Missouri, 1819.

SCHREIBER (*Charlotte Elizabeth*), married sir Josiah John Guest, 1812–   . Translated the *Mabinogion*, 1838–49.

SCHREINER (*Olive*), (Mrs. *Cronwright*), pseudonym "Ralph Iron," born early in the sixties. Dreams, 1892 ; Story of an African Farm, 1891 ; The Political Situation, 1897 (in collaboration with C. S. Cronwright Schreiner) ; Trooper Halket of Mashonaland, 1897.

SCOGIN (*John*), court jester to Edward IV. Jests, gathered together by Andrew Boord, M.D., 1626.

SCORESBY, D.D. (*William*), Whitby, in Yorkshire, 1790–1857. Account of the Arctic Regions (*An*), 1820 (a capital book) ; Discourses to Seamen, 1812 ; Journal of a Voyage to the Northern Whale Fisheries, 1823 ; Magnetical Investigations, 1839–52 ; Memorials of the Sea ; Records of the Adventurous Life of the Late William Scoresby (*i.e.* his father), 1830 ; Records of the Sea. His Life, by Scoresby-Jackson, 1861.

SCOT (*Reginald*), Scotshall, near Smeethe, in Kent, 1545–1599. Discoverie of Witchcraft (*The*), 1584 (his great work, demonstrating the absurdity of the popular belief in witches ; this book called forth James's *Dæmonology*, and Scot's book was ordered to be burnt by the common hangman) ; Perfite Platforme of a Hoppe-Garden (*The*), printed 1574.

SCOTSMAN (*The*), a newspaper, first started 1817.

SCOTT (*Clement*), 1841–   . Dramatic Critic of *Daily Telegraph*, 1872, having before been dramatic critic of *Sunday Times*, *Weekly Despatch*, *London Figaro*, *The Observer*, etc. *Publications:* Among the Apple Orchards ; Blossom Land ; From the Bells to King Arthur ; Pictures of the World ; Poppy Land, 1885 ; Land of Flowers (*The*) ; Lays and Lyrics, 1888 ; Lays of a Londoner, 1882 ; Round about the Islands, 1873 ; Thirty Years at the Play.

SCOTT (*John*), Amwell, in Hertfordshire, 1730–1783. Amwell, 1776 ; Critical Essays on the English Poets, 1785, posthumous ; Poems, 1782. His Life, by John Hadley, 1785 ; R. A. Davenport, 1822.

SCOTT (*Michael*), Glasgow, Scotland, 1789–1835. Cruise of the *Midge* (appeared in *Blackwood's Magazine*) ; Tom Cringle's Log (appeared in *Blackwood's Magazine*).

SCOTT (Sir *Michael*), died 1290. Avicennæ de Animalibus, ex Arabico in Latinum, translatio ; De Procreatione et Hominis Phisionomia Opus, printed 1477 ; Mensa Philosophica, translated into English and printed 1633 ; Quæstio Curiosa de Natura Solis et Lunæ, printed 1622. (Dante places him with magicians in his *Inferno*, in the fifth part of the Malêbolgê. See HANDBOOK, p. 524, col. 1.)

SCOTT (Rev. *Thomas*), English minister at Utrecht, murdered at Utrecht by John Lambert, a garrison soldier, 1626. Aphorismes of State, 1624; Belgicke Pismire (*The*), 1622; Belgicke Souldier (*The*), 1624; Christ's Politician, and Solomon's Puritan, 1616; Discoverie of Spanish Practices (*A*), 1623–24; England's Joy for suppressing the Papists, 1624; Ghost of Robert, Earl of Essex, 1624; Ghost of Sir Walter Rawleigh, 1626; Highwaies of God and the King (*The*), 1620; Newes from Parnassus, 1622; Spanish Designes to an Universall Monarchie, 1624; Symmachia, or True Love-knot (no date); Tongue Combat (*A*), 1623 (useful for a wordbook); Votivæ Angliæ, 1624; Vox Cœli, 1624 (a consultation held in heaven by Henry VIII., queen Elizabeth, and others, on Spain's designs against England); Vox Dei, 1624; Vox Populi (a warning against Spain), 1620, 1624; Vox Regis, 1624.

SCOTT (Rev. *Thomas*), Braytoft, in Lincolnshire, 1747–1821. Commentary on the Bible, 1796 (generally called "Scott's Family Bible"); Essays on the Most Important Subjects of Religion, 1793; Force of Truth, 1799; Quotations from the Old Testament in the New, 1810–11; Vindication of the Inspiration of Scripture, 1796. His Life, by his son, 1824.

SCOTT (Sir *Walter*), Edinburgh, 1771–1832.

Novels and Prose Romances: Abbot (*The*), 1820 (time, Elizabeth); Anne of Geierstein, 1829 (time, Edward IV.); Antiquary (*The*), 1816 (time, George III.); Aunt Margaret's Mirror, a tale (time, William III.); Betrothed (*The*), 1825 (time, Henry II.); Black Dwarf (*The*), 1816 (time, Anne); Bride of Lammermoor, 1819 (time, William III.), (his best novel); Castle Dangerous, 1831 (time, Henry I.); Chronicles of Canongate (*see* p. 207); Count Robert of Paris, 1831 (time, Rufus); Fair Maid of Perth, 1828 (time, Henry IV.); Fortunes of Nigel, 1822 (time, James I.); Guy Mannering, 1815 (time, George II.); Heart of Midlothian, 1818 (time, George II.); Highland Widow (*The*), a tale, 1827 (time, George II.); Ivanhoe, 1819 (time, Richard I.); Kenilworth, 1821 (time, Elizabeth), (the best of his three Elizabethan novels); Laird's Jock (*The*), 1827 (time, Elizabeth); Legend of Montrose (*The*), 1819 (time, Charles I.); Monastery (*The*), 1820 (time, Elizabeth); Old Mortality, 1816 (time, Charles II.), (the best of his historic novels); Peveril of the Peak, 1823 (time, Charles II.); Pirate (*The*), 1821 (time, William III.); Quentin Durward, 1823 (time, Edward IV.); Redgauntlet, 1824 (time, George III.); Rob Roy, 1817 (time, George I.); St. Ronan's Well, 1825 (time, George III.); Surgeon's Daughter (*The*), 1827 (time, George II.); Tales of my Landlord (*see* p. 1073); Talisman (*The*), 1825 (time, Richard I.); Tapestried Chamber (*The*), a tale (time, George III.); Two Drovers (*The*), a tale, 1827 (time, George III.); Waverley, 1814 (time, George II.); Waverley Novels (*The*), (*see* p. 1199); Woodstock, 1826 (time, Commonwealth).

Poetry, Dramatic Sketches, etc.: Auchindrane, 1830, an Ayrshire tragedy; Ballads and Lyrical Pieces, 1806; Battle of Sempach, 1818; Border Minstrelsy (in three parts), 1802–5 (Thomas the Rhymer); Bridal of Triermain (in three cantos), 1813; Doom of Devorgoil, 1830, a melodrama, blank verse; Ettricke Garland (*The*), 1815, two songs; Field of Waterloo (*The*), 1815, a poem; Fire King (*The*), 1801, a ballad, in Alexandrines; "For a' that an' a' that," 1814 (song); Frederick and Alice, 1801, a ballad; Halidon Hall, 1822, a dramatic sketch; Harold the Dauntless (in six cantos), 1817; Helvellyn, 1805, a ballad, in Alexandrines; House of Aspen (*The*), 1829, a prose dramatic sketch; Hunting Song (*A*), in sevens, 1808; Lady of the Lake (*The*), (in six cantos), 1809; Lay of the Last Minstrel (*The*), (in six cantos), 1805; Lord of the Isles (*The*), (in six cantos), 1814; Macduff's Cross, 1830, a dramatic sketch; Marmion (in six cantos), 1808; Noble Moringer (*The*), 1819, a ballad, in Alexandrines; Rokeby (in six cantos), 1813; Sir Tristram, edited 1804, a romance; Vision of Don Roderick (Spenserian), 1811; Wild Huntsman (*The*), 1796, a balled, in eights; William and Helen, 1796, a ballad, in eight and six.

Prose Works (*not novels*): Border Antiquities of Scotland, 1818, essays; Demonology and Witchcraft, 1830, letters; History of Scotland, 1830; Letters of Malachi Malagrowther, 1826; Life of Dryden, 1808; Life of Napoleon Buonaparte, 1827; Life of Swift, 1814; Lives of British Novelists, 1825; Memoirs of the Earl of Montrose, 1808; Paul's Letters to his Kinsfolk, 1815; Provincial Antiquities, etc., 1826; Regalia of Scotland (*The*), 1819; Tales of a Grandfather (in three series), 1827–1830 (a history of Scotland).

Edited: Minstrelsy of the Scottish Border; Dryden, 1808; Swift, 1814; Strutt's *Queenhoo Hall*, 1808; etc.

His Life, by W. Weir, 1832; J. Hogg, 1834; Lochart, 1837–39; G. Grant, 1849; Gilfillan, 1870; Rossetti, 1870; Chambers, 1871; Hutton, 1878.

SCOTT (*William Bell*), Scotland, 1811–1889. Hades, or the Transit, 1838; Life, etc., of Albert Durer, 1869; Little Masters (*The*), 1879; Memoir of David Scott, 1850; Poems, 1855, 1864; Year of the World (*The*), 1846, a poem.

SCOTUS (*John Duns*), called "The Subtile Doctor," and "The Prince of Divines," 1265–1308. Idiota's, or Duns's Contemplations of Divine Love, printed 1662; Opera Omnia, Notes, etc., printed 1639. His Life, by L. Waddingus, editor, 1639.

SCOUGAL (*Henry*), 1650–1678. De Objectu Cultus Religiosi, 1664; Life of God in the Soul, 1677; New Discourses, etc., 1735; Occasional Meditations, 1740.

SCRIVENER, LL.D. (Rev. *Frederick Henry Ambrose*), Bermondsey, Surrey, 1813–1891. Plain Introduction to . . . the New Testament, 1861; Six Lectures on the Text of the New Testament, 1874; Supplement to the New Testament, 1845.

SCROPE (*George Poulett*), 1797–1876. Considerations on Volcanoes, 1825; Geology of Central France, 1827; Principles of Political Economy, 1833.

SEDGWICK (Rev. *Adam*), Dent, in Yorkshire, 1787–1873. Discourse on the Studies of the University of Cambridge, 1850 (the bearing of physics on religion); Geology of the Lake Districts, 1853.

SEDGWICK (*Catherine Maria*), Stockbridge, U.S., 1799–1867. Clarence, 1830, a tale of our own times; Home, 1840, a tale on domestic economy; Hope Leslie, 1827, a tale of early times in America; Le Bossu, 1835, a novel; Letters from Abroad, 1841; Linwoods (*The*), 1835, a novel; Live and Let Live 1837, Married and Single 1849, Means and Ends 1838, Morals and Manners 1847, tales on morals and domestic economy; New England Tale (*A*), 1822; Poor Rich Man and Rich Poor Man (*The*), 1836; Redwood, 1824, a novel; Wilton Hervey, and other Tales, 1845.

SEDGWICK (Mrs.), maiden name *Susan Ridley Livingston*), 1788–1868. Alida, 1844; Allan Prescott, 1834, a novel; Children's Week (*The*), 1830; Morals of Pleasure (*The*), 1829; Walter Thornby, 1859, a novel; Young Emigrants (*The*), 1831.

SEDLEY (Sir *Charles*), Kent, 1639–1701. Antony and Cleopatra, 1677, a tragedy; Beauty the Conqueror, or Death of Mark Antony, 1702, a tragedy; Bellamira, 1687, a comedy; Grumbler (*The*), 1702, a comedy; Mulberry Garden (*The*), 1668, a comedy; Tyrant King of Crete (*The*), 1702; Works, consisting of Poems and Plays, 1719, posthumous.

∴ The duke of Buckingham called his poems "Sedley's Witchcraft."

SEELEY (Sir *John Robert*) London, 1834–1895. Ecce Homo, 1866 (his best-known work); Expansion of England (*The*), 1883; Greatest of all the Plantagenets (*The*), 1860 (new edition, entitled "Life of Edward I.," 1872); Horace Walpole, 1883; Lectures and Essays, 1870; Life, etc., of Stein, 1878; Napoleon, 1886; Natural Religion, 1882; Our Colonial Empire, 1887; Our Colonial Expansion, 1887; Short History of Napoleon I., 1886.

SELDEN (*John*), Salvington, in Sussex, 1584–1654. Analecton Anglo-Britannicon, 1615; De Diis Syris, 1617; De Jure Naturali et Gentium, etc., 1640; De Successionibus, 1631; Duello (*The*), 1610; England's Epinomis, 1610; History of Tithes, 1618; Jani Anglorum Facies Altera, 1610; Mare Clausum, 1635; Marmora Arundeliana, 1628; Notes on Drayton's *Polyolbion*, 1613; Table Talk, 1689, posthumous; Titles of Honour, 1614. His Life, by Wilkins, 1726; Dr. J. Aikin, 1773; G. W. Johnson, 1835.

SELOUS (*Frederick Courtenay*), 1851– . Hunter's Wanderings in Africa (*A*), 1881; Travel and Adventure in South-East Africa, 1893; Sunshine and Storm in Rhodesia, 1896.

SELWYN (Rev. *William*), 1806–1875. Horæ Hebraicæ, 1848–60; Two Charts of Prophecy.

SENIOR (*Nassau William*), Compton, in Berkshire, 1790–1864. Biographical Sketches, 1863; Conversations with Thiers, Guizot, etc., 1878; Essays on Fiction, 1864; His-

torical and Philosophical Essays, 1865; Journal in Turkey and Greece, 1859; Journals, etc., relating to Ireland, 1868; Political Economy, 1848.

SETTLE (*Elkanah*), Dunstable, in Bedfordshire, poet laureate, 1648–1724. Cambyses, 1671, a tragedy; City Ramble (*The*), 1712, a comedy; Conquest of China, 1676, a tragedy; Empress of Morocco (*The*), 1673, a tragedy; Fatal Love, 1678, a tragedy; Female Prelate (*The*), 1680, a tragedy (Pope Joan); Ibraham, 1680; Love and Revenge, 1675, a tragedy; Poems, chiefly Laudatory, 1681, 1685, 1714, 1716, 1722; Siege of Troy (*The*), 1715, a drama; Triumphs for Lord Mayor's Day, 1691–1708.

SEWARD (*Anna*), Derbyshire, 1747–1809. Letters, 1811, posthumous; Louisa, 1782; Memoirs of Dr. Darwin, 1804; Poems, 1816, posthumous; Visions (*The*), 1810, posthumous. Her Life, by sir Walter Scott, 1810.

SEWARD (*William*), London, 1746–1799. Anecdotes of Distinguished Persons, 1795; Biographiana, 1799.

SEWARD (*William Wenman*), eighteenth century. Topographia Hibernica, 1795 (meritorious).

SEWELL (*Elizabeth Missing*), Isle of Wight, 1815– . Amy Herbert, 1844, a novel; Clove Hall, 1847, a tale; Earl's Daughter (*The*), 1845, a tale; Gertrude, 1847, a novel; Homely Ballads and Stories in Verse, 1865; Ivors, 1856, a novel; Katherine Ashton, 1854, a tale; Margaret Percival, 1858, a novel; Rose of Cheriton, 1872, a ballad; Sketches, 1847, three tales; Ursula, 1858, a tale of country life.

SEWELL (*William*), 1650–1725. History of the Quakers, 1722.

SEWELL (Rev. *William*), 1805–1874. Christian Morals, 1840; Christian Politics, 1844; Christian Vestiges of Creation, 1861; Hawkestone, 1845, a tale; Hora Philologica, 1830; Rodolph the Voyager, 1844; Sacred Thoughts in Verse, 1835.

SEYMOUR (Rev. *Michael Hobart*), 1802–1874. Evenings with the Romanists, 1854; Mornings among the Jesuits, 1850.

SHADWELL (*Thomas*), Norfolk, poet laureate, 1640–1692. *He wrote* 17 *plays:* |Amorous Bigot (*The*), 1690, a comedy; Bury Fair, 1680, a comedy; Epsom Wells, 1673, a comedy; Humourist (*The*), 1671, a comedy; Lancashire Witches (*The*), 1682, a comedy; Libertine (*The*), 1676, a comedy; Miser *The*), 1672, a comedy; Psyche, 1675; Royal Shepherdess (*The*), 1669, a comedy; Scowerers (*The*), 1691, a comedy; Squire of Alsatia (*The*), 1688, a comedy, to which sir W. Scott is indebted in his *Fortunes of Nigel*; Sullen Lovers (*The*), 1668 (his first comedy); Timon of Athens, 1678; True Widow (*The*), 1679, a comedy; Virtuoso (*The*), 1676 (his best comedy); Volunteers (*The*), 1693, a comedy; Woman Captain, 1680, a comedy.

Dryden satirized Shadwell under the name of "MacFlecknoe," and says that he

In prose and verse was owned without disput:
Through all the realms of nonsense absolute.

And again—

But Shadwell never deviates into sense.

Yet, without doubt, he had considerable comic humour, and *The Virtuoso* is a good comedy. He superseded Dryden as poet laureate.

SHAFTESBURY(*Anthony Ashley Cooper*, earl of), London, 1671-1713. Characteristics of Men, Manners, Opinions, and Times, 1711, 1713; containing the Inquiry Concerning Virtue, 1691, 1699; Judgment of Hercules, 1713; Letter concerning Enthusiasm, 1708; Moralists, 1709; Sensus Communis, 1709; Soliloque, or Advice to an Author, 1710. His Life, by B. Martyn, revised by Dr. Kippis, 1830.

SHAIRP, LL.D. (*John Campbell*), Houstoun House, in Scotland, *-1885. Kilmahoe, and other Poems, 1864; Lectures on Culture and Religion, 1870; Poetic Interpretation of Nature (*The*), 1877; Studies in Poetry and Philosophy, 1868.

SHAKESPEARE (*William*), Stratford-upon-Avon, in Warwickshire, 1564-1616. *He wrote 36 plays; some say 37.* The dates are *about* as follows :—All's Well that Ends Well, 1598, a comedy; Antony and Cleopatra, 1608, a tragedy; As You Like It, 1600, a comedy; Comedy of Errors (*The*), 1593, a comedy; Coriolanus, 1616, a tragedy; Cymbeline, 1605, a tragedy; Hamlet Prince of Denmark, 1596, a tragedy; Henry IV., part i. 1597, part ii. 1598, historical plays; Henry V., 1599, an historical play; Henry VI., part i. 1591, part ii. 1594, part iii. 1595, historic plays; Henry VIII., 1613, an historic play; Julius Cæsar, 1607, printed 1623, an historic tragedy; King John, 1596, an historic tragedy; King Lear, 1605, a tragedy; Lover's Complaint (*The*), 1609, a poem in 7-line stanzas; Love's Labour's Lost, 1594, a comedy; Macbeth, 1606, a tragedy; Measure for Measure, 1603, a comedy; Merchant of Venice (*The*), 1598, a tragi-comedy; Merry Wives of Windsor (*The*), 1596, a comedy; Midsummer Night's Dream, 1592, a fairy comedy; Much Ado about Nothing, 1600, a comedy; Othello, the Moor of Venice, 1602, a tragedy; Pericles Prince of Tyre, 1609, a tragedy; Passionate Pilgrim (*The*), 1599, a poem in 14-line stanzas; Rape of Lucrece (*The*), 1594, a poem in 7-line stanzas; Richard II., 1597, an historic play; Richard III., 1597, an historic tragedy; Romeo and Juliet, 1595, a tragedy; Sonnets (154 in number), 1598; Taming of the Shrew (*The*), 1593, a comedy; Tempest (*The*), 1609, a comedy; Timon of Athens, 1609, a tragedy; (?) Titus Andronicus, 1593, a tragedy; Troilus and Cressida, 1602, a tragedy; Twelfth Night, or What you Will, 1602, a comedy; Two Gentlemen of Verona (*The*), 1595, a comedy; Venus and Adonis, 1593, a poem in 6-line stanzas; Winter's Tale, 1604, a comedy. There is considerable doubt as regards the dates of the composition of his plays; Malone, Chalmers, and Drake all differ.

N.B.—Mary Cowden Clarke published in 1845 an admirable "Concordance to Shake-speare," which has wholly superseded the very imperfect one of Samuel Ayscough, 1827.

His Life, by N. Rowe, 1709; Hanmer, 1745; Dr. H. Blair, 1753; [Francis] Gentleman, 1774; Malone, 1790; Alex. Chalmers, 1805; Wheler, 1806; John Britton, 1814; Drake, 1817, 1828; Skottowe, 1824; Wheeler, 1824; Moncreiff, 1824; Rev. W. Harness, 1825; W. Harvey, 1825; C. Symmons, D.D., 1826; C. Knight, 1838; Campbell, 1838; Barry Cornwall, 1839-43; J. P. Collier, 1841; Baudry's (French edition) contains "a new Life," 1842; Dr. G. C. Verplanck, U.S., 1847; J. O. Halliwell, 1851; Rev. H. N. Hudson, 1852; W. W. Lloyd, 1856; H. Staunton, 1858; Neill, 1861; S. W. Fullom, 1861; Kenney, 1864; Richard Grant-White, U.S., 1865. *In one or two instances the biographer's name is not known, but a "Life" is prefixed to an edition of the Works.*

SHARP (*Granville*), Durham, 1734-1813. Injustice, etc., of tolerating Slavery in England (*The*), 1772; Uses of the Definite Article in the Greek Testament, 1798. His Life, by Prince Hoare, 1820.

SHARP (*Richard*), called "Conversation Sharp," 1759-1835. Letters and Essays, 1834.

SHARP (*Samuel*), called "Mundungus" by Sterne, for his scandalous "Letters from Italy," *-1778. Critical Inquiry into the Present State of Surgery, 1750; Letters from Italy, 1766; Operations of Surgery, 1739.

SHARP (*William*), 1855-   . Conqueror's Dream, and other Poems, 1878; Dante Gabriel Rossetti, 1882; Earth's Voices, 1884, poems; Euphrenia, 1885; Heine, 1888; Human Inheritance (*The*), 1882; Humanity and the Man, 1878; Romantic Ballads, 1888; Shakespeare's Songs, 1885; Shelley, 1887; Sonnets of this Century, 1886 (the sale of this book has exceeded 30,000 copies).

SHARPE (*Charles Kirkpatrick*), Hoddam, in Scotland, 1781-1851. Ballad Book, 1822; Etchings and Literary Remains, 1869, posthumous; Genealogy of the House of Seton, 1830; Life of Lady Margaret Cunninghame, 1828; Metrical Legends, and other Poems, 1807; Portraits by an Amateur, 1833; Sargundo, or the Valiant Christian, 1837.

SHARPE, D.D. (*Gregory*), Yorkshire, 1713-1771. Argument in Defence of Christianity, 1755, 1762; Defence of Dr. Clarke, 1744; Review of the Controversy about Demoniacs, 1738; Two Dissertations on Languages and Letters, 1751.

SHAW (*Flora*). Castle Blair, 1877 (a book much praised by Ruskin); Hector, 1882; Sea Change (*A*), 1885.

SHAW, M.D. (*George*), Bierton, in Buckinghamshire, 1751-1813. Catalogue of the Leverian Museum, 1792-96; Naturalist's Miscellany (*The*), 1789-1813; Zoölogy, 1800-16.

SHAW (*George Bernard*), Dublin, prominent leader of the Fabian Society, 1856-   .
Plays: Arms and the Man, 1894; Widowers' Houses, 1892.

Publications: Four early novels, *i.e.* Cashel Byron's Profession, Irrational Knot (*The*), Love among the Artists, Unsocial Socialist (*An*), 1880–1883.

He also wrote various essays and weekly articles on music in *The World* from 1891 to 1894.

SHAW, M.D. (*Peter*), 1695–1763. Abridgment of Bacon's Philosophical Works, 1725; Chemical Lectures, 1734; New Practice of Physic, 1726.

SHAW (Rev. *Stebbing*), Staffordshire, 1762–1802. History of Staffordshire, 1798–1801; Topographer (*The*), 1789.

SHEA (*Daniel*), Dublin, 1772–1836. Translation of Mirkhond's *History of the Kings of Persia*, 1843.

SHEBBEARE, M.D. (*John*), Bideford, in Devonshire, 1709–1788. History of the Sumatrans, 1760; Letters on the English Nation, 1755; Letters to the People of England, 1756–58; Marriage Act (*The*), 1754; Origin and Progress of National Society, 1776.

SHEE, R.A. (Sir *Martin Archer*), Dublin, 1770–1850. Alasco, 1824, a tragedy; Commemoration of Reynolds, 1814; Elements of Art (a poem in six cantos), 1809; Oldcourt, 1829, a novel; Rhymes on Art, 1805. His Life, by his son, 1860.

SHEFFIELD (*John Baker Holroyd*, lord), 1741–1821. Letter on the Corn Laws, 1815; Observations on the Commerce of American States, 1783; On the Manufactures, etc., of Ireland, 1785; On the Project for Abolishing the Slave Trade, 1789; Orders in Council, etc., 1809.

SHEIL (*Richard Lalor*), near Waterford, in Ireland, dramatist, 1791–1851. Adelaide, 1814; Apostate (*The*), 1817, a tragedy; Bellamira, 1818, a comedy; Evadne, 1819; Huguenot (*The*), Montoni, 1820; Sketches of the Irish Bar, 1822. His Life, by Macnevin, 1854; T. W. MacCulloch, 1855.

SHELLEY (Mrs.), maiden name *Mary Wollstonecraft Godwin*, second wife of Percy Bysshe Shelley, London, novelist, 1797–1851. Biography of her Husband, 1839; Falkner, 1837; Frankenstein, 1818 (her best novel); Last Man (*The*), 1824; Lodore, 1835; Perkin Warbeck, 1830, an historical novel; Rambles in Germany and Italy, 1844; Valperga, 1823.

SHELLEY (*Percy Bysshe*), Field Place, in Sussex, poet, 1792–1822. Adonais, 1821, a monody on Keats; Alastor, or the Spirit of Solitude, 1816, blank verse; Arethusa, 1820, an ode; Cenci (*The*), 1819, a tragedy; Clouds (*The*), 1820, an ode; Epipsichidion, 1821; Hellas, 1821, a lyrical drama; History of a Six Weeks' Tour in France, etc., 1817; Julian and Maddalo, 1818, a conversation in verse; Laon and Cynthia (Spenserian), 1818; Nightmare (*The*), 1809; Ode to the West Wind, 1820; Œdipus Tyrannus, 1820, a classical play; Peter Bell III., 1819; Prometheus Unbound, 1821, a classical play; Prometheus Unmasked, 1823; Queen Mab, 1813 (written at the age of 18); Revolt of Islam (in 12 cantos, in 5-line stanzas), 1818; Rosalind and Helen, 1819, a dialogue in verse; St. Irvyne, 1818, a novel; Shelley

Papers (*The*), 1815; Skylark (*The*), 1820 (his best ode); Witch of Atlas (*The*), 1820 (composed in three days); "We pity the Plumage, but forget the Dying Bird," 1817 (an address on the death of the Princess Charlotte); Zastrozzi, 1809, a novel. His Life, by captain T. Medwin, 1847; T. J. Hogg, 1858; his widow, 1859; C. S. Middleton, 1858; Thornton Hunt, 1863; Barnett Smith, 1877; W. M. Rossetti, 1878; J. C. Jeaffreson, 1880.

SHENSTONE (*William*), Hales Owen, in Shropshire, 1714–1763. (26) Elegies, 1743–46; Essay on Men and Manners, 1764, posthumous; Jemmy Dawson, 1745, a ballad; Judgment of Hercules, 1741, a dramatic poem; Odes, Songs and Ballads, 1750–54; Pastoral Ballad (in four parts), 1743; Poems on Several Occasions, 1737; Progress of Taste (in four parts), 1764, posthumous; Schoolmistress (*The*), 1737–42, in Spenserian metre (his best poem); Written at an Inn at Henley, 1741. His Life, by Greaves, 1764; Gilfillan, 1854.

SHEPPARD (*John George*), Killarney, in Ireland, 1818–1869. Aids to Classical Study, 1868 (with Dr. D. W. Turner); Fall of Rome and Rise of New Nationalities, 1861; Notes on Thucydides, 1857 (with Evans); St. Paul at Athens, 1851, a poem; Theophrasti Characteres, with Notes, 1852.

SHERBURNE (Sir *Edward*), London, 1618–1702. Forsaken Lydia, 1651; Lyrian and Silvia, 1651; Poems, 1651; Rape of Helen (*The*), 1651; Salamis, 1651; Sphere of Marcus Mamilius (*The*), 1675.

SHERIDAN (Mrs.), maiden name *Frances Chamberlayne*, mother of Richard Brinsley Sheridan, 1724–1766. Discovery (*The*), 1763, a comedy; Dupe (*The*), 1765, a comedy; Miss Sidney Biddulph, 1761, a novel; Nourjahad, 1767, a romance. Her Memoirs, by Alicia Lefanu, 1824.

SHERIDAN (*Richard Brinsley Butler*), Dublin, 1751–1816. Clio's Protest, and other Poems, 1819; His Speech for the Impeachment of Warren Hastings, 1786.

Plays: Critic (*The*), 1779, a farce; Duenna (*The*), 1775, an operatic comedy; Pizarro, 1799, a tragedy; Rivals (*The*), 1778, a comedy; School for Scandal (*The*), 1777, a comedy; St. Patrick's Day, 1775, a farce; Stranger (*The*), 1798 (see APPENDIX II.); Trip to Scarborough (*A*), 1777 (see APPENDIX II.).

N.B.—Sheridan is credited with the best speech (*Warren Hastings*), the best comedy (*The School for Scandal*), and the best drinking song ("Here's to the Maiden of Bashful Fifteen"), in the language.

His Life, by Watkins, 1817; T. Moore, 1825; W. Smyth, 1840; Browne, 1873.

SHERIDAN (*Thomas*), Quilca, in Ireland, 1721–1788. Pronouncing Dictionary of the English Language, 1778.

SHERINGHAM (*Robert*), died 1677. De Anglorum Gentis Origine, 1670 (highly praised by Nicolson).

SHERLEY (Sir *Anthony*), Weston, in Sussex, 1565–1631. Travele into Persia, edited by W. Parry, 1601, by G. Manwaring, 1613.

N.B.—Sir Thomas, sir Anthony, and Robert Sherley, called "the three English brothers," were all eminent in their day—sir Thomas for his travels and imprisonment in Turkey, and Robert for his wars against the Turks and his marriage with the niece of the shah of Persia.

SHERLOCK, D.D. (*Thomas*), bishop of London, born in London, 1678-1761. Discourses at the Temple Church, 1754-58 ; Sermons, 1755, etc. ; Trial of the Witnesses of the Resurrection of Jesus Christ, 1729 ; Use and Intent of Prophecy, 1725.

SHERLOCK, D.D. (*William*), London, 1641-1707. Divine Providence (*The*), 1694 ; Future Judgment (*A*), 1692 ; Treatise on Death, 1690 ; Vindication of the Doctrine of the Trinity, 1691.

SHERRINGHAM (*Robert*). See above, SHER-INGHAM.

SHERWOOD (Mrs.), maiden name *Mary Martha Butt*, Stanford, in Worcestershire, 1775-1851. Arzomund ; Ayah and Lady (*The*) ; Charles Lorraine, the Young Soldier ; Emily and her Mother ; Ermina, a Calcutta Tale ; Fairchild Family (*The*) ; George Desmond ; Gipsy Babes (*The*) ; Indian Pilgrim (*The*) ; Infant's *Pilgrim's Progress* (*The*) ; Juliana Oakley ; Lady of the Manor (*The*), a series of tales, etc., about confirmation ; Little Henry and his Bearer ; Little Lucy and her Dhaye ; Little Woodman (*The*) and his Dog ; Lucy Clare ; My Aunt Kate ; Père la Chaise ; Potter's Common (*The*) ; Re-captured Negro (*The*) ; Roxobel, or English Manners Seventy Years Ago ; Sergeant Dale ; Story to explain the Church Catechism ; Stranger at Home (*The*) ; Susan Gray ; Waste Not, Want Not.

SHIELD (*William*), operatic composer, Durham, 1749-1829, buried in Westminster Abbey. Introduction to Harmony, 1800 (esteemed). (*He composed* 34 *operas, besides canzonets, ballads, rounds, etc.*) Farmer (*The*), 1785, an opera ; Flitch of Bacon (*The*), 1778 (his first opera) ; Hartford Bridge, a musical farce ; Lock and Key (*The*) ; Poor Soldier (*The*), 1783, an opera ; Robin Hood, 1784, an opera ; Rosina, 1783, an opera.

SHIPTON ("Mother"), time of Henry VIII. Fourteen Strange Prophecies, 1648 (with J. Saltmarsh) ; Prophesie Fortelling the Death of Cardinal Wolsey and Others, 1641 ; Two Strange Prophesies predicting Wonderfull Events to betide this Yeare, 1642 ; Yorkshire Prophecy preserved in the Noble Family of the P—'s, first printed 1740. Her Life, by R. Head, 1677 ; others anonymous, 1687, 1797, etc

SHIRLEY (Sir *Anthony*). See SHIRLEY.

SHIRLEY (*Evelyn Philip*), Ettingham Park, in Warwickshire, 1812-1882. Historical Memoirs of the Lives of the Shirley Brothers, 1848 ; History of the Church of Ireland, 1851 ; History of the County of Monaghan, 1877 ; Noble and Gentle Men of England, and their Arms, 1863 ; Some Account of Deer and Deer Parks, 1867 ; Some Account of the Territory of Farney, in Ulster, 1846 ; Stemmata Shirleiana, 1841.

SHIRLEY (*James*), London, 1594-1666. Admiral of France (*The*), 1639 ; Andromana, or the Merchant's Wife, 1660 (? Shirley) ; Arcadia, 1640, a pastoral ; Ball (*The*), 1639, a comedy ; Bird in a Cage (*The*), 1633, a comedy ; Brothers (*The*), 1652, a play ; Cardinal (*The*), 1652 (Shirley himself considered this his best play) ; Changes (*The*), 1632, a comedy ; Constant Maid (*The*), 1640, a comedy ; Contention for Honour and Riches (*A*), 1633, an interlude ; Contention of Ajax and Achilles (*The*), 1659 ; Coronation (*The*), 1640, a comedy ; Court Secret (*The*), 1653 ; Cupid and Death, 1653, a masque ; Doubtful Heir (*The*), 1652, a comedy ; Duke's Mistris (*The*), 1638, a tragedy ; Eccho, or the Un-fortunate Lovers, 1618 (his best poem) ; Example (*The*), 1637, a comedy ; Gamester (*The*), 1637, a comedy (good) ; General (*The*), 1653, a tragi-comedy ; Gentleman of Venice (*A*), 1655, a tragi-comedy ; Grateful Servant (*The*), 1630, a comedy ; Honoria and Mammon, 1659 ; Humourous Courtier (*The*), 1640, a comedy ; Hide Parke, 1637, a comedy (excellent) ; Imposture (*The*), 1652 ; Lady of Pleasure (*The*), 1637, a comedy ; Love's Crueltie, 1640, a tragedy ; Love's Victorie, 1653, a pastoral drama ; Love Tricks, or the Schoole of Complement, 1625 (his first play) ; Maides Revenge (*The*), 1639, a tragedy ; Narcissus, or the Self-Lover, 1646, a poem ; Night-Walkers (*The*), 1633 (altered from Fletcher) ; Opportunitie (*The*), 1640, a comedy ; Phillis of Scyros, 1655, a pastoral from the Italian ; Poems, 1646 ; Politician (*The*), 1655, a tragedy ; Royal Master (*The*), 1638, a comedy ; St. Patrick for Ireland, part i., 1640 ; Schoole of Complement (*The*), 1631, a comedy ; Sisters (*The*), 1652, a play ; Tragedie of Chabot (*The*), 1639 (? Chapman) ; Traytor (*The*), 1631, a tragedy (by far his best play) ; Triumph of Beauty (*The*), 1646, a masque ; Triumph of Peace (*The*), 1633, a masque ; Wedding (*The*), 1629, a comedy ; Wittie Faire One (*The*), 1633, a comedy ; Young Admirall (*The*), 1633, a poem. His Life, by Dyce, 1833.

SHORT, M.D. (*Thomas*), 1708-1772. Chronological History of the Air, Weather, etc., 1749 ; Comparative History of the Increase and Decrease of Mankind in England, 1767 ; Mineral Waters of Derbyshire, etc. (*The*), 1725.

SHORT (*Thomas Vowler*), bishop of St. Asaph, born at Dawlish, in Devonshire, 1790-1872. Parochialia, 1842 ; Sketch of the History of the Church of England, 1854.

SHORTER (*Clement*), 1858- . Charlotte Brontë and her Circle, 1896 ; History of Victorian Literature (*A*), 1886 ; Nineteenth Century Classics (*The*), (edited by C. Shorter) ; Select Poems of Wordsworth (edited), 1886.

SHORTER (*Dora Sigerson*), wife of the above. Fairy Changeling, and other Poems (*The*), 1897 ; Verses, 1894.

SHORTHOUSE (*John Henry*), 1834- . Blanche Lady Falaise, 1891 ; Countess Eve (*The*), 1888 ; Golden Thoughts of Molinos, 1883 ; John Inglesant, 1881 ; Little Schoolmaster Mark (*The*), 1883; Platonism of Wordsworth (*The*), 1882; Sir Percival, 1886; Teacher of the Violin (*A*), 1888.

SHUCKFORD, D.D. (*Samuel*), 1695-1754. Creation and Fall of Man, 1753; History of the World, 1728 (esteemed).

SIBBALD, M.D. (Sir *Robert*), Edinburgh, 1643-1712. Collection of Treatises concerning Scotland, 1739 (valuable); History of Fifeshire and Kinross-shire, 1710; History of Linlithgow and Stirling, 1710; Portus Coloniæ, etc., 1711; Roman Antiquities in Scotland, 1707; Scotia Illustrata, 1684 (of great merit); Treatises concerning Scotland, 1739. His Autobiography, 1837.

SIBBS, D.D. (*Richard*), 1577-1635. Beames of Divine Light (21 sermons), 1639; Bruised Reede and Smoaking Flax (*The*), 1631; Divine Meditation, 1638; Fountaine Sealed (*The*), 1627; Light from Heaven, 1638; Riches of Mercie, 1638; Saints' Cordials, etc., 1629; Soules Conflict with itselfe, 1635; Yea and Amen, 1638.

SIBTHORP, M.D. (*John*), Oxford, 1758-1796. Flora Græca, 1806-40, posthumous (superb); Flora Oxoniensis, 1794.

SIDGWICK, D.C.L. (*Henry*), Skipton, in Yorkshire, 1838- . Elements of Politics, 1891; Ethics of Conformity and Subscription, 1870; Methods of Ethics (*The*), 1874, Supplement 1877; Outlines of the History of Ethics, 1886; Principles of Political Economy, 1883; Scope and Method of Economic Science (*The*), 1885.

SIDNEY (*Algernon*), London, 1622-1683. Discourses on Government, 1698. His Life, by Willis, 1751; S. W. Meadley, 1813; R. C. Sidney, 1835; G. van Santvoord, U.S., 1851.

SIDNEY (Sir *Philip*), Penshurst, in Kent, 1554-1586. Apologie for Poetrie (*An*), 1595; Arcadia, 1580, published 1590-93, an heroic romance; Astrophel and Stella, 1591, posthumous, a collection of songs; Defence of Poesic, 1583, published 1595. His Life, by sir Fulke Greville, 1652; lord Brook, 1652; Dr. Zouch, 1808; Julius Lloyd, 1862; H. R. Fox-Bourne, 1862; A. J. Symonds.

SIGOURNEY (Mrs.), maiden name *Lydia Huntly*, "The American Hemans," born at Norwich, U.S., 1791-1865. Lays of the Heart; Pleasant Memories of Pleasant Lands, 1842; Pocahontas, and other Poems; Sketch of Connecticut, 1824; Tales in Prose and Verse; Traits of the Aborigines, 1822, a poem.

SIMEON (Rev. *Charles*), Reading, in Berkshire, 1759-1836. Appeals to Men of Wisdom and Candour, 1839, posthumous; Christian's Armour (*The*), 1840, posthumous; Discourses on behalf of the Jews, 1839, posthumous; Excellence of the Liturgy (*The*), 1812; Helps to Composition (600 skeleton sermons), 1802; Horæ Homileticæ (21 vols.), 1832; Humiliation of the Son of God, 1839, posthumous; Offices of the Holy Spirit (*The*), 1838, posthumous. His Memoirs, by M. M. Preston, 1840; Rev. W. Carus, 1847; Rev. J. Williamson, 1848.

SIMEON OF DURHAM, 1061-1131. Historia Ecclesiæ Dunhelmensis, printed 1732; History of England from the Danish Invasion, 1130 (continued by John, prior of Hexham).

SIMMS (*William Gilmore*), Charleston, in South Carolina, U.S., 1806-1870. American Loyalists of the Revolution; Areytos, or Songs of the Soul, 1860; As Good as a Comedy, 1852; Atalantis, 1832, a drama of the sea (his best); Beauchampe, 1842, a local tale, in prose; Book of my Lady (*The*), 1853, a novel; Border Beagles, 1840, a local tale in prose; Border Romances, 1859; Cain, and other Poems, 1829; Carl Werner, 1838, a novel; Cassique of Klawah, 1859, an historical novel; Castle Dismal, 1844, a novel; Charlemont, 1856, a local tale, in prose; Civil War in the South (*The*); Confession, or the Blind Heart, 1842, a novel; Count Julian, 1845, an historical novel; Damsel of Darien (*The*), 1839, an historical novel; Donna Anna, 1843, in verse; Early Lays, 1833; Eutaw, 1856, a story of the war, in prose; Forayers (*The*), 1855, a story of the war, in prose; Golden Christmas, 1852, a local tale, in prose; Grouped Thoughts 1845, in verse; Guy Rivers, 1834, a local tale, in prose; Helen Halsey, 1845, a local tale, in prose; History of South Carolina (*The*); Katharine Walton, 1851, a revolutionary story, in prose; Kinsman (*The*), 1841, a story of the war, in prose (afterwards called "The Scout"); Lays of the Palmetto, 1848; Lily (*The*), and the Totem, 1850 (Huguenots), in prose; Lives of Captain John Smith, of Chevalier Bayard, of General Greene, of General Marion; Lyrical and other Poems, 1825; Marie de Bernière, 1853, a novel; Maroon (*The*), and other Tales, 1858, in prose; Martin Faber, 1833, a story, in prose; Mellichampe, 1836, a revolutionary story, in prose; Michael Bonham, a drama; Morals of Slavery; Norman Maurin, a drama; Partisan (*The*), 1835, a revolutionary story, in prose; Pelayo, 1839, an historical novel; Poems, 1853; Richard Hurdis, 1838, a local story, in prose; Scout (*The*), 1841, a story of the war, in prose (same as "The Kinsman"); South Carolina in the Revolution; Southern Passages and Pictures, 1839, verse; Tricolour (*The*), in verse, 1830; Vasconcelos, 1853, an historical novel; Views and Reviews of American Literature; Visions of Cortes (*The*), 1829, in verse; Wigwam (*The*), and the Cabin, 1845-46, a novel; Woodcraft, 1854, a story of the war, in prose; Yemassee, 1835, an historical novel.

N.B.—Several of these works are of great excellence.

SIMPSON (*John Palgrave*), Norfolk, 1810-1888. Gisella, 1847, a novel; Letters from the Danube, 1847; Life of Karl Maria von Weber, 1865; Lily of Paris, or the King's Nurse, 1848; Pictures of Revolutionary Paris, 1848; Second Love, and other Tales, 1846; Sybilla, or Step by Step, a drama; World (*The*), and the Stage, a drama.

SIMPSON (*Thomas*), Market Bosworth, in Leicestershire, 1710-1761. Doctrine and Applications of Fluxions, 1750; Elements of Geometry, 1747; Mathematical Dissertations, 1743; Miscellaneous Tracts, 1754;

Nature and Laws of Chance, 1740; New Treatise of Fluxions, 1737; Trigonometry, Plane and Spherical, 1748.

SIMS (*George Robert*), London, pseudonym "Dagonet," novelist and dramatist, etc., 1847- . Ballads of Babylon, 1880; Case of George Candlemas (*The*), 1890; Coachman's Club (*The*), 1897; Crutch and Toothpick, 1879, a burlesque (his first play); Dagonet Abroad, 1895; Dagonet Ballads, 1879; Dagonet Ditties, 1891; Dagonet Reciter and Reader, 1888, in prose and verse; Dramas of Life, 1890; Gay City (*The*), 1882, a comedy; Half-way House (*The*), 1882; How the Poor Live, 1883 (and, with Horrible London added, 1889); Land of Gold (*The*), 1888, poems; Lights of London (*The*), 1882, a comedy (which had a great run); Mary Jane Married, 1888; Mary Jane's Memoirs, 1888; Member for Slocum (*The*), 1881, a farce; Memoirs of a Landlady, 1894; Merry Duchess (*The*), 1883, a comedy; Mother-in-Law (*The*), 1881, a comedy; My Two Wives, 1894; Ring o' Bells (*The*), 1886; Rogues and Vagabonds, 1885; Romany Rye, 1883, a comedy; Scenes from the Show, 1894; Social Kaleidoscope, 1880; Stories in Black and White, 1885; Tales of To-day, 1889; Ten Commandments (*The*), 1896, stories; Theatre of Life (*The*), 1881; Three Brass Balls, 1880; Tinkletop's Crime, 1891; Zeph, 1880, a circus story.

SIMS (*Richard*), Oxford, 1816- . Autograph Miscellany, 1860-61; Handbook to Autographs, 1864-65; Handbook to the Library of the British Museum, 1856; Index to the Heralds' Visitations, 1854; Manual for the Genealogist, Topographer, Antiquary, etc., 1855 (with Netherclift).

SIMSON (*Robert*), Kirton Hall, Scotland, 1687-1768. Edits Euclid's *Elements of Geometry*, 1758; *Loci Plani* of Apollonius restored, 1746. His Life, by Dr. W. Trail, 1812.

SINCLAIR (Miss *Catherine*), Edinburgh, 1800-1864. Beatrice, 1850, a novel; Business of Life (*The*); Charlie Seymour, a novel; Heirs of the Cæsars (*The*), a novel; Hill and Valley, 1840, a tour in Wales; Holiday House (*The*), 1839, a novel; Journey of Life, 1847, a novel; Lord and Lady Harcourt, a novel; Memoirs of the English Bible, 1858; Modern Accomplishments, 1836; Modern Flirtations, 1855; Modern Society, 1837; Scotland and the Scots, 1840; Shetland and the Shetlanders, 1840; Tour in Wales, 1853.

SINNETT (*Alfred Percy*), 1840- . Esoteric Buddhism, 1883; Karma, 1885, a novel; Occult World (*The*), 1881; Our Policy in China, 1869; United, 1886, a novel.

SKEAT (Rev. *Walter William*), London, 1835- . Dictionary of Middle English, 1888 (with A. C. Mayhew); Etymological Dictionary of the English Language, 1879-81 (his chief work); Mæso-Gothic Glossary (*A*), 1868; Principles of English Etymology, 1887, 1891; Tale of Ludlow Castle (*A*), 1866, a poem.

∴ He has edited several works for the Early Text Society.

SKELTON (Rev. *John*), Norfolk, poet laureate, 1460-1529. Agaynste a Comely Croystrowne (printed by R. Pynson, no date); Bowge of Courte (*The*), a poetic invective (printed by Wynkyn de Worde, no date); Collyn Cloute (a satire on the clergy); Elegy on the Earl of Northumberland, 1489; Goodly Garland (*A*), 1523; Magnyfycence, 1530, a play in rhyme; Maner of the World Nowadays (*The*), no date; Manerly Maistresse Margery, a ballad; Merie Tales, 1576; Nigramansir (*The*), 1504; On the Death of Kynge Edward IV., 1484; Phyllyp Sparowe (a poem of 1400 lines on a sparrow killed by a cat), no date; Speke Parot (*The*), no date; Speculum Principis, no date; Tunnyng of Elynor Rummyn (alewife at Leatherhead, in Surrey) a poem, no date; Ware the Hawke, no date; Why come ye not to Courte? (an attack on Wolsey, in verse, running to 1300 lines). Memoir, by Rev. Alexander Dyce, 1843.

SKELTON, LL.D. (*John*), Edinburgh, pseudonym "Shirley," 1831- . Benjamin Disraeli, 1868; Crookit Meg, 1880; Essays in History and Biography, 1882; Essays in Romance, 1878; Impeachment of Mary Stuart (*The*), 1875; Maitland of Lethington and the Scotland of Mary Stuart, 1887-88; Mary Stuart, 1893.

SKENE (*William Forbes*), Inverie, in Scotland, 1809- . Celtic Scotland (ancient Alban), 1876; Chronicles of the Picts and Scots, 1868; Church and Culture, 1877; Coronation Stone (*The*), 1869; Dean of Lismore's Book, etc., 1862; Four Ancient Books of Wales, 1869, Cymric poetry; Highlanders of Scotland (*The*), 1837; History of Ethnology, 1876; Land and the People (*The*), 1880.

SKETCHLEY (*Arthur*). See ROSE (Rev. *George*).

SKINNER (Rev. *John*), Scotland, 1721-1807. Dissertation on Job's Prophecy, 1757; Ecclesiastical History of Scotland, 1788; Tullochgorum (a song in praise of the Scotch reel). His Memoirs, by his son, 1809; H. G. Reid, 1859.

SKINNER, M.D. (*Stephen*), London, 1623-1667. Etymologicon Linguæ Anglicanæ, 1671.

SLADEN (*Douglas*), (Brooke Wheelton), London, 1856- . Editor of *Who's Who*. Australian Ballads, 1888; Australian Lyrics, 1882; Brittany for Britons, 1896; Century of Australian Song (*A*), 1888; Edward the Black Prince, 1886; Frithjof and Ingebjorg, 1882; In Cornwall and across the Sea, 1885; Japs at Home (*The*), 1892; Japanese Marriage (*A*), 1895; On the Cars and off, 1895; Lester the Loyalist, 1890; Poetry of Exiles (*A*), 1883; Spanish Armada (*The*), 1888; Summer Christmas (*A*), 1884; Younger American Poets, 1891.

SLEEMAN (Sir *William Henry*), Cornwall, 1788-1856. Diary in Oude, 1852; Rambles and Recollections of an Indian Officer, 1843.

SLOANE, M.D. (Sir *Hans*), Ireland, 1660-1753. Natural History of Jamaica, 1707-25.

∴ The collection of sir Hans Sloane was purchased by the State, and was the nucleus of the British Museum. There were 50,000 books, 3560 MSS., besides his vast museum of natural history.

SMART (*Benjamin Humphrey*), 1787-1872. Edits Walker's *Pronouncing Dictionary*, 1836; Introduction to Grammar, 1858; Manual of Logic, 1849; Outlines of Sematology, 1831, 1837, 1839; Thought and Language, 1855.

SMART (*Christopher*), Kent, 1722-1770. Grateful Fair (*The*), 1747 (the last play ever performed before either of the universities); Hannah, 1764; Hilliad (*The*), 1753, a satire on John Hill; Hop Garden (*The*), two Georgics in Miltonic verse; *Horace* translated, 1756; Hymn to the Supreme Being, 1756; Ode to the Earl of Northumberland, 1764; Parables in Familiar Verse (*The*), 1768; *Phædrus* translated into verse, 1765; Poems, 1752, 1763, and a mass of religious poetry; Poetical Essays on the Divine Attributes, 1750-1755 (*Eternity* 1750, *Immensity* 1751, *Omnipresence* 1752. *Omnipotence* 1753, *Goodness* 1755); Smartiad (*The*), 1753; Song to David, 1763; Trip to Cambridge, 1747.

SMART (*Hawley*), novelist, *- . At Fault, 1883; Bitter is the Rind, 1870; Bound to Win, 1877; Breezie Langton, 1869; Broken Bonds, 1874; Cecile, 1871; Courtship (in 1720 and 1860), 1876; False Cards, 1872; Great Tontine (*The*), 1881; Hard Lines, 1883; Play or Pay, 1877; Pride of the Paddock, 1886; Race for a Wife, 1870; Social Sinners, 1880; Sunshine and Snow, 1879; Two Kisses, 1875.

SMEDLEY (Rev. *Edward*), 1789-1836. Erin, 1814, a descriptive poem; History of the Reformed Religion in France, 1832-34; Jephtha, 1815, a poem; Jonah, 1815, a poem; Marriage in Cana, 1828, a poem; Poems (with a memoir of his life), 1837; Prescience, 1828, a poem; Religio Clerici 1818, a poem; Sketches from Venetian History, 1831-32.

SMEDLEY (*Francis Edward*), Marlow, in Buckinghamshire, novelist, 1818-1864. Frank Fairleigh, 1850; Gathered Leaves, 1865; Harry Coverdale's Courtship, 1854; Lewis Arundel, 1852; Miles Coverdale's Courtship.

SMEDLEY (*Menella Bute*), *- . Linnet's Trials, 1864; Mere Story (*A*), 1869; Other Folks' Lives, 1869; Poems, 1869; Twice Lost, and other Tales, 1863; Two Dramatic Poems, 1874.

SMEETON (*George*), about 1785-1830. Biographia Curiosa, 1820; Lives, etc., of Remarkable Characters, 1814; Reprint of Rare and Curious Tracts, 1820.

SMILES, LL.D. (*Samuel*), Haddington, in Scotland, 1816- . Baker of Thurso (*The*), 1878; Character, 1871 (sequel to "Self-Help"); Duty, 1880; George Moore, Philanthropist, 1878; Huguenots in England and Ireland, 1867; Huguenots in France, 1873; Industrial Biography, 1863; Jasmin, 1891; Josiah Wedgwood, 1891; Life and Labour, 1887; Life of George Stephenson, 1859; Life of Robert Dick, Geologist, etc., 1878; Lives of Boulton and Watt, 1865; Lives of the Engineers, 1862; Men of Invention, 1884; Physical Education, 1837;

Publisher (*A*) [J. Murray] and his Friends, 1891; Railway Property, 1849; Robert Dick, 1878; Scotch Naturalist, 1876; Self-Help, 1860; Thrift, 1875; Workmen's Earnings, Strikes, and Wages, 1861.

SMITH, LL.D. (*Adam*), Kirkaldy, in Scotland, 1723-1790. Dissertation on the Origin of Languages; Essay on Philosophical Subjects, 1795; Letter to Mr. Strahan, 1777; Rights of Great Britain asserted against the Claims of America, 1776; Theory of Moral Sentiments, 1759; Wealth of Nations, 1776 (his great work). His Life, by Smellie, 1800; Playfair, 1805; Dugald Stewart, 1812; lord Brougham, 1845.

SMITH (*Albert Richard*), Chertsey, in Middlesex, 1816-1860. Adventures of Mr. Ledbury, 1844, a novel; Ascent of Mont Blanc, begun 1852 (an entertainment repeated till his death); Ballet Girl (*The*), 1847; Bowl of Punch (*A*), 1848; Christopher Tadpole, 1848, a novel; Comic Sketches, 1848; Evening Parties, a sketch; Flirt (*The*), 1849, a sketch; Gavarni in London, 1849; Gent (*The*), 1847, a sketch; History of Kasperi, 1857; Idler upon Town (*The*), 1848; Marchioness of Brinvilliers, 1846, a novel; Month at Constantinople (*A*), 1850; Overland Mail (*The*), 1850; Physiology of Evening Parties, 1843; Physiology of the Medical Student, 1861; Pottleton Legacy (*The*), 1849, a novel; Scattergood Family (*The*), 1845, a novel; Stuck-up People, 1847; To China and back, 1859; Wassail Bowl (*The*), 1843; Wild Oats, 1860.

SMITH (*Alexander*), Kilmarnock, in Scotland, 1830-1867. Alfred Hagarth's Husband, 1865, a novel; City Poems, 1857; Dreamthorpe, 1863, in prose; Edwin of Deira, 1861; Last Leaves, 1868, posthumous; Life-drama (*A*), and other Poems, 1853; Sonnets on the Crimean War, 1855 (with S. Dobell); Summer in Skye 1865, in prose. His Life, by P. P. Alexander, 1868.

SMITH (*Charles Roach*), Landguard, in the Isle of Wight, 1804-1889. Antiquities of Richborough, etc., 1850, with Supplements on Pevensey, etc., 1852-58; Collectanea Antiqua, 1843-63; Roman London, 1859.

SMITH (Mrs. *Charlotte*), maiden name *Charlotte Turner*, 1749-1806. Banished Man (*The*), 1794, a novel; Celestina, 1791, a novel; Desmond, 1792, a novel; Elegiac Sonnets, 1784; Emigrants (*The*), 1793, a poem; Emmeline, 1788, a novel; Ethelinda, 1789, a novel; Marchment, 1796, a novel; Montalbert, 1802, a novel; Old Manor House (*The*), 1793, a novel; Romance of Real Life, 1786; Rural Walks (in dialogue), 1795; Solitary Wanderer (*The*), 1799; Wanderings of Warwick (*The*), 1794; Young Philosopher (*The*), 1798.

SMITH, LL.D. (*Goldwin*), Reading, in Berkshire, 1823- . Bay Leaves, 1893; Canada and the Canadian Question, 1891; Conduct of England to Ireland (*The*), 1882; Does the Bible sanction American Slavery? 1864; Empire (*The*), 1863; England and America, 1865; Essay on Questions of the Day, 1893; False Hopes, 1883; Foundation of the American Colonies (*The*), 1861; Irish History and Irish Characteristics, 1861; Lectures and Essays, 1881; Lectures on Modern History, 1869; Life of Jane Austen, 1890; Loyalty, Aristocracy, and Jingoism, 1891; Moral Crusader (*The*), 1892 (W. Lloyd Garrison): Oxford and her Colleges, 1894; Rational Religion, etc., 1858; Short History of England to the Reformation, 1869; Specimens of Greek Tragedy, 1893; Three English Statesmen (Pym, Cromwell, and Pitt), 1867; Trip to England (*A*), 1888; United States (*The*), 1893.

SMITH (*Horace*), London, 1779–1849. Adam Brown, the Merchant, 1843, a novel; Arthur Arundel, 1844, a novel; Brambletye House, 1826, a novel; Festivals, Games, etc., of all Nations, 1831; First Impressions, 1813, a comedy; Gaieties and Gravities, 1825; Gale Middleton, 1833, a novel; Horace in London, 1813; Horatio, or Memoirs of the Davenport Family, 1807, a novel; Involuntary Prophet (*The*), 1835; Jane Lomax, or a Mother's Crime, 1837; Love's Mesmerism, 1845, a novel; Midsummer Medley, 1830; Moneyed Man, etc. (*The*), 1841, a novel; New Forest (*The*), 1829, a novel; Oliver Cromwell, 1840, a novel; Poetical Works (collected), 1840; Rejected Addresses, 1812 (with his brother James); Reuben Apsley, 1827, a novel; Runaway (*The*), 1813, a novel; Tales of the Early Ages, 1832; Tin Trumpet (*The*), 1836; Tor Hill, 1827, a novel; Trevanion, or Matrimonial Errors, 1813, a novel; Walter Colyton, 1830, a tale of 1688; Zillah, a Tale of the Holy City, 1828.

SMITH (*James*), Glasgow, in Scotland, 1789–1850. Thorough Draining and Deep Ploughing, 1831.

SMITH (*James*), brother of "Horace Smith," London, 1775–1839. Horace in London, 1815; Rejected Addresses, 1812 (with his brother Horace). His Memoirs, Comic Miscellanies, etc., edited and published by his brother Horace.

SMITH, M.D. (Sir *James Edward*), Norwich, 1759–1828. English Botany, 1792–1807; Exotic Botany, 1804–5; Flora Britannica, 1800–4; Grammar of Botany (*A*), 1821; Icones Pictæ Plantarum Rariorum, 1790–93; Introduction to Physiological Botany, 1807; Plantarum Icones Hactenus Ineditæ, 1789–90; Specimens of the Botany, etc., of New Holland, 1793–94; Spicilegium Botanicum, 1792; Tour on the Continent, 1793. His Memoirs, by lady Smith, 1832.

SMITH (Captain *John*), Lincolnshire, one of the founders of Virginia, 1579–1631. Generall Historie of Virginia, etc., 1626; Travels, 1630; True Relation of Occurrences in Virginia, 1608. His Life, by W. C. Simms, U.S., 1846; Hill, 1858.

SMITH, D.D. (*John*), Argyllshire, 1747–1807. Dissertation on the Authenticity of Ossian's Poems, 1782; Essay on Gaelic Antiquities, 1780; Last Judgment (*The*), 1783; Life of St. Columba, 1798.

SMITH (*John Pye*), Sheffield, in Yorkshire, 1774–1851. First Lines of Christian Theology, 1854; Letters to Belsham, 1804; Mosaic Account of the Creation and the Deluge, illustrated by the Discoveries of Modern Science, 1830; On the Sacrifice and Priesthood of Jesus Christ, 1828; Relation between Holy Scriptures and Some Parts of Geological Science, 1834; Scripture and Geology, 1839; Scripture Testimony to the Messiah, 1818–21. His Life, by Medway, 1853; Dr. Eadie, 1859.

SMITH (*John Thomas*), London, 1766–1833. Ancient Topography of London, 1810–15; Antiquities of London and its Environs, 1791–1800 (his chief work); Antiquities of Westminster, 1807; Book for a Rainy Day, 1845; Cries of London, 1839; Nollekens and his Times, 1828; Tag, Rag, and Bobtail, 1800; Vagabondiana, or Anecdotes of London Vagabonds, 1820.

SMITH (*Joseph*), Sharon, U.S., founder of the Latter-day Saints, 1805–1844. Book of Mormon, 1830 (said to be a plagiarism of Solomon Spalding's romance *The Manuscript Found*).

SMITH (Rev. *Joseph Denham*), Romsey, in Hampshire, 1816– . Connemara, 1853; Life Truths, 1866; Oliver Cromwell, 1850; Rhine and the Reformation (*The*), 1852; Voice from the Alps (*A*), 1854; Winnowed Grain, 1862.

SMITH (*Reginald Bosworth*), Dorchester, 1839– . Carthage and the Carthaginians, 1878; Life of Lord Laurence, 1883; Mohammed and Mohammedanism, 1874; Rome and Carthage, 1881.

SMITH, D.D. (*Robert*), 1689–1768. Complete System of Optics, 1738; Harmonia Mensurarum, 1722; Harmonics, 1748.

SMITH, Phil.Doc. (*Robert Angus*), Glasgow, in Scotland, 1817–1883. Air and Rain, 1872; History of the Atomic Theory; Life of Dalton.

SMITH, D.D. (*Robert Payne*), Gloucestershire, 1818–1894. Messianic Interpretation of the Prophecies of Isaiah, 1862; Prophecy as a Preparation for Christ, 1869, a Bampton lecture.

SMITH (Rev. *Sydney*), Woodford, in Essex, a wit, 1769–1845. Peter Plymley's Letters, 1807; Sermons, 1800, 1809, 1846; Sketches of Moral Philosophy, 1849, posthumous; Wit and Wisdom of Sydney Smith, 1861, posthumous; Works, 1839–40. His Life, by lady Holland, 1858.

SMITH, D.D. (*Thomas*), London, 1638–1710. Account of the Greek Church, 1680; Catalogus Librorum MSS. Bibliothecæ, Cottonianæ, 1696; Diatriba de Chaldaicis Paraphrastis, 1662; Inscriptiones Græcæ Palmyrenorum, 1698; Manners, etc., of the Turks, 1678; Miscellanea, 1686–92; Syntagma de Druidum Moribus, 1664; Vitæ Quorumdam . . . Illustrium Virorum, 1707.

SMITH, M.D. (*Thomas Southwood*), Somersetshire, 1788–1861. Animal Physiology; Divine Government (*The*), 1814; Philosophy of Health (*The*), 1834; Treatise on Fever, 1830.

SMITH (*Toulmin*), Birmingham, in Warwickshire, 1816–1869. Discovery of America by Northmen, 1839; English Guilds, 1870; Parallels between the Constitutional History of England and Hungary, 1840; Parish (*The*), 1854.

SMITH, D.D. (*William*), Worcester, 1711-1787. Poetical Works, 1791, posthumous; Sermons on the " Beatitudes," 1782. Translated *Longinus*, 1739; *Thucydidês*, 1753.

SMITH, LL.D. (*William*), Oxfordshire, 1769-1839. Geological Map of England and Wales, etc., 1815; Strata identified by . . . Fossils, 1816-19; Stratigraphical System of . . . Fossils, 1817. His Life, by John Phillips, 1844.

SMITH (Sir *William*), better known as " Dr. Smith," London, 1814-1893. *Editor of:* Atlas of Biblical and Classical Geography, 1875; Dictionary of Christian Biography, 1876-81 (with Wace); Dictionary of Greek and Roman Antiquities, 1840-42; Dictionary of Greek and Roman Biography and Mythology, 1843-49; Dictionary of Greek and Roman Geography, 1852-57; Dictionary of the Bible, 1860-63; New Classical Dictionary, 1850.

SMITH (*William Robertson*), Keig, Aberdeenshire, joint editor of the *Encyclopædia Britannica* (ninth edition), 1846-1894. Kinship and Marriage in Early Arabia, 1885; Lectures on the Religion of the Semites, 1889; Old Testament in the Jewish Church (*The*), 1881; Prophets of Israel (*The*), 1882.

SMOLLETT, M.D. (*Tobias George*), Cardross, in Scotland, 1721-1771. Adventures of an Atom, 1749, a political satire; Adventures of Ferdinand Count Fathom, 1753, a novel; Adventures of Peregrine Pickle (*The*), 1751, a novel; Adventures of Roderick Random (*The*), 1748, a novel (his first); Adventures of Sir Launcelot Greaves, 1760-62, a novel; Advice, 1746, a satire; Alceste, 1747, an opera; Compendium of Voyages and Travels, 1757; Essay on the External Use of Water, etc., 1752; History of England, from the Landing of Cæsar to the Treaty of Aix-la-Chapelle 1757, continuation to the last year of publication, 1761-65; Humphry Clinker, 1771 (his last work and best novel); Ode to Independence, 1773; Present State of all Nations, 1764; Regicide (*The*), 1749, a tragedy; Reprisals, or the Tars of Old England, 1757, a comedy in two acts; Reproof (*The*), a satire, 1747; Tears of Caledonia, 1746; Translation of *Don Quixote*, 1755; Travels through France and Italy, 1766. His Life, by Dr. Anderson, 1797; W. Roscoe, 1845; Dr. J. Moore, 1872; sir W. Scott; R. Chambers, etc.

SMYTH (*William*), Liverpool, 1764-1849. English Lyrics, 1806; Evidences of Christianity, 1845; French Revolution (*The*), 1840; Lectures on Modern History, 1840; Memoirs of Sheridan, 1840.

SMYTH (*William Henry*), Westminster, 1788-1865. Cycle of Celestial Objects, 1844; Mediterranean (*The*), 1854; Nautical Dictionary, 1867.

SNOW, M.D. (*John*), York, 1813-1858. Chloroform and other Anæsthetics, 1858; Mode of Communication of Cholera, 1849.

SOANE (Sir *John*), Reading, in Berkshire, founder of the Soane Museum, 1753-1837.

Civil Architecture, 1829; Designs for Public and Private Buildings, 1828; Designs in Architecture, 1793; Plans of Buildings executed, 1788.

SOMERVILLE (Mrs.), maiden name *Mary Fairfax*, Roxburghshire, Scotland, 1780-1872. Connection of the Physical Sciences (*The*), 1834 (her chief work); Mechanism of the Heavens, 1831 (summary of La Place's work); Molecular and Microscopic Science, 1851; Personal Recollections, etc., 1873, posthumous; Physical Geography, 1848.

SOMERVILLE (*William*), Edston, in Warwickshire, 1692-1742. Chase (*The*), 1735, in blank verse; Field Sports, 1742; Hobbinolia, 1740, a burlesque, in blank verse; Two Springs (*The*), 1725.

SOMNER (*William*), Canterbury, 1606-1669. Antiquities of Canterbury, 1640 (excellent); Dictionarium Saxonico - Latino - Anglicum, 1659; Julii Cæsaris Portus Iccius, 1694; Roman Ports and Forts in Kent, 1693; Treatise on Gavelkind, 1660. His Life, by bishop Kennett, 1693.

SOTHEBY (*Sammel Leigh*), 1806-1861. Principia Typographica, 1858.

SOTHEBY (*William*), London, poet, 1757-1833. Battle of the Nile (*The*), 1799, a poem; Constance de Castile, 1810, a poem; Farewell to Italy, and other Poems, 1818; Italy, and other Poems, 1828; Julian and Agnes, 1801, a tragedy; Orestes, 1802, a tragedy; Saul, 1807, a poem, in blank verse; Tour through Parts of Wales (*A*), 1789. Translated in English verse, Homer's *Iliad*, 1831; Virgil's *Georgics*, 1800; Wieland's *Oberon*, 1798.

SOUTH, D.D. (*Robert*), Hackney, near London, 1633-1716. Animadversions on Dr. Sherlock's *Vindication of the Doctrine of the Trinity*, 1693; Laitie instructed (*The*), 1660; Musica Incantans, 1655; Posthumous Works, 1717; Sermons, 1678-1715.

SOUTHCOTT (*Joanna*), Devonshire, 1750-1814. Book of Wonders (in five parts), 1813-14; Warning to the Whole World, 1803.

SOUTHERNE (*Thomas*), Oxmantown, in Ireland, 1660-1746. Cleomenes, 1692 (with Dryden); Disappointment, 1684, a comedy; Isabella, or the Fatal Marriage, 1695, a tragedy (good); Oronooko, 1696, a tragedy (good); Persian Prince (*The*), 1682, a tragedy; Rambling Lady (*The*), 1698, a comedy; Spartan Dame (*The*), 1721, a tragedy; Wife's Excuse (*The*), 1692, a comedy.

SOUTHESK (The earl of), 1827- . Greenwood's Farewell, and other Poems, 1875; Jonas Fisher, 1875, a poem; Meda Maiden (*The*), and other Poems, 1877; Saskatchewan and the Rocky Mountains, 1875.

SOUTHEY, LL.D. (*Robert*), Bristol, poet laureate, 1774-1843.

Poetical works: All for Love, or a Sinner Well Saved (in nine parts), 1829; Battle of Blenheim, 1798, a ballad; Bishop Bruno, 1798, a ballad; Bishop Hatton (eaten by rats), 1799, a ballad; Botany Bay Eclogues (four in number), 1794; Carmen Aulica, 1814; Carmen Triumphale, 1814; Cataract of Lodore, 1820, word-painting; Curse of Kehama (in 24 subdivisions), 1810; Devil's

4 Y

Walk (*The*), 1820, a ballad ; English Eclogues (nine in number), 1798-1803, blank
verse ; Holly Tree (*The*), 1798, an ode ; Inch-
cape Rock (*The*), 1802, a ballad ; Joan of
Arc, 1796, an epic in 10 books ; Lay of the
Laureate, 1816 ; Madoc, 1805, an epic in
two parts (part i. contains 18 subdivisions,
part ii. 27) ; Mary, the Maid of the Inn,
1796, a ballad ; Metrical Tales, 1805 ; Minor
Poems, 1797-99, 1815 ; Odes, 1814 ; Old
Woman of Berkeley, 1798, a ballad ; Oliver
Newman, and other poetical remains, 1845 ;
Pig (*Defence of the*), 1798, a colloquial poem,
in blank verse ; Pilgrim of Compostella
(*The*), in four parts, 1829 ; Poems, 1795, 1797,
1801 ; Poet's Pilgrimage to Waterloo, 1816 ;
Robin Hood, 1847, a fragment ; Roderick,
the Last of the Goths (in 24 subdivisions,
blank verse), begun 1809, and finished
1807 ; St. Patrick's Purgatory, 1801, a ballad ;
Specimens of the later English Poets, 1814 ;
Tale of Paraguay (*A*), in four cantos, Spenserian metre, 1825 ; Thalaba the Destroyer
(an epic in 12 books, in rhythm, irregular
metre), 1801 ; Vision of Judgment (in 12
subdivisions, hexameters), 1821 (the apo-
theosis of George III.); Wat Tyler, 1817,
a drama ; Well of St. Keyne (*The*), 1798, a
ballad.

Prose works: Amadis de Gaul, 1803 ;
Book of the Church, 1824 ; Byrth and Lyf of
Kyng Arthur, 1817 ; Chronicle of the Cid,
1808 ; Commonplace Book, 1849-51 ; Corre-
spondence, 1849-50, posthumous ; Doctor
(*The*), 1834, a novel ; Essays, 1832 ; Henry
Kirke White, 1807 ; History of Brazil,
1810-23 ; History of the Expedition of
Orsua, 1821 ; History of the Peninsular War,
1823-27-32 ; Letters from England, 1807; Life
of Dr. Andrew Bell, 1844 ; Life of Bunyan,
1830 ; Life of Cromwell, 1844 ; Life of Lord
Nelson, 1813 ; Life of John Wesley, 1820 ;
Lives of the English Admirals, 1833-40 ;
Naval History of England, 1833-40 ; Oliver
Newman, 1845 (unfinished) ; Omniana, 1812 ;
Palmerin of England, 1807 ; Pilgrimage to
Waterloo, 1816 ; Robin Hood, 1847 ; Sir
Thomas More, 1829 ; Spanish and Portu-
guese Poetry, 1797 ; Vindiciæ Ecclesiæ
Anglicanæ, 1826. His Life, by his son, C.
C. Southey, 1849-50 ; Browne, 1854 ; Dow-
den, 1880.

SOUTHEY (Mrs. *Robert*), the poet's second
wife, maiden name *Caroline Anne Bowles*,
poetess, 1786-1854. Chapters on Churchyards, 1829 ; Ellen Fitzarthur, 1820 ; Solitary
Hours, 1839 ; Widow's Tale (*The*).

SOUTHWELL (*Robert*), St. Faith's, Norfolk,
1560-1595. Epistle of Comfort, etc., 1605, posthumous ; Mæoniæ, 1595 ; Marie Magdalen's
Funerall Teares, 1594 ; St. Peter's Complaynt, and other Poems, 1595 ; Short Rule
of Good Life, 1606, posthumous ; Supplication to Queen Elizabeth, 1593 ; Triumphs
over Death, 1595.

SOWERBY (*George Brettingham*), London,
1788-1854. Genera of Recent and of Fossil
Shells, 1820-24 ; Manual of Conchology,
1839 ; Popular British Conchology, 1854 ;
Species Conchyliorum, 1830.

SOWERBY (*George Brettingham*), son of the

preceding, 1812-   . Conchological Illustrations, 1841-45 ; Illustrated Index of
British Shells, 1859 ; Popular British Conchology, 1855 ; Popular Guide to the
Aquarium, 1857 ; Thesaurus Conchyliorum,
1842-82.

SOWERBY (*James*), London, 1757-1822. British
Mineralogy, 1804-17 ; English Botany, 1790-
1820 (with sir J. E. Smith) ; English Fungi,
1797-1809 ; Genera of . . . Shells, 1822-34 ;
Mineral Conchology of Great Britain,
1812-41.

SPALDING (*Samuel*), London, 1807-1834.
Philosophy of Christian Morals, 1834.

SPECTATOR (*The*), a review and newspaper,
issued weekly, started 1828.

SPEDDING (*James*), 1810-1881. Evenings
with a Reviewer, 1881 ; Francis Bacon,
1857-74 ; Life and Times of Bacon, 1878 ;
Macaulay and Bacon, 1882 ; Publishers and
Authors, 1867 ; Reviews, etc., not relating
to Bacon, 1879.

SPEED (*John*), Cheshire, 1542-1629. Clowd of
Witnesses (*A*), 1616 ; Genealogies of Scripture, 1640 ; History of Great Britaine under
the Romans, Saxons, Danes, and Normans,
1611 ; Prospect of the most Famous Parts
of the World (*A*), 1631 ; Theatre of the
Empire of Great Britaine, 1611.

SPEKE (Captain *John Hanning*), near Bideford, in Devonshire, 1827-1864. Journal of
the Discovery of the Source of the Nile,
1863 ; What led to the Discovery of the
Source of the Nile, 1864.

SPELMAN (Sir *Henry*), Norfolk, 1562-1641.
Concilia, Decreta, etc., in re Ecclesiastica
Orbis Britannici, 1639-64 ; De Sepultura,
1616 ; Glossarium Archaiologicum, 1626 ;
Reliquiæ, 1698. His Life, by Edmund
Gibson, 1723.

SPENCE (Rev. *Joseph*), Kingsclere, in Hampshire, 1698-1768. Essay on Pope's *Odyssey*,
1727 ; Life of Blacklock, 1754 ; Moralities
(essays, fables, translations, etc.), 1753 ;
Observations, Anecdotes, etc. (men and
books), 1820 ; Parallel between Magliabecchi
and Robert Hill, 1758 ; Polymetis, 1747.
His Life, by Singer, 1820.

SPENCE (*William*), 1783-1860. Introduction
to Entomology, 1815-26.

SPENCER (*Herbert*), Derby, 1820-   . Cere-
monial Institutions, 1879 ; Classification of
the Sciences, 1864 ; Coming Slavery (*The*),
1884 ; Data of Ethics, 1879 ; Descriptive
Sociology, 1874-82 ; Ecclesiastical Institutions, 1885 ; Education, 1861 ; Essays,
1858-63-74 ; Factors of Evolution (*The*),
1887 ; First Principles, 1862 ; Inadequacy of
Natural Selection, 1893 ; Man *v*. the State,
1884 ; Principles of Biology, 1864 ; Principles
of Ethics (*The*), 1892 ; Principles of Psychology, 1855 (enlarged 1870-72) ; Principles of
Sociology, 1877 ; Proper Sphere of Government, 1842 ; Recent Discussions in Science,
Philosophy, and Morals, 1871 ; Rejoinder to
Professor Weismann, 1893 ; Sins of Trade
and Commerce, 1875 ; Social Statics, 1851 ;
Spontaneous Generation, 1870 ; Study of
Sociology, 1873 ; Weismannism Once More,
1894.

SPENCER, D.D. (*John*), Bocton, in Kent,

1630-1695. De Legibus Hebræorum Ritualibus, 1685 (to show that the Mosaic laws were Egyptian); De Urim et Thummim, 1678; Discourse concerning Prodigies, 1663.

SPENSER (*Edmund*), London, 1553-1599. Amoreti, 1595; Astrophel, 1594, a pastoral elegy; Britain's Ida, 1628; Colin Clout's come Home againe, 1595; Complaints, 1591; Court of Cupid (lost); Daphnaiada (an elegy, in seven fits), 1592; Dreams, 1580 (lost); Dying Pelican, 1580 (lost); Epithalamium, 1595, a marriage song; Faërie Queene (in six allegories, partly connected), i.-iii. 1590, iv.-vi. 1596 (his great work); Fowre Hymns, viz. Love, Beauty, Heavenly Love, and Heavenly Beauty, 1596; Legends (lost); Mother Hubberd's Tale, 1591, in rhyme; Muiopotmos, or the Fate of the Butterfly (in 55 stanzas, eight lines each), 1590; Prothalamion, 1596, spousal verses; Purgatory of Lovers (lost); Ruins of Rome (the 33 sonnets of Bellay translated), 1590; Ruins of Time (in 97 Spenserian stanzas), 1590; Shepheardes Calendar (in 12 eclogues), 1579; Slomber, 1579 (lost); Sonnets, 1592-93 (lost); Tears of the Muses (in 6-line stanzas), 1590; View of the State of Ireland, 1633, posthumous; Virgil's Gnat, 1588 (*Culex*); Visions of the World's Vanity (in 12 sonnets), 1590. Nine comedies, all lost. His Life, by Hughes, 1715; Birch, 1751; Church, 1758; Upton, 1758; Todd, 1805; Dr. Aikin, 1806; Robinson, 1825; J. Mitford, 1829; Hillard, 1839; G. L. Craik, 1845; Masterman, 1848; Child, 1855; Gilfillan, 1859; J. P. Collier, 1862; Morris, 1869.

SPOTTISWOODE (*John*), archbishop of St. Andrews, born in Scotland, 1565-1639. History of the Church of Scotland, 1655; Refutatio Libelli de Regimine Ecclesiæ Scoticanæ, 1620. His Life, by bishop Russell, 1847.

SPOTTISWOODE, LL.D. (*William*), London, 1825-1883. Polarisation of Light, 1874.

SPRAT (*Thomas*), bishop of Rochester, born at Tallaton, in Devonshire, 1636-1713. Accounts of the Rye-house Plot, 1685; History of the Royal Society, 1667; Life of Cowley; Plague of Athens, 1659; Poem on the Death of Cromwell, 1659.

SPURGEON (Rev. *Charles Haddon*), Kelvedon, in Essex, 1834-1892. Birthday Book (*Spurgeon's*), 1879; Comments and Commentaries, 1876; Evening by Evening, 1868; Feathers for Arrows, 1870; Flashes of Thought, 1874; Gleanings among the Sheaves, 1859; Interpreter (*The*), 1873; John Ploughman's Pictures, 1881; John Ploughman's Talk, 1869; Lectures to my Students, 1875, 1877; Memorial Volume, 1879; Metropolitan Tabernacle (*The*), its History and Work, 1875; Metropolitan Tabernacle Pulpit (*The*), a periodical, started 1855; Morning by Morning, 1865; Our Own Hymn-book, 1866; Saint and his Saviour (*The*), 1857; Shilling Series, 1877-1882; Smooth Stones; Speeches, 1878; Spurgeon's Gems, 1859; Sword and the Trowel (*The*), a periodical, started 1865; Treasury of David (*The*), 1869-85; Trum-

pet Calls, etc., 1875; Types and Emblems, 1873.
N.B.—About 2000 sermons published, not under the sanction or supervision of the preacher.

SQUIER (*Ephraim George*), Bethlehem, in New York, U.S., 1821- . Aboriginal Monuments of New York; Authors who have written on the Aboriginal Languages of Central America, 1861; Nicaragua, etc., 1852; Peru . . . Explorations in the Land of the Incas, 1850; Smithsonian Contribution, etc., 1840; States of Central America, 1857; Tropical Fibres, 1861; Waikna, 1855, a story.

STACKHOUSE (*John*), died 1819. Nereis Britannica, 1795; edited Theophrastus on *Plants*, 1811.

STACKHOUSE (Rev. *Thomas*), 1680-1752. Comment on the Apostles' Creed, 1747; Complete Body of . . . Divinity, 1743; History of the Bible, 1732 (esteemed); Memoir of Bishop Atterbury, 1727.

STAFFORD (*Anthony*), 1570-1641. Day of Salvation (*The*), 1635; Female Glory, 1635 (the Virgin Mary); Guide to Honour (*The*), 1634; Heavenly Dogge (*The*), 1605 (Diogenes); Life of Lord Stafford, 1640; Meditations, etc., 1612; Niobe, or the Age of Teares, 1611.

STAINER, Mus.D. (*John*), London, 1840- . Theory of Harmony (*The*), 1871.

STAIR (Sir *James Dalrymple*, first viscount of), born in Ayrshire, Scotland, 1619-1695. Decisions of the Court of Sessions, 1684-87; Institutions of the Laws of Scotland, 1681; Phisiologia Nova Experimentalis, 1686; Vindication of the Divine Perfections, 1695.

STALKER, D.D. (*James*), Crieff, in Perthshire, 1848- . Atonement (*The*), 1894; Four Men (*The*), 1890; Imago Christi, 1889; Life of Jesus Christ, 1879, 1884; Life of St. Paul, 1884-85; New Song (*The*), 1882, sermons; Preacher and his Models (*The*), 1891; Richard Baxter, 1883.

STANHOPE (*Charles*, third earl), London, 1753-1816. Treatise on Electricity, 1779.

STANHOPE, D.D. (*George*), Hartshorne, in Derbyshire, 1660-1728. Boyle Lectures, 1706; Paraphrase, etc., on the Epistles and Gospels, 1705. Translated *Imitatio Christi*, 1696; Marcus Aurelius's *Meditations*; and *Epictetus*, 1700.

STANHOPE (*Philip Henry*, earl), Walmer, in Kent, 1805-1875. Court of Spain under Charles II. (*The*), 1844; Historical Essays, 1848; History of England, from the Peace of Utrecht to the Peace of Versailles, 1836-52 (his best work); History of the Reign of Queen Anne to the Peace of Utrecht, 1870; History of the Rise of our Indian Empire, 1858; History of the War of Succession in Spain, 1832; Life of Belisarius, 1848; Life of Jeanne d'Arc; Life of Louis, Prince of Condé, 1845; Life of Sir R. Peel, 1856-57; Life of W. Pitt.

STANLEY, D.D. (*Arthur Penrhyn*), Alderley, in Cheshire, 1815-1881. Athanasian Creed (*The*), 1871; Christian Institutions, 1881; Edward and Catherine Stanley, 1879·

Epistles to the Corinthians (*The*), 1854; Essays on Church and State, 1870; Historical Memorials of Canterbury, 1854; Historical Memorials of Westminster Abbey, 1867; History of the Eastern Church, 1861; History of the Jewish Church, 1863, 1865; Lectures on the Church of Scotland, 1872; Life of Dr. Arnold, 1844; Life of Bishop Stanley (his father), 1850; Sermons and Essays on the Apostolic Age, 1846; Sermons preached before the University of Oxford, 1860-63; Sermons preached in the East, 1862; Sinai and Palestine, 1855; Stories and Essays on the Apostolic Age, 1846; Three Irish Churches (*The*), 1869; Unity of Evangelical and Apostolic Teaching, 1859. His Life, by R. E. Prothero and dean Bradley, 1893.

STANLEY (*Edward*), bishop of Norwich, born in London, 1779-1849. Familiar History of Birds, 1835. His Life, by A. P. Stanley, his son, 1850.

STANLEY, LL.D. (*Henry Morton*), Denbigh, in Wales, 1841– . Congo (*The*), and the founding of its Free States, 1885; Coomassie and Magdala, 1874; How I found Livingstone, 1872; In Darkest Africa, 1890; My Dark Companions, etc., 1893; My Early Travels and Adventures, 1895; My Kalulu: Prince, King, and Slave, 1873, a story; Through the Dark Continent, etc., 1878.

STANLEY (*Thomas*), Hertfordshire, 1625-1678. Don Juan P. de Montalvan's *Aurora* translated, 1650; Europa (Cupid crucified, etc.), 1649; History of Chaldaic Philosophy, 1662; History of Philosophy, 1655-62; Poems, 1649; Psalterium Carolinum, 1657. His Life, by sir E. Brydges, 1814.

STAPLETON (*Augustus Granville*), 1800– . French Case (*The*), 1871 (showing how they were beguiled into the Prussian war); George Canning and his Times, 1859; Intervention and Non-intervention, 1866; Origin of Fenianism, 1868; Political Life of G. Canning, 1830; Real Monster Evil of Ireland (*The*), 1843.

STAPLETON, LL.D. (Sir *Robert*), died 1669. Translated *Juvenal*, 1647; *Musæus*, 1647; and Strada's *History of the Belgic War*, 1650.

STAPLETON, D.D. (*Thomas*), Henfield, in Sussex, defender of Philip of Spain!! 1535-1598. Antidota Apostolica, 1595; Apologia pro . . . Philippo II. Hispaniæ, 1592; Fortresse of the Faith planted in England, 1565; Life of Sir Thomas More, 1589; Tres Thomæ, 1588 (that is, Thomas the Apostle, Thomas Cranmer, and Thomas More).

STAUNTON (Sir *George Leonard*), Cargin, in Ireland, 1737-1801. Embassy to the Emperor of China, 1797. His Memoirs, by sir G. T. Staunton, 1823.

STAUNTON (Sir *George Thomas*), Salisbury, 1781-1859. Narrative of the Chinese Embassy to Kan Tourgouth, 1821; Penal Code of the Chinese Empire, 1810; Translated Mendoza's *History of China*, 1853.

STEAD (*William Thomas*), Embleton, in Northumberland, 1849– . Character Sketches, 1892; "General" Booth, 1891; If Christ came to Chicago, 1893; Labour War in the United States (*The*), 1894;

MaidenTribute (*The*), 1885; No Reduction, No Rent, 1886; Pope (*The*) and the New Era, 1889; Sketch of Josephine Butler, 1887; Story that transformed the World (*The*), 1890; Truth about the Navy (*The*), 1884; Truth about Russia (*The*), 1888. Founded *Review of Reviews*, 1890; is editing Library of Penny Poets, Novels and Prose Classics, begun 1895.

STEBBING, D.D. (*Henry*), the opponent of bishop Hoadly, died 1763. Christianity Justified, 1750; Polemical Tracts, 1727.

STEBBING, D.D. (*Henry*), 1799-1883. Christian Graces in the Olden Time, 1852; History of Chivalry and the Crusades, 1830; History of Christ's Universal Church in Primitive Times, 1845; History of the Church of Christ from the Reformation to the Eighteenth Century, 1839; History of the Reformation, 1836; Lives of the Italian Poets, 1831.

STEDMAN (*Edmund Clarence*), poet, etc., United States, 1833– . Alice of Monmouth, and other Poems, 1864; Blameless Prince (*The*), and other Poems, 1869; Complete Poetical Works, 1874; Edgar Allan Poe, 1880; Hawthorne, and other Poems, 1877; Lyrics and Idylls, 1879; Octavius Brooks Frothingham, 1876; Poetical Works, 1874; Poets of America, 1885; Star-bearer, 1888; Victorian Poets (*The*), 1875.

STEEL (*Flora Annie*). Flowers of Forgiveness, 1894; From the Five Rivers, 1893; Miss Stuart's Legacy, 1893; On the Face of the Waters, 1896; Potter's Thumb (*The*), 1894; Tales from the Punjab, 1894.

STEELE (Sir *Richard*), pseudonym "Isaac Bickerstaff," Dublin, 1671-1729. Christian Hero (*The*), in four parts, prose, 1701; Conscious Lovers (*The*), 1722, a comedy; Crisis (*The*), 1714, a pamphlet; Grief à-la-Mode, 1702, a comedy; Lying Lover (*The*), 1704, a comedy; Poetical Miscellanies, 1694; Tender Husband (*The*), 1703, a comedy.

  ∴ Began the *Tatler*, 1709; the *Spectator* (with Addison), 1711; the *Guardian*, 1713; and the *Englishman*, 1713. His Life, by Forster, 1859; Montgomery, 1865.

STEPHEN (Sir *George*), 1794-1879. Adventures of an Attorney in Search of Practice, 1839; Adventures of a Gentleman in Search of a Horse, 1840; Anti-Slavery Recollections, 1854; Digest of County-Court Cases, 1855; Juryman's Guide (*The*), 1845; Principles of Commerce and Commercial Law, 1853.

STEPHEN (*Henry John*), 1788-1864. New Commentaries on the Laws of England, 1848; Principles of Pleading in Civil Actions, 1830; Summary of Criminal Law, 1834.

STEPHEN (Sir *James*), Lambeth, London, 1789-1859. Essays on Ecclesiastical Biography, 1849; Lectures on the History of France, 1851. His Life, by his son, 1860.

STEPHEN (Sir *James Fitzjames*), London, 1829-1894. Digest of the Law of Evidence, 1876; Essays by a Barrister, 1862; General View of the Criminal Law of England, 1863; Horæ Sabbaticæ, 1892; Liberty, Equality, and Fraternity, 1873; Story of Nunamar (*The*), 1885. His Life, by his brother Leslie Stephen, 1895.

STEPHEN (*James Kenneth*). International Law, and International Relations, 1884 ; Lapsus Calami, 1891 ; Living Languages (*The*), 1891 ; Quo Musa Tendis, 1891.

STEPHEN (*Leslie*), 1832– . Agnostic's Apology (*An*), 1893 ; Dictionary of National Biography, i.-xxv., 1885–91; Essays on Free Thinking and Plain Speaking, 1873; History of English Thought in the Eighteenth Century, 1876; Hours in a Library, 1874–79 ; Life of Dr. Johnson, 1878 ; Life of Henry Fawcett, 1885 ; Life of James Fitzjames Stephen (his brother), 1895 ; Lives of Pope 1880, and Swift 1882 ; Playground of Europe, 1871; Science of Ethics (*The*), 1882 ; Works of Henry Fielding, 1882.

STEPHENS (*Alexander*), Elgin, in Scotland, 1757–1821. Annual Biography, 1817–21 ; Memoirs of John Horne Tooke, 1813 ; Public Characters, 1799–1808.

STEPHENS (Dr. *George*). Handbook of the Old Northern Runic Monuments of Scandinavia and England, 1884 ; Macbeth, etc., from the Rune-finds of Scandinavia, 1870 ; Queen Dagomar's Cross, 1863 ; Thunor the Thunderer, 1878.

STEPHENS (*Henry*), Keerpoy, in Bengal, 1795–1874. Book of the Farm (*The*), 1844 ; Drainage of Land (*The*), 1846 ; Yester Deep Land Culture (*The*), 1855.

STEPHENS (*James Francis*), Shoreham, in Sussex, 1792–1852. Illustrations of British Entomology, 1829 ; Manual of British Coleoptera, 1839 ; Nomenclature of British Insects, 1829 ; Systematic Catalogue of British Insects, 1829.

STEPHENS (*Walter*), London, 1832– . Blackfriars, or the Monks of Old, 1844 ; Vendetta, 1846, a drama.

STERLING (*John*), Bute Island, 1806-1844. Arthur Coningsby, 1830, a novel ; Election (*The*), 1841 ; Essays and Tales, 1848 ; Poems, 1839 ; Strafford, 1843, a tragedy. His Life, by archdeacon Hare, 1848 ; Thomas Carlyle, 1851.

STERNE (Rev. *Laurence*), pseudonym "Mr. Yorick," Clonmel, in Ireland, 1713–1768. History of a Warm Watchcoat, 1769 ; Letters, 1775, 1788, 1844, posthumous ; Sentimental Journey, 1768 (it was intended to be jottings of a tour though France and Italy, but he never reached Italy) ; Sermons of Mr. Yorick, 1760, 1766, 1769 ; Tristram Shandy, Gent., 1759-67, a novel. His Life, by Blanchard, 1857 ; Fitzgerald, 1860–64 ; Stapfer, 1878.

STERNHOLD (*Thomas*), Hampshire, died 1549. Metrical Version of the Psalms, 1549 (with Hopkins). These Psalms were at one time bound up with the Book of Common Prayer.

STERRY (Rev. *Peter*), died 1672. Discourse on the Freedom of the Will, 1675 ; Remains, 1710, posthumous ; Rise, Race, and Royalty of the Kingdom of God in the Soul of Man, 1683.

STEVENS (*George Alexander*), 1720-1784. Adventures of a Speculist, 1788 ; Law Cases, 1755 ; Lecture on Heads, 1753 ; Songs, Comic and Satirical, 1772 ; Tom Fool, 1760,

a farce Trip to Portsmouth (*A*), an operatic comedy.

STEVENSON (*John Hall*), the "Eugenius" of Sterne, 1718–1785. Crazy Tales, 1762 (once very popular).

STEVENSON (*Matthew*), Norfolk, seventeenth century. Bellum Presbyteriale, 1661 ; Florus Britannicus (from William I. to Charles II.), 1662 ; Norfolk Drollery, 1673, songs ; Occasion's Offspring, 1654, poems ; Poems, 1665, 1673 ; Twelve Moneths (*The*), 1661 ; Wits (*The*), 1685, poems and songs.

STEVENSON (*Robert Louis*), Edinburgh, 1850–1894. Across the Plains, 1892 ; Amateur Emigrant (*The*), 1883 (published originally in *Longman's Magazine*); Black Arrow (*The*), 1888 (published as a serial in *Young Folks*, 1883); Ballads, 1890; Catriona, 1893 ; Child's Garden of Verse (*A*), 1885 ; Dr. Jekyll and Mr. Hyde, 1886 ; Dynamiter (*The*): more new Arabian Nights, 1885 (with Mrs. Fanny van de Grift Stevenson) ; Ebb Tide (*The*), 1894 (with Lloyd Osbourne), (originally published in *To-day*, 1893-94) ; Edinburgh, Picturesque Notes, 1878 (first published in the *Portfolio*) ; Epilogue to an Inland Voyage, 1888 (in *Scribner*) ; Fables, 1897 ; Familiar Studies of Men and Books, 1882 ; Family of Engineers (*A*), 1896 (published in the new Edinburgh edition, vol. xviii., for the first time) ; Father Damien, 1890 ; Fleeming Jenkin (*Memoirs of*), 1887 ; Footnote to History (*A*) ; Inland Voyage (*An*), 1878 ; In the South Seas, 1891 (selected from a series published in *Black and White* partly, and fully in the *New York Sun*): Island Night's Entertainment (*An*), 1893 (published originally under the title of "Uma," 1891-93); Juvenilia, and other Papers (drawn from unpublished MSS. and various pamphlets, [reviews, and periodicals, first published in vol. xxi. Edinburgh edit., 1896); John Nicholson, 1887 (originally published in *Yuletide*, 1887) ; Kidnapped, 1886 ; Later Essays, 1895 (vol. xi. Edinburgh edit.) ; Lay Morals (first chapters of a projected treatise on Ethics, printed for the first time in vol. xxi. Edinburgh edit., 1896) ; Master of Ballantrae, 1889 (originally published in *Scribner*, 1888–89) ; Memories and Portraits, 1887 ; Merry Men (*The*), 1887 ; New Arabian Nights (*The*), 1882 ; Old and New Pacific Capitals, 1883 ; Prayers Written for Family Use at Vailima, 1896 (vol. xxi. Edinburgh edit.) ; Prince Otto, 1885 (in *Longman's Magazine*, 1885) ; Saint Ives, 1897 ; Silverado Squatters (*The*), 1883 ; Story of a Lie (*The*) (in the *New Quarterly Magazine*, 1879) ; Songs of Travel, 1896 ; Travels with a Donkey in the Cevennes, 1879 ; Treasure Island, 1883 (originally published as a serial in *Young Folks*, October, 1881, to January, 1882) ; Underwoods, 1887 ; Vailima Letters, 1896 ; Virginibus Puerisque, 1881 ; Weir of Hermiston, 1896 ; Wrecker (*The*), 1892 (with Lloyd Osbourne), (originally published in *Scribner*, 1891-92) ; Wrong Box (*The*), 1889 (with Lloyd Osbourne).

Moral Emblems, a collection of cuts and verses, issued about 1881 ; later on a third volume appeared, "The Graver and the Pen, or Scenes from Nature," with appropriate verse. Other little books appeared, all written by Stevenson and Lloyd Osbourne, illustrated mainly by Stevenson. See *The Studio* winter number, 1896–97, for most interesting article on "R. L. Stevenson, Illustrator," by Joseph Pennell.

STEWART, LL.D. (*Balfour*), Edinburgh, 1828–1887. Conservation of Energy, 1874; Lessons in Elementary Physics, 1871; Physics, 1872; Researches in Solar Physics (with De la Rue).

STEWART (*Dugald*), Edinburgh, 1753–1828. Elements of the Philosophy of the Human Mind, 1792–1827 (excellent); History of Ethical Philosophy, 1815, 1821; Lectures on Political Economy, 1855, posthumous; Life of Adam Smith, 1811; Life of Thomas Reid, D.D., 1803; Life of W. Robertson, D.D., 1801; Outlines of Moral Philosophy, 1793; Philosophical Essays, 1810; Philosophy of the Active and Moral Powers, 1828; Progress of Metaphysical . . . Philosophy, etc., 1815, 1821; View of the Active and Moral Powers, 1828. His Life, by sir W. Hamilton, 1855.

STEWART, D.D. (*Matthew*), Rothsay, in Scotland, 1717–1785. Geometrical Theorems, 1746; Tracts, Physical and Mathematical, 1761.

STIGAND (*William*), Devonport, in Devonshire, 1827–   . Athenais, or the First Crusade, 1866; Life, etc., of Heinrich Heine, 1875; Vision of Barbarossa (*A*), and other Poems, 1860.

STILL (*John*), bishop of Bath and Wells, 1543–1607. Gammer Gurton's Nedle, printed 1575 (our second comedy).

∴ Said to be written in 1551 by Mr. S., Master of Arts. If the date given is correct, it is plain that bishop Still was not the author, as he would have been under eight years of age at the time.

STILLINGFLEET (*Benjamin*), 1702–1771. Calendar of Flora (*The*), 1765; Principles and Power of Harmony, 1771; Tracts on Natural History, 1759. His Life, by Coxe, 1811.

STILLINGFLEET, D.D. (*Edward*), bishop of Worcester, born at Cranborne, in Dorsetshire, 1635–1699. Directions for the Conversations of the Clergy, 1710, posthumous; Irenicum, 1659 (his first publication); Miscellaneous Discourses, etc., 1735, posthumous; On the Amusements of Clergymen; Origines Britannicæ, 1685; Origines Sacræ (generally called "Stillingfleet's *Revealed Religion*"), 1662 (good); Rational . . . Grounds of the Protestant Religion, 1665; Reasons of Christ's Sufferings, 1678; Sermons, 1696–98; Unreasonableness of Separation, 1688; Vindication of the Doctrine of the Trinity, 1697. His Life, by T. Goodwin, 1710.

STIRLING, LL.D. (*James Hutchinson*), Glasgow, 1820–   . Address on Materialism, 1868; Philosophy of Law, etc. (*The*), 1873; Protoplasm, 1869; Schwegler's *History of Philosophy*, 1867; Secret of Hegel (*The*), 1865; Sir W. Hamilton on the *Philosophy of Perception*, 1865.

STIRLING (*Patrick James*), Dumblane, in

Scotland, 1809–   . Australian and Californian Gold Discoveries, 1852; Philosophy of Trade, 1846.

STIRLING (*William Alexander*, earl of), 1580–1640. Alexandrian (*The*), 1605, a tragedy; Aurora, 1604; Doomsday, 1614; Elegie on Prince Henrie, 1613; Julius Cæsar, 1607, a tragedy; Monarchicke Tragedies (*The*), 1604 (Crœsus, etc.); Paraenesis to Prince Henrie (*A*), 1604; Recreations with the Muses, 1637; Tragedy of Darius, 1603, published 1607.

STIRLING-MAXWELL (Sir *William*), Kenmure, in Scotland, 1818–1877. Cloister-life of Charles V., 1852; Velasquez and his Works, 1855.

STOCKDALE (Rev. *Percival*), 1736–1811. Autobiography, 1808; Lectures on the Eminent English Poets, 1807; Life of Waller (the poet), 1808.

STODDARD (*Richard Henry*), Hingham, U.S., 1825–   . Adventures in Fairyland, 1853; Anecdote Biography of Percy Bysshe Shelley, 1876; Book of the East (*The*), and other Poems, 1871; Century After (*A*), 1876; Children in the Wood, 1866; Female Poets of America, 1874; Footprints, 1849; Henry E. Longfellow, 1882; King's Bell (*The*), 1863; Late English Poets, 1865; Life of Alexander von Humboldt, 1859; Loves and Heroines of the Poets, 1860; Melodies and Madrigals, 1865; Memoir of Edgar Allan Poe, 1875; Poems, 1852–1880; Poets and Poetry of England (nineteenth century), 1875; Putnam the Brave, 1869; Songs of Summer, 1857; Story of Little Red Riding Hood, 1864; Town and Country, 1857; Under Green Leaves, 1865; William Bryant, 1879.

STORER (*James Sargant*), 1771–1853. Ancient Reliques, 1812; Antiquarian and Topographical Cabinet, 1806–1812 (500 views of objects of curiosity in Great Britain); Cathedrals of Great Britain, 1814–19 (much praised by Pugin); Fonthill Abbey, 1812; Graphic Description of Edinburgh, 1820.

STORER (*Thomas*), poet, died 1604. Wolsey, in Three Parts: his Aspiring, his Triumph, and his Death; 1599.

STORY, D.D. (*Robert Herbert*), Roseneath Manse, in Scotland, 1835–   . Christ the Consoler, 1864; Life of the Rev. Robert Story (his father), 1862; Manual of Scripture, with Hymns and Prayers, 1868; Memoirs of R. Lee, D.D., 1870; William Garstares, 1874.

STORY (*William Wetmore*), Salem, U.S., 1819–   . American Question (*The*), 1862; Graffiti d'Italia, 1869, poems; Life of Joseph Story (his father), 1851; Nero, 1875, an historical play; Phi Beta Kappa, 1844, a poem; Poems, 1847; Proportions of the Human Figure, 1866; Roba di Roma, 1863, in prose; Roman Lawyer in Jerusalem (*The*), 1870, a poem; Stephanie, 1877, a tragedy.

STOTHARD (*Charles Alfred*), London, 1786-1821. Death of Richard II., 1810; Monumental Effigies of Great Britain, 1811–23 (highly esteemed). His Memoirs, by his widow, 1823.

STOUGHTON, D.D. (*John*), Norwich, 1807- .
Ages of Christendom, 1856; Church and
State Two Hundred Years Ago, 1862;
Ecclesiastical History of England (*The*),
1867–74; Footprints of Italian Reformers,
1881; Haunts and Homes of Martin Luther
(*The*), 1875; Lights and Shadows of Church
Life, 1895; Lights of the World (*The*), 1876;
Our English Bible, 1878; Progress of Divine
Revelation (*The*), 1878; Religion in Eng-
land from the Long Parliament to the
Eighteenth Century, 1881; from 1800 to 1850,
1884; Spanish Reformer (*The*), 1884; Spiri-
tual Heroes, 1848; William Penn, 1882;
Windsor in the Olden Time, 1844.
STOW (*John*), London, 1525–1605. Annales
of England, 1580; Flores Historiarum,
1606; Successions of the History of
England, 1638; Summarie of Englysh
Chronicles, 1561; Survay of London, 1598
(his chief work). His Life, by Strype, and
by W. J. Thoms, 1842.'
STOWE. See BEECHER-STOWE.
STRADLING (Sir *John*), contemporary with
Shakespeare. Beati Pacifici, 1623, a poem;
De Vita et Morte Contemnenda, 1597; Divine
Poems (in seven classes), 1625; Epigrammatum, libri iv. 1607.
STRATFORD DE REDCLIFFE (*Stratford Canning*, viscount), London, 1788–1880. Alfred
the Great in Athelney, 1876, a tragedy; Why
am I a Christian? 1873.
STREET, R.A. (*George Edmund*), Woodford,
in Essex, 1824–1881. Brick and Marble Architecture of North Italy in the Middle Ages,
1855; Gothic Architecture in Spain, 1865.
STRETTON (*Hesba*), i.e. *Sarah Smith*. She
writes tales for young people.
STRICKLAND (*Agnes*), Reydon Hall, in Suffolk,
1806–1874. Alda, the British Captive, 1841,
a novel; Broken Heart (*The*), 1835; De-
metrius, 1833, a poem in three cantos; Floral
Sketches, and other Poems, 1836; Guthred,
1875; Historical Tales of Illustrious British
Children, 1847; Historic Scenes and Poetic
Fancies, 1850; How will it End? 1865, a
novel; Life of Mary Queen of Scots, 1873;
Lives of the Bachelor Kings of England,
1861; Lives of the Last Four Princesses of
the Royal House of Stuart, 1872; Lives of
the Queens of England, 1840–48 (her great
work); Lives of the Queens of Scotland, etc.,
1850–59; Lives of the Seven Bishops, 1866;
Old Friends and New Acquaintances (in
two series), 1860–61; Patriotic Songs, 1825
(with her sister Susanna); Pilgrims of
Walsingham, 1835, an historical romance;
Rival Crusoes (*The*), 1834, a tale; Royal
Brothers (*The*), 1875; Seaside Offering
(*The*), 1856; Seven Ages of Woman (*The*),
and other Poems, 1827; Tales and Stories
from History, 1836; Worcester Field, or the
Cavalier, 1826, a poem in four cantos.
STRICKLAND (*Hugh Edwin*), Yorkshire,
1811–1853. Dodo and its Kindred (*The*), 1848.
STRUTHERS (*John*), 1776–1853. Deckmont,
1836; History of Scotland since the Union,
1828, prose; Peasant's Death (*The*), 1806;
Plough (*The*), 1816; Poems, Moral and
Religious, 1814; Poor Man's Sabbath (*The*),
1804; Winter's Day (*The*), 1811.

STRUTT (*Jacob George*), *-*. Deliciæ Sylvarum, 1828 (the romantic forest scenery of
Great Britain); Sylva Britannica, 1826
(excellent).
STRUTT (*Joseph*), Springfield, in Essex, 1742–
1802. Ancient Times, 1808, posthumous;
Biographical Dictionary of Engravers, 1785–
86; Bumpkin's Disaster, 1808, posthumous;
Chronicle of England, from the Landing of
Cæsar to the Conquest (*The*), 1777–78; Complete View of the Manners, Customs, Arms,
etc., of the English, 1774–76; Complete
View of the Dress and Habits of the English,
1796–99; Queenhoo Hall, 1808, posthumous,
a romance; Regal and Ecclesiastical Antiquities of England, 1773; Sports and
Pastimes of the People of England, 1801
(his best-known work); Test of Guilt, 1808,
posthumous, a dramatic tale.
STRYPE (*John*), London, 1643–1737. Annals
of the Reformation, 1709–31; Ecclesiastical
Memorials, 1721–33; Life of Bishop Aylmer,
1701; Life of Sir John Cheke, 1705; Life of
Sir Thomas Smith, 1698; Lives of Archbishops Grindall 1710, Parker 1711, Whitgift
1718; Memorials of Thomas Cranmer, 1694.
STUART, LL.D. (*Gilbert*), Edinburgh, 1742–
1786. History of Scotland, 1782; View of
Society in Europe, 1778.
STUART (*James*), called "Athenian Stuart,"
London, 1713–1788. Antiquities of Athens,
1762–1815 (with Revett), (excellent)
STUART (*James*), "of Duncarn," 1776–1849.
Three Years in North America, 1833.
STUART (*Moses*), Wilton, in Connecticut, U.S.,
1780–1852. Commentary on the Apocalypse,
1845; Commentary on the Book of Proverbs,
1852; Commentary on Ecclesiastes, 1851;
Commentary on the Epistle to the Hebrews,
1827–28 (masterly); Commentary on the
Episle to the Romans, 1832; Elements of
Biblical Criticism, etc., 1827; Grammar of
the New Testament Dialect, 1834; Hebrew
Chrestomathy, 1832; Hebrew Grammar,
1813, 1821; Hints on the Interpretation of
Prophecy, 1842.
STUART-WORTLEY (Lady *Emmeline*), 1806–
1855. Etcetera, 1853; Portugal and Madeira,
1854; Travels in the United States, 1851.
STUBBES (*Philip*), died 1592. Anatomie of
Abuses, 1583 (very popular); Christall Glasse
for Christian Women, 1592; Motive to Good
Works, 1592, posthumous; Perfect Path to
Felicitie (*The*), 1592; Rosarie of Christian
Praiers, 1583; Theatre of the Pope's
Monarchie (*The*), 1584; Two Judgments of
God, 1581; View of Vanitie, etc. (*A*), 1582.¶
STUBBS, D.D. (*Charles William*), Liverpool,
1845- . Christ and Democracy, 1883;
Christ and Economics, 1893; Church in the
Villages (*The*), 1887; Conscience (*The*), and
other Poems, 1884; For Christ and City,
1890; Glebe Allotments, 1880; God's
Englishmen, 1887; International Morality,
1869; Land (*The*) and the Labourers,
1884; Mythe of Life (*The*), 1880; Urgent
Questions, 1888; Village Politics, 1878.
STUBBS (*George*), Liverpool, 1724–1806.
Anatomy of the Horse, 1786.
STUBBS (*John*), 1541–1599. Discovery of a
Gaping Gulf, 1579.

STUBBS, D.D. (*William*), bishop of Oxford, Knaresborough, in Yorkshire, 1825– . Constitutional History of England, 1874–78; Early Plantagenets (*The*), 1876; Memorials of St. Dunstan, 1874; Registrum Sacrum Anglicanum, 1858; Seventeen Lectures on Church History, 1887.

∴ He has edited several historical and other works; and the *Gesta Regum* of William of Malmesbury, one of the "Rolls Series," 1887–89.

STUKELEY, M.D. (*William*), Holbeach, in Lincolnshire, 1687–1765. Abury, 1743; Centuria, 1776; Itinerarium Curiosum, 1724; Medallic History of Carausius, 1757–1759; Palæographia Britannica, 1743–52; Palæographia Sacra, 1736–63; Richard of Cirencester, 1757; Stonehenge, 1740.

STURGEON (*William*), Lancashire, 1783–1850. Experimental Researches in Electro-Magnetism, 1830.

SUCKLING (Sir *John*), Whitton, in Middlesex, 1609–1641. Account of Religion by Reason (*An*); Aglaura, 1637, a tragi-comedy; Brennoralt, a tragedy; Four Plays, 1646, posthumous; Goblins (*The*), 1636, a comedy; Session of the Poets (*A*), 1636, a satire; Songs and Ballads (that called "The Wedding" contains the exquisite verse—

Her feet beneath her petticoat,
Like little mice, stole in and out,
As if they feared the light;
But oh! she dances such a way,
No sun upon an Easter day
Is half so fine a sight).

∴ All compiled and published in 1770. His Memoirs, by the Rev. A. Suckling, 1836.

SUGDEN (*Edward Burtenshaw*, baron St. Leonard's), 1781–1875. Handybook of Property Law, 1849; Law of Vendors and Purchasers, 1830; Real Property Statutes, 1852.

SULLIVAN, Mus.D. (*Arthur*), 1844– . He composed the music of *Box and Cox*; *The Light of the World*; *H.M.S. Pinafore*, 1878; *The Prodigal Son*; *Pygmalion and Galatea*, 1871; Shakespeare's *Tempest*; *Trial by Jury*, 1875; *The Sorcerer*, etc. See GILBERT.

SULLIVAN (*William*), Maine, U.S., 1774–1839. Historical Causes and Effects, 1838; Public Men of the Revolution, 1847.

SULLY, LL.D. (*James*), Bridgwater, 1842– . Human Mind (*The*), 1892; Illusions, 1881; Outlines of Psychology, 1884; Pessimism, 1877; Sensation and Intuition, 1874; Teacher's Handbook of Psychology, 1886.

SUMNER, D.D. (*Charles Richard*), bishop of Winchester, 1790–1874. Ministerial Character of Christ (*The*), 1822. His Life, by the Rev. G. H. Sumner, 1876.

SUMNER, D.D. (*John Bird*), archbishop of Canterbury, 1780–1862. Apostolic Preaching, 1815; Evidences of Christianity, 1824; Practical Exposition of the Gospels, etc., 1833–40; Practical Reflections, 1859; Records of Creation, 1816; Sermons on Christian Charity, 1841; Sermons on the Christian Faith, etc., 1821; Sermons on the Church Festivals, 1817.

SUTCLIFFE, D.D. (*Matthew*), died 1629. De Presbyterio, 1591; De Vera Christi Ecclesia, 1600; Ecclesiastical Discipline, 1591.

SWAIN (*Charles*), Manchester, 1803–1874. Art and Fashion, 1863; Dramatic Chapters, Poems, and Songs, 1847; Dryburgh Abbey (an elegy on sir W. Scott), 1834; English Melodies, 1849; Letters of Laura d'Auverne, and other Poems, 1853; Metrical Essays, 1827; Mind (*The*), and other Poems, 1831; Songs and Ballads, 1868.

SWAINSON (*William*), 1789–1855. Animals in Menageries, 1838; Birds of Western Africa, 1844; Exotic Conchology, 1841; Fauna Boreali Americana, 1829; Fly-Catchers, 1854; Geography and Classification of Animals, 1835; Habits and Instincts of Animals, 1839; History of Insects, 1841; Malacology, or Shells and Shellfish, 1840; Natural History of Birds, 1836–37; Natural History of Fishes and Reptiles, 1835; Natural History of Quadrupeds, 1835; Naturalist's Guide (*The*), 1822; Ornithological Drawings, 1841; Preliminary Discourse on the Study of Natural History, 1834; Taxidermy, with the Biography of Zoologists, 1840; Zoological Illustrations, 1820–33.

SWEET (*Robert*), nineteenth century. Botanical Cultivator, etc. (*The*), 1821; British Flower Garden (*The*), 1823–38; British Warblers (*The*), 1823; Cistineæ, or Natural History of the Rock Rose, 1825–30; Flora Australasiæ, 1827–32; Geraniaceæ, or Natural History of Gerania, 1820–30; Hortus Britannicus, 1827; Hortus Suburbanus Londonensis, 1818; Hothouse and Greenhouse Manual (*The*), 1823.

SWIFT, D.D. (*Jonathan*), Dublin, 1667–1745. Arguments against the Abolition of Christianity, 1708, a satire; Battle of the Books, 1704, a burlesque allegory; Baucis and Philemon (a poem on two yew-trees), 1710; Bella Punica, or the Art of Punning, 1719; Cadenus and Vanessa, 1713, in verse; City Shower described, 1710, in verse; Conduct of the Allies (*The*), 1712; Directions to Servants, 1729, a satire; Drapier's Letters (against Wood's halfpence, etc.), 1724; Gulliver's Travels, 1726, satirical tales; History of the Last Four Years of Queen Anne, 1728; Law, a Bottomless Pit, 1712; Meditations on a Broomstick, 1710; Polite Conversation, 1738; Predictions of Isaac Bickerstaff, 1708, a *jeu d'esprit*; Public Spirit of the Whigs (*The*), 1714; Riddles (26 in number, in verse), 1724; Stella (*To*), seven birthday odes, 1720–26; Tale of a Tub (satire on Calvin, Luther, and the pope), 1704; Trip to Dunkirk (*A*), 1708. His Life, by John Boyle, earl of Orrery, 1751; D. Swift, 1753; John Hawkesworth, 1755; T. Dilworth, 1760; Johnson, in his *Lives of the Poets*, 1779–81; T. Sheridan, 1784; John Berkeley, 1789; Madame Montmorency, 1800; John Barrett, D.D., 1808; sir W. Scott, 1814; T. Roscoe, 1848; J. Forster, 1876, unfinished; H. Craik, 1881. Mrs. Lætitia Pilkinton's *Memoirs*, by herself, contain numerous anecdotes of dean Swift, 1748.

SWINBURNE (*Algernon Charles*), London,

1843- . Astrophel, etc., 1894; Atalanta in Calydon, 1865; Blake (*William*), 1868; Bothwell, 1874; Century (*A*) of Roundels, 1883; Charlotte Brontë (*A Note on*), 1877; Chastelard, 1865; Dead Love, 1864; Erechtheus, 1876; Essays and Studies, 1875; George Chapman, 1875; Heptalogia (*The*), or The Seven against Sense, 1880; Laus Veneris, 1866; Locrine, 1887; Marino Faliero, 1885; Mary Stuart, 1881; Midsummer Holiday (*A*), 1884; Miscellanies, 1886; Note of an English Republican on the Muscovite Crusade, 1876; Notes on Poems and Reviews, 1866; Ode on the Proclamation of the French Republic, 1870; Poems and Ballads, first series 1866, second series 1878, third series 1889; Queen Mother (*The*) and Rosamond, 1860; Selections from Mr. Swinburne's Poems, 1887; Sisters (*The*), 1892; Song (*A*) of Italy, 1867; Songs before Sunrise, 1871; Songs of the Springtides, 1880; Songs of Two Nations, 1875; Study (*A*) of Ben Jonson, 1889; Study (*A*) of Shakespeare, 1880; Study (*A*) of Victor Hugo, 1886; Studies in Prose and Poetry, 1894; Studies in Song, 1880; Tale (*The*) of Balen, 1896; Tristram of Lyonesse, etc., 1882; Under the Microscope, 1872; Word (*A*) for the Navy, 1887.

SWINBURNE (*Henry*), 1752–1803. Courts of Europe at the Close of the Eighteenth Century, 1841, posthumous; Travels in the Two Sicilies, 1783-85; Travels through Spain, 1779.

SWINDEN (*Henry*), *-*. History and Antiquities of Yarmouth in Norfolk, 1778.

SWINDEN (Rev. *Tobias*), died 1720. On the Nature and Place of Hell, 1727.

SYKES, D.D. (*Arthur Ashley*), London, 1684-1756. Case of Subscription to the "Articles" considered, 1721; Credibility of Miracles, etc., 1742; Essay on the Truth of the Christian Religion, 1725; Examination of Newton's Chronology, 1744; Innocence of Error asserted, 1715; Inquiry on the Meaning of Demoniacs, 1737; Nature, Design, and Origin of Sacrifices, 1748; Paraphrase, etc., of the Epistle to the Hebrews, 1755; Principles and Connexion of Natural and Revealed Religion, 1740. His Life, by J. Disney, D.D., 1785.

SYLVESTER (*Joshua*), surnamed "Silvertongued," 1563-1618. Lachrymæ Lachrymarum (lament on the death of prince Henry), 1612; Maiden's Blush (*The*), 1620 (Joseph); Monodia, 1594; Parliament of Vertues Royal, 1614, poetry, second series, 1620; Poems against Tobacco, 1672; Tobacco battered and the Pipes shattered, 1615, a poem; Translation of Du Bartas's *Week of Creation*, and *The Second Week* (New Testament History), to which Milton is indebted; Woodman's Bear (*The*), 1620, a poem.

SYME (*James*), of Scotland, 1799-1870. Contributions to Pathology and Practice of Surgery, 1847; Excision of Diseased Joints, 1831; Principles of Surgery, 1832.

SYMMONS, D.D. (*Charles*), Cardigan, in Wales, 1749-1826. Life of Milton, 1806; Poems, 1813; Translated the *Æneid* of Virgil, 1817.

SYMONDS, M.D. (*John Addington*), Oxford, 1807-1871. Miscellanies, 1871; Principles of Beauty, 1857.

SYMONDS (*John Addington*), 1840-1893. Animi Figuræ, 1882; Ben Jonson, 1886; Blank Verse, 1894; Brown (*Horatio F.*), Life of, 1895; Essays, 1890; Giovanni Boccaccio as Man and Author, 1894; In the Key of Blue, 1893; Introduction to the Study of Dante, 1872; Italian Byeways, 1883; Many Moods, 1878; Michael Angelo (*Life of*), 1892; New and Old, 1880; Our Life in the Swiss Highlands, 1892; Renaissance in Italy (*The*), 1875, 1877, 1881, 1886; Shakespeare's Predecessors, 1884; Shelley, 1878; Short History of the Renaissance in Italy (*A*), taken from the work of J. A. Symonds, by lieut.-col. Alfred Pearson; Sir Philip Sidney, 1886; Sketches and Studies in Italy, 1879; Sketches in Italy and Greece, 1874; Sonnets of Michael Angelo Buonarotti, etc., 1878; Studies of the Greek Poets, 1873-76; (Translated) Life of Benvenuto Cellini, 1887; Vagabunduli Libellus, 1884; Walt Whitman, 1893; Wine, Woman, and Song, 1884.

SYMONS (*Arthur*). Milford Haven, in Pembroke, Wales, 1865- . Editor of *The Savoy*. Amoris Victima, 1897; Days and Nights, 1888; Introduction to the Study of Browning, 1886; London Nights, 1895; Silhouettes, 1892.

TAINE (*Hippolyte Adolphe*), Vouzieres, Ardennes, 1828-1893. History of English Literature, 1864.

TAIT, D.D. (*Archibald Campbell*), archbishop of Canterbury, Edinburgh, 1813-1882. Dangers and Safeguards of Modern Theology, 1861; Harmony of Revelation and the Sciences, 1864; Present Position of the Church of England, 1872; Word of God (*The*), and the Ground of Faith, 1863.

TALBOT (*Matthew*), *-*. Analysis of the Holy Bible, 1800 (excellent).

TALBOT (*William Henry Fox*), Locock Abbey, in Wiltshire, inventor of talbotype, 1800-1877. English Etymologies, 1853; Hermes, or Classical and Antiquarian Researches, 1850; Illustrations of the Book of Genesis, 1852; Legendary Tales; Pencil of Nature, 1844.

TALFOURD (Sir *Thomas Noon*), Doxey, in Staffordshire, 1795-1854. Athenian Captive (*The*), 1838, a tragedy; Castilian (*The*), 1853, a tragedy; Final Memorials of Charles Lamb, 1849-50; Glencoe, etc., 1839, a tragedy; Ion, 1835, a tragedy; Recollections of a First Visit to the Alps, 1841; Vacation Rambles and Thoughts, 1844, Supplement 1846.

TALLIS (*Thomas*), called "The Chaucer of Cathedral Quires," 1529-1585. Cantiones Sacræ, 1575 (with Bird).

TANNER, D.D. (*Thomas*), bishop of St. Asaph, born at Market Lavington, in Wiltshire, 1674-1735. Bibliotheca Britannico-Hibernica, 1748, posthumous; Notitia Monastica, 1695 (admirable).

TARLTON (*Richard*), Shropshire, jester, died

1588. Newes out of Purgatorie, 1630, posthumous; Seven Deadly Sins (*The*), a comedy (lost); Tarlton's Jests (in three parts), 1611, posthumous.

TATE (*Nahum*), Dublin, poet laureate, who succeeded Shadwell ! ! 1652–1715. (Tate wrote ten dramas.) Brutus of Alva, a drama; Characters of Virtue and Vice, 1691; Elegies, 1699; Injured Love, a drama; Innocent Epicure (*The*), 1697, a poem on angling; Loyal General (*The*), a drama; Memorials for the Learned, 1686; Miscellanea Sacra, 1698; Panacea, a poem on tea; Psalms turned into Rhyme, 1696 (with Brady; these supplanted the rhyming psalms of Sternhold and Hopkins); Poems, 1677; Richard II., a drama.

N.B.—Pope says of him, His

. . . fustian is so sublimely bad,
It is not poetry, but prose run mad.

Yet Dryden allowed him to write the second part of his unrivalled satire of *Absalom and Achitophel*, and showed his approval by adding a few lines here and there. His (and Brady's) Psalms were bound up with the Book of Common Prayer, and used as late as 1850.

TATHAM (*John*), city-laureate, 1609–1672. Distressed State (*The*), 1641, a tragedy; Fancies Theater, 1640, poems, epigrams, etc.; Knavery in All Trades, 1664, a comedy; Love Crowns the End, 1657, a tragi-comedy; Ostella, or the Faction of Love and Beauty reconciled, 1650; Rump (*The*), 1660, a comedy; Scots Figaries (*The*), 1652, a comedy; "Triumphs," arranged for the Lord Mayor's day from 1657 to 1664.

TAYLER (Rev. *John James*), Nottingham, 1798–1869. Attempt to ascertain the Character of the Four Gospels, 1867; Christian Aspects of Faith and Duty, 1851; Retrospect of the Religious Life of England, 1845.

TAYLOR, M.D. (*Alfred Swaine*), Northfleet, in Kent, 1806–1880. Elements of Chemistry, 1831 (with Brande); Elements of Medical Jurisprudence, 1838; Manual of Medical Jurisprudence, 1844; Principle and Practice of Medical Jurisprudence, 1865.

TAYLOR (*Ann*), afterwards Mrs. *Gilbert*, sister of Isaac and Jane Taylor, and daughter of the Rev. Isaac Taylor, of Ongar, 1782–1866. Original Poems, 1806 (with her sister Jane). Memorials, by Josiah Gilbert, 1874.

TAYLOR (*Bayard*), Kennett Square, Chester, U.S., 1825–1878. At Home and Abroad, 1859, 1862, a sketch of life, scenery, and men; Beauty and the Beast, 1872; Book of Romances, Lyrics, and Songs, 1851; Boys of Other Countries, 1876; Byeways of Europe (*The*), 1869; Diversions of the Echo Club, burlesques of modern authors; Dramatic Works, 1889; Egypt and Iceland in 1874; El Dorado, or Adventures in the Path of Empire, 1850; Essays on German Literature, 1880; Home Pastorals, and other Poems, 1875; Illustrated Library of Travel, 1872–74; John Godfrey's Fortunes, 1864, a novel; Joseph and his Friend, 1870; Journey to Central Africa, etc., 1853; Lands of the Saracen (*The*), 1854; Laro, 1873; Lyrics of

the War of Secession, 1865; Masque of the Gods (*The*), 1872, a poem; National Ode (*The*), 1876; Northern Travel, or Summer and Winter Pictures of Sweden, Denmark, and Lapland, 1856; Poems of Home and Travel, 1855; Poems of the Orient, 1854; Poetical Works, 1880; Poet's Journal (*The*), 1862, a novel of American life; Prince Deukalion, 1879, a drama; Prophet (*The*), 1874, a tragedy; Rhimes of Travel, Ballads, and other Poems, 1848; School History of Germany, 1871; Story of Kennet (*The*), 1866, a tale; Studies in German Literature, 1879; Travels in Greece and Russia, etc., 1857; Views Afoot, or Europe seen with Knapsack and Staff, 1846; Visit to India, China, Japan, etc., 1855; Voyage to California, 1850; Ximena, and other Poems, 1844.

TAYLOR, LL.D. (*Brook*), Edmonton, in Middlesex, 1685–1731. Linear Perspective, 1719; Method of Approximation to the Roots of Equations, 1717; Methodus Incrementorum, 1715 (Taylor's theorem); New Principles of Linear Perspective, 1719.

TAYLOR (Sir *Henry*), Wilton Hall, Durham, 1800–1886. Autobiography of Henry Taylor, 1885; Correspondence of Henry Taylor, 1888; Edwin the Fair, 1842, an historic play; Eve of the Conquest (*The*), and other Poems, 1847; Isaac Comnenus, 1827, a play in verse; Notes from Books, 1849; Notes from Life, 1847; Philip van Artevelde, 1834, a dramatic romance; St. Clement's Eve, 1862, a drama; Sicilian Summer (*A*), 1850, a comedy; Statesman (*The*), in prose, 1836; Virgin Widow (*The*), 1854, a comedy; Way of the Rich and Great (*The*), 1852; Works, 1877.

TAYLOR (Rev. *Isaac*), of Ongar, father of Isaac and Jeffereys, Ann and Jane Taylor, died 1829. Advice to the Teens, 1828; Beginnings of European Biography, 1828–29; Bunyan explained to a Child, 1824; Character Essential to Success in Life, 1820; Scenes in Africa and America 1821, in England 1829, in Europe 1829, in Foreign Lands 1829; Scenes of British Wealth 1826, of Commerce by Land and Sea 1830; Self-Cultivation recommended, 1818.

TAYLOR (Mrs. *Isaac*), of Ongar, wife of the preceding, maiden name *Ann* ——, died 1830. Advice to Mothers, 1814; Family Mansion (*The*), 1819, a tale; Itinerary of a Traveller in the Wilderness, 1825; Maternal Solicitude, etc., 1816 (her best); Practical Hints on the Duties of Wives, etc., 1815; Reciprocal Duties of Parents and Children, 1818; Retrospection, 1820, a tale.

TAYLOR (*Isaac*), brother of Jeffereys, Ann, and Jane Taylor, and son of the Rev. Isaac Taylor, of Ongar, born at Lavenham, in Suffolk, 1787–1865. Ancient Christianity v. the Tracts for the Times, 1839–40; Characters of Theophrastus (with his own etchings), 1824; Elements of Thought (*The*), 1822–27; History of the Transmission of Ancient Books, 1827; Home Education, 1838; Lectures on Spiritual Christianity, 1841; Logic of Theology, 1849; Loyola and Jesuitism, 1849; Man Responsible for his Dispositions, 1840; Memoirs of Jane Taylor (his sister), 1825;

Natural History of Enthusiasm, 1829 (his best work); Natural History of Fanaticism, 1833; New Model of Christian Missions, 1829; Physical Theory of Another Life, 1836; Process of Historical Proof, 1828; Restoration of Belief, 1855; Saturday Evening, 1832; Spirit of Hebrew Poetry, 1860; Spiritual Despotism, 1835; Temple of Melekartha, 1831; Translation of *Herodotus*, 1829; Ultimate Civilization, 1860; Wesley and Methodism, 1851; World of Mind (*The*), 1857. Memorials of the Taylor family, of Ongar, by canon Taylor, 1867.

TAYLOR (Rev. *Isaac*), generally called "Canon Taylor," son of the preceding, and grandson of the Rev. Isaac Taylor of Ongar, 1829–   . Alphabet (*The*), 1883; Etruscan Languages, 1876; Etruscan Researches, 1874; Family Pen (*The*), memoirs of the family, 1867; Greeks and Goths, 1879; Leaves from an Egyptian Note-book, 1888; Manx Runes (*The*), 1886; Names and their Histories, 1896; Origin of the Aryan Family, 1890; Words and Places, 1865 (his speciality).

TAYLOR (*Jane*), sister of Isaac, Jeffereys, and Ann Taylor, and daughter of the Rev. Isaac Taylor, of Ongar, born in London, 1783–1824. Contributions to Q. Q. to the *Youth's Magazine*, 1824; Correspondence, 1825, posthumous; Display, 1815, a tale; Essays in Rhyme, 1816; Hymns for Infant Minds, 1818 (her best production); Poems for Infant Minds, 1806 (with her sister Ann); Rhymes for the Nursery, 1807. Her Memoirs, by Isaac Taylor, her brother, 1825.

TAYLOR (*Jeffereys*), brother of Isaac (not the canon), Ann, and Jane Taylor, and son of the Rev. Isaac Taylor, of Ongar, *-*. Æsop in Rhyme, 1822; Barn (*The*) and the Steeple, 1834; Earth as a Residence for Man (*The*), 1832; Farm (*The*), or Rural Toil and Produce, 1834; Forest (*The*), or History of Trees, 1834; Old English Sayings, 1827; Parlour Commentaries on the Laws of England, 1825; Ralph Richards, the Miser (no date); Tales in Prose and Verse, 1822; Young Islander (*The*), 1841, a tale.

TAYLOR, D.D. (*Jeremy*), bishop of Down and Connor, called "The Modern Chrysostom," born at Cambridge, 1613–1667. Baptism, its Institutions and Efficacy, 1652; Catechism, and Exposition of the Creed, 1652; Clerus Domini, 1651; Deus Justificatus (on original sin), 1656; Discourses concerning Extempore Prayers, 1646; Dissuasive from Popery (*A*), 1647; Ductor Dubitantium, 1660 (his most famous discourse); Episcopacy a Divine Institution, 1642; Friendship, its Measures and Offices, 1657; Golden Grove (*The*), 1655; Grammar, 1647; Great Exemplar (*The*), 1649; Guide of Infant Devotion, or the Golden Grove, 1655; Holy Living and Dying, 1651 (well-known); Liberty of Prophesying, 1647; Life of Christ, 1650 (popular); Martyrdom of King Charles (*The*), 1649; Polemical and Moral Discourses, 1657; Prayers before and after Sermon, 1651; Psalter, with Titles and Collects, 1644; Real Presence (*The*), 1654; Rules and Advice given to the Clergy,

1661; Sermons for the Year, 1651–53; Sermons on Gunpowder Treason, 1638; Unum Necessarium (repentance), 1655; Worthy Communicant (*The*), 1660. His Life, by Wheeldon, 1793; Rev. K. Bonney, 1815; bishop Heber, 1822; Hughes, 1831; Croly and Stebbing, 1834; Rev. R. A. Wilmott, 1847; Rogers, 1851; Duychinck, 1860.

TAYLOR (*John*), Gloucester, "The Water Poet," 1580–1654. Penniless Pilgrimage, 1618; Praise of Hempseed (*The*), 1623; Travels in Germany, 1617.

TAYLOR, D.D. (*John*), Lancashire, 1694–1761. Hebrew-English Concordance, 1754–57 (very valuable to Hebrew students); Key to the Apostolic Writings (*A*), 1805, posthumous; Paraphrase, etc., on the Epistle to the Romans, 1745; Scripture Doctrine of the Atonement, 1750; Scripture Doctrine of Original Sin, 1740.

TAYLOR, LL.D. (*John*), Shrewsbury, 1704–1766. De Debitore Dissecando, 1742 (excellent); Elements of Civil Law, 1755.

TAYLOR (*Joseph*), *-*. English and Hindoostanee Dictionary, 1808.

TAYLOR (*Richard*), 1789–1851. Index Monasticus, 1821.

TAYLOR (*Robert*), contemporary with Shakespeare. Hogge hath lost his Pearle (*The*), 1614, a comedy; Sacred Hymns, 1615.

TAYLOR (Rev. *Robert*), nineteenth century. Devil's Pulpit (*The*), 1831 (the sale was prohibited, and all copies not in circulation destroyed); Diegesis (the early history of Christianity), 1833.

TAYLOR (*Silas*), Shropshire, 1624–1678. History of Gavelkind, 1663.

TAYLOR (*Thomas*), "The Platonist," London, 1758–1835. Arguments of the Emperor Julian against the Christians, 1809; Elements of a New Arithmetical Notation, 1823; Elements of a New Method of Reasoning in Geometry, 1780; Elements of the True Arithmetic of Infinities, 1809; History of the Restoration of the Platonic Theology; On the Eleusinian and Bacchic Mysteries, 1791; On Nullities and Diverging Series, 1801; On the Philosophy of Aristotle, 1812; Theoretic Arithmetic. *Translated:* Apuleius, Arsitotle, Hierocles, Iamblicus, Julian, Maximus Tyrius, Pausanias, Plato, Plotinus, Porphyry, Sallust, etc.

TAYLOR (*Tom*), (editor of *Punch* 1874–80), Sunderland, in Cumberland, dramatist, 1817–1880. Anne Boleyn, 1876, an historic play; Arkwright's Wife, 1873, an historic play; Babes in the Wood (*The*), 1860; Barefaced Impostors, 1854 (joint author); Blighted Being (*A*), 1854; Clancarty, 1873, an historic play; Contested Election (*The*), 1859; Diogenes and his Lantern, 1849; Fool's Revenge (*The*), 1859, an historic play; Going to the Bad, 1858; Harlequin Columbus, 1853; Helping Hands, 1855; Henry Dunbar, 1865; Hidden Hand (*The*), 1864; Historical Plays, 1877; House or the Home (*The*), 1859; Jeanne d'Arc, 1871, an historic play; King's Rival, 1854 (joint author); Lady Clancarty, 1873; Little Red Riding Hood, 1851; Masks and Faces, 1852 (joint author); New Men and Old Acres, 1869 (joint author); Nice Firm (*A*), 1853; Nine Points of the Law, 1859; Our American Cousin, 1858; Our Clerks, 1852; Overland Route (*The*), 1860; Payable on Demand, 1859; Philosopher's Stone (*The*), 1850; Plot and Passion, 1852 (joint author); Prince Dorus, 1850; Retribution, 1856 (joint author); Sense and Sensation, 1864; Serf (*The*), 1864; Settling Day, 1865; Sheep in Wolf's Clothing (*A*), 1857; Sir Roger de Coverley, 1851; Sister's Penance, 1866 (joint author); Slave Life, 1852 (joint author); Still Waters Run Deep, 1855; Tale of Two Cities (*A*), 1860 (from Dickens); Ticket of Leave Man (*The*), 1863; To oblige Benson, 1854; To Parents and Guardians, 1846; Trip to Kissengen (*A*), 1844; 'Twixt Axe and Crown, 1870, an historic play; Two Loves and a Life, 1854 (joint author); Unequal Match (*An*), 1857; Up at the Hills, 1860; Vicar of Wakefield, 1850; Victims, 1856; Webster at Home, 1853 (joint author); Wittikind and his Brothers, 1852. His plays were published in two vols.; the first (December, 1854) contains nearly all his early ones.

Not Dramatic Works: Autobiography of Haydon, 1853; Autobiography of Leslie, R.A., 1860; Leicester Square, 1874; Life and Times of Sir J. Reynolds, 1865; Local Government Acts, 1858; Songs and Ballads of Brittany, 1865.

TAYLOR (*William*), Norwich, 1765-1836. English Synonyms, 1813; Survey of German Poetry, 1828-30. His Memoirs, by J. W. Robberds, 1843.

TAYLOR, LL.D. (*William Cooke*), Youghal, in Ireland, 1800-1849. Historical Miscellany, 1829; History of France and Normandy, 1830; History of Mohammedanism, 1845; History of the House of Orleans, 1849; History of the Overthrow of the Roman Empire, etc., 1836; History of the Revolutions and Conspiracies of Europe, 1843; Life and Times of Sir Robert Peel, 1846-48; Manual of Ancient History, 1836; Manual of Modern History, 1839; Modern British Plutarch, 1846; Popular History of British India, 1842; Revolutions and Remarkable Conspiracies of Europe, 1847; Romantic Biography, etc., 1842.

∴ A copy of Lowndes's list of books given under the name "Taylor" would occupy eight pages of this Appendix.

TEIGNMOUTH (*John Shore*, lord), 1751-1834. Memoirs of Sir W. Jones's Works, 1804. His Life, by his son, Charles James, 1842.

TEMPLE, D.D. (*Frederick*), archbishop of Canterbury, 1821- . The first of the seven *Essays and Reviews*, 1860; Relation between Religion and Science, 1885.

TEMPLE (Sir *William*), London, 1628-1698. Ancient and Modern Learning (*On*), posthumous; Garden of Epicurus (*The*), posthumous; Heroic Vertue and Poetry, 1705, posthumous; Letters, 1700-25, posthumous; Letters to King Charles II., 1703, posthumous; Memoirs of what passed (1672-1679) in Christendom, 1693; Miscellanea, 1680-90; Observations on the Netherlands, 1673. His Life, by T. P. Courtenay, 1836.

TENISON, D.D. (*Thomas*), archbishop of Canterbury, born at Cottenham, in Cambridgeshire, 1636-1715. Baconiana, 1679; Creed of Mr. Hobbes examined, 1670; Discourse of Idolatry, 1678.

TENNANT (*James*), geologist, etc., *- . Art Gems and Precious Stones, 1859; Catalogue of Fossils found in the British Isles, 1858; Description of the Imperial Crown Jewels in the Tower of London, 1858; Iceland Spars; Stratigraphical List of British Fossils, 1847; Treatise on Geology, Mineralogy, and Crystallography, 1857 (with Ansted and Mitchell).

TENNANT (*William*), Anstruther, in Scotland, 1785-1848. Anster Fair (in ottava rima), 1812 (his best); Cardinal Beaton, 1823, a tragedy; Hebrew Dramas, 1845; John Baliol, 1825, a drama; Papistry stormed, 1819; Synopsis of Syriac and Chaldee Grammar, 1840; Thane of Fife (*The*), 1822, a poem. His Memoirs, by M. F. Conolly, 1861.

TENNYSON (*Alfred*, baron), Somersby, in Lincolnshire, poet laureate, 1809-1892. A complete single-volume edition of his works issued in 1894. Achilles over the Trench (*Nineteenth Century*, Aug., 1877); Aylmer's Field, 1864; Ballads, 1880; Becket, 1884; Carmen Sæculare, 1887; Charge of the Light Brigade (*The*), 1854; Coll. Sonnets, 1880; Cup (*The*), 1881, a drama; Death of Ænone, Abbar's Dream, and other Poems, 1892; Defence of Lucknow, with Dedicatory Poem to Princess Alice (*Nineteenth Century*, April, 1879); Demeter, 1889; De Profundis, 1880 (*Nineteenth Century*, May); Despair, 1881 (*Nineteenth Century*, Nov.); Dying Swan (*The*), in three subdivisions, 1830; Elaine, 1859, an idyll; Enid, 1859, an idyll; Enoch Arden, 1864, a tale in verse; Epitaph on the Duchess of Kent, 1864; Falcon (*The*), 1884, a dramatic poem in one act; Foresters (*The*), 1892; Frater Ave atque Vale, 1883 (*Nineteenth Century*, March); Gareth and Lynette, 1872, an idyll; Geraint and Enid, 1859, an idyll; Grandmother's Apology (*The*), 1859; Guinevere, 1859, an idyll; Harold, 1877, a drama; Hero and Leander, 1830; Holy Grail (*The*), 1869, an idyll; Idylls of the King, begun in 1859 (Coming of Arthur, Gareth and Lynette, Geraint and Enid, The Holy Grail, Lancelot and Elaine, The Last Tournament, Merlin and Vivien, The Passing of Arthur, and Pelleas and Etarre); In Memoriam, in 131 subdivisions, 1850, in memory of Arthur Hallam, son of Hallam the historian; Jubilee Poem (*The*), 1887; Lady Clara Vere de Vere, 1833; Last Tournament (*The*), 1871, an idyll; Lilian, 1830; Locksley Hall (in two-line stanzas), 1833; Locksley Hall Sixty Years After, 1886; Lotus Eater (*The*), 1833; Lover's Tale (*The*), 1833, recast 1879; Mariana (in two parts), 1830; Maud (in three parts), and other Poems, 1855; May the First, 1862, an ode; Mermaid (*The*), 1830; Miller's Daughter (*The*), 1833; Montenegro (*Nineteenth Century*, May, 1877); New Timon (*The*), and the Poets, 1846; Ode for the

Opening of the International Exhibition, 1862 ; On the Death of the Duke of Clarence, 1892 (*Nineteenth Century*, Feb.); Oriana, 1830, a ballad ; Passing of Arthur (*The*), an idyll ; Peleas and Etarre, an idyll ; Poems, 1830, 1832, 1842, 1848, 1850, 1851, 1853, 1857 ; Poems by Two Brothers (*i.e.* Alfred and Charles), 1827 ; Prefatory Sonnet, 1877 (*Nineteenth Century*, March); Princess (*The*), 1847, a medley in seven parts ; Promise of May (*The*), 1882, a drama in three acts ; Queen Mary, 1875-77, a drama ; Relief of Lucknow (*The*), 1879 ; Revenge (*The*), 1878, a naval song (*Nineteenth Century*, March); Sailor Boy(*The*), 1861; Silent Voices (*The*), 1892; Sonnets, 1877, 1880 ; Timbuctoo, 1829 (obtained the Chancellor's medal) ; Tiresias, 1885 ; Tithonus, 1860 (one of his best) (*Cornhill Magazine*, February, 1860) ; To Victor Hugo, 1877 (*Nineteenth Century*, June) ; To Virgil, 1882 (*Cornhill Magazine*, September, 1882) ; Two Northern Farmers ; Victim (*The*), 1867 ; Vivien, 1859, an idyll ; Welcome (*A*), 1863 (originally published in the London *Times*) ; Welcome to Marie Alexandrovna, 1874 ; Wellington (*The Death of the Duke of*), 1852, an ode ; Window (*The*), or Songs of the Wrens, 1870 (music by Sullivan). His Life, by Shepherd ; Walter G. Wace, 1881 ; Jennings, 1884. Tennyson, a Memoir by Hallam, lord Tennyson, 1897.

∴ A concordance to Tennyson was published in 1869.

TENNYSON (*Frederick*), brother of the late poet, 1840-1898. Daphne and other Poems, 1891 ; Days and Hours, 1854, poems ; Isles of Greece (*The*), 1890 ; Poems of the Day and Year, 1895.

THACKERAY (*Anne Isabella*), Mrs. *Ritchie*, daughter of W. M. Thackeray, the novelist, 1839– . Alfred Lord Tennyson and his Friends, 1893 ; Anne Evans, 1880 ; Bluebeard's Keys, and other Stories, 1874 (the old tales made into allegories of modern life); Book of Sibyls (*A*), 1883; Chapters from some Memoirs, 1894 ; Esther (*To*), and other Sketches, 1869 ; Five Old Friends and a Young Prince, 1868 ; Madame de Sévigné, 1881 ; Miss Angel, 1875 ; Miss Williamson's Divagations, 1883 ; Mrs. Dymond, 1885 ; Old Kensington, 1871 ; Portraits and Reminiscences, 1893 ; Records of Tennyson, Ruskin, and Browning, 1892; Story of Elizabeth, 1863 ; Toilers and Spinsters, with other Essays, 1873 ; Village on the Cliff (*The*), 1866 ; Works, 1875-76.

THACKERAY (*William Makepeace*), pseudonyms " Michael Angelo Titmarsh " and "FitzBoodle," Calcutta, 1811-1863. Adventures of Philip, 1862, a novel ; Barber Cox, 1840 ; Barry Lyndon, 1844, a novel (in *Fraser's Magazine*, (a sharper); Bedford Row Conspiracy (*The*), 1840 ; Book of Snobs (*The*), 1848 ; Box of Novels (*A*), 1844 ; Catherine [Hayes] by Ikey Solomon, 1839-40 ; Chronicle of the Drum (*The*), 1841 ; Comic Tales and Sketches, 1841 ; Denis Duval, 1867 (unfinished at his death); Dr. Birch and his Young Friends, 1849 ; English Humorists (*The*), 1853 ; Esmond, 1852, a

novel ; FitzBoodle's Confessions, 1842-43 ; Flore et Zephyr (London and Paris), 1836 ; Four Georges (*The*), 1864, lectures ; From Cornhill to Grand Cairo, 1845 ; History of the next French Revolution, 1844 ; Hoggarty Diamond (*The Great*), (published in *Fraser's Magazine*), 1841 ; Irish Sketch-book (*The*), 1843 ; Jeames's Deary, (in *Punch*); Kickleburys on the Rhine (*The*), 1851 ; L'Abbaye de Penmarch, 1840 ; Lovel the Widower (in *Cornhill Magazine*), 1860; Mary Ancel (*Story of*), 1838; Men's Wives, 1843 ; Mrs. Perkins's Ball, 1847, a Christmas tale ; Newcomes (*The*), 1854-55, a novel; Novels by Eminent Hands (parodies on Bulwer, Disraeli, Lever, Bret Harte, James, Cooper, etc.); Orphan of Pimlico, 1876 ; Our Street, 1848 ; Paris Sketch-book (*The*), 1840 ; Pendennis, 1849-50, a novel; Rebecca and Rowena, 1850 ; Rose and the Ring (*The*), 1855; Roundabout Papers(*The*), (in *Cornhill Magazine*), 1860-63 ; Second Funeral of Napoleon (*The*), 1841 ; Shabby Genteel Story, 1840 ; Snob Papers (in *Punch*); Snob (*The*), a Literary and Scientific Journal, 1829 ; Some Passages in the Life of Major Gahagan, 1838-39 ; Strictures on Pictures (*Fraser's Magazine*, June, 1838) ; Stubb's Calendar, 1839 ; Vanity Fair, 1847-48 (his best novel); Virginians (*The*), 1857-59, a novel ; Yellow Plush Correspondence, 1837-38. And many other sketches and articles. His Life, by Trollope, 1879; Shepherd.

THEOBALD (*Lewis*), called in the *Dunciad* " Piddling Theobald," Sittingbourne, in Kent, 1688-1744. Double Falsehood, 1728, a tragedy ; Electra, 1714, a tragedy ; Life of Raleigh, 1719 ; Persian Princess (*The*), 1711.

∴ His chief work is an edition of *Shakespeare*, 1733.

THIRLWALL (*Connop*), bishop of St. David's, 1797-1875. Essay on St. Luke, 1825 ; Essays and Reviews, 1863 ; Gorham Case (*The*), 1851 ; History of Greece, 1834-47 (his chief work) ; Newman (*Dr.*) on Development, 1848 ; Tractarian Controversy (*The*), 1842 ; Vatican Council (*The*), 1872.

THOM (*William*), 1799-1850. Rhymes and Recollections of a Handloom Weaver, 1841.

THOMAS À BECKET, called "St. Thomas of Canterbury," London, 1117-1170. Opera, printed 1682 (here I unexpectedly found those articles in Rymer's *Fœdera* inserted by Dr. Clarke, under Henry I., without marginal "authorization"). His Life, by A. B. Coloniæ, 1639 ; F. Christian Lupus, *Iprensis*, 1862.

THOMAS (*Annie*), married name Mrs. *Pender Cudlip*, novelist, 1838– . Has written upwards of 100 novels. Blotted Out, 1876 ; Cross of Honour (*The*), 1863 ; Eyre of Blendon, 1880 ; False Colours, 1869 ; False Pretences, 1885 ; Four Women in the Case, 1896 ; Friends and Lovers, 1883 ; Girl's Folly (*A*), 1894 ; He Cometh Not, 1873 ; Honourable Jane(*The*), 1892 ; Kate Valiant, 1884 ; London Season (*A*), 1879 ; Love of a Lady (*The*), 1890 ; Love's a Tyrant, 1888 ; No Alternative, 1875 ; No Hero, but a Man, 1894 ; No Medium, 1885 ; Old Dacre's

Darling, 1892; On the Children, 1890; Passion in Tatters (*A*), 1872; Sloane Square Scandal (*The*), 1890; Society's Puppets, 1882; Tenifer, 1883; That Affair, 1891; That Other Woman, 1889; Utterly Mistaken, 1893.

THOMAS, D.D. (*David*), Tenby, in South Wales, 1813– . Genius of the Gospel (*The*), 1864; Homiletic Commentary on *The Acts*, 1870; Practical Philosopher (*The*), 1873; Resurrections, etc., 1862.

THOMAS (*Edward*), London, 1813– . Ancient Indian Weights, 1877; Chronicles of the Pathán Kings of Delhi, 1871; Early Sassanian Inscriptions, etc., 1868; Essays on Indian Antiquities, 1858; Indian Numerals, 1863; On the Epoch of the Gupta Dynasty, 1855.

THOMAS (*Isaiah*), Worcester, U.S., 1749-1831. History of Printing in America, with Biography of Printers, and an Account of American Newspapers, 1810 (very interesting).

THOMAS OF ERCILDOUNE.   See RHYMER (*Thomas the*).

THOMAS OF READING, called "The Great Ballad Maker," real name *Thomas Deloney (q.v.)*.

THOMAS (*William*), 1509-1553. Defence of Henry VIII. (*A*); History of Italie (*The*), 1549 (this book was publicly burnt); Vanitee of this World (*The*), 1549.

THOMAS, D.D. (*William*), 1670-1738. Survey of the Cathedral of Worcester, with a Biography of its Bishops, 1736.

THOMPSON (*Edward*), 1738-1786. Court of Cupid (*The*); Courtezan (*The*), 1765, a poem; Demirep (*The*), 1765, a poem; Fair Quaker (*The*), 1773 (Shadwell's play re-cast); Meretriciad (*The*), a poem; Muse's Mirror (*The*); Sailor's Letter (*A*), 1767; Soldier (*The*), 1764.

THOMPSON (*Francis*), *– . Poems, 1893, 1897; Sister Songs, 1895.

THOMPSON (Sir *Henry*), pseudonym "Pen Oliver," Framlingham, in Suffolk, 1820– . All But, 1886; Catalogue of Blue and White Nankin Porcelain, 1878; Charley Kingston's Aunt, 1884; Modern Cremation, 1889; Pathology and Treatment of Stricture, etc., 1860 (which gained the Jacksonian prize); Practical Lithotomy and Lithotrity, 1860.

THOMPSON (Rev. *Henry*), 1797-*. Concionalia, or Outline Sermons, 1853; Davidica, or Sermons on David, 1827; Life of Hannah More, 1838; Pastoralia, a Manual for the Parochial Clergy, 1830.

THOMPSON (*Thomas Perronet*), Hull, 1783-1869. Audi Alteram Partem, 1857-61; Corn-law Catechism, 1827; Geometry without Axioms, 1830.

THOMPSON (Very Rev. *William*), died 1767. Sickness, 1746; Poems, 1757.

THOMPSON (*William*), Belfast, Ireland, 1805-1852. Natural History of Ireland, 1849-56.

THOMS (*William John*), Westminster, 1803-1885. Book of the Court, 1838; Death-warrant of Charles I., 1881; Early Prose Romances, 1828; Exceptional Longevity, 1881; Lays and Legends of Various Nations, 1834; Longevity of Man (*The*), 1873;

Hannah Lightfoot, Queen Charlotte, and the Chevalier d'Eon, 1867. ∴ He founded *Notes and Queries*, 1849, and acted as editor till 1872.

THOMSON (*Alexander*), 1762-1803. Paradise of Taste (*The*), in five cantos, 1790.

THOMSON, M.D. (*Anthony Todd*), Edinburgh, 1778-1849. Conspectus Pharmacopiæ, 1810 (his chief work); Diseases of the Skin, 1839-40; Domestic Management of the Sick Room, 1841; Elements of Botany, 1822; Elements of Materia Medica, 1832; London Dispensatory, 1811; Philosophy of Magic, etc., 1846.

THOMSON (Mrs. *Anthony Todd*), maiden name *Katherine Byerley*, died 1862.   Anne Boleyn, 1842, an historical romance; Celebrated Friendships, 1861; Chevalier (*The*), 1845, a romance; Constance, 1854, a novel; Court Secrets, 1857; Faults on Both Sides, 1858, a novel; Lady Annabetta (*The*), 1817, a novel; Lady of Milan (*The*), 1845; Life and Times of George Villiers, 1860; Memoirs of Sarah Duchess of Marlborough, 1838; Memoirs of the Court of Henry VIII., 1826; Memoirs of the Jacobites, 1715; Memoirs of the Life of Sir W. Raleigh, 1830; Memoirs of the Viscountess of Lundon, 1847; Private Correspondence of the Duchess of Marlborough, 1838; Ragland Castle, 1843, a novel; Recollections of Literary Characters, 1854; Rosabel, 1835, a novel; Tracey, or the Apparition, 1847; White Mask (*The*), 1844; Widows and Widowers, 1842.

THOMSON (Sir *Charles Wyville*), Bonsyde, in Scotland, 1830– . Depths of the Sea, 1872.

THOMSON (*James*), pseudonym "B.V." (*Bysshe Vanolis*), poet, 1834-1882. City of Dreadful Night, 1880 (his best-known work); Essays and Phantasies, 1881; Shelley, 1884; Vane's Story, 1880; Voice from the Nile (*A*), 1884. He wrote quantities of pamphlets, poems, reviews, etc.

THOMSON (*James*), Ednam, in Scotland, poet, 1700-1748. Agamemnon, 1738, a tragedy; Alfred, 1740, a masque, which contains the song "Rule, Britannia;" Autumn, 1730, in blank verse (The Seasons); Britannia, 1727, in blank verse; Castle of Indolence, in two cantos, 1748, Spenserian metre (most excellent); Coriolanus, 1749, a tragedy; Edward and Leonora, 1739, a tragedy; Liberty, in five parts, blank verse, 1734 (thought by Thomson himself to be his best poem); Rule, Britannia, 1740 (see above, "Alfred."); Seasons Complete (*The*), 1730 (excellent); Sophonisba, 1729, a tragedy; Spring, in blank verse, 1728 (The Seasons); Summer, in blank verse, 1727 (The Seasons); Tancred and Sigismund, 1745, a tragedy; Winter, in blank verse, 1726 (The Seasons).   His Life, by Murdock, 1762; David E. Buchan, 1729; sir Harris Nicolas, 1830; Gilfillan, 1853; and R. Bell, 1855.

THOMSON (*Richard*), 1795-1865. Account of Processions and Ceremonies observed in [our] Coronations, 1820; Book of Life, 1820, a bibliographical melody; Chronicles of London Bridge, 1827 (his best book); Historical

Essay on the Magna Charta, 1856 ; Illustrations of British History, 1828 ; Legends of London, 1832 ; Tales of an Antiquary, 1828.

THOMSON (*Thomas*), Crieff, Scotland, 1773-1852. Annals of Philosophy, 1813-26 ; Attempt to establish First Principles of Chemistry, 1825 ; Chemistry of Organic Bodies, 1838 ; Elements of Chemistry, 1810 ; Heat and Electricity, 1830 ; History of Chemistry, 1830-31 ; History of the Royal Society, 1812 ; Outlines of Mineralogy and Geology, 1836 ; System of Chemistry, 1802 (esteemed) ; Travels in Sweden, 1813.

THOMSON, D.D. (*William*), archbishop of York, born at Whitehaven, in Cumberland, 1819-1891. Atoning Work of Christ (*The*), 1853, a Bampton lecture ; Crime and its Excuses, 1855 ; Design in Nature, 1871 ; Life in the Light of God's Word, 1870 ; Limits of Philosophical Inquiry, 1868 ; Necessary Laws of Thought (*The*), 1849 ; Sermons, 1861 ; Seven Years, 1870 ; Word, Work, and Will, 1879. His Biography, by C. Bullock, 1891.

THOMSON (Sir *William*), lord Kelvin, Belfast, in Ireland, 1824– . Distribution of Electricity on Spherical Conductors, 1848 ; Electro-dynamic Properties of Metals, 1855, a Bakerian lecture ; Electrostatics and Magnetism, 1872 ; Linear Motion of Heat (*The*), 1842 ; Mathematical and Physical Papers, 1882 ; Popular Lectures, etc., 1872-94 ; Secular Coating of the Earth, 1852 ; Tables for "Sumner's Method at Sea," 1876 ; Thermal Effects of Fluids in Motion ; Treatise on Natural Philosophy, 1867.

THORESBY (*Ralph*), Leeds, 1658-1725. Diary, 1674-1724 ; Ducatus Leodiensis (the Topography of Leeds), 1715 ; Letters of Eminent Men addressed to him, 1832, posthumous ; Vicaria Leodiensis (the Church of Leeds), 1725.

THORNBURY (*George Walter*), London, 1828-1876. Art and Nature at Home and Abroad, 1856 ; British Artists from Hogarth to Turner, 1861 ; Criss-cross Journeys, 1873 ; Every Man his own Trumpeter, 1858, a novel ; Greatheart, 1866, a novel ; Haunted London, 1865 ; Historical and Legendary Ballads and Songs, 1875 ; Lays and Legends of the New World, 1851 ; Life in Spain and in Turkey, 1859 ; Life of Turner (the artist), 1862 ; Monarchs of the Main, 1855 ; Old and New London (the first two vols. 1875, the rest by Walford) ; Old Stories Retold, 1869 ; Shakespeare's England, 1856 ; Songs of the Cavaliers and Roundheads, 1857 ; Tales for the Mariner, 1865 ; Tour round England, 1870 ; True as Steel, 1863, a novel ; Vicar's Courtship (*The*), 1869, a novel ; Wildfire, 1864, a novel.

THORNDIKE (Rev. *Herbert*), 1620-1672. De Ratione ac Jure Finiendi Controversias, etc., 1670 ; Epilogue to the Tragedy of the Church of England (in three books : Truth, Grace, and Church Government), 1659 (his great work) ; Just Weights and Measures (the state of religion weighed in the balance of the sanctuary), 1662 ; On Religious Assemblies, 1642 ; On the Government of the Church, 1641 ; On the Right of a Church in a Christian State, 1649.

THORNTON (*Bonnel*), London, 1724-1768. Battle of the Wigs, 1768, a burlesque supplement to Garth's *Dispensary*; Connoisseur (*The*), 1754 ; Have at ye All, 1752, a periodical ; Ode on St. Cecilia's Day (*An*), 1765, a burlesque.

THORNTON, M.D. (*Robert John*), 1758-1837. British Flora, 1812 (his chief work) ; Elements of Botany, 1812 ; New Family Herbal, 1810 ; New Illustrations of the Sexual System of Plants, 1799-1807 ; Philosophy of Botany, 1809-10 ; Philosophy of Medicine, 1798 ; Philosophy of Politics, 1799 ; Practical Botany, 1809.

THORNTON (*William Thomas*), Burnham, in Buckinghamshire, 1813–1880. Modern Manicheism, and other Poems, 1856 ; Old-fashioned Ethics, etc., 1873 ; On Labour, 1869 ; Over-population and its Remedy, 1845 ; Plea for Peasant Proprietors, 1848 ; Zohrab, and other Poems, 1854.

THOROTON, M.D. (*Robert*), seventeenth century. Antiquities of Nottinghamshire, 1677.

THORPE (*Benjamin*), antiquary, 1808-1870. Ancient Laws and Institutes of England, 1848 ; Analecta Anglo-Saxonica, 1834 ; Diplomaticum Anglicum Ævi Saxonici, 1865 ; Northern Mythology, 1852 ; Yuletide Stories, 1853. Edited Anglo-Saxon Chronicle, with translation, 1858 ; and Rask's *Grammar of Anglo-Saxon*. Translated Pauli's *Life of Alfred the Great*, 1847 ; and Lappenberg's *History of England*, 1845-57.

THORPE, M.D. (*John*), Rochester, 1682-1750. Registrum Roffense, etc., 1769.

THORPE (*John*), son of the preceding, Rochester, 1714-1792. Custumale Roffense, 1788.

THRALE (Mrs.). See PIOZZI.

THROSBY (*John*), Leicester, 1740-1803. History and Antiquities of Leicester, 1791 ; Memoirs of the Town and County of Leicester, 1777 ; Select Views in Leicestershire, 1789-90.

THURLOE (*John*), Essex, 1616-1668. State Papers, 1742, posthumous.

THURLOW (*Edward*, lord), Stowmarket, in Suffolk, 1732-1806. Carmen Britannicum, 1814 ; Poems, 1813, 1821.

TICKELL (*Thomas*), Bridekirk, in Cumberland, 1686-1740. Colin and Lucy, 1720 (Gray calls it "the prettiest ballad in the world ") ; Elegy of Addison, 1719 (Dr. Johnson says, "A more sublime and elegant funeral poem is not to be found ") ; Imitation of the Prophecy of Nereus, 1715 (on the Jacobite outbreak) ; Kensington Gardens, 1730, a fairy romance in verse.
∴ He translated Homer's *Iliad*, book i. Many prefer it to Pope's version.

TICKNOR (*George*), Boston, in Massachusetts, U.S., 1791-1871. History of Spanish Literature, 1849 ; Life of Lafayette, 1825 ; Life of W. H. Prescott, 1863.

TIGHE (Mrs. *Henry*), maiden name *Mary Blackford*, Dublin, 1773-1810. Psyche (in six cantos), 1805.

TILLOTSON, D.D. (*John*), archbishop of Canterbury, born at Sowerby, in Yorkshire, 1630–1694. On the Wisdom of being Religious, 1664; Protestant Religion vindicated, 1680 (he says no man ought to oppose a national religion, whether it be true or false); Rule of Faith (*The*), 1666; Sermons, 1671, 1678, 1682, 1694; Works collected after his death, 1707-12. His Life, by Young, 1717; Dr. T. Birch, 1752.

TIMBS (*John*), 1801–1875. Curiosities of London; Curiosities of History; English Eccentrics and Eccentricities; History of Clubs, and Club-life in London; Things not Generally Known; Year-book of Facts (*The*).

TIMES (*The*), a daily London newspaper, started by John Walter, 1785 (see p. 1110).

TINDAL, LL.D. (*Matthew*), "The Christian Deist," born at Beer-Ferris, in Devonshire, 1657-1733. Christianity Old as Creation, 1730 (his best); Defence of the "Rights of the Christian Church," i. 1707, ii. 1708 (burnt by order of the House of Commons); Jacobitism, Perjury, and Popery, 1710; Laws of Nations and Rights of Sovereigns, 1695; On Obedience to the Supreme Powers, 1694; Rights of the Christian Church, 1706.

TINDAL (Rev. *Nicholas*), Devonshire, 1687–1774. History of Essex, 1726; Rapin's *History of England* continued, 1757.

TITE (*William*), 1800–1873. Descriptive Catalogue of the Antiquities found in the Excavations at the New Royal Exchange, 1848.

TOBIN (*John*), 1770–1804. Curfew (*The*), published 1820, a comedy; Faro-table (*The*), published 1820, a comedy; Honeymoon (*The*), 1805, a comedy (good); Indian (*The*), published 1820, a comedy; School for Authors (*The*), published 1820, a comedy; Undertaker (*The*), published 1820, a comedy. His Memoirs, by E. S. Benger, 1820.

TOD (*James*), 1782–1835. Annals of Rajast'han, 1829-32; Travels in Western India, 1839.

TODD (Rev. *Henry John*), 1763-1845. Accomplishment of Prophecy in the Life of Christ, 1810; Deans of Canterbury (*The*), 1793; Dictionary, 1814 (Dr. Johnson's, edited); History of the College of Bonhommes, in Buckinghamshire, 1812; Life of Cranmer, 1831; Lives of Gower and Chaucer, 1810; Memoirs of Brian Walton, 1821; Vindication of Cranmer, 1826.

TODD (*James Henthorne*), Dublin, 1805–1869. Book of the Hymns of the Ancient Church of Ireland, 1855; Books of the Vaudois, 1866; Memoir of St. Patrick, 1863; Testimony of the Fathers to the Dogma of Infallibility, 1848; Wars of the Danes in Ireland, 1866.

TODHUNTER (*Isaac*), Rye, in Sussex, 1820–1884. Analytical Statics, 1861; Differential Calculus, 1861; History of the Mathematical Theories of Attraction, etc., 1873; Integral Calculus, 1861; Mensuration for Beginners, 1869; Researches on the Calculus of Variations, 1872 (an Adams prize essay); Trigonometry for Beginners, 1869.

TODHUNTER, M.D. (*John*), 1839- . Alcestis, 1879; Banshee (*The*), and other Poems, 1888; Black Cat (*The*), 1895; Comedy of Sighs (*A*), 1894; Helena in Troas, 1885; Poison Flower (*The*), 1891; Sicilian Idyll (*A*), 1890; Study of Shelley (*A*), 1880; Three Irish Bardic Tales, 1896; True Tragedy of Rienzi, 1881.

TOLAND (*Janus Junius*), generally called "John Toland," Redcastle, Ireland, 1669–1722. Adeisidæmon, 1709(Livy vindicated); Amyntor, 1699; Anglia Liberia, 1701; Art of Restoring (*The*), 1714 (on general Monk); Christianity not Mysterious, 1696 (burnt by the hangman); Courts of Prussia and Hanover (*The*), 1706; History of the Druids (*A*), 1814; Letters to Serena, 1704; Life of Milton, 1698; Memoirs of Denzil, Lord Holles, 1699; Nazarenus, 1718; Pantheisticon, 1720; Socinianism Truly Stated, 1705; Tetradymus, 1720. His Life, by Des Maizeaux, 1723; Mosheim.

TOMLINE, D.D. (*George Pretyman*), bishop of Winchester, born at Bury St. Edmund's, in Suffolk, 1753-1827. Elements of Christian Theology, 1799; Introduction to the Study of the Bible, 1813; Life of Pitt, 1821 (Macaulay says "the worst biographical work in the world"); Refutation of the Charge of Calvinism against the Church of England, 1812.

TONSTALL (*Cuthbert*), bishop of Durham, born at Hatchford, in Yorkshire, 1474-1559. Contra Impios Blasphematores Dei Prædestinationis Opus, 1555; De Arte Supputandi, libri iv., 1522; De Veritate Corporis et Sanguinis Domini in Eucharistia, 1554.

TOOKE (*John Horne*), Westminster, 1736–1812. Diversions of Purley, 1786-1805 (on the etymology of English words, his great work); Letter on the Reported Marriage of the Prince of Wales, 1787; Letter to Mr. Dunning, 1778; Petition of an Englishman, 1765. His Life, by Hamilton, 1812; Stephens, 1813; W. H. Reid.

TOOKE (Rev. *William*), Islington, London, 1744–1820. General Biographical Dictionary, 1798 (with others); History of Russia, 1800; Life of Catherine II., 1797; View of the Russian Empire, 1799.

TOOKE (*William*), 1777–1863. Monarchy of France (*The*), 1855.

TOPLADY (Rev. *Augustus Montague*), Farnham, in Surrey, 1740-1778. Calvinism of the Church of England, 1774; Christian and Philosophical Necessity asserted, 1775; Hymns and Sacred Poems, 1776; Psalms and Hymns, 1776. N.B.—Toplady is the author of "Rock of Ages," admirably rendered into Latin by W. E. Gladstone. His Memoirs were published in 1778, 1794, 1860.

TORRENS (*William Torrens MacCullagh*), 1813–1894. Empire in Asia (how we came by it), 1872; History of Cabinets, 1894; Industrial History of Free Nations, 1846; Life and Times of Sir J. R. G. Graham, 1863; Memoirs of Lord Melbourne, 1878; Memoirs of R. L. Shiel, 1855; On the Uses and Study of History, 1842; Proconsul and Tribune (Wellesley and Cromwell), 1879;

Reform of Precedent in Parliament, 1881 ; Twenty Years in Parliament, 1893

TOURNEUR (*Cyril*), poet, seventeenth century. Atheist's Tragedie (*The*), 1611, a tragedy ; Funerall Poem on . . . Sir Francis Vere, 1609 ; Griefe on the Death of Prince Henrie (*A*), 1613 ; Laugh and Lie Down, 1605, a comedy ; Revenger's Tragedie (*The*), 1607, a tragedy.

TOWERS, LL.D. (Rev. *Joseph*), London, 1737–1799. British Biography, 1766–72 ; General Doctrines of Christianity, 1763 ; Life, etc., of Frederick III. of Prussia, 1788.

TOWNLEY (Rev. *James*), 1715–1778. False Concord, 1760, a comedy ; High Life Below Stairs, 1759, a burlesque ; Tutor (*The*).

TOWNSHEND (*Chauncy Hare*), poet, 1800–1868. Mesmerism proved True, 1855 ; Sermons in Sonnets, 1851 ; Three Gates (*The*), 1859.

TOWNSHEND (*George Herbert*), died 1869. Handbook, 1869 (for the year 1868) ; Manual of Dates, 1862.

TRACT SOCIETY (*The Religious*), of London, established 1799 ; of Scotland, 1793 ; of New England, 1814.

TRAILL, D.C.L. (*Henry Duff*), Blackheath, London, 1842– . Central Government, 1882 ; Coleridge, 1884 ; From Cairo to the Soudan Frontier, 1896 ; Life of Sir John Franklin, 1896 ; Marquis of Salisbury, 1890 ; New Lucian (*The*), 1884 ; Number Twenty, 1892, fables and fantasies ; Recaptured Rhymes, 1882 ; Saturday Songs, 1890 ; Shaftesbury, 1886 ; Sterne, 1882 ; Strafford, 1889 ; William III., 1888.

TRAPP, D.D. (*Joseph*), 1679-1747. Defence of the Church of Eng'and, 1727; Notes on the Gospels, 1747-48 (good); Prælectiones Poeticæ, 1711-19.

TREDGOLD (*Thomas*), Brandon, in Durham, 1788-1829. Elementary Principles of Carpentry, 1820 ; Principles of Warming and Ventilating Public Buildings, 1824 ; Railroads and Carriages, 1825 ; Steam Engine (*The*), 1827; Strength of Cast Iron and other Metals, 1821.

TRENCH, D.D. (*Richard Chenevix*), archbishop of Dublin, born in Dublin, 1807–1886. Elegiac Poems: Genoveva ; Poems from Eastern Sources ; Sabbation, H. Neale, and other Poems ; Story of Justin Martyr, 1837-38, collected 1864. English, Past and Present, 1855 ; Epistles to the Seven Churches, 1859 ; Lessons in Proverbs, 1853 ; Mediæval Church History, 1878 ; Notes on the Miracles, 1846 ; Notes on the Parables, 1841 (his best book) ; Remains of Mrs. Trench (his mother), 1862 ; Sacred Latin Poetry, 1849 ; St. Augustine, etc., 1851 ; Sermon on the Mount, 1844 ; Social Aspect of the Thirty Years' War ; Study of Words, 1851 (the largest circulation of all his works) ; Synonyms of the New Testament, 1854.

TRENCHARD (*John*), Dorsetshire, 1662–1723. Cato's Letters, 1720-23 ; History of Standing Armies, 1698 ; Independent Whig (*The*), 1720-23.

TREVELYAN (Sir *George Otto*), Rothley Temple, in Leicestershire, 1838– . Cawnpore, 1865; Fox (*Charles James*), 1880 ;

Horace at the University of Athens, 1862 ; Ladies in Parliament, 1869 ; Letters of a Competition Wallah, 1864 ; Macaulay (his Life, etc.), 1876 ; Speeches on Army Reform, 1870.

TREVOR (Rev. *George*), 1809– . Ancient Egypt, 1864 ; Christ in His Passion, 1847 ; Doctrines and Means of Grace, 1851 ; Egypt from Alexander to Napoleon, 1866 ; India, 1858, an historical sketch ; Origin, Constitution, and Form of Procedure in Convocation, 1852 ; Rome since the Fall of the Western Empire, 1869 ; Russia, Ancient and Modern, 1862 ; Sacrifice of the Eucharist (*The*), 1869 ; Story of the Cross (*The*), 1866 ; Types and Antitypes, 1864.

TRIMMER (Mrs.), maiden name *Sarah Kirby*, Ipswich, Suffolk, 1741-1810. Catechism of the Church of England Familiarized, 1791 ; Companion to the Book of Common Prayer, 1791 ; Easy Introduction to the Knowledge of Nature, 1780 ; Economy of Charity, 1788 ; Fabulous Histories, 1785 ; Instructive Tales, collected, 1814 ; Sacred History, 1782-85 (her chief work).

TROLLOPE (*Anthony*), novelist, 1815-1882. (*Those marked thus * are not novels.*) American Senator (*The*), 1877; *Australia and New Zealand, 1873 ; *Autobiography (*An*), 1883; Ayala's Angel, 1881 ; Barchester Towers, 1857 (his best novel, the continuation of "The Warden ") ; Belton Estate (*The*), 1865 ; Bertrams (*The*), 1859 ; *British Sports and Pastimes, 1868 ; Can you Forgive her ? 1864 ; Castle Richmond, 1860 ; Claverings (*The*), 1867 ; *Clergymen of the Church of England, 1866, sketches ; Cousin Henry, 1879 ; Doctor Thorn, 1858 ; Doctor Wortle's School, 1881 ; Editor's Tales (*An*), 1870 ; Eustace Diamonds, 1872 ; Eye for an Eye (*An*), 1879 ; Fixed Period (*The*), 1882 ; Framley Parsonage, 1861 ; Frau Frohmann, 1881 ; Golden Lion of Grandpère, 1872 ; Harry Heathcote, 1874 ; He knew he was Right, 1869 ; *Hunting Sketches, 1865 ; Is he Popenjoy ? 1878 ; John Caldigate, 1879 ; Kellys (*The*) and the O'Kellys, 1848 ; Kept in the Dark, 1871 ; Lady Anna, 1874 ; Land Leaguers (*The*), 1883 ; Last Chronicles of Barset, 1867 ; La Vendée, 1850, an historical romance ; *Life of Cicero, 1880 ; Lotta Schmidt, and other Stories, 1867 ; Macdermots of Ballycloran (*The*), 1847 ; Marion Fay, 1882 ; Mary Gresly, 1871 ; Miss Mackenzie, 1865 ; Mr. Scarborough's Family, 1883 ; *New South Wales and Queensland, 1874 ; Nina Balatka, 1867 ; *North America, 1862 ; Old Man's Love (*An*), 1884 ; Orley Farm, 1862 ; *Palmerston, 1882 ; Phineas Finn, the Irish Member, 1869 ; Phineas Redux, 1873 ; Prime Minister (*The*), 1875-76 ; Rachel Ray, 1863 ; Ralph the Heir, 1871 ; Sir Harry Hotspur, 1870 ; Small House at Allington, 1864 ; *South Africa, 1877 ; *South and Western Australia, 1874 ; Struggles of Brown, Jones, and Robinson (*The*), 1870 ; *Tales of All Countries, 1861 ; Thackeray, 1879, a biographical sketch ; Three Clerks (*The*), 1857 ; *Travelling Sketches, 1866 ; Vicar of Bullhampton (*The*), 1870 ; *Victoria and Tasmania, 1874 ; Warden (The), 1855 (see above, "Barchester Towers"); Way we Live now (The), 1875; *West Indies and the Spanish Main, 1859. His Autobiography was published 1883.

TROLLOPE, D.D. (Edward), bishop suffragan of Nottingham, antiquary, 1817–1893. Battle of Bosworth Field (The), 1862; Boston and other Churches, 1870; Captivity of John, King of France, 1857; Church Spires, 1874; Danes in Lincolnshire (The), 1859; Fens and Submarine Forests, 1862; Gainsborough and other Churches, 1866; Grantham and other Churches, 1867; History of Anne Askewe, 1859; History of Worksop, 1860; Holbeach and other Churches, 1872; Illustrations of Ancient Art, 1854; Introduction of Christianity into Lincolnshire, 1857; Labyrinths, Ancient and Modern, 1858; Life of Hereward the Saxon, 1861; Life of Pope Adrian IV., 1856; Louth Park Abbey and other Churches, 1873; Memorabilia of Grimsby, 1859; Monastic Gatehouses, 1860; Norman and Early English Styles of Gothic Architecture, 1869; Norman Sculpture of Lincoln Cathedral, 1866; Raising of the Royal Standard at Nottingham, 1864; Roman Ermine Street, 1868; Roman House at Apethorpe (The), 1859; Sepulchral Memorials, 1858; Shadows of the Past, 1863; Sleaford and the Wapentakes of Flaxwell, etc., 1872; Spilsby and other Churches, 1865; Use and Abuse of Red Bricks, 1859.

TROLLOPE (Mrs. Frances), Heckfield, in Hampshire, novelist, 1790–1863. (Those marked thus * are not novels.) Abbess (The), 1833; Adventures of Jonathan Jefferson Whitlaw, 1836; Anne Furness; Attractive Man (The), 1843; Barnabys in America (The), 1843; *Belgium and Western Germany, 1833–34; Blue Belles of England (The), 1841; Charles Chesterfield, 1841; *Domestic Manners of the Americans, 1832; Father Eustace, 1846; Hargrave, 1843; Jessie Phillips, 1843; Lauringtons (The), or Superior People, 1843; Life and Adventures of a Clever Woman, 1846; Like Ships upon the Sea; Mabel's Progress; Michael Armstrong, the Factory Boy, 1839; One Fault, 1839; *Paris and London, 1856; *Paris and the Parisians, 1835; Petticoat Government, 1846; *Refuge in America (The), 1832; Robertses on their Travels (The), 1843; Romance of Vienna (A), 1838; Three Cousins (The), 1847; Town and Country, 1844; Tremordyn Cliff, 1838; Uncle Walter, 1852; Vicar of Wrexhill (The), 1837; *Vienna and the Austrians, 1837; *Visit to Italy (A), 1842; Ward of Thorpe Combe (The), 1842; Widow Barnaby, 1838 (her most popular novel); Widow Married (The), 1840; Young Love, 1844.

TROLLOPE (Thomas Adolphus), son of Mrs. Frances Trollope, the novelist, 1810–1892. Artingall Castle, 1867, a novel; Beppo the Conscript, 1864, a novel; Decade of Italian Women (A), 1849; Diamond cut Diamond, 1875; Dream Numbers (The), 1868, a novel; Durnton Abbey, 1871; Family Party at the Piazza of St. Peter's, 1877; Filippo Strozzi, 1860; Garstangs of Garstang Grange (The),

1869; Gemma, 1866, a novel; Girlhood of Catherine de' Medici, 1856, a tale; Giulio Malatesta, 1863, a novel; History of the Commonwealth of Florence, 1865 (his chief work); Impressions of a Wanderer in Italy, etc., 1850; La Beata, 1861 (an Italian tale, well told); Lenten Journey in Umbria, etc., 1862; Leonora Casoloni, 1868, a novel; Life of Filippo Strozzi, 1860; Life of Pope Pius IX., 1877; Lindisfarn Chase, 1864, a novel; Marietta, 1862, a novel; Papal Conclaves (The), 1876; Paul the Pope and Paul the Friar, 1860; Peep Behind the Scenes at Rome, 1877; Siren (A), 1870; Sketches from French History, 1878; Summer in Brittany (A), 1840; Summer in Western France (A), 1841; Tuscany, 1859; What I remember, 1887–89.

TROTTER, M.D. (Thomas), Edinburgh, 1788–1832. Medica Nautica, 1799; Medical and Chemical Essays, 1796; Treatise on Scurvy, 1786; Tuscany in 1849 . . . 1859.

TRUMAN (Rev. Joseph), Nottinghamshire, 1631–1671. Discourse of Natural and Moral Impotency, 1671; Great Propitiation (The), 1669. His Life, by H. Rogers, 1834.

TUCKER (Abraham), London, 1705-1774. Advice to his Son (on clubs), 1755; Cuthbert Commet's Man in Quest of himself, 1763; Free Will, Foreknowledge, and Fate, 1763; Light of Nature pursued, 1765 (excellent); Vocal Sounds, 1781.

TUCKER, D.D. (Josiah), Wales, 1711-1799. Apology for the Church of England, 1772; Reflections on the Matters of Dispute between England and Ireland, 1785; Religious Intollerance [condemned], 1773; Treatise concerning Civil Government, 1781.

TUCKER (Miss), her assumed signature "A.L.O.E." (i.e. A Lady of England), 1821-1893. Cyril Ashley, 1870; Exiles in Babylon; Fairy Know-a-bit, 1872; Giant-killer (The), 1868; House Beautiful (The); Jewish History (Stories from), 1868; Lady of Provence (The); Pride and his Prisoners, 1882; Rescued from Egypt, 1865; Shepherd of Bethlehem, 1864; Silver Key (The), 1872; Triumph over Midian, 1866. And many other stories.

TUCKERMAN (Henry Theodore), Boston, in Massachusetts, U.S., 1813-1871. Artist's Life (An), 1847; Biographical Essays, 1857; Characteristics of Literature, 1849, 1851; Italian Sketch-book, 1835; Leaves from the Diary of a Dreamer, 1853; Memorial of Horatio Greenough, 1853; Month in England (A), 1853; Optimist (The), 1850; Spirit of Poetry (The), 1851; Thoughts on the Poets, 1846.

TUCKEY (James Hingston), Cork, Ireland, 1778-1816. Maritime Geography and Statistics, 1815.

TULLOCH, D.D. (John), Perthshire, Scotland, 1822-1886. Beginning Life, 1862; Christ of the Gospels (The), and the Christ of Modern Criticism, 1864; Christian Doctrine of Sin, 1876; Church of the Eighteenth Century (The), 1881; English Puritanism and its Leaders, 1861; Leaders of the Reformation, 1859; Modern Theories in Philosophy and Religion, 1884; National Religion in Theory and Fact, 1886; Pascal, 1878; Rational Theology and Christian Philosophy, 1872; Religion and Theology, 1875; Religious Thought, 1885; Some Facts of Religion and of Life, 1877; Theism, 1855 (second Burnett prize essay); Unity and Variety in the Churches of Christendom, 1884. Memoir, by Mrs. Oliphant, 1888.

TUPPER, D.C.L. (*Martin Farquhar*), 1810-1889. Author's Mind (*An*), 1841; Ballads for the Times, and other Poems 1852, Twenty-one ballads 1868, Fifty ballads 1874; Cithara, 1863, lyrics; Creed (*A*) and Hymns, 1870; Crock of Gold (*The*), 1844; Dirge for Wellington, 1852; Farley Heath, 1851; Geraldine, 1838 (a continuation of Coleridge's *Christabel*), and other Poems; Greeting to Princess Alexandra, 1863; Hactenus, a Budget of Lyrics, 1848; Heart, 1844, a tale; Hymns for All Nations, in Thirty Languages, 1851; King Alfred's Poems in English Metre, 1850; Lyrics, 1855; Modern Pyramid (*The*), 1839; My Life as an Author, 1886; Our Canadian Dominion, 1868; Probabilities, an Aid to Faith, 1847; (21) Protestant Ballads 1868, Fifty more 1874; Proverbial Philosophy, 1838, 1842, 1867 (a book of almost unparalleled sale); Ralcigh, 1866, an historical play; Rides and Reveries of Mr. Æsop Smith, 1861; Stephen Langton, or the Days of King John, 1858; Surrey, its Persons and Places, 1849; Thousand Lines (*A*), 1845; Three Hundred Sonnets, 1860; Twenty-one Protestant Ballads, 1868; Twins (*The*), 1844, a tale; War Ballads, 1854; Washington, 1877, a drama.

TURBERVILLE (*George*), Dorsetshire, 1530-1595. Booke of Faulconrie, 1575; Epitaphs, Epigrams, Songs, etc., 1570; Noble Art of Venerie (*The*), 1576; Songs and Sonnets, 1567; Tragical Tales (from Italian authors), 1576.

TURNER (*Charles Tennyson*), brother of Alfred lord Tennyson. The two brothers published a book of poems in conjunction in 1827. Charles, the elder brother, 1808-1879 (Alfred, 1809-1892). Small Tableaux, 1868; Sonnets, 1864; Sonnets, etc., 1873.

TURNER (*Dawson*), Great Yarmouth, 1775-1858. Botanist's Guide (*The*), 1805; Fuci, (*The*), 1808-18; Muscologiæ Hibernicæ Spicilegium, 1804; Sepulchral Reminiscences of Yarmouth, 1848.

TURNER (*Edward*), Scotland, 1798-1839. Elements of Chemistry, 1828.

TURNER (*Sharon*), London, 1768-1847. Ancient British Poems, with Specimens, 1803; History of the Anglo-Saxons, 1799-1805; History of England (from the Conquest to 1509), 1814-23; History of the Reign of Henry VIII., 1826; History of the Reigns of Edward VI., Mary, and Elizabeth, 1829; Prolusions, 1819; Richard III., 1845, a poem; Sacred History of the World, 1832.

TURNER (*Thomas Hudson*), London, 1815-1852. Account of the Domestic Architecture of England (*An*), 1851.

TURNER, M.D. (*William*), Morpeth, in Northumberland, 1510-1568. Avium . . . Historia, 1554; Herball (*The*), 1551-62; Huntyng and Fynding out of the Romishe

Foxe, etc. (*The*), 1543; Huntyng of the Romishe Wolfe, 1554; Preservative or Triacle against the Poyson of Pelagius, 1551; Rescuyinge of the Romishe Foxe, etc. (*The*), 1545.

TUSSER (*Thomas*), Essex, poet, 1515-1580. Dialoge of Wyvinge and Thryvinge, 1562; Five Hundred Points of Good Husbandry (in 57 chapters), 1557; Metrical [Auto]biography, 1573; Points of Housewifery, 1563.

TWINING, M.D. (*William*), died 1835. Clinical Illustrations of the More Important Diseases of Bengal, etc., 1832-35.

TWISS (*Horace*), 1786-1849. Life of Lord Eldon, 1844.

TWYSDEN (Sir *Roger*), Kent, 1597-1672. Anglicanæ Historiæ Scriptores Decem, 1652 (see SCRIPTORES DECEM, p. 973); Historical Defence of the Church of England, 1675.

TYNAN (*Katharine*). See HINKSON.

TYLOR (*Edward Burnett*), born at Camberwell, in Surrey, 1832- . Anahuac, or Mexico and the Mexicans, 1861; Anthropology, 1881; Primitive Culture, etc., 1871; Researches into the History of Mankind, 1865.

TYNDALE (*William*), Nibley, in Gloucestershire, 1485-1536. Exposicion of 1 Ep. of S. John, 1531; Exposicion on 1 Cor. vii., etc., 1529; Exposicion upon v. vi. vii. Mathew, 1548; Fyrst Boke of Moses (*The*), 1530; Letter to More against John Fyrth, 1533; Obedyence of a Christen Man, etc., 1528; Parable of the Wicked Mammon, 1528; Pathway to Scripture, 1526; Preface unto the Pistle to the Romayns, 1530; Sacrament of the Lord's Supper, 1533 (John vi. and 1 Cor. xi.); Sacraments (*The*), 1538; Translation of Deuteronomy, printed 1830 (with Coverdale) of the New Testament, 1526 (burnt 1529), new and revised edition, 1534; of the Pentateuch, 1529. (Tyndale also translated *Jonah* and *Nehemiah*; Tyndale's version is far superior to Coverdale's). His Life, by Offor, 1836; Demaus, 1871.

TYNDALL, LL.D. (*John*), Leighton Bridge, in Ireland, 1820-1893. Absorption and Radiation of Heat by Gases and Vapours, 1861; Address to the British Association, 1874; Calorescence, 1865; Contributions to Molecular Physics, 1872; Faraday as a Discoverer, 1868; Fermentation, 1877; Floating Matter of the Air, 1881; Forms of Water in Clouds and Rivers, Ice and Glaciers, 1873; Fragments of Science for the Unscientific, 1871, 1891; Free Molecules and Radiant Heat, 1882; Glaciers of the Alps, 1860; Heat as a Mode of Motion, 1863; Hours of Exercise in the Alps, 1871; Imagination in Science, 1870; Invisible Radiation of the Electric Light, 1865; Lectures on Light, 1869, 1872-73; Lectures on Sound, 1867; Lessons on Electricity, 1875-76; Mountaineering, 1861; Nature of the Force by which Bodies are repelled from the Poles of a Magnet, 1855; Notes on Electricity, 1870; Notes on Light, 1871; On Molecular Influences, 1853; On the Vibrations and Tones produced by Bodies in

Contact having Different Temperatures, 1854; Physical Connection of Absorption and Radiation, etc., 1861; Physical Phenomena of Glaciers, 1857; Physical Properties of Ice, 1858–59; Radiation, 1861–65; Researches on Diamagnetism and Magne-Crystallic Action, 1888; Sounding and Sensitive Flames, 1867; Transmission of Heat through Gaseous Bodies, 1859; Transmission of Heat through Organic Structures, 1853; Transmission of Sound by the Atmosphere, 1874; Vacation Tour, 1862.

TYRRELL (*James*), London, 1642–1718. Bibliotheca Politica, 1692–95; General History of England, 1700–4.

TYRWHITT (*Thomas*), London, 1730–1786. Dissertatio de Babrio, 1776; Edited Chaucer's *Canterbury Tales*, 1773; Epistle to Florio, 1749.

TYSON, M.D. (*Edward*), Somersetshire, 1649–1708. Orangoutang (*The*), 1699.

TYTLER (*Alexander Fraser*, lord Woodhouselee), Edinburgh, 1747–1813. Elements of General History, 1801 (his best-known work); Life, etc., of Petrarch, 1810; Memoirs of Lord Kames, 1807; On Military Law, etc., 1800; On the Principles of Translation, 1791; Outlines of . . . Universal History, 1782.

TYTLER (*C. C. Fraser*), poet and novelist, *– . Jasmine Leigh, 1871; Jonathan,1876; Making or Marring, 1877; Margaret, 1872; Mistress Judith, 1873; Rose and a Pearl (*A*), 1869; Sweet Violet, and other Stories, 1868.

TYTLER (*Patrick Fraser*), son of Alexander Fraser Tytler, Edinburgh, 1791–1849. England under Edward VI. and Mary, 1839; Historical View of the . . . Discovery of America, 1840; History of Scotland, 1828–43 (his chief work); King Henry VIII. and his Contemporaries, 1837; Life and Character of Henry VIII., 1838; Life of the Admirable Crichton, 1819; Life of Sir Thomas Craig, 1823; Life of Sir Walter Raleigh, 1833; Life of Wicklyff, 1826; Lives of Scottish Worthies, 1831–33. His Life, by J. W. Burgon, D.D., 1859.

TYTLER (*Sarah*), a name assumed by Miss *Henrietta Keddie*, 1827– . Beauty and the Beast, 1884; Blackhall Ghosts, 1888; Bride's Pass (*The*), 1881; Buried Diamonds, 1886; By the Elbe, 1876; Childhood a Hundred Years Ago, 1876; Citoyenne Jacqueline, 1865; Comrades, 1886; Disappeared, 1887; French Janet, 1884; Heroines in Obscurity, 1871; Huguenot Family (*The*); Jane Austen and her Works, 1880; Lady Bell, 1873; Macdonald Lass (*The*), 1895; Marie Antoinette, 1883; Meg of Ellibank, 1860; Modern Painters, 1873; Mrs. Carmichael's Goddess, 1898; Musical Composers, 1875; Noblesse Oblige; Nut Brown Maids, 1860; Old Masters (*The*); Papers for Thoughtful Girls, 1862; Rachel Langton, 1896; St. Mungo's City, 1885; Sisters and Wives, 1871; Vashti Savage, 1888; What she Came through, 1876; Witch-Wife (*The*), 1897.

TYTLER (*William*), Edinburgh, 1711–1792. Historical and Critical Inquiry into the Evidence against Mary Queen of Scots, 1759; Poetical Remains of James I., 1783.

UDAL (*Nicholas*), Hampshire, 1506–1556. Ezechias, 1564; Floures for Latine Spekynge, 1533; Ralph Royster Doyster, 1534, printed 1565 (the first English comedy).

URBAN (*Sylvanus*), the pseudonym adopted by *Edward Cave*, the original editor and founder of the *Gentleman's Magazine*, 1731. The name is still retained by the present editor.

URE, M.D. (*Andrew*), Glasgow, 1778–1857. Cotton Manufactures of Great Britain, 1831; Dictionary of Arts and Manufactures, 1839; Dictionary of Chemistry, 1821; New System of Geology, 1829; Philosophy of Manufactures, 1835.

URQUHART (Sir *Thomas*), Cromarty, in Scotland, 1613–1654. Epigrams, Divine and Moral, 1641; Jewel (*The*), in praise of Scotland and Scotchmen, 1651; Longapandecteision (in six books), 1653; Translation of *Rabelais*, 1653; Trigonometry, 1645; Trissotetras (*The*), for resolving triangles, 1649.

USHER, D.D. (*James*), archbishop of Armagh, born in Dublin, 1580–1656. Annales Veteris et Novi Testamenti, 1650–54 (a chronological work); Britannicarum Ecclesiarum Antiquitates, 1639; Chronologia Sacra, 1660, posthumous (well known); De Ecclesiarum Christianarum Successione et Statu, 1613 (his first publication); De Græca Septuagenta, etc., 1654 (excellent); De Romanæ Ecclesiæ Symbolo, 1647; Discourses on the Religion anciently held by the Irish and British, 1622; Dissertatio de Macedonum et Asianorum Anno Solari, 1648; Episcopal and Presbyterian Government enjoyned, 1679; Historia Dogmatica Controversiæ . . . 1689, posthumous; Immanuel, 1638 (on the Incarnation); Letters, 1686, posthumous; Original of Bishops, 1641; Power of the Prince and the Obedience of the Subject (*The*), 1641; Principles of the Christian Religion (*The*), 1644; Veterum Epistolarum Hibernicarum Sylloge, 1632; Vox Hiberniæ, 1642. His Life, by Dr. N. Bernard, 1656; Dr. R. Parr, 1686; Dillingham, 1700; T. Smith, 1722; Dr. J. Aikin, 1773; Dr. Elrington, 1847.

VALPY, D.D. (*Richard*), Jersey, 1754–1836. Greek Grammar, 1805; Latin Grammar, 1782.

⁂ Valpy's Grammars, and editions of the Greek and Latin classics, were once in very general use.

VANBRUGH (Sir *John*), 1666–1720. Æsop, 1697, a comedy; Confederacy (*The*), 1705, a comedy; False Friend (*The*), 1699, a comedy; Journey to London, afterwards called "The Provoked Husband" (*q.v.*); Pilgrim (*The*), 1700; Provoked Husband (*The*), 1726 (finished by Cibber); Provoked Wife (*The*), 1697, a comedy; Relapse (*The*), 1697, a comedy, famous for "lord Fopping-

ton" and "Miss Hoyden." His Life, by
E. W. Swaen, 1896.
VANCOUVER (*George*), 1750-1798. Voyage of
Discovery to the North Pacific Ocean, etc.,
1798.
VANE (Sir *Henry*), 1612-1662. Healing
Question propounded and resolved (*A*),
1656; Retired Man's Meditations (*The*),
1653; Two Treatises, 1662. His Life, by
G. Sikes, 1662; Knight, 1662; Birch; E.
Ludlow, 1771.
VAUGHAN, D.D. (*Charles James*), Leicester,
1816-   Christ satisfying the Instincts
of Humanity, 1870; Church of the First Days
(*The*), 1864-65; Half-hours in the Temple
Church, 1871; Heroes of Faith, 1876; Last
Words in the Temple Church, 1894;
Memorials of Harrow Sundays, 1859;
Prayers of Jesus Christ, 1891; Restful
Thoughts in Restless Times, 1893; Solidity
of True Religion (*The*), 1874; Sundays in
the Temple, 1871; Temple Sermons, 1881;
Twelve Discourses on Liturgy, etc., 1867;
University Sermons, 1888.
VAUGHAN (*Henry*), "Silurist," Brecon, in
Wales, poet, 1621-1695. Flores Solitudinis,
1654; Mount of Olives (*The*), 1652; Olor
Iscanus, 1651; Poems, 1646, 1647; Silex
Scintillans, 1650-55, sacred poems; Thalia
Rediviva, 1678, divine poems. His Life, by
H. F. Lyte.
VAUGHAN, D.D. (*Robert*), 1795-1868. Age of
Great Cities, 1843; Christian Warfare illus-
trated, 1833; Congregationalism, 1842;
English Nonconformity, 1862; Essays, 1849;
History of England under the House of
Stuart, 1848; John de Wycliffe, 1828, 1853;
Lectures on the Age and Christianity, 1849;
Lectures on the Corruption of Christianity,
1834; Letter and Spirit, or Spiritualism and
Christianity, 1849; Life of the Rev. Robert
Alfred Vaughan (his son), 1858; Life-search
after Religious Truth, 1866; Memorials of
the Stuart Dynasty, 1831; Modern Pulpit
(*The*), 1842; Popular Education in England,
1846; Protectorate of Cromwell, 1838;
Protestant Nonconformity, 1843; Religious
Parties in England, 1839; Revolutions in
English History, 1859-63; Ritualism in the
English Church, 1866; Sermons on Prophecy,
1629; Way to Rest, 1866.
VAUGHAN (Rev. *Robert Alfred*), son of the
preceding, Worcester, 1823-1857. Essays
and Remains, 1858, posthumous; Hours with
the Mystics, 1856. His Life, by his father,
Robert Vaughan, D.D., 1858.
VAUX (*Thomas*, lord), 1510-1557. "I loath
that I did love," 1550 (this poem is very
interesting, because the Gravedigger in
Hamlet quotes it—

A pickaxe and a spade,
And eke a shrouding sheet,
A house of clay for to be made
For such a guest most meet).

VAUX (*William Sandys Wright*), 1818-   .
Greek Cities, etc., of Asia Minor, 1877;
Handbook to the Antiquities in the British
Museum, 1851; Nineveh and Persepolis,
1848; Persia from the Earliest Period, 1875.
VEITCH, LL.D. (*John*), Peebles, Scotland,

1829-1894. Dugal Stewart and Sir William
Hamilton, 1896; Dualism and Monism,
1895; Essays, 1889; Feeling for Nature in
Scotch Poetry, 1887; History and Poetry of
the Scottish Border, 1877; Institutes of
Logic, 1885; Lucretius and the Atomic
Theory, 1875; Memoir of Sir W. Hamilton,
1869; Merlin, and other Poems, 1889; Tweed
(*The*), and other Poems, 1875.
VENN (Rev. *Henry*), Barnes, Surrey, 1725-
1797. Compleat Duty of Man (a sequel to
The Whole Duty of Man), 1764; Mistakes
in Religion exposed, 1774. His Life, by his
grandson, the Rev. John Venn, 1834.
VENNER, M.D. (*Tobias*), 1577-1660. Baths
of Bath (*The*), 1628; Taking of the Fume
of Tobacco (*The*), 1621; Via Recta ad
Vitam Longam, 1620.
VERE (*Aubrey Thomas de*), 1814-   . Antar
and Rora, 1877; Fall of Rora (*The*), and
other Poems, 1877; Infant Bridal (*The*),
and other Poems, 1874; Saxon Saints (*The*),
1879; Search after Proserpine (*The*), and
other Poems, 1843; Sketches of Greece and
Turkey, 1850; Waldenses (*The*), and other
Poems, 1842.
VERE (Sir *Aubrey de*), 1807-1846. Duke of
Mercia (*The*), 1823; Julian the Apostate,
1822; Mary Tudor, 1847, a drama; Song of
Faith (*A*), and other Poems, 1842.
VERE (Sir *Francis*), 1554-1608. Bloody
Battel of Nieuport, in Flanders (*The*), 1641;
Commentaries, 1657, posthumous.
VERTUE (*George*), London, 1684-1756. Anec-
dotes of Painting in England, 1762, post-
humous; Catalogue of the Pictures of
Charles I., James II., and the Duke of
Buckingham, 1757, 1758, 1759.
VICTORIA (queen of Great Britain and Ireland,
and empress of India), born at Kensington
Palace, 1819-   . Early Days of H.R.H.
the Prince Consort, 1867 (compiled by the
Hon. C. Grey, under her Majesty's direc-
tion); Leaves from the Journal of Our Life
in the Highlands, 1869; Life of H.R.H. the
Prince Consort, 1874-78 (under the direction
of her Majesty and the charge of sir
Theodore Martin).
VINCE (Rev. *Samuel*), died 1821. Complete
System of Astronomy, 1797-1808; Confuta-
tion of Atheism, 1807; Elements of Conic
Sections, 1781; Principles of Fluxions, 1795;
Propagation of the Gospel (Harleian prize
essay), 1807.
VINCENT, D.D. (*William*), London, 1739-
1815. Commerce and Navigation of the
Ancients, 1807; Origination of the Greek
Verb, 1794; Periplus of the Erythræan Sea,
1800-5; Voyage of Nearchus, 1797.
VOYSEY (Rev. *Charles*), London, 1828-   .
Dogma *v*. Morality, 1866; Humanity *v*.
Barbarism, 1868; Is every Statement in the
Bible . . . True? 1864; Sling and the
Stone (*The*), 1865-69.

WACE, D.D. (*Henry*), London, 1836-   .
Christianity and Morality, 1874-75 (Boyle
lectures); Ethics of Belief, 1877; Foundations of Faith, 1879 (Bampton lecture);
Gospel and its Witnesses (*The*), 1883; Prin-

cipal Facts in the Life of our Lord, 1881; Some Central Points of our Lord's Ministry, 1890.

WACE (*Maistre Robert*), Jersey, a Norman poet, about 1112-1183. Roman de Brut (*Le*), 1155, printed 1836-38 (*i.e.* Brute or Brutus, the hypothetical king of England); Roman de Rou (*Le*), part i. 1160, part ii. 1170, first printed 1827, new edition 1876 (Rou, *i.e.* Rollo, duke of Normandy: part i. is in Alexandrine verse, part ii. is in eights).
  ∴ Attributed to him: Chroniques des Ducs de Normandie, published 1825; Vie de S. George, published 1829; Vie de S. Nicolas, published 1850; Vie de la Vierge Marie, published 1829.

WADDING (*Luke*), Waterford, in Ireland, 1588-1657. Annales Ordinis Minorum, 1647-54.

WADDINGTON, D.D. (*George*), 1793-1869. History of the Church to the Reformation, 1833; History of the Reformation on the Continent, 1841; Present Condition, etc., of the Greek Church, 1829; Visit to Ethiopia, 1822; Visit to Greece, 1825.

WADDINGTON, D.D. (*John*), Leeds, in Yorkshire, 1810-1880. Bicentenary Prize Essay, 1862; Black Bartholomew, 1862; Congregational History, 1869, 1874-78 (his chief work); Emmaus, 1846; Hebrew Martyrs (*The*), 1846; Historical Papers, 1861; Life of John Penry, 1854; Surrey Congregational History, 1860; Track of the Hidden Church, 1863; Wolf in the Fold (*A*), 1867.

WAKE (Sir *Isaac*), 1575-1632. Rex Platonicus, etc., 1607.

WAKE, D.D. (*William*), archbishop of Canterbury, born at Blandford, in Dorsetshire, 1657-1737. Defence of the Power of Christian Princes over Ecclesiastical Synods, 1697; Doctrines of the Church of England, 1686; English Version of the Epistles of the Apostolic Fathers, 1693; State of the Church and Clergy of England, 1703. His Life, by dean Hook.

WAKEFIELD (*Edward*), 1768-1854. Account of Ireland (*An*), 1812 ("No eulogium can be too high," *Edin. Review*).

WAKEFIELD (*Edward Gibbon*), 1786-1862. England and America, 1833; Letters from Sydney, 1829; View of the Art of Colonization, 1833.

WAKEFIELD (Rev. *Gilbert*), Nottingham, 1756-1801. Essay on Inspiration, 1781; Evidences of Christianity, 1793; Expediency, etc., of Public . . . Worship, 1792; Internal Evidence of the Christian Religion, 1789; Memoirs of himself, 1804, posthumous; Nature of Baptism, 1781; Observations on Pope, 1796; Opinions of the First Three Centuries concerning . . . Christ, 1784; Poemata, etc., 1776; Silva Critica, 1789-95; Thomas Paine's *Age of Reason* examined, 1794-95. His Memoirs, by himself, 1792.

WAKEFIELD PLAYS (*The*), a collection of ancient plays by various authors, published by the Surtees Society in 1836, and called the "Townley Mysteries," because the MS. belongs to the Townley family.

WALCOTT (*John*), pseudonym "Peter Pindar." See WOLCOT.

WALCOTT (Rev. *Mackenzie Edward Charles*), Bath, in Somersetshire, 1822-1880. Ancient Church of Scotland (*The*), 1874; Cathedralia, etc., 1865; Cathedral Cities of England and Wales, 1865; Cathedrals of the United Kingdom (*The*), 1858; Constitutions and Canons of the Church of England, 1874; Double Choir (*The*), 1869; Four Minsters round the Wrekin (*The*), 1877; Handbook for St. James's, Westminster, 1850; History of Battle Abbey, 1866; History of Christchurch Priory, Hampshire, 1861; History of St. Margaret's Church, Westminster, 1847; History, etc., of the English Ordinal, 1851; Memorials of Stamford, 1867; Memorials of Westminster, 1849; Minsters and Abbey Ruins of the United Kingdom, 1860; Plain Persuasive to Holy Communion (*A*), 1849; Sacred Archæology, 1869; William of Wykeham and his Colleagues, 1852.

WALFORD (*Edward*), 1823- . Handbook of the Greek Drama, 1856; Life of Lord Palmerston, 1867; Life of Louis Napoleon, 1873; Life of the Prince Consort, 1862; Old and New London (the first two were by G. W. Thornbury), no date; Tales of our Great Families, 1877.

WALKER (*Clement*), Cliffe, in Dorsetshire, 1595-1651. High Court of Justice, or Cromwell's Slaughter-house, 1654; History of Independency, 1648-51 (Cromwell committed him to the Tower for this book).

WALKER (Sir *Edward*), 1610-1677. Coronation of Charles II., 1661; Historical Discourses, 1705; Iter Carolinum, 1660.

WALKER (*George*), died 1690. True Account of the Siege of Londonderry, 1689.

WALKER (*George Alfred*), Nottingham, 1807- Actual Condition of the Metropolitan Graveyards, 1846; Burial-ground Incendiarism, 1846; Gatherings from Graveyards, 1839; Grave Reminiscences, 1875; Graveyards of London (*The*), 1840; Interment and Disinterment, 1843; Past and Present State of Intramural Burial-places, 1851; Practical Suggestions for Extramural Cemeteries, 1849.

WALKER, D.D. (*John*), died 1730. Sufferings of the Clergy . . . in the Grand Rebellion, 1714.

WALKER (*John*), Colney Hatch, Middlesex, 1732-1807. Critical Pronouncing Dictionary, 1791; Elements of Elocution, 1781; Rhyming Dictionary, 1775; Speaker (*The*), 1801.

WALKER (*William Sidney*), 1795-1846. Critical Examination of the Text of *Shakespeare*, 1860; Poetical Remains, 1852; Shakespeare Versification, 1854.

WALL, D.D. (*William*), 1646-1728. Defence of the History of Infant Baptism, 1719 (highly commended by bishop Watson and bishop Tomline); History of Infant Baptism, 1707.

WALLACE (*Alfred Russel*), Usk, in Monmouthshire, 1822- . Contributions to the Theory of Natural Selection, 1870; Darwinism, 1889; Forty-five Years of Registration Statistics, 1884; Geographical Distribution of Animals (*The*), 1876 (his great work); Island Life, 1880; Land Nationalization, 1882; Malay Archipelago (*The*),

1869; On Miracles and Spiritualism, 1875; Psycho-Physiological Sciences, etc., 1878; Travels on the Amazon and Rio Negro 1853; Tropical Nature, 1878.

WALLACE (*William Vincent*), Waterford, in Ireland, 1814-1865. Amber Witch (*The*), 1861, an opera; Desert Flower (*The*), 1863, an opera; Estrella, an opera (not completed at his death); Love's Triumph, 1860, an opera; Lurline, 1860, an opera, and Maritana, 1845, an opera (his two best); Matilda of Hungary, 1847, an opera.

WALLER (*Edmund*), Coleshill, in Herefordshire, poet, 1605-1687. Divine Love (in six cantos), 1685; Fear of God (in two cantos), 1686; Instructions to a Painter, 1665; Invasion and Defeat of the Turks, 1683; Poems, 1645; To my Lord Protector, 1656, a panegyric on Cromwell; To the King Charles II., 1660, on his restoration; Welcome to the Prince of Orange, 1677. His Life, by Bell, 1871.

WALLER, LL.D. (*John Francis*), 1810- . Dead Bridal (*The*), 1856; Festival Tales, 1873; Pictures from English Literature, 1870; Poems, 1854; Revelations of Peter Brown (*The*), 1870; Slingsby Papers (*The*), 1852. Also editions of Goldsmith, Moore, and Swift, with biographies.

WALLER (Sir *William*), Kent, 1597-1668. Divine Meditations, 1680, posthumous; Vindication . . . for taking up Arms against Charles I., first published in 1793.

WALLIS, D.D. (*John*), Ashford, in Kent, 1616-1703. Hobbius Heauton-timorumenos, 1662; Mathesis Universalis, 1657; Mechanica, sive de Motu, 1670; Mnemonica, or the Art of Memory, 1661; Treatise on Logic, 1687.

WALPOLE (*Horace*). See ORFORD.

WALPOLE, LL.D. (*Spencer*), 1839- . History of England from 1815, 1878-80; Land of Home Rule (*The*), 1893; Life of Lord John Russell, 1889; Life of Spencer Perceval, 1874.

WALSH, M.D. (*Walter Hayle*), Dublin, 1816- . Diseases of the Heart and Great Vessels, about 1850; Nature and Treatment of Cancer, 1846; Practical Treatise on the Lungs, 1842.

WALSINGHAM (Sir *Francis*), Chiselhurst, in Kent, 1536-1590. Complete Ambassador (*The*), 1655.

WALSINGHAM (*Thomas of*), monk of St. Albans, chronicler, fifteenth century. Historia Brevis (continuation of Matthew Paris from the death of Henry III. to Henry VI.), about 1423, printed 1603; Ypodigma Neustriæ, fifteenth century, printed 1574; and again 1603.

WALTON, D.D. (*Brian*), bishop of Chester, born at Cleveland, in Yorkshire, 1600-1661. Biblia Polyglotta, 1657 (a monumental work). His Life, by Todd, 1821.

WALTON (*Izaak*), Stafford, 1593-1683. Compleat Angler (*The*), 1653 (his best-known work); Elegy on the Death of Donne, 1633; Life of Donne, 1640 (his first publication); Life of Herbert, 1670; Life of Hooker, 1665; Life of Sanderson, 1678; Life of Wotton, 1651. His Life, by sir J. Hawkins, 1760; Dr. T. Zouch, 1796; sir H. Nicolas, 1833-

36; Dr. G. W. Bethune, U.S., 1847; W. Dowling.

WANKLYN (*James Alfred*), 1834- . Treatise on Milk Analysis, 1873; Treatise on Tea, Coffee, and Cocoa, 1874; Treatise on Water Analysis, 1871.

N.B.—These are text-books and standard works.

WARBURTON (*Eliot Bartholomew George*), Ireland, 1810-1852. Crescent and the Cross (*The*), 1845; Darien, or the Merchant Prince, 1852, posthumous; Life of the Earl of Peterborough, 1853; Prince Rupert and the Cavaliers, 1849; Reginald Hastings, 1850, a novel.

WARBURTON (*William*), bishop of Gloucester, born at Newark, in Notts., 1698-1779. Alliance between Church and State, 1736; Commentary on Pope's *Essay on Man*, 1742; Divine Legation of Moses, 1737-41 (his great work); Doctrine of Grace (*The*), 1762; Inquiry into the Prodigies and Miracles related by Historians, 1727; Julian, 1750; Lord Bolingbroke's Philosophy, 1756; Miscellaneous Translations, 1714; Natural and Revealed Religion, 1753-54; Pope's *Essay on Man* vindicated, 1739-40. His Life, by bishop Hurd, 1788; Rev. J. S. Watson, 1863.

WARD, LL.D. (*Adolphus William*), Hampstead, London, 1837- . Chaucer, 1879; Counter-Reformation (*The*), 1889; Dickens, 1882; History of English Dramatic Literature to the Death of Queen Anne, 1875.

WARD (*Artemus*). See BROWNE (*C. F.*).

WARD (*Edward*), usually called "Ned Ward," Hudibras poet, 1667-1731. Adam and Eve stripped of their Furbelows, 1714; Bacchanalia, 1698, a poem; Delights of the Bottle, 1720, a poem; History of the Grand Rebellion, 1713 (in verse); Hudibras Redivivus, 1705-7, a burlesque poem; Hudibrastic Brewer (*The*), 1714, a poem; London Spy (*The*), 1698-1700; Miracles performed by Money, 1692, a poem; News from Madrid, 1726; Nuptial Dialogues, etc., 1710; Poet's Ramble after Riches (*The*), 1699, in verse; Revels of the Gods, 1701; Secret History of the Clubs (*The*), 1709; Sot's Paradise (*The*), 1700, a satire on ale; Trip to Ireland (*A*), 1699; Trip to Jamaica (*A*), 1698; Vulgus Britannicus (in 15 cantos), 1710; Wandering Spy (*The*), 1722; Whigs Unmasked (*The*), 1713.

WARD (Mrs. *Humphry*), maiden name *Mary Augusta Arnold* (niece of Matthew Arnold), Hobart, Tasmania, novelist, 1851- . Amiel's Journal, 1885; David Grieve, 1892; Marcella, 1894; Milly and Olly, 1881; Miss Bretherton, 1884; Robert Elsmere, 1888; Sir George Tressady, 1896; Story of Bessie Costrell, 1895; Unitarians and the Future, 1894.

WARD, LL.D. (*John*), London, 1679-1758. Lives of the Gresham Professors, 1740. His Life, by T. Birch, 1766.

WARD (*Robert Plumer*), 1765-1846. Chatsworth, or the Romance of a Week, 1844; De Clifford, 1841, a novel; De Vere, 1827, a novel; Historical Essay on the (1688) Revolution, 1800; History of the Law of Nations in Europe, 1795; Illustrations of Human

Life, 1837; Pictures of the World at Home and Abroad, 1838; Revolution of 1688 (*The*), 1838; Tremaine, 1825, a novel. His Life, by E. Phipps, 1850.

WARD, D.D. (*Seth*), bishop of Salisbury, born at Buntingford, in Hertfordshire, astronomer, 1617-1689. Being and Attributes of God, 1662; Geometrical Astronomy, 1656; Lecture on Comets, 1653; On Hobbes, 1659; On the Immortality of the Soul, 1652. His Life, by Dr. Walter Pope, 1697.

WARD (*Thomas Humphry*), 1845- . Brasenose Ale, 1878; English Poets (selections), 1880-83; English Art in the Public Galleries of London, 1886-88; Humphry Sandwith, 1884; Men of the Reign, 1885; Reign of Queen Victoria, 1887 (25 chapters, by 22 different authors).

WARD (*Wilfrid*). Clothes of Religion (*The*), 1886; W[illiam] G[eorge] Ward, and the Catholic Revival, 1893; W[illiam] G[eorge] Ward, and the Oxford Movement, 1889; Wish to Believe (*The*), 1884; Witness to the Unseen, 1893.

WARD, D.D. (*William George*), 1812-1882. Essays on the Philosophy of Theism, 1884; Ideal of a Christian Church, 1844.

WARDLAW, D.D. (*Ralph*), Dalkeith, in Scotland, 1779-1853. Assurance of Faith (*The*), 1830; Christian Ethics, 1834; Congregational Independency, 1848; Female Prostitution, 1842; Infant Baptism, 1846; Lectures on Ecclesiastes, 1821; Life of Joseph (*The*), 1845; National Church Establishments considered, 1839; On the Atonement, 1843; On Faith and Atonement, 1832; On Miracles, 1853; On the Nature and Extent of the Atonement, 1843; On Pardon and Assurance, 1831; Sabbath (*The*), 1832; Socinian Controversy (*The*), 1813; Systematic Theology, 1854; Unitarianism Indefensible, 1816. His Life, by Dr. W. L. Alexander, 1856.

WARE (Sir *James*), "The Camden of Ireland," Dublin, 1594-1666. De Hibernia et Antiquitatibus ejus Disquisitiones, 1654-58; De Præsulibus Hiberniæ Commentarius, 1665; Rerum Hibernicarum Annales, 1662.

WARING, M.D. (*Edward*), near Shrewsbury, 1736-1798. Meditationes Algebraicæ, 1770; Meditationes Analyticæ, 1773-76; Miscellanea Analytica, 1762; Proprietates Algebraicarum Curvarum, 1772.

WARNER (*Susan*), pseudonym "Miss Wetherell," New York, U.S., 1819-1885. Hills of the Shatemuc, 1856; Melbourne House, 1864; Old Helmet (*The*), 1863; Queechy, 1851; Wide, Wide World (*The*), 1849. And many others.

WARNER (*William*), Oxfordshire, 1558-1609. Albion's England, 1586-1606 (Campbell says the episode of "Argentile and Curan" is the best pastoral in the language); Pan, his Syrinx, 1584.

WARREN (*Henry*), London, 1798- . Artistic Anatomy; Hints upon Hints; Notes upon Notes; On the River Ravensbourne; Water-colour Painting.

WARREN (*John Leicester*), poet, *- . Orestes, 1871, a metrical drama; Philoctetes, 1871, a metrical drama; Rehearsals, 1870, a book of verses; Searching the Net, 1873, a book of verses.

WARREN, D.C.L. (*Samuel*), Denbighshire, North Wales, 1807-1877. Diary of a Late Physician, 1832; Lily and the Bee (*The*), 1851; Miscellanies, 1854; Moral and Intellectual Development of the Age, 1854; Now and Then, 1847, a novel; Ten Thousand a Year, 1839-41, a novel (his chief work).

WARTON, D.D. (*Joseph*), Dunsfold, in Surrey, 1722-1800. Odes on Several Subjects, 1746; On the Writings and Genius of Pope, 1756-82; Translation of *Virgil*, 1753. His Life, by the Rev. John Wooll, 1806.

WARTON (*Thomas*), brother of Dr. Joseph Ward, Basingstoke, in Hampshire, poet laureate, 1728-1790. Companion to the Guide and *v.v.*, 1762; History of English Poetry, 1774, 1778, 1781 (his great work, and wholly unrivalled); History of Kiddington Parish, 1781; Life, etc., of Ralph Bathurst, 1761; Life of Sir Thomas Pope, 1760; Observations on Spenser's *Faërie Queene*, 1753; Observer Observed (*The*), 1756; Ode for Music (*An*), 1751; Oxford Sausage (*The*), 1764; Panegyric on Ale (*A*); Pastoral Eclogues (*Five*), 1745; Pleasures of Melancholy, 1745; Poetical Works, 1802, posthumous; Triumph of Isis, 1749, a poetic reply to Mason; Union (*The*), 1753, select English and Scotch poems. His Life, by R. Mant, 1802.

WATERLAND, D.D. (*Daniel*), Waseley, in Lincolnshire, 1683-1740. Advice to a Young Student, 1714; Arian Subscription considered, 1721; Critical History of the Athanasian Creed, 1723; Doctrine of the Trinity asserted (*The*), 1734; Nature . . . and Efficacy of the Sacraments, 1730; Review of the Doctrine of the Eucharist (*A*), 1734; Scripture vindicated, 1734; Vindication of Christ's Divinity, 1719, 1723. His Life, by bishop Van Mildert, 1823.

WATER-POET (*The*). See TAYLOR (*John*).

WATERTON (*Charles*), 1782-1865. Essays on Natural History, 1838, 1844, 1857; Wanderings in South America, 1825.

WATKINS, D.D. (*Henry William*), 1844- . Modern Criticisms [of] the Fourth Gospel, 1890; Religion and Science, 1879.

WATKINSON (Rev. *William L.*), Hull, 1838- . Influence of Scepticism on Character, 1886; John Wicklif, 1884; Lessons of Prosperity, 1890; Mistaken Signs, 1882; Noonday Addresses, 1890; Transfigured Sackcloth, 1891.

WATSON (*Hewett Cottrell*), 1804-1884. Cybele Britannica, 1847-59, supplement 1863, compendium 1870; Geographical Distribution of British Plants, 1843; New Botanist's Guide, 1835-37; On the Geographical Distribution of Plants, 1835; also "The London Catalogue of British Plants."

WATSON (*H. R. Marriott*), 1863- . At the First Corner; Diogenes of London, 1893; Lady Faintheart, 1890; Marahuna, 1888; Web of the Spider (*The*), 1891.

WATSON, D.D. (*Richard*), bishop of Llandaff, born near Kendal, in Westmoreland, 1737-1816. Apology for the Bible (in answer to T. Paine), 1796; Apology for Christianity (addressed to Gibbon), 1776; Chemical Essays, 1781, 1786; Institutiones Metallurgicæ, 1768; On Church Revenues, 1785; Principles of the Revolution vindicated, 1815. His Life, by himself, 1817, posthumous.

WATSON (Rev. *Richard*), 1781–1833. Biblical and Theological Dictionary, 1832; Conversations for the Young, 1830; Expositions of Scripture, 1835; Life of John Wesley, 1831; Sermons, 1834; Theological Institutes, 1814; Universal Redemption, 1830. His Life, by the Rev. T. Jackson, 1834.

WATSON, LL.D. (*Robert*), St. Andrews, in Scotland, 1730–1780. History of Philip II., 1777; History of Philip III., 1783; Life of the Duke of York, 1779.

WATSON, D.D. (*Thomas*), Catholic bishop of Lincoln, 1557–1582. Holsome and Catholyke Doctrine of the Seven Sacraments, 1558; Reall Presence (*The*), 1554.

WATSON (*Thomas*), poet, 1560–1592. Amyntæ Gaudia, 1592; Amyntas, 1585; Eclogue on the Death of Walsingham, 1590; Hecatompathia (in two parts), 1582; Madrigals, 1590; Melibæus, 1590; Tears of Fancie, 1593.

WATSON (*William*), Wharfedale, Ripon, in Yorkshire, *– . Eloping Angels (*The*), 1893; Epigrams of Art, etc., 1881; Excursions in Criticism, 1893; Father of the Forest, and other Poems, 1895; Lacrymæ Musarum, and other Poems, 1892; Lyric Love, 1892, an anthology; Odes, and other Poems, 1894; Poems, 1892; Prince's Quest, and other Poems (*The*), 1880; Wordsworth's Grave, 1889.

WATSON, M.D. (Sir *William*), London, 1715–1787. Experiments, etc., in Electricity, 1745.

WATT, M.D. (*Robert*), Ayrshire, Scotland, 1774–1819. Bibliotheca Britannica, 1819–24; Catalogue of Medical Books, 1812; Rules of Life, 1814.

WATTS (*Alaric Alexander*), London, 1799–1864. Lyrics of the Heart, 1851; Poetical Sketches, 1822; Scenes of Life and Shades of Character, 1831.

WATTS, D.D. (*Isaac*), Southampton, 1674–1748. Divine and Moral Songs, 1720; Horæ Lyricæ, 1706; Hymns, 1707; Moral Songs, 1730; Palinode (*A*), 1721; Psalms of David, 1719.

In Prose: Catechisms, 1730; Doctrine of the Trinity, 1726; Glory of Christ as God-Man, 1746; Guide to Prayer, 1715; Improvement of the Mind, 1741; Logic, 1725; On the Love of God, 1729; Orthodoxy and Charity United, 1745; Philosophical Essays, 1734; Reliquiæ Juveniles, 1734; Ruin and Recovery of Mankind, 1740; Sermons, 1721–23, 1747, and 1812 posthumous; Short View of Scripture History, 1730; Strength and Weakness of Human Reason (*The*), 1737; Use and Abuse of the Passions, 1729; World to Come (*The*), 1738. His Life, by Dr. Johnson, 1779–81; S. Palmer, 1785; Milner, 1834; R. Southey, 1837; Mills, 1839; T. Gibbons; E. P. Hood, 1875.

WAUGH (*Edwin*), Rochdale, in Lancashire, 1818–1890. Around the Yule Log, 1879, fireside stories; Ben an' the Bantam, 1866, sequel to "Besom Ben," 1865; Birthplace of Jim Bobbin, 1867; Chimney Corner, 1879; Chirrup, 1858, a song; Come Whoam to thy Childer and Me, 1856, a ballad; Dulesgate,

etc., 1868; Fourteen Days in Scotland, 1864; Goblin's Grave (*The*), 1869; Grand Comic Christmas Pantomime, etc., 1866; Guide to Castletown, 1869; Hermit Cobbler (*The*), 1878, a tale; Home Life of the Lancashire Factory Folk during the Cotton Famine, 1867; Irish Sketches, 1869; Jannock, 1873; Johnny o' Wobblers an' th' Two-Wheeled Dragon, 1869; Lancashire Anecdotes, 1872; Lancashire Sketches, 1871; Lancashire Songs, 1863; Nomination (*The*), or a Striking Story, 1878; Old Coal-Man (*The*), 1873, a sketch; Old Nest (*An*), 1869; Owd Bodle, 1865, a tale; Poems and Lancashire Songs, 1859; Poesies from a Country Garden, 1866; Port Erin, etc., 1869; Rambles and Reveries, 1872; Rambler in the Lake Country, 1861; Samples of Lancashire Wares, 1879, prose and verse; Sketches of Lancashire Life and Localities, 1855; Sneck Bant, or th' Owd Tow-bar, 1868; Snowed up, 1869; Th' Owd Blanket, 1867; Tufts of Heather, etc., 1864; What ails thee, my Son Robin? 1856, a ballad; Yeth Bobs an' Scaplins, 1868.

WEAVER (*John*), Lancashire, 1576–1632. Ancient Funeral Monuments of Great Britain and Ireland, 1631.

WEBSTER (Mrs. *Augusta*), maiden name *Augusta Daviss*, died 1894. Auspicious Day (*The*), 1872; Disguises, 1880; Dramatic Studies, 1866; Mother and Daughter, 1895, posthumous; Sentence (*The*), 1887; Woman Sold (*A*), and other Poems, 1866.

WEBSTER (*Daniel*), Salisbury, U.S., statesman, 1782–1852. Writings and Speeches (in six vols.), 1851; and his Correspondence in 1855.

WEBSTER (*John*), dramatist, seventeenth century. (Either with Dekker or with Rowley.) Appius and Virginia, 1659, a tragedy; Cure for a Cuckold, 1661, a comedy; Devil's Law Case (*The*), 1623, a comedy; Duchess of Malfy (*The*), 1623, a tragedy; Famous History of Sir Thomas Wyat, 1607, a tragedy; Monumental Column in Memory of Henry Prince of Wales, 1613; Monument of Honour (*The*), 1624; Thracian Wonder (*The*), 1661, a comedy; White Devil (*The*), 1612, a tragedy. His Life, by Dyce, 1830; W. Hazlitt, 1857.

WEBSTER, LL.D. (*Noah*), Hartford, U.S., 1758–1843. Dictionary of the English Language, 1828; Grammar of the English Language, 1807; Sketches of American Policy, 1785.

WEBSTER (*Thomas*), the Orkneys, 1773–1844. Encyclopædia of Domestic Economy, 1844.

WEDMORE (*Frederick*), Richmond Hill, Clifton, in Gloucestershire, 1884. Four Masters of Etching, 1883; Life of Balzac, 1889; Masters of Genre Painting (*The*), 1879; Pastorals of France, 1877, poetical prose fiction; Renunciation, 1890; Snapt Gold Ring (*A*), 1871, a novel; Studies in English Art, 1876–1880; Two Girls, 1873, a novel; Wilfrid Harris, 1868, biographical.

WELLDON, D.D. (*James Edward Cowell*), 1854– . Future and the Past (*The*), 1885–86; Gerald Eversley's Friendship, 1893; Politics of Aristotle, 1885; Rhetoric of

Aristotle (*The*), 1886 ; Sermons preached to the Harrow Boys, 1887, 1891 ; Spiritual Life (*The*), 1880.

WELLESLEY (*Richard Colley*), marquis Wellesley and earl of Mornington, born in Dublin, 1760–1842. Despatches, Minutes, and Correspondence, 1836, 1838 ; History of the Events, etc., in India . . . in the Late War, 1805. His Life, by R. R. Pearce, 1846.

WELLINGTON (*Arthur Wellesley*, duke of), called "The Iron Duke," was born at Dangan Castle, in Ireland, 1769–1852. Correspondence and Memoranda, edited by his son, 1859 ; Despatches, published by Colonel Gurwood (in 13 vols.), 1834–39. His Life, by G. Elliott, 1814 ; Southey, 1816 ; Bourrienne, Napoleon's secretary (in French) ; G. Soane, 1839 ; sir J. E. Alexander, 1839 ; W. H. Maxwell, 1839–41 ; B. Jackson and C. R. Scott, 1840 ; A. Vieusseux, 1841 ; G. H. Francis, 1845 ; J. Macgill, 1850 ; Macfarlane, 1851 ; J. M. Wilson, 1853–55 ; Brialmont, 1858–59 (in French : it was translated by Greig) ; C. D. Yonge, 1860 ; H. Clark, no date ; Williams, etc.

WELLS, M.D. (*Charles William*), Charleston, U.S., 1757–1817. Essay on Dew, etc., 1814 (excellent) ; Single Vision with Two Eyes, 1818. His Life, by himself, 1818.

WELLS (*H. G.*). Island of Doctor Moreau (*The*), 1896 ; Plattner Story (*The*), 1897 ; Stolen Bacillus (*The*), 1895 ; Time Machine (*The*), 1895 ; War of the Worlds, 1898 ; Wheels of Chance, 1896 ; Wonderful Visit (*The*), 1895.

WELSH, D.D. (*David*), Dumfriesshire, Scotland, 1793–1845. Elements of Church History, 1844 ; Life of Dr. Thomas Brown, 1825.

WELSTED (*Leonard*), 1689–1747. Apple Pie ; Dissembled Wanton (*The*) ; Epistles, Odes, etc., 1724 ; Genius (*The*), a poem in honour of the duke of Marlborough ; Triumvirate (*The*), a satire on Pope, for which he was placed in the *Dunciad*. His Memoirs, by J. Nichols, 1787.

WESLEY (Rev. *Charles W.*), brother of John Wesley, Epworth, in Lincolnshire, 1708–1788. Funeral Hymns, 1753 ; Gloria Patri, 1753 ; Hymns and Sacred Poems, 1749 ; Hymns for Ascension Day, 1753 ; Hymns for the Nativity, 1750 ; Hymns for the Resurrection, 1754 ; Hymns for the Watch Night, 1780 ; Hymns for the Year, 1756 ; Sacred Poetry, Sermons, etc. ; Works, 1829–31. His Life, by J. Whitehead, 1793–96 ; Rev. H. Moore, 1824 ; Southey, 1820 ; Jackson, 1841 ; Wedgwood, 1870. See also Tyerman's vols. on the Wesley family.

WESLEY (Rev. *John*), founder of the "Wesleyan Methodists," brother of Charles Wesley, Epworth, in Lincolnshire, 1703–1791. Account of the People called "Methodists," 1749 ; Collection of Psalms and Hymns, 1738 (with Charles Wesley) ; Doctrine of Original Sin (*The*), 1757 ; Earnest Appeal, 1745 ; Ecclesiastical History, 1781 ; History of England from the Death of George II., 1776 ; Hymns for the Lord's Supper, 1748 (with Charles Wesley) ; Hymns of Petition and Thanksgiving, 1753 ;

Letters, 1816 ; Life of the Rev. J. Fletcher, 1786 ; Notes on the New Testament, 1755 ; Notes on the Old and New Testaments, 1764 ; Select Hymns with Tunes, 1764 ; Sermons, 1787 ; Survey of God's Wisdom in Creation, 1763. His Life, by J. Hampson, 1791 ; J. A. Colet, 1791 ; Dr. T. Coke and H. Moore, 1792 ; J. Whitehead, M.D., 1793–96 ; R. Southey, 1820 ; Rev. R. Watson, 1831 ; Rev. S. Bradburn, 1837 ; J. Beecham, 1847 ; G. Smith ; Miss Wedgwood, 1870 ; Rev. Luke Tyerman, 1870.

WESLEY (Rev. *Samuel*), father of John and Charles, Dorsetshire, 1662–1735. Dissertations (53 in number), 1736 ; History of the Old and New Testaments, 1704, in verse ; Life of Christ (*The*), 1693, an heroic poem ; Maggots, or Poems on Several Subjects, 1685 ; Pious Communicant (*The*), 1700. His Life, by the Rev. Luke Tyerman, 1870.

WESLEY (*Samuel*), poet, born at Epworth, in Lincolnshire, 1690–1739. Poems, 1736.

WEST, R.A. (*Benjamin*), the artist, Springfield, in Pennsylvania, U.S., 1738–1820. His Life, by John Galt, 1816–20.

WEST, LL.D. (*Gilbert*), 1705–1756. Institution of the Garter, 1742, a dramatic poem ; Observations on the Resurrection of Christ, 1747 ; translated *Pindar*, 1749. His Life, by lord Lyttleton, 1757. See Johnson's *Lives*.

WESTCOTT, D.D. (*Brooke Foss*), near Birmingham, bishop of Durham, 1825– . Bible and the Church (*The*), 1864 ; Characteristics of the Gospel Miracles, 1859 ; Christian Consummation, 1886 ; Christian Life Manifold and One (*The*), 1869 ; Elements of Gospel Harmony, 1851 (Norrisian Essay) ; Epistles of St. John, 1883 ; Epistle to the Hebrews (*The*), 1892 ; Gospel of Life (*The*), 1892 ; Gospel of St. John, 1882 ; Gospel of the Resurrection (*The*), 1866 ; Historic Faith (*The*), 1883 ; History of the Canon of the New Testament, 1855 ; History of the English Bible, 1869 ; Incarnation and Common Life (*The*), 1893 ; Introduction to the Study of the Gospels, 1860 ; New Testament in Greek (*The*), 1885 ; On the Religious Office of the Universities, 1873 ; Religious Thought in the West, 1891 ; Revelation of the Father (*The*), 1884 ; Revisers of the New Testament, 1882 ; Social Aspects of Christianity, 1887 ; Steps in the Christian Life, 1880 ; Victory of the Cross, 1888.

WESTMINSTER REVIEW (*The*), started 1824.

WESTON (Rev. *Stephen*), Exeter, 1747–1830. Letters from Paris, 1792–93 ; Specimen of a Chinese Dictionary, 1812 ; Specimen of a Conformity of European Languages with the Oriental, 1802.

WESTON (Rev. *William*), Campden, in Gloucestershire, died 1760. Dissertation on the Wonders of Antiquity, 1748 ; Enquiry into the Rejection of Christian Miracles, 1746.

WESTWOOD (*John Obadiah*), Sheffield, 1805– . Arcana Entomologica, 1845 ; British Butterflies and their Transformations, 1841 ; British Moths and their Transformations, 1845 ; Cabinet of Oriental Entomology, 1848 ;

Entomologist's Text-Book (*The*), 1838; Illuminated Illustrations of the Bible, 1849; Introduction to the Modern Classification of Insects, 1838; Palæographia Sacra Pictoria, 1845.

WESTWOOD (*Thomas*), poet, 1814-1888. Beads from a Rosary, 1843; Berries and Blossoms, 1855; Burden of the Bell (*The*), 1850; Quest of the Sanctgreal, 1868.

WETHERELL (Miss). *See* WARNER (*Susan*).

WEYMAN (*Stanley John*), Ludlow, in Shropshire, 1855– . Gentleman of France (*A*), 1893; House of the Wolf (*The*), 1890; Man in Black (*The*), 1894; Memoirs of a Minister of France, 1895; My Lady Rotha, 1894; New Rector (*The*), 1891; Red Cockade (*The*), 1895; Shrewsbury, 1898; Story of Francis Cludde (*The*), 1891; Under the Red Robe, 1894.

WHARTON (*Grace* and *Philip*), real names Mrs. *Katherine Thomson* and her son *J. C. Thomson*, *–* . Literature of Society (*The*), 1862; Queens of Society (*The*), 1860; Wits and Beaux of Society (*The*), 1860.

WHARTON (Rev. *Henry*), Norfolk, 1664-1695. Anglia Sacra, 1691-95 (his chief work); Troubles and Trials of Archbishop Laud, 1695.

WHARTON (*Philip Wharton*, duke of), poet, 1698-1731. Poetical Works, 1727. His Life and Writings were published 1732. Pope calls him "the scorn and wonder of our days"—*scorn* for his political follies, *wonder* for his extraordinary genius.

WHARTON, M.D. (*Thomas*), Yorkshire, 1610-1673. Adenographia, 1656 (*i.e.* a treatise on the glands).

WHATELY, D.D. (*Richard*), archbishop of Dublin, born in London, 1787-1863. Christian's Duty with Respect to the Established Church, 1819; Collection of English Synonyms (*A*), 1852; Dangers of the Christian Faith, 1839; Elements of Logic, 1826; Elements of Rhetoric, 1828; English Synonyms, 1851; Errors of Romanism, 1830; Historic Doubts, 1819 (a capital satire); History of Religious Worship, 1847; Introductory Lectures on Political Economy, 1831; Party Feeling in Matters of Religion, 1822; Revelations concerning a Future State, 1829; Some of the Difficulties in the New Testament, 1828; Some of the Peculiarities of the Christian Religion, 1825; Thoughts on Secondary Punishment, 1832; Thoughts on the Sabbath, 1830. His Life, by Fitzpatrick, 1864; and by his daughter, E. Jane Whately, 1866.

WHEATLEY (Rev. *Charles*), London, 1686-1742. On the Book of Common Prayer, 1720.

WHEATON, LL.D. (*Henry*), Providence, in Rhode Island, U.S., 1785-1848. Digest of the Law of Maritime Captures, 1815 (a standard work); Elements of International Law, 1836 (his chief work); Histoire du Droit des Gens (prize of the French Institute), 1841 (a standard work); History of the Law of Nations, 1845; History of the Northmen, 1831; Life of William Pinckney, 1826; Reports (in 12 vols.), "the Golden Book of American Law."

WHEATSTONE (Sir *Charles*), Gloucester, 1802-1875. Experiments to measure the Velocity of Electricity, 1834; On Acoustic Figures, 1833.
N.B.—His scientific writings and inventions are so numerous that a mere list of them would require several pages of this APPENDIX.

WHELER (Rev. sir *George*), 1650-1724. Travels in Dalmatia, Greece, and the Levant, 1682.

WHETSTONE (*George*), in Elizabeth's reign. Addition (*An*), or Touchstone of the Time, 1584; Amelia, 1593; Enemie to Unthriftynesse, 1586; English Myrror (*The*), 1586; Heptameron, 1582; Honourable Reputation of a Souldier (*The*), 1586; Mirur for Magestrates of Cyties, 1584; Promos and Cassandra, 1578, a comedy (the quarry of Shakespeare's *Measure for Measure*); Remembrances of Sir Philip Sidney, Sir Nicholas Bacon, George Gascoigne, etc.; Rocke of Regard, 1576.

WHEWELL, D.D. (*William*), Lancashire, 1794-1866. Analytical Statics, 1833; Astronomy and General Physics, 1833 (a Bridgewater treatise); Dynamics, 1823; Elements of Morality, 1845; History of the Inductive Sciences, 1837; History of Moral Philosophy in England, 1852; Mechanics, 1819; Mechanics of Engineering, 1841; Philosophy of the Inductive Sciences, 1840; Plurality of Worlds, 1853 (the negative, against Brewster, who maintained the affirmative); Systematic Morality, 1846; Todhunter, 1876.

WHICHCOTE, D.D. (*Benjamin*), Shropshire, 1610-1683. Moral and Religious Aphorisms, 1703, posthumous; Sermons, 1702-7, posthumous.

WHISTON (*William*), Norton, in Leicestershire, 1667-1752. Autobiography, 1749; *Josephus* translated, 1737 (well known); Primitive Christianity, 1711; Theory of the Earth, 1696.

WHITAKER (Rev. *John*), Manchester, 1735-1808. Course taken by Hannibal over the Alps, 1794; Genuine History of the Britons, 1772; History of Manchester, 1774-75; Life of St. Neot, brother of King Alfred, 1809; Origin of Arianism disclosed, 1791; Queen Mary of Scots vindicated, 1788.

WHITAKER, LL.D. (Rev. *Thomas Dunham*), Rainham, in Norfolk, 1759-1821. History and Topography of Leeds, 1816; History of Richmondshire, in Yorkshire, 1823; History of the Parish of Whalley, 1801; *Piers Ploughman* edited, 1810.

WHITAKER'S ALMANACK, started 1869.

WHITBY, D.D. (*Daniel*), Northamptonshire, 1638-1726. Disquisitiones Modestæ, 1718; Five Points of Calvinism (*The*), 1735 (against Calvinism); Last Thoughts, 1727; Paraphrase, etc., on the New Testament, 1703; Protestant Reconciler, 1683 (burnt by order of the Oxford University).

WHITE (Rev. *Edward*), London, 1819– . Higher Criticism (*The*), 1892; Life and Death, 1877; Life in Christ, 1846; Modern Spiritualism, 1893; Mystery of Growth, 1867; Some of the Minor Moralities, 1868.

WHITE (Rev. *Gilbert*), Selborne, in Hampshire, 1720-1793. Natural History of Selborne, 1789 (excellent); Naturalist's Calendar (*The*), 1795. His Memoir, by Jesse, 1850.

WHITE (*Henry Kirke*), Nottingham, 1785–1806. Clifton Grove, and other Poems, 1803; Poems, 1804; Remains, 1807, posthumous. His Life, by Southey, 1807; sir Harris Nicolas, 1837.

WHITE (Rev. *James*), near Edinburgh, vicar of Bonchurch, in the Isle of Wight, 1785–1862. Earl of Gowrie (*The*), a drama; Eighteen Christian Centuries, 1858 (his best book); Feudal Times, a drama; History of England, 1860; History of France, 1859; King of the Commons, a drama; Landmarks of English History, 1855; Landmarks of Grecian History, 1857; Village Poorhouse (*The*), 1832, a poem.

WHITE (Rev. *Jeremiah*), chaplain to Cromwell, 1630-1707. Persuasion to Moderation, 1708; Restoration of all Things, 1712 (his principal work).

WHITE, D.D. (*Joseph*), Stroud, in Gloucestershire, 1746-1814. Ægyptiaca, 1801; Diatessaron, 1800; Novum Testamentum Græce, 1808; Sacrorum Evangeliorum versio Syriaca Philoxeniana, 1778; View of Christianity and Mahometanism, 1783.

WHITE (Rev. *Joseph Blanco*), Seville, in Spain, of Irish parents, 1775-1841. Letters from Spain, 1822 (valuable); Practical and Internal Evidence against Catholicism, 1825; Poor Man's Preservative against Popery (*The*), 1825; Second Travels of an Irish Gentleman in Search of a Religion, 1833; Sonnet to Night (called by Coleridge "the finest in the language"). His Life, by himself, edited by J. H. Thom, 1845.

WHITE (Rev. *Thomas*), 1582-1676. De Medio Animarum Statu, 1659 (censured by the House of Commons); Institutiones Peripateticæ, 1646; Institutiones Theologicæ, 1652; Sonitus Buccinæ, 1659.

WHITE (*Walter*), Reading, in Berkshire, 1810-1892. All Round the Wrekin, 1860; Eastern England from the Thames to the Humber, 1865; July Holiday in Saxony, etc. (*A*), 1857; Londoner's Walk to the Land's End (*A*), 1855; Month in Yorkshire (*A*), 1858; Northumberland and the Border, 1859; On Foot through the Tyrol, 1856; To Switzerland and Back, 1854.

WHITE (*William Hale*), Bedford, 1831– . Autobiography of Mark Rutherford, 1881; Catherine Furze, 1893; De Emendatione Intellectus, 1895; Mark Rutherford's Deliverance, 1885; Miriam's Schooling, 1889; Revolution in Tanner's Lane, 1887.

WHITEFIELD (Rev. *George*), Gloucester, 1714-1770. Journals, 1756; Sermons, etc., 1771, posthumous. His Life, by Rev. L. Tyerman, 1771; J. Gillies, D.D., 1772; S. Drew, 1828; R. Philip, 1838; T. Robert, 1860.

WHITEHEAD (*Charles*), 1804-1862. Autobiography of Jack Ketch, 1834; Earl of Essex, 1843; Life of Sir Walter Raleigh, 1854; Richard Savage, 1842; Smiles and Tears, 1847.

WHITEHEAD (*Paul*), London, poet, 1710-1774. Gymnasiad, a mock heroic poem in ridicule of boxing. His *Works* were published 1777;

but he is better known by the two lines of Churchill—

May I (can more disgrace on manhood fall)
Be born a Whitehead, and baptized a Paul.

His Life, by E. Thompson, 1777.

WHITEHEAD (*William*), Cambridge, poet laureate, 1715-1788. Atys and Adrastus, 1743; Charge to the Poets (*A*), 1762; Creusa, 1754, a tragedy; Essay on Ridicule (*An*), 1743; On the Danger of Writing Verse, 1741, a poem; Poems, 1754; Roman Father (*The*), 1750, a tragedy; School for Lovers, 1762, a comedy; Trip to Scotland (*A*), 1770; Variety, 1754 (his best production). His Life, by W. Mason, 1774.

WHITEHURST (*John*), Congleton, in Cheshire, 1713-1788. Inquiry into the Original State and Formation of the Earth, 1778. His Life, by Dr. Hutton, 1792.

WHITELOCKE (*Bulstrode*), London, 1605-1676. Journal of the Swedish Embassy of 1653-54, published 1772; Memorials of English Affairs, 1682 (from 1625 to 1666, and from "Brute" to James II., both valuable).

WHITMAN (*Walt*), American poet, 1819-1892. Democratic Vistas, 1888; "Leaves of Grass," 1855 (first edition); Specimen Days in America, 1887.

WHITTIER (*John Greenleaf*), Haverhill, in Massachusetts, U.S., 1807-1892. Among the Hills, and other Poems, 1868; Ballads, 1838; Ballads of New England, 1870; Centennial Hymn (*A*), 1876; Chapel of the Hermits, and other Poems, 1853; Child Life, 1871; Collected Poems, 1850; Home Ballads, and other Poems, 1859; In War Time, and other Poems, 1863; Lays of my Home, and other Poems, 1843; Leaves from Margaret Smith's Journal, 1836, poems; Legends of New England, 1831 (these legends were afterwards versified under the titles of "Bridal of Pennacook," "Cassandra Southwick," "Mary Garvin," and "Mogg Megone"); Literary Recreations, 1854; Maud Müller, 1865; Miriam, and other Poems, 1870; Moll Pitcher, 1833, a poem; National Lyrics, 1865-66; Old Portraits and Modern Sketches (biographical), 1850; Panorama (*The*), and other Poems, 1856; Pennsylvanian Pilgrims (*The*), and other Poems, 1872; Sabbath Verse (*A*), 1853; Snow-bound, a Water Idyll, 1866; Songs of Labour, and other Poems, 1851; Stranger in Lowell (*The*), 1845, prose essays; Supernaturalism in New England, 1847; Tent on the Beach, and other Poems, 1867; Vision of Echard, etc. (*The*), 1878; Voices of Freedom, 1849.

WHITTINGTON (*Robert*), Lichfield, in Hampshire, poet laureate, 1480-1531. Epigrammata, 1519.

WHYTE, D.D. (*Alexander*), Kirriemuir, in Forfarshire, Scotland, 1837– . Bunyan's Characters, 1893, etc.; Characters and Characteristics (of W. Law), 1893; Jacob Behmen, 1894; Samuel Rutherford, etc., 1894; Shorter Catechism (*The*), 1883.

WHYTE-MELVILLE (*George John*). See MELVILLE (*George John Whyte*).

WHYTT, M.D. (*Robert*), Edinburgh, 1714-1766. Nervous Disorders, 1764; On the

Vital and other Involuntary Motions of Animals, 1751; Physiological Essays, 1755.

WICLIFFE. See WYCLIFFE.

WIFFEN (*Jeremiah Holme*), near Woburn, in Bedfordshire, 1792-1836. Aonian Hours, 1819; Historical Memoirs of the House of Russell, 1833; Julia Alpinula, and other Poems, 1820; Translated Tasso's *Jerusalem Delivered*, 1830.

WILBERFORCE (Rev. *Robert Isaac*), London, brother of Samuel Wilberforce, 1802-1857. Doctrine of Holy Baptism, 1849; Doctrine of the Eucharist, 1853; Doctrine of the Incarnation, 1848; Principles of Religious Authority, 1854.

WILBERFORCE, D.D. (*Samuel*), bishop of Winchester, place of birth, Clapham Common, London, son of William Wilberforce, 1805-1873. Agathos, and other Stories, 1840, religious allegories; Essays, 1874; Eucharistica, 1840; Hebrew Heroes, 1870; History of the American Church, 1844; Life of William Wilberforce (his father), 1838; Rocky Island (*The*), 1840. His Life, vol. i. by canon Ashwell, 1880, vol. ii. by R. G. Wilberforce, 1881; G. W. Daniel.

WILBERFORCE (*William*), Hull, the resistless advocate of the abolition of slavery, 1759-1833. Practical View of Christianity, 1797 (six editions exhausted in five months). His Life, by his sons, 1838.

WILDE (Lady), maiden name *Jane Francesca Speranza Elgee*. Ancient Cures, Charms, and Usages of Ireland, 1890; Ancient Legends of Ireland, 1886; Driftwood from Scandinavia, 1884; Notes on Men, Women, and Books, 1891; Poems, 1864; Social Studies, 1893; Ugo Bassi, 1837.

WILDE (*Oscar Fingall O'Flahertie Wills*), Dublin, 1858- . Dorian Grey, 1891; Happy Prince (*The*), 1888; House of Pomegranates (*A*), 1891; Intentions, 1891; Lady Windermere's Fan, 1893; Lord Arthur Savile's Crimes, 1891; Poems, 1881; Ravenna, 1878, Newdigate Prize poem; Salomé (in French), 1893; Sphinx (*The*), 1894; Woman of No Importance (*A*), 1894.

WILKES (*John*), founder and editor of the *North Briton*, 1762, Clerkenwell, London, 1727-1797. Essay on Woman, 1763; Letters, 1767-69; Letters to his Daughter, 1804; Speeches, 1777-79, 1786. His Life, by Baskerville, 1769; Cradock, 1772; Almon, 1805; Watson, 1870; W. F. Rae, 1873.
·.· In No. 45 of the *North Briton*, the king is charged with uttering a deliberate lie (for which charge Wilkes was sent to the Tower).

WILKIE, R.A. (Sir *David*), Cults, in Fifeshire, Scotland, 1785-1841. His Life, by Allan Cunningham, 1843.

WILKIE, D.D. (*William*), called "The Scottish Homer," Scotland, 1721-1772. Dream (*A*), in the manner of Spenser, 1759; Epigoniad (an epic in rhyme, in nine books), 1757; Fables, 1768.

WILKINS (Sir *Charles*), Frome, in Somersetshire, 1749-1836. Sanscrit Grammar, 1808; Translated the *Bhagasad-Gita*, 1785; the *Hitopadesa*, 1787.

WILKINS, D.D. (*David*), 1685-1745. Concilia

Magnæ Britanniæ, 1736 (a standard work); Leges Anglo-Saxonicæ, 1721.

WILKINS, D.D. (*John*), bishop of Chester, born in Northamptonshire, 1614-1672. Discovery of a New World, 1638 (Is the Moon inhabited?); Essay towards a Real Character, etc., 1668; Mathematical Magick, 1648; Mercury, 1641; Our Earth one of the Planets, 1640; Principles and Duties of Natural Religion, 1675.

WILKINS, R.A. (*William*), Norwich, 1778-1839. Antiquities of Magna Græcia, 1807; Prolusiones Architectonicæ, 1837.

WILKINSON, M.D. (*James John Garth*), London, 1812- . Human Body and its Connection with Man (*The*), 1851; Improvisations from the Spirit, 1857; Ministry of Health (*The*), 1856; On Social Health, 1865; Swedenborg, 1849, a biography.

WILKINSON (Sir *John Gardner*), Hardendale, in Westmoreland, Egyptologist, 1797-1875. Architecture of Ancient Thebes, 1850; Dalmatia and Montenegro, 1848; Egyptians in the Time of the Pharaohs, 1857; Extracts from Hieroglyphical Subjects found at Thebes, etc., 1830; Fragments of an Hieratic Papyrus found at Turin, containing the Names of Egyptian Kings, 1851; Handbook for Travellers in Egypt, 1847; Manners and Customs of the Ancient Egyptians, derived from Paintings, Sculptures, and Monuments still existing, 1837-41, a second series, 1841 (a standard work); Materia Hieroglyphica, 1828; Modern Egypt and Thebes, 1843; On Colour . . . and laying out Geometrical Gardens, 1858; Popular Abridgment of "Manners and Customs of the Ancient Egyptians," 1854; Topographical Survey of Thebes, etc., 1830; Topography of Thebes, and General View of Egypt, 1835.

WILLIAM OF MALMESBURY. See MALMESBURY.

WILLIAM OF NEWBURY, chronicler, born at Bridlington, 1136-1208. Rerum Anglicarum (in five books), first printed 1597.

WILLIAM OF OCCAM. See OCCAM.

WILLIAMS (Rev. *George*), 1814-1878. Holy City (*The*), or Historical and Topographical Notices of Jerusalem, 1845.

WILLIAMS (*Helen Maria*), 1762-1828. Julia, 1790, a novel; Letters from France (in favour of the Girondists), 1790-93; Manners and Opinions of the French Republic, 1801; Miscellaneous Poems, 1786; Narrative of Events in France, 1815; Poems, 1823; [Present] Politics of France, 1795; Tour in Switzerland (*A*), 1798.

WILLIAMS (Rev. *Isaac*), poet, 1802-1865. Baptistery (*The*), 1842; Cathedral (*The*), 1838; Christian Scholar (*The*), 1849; Christian Seasons (*The*), 1854; Study of the Gospels, 1841-50; Thoughts in Past Years, 1838.

WILLIAMS (*John*), Tottenham, 1796-1839. Missionary Enterprises in the South Sea Islands, 1837. His Life, by Prout.

WILLIAMS (*John*), Denbighshire, Wales, 1811-1862. Ecclesiastical Antiquities of the Kymry, 1844. Edited *Annales Cambriæ*, 1850; *Barddas*, 1862; *Brut y Tywysogion*, 1850.

WILLIAMS (*Monier*), Bombay, 1819-
Buddhism, 1890; Bāgh of Bahār, text, 1859;
English and Sanskrit Dictionary (*An*), 1851;
Hindúism, 1877; Indian Epic Poetry, 1863,
a lecture; Indian Wisdom, 1875-1893;
Introduction to the Study of Hindúism, 1859;
Nalopākhyāna, 1879; Modern India and
the Indians, 1878; Practical Grammar of
Sanskrit, 1846; Religious Thought and Life
in India, 1883; Roman Letters applied to
the Indian Languages, 1859; Rudiments of
Hindústáni, 1858; Sanskrit and English
Dictionary, 1872; Sanskrit in Relation to
Missionary Work in India, 1861; Story of
Nala, 1861, a Sanskrit poem. Edited
S'akuntalá, 1853, a drama, which he trans-
lated into prose and verse, 1855; *Vikra-
morvasi* 1849, the Sanskrit drama.

WILLIAMS (Rev. *Roger*), Conwyl Cayo, in
Wales, 1606-1683. Bloudy Tenent of Perse-
cution for Cause of Conscience, 1645; Bloudy
Tenent of Persecution yet more Bloudy by
Cotton's Endeavour to Wash it White in the
Blood of the Lamb, 1653; Experiments of
Spiritual Life and Health, 1651; George Fox
digged out of his Burrows, 1655; Hireling
Ministry none of Christ's (*A*), 1650; Key to
the Languages of America, 1642.

WILLIAMS, D.D. (*Rowland*), Wales, 1817-
1870. Broad-Chalke Sermon-Essays, 1867;
Christian Freedom in the Council of Jerusalem, 1858; Christianity and Hinduism
compared, 1856; Hebrew Prophets retranslated, 1872; Owen Glendower, 1870, a dramatic biography; Persecution for the Word
of God, 1862; Prophets of Israel and Judah,
1866; Rational Godliness, 1855; Review of
Bunsen, 1860 (*Essays and Reviews*).

WILLIAMS (*W. Mattieu*), 1819-1892. Chemistry of Cookery (*The*), 1885; Chemistry
of Iron and Steel Making (*The*), 1890; Fuel
of the Sun (*The*), 1870; Science in Short
Chapters, 1882; Simple Treatise on Heat
(*A*), 1880; Through Norway with Ladies,
1877; Vindication of Phrenology (*A*), 1894.

WILLIAMSON, M.D. (*Hugh*), Pennsylvania,
U.S., 1735-1819. History of New Carolina,
1812.

WILLIS, LL.D. (*Browne*), Blandford, in Dor-
setshire, 1682-1760. Gold Coins of the
Kings of England and Wales, 1733; Notitia
Parliamentaria, 1715-30; Survey of the
Cathedrals of England, 1717-33. His Me-
moirs, by Dr. Ducarel, 1760.

WILLIS (*Nathaniel Parker*), Maine, U.S.,
1807-1867. Absalom (*The Death of*), 1846,
a poem in blank verse; Bianca Visconti,
1843, a play; Convalescent (*The*), 1860;
Corsair (*The*), 1840; Dashes at Life with a
Free Pencil, 1845; Famous Persons and
Places, 1854; Fun Jottings, 1853; Hagar in
the Wilderness, 1846, a poem in blank verse;
Health Trip to the Tropics, 1852; Hurry-
graphs, 1851; Inklings of Adventure, 1839;
Leper (*The*), 1846, a poem in blank verse;
Letters from under a Bridge, 1840; Life
Here and There, 1850; Loiterings of Travels,
1839; Memoranda of Jenny Lind, 1851;
Paul Fane, 1856; Pencillings by the Way,
1835; People I have met, 1850; Poems,
1828-31; Summer Cruise in the Mediterra-

nean, 1853; Tortesa, the Usurer, 1841, a
play; Two Ways of dying for a Husband,
1839.

WILLIS (Rev. *Robert*), London, 1800-1875.
On the Architecture of the Middle Ages, etc.,
1840; Principles of Mechanism, 1841.

WILLIS, M.D. (*Thomas*), Great Bedwin, in
Wiltshire, 1621-1675. Cerebri Anatome,
1664; De Anima Brutorum, 1672; Patholo-
giæ Cerebri et Nervosi Generis Specimina,
1667.

WILLMOTT (*Robert Aris*), Wiltshire, 1809-
1863. Biography of Jeremy Taylor, 1846;
Lives of English Sacred Poets, 1832; Pleasures of Literature, 1851; Summer-time in
the Country, 1849.

WILLS (*William Gorman*), Kilkenny, in Ireland, 1828- . Buckingham, 1875; Charles
I., 1872, an historic play (Mr. Irving's
Charles I.); David Chantery, a novel; Eng-
land in the Days of Charles II., 1877, a
drama; Eugene Aram, 1873, a play; Hinko,
1871, a play; Jane Shore, 1875; Juana;
Man o' Airlie (*The*), 1866, a play; Mary
Queen of Scots, 1874; Nell Gwynne, 1878;
Ninon, 1880, a play; Notice to Quit, a novel;
Olivia, 1878, a play, founded on the *Vicar
of Wakefield*; Pace that kills (*The*), a
novel; Vanderdecken, 1878 (with Fitzgerald);
Wife's Evidence (*The*), a novel.

WILMOT (*John Wilmot Eardley*), Derby,
1748-1815. Laws and Customs of England;
Life of Sir John Eardley Wilmot (his father),
1793.

WILSON (*Alexander*), Paisley, in Scotland,
1766-1813. American Ornithology, 1808-14;
Foresters (*The*), 1825, a poem (descriptive of
a pedestrian journey to the Falls of Niagara);
Laurel disputed (*The*), 1791; Watty and
Meg, 1792, a ballad. His Life, in his "Ornithology," and by G. Ord, 1828.

WILSON (*Andrew*), *- . Abode of Snow,
1875; Ever-Victorious Army (the Taiping
rebellion).

WILSON (*Arthur*), 1596-1652. History, etc.,
of James I., 1653; Inconstant Lady (*The*),
printed 1814, a comedy.

WILSON (Sir *Daniel*), Edinburgh, 1816-1892.
Archæology and Prehistoric Annals of Scot-
land (*The*), 1851 (his chief work); Caliban,
1873; Chatterton, 1869; Lost Atlantis (*The*),
1892; Memorials of Edinburgh in the Olden
Times, 1846-48; Oliver Cromwell and the
Protectorate, 1848; Prehistoric Man, 1863;
Spring Wild Flowers, 1875.

WILSON (*Florence*), Scotland, 1500-1546. De
Animi Tranquillitate, 1543.

WILSON, M.D. (*George*), Edinburgh, 1818-
1859. Chemistry, 1850; Colour Blindness,
1855; Five Gateways of Knowledge (*The*),
1857 (his chief work); Life, etc., of Henry
Cavendish, 1851; Life of Edward Forbes,
1861; Life of Reid, 1852. His Life, by his
sister, 1866.

WILSON (Rev. *Henry Bristow*), 1803-1875.
National Church (*The*), in *Essays and
Reviews*, 1860; Schemes of Christian Com-
prehension (in *Oxford Essays*), 1857.

WILSON (*Horace Hayman*), London, 1786-
1860. Ariana Antiqua, 1841 (on the coins
and "Topes" of Afghanistan); Burmese

War (*The*), 1827, 1852; Dictionary of Sanskrit-English, 1819-40; External Commerce of Bengal (between 1813 and 1828), 1830; Glossary of Arabic, Persian, Hindustáni, etc., Judicial and Revenue Terms, 1855; Hindu and Mohammedan Law, 1860; History of British India (between 1805 and 1835), 1841; History of Cashmere, 1825-27; Manual of Universal History and Chronology, 1835; Oriental MSS., 1828; Present State of Oriental Literature, 1852; Proverbs (Persian and Hindu), 1824; Sanskrit Grammar for Students, 1841; Sanskrit-English Dictionary, 1849.

Translations: Mahâbhârata (selections), 1842; *Mégha Dúta* of Kâlidâsa, 1813, in verse; *Raghu Vansa* of Kâlidâsa, 1832, in verse; *Rig Veda*, 1850-66; *Theatre of the Hindus* (selections), 1827, 1835; *Vishn'u Parân'a* (Hindu mythology), 1840.

WILSON (*James*), Scotland, 1805-1860. Capital, Currency, and Banking, 1846; Economist (*The*), started 1843; Fluctuations of Currency, etc., 1840; Influences of the Corn Laws, 1839; Revenue (*The*), 1841.

WILSON (*John*), best known as "Christopher North," Paisley, in Scotland, 1785-1854. (Burns, sir W. Scott, and Wilson are called " The Scottish Trinity.") City of the Plague, 1816, poetry; Dies Boreales, 1836-46; Forester (*The*), 1824; Isle of Palms (*The*), 1812, poetry; Life, etc., of Burns, 1841; Lights and Shadows of Scottish Life, 1822; Noctes Ambrosianæ, 1822-36, in dialogue and prose (his chief literary production); Poems and Dramatic Works, 1825; Recreations of Christopher North, 1842; Trials of Margaret Lindsay, 1823, a novel. His Life, by Mrs. Gordon, his daughter, 1862.

WILSON (Sir *Robert Thomas*), London, 1777-1849. Historical Account of the British Expedition to Egypt, 1802; Journals of the Russian Campaigns against Napoleon, 1861; Military and Political Power of Russia (*The*), 1817.

WILSON, LL.D. (*Thomas*), Stroby, in Lincolnshire, 1520-1581. Art of Rhetorique, 1553; Rule of Reason, 1551.

WILSON, D.D. (*Thomas*), bishop of Sodor and Man, 1663-1755. Instructions, etc., for the Lord's Supper, 1736; Maxims of Piety and Christianity, 1791, posthumous; Parochialia, 1791, posthumous; Principles and Duties of Christianity (*The*), 1707; Sacra Privata, 1800, posthumous. His Life, by Cruttwell, 1808; Rev. H. Stowell, 1819; Rev. John Keble, 1852.

WILSON, LL.D. (*William Rae*), Paisley, in Scotland, 1772-1849. Travels in Egypt and the Holy Land, 1823; Travels in Norway, etc., 1826; Travels in Russia, 1828.

WING (*Vincent*), died 1669. Astronomia Britannica, 1669; Ephemerides, 1659-71; Harmonicon Cœleste, 1651. His Life, by J. G., 1670.

WINGATE (*David*), 1828- . Annie Weir, and other Poems, 1866; Lily Neil, 1879, in verse; Poems, 1866.

WINSLOW, M.D. (*Forbes Benignus*), Pentonville, London, 1810-1874. Anatomy of Suicide (*The*), 1840; Lectures on Insanity,

1854; Obscure Diseases of the Brain, 1860; On Cholera, 1831; Physic and Physicians, 1839; Physiology and Pathology of the Human Mind, 1831; Plea of Insanity in Criminal Cases (*The*), 1840.

WINSLOW, D.D. (*Miron*), Vermont, U.S., 1789-1864. Tamil-English Lexicon, 1862.

WINSTANLEY (*William*), about 1625-1684. England's Worthies, 1600; Historical Rarities, 1684; Honours of the Merchant Taylors (*The*), 1668; Lives of the Most Famous English Poets, 1687; Loyall Martyrology (*The*), 1663; Muses' Cabinet (*The*), 1655.

WINSTON (*Charles*), Kent, 1814-1864. Inquiry into the Difference of Style in Ancient Glass-painting, 1847; Memoirs Illustrative of Glass-painting, 1865.

WINTER (*John Strange*), real name Mrs. Henrietta Eliza Vaughan Stannard, York, 1856-1897. Aunt Johnnie, 1893; Bootles' Baby, 1885; Bootles' Children, 1888; Born Soldier (*A*), 1894; Buttons, 1889; Cavalry Life, 1881; Confessions of a Publisher, 1888; Dinna Forget, 1890; Ferrer's Court, 1890; Harvest, 1891; He went for a Soldier, 1890; Houp-la, 1886; Lumley the Painter, 1891; Magnificent Young Man (*A*), 1895; Man's Man (*A*), 1893; Mignon's Husband, 1887; Mignon's Secret, 1886; Mrs. Bob, 1889; Only Human, 1892; On March, 1886; Other Man's Wife (*The*), 1891; Pluck, 1886; Seventh Child (*A*), 1894; Soul of a Bishop (*The*), 1893; That Imp, 1887; That Mrs. Smith, 1893; Truth-teller (*The*), 1896.

WISE (Rev. *Francis*), Oxford, 1695-1767. Catalogue of Coins in the Bodleian Library, 1750; Enquiries concerning the Aborigines of Europe, 1758; History and Chronology of the Fabulous Ages, 1764; Nummorum . . . Scriniis Bodleianis Reconditorum Catalogus, 1750.

WISEMAN (*Nicholas Patrick Stephen*), cardinal, archbishop of Westminster, 1802-1865. Ceremonies of Holy Week, 1839; Connection between Science and Revealed Religion, 1836; Doctrines of the Catholic Church (*The*), 1836; Essays, 1853; Fabiola, or the Church of the Catacombs, 1868; Horæ Syriacæ, 1828; Points of Contact between Science and Art, 1863; Real Presence (*The*), 1836; Recollections of the Last Four Popes, etc., 1858; Rome and the Catholic Episcopate, 1862; Sermons, etc., 1859, 1864; William Shakespeare, 1865. His Life, by Wilfrid Ward, 1897.

WISHART, D.D. (*George*), bishop of Edinburgh, born in Forfarshire, Scotland, 1609-1671. De Rebus sub Imperio Jacobi Montisrosarum Marchionis Commentarius, 1647 (the wars of the marquis of Montrose).

WITHER (*George*), Bentworth, in Hampshire, 1588-1667. Abuses Stript and Whipt, 1613, satirical essays; Britain's Remembrancer, 1628, the Plague; Campo Musæ, 1643; Collection of Emblems, 1635; Emblems, Ancient and Modern, 1635; Epithalamia, 1613; Exercises upon the First Four Psalms, 1620, in verse and prose; Fidelia, 1617; Great Assizes holden in Parnassus (*The*), 1645; Hallelujah, 1641; Hymns and Songs of the Church, 1623; Juvenilia, 1622 · Letters of Advice, 1644; Mercurius Rusticus, 1643; Mistress of Philarete (*The*), 1622, poems; Nature of Man, 1636; Preparation to the Psalter (*A*), 1619; Prince Henry's Obsequies, 1612, an elegy; Prophecy (*A*),1641; Psalms versified, 1620, 1638; Read and Wonder, 1641; Satyre to the King, 1614; Scholler's Purgatory (*The*), 1624–26; Se Defendendo, 1643; Shepheard's Hunting, 1615 (his best); Shepheard's Pipe, 1614 (with Browne); Songs of the Old Testament versified, 1621; Speech without Doore, 1644; Vox Pacifica, 1645; Wither's Motto, 1618.

⁂ About 80 more publications. See Park's *British Biographer*. His Life, in Wilmott's *Lives of the Sacred Poets*, 1834.

WITHERING, M.D. (*William*), Wellington, in Shropshire, 1741–1799. Botanical Arrangement of British Plants, 1776.

WODROW (Rev. *Robert*), Glasgow, 1679–1734. Analecta (published by the Maitland Club), 1842–43; History of the Sufferings of the Church of Scotland, 1721–22 (in high esteem); Lives of the Scottish Reformers (published by the Maitland Club), 1834–45. His Life, by Dr. R. Burns, 1828.

WOLCOT, M.D. (*John*), better known as "Peter Pindar," Dodbrooke, in Devonshire, 1738–1819. Birthday Ode (irregular metre), 1786 (the visit of George III. to Whitbread's brewery); Bozzy and Piozzi, 1796, a town eclogue in two parts; Lousiad (*The*), in five cantos, 1786–89 (a lampoon on George III., who saw a louse in his green peas served at table, and ordered his cooks to have their heads shaved in future); Lyric Odes (15 in number), 1782, satires on the Royal Academicians; Ode upon Ode, 1785, irregular metre (the collection contains "King George III. and the Apple Dumplings"), (one of his best); Orson and Ellen, 1796, a legendary tale, in five cantos; Pilgrims and the Peas (*The*), 1782, irregular metre (one of the "Lyric Odes"); Pindariana, or Peter Pinder's Portfolio, 1796; Razor Seller (*The*), 1782, irregular metre (one of the "Lyric Odes"); Tristia, or the Sorrows of Pindar, 1796; Whitbread's Brewery visited by their Majesties (see above, "Birthday Ode").

⁂ A Biography is affixed to his *Works*, collected in 1809.

WOLFE (Rev. *Charles*), Dublin, 1791–1823. Burial of Sir John Moore, 1817 ("Not a drum was heard," etc.), (one of the best poems in the language).

⁂ Remains, published by Rev. John A. Russell, 1826. His Memoir, by the Rev. J. A. Russell, 1825.

WOLLASTON (Rev. *William*), Staffordshire, 1659–1724. Part of Ecclesiastes, as a Poem, 1691; Religion of Nature delineated, 1722.

WOLLSTONECRAFT (*Mary*), afterwards Mrs. *William Godwin*, Beverley, in Yorkshire, 1759–1797. Female Reader, 1789; French Revolution (*The*), 1790; Letters from Norway, etc., 1796; Letters to Edmund Burke, 1790; On the Education of Daughters, 1787; Origin and Progress of the French Revolution, and its Effects on Europe, 1795; Original Stories from Real Life, 1791; Posthumous Works, 1798; Vindication of the Rights of Women, 1792. Her Memoir, by W. Godwin, her husband, 1798; Kegan Paul, 1878.

WOLSELEY (*Garnet Joseph*, viscount), Golden-Bridge House, Dublin, 1833- . Decline and Fall of Napoleon, 1895; Field Pocketbook, 1873; France as a Military Power, 1870, 1878; Life of John Churchill, 1894; Marley Castle, 1877, a novel; Narrative of the War with China (in 1860), 1861; Soldier's Pocket-book for Field Service (*The*), 1869; System of Field Manœuvres (*The*), 1872.

WOLSEY (*Thomas*), Ipswich, in Suffolk, cardinal, 1471–1530. Rudimenta Grammatices et Docendi Methodus, 1534. His Life, by T. Storer, 1599; R. Fiddes, 1724; Jos. Grove, 1742–44; sir W. Cavendish, 1607; John Galt, 1818; C. Howard, 1824; George Cavendish, 1825.

WOOD (*Anthony à*), Oxford, 1632–1695. Athenæ Oxonienses, 1691–92; Fasti, 1693; Historia et Antiquitates Universitatis Oxoniensis, 1674; History and Antiquities of Oxford, 1669. His Life, by himself; by Huddersford, 1772; Rawlinson, 1811; Bliss, 1848.

WOOD (Mrs. *Henry*), maiden name *Ellen Price*, Worcester, novelist, 1820–1887. About Ourselves, 1883; Adam Grainger, 1876; Anne Hereford, 1868; Bessy Rane, 1870; Channings (*The*), 1862; Court Netherleigh, 1881; Danesbury House, 1860, a prize temperance tale (her first); Dene Hollow, 1871; East Lynne, 1861 (her most reputed novel); Edina, 1876; Elster's Folly, 1866; Foggy Night at Offord (*The*), 1863; George Canterbury's Will, 1870; Johnny Ludlow, 1874–85; Lady Adelaide; Life Secret (*A*), 1867; Lord Oakburn's Daughters, 1864; Master of Greylands, 1873; Mildred Arkell, 1865; Mrs. Halliburton's Troubles, 1862; Oswald Cray, 1864; Orville College; Parkwater; Pomeroy Abbey, 1878; Red Court Farm; Roland Yorke, 1869; St. Martin's Eve, 1866, a novel; Shadow of Ashlydyat (*The*), 1863; Told in the Twilight, 1875; Trevlyn Hold, 1864; Verner's Pride, 1863; William Allair, 1863, a story for boys; Within the Maze, 1872.

WOOD (Rev. *John George*), London, 1827–1889. Bible Animals; Boy's Own Natural History (*The*); Common Beetles of England; Common Moths of England; Common Objects of the Country; Common Objects of the Microscope; Common Objects of the Sea Shore,1857;Common Shells of England; Field Naturalist's Handbook(*The*),1880; Glimpses into Petland; Here and Hereafter, 1874; Homes without Hands (excellent); Insects Abroad, 1874; Insects at Home, 1885; Lane and the Field (*The*), 1879; Man and Beast, 1873; My Feathered Friends; Natural History of Man (his chief work); Natural History Ramble, 1879; Natural History Readings for Schools, 1882; Nature's Teaching; Our Garden Friends and Foes; Out of Doors, 1874; Popular Natural History, 1874; Sketches, etc., of Animal Life; Sketch-Lectures on Zoology, 1879; Wanderings in South America, 1879.

WOOD (*Robert*), Ireland, 1716-1771. Essay on the Genius of Homer, 1775, posthumous; Ruins of Balbek, 1757 ; Ruins of Palmyra, 1753.

WOODDESON (Dr. *Richard*), born at Kingston, in Surrey, 1745-1822. Elements of Jurisprudence, 1789 ; Systematic View of the Laws of England, 1792-93.

WOODHEAD (*Abraham*), 1608-1690. Brief Account of Church Government, 1662-87 ; Catholick Theses, 1689; Life of St. Tereza (no date) ; Motives for Holy Living, 1688 ; On the Adoration of our Blessed Saviour in the Eucharist, 1687 ; On the Spirit of Luther, 1687; Paraphrase of the Apocalypse (no date) ; Pietas Romana (no date).

WOODHOUSE (*Robert*), Norwich, 1773-1827. Elements of Trigonometry, 1809 ; Principles of Analytical Calculation, 1803 ; Treatise on Astronomy, 1812 ; Treatise on Isoperimetrical Problems, and the Calculus of Variations, 1810.

WOODWARD, M.D. (*John*), Derbyshire, 1665-1728. Attempt towards a Natural History of the Fossils of England, 1728-29 ; Natural History of the Earth, 1695.

WOODWARD (*Samuel Peckworth*), Norwich, 1821-1865. Manual of Recent Fossils and Shells, 1851-56.

WOOLNER, R.A. (*Thomas*), Hadleigh, in Suffolk, sculptor and poet, 1825 - 1892. My Beautiful Lady, 1887, a poem (his best); Nelly Dale, 1887, a poem ; Pygmalion, 1881, a poem ; Silenus, 1884, a poem ; Tiresias, 1886, a poem.

WOOLRYCH (*Humphrey William*), 1795-1871. Judge Jeffreys, 1827; Life of Sir Edward Coke, 1826 ; Lives of Eminent Serjeants-at-Law, 1869; Treatises on various legal subjects.

WOOLSTON (Rev. *Thomas*), Northampton, 1669-1733. Free Gifts to the Clergy, 1723-24; Moderator between the Infidel and the Apostate, 1721 ; Old Apology for the Truth of the Christian Religion revived (*The*), 1705 (to show that Moses was an allegorical person, and all history typical of Christ); On the Miracles, 1727-28 (to show they are not to be taken as literal facts, but only as allegories).

WORBOISE (*Emma Jane*), 1825- . Alice Cunninghame ; Amy Wilton, 1855 ; Brudenells of Brude (*The*), 1879 ; Canonbury Hold, 1872; Chrystabel, 1872 ; Emilia's Inheritance, 1874-75 ; Father Fabian, 1875 ; Grace Hamilton's School-days, 1856 ; Grey and Gold, 1870; Heir of Errington (*The*), 1881 ; Helen Bury, 1850; House of Bondage (*The*), 1873 ; Husbands and Wives, 1873 ; Joan Carisbroke, 1880; Kingsdown Lodge, or Seed-time and Harvest, 1858; Labour and Wait, or Evelyn's Story, 1864 ; Lights and Shades of Christian Life, 1855 ; Lillingstones of Lillingstone, 1864 ; Lottie Lonsdale, 1863 ; Margaret Torrington, 1867; Married Life, or Philip and Edith, 1863 ; Maud Bolingbroke ; Millicent Kendrick, 1862 ; Mr. Montmorency's Money, 1871; Nobly Born, 1871 ; Oliver West, 1876 ; Overdale, 1860 ; Robert Wreford's Daughter, 1877 ; St. Beetha's, or the Heiress of Arne, 1865 ; Singlehurst Manor, 1869 ; Sir Julian's

Wife, 1866 ; Story of Penelope (*The*), 1882 ; Thornycroft Hall, 1864 ; Violet Vaughan, 1866 ; Wife's Trials (*A*), 1858, a tale ; Woman's Patience (*A*), 1874.

WORCESTER (*Edward Somerset*, earl and marquis of), 1601-1667. Century of Inventions, 1663 (useful). His Life, by Dircks, 1805 ; C. F. Partington, 1825.

WORCESTER (*Joseph Emerson*), United States, 1784-1865. Dictionary of the English Language, 1860 ; Universal and Critical Dictionary of the English Language, 1846.

WORDE (*Wynkyn de*), printer, died 1534. Passetyme of Plesure, 1517 ; Polycronicon, 1495.

WORDSWORTH, D.C.L. (*Charles*), bishop of St. Andrews, son of Dr. Christopher Wordsworth master of Trinity, and brother of Dr. Christopher Wordsworth bishop of Lincoln, born at Bocking, in Essex, 1806-1885. Annals of my Life, 1891 ; Catechesis, 1860 ; Christian Boyhood at a Public School, 1846 ; College of St. Mary, Winton (*The*), 1848; Græcæ Grammaticæ Rudimenta, 1839 ; Manual of Reformation Facts, etc., 1860 ; Notes on the Eucharistic Controversy ; Outlines of the Christian Ministry, etc., 1872 ; Primary Witness to the Truth of the Gospels, 1892 ; Shakespeare's Knowledge and Use of the Bible, 1854 ; United Church for a United People (*A*), 1860.

WORDSWORTH, D.D. (*Christopher*), master of Trinity, born at Cockermouth, in Cumberland, 1774-1846. Ecclesiastical Biography (from the Reformation to the Revolution), 1809 ; Sermons, 1815.

WORDSWORTH, D.D. (*Christopher*), bishop of Lincoln, son of Dr. Christopher Wordsworth master of Trinity, and brother of Dr. Charles Wordsworth bishop of St. Andrews, born at Bocking, in Essex, 1807-1885. Ancient Writings from the Walls of Pompeii, 1837 ; Apocalypse, 1848, a Hulsean lecture; Athens and Attica, 1854 ; Confession and Absolution ; Cremation (*On*) ; Diary in France from 1844 to 1848 ; Discourses on Public Education, 1844; Ethica et Spiritualia, 1877 ; Fellowships and Endowments, 1872 ; Greece, Historical, Pictorial, and Descriptive; Greek Testament, with Notes ; Hippolytus, etc., 1853; Holy Year (*The*), hymns ; Irenicum Wesleyanum, 1876 ; Lectures on Art, 1875 ; Lectures on Inspiration ; Memoirs of Wordsworth [the poet, his uncle], 1851 ; Millennium (*On the*); Newtonian System (*The*), 1877 ; Procession of the Holy Spirit, 1872 ; Scripture Inspiration, 1847, a Hulsean lecture ; Sermons, 1841, 1850-68, 1871 ; State of the Soul after Death ; Theophilus Anglicanus, 1857; Visitation Addresses, 1873, 1879.

WORDSWORTH (*Dorothy*), 1855- . Recollections of a Tour in Scotland, 1874.

WORDSWORTH, D.D. (*John*), bishop of Salisbury, born at Harrow, 1843- . Church and the Universities (*The*), 1880 ; Four Addresses to the Clergy and Churchwardens of Salisbury, 1888 ; Fragments and Specimens of Early Latin, 1874 ; History of Latin Literature, 1870 ; Keble College, etc., 1860 ; Love and Discipline, 1885, a sermon ; One Religion (*The*), 1881, a Bampton lecture ; Prayers for

Use in College, 1883; Roman Conquest of S. Britain, 1889; University Sermons, 1879.

WORDSWORTH, D.C.L. (*William*), Cockermouth, in Cumberland, poet laureate, 1770–1850. Borderers (*The*), 1842; Descriptive Sketches in Verse, 1793; Ecclesiastical Sketches (in three parts, sonnets), 1822; Evening Walk (*An*), 1793; Excursion (in nine books), 1814 (his principal poem); Goody Blake and Harry Gill, 1798, a ballad; Idiot Boy (*The*), 1819; Lyrical Ballads, 1798 (with Coleridge); Memorials of a Tour in Scotland, 1803, 1814; Memorials of a Tour on the Continent, 1820; Odes, 1803–6; Pet Lamb (*The*), 1793, a pastoral ballad; Peter Bell (in three parts), 1819; Prelude, 1850; Sonnets to Liberty, 1802–16; Waggoner (*The*), (in four cantos), 1819; We are Seven, 1790, a ballad; White Doe of Rhylstone (in seven cantos), 1815; Yarrow revisited, and other Poems, 1835.

The poems of Wordsworth are arranged thus: 1, Poems referring to the period of Childhood (15 in number); 2, Juvenile Pieces (4); 3, Poems of the Imagination (31); 4, Miscellaneous Sonnets (93); 5, Memorials of a Tour in Scotland in 1803 (15); 6, Memorials of a Tour in Scotland in 1814 (4); 7, Poems on the Naming of Places (6); 8, Inscriptions (13); 9, Sonnets to Liberty (25); 10, Odes (44); 11, Memorials of a Tour on the Continent (36); 12, Ecclesiastical Sketches (part i. contains 37, part ii. 36, part iii. 33); 13, The River Duddon Sonnets (35); 14, Poems of Sentiment and Affection (35); 15, Poems referring to the period of Old Age (5); 16, Epitaphs and Elegiac Poems (14); 17, The Waggoner; 18, Peter Bell; 19, The White Doe; 20, The Excursion. His Life, by Dr. [bishop] Wordsworth, 1851; G. S. Phillips; Rev. E. Paxton Hood, 1856; F. W. E. Myers, 1881.

WORLIDGE (*Thomas*), Peterborough, 1700–1766. Collection of Designs from Antique Gems, 1768.

WORNUM (*Ralph Nicholson*), Durham, 1812–1877. Epochs of Painting, 1864; History of Ancient and Modern Painting, 1847.

WORSLEY (*Philip Stanhope*), 1831–1866. Poems and Translations, 1863; Translated Homer's *Iliad* 1865, *Odyssey* 1853.

WORSLEY (Sir *Richard*), born in the Isle of Wight, 1751–1805. History of the Isle of Wight, 1781; Musæum Worsleianum, 1794–1803.

WOTTON, M.D. (*Edward*), 1492–1555. De Differentiis Animalium, 1552.

WOTTON (Sir *Henry*), Bocton Hall, in Kent, 1568–1639. Ad Regem, etc., 1633; Elements of Architecture, 1624; George Villiers, Duke of Buckingham, 1642, posthumous; Panegyrick on King Charles; Parallel between Robert, Earl of Essex, and George Villiers, Duke of Buckingham, 1641, posthumous; Poems (published by the Percy Society, 1845); Reliquiæ Wottonianæ, 1651, posthumous; State of Christendom, 1657, posthumous. His Life, by Izaak Walton, 1670.

WOTTON, D.D. (*William*), Suffolk, 1666–1726. History of Rome, 1701; Leges

Walliæ, 1730; On Ancient and Modern Learning, 1694; On the Confusion of Tongues at Babel, 1730; Traditions and Usages of the Scribes and Pharisees, 1718.

WRANGHAM (Rev. *Francis*), Chester, 1769–1843. British Plutarch (*The*), 1812, 1816; Pleiad (*The*), 1828 (seven abridgments of "Christian Evidences"); Poems, 1795; Scraps, 1816; Sermons, 1816; Sertum Cantabrigiense, 1824; Tracts, 1816.

WRAXALL (Sir *Nathaniel William*), Bristol, 1751–1831. History of France, 1795 (from Henri III. to Louis XIV.); Memoirs of his own Time, 1815, 1836; Memoirs of the Courts of Berlin, Dresden, Warsaw, and Vienna, 1797; Memoirs of the Kings of France of the House of Valois, 1777.

WREN (Sir *Christopher*), East Knoyle, in Wiltshire, architect, 1632–1723. *He built:* Ashmolean Museum, Oxford, 1683; Buckingham House, London, 1703; Chelsea Hospital, 1682–90; College of Physicians, London, 1674–98; Custom House, London, 1668; Gateway Tower, Christchurch, Oxford, 1681–82; Greenwich Hospital, 1696; Hampton Court, 1690; Marlborough House, 1709; Monument, London, 1671–77; Morden College, Blackheath, 1692; Nevil's Court, Inn, College, Cambridge, 1664; Pembroke College Chapel, Cambridge, 1663 (his first work); Royal Exchange, London, 1667 (destroyed by fire 1838); Royal Observatory, Greenwich, 1675; St. Paul's Cathedral, 1675–1710 (his great work); Sheldonian Theatre, Oxford, 1664–69; Temple Bar, London, 1670 (taken down as an obstruction, 1878); Tower and Spire of St. Dunstan-in-the-East; Towers of the West Front of Westminster Abbey, 1713; Trinity College Library, Cambridge, 1666.

The following churches of London also: St. Andrew's, Holborn; St. Antholin's, Watling Street; St. Bennet Fink; St. Bride's, Fleet Street; Christ Church, Newgate; St. Clement's, Eastcheap; St. James's, Westminster; St. Lawrence's, Jewry; St. Martin's, Ludgate; St. Mary-at-Hill; St. Mary-le-Bow; St. Michael's, Cornhill; St. Sepulchre's, Newgate; St. Stephen's, Walbrook; St. Swithin's.

WRIGHT (*Thomas*), Cowper School, Olney, in Buckinghamshire, 1859– . Acid Sisters, 1897, poems; Blue Firedrake (*The*), 1892; Chalice of Carden (*The*), 1889; Hind Head, or the English Switzerland, 1898; Ianthe of the Jumps, a story of West Surrey in the old smuggling days, 1898; John Valiant, a story of Cobden's days, 1898; Life of Charles Dickens (*The*), 1898; Life of Daniel Defoe (*The*), 1894; Life of William Cowper (*The*), 1892; Loved Haunts of Cowper (*The*), 1894; Mystery of St. Dunstan's (*The*), 1892; Olney and Dr. Carey, 1892; Town of Cowper (*The*), 1886; Turvey and Legh Richmond, 1892.

WRIGHT (*Thomas*), Ludlow, in Shropshire, 1810–1877. Archæological Album, 1845; Biographia Britannica Literaria, 1842, 1846; Celt (*The*), the Roman, and the Saxon, 1852; Dictionary of Obsolete and Provincial English, 1857; Domestic Manners in England during the Middle Ages, 1861 ; England under the House of Hanover, 1848 ; Essays on Archæological Subjects, 1861 ; Essays on Popular Superstitions, etc., 1846 ; History of Caricature, etc., 1865 ; History of France, 1856–62 ; History of Ireland, 1854 ; History of Ludlow, 1852 ; Narratives of Sorcery and Magic, 1851 ; Political Poems and Songs, etc., 1859–61 ; Queen Elizabeth and her Times, 1838 ; Wanderings of an Antiquary, 1854 ; Womankind in Western Europe, 1869.

WRIGHT, LL.D. (*William*), Bengal Presidency, 1830 . Analectes sur l'Histoire, etc., des Arabes d'Espagne, 1855 ; Apocryphal Acts of the Apostles, 1871 ; Arabic Grammar, 1859–62 ; Arabic Reading-book (*An*), 1870 ; Book of Jonah (*The*), 1857, in four Oriental versions ; Catalogue of the Syriac MSS. in the British Museum, 1870–72 ; Contributions to the Apocryphal Books of the New Testament, 1865 ; Homilies of Aphraates (*The*), 1869 ; Opuscula Arabica, 1859 ; Travels of Ibn Jubair, 1852.

WYATT (Sir *Thomas*), Allington Castle, in Kent, 1503–1542. Poems, 1557, posthumous. His Life, by Dr. Nott, 1831.

WYCHERLY or WYCHERLEY (*William*), Clive, in Shropshire, dramatist, 1640–1715. Country Wife (*The*), 1675, a comedy ; Gentleman Dancing-master (*The*), 1673, a comedy ; Love in a Wood, 1672, a comedy ; Poems, 1704 ; Plain Dealer (*The*), 1677, a comedy. ∴ At the age of 80 he married a young lady (his second wife), and survived only eight days. His first wife was the countess of Drogheda, who died shortly afterwards, and left him all her property.

WYCLIFFE, D.D. (*John de*), called " The Morning Star of the Reformation," born at Spresswall, in Yorkshire, 1324–1384. Apology for Lollard Doctrines, printed 1842 ; Dialogorum, libri iv., printed 1525 ; Last Age of the Church (edited by Dr. Todd), 1840 ; Põre Caitiff (*The*) ; Prolog (*A*), etc., 1550 (found in an old English Bible) ; Tracts and Treatises, printed 1845 ; Translation of the Bible, 1380, first printed 1850 ; Two Treatises against the Order of Begging Friars (edited by Dr. James), printed 1608 ; Wycliffe's Wycket, first printed 1546. His Life, by Foxe, 1563 ; Rev. J. Lewis, 1719 ; Rev. C. W. Lebas, 1823 ; P. F. Tytler, 1826 ; Dr. Robert Vaughan, 1828 ; the Prayer-book and Homily Society, 1841.

WYNTER, M.D. (*Andrew*), 1819–1876. Curiosities of Civilization ; Our Social Bees, 1861 (same as "Sketches") ; Sketches of Town and Country Life, 1855 ; Subtle Brains and Lissom Fingers.

WYNTOUN (*Andrew*), 1390–1420. Orygynale Cronykil of Scotland (*The*), first printed 1795.

YALDEN, D.D. (*Thomas*), Exeter, 1671–1736. Hymn to Light ; Hymn to Darkness, with other Hymns, Odes, Elegies, and Fables (in Johnson's *Poets*). His Life, by Dr. Johnson.

YARRELL (*William*), Westminster, 1784–1856. History of British Birds, 1843 ; History of British Fishes, 1836.

YATES (*Edmund Hodgson*), novelist, 1831–1894. After Office Hours, 1861 ; Black Sheep, 1866–67 ; Broken to Harness, 1864 ; Business of Pleasure, 1865 ; Castaway, 1872 ; Dr. Wainwright's Patent, 1871 ; Edmund Yates, his Recollections, 1884 ; For Better for Worse, 1876 ; Forlorn Hope, 1867 ; Impending Sword (*The*), 1874 ; Kissing the Rod, 1866 ; Land at Last, 1866 ; Life of Charles Mathews the Elder, 1860 ; Memoir of Albert Smith, 1860 ; Mirth and Metre, 1854 (with F. E. Smedley); My Haunts and their Frequenters, 1854 ; Nobody's Fortune, 1871 ; Pages in Waiting, 1865 ; Righted Wrong (*A*), 1870 ; Rock Ahead (*A*), 1868 ; Running the Gauntlet, 1865 ; Silent Witness, 1875 ; Two by Tricks, 1874 ; Two Merry Men, 1854 (with F. E. Smedley) ; Waiting Race, 1872 ; World (*The*), a periodical, started 1874 ; Wrecked in Port, 1869 ; Yellow Flag (*The*), 1872.

YEAR-BOOKS from Edward I. to Henry VIII., 1678–79.

YEARSLEY (*Anna*), a milkwoman of Bristol, patronized by Mrs. H. More, 1756–1806. Earl Godwin, a tragedy ; Poems on Various Subjects, 1785 ; Royal Captives (*The*), a romance.

YEATES (*Thomas*), London, 1768–1839. Hebrew Grammar, 1812 ; Syriac Grammar, 1819.

YEATS (*William Butler*), Sandymount, Dublin, 1865– . Book of Irish Verse (*A*), 1895 ; Celtic Twilight (*The*), 1893 ; Countess Kathleen (*The*), 1892 ; Fairy and Folk Tales of the Irish Peasantry, 1869 ; John Sherman, 1891 ; Land of the Heart's Desire (*The*), 1894 ; Poems, 1895 ; Poems of William Blake, 1894 ; Representative Irish Tales, 1890 ; Stories from Carleton, 1891 ; Wanderings of Oisin (*The*), 1889 ; Works of W. Blake, 1893.

YENDYS (*Sydney*). See DOBELL (*Sydney*).

YONGE (*Charles Duke*), 1810– . History of England, 1857 ; History of France under the Bourbons, 1866 ; History of the British Navy, 1864 ; History of the English Revolution, 1874 ; Life of the Duke of Wellington, 1860 ; Parallel Lives : Epaminondas and Gustavus Adolphus, Philip and Frederick the Great, 1858 ; Three Centuries of Modern History, 1872.

YONGE (*Charlotte Mary*), Otterbourne, in Hampshire, novelist, 1823– . Aunt Charlotte's Stories of English History 1873, Stories of French History 1874, Stories of Bible History 1875, Stories of Greek History 1876, Roman History 1877, German History 1877 ; Beechcroft at Rockstone, 1893 ; Burnt out, 1879 ; Catherine of Aragon, 1881 ; Chaplet of Pearls (*The*), 1868 ; Christian Names (their history and derivation); Clever Woman of the Family (*The*), 1865 ; Constable's Tower (*The*), 1891 ; Cross Roads (*The*), 1892 ; Cunning Woman's Grandson (*The*), 1890 ; Daisy Chain (*The*), 1856 (see below, "The Trial"); Dove in the Eagle's Nest (*The*), 1866 ; Dynevor Terrace, 1857 ; Frank's Dog, 1882 ; Gold Dust, 1880 ; Grisly Grisell, 1893 ; Heartsease, 1854 ; Heir of Redclyffe (*The*), 1853 (her first and best) ; Lads and Lasses of Langley, 1881 ; Lady Hester,

1873 ; Lances of Lynwood (*The*); Landmarks of History ; Life of Bishop Patteson, 1873 ; Life of the Prince Consort, 1889 ; Love and Life, 1880 ; Magnum Bonum, 1879 ; Modern Telemachus (*A*), 1886 ; More By-ways, 1890 ; My Young Alcides, 1875 ; Old Woman's Outlook (*An*), 1892 ; Pillars of the House, 1873 ; Reputed Changeling (*A*), 1889 ; Slaves of Sabinus (*The*), 1890 ; Sowing and Sewing, 1882 ; Stick (*The*), 1892 ; Stray Pearls, 1883 ; Three Brides (*The*), 1876 ; Treasures in the Marshes (*The*), 1893 ; Trial (*The*), 1864 (a continuation of the "Daisy Chain"); Two Pennyless Princesses, 1891 ; Two Sides of a Shield (*The*), 1885 ; Under the Storm, 1887 ; Unknown to History, 1882 ; Wolf, 1882 ; Womankind, 1876 ; Young Stepmother (*The*), 1864. And many other books.

YOUATT (*William*), *-*. Cattle, their Breed, Management, and Diseases, 1834 ; Complete Grazier (*The*), 1850 ; Farmer's Library (*The*), 1849 (with Martin); Horse (*The*), 1831 (his best-known book) ; Pig (*The*), 1860 ; Treatise on Sheep (*A*), 1832.

YOUNG (*Arthur*), Bradfield, in Suffolk, 1741-1820. Agricultural Survey of France, 1792 ; Annals of Agriculture, 1784-1807 ; Busiris, King of Egypt, 1719, a tragedy ; Farmer's Calendar (*The*), 1770 ; Six Months' Tour through the North of England, 1771 ; Six Weeks' Tour through the Southern Counties, 1768.

YOUNG, D.C.L. (Rev. *Edward*), Upham, in Hampshire, poet, 1684-1765. Apology for Princes, 1729 ; Brothers (*The*), 1728, a tragedy ; Centaur not Fabulous (*The*), 1754, in prose ; Complaint (*The*) (see below, "Night Thoughts") ; Consolation (*The*), 1745 ; Death of Queen Anne, 1714, poetry ; Epistle to George, Lord Lansdowne, 1713, in verse (his first production) ; Epistles to Pope (*Two*), 1630, poetry ; Essay on Pope, 1756 ; Estimate of Human Life, 1728 ; Force of Religion, or Vanquished Love, 1713,

poetry (on the execution of lady Jane Grey); Foreign Address (*The*), 1734 ; Imperium Pelagi (in five stanzas), 1730 ; Instalment (*The*), 1726, a poem ; Last Day (*The*), 1713, poetry ; Love of Fame (*The*), 1725, a satire ; Night Thoughts (in nine Nights), 1742-46 (on Life, Death, and Immortality) (his chief work) ; Ocean, 1728, an ode ; Paraphrase of the Book of Job, 1719 ; Resignation (in two parts), 1761 ; Revenge (*The*), 1721, a tragedy ; Universal Passion (*The*), 1725-26, a satire. His Life, by J. Mitford, 1834 ; Doran, 1851 ; Thomas, 1852.

YOUNG (*John Radford*), London, 1799- . Modern Scepticism viewed in Relation to Modern Science, 1865 (referring to the writings of Colenso, Huxley, Lyell, and Darwin); On the Origin of Speech, 1866 ; Science Elucidative of Scripture, 1863 (on the Mosaic cosmogony and the theories of geology).

YOUNG (*Matthew*), bishop of Clonfert, in Galway, born in Ireland, 1750-1800. On the Phenomena of Sounds and Musical Strings, 1784 ; Principles of Natural Philosophy, 1800.

YOUNG, M.D. (*Thomas*), noted for his theory of light, was born at Milverton, in Somersetshire, 1773-1829. Account of the Discoveries in Hieroglyphical Literature (*An*), 1820 ; Lectures on Natural Philosophy and Mechanical Arts, 1807 ; Miscellaneous Works, 1855, posthumous His Life, by dean Peacock, 1855.

ZANGWILL (*Israel*), London, 1864- . Bachelors' Club (*The*), 1891 ; Big Bow Mystery (*The*), 1892 ; Children of the Ghetto, 1892 ; Ghetto Tragedies, 1893 ; King of Schnorrers, 1894 ; Master (*The*), 1895 ; Merely Mary Ann, 1893 ; Old Maids' Club (*The*), 1892 ; Premier and the Painter (*The*), 1888 ; Without Prejudice, 1896.

ZOUCH, D.D. (*Thomas*), Yorkshire, 1737-1815. Life of Sir Philip Sidney, 1808.

NOTE.

No one will for a moment suppose that the above Appendix is wholly, or anything like wholly, an original compilation, although several living authors and publishers have rendered great assistance when other sources of information have failed. The main part of the Appendix has been selected from Watt's *Bibliotheca Britannica;* Darling's *Cyclopædia Bibliographica;* Brunet's *Manuel du Libraire;* Lowndes's *Bibliographical Manual;* Allibone's *Critical Dictionary of English Literature* (largely taken from Watt's book) ; Bouillet's *Dictionnaire d'Histoire;* Cates's and Cooper's *Dictionaries;* Woodward and Cates's *Encyclopædia of Chronology;* the several volumes of *Men of the Time;* Crockford's *Clerical Directories;* Martin's *Contemporary Biography;* *The Encyclopædia Britannica;* Chambers's *Encyclopædia;* Craik's *Literature and Learning;* Chambers's *Cyclopædia of English Literature;* Hole's *Biographical Dictionary;* Phillips's *Dictionary of Biographical Reference;* the Catalogues of the British Museum ; *The Oracle;* Mr. Douglas Sladen's *Who's Who* (1897); and in some cases *Notes and Queries.* When all these authorities have failed, various booksellers' catalogues have been searched. By means of the American and English *Publishers' Circulars,* dates otherwise unknown have often been eliminated, and sometimes a biographical dictionary containing lives *in extenso* has furnished useful information. The standard poets published by Bell, Johnson and Chalmers, Southey, Bohn, etc., have been used for the dates and works of the poets contained in their collections, and the possession of an extensive library has been of some service, though not much, as the first edition has been the one required, but not often the one possessed. Whitaker's Almanacks (from the beginning) have supplied the obituaries of many recent authors, and a gentleman in the British Museum has assisted in obtaining dates to long lists submitted to him. With all this search and toil, the difficulty has not in all cases been surmounted; for some modern publishers omit to date their books, and even in their catalogues observe no chronological order.

It was found practically impossible to sign each article with the authority, because few have been taken in their entirety from any one source; almost all have been supplemented, corrected, or otherwise altered; and such an addition would have materially enlarged the bulk of the Appendix.

LIST OF ABBREVIATIONS IN APPENDIX II.

A.	=	*Afterpiece.*
Alleg.Pl.	=	*Allegorical play.*
B.	=	*Burlesque.*
B.C.	=	*Burlesque comedy.*
B.O.	=	*Burlesque opera.*
B.T.	=	*Burlesque tragedy.*
Bd.	=	*Ballad.*
Bd.F.	=	*Ballad farce.*
Bd.O.	=	*Ballad opera.*
Bl.	=	*Ballet.*
Blta.	:=	*Burletta.*
C.	=	*Comedy.*
C.Bf.	=	*Comédie bouffe.*
C.D.	=	*Comic drama.*
C.H.	=	*Comédie historique.*
C.O.	=	*Comic opera.*
Cdta.	=	*Comedietta or comedetta.*
Cl.C.	=	*Classical comedy.*
Cl.Cdta.	=	*Classical comedietta.*
Cl.D.	=	*Classical drama.*
Cl.Pl.	=	*Classical play.*
Cl.T.	=	*Classical tragedy.*
Ct.E.	=	*Court entertainment.*
Ct.S.	=	*Court show.*
D.	=	*Drama.*
D.Dia.	=	*Dramatic dialogue.*
D.E.	=	*Dramatic entertainment.*
D.Fab.	=	*Dramatic fable.*
D.H.	=	*Drama historique.*
D.Mon.	=	*Dramatic monologue.*
D.N.	=	*Dramatic novel.*
D.O.	=	*Dramatic opera.*
D.Pc.	=	*Dramatic piece.*
D.Pm.	=	*Dramatic poem.*
D.R.	=	*Dramatic romance.*
D.S.	=	*Dramatic satire.*
D.Sk.	=	*Dramatic skit.*
Dom.D.	=	*Domestic drama.*
E.	=	*Entertainment.*
Ex.	=	*Extravaganza.*
F.	=	*Farce.*
F.C.	=	*Farce comedy.*
Fy.C.	=	*Fairy comedy.*
Fy.P.	=	*Fairy pastoral.*
G.E.Mel.S.	=	*Grand Eastern melodramatic spectacle.*
G.O.R.	=	*Grand operatic romance.*
H.C.	=	*Historic comedy.*
H.D.	=	*Historic drama.*
H.O.	=	*Historic opera.*
H.Pc.	=	*Historic piece.*
H.Pl.	=	*Historic play.*
H.R.	=	*Historic romance.*
H.T.	=	*Historic tragedy.*
He.Pl.	=	*Heroic play.*
Int.	=	*Interlude.*
I.D.	=	*Irish drama.*
L.D.	=	*Lyrical drama.*
L.Pl.	=	*Lyrical play.*
LowC.	=	*Low comedy.*
M.	=	*Masque.*
Mel.	=	*Melodrama.*
Mel.O.	=	*Melodramatic opera.*
Mel.R.	=	*Melodramatic romance.*
Met.D.	=	*Metrical drama.*
Mir.Pl.	=	*Miracle play.*
Mo.	=	*Morality.*
MockPl.	=	*Mock play.*
MockT.	=	*Mock tragedy.*
Mu.C.	=	*Musical comedy.*
Mu.D.	=	*Musical drama.*
Mu.E.	=	*Musical entertainment.*
Mu.F.	=	*Musical farce.*
Mu.Int.	=	*Musical interlude.*
Mu.Pl.	=	*Musical play.*
Mu.Sp.	=	*Musical spectacle.*
Mu.Tr.	=	*Musical trifle.*
Mys.	=	*Mystery.*
Myt.C.	=	*Mythological comedy.*
Myt.D.	=	*Mythological drama.*
N.Blta.	=	*Nautical burletta.*
N.C.O.	=	*Nautical comic opera.*
N.C.Opta.	=	*Nautical comic operetta.*
N.D.	=	*Nautical drama.*
N.O.	=	*Nautical opera.*
N.Pl.	=	*Nautical play.*
O.	=	*Opera.*
O.Bf.	=	*Opéra bouffe.*
O.Blta.	=	*Operatic burletta.*
O.C.	=	*Opéra comique.*
O.D.	=	*Operatic drama.*
O.E.	=	*Operatic entertainment.*
O.Ex.	=	*Operatic extravaganza.*
O.F.	=	*Operatic farce.*
Op.C.	=	*Operatic comedy.*
Opta.	=	*Operetta.*
Or.	=	*Oratorio.*
P.	=	*Pastoral.*
P.C.	=	*Pastoral comedy.*
P.O.	=	*Pastoral opera.*
P.T.	=	*Pastoral tragedy.*
P.T.C.	=	*Pastoral tragi-comedy.*
Pl.	=	*Play.*
Pn.	=	*Pantomime.*
Pn.Bl.	=	*Pantomimic ballet.*
Po.D.	=	*Poetic drama.*
Pol.D.	=	*Political drama.*
Pr.C.	=	*Prize comedy.*
Pr.T.	=	*Prize tragedy.*
Pt.C.	=	*Petit comedy.*
Pt.Pc.	=	*Petit piece.*
R.D.	=	*Romantic drama.*
R.T.	=	*Romantic tragedy.*
Rel.Pl.	=	*Religious play.*
S.D.	=	*Sacred drama.*
S.T.	=	*Sacred tragedy.*
Sat C.	=	*Satiric comedy.*
Sat.D.	=	*Satiric drama.*
Sen.D.	=	*Sensational drama.*
Ser.	=	*Serenata.*
Sol.	=	*Solemnity.*
Sp.T.	=	*Spasmodic tragedy.*
T.	=	*Tragedy.*
T.C.	=	*Tragi-comedy.*
T.C.P.	=	*Tragi-comic pastoral.*
T.L.	=	*Tragedie lyrique.*
T.O.	=	*Tragedy-opera.*
V.	=	*Vaudeville.*
*	=	*Unknown.*
Etc.	=	*With some other author or authors.*

Notwithstanding the length of this list, there are some dramatic pieces very difficult to classify.

APPENDIX II.

AUTHORS AND DATES OF DRAMAS AND OPERAS.

If any discrepancy is observed between the dates given in this list and those in the body of the book, the dates here given are to be preferred. It must be borne in mind that the date of some plays is purely conjectural, and can be assigned only approximately ; and in not a few instances authorities differ. Great labour has been bestowed on this list, which is wholly original.

Abdelazer or The Moor's Revenge, 1677, Mrs. Behn. C.
Abel, 18th cent., Alfieri. T.O. (translated by C. Lloyd, 1815).
About Town, 1873, A. W. A'Beckett. C.
Abraham's Sacrifice, 1550, T. Beza (French). Rel.Pl. (translated by A. Golding, 1575).
Abroad and at Home (1764-1817), Holman. C.O.
Absalon, printed 1599, Peele. T.
Absent Man (*The*), 1768, Bickerstaff. C.
Accomplices (*The*), about 1790, Goethe. C.
Acharnanians, B.C. 425, Aristophanes. C. (Greek). Translated by Mitchell, 1820–1822 ; Hickie, 1853 ; Rudd, 1867.
Achille in Sciro, 1736, Metastasio. O. (written in eighteen days ; music by Leo).
Achilles, 1732, Gay. O.
Acis and Galatea, 1683, Camistron. O.(music by Lulli).
Acis and Galatea, 1732, Gay. Ser. (music by Handel).
Adelaide, 1814, Sheil.
Adelaide du Guesclin, 1734, Voltaire. T.
Adelaide of Wulfingen, 1799. B. Thompson. T. (from Kotzebue).
Adelazar, 1677, Mrs. Behn. C.
Adelgitha, 1806, Lewis. Pl.
Adelmorn or The Outlaw, 1801, Lewis. D.
Adelphi or The Brothers, B.C. 160, Terence. C. (Latin). Translated by Bentley, 1726 ; Colman the Elder, 1765 ; Barry, 1857 ; etc.
Adherbal, 1687, Lagrange. T.
Adopted Child, *, Birch. Mu.D.
Adrasta or Woman's Spleen, 1635, J. Jones. Pl.
Adriano in Siria, 1731, Metastasio. O. (music by Caldara).
Adrienne Lecouvreur, 1849, MM. Legouvé and Scribe. C.
Adventures of Five Hours (*The*), 1663, Tuke. T.C. (It contains the famous lines—

He is a fool who thinks by force or skill
To turn the current of a woman's will.)

Ælla, posthumous 1777, Chatterton. T.
Æsop, 1697, Vanbrugh (borrowed from Boursault's *Esope*, 1696).
Afflicted Father (*The*), 1745-1820, Hayley. D.

Africaine (*L'*), 1865, Meyerbeer. O.
Africans (*The*), 1808, Colman. Pl.
After Dark, 1868, Boucicault.
Agamemnon, B.C. 458, Æschylus. T. (Greek). Translated by Potter, 1777 ; Symons, 1824; Boyd, 1824 ; Buckley, 1849 ; Davies, 1868 ; Plumptre, 1869.
Agamemnon (B.C. 58-32), Seneca. T. (Latin). Adapted in Alexandrines by J. Studly, 1566 ; translated by T. Newton, 1581.
Agamemnon, 1738, Thomson. T.
Agamemnon, printed 1783, Alfieri. T. (translated by C. Lloyd, 1815).
Agathocles or The Sicilian Tyrant, 1676, R. Perrinchief. T.
Ages Ago, 1869, Gilbert.
Agésilas, 1666, Corneille. T.
Agis, 1758, Home. T.
Agis (*Agide*), printed 1783, Alfieri. T. (translated by C. Lloyd, 1815).
Aglaura, 1637, sir J. Suckling. T.C.
Agnes de Castro (1679-1749), Mrs. Cockburn D.
Agnes de Vere, 1834, Buckstone. D.
Agnese, about 1820, Paer. O.
Agnola Diora, nineteenth century, Herand.
Agreeable Surprise, 1798, O'Keefe. C.
Agrippina, 1771, T. Gray. T. (unfinished).
Ah ! que l'Amour est Agréable, 1862, Delaporte. C.
Aïda, 1872, Verdi. O.
Ajax, about B.C. 420, Sophocles. T. (Greek). Translated by L. Theobald, 1714 ; G. Adam, 1729 ; Potter, 1788 ; Dale, 1824 ; G. Burges, 1849 ; Plumptre, 1865.
Aladdin, 1824, Bishop. O.
Aladdin, 1859, H. J. Byron.
Alaham Mustapha, 1609, T. Grenville. T.
Alarcos, 1839, Disraeli. T.
Alarkas, 1802, F. C. Schlegel. T.
Alarming Sacrifice, about 1849, Buckston. F.
Alarum for London or The Siege of Antwerp, 1602, Anon. T.
Alasco, 1824, Shee. T.
Alba, 1583, performed at Oxford before Albertus de Alasco, a Polish prince.
Albertus Wallenstein, 1639, Glapthorne. T.
Albian and Albanus, 1684, Dryden.

Albovine King of Lombardy, 1629, sir W. Davenant. T.
Albumazar, 1634. B. (a comedy).
Albumazar the Astronomer, 1614, Tomkis. C.
Albyon Knight (The), 1565, Anon. Alleg.Pl.
Alcazar (Battle of), 1594, Peele. T.
Alceste, 1690, Lagrange. T.
Alceste, 1747, Smollett. O.
Alceste, 1769, Glück. O. (libretto by Calzabigi).
Alcestis, B.C. 438, Euripides. T. (Greek). Translated by Potter, 1781 ; Wodhull, 1782 ; Edwards, 1824 ; Nevins, 1870 ; Williams, 1871 ; with Buckley's prose translation.
Alchemist (The), 1610, Jonson. C. (altered into The Tobacconist, 1780, by F. Gentleman).
Alcibiade, 1688, Campistron. T.
Alcibiades, 1675, Otway. T.
Alcida, 1588, Greene.
Alessandro nell' Indie, 1729, Metastasio. O.
Alexander and Campaspê, etc., 1591, J. Lyly. Myt.D.
Alexander and the King of Egypt, 1788, Anon. MockPl.
Alexander the Great (second title of The Rival Queens), 1671, Lee. T.
Alexandre, 1665, Racine. T. (translated by Ozell, 1714).
Alexandrians (The), 1605, lord Stirling. T.
Alexina, 1866, Knowles. Pl.
Alexius or The Chaste Lover, 1639, Massinger. C.
Alfonso King of Castile, 1801, Lewis. H.Pl.
Alfred, 1724, Arne or his pupil Burney. O.
Alfred, 1778, Home. H.Pl.
Alfred or The Roast Beef of Old England, 1740, J. Thomson and Mallet. M. (Afterwards coverted into a play by Mallet, 1751. It contains the famous song of Rule, Britannia.)
Alfred the Great, 1831, Knowles.
Alfred the Great at Athelney, 1876, Stratford de Redcliffe. T.
Ali Baba, 1833, Cherubini. O.
Aline Reine de Golconde, 1767, Sedaine. O.
All Alive and Merry, 1737, S. Johnson. C.
All Fools, 1605, Chapman. C. (based on the Heautontimorumenos of Terence).
All for Fame, 1805, Cherry. C.
All for Love or The World Well Lost, 1668, Dryden. T.
All for Money, 1578, Lupton. T.C.
All in the Wrong, 1761, Murphy. C. (from Destouches).
All is Vanity or The Cynic's Defeat, *, Alfred Thompson. Cl.Cdta.
All's Fair in Love, 19th cent., J. Brougham. D.Pc.
All's Lost by Lust, 1633, Rowley. T.
All's Well that Ends Wells, 1598, Shakespeare. C.
All the World's a Stage, 1777, Jackman. F.
Almahide and Hamet, 1804, Malkin. T.
Almansor. (See "Conquest of Granada.")
Almeria, 1698, Handel. O.
Almeyda Queen of Grenada, 1796, Miss Lee. T.
Alonzo, 1773, Home. T.
Alphonsus Emperor of Germany, 1654, Capman. T.

Alphonsus King of Arragon, posthumous 1594, Greene. C.
Alsatia (The Squire of), 1688, Shadwell. C. (often called The Gentleman of Alsatia).
Alzire, 1736, Voltaire. T. (done into English by Hill, Alzira, 1738).
Amadis de Grèce, 1704, Lamotte. O.
Amant Difficile (L'), 1672-1731, Lamotte. C.
Amant Jaloux (L'), 1778, Grétry. O.
Amants Magnifiques, 1670, Molière. C.
Amasis (1677-1758), Lagrange. T.
Ambassadrice, 1837, Scribe. O.C.
Amber Witch (The), 1861, Wallace. O.
Ambitious Stepmother (The), 1698, Rowe. T.
Ambitious Vengeance (1755-1798), Merry.
Amboyna, 1673, Dryden.
Amelia and Teraminta, 1732, H. Carey.
Amelia, 1768, Cumberland. (This is The Summer's Tale cut down into an after-piece.)
Amends for Ladies, 1611, Field. C. (The second part of his Woman's a Weather-cock, 1610.)
American Cousin (Our), 1858, Tom Taylor and Sothern. C.
American Lady (An), 1874, H. J. Byron. C.
Americans (The), about 1770, Arnold. O. (music by Braham).
Ami de la Maison, 1772, Marmontel. O. (music by Grétry).
Amoroso King of Little Britain, 1818, Planché. B.
Amorous Bigot, 1690, Shadwell. C.
Amorous Fantasms, 1660, Lower. T.C.
Amorous Gallant (The), 1675 (from Corneille).
Amorous Old Woman (The), 1674, Duffet. C.
Amorous Orontus or Love in Fashion, 1665, J. Bulteel. C. (from Corneille. Same as Amorous Gallant).
Amorous Prince (The), 1671, Mrs. Behn. C.
Amorous Warre, 1648, Mayne. T.C.
Amorous Widow (The), 1706, Betterton. C.
Amour (L') et l'Opinion (1781-1857), Brifaut. C.
Amour Médecin, 1665, Molière. C.
Amours de Diable, 1852, St. Georges. O.C.
Amphitruo (B.C. 254-184), Plautus. C. (Latin). Translated into blank verse by Messrs. Thornton, Rich, Warner, and Colman, 1769-74.
Amphitryon, 1668, Molière. C. (adapted from Plautus).
Amphitryon, 1690, Dryden. C.
Amphitryon, 1781, Sedaine. O. (See "Jacke Juggler.")
Amphitryon, 1782, Andrieux. C.
Amy Robsart (1830-1877), Halliday.
Amyntas or The Impossible Dowry, 1638, Randolph. Fy.P.
Amyntas, 1698, Oldmixon. C.
Anacreon, 1766, Sedaine. C.O.
Anacreon, 1832, Cherubini. O.
Anatomy of Wit, 1579, Lilly.
Anaxandre, 1782, Andrieux. C.
Andrew of Hungary, 1839, Landor. T.
Andria (The Woman of), B.C. 166, Terence. C. (Latin). Translated 1520; by T. Newman, 1556; M. Kyffin, 1588; G. Webb, 1629; Bentley, 1726; Colman, 1765; Good-

luck, 1810; sir H. Englefield, 1814; Dr. W. Gardiner, 1821; J. A. Phillips, 1836; Barry, 1857; etc.

Andromachê, B.C. 417, Euripides. T. (Greek). Translated by Potter, 1781; Wodhull, 1782; Edwards and Hawkins, 1868; with Buckley's prose translation in Bohn's series.

Andromana or The Merchant's Wife, 1660, Shirley. T. (quarried from Sidney's *Arcadia*. The play called *Cupid's Revenge*, by Beaumont and Fletcher, is also from Sidney's romance).

Andromaque, 1667, Racine. T. (See "Distressed Mother.")

Andromaque, 1683, Campistron. T.

Andronic, 1686, Campistron. T.

Andronicus or Heaven's Late Revenge, 1661, Anon. T. (An attack on the Cromwell party.)

Angelica, 1722, Metastasio. O. (music by Porpora).

Anglais à Bordeaux (L'), 1763-72, Favart. O.C.

Anglomane, 1752, Saurin. C.

Animal Magnetism, 1785, Inchbald. F.

Ann Blake, 1852, W. Marston. Pl.

Anna Bolena, 1830, Donizetti. O.

Anna Boleyn, about 1680, Banks. T.

Anna Boleyn, 1877, Miss Dickenson. H.P.

Anne Boleyn, 1826, Milman. D.Pm.

Anne Boleyn, 1850, G. H. Boker. T.

Anne Boleyn, 1876, T. Taylor.

Annette et Lubin, 1763-72, C. N. Favart. O.C.

Año Despues de la Boda, 1825, Gil y Zarate.

Antidote (The), posthumous 1805, Alfieri. C. (on mixed governments). Translated by C. Lloyd, 1815.

Antigonê, about B.C. 441, Sophocles. T. (Greek). Translated by G. Adams, 1729; Potter, 1788; Dale, 1824; W. Bartholomew, 1844; Plumptre, 1865.

Antigone, 1631, May. Cl.D.

Antigone, 1633, Rotrou. Cl.D. (imitated from the *Antigonê* of Sophoclês).

Antigone, 1756, Glück. O.

Antigone, 1783, Alfieri. T. (translated by C. Lloyd, 1815).

Antiochus et Cléopâtre, 1717, Deschamps. T.

Antipodes (The), 1633, Brome. C.

Antiquary (The), 1633, Marmion. C.

Antonio and Mellida, 1602, Marston. T.

Antonio and Vallia, posthumous 1660, Massinger.

Antonio or The Soldier's Return, 1801, Godwin. T.

Antonio's Revenge, 1602, Marston. T. (the second part of *Antonio and Mellida*).

Antony, 1590, published 1595, lady Pembroke. T. (from Garnier).

Antony, 1831, Dumas. T.

Antony and Cleopatra, 1608, Shakespeare. T.

Antony and Cleopatra, 1677, Sedley. T. (See "Cleopatra.")

Anything for a Quiet Life, 1662, Middleton. C.

Apocryphal Ladies (The), 1624-1673, Margaret duchess of Newcastle. C.

Apollo and Daphne, 1716, Hughes. M. (music by Pepusch).

Apollo Shroving, 1626, Hawkins. C.

Apostate (The), 1817, Sheil. T.

Appearance is.Against Them, *, Anon. F.

Appius and Virginia, 1574, R. B—. Mo.

Appius and Virginia, 1654, Webster. T. Revised by Betterton, 1679, and entitled *The Roman Virgin or The Unjust Judge.* (See "Virginia.")

Appius and Virginia, 1705, acted 1709, Dennis. T.

Apprentice (The), 1751 or 1756, Murphy. F.

April Day, 1766, O'Hara.

Arab (The), 1783, Cumberland. T.

Arcades, 1636, Milton. M.

Arcadia, 1640, Shirley. Pl. (based on Sidney's *Arcadia*).

Archipropheta, 1547, Grimbold. T. (Latin. John the Baptist).

Arden of Feversham, 1592, Anon. H.T.

Arden of Feversham, 1762, Lillo. T.

Argalus and Parthenia, 1639, Glapthorne. Pl.

Ariadne, 1721, D'Urfey. O.

Ariane, 1672, T. Corneille. T.

Ariodante and Ginevra, 1582, Anon. Pl. (founded on a story in *Orlando Furioso*, by Ariosto).

Aristodemus, 1825, Monti. T. (rendered into French, 1854, by Duplissis).

Aristomène, 1749, Marmontel. T.

Arkwright's Wife, 1873, T. Taylor.

Armgart, 1874, "George Eliot" (Mrs. Cross). D.Pm.

Armida, 1774, Glück. O. (libretto by Calzabigi).

Arminius, 1684, Campistron. T.

Arminius, 1798, Murphy. T.

Armourer (The), 1793, Cumberland. C.O.

Armourer of Nantes, 1863, Balfe. O.

Arrah na Pogue, 19th cent., Boucicault. I.D.

Arraignment of Paris, 1584, Peele. Ct.S. or M.

Art of Management (The), 1735, C. Clarke. D.Pc.

Artaserse, before 1730, Metastasio. O.

Artaxerxes, 1741, Glück. O.

Artaxerxes, 1761, Arne. O. (from Metastasio).

Artaxerxes, 1831, Dorn. O.

Artémire, 1720, Voltaire. T.

Arthur (King), 1691, Dryden. O. (music by Purcell).

Arthur King of England, 1598, Hathaway. Pl. (See "Misfortunes of Arthur.")

Artifice, 1721, Centlivre. C.

As Cool as a Cucumber, 1851, W. B. Jerrold. F.

As You Find It, 1703, Boyle. C.

As You Like It, 1600, Shakespeare. C. (The quarry of this play was Lodge's novel called *Rosalynde*, 1590.)

Asdrubal, 1647, Jacob Montfleury. T.

Asinaria or The Ass Comedy (B.C. 254-184), Plautus. C. (Latin). Translated into blank verse by Messrs. Thornton, Rich, Warner, and Colman, 1769-74.

Assignation (The), 1672, Dryden. C.

Assignation (The), 1807, Miss S. Lee. C.

Assommoir (L'), 1878, Zola. D. (See "Drink.")

Astræa Appeased, 1797, Olivari (translated from Metastasio).

At Home, 1818, C. Mathews. E.

Atalanta in Calydon, 1864, Swinburne. D.Pm.

Athalia, 1733, Handel. O.

Athalia, 1844, Mendelssohn. O.

Athalie, 1690, Racine. T. (translated by J. C. Knight, 1822).

Atheist's Tragedy (*The*), 1611, Tourneur. T.
Athelwold, 1732, Hill. T.
Athelwold, 1842, W. Smith. T.
Athénais (1677–1758), Lagrange. T.
Athenian Captive, 1838, Talfourd. Cl. Pl.
Atonement or Branded for Life, 1863, Muskerry. D. (*Les Misérables* of Victor Hugo dramatized).
Attila, 1667, Corneille. T.
Attila, 19th cent., Verdi. O.
Attilio Regolo, 1740, Metastasio. O.
Atys, 1780, Piccini. O.
Auchindrane. (See "Ayrshire Tragedy.")
Auction of Pictures, 1748, Foote. F.
Auction (*The*), 1757, T. Cibber. F.
Augusto (*L'*), 1665, Amore. T.
Aulularia (B.C. 254–184), Plautus. C. (Latin). Translated into blank verse by Messrs. Thornton, Rich, Warner, and Colman, 1769–74.
Aureliano in Palmira, 1814, Rossini. O.
Aurengzebe, 1675, Dryden. He. Pl.
Author (*The*), 1757, Foote, F.
Author's Farce (*The*), 1731, Fielding. F.
Avant, Pendant, et Aprés, before 1822, Scribe. C.
Avare (*L'*), 1667, Molière. C. (indebted to the *Aulularia* of Plautus).
Avocat Patelin (*L'*), 1706, De Brueys. F. (This was a reproduction of a comedy attributed to Blanchet, who died 1519; but Bouillet says it was more ancient still.)
Ayrshire Tragedy, 1830, sir W. Scott. T.

Babes in the Wood, 1860, Tom Taylor. (Rob. Yarrington, in 1601, wrote *Two Lamentable Tragedies*, one of which was about a young child murdered in a wood by two ruffians by command of its uncle.)
Babes in the Wood, H. J. Byron.
Bacchæ (B.C. 480–407), Euripides (Greek). Translated by Potter, 1781; Wodhull, 1782; Buckley, pr. in Bohn's library.
Bacchides (B.C. 254–184), Plautus. C. (Latin, based on a Greek comedy by Menander). Translated into blank verse by Messrs. Thornton, Rich, Warner, and Colman (1769–74).
Bacon and Frier Bongay (*The Honourable History of Frier*), 1594, R. Greene. C.
Bad Lovers, 1836, Coyne. C.
Bague de Thérèse, 1861, Carmouche. C.
Bajazet, 1672, Racine. T.
Balder's Död, 1773, Evald or Ewald. D.
Ball (*The*), 1632, Chapman and Shirley. C.
Ballo in Maschera (*Un*), 1861, Verdi. O.
Banditti (*The*) or Lady's Distress, 1686, D'Urfey. Pl.
Banishment of Cicero, 1761, Cumberland. D. Pm.
Banker's Daughter (*The*), 1879, B. Howard. D.
Bankrupt (*The*), 1776, Foote. F.
Baptistes (1506–1582), G. Buchanan. T. (Latin).
Barbarossa, 1755, Brown. T.
Barbe Bleue, 1866, Offenbach. C. Bf.
Barbier de Séville (*Le*), 1775, Beaumarchais. C.
Barbiere di Siviglia, 1870, Paisiello. O.

Barbiere di Siviglia, 1816, Rossini. O. (sir H. Bishop altered it).
Barefaced Impostors, 1854, T. Taylor.
Barmecides (*Les*), 1778, Laharpe. T.
Barnwell. (See "George Barnwell.")
Barry (*Mde. du*), 1836, Ancelot. V.
Bartholomew Fayre, 1614, Jonson. C.
Bashful Lover, 1636, printed 1655, Massinger. C.
Bashful Man (*The*), *-1857, Moncrieff. C.D.
Basil (*Count*), 1798, printed in the "Series," 1802, J. Baillie. T. (the passion of "love").
Basset Table, 1706, Centlivre. C.
Bastard (*The*), 1652, C. Manuche. T.
Bastien et Bastienne (1749–1806), Favart. O.C.
Bath (*The*) or The Western Lass, 1701, D'Urfey. C.
Bataille de Danes, 1851, Scribe and Legouvé. C.
Battle of Alcazar, 1594, Peele. T.
Battle of Hastings, 1778, Cumberland. T.
Battle of Hermann (1776–1811), Kleist. H.D.
Battle of Hexham, 1789, Colman. C.
Battle of Sedgmoor, about 1675, duke of Buckingham. F.
Bear-Hunters (1802–1879), Buckstone.
Beatrice di Tenda, 1833, Bellini. O.
Beau Brummel, 1858, W. B. Jerrold. C.
Beau's Duel, 1703, Centlivre. C.
Beauty, 1616, Jonson. C.
Beauty in a Trance, 1653, Ford. C.
Beauty in Distress, 1698, Motteux. T.
Beauty the Conqueror or The Death of Mark Antony, 1702, Sedley. T. (See "Antony and Cleopatra.")
Beauty's Triumph, 1676, Duffett. M.
Beaux' Stratagem, 1707, Farquhar. C.
Becket. (See "Thomas à Becket.")
Beggar of Bethnal Green, 1828, Knowles. C. (See "Blind Beggar of Bethnal Green.")
Beggars' Bush, 1622, Fletcher (Beaumont died 1616). Folio edition 1647. C.
Beggar's Opera, 1727, Gay. C.O. (music by Linley. Dr. Pepusch adapted music to this opera).
Believe as you List, posthumous 1653, Massinger. C.
Bélisaire, 1645, Rotrou. T.
Belisarius (1757–1823), Kemble.
Bellamere Earl of Carlisle, 1807. T.
Bellamira or The Mistress, 1687, sir C. Sedley. C.
Bellamira, 1818, Sheil. C.
Belle Arsène (*La*), 1775, Favart. O.C. (music by Monsigny).
Belle Hélène (*La*), 1865, Offenbach. O.Bf.
Belle's Stratagem (*The*), 1780, Mrs. Cowley. C.
Bells (*The*), 1874, Erckmann-Chatrian, adapted from *The Polish Jew* (*q.v.*).
Belphegor, 1856, C. Webb and L. Buckingham. D. (translated from the French of Dennery and Fournier).
Belshazzar, 1822, Milman. D. Pm.
Ben Nazir, 1827, Grattan. T.
Benevolent Tar (*The*), *, Cross. Mu. E
Benyowski, 1811, Kotzebue. (The English version is called *The Virgin of the Sun*.)
Bérenice, 1670, Racine. T. (the hero and heroine meant for Louis XIV. and Henrietta of England).

Bertram, 1816, Maturin. T. (copyright was £525).
Bertrand et Raton, 1833, Scribe. C.
Betrothal (*The*), 1852, G. H. Boker.
Betsy, 1879, Burnard (from the French).
Better Late than Never, before 1814, Andrews. C.
Beverley, 1748, Saurin. D.
Bianca, 1817, Ingemann. T.
Bianca, 1859, Balfe. O.
Bianca Visconti, 1843, Willis. T. (Greek).
Bickerstaff's Burying, 1710, Centlivre. C.
Bijou Perdu, 1855, Adam. Pt.Pc. (libretto by Deforges).
Billy Taylor (1802–1879), Buckstone.
Biorn, 1873, Marshall. R.D.
Bird in a Cage (*The*), 1633, Shirley. C.
Birds (*The*), B.C. 409, Aristophanes. C. (Greek). Translated by Mitchell, 1820–22; Carey, 1824; Hickie, 1853; Rudd, 1867.
Biron's Conspiracie, 1604, Chapman. T.
Biron's Tragedy, 1605, Chapman. T.
Birth (1829–1871), Robertson. C.
Birth of Jupiter, 1797, Olivari (translated from Metastasio).
Birth of Merlin, 1662, Rowley. C.
Birthday (*The*), 1801. C. (from Kotzebue).
Biter (*The*), 1705, acted 1706, Rowe. C.
Black and White, 19th cent., Wilkie Collins. C.
Black Domino, 1841 (an English version of Scribe's *Le Domino Noir*, 1837). O.C.
Black-Eyed Susan, 1822, D. Jerrold. N.D.
Black Horse (*The*), before 1620, Fletcher. Pl. (See "Palamon and Arcyte.")
Black Prince, 1669, lord Orrery. H.Pl.
Black Sheep (1805–1868), Coyne.
Blackness, 1616, Jonson. C.
Blanche of Navarre, 1839, James. Pl.
Blazing Comet (*The*), 1732, S. Johnson. C.
Blighted Being (*A*), 1854, Tom Taylor.
Blind Bargain (1765–1841), Reynolds. C.
Blind Beggar of Alexandria, 1559, Chapman. Pl.
Blind Beggar of Bethnal Green, 1592, acted 1600, Day. C. (See "Beggar of Bethnal Green.")
Blind Beggar of Bethnal [Bednal] Green (*The*), 1745, Dodsley. C.
Blind Girl, 1801, Morton. C.
Blind Lady (*The*), 1660, Howard. C.
Bloodie Banquet (*The*), 1639, R. Davenport. T.
Bloody Brother, published 1639, Beaumont. T.
Blot on the 'Scutcheon, 1843, R. Browning. T.
Blue Beard, 1797, Sedaine. C.O. (music by Grétry); 1866.
Blue Beard, 1798, Colman. Mu.Sp. (music by Kelly).
Blue Beard, 1868, Offenbach. O.Bf.
Blurt, Master Constable, 1602, Middleton. C.
Boadicea, 1611, Fletcher. T.
Boadicea, 1753, Glover. T.
Bohemian Girl, 1844, Balfe. O. (burlesqued by H. J. Byron in *The Bohemian Gyurl*).
Bohemians or Rogues of Paris, 1863, Stirling. D.
Bohemienne, 1862, St. Georges. O.C.
Boite d'Argent, 1858, Dumas *fils*. C.
Bold Stroke for a Husband, 1782. Mrs. Cowley. C.
Bold Stroke for a Wife, 1717, Centlivre. C.
Bombastes Furioso, 1790, W. B. Rhodes. F.
Bon Fils, 1785, Florian. C.

Bon Ménage, 1782, Florian. C.
Bon Père, 1783, Florian. C.
Bon Ton, 1760, Burgoyne. C.
Bon Ton, 1776, Garrick. F. (the above curtailed).
Bondman (*The*), 1624, Massinger and Field. T.
Bondman (*The*), 1780, Cumberland.
Bondman (*The*), 1846, Balfe. O.
Bondman (*The*) or Love and Liberty, 1719, Betterton. C.
Bonduca, published 1647, Beaumont and Fletcher. T. (converted by Thomas Sheridan into a spectacle).
Bonne Mère, 1784, Florian. C.
Book of the 400 Lovers, 17th cent., Rowley. C.
Boots at the Swan, 1857, Selby. F. (Dickens's tale dramatized).
Borderers (*The*), 1795–96, printed 1842, Wordsworth. T.
Bothwell, *, Ware, T.
Bothwell, 1874, Swinburne. T.
Bourgeois Gentilhomme, 1670, Molière. C.
Bourgeoises à-la-Mode, 1654, Dancourt. C.
Bourse (*La*), 1856, Ponsard. F.
Bow Bells, 1880, Mr. Byron. D.
Box and Cox, Frank Burnand and A. Sullivan. F.
Box Lobby Challenge (*The*), 1794, Cumberland. C.
Bradamante, 1580, Garnier. T.
Braganza (*The Duke of*), 1775, Jephson. T.
Bravo (*The*), 1833, Buckstone. Mel. (Cooper's novel dramatized).
Brazen Age (*The*), 1603, T. Heywood. C.
Breach of Promise (1829–1871), Robertson. C.
Brennoralt (1609–1641), sir J. Suckling. T.
Brian Boroihme, 1814, Knowles.
Bride (*The*), 1640, Nabbes C.
Bride (*The*), 1808, Korner. C.
Bride of Messina, 1803, Schiller. T.
Bride's Tragedy (*The*), 1822, Beddoes. T.
Brides of Aragon (*The*), 1823, Beer. T.
Brier Cliff, 1842, George Morris. D.
Brigand (*The*), 1829, Planché.
Brighton. (See "Saratoga.")
Bristowe Merchant (*The*), *, Ford and Dekker.
Britannia Triumphans, 1637, Davenant. M.
Britannicus, 1669, Racine. T.
British Enchanters (*The*), 1701, G. Granville. D.Pm.
Briton (*The*), 1722, Philips. T.
Broken Heart, 1633, Ford. T. (His best.)
Broken Hearts, 1876, Gilbert. T.C.
Broker of Bogota (1803–1854), Bird. T.
Brother and Sister, 1633, Ford. T.
Brother Sam, 19th cent., Oxenford, Sothern, and Buckstone. C.
Brothers (*The*), 1652, Shirley. Pl.
Brothers (*The*), 1728, Young. T.
Brothers (*The*), 1769, Cumberland. C. (based on "The Little French Lawyer," *q.v.* See "Adelphi.")
Brutus, about 1690, Miss Bernard. T.
Brutus, 1730, Voltaire. T.
Brutus (*Junius*), 1783, Alfieri. T. (translated by C. Lloyd, 1815).
Brutus (*Junius*), 1828, Andrieux. T.
Brutus (*Lucius Junius*), 1679, Lee. T.
Brutus (*Lucius Junius*), 1784, Duncombe. T.

Brutus (*Marcus*), 1783, Alfieri. T. (translated by C. Lloyd, 1815).
Brutus and Cassius (1764–1811), Chénier. T. (See "Conspiracy of Brutus.")
Brutus of Alva, Tate.
Brutus or The Fall of Tarquin, 1820, Payne. T.
Bubbles of the Day, 1842, Jerrold. C.
Buckingham, 1875, Wills. H.Pl.
Buffoon (*Sir Hercules*), 1622–1681, Lacy. C.
Bull. (See "John Bull.")
Bury Fair, 1689, Shadwell. C.
Busiris, 1719, Young. T. (copyright was £84).
Bussy d'Ambois, 1607, Chapman. T.
Bussy d'Ambois, 1691, D'Urfey. T.
Busybody (*The*), 1708, Centlivre. C. (based on Dryden's *Sir Martin Marall*, 1667).
By Royal Command, 19th cent., Stirling. C.O.
Byron's Conspiracy. (See "Biron's Conspiracie.")

Cabal and Love, 1783, Schiller. T.
Cadi Dupé (*Le*), 1761, Monsigny. O.C.
Cælina or L'Enfant du Mystère, 1800, Guilbert de Pixérécourt. Mel.
Cæsar and Pompey, 1631, Chapman. T.
Cæsar and Pompey or Cæsar's Revenge, 1607, acted by the students of Trinity College, Oxford.
Cain, 1821, Byron. Mys.
Caio Gracco, 1720, Leo. O. (See "Gracchus.")
Caius Gracchus, 1815, Knowles. H.T.
Caius Gracchus, 1825, Monti. H.T. (rendered into French by Duplissis, 1854; and into English by lord John Russell, 1830).
Caius Marius, 1680, Otway. T. (This is Shakespeare's *Coriolanus* reset.)
Calandria (*La*), 1490, Bibbi. C. (the first Italian comedy).
Calaynos, 1848, G. H. Boker. T.
Caleb Quotem, *, H. Lee.
Calife de Bagdad, 1799, Boieldieu. O.
Calisto, about 1679, Crowne. M.
Calistus, 1530, Anon. T.C.
Callisthène, 1780, Piron. T.
Calypso, 1779, Cumberland.
Calypso, 1803, Winter. O. (See "Gracchus.")
Calypso and Telemachus (1677–1720), Hughes. O.

Camaraderie (*La*), 1837, Scribe. C.
Cambises (*King*), 1569, Preston. T. (Referred to by Shakespeare, 1 *Henry IV.*, act ii. sc. 4.)
Cambyses, 1671, Settle.
Cameralzaman, 1848, James. Fy.C.
Camma, 1661, T. Corneille. T.
Camp (*The*), 1780, Sheridan. Mu.D.
Campaigners (*The*) or Pleasant Adventures in Brussels, 1698, D'Urfey. C.
Campaign or Love in the East, 1783, Jephson. O.
Campaspê. (See "Alexander and Campaspê," "Cupid and Campaspê.")
Candidate (*The*), about 1781, Dent. F. (See "Rival Candidates.")
Caprices of a Lover (*The*), 1769, Goethe. C.
Capricious Lovers (*The*), 1764, R. Lloyd. C.O. (from the *Caprices d'Amour* of Favart).
Captain (*The*), 1613, Beaumont and Fletcher. C.
Captain Mario, 1577, Gosson. C.

Captifs (*Les*), 1635, Rotrou. C. (imitated from the *Captivi* of Plautus).
Captive (*The*), 1839, Lewis. Mel.
Captive (*The*), 1769, Bickerstaff.
Captives (*The*), 1723, J. Gay. T.
Captivi (B.C. 254–184), Plautus. C. (Latin). Translated into blank verse by Messrs. Thornton, Rich, Warner, and Colman, 1769–74. (See "Captifs.")
Captivity (*The*), 1728–1744, Goldsmith. Or Capuchin (*The*), 1776, Foote.
Caractacus, 1759, Mason. D.Pm.
Caractacus, 1808, Bishop. Pn.Bl.
Caravanne (*La*), 1783, Grétry. O.
Card of Fancy, 1601, Greene. C.
Cardinal (*The*), 1652, Shirley. D.
Cardinal Beaton, 1823, Tennant. T.
Careless Husband (*The*), 1704, Cibber. C.
Careless Shepherdess (*The*), 1656, T. G[offe]. T.C.
Carlos (*Don*), 1676, Otway. T.
Carlos (*Don*), 1787, Schiller. T.
Carmelite (*The*), 1785, Cumberland. T.
Carnival (*The*), 1663, Porter. C.
Carnival of Venice, 1781, Tickell. C.O.
Cartesmunda, the Fair Nun of Winchester, 1655, Brewer. T.
Case is Altered (*The*), 1609, Jonson. C.
Case of Conscience (*The*), 1753–1821, Inchbald. C.
Casini (B.C. 254–184), Plautus. C. (Latin, based on a Greek comedy by Diphilos). Translated to blank verse by Messrs. Thornton, Rich, Warner, and Colman, 1769–74.
Cassandre, 17th cent., Calprenède. T. (translated by sir C. Cotterell, 1652).
Cassandre (1677–1758), Lagrange. O.
Cassius (1677–1758), Lagrange. T.
Caste, 1867, Robertson. C.
Castilian (*The*), 1853, Talfourd. T.
Castle of Andalusia, 1798, O'Keefe. C.O.
Castle of Sorento, *, Heartwell. Mu.E.
Castle of Perseverance (*The*). (One of the oldest Morality plays in the language.)
Castle Spectre, 1797, Lewis. D.R.
Castor and Pollux, 1770, Bernard. O.
Catch Him Who Can, 1808, Hook.
Catching an Heiress, C. Selby. C.
Caterino Conara, 1844, Donizetti. O.
Catherine Douglas, 1843, Helps. T.
Catherine Grey, 1837, Balfe. O.
Catherine of Heilbronn (1776–1811), Kleist. C.
Catiline, 1822, Croly. T.
Catiline's Conspiracies, 1611, Jonson. T.
Catiline's Conspiracy (1554–1623), Gosson. H.D.
Cato, 1713, Addison. T.
Caton d'Utique, 1715, Dechamps. O. (music by Vinci).
Catone in Utica, 1726, Metastasio. T. (music by Leo).
Catspaw, 1850, Jerrold.
Ce qui Plait aux Femmes, 1860, Ponsard. C.
Cecchina (*La*), 1760, Piccini. O.
Celestina. (See "Spanish Bawd.")
Cenci (*The*), 1819, Shelley. T.
Cenerentola (*La*), 1817, Rossini. O.
Chabot, Admiral of France, 1639, Chapman. T.
Chaîne (*Une*), 1841, Scribe. C.

Cléopâtre, 1750, Marmontel. T.
Cléopâtre Captive, 1550, Jodelle. T. (*Antony and Cleopatra*, by Shakespeare, 1608. T.)
Clifford, 1817, Clifford, T.
Clitandre, 1632, Corneille.
Closerie des Genêts (*La*), 1846, Soulié. D.
Clotilde, 1832, Soulié. T.
Clouds (*The*), B.C. 423, Aristophanes. C. (Greek). Translated by Stanley, 1687; White, 1759; Cumberland, 1797; Mitchell, 1820-22; Hickie, 1853; Rudd, 1867.
Clytemnestra, 1823, Beer. T.
Clytie (a novel dramatized), 1874, Hatton.
Cobbler's Prophecy (*The*), 1594, Wilson. D.
Cocalus, B.C. 387, Aristophanes. C. Translated by Mitchell, 1820-22; Hickie, 1853; Rudd, 1867.
Cockle. (See " Sir John Cockle at Court.")
Cocu Imaginaire, 1660, Molière. C.
Cœlum Britannicum, 1633, Carew. M.
Coffee-house Politicians, 1732, Fielding. C.
Colinette à la Cour (1774-1826), Grétry. O.
Colleen Bawn, 1860, Boucicault. C.
Columbus, 1798, Morton. H.Pl.
Combat of Love and Friendship (*The*), 1654, Mead. C.
Combat of the Tongue, 1607, Brewer. C. (Cromwell acted the part of *Tactus* in this play.)
Comédienne (*La*), 1816, Andrieux. C.
Comédiens (*Les*), 1819, Delavigne. C.
Comedy of Errors, 1593, Shakespeare. C. (first mention 1598).
Comical Gallant, 1702, Dennis. C. (This is *The Merry Wives of Windsor*, by Shakespeare, 1596, new set.)
Comical Hash (*The*), 1625-1673, Margaret duchess of Newcastle. C.
Comical History of Don Quixote, in three parts, 1694-96, D'Urfey. C.
Comical Lovers (*The*), 1671-1757, C. Cibber. C. (copyright was £10 15s.).
Comical Revenge or Love in a Tub, 1664, Etherege. C.
Commissary (*The*), 1765, Foote. F.
Committee (*The*), 1670, Howard. C. (See " Honest Thieves.")
Common Conditions, 1576, *. C.
Commonwealth of Women (*The*), 1686, D'Urfey. T.C. (based on Fletcher's *Sea Voyage*).
Complaint of Rosamond (1562-1619), Daniel. T.
Comte d'Ory (*Le*), 1828, Scribe. C.
Comtesse d'Escarbagnas, 1672, Molière. C.
Comus, 1634, Milton. M. (music by Lawes).
Comus, 1738, Arne. O.
Confederacy (*The*), 1705, Vanbrugh. C.
Confederates (*The*), 1717, Jos. Gay. F.
Confederates (*The*), about 1720, Breval. Sat.D.
Conflict of Conscience (*The*), 1581, Woodes. Mo.
Conquest of China, 1676, Settle. T.
Conquest of Granada, 1672, Dryden. T.
Conrad, 1772, Magnocavallo. Pr.T.
Conscience or The Bridal Night, 1823, Haynes.
Conscious Lovers (*The*), 1722, Steele. C.
Conseiller Rapporteur (*Le*), 1841, Delavigne. C.
Conspiracy (*The*), 1638, H. Killigrew. T.
Conspiracy (*The*), 1796, Jephson. T. (Metastasio's *Clemenza di Tito*).

Conspiracy of Brutus, 1691, Antoni. T. (See " Julius Cæsar.")
Conspiracy of the Pazzi, 1783, Alfieri. T. (translated by C. Lloyd, 1815).
Constant Couple (*The*), 1700, Farquhar. C.
Constant Maid (*The*), 1640, Shirley. C. (altered into *Love will find out a Way*, 1661).
Contention (*The*), 1640, Shirley. C.
Contention between Liberality and Prodigality, 1602, (?) Greene. Mo.
Contention between the Houses of Lancaster and York, 1600, Anon. H.Pl. (Shakespeare's part ii. of *Henry VI.*, published 1623, is very like it indeed.)
Contes de la Reine de Navarre (*Les*), 1850, Scribe and Legouvé.
Contested Election (*The*), 1859, Tom Taylor.
Contract (*The*), 1780, T. Franklin. C.
Contrivances (*The*), 1715, Carey. Pd.F.
Convict (*The*), 1816, J. Wilson. D.Pm.
Convivado de Piedra, 1626, Tirso de Molino, whose name was Tellez. C. (This is the original of all the *Don Juans.*)
Cool as a Cucumber, 1851, W. B. Jerrold. F.
Cophte (*The Grand*), 1792, Goethe. C.
Coquette (*The*), 1706-1767, Molloy. C.
Coquette du Village, 1715, Dufresny. C.
Corésus et Callirhoe, 1696, Lafosse. T.
Coriolan, 1781, Laharpe. T.
Coriolanus, 1610, Shakespeare. T. (See " Invader of His Country.")
Coriolanus, 1723, founded on Haym's drama of *Cajo Marzio Coriolano* (music by Attilo Ariosti).
Coriolanus, 1749, Thomson. T.
Cornelia, 1594, Kyd. T. (from Garnier's tragedy *Cornélie*).
Cornélie, 1591, Garnier. T. (See above.)
Cornélie, 1768, Henault and Fuscher. T.
Cornette Jaune, 1864, Carmouche. C.
Coronation (*The*), printed 1640, Beaumont and Fletcher (posthumous).
Coronation (*The*), 1640, Shirley. C.
Corsaire (*The*), 1856, Adam. B.
Corsican Brothers, 1848, Boucicault. D.
Corsicans, 1799. D. (from Kotzebue).
Cosa Rara (*La*), 1786, Martini. O. (The English version is called *The Siege of Belgrade*.)
Cosi Fan Tutte, 1788, Mozart. O.
Cosmo de Medici, 1837, Horne. T.
Costlie Whore (*The*), 1633, Anon. C.
Count Egmont, 1788, Goethe. T. (translated 1848).
Count of Burgundy, 1798, Anne Plumtree. Pl. (from Kotzebue).
Count of Narbonne, 1781, Jephson. T. (Walpole's *Castle of Otranto* dramatized).
Counterfeit Presentment, 1876, Howells. C.
Counterfeits, 1677, Leanerd. C.
Countess of Salisbury, 1767, Hartson. T.
Country Attorney (*The*), 1793, Cumberland. C.
Country Captain (*The*), 1649, duchess of Newcastle. C.
Country Girle (*The*), 1647, Brewer. C.
Country Girle (*The*), 1716-1779, Garrick. C. (altered from *The Country Wife*, by Wycherly).
Country House, 1715, Vanbrugh. F.
Country Innocence, 1677, Leanerd. C. (a plagiarism of *The Country Girle*).

Country Wake (*The*), 18th cent., Dogget. C.
Country Wife, 1675, Wycherly. C. (largely borrowed from *L'École des Maris* and *L'École des Femmes*, by Molière, *q.v.*).
Courageous Turk (Aurath I.), 1632, Goff. T.
Courier of Lyons, 1852, Stirling. D.
Couronne de Bluets, 1836, Houssaye.
Court Beauties, 1835, Planché. C.
Court Beggar (*The*), 1653, Brome. C.
Court Secret (*The*), 1653, Shirley. C.
Courtley Nice (*Sir*), 1685, Crowne. C. (based on Moreto's *No Puede Ser*, which was borrowed from Lope de Vega's *Mayor Impossibile*).
Courtly Masque (*A*), 1620, Middleton. M.
Covent Garden, 1632, printed 1638, Nabbes. C.
Covent Garden Weeded, 1653, Brome. C.
Coventry Plays (*The*), in MS., 1468.
Covivando de Piedro. (See "Convivado," etc.)
Coxcomb (*The*), 1612, Beaumont and Fletcher. C.
Cozeners (*The*), 1774, Foote. F.
Creation (*The*), 1798, Haydn. Or.
Creatures of Impulse, 1869, Gilbert.
Creole (*The*), 1815–1874, C. S. Brooks. D.
Creusa, 1754, Whitehead. T.
Crispin Gentilhomme (1640–1685), Ant. J. Montfleury. C.
Critic (*The*), 1779, Sheridan. F. ("Sir Fretful Plagiary" is meant for Cumberland.)
Critique (*La*), 1662, Molière. C.
Crochets du Père Martin (*Les*), 1858, Cormon and Grange. (This is the original of Oxenford's *Porter's Knot*, and Boucicault's *Daddy O'Dowd*.)
Crociato in Egitto (*Il*), 1825, Meyerbeer. O.
Crœsus, 1604, W. Alexander, earl of Stirling. T.
Crœsus, 1845, Richards. T.
Cromwell (*Lord*), 1602, Anon. H.Pl.
Cromwell, 1827, Victor Hugo. H.Pl. (See "Charles I.")
Cromwell, 1847, Richards. H.Pl.
Cross Purposes, 1654, Brome. C.
Crown Diamonds, 1842 (English version of *Diamants de la Couronne*, *q.v.*).
Crowne for a Conqueror (*A*), 1639, R. Davenport. D.
Cruel Brother (*The*), 1630, Davenant. T.
Cruel Gift, 1707, Centlivre. C.
Crusaders (*The*), 1893, H. A. Jones.
Crutch and Toothpick, 1879, Sims. B.
Cry (*The*), 1754, Mesd. Fielding and Collier. D.Fab.
Cuck Queanes, etc., 1824, Percy. C.
Cuculio or The Hood (B.C. 254–184), Plautus. C. (Latin). Translated into blank verse by Messrs. Thornton, Rich, Warner, and Colman, 1769–74.
Cunning Lovers (*The*), 1654, Brome. C.
Cup (*The*), 1881, Tennyson. T.
Cupid and Campaspê, 1583, Lyly. L.D.
Cupid and Death, 1653, Shirley. M.
Cupid and Psychê, 19th cent., Müller. L.D.
Cupid in Waiting, 1871, W. B. Jerrold. C.
Cupid's Revenge, 1615, Beaumont and Fletcher. C. (The quarry of this play was Sidney's *Arcadia*.)
Cure for a Cuckold (*A*), 1661, Webster and Rowley. C.
Cure for Romance, 1819, Thomson. C.

Cure for the Heartache, 1811, Th. Morton. C.
Cure of Saul, 1770, Arnold. O.
Curfew (*The*), 1770–1804, Tobin. C.
Custom of the Country, posthumous 1647, Beaumont and Fletcher. T.
Cutter of Coleman Street, 1663, Cowley. C.
Cyclops (B.C. 480–407), Euripides. Sat.D. (Greek). Translated by Potter, 1781; Wodhull, 1782; Shelley; with Buckley's prose translation in Bohn's series.
Cymbeline, 1605, Shakespeare. T.
Cymon (1716–1779), Garrick. D.R.
Cymon and Iphigenia (1631–1701), Dryden.
Cynthia and Cyrus, 1768, Hoole. T.
Cynthia and Edymion, 1697, D'Urfey. D.O.
Cynthia's Revels, 1600, Jonson. Sat.C.
Cyril's Success, 19th cent., H. J. Byron.
Cyrus, 1768, Hoole. T.
Cyrus the Great, 1696, Banks. T.

Dacre of the South, 1841, Mrs. Gore.
Daddy O'Dowd, 1858-9, Boucicault. I.D. (See "Crochets du Père Martin.")
Daisy Farm (*The*), 1871, H. J. Byron. Dom.D.
Dame Blanche (*La*), 1829, Boieldieu. O.C. (libretto by Scribe).
Dame Médecin (*La*), 1640–1685, Ant. J. Montfleury. C.
Dame Voilée, 1838, Balfe. O.
Dame aux Camélias, 1848, Dumas *fils*. C.
Dames Capitaines (*Les*), 1857, Reber. O.
Damoiselle, 1653, Brome. C.
Damoiselle à Marier (*La*), before 1822, Scribe.
Damoiselles à-la-Mode, 1667, Flecknoe. C.
Damon and Pythias, 1571, R. Edwards. T. (See "Ferrex and Porrex.")
Damon and Pythias, 1825, Banim. Pl.
Dancing Devils (*The*), 1724, E. Ward. C.
Dan'l Druce, 1876, Gilbert, a play in three acts. D.
Daphne and Amintor, 1765, Bickerstaff.
Daranes, 1743, Hill.
Darius (*King*), 1565, Anon. Mir.Pl.
Darius, 1603, published 1607, lord Stirling. T.
Dark Glen of Ballyfoill (*The*), 19th cent., Stirling. I.D.
Dark Night's Work, 1870, Boucicault.
Daughter (*The*), 1836, Knowles. D.
Daughter of St. Mark, 1844, Balfe. O.
Daughter of the Isles, 1861, Leslie. O.
Daughter of the Stars (*The*), 1815–1874, C. S. Brooks. D.
Daughter to Marry (*A*), 1828, Planché. C.
David (1724–1803), Klopstock. S.D.
David, 1834, Neukomm. Or.
David (*King*), 1874, Armstrong. O.
David Garrick. (See "Garrick.")
Days of Jezebel (*The*), 1872, P. Bayne. H.D.
Days of Yore, 1796, Cumberland. C.
De Christo Triumphante, 1551, Foxe. S.D.
De Montfort, 1798, Baillie. T.
De Paris à Corbell, etc., 1854, Demolière. C.
Dead Secret, 1878, Boucicault.
Deaf and Dumb, 1785, Holcroft. H.D.
Death Fetch, 1830, Horne. D.
Death of Adam (1724–1803), Klopstock. S.D.
Death of Marlowe, 1838, Horne. T.
Death of Nero, 1690, Pechantre. T.
Death of Robert Earl of Huntington, in two parts, 1601, Heywood. Pl. (See "Robin

Hood.") This play is by some attributed to Ant. Munday and Chettle.

Death's Jest-book or The Fool's Tragedy, 1850, Beddoes. D.

Debates in the Police Friend, 19th cent., Herz. V.

Debauchee (*The*), 1677, Mrs. Behn. C.

Deborah, 1733, Handel. Or.

Deformed Transformed, 1824, Byron. D. (founded partly on *The Three Brothers*, a novel, and partly on Goethe's *Faust*. The "Wood Demon," by M. G. Lewis, was from the same novel).

Dégel (*Le*), 1864, Sardou.

Delinquent (*The*), 1765-1841, Reynolds. C.

Demafoonte, 1719, Metastasio. O. (music by Leo).

Demetrio, 1731, Metastasio. O. (music by Caldara).

Demetrio, 1742, Glück. O.

Démocrite, 1700, Régnard. C.

Démophon, 1791, Cherubini. O.

Dependant (*The*), 1798, Cumberland. C.

Dépit Amoureux, 1654, Molière. C.

Der Freischütz, 1822, Weber. O. (libretto by Kind).

Der Freischütz, H. J. Byron. A travestie.

Dervis (*Le*), 1811, Scribe. O.

Desert Flower (*The*), 1863, Wallace. O.

Desert Island (*The*), 1760, Murphy. D.Pc. (from Metastasio).

Deserted Daughter, 1785, Holcroft. C. (altered into *The Steward*).

Deserter (*The*), 1770, Dibdin. Mu.D. (from *Le Déserteur*).

Déserteur (*Le*), 1769, Sedaine. C.O. (music by Monsigny).

Destruction of Jerusalem, 1677, Crowne. T. (Milman wrote *The Fall of Jerusalem*, 1820. Cl.T.)

Destruction of Troy (*The*), 1679, Banks. T.

Deuce is in Him (*The*), 1763, Colman the Elder. F.

Deux Amis (*Les*), 1770, Beaumarchais. D.

Deux Aveugles (*Les*), 1855, Offenbach. O.Bf.

Deux Billets (*Les*), 1779, Florian. C.

Deux Hommes pour un Placard, 1860, Desarbres. F.

Deux Journées, 1800, Cherubini. O.

Deux Jumeaux de Bergame, 1781, Florian. C.

Deux Papas Très-Bien, 1845, Labiche. C.

Deux Précepteurs (*Les*), before 1822, Scribe. Pt.Pc.

Devil of a Wife (*The*), 1686, Jevon. C.

Devil to Pay (*The*), 1731, Coffey. Bd.F.

Devil upon Two Sticks, 1768, Foote. F.

Devil's an Ass (*The*), 1616, Jonson. C.

Devil's Charter, 1607, Barnes. T. (chief character, pope Alexander VI.).

Devil's Law-Case, 1613, Webster. C.

Devil's Opera (*The*), 1838, Macfarren. O.

Devin du Village (*Le*), 1752, words and music by Rousseau. Opta.

Diable à l'École, 1842, Boulanger. C.O.

Diable à Quatre (*Le*), 1756, Sedaine. C.O.

Diamants de la Couronne (*Les*), 1841, Auber. O. (See "Crown Diamonds.")

Diane et Endymion, 1787, Piccini. O.

Dido, 1734, Reed. T.

Dido, 1783, Marmontel. O. (music by Piccini).

Dido Queen of Carthage, 1594, Marlowe and Nash. T.

Dido and Æneas, 1657, Purcell. O.

Dido and Æneas, 1727, D'Urfey. D.E.

Didone Abbandonata, 1724, Metastasio. O. (music by Sarro and by Vinci).

Die Zauberflöte. (See "Zauberflöte.")

Dieu et la Bayadère, 1830, Scribe. O.

Dinorah, 1859, Meyerbeer. O.

Dioclesian, 1690, Purcell. O.

Diogenes and His Lantern, 1849, Tom Taylor. C.

Dione, 1720, J. Gay. P.T.

Dionysius, 1748, Marmontel. T. (*Denys le Tyrant*).

Diplomate (*Le*), 1827, Delavigne and Scribe. Pt.Pc.

Disappointed Gallant (*The*), 1738, A. Thomson. Bd.O.

Disappointment (*The*), 1684, Southerne. C.

Discarded Son (*The*), 1854, Godfrey. C. (This is an English version of *Un Fils de Famille*; see "Queen's Shilling.")

Discontented Colonel, 1638, Suckling. C.

Discovery (*The*), 1763, Mrs. Sheridan. C.

Disobedient Child (*The*), 1575, Ingleand. Mo.

Distrait (*Le*), 1697, Régnard. C.

Distressed Mother (*The*), 1725, Philips. T. (Racine's tragedy *Andromaque* Anglicized).

Distressed Wife (*The*), 1743, J. Gay. C.

Diversions of the Morning, 1747, Foote. F.

Divine Olimpiade, 1719, Metastasio. O. (music by Leo).

Divorce (*The*), posthumous 1805, Alfieri. C. (translated by C. Lloyd, 1815).

Djengis Khan ou La Conquête de la Chine, 1837, Anicet Bourgeois. T.

Dr. Last in His Chariot, 1769, Foote and Bickerstaff. F. (based on *Le Malade Imaginaire*, by Molière, 1673).

Dr. Magnus, 1864, Cormon. D.

Dodypoll (*Dr.*), 1600, Lyly. Pl.

Dog of Montargis, 1815. Mel. (an English version of the *Chien de Montargis*, of Guilbert de Pixérécourt). (There is another French drama, called *Le Chien d'Aubry*, on the same subject.)

Doigts de Fee (*Les*), 1858, Scribe and Legouvé. O.C.

Domino Noir (*Le*), 1837, Auber. O.C. (libretto by Scribe). (See "Black Domino.")

Don Cæsar de Bogan, 19th cent., Boucicault.

Don Carlos, 1676, Otway. T.

Don Carlos, 1787, Schiller. T. (translated by Calvert, 1836).

Don Carlos, 1822, lord J. Russell. T.

Don Carlos, 1844, Michael Costa. O.

Don Carlos, 1867, Verdi. O.

Don Felix, 1714, Centlivre. C. (same as *The Wonder*).

Don Garcia, 1785, Alfieri. T. (translated by C. Lloyd, 1815).

Don Giovanni, 1787, Mozart. O. (libretto by L. da Ponte). (Sir H. Bishop recast this opera.) (See "Giovanni" and "Convivado.")

Don Juan, 1665, Glück. O.

Don Juan, 1665, Molière. C. (imitated from the "Convivado," *q.v.*).

Don Juan, 1673, Thomas Corneille. C. (from the Spanish comedy "Convivado," *q.v.*).

Don Juan, 1802, Kalkbrenner. O.
Don Juan d'Autriche, 1835, Delavigne. C.
Don Pasquale, 1843, Donizetti. O.
Don Pédre, 1857, Cormon. D.
Don Pedro, 1795, Cumberland. D.
Don Pedro de Portugal, 1828, Gil y Zarate. D.
Don Quixote, 1846, Macfarren. O.
Don Quixote in England, 1736, Fielding. C.
Don Sebastian, 1690, Dryden. T.
Don Sebastiano, 1843, Donizetti. O. (composed in two months).
Donna Diana, 1864, W. Marston. C.
Donna del Lago (La), 1821, Rossini. O.
Doom of Devorgoil, 1829, sir W. Scott. Pl.
Dot, 19th cent., Boucicault.
Double Dealer (The), 1694, Congreve. C.
Double Deceit (The), 1736, W. Popple. C.
Double Disguise (The), 1783, Murdoch. C.
Double Falsehood, 1728, Theobald. T.
Double Gallant, 1707, Cibber. C. (copyright was £16 2s. 6d.).
Double Marriage, printed 1647, Fletcher (posthumous).
Double Veuvage, 1701, Dufresny. C.
Double or Quits. (See " Quitte," etc.)
Doubtful Heir (The), 1652, Shirley. C.
Douglas, 1756, Home. T. (based on the tale of Gil Morice).
Dowager (The), 1803–1878, C. J. Mathews.
Dragon of Wantley, 1737, Carey. B.O. (Its sequel is called Margery or The Dragoness.)
Dragons de la Reine, 1841, Decourcelle. C.
Dragoons (The), 1879, Hersee. (This is an English version of Des Dragons de Villars, a comic opera by Maillart.)
Drama of Exile, 1850, E. B. Browning.
Dramatist (The), 1789, Reynolds. C.
Drames du Cabaret, 1864, Dumanoir. D.
Dream at Sea, before 1838, Buckstone. Mel.
Dream of Scipio (The), 1797, Olivari. F. (from Metastasio).
Dreams (1829–1871), Robertson. C.
Drink, 1879, C. Reade. D. (from L'Assommoir, by Mons. Zola, 1878).
Druid or The Vision of Fingal, 1815, Thomson.
Drummer (The), 1715, Addison. C. (founded on a tradition of Hurstmonceux House).
Duchess de la Vallière, 1836, Lytton. T.
Duchess of Guise, 1838, Flotow. O.
Duchess of Malfy, 1623, Webster. T.
Duenna (The), 1775, Sheridan. Op.C. (music by Linley).
Duke of Braganza, 1785, Jephson. T.
Duke of Guise, 1682, Dryden. T.
Duke of Lerma, 1665, sir Robert Howard.
Duke of Millaine, 1623, Massinger. T. (imitation of Shakespeare's Othello).
Duke's Mistress, 1638, Shirley.
Dulcamara, 1866, Gilbert. D.P.
Dumb Knight, 1608, Machin. C.
Dumb Lady, 1672, Lacy. C.
Dundreary Married and Done for (Lord), 1859, H. J. Byron and Sothern. C. (See " Our American Cousin.")
Dupe (The), 1765, Mrs. Sheridan. C.
Dupe. (See "Who's the Dupe?")
Duplicity, 1781, Holcroft. C.
Dutch Courtesan (The), 1605, Marston. C. (Revived in 1680, and called The Revenge.

Revived again in 1746, and called The Vintner Tricked.)
Dutch Lover (The), 1673, Mrs. Behn. C.

Earl Godwin, 1796, Anne Yearsley. T.
Earl of Essex (1610–1663), La Calprenède. T.
Earl of Essex, 1678, Th. Corneille. T. (Essex).
Earl of Essex, 1682, Banks. T.
Earl of Essex, 1753, Jones. T.
Earl of Essex, 1760, Brooke. T.
Earl of Gowrie (1785–1862), White. Pl.
Earl of Huntingdon. (See " Death of Robert . . .")
Earl of Warwick, 1767, Dr. T. Franklin. T. (See " Warwick.")
Earl of Westmoreland, 1748, H. Brooke. T.
East Indian, 1800, Lewis. C. (from Kotzebue).
Eastward Hoe ! 1605, Jonson, Chapman, etc. Sat.D. to ridicule the Scotch. (Revived by Tate, and called The Cuckold's Haven, 1685. Revived again by Mrs. Lennox, and called Old City Manners, 1777.)
Eccentric Love, 1799, Cumberland. C.
Echo et Narcisse, 1778, Glück. O.
Eclair. (See "L'Éclaire.")
Ecole. (See "L'École.")
Ecossaise (L'), 1764, Voltaire. C. (in which Fréron is gibbeted).
Edgar, the English Monarch, 1677, Thomas Rymer. H.Pl.
Edith (1740–1809), Downman. T.
Edward I., 1593, Peele. H.Pl.
Edward II., 1592, Marlowe. H.T. (Shakespeare's Richard II. is in imitation of it, 1597.)
Edward IV., in two parts, 1600, Thomas Heywood. H.Pl.
Edward and Leonora, 1739, Thomson. T.
Edward the Black Prince, 1640, Shirley. H.T.
Edwin (1678–1755), Jefferys. T.
Edwin and Elgitha, 1795, Mme. D'Arblay. T.
Edwin and Merope, 17th cent., G. Jeffreys. T.
Edwin the Banished Prince, 1784, Douglas. T.
Edwin the Fair, 1842, Taylor. H.D.
Egmont (Count), 1788, Goethe. T. (translated 1848).
Elavi, 1816, Bishop. O.
Elder Brother, 1637, Fletcher. C.
Election (The), 1774, Andrews. Int.
Election of the Managers (The), 1784, G. Colman. D.Skit.
Electra, about B.C. 439, Sophocles. T. (Greek). Translated by C. W[ase], 1649 ; L. Theobald, 1714 ; G. Adams, 1729 ; Potter, 1788 ; Dale, 1824 ; Plumptre, 1865.
Electra, B.C. 413, Euripides. T. (Greek). Translated by Potter, 1781 ; Wodhull, 1782.
Electra, 1714, Theobald. T.
Elfrid or The Fair Inconstant, 1710, Hill.
Elfrida, 1752, acted 1753, Mason. T.
Elfrida, 1856, Balfe. O.
El Hyder, *, Barrymore. G.E.Mel.S.
Eli, 1855, M. Costa. Or.
Elijah, 1846, Mendelssohn. Or.
Elisa, 1794, Cherubini. O.
Elisca (1741–1813), Grétry. O.
Elixir d'Amour (L'), 1845, Donizetti. O.
Eliza (1710–1778), Dr. Arne. Op.

5 B

Ella Rosenberg, 1807, Kenney. C.
Ellen Wareham, about 1834, Buckstone. D. (written for Mrs. Yates).
Elmerick, 1739, Lillo. T.
Eloisa, 1786, Reynolds. C.
Elves (*The*), 1835, Heiberg. Fy.C.
Elvira, 1760, Mallet. T.
Emillia Galotti, 1772, Lessing. T.
Emma, 19th cent., Herz. D.
Emma di Resburgo, 1820, Meyerbeer. O.
Empedocles on Etna, 1853, M. Arnold. D.Pm.
Emperiques (*Les*), 1698, De Brueys. C.
Emperor of the East, 1632, Massinger.
Emperor of the Moon, 1687, Mrs. Behn. C.
Empress of Morocco, 1673, Settle. T.
Empress of Morocco, 1674, Duffett. T.
En Avant les Chinois! 1858, Labiche. C.
Enchanted Lovers (*The*), 1663, Lower. P.
Enchantress (*The*), 1849, Balfe. O.
Endimione, 1721, Metastasio. Mu.D.
Endymion, the Man in the Moon, 1591, J. Lyly. Myt.D.
Enfant du Peuple (*Un*), 1847, Labrousse. C.
Enfants d'Edouard (*Les*), 1833, Delavigne. H.D.
Engaged, 1878, Gilbert. F. (in two acts).
England in the Days of Charles II., 1877, Wills. C.
English Fleet (1739-1802), Arnold. Mu.D.
English Gentleman (*The*), 19th cent., H. J. Byron. C.
English Merchant, 1767, Colman. C.
English Moor (*The*), 1653, Brome. C.
English Rogue (*The*), 1668, Thompson. C.
English Rogue (*The*), 1671, Head. Ex.
English Princess or Death of Richard III. 1667, Caryl. T.
English Travellers (*The*), 1633, Th. Heywood. C.
Englishman in Paris, 1753, Foot. F.
Englishman returned from Paris, 1756, Foote. F.
Englishmen for my Money, 1596, Haughton. C.
Enrico di Borgogna, 1818, Donizetti. O.
Enrico IV., 1834, Balfe. Op.
Enseignement Mutuel, 1846, Nus. C.
Envies de Mde. Godard, 1848, Carmouche. C.
Ephesian Matron (*The*), 1769, Bickerstaff.
Epicharis et Néron, 1793, Legouvé. T.
Epicœne or The Silent Woman, 1609, Jonson. C.
Epidicus (B.C. 254-184), Plautus. C. (Latin). Translated into blank verse by Messrs. Thornton, Rich, Warner, and Colman, 1769-74.
Epsom Wells, 1673, Shadwell. C.
Erechtheus, 1876, Swinburne. T.
Erigone (1677-1758), Lagrange. T.
Erik (*King*), 1876, Gosse. T.
Erik VII., 19th cent., Bojé. T.
Eriphyle, 1732, Voltaire. T.
Erminia or The Chaste Lady, 1665, Flecknoe. T.C.
Ernani [Hernani], 1830, Victor Hugo. R.T.
Ernani, 1841, Verdi. O.
Esclave de Camoëns, 1843, Flotow. O.
Esmeralda, 1833, Victor Hugo. R.D. (An English version by H. J. Byron.)
Esperidi (*Gli Orti*), 1722, Metastasio. O. (music by Porpora).

Esprit de Contradiction, 1700, Dufresny. F.
Essex. (See "Earl of Essex.")
Esther, 1689, Racine. S.T.
Esther, 1720, Handel (first performance 1732). Or.
Estrella, 1865, Wallace. O. (left incomplete).
Esule di Granada, 1823, Meyerbeer. O.
Etéocle, 1799, Legouvé. T.
Etoile de Nord (*L'*), 1854, Meyerbeer. O. (libretto by Scribe).
Etoile de Seville (*L'*), 1842, Balfe. O.
Etourdis (*Les*), 1788, Andrieux. C.
Eugene Aram, 1873, W. G. Wills. D. (lord Lytton's novel dramatized).
Eugénie, 1767, Beaumarchais. D.
Eugenie, One Drama of a Trilogy (1749-1832), Goethe. T.
Eumenides, B.C. 458, Æschylus. T. (Greek). Translated by Potter, 1777; Buckley, 1849; Dalton, 1868; Plumptre, 1869.
Eunuchus or The Eunuch, B.C. 162, Terence. C. (Latin). Translated by Bentley, 1726; Colman the Elder, 1765; Barry, 1857; etc.
Euphosine et Coradin, 1790, Hoffmann. O.C. (music by Méhul).
Euryanthe, 1825, Weber. O.
Eurydice, 1731, Mallet. T.
Evadne or The Statue, 1819, Sheil (*The Traitor*, by Shirley, 1631, reset).
Evasion de Marie Stuart, 1822, Guilbert de Pixérécourt. D.
Eve of the Conquest (*The*), 1847, sir H. Taylor.
Evening's Love (*An*), 1668, Dryden.
Every Man (written in the reign of Edward IV.), Anon. Mo. (printed by Pynson).
Every Man in His Humour, 1596, improved 1598, Jonson. C. (Garrick reset this comedy.)
Every Man out of His Humour, 1599, Jonson. C.
Every One has His Fault, 1794, Inchbald. C. (realized £700).
Example (*The*), 1637, Shirley. C.
Excommunicated Prince (*The*), 1679, Bedlow. T.
Exiles of Siberia, 1789, Aude. D.
Extravagant Shepherd (*The*), 1654. T.R. (from Corneille).
Extremes or Men of the Day, 1859, O'Rourke (*i.e.* E. Falconer).
Ezechias, 1564, Udal. S.D.
Ezio, 1728, Metastasio. O.

Fabii (*The*), 1573, Anon. H.Pl.
Facheux (*Les*), 1661, Molière. C.
Faded Flowers, 1874, A. W. A'Beckett. C.
Fair Anchoress of Pausilippo, 1640, Massinger. C.
Fair Circassian (*The*), 1720, Dr. Croxall. D.Pm. (This is *Solomon's Song* dramatized.)
Fair Circassian (*The*), 1749-1814, S. J. Pratt. T.
Fair Maid of the Exchange, 1607, Heywood.
Fair Maid of the Inn, posthumous 1647, Beaumont and Fletcher. C.
Fair One with the Golden Locks (*The*), 1843, Planché.
Fair Penitent (*The*), 1703, Rowe. T. (quarried from *The Fatal Dowry* by Massinger).

Fair Quaker of Deal, 1617, Ch. Shadwell. C. (altered by Ed. Thompson).
Fair Quarrel, 1617, Middleton and Rowley. C.
Fair Rosamond. (See "Rosamond.")
Fair Rosamond, 1836, Barnett. H.O.
Fairy Knight (*The*), 19th cent., Ford and Dekker.
Faithful Friend, 1647, Beaumont and Fletcher.
Faithful Shepherdess, 1610, Fletcher. P. (in imitation of *Il Pastor Fido*, 1590, *q.v.*).
Falcon (*The*), 1879, Tennyson. V. (in one act). (The story is from Boccaccio's *Decameron*.)
Fall of Jerusalem, 1820, Milman. D.Pm. (Crowne wrote, in 1680, *The Destruction of Jerusalem*. T.)
Fall of Mortimer, 1731, Mortimer. H.Pl.
Fall of Portugal, 1808, Dr. Wolcot (Peter Pindar). T.
Fall of Robespierre, 1794, Coleridge. H.Pl.
Fall of the Giants, 1745, Glück. O.
False Alarms, 1807, Kenney. Opta. (music by King and Braham).
False Appearances (1720-1795), W. S. Conway.
False Concord, 1760, Townley. C. (See "Clandestine Marriage.")
False Count (*The*), 1682, Mrs. Behn. C.
False Delicacy, 1763, Kelly. C.
False Friend, 1699, Vanbrugh. C.
False Impressions, 1796, Cumberland. C.
False One (*The*), 1619, Fletcher (Beaumont died 1616). T. (That is Cleopatra and J. Cæsar.)
False Shame, 1872, Marshall. C.
Falstaff, 1838, Balfe. O.
Falstaff's Wedding, 1766, Mortimer. H.Pl.
Famille Benoiton (*La*), 1865, Sardou. D.
Famille Poisson (*La*), 1633-1690, Poisson. C.
Famille Renneville (*La*), 1802, Demolière. D.
Famille au Temps de Luther (*Une*), 1836, Delavigne. T.
Famille de Lusigny (*La*), 1830, Soulié. D.
Family Honours, 1878, Marshall. Pl.
Family Legend (*The*), 1810, Joanna Baillie. T.
Family of Love (*The*), 1608, Middleton. C.
Famous History of Sir Thomas Wyat (*The*), 1607, Webster. H.Pl.
Famous Victories of Henry V. (*The*), 1578, Anon. H.Pl. (This was the quarry of Shakespeare's *Henry V*.)
Fanatico per la Musica, 1799, Mayer. O.
Fancies Chaste and Noble, 1638, Ford. T.C.
Fancy's Festival, 1657, Jordan. M.
Fanisca, 1805, Cherubini. O.
Farinelli 1837, Barnett. O.
Farm-House (*The*), 1757-1823, Kemble. F.
Farmer (*The*), 1785, Shield. O.
Farmer's Wife (*The*), 1780, Dibdin, junior. C.O.
Faro Table (*The*), printed 1820, Tobin.
Fashion, 1845, Mowatt. C.
Fashionable Levites (1752-1820), Macnally. C.
Fashionable Lover (*The*), 1772, Cumberland. C.
Fast and Welcome, posthumous 1660, Massinger. C.
Fata Morgana, 1838, Heiberg. Fy.C.
Fatal Contract (*The*), 1653, Hemmings. T. (from the French).
Fatal Curiosity, 1737, Lillo. T.
Fatal Discovery, 1769, Home. T.

Fatal Dowry, 1632, Massinger and Field. T. (See "Fair Penitent.")
Fatal Extravagance, 1721, Mitchell. T. (altered by Hill, in 1746).
Fatal Falsehood, 1779, H. More. T.
Fatal Friendship (1679-1749), Mrs. Cockburn. T.
Fatal Love, 1678, Settle. T.
Fatal Marriage, 1695, Southerne. T. (See "Isabella or The Fatal Marriage.")
Fatal Vision, 1716, Hill. T.
Fate of Villainy (*The*), 1730, T. Walker. T.
Father Baptiste, 19th cent., Stirling. D.
Father's Revenge (*A*), 1783, earl of Carlisle. T.
Faucon (*Le*), 1772, Sedaine. O.C. (music by Monsigny).
Faulkner, 1808, W. Godwin. T.
Faussaires Anglaises (*Les*), 1833, Cormon. D.
Fausse Magie (*La*), 1775, Marmontel. O. (music by Grétry).
Faust, pt. i. 1798, ii. 1828, Goethe. T. or rather a dramatic poem. English versions by Leveson-Gower 1823 ; A. Hayward, 1833 ; J. S. Blackie, 1834 ; Anster, 1835 ; R. Talbot, 1835 ; J. Birch, 1839 ; J. Hills, 1840 ; L. Filmore, 1841 ; MacDonald, 1842 ; Gurney, 1843 ; C. H. Knox, 1847 ; sir W. Scott, 1851 ; Grant, 1868 ; Martin, 1870 ; Taylor, 1871 ; B. Bernard ; Scoones ; Swanwicke ; etc.
Faust and Marguerite, 1877, Boucicault.
Faust e Margherito, 1859, Gounod. O.
Faustus (*Dr.*), 1604, Marlowe. T.
Favorita, 1843, Donizetti. O.
Favourite of Fortune (*The*), 1866, W. Marston. C.
Fazio, 1815, Milman. T.
Fée Urgèle (*La*), 1749-1806, Favart. O.C.
Feigned Courtezan (*The*), 1679, Mrs. Behn. C.
Feinte par Amour (*La*), 1734-1780, Dorat. C.
Félix, 1777, Sedaine. O.C. (music by Monsigny).
Felix (*Don*). (See "Wonder.")
Felton (*John*), 1852, Stirling. H.Pl.
Female Academy (*The*), 1624-1673, Margaret duchess of Newcastle. C.
Female Dramatist, 1782, Colman. Mu.F.
Female Officer (1757-1823), Kemble. F.
Female Parricide (*The*), 1761, Crane. T.
Female Prelate (*The*), 1680, Settle. T.
Female Volunteer (*The*), 1801, Hallorom. D.
Femme à Deux Maris (*La*), 1802, Guilbert de Pixérécourt. V.
Femme Jalouse (*La*), 1726, Joly. C.
Femme Juge et Partie (*La*), 1666, Montfleury. C. (reduced to three acts by Leroy, 1821).
Femmes et le Mérite des Femmes, 1824, Antier. C.
Femmes et le Secret, 1843, Déaddé. C.
Femmes Savantes (*Les*), 1672, Molière. C.
Femmes Soldats (*Les*), 1809, Dartois. C.
Femmes Terribles (*Les*), 1858, Dumanoir. D.
Fénelon, 1793, Chénier. T. (An English version by Merry.)
Fernande, 1868, Sardon. C. (adapted by S. Edwards).
Ferrex and Porrex, 1561-62, Buckhurst. T. (called *Gorboduc* by sir P. Sidney. The first three acts by Norton, the last two by Sackville lord Buckhurst. First English

tragedy). (See "Damon and Pythias" and "Ralph Roister Doister.")

Festin de Pierre. (See "Don Juan.")

Festus, 1839, Bailey. D.Pm.

Feudal Times (1785–1862), White. Pl.

Few (*The*), posthumous 1805, Alfieri. C. (on the subject of Oligarchies).

Fidèle Berger (*Le*), 1837, Adam. O.C.

Fidelio, 1791, Beethoven. O.

Fiesco, 1783, Schiller. T.

Fiesco, 1850, H. Elliott. T.

Fiesque, 1824, Ancelot. T. (a French version of the above).

Figaro. (See "Mariage de..." and "Nozze...")

Filippo II., 1783, Alfieri. T. (translated by C. Lloyd, 1815).

Fille de Jephte, 1814, Meyerbeer. Or. (See "Jephte.")

Fille de l'Exilé (*La*), 1819, Guilbert de Pixérécourt. D.

Fille des Bois, 1800, Weber. O.

Fille du Cid (*La*), 1840, Delavigne. T.

Fille du Diable, 1860, Thiboust. D. (See "Fils du Diable.")

Fille du Régiment, 1840, Donizetti. O.C.

Fille du Tambour-Major, 1879, Offenbach. C.Bf.

Filles de Marbre (*Les*), 1853, Barrière. D.

Fils de Famille (*Un*), 1853, Bayard and Bieville. C. (See "Discarded Son.")

Fils de la Nuit, 1857, Sejour. D.

Fils du Diable, 1860, Déaddé. D. (See "Fille du Diable.")

Fils Ingrats ou D'École des Pères, 1728, Piron. C.

Fils Naturel, 1757, Diderot. C. (See "Natural Son.")

Financier et le Savetier (*Le*), 1819–1880, Offenbach. O.Bf.

Fine Companion (*A*), 1633, Marmion. Pl.

Finestrina (*La*), posthumous 1805, Alfieri. C. (scene laid in hell. Translated by C. Lloyd, 1815).

Finta Giadiniera (*La*), 1774, Mozart. O.

Fiole de Cagliostro (*La*), 1835, Brisebarre. D.

Firmilian, 1854, T. P. Jones (*i.e.* Aytoun). Sp.T.

First Floor (*The*), 1756–1818, Cobb. F.

First Impressions, 1813, H. Smith. C.

First Love, 1795, Cumberland. C.

Fleurette, 1833, Labrousse. C.

Flitch of Bacon, 1778, Dudley. Mu.F. (music by Shield).

Flitting Day (*The*), 19th cent., Herz. D.

Floating Island (*The*), 1655, Strode. T.C. (music by Lawes).

Florinda, 1699, Handel. O.

Flowers of the Forest, 1847, Buckstone. R.D.

Flying Dutchman, about 1830, Fitzball. Mel.

Flying Scud, 1866, Boucicault. D.

Foggarty's Fairy, 1877, Gilbert.

Folies Amoureuses, 1704, Régnard. C.

Follies of a Day (*The*), 1745–1809, Holcroft. C.

Follies of the Night, 1842, Planché. C.

Folly as it Flies (1765–1841), Reynolds. C.

Fond Husband (*The*), 1676, D'Urfey. C.

Fontainbleau, 1798, O'Keefe. C.

Fool made Wise, 1741, S. Johnson. C.O.

Fool of Quality (1633–1690), Poisson. C.

Fool turned Critic (*The*), 1678, D'Urfey. C.

Fool without Book, 17th cent., Rowley. C.

Fool would be a Favourite (*The*), 1657, Carlell. Pl.

Fool's Opera, 1731, Aston. O.

Fool's Preferment (*The*), 1688, D'Urfey. C. (Fletcher's play *The Two Noble Kinsmen*. The songs are by Purcell.)

Fool's Revenge (*The*), 1859, Tom Taylor. H.D.

Fopling Flutter (*Sir*), 1676, Etherege. C. (second title of *The Man of Mode*).

Forced Marriage (*The*), 1770, Armstrong. T. (See "Mariage Forcé.")

Forest (*The*), 1616, B. Jonson.

For Love or Money (1830–1877), Halliday. C.

Forgery, 1832, Buckstone. Mel.

Formosa, 19th cent., Boucicault.

Fortresse du Danube (*La*), 1805, Guilbert de Pixérécourt. Mel.

Fortunate Isles (*The*), 1626, B. Jonson. M.

Fortunate Isles (*The*), 1840, Planché.

Fortunatus (*Old*) or The Wishing-Cap, 1600, Dekker. C.

Fortune by Land and Sea, 1655, Th. Heywood. T.C.

Fortune's Fool (1765–1841), Reynolds. C.

Fortune's Frolic, about 1800, Allingham. F.

Fortunes of Nigel, sir W. Scott's novel 1822, dramatized by A. Halliday.

Fortunis, 1842, Planché.

Forza del Destino (*La*), 1869, Verdi. O.

Foscari (*I due*), 19th cent., Verdi. O.

Foscari (*The*), 1826, Miss Mitford. H.T.

Foscari (*The Two*), 1821, Byron. H.T.

Foul Play, 19th cent., C. Reade and Boucicault.

Foundling (*The*), 1748, E. Moore. C.

Foundling of the Forest, *, Dimond. Pl.

Four Elements (*The*), before 1536, Rastell. Int.

Four Fine Gallants, 1607, Middleton. C.

Four P's (*Palmer, Pardoner, Poticary, Pedlar*), 1530, printed 1569, J. Heywood. Int.

Four Plays in One, posthumous 1647, Beaumont and Fletcher. C.

Four 'Prentices of London, 1632, Heywood. H.Pl.

Four Sons of Aymon, 1843, Balfe. O.

Fourberies de Scapin, 1671, Molière. C. (See "Cheats of Scapin.")

Fox. (See "Volpone.")

Fra Diavolo, 1830, Auber. O.C. (libretto by Scribe). (*Fra Diavolo*, by H. J. Byron. His first play.)

Francesca da Rimini, 1816, Hunt. D.Pm.

Francis I., 1830, F. A. Kemble. H.Pl.

François I. à Madrid, 1826, Brifaut. T.

Fredolpho, 1818, Maturin.

Freethinker (*The*), 1774, Lessing. D.

Freischütz (*Der*), 1822, Weber. O. (libretto by Kind).

French Refugée (*The*), 1836, Mrs. S. C. Hall. Pl.

Friar Bacon and Friar Bungay, 1588, Greene. C. (first acted in 1591, first printed 1594).

Friendship in Fashion, 1683, Otway. C.

Frogs (*The*), B.C. 405, Aristophanes. C. (Greek). Translated by Dunster, 1812; Mitchell, 1820–22; Hickie, 1853; Rudd, 1867.

Frozen Deep (*The*), 1857, Wilkie Collins. D.

Fugitive (*The*), 1758–1803, J. Richardson. C.

Funeral or Grief à-la-Mode, 1701, Steele. C.

Gabrielle de Vergy, 1768, De Belloy. T. (This is the story of Raval de Courcy and the Dame de Fayel, whose history was written by G. A. Crapelet, and published in 1829.)
Gageure Imprévue (La), 1772, Sedaine. C.
Galant Jardinier, 1667, Dancourt. C.
Galathea, 1592, J. Lyly. Pl.
Gallant (The), 1765, O'Keefe. C.
Gallants (The), 1696, G. Granville. C.
Galotti. (See " Emilia Galotti.")
Game at Chesse, 1624, Middleton. C.
Game of Life (The), 19th cent., J. Brougham. D.Pc.
Game of Love (The), 19th cent., J. Brougham. D.Pc.
Game of Speculation, 19th cent., Slingsby Laurence (i.e. G. H. Lewes). Adapted from Balzac's Mercadet le Faiseur. (See " Speculation.")
Gamester (The), 1637, Shirley. C. (Altered by C. Johnson into The Wife's Relief, 1711; The Gamesters, by Garrick, 1758 ; The Wife's Stratagem, by J. Poole, 1827. It was founded on a tale by Malespini.)
Gamester (The), 1709, Centlivre. T.
Gamester (The), 1753, E. Moore. T.
Gamesters (The), 1758, Garrick. C. (See above, " Gamester.")
Gammer Gurton's Needle, 1551, Mr. S. Master of Arts (said to be bishop Still ; but he was under nine years of age at the date given. It was printed in 1575, when Still was 32. This was our second comedy). (See " Roister Doister" and " Mesogonus.")
Garçon de Ferme (Le), 1861, Brisebarre. D.
Garrick (David), 1864, Robertson. C. (adapted from the French).
Gay City (The), 1882, Sims.
Gay Deceivers, 1804, Colman. F.
Gazza Ladra (La), 1817, Rossini. C.O.
Gemma di Vergi, 1835, Donizetti. O.
General (The), 1653, Shirley. T.C.
Generous Conqueror, 1702, Higgons.
Geneviève de Brabant, 1860, Offenbach. O.Bf.
Gentle Shepherd, 1725, Ramsay. P. (altered by Tickell in 1786).
Gentleman Cully (The), 1702, C. Johnson. Pl.
Gentleman Dancing-Master, 1673, Wycherly. C.
Gentleman Usher, 1606, Chapman. C.
Gentleman of Alsatia (The), 1688, Shadwell. C. (sometimes called The Squire of Alsatia).
Gentleman of Venice (A), 1655, Shirley. T.C.
Genvière, before 1822, Scribe. Pt.Pc.
George Barnwell, 1730, Lillo. T.
George Dandin, 1668, Molière. C.
George-a-Green, 1599, Greene. C. (a ballad bearing the same title is amongst Greene's Dramatic Works).
Geta, 1687, Pechantre. T.
Gibraltar, 1704, Dennis. D.
Gil Blas, 1750, E. Moore. C.
Gilden Age (The), 1874, Clemens (" Mark Twain "). C.
Giovanni (Don), 1787, Mozart. O. (libretto by L. da Ponte). (See " Don Juan.")
Giovanni in London, 1829, Moncrieff. O.Ex.
Giovanni of Naples, 1839, Landor. (See " Don Giovanni.")
Giovanno-d'Arco, 1868, Verdi. O.

Gipsies Metamorphosed (The),*, B. Jonson. M.
Gipsy Warning, 1838, Benedict. O.
Giralda, 1850, Adam. O.C.
Girl's Romance (A), 1879, Boucicault. D.
Girls (The), 1879, H. J. Byron. C.
Gisèle, 1841, Adam. B.
Gisipus, 1842, Griffin. T.
Giulio Sabino, 1781, Sarti. O.
Giulio Sabino, 1784, Cherubini. O. (a pupil of Sarti).
Giuseppe, 1732, Metastasio. O.
Giustino, 1712, Metastasio. T. (aged 14).
Give a Dog a Bad Name, *, J. M. Morton. C.
Gladiateur, 1841, Altenheim. T.
Gladiator (The), 1803-1854, Bird. T.
Glass of Government (The), 1575, Gascoigne. T.C.
Glencoe, 1839, Talfourd. T.
Gli Orti Esperidi. (See "Orti . . .")
Goblins (The), 1636, Suckling. C. (a wretched imitation of Miranda and Ariel in The Tempest).
Godly Queen Hester, 1561, Anon. Mir.Pl.
Goetz von Berlichengen, 1773, Goethe. H.D. (English versions by Rose d'Aguilar, 1795 ; sir W. Scott, 1799.)
Going to the Bad, 1858, Tom Taylor. C.
Gold-Mine or Miller of Grenoble, 1854, Stirling. D.
Golden Age (The), 1611, Th. Heywood. C.
Golden Branch (The), 1847, Planché.
Golden Fleece (The), 1845, Planché.
Golden Legend (The), 1851, Longfellow. D.Pm.
Golden Pippin, 1765, O'Hara.
Good-Natured Man (The), 1768, Goldsmith. C.
Good Soldier (The), about 1680, from R. Poisson.
Good for Nothing, 1851, Buckstone. C.D.
Gorboduc. (See "Ferrex and Porrex.")
Gotham Election, 1715, Centlivre. C.
Governor of Cyprus, 1703, Oldmixon.
Gracchus, 1792, Chénier. T. (See " Caio Gracco.")
Gracchus (Caius), 1815, Knowles. H.T.
Gracchus (Caius), 1825, Monti. H.T.
Grande Duchesse de Gérolstein (La), 1867, Offenbach. O.
Grasshopper (The), 1877, Hollingshead. C. (from the French).
Grateful Fair (The), 1747, C. Smart. Pl.
Grateful Servant, 1630, Shirley. Pl.
Gray. (See " Grey.")
Great Casimir (The), 1879, Leigh. Mu.D. (music by Lecocq ; from the French).
Great City (The), 1830-1877, Halliday. C.
Great-Duke of Florence, 1636, Massinger. C.
Grecian Daughter, 1772, Murphy. T.
Grecian Heroine (The), 1721, D'Urfey. O.
Green Bushes, 1845, Buckstone. D.
Green Domino, 1810, Korner. C.
Green-Eyed Monster (The), 1828, Planché.
Gregory VII., 1840, Horne. T.
Gretchen, 1879, Gilbert. (Based on the Conquest by Faust.)
Grey (Lady Jane), 1638, Calprenède. T.
Grey (Lady Jane), 1715, Rowe. T. (copyright was £75 5s.).
Grey (Lady Jane), 1876, Tennyson. T.
Grief à-la-Mode, 1702, Steele. C.
Grim, the Collier of Croydon, 1662. C. by J. T.

Grin Bushes, H. T. Byron. A travestie.
Griselda (1774–1839), Paer. O.
Griṣelda, 1856, E. Arnold. D. (See "Patient Griṣṣel.")
Griselda, 1873, M. E. Braddon. T.
Grondeur (Le), 1691, De Brueys. C.
Grotius (1761–1819), Kotzebue.
Grotto on the Stream (The), 19th cent., Stirling. D.
Grove (The) or Lovers' Paradise, 1700, Oldmixon. C.
Grumbler (The), 1702, Sedley. C.
Guardian (The), 1637, printed 1655, Massinger. C. (altered by Garrick in 1759).
Guardian (The), 1650, Cowley. C.
Guèbres, 1762, Voltaire. T.
Gul's Hornbook, 1609, Dekker. C.
Gustave III., 1833, Scribe. O.
Gustave or Le Napolitain, 1825, Anicet Bourgeois. D.
Gustavus Erikson (1679–1749), Mrs. Cockburn.
Gustavus Vasa, 1733, Piron. T.
Gustavus Vasa, 1739, Brooke. T.
Gustavus Vasa, 1797, Kotzebue. T.
Guy Mannering, 1816, Terry. Mu.Pl. (music by Bishop). (This is a dramatized version of sir W. Scott's novel so called, 1815.)

H. (Mr.), 1806, C. Lamb. F.
Habit de Cour, 1818, Antier. D.
Haine d'Une Femme (La), before 1822, Scribe. Pt.Pc.
Half-Pay Officer (1706–1767), Molloy. C.
Half-Way House (The), 1882, Sims. C.
Halidon Hill, 1822, sir W. Scott. A dramatic sketch, in three acts.
Hamlet Prince of Denmark, 1596, Shakespeare. T. (printed 1603).
Hamlet Travestied, 1811, Poole. F.
Hampstead Heath, 1706, Baker. C.
Handsome Hernani, 1879, H. J. Byron. B.
Hanging and Marriage, 1722, Carey. F.
Hannibal and Scipio, 1635, acted in 1637, Nabbes. T.
Happiest Day of My Life (The), 1802–1879, Buckstone.
Happy Arcadia, 1869, Gilbert.
Happy Family (The), 1799, Thompson. Pl. (from Kòtzebue).
Happy Man (The), 1797–1868, Lover. O.
Happy Pair, 1868, S. T. Smith. Cdta.
Hard Struggle (A), 1858, W. Marston. Pl.
Harlekin Patriot (The), 1772, Ewald. D.
Harlequin Columbus, 1853, Tom Taylor.
Harlot's Progress (The), 1733, T. Cibber. Ex.
Harold, 1876, Tennyson. H.Pm.
Harry Gaylove (Sir), 1772, Miss Marshall. C.
Hartford Bridge (1754–1829), Shield. Mu.F.
Haunted Tower (The), 1793, Cobb. Mu.D. (music by Storace).
Haydee, 1847, Auber. O.
He Would if He Could, 1771, Bickerstaff. C.
He's Much to Blame, 1790, Holcroft. C.
Heart (The) and the World, 1847, W. Marston. Pl.
Heart's Delight (The), 1830–1877, Halliday. C.
Heauton-timoroumenos or The Self-Tormentor, B.C. 163, Terence. C. (Latin). Translated by Bentley, 1726; Colman the Elder, 1765; Barry, 1857; etc.

Heaven and Earth, 1822, Byron. Mys.
Hector, his Life and Death, 1614, Thomas Heywood. H.Pl.
Hecuba, B.C. 423, Euripides. T. (Greek). Translated by Potter, 1781; Wodhull, 1782; Morgan, 1865; Giles, 1866.
Hecyra or The Stepmother, B.C. 165, Terence. C. (Latin). Translated by Bentley, 1726; Colman the Elder, 1765; Barry, 1857.
Heir (The), 1622, May. C.
Heir-at-Law (The), 1797, Colman. C. (See "Lord's Warmingpan.")
Heir of Vironi, 1817, Pocock. Mu.D. (music by Whittaker).
Heiress (The), 1786, Burgoyne. C.
Heiress of Bruges (The), C. Selby. C. (from the French).
Helen and Paris, 1768, Glück. O. (libretto by Calzabigi).
Helena, B.C. 412, Euripides. T. (Greek). Translated by Potter, 1781; Wodhull, 1782.
Hellas, 1821, P. B. Shelley. L.D.
Helping Hands, 1855, Tom Taylor. C.
Helter Skelter, 1704, E. Ward. C.
Helvellyn, 1864, Macfarren. O.
Helvétius, 1802, Andrieux. C.
Henri III., 1829, Dumas. H.D.
Henri IV., 1725, Beckingham. H.D.
Henri IV., 1834, Balfe. O. (Enrico IV.).
Henri IV., en Famille, 1828, Deforges. D.
Henriette the Forsaken, about 1835, Buckstone. C.
Henriette Deschamps, 1863, Carré. D.
Henry II., 1773, a drama produced by adding together the two subjoined.
Henry II. King of England, with the death of Rosamond, 1693, ascribed both to Bancroft and to Mountford. H.T.
Henry and Rosamond, 1749, Hawkins. H.T.
Henry II., 1799, Ireland. H.D.
Henry II., 1843, Helps. H.D.
1 Henry IV., 1598, Shakespeare. H.Pl. (printed 1597).
2 Henry IV., 1598, Shakespeare. H.Pl. (printed 1598).
Henry IV. with ... Sir John Falstaff, 1700, Betterton. C. (the sequel in 1719).
Henry V., 1599, Shakespeare. H.Pl. (printed 1600). (This play was suggested by that called The Famous Victories of Henry V.)
Henry V., 1723, Hill. H.Pl.
1 Henry VI., 1592, Shakespeare. H.Pl. (alluded to by Nash, in Pierce Penniless, 1592).
2 Henry VI., 1594, Shakespeare. H.Pl.
3 Henry VI., 1595, Shakespeare. H.Pl.
Henry VII., 1812, Chenevix. H.Pl.
Henry VIII., 1601, Shakespeare. H.Pl. (Knight, 1613).
Henry VIII., 1791, Chénier. D.H. (Henri VIII.)
Henry Dunbar, 1865, Tom Taylor.
Heraclidæ, B.C. 421, Euripides. T. (Greek). Translated by Potter, 1781; Wodhull, 1782.
Héraclides (Les), 1752, Marmontel. T.
Heraclius Emperor of the East, 1664, L. Carlell. T. (from Corneille).
Hercule, 1643, Rotrou. Cl.T. (imitated from the Herculês Furens of Euripidês. T. Greek). Translated by Potter, 1781; Wodhull, 1782.

Hercules Furens (B.C. 58–32), Seneca. T. (Latin). Adapted by T. Heywood, 1561 ; T. Newton, 1581.
Hercules Etæus (B.C. 58–32), Seneca. T. (Latin). Adapted in English hexameters by J. Studley, 1587.
Hernani. (See " Ernani " and " Handsome Hernani.")
Hero and Leander, 1598, Marlowe. T.
Hero and Leander, 1669, Stapleton. T.
Hero and Leander, 18th cent., Jackman. O. Blta.
Hero of Romance (A), 1867, W. Marston (from the French).
Herod and Antipas, 1622, Markham. T.
Herod and Mariamne, 1673, Pordage. T.
Heroic Love, 1686, G. Granville. T.
Heroine of the Cave (1719–1777), Hiffernan. D.
Herr Burckhurd and His Family, 1827, Herz. Dom.D.
Hertford Bridge. (See " Hartford Bridge.")
Hey for Honesty, 1638, Randolph. C. (the Plutus of Aristophanes). Sir C. Wren performed in this play the character of Nœnias.
Hic et Ubique, 1663, Head. C.
Hick Scorner (*–*). Mo. (printed by Wynkyn de Worde).
Hidden Hand (The), 1864, Tom Taylor.
Hide Park. (See " Hyde Park.")
Hieronimo. (See " Jeronimo.")
High Life Above Stairs, 1776, Garrick. F.
High Life Below Stairs, 1759, Townley. F.
High-Mettled Racer (1771–1841), Dibdin. Mu.Tr.
Highland Fair, 1729, Mitchell. Bd.O.
Highland Reel, 1798, O'Keefe.
Hinko, 1871, Wills. D.
Hints for Husbands, 1806, Cumberland. C.
Hippolyte et Aricie, 1732, Rameau. O.
Hippolytus, B.C. 428, Euripides. T. (Greek). Translated by Potter, 1781 ; Wodhull, 1782 ; Fitzgerald, 1867 ; Williams, 1871.
Hippolytus or Phædra (B.C. 58–32), Seneca. T. (Latin). Adapted in Alexandrine verse by J. Studley, 1581; translated by E. Prestwich, 1651. (See " Phædra.")
Hiren the Faire Greek, 1584, Peele. C. (The title of this play is The Turkish Mahomet and . . .)
His Last Legs (1808–1875), W. B. Bernard.
Historical Register, 1738, Fielding. C.
History of Madoc, 1647, Beaumont and Fletcher.
History of Orlando Furioso, posthumous 1594, Greene. C.
History of the Two Valiant Knights, Sir Clyomon and Sir Clamydes, 1599, Peele. T.
Hit or Miss (1782–1835), Pocock. C.
H.M.S. Pinafore, 1878, Gilbert and Sullivan. N.C.Opta.
Hoffman, 1631, Chettle. T.
Hog hath lost His Pearl (The), 1613, R. Tailor. C.
Hollander (The), 1640, Clapthorne. G.
Holland's Leaguer, 1622, Marmion. C.
Holofernes, 1554, Anon. T.
Home (1829–1871), Robertson.
Home for Home, 1879, Lee. V.
Homme à Trois Visages (L'), 1801, Guilbert de Pixérécourt V.
Homo (*–1639), Atkinson. T. (Latin).

Honest Cheats, 1836, Coyne. C.
Honest Lawyer, 1616, S.S. T.
Honest Man's Fortune, 1613, Beaumont and Fletcher. C.
Honest Thieves (The), 1774–1826, Knight. F. (The Committee, C., reset.)
Honest Whore (The), 1602, Dekker. C. (published under the title of The Converted Courtezan, 1604).
Honest Yorkshireman, 1736, Carey. F.
Honeycombe (Polly), 1760, Colman. D.N.
Honeymoon (The), 1805, Tobin. C. (suggested by Shakespeare's comedy The Taming of the Shrew). In this play occur the lines—

The man that lays his hand upon a woman, Save in the way of kindness, is a wretch Whom 'twere base flattery to call a coward.

Honneur de Mamère, 1837, Boule.
Honoria and Mammon, 1659, Shirley. Pl.
Honour of Women (The), Massinger.
Honourable Ambition, 1751, Holberg. C.
Honourable Delinquent (1749–1811), Jovellanos. C.
Honours and Tricks (1815–1874), C. S. Brooks. C.
Hood. (See " Robin Hood.")
Hop o' my Thumb, 1864 *. O.
Hope of the Family (The), 1805–1868, Coyne.
Horace, 1639, Corneille. T. Translated by sir W. Lower, 1656 ; C. Cotton, 1671.
Horatius, 1657, sir W. Lower (from Corneille).
Hotel (The), 1783, Jephson. Pl.
House or the Home (The), 1859, Tom Taylor.
Housekeeper (The), 1835, Jerrold. C. (a story of Jacobite times).
How She Loves Him ! 1867, Boucicault. C.
How to Grow Rich (1765–1841), Reynolds. C.
How to Settle Accounts with your Laundress, 1847, Coyne.
Huguenot (The), 1791–1851, Sheil.
Huguenots (Les), 1833, Meyerbeer. O. (libretto by Scribe).
Huitre et les Plaideurs (Le), 1769, Sedaine. O.C.
Humour out of Breath, 1608, Day. C.
Humourist (The), 1671, Shadwell. C.
Humourous Courtier (The), 1640, Shirley. C.
Humourous Dayes Myrth (An), 1599, Chapman. C.
Humourous Lieutenant, posthumous 1647, Beaumont and Fletcher. C.
Humourous Lovers (The), 1677, duchess of Newcastle. C.
Humours of an Election (The), 1780, *. C.
Humphrey Duke of Gloucester, 1725, Philips. T.
Hunchback (The), 1832 Knowles. C.
Hundred-thousand Pounds (A), H. T. Byron. C.
Hunting of Cupid (The), 1591, George Peele. P.
Hurlo-Thrumbo, 1729, S. Johnson. Ex.
Huron (Le), 1769, Marmontel. O. (music by Grétry).
Husband His Own Cuckold, before 1704, C. Dryden. C.
Husband at Sight (1802–1879), Buckstone.
Hussard de Feltheim, 1827, Dupenty.
Hussites (The), 1761–1819, Kotzebue. D.
Hyde Park, 1637, Shirley. C.

Hymenæi, 1606, Jonson. M.
Hymen's Triumph, 1615, S. Daniel. P.T.
Hypocrite (The), 1768, Bickerstaff. C. (This is The Nonjuror, 1717, modernized; and The Nonjuror is an English version of Molière's Tartuffe, 1664.)
Hyppolytus. (See "Hippolytus.")
Hyrden af Tolosa, 19th cent., Ingemann.
Hyren the Fair Greek, 1584, Peele. C.

Ibraham, 1680, Settle.
Idle Business or Man who has no Time, 1750, Holberg. C.
Idomeneo, 1781, Mozart. O.
If I had a Thousand a Year (1764-1838), Morton. C.
If it is not Good the Divel is in It, 1612, Day. C.
Ifigenia in Aulide, 1788, Cherubini. O. (See "Iphigenia.")
Ignoramus, 1611, printed 1662, G. Ruggle. C. (Latin).
Ildegerte Queen of Norway, 1799, B. Thompson. Pl. (from Kotzebue).
Ill Beginning has a Good End (An), 1613, Ford. C.
Ill-Treated Il Trovatore, 1865, H. J. Byron. F.
Illustrious Stranger (The), 1827, Kenney. Mel.
Immanuel, 1853, Leslie. Or.
Imperial Captives (1692-1750), Mottley. D.
Imperial Tragedy (The), 1669, sir W. Killigrew. T.
Impertinent (The), 1750, Desmahis. F.
Important de Cour (L'), 1693, De Brueys. C.
Impostor (The), 1789, Cumberland. C.
Impromptu de Campagne (L'), 1633-1690, R. Poisson. C.
Impromptu de l'Hôtel de Condé, 1664, Montfleury. C. (written in rivalry of Molière's Impromptu de Versailles).
Impromptu de Versailles, 1663, Molière. C.
In Quarantine, *, Ware. C.
Inconstant (The), 1703, Farquhar. C.
Inconstant Lady (The), 16th cent., Wilson. C. (printed 1814).
Independent, 1782, MacDonald.
Indian Emperor, 1665, Dryden. He.Pl.
Indian Queen (The), 1664, Dryden and Howard. He.Pl.
Indians (The), printed 1820, Tobin (posthumous).
Indians in England (The), 1761-1819, Kotzebue. D.
Indiscret (L'), 1725, Voltaire. C.
Inès de Castro, 1723, Lamotte. T.
Inès de Cordoue, 1696, Bernard. T.
Inez de Castro, 1590, Ferreira. T.
Inflexible Captive (The), 1774, H. More. T. (adapted from Metastasio's Attilio Regolo).
Ingranno Infelice, 1812, Rossini. O.
Injured Love, *, Tate.
Injured Princess (The), 1682, D'Urfey. T.C. (a version of Shakespeare's Cymbeline).
Inkle and Yarico, 1742, Weddle. T.
Inkle and Yarico, 1787, Colman. Mu.Pl.
Innocent Usurper (The), 1694, Banks. T.
Ino et Melicerte (1677-1758), Lagrange. T.
Insatiate Countess (The), 1613, Marston. T.
Insolvent (The), 1738, Hill.

Institution of the Garter (The), 1742, West. D.Pm.
Intrigue and Love, 1783, Schiller. T. (Kabale und Liebe).
Intrigues of Versailles, 1697, D'Urfey. C.
Intriguing Chambermaid, 1734, Fielding. F.
Invader of His Country, 1705, Dennis. T. (This is Shakespeare's Coriolanus reset.)
Invincibles (The), 1820, Morton. C.
Invisible Prince (The), 1846, Planché.
Iolanthe, Gilbert.
Ion (B.C. 480-406), Euripides. T. (Greek). Translated by Potter, 1781; Wodhull, 1782; Cooke, 1869.
Ion, 1803, Schlegel. Cl.T.
Ion, 1835, Talfourd. Cl.T.
Ipermnestra, 1742, Glück. O.
Ipermnestra, 1744, Metastasio (written in nine days).
Iphigenia, 1702, Dennis. T.
Iphigenia at Tauri (B.C. 480-406), Euripides. T. (Greek). Translated by Potter, 1781; Wodhull, 1782.
Iphigenia in Aulis (B.C. 480-406), Euripides. T. (Greek). Translated by Banister, 1780; Potter, 1781; Wodhull, 1782.
Iphigenia in Aulis, 1776, Glück. O. (libretto by Calzabigi).
Iphigenia in Tauris, 1779, Glück. O. (libretto by Calzabigi).
Iphigenia in Tauris, 1786, Goethe. Cl.D. (translated by Taylor, 1793).
Iphigenia in Tauris, 1792, Piccini. O.
Iphigénie, 1637, Rotrou. Cl.D. (imitated from the Iphigenia of Euripidês).
Iphigénie, 1674, Racine. Cl.D. (in imitation of Euripidês).
Iphigénie (Sacrifice d'), 1861, Dennery. Cl.D.
Irato (L'), 1807, Méhul. O.B.
Irene, 1658, Swinhoe. T.
Irene, 1737, Dr. Johnson. T.
Irish Lion (The), 1802-1879, Buckstone.
Irish Widow (The), 1757, Garrick. F.
Irlandais (L') ou L'Esprit National, 1831, Antier.
Iron Age (The), in two parts, 1632, Thomas Heywood. C.
Iron Chest, 1796, Colman. Mu.D. (music by Storace). A dramatic version of Godwin's novel called Caleb Williams.
Isaac Comnenus, 1827, H. Taylor.
Isabella or The Fatal Marriage, 1695, Southerne. T. (same as Fatal Marriage).
Isabelle et Gertrude (1741-1813), Grétry. O.
Isabelle or Woman's Life, about 1836, Buckstone. D.
Island Princess, posthumous 1647, Beaumont and Fletcher.
Island Queens (The), 1684, Banks. T.
Isle of Dogs, 1597, Nash. Sat.C.
I[s]le of Guls, 1606, Day. C.
Isle of Palms (The), 1812, Wilson.
Israel in Egypt, 1738, Handel. Or.
Issé, 1699, Lamotte. P.O.
Issipile, 1732, Metastasio. O.
Istamine, 1817, Victor Hugo. Cl.T.
Italiana en Algeri, 1813, Rossini. O.
It's Never too Late to Mend, 1878, Reade. C. (the novel so called dramatized).
It is only My Aunt, 1832, Anne C. Bartholomew. F.

Jack Drum's Entertainment, 1601, Anon. C.
Jack the Giant-killer, H. J. Byron. Pn.
Jacke Juggler, 1562, Anon. Int. (based on the *Amphitruo* of Plautus.) (See "Amphitryon.")
Jaloux (*Le*), 1708, Dufresny. C.
Jaloux Désabusé (*Le*), 1700, Campistron. C.
James IV., posthumous 1594, Greene. H.Pl.
Jamie and Bess, 1787, Shirrefs. C.
Jane Grey (*Lady*). (See "Grey.")
Jane Shore, 1713, Rowe. T. (copyright was £50 15s.). (His best drama.)
Jane Shore, 1876, W. G. Wills. H.Pl.
Janet Pride, 19th cent., Boucicault. Sen.D.
Janetta, 1840, Auber. O.
Jardinier (*Le*), 1771, Sedaine. O.C.
Jason, 1799, Glover. T. (suppressed).
Jealous Lovers (*The*), before 1630, Randolph. C.
Jealous Wife (*The*), 1761, Colman the Elder. C. (suggested by Fielding's *Tom Jones*).
Jean Dacier, 1876, Lomon. T.
Jean de Paris, 1812, Boieldieu. O.
Jeannot et Colin, 1780, Florian. C.
Jephte (*Fille de*), *, Plessis Mornay.
Jephte (*Fille de*), 1814, Meyerbeer. Or.
Jephtha, 1546, Christopherson. T.
Jephtha, 1554, Buchanan. T.
Jephtha, 1751, Handel. Or,
Jeronimo, 1588, Kyd. T. (See "Spanish Tragedy.")
Jessy Lea, 1863, Macfarren. O.
Jeune Dacier, 1797, Méhul. O.C.
Jeunesse de Luther, 1843, Carré. H.D.
Jeunesse de Richelieu (*La*), 1833, Ancelot. V.
Jew (*The*), 1795, Cumberland. C.
Jew and Doctor (1771-1841), Dibdin. Mu.Tr.
Jew of Malta (*The Rich*), 1586, printed 1633, Marlowe. T. (Shakespeare's *Merchant of Venice* is 1598. The two plays are evidently allied.)
Jeweller of Amsterdam (*The*), posthumous 1647, Beaumont and Fletcher.
Jewess (*The*), 1835, Balfe. O.
Jilt (*The*), 1885, Boucicault. C.
Joan of Arc, 1801, Schiller. T. (*Jungfrau von Orleans*).
Joan of Arc, 1839, Balfe. O.
Joan of Arc, 1870, T. Taylor. H.D.
Joan of Hedington, 1712, King. T.C.
Joanna Montfaucon, 1799. D.R. (from Kotzebue).
Joanna Montfaucon, 1808, Cumberland. D.R.
Jocasta, 1566, Gascoigne and Kinwelmarsh. T. (from the *Phœnissœ* of Euripidès ; one of our earliest dramas).
John (*King*), 1596, Shakespeare. H.T. (first mentioned 1598). This play was suggested by that entitled *The Troublesome Reign of King John.* (See "Kynge Johan.")
John (*King*) and Matilda, 1655, R. Davenport. T.
John Baliol, 1825, Tennant. H.D.
John Bull, 1805, Colman. C.
John Cockle at Court (*Sir*), 1737, Dodsley. F.
John Felton, 1852, Stirling. H.Pl.
John Jones (1802-1879), Buckstone. C.
John Oldcastle (*Sir*), printed 1600, Munday and Drayton (printed in 1601, with the name of Shakespeare on the title-page, and contained in Pope's edition of Shakespeare).

John Street (1802-1879), Buckstone. C.
John the Baptist, 1548, Grimbold. S D.
John Woodvil, 1801, Lamb. T.
John-a-Kent, etc., 1595, Munday. C.
John of Paris (1782-1835), Pocock. C.
John of Procida, 1840, Knowles. T.
Joseph, 1816, Méhul. Or.
Joseph and His Brethren, 1747, J. Miller (music by Handel).
Joseph and His Brethren, 1785, J. Platt. S.D.
Joseph and His Brethren, 1802, W. F. Procter. S.D.
Joseph and His Brethren, 1876, C. Wells. S.D.
Joseph made known to His Brethren, *, Mme. Genlis (translated by Holcroft, 1789).
Joshua, 1747, Handel. Or.
Joueur (*Le*), 1696, Régnard. C.
Journée à Versailles, 1814, Duval.
Journey to London. (See "Provoked Husband.")
Jovial Crew, 1652, Brome. C.
Juan. (See "Don Juan.")
Jube the Sane [Job], time Edward VI., Anon. S.D.
Judah, 1894, H. A. Jones.
Judas Iscariot, 1848, Horne. Mir.Pl.
Judas Maccabæus, 1746, Handel. Or.
Judith, 1764, Bickerstaff. Or. (music by Arne).
Judith, 1857, Leslie. Or.
Judge (*The*), Massinger.
Judge Not or The Scales of Justice, 19th cent., Stirling. D.
Jugement de Midas (1741-1813), Grétry. O.
Jugglers (*The*), *, Ware. D.
Jugurtha, 1689, Pechantre. T.
Jugurtha (1677-1758), Lagrange. T.
Juif Errant (*Le*), 1799-1862, Halévy. O. (libretto by Scribe).
Juive (*La*), 1835, Halévy. O. (libretto by Scribe).
Julia Agrippina Empress of Rome, 1639, May. H.D.
Julia or The Italian Lover, 1786, Jephson. T.
Julian, 1823, Miss Mitford. T.
Julian and Agnes, 1800, Sotheby.
Juliana, 1671, Crowne. D.
Julius Cæsar, 1601, printed 1623, earl of Stirling. H.T.
Julius Cæsar, 1607, printed 1623, Shakespeare. H.T. (See "Conspiracy of Brutus.")
Junius Brutus, 1828, Andrieux. T. (See "Brutus.")
Jupiter, 1771, Sheridan and Halhed. Blta.
Just Italian (*The*), 1630, Davenant.

Killing no Murder, 1811, Hook.
Kindheart's Dream, 1592, Chettle. C.
King (*The*) and the Subject, Massinger.
King (*The*) or The Farmer's Daughter, 1829, Anne C. Bartholomew.
King Arthur, 1691, Purcell. O. (words by Dryden).
King Charming, 1850, Planché.
King Christmas, 1871, Planché.
King David and Absalom, printed 1599, Peele. S.D.
King John and Matilda, 1651, Davenport. T.
King Réné's Daughter, 19th cent., Herz L.D. (an English version by Martin).
King Sigurd, 19th cent.. Bojé. T.

King and No King, 1619, Fletcher. T.
King and the Miller (1791–1852), Murray. F.
King and the Miller of Mansfield, 1737, Dodsley. F. (See "Sir John Cockle at Court.")
King of the Alps, 1832, Buckstone (adapted from the German).
King of the Commons (*The*), 1785–1862,White.
King o' Scots (1830–1877), Halliday.
King's Rival (*The*), 1854, Tom Taylor, etc.
Kinkvervankots - dor - sprakengotchdern (*The Baron*), 1781, Andrews. C.
Kiolanthe, 1840, Balfe. O.
Knave in Print (*A*), 17th cent., Rowley. C.
Knavery in All Trades, 1664, Tatham. C.
Knight of Malta, 1647, Beaumont and Fletcher.
Knight of the Burning Pestle, 1611, Beaumont. C.
Knights (*The*), B.C. 424, Aristophanes. C. (Greek). Translated by Mitchell, 1820–22 ; Hickie, 1853 ; Rudd, 1867.
Knights (*The*), 1754, Foote. F.
Knights Conjuring . . . 1607, Day. C.
Know Your Own Mind, 1777, Murphy. C.
König Saul, 1839, Gutzikow. O. (See "Saul.")
Koranzzo's Feast, 1811, Hayes. T.
Kynge Johan, 1550, *. T. (See "John.")

Labyrinth (*The*) or Fatal Embarrassment,1795. T. (from Corneille).
Ladies' Battle, 1851, Robertson. C. (from the French of Scribe and Legouvé, 1851).
Ladies' Privilege (*The*), 1640, Glapthorne. C.
Lady Clancarty, 1873, T. Taylor.
Lady Contemplation (1624–1673), Margaret duchess of Newcastle. C.
Lady Errant (*The*), 1651, Cartwright. C.
Lady Jane Grey. (See "Grey.")
Lady of Lyons, 1838, lord Lytton. C.
Lady of Lyons (*The*), 1861, H. J. Byron. Travestie.
Lady of Pleasure (*The*), 1637, Shirley. C.
Lady of the Desert (*The*), 1859, Stirling. D.
Lady of the Lake (*The*), 1830–1877, Halliday.
Lady's Frolic, before 1774, Love.
Lady's Last Stroke (*The*), 1703–1758, Theo. Cibber. C. (copyright was £32 5s.).
Lady's Revenge (*The*), 1734, W. Popple. C.
Lady's Trial (*A*), 1638, printed 1639, Ford. D.
Lame Lover, 1770, Foote. F.
Lancashire Witches (*The*), 1634, T. Heywood. C.
Lancashire Witches (*The*), 1682, Shadwell. C.
Laodamia, 1689, Miss Bernard. T.
La Perouse. (See "Perouse.")
Lara, 1864, Cormon.
Last Days of Pompeii, 1835, Buckstone. D. (lord Lytton's novel dramatized).
Last Year (1802–1879), Buckstone.
Last of the Family (*The*), 1795, Cumberland. C.
Late Murther of the Sonne upon the Mother (*The*), *, Ford and Webster. T.
Latude, 1834, Guilbert de Pixérécourt.
Laugh and Lie Down, 1605, Tourneur. C.
Laugh When You Can (1765–1841), Reynolds. C.
Law of Java (*The*), 1822, Colman. Mu.D.
Law of Lombardy (*The*), 1779, Jephson. T.
Law Tricks or Who Would Have Thought It? 1603, Day. C.

Laws of Candy, printed 1647, Beaumont and Fletcher.
Leah the Jewish Maiden, *, Dr. Mosenthal. T.
Leap in the Dark (*A*), 1850, Buckstone. Dom.D.
Leap-Year or The Ladies' Privilege, 1850, Buckstone. C.
Lear (*King*), 1605, Shakespeare. T. (printed 1608). (This play was suggested by one called *The Chronicle History of Leir King of England*, 1578.)
L'Éclair (1799–1862), Halévy. O.C.
L'École des Amants, 1718, July. C. (See "School for Lovers.")
L'École des Femmes, 1662, Molière. C. (See "School for Wives.")
L'École de Jaloux (1640–1685), A. J. Montfleury. C.
L'École des Maris, 1661, Molière. C.
L'École des Vieillards, 1823, Delavigne. C. (See "School.")
Led Astray, 1873, Boucicault. C.
Légataire Universel, 1708, Régnard. C.
Legend of Florence, 1840, Hunt. D.R.
L'Élisire d'Amour, 1832, Donizetti. O.
Lend Me Five Shillings (1764–1838), Morton. F.
Leo or The Gipsy, 1813, Knowles.
Léonard, 1863, Brisebarre. D.
Les 20,000 Francs, 1832, Boule. D.
Lesson (*A*) for Ladies (1802–1879), Buckstone. C.
Lethe, 1743, Garrick.
L'Étoile de Seville, 1842, Balfe. O.
L'Étourdi, 1653, Molière. C.
Leucothe, 1756, Bickerstaff. C.
Liar (*The*), 1762, Foote. F. (See "Menteur.")
Libertine (*The*), 1676, Shadwell. C.
Liberty Asserted, 1704, Dennis. D.
Life (1765–1841), Reynolds. C.
Life-Buoy (*The*), 1566–1638, Hoskins. D.
Life-Drama (*The*), 1852, A. Smith. D.Pm.
Light Heart (1574–1637), Jonson.
Lights of London (*The*), 1882, Boucicault. C. (Had a great run.)
Lighthouse (*The*), 1855, Wilkie Collins. D.
Like will to Like, 1568, Fulwel. Int.
L'Ille du Prince Touton, 1854, Dennery.
Lily of Killarney, 1862, Benedict. O.
Lily of the Desert (*The*), 1859, Stirling. R.D.
Limherham, 1679, Dryden.
Linda di Chamourini, 1842, Donizetti. O.
Lindamira, posthumous 1805, Foote.
Lingua or The Five Senses, 1580, printed 1607. Brewer. Alleg.Pl. (Cromwell, on one occasion, acted the part of Tactus. In it occur these lines—

Roses and bays pack hence ! This crown and robe . . .
How gallantly it fits me !)

Lionel and Clarissa, 1768, Bickerstaff. O. (music by Dibdin).
Little Don Giovanni, H. J. Byron.
Little Em'ly (1830–1877), Halliday.
Little French Lawyer, posthumous 1647, Beaumont and Fletcher. C.
Little Rebel (*The*), 1805–1868, Coyne. C.
Little Red Riding-Hood, 1851, Tom Taylor.
Little Toddlekins (1803–1878), C. T. Mathews.
Loan of a Lover (*The*), 1833, Planche. V.

Lock and Key (1755-1834), Hoare (music by Shield).
Locrine, 1595, Tylney. T.
Locrine, 1887, Swinburne. T.
Lodoiska, 1791, Kemble. Mu.D. (music by Storace).
Lodoiska, 1800, Mayer. Mu.D.
Lodowick Sforza, 1628, Gomersall. T.
Lohengrin, 1848, Wagner. O.
Lola, 1874, Marshall. C.O. (music by Sig. Antonio).
Lombardi, 1843, Verdi. O.
London Assurance, 1841, Boucicault. C.
London Florentine (The), 1602, Chettle and Heywood. Pl.
London Prodigal (The), 1605 (ascribed by some to Shakespeare).
Long Strike, 19th cent., Boucicault. D.
Longer Thou Livest the More Foole Thou Art (time, Queen Elizabeth), Wager. C.
Looking-Glasse for London, etc., 1594, Greene and Lodge. T.C. (The Looking-Glass is Nineveh.)
Lord Cromwell, 1602, Anon. H.Pl. (See "Cromwell.")
Lord Dacre, *, Mrs. Gore.
Lord Dundreary Married and Done For, 1859, H. J. Byron and Sothern. C.
Lord of the Manor, before 1833, C. Dibdin, junior. C.O. (altered from Burgoyne, 1783; music by Jackson).
Lord of the Manor, 1783, Burgoyne. C.
Lord's Warmingpan (The), 1825 (same as Colman's Heir-at-Law).
Lorenzo (1755-1798), Merry. T.
Lost Lady (The), 1639, Berkley. T.C.
Lost at Sea, 19th cent., Boucicault. D.
Louis IX., 1819, Ancelot. T.
Louis XI., 1832, Delavigne. H.D. (An English version in 1846 by Boucicault.)
Louise de Lingerolles, 1838, Legouvé. D.
Love, 1840, Knowles. D.
Love-Chase (The), 1837, Knowles. C.
Love Crowns the End, 1657, Tatham. T.C.
Love Laughs at Locksmiths, 1803, Colman. F.
Love, Law, and Physic (1772-1849), Kenney. C.
Love Makes a Man, 1700, Cibber. C.
Love-Riddelig (chivalrous love), 1816, Ingemann. D.
Love Tricks, 1667, Shirley. C. (originally called The Schoole of Complement, 1631).
Love Triumphant, 1694, Dryden. C.
Love à-la-Mode, 1759, Macklin. C.
Love and a Bottle, 1698, Farquhar. C.
Love and Fortune, 1859, Planché. C.
Love and Friendship, 1666, sir W. Killigrew. Pl.
Love and Honour, 1649, Davenant. C.
Love and Police, 19th cent., Herz. V.
Love and Revenge, 1675, Settle. T.
Love and War, 1658, Meriton. T.
Love and War, 1792, Jephson. F.
Love at First Sight (1730-1805), King. C.
Love at a Loss (1679-1749), Mrs. Cockburn. C.
Love at a Venture, 1706, Centlivre. C.
Love for Love, 1695, Congreve. C.
Love for Money or The Boarding School, 1691, D'Urfey. C.
Love in a Blaze, 1800, Atkinson. C.

Love in a Camp, 1798, O'Keefe. C.
Love in a Forest, 1721, C. Johnson. C. (based on Shakespeare's As You Like It).
Love in a Hurry, 1709, Aston. C.
Love in a Maze, 1844, Boucicault. C.
Love in a Riddle (1671-1757), C. Cibber. C.
Love in a Tub, 1664, Etherege. C.
Love in a Veil, 1718, Savage. C.
Love in a Village, 1762, Bickerstaff. O.F. (music by Arne). (Based on Jonson's Village Opera.)
Love in a Wood, 1672, Wycherly. C.
Love in a Wood (1686-1744), G. Jacob. C.
Love in Several Masques, 1728, Fielding. C.
Love in the City, 1767, Bickerstaff. C. (See "The Romp.")
Love of Arcadia, 1860, Miss Braddon. Cdta.
Love of King David, etc., 1599, Peele. S.D.
Love will find out the Way, 1661, by T. B. (Shirley's Constant Maid reset). C.
Love's Contrivances, 1703, Centlivre. C.
Love's Cruelty, 1640, Shirley. C.
Love's Cure, printed 1647 (posthumous), Beaumont and Fletcher. C.
Love's Disguises, 1838, Knowles. C.
Love's Dominion, 1654, Flecknoe. D.
Love's Kingdom, 1664, Flecknoe. P.T.C. (same as Love's Dominion, slightly altered).
Love's Labour's Lost, 1594, Shakespeare. C. (printed 1598).
Love's Last Shift, 1695, Cibber. C.
Love's Metamorphosis, 1601, J. Lyly. Myt.D.
Love's Mistress, 1636, Heywood. C.
Love's Pilgrimage, printed 1647 (posthumous), Beaumont and Fletcher. C.
Love's Riddle, 1638, A. Cowley. P.C.
Love's Sacrifice, 1633, Ford. T. (It resembles Shakespeare's Othello.)
Love's Stroke of Genius, 19th cent., Herz. V.
Love's Triumph, 1630, Johnson. M.
Love's Triumph, 1860, Wallace. O.
Love's Victorie, 1653, Shirley. Pl.
Love's Victory, 1658, Chamberlayne. T.C.
Loves of Arcadia (The), 1860, Miss Braddon. Cdta.
Lover (The), 1730, T. Cibber. C.
Lover Lost (The), 1696, Mrs. Manley. C.
Lover's Melancholy (The), 1628, Ford. T. (This play contains the exquisite description of a contest of song between a musician and a nightingale.)
Lovers' Progress, printed 1647 (posthumous), Beaumont and Fletcher. C.
Lovers' Quarrels (1730-1805), King. Int. (See "Mistake.")
Lovers' Vows, 1800, Inchbald. Pl. (Kotzebue's play, 1798, Anglicized). By this play Mrs. Inchbald cleared £150.
Lover's Watch (The), 1686, Mrs. Behn. C.
Lovesick Court (The), 1653, Brome. C.
Lovesick King (The), 1655, Brewer. C.
Loyal Brother (The), 1682, Southerne. T.
Loyal General (The), *, Tate.
Loyal Subject, 1618, Fletcher (Beaumont died 1616). (Based on Heywood's Royal King and Loyal Subject.)
L.S.D., 1872, A. W. A'Beckett. C.
Lucia di Lammermoor, 1835, Donizetti. O. (composed in six weeks).
Lucidi (I), 1539, Angelo. C.

Lucio Silla, 1773, Mozart. O.
Lucius, 1717, Mrs. Manley. T.
Lucius Junius Brutus. (See " Brutus.")
Lucky Chance (The), 1687, Mrs. Behn. C.
Lucretia Borgia, 1831, Victor Hugo. R.T.
Lucretius, 19th cent., Tennyson. D.Mon.
Lucrezia di Borgia, 1834, Donizetti. O.
Luisa Miller, 19th cent., Verdi. O.
Luke the Labourer, 1828, Buckstone. Mel.
Luria, 19th cent., R. Browning. T.
Lurline, 1860, Wallace. O.
Lust's Dominion, 1593, Marlowe. T. (finished by Dekker, 1617).
Lusty Juventus (time, Henry VIII.), Anon. Mo.
Lying Lover (The), 1704, Steele. C.
Lying Valet, 1740, Garrick. F.
Lysistrata, B.C. 411, Aristophanes. C. (Greek). Translated by Mitchell, 1820-22 ; Hickie, 1853 ; Rudd, 1867.

Ma Tante Aurore, 1802, Boieldieu. O.
Macbeth, 1606, Shakespeare. T. (music by Lock, 1672).
Macbeth, 19th cent., Verdi. O.
Mad as a Hatter, 1863, Marshall. F.
Mad Couple well matched (The), 1653, Brome. C.
Mad Lover, 1617, Fletcher (Beaumont died 1616).
Mad Lover, 1637, Massinger.
Mad Lovers (The), 1732, S. Johnson. C.
Mad World, 1608, Beaumont and Fletcher.
Mad World, My Masters (A), 1608, Middleton. C.
Madam Fickle, 1677, D'Urfey. C.
Madame Diogène, etc., 1854, Desarbres. C.
Madame Favart, 1878, Offenbach. C.O.
Madame du Barry, 1836, Ancelot. V.
Madame du Châtelet, about 1834, Ancelot. V.
Madcap Prince (A), 1874, *.
Maestro di Capella, 1797, Dellamaria.
Magician no Conjuror (1755-1798), Merry. C.
Magicienne (La), 1799-1860, Halévy. O.
Magnetic Lady, 1632, Jonson. C.
Magnifique (Le), 1672-1731, Lamotte. C.
Magnifycence (time, Henry VII.), Skelton. Mo.
Mahomet, 1738, Voltaire. T. (done into English by Miller, 1740).
Maid Marian (The), 1822, Bishop. O. (libretto by Planché).
Maid and the Magpie (The), 1792-1852, Payne. C.
Maid and the Magpie (The), H. J. Byron.
Maid in the Mill, printed 1647, Beaumont and Fletcher, or Rowley and Fletcher. C. (posthumous).
Maid of Artois, 1836, Balfe. O.
Maid of Bath, 1771, Foote. F.
Maid of Honour, 1632, Massinger. T.C.
Maid of Honour, 1847, Balfe. O.
Maid of Lockling, 1801, W. Richardson. L.D.
Maid of Mariendorpt, 1838, Knowles. D.
Maid of Milan (Clari, the), 1822, Payne. Mu.D. (music by Bishop).
Maid of Orleans, 1801, Schiller. T. (See " Joan of Arc.")
Maid of Saxony, 1842, George Morris. O.
Maid of the Mill, 1765, Bickerstaff. O.F.

(music by Arnold). (See " Maid in the Mill.")
Maid of the Oaks (The), 1779, Burgoyne. D.E.
Maid's Metamorphoses. (See " Maydes Metamorphoses.")
Maid's Revenge (The), 1639, Shirley. T.
Maid's Tragedy, 1610, Beaumont and Fletcher. T. (Waller altered the fifth act). (One of their best.)
Maids and Bachelors (1768-1850), Skeffington. C.
Maids as They Are, etc., 1797, Inchbald. C.
Maiden Queen (The), 1667, Dryden. H.Pl.
Maidenhead. (See " Maydenhead.")
Maire du Palais (Le), 1823, Ancelot. T.
Maître en Droit (Le), 1760, Monsigny. O.C.
Major Maximilian, 1896, Havard.
Malade Imaginaire (Le), 1673, Molière. C. (See " Dr. Last in His Chariot," and " Robert the Invalid.")
Malati and Madhava, 8th cent., Bhavabhouti. R.T. (translated by Wilson, in his Indian Theatre).
Malcontent (The), 1604, Marston and Webster. T.C.
Male Coquette, 1758, Garrick. F.
Mamilia, 1593, Greene.
Man Bewitched, 1710, Centlivre. C.
Man o' Airlee, 1866, Wills. Pl.
Man of Honour (The), 19th cent., Boucicault. C.
Man of Mode (The), 1676, Etherege. C.
Man of Reason (The), 1776, Kelly.
Man of the World, 1764, Macklin. C. (Its original title was The Freeborn Scotchman.)
Man's the Master (The), 1668, Davenant. C.
Management (1765-1841), Reynolds. C.
Manfred, 1817, Byron. T.
Manfredi, 1825, Monti. T. (a version in French, by Duplissis, 1854).
Maniac (The), 1810, Bishop. O.
Mankind (time, Henry VI.), Hynghus. Mo.
Manlius Capitolinus, 1684, Lafosse. T. (imitated from Otway's Venice Preserved).
Manteau (Le), 1826, Andrieux. C.
Mantuan Revels, 1812, Chenevix. C.
Manuel, 1817, Maturin. T.
Maometto Secundo, 1822, Rossini. O
Marble Heart (The), Selby (from the French).
Marciano or The Discovery, 1663, W. Clerke. T.C.
Maréchal Ferrent (Le), 1726-1795, Philidor. O.C.
Maréchaux de l'Empire (Les), 1856, Anicet Bourgeois. D.
Margaret of Anjou (1727-1812), Jerningham. T.
Margery or The Dragoness, 1738, Carey. F. (sequel to The Dragon, q.v.).
Margherita d'Anjou, 1822, Meyerbeer. O. (See " Margaret . . .")
Marguerite d'Anjou, 1810, Guilbert de Pixérécourt. D.
Mari dans du Coton, 1862, Thiboust. C.
Mari Impromptu, 1836, Duval. C.
Mari Retrouve, 1662, Dancourt. C.
Mari qui Lance sa Femme, 1864, Deslande or Labiche (it is attributed to both). C.
Maria Padilla, 1838, Ancelot. T.
Maria Stuarda, 1785, Alfieri. T. (translated by C. Lloyd, 1815). (See " Mary Stuart.")

Maria Stuart, 1800, Schiller. T. (See "Mary Queen of Scots," "Mary Stuart," etc.)
Mariage Fait et Rompu, 1721, Dufresny. C.
Mariage Forcé, 1664, Molière. C. (See "Forced Marriage.")
Mariage Infantin (Le), before 1822, Scribe. Pt.Pc.
Mariage d'Argent (Le), 1827, Scribe. C.
Mariage de Figaro, 1784, Beaumarchais. C. (See "Nozze . . .")
Mariage de Rien (Le), 1640–1685, Ant. J. Montfleury. C.
Mariages Samnites (Les), 1741–1813, Grétry. O.
Mariamne, 1623, Hardy. T.
Mariamne, 1640, P. T. L'Ermite. T.
Mariamne, 1724, Voltaire. T.
Marian, the Faire Queene of Jewry, 1613, lady Elizabeth Carew. T.
Marian, 1788, Miss Brooke. Pl.
Marian (1754–1829), Shield. O.
Marianne, 1718, Fenton. T.
Marie de Brabant, 1825, Ancelot. D.Pm.
Marino Faliero, 1821, Byron. T.
Marino Faliero, 1829, Delavigne. T.
Marino Faliero, 1835, Donizetti. O.
Marino Faliero, 1885, Swinburne. T.
Marion Delorme, 1829, Victor Hugo. R.D.
Maritana (a mosaic, by Wallace, of Ruy Blas and Notre Dame), 1845. O.
Marius, 1791, Arnault. T.
Marius (Caius), 1680, Otway. T.
Marius and Sylla, 1594, Lodge. H.Pl.
Marmaduke Maxwell (Sir), 1827, Cunningham. C.
Marplot, 1711, Centlivre. C.
Marquis Caporal, 1864, Sejour. D.
Marquis d'Argencourt, 1857, Dupenty. D.
Marquis de Kénilis, 1879, Lomon. D.
Marriage, 1842, R. Bell. C.
Marriage-à-la-Mode, 1672, Dryden. C.
Marriage-Hater Matched (The), 1692, D'Urfey. C.
Marriage-Night (The), 1664, H. Carey, lord Falkland. T.
Marriage of Witte and Science (The), about 1559, Anon. Mo.
Married for Money (1803–1878), C.J.Mathews. C.
Married in Haste, 16th cent., H. J. Byron. C.
Married Libertine (The), 1761, Macklin. F.
Married Life, 1834, Buckstone. C.
Married Man (The), 1789, Inchbald. C. (realized £100).
Martha, 1858, Flotow. O.
Martyr of Antioch, 1822, Milman. T.
Martyrs (Les), 1840, Donizetti. O. (from Corneille's Polyeucte).
[Mary] Queen of Scots, 1684, Banks. T.
Mary Queen of Scots, 1807, Grahame. T.
Mary Queen o' Scots, 1874, Wills. H.Pl.
Mary (Queen), 1877, Tennyson. T.
Mary Stuart, queen of Scots, 1840, Haynes. T.
Mary Stuart, 1881, Swinburne. T. (See "Maria . . ." and "Evasion de . . .")
Mary Tudor, 1833, Victor Hugo. T.
Mary Tudor, 1847, Aubrey de Vere. T.
Mary Tudor, 1876, Miss Dickenson. H.Pl.
Masaniello, 1814, Ingemann. T.
Masaniello, about 1820, Carafa. O.
Masaniello, 1828, Auber. O. (libretto by Scribe). Often called La Muette de Portici. (See "Massaniello.")

Masks and Faces, 1852, Tom Taylor. C.
Masnadieri (I), 1847, Verdi. O.
Masque (The), 1612, Beaumont. C.
Masque de Velours, 1860, Delaporte. D.
Masque of Calisto, 1676, Crowne. M.
Masque of Heroes, 1619, Middleton. M.
Masqueraders (The), 1894, H. A. Jones.
Massacre of Paris, 1590, Marlowe. T.
Massacre of Paris, 1690, Lee. T.
Massacre de Syrie, 1860, Sejour. T.
Massaniello, 1699, D'Urfey. T. (Originally two plays, but compressed into one by T. Walker, in 1700.)
Massaniello, 1829, Kenney. (See "Masaniello.")
Match at Midnight, 1633, Rowley. C.
Match for a Widow (A), 1787, Atkinson. C.
Match mee in London, 1631, Day. T.C.
Matilda, 1775, T. Franklin. T.
Matilda of Hungary, 1847, Wallace. O.
Matrimonial Troubles, pt. i. (1624–1673), Margaret duchess of Newcastle. C. But pt. ii. T.
Matrimonio Segreto (Il), 1793, Cimarosa. O.
Matrimony, 1804, Kenney. C.
Maud, 1855, Tennyson. D.Pm.
Maures d'Espagne (Les), 1804, Guilbert de Pixérécourt. D.
Maximian, 1800, lady S. Burrell. T. (from Corneille).
May Day, 1611, Chapman. C.
May Queen (1802–1879), Buckstone.
Maydenhead Well Lost (A), 1634, T. Heywood. C.
Maydes Metamorphoses, 1600, J. Lyly. Myt.D.
Mayor of Garratt, 1763, Foote. F.
Mayor of Quinborough (The), 1661, Middleton. C.
Mazeppa, a travestie. H. J. Byron.
Meadows of St. Gervaise (The), *, Ware. F.C. (translated from the French).
Measure for Measure, Shakespeare. C. (based on Promos and Cassandra, 1578, by Whetstone; acted at Whitehall, 1604).
Medea, B.C. 431, Euripides. T. (Greek). Translated by Potter, 1781; Wodhull, 1782; Morgan, 1865; Giles, 1865; Lee, 1867; Webster, 1868; Williams, 1871.
Medea (B.C.58–32), Seneca. T. (Latin). Adapted by J. Studley, 1566; translated by E. Sherburne, 1648.
Medea, 1761, Glover. T.
Medea, 1795, Cherubini. O.
Medea, about 1820, Mayer. O.
Médecins Malgré Lui, 1666, Molière. C. (See "Mock Doctor.")
Médecins (Les), 1863, Nus. D.
Médée, 1635, Corneille. T.
Médée, 1695, Longepierre. T
Médée, 1853, Legouvé. T.
Médus, 1739, Deschamps. T.
Méduse (1677–1758), Lagrange. O.
Mélanie, 1770, Laharpe. T.
Melanthe, 1614, printed 1615, Brookes. P.
Méléagre (1677–1758), Lagrange. T.
Mélicerte, 1666, Molière. C.
Mélite, 1629, Corneille. C. (translated 1776).
Memorable Maske of the Two Hon. Inns-of-Court (The), 1614, Chapman. M.
Menæchmi or The Brothers Menæchmus who

were Exactly Alike (B.C. 254-184), Plautus. C. (Latin). Translated into blank verse by Messrs. Thornton, Rich, Warner, and Colman, 1769-74. It was translated by W. W[arner] in 1595, and furnished Shakespeare with the scheme, etc., of his *Comedy of Errors*. (See below.)

Ménage en Ville, 1864, Barrière. Pl.

Ménechmes, 1637, Rotrou. C. (imitated from the *Menæchi* of Plautus).

Ménechmes (*Les*), 1705, Régnard. C.

Menteur, 1642, Corneille. C. (See "Liar.")

Mercator or The Merchant (B.C. 254-184), Plautus. C. (Latin, adapted from a Greek play by Philemon). Translated into blank verse by Messrs. Thornton, Rich, Warner, and Colman, 1769-74.

Merchant Pirate, 19th cent., Stirling. D.

Merchant of Bruges, before 1830, Kinnaird. Pl. (altered from Beaumont and Fletcher).

Merchant of Venice, 1598, Shakespeare. D. (See "Jew of Malta.")

Mercurius Britannicus, 1641, Braithwait. T.C. (from the French. A political play about ship-money).

Mère Coupable (*La*), 1792, Beaumarchais. D.

Méridien, 1852, Deslandes. D.

Merlin in Love, 1759, Hill. C.

Mérope, 1713, Maffei. T.

Mérope, 1738, Voltaire. T.

Merope, 1749, Jefferys or Hill (ascribed to both). T.

Merope, 1783, Alfieri. T. (translated by C. Lloyd, 1815).

Merope, 1858, Matthew Arnold. Cl.T.

Merry Devil of Edmonton (*The*), 1608, Brewer. C.

Merry Play between Johan. . . , Tyb. . . , and Johan the Prester, 1533, Heywood. C.

Merry Wives of Windsor, 1596, Shakespeare. C. (printed 1602). (See "Comical Gallant.")

Mery Play between the Pardoner and the Frere (*A*), 1533, J. Heywood. C.

Mesogonus, 1560, Thomas Rychardes. C. (only four acts extant).

Messalina, 1640, Richards. T.

Messiah (*The*), 1741, Handel. Or. (libretto by Jennens).

Metamorphosed Gipsies (1574-1637), Jonson. C.

Métamorphoses de l'Amour, 19th cent., Brohan. C. (See "Love's Metamorphosis.")

Metamorphosis of Pygmalion's Image, 1598, Marston. C.

Métromanie ou Le Poete, 1738, Piron. C. (said to be the best comedy in the French language).

Michael and His Lost Angel, 1896, H. A. Jones. P.

Michaelmas Term, 1607, Middleton.

Michel et Cristine, before 1822, Scribe. Pt.Pc.

Microcosmus, 1637, Nabbes. M.

Midas, 1592, J. Lyly. Myt.D.

Midas, 1764, O'Hara. Blta.

Midas (*Jugement de*), 1741-1813, Grétry. O.

Middleman (*The*), 1889, H. A. Jones.

Midnight Hour (*The*), 1793, Inchbald. Pt.C. (realized £130).

Midsummer Night's Dream, 1592, Shakespeare. Fy.C. (printed 1600).

Midsummer Night's Dream, 1843, Mendelssohn.

Mikado (*The*), Gilbert.

Milês (B.C. 254-184), Plautus. C. (Latin). Translated into blank verse by Messrs. Thornton, Rich, Warner, and Colman, 1796-74.

Milesdan (*The*), Jackman.

Milkmaid (*The*), 1771-1841, Dibdin. Mu.D.

Miller and His Men, 1813, Pocock. Mel. (music by Bishop). ?

Miller of Mansfield (*The*), 1737, Dodsley. D.E. (The second part is *Sir John Cockle at Court*.)

Mind, Will, and Understanding (time, Henry VI.), Anon. Mo. (In MS. only.)

Minerva's Sacrifice, posthumous 1653, Massinger.

Mines de Pologne (*Les*), 1803, Guilbert de Pixérécourt.

Minister (*The*), 1797, Lewis. T. (adapted from Schiller).

Minna von Barnhelm, 1767, Lessing. C.

Minor (*The*), 1760, Foote. F.

Mirandola, 1821, Procter. T. (copyright was £525).

Mirra, 1783, Alfieri (translated by C. Lloyd, 1815).

Mirror. (See "Myrrour.")

Mirza, 17th cent., R. Baron. T.

Misanthrope, 1666, Molière. C.

Misanthropy and Repentance, 1797, Kotzebue. D. (called in English *The Stranger*).

Miser (*The*), 1672, Shadwell. (See below.)

Miser (*The*), 1732, Fielding. C. (from *L'Avare*, by Molière, 1667).

Misérables (*Les*), 1864, Hugo, junior. D. (his father's novel, 1863, dramatized).

Misfortunes of Arthur, 1587, Hughes. T.

Misogonist (*The*), 1780, Lessing. D.

Misogonus, 1560, printed 1577, Rychardes. C. (one of his earliest plays).

Miss Eily O'Connor, H. J. Byron.

Miss Sarah Samson, 1755, Lessing. T. (music by Mendelssohn and Nicolay).

Miss in Her Teens, 1747, Garrick. F.

Mistake (*The*), 1672-1726, Vanbrugh. C. (altered by King into *Lovers' Quarrels*).

Mistakes (*The*) or The Happy Resentment, 1758, lord Hyde. C.

Mithridate, 1673, Racine. T. (imitated from Euripidês).

Mithridate, 1770, Mozart. O.

Mithridates, 1674, Lee. T.

Mock Doctor (*The*), 1732, Fielding. F. (This is *Le Médecin Malgré Lui* of Molière, 1666, converted into a farce.)

Mock Officer (*The*), 1733, T. Cibber. C.

Mock Tempest (*The*), 1675, Duffett. C.

Modern Antiques, 1798, O'Keefe. C.

Modern Husband (*The*), 1735, Fielding. C.

Modern Prophets, 1709, D'Urfey. C.

Mœurs de Temps (*Les*), 1750, Saurin. C.

Mogul Tale (*The*), 1784, Inchbald. F.

Moise in Egitto, 1818, Rossini. O.

Mon Gigot et Mon Gendre, 1861, Antier.

Monastère Abandonna, 1816, Guilbert de Pixérécourt.

Money, 1840, Lytton. C.

Money is an Asse, 1668, Jordan. C.

Mons. D'Olive, 1606, Chapman. C.

Mons. le Duc, 1879, Val Prinsep. Pl.
Mons. Ragout, about 1669, Lacy. C.
Mons. Thomas, 1619, Fletcher (Beaumont died 1616). C.
Mons. Tonson, 1767, Moncrieff or Taylor (attributed to both : Moncrieff died 1857). F.
Montargis. (See " Chien.")
Montezuma, 1772, Sacchini. O.
Montezuma, 1878, Verdi. O.
Montfort (De), 1798, Baillie. T. (the passion of " hate ").
Montoni, 1820, Sheil.
Montrose (1782-1835), Pocock.
Monument of Honour (The), 1624, Webster.
Moonstone (The), 1877, Wilkie Collins (his novel dramatized).
Morando, 1584, Greene.
More Dissemblers besides Women, 1657. Middleton. C.
More Ways than One, 1785, Mrs. Cowley. C.
Mort d'Abel, 1792, Legouvé. T. (imitated from Gesser and Klopstock).
Mort de Calas, 1791, Chénier. T.
Mort de Henri IV., 1806, Legouvé. T.
Mostellaria or The Haunted House (B.C. 254-184), Plautus. C. (Latin). Translated into blank verse by Messrs. Thornton, Rich, Warner, and Colman, 1769-74 ; and imitated by Regnard, Addison, and others.
Mother and Daughter (The), 1843, R. Bell.
Mother Bombie, 1594, J. Lyly. Ct.E.
Mother Goose (1771-1841), Dibdin. Pn.
Mother Pantom (1771-1841), Dibdin. C.
Mother Shipton (no date), about 1670, Thompson. C.
Mother-in-Law, 1881, Sims. C.
Mount Sinai, 1831, Neukomm. Or.
Mountain Sylph (The), 1834, Barnett. O.
Mountaineers (The), 1793, Colman. C.
Mountebank (The), Gilbert.
Mourning Bride, 1697, Congreve. T.
Mousquetaires (Les), 19th cent., Halévy. O.C.
M.P., 1870, T. W. Robertson. C.
M.P. or The Blue Stocking, 1811, Moore. Mu.C.
Mucedorus (no date), about 1590, Greene. F.
Much Ado about Nothing, 1600, Shakespeare. C.
Muet (Le), 1691, De Brueys. C.
Muette de la Fôret, 1828, Antier.
Muette de Portici (La). (See " Masaniello.")
Mulberry Garden (The), 1668, Sedley. C.
Murderous Michael, 1578, Anon. T.
Muse in Livery, 1732, Dodsley. C.
Muses in Mourning, 1749, Hill. C.
Muses' Looking-Glass (The), 1638, Randolph. C.
Mustapha, 1609, F. Greville, lord Brooke. T.
Mustapha, 1739, Mallet. Pl.
Mutius Scævola, 1801, Ireland. H.D.
Mutual Deception, 1795, Atkinson. C. (altered by Colman into Tit for Tat).
My Awful Dad (1803-1878), C. J. Mathews.
My Grandmother and Other Fairies (1755-1834), Hoare.
My Lord and My Lady, 1861, Planché.
My Spouse and I (1771-1841), Dibdin. O.F.
My Wife's Daughter (1805-1868), Coyne.
My Wife's Mother (1803-1878), C. J. Mathews.
Myrrha, 1783, Alfieri. T. (translated by C. Lloyd, 1815).

Myrrour for Magistraytes, 1557, Sackville and others. Po.D.
Mystères d'Udolphe (Les), 1798, Guilbert de Pixérécourt. Mel.
Mysterious Husband (The), 1783, Cumberland. C.
Mysterious Marriage (The), 1795, Miss H. Lee.
Mysterious Mother, 1788, Walpole. T.
Mysterious Stranger (The), founded on the French, Selby. C.

Naaman, 1864, Costa. Or.
Nabob (The), 1772, Foote. F.
Nabob (The), 1879, Burnard (an English version of Les Trente Millions de Gladiateurs, by Labiche and Gille).
Nabucco, 1842, Verdi. O.
Nabucodonosor, 19th cent., Verdi. O.
Nancy, 1739, Carey. Int.
Nanine, 1749, Voltaire. C.
Narbonne. (See " Count of Narbonne.")
Nathan the Sage, 1779, Lessing. D.
Nations (Les), 1851, Banville. O.
Native Land, 1823, Bishop O.
Natural Daughter (The), 1792, Goethe. C.
Natural Son (The), 1786, Cumberland. C. (See " Fils Naturel.")
Natural Son (The), 1799, Anne Plumtree. Pl. (from Kotzebue).
Nature, 1490, H. Medwell. Int.
Naufragium Joculare, 1638, Cowley. C. (translated by C. Johnson, and called Fortune in her Wits, 1705).
Neck or Nothing, 1766, Garrick or King (ascribed to both). F.
Ne'er-do-Weel (The), 1878, Gilbert. C.
Negro Slaves, 1796, Halliday. H.Pc. (from Kotzebue).
Nell (1830-1877), Halliday. C.
Nell Gwynne, 1832, Jerrold. C.
Nero, 1675, Lee. T.
Nerone, 1700, Handel. O.
Nervous Man, 19th cent., B. Bernard. C.
Nest of Ninnies (A), 1608, Armyn. C.
Never too Late, 1590, Greene. C.
Never too Late to Mend (It's), 1878, Reade. C.
New Academy (The), 1653, Brome. C.
New Droll (A), 1660, Jordan. M.
New Hippocrates (The), 1761, Hiffernan. D.
New Inn (The), 1630, Jonson. C.
New Men and Old Acres, 1869, T. Taylor. C.
New Peerage (The), 1830, Miss H. Lee. C.
New Tricke to Cheat the Divell, 1639, R. Davenport. C.
New Way to Pay Old Debts, 1625, printed 1633, Massinger. C.
New Woman (The), 1894, Sydney Grundy.
New Wonder, a Woman Never Vext, 1632, Rowley. C.
Nice Firm (A), 1853, Tom Taylor.
Nice Valour (The), 1647, Beaumont and Fletcher. C.
Nice Wanton (The), 1560, Anon. Mo.
Nicholas Flam, 19th cent., Buckstone.
Nicholas Nickleby (1830-1877), Halliday (C. Dickens's novel dramatized).
Nicodemus (time, Edward III.), Anon. Mir.Pl. (founded on chap. xvi. of the Gospel of Nicodemus).
Nicomède, 1670, P. Corneille. T.C.
Nicomedes, 1671, J. Dancer. T.C. (from the Nicomède of Corneille).
Niebelungen, 1850, Wagner. O.

Night Walkers, printed 1633, (?) Beaumont and Fletcher. C.
Night Watcher (*The*), *, Körner. C.
Nine Points of the Law, 1859, Tom Taylor.
Ninette à la Cour (1710-1792), Favart. O.C.
Ninus II., 1814, Brifant. T.
No Cure no Pay, 1794, H. Rowe. Mu.F.
No Song no Supper, 1790, Hoare. Mu.E. (music by Storace).
No Wit, no Help, like Woman's, 1657, Greene or Middleton. C.
Noah's Flood, 1679, Ecclestone. Or.
Noble Choice, 1653, Massinger.
Noble Gentleman, printed 1647, (?) Beaumont and Fletcher.
Noble Heart (*The*), 1850, Lewes. T.
Noble Ingratitude, 1659, Lower. P.T.
Noble Valour, (?) Beaumont and Fletcher.
Nobleman (*The*), 17th cent., Tourneur. T.C. (The manuscript of this play was destroyed by the cook of Mr. Warburton the Somerset herald.)
Nobody and Somebody, 1606, Trundell. C.
Noces de Gamache, 1827, Mendelssohn. O.
None Such, 17th cent., Rowley. C.
Nonjuror (*The*), 1717, Cibber. C. (from Molière's *Tartuffe;* copyright £105). (See "Hypocrite.")
Nonne Sanglante, 1854, Delavigne. O. (music by Gounod).
Norma, 1831, Bellini. O. (libretto by Romani).
Northern Lass (*The*), 1632, Brome. C.
Northward Hoe ! 1607, Dekker.
Not so Bad as we Seem, 1851, lord Lytton. C.
Not such a Fool as he Looks, 1869, H. J. Byron. C.
Notaire Obligeant, 1650, Dancourt. C.
Note of Hand or Trip to Newmarket, 1777, Cumberland. C.
Notoriety (1765-1841), Reynolds. C.
Notorious Mrs. Ebbsmith (*The*), A. Pinero. C.
Notre Dame, 19th cent., Victor Hugo. D.
Notre Dame (1850-1877), Holliday.
Nouveau Pourceaugnac, before 1822, Scribe. Pt.Pc.
Nouveau Seigneur du Village, 1813, Boieldieu. O.
Novella, 1653, Brome. C.
Nozze di Bigaro, 1786, Mozart. O. (See "Mariage de Figaro.") Sir H. Bishop altered this opera.
Nuit Blanche (*Une*), 19th cent., Offenbach. O.Bf.
Nuit de Noël (*La*), 1848, Reber. O.
Nuits Terribles, 1821, St. Georges. O.C.
Nuptials of Peleus and Thetis, 1654, Howell. M. and C.

Oberon, 1616, Jonson. C.
Oberon, 1826, Weber. O. (libretto by Planché).
Oberto di Bonifazio, 1839, Verdi. O.
Obstinate Lady (*The*), 1657, Cokaine. C.
Octavia (B.C. 58-32), Seneca. T. (Latin. The cruelty of Nero to his wife). Adapted by T. Nuce, 1566 ; acted 1581.
Octavia, 1783, Alfieri. T. (translated by C. Lloyd, 1815). (See "Virtuous Octavia.")
Octavius (1761-1819), Kotzebue. H.D.
Octoroon, 1861, Boucicault. D.
Oden (1756-1829), Léopold. T.
Odette, 1832, Déaddé. D.

O'Dowd (*The*), 1880, Boucicault (a version like "The Porter's Knot" of *Les Crochets du Père* by Cormon and Grange).
Œdipe, 1659, Corneille. T.
Œdipe, 1718, Voltaire. T.
Œdipe, 1781, Sacchini. O.
Œdipe Roi, 1798, Chénier. T.
Œdipe à Colone, 1796, Chénier. T.
Œdipe chez Admète, 1778, Ducis. T.
Œdipus (B.C. 58-32), Seneca. T. (Latin). Adapted by A. Nevyle, 1560.
Œdipus, 1679, Dryden and Lee. T.
Œdipus et Colonus, about B.C. 407, Sophocles. T. (Greek). Translated by. G. Adams, 1729 ; Potter, 1788 ; Dale, 1824 ; Plumptre, 1865.
Œdipus Tyrannus, about B.C. 425, Sophocles. T. (Greek). Translated by L. Theobald, 1715 ; G. Adams, 1729 ; Potter, 1788 ; G. S. Clarke, 1791 ; Dale, 1824 ; F. H. Doyle, 1849 ; Plumptre, 1865.
Œdipus Tyrannus, etc., 1820, P. B. Shelley. T.
Œnone, 1804, Kalkbrenner. O.
Œuvres du Démon (*Les*), 1854, Boule. D.
Of Age To-morrow, 1800.
Old Bachelor, 1693, Congreve. C.
Old City Manners, 1717, Mrs. Lennox. C. (This is *Eastward Hoe* reset.)
Old Couple, before 1641, May. C.
Old Fortunatus. (See "Fortunatus.")
Old Heads and Young Hearts, 1843, Boucicault. C.
Old Law (*The*), 1599, printed 1656, Middleton and Rowley. C. (altered by Massinger).
Old Maid (*The*), 1761, Murphy. F.
Old Maids, 1841, Knowles. C.
Old Martin's Trials, 19th cent., Stirling. Dom.D.
Old Mode (*The*) and the New, 1709, D'Urfey. C.
Old Sailors, 1874, H. J. Byron. C.
Old Score (*An*), 1867, Gilbert. C.
Old Story (*An*), H. J. Byron. C.
Old Troop, 1672, Lacy. C.
Old Wives' Tale, 1590, Peele. C. (Milton's *Comus* is indebted to this comedy.)
Oldcastle (*Sir John*), 1600, Munday and Drayton. T. (one of the "spurious plays" of Shakespeare).
Olimpiade, 1719, Leo. O.
Olive (*D'*) (See "Mons. D'Olive.")
Olivia, 1878, W. G. Wills. C. (a dramatic version of Goldsmith's *Vicar of Wakefield*).
Ollanta, 1871, Markham. D.
Olympiade, 1761, Piccini. O.
Olympic Revels, 1831, Planché.
Olympie, 1800, Kalkbrenner. O.
Olympie, 1820, Brifaut. O. (music by Spontini).
Omba, 1853, Bigsby. D.R.
Oncle Valet, 1798, Dellamaria. O.C.
Ondine, 1816, Hoffmann. O.
On Bail, 1877, Gilbert (adapted from *Le Réveillon*). C.
On Strike, 1873, A. W. A'Beckett.
One or a Monarchy, posthumous 1805, Alfieri. C. (subject, Darius chosen king by the neighing of his horse). Translated by C. Lloyd, 1815.

One o'clock or The Wood Demon, 1811, Lewis. G.O.R.
One Snowy Night, *, Ware. C. (translated from the French).
Opera Comique, 1799, Dellamaria. O.C.
Opera di Camera of Jessy Lea, 1863, Macfarren. O.
Opportunity (The), 1640, Shirley. C.
Oraloosa (1803-1854), Bird. T.
Orator (The), Massinger.
Orators (The), 1672, Foote. F.
Ordeal by Touch (The), 1872, R. Lee. D.
Order of the Garter (The), 1742, West. D.Pm.
Ordinary (The), 1647, printed 1651, Cartwright. C.
Oreste, 1750, Voltaire. T.
Oreste et Pylade, 1695, Lagrange. T.
Orestes, B.C. 408, Euripides. T. (Greek). Translated by Banister, 1780 ; Potter, 1781 ; Wodhull, 1782.
Orestês, 1783, Alfieri. T. (translated by C. Lloyd, 1815).
Orestes, 1802, Sotheby. T.
Orestes, 1871, Warren. Met.D.
Orfeo, 1483, Poliziano. (See " Orpheus.")
Orfeo, 1764, Glück. O. (libretto by Calzabigi).
Orientales (Les), 1828, V. Hugo. R.D.
Originaux (Les), 1693, Lamotte.
Orlandino, 1526, Folengo. B.
Orlando Furioso, 1594, Greene. (See " Bombastes Furioso.")
Ormasdes (1612-1690), Henry Killigrew.
Oronooko, 1696, Southerne. T. (Mrs. Behn's novel dramatized).
Orphan (The), 1680, Otway. T.
Orphan of China (The), 1761, Murphy. T. (Voltaire's Orphelin de la Chine).
Orphan of the Frozen Sea, 1856, Stirling. N.D.
Orphée (1677-1758), Lagange. O.
Orphée aux Enfers, 1858, Offenbach. O.Bf.
Orphelin de la Chine (L'), 1760, Voltaire. T.
Orpheus and Eurydice, 1705, Dennis. T. (See " Orfeo.")
Orpheus and Eurydice (1730-1805), King.
Orti Esperidi (Gli), 1722, Metastasio. O. (music by Porpora).
Oscar and Malvina (1754-1829), Shield. O.
Osmond the Great Turk, 1657, Carlell. Pl.
Otello, 1816, Rossini. O.
Othello, 1602, Shakespeare. T.
Otho the Great (1796-1821), Keats and Brown. T.
Othon, 1664, Corneille. T.
Oulita the Serf, 1858, Helps. Pl.
Our American Cousin, 1858, Tom Taylor. C. (It was greatly altered by Sothern.)
Our Boys, 1878, H. J. Byron. C. (It had a continuous run for 4 years and 3 months.)
Our Clerks, 1852, Tom Taylor. C.
Our Mary Anne (1802-1879), Buckstone. C.
Our New Governess (1815-1874), C. S. Brooks. D.
Ours, 1866, Robertson. C.
Ours et la Pacha (Les), before 1822, Scribe. Pt.Pc.
Outtara-Rama-Tscheritra, 8th cent., Bhavabhouti. Myt.D. (translated by Wilson in his Indian Theatre).
Overland Route, 1860, Tom Taylor. C.
Ovid, 1662, Cockaine. T.

Padlock (The), 1768, Bickerstaff. O.F.
Page (The), 1765-1841, Reynolds. C.
Page of Plymouth (time, Queen Elizabeth), Anon. T.
Palace of Truth, 1870 (3 acts), Gilbert. Fy.C.
Palamon and Arcyte, 1566, Edwards. C.
Palestine (1775-1847), Crotch. Or.
Pallantus and Eudora, 1653, T. Killigrew. T. (same as The Conspiracy).
Pamela, 1742, Love. C.
Pammachius, 1544, Anon. C. (Latin).
Pandora, 1664, sir W. Killigrew. Pl.
Panel (The), 1757-1823, Kemble. (This is Bickerstaff's comedy of 'Tis Well 'tis no Worse reset.)
Pan's Anniversary, 1625, B. Jonson. M.
Panurge, 1785, Grétry. O.
Pap with a Hatchet, 1589, Lilly.
Papal Tyranny, 1745, Cibber. T.
Paracelsus, 1836, R. Browning. D.Pm.
Parasitaster or The Fawn, 1606, Marston. C.
Paria (Le), 1821, Delavigne. T.
Paria (The), 1826, Beer. T. (the above in English).
Paride e Elena, 1770, Glück. O. (libretto by Calzabigi).
Paris and Pleasure (from the French), C. Selby. C.
Paris et Londres, 1827, Dartois. C.
Parisien (Le), 1838, Delaporte. C.
Parisina, 1833, Donizetti. O.
Parliament of Love, 1625, Massinger. C.
Parolle et Izidora (1703-1758), Theo. Cibber. C. (copyright was £36 10s.).
Parson's Wedding (The), 1663, Killigrew. C.
Parted (1799-1838), Reeve. C.
Pasquale (Don), 1843, Donizetti. O.
Pasquin, 1736, Fielding. C.
Passionate Lovers (The), 1655, Carlell. T.C.
Passions (Plays of the), 1798-1812, J. Baillie. C. and T.
Past Ten o'clock (1771-1841), Th. Dibdin. F.
Pastorale Comique, 1666, Molière.
Pastor Fido (Il), 1590, Guarini. P. (See " Faithful Shepherdess.")
Pathomachia or The Battle of the Affections, 1630, Constable. D.
Patience, Benethorne's Bride, 1881, Gilbert and Sullivan. Opta.
Patient Grissel, 1607, Middleton.
Patient Grizzell, 1603, Chettle and Dekker. C. (drawn from a novel by Boccaccio).
Patrician and Parvenu (The), 1835, Poole. C.
Patrician's Daughter, 1841, W. Marston. T.
Patriot (The), 1784, Charles Hamilton. T. (from Metastasio).
Patron (The), 1764, Foote. F.
Patter v. Clatter (1803-1878), C. J. Mathews.
Pattie and Peggie, 1730, Th. Cibber. Bd.O. (This is Allan Ramsay's Gentle Shepherd reset.)
Paul, 1836, Mendelssohn. Or.
Paul Lafarge, 1870, Boucicault.
Paul Pry, 1825, Poole. F.
Paul and Virginia (1756-1818), Cobb. Mu.E.
Paul and Virginia (1755-1837), Favieres. T.
Paul and Virginia (1768-1844), Mazzhingi. O.
Pauline, 1841, Labrousse. C.
Payable on Demand, 1859, Tom Taylor.
Peace, B.C. 419, Aristophanes. C. (Greek).

Translated by Mitchell, 1820–22 ; Hickie, 1853 ; Rudd, 1867.

Pédre (*Don*), 1857, Cormon. D.

Pedro de Portugal (*Don*), 1828, Gily Zarate. D.

Peep Behind the Curtain, 1767 (ascribed to Garrick and to King). F.

Pelayo (1749–1811), Jovellanos. T.

Pèlerin Blanc (*Le*), 1811, Guilbert de Pixéré-court.

Pélopides, 1763, Voltaire. T.

Pénélope, 1785, Marmontel. O. (music by Piccini).

Percy, 1777, Hannah More. T. (copyright £150).

Père de Famille, 1758, Diderot. C.

Pericles Prince of Tyre, 1609, Shakespeare. T.

Perjured Husband, 1700, Centlivre. C.

Perkin Warbeck, 1634, Ford. H.D.

Perle Noire, 1862, Sardou.

Perouse (*La*), 1799, B. Thompson. D. (from Kotzebue).

Perplexed Couple (*The*), 1706–1767, Molloy. C.

Perplexed Loves, 1712, Centlivre. C.

Perplexities (*The*), 1767, Hull. C. (This is Tuke's play *The Adventures of Five Hours*, 1663, reset.)

Persa or The Persian (B.C. 254–184), Plautus. C. (Latin). Translated into blank verse by Messrs. Thornton, Rich, Warner, and Colman, 1769–74.

Persian Prince (*The*), 1682, Southerne. T.

Persian Princess (*The*), 1711, Theobald. T.

Persians (*The*), B.C. 472, Æschylus. T. (Greek). Translated by Potter, 1777 ; Buckley, 1849 ; Plumptre, 1869.

Pertharite, 1693, Corneille. T.

Peter and Paul (1788–1841), Hook.

Pewterer (*The*), 1747, Holbery. B.C.

Phædra and Hippolytus, 1708, E. Smith. T. (realized £501). (See "Hippolytus.")

Phaëton, 1597, Daniel or Dekker. T.

Pharamond, 17th cent., Calprenède. T. (translated by Phillips, 1677).

Pharamond, 1736, Cahusac. T.

Phèdre, 1677, Racine. T. (imitated from Euripidês).

Phèdre et Hippolyte, 1677, Pradon. T. (a rival play).

Phenomenon in a Smock Frock (*A*), T. M. Morton. F.

Philaster or Love Lies a-Bleeding, 1620, John Fletcher (excellent). T.

Philenzo and Hippolyta, posthumous 1653, Massinger.

Philip II., 1783, Alfieri. T. (translated by C. Lloyd, 1815).

Philip von Artevelde, 1834, H. Taylor. D.Pm.

Philip Chabot, 1639, Chapman. T.

Philippe II. (1764–1881), Chénier. D.

Phillis of Seyros, 1655, Shirley. Pl. (from the Italian).

Philoctète, 1783, Laharpe. T.

Philoctetes, about B.C. 415, Sophocles. T. (Greek). Translated by T. Sheridan, 1725 ; G. Adams, 1729 ; Potter, 1788 ; Dale, 1824 ; Plumptre, 1865.

Philoctetes, 1871, Warren. Met.D.

Philosophe sans le Savoir (*Le*), 1765, Sedaine. C.

Philosopher's Stone (*The*), 1850, Tom Taylor.

Philotas, 1597, acted 1607, Daniel. T.

Philtre (*Le*), 1830, Scribe. O.

Phœnissæ (B.C. 480–406), Euripides. T. (Greek). Translated by Banister, 1780 ; Potter, 1781 ; Wodhull, 1782 ; Morgan, 1805 ; Giles, 1865. (See "Thebaïs.")

Phœnix (*The*), 1607, Middleton.

Phœnix in Her Flames (*The*), 1639, Lower. T.

Phormio, B.C. 162, Terence. C. (Latin). Translated by Bentley, 1726 ; Colman the Elder, 1765 ; Barry, 1857 ; etc.

Phrenologist, 1835, Coyne. C.

Phrontisterion or Oxford in the Nineteenth Century, 1852, Mansel. D. (unfinished).

Phrosine et Mélidor, 1794, Méhul. O.C.

Physic Lies a-Bleeding, 1697, Th. Brown. C.

Piccolino, 1875, Guiraud. O. (libretto by Sardou).

Picture (*The*), 1630, Massinger. T.C.

Pierce Penniless (*Supplication of*), 1592, Nash.

Pierre et Catherine, 1829, St. Georges.

Pierre le Grand, 1854, Meyerbeer. O.

Piety in Pattens, 1773, Foote. F.

Pilgrim (*The*), 1621, Fletcher (Beaumont died 1616). Altered by Vanbrugh in 1699.

Pilot (*The*), 19th cent., Fitzball. N.Blta.

Pinafore (*H.M.S.*), 1878, Gilbert and Sullivan. N.C.Opta.

Pinner of Wakefield (*The*), 1560–1592, R. Greene. C.

Piperman's Predicaments, *, Ware. F. (translated).

Pippa Passes, 1842, R. Browning, 1842. D.

Pirata (*Il*), 1806–1835, Bellini. O.

Pirate (*The*), 1792–1851 (never printed), Davenport. Pl.

Pirates (1763–1796), Storace. Mu.D.

Pirates of Penzance (*The*), 1880, Gilbert and Sullivan. Opta.

Piso's Conspiracy, 1676, Lee. T. (same as *Nero*).

Pizarro, 1799, Sheridan. T. (from Kotzebue's drama *The Spaniard in Peru*, 1797).

Plaideurs (*Les*), 1668, Racine. C. (imitated from the *Wasps* of Aristophanês).

Plain Dealer, 1677, Wycherly. C.

Plain Dealer (*The*), 1766, Bickerstaff. C.

Platonic Love, 1707, Centlivre. C.

Platonic Lovers, 1636, Davenant. T.C.

Play (1829–1871), Robertson. C.

Play betwene the Pardoner and the Frere, printed 1533, J. Heywood. Int.

Play called the Four P's (*The*), printed 1569, J. Heywood. Pl.

Play of Love (*The*), 1533, Heywood. Int.

Play of the Wether (*The*), 1533, Heywood. Int.

Playing Comet (*The*), 18th cent., S. Johnson.

Plays of the Passions (1798–1836), J. Baillie. T. and C.

Plot and No Plot (*A*), 1697, Dennis. C.

Plot and Passion, 1852, Tom Taylor, etc.

Plotting Sisters (*The*), 1676, D'Urfey. C.

Plus Beau Jour de la Vie (*Le*), before 1822, Scribe. Pl.Pc.

Plutus, B.C. 408, Aristophanes. C. (Greek). Translated by Randolph, 1651 ; Fielding and Young, 1812 ; Mitchell, 1820–22 ; Cunningham, 1826 ; Rudd, 1857.

Pœrulus (B.C. 254–184), Plautus. C. (Latin). Translated into blank verse by Messrs. Thornton, Rich, Warner, and Colman, 1769–74.

Poetaster (*The*), 1601, Jonson. Sat.C. (in which Dekker is satirized as "Crispinus").
Poet made Wise (*A*), 18th cent., S. Johnson. C.
Poets (*The*), 1774, Alfieri. F. (translated by C. Lloyd, 1815).
Polidoro, 1788, Bandettini.
Polinice, 1783, Alfieri. T. (translated by C. Lloyd, 1815).
Polish Jew (*The*), *, Ware. D. (altered into *The Bells*, 1874).
Politician (*The*), 1655, Shirley. T.
Politician Cheated (*The*), 1663, Greene. C.
Polly Honeycombe, 1760, Colman the Elder. D.N.
Polyeucte, 1640, Corneille. T.
Polyxène, 1686, Lafosse. T.
Pompadour (*The*), 1888, Sydney Grundy.
Pompée, 1592, Garnier. T.
Pompée, 1641, Corneille. T.
Pompey, 1663, Mrs. C. Philips. T. (from Corneille).
Pompey the Great, 1595, Kyd. T. (translated from the *Pompée* of Garnier).
Pompey the Great, 1664, E. Waller. T. (from Corneille).
Pompey the Great (1705–1773), never printed, S. Johnson. T.
Poor Gentleman (*The*), 1802, Colman. C.
Poor Jack (1802–1879), Buckstone. C.
Poor Man's Comfort (*The*), 1655, Daborn. C.
Poor Soldier (*The*), 1783, O'Keefe. O. (music by Shield).
Pope als Metaphysiker, 1754, Lessing (music by Mendelssohn).
Pope Joan. (See "Female Prelate.")
Popping the Question (1802–1879), Buckstone. C.
Popularité, 1838, Delavigne. C.
Porter's Knot (*The*), 1858, Oxenford. D. (Like *O'Dowd*, it is an adaptation of *Les Crochets du Père*, by Cormon and Grangé.)
Postillon de Lonjumeau (*Le*), 1836, Adam. O.C.
Poulet et Poulette, 1878, Hervé. B.O.
Pourceaugnac (*Mons.*), 1669, Molière. C.
Pragmatical Jesuit New-Leven'd (*The*), 1657, Carpenter. C.
Precieuses Ridicules, 1659, Molière. C.
Premier Jour de Bonheur (*Le*), 1868, Auber. O.
Presence (1624–1678), Margaret duchess of Newcastle. C.
Presented at Court, 1848, Coyne. C.
Presumptive Evidence (1802–1879), Buckstone.
Pretty Esmeralda and Captain Phœbus of Ours, 1879, H. J. Byron. B.
Pride shall have a Fall, 1825, Croly. C.
Priestess (*The*), 1855, Sargent.
Prince Deukalion, 1879, B. Taylor. D.
Prince Dorus, 1850, Tom Taylor.
Prince of Homburg (1776–1811), Kleist. D.
Princess (*The*), 1868, Gilbert. D.
Princess of Cleves, 1689, Lee.
Princesse Aurélie (*Le*), 1828, Delavigne. C.
Princess Ida, Gilbert.
Princesse d'Élide, 1664, Molière. C.
Princesse de Navarre, 1743, Voltaire. O.
Princesse de Navarre, 1747, Rameau. O.
Princesse de Trébizonde, 1870, Offenbach. O.
Prisoner of State, 1847, Stirling. D.
Prisoner of War, 1837, Jerrold. C.
Prisoner (*The*), 1641, Killigrew. T.C.
Prisonnier (*Le*), 1796, Dellamaria. O.C.

Procureur Arbitre (*Le*), 1633–1690, R. Poisson. C.
Prodigal Son (*The*), 1739–1802, Arnold. O. (music by Sullivan).
Profligate (*The*), 1820, G. W. Taylor. C.
Profligate (*The*), A. Pinero.
Prometheus Bound, B.C. 460, Æschylus. T. (Greek). Translated by Potter, 1777; Buckley, 1849; Webster, 1866; Plumptre, 1869; Lang, 1870.
Prometheus Bound, 1838, recast in 1850, E. Browning. T.
Prometheus Unbound, 1821, Shelley. L.D.
Promos and Cassandra, 1578, Whetstone. C. (This is the quarry of Shakespeare's *Measure for Measure*.)
Prôneurs (*Les*) or La Tartuffe Littéraire (1734– 1780), Dorat. Sat.D. (directed against D'Alembert and his set).
Proof, 1878, Burnand (an English version of *Une Cause Célèbre*).
Prophet (*The*), 1874, B. Taylor. T.
Prophète (*Le*), 1849, Meyerbeer. O. (libretto by Scribe).
Prophetess (*The*), printed 1647, (?) Beaumont and Fletcher.
Prophetess (*The*) or History of Dioclesian, 1690, Betterton.
Proserpina, 1804, Winter. O.
Proserpine, 1801, Paisiello. O.
Protecteur (*Le*), 1781–1857, Brifaut. C.
Provoked Husband, 1726, Vanbrugh. C. (left unfinished by Vanbrugh, and called *The Journey to London*. Cibber finished the play, and changed the name).
Provoked Wife, 1697, Vanbrugh. C.
Provost of Bruges, 1836, Knowles. T.
Prude's Progress (*The*), 1895, Jerome. C.
Pseudolus or The Cheat (B.C. 254–1849), Plautus. C. (Latin). Translated into blank verse by Messrs. Thornton, Rich, Warner, and Colman, 1769–74.
Psyché, 1671, Molière. C.
Psyché, 1675, Shadwell.
Psyché Debauched, 1678,
Public Wooing (1624–1673), Margaret duchess of Newcastle. C.
Pulchérie, 1672, Corneille.
Puritan Maid (*The*), 1602, Middleton. Pl. (lost).
Puritan (*The*) or The Widow of Watling Street, 1607, W[entworth] S[mith].
Puritani (*I*), 1834, Bellini. O. (libretto by Pepoli).
Puritan's Daughter, 1861, Balfe. O.
Purse (*The*) or The Benevolent Tar, *, Cross. Mu.E.
Pygmalion, 1748, Rameau. O.
Pygmalion, 1809, Cherubini. O.
Pygmalion and Galatea, 1871, Gilbert. Myt.D.
Pyrame et Thisbé (1632–1698), Pradon. T.
Pyrame et Thisbé (1677–1758), Lagrange. O.
Pyrrhus King of Egypt, 1695, Hopkins. T.

Q.E.D., 1871, Marshall. Cdta.
Quaker (*The*), 1777, Dibdin. C.O.
Quaker's Opera (*The*), 1728, Th. Walker.
Quarantine (*The*), *, Ware. C.
Queen and Concubine (*The*), 1653, Brome. D.
Queen Elizabeth's Troubles, in two parts, 1606–1609, Thomas Heywood. H.Pl.

Queen Juta of Denmark, 19th cent., Bojé. T.
Queen Mab, 1760, Burney. O.
Queen Mary [of England], 1875, Tennyson. T. (See "Mary Tudor.")
Queen Mother (*The*), 1861, Swinburne. T.
Queen of Arragon, 1635, Habington. T.C.
Queen of Connaught (*The*), 1870, Harriet Jay. (This is her novel dramatized.)
Queen of Corinth, printed 1647, (?) Beaumont and Fletcher.
Queen of Scots (*The*), 1684, Banks. T.
Queen's Arcadia (*The*), 1606, Daniel. P.T.
Queen's Exchange, printed 1659, Brome.
Queen's Shilling (*The*), 1879, Godfrey. C. (an English version of *Un Fils de Famille*; see also "Discarded Son.")
Queens, 1616, Jonson.
Queer Subject (*The*), 1837, Coyne. C.
Qui Femme a, Guerre a, about 1830, Brohan. C.
Quintus Fabius, 1573, Anon. H.Pl.
Quip for an Upstart Courtier (*A*), 1592, Greene. C.
Quitte ou Double, about 1830, Brohan. C. (The English adaptation is called *Double or Quits*.)

Rabages, 1872, Sardou. C.
Rage (1765-1841), Reynolds. C.
Raging Turk (*The*), 1631, Goffe. T. (Bajazet II.).
Ragout. (See "Mons. Ragout.")
Raising the Wind, 1803, Kenney. F.
Rake and His Pupil (*The*), 1834, Buckstone. C.
Ralph Roister Doister, 1534, Udal (the first English comedy). (See "Gammer Gurton's Needle" and "Mesogonus.")
Ram Alley or Merry Tricks, 1611, Barry. C.
Rambling Justice, 1677, Leanerd. C.
Rambling Lady, 1698, Southerne. C.
Randall's Thumb, 1870, Gilbert.
Rape of Lucrece (*The*), 1608, Th. Heywood. T. (See "Lucretia.")
Rapparee (*The*) or The Treaty of Limerick, 1870, Boucicault.
Rare Triumphs of Love and Fortune (*The*), 1580, Anon. Pl.
Re Teodoro, 1785, Paisiello. O.
Ready-Money Mortiboy, 1872, Besant and Rice. C.
Rebecca (1830-1877), Halliday. D.
Rebellion (*The*), 1640, Rawlins. T.
Rebellion Defeated or The Fall of Desmond, 16th cent., Cutts. T.
Rebels (*The*), 1749-1832, Goethe. C.
Recess (*The*), 1785, Miss Lee.
Réconciliation Normande, 1719, Dufresny. C.
Reconciliation or The Two Brothers, 1799. C. (from Kotzebue).
Recruiting Officer (*The*), 1706, Farquhar. C.
Recruiting Sergeant (*The*), 1770, Bickerstaff. Mu.E.
Reculer pour Mieux Sauter, 1854, Dartois. C.
Red Cross Knight, 1794, Holman.
Red Mask (*The*), 1834, Planché.
Regent (*Le*), 1831, Ancelot. V.
Regicide (*The*), 1747, acted 1749, Smollett. T.
Register Office (*The*), 1723-1787, Reed. F.
Regolo (*Attilio*), 1740, Metastasio. O. (See "Régulus.")

Regular Fix (1764-1838), Morton. C.
Régulus (1632-1698), Pradon. T.
Régulus (1734-1780), C. J. Dorat. T.
Regulus, 1774, Mrs. H. More. T.
Rehearsal (*The*), 1671, duke of Buckingham. B.
Reinald (1789-1862), Ingemann.
Reine de Chypre (*La*), 1799-1862, Halévy. O.
Reine de Golconde. (See "Aline," etc.)
Reine de Saba, 1862, Gounod. O. (libretto by Curré).
Relapse (*The*), 1697, Vanbrugh. C. (altered by Sheridan into *The Trip to Scarborough*, 1777).
Religious (1624-1673), Margaret duchess of Newcastle. T.C.
Remorse, 1797, acted 1813, Coleridge. T.
Réncontre (*The*), 1827, Planché.
Rendezvous Bourgeois (*Les*), 1794, Hoffmann. O.C. (music by Méhul).
Renegado (*The*), 1624, printed 1630, Massinger. T.C.
Rent Day, 1832, Jerrold. C. (His offer of the copyright for £5 was revived.)
Reprisals or The Tars of Old England, 1757, Smollett. F.
Rescued, 1879, Boucicault. Sen.D.
Retaliation (1752-1820), Macnally. F.
Retour de Nepoléon, 1841, Sejour. D.
Retribution, 1856, Bennett and Tom Taylor. H.P.
Return from Parnassus (*The*), 1606, Anon. Pl.
Return of the Druses, 1865, R. Browning. T.
Revenge (*The*), 1680, Anon. C. (This is the *Dutch Courtezan* revived.)
Revenge (*The*), 1721, Young. T.
Revenge or A Match at Newgate, 1680, Betterton.
Revenge for Honour, 1654, Chapman. T.
Revenge of Bussy d'Amboise, 1613, Chapman. T.
Revenger's Tragedie (*The*), 1607, Tourneur. T.
Revers de la Medaille (*Le*), 1861, Demolière. C.
Review (*The*) or Wags of Windsor, 1798, Colman. F.
Rewards of Vertue (*The*), 1661, Fountaine. C. (altered by Shadwell, and called *The Royal Shepherdess*, 1669).
Rich Jew of Malta, 1586, Marlowe. T.
Rich and Poor, 1812, Lewis. C.O.
Richard Cœur de Lion, 1781, Sedaine. O. (music by Grétry).
·Richard Cœur de Lion, 1782, Burgoyne. H.R. (the above Anglicized).
Richard Cœur de Lion (1752-1820), Macnally. O.
Richard Cœur de Lion (1830-1877), Halliday. H.D.
Richard Cœur de Lion, 1863, Benedict. O.
Richard I., 1728, Sewell. T.
Richard II., 1597, Shakespeare. H.D. (imitated from Marlowe's *Edward II.*, 1592).
Richard II., Tate.
Richard III., 1597, Shakespeare. H.T.
Richard Duke of York, 1595, Marlowe. T.
Richelieu, 1839, lord Lytton. H.Pl.
Richelieu (*La Jeunesse de*), 1833, Ancelot. V.
Richmond Heiress (*The*), 1693, D'Urfey. C.
Rienzi, 1828, Miss Mitford. T.
Rienzi, 1841, Wagner. O. (libretto by Jackson).
Right Woman (*A*), 1615, Beaumont and Fletcher. C.

Rightful Heir (*The*), 1868, lord Lytton. T.

Rigoletto, 1852, Verdi. O. (libretto from Victor Hugo).

Rimini (*Francesca di*), 1819, Pellico. T. (an episode in Dantè's *Inferno*).

Rinaldo, 1711, Hill. O. (music by Handel; this was the first piece he set to music).

Rinaldo and Armida, 1699, Dennis. D.

Riquet, 1836, Planché.

Rival Candidates, 1774, Dudley. Mu.Int.

Rival Friends (*The*), 1632, Hausted. C.

Rival Kings (*The*), 1677, Banks.

Rival Ladies, 1663, Dryden. C.

Rival Modes, 1726, Moore. C.

Rival Queens, 1671, Lee. (See "Alexander the Great.")

Rivals (*The*), 1668, Davenant. C.

Rivals (*The*), 1778, Sheridan. C.

Rivals (*The*), 1830, Balfe. O. (*I Rivali*).

Road to Ruin, 1792, Holcroft. C.

Roaring Girl (*The*), 1611, Middleton. C. (*i.e.* Moll Cutpurse).

Rob Roy, 1832, Flotow. O.

Rob Roy MacGregor (1782-1835), Pocock. O.D. (from sir W. Scott's novel).

Robbers (*The*), 1781, Schiller. D.

Robbers of Calabria, *, Lane. D. (adapted).

Robert le Diable, 1831, Meyerbeer. O. (libretto by Scribe).

Robert the Invalid, 1870, C. Reade. C. (a version of Molière's *Le Malade Imaginaire*).

Robert Macaire, C. Selby. C. (from the French).

Robin Hood, pt. i. 1597, Munday. D.

Robin Hood, pt. ii. 1598, Chettle. D.

Robin Hood, 1741, Dr. Arne and Burney. O.

Robin Hood, 1784, O'Keefe. O. (music by Shield).

Robin Hood (1752-1820), Macnally. C.O. (See "Death of Robert Earl of Huntington.")

Robin Hood, 1860, Macfarren. O.

Robin des Bois, 1824, Weber. O.

Robinson Crusoé, 1805, Guilbert de Pixérécourt. V.

Robinson Crusoe, 1806, Pocock (the above in English).

Rock of Rome, 1849, Knowles. H.Pl.

Roderigo, 1706, Handel. O.

Rodogune, 1646, Corneille. T.

Rodogune or The Rival Brothers, 1765, Aspinwall. T. (from T. Corneille).

Rodolphe, before 1822, Scribe. Pt.Pc.

Roef-Krage, 1770, Ewald. D.

Rogue's Comedy (*The*), H. A. Jones. C.

Roi Fainéant (*Le*), 1830, Ancelot. T.

Roi d'Yvetot (*Le*), 1842, Adam. O.C. (suggested by Béranger's song).

Roi et le Fermier, 1762, Sedaine. O.C. (music by Mosigny).

Roister Doister (*Ralph*), 1534, printed in 1566, Udal. C. (This was the first English comedy. For the first European comedy, see "Calandria.")

Roland, 1778, Piccini. O.

Roland for an Oliver, 1819, Th. Morton. C.

Rolla, 1798, Kotzebue. T.

Rolla, 1799, Lewis. T. (from the above).

Rollo, posthumous 1639, Beaumont and Fletcher.

Roman (*The*), 1550, S. Dobell. D.Pm.

Roman Actor (*The*), 1629, Massinger.

Roman Brother (*The*), 19th cent., Heraud. T.

Roman Comique (*Le*), 1861, Offenbach. O.Bf.

Roman Empress (*A*), 1622-1706, Joyner. D.

Roman Father (*The*), 1750, Whitehead. T. (based on the *Horace* of Corneille).

Roman Revenge, 1753, Hill.

Roman d'Une Heure or La Folle Gageure, 1803, Hoffmann. C.

Roman Virgin (*The*) or The Unjust Judge, 1679, Betterton. T. (the tale of Virginius).

Romance and Reality, 19th cent., J. Brougham. D.Pc.

Romance for an Hour, 1771, Kelly. C.

Romany Rye, 1883, Sims. C.

Rome Sauvée, 1752, Voltaire. T.

Romeo and Juliet, 1595, Shakespeare. T. (printed 1597).

Roméo et Juliette, 1828, Soulié. T. (imitated from the above).

Romildare Constanza, 1819, Meyerbeer. O.

Romp (*The*), *, Anon. C.O. (altered from Bickerstaff's *Love in the City*).

Rosalinda, 1762, Lockman. Mu.D.

Rosamond, 1706, Addison. O. (music by Arne).

Rosamond, 1861, Swinburne. Po.D.

Rosamond (*Fair*), 1879, Tennyson. T.

Rosamond (*The Fair*), 1812, Korner. T. (See "Rosmonda.")

Rosamond the Fair, 1836, Barnett. H.O.

Rose (*The*), 1710-1778, Arne. C.O. (from the French).

Rose Blanche (*La*) et La Rose Rouge, 1809, Guilbert de Pixérécourt. D. (See "Two Roses.")

Roses de St. Fleur (*La*), 19th cent., Offenbach. O.Bf.

Rose et Colas, 1764, Sedaine. O.C.

Rose of Aragon, 1842, Knowles. D.

Rose of Castile, 1857, Balfe. O.

Rosencrantz and Guilderstein, Gilbert.

Rosière de Salency (*La*), 1774, Grétry. O.

Rosière et Norrice, 1842, Barrière. D.

Rosina, 1782, Miss Brooke. Pl.

Rosina, 1783, Shield. O.

Rosmonda, 1525, Rucelleri. T.

Rosmunda, 1783, Alfieri. T. (based on Bandello's novel). Translated by C. Lloyd, 1815.

Rosmunda, 1840, Gil y Zarate. (See "Henry" and "Complaint.")

Rösten i Oerken, 1815, Ingemann.

Rough Diamond (1802-1879), Buckstone. Cdta.

Roundheads (*The*), 1682, Mrs. Behn. C.

Rover (*The*), 1677, Mrs. Behn; pt. ii. 1681. C.

Roving (*The*), 17th cent., Middleton. C.

Roxana, 1592, printed 1632, Alabaster. T. (Latin).

Roxana, 1772, Magnocavallo. T. (a prize play).

Royal Captive (*The*), 1745, J. Maxwell. T.

Royal Combat, 17th cent., Ford and Dekker.

Royal Command (*By*), 19th cent., Stirling. C.O.

Royal Convert, 1708, Rowe. T. (*i.e.* Rodogune).

Royal Exchange (*The*), printed 1853, Brome.

Royal Garland, 1768, Bickerstaff.

Royal King and Loyal Subject (*The*), 1737, Th. Heywood. T.C.

Royal Martyr (*The*), 1669, Dryden. T.
Royal Master (*The*), 1638, Shirley. C.
Royal Mischief, 1696, Mrs. Manley.
Royal Mistress (*The*), 1696, Mrs. Manley.
Royal Shepherd (*The*), 1764, R. Holt. O. (from Metastasio).
Royal Shepherdess, 1669, Shadwell. C. (This is Fountain's comedy *The Reward of Vertue*, 1661, altered.)
Royal Slave (*The*), 1637, printed 1639, Cartwright. T.C.
Royalist (*The*), 1682, D'Urfey. C.
Rubans d'Ivonne, 1850, Thiboust.
Rudens or The Rope (B.C. 254-184), Plautus, C. (Latin, adapted from a Greek play by Diphulos). Translated into blank verse by Messrs. Thornton, Rich, Warner, and Colman, 1769-74.
Rugantio, 1805, Lewis. Mel.
Ruines de Babylone (*Les*), 1819, Guilbert de Pixérécourt.
Ruines de Vaudemont, 1845, Boule.
Rule 'a Wife and Have a Wife, 1624, John Fletcher. C. (altered by Garrick).
Rump (*The*), 1660, Tatham. C.
Runantio, 1806, Lewis.
Runaway (*The*), 1776, Mrs. Cowley. C.
Runnimede, 1783, J. Logan. T.
Rural Felicity, 1834, Buckstone. C.
Ruy Blas, 1840, Victor Hugo. R.D. (Fechter produced a bad English version about 1863.)

Sabots de la Marquis, 1854, Boulanger. O.C.
Sackfull of News (*The*), 1557, Anon. Pl.
Sacrifice d'Iphigénie, 1861, Dennery. T. (See "Iphigénie.")
Sad One (*The*), 1609-1641, Suckling. T.
Sad Shepherd (*The*), left at death unfinished, 1637, Jonson. P.
Sailor's Daughter (*The*), 1800, Cumberland. C.
St. Clement's Eve, 1862, sir H. Taylor. D.
St. Genest, 1641, Rotrou. T.
St. Patrick for Ireland, 1640, Shirley. C.
St. Patrick's Day, 1775, Sheridan. F.
St. Peter, 1866, Benedict. Or.
Saint's Tragedy, 1846, Kingsley. D.Pm. (based on the story of *St. Elizabeth of Hungary*).
Saints and Sinners, 1884, H. A. Jones.
Salmacida Spolia, 1639, Davenant. M.
Salvator, 19th cent., Herault. T.
Samor, 1818, Milman.
Samson, 1742, Handel. Or.
Samson Agonistes, 1671, Milton. D.Pm.
Sapho, 1850, Gounod. O.
Sappo and Phao, 1591, J. Lyly. Myt.D.
Saratoga, 1874, Marshall (brought out in London under the title of *Brighton*).
Sardanapalus, 1821, Byron. T.
Satanella, 1858, Balfe. O.
Satiro-mastix, 1602, Dekker. Sat. C. (in which Ben Jonson is satirized under the name of "Horace, Junior").
Saucy Valets (1730-1805), King.
Saul, 1738, Handel. Or.
Saul, 1739, Hill. T.
Saul, 1782, Alfieri. T. (translated by C. Lloyd, 1815).
Saul, 1801, Kalkbrenner. Or.

Saul (*King*), 1872, Armstrong. T.
Saul (*König*), 1839, Gutzkow. D.
Sauney the Scot, 1698, Lacy. C.
Savage (*Richard*), 19th cent., Gutzkow. D.
Savonarola, 1881, Austin. T.
Scapegoat (*The*), about 1840, Poole. F.
Scholar (*The*), 1649, Lovelace. C.
Scholar (*The*), 1802-1879, Buckstone. C.
School, 1869, Robertson. C.
School for Arrogance (1745-1809), Holcroft. C.
School for Authors, printed 1820, Tobin. C.
School for Coquettes (1799-1861), Mrs. Gore, Prose C.
School for Fathers (*The*), 1770. Bickerstaff. C.
School for Grown Children, 1826, Morton. C.
School for Grown Gentlemen, 1827, Morton. C.
School for Lovers, 1762, Whitehead. C. (See "L'École des Amants.")
School for Scandal, 1777, Sheridan. C. ("Charles" and "Joseph Surface" are copies of Fielding's "Tom Jones" and "Blifil.")
School for Wives, 1774, Kelly. C. (See "L'École des Femmes.")
School of Complement, 1631, Shirley. C.
School of Reform, 1817, Thomas Morton. C. (See "L'École.")
Scipio Africanus, 1729, Beckingham. T. (from Pradon's *Scipion l'Africain*).
Scipion l'Africain (1632-1698), Pradon. T.
Scornful Lady, 1616, Beaumont and Fletcher. C.
Scots Figaries (*The*), 1652, Tatham. C.
Scowerers (*The*), 1691, Shadwell. C.
Scythes, 1761, Voltaire. T.
Sea-Captain (*The*), 1839, Lytton. T. (often called *The Rightful Heir*).
Sea-Voyage (*The*), printed 1647, (?) Beaumont and Fletcher. C.
Search after Happiness, 1773, H. More. P. (Her first production. Aged 17.)
Search for Money (*A*), 1609, Rowley. C.
Seasons (*The*), 1800, Haydn. O.
Sebastian. (See "Don Sebastian.")
Second Maiden's Tragedy, before 1620, Anon. T. (ascribed to Chapman). The heroine has no name.
Second Mrs. Tanqueray (*The*), A. W. Pinero.
Second Thoughts, 19th cent., Buckstone.
Secret (*Le*), 1793, Hoffmann. O.C. (music by Méhul).
Secret Love, 1667, Dryden. C.
Secrétaire et le Cuisinier (*Le*), before 1822, Scribe. Pt.Pc.
Secretary (*The*), 1843, Knowles.
Secrets Worth Knowing, 1798, Th. Morton. C.
See Me and See Me Not, 1618, Belcher. C. (adapted from a play by Hans Beerpot).
Sejanus, 1603, Jonson. T.
Séjour Militaire, 1813, Auber. O.
Self-Immolation or The Sacrifice of Love, 1799, Newman. Pl. (from Kotzebue).
Selindra, 1665, sir W. Killigrew. Pl.
Semele, 1698, Congreve. Mu.D. (music by Handel).
Semiramide, 1729, Metastasio. O.
Semiramide, 1819, Meyerbeer. O.
Semiramide, 1823, Rossini. O.
Sémiramis, 1748, Voltaire. T.

Semiramis, 1776, G. E. Arcough.
Senile Odium, 1633, Hausted. C.
Sense and Sensibility, 1864, Tom Taylor.
Serail, 1782, Mozart. O.
Serf (The), 1865, Tom Taylor.
Serious Family (A), about 1850, Buckstone (music by Barnett).
Sertorius, 1662, Corneille. T.
Servius Tullius, 1826, Bouzique. T.
Sesostris, 1667, Amore. T.
Settling Day (The), 1865, Tom Taylor.
Seven against Thebes (The), B.C. 471, Æschylus. T. (Greek). Translated by Potter, 1777 ; Buckley, 1849 ; Davies, 1864 ; Plumptre, 1869.
Shaughraun, 1874, Boucicault. D.
She Stoops to Conquer, 1773, Goldsmith. C.
She Stoops to Conquer, 1864, Macfarren. O.
She Would and SheWould Not, 1703, Cibber. C-
She Would if She Could, 1668, Etherege. C.
Sheep in Wolf's Clothing, 1857, Tom Taylor.
Shepherd of Tolosa, 1829, Ingemann.
Shepherd's Artifice, 1761, Dibdin. O.
Shepherd's Holiday (The), 1635, Rutten. P.T.C.
Shoemaker a Gentleman (A), 1638, Rowley. C.
Shoemaker's Holiday (The), 1600, Dekker. C.
Shore. (See " Jane Shore.")
Si j'étais Roi, 1854, Adam. Pt.Pc.
Sicilian Summer (A), 1850, Henry Taylor. C.
Sicilian Vespers, 1840, Kenney.
Sicilian Vespers, 1819, Delavigne. T. (See " Vespers of Palermo.")
Sicilien ou L'Amour Peintre, 1667, Molière. C.
Siege (The) or Love's Convert, 1651, Cartwright. C.
Siege of Aguileia, 1760, Home.
Siege of Babylon (The), 1678, Pordage. T.
Siege of Belgrade, 1796, Cobb. C.O. (music by Storace ; an English version of La Cosa Rara).
Siege of Berwick, 1806, Jerningham. T.
Siege of Damascus, 1720, Hughes. T.
Siege of Grenada, 1671, Dryden. H.Pl.
Siege of Ischia (1778-1824), Kemp. O.
Siege of Memphis (The), 1676, D'Urfey. T.
Siege of Rhodes, 1663, Davenant. Pl.
Siege of Rochelle, 1835, Balfe. O.
Siege of Sinope, 1781, Miss Brooke. T.
Siege of Troy (The), 1715, Settle. D.
Siege of Urbin, 1666, sir W. Killigrew. Pl.
Sigurd (King), 19th cent., Bojé. T.
Silent Woman (The), 1609, Jonson. C.
Silver Age (The), 1613, Thomas Heywood. C. (The Brazen Age was 1613 ; and The Iron Age in 1632.)
Silver King (The), 1882, H. A Jones.
Silver Shield (The), 1885, S. Grundy.
Silvia, 1731, Lillo.
Single Life, about 1835, Buckstone. C.
Sir Barnaby Whigg, 1681, D'Urfey. C.
Sir Courtley Nice, 1685, Crowne. C. (from the Mayor Imposible of Lope de Vega).
Sir Fopling Flutter, 1676, Etherege. C. (the second title of The Man of Mode).
Sir George Etherege's Comical Revenge (1642-1689), Mrs. Behn. C.
Sir Harry Gaylove, 1772, Miss Marshall. C,
Sir Harry Wildair, 1701, Farquhar. C.
Sir Hercules Buffoon, 1684, Lacy. C.
Sir John Cockle at Court, 1737, Dodsley. F.

Sir John Falstaff in Masquerade, 1741, S. Johnson. C.
Sir John Oldcastle. (See " Oldcastle.")
Sir Marmaduke Maxwell, 1827, Cunningham. C.
Sir Martin Marplot (1592-1670), William duke of Newcastle. C. (founded on Molière's L'Etourdi).
Sir Martin Marrall, 1667, Dryden. C. (This is Sir Martin Marplot adapted for the stage.)
Sir Patient Fancy, 1678, Mrs. Behn. C.
Sir Richard Grinvile, 1595, Markham. T.
Sir Roger de Coverley, 1861, Tom Taylor. C.
Sir Solomon or The Cautious Coxcomb, 1671, Caryl. C.
Sir Thomas More, 1792, Hurdis. T.
Sir Thomas Overbury, 1726, Savage. T. (brought him £200).
Sir Thomas Overbury's Life and Untimely Death, 1614, Ford. T.
Sir Thomas Wyat, 1607, Webster and Dekker. T.
Sir Walter Raleigh, 1720, Sewell. T,
Sirène (La), 1844, Scribe. O.C.
Siroe (Il), 1728, Metastasio. O.
Sister's Penance, 1866, Tom Taylor.
Sisters (The), 1652, Shirley. C.
Sisters (The), 1769, Mrs. Lennox. C.
Sisters (The), 1890, Swinburne.
Slanderer (The), posthumous 1778, Foote.
Slave (The), 1816, Bishop. O.
Slave Life, 1852, Tom Taylor, etc.
Slaves of the Ring, 1894, S. Grundy.
Sleeping Beauty, 1805, Skeffington. Pn.
Sleeping Beauty, 1840, Planché.
Slighted Maid (The), 1663, Stapylton. C.
Snake in the Grass, 1759, Hill. C. (altered by Buckstone, 19th cent.).
Snowball (The), 1879, S. Grundy.
Society, 1865, Robertson. C.
Sofonisbe, 1718, Leo. O. (See " Sophonisba.")
Soirée à la Bastille, 1845, Decourcelle. C.
Soirée d'Auteuil (La), 1804, Andrieux. C.
Soldier (The), 1649, Lovelace. T.
Soldier's Daughter (The), 1804, Cherry. C.
Soldier's Fortune, 1681, Otway. C.
Soldier's Last Stake (The), 1686-1744, G. Jacob.
Soldier's Return, 1805, Hook. C.
Soliman and Persida, 1599, Anon [? Kyd]. T.
Soliman II. (1710-1792), Favart. O.C.
Solliciteur (Le), before 1822, Scribe. Pt.Pc.
Solomon, 1748, Handel. Or.
Solomon, 1748, Klopstock. S.D. (translated by R. Huish, 1809).
Solomon (King), 1876, Armstrong. T.
Somnambule (La), 1819, Delavigne. D.
Sonnambula, 1831, Bellini. O. (libretto by Scribe).
Sonnambula (a travestie), H. J. Byron.
Sophi (The). (See " Sophy.")
Sophister (The), 1639, Zouch. C.
Sophonisba, 1514, Trissino. T. (the first Italian tragedy). (See " Ferrex," etc.)
Sophonisba or The Wonder of Women, 1606, Marston. T. (See " Sofonisbe.")
Sophonisba, 1729, Thomson. T.
Sophonisba, 1783, Alfieri. T. (translated by Lloyd, 1815).
Sophonisbe, 1630, Mairet. T. (imitated from Trissino ; the first French tragedy).

Sophonisbe (1606-1684), Corneille. T.
Sophonisbe (1677-1758), Lagrange-Chancel. T.
Sophonisbe, Voltaire. T.
Sophonisbe in German, Gaspar Lohenstein. T.
Sophy (The), 1641, printed 1642, Denham. T.
Sorcerer (The), 1877, Gilbert and Sullivan. Opta.
Sorcière (La), 1863, Bourgeois and Barbier. C.
Sordello, 1839, R. Browning.
Sosies, 1639, Rotrou. C.
Sot toujours Sot, 1693, De Brueys. C.
Sowing the Wind, 1893, S. Grundy.
Spaniard in Peru (The), 1797, Kotzebue. T. (The English version is called Pizarro).
Spanish Bawd (The), 1631, Fernando de Roias. C. (the longest play ever published).
Spanish Curate (The), 1622, Fletcher (Beaumont died 1616). C. (based on The Unfortunate Spaniard by Gonsalvo de Cespides).
Spanish Dollars, 1807, Cherry. C.
Spanish Father (The), 1745-1831, H. Mackenzie. T.
Spanish Fryar (The), 1680, Dryden. C.
Spanish Gipsy, 1653, Middleton and Rowley. C.
Spanish Gipsy, 1865, rewritten 1867, and published 1868, "George Eliot" (Mrs. Cross). D.Pm.
Spanish Masquerado, 1589, Greene. C.
Spanish Rogue (The), 1674, Duffett. C.
Spanish Student (The), 1845, Longfellow. D.Pm.
Spanish Tragedy (The) or Jeronimo Mad Again, 1603, Kyd. T. (forming pt. ii. to Jeronimo).
Spanish Viceroy, posthumous 1653, Massinger.
Spartacus, 1746, Saurin. T.
Spartan Dame (The), 1721, Southern. T.
Speculation (1765-1841), Reynolds. C.
Speed the Plough, 1798, Thomas Morton. C.
Spoilt Child (The), 1805 (?) Bickerstaff. C.
Spouter (The), 1756, Murphy. F.
Sprigs of Laurel, 1798, O'Keefe. M.F. (music by Shield).
Spring and Autumn, 1827, Kenney. C.
Spring's Glory (The), 1638, Nabbes. M.
Squeeze to the Coronation, 1821, Thomson. C.
Squire of Alsatia (The), 1688, Shadwell. C. (same as The Gentleman of Alsatia).
Squire Oldsapp, 1679, D'Urfey. C.
Stage Beaux toss'd in a Blanket, 1704, Thomas Brown. C.
Stage Coach, 1704, Farquhar. C.
Staple of News (The), 1625, Jonson. C.
Star of Seville, 1837, Mrs. Butler (born Kemble).
State of Innocence, 1673, Dryden. D.Pm. (a dramatic version of Milton's Paradise Lost).
State Prisoner, 1847, Stirling.
Statira (1632-1698), Pradon. T.
Stella, 1776, Goethe. D.
Stella, 1843, Anicet Bourgeois. D.
Stephanie, 1877, Story. T.
Stepmother (The), 1664, Stapylton. T.C. (See "Hecyra.")
Stepmother (The), 1800, earl of Carlisle (Byron's uncle). T.
Steward (The). (This is merely The Deserted Daughter of Holcroft, 1785, reset.)
Stichus (B.C. 254-184), Plautus. C. (Latin, adapted from a Greek play by Menander).

Translated into blank verse by Messrs. Thornton, Rich, Warner, and Colman, 1769-74.
Stilicon, 1660, Thomas Corneille. T.
Still Waters Run Deep, 1855, Tom Taylor. C.
Stolen Heiress, 1703, Centlivre. C.
Stolen Kisses, 19th cent., Merritt. C.
Strafford, 1837, R. Browning. H.T.
Strafford, 1843, Sterling. H.T.
Strange Discovery (The), 1640, Gough. T.C.
Strange Gentleman (The), 1836, Dickens. Blta.
Stranger (The), 1797, B. Thompson. D. (from Misanthropy and Repentance, by Kotzebue). (Thompson's version was greatly altered in 1798 by Sheridan. It is the latter alone which is acted.)
Straniera (La), 1806-1835, Bellini. O.
Strathmore, 1849, W. Marston. T.
Stratonice, 1792, Hoffmann. O.C. (music by Méhul).
Streets of London, 1862, Boucicault. D.
Struensee, 1827, Beer. T.
Success or A Hit if You Like It, 1825, Planché. F.
Such a Good Man, 1874, Besant and Rice. C.
Such Things Are, 1787, Inchbald. Pl. (realized £410 12s.).
Suite du Mentuer (La), 1803, Andrieux. C.
Sullen Lovers, 1668, Shadwell. C.
Sultan (The), 1775, Bickerstaff. F.
Summer's Last Will, etc., 1600, Nash. C.
Summer's Tale, 1768, Cumberland. C.O. (music by Bach, Arne, and others. It was cut down by Cumberland into Amelia, an afterpiece).
Sun in Aries (The), 1621, Middleton. C.
Sun's Darling (The), 1656, Ford. M.
Superiority, 1607, Ant. Brewer. C.
Suppliants (The), B.C. 461, Æschylus. T. (Greek). Translated by Potter, 1777; Buckley; 1849; Plumptre, 1869.
Supplication of Pierce Penniless, etc., 1592, Nash.
Supplice d'un Homme, 1865, Thiboust.
Supplices, B.C. 421, Euripides. T. (Greek). Translated by Potter, 1781; Wodhull, 1782.
Supposes (The), 1566, Gascoigne. C. (from Gli Suppositi, of Ariosto; one of our earliest dramas).
Suréna, 1674, Corneille. T.
Surprise (Agreeable), 1798, O'Keefe. C.
Surrender of Calais, 1791, Colman. C.
Suspicious Husband (The), 1747, Hoadly. C.
Sutcliffe (Dr.), Robertson. C.
Svend Dyring's House, 19th cent., Herz. R.D.
Svend Grathe, 19th cent., Bojé. T.
Sweethearts, 1874, Gilbert. D.Pc. (in two acts).
Sweethearts and Wives (1772-1849), Kenney. Mu.C. (music by Nathan).
Sweet Lavender, A. Pinero.
Sweetman, the Woman-Hater, 1640, Anon. C.
Swindler (The), 1764-1838, Morton. C.
Sword and the Hand, 1832, Beer. T.
Sylvain, 1770, Marmontel. O.C. (music by Grétry).
Sylvana, 1809, Weber. O. (This is The Woodgirl altered).
Sylvester Daggerwood, 1795, Colman. C.
Sylvia, 1731, Lillo.

Tableau Parlant (*Le*), 1769, Grétry. O.
Tailors (*The*), *, Anon. B.T.
Tale of Mantua, 1830, Knowles.
Tale of Mystery (1745–1809), Holcroft. Mel.
Tale of a Tub, 1633, Jonson. (His last comedy. Its object was to hold up Inigo Jones to ridicule.)
Tale of Two Cities (*A*), 1840, Tom Taylor. (Dickens's novel dramatized.)
Tamburlaine, 1590, Marlowe, T. In Two parts. (See " Timour.")
Tamerlan (1632–1698), Pradon. T.
Tamerlan et Bajazet, 1806, Bishop. Bl.
Tamerlane, 1702, Rowe. T. (Tamerlane is meant for William III., and Bajazet for Louis XVI.)
Tamerlane, 1722, Leo. O.
Taming a Tartar, C. Selby. C.
Taming of the Shrew, 1593, Shakespeare. C. (See " Honeymoon.")
Tancred and Gismunda, 1568, by Hatton and four other members of the Inner Temple. (Based on an Italian novel.)
Tancred and Sigismunda, 1745, Thomson. T.
Tancréde, 1760, Voltaire. T.
Tancredi, 1813, Rossini. O.
Tannhäuser, 1845, Wagner. O.
Tante (*La*) et le Neveu(1781–1857), Brifaut. C.
Tarare, 1787, Beaumarchais. O.
Tartuffe, 1664, Molière. C. (See " Nonjuror.")
Tasso (*Torquato*), 1790, Goethe. T.
Tasso Refriede, 1819, Ingemann. D.
Taste, 1752, Foote. F.
Tatlers (*The*), 1797, Hoadly. C.
Taverne des Étudiants (*La*), 1854, Sardou. C.
Technogamia or Marriage of the Arts, 1630, Holyday. C.
Tekeli, 1803, Guilbert de Pixérécourt. Mel. (done into English by Hook).
Tell (*Guglielmo*), 1829, Rossini. O. (Sir H. Bishop altered this opera.)
Tell (*Guillaume*), 1766, Lemière. T.
Tell (*Guillaume*), 1772, Sedaine. O.
Tell (*Wilhelm*), 1804, Schiller. T.
Tell (*William*), 1825, Knowles. T.
Tell (*William*), 1827–1862, Talfourd. F.
Temistocle, 1738, Metastasio. D.
Temper, 1847, R. Bell.
Tempest (*The*), 1609, Shakespeare. C. (first mentioned 1611. Music by Sullivan).
Tempest (*The*), 1668, Dryden. C. (the above altered).
Temple Beau (*The*), 1738, Fielding. C.
Temple de la Gloire, 1744, Voltaire. O.
Temple of Love (*The*), 1634, Davenant. M.
Temptatyon of Our Lorde and Saver (*The*), 1538, Bale. Int.
Tempter (*The*), 1893, H. A. Jones.
Tender Husband (*The*), 1703, Steele. C.
Teraminta, 1732, H. Carey.
Tête de Mort (*La*), 1827, Guilbert de Pixérécourt. V.
Théagène et Chariclée, 1662, Racine. T.
Thébaïde (*La*), 1664, Racine. T.
Thebaïs or The Phœnissæ(B.C. 58–32), Seneca. T. (Latin). Adapted in Alexandrine metre by T. Newton, 1581.
Themistocle. (See " Temistocle.")
Theodosius or The force of Love, 1680, Lee. T. (One of his best.)

Therese, the Orphan of Geneva, 19th cent., Kerr. Mel.R. (adapted).
Thersytes, 1537, Anon. Int.
Thésée, 1690, Lafosse. T.
Theseus, 1715, Handel. O.
Theseus and Ariadne, 1848, Planché.
Thesmophoriazusæ, B.C. 410, Aristophanes. C. (Greek). Translated by Mitchell, 1820–22 ; Hickie, 1853 ; Rudd, 1867.
Thespis, 1762, Kelly.
Thierry and Theodoret, 1621, Fletcher (Beaumont died 1616). T.
Thieves of Paris, 1856, Stirling. D.
Thimble Rig (*The*), 1802–1879, Buckstone. F.
Thirty Years of a Woman's Life, before 1834, Buckstone.
Thomas. (See " Mons. Thomas.")
Thomas à Becket, 1780, Tennyson. T.
Thomas and Sally (1696–1743), Carey. Mu.E.
Thomas and Sally, 1760, Carey. C.O.
Thracian Wonder, 1661, Webster. C.
Three Black Seals (*The*), 1864, Stirling. H.D.
Three Hours after Marriage, 1716, Gay. F. (with Pope and Arbuthnot).
Three Ladies of London (*The*), 1584, Anon. Mo.
Three Lords and Three Ladies of London, 1590, Anon. Mo.
Three Strangers (*The*), 1835, Miss H. Lee. C.
Three Weeks after Marriage, 1776, Murphy. F.
Thyestes (B.C. 58–32), Seneca. T. (Latin). Translated by J. Heywood, 1560 ; J. Wright, 1674.
Thyestes, about 1680, Crowne. T.
Tibère (1764–1811), Chénier. T.
Ticket-of-Leave Man, 1863, Tom Taylor.
Timanthes, 1769, Hoole. T.
Time Works Wonders, 1845, Jerrold. C.
Times (*The*), H. Pinero. C.
Timocrate, 1656, Thomas Corneille. T.
Timocrate, 1723, Leo. O.
Timoléon, 1783, Alfieri. T. Translated by C. Lloyd, 1815.
Timoléon, 1794, Chénier. T.
Timon of Athens, 1609, Shakespeare. T.
Timon of Athens, 1778, Cumberland. T. (the above altered).
Timon of Athens, 1672, Shadwell.
Timon the Manhater, 1678, Shadwell. T. (Shakespeare's play reset).
Timour the Tartar, 1812, Lewis. Mel. (See " Tamerlane.")
Tipperary Legacy, 1847, Coyne. C.
'Tis Pity She's a Whore, 1633. Ford. T. (an exquisite play with a repulsive title).
'Tis Well 'tis no Worse, 1770, Bickerstaff. C. (See " Panel.")
Tit for Tat, *, Colman. C. (This is Atkinson's *Mutual Deception* reset.)
Tito, 1791, Mozart. O.
Titus Andronicus, 1593, (?) Shakespeare. T. (first mentioned 1600).
Titus Andronicus, 1687, Ravenscroft. T.
Titus and Berenice, 1672, Otway. T.
To Marry or Not to Marry (1753–1821), Inchbald. C.
To-Night, Uncle, 1878, H. J. Byron.
To Oblige Benson, 1854, Tom Taylor.
To Parents and Guardians, 1846, Tom Taylor.

Tobacconist (*The*), before 1170, Gentleman. F. (This is merely Jonson's comedy, *The Alchemist*, 1610, altered and reduced).

Tom Cobb, 1876, Gilbert. F.

Tom Essence or The Modish Wife, 1677, Rawlins. C.

Tom Fool, 1760, Stevens. F. (in three acts).

Tom Jones, 1740, Reed. C.O.

Tom Thumb, 1733, Fielding. C.O. (music by Dr. Arne; altered in 1778 by O'Hara).

Tom Thumb, 1766, O'Hara.

Tom Tyler and his Wife, about 1569, published in 1578, Anon. Mo.

Tonson. (See "Mons. Tonson.")

Tony Lumpkin in Town, 1778, O'Keefe. C.

Too Late to Call Back Yesterday, 1639, R. Davenport. C.

Too Many or Democracy, posthumous 1805, Alfieri. C.

Toréador (*Le*), 1849, Adam. O.C.

Tortesa the Usurer, 1841, Willis. C.

Tottenham Court, 1633, printed 1638, Nabbes. C.

Tour de Londres, 1855, Nus. D.

Tower of Babel(*The*), 1871, A. Austin. Dc.Pm.

Town and Country, 1807, Morton. C. (brought him in £1000).

Town Fop (*The*), 1677, Mrs. Behn. C.

Toy-Shop, 1735, Dodsley. D.S.

Trachiniæ, about B.C. 430, Sophocles. T. (Greek). Translated by G. Adams, 1729; Potter, 1788; Dale, 1824; Plumptre, 1865.

Tragedy of Cleander (*The*), 1614, Massinger.

Traitor (*The*), 1635, Shirley. T. (See "Evadne.") (Reset by Rivers in 1692.)

Travailes of Three English Brothers, 1607, Rowley with Day. T.C.

Travellers (*The*), 1806, Cherry. C.

Traviata (*La*), 1856, Verdi. O.

Trente Millions de Gladiateurs (*Les*), 19th cent., Labiche and Gille. (See "Nabob.")

Trésor (*Le*), 1803, Andrieux. C.

Trial. (See "Tryal.")

Trial by Jury, 1876, Gilbert and Sullivan. Opta.

Trial of Pleasure (*The*), 1567, Skelton. Mo.

Trick for Trick, 1678, D'Urfey. C. (based on Fletcher's *Mons. Thomas*, 1619).

Trick upon Trick, 1710, Hill. C.

Tricke to Catch the Old One (*A*), 1608, Middleton. C.

Trilby, 1895, Du Maurier. (This is his novel *Trilby* dramatized.)

Trinummus (B.C. 254–184), Plautus. C. (Latin, adapted from a Greek play by Philemon). Translated into blank verse by Messrs. Thornton, Rich, Warner, and Colman, 1769–1774. (Lessing's *Scatz* is borrowed from this play.)

Trinuzzia (*La*), 1540, Angelo. C.

Triomphe des Arts (*Le*), 1672–1731, Lamotte. O.

Trip to Calais (*A*), 1777, Foote. F.

Trip to Kissengen (*A*), 1844, Tom Taylor.

Trip to Portsmouth (*A*), 1720–1784, Stevens. O.C.

Trip to Scarborough (*A*), 1777, Sheridan. This is *The Relapse* of Vanbrugh altered.)

Trip to Scotland (*A*), 1770, Whitehead. F.

Tristan and Isolde, 1865, Wagner. O.

Triumph of Oriana, 1601, Morley. Q.

Triumph of Peace (*The*) 1633, Shirley. M.

Triumph of the Philistines, 1895, H. A. Jones.

Triumph of Truth (*The*), 17th cent., G. Jeffreys. O.

Triumphs of Beautie (*The*), 1646, Shirley. M.

Triumphs of Health and Prosperity, 1626, Middleton. Sol.

Triumphs of Honour and Industry, 1617, Middleton. Sol.

Triumphs of Honour and Virtue, 1622, Middleton. Sol.

Triumphs of Integrity, 1623, Middleton. Sol.

Triumphs of Love and Antiquity, 1619, Middleton. Sol.

Triumphs of Love and Fortune, 1589, by E. A. Sol.

Triumphs of Truth, 1613, Middleton (and scores more for Lord Mayor's Day).

Triumphs of the Prince D'Amour, 1635, Davenant. M.

Triumphant Widow (*The*), 1677, the duchess of Newcastle. O.

Troade (*La*), 1632–1698, Pradon. T.

Troades (B.C. 415), Euripides. T. (Greek). Translated by Banister, 1780; Potter, 1781; Wodhull, 1782.

Troas or Hecuba (B.C. 58–32), Seneca. T. (Latin). Translated by J. Heywood, 1559; S. P[ordage], 1660; E. Sherburne, 1679; J. T[albot], 1686.

Troilus and Cressida, 1602, Shakespeare. T. (printed 1609).

Troilus and Cressida, 1679, Dryden. T. (the above altered).

Trois Cousins, 1664, Dancourt. C.

Trois Rivaux (*Les*), 1758, Saurin. C.

Trois Sultanes (*Les*), 1710–1792, Favart. C.

Troja Distrutta, 1663, Andrea. T.

Troublesome Reign of King John, 1578, Anon. H.Pl. (the quarry of Shakespeare's *King John*).

Trovatore (*Il*), 1853, Verdi. O. (based on the drama of *Gargia Guttierez*, 15th cent.).

Truculentus (B.C. 254–184), Plautus. C. (Latin). Translated into blank verse by Messrs. Thornton, Rich, Warner, and Colman, 1769–74.

True Love can ne'er Forget (1797–1868), Lover. O.

True Widow, 1679, Shadwell. C.

Tryal of Samuel Foote, 1763, Foote. F.

Tu Quoque, 1599, Greene.

Tunbridge Wells, 1678, Rawlins. C.

Turcaret, 1708, Lesage. C.

Turco in Italia, 1814, Rossini. O.

Turk and No Turk, 1785, Colman. Mu.C.

Turke (*The*), 1610, J. Mason. T.

Turkish Court (*The*), 1748, L. Pilkington. Pl.

Turkish Mahomet, 1584, Peele.

Turnpike Gate (1774–1826), Knight. F.

Tutor (*The*), Hownley.

Twelfth Night, etc., 1602, Shakespeare. C.

Twin Rivals, 1705, Farquhar.

'Twixt Axe and Crown, 1870, Taylor. H.Pl.

Two Foscari (*The*), 1821, Byron. (*The Foscari*, 1826, Miss Mitchell.)

Two Gentlemen of Verona, 1595, Shakespeare. C. (first mentioned 1598).

Two Italian Gentlemen (*The*), 1584, Munday. D. (afterwards called *Fidele and Fortunio*).

Virginius, 1820, Knowles. T.
Virtue Betrayed, 1682, Banks. T.
Virtuoso (*The*), 1676, Shadwell. C.
Virtuous Octavia, 1598, Brandon. H.Pl.
Virtuous Wife (*The*) or Good Luck to the
    Last, 1680, D'Urfey. C.
Visite à Bedlam (*Une*), before 1822, Scribe.
    Pt.Pc.
Vologese, 1744, Leo. O.
Volpone or The Fox, 1605, Jonson. C.
Volunteers (*The*), 1693, Shadwell. C.
Vortigern and Rowena, 1796, Ireland. T.
Votary of Wealth (*The*), 1792, Holman. C.

Wags of Windsor. (See " Review.")
Wakefield Plays (*The*), 32 in number, printed
    by the Surtees Society in 1836. The only
    MS. belongs to the Townley family. Mys.
Walking Statue, 1710, Hill.
Wallace, 1799, Grahame. T.
Wallace. (See " Valsei.")
Wallenstein (*Albertus*), 1639, Glapthorne.
    H.D.
Wallenstein, 1799, Schiller. (An English
    version by Coleridge, 1800.)
Walloons (*The*), 1782, Cumberland.
Walpole, 1869, lord Lytton. C.
Walter Raleigh (*Sir*), 1720, Sewell. T.
Wandering Lover (*The*), 1653, Massinger.
    T.C.
Wandering Minstrel (*The*), 1841, Mayhew and
    Beckett. F.
War (1829-1871), Robertson. C.
War to the Knife, 1865, H. J. Byron. C.
Warning to Fair Women (*The*), 1599, Anon.
    T.
Warwick, 1763, Laharpe. T. (In 1767 ap-
    peared the English version by Franklin.)
Washington, 1877, Tupper. D.
Wasps (*The*), B.C. 422, Aristophanes. C.
    (Greek). Translated by Mitchell, 1820-22;
    Hickie, 1853 ; Rudd, 1867; Rogers, 1876.
Wat Tyler, 1794, Southey. Pol.D.
Wat Tyler, 1869, Sala. B.
Water Witches (*The*), 1805-1868, Coyne.
Waterman (*The*), 1774, Dibdin. Bd.O.
Way of the World (*The*), 1700, Congreve. C.
Way to get Married (*The*), 1796, Morton. C.
Way to Keep Him (*The*), 1760, Murphy. C.
Ways and Means, 1788, Colman. C.
We Fly by Night, 1806, Colman. F.
Weak Points (1802-1879), Buckstone.
Weathercock (*The*), about 1810, Allingham.
    C.
Webster at Home, 1853, Tom Taylor. C.
Wedding (*The*), 1629, Shirley. C.
Wedding Day (*The*), 1740, Fielding. C.
Wedding Day, 1790, Inchbald. F. (realized
    £200).
Wedding March (*The*), 1873, Gilbert.
Welcome and Farewell, 1837, Harness. D.
Wenceslaus. (See " Venceslas.")
Werner, 1822, Byron. T. (based on one of
    Miss Lee's *Canterbury Tales*).
Werter, 1786, Reynolds.
Werther, 1817, Duval. F.
West Indian, 1771, Cumberland. C.
Westward Hoe ! 1607, Dekker and Webster. C.
What a Blunder ! (1764-1817), Holman. C.
What d'ye Call It ? 1714, Gay. T.C.P,

What Next ? (1771-1841), Dibdin. F.
What You Will, 1607, Marston. C. (*What You
    Will* is the second title of Shakespeare's
    comedy of *Twelfth Night*.)
Wheel of Fortune (*The*), 1779, Cumberland. C.
Which is the Man ? (1743-1809), Mrs. Cowley.
    C.
White Devil (*The*), 1612, Webster. T.
White Elephant (*The*), 1896, Carton. C.
White Lady of Berlin Castle, 1875, C. Win-
    chester. T.
Who is She ? 19th cent., Stirling. Pt.C.
Who wants a Guinea ? 1805, Colman. F.
Whore of Babylon (*The*), 1603, Day.
Who's the Dupe?(1743-1809), Mrs. Cowley. F.
Wicked World (*The*), 1873, Gilbert. Fy.C.
Widow (*The*), 1628, Middleton. C.
Widow (*The*), printed 1652, Jonson, Fletcher,
    and Middleton. C.
Widow Ranter (*The*), 1690, Mrs. Behn. C.
Widow of Delphi, 1780, Cumberland. O.
Widow's Tears (*The*), 1612, Chapman. C.
Wife (*The*), 1833, Knowles. D.
Wife for a Month, 1624, Fletcher (Beaumont
    died 1616). T.C.
Wife of Bath, 1713, altered 1730, J. Gay. C.
Wife or No Wife, 19th cent., Heraud. C.
Wife Well Managed, 1715, Centlivre. C.
Wife's Excuse, 1692, Southerne. C.
Wife's Relief (*The*), 1711, Johnson. C. (See
    " Gamester.")
Wife's Stratagem (*The*), 1827, Poole. C. (See
    " Gamester.")
Wives as They Were, etc., 1797, Inchbald. C.
Wild Gallant, 1663, Dryden. C.
Wild-Goose Chase, 1619, Fletcher. C. (first
    published 1652).
Wild Oats, 1798, O'Keefe. C.
Wildair (*Sir Harry*), 1701, Farquhar. C.
Wilhelm Tell. (See " Tell.")
Will (*The*), 1765-1841, Reynolds. C.
Willow Copse (*The*), 19th cent., Boucicault.
Wily Beguilede, 1606, Anon. C.
Winning a Husband (1802-1879), Buckstone. C.
Winter's Tale, 1604, Shakespeare. C. (first
    mentioned 1611). The source of this
    play was a novel called *Pandosto or The
    Triumph of Time*, 1588, by Robert Greene.
    (See " Zapolya.")
Wisdom of Dr. Dodypoll, 1600, Lyly. C.
Wise Man of the East (*A*), 1799, Inchbald.
    Pl. (from Kotzebue).
Wise Woman of Hogsdon, 1638, T. Heywood.
    C.
Wit at Several Weapons, 1614, Beaumont and
    Fletcher. C.
Wit in a Constable, 1640, Glapthorne. C.
Wit Restored, 1621 or 1623, printed 1658.
Wit without Money, posthumous 1639, Beau-
    mont and Fletcher. C.
Witch (*The*), 1604, Middleton. T.C. (Shake-
    speare borrowed his witches in *Macbeth*
    from this play.)
Witch of Edmonton, 1658, Rowley, Tourneur,
    etc. T.C. (The witch was Mother Sawyer.)
Witch-Finder (*The*), 19th cent., R. Buchanan.
    T.
Within and Without, 1856, McDonnell. D.Pm.
Wits (*The*), 1636, Davenant. C.
Wit's Cabal (1624-1673), Margaret duchess of
    Newcastle. C.

Wit's Last Stake (1730–1805), King.　C.

With Kin and Brothers, 1852, Tom Taylor.

Wittie Faire One (*The*), 1633, Shirley.　C.

Wives.　(See under "Wife.")

Woman Captain, 1680, Shadwell.　C.

Woman-Hater, 1607, Beaumont and Fletcher.　C.

Woman in Red (*The*), 1849, Coyne.

Woman in the Moon, 1597, J. Lyly.　Myt.D. (The woman is Pandora.)

Woman Kilde with Kindnesse (*A*), before 1603, third edition 1617, Heywood.　T.

Woman made Justice (*A*), 1720, Betterton.　C.

Woman will have her Will (*A*), 1616, Haughton.

Woman's Place, posthumous 1647, Beaumont and Fletcher.　C.

Woman's Prize, posthumous 1647, Beaumont and Fletcher.　C.

Woman's Wit, 1697, C. Cibber.　C.

Woman's Wit, 1838, Knowles.　C.

Woman's a Weathercock, 1609, printed 1612, Field.　C. (The second part, called *Amends for Ladies*, was acted in 1610.)

Women, Beware of Women, 1657, Middleton.　C. (from the Italian).

Women Pleased, printed 1647, (?) Beaumont and Fletcher.　C.

Wonder (*A*) or An Honest Yorkshireman, 1736, Carey.　Bd.O.

Wonder (*A New*) or A Woman Never Vext, 1632, Rowley.　C.

Wonder (*The*) or A Woman keeps a Secret, 1713, Centlivre.　C.

Wonder of Women.　(See "Sophonisba," Marston.)

Wonderful Year, 1603, Dekker.　C.

Wonders in the Sun, 1706, D'Urfey.　C.O.

Wood Demon (*The*), 1811, Lewis.　Mel.

Woodgirl (*The*), 1800, Weber.　O. (See "Sylvana.")

Woodman (*The*), 1771, Dudley.　C.O.

Woodvil.　(See "John Woodvil.")

Word of Nature (*The*), 1797, Cumberland.　C.

Word to the Wise, 1765, Kelly.　C.

Works for Cutlers, 1615, Anon.　D.Dial.

World (*The*), 1808, Kenney.　C.

Worlde and the Chylde (*The*), printed 1522, Anon.　Mo.

World's Idol (*The*), 1659, by H. H. B. (adapted from the Greek comedy of *Plutus* by Aristophanes).

Wounds of Civil War, 1594, Lodge.　H.Pl.

Wreck Ashore, 1830, Buckstone.　Mel.

Writing Desk (*The*) or Youth in Danger, 1799. Pl. (from Kotzebue).

Xerxes, 1699, C. Cibber.　H.D.

X.Y.Z., 1810, Colman.　F.

Yellow Dwarf (*The*), 1854, Planché.

Yeoman of the Guard (*The*), Gilbert.

Yorkshire Tragedy (*The*), 1604, Anon. (at one time printed with the name of Shakespeare).

Young Hypocrite (*The*), posthumous 1778, Foote.

Young King (*The*), 1683, Mrs. Behn.

Younger Brother (*The*), 1696, Mrs. Behn.

Your Five Gallants, 1607, Middleton.　C.

Youth, 1549, Anon.　Mo.

Youthful Martyrs of Rome, 1856, Oakley.

Youth's Glory and Death's Banquet, in two parts (1624–1673), Margaret duchess of Newcastle.　T.

Zaïre, 1733, Voltaire.　T.

Zaïre, 1815, Winter.　O.

Zapolya, 1817, Coleridge.　T. (founded on *The Winter's Tale*, by Shakespeare).

Zara, 1735, Hill.　T. (an English version of Voltaire's *Zaïre*).

Zauberflöte (*Die*), 1791, Mozart.　O.

Zelinda, 1772, Calini.　C. (a prize play).

Zémire et Azor, 1771, Marmontel.　O. (music by Grétry).

Zenobia, 1758, Piccini.　O.

Zenobia, 1768, Murphy.　T.

Zobeide, 1772, Craddock.

Zoraïde di Granata, 1822, Donizetti.　O.

Zorinski, 1809, Thomas Morton.